DICTIONARY OF MING BIOGRAPHY
Volume II
M-Z

There is properly no History: only Biography.
—Ralph Waldo Emerson
Essays, first series (1841)

国人紀事
叺事傳人

房兆楹述
杜聯喆書

Dictionary
of
MING BIOGRAPHY
1368-1644

明代名人傳

THE MING BIOGRAPHICAL HISTORY PROJECT
OF THE
ASSOCIATION FOR ASIAN STUDIES

L. Carrington Goodrich, EDITOR
Chaoying Fang, ASSOCIATE EDITOR

Volume II
M-Z

1976
COLUMBIA UNIVERSITY PRESS
New York and London

Library of Congress Cataloging in Publication Data

Association for Asian Studies. Ming Biographical
History Project Committee.
Dictionary of Ming biography, 1368–1644.

Added title: Ming tai ming jen chuan.
Bibliography: p. 1695.
Includes index.
1. China—History—Ming dynasty, 1368–1644—
Biography. 2. China—Biography. I. Goodrich,
Luther Carrington, 1894–   II. Fang, Chao-ying,
1908–   III. Title.
DS753.5.A84 1976   951′.026′0922 [B]   75-26938
ISBN 0-231-03801-1 (v. 1)
ISBN 0-231-03833-X (v. 2)

Eighty-nine Collections of Ming Dynasty Biographies

(yin-te ♯24)

種數	書　　　　名	纂　輯　者	種數	書　　　　名	纂　輯　者
1	明史（列傳之部）	張 廷 玉 等	46	皇明將略	李 同 芳
2	明史（列傳之部）	萬 斯 同	47	造邦賢勳錄略	王 禕
3	明史稿（列傳之部）	王 鴻 緒	48	靖難功臣錄	朱 當 㴐
4	皇明通紀直解	張 嘉 和	49	勝朝粵東遺民錄	陳 伯 陶
5	國朝獻徵錄	焦 竑	50	甲申後亡臣表	彭 孫 貽
6	國朝名世類苑	凌 廸 知	51	建文忠節錄	張 芹
7	今獻備遺	項 篤 壽	52	熹朝忠節死臣列傳	吳 應 箕
8	明名臣言行錄	徐 開 江	53	前明忠義別傳	汪 有 典
9	皇明名臣琬琰錄	徐 紘	54	崇禎忠節錄	高 承 埏
10	皇明名臣言行錄	王 宗 沐	55	勝朝殉節諸臣錄	舒 赫 德 等
11	國朝名臣言行略	劉 廷 元	56	南都死難紀略	顧 苓
12	皇明名臣言行錄	沈 應 魁	57	明季南都殉難記	屈 大 均
13	昭代明良錄	童 時 明	58	天問閣集	李 長 祥
14	皇明人物考	焦 竑	59	小腆紀傳	徐 鼒
15	皇明應謚名臣備攷錄	林 之 盛	60	小腆紀傳補遺	徐 鼒
16	國朝列卿記	雷 禮	61	明書	傅 維 鱗
17	嘉靖以來首輔傳	王 世 貞	62	明史分稿殘編	方 象 瑛
18	國朝內閣名臣事略	吳 伯 與	63	續藏書	李 贄
19	內閣行實	雷 禮	64	明詩紀事	陳 田
20	皇明開國功臣錄	黃 金	65	明畫錄	徐 沁
21	蘭臺法鑒錄	何 出 光 等	66	遜國記	未 詳
22	皇明詞林人物考	王 兆 雲	67	滄江野史	未 詳
23	明名人傳	未 詳	68	海上紀聞	未 詳
24	明人小傳	曹 溶	69	沂陽日記	未 詳

Emperors of the Ming Dynasty

Name	Temple Name	Birth	Death	Enthroned	Reign title and dates in effect
Chu Yüan-chang	T'ai-tsu	10/21/1328	6/24/1398	1/23/1368	Hung-wu (1/23/1368–2/5/1399)
Chu Yün-wen	(Hui-tsung)	12/5/1377	7/13/1402?	6/30/1398	Chien-wen (2/6/1399–7/13/1402)
Chu Ti	T'ai-tsung Ch'eng-tsu (conferred 10/3/1538)	5/2/1360	8/12/1424	7/17/1402	Yung-lo (1/23/1403–1/19/1425)
Chu Kao-chih	Jen-tsung	8/16/1378	5/29/1425	9/7/1424	Hung-hsi (1/20/1425–2/7/1426)
Chu Chan-chi	Hsüan-tsung	3/16/1399	1/31/1435	6/27/1425	Hsüan-te (2/8/1426–1/17/1436)
Chu Ch'i-chen	Ying-tsung	11/29/1427	2/23/1464	2/7/1435 restored 2/11/1457	Cheng-t'ung (1/18/1436–1/13/1450) T'ien-shun (2/11/1457–1/26/1465)
Chu Ch'i-yü	(Tai-tsung) (captive 9/1/1449–9/20/1450)	9/11/1428	3/14/1457	9/22/1449	Ching-t'ai (1/14/1450–2/11/1457)
Chu Chien-shen	Hsien-tsung	12/9/1447	9/9/1487	2/28/1464	Ch'eng-hua (1/27/1465–1/13/1488)
Chu Yu-t'ang	Hsiao-tsung	7/30/1470	6/8/1505	9/22/1487	Hung-chih (1/14/1488–1/23/1506)
Chu Hou-chao	Wu-tsung	10/26/1491	4/20/1521	6/19/1505	Cheng-te (1/24/1506–1/27/1522)
Chu Hou-ts'ung	Shih-tsung	9/16/1507	1/23/1567	5/27/1521	Chia-ching (1/28/1522–2/8/1567)
Chu Tsai-hou	Mu-tsung	2/4/1537	7/5/1572	2/4/1567	Lung-ch'ing (2/9/1567–2/1/1573)
Chu I-chün	Shen-tsung	9/4/1563	8/18/1620	7/19/1572	Wan-li (2/2/1573–1620)
Chu Ch'ang-lo	Kuang-tsung	9/29/1582	9/26/1620	8/28/1620	T'ai-ch'ang (8/28/1620–1/21/1621)
Chu Yu-chiao	Hsi-tsung	12/23/1605	9/30/1627	10/1/1620	T'ien-ch'i (1/22/1621–2/4/1628)
Chu Yu-chien	Ssu-tsung	2/6/1611	4/24/1644	10/2/1627	Ch'ung-chen (2/5/1628–1/27/1645)
Chu Yu-sung	(An-tsung)	12/12/1607	5/?/1646	6/7/1644	Hung-kuang (1645)
Chu Yü-chien	(Shao-tsung)	5/25/1602	10/?/1646	7/29/1645	Lung-wu (1646)
Chu Yu-lang		11/?/1623	6/?/1662	11/20/1646	Yung-li (2/5/1647–1661)

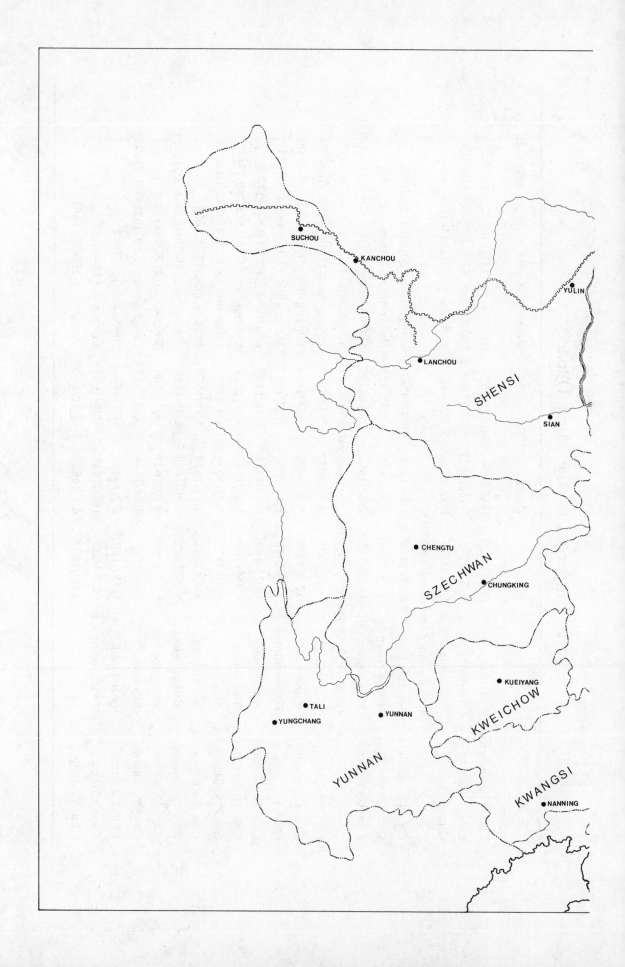

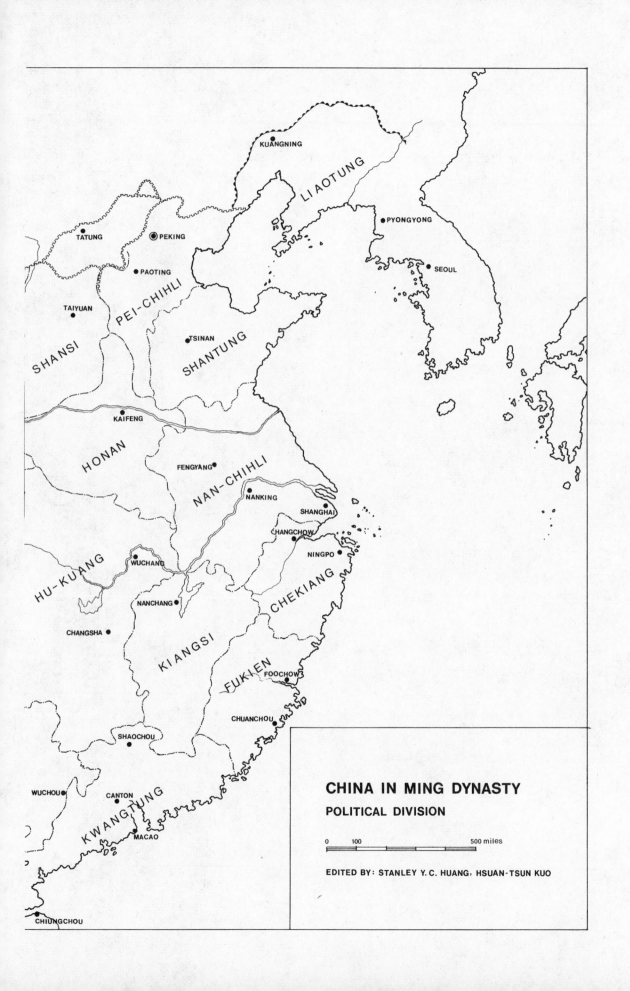

CHINA IN MING DYNASTY

POLITICAL DIVISION

0   100   500 miles

EDITED BY: STANLEY Y. C. HUANG, HSUAN-TSUN KUO

DICTIONARY OF MING BIOGRAPHY
Volume II
M-Z

There is properly no History: only Biography.
—Ralph Waldo Emerson
Essays, first series (1841)

国人紀事
叺事傳人
房兆楹述
杜聯喆書

MA 馬, Empress, August 9, 1332–September 17, 1382, born in Su-chou 宿州 (Anhwei), became the wife of Chu Yüan-chang and eventually his empress. Her father, whose personal name is not even given in the records, left home because of a murder, taking his family to Ting-yüan 定遠 in the same province. As the political situation worsened towards the close of the Yüan dynasty, several areas in the region became the locale of rebellious bands; so her father and her mother, née Cheng 鄭, were obliged to move again. This time their baby daughter was entrusted to her father's close friend, Kuo Tzu-hsing (*q.v.*), who accepted her in his household and brought her up as a foster child. In 1369 her parents were granted the posthumous titles of prince and princess of Hsü (徐王 and 徐王夫人) and were honored in Su-chou by the erection of tombs and a shrine. The empress mourned her parents and welcomed the honors accorded them, but she dissuaded the emperor from extending the honor of official posts to surviving members of her clan.

Her shrewd good sense was already evident in the years before she became empress. As a child she had worked in the fields; so her feet remained unbound. Though largely self-taught, she reportedly became not only literate, but even well read. In 1352, when Kuo Tzu-hsing was occupying Hao-chou 濠州 (Anhwei) with the army he had raised against the Mongols, he and his concubine, née Chang 張, gave her in marriage to Chu Yüan-chang, then serving as Kuo's bodyguard. She was twenty years of age and Chu twenty-five. During the subsequent events which led to his emergence as rebel-leader, she served him as secretary in charge of his documents and records as well as manager of his household. By retaining the friendship of Kuo Tzu-hsing's consort, she secured an advocate for Chu Yüan-chang against General Kuo's rising doubts as to Chu's loyalty. When the general ordered Chu confined and denied food, in the hope of starving him to death or making him more docile, she prepared food secretly, taking up cakes so hot from the stove and hiding them in her clothes so that she burned her breasts severely. During Chu's later occupation of T'ai-p'ing 太平 (Anhwei), she, on her own initiative, rescued the families of his officers by moving them across the Yangtze ahead of the attacking Mongols. She made and distributed clothes and shoes to Chu's troops. During a critical battle in 1360, she increased the devotion of his soldiers by sending to the front all Chu's reserves of gold and silver, to be given as rewards for loyalty and bravery. She also is said to have persuaded Chu to restrain his troops from random and unnecessary slaughter.

When he was enthroned in January, 1368, he reminded the court of her role in his rise to power, comparing her services to those of General Feng I (d. A.D. 34), who sustained with porridge and wheatcakes Liu Hsiu, the future emperor of the Eastern Han (r. A.D. 25–57), and her steadfastness to that of Empress Chang-sun, wife of Li Shih-min (r. 626–49) of the T'ang. To such praise the new empress made the tart reply, "It is easy for husband and wife to cherish each other, but hard for an emperor and his courtiers to maintain lasting devotion. I am glad the emperor does not forget that his comrades endured the years of hardship also." She showed similar astuteness when Chu's officers, who had occupied the Mongol capital, presented him with jewels seized from the Mongol palaces. Examining them and noting their worth, she inquired if they could be compared with what was of even greater value to an emperor. He sensed her thought and remarked, "A man of virtue and ability, you mean, is the most valuable possession of state." She bowed in assent, reminding him of the dangers inherent in their sudden rise from obscurity to power. On another occasion she spoke of the confusion that might result from a frequent modification of the laws. Considering her comments worthy of preservation, the emperor had one of the literary women at court make a record of them.

The empress often advised Chu in specific cases, and sometimes succeeded in restraining him from hasty decisions. When he was about to order the execution of the son of a military administrator solely because of a rumor that the son was extremely unfilial the empress insisted on investigation of the rumor, which proved to be false. The emperor acknowledged that her intervention had been timely and wise. In another case she prevented the emperor from unjustly demoting his nephew and adopted son, Li Wen-chung (*q.v.*), whom Yang Hsien 楊憲 (T. 希武, early *ming* 慈, executed 1370) had falsely accused. She also managed to save the life of Shen Fu (*q.v.*), a wealthy commoner who, having already subscribed a third of the cost for the Nanking city wall, offered also to contribute funds for further reimbursement of the troops. This offer aroused the emperor who suspected that Shen Fu might, by buying favor of the troops, be plotting rebellion. Through the appeal of the empress, who argued that Shen had broken no law in making his offer, the emperor desisted from his original intent to have Shen executed and exiled him to Yunnan instead. She also intervened on behalf of prisoners who, ordered to labor on the city wall, were being driven beyond their strength.

Her persuasions likewise improved the lot of metropolitan officials. Pointing out to the emperor that these officials, along with wives and servants, had suffered hardship in moving from their former homes, she secured for them additional allowances. Discovering that several thousand students at the National Academy received a grain allowance for themselves but no provision for their wives, she brought about the institution of a special granary from which the government issued allowances to them. When the emperor once rebuked her for inquiring about the prosperity and contentment of the people, saying that this was not

her province, she countered by reminding him that she was as much the mother of the people as he was their father. During periods of drought she herself and all the ladies of the palace took only frugal meals and prayed for rain. During famines she distributed wheat, rice, and soup to the people. Though the emperor approved such measures as a temporary expedient, she urged him also to build up grain reserves in good years to anticipate emergencies.

Within the palace she was equally astute and active. She wore clothes of coarse silk, much washed, patched, and mended. Learning that Qubilai's empress had recovered silk thread by boiling the strings of old bows, she and her women also recovered thread by this method. Some of it they wove into quilts which were given to old people who had no children, and some they used to make garments for the princesses and the princes' consorts, not only as an economy but also to remind the young people of the work involved in producing cloth. But the empress' economies were not due to parsimony; in such matters as proper food for courtiers and other palace guests, she tested dishes from the kitchens and insisted that all the food be palatable and well served. When her ladies in waiting protested her giving personal attention to all the emperor's meals, she replied that he was a hotheaded man and his temper might get out of hand unless his food were well prepared. When on one occasion the emperor, objecting that the soup was not hot enough, angrily upset the bowl and spilled it on her, she scolded no one but quietly had a warmer serving brought in. Toward all residents of the palace she was well disposed, cordial to women whom the emperor favored and who had borne him sons, and friendly to the wives of courtiers. On one occasion, finding the emperor in a fit of anger directed against one of the palace women, the empress pretended to be even more angry and ordered the woman off to the staff surveillance office. When the emperor asked why the empress had interfered with his punishing the woman then and there, the empress replied, "When you are in a temper, your punishments tend to be excessive. The staff officials will deal justly with her case. Even a criminal, I think, should not be judged by you but should be turned over to the proper officials." The emperor then asked why she too had upbraided the woman; she replied, "To reduce your anger." Her consideration, however, did not countenance lack of discipline. When the emperor objected because a teacher of the princes struck one of them over the head for inattention, the empress prevented the emperor from interfering. Remarking that a teacher's function in the palace was different from that of palace women or eunuchs, she added, "As brocade, in the process of weaving, needs shearing, so do children, undergoing instruction, require punishment. Indulging children does no good."

The empress herself also continued to study, gathering around her a group of women of like interests, with whom she read ancient texts. One day in discussing Taoism, which had been much admired by Empress Tou (d. 135 B.C.) of the Han dynasty, the empress suggested that the virtues of filial piety, tenderness, benevolence, and justice must have been interdependent and inseparable. She particularly admired several Sung dynasty empresses and had their household rules written down for special study. When one of her associates criticized the Sung as too merciful, the empress retorted, "Better too merciful than too oppressive." She showed her own sense of mercy notably in the case of Chancellor Sung Lien (*q. v.*), whom the emperor was about to condemn to death because of the involvement of Sung's grandson, Sung Shen (*see* Sung Lien) in the case of Hu Wei-yung (*q.v.*). The empress protested the death sentence against Sung Lien, reminding the emperor that Sung had taught their children for a number of years, and that an emperor should show no less concern

for his children's instructor than ordinary people for theirs. She argued further that the elderly gentleman had long since retired to his native place and was unlikely to have any knowledge of the affairs of his grandson. When the emperor refused to be moved by her pleas, she in her turn refused to eat. Asked to explain, she replied that she was keeping fast and praying to the gods for a show of mercy on his part. The emperor was sufficiently moved that, though Sung Lien was banished to Szechwan, he remitted the death penalty.

The empress retained interest in the national welfare even on her deathbed. When the emperor and his court wished to order sacrifices and to summon doctors to attend her, she rejected the sacrifices, saying, "Death and life are decreed," and especially forbade the calling of physicians because, she added, "If their treatments are of no avail, you will blame them and so bring hardship upon them." When the emperor asked her for a final message, she replied, "May you always seek out virtuous and able men, listen to their advice, and not act hastily. May our descendants be worthy and our subjects obedient." At her death the emperor is said to have mourned her deeply, and no new empress was designated. Ladies of the palace, who were devoted to her, sang an ode composed to her memory.

How many children the empress had is a matter of controversy. According to the official account she bore five sons and two daughters. The sons were the heir apparent Chu Piao (*q.v.*), Chu Shuang, Chu Kang (for both *see* Chu Yüan-chang), Chu Ti and Chu Su (*qq.v.*). The daughters were An-ch'ing kung-chu and Ning-kuo kung-chu (*q.v.*). The unofficial view is quite different. The extreme one is that she had no sons at all, and that the twenty-six sons of Chu Yüan-chang —including the heir apparent and Chu Ti—were all born to various concubines. The empress was interred at Hsiao-ling 孝 陵 at Nanking on October 31, 1382. In 1403 she was canonized as Hsiao-tz'u Kao-huang-hou 孝慈高皇后. A portrait of her is preserved in the Palace Museum, Peking.

All records agree that Empress Ma was a woman of much native good sense, who exercised considerable influence on the first emperor. She contributed in various ways during the early days to the founding of the dynasty, and later she often acted as a restraining force upon her husband's highly suspicious and ruthless nature. Of the many stories told about her, factual as well as fictional, most have happy endings with some one or some people being saved or benefited. One anecdote, however, ends differently. If it really happened, in all likelihood it was without her knowledge. The story relates that one year during the festival celebrating the first full moon of the first month, Chu Yüan-chang went out of the palace incognito to see the capital. As was the custom in Nanking and in many other places throughout the empire, the Shang-yüan 上元 celebration was a time not only to display lanterns of all shapes and colors, but also to post riddles in the streets. One riddle which Chu noticed was a picture of a barefoot woman carrying a watermelon in her bosom. In Chinese the watermelon is known as hsi-kua 西瓜, and to carry something in one's bosom is huai 懷. He immediately guessed the answer of this riddle to be "the woman of Huai-hsi 淮西 with big feet." Huai-hsi is the geographical term for the region from which the empress came, while Huai 淮 for the Huai River and huai for bosom are of course homophonous. The emperor, incensed by this joke at his wife's expense, took vengeance by ordering the execution of many people in that neighborhood on the following day. The degree of reliability of this story may be questioned, but it does support the contention that the empress was physically strong and had unbound feet. [Editors' note: The story of Empress Ma's life can not be fully ascertained because the records of the early years of the Ming dynasty have been altered and rewritten a number of times. According to T'an Ch'ien (q. v.), when her father brought her to Ting-yüan, there was a famine and her parents were forced by hunger to sell her. Hence her early status in Kuo's home was probably that of a slave girl serving one of Kuo's concubines. It was because Kuo wanted to secure the loyalty of Chu Yüan-chang that he gave her to him as wife and, to make the relationship more intimate and binding, raised her to the status of a foster daughter. This seems to be the true story, and it does not detract at all from her good name. On the contrary, it shows that she learned early how to overcome difficulties and master any kind of situation.]

Bibliography

1/113/3a, 300/4a; 3/106/3a; 5/3/4a; 61/20/1a; 81/x/16; MSL (1962), T'ai-tsu, *ch.* 147; KC (1958), 352, 624; Hsia Hsieh 夏燮, *Ming t'ung-chien* 明通鑑 (*ca.* 1870), 7/402; Wu Han (BDRC), *Ming T'ai-tsu*, Chungking, 1944; *id.*, *Chu Yüan-chang chuan* (Shanghai, 1949), with a portrait of Empress Ma reproduced from *Ku-kung chou-k'an* 故宮週刊 (Palace Museum Weekly), Vol. 16, no. 368 (July 18, 1934), 1; Hsieh Chin, *T'ien-huang yü-tieh* in *Sheng-ch'ao i-shih ch'u-pien* 勝朝遺事初編, compiled by Wu Mi-kuang 吳彌光, published 1883; Hsü Chen-ch'ing, *Chien-sheng yeh-wen* in *Sheng-ch'ao i-shih ch'u-pien*.

Chou Tao-chi

MA Huan 馬歡 (T. 宗道, H. 會乩山樵), fl. 1413-51, Muslim interpreter, who voyaged on several of the expeditions to the Indian Ocean organized by Cheng Ho (*q. v.*), was a native of K'uai-chi 會稽, Chekiang. He came of humble origin, but was sufficiently literate, both in Chinese and Arabic, to qualify for a post on at least three of Cheng's voyages, the fourth (1413-15), sixth (1421-22), and seventh (1431-33). When he took off for the first time, he must have felt elated at the sight of strange lands and peoples, writing down what he saw and heard. Beginning in 1415, he began to edit the notes, perhaps consulting some earlier works on south Asian countries such as the *Tao-i chih-lüeh* 島夷志畧 by Wang Ta-yüan

汪大淵 (mid-14th century). About 1416 he had apparently completed the first version of his account, which he named the *Ying-yai sheng-lan* 瀛涯勝覽 (Captivating views of the ocean's shores), 1 *ch.* Then he made additions and corrections after the two subsequent voyages. Conceivably there existed at least three original versions of this work in manuscript. In 1451 he wrote a colophon to the final draft which was probably printed in the same year by a fellow Muslim, Kuo Ch'ung-li (*see* Cheng Ho), who had also served as an interpreter on the same voyages. Unfortunately, this first printed edition is no longer extant. The work must have circulated in several versions in manuscript, for it appears that each available printed edition differs more or less from the others, depending on the particular manuscript copy from which it came. The best known versions are the two printed by Shen Chieh-fu (*q.v.*) in his *Chi-lu hui-pien* of 1616; this includes besides Ma's text an abridged and reworded version edited by Chang Sheng 張昇 (T. 啓昭, H. 柏崖, Pth. 文僖, 1442–1517, optimus 1469). Among the other versions may be mentioned the one in the *Kuo-ch'ao tien-ku* 國朝典故, edited by a Ming imperial clansman, Chu Tang-mien 朱當㴐 (H. 望洋子, fl. 1522–44, a great-great-grandson of Chu T'an, tenth son of Chu Yüan-chang. Making use of these and later texts, Feng Ch'eng-chün (BDRC) compiled his collated edition *Ying-yai sheng-lan chiao-chu* 校注 (1935). Thirty-five years later appeared the English translation with extensive notes by J. V. G. Mills.

Ma asserts that he visited twenty of the countries mentioned in his book. These included Champa, several ports in Java, Malacca, various countries in Sumatra, Bengal, Ceylon, southwest India (the Malabar coast), Hormuz, and southern Arabia, and it is quite likely that he made the pilgrimage to Mecca.

For other contemporary accounts of Cheng Ho's voyages, see Fei Hsin (*q.v.*).

Bibliography

1/97/29b; *T'ai-ts'ang-chou chih* (1500, repr. 1909), 8/12b; SK (1930), 78/4b; Fei Hsin, *Hsing-ch'a sheng-lan* (various editions in collections and the recent *chiao-chu* edition of Feng Ch'eng-chün, 1935); Kung Chen, *Hsi-yang fan-kuo chih* (the edition annotated by Hsiang Ta 向達, 1961); Ma Huan, *Ying-yai sheng-lan: The overall Survey of the Ocean's Shores (1433)*, tr. and ed. by J. V. G. Mills (Cambridge, 1970); J. J. L. Duyvendak, *Ma Huan Re-examined* (Amsterdam, 1933); *id.*, "The True Dates of the Chinese Maritime Expeditions in the Early Fifteenth Century," TP, 34 (1938), 341; P. Pelliot, "Les grands voyages maritimes chinois au début du XVe siècle," TP, 30 (1933), 237; *id.*, "Notes additionelles sur Tcheng Houo et sur ses voyages," TP, 31 (1935), 274; *id.*, "Encore à propos des voyages de Tcheng Houo," TP, 32 (1936), 210; W. W. Rockhill, "Notes on the Relations and Trade of China with the Eastern Archipelago and the Coasts of the Indian Ocean during the Fourteenth Century," TP, 16 (1915), 61; Joseph Needham, *Science and Civilization in China*, IV: 3 (Cambridge, England, 1971), 492.

Wang Gungwu

MA Wen-sheng 馬文升 (T. 負圖, H. 約齋, 三峯居士, 友松道人, Pth. 端肅), 1426–July 13, 1510, an official, was a native of Chün 鈞 sub-prefecture, Honan. A *chin-shih* of 1451, he attracted the attention of Wang Chih 王直 (*q.v.*), then minister of Personnel, and was appointed a censor in 1452. He served as an investigating censor in Shansi (1454) and Hukuang (1456). From 1459 to 1462 he remained at home mourning the loss of his mother. In 1463 he was sent to Fukien as surveillance commissioner. Two years later he became chief minister of the Grand Court of Revision in Nanking, his duties in the post being soon interrupted by the death of his father.

In 1468 the natural fortress of Shih-ch'eng 石城, northwest of Ku-yüan 固原 in northeast Kansu, was captured by a local bandit known as Man-ssu (*see* Hsiang Chung). When local authorities proved unable to cope with the situation, Ma Wen-sheng was brought in as vice censor-in-chief of the right and governor of Shensi. He accompanied the supreme commander Hsiang Chung to the scene and was largely responsible for the strategem of isolating the fortress by burning the grass around it and cutting off its access to water. The city fell with the destruction of a large number of the enemy, and Ma was promoted to vice censor-in-chief of the left, retaining the post of governor.

He served on the northwest frontier for eight years with distinction, rebuffing numerous invasion attempts by the Mongols, and in 1476 was brought into the ministry of War as vice-minister of the right. In the eighth month of the same year Ma went to Liaotung to clean up the corrupt local administration of Ch'en Yüeh (see Wang Chih). In the accomplishment of the task he earned the enmity not only of Ch'en Yüeh but also of Ch'en's protector, the powerful palace eunuch, Wang Chih 汪直 (q.v.). The two men conspired to blacken Ma's record in Liaotung by accusing him of stirring up border difficulties unnecessarily, specifically by refusing to trade agricultural implements with the Jurchen. Despite his defense that he had refused them not agricultural tools but (potential) iron weapons, Ma was removed from Liaotung (in 1479) and sent out to garrison Chungking. After both the eunuch Wang Chih and Ch'en Yüeh fell from their positions of influence Ma was vindicated and returned to Liaotung in 1483 as vice censor-in-chief of the left and governor. The people welcomed him back for a year's administration characterized by stability and justice after which he was made supreme commander of the Grand Canal.

On December 30, 1485, he was called to the capital to become minister of War but was transferred (October 13, 1486) to Nanking due to the machinations of the clever Li Tzu-sheng (see Liang Fang), an adept who enjoyed a position of trust and influence with the emperor, Chu Chien-shen, (q. v.). With the ascent to the throne of Chu Yu-t'ang (q.v.), however, Ma was restored to office as head of the Censorate near the close of 1487. In March, 1489, he once again became minister of War. Ma set about tightening up the mili-

tary bureaucracy, which had become lax in the period of relative peace immediately preceding, thereby making many enemies among families whose members were victims of his personnel reforms. So great became the threat to his safety that the emperor felt impelled to assign a bodyguard to protect him, much to his discomfiture.

In his tenure as minister of War in the last decade of the 16th century Ma emphasized prudence in the use of armed force, preferring always to achieve submission of hostile elements through the application of pressure and threat combined with willingness to negotiate the resumption of peaceful relations. When direct military action was clearly the most efficient means of securing the end in view, he applied it as a specific; he would dispatch a punitive expedition of appropriate strength to the spot where it would have maximum effect. An instance was his handling of the sultan of Ili, Youldang, and the Turfan khanate, Ahmad (q.v.), who seized the city of Hami in 1488. The situation was this: Hami had been taken in 1482 by the native chieftain Han-shen (see Ahmad), whom the Chinese promptly recognized as regent. In 1488 Ahmad attacked Hami and slew Han-shen. The following year the Chinese, under the direction of Ma, retook the stronghold. An uneasy truce ensued. Three years later, on the advice of Ma, who clearly recognized the ascendancy of the Mongols in the region, the Chinese court conferred the title, Chung-shun wang 忠順王, on Shan-pa 陝巴 (grandnephew of Toγtō 脱脱, d. 1410). In 1493 Ahmad seized Hami again, captured Shan-pa, and put the Turfan khanate in firm control of the entire region. Ma Wen-sheng, dissatisfied with the government's handling of the affair, set in motion a campaign to retake Hami (see Hsü Chin), as a result of which the Turfan people fled and Hami once more came under Chinese influence, but not for long.

In matters other than military, Ma also had the ear of the emperor; it was largely due to his advice that the heir apparent's education emphasized traditional Confucian values to the exclusion of Buddhist and Taoist influences. He saw it as his duty not merely to put down rebellion but also to prevent it. He frequently promoted distribution of relief supplies to areas of economic distress, and he was always quick to decry excessive imposts which would cause discontent and restiveness among the people. On March 29, 1501, Ma became minister of Personnel and stood as one of the most highly regarded and respected ministers of state. He rose from grand protector of the heir apparent to junior protector and grand tutor of the heir apparent.

The emperor (Chu Yu-t'ang) continued to rely heavily upon Ma up to the close of his reign in 1505. It is recorded, for example, that the emperor met with him privately one day in 1504 to request a survey and evaluation of the officials of the empire. Ma was nearly eighty at the time, but the emperor spoke with voice raised to compensate for the old man's increasing deafness. He had his attendants brace Ma as he descended the stairs on his departure from the consultation. Ma's recommendations, drawn from his own sources of information, apparently tallied well with the special evaluation reports which appeared the following year, an indication of his comprehensive grasp of the problems of personnel. He was rewarded with the title junior preceptor and grand preceptor of the heir apparent. When the emperor died, the loyal courtier followed the funeral cortege on foot for a distance of 20 *li*.

The new emperor, Chu Hou-chao (*q. v.*), was under the influence of eunuchs in the early part of his reign, and the narrowly righteous and still influential Ma Wen-sheng stood as an obstacle to their ambitions. In 1506, being allowed to resign, he was removed from office to make room for Chiao Fang (*q.v.*) as minister of Personnel. In October, 1508, the eunuch Liu Chin (*q.v.*) had become so

powerful that he was able to bring Ma to trial and revoke his liberal pension. Two years later, the latter died at the age of eighty-five, just after Chiao Fang himself had been cashiered (July 4).

A year later Ma Wen-sheng's honors were restored. He was praised for his talents in both civil and military affairs; his greatest gift lay in his deft selection of means most appropriate to the end. Stern and taciturn by nature, he would often sit silently through lengthy court discussions and then with a word or two provide decisive resolution of the dispute.

Among the writings of Ma Wen-sheng still extant are *Ma Tuan-su san-chi* 馬端肅三記 in 3 *chüan*, and *Ma Tuan-su tsou-i* 奏議 in 16 *chüan*. The *San-chi*, first printed about 1520 and reprinted in several editions, records three highlights in the author's career. These are the *Hsi-cheng shih-ch'eng chi* 西征石城記 about his campaign against Man-ssu, the *Fu-an tung-i chi* 撫安東夷記 on his reforms in Liaotung, and the *Hsing-fu Ha-mi chi* 興復哈密記 about his restoration of Hami. The *Ssu-k'u* catalogue records these titles but the works were listed among the prohibited books because of the anti-Jurchen expressions. The *Tsou-i* contains 55 memorials of Ma Wen-sheng, together with some commemorative pieces, brought together by his grandson Ma T'ien-yu 馬天祐 in 1547. This too was prohibited in the 18th century, but has survived.

Bibliography

Hsing-lüeh 行畧 and *Mu-chih-ming* 墓誌銘 in the 19th-century reprint of the *Ma Tuan-su tsou-i*; 1/182/8b; 3/165/7b; 5/24/87a; 40/21/7b; 63/16/331; 84/丙/12b; KC (1958), 2479; Sun Tien-ch'i (1957), 134; D. Pokotilov, *History of the Eastern Mongols during the Ming Dynasty from 1368 to 1634*, tr. by R. Loewenthal (Chengtu, 1947), 90: P. Pelliot, *TP*, 38 (1950), 137: W. Franke, *Sources*, 5. 4. 12, 7. 3. 5, 4.3, 10. 2.

Benjamin E. Wallacker

MAC Dang-dung 莫登庸, December 22, 1483–September 11, 1541, who rose to be a powerful Annamite minister and foun-

der of the Mac dynasty—this act leading
to a crisis in relations with the Ming—,
was a native of the coastal regions of
Hai-duong 海楊 province deep in the Red
River delta to the east of the Annamite
capital of Thang-long 昇龍 (Hanoi).
His dynasty lasted sixty-five years (to
1592) before being overturned in the
great restoration of the Lê dynasty (*see*
Lê Lọ'i), which Mac Dang-dung had overthrown. Though remnants of the Mac
clan survived thereafter in the northern
hills of Annam, on the Chinese border
protected by the Ming, for another
eighty-five years (until 1677), they had
come to be seen as usurpers, and little
documentary material on which they may
be judged has come down. Two major
sources now exist for reconstructing Mac
Dang-dung's career: first, that section of
Ngo Si-lien 吳士蓮, *Dai-Viet su ky toan
thu* 大越史記全書 (hereafter known as
TT) covering the years up to 1527, and
probably compiled by Mac historians
assigned to write the history of the then
defunct Lê dynasty; second, a chapter in
the section on "rebels" which the 18th
century Annamite historian Lê Quy-don
黎貴惇 included in his *Dai-Viet thong su
通史* (hereafter known as TS), written
under Lê/Trinh 鄭 rule. (The Trinh, one
of two major families which supported
the Lê in their restoration, had come to
hold the major power in the realm.)

From these two sources, one favorable, the other hostile, one may sort out
the major lines of Mac Dang-dung's life.
Both sources relate that he came from an
impoverished fisherman's family descended
from the great Confucian minister of the
early 14th century, Mac Dinh-chi 梃之.
[Editors' note: A Chinese source asserts
that he was descended from a Tanka 蛋
家 (boat population) family in Tung-kuan
東莞, Kwangtung.] According to the TS
(but not the TT), the decline of the
family had taken place because, four
generations earlier, the Mac had actively
aided and served the Ming invaders of
the early 15th century, and, on Lê Lọ'i's

great success, had had to move deeper
into the Red River delta of Hai-duong
province. Mac Dang-dung's grandfather
moved all the way to the coast, and
there the boy was born and grew up, fishing for a living. A strong and courageous
youth, who may well have benefited
from the strong Confucian tradition of
his family, he was recruited for a military
examination, in which he excelled, during
the turbulent reign of Lê Tuan 濬 (1505-
9). Initially stationed near the emperor,
Mac moved rapidly up the ranks until,
in 1508, he was named to the command
of one of the capital units (天武衛). This
period, following the peaceful reigns of
Lê Hao 灝 (1460-97) and his son Lê
Huy 暉 (1498-1504), during which the
Chinese model had been fully adopted,
marked the return of regional factionalism and bloodshed to the court. The
opposing faction of the Nguyen 阮 family
had taken refuge in its home province of
Thanh-hoa 清化 to the south. Mac survived the fall of the hated Lê Tuan, and
in 1511 received the title of earl of Vu-
xuyen 武川伯 from the latter's successor
Lê Oanh 瀅 (1510-16), backed by the
Thanh-hoa group. He thus became a member of the nobility. About this time the
TT records a unanimous prophecy of "imperial air" rising in the east, no doubt a
device of the Mac historians in later
decades. Soon afterwards, it would
appear, his father died, and we hear no
more of Mac until 1516 or 1517. The
young officer had probably retired to his
home for the required mourning period;
in all likelihood he took advantage of
the time to increase his Confucian knowledge, being close friends with a scholar
who "perfected" him, as the TS notes.

Weakened by the earlier court conflict
and, we are told, by licentiousness in the
capital, the country fell into a state of
rebellion, chaos, and warfare from 1515
on. In this climate, Mac Dang-dung, "inside, hiding his treachery, while outside
professing simplicity and straightforwardness" (according to Lê Quy-don), began

a steady rise in power until, by 1527, he sat on the throne. His way was paved for him by the destructive intrigue of the two major families, the Nguyen and the Trinh, both established from the previous century and neighbors of the imperial home in Thanh-hoa. By 1516 Trinh Duy-san 惟憻 and Nguyen Hoang-du 弘裕 were both major figures in Lê Oanh's court. The great rebellion of Tran Cao 陳高, who claimed descent from the Tran dynasty of the 14th century and to be a reincarnation of Indra, shook the capital, and led to Lê Oanh's removal by the Trinh, against the wishes of the Nguyen. The threat of Tran Cao, however, caused the two families to unite and place the fourteen-year-old Lê Y 椅 (1516 -22) on the throne. In the following campaign against Tran Cao, Trinh Duy-san was killed, and his adopted son Tran Chan 眞 took his place. At this time, Mac Dang-dung received the appointment of defender of Son-nam 山南 province south of the capital and also that of assistant general and left commissioner-in-chief. As the political atmosphere in the court heated up, particularly with the continued rivalry of the two great families, Mac attempted to make his own way amidst the intrigue. In a battle between the Trinh and the Nguyen in mid-1517, Tran Chan drove Nguyen Hoang-du south to his home in Thanh-hoa, and took the preeminent role in the court. Mac appears to have tried to avoid joining either side, instead making himself a servant of the throne. He became involved in civil matters in the court, apparently for the first time, and submitted two lengthy memorials to the throne, one against preachers of heterodox doctrines, and the other against a traitor, formerly a major figure, who he thought deserved punishment. Using orthodox Confucian phraseology, beginning with humaneness 仁 and righteousness 義 against the heterodox, and the three great rules 綱 and five virtues 常 against the traitor, Mac gave the emperor the advice that was followed, and Lê Y

honored him for his direct and forthright approach to affairs. By early 1518 Mac had become a marquis 侯 of Vu-xuyen.

Now the king's man, Mac became Lê Y's instrument against the families; yet he was also cautious when acting against either one. Fearing the power of Tran Chan at court, Mac betrothed the latter's daughter to his son, Mac Dang-doanh 瀛. On the other hand, when sent to pursue Nguyen Hoang-du into Thanh-hoa, Mac Dang-dung made a deal with him and allowed him to escape. In the autumn of 1518, however, the pattern changed as Lê Y decided to rid himself of Tran Chan and his followers. Tran Chan was killed at the walls of the palace, but the counterattack of his followers devastated the capital, and drove Lê Y north into Kinh-bac 京北 province as his support crumbled. Lê Y called on Nguyen Hoang-du for aid, but he did not respond. As a Mac historian noted in the TT, "Seeing this situation was quite sufficient to know that the Lê dynasty would not rise again."

During this period, Mac Dang-dung had been consolidating his home base in Hai-duong and gathering local troops. He was therefore ready when Lê Y, seeing that he had no alternative, sent envoys to call him and his naval force back from the east. The next three years (to mid-1521) mark Mac's rise to power (and his evil scheming, as Lê Quy-don puts it, using bandits and local powers to kill the high ministers and to weaken the authority of the emperor). Mac and his supporters immediately began to take control of the government and to eliminate the opposition, while they maneuvered Lê Y back into power in the capital. In the process, Mac steadily rose in rank, becoming Minh quan-cong 明君公, Nhan quoc 仁國-cong, and commander of the military and naval posts throughout the thirteen provinces. The elite military units came under his control, and the generals joined his side. Yet Lê Y continued to trust him, and made an imperial visit to his home in mid-1521, there giving him the high position of Grand Tutor 太傅.

While Mac's influence expanded in the capital, the control of the government over the countryside increased as he crushed the remnants of the earlier revolts and other opposition. His power "grew day by day," reaching into all parts of the capital, and he was able "to observe the emperor both in action and in repose." His younger brother, the Dong quan-cong Mac Quyet 橛, took charge of the army, and his eldest son, Mac Dang-doanh, became Duc-mi 毓美 marquis. As Lê Y became increasingly isolated, he secretly sought aid from his kin the Trinh family and fled the capital, going west to Son-tay 山西 province, leaving his queen and younger brother Lê An 安 behind. Bloody fighting erupted as Mac Dang-dung's forces pursued the emperor. Mac immediately began to plan to put Prince Lê An on the throne. Gradually the government fell behind Lê An (1522–27) and he became the ruler, later to receive the posthumous title of Cung Hoang De 恭皇帝. Lê Y's forces, however, held the territory north, west, and south of the capital, while Mac fell back to his base in the east and northeast. Despite considerable pressure for several months, Mac was finally able to establish Lê An in the capital and gain control of the countryside as Lê Y's support ebbed away, and he was taken back to Thanh-hoa by the Trinh family.

Almost immedately, from the beginning of 1523, Mac began to put the Annamite state back into order again. The Confucian examinations were held, after a delay due to the civil strife, and an order went out to record and worship the spirits in the local temples. Meanwhile Mac kept up the military pressure on Thanh-hoa, forcing the Trinh to take Lê Y into the mountains while reducing his rank to that of prince 王. The next three years (1524–26) saw Mac completely consolidate his position. The young emperor made him prime minister (平章軍國重事), established the land and population regis-

ters, and honored the former emperors and their consorts. The harvests were good, and Mac Dang-dung made steady progress against the Trinh in Thanh-hoa, leading an expedition south himself, defeating them, and capturing Lê Y. Though a stalwart, last-ditch Confucian loyalty sprang up on the former emperor's return, Mac put it down bloodily, and justified his action in an imperial edict proclaiming the need for a peace and security denied by the preceding emperors, and citing the actions of the earliest Lê rulers (with a comparison also to the Chou and the Han of China). Regulations were promulgated for maintaining the capital and for fair procedures in selecting officials, the examinations were held again, and the dikes repaired. Mac, behind the throne, was bringing the state once more to the Confucian order established by Lê Hao less than a hundred years before.

By 1527 Mac Dang-dung was prepared to move. Lê Y was quietly killed; then Lê An came amid pomp and ceremony to Mac's home village in Hai-duong, and made him a prince (An-hung 安興 vuong), later presenting him with a poem comparing him to the Duke of Chou. Mac repaid the visit, and the following month forced Lê An to abdicate, taking the throne himself amid, according to reports (by both the TT and the TS), the acclamation of the people. Lê An, like his elder brother before him, was demoted, jailed, and slain.

Mac Dang-dung in 1527–29, having set up his new dynasty, continued his efforts to maintain a strong Confucian state in Annam. He held the Nam-giao 南郊 ceremony of worship of Heaven, established his ancestral temple honoring seven generations of his paternal line (back to Mac Dinh-chi), and gave his home village and province special recognition. His eldest son, Mac Dang-doanh, became heir apparent, his brothers were made princes, and his entire family was placed within the imperial context. Loyal followers received the name Mac, and all of them were rewarded. Mac Dang-dung's birthday became an imperial festival (乾寧聖節). The writings of the later Lê historians (those in the second half of the 17th century who continued the TT from 1528, and Le Quy-don) have portrayed the Mac as having had no alternative to maintaining the Lê institutions if they were to survive. ("The ministers and the people were losing hope; there was much discontent throughout the land.") This was probably not the case. Mac Dang-dung would seem to have had a firm personal belief in maintaining what the Lê had established. Indeed, the first two decades of his dynasty show a strong commitment not only to adapting but to improving the use of the Chinese model as adopted by the Lê. The history appears to have been written, as was proper, covering the previous dynasty (1428-1527), and, while the first five reigns of the Lê (1428-1504) were seen as exemplary, the last four reigns (1505-27) were felt to have demonstrated that the dynasty had lost all effectiveness. The examination system was maintained with sessions faithfully every three years, strictly following the Lê regulations. In 1529 a stele commemorating the first examinations of the dynasty was erected ("this marks the beginning of the civilization of the empire"), and the Mac seem to have carried out their duties with regard to the cult of learning throughout the sixty-five years of their rule in Thang-long. Laws from the reign of Lê Hao were compiled into a code, the *Hong-duc thien-chinh thu* 洪德善政書, and supplemented, particularly for matters dealing with ancestral land. The bureaucratic structure was maintained for administration, and an up-to-date edition of the 1471 administrative document of Lê Hao appears to have been published in these years—the *Hoang-trieu quan-che dien-le* 皇朝官制典例—, including a list of the administrative units and the villages of the realm differing from that of fifty years before. Basically, Mac kept the structure and recruiting pattern

of the Lê government, changing only the military, land, and salary patterns.

Mac Dang-dung abdicated in 1530, making his son Mac Dang-doanh emperor, (1530-40) and taking the title Thai Thuong Hoang 太上皇. Through the 1530s and beyond, the historical records reflect more the history of the Lê, as written by their historians, than of the Mac. The latter tried time and again to wipe out their opposition, the partisans of the Lê, in Thanh-hoa (1530, 1531, 1532). Out of the varied revolts arose the beginning of the Lê restoration. Nguyen Kim 淦, of the same family as Nguyen Hoang-du, set up Lê Y's son, Lê Ninh (*see* Mao Po-wen), as the Lê claimant, in the Lao hills 哀牢 in 1532. Nguyen Kim was joined by his son-in-law, Trinh Kiem 檢, of the former rival family. Together the forces of the Nguyen and Trinh families were eventually able to put the Lê back on the throne (1592), and their descendants were to be dominant throughout Annam, in one manner or another, until the end of the monarchy in 1945.

During Mac Dang-dung's lifetime, the Lê forces in Thanh-hoa were more a nuisance than a threat. The battlefield was rather the court of China where the Mac sought recognition, and the Lê sought to damn the Mac. In 1528, Mac Dang-dung had sent an envoy to Peking with the message that no heir of the Lê existed, and that the Mac had temporarily taken over the affairs of the country. The Ming seem to have paid little attention, though the Lê historians assert that the Chinese had sent a secret envoy to check on the situation, and that the Mac had used smooth words, gold, and territory to protect themselves; this, of course, being a Lê explanation for the tolerance shown the Mac in Peking. In this way, we are told, were adherents of the Lê put aside. Only in 1533, when Lê Ninh had officially claimed the throne, did the Lê send an envoy to Peking with immediate recognition on the Chinese part and the dispatch of an army—again according to the Lê historians—, this probably reflecting later events. In reality the question did not come up in Peking until 1536, with the birth of the Chinese heir apparent and the matter of sending missions announcing the fact to the tributary states. Hsia Yen (*q.v.*), minister of Rites and new grand secretary, argued against the Mac regime and called for its suppression.

The affair promptly became part of court politics as the parties argued whether the Ancestral Instructions of the first emperor not to attack small countries were or were not applicable to the case. In addition, when mobilization plans were drawn up for the campaign, argument also raged over the feasibility of such direct action. Those against it pointed to the prohibitive cost, not to mention the potential danger from the northern border. Then in 1537 an envoy from Lê Ninh arrived (sent the year before), and eloquently presented his case. Yen Sung (*q.v.*), new minister of Rites and enemy of Hsia Yen, attacked the Lê position and drew support from the anti-war faction, at least until the emperor, Chu Hou-ts'ung (*q.v.*), expressed himself in favor of Hsia Yen; whereupon Yen Sung changed sides. The emperor, however, suspended the war preparations. From 1537 to 1539 differing border officials urged varying courses of action. The Ming court was split and indecisive.

At first the Mac attempted to explain how they had come to the throne, insisting again that the Lê had left no successors, and that Lê Ninh was in reality a son of Nguyen Kim who had taken the Lê name. Then, in 1538, Mac Dang-dung began to grope for terms whereby his dynasty and the Chinese could live together. The following year his octogenarian mother died, and he went into mourning for three years in accordance with the "old regulations." He rejected the Chinese demand, however, that he recognize Lê Ninh as his sovereign. This seems finally to have sparked the Ming to action, and by mid-1540 over 110,000 Chinese troops stood on the border in Kwangsi ready to invade. This period represented the first sustained interest China had taken in Annam in over a century, ever since Lê Lợi's victory. This also meant that little documentary material had been collected vis-à-vis Annam for some time, a lack which was promptly filled by the *Yüeh ch'iao shu* 越嶠書 of Li Wen-feng 李文鳳 (T. 廷儀, H. 月山子, cs 1532). With a preface dated July 18, 1540, this work predated the resolution of the problem by five months, and in fact laid out the conditions of Mac acquiescence: "If the Mac, regretting their crime, abandon their imperial title, reform their hierarchy, and come to the frontier (with long cords around their necks), leading their officers and their people, to await with submisson the decision of China, ..." they would be absolved.

That is what happened. Mac Dangdoanh had died at the beginning of the year, and Mac Dang-dung had placed the latter's son, Mac Phuc-hai 福海 (1541-46), on the throne. With this threat facing him, Mac Dang-dung led a number of ministers to the border on foot and with lengths of cord around their necks. On reaching the Ming camp, they crawled in barefoot and, kneeling towards the north, presented their statement of acquiescence, together with records of their land, population, and administrative and military organization to the Ming general. The Mac also gave up land on their northeastern border and sent an embassy to Peking, Mac Dang-dung pleading ill health for his inability to make the trip. A request was sent for the proper calendar, and a gold and silver figure of a man offered in tribute. All this was given in exchange for permission to administer the territory of Annam. The Ming allowed this, and Annam technically ceased to be an independent vassal state, becoming instead An-nan tu-t'ung shih-ssu 安南都統使司, with the Mac ruler as tu-t'ung shih 使. The names of administrative offices were changed to accord with the desired Chinese pattern.

Protest as the Lê faction might, the Ming dynasty had made its decision and continued to recognize the Mac until the Manchu conquest a century later, helping to protect them even after the Lê restoration, when they had been forced up into the northern hills of Cao-bang 高平 province. Meanwhile Mac Dang-dung died in September of the year following the settlement, leaving a relatively stable situation for his line. His last instructions were, "Don't do anything heterodox 不作 仸事." The reign of his son, Mac Dang-doanh, had been peaceful, prosperous, and efficient. His grandson, Mac Phuc-hai, liked the theater and cockfighting, and staffed his government with relatives and in-laws until power had come to reside with the latter. Mac Phuc-nguyen 源 (r. 1547-61), Mac Dang-dung's great-grand-son, came to the throne as a child, and his uncle Mac Kinh-dien 敬典 was preeminent in the court until the young emperor's favorites sowed doubt in his mind and split the court. One element went over to the Lê, and the Lê forces under Trinh Kiem put great pressure on the capital, forcing Mac Phuc-nguyen to flee to Hai-duong and then Son-nam province, where he died of smallpox. Mac Mau-hop 茂洽 (r. 1562-92), Mac Dang-dung's great-great-grandson, was the last of the line to rule in Thang-long. Since Mac Mau-hop was only one or two years old when he came to the throne, the prince Mac Don-nhuong 敦讓 wielded the major influence in the court, and Mac Kinh-dien was reinstated. In 1578, however, the young ruler staged a coup and took power himself, only to fall victim to cataracts and cloudy vision, though he recovered after several years. With the arrival of the Lê forces in the delta in 1592, Mac Mau-hop abdicated, placing a son on the throne, and took command of the Mac forces, only to be beaten and executed while most of the family fled north into the mountains. The young ruler vanished, but Mac Kinh-cung 恭 ruled in Cao-bang until 1625, and then Mac Kinh-

khoan 寬 and Mac Kinh-vu 宇 ruled until 1677 with Ming support as long as the Ming survived.

Bibliography

1/321/24a; MSL (1965), Shih-tsung, 4070, 4115, 4156, 4221, 4849, 4966, 5283, 5295, 5366, 5445; KC (1958), 3601, 3616, 3645, 3688, 3777, 4007; *Tung-kuan-hsien chih* (1911), 64/16b; Li Wen-feng, *Yüeh ch'iao shu*, "Preface"; Yen Ts'ung-chien 嚴從簡 (cs 1559), *Shu-yü chou-tzu lu* 殊 域周咨錄, *ch.* 6; Ngo Si-lien, *Dai-Viet su ky toan thu* (1798), *quyen* 14–16; Lê Quy-don, *Dai-Viet thong-su*, *quyen* on "rebels"; Phan Huy-chu 潘輝 注, *Lieh-trieu hien chuong loai-chi* 歷朝憲章類誌, *quyen* 6, 26, 46; *Kham-dinh Viet su thong-giam cuong-muc* 欽定越史通鑑綱目, *quyen* 25, 27; Trân Hàm-tan, "Etude sur la Văn Miêu (Temple de la Litérature) de Hà-nội", BEFEO, 45 (1951–52), 114, pls. 12, 13; L. Aurousseau, BEFEO, 20, 4 (1920), 98; E. Gaspardone, "La géographie de Li Wen-fong," BEFEO, 29 (1929), 63; Lo Jung-pang, "Policy Formulation and Decision-making on Issues Respecting Peace and War," in Charles O. Hucker, ed., *Chinese Government in Ming Times* (New York, 1969), 63; Bui Quang Tung, "Tables synoptiques de chronologie vietnamienne," BEFEO, 51: 1 (1963), 55.

John K. Whitmore

MAḤMŪD (Ma-ha-mu 馬哈木), died 1416?, Mongol chieftain whose pasture land was a vast area extending north and north-west of Tatung, was the first prominent Oirat to have relations with the Ming. The written sources concerning him, however, are meager compared to those about his son Toγon and particularly his grandson Esen (*q.v.*). His background and ancestry are unknown. Similarly the origin of his people, the Oirat, is uncertain and has been the subject of much scholarly speculation and controversy. The earliest Oirat leader to appear in the Ming annals is Meng-k'o T'ieh-mu-er 猛哥帖木兒 (not to be confused with the Odoli chieftain Menggetimur), who lived during the reign of the first Ming emperor, but little is known about him. After his death, the Oirat apparently split into three separate groups. Maḥmūd, also known as Batula Tsching ssang (Tsching ssang is

equivalent to Chinese ch'eng-hsiang 丞相),
was the leader of the strongest contingent
and as such merited special attention. On
April 26, 1403, Emperor Chu Ti (*q.v.*),
who initiated relations with numerous foreign states, sent an envoy to the Oirat
camp. Maḥmūd briefly detained the
envoy and refused to pay tribute. But
the emperor, undeterred, again dispatched
embassies on May 9, 1404, and June 18,
1407, with gifts. These overtures finally
elicited a favorable response from Maḥmūd, who sent a tribute mission in
October, 1408. Chu Ti, concerned about
the hostility of the Eastern Mongol leaders, Bunyaširi and Aruɣtai (*q.v.*), bestowed
titles and gave seals to the chiefs of all
three Oirat groups. Maḥmūd received the
title Shun-ning wang 順寧王, and the
chiefs T'ai-p'ing 太平 and Pa-t'u-po-lo
把禿孛羅 became Hsien-i 賢義 wang and
An-lo 安樂 wang respectively. Maḥmūd
was so pleased that he immediately sent
a tribute offering of horses. Even more
important, he repaid the emperor by attacking and defeating the forces of
Aruɣtai and the khan Bunyaširi, capturing
and killing the latter. He named Bunyaširi's son, Delbek (Ta-li-pa 答里巴), to
succeed his father, but sharply circum-
scribed his power.

The cordiality that characterized the
initial relations between Maḥmūd and
China was shortlived. After the defeat of
the Eastern Mongol forces, Chu Ti became
concerned lest Maḥmūd accumulate too
much power. He sought to restore Aruɣtai's influence in order to couteract the
might of the Oirat. On the other hand,
Maḥmūd feared the ever-growing intima-
cy between Chu Ti and Aruɣtai. In 1412
he sent an envoy to demand Chinese gifts
for his troops, who had defeated Aruɣtai,
and Chinese armament for the destruction of the Eastern Mongol chieftain. The
emperor provided gifts and banquets for
the envoy but rejected his other requests.
As a result, later that year Maḥmūd detained a few Chinese envoys and made
known his intention of repatriating, per-

haps through force, the Mongols in Kansu
and Ninghsia. On February 26, 1413, the
emperor sent the eunuch Hai T'ung 海童
to rebuke the Oirat and to effect the
release of the envoys. Hai's mission failed,
as Maḥmūd refused to compromise.

The outbreak of hostilities between
the Oirat and the Chinese was partly
precipitated by Maḥmūd's fear of a Sino-
Eastern Mongol alliance against him. Noting
that Chu Ti showered Aruɣtai with presents
and a title, he decided upon an offensive, and late in 1413 marched with thirty
thousand troops to the Kerülen River.
The Chinese border officials informed the
emperor that Maḥmūd intended to invade
China. During 1413 and early 1414, therefore, Chu Ti planned and organized a
punitive expedition against Maḥmūd, and
in the summer of 1414 he and his grandson
led their troops in pursuit of the Oirat.
The opposing forces met at Hu-lan-hu-
shih-wen 忽蘭忽失溫, between the upper
courses of the Tula and Kerülen Rivers,
and, according to the Chinese sources,
the imperial army (one of the more prominent officers being Liu Jung 劉榮
[1360–1420, Pth. 忠武]), soundly defeated
the Oirat. Actually both sides suffered
heavy losses, and the Chinese were unable
to pursue Maḥmūd and his troops when
they fled across the Tula River. Aruɣtai.
who could have been extremely helpful
to the Chinese, asserted that he was ill
and took no part in the campaign. Even
so, Chu Ti, unwilling to alienate him,
accepted this explanation, gave him 100
shih of rice, 100 sheep, and 100 donkeys,
and gave 5,000 *shih* of rice to his people.

Early in the following year Maḥmūd
sought a reconciliation with the Chinese. He released the envoys whom he
had detained, offered horses as tribute,
and humbly asked for the normalization
of relations. Chu Ti lodged and entertained Maḥmūd's envoy, but was apparently suspicious of the latter's motives. He
warned his border officials to maintain
strong defenses. Perhaps the two leaders
might have effected a rapprochement, but

the struggle between Aruɣtai and Maḥmūd precluded such a possibility. Aruɣtai, planning to attack the Oirat, took advantage of their temporary weakness after their war with the Chinese, and late in 1415 or early in 1416 succeeded in defeating and killing Maḥmūd and the khan Delbek. Learning of Maḥmūd's death, Chu Ti sent Hai T'ung to propose a peaceful settlement to the two remaining Oirat chiefs and to enfeoff Maḥmūd's son Toɣon as his successor.

Part of the blame for China's troubles with the Mongols lay with the policy of divide and rule. The imperial court discouraged the rise of any particularly powerful tribe or state on China's borders. It rewarded the weaker rulers in these areas, and bestowed titles upon them; such favoritism inevitably fostered conflict. Chu Ti's shifting of support from Maḥmūd to Aruɣtai and vice versa illustrates the pitfalls of this policy.

Bibliography

1/6/8a, 7/1b, 155/6b, ch. 328; Ku Ying-t'ai (EC CP), *Ming-ch'ao chi-shih pen-mo* (1658), *ch.* 21; Hsü Hsüeh-chü, *Kuo-ch'ao tien-hui* (Taipei, 1965), 159/5b, 170/9b; Hsia Hsieh (1799–1875?), *Ming t'ung-chien* (Peking-Shanghai, 1959), 678, 709, 715, 728; H. H. Howorth, *History of the Mongols* (London, 1876), 355; L. Hambis, *Documents sur l'histoire des Mongols à l'époque des Ming* (Paris, 1969), 22, 94; D. Pokotilov, *History of the Eastern Mongols during the Ming Dynasty from 1368 to 1634*, tr. by R. Loewenthal, *Studia Serica*, ser. A, no. 1 (Chengtu, 1947), pt. 1, 25; W. Franke, "Addenda and Corrigenda," *Studia Serica*, ser. A, no. 3 (1949), pt. 2, 21; *id.*, "Chinesische Feldzuge durch die Mongolei im frühen 15. Jahrhundert," *Sinologica*, III (1951–1953), 81; H. Serruys, "Sino-Mongol Relations with the Ming: The Tribute System and Diplomatic Missions (1400–1600)," MCB, XIV (1967), 32, 52, 172, 562.

Morris Rossabi

MAI-LU, *see* **WU Ch'eng**

MANṢŪR (Man-su-er 滿速兒), 1484/85–1545/46, chief of Turfan and part of Eastern Moghulistan, was China's main foe in central Asia during the early 16th century. Little is known of his childhood and education except that his father trained him in the martial arts. He was, according to one Persian account, a devout Muslim, and apparently memorized the contents of the Koran. He abhorred luxuries and thus lived simply and ascetically.

In 1503 his father Aḥmad (*q.v.*) left Eastern Moghulistan to attack the newly active Uzbeg tribes, and named him sultan of Aksu and Turfan. Within a year, Aḥmad was captured and died. When Manṣūr attempted to assert his authority as sultan, his uncle and his younger brothers rebelled. His uncle, Mir Jabar Birdi, called on Abu-Bakr, the powerful ruler of Kashgar, for assistance, and the latter conquered Aksu, forcing Manṣūr to flee eastward to Turfan. Shortly thereafter, however, Manṣūr and his uncle reached a reconciliation and united to suppress Manṣūr's brothers. Their alliance proved successful, and by 1508 he was the undisputed ruler of Turfan and the surrounding area. He could now turn his attention to Hami, the oasis which his father and his grandfather had attempted to annex. In the early 1500s Aḥmad had supported some rebel chieftains in Hami on the condition that they proclaim his younger son, Chen Timür (*see* Aḥmad), the prince of Hami. The authorities, however, of that city, with the aid of the Ming court, crushed the rebellion, and in 1505 named Pai-ya-chi 拜牙即, a descendant of the original Hami royal family, as their new ruler. Manṣūr, who by this time had succeeded his father, now demanded the return of Chen Timur, but the latter, fearing that his elder brother desired an uncontested claim to the sultanate of Turfan and thus might harm him, sought and received asylum in Hami.

Manṣūr soon discovered that Pai-ya-chi and the Chinese court were not on good terms. Pai-ya-chi repeatedly evaded the Ming tribute and trade regulations. The court frequently rebuked him, but such reprimands failed to deter him. In 1513

Manṣūr took advantage of the dispute to persuade Pai-ya-chi to migrate to Tur-fan. He then quickly sent troops to oc-cupy Hami, confiscated its seal, and cap-tured but did not injure his younger brother. Two decades earlier, the Chinese court had twice dispatched troops to recover Hami, but its efforts now were feeble. It sent in July, 1514, rather than a general, the censor-in-chief P'eng Tse 彭澤 (T. 濟物, H. 幸庵, Pth. 襄敏, cs 1490, a native of Lan-chou 蘭州, Kansu), to secure the release of Pai-ya-chi and to obtain Hami's seal. As P'eng was setting forth for the northwestern border, Man-ṣūr raided the guard of Sha-chou 沙州 (Kansu) and lands even closer to the cen-tral plain. The ruler of Turfan demanded gold, silver, and other gifts for the return of Pai-ya-chi and the seal. P'eng provided some of the ransom, but Manṣūr failed to carry out his end of the bargain. The court retaliated by prohibiting his tribute embassies from entering China. He in turn responded with an attack on Su 肅 -chou. By 1517 he had occupied Sha-chou and was threatening areas still farther east. The court finally relented and allow-ed his embassies to reach Peking even though some officials objected. As a result, a Persian historian writes: "Anyone, for example, could travel alone from Kámul [Hami] in Khitái, to Andiján without hav-ing duties levied on him; and could be taken every night, as a guest, into some home."

A period of relative calm followed, but the succession to the throne of Em-peror Chu Hou-ts'ung (q.v.) in 1521 dis-rupted the peace. The emperor ordered the execution of the former Muslim chief of Hami, Sayyid Ḥusain (q.v.), who was a confidant of the previous ruler and ap-parently a spy for Manṣūr. He also de-tained some tribute envoys from Turfan. In 1524 Manṣūr with, according to the perhaps exaggerated account of the Ming-shih, twenty thousand cavalry launched an attack on Kan甘-chou to induce China to free his envoys. Ch'en Chiu-chou 陳九疇

(T. 禹學, Pth. 忠襄, cs 1502), the governor of Kansu, successfully routed Manṣūr from Kan-chou and forced him to flee. In the next year, however, the chief of Turfan again invaded the area. The dispute between him and the Chinese court was exacerbated by the defection of Ya-lan 牙蘭, one of his generals, in 1528. When the emperor rejected his de-mand for the return of Ya-lan, he joined with the Oirat for a raid on Su-chou. Both sides sustained heavy losses, but in the end the Chinese forces repelled the aggressor. Manṣūr then abandoned large-scale military expeditions, though he continued to sanction raids on China to attain his objectives. Instead he offered tribute, occasionally dispatching a dozen or more embassies a year. He was appar-ently eager to obtain the Chinese gifts granted to foreign embassies, and there-fore limited his incursions. On the other hand, the Chinese court acknowledged his *de facto* control of Hami. It recognized that it could no longer control that important oasis on the caravan route, and sought an accommodation with the ruler of the area. By 1530 it released Manṣūr's envoys and made few further efforts to bar his embassies from China. An uninterrupted flow of tribute missions from Turfan, frequently making such ex-otic offerings as lions, reached China until Manṣūr's death some fifteen years later. Though a succession crisis temporarily clouded the future of the sultanate of Turfan, Manṣūr's son Sultan Sha 沙 finally emerged to consolidate and rule the state.

Bibliography

1/329/11b; MSL (1965), Wu-tsung, 0192, 1024, 2185; Fu Wei-lin, *Ming shu* (Shanghai, 1937), 3298; Ho Ch'iao-yüan, *Ming-shan-ts'ang* (Taipei repr., 1971), 6329; V. V. Barthold, *Four Studies on the History of Central Asia*, tr. by V. and T. Minorsky, I (Leiden, 1956), 152; R. Grousset, *L'empire des steppes* (Paris, 1939), 577; N. Elias (ed.), *The Tarikh-i-Rashidi of Mirza Muhammad Haidar, Dughlat: A History of the Moghuls of Central Asia*, tr. by E. D. Ross (London, 1895),

123; E. Bretschneider, *Mediaeval Researches from Eastern Asiatic Sources*, II (London, 1910), 182, 195.

Morris Rossabi

MAO Chung 毛忠 (T. 允誠), July 19, 1394–October 26, 1468, military officer, was one of several commanders of Mongol descent ennobled during the early years of the Ming dynasty for distinguished service. He was first known by his Mongol name Qara 哈喇; it was only after 1448 that he adopted his Chinese name. The early history of the family is rather obscure. The author of Mao's tomb inscription states that he was a man from Szechwan, but the *Ming-shih* calls him "a man from the western frontier," presumably Kansu. His great-grandfather surrendered to the Ming court at the beginning of the dynasty, settled in Lanchou 蘭州, became a chiliarch commander in the Chinese army, and was killed in action in 1376. His grandfather also perished during a war against Hami. His father, the first to use the Chinese surname Mao, rose to the rank of battalion commander in the Yung-ch'ang 永昌 guard, Kansu. Mao Qara later inherited his father's rank and is known for his vigorous physique and skill at shooting on horseback.

From his garrison in Kansu, Mao Qara was chosen to take part in expeditions led by Emperor Chu Ti (*q.v.*) against both the Western and Eastern Mongols, and distinguished himself in battle. In 1430 he joined a campaign led by General Shih Chao (*see* Wang Chin) against the recalcitrant tribesmen at Ch'ü-hsien 曲先, and received promotion to be a deputy chiliarch commander in March of the following year. Between 1433 and 1435 he saw action against rebellious Mongol tribesmen to the north of Kansu during which he proved his bravery and was awarded the rank of vice commander of the Kan-chou 甘州 guard. Early in 1438, in a campaign against the Mongol

rebel To-er-chih-po (*see* Wang Chi), Mao Qara assisted Commander-in-chief Wang Chi, and was promoted in May to be the assistant commander of the Shensi regional military commission. In the following years he continued to distinguish himself in skirmishes against the Mongol tribesmen, receiving several rewards and eventually advancing to the rank of vice commander of the same regional military commission early in 1445.

Following the outbreak of an uprising among the Turkish tribesmen in Shachou 沙州 (October, 1446), the court dispatched Jen Li 任禮 (T. 尚儀, d. 1465, Pth. 僖武) in command of an expeditionary force against the tribesmen and appointed Mao his deputy commander. Mao succeeded in resettling the chieftain Nanko (*see* Kunjilai) and his people inside the Chinese borders; he received further promotion in rank. Nan-ko's younger brother, So-nan-pen (*see* Kunjilai), however, made an alliance with the Oirat who by then were steadily expanding their power over all of Mongolia. Mao Qara continued his pursuit of So-nan-pen and succeeded in capturing him in August, 1448. As a reward Mao Qara received the rank of assistant commissioner, after which he used the Chinese name Mao Chung. Following this he was made a deputy commander of the area of Kansu.

The year 1449 saw the Oirat invasion and, following the T'u-mu debacle in September, the capture of Emperor Chu Ch'i-chen (*q.v.*) and his imprisonment in Mongolia. In the following months, tense relations between the Oirat and the Chinese caused difficulties for many of the Chinese army officers of Mongol descent. A Chinese envoy by the name of Li Shih (*q.v.*), who went to the camp of Esen (*q. v.*) in 1450 in order to negotiate the emperor's release, accused Mao of having repeatedly connived with the enemy. The origin of this charge seems to have been due to Mao's capture of a lama whom he brought back as a prisoner. Later the lama escaped and fled to Esen's camp, where he was no doubt employed because of his knowledge of Chinese affairs. The lama bore a grudge against Mao and waited for an opportunity to ruin him. It would appear that on the basis of the lama's false charges Li made his accusation. The new emperor, Chu Ch'i-yü (q.v.), subsequently ordered Mao arrested and brought back to the capital for trial and punishment. The ministry of War demanded the death penalty, but the emperor refused. Instead, he sent Mao into exile in Fukien where he was put in charge of the suppression of local bandits. He was allowed to keep his rank and given a chance to qualify for a pardon. His family and dependants, however, were kept as hostages at the capital. Shortly after Chu Ch'i-chen regained his throne early in 1457, he recalled Mao from exile and in July made him a commander of the Kansu army with the rank of vice commissioner.

Early in 1458 the Mongol chieftain, Po-lai 孛來, launched a series of offensives against the Chinese defense in Liang-chou 涼州 on the Kansu frontier. Mao suffered an initial setback and was accused of neglect of duty; he soon cleared his name, however, and became a full commissioner in May, 1459. During the next two years he successfully warded off several Mongol incursions, and scored a decisive victory in June, 1461, over Po-lai, who had hoped to gain control of the Kansu corridor. Mao led several punitive expeditions in August, 1463, against the rebellious tribesmen in the Yung-ch'ang, Liang-chou, and Chuang-lang 莊浪 border areas. He efficiently subdued the larger tribes, including some whom other officers had attempted to suppress. As a reward for this service Mao received an increase in salary of only one hundred shih of rice while other commanders fared remarkably better. Probably as a protest against the unfair treatment, Mao submitted (March, 1465) a request for permission to retire as he was over seventy years of age, but his

superior, thinking he was still strong, recommended his retention. Finally, on April 23, 1467, the court awarded him the hereditary rank of earl of Fu-ch'iang 伏羌伯 (subduer of the Ch'iang tribe) with an annual stipend of 1,000 shih of rice.

Mao's career, however, ended in tragedy. In October, 1468, at the height of the rebellion of the Mongol chieftain, Man-ssu, in the Shensi and Kansu area, Mao Chung received a summons to join the expedition led by Hsiang Chung (q.v.). At the battle of Shih-ch'eng 石城 on the 25th, in which the Chinese attempted to capture the town from Mongol hands, they suffered a defeat during which Mao was struck by an arrow and died the following day. His nephew, Mao Hai 海, and his grandson, Mao K'ai 愷, perished in the same battle. Mao Chung was then seventy-four.

Mao Chung has been hailed as a brave warrior and a strict disciplinarian who was good to his soldiers, but he was not an able strategist, which probably accounted for his several setbacks. In November, 1468, when a report of his death reached the court, Emperor Chu Chien-shen (q.v.) conferred on him the posthumous rank of marquis and the canonized name Wu-yung 武勇. Twenty-six years later (August, 1494) Emperor Chu Yu-t'ang (q.v.) granted the honorific name Chung-i fang 忠義坊 to his former living quarters in Lan-chou. Then in January, 1497, acting on the recommendation of the governor of Kansu, Hsü Chin (q.v.), the emperor ordered the erection of a shrine in Kan-chou, to be called Wu-yung tz'u 祠.

Mao Chung's eldest son did not survive him; hence in May, 1469, Emperor Chu Chien-shen ordered that his surviving grandson Mao Jui 銳 (T. 穎夫) inherit his hereditary earldom. An able military officer, Mao Jui served as area commander of Hukuang (1488) and of Kwangtung and Kwangsi (1498). In 1504 he was made a grand protector of the heir apparent and was later put in charge of the supervision of the tribute grain transportation (1509). Early in 1521 he was reinstated as area commander of Hukuang, where he died two years later and was awarded the posthumons name Wei-hsiang 威襄. His descendants successively inherited this title to the end of the dynasty.

Another military officer, possibly also of Mongol descent, known by the name Mao Qara was a contemporary of Mao Chung. He held the rank of commander and served, *inter alia*, as interpreter and envoy to the Oirat court between 1418 and 1428. The last of such missions in which he took part occurred in April, 1428.

Bibliography

1/207/28a, 156/8b; 5/9/45a; MSL (1963), Hsüantsung, 1759, Ying-tsung (1964), *ch.* 41–361, Hsien-tsung (1964), *ch.*1–59, Hsiao-tsung (1964), 198, 699, 2155, 4004, Wu-tsung (1965), 1256, 1509, Shih-tsung (1965), 329, 765, 1109; Wang Ao 王鏊, *Chen-tse hsien-sheng chi*, 18/1a; Chang Hung-hsiang 張鴻翔, "*Ming-shih* chüan i-wu-liu chu-ch'en shih-hsi piao" 明史卷一五六諸臣世系表, *Fu-jen hsüeh-chih* 輔仁學誌, 5: 1–2 (December, 1936), 30; Henry Serruys, "Mongols Ennobled during the Early Ming," HJAS, 22 (December, 1959), 239. For MAO Qara II: MSL (1963), T'ai-tsung, 2077, 2139, 2168, Jen-tsung, 221, Hsüan-tsung, 1003, 1191, 1210.

Hok-lam Chan

MAO Fu-shou, *see* **MAO Sheng**

MAO Jui-cheng 茅瑞徵 (T. 伯符, H. 苕上愚公, 澹泊居士, 浣花主人, 五芝), fl. 1597-1636, official, writer on foreign relations and military affairs, and also a poet, was the grandnephew of Mao K'un and cousin of Mao Yüan-i (*qq.v.*), and like them a native of Kuei-an 歸安, Chekiang. In a short autobiographical sketch he relates that his ancestors were farmers, but that he himself liked to study, and was never so happy as when he was poring over the books his family possessed. These are known to have been considerable, especially in the fields that interested him. It is no surprise to find, therefore, that he cut short his official career to give his full attention to scholarship.

Following his acquisition of the *chü-jen* in 1597 and *chin-shih* in 1601, Mao was assigned (1603) the magistracy of Ssu-shui 泗水, Shantung, and then, from 1604 to 1609, he served as magistrate of Huang-kang 黃岡, Hukuang. While there he edited the local history, *Huang-kang-hsien chih*, 10 ch. (published 1608). An incomplete copy is in the Rare Books Collection of the Peiping Library, now located in Taipei. In his preface he writes that three tenths of it was based on local records and geographical materials, and seven tenths on fast disintegrating books and broken tablets bearing inscriptions. He reports that he revised it three times. About 1609 he was summoned to Peking and appointed a secretary in the ministry of War, where he was later raised to be director of the bureau of operations. His subsequent appointments were as administration vice commissioner in Fukien, right administration commissioner in Hukuang, and director of the Court of Imperial Entertainments at Nanking. On December 7, 1621, Mao was cashiered, being held partly responsible for the defeat of Chinese arms in 1618-19, by the forces of Nurhaci (ECCP). At his death he was awarded the posthumous rank of director of the Grand Court of Revision.

Mao is remembered for his publications. He left two works on the Book of History, both written in 1632. These are the *Yü-shu chien* 虞書箋, 2 *ch.*, and the *Yü-kung hui-shu* 禹貢滙疏, 12 *ch.*, to which are appended maps in 2 *chüan* and a *pieh-lu* 別錄, 1 *ch.* A copy of the latter is in the Library of Congress. His real contributions to scholarship are three works based on documents in the ministry of War. All three appear on the list of banned books of the 18th century. The first, *Huang Ming hsiang-hsü lu* 象胥錄, 8 *ch.*, written in 1629, is a treatise on tribute peoples on the periphery of the Ming empire. It was reproduced in 1936 by the National Peiping Library in the series *Shan-pen* 善本 *ts'ung-shu*. The second is the *Wan-li san ta-cheng k'ao* 萬曆三大征考, *5 ch.*; it treats of the conflicts in the Ning-hsia area with the Mongol commander Pübei (*see* Li Ju-sung), with the Japanese in the Korean peninsula, and with the Miao tribesmen in Kweichow (*see* Li Hua-lung, Kuo Tzu-chang, and Yang Ying-lung), and is supplied with maps and descriptions of these regions. In 1934 the Yenching University library published it from a manuscript copy; actually original editions are extant in China and Japan. The third is the *Tung-i k'ao-lüeh* 東夷考略, which has to do with Liaotung and its people (the Jurchen), and also includes maps. It concludes with Mao's brief autobiographical sketch. The original edition of 1621 was reprinted in 1940 in the *Hsüan-lan-t'ang* 玄覽堂 *ts'ung-shu*. Walter Fuchs wrote in 1936: "Of these proscribed books, the first in importance is Mao Jui-cheng's *Tung-i k'ao-lüeh*." Mao is also credited with the publication of an edition of the *Hua-i i-yü*, 13 *ch.*, a complete reworking of the book with the same title brought out over two centuries earlier by Qoninči (*q.v.*) and others. Léonard Aurousseau acquired a manuscript copy of this (*ca.* 1912) from the collection of Yang Shou-ching (BD RC), and describes it as a work in 13 volumes, with 13 vocabularies: Korean, Liu-ch'iu, Japanese, Annamite, Cham, Siamese, Mongol, Uighur, Tibetan, Muslim (Persian ?), Malay, Jurchen, Pai-i (Yunannese Thai). The preface was composed by the optimus of 1595, Chu Chih-fan (*q.v.*). It was doubtless prepared for the College of Translators of his day (*see* Wang Tsung-tsai). Copies of Mao's edition of the *Hua-i i-yü* are known to be preserved in Berlin, London, Hanoi, and Tokushima (Japan).

Another rare work which Mao compiled is the *Chih-yüan pi-lu* 芝園祕録, 14 *ch.*, a collection of writings of seven scholars; a copy belonging to the National Library of Peiping is available on microfilm. Mao made no contribution of his own except his preface of 1636. According to the local history he was responsible for at least six other works which seem not to have survived.

Bibliography

1/96/9a, 97/7a, 31a; 40/59/10b; 86/16/33b; MSL (1966), Hsi-tsung, 0772; *Kuei-an-hsien chih*(1881), 21/2b, 31/10a, 32/6a, 36/23b; *Ssu-shui-hsien chih* (1892), 3/4b; *Huang-kang-hsien chih* (1881), 6/14a; *Fu-chou-fu chih* 福州府志 (1754, reprinted 1967), 29/23b; *Shantung t'ung-chih* (1934), 2493; SK (1930), 14/1b; Sun Tien-ch'i (1957), 91, 186; Hsüeh Ying-po 薛瀛伯, "*Wan-li san ta-cheng k'ao tung-i k'ao-lüeh* ho-pa 合跋," *Yenching University Library Bull.*, 109 (January 15, 1938), 2; Isson Shomoku 佚存書目 (Tokyo, 1933), 75; Yeh Ch'ang-ch'ih 葉昌熾, *Ts'ang-shu chi-shih shih* 藏書紀事詩 (Shanghai, 1958), 118; W. Franke, *Sources*, 7. 1. 1, 12, 2. 9, 10. 5; L. Aurousseau, BEFEO, 12 (1912), 9, 198; W. Fuchs, "The Personal Chronicle of the First Manchu Emperor," PA, IX (1936), 84; *id.*, MS, III (1938), 306; *id.*, Bulletin no 8, Catholic University of Peking (1931), 94; L. Ligeti, "Un vocabulaire sino-ouigour des Ming," *Acta Orientalia Hung*, 19 (1966), 121.

Yang Chin-yi and L. Carrington Goodrich

MAO K'un 茅坤 (T. 順甫, H. 鹿門, 髯翁) August 30, 1512-December 22, 1601, a celebrated essayist better known by his sobriquet Mao Lu-men 鹿門, was born into a wealthy family in Kuei-an 歸安, Chekiang, situated about forty miles north of Hangchow. According to his family records, an ancestor who was a deputy prefect under the Mongols concealed his identity after the Ming conquest and became a trader in bamboo used for rafts. It is possible that he was not of Chinese origin and perhaps assumed the surname Mao after settling in Kuei-an. There are stories about some miraculous phenomena after his death, resulting in his being regarded locally as a minor deity, and certain people may have associated his name with the Taoist immortals, the San Mao-chün 三茅君 (the three brothers

Mao). In any case, his descendants prospered, owning farmland and engaging
in the silk industry.

Mao K'un was the first in his family
to pass the civil examinations and enter
officialdom. A *chü-jen* of 1534, he became
a *chin-shih* in 1538 in the same class as
Shen Lien and Hu Tsung-hsien (*qq.v.*).
His first assignment was to the magistracy
of Ch'ing-yang 青陽, about thirty-five
miles east of Anking, where he served
for only two months in 1540 before
being obliged to retire to mourn his father's and later his mother's death. During
the two months in office, however, he
gave aid to the registered coppersmiths
of the district by closing those shops
illegally operated by nonresidents. He
also chastised several notorious bullies.
After his departure a shrine was erected
in his honor.

His next assignment was as magistrate
of Tan-t'u 丹徒, northwest of Soochow.
Arriving in March, 1544, he soon found
the district suffering from a serious drought.
By rearranging the procedure of tax collection he granted the owners of higher
dry land exemption from taxes, while
collecting enough revenue from irrigated
land to fulfill the quota. The regulations
drafted by him for the distribution of
food to the famine stricken came to be
followed in other districts. Early in 1546
he was recommended for promotion. It
happened that the minister of Personnel,
a fellow provincial named T'ang Lung 唐
龍 (T. 虞佐, H. 漁石, 1477-1546, cs 1508,
Pth. 文襄), had long been aware of Mao's
ability and, soon after appointing him a
secretary in the ministry of Rites, transferred him to Personnel. A few months
later (July), T'ang and some of his subordinates were accused and convicted of
forming a clique for private gain. T'ang
suffered discharge, was reduced to the
status of a commoner, and died on his
way home. Mao was demoted to assistant
prefect of Kuang-p'ing 廣平, south of
Peking. According to Mao's own account,
this demotion was due to a grudge held

against him by Grand Secretary Hsia Yen
(*q. v.*). There seems to be some truth in
this because, just after the fall of Hsia
in 1548, Mao was restored to his former
rank and sent to the Nanking ministry
of War.

In 1551, while serving in Nanking as
a bureau director in the ministry of
Rites, Mao received promotion to assistant surveillance commissioner of Kwangsi. The transfer was regarded by Mao as
a punishment, as it put him farther away
from the throne; this time he suspected
the minister of Rites, Hsü Chieh (*q.v.*),
as the one responsible for the shift. He
gave several reasons why Hsü should find
him at fault, all of them seeming to be
either for trivial matters of etiquette or
based on suspicion only. At any rate he
accepted the appointment after receiving
a memorandum from the governor of
Kwangsi, Ying Chia 應檟 (T. 子材, 1494-
1554, cs 1526), urging him to come there
to help in dealing with the aborigines.
When Mao arrived early in 1552, he was
assigned to be acting intendant of Fu-
chiang 府江 circuit (official name: Kuei-
p'ing tao 桂平道, to which the Kweilin and
P'ing-lo 平樂 prefectures in northeastern
Kwangsi were subordinate). Fu-chiang is
another name for the river Kuei that ran
from Kweilin southeast to the West River.
Along the gorges at Yang-shuo 陽朔 were
strongholds of Yao tribesmen, who had
for centuries harassed travelers on the
river and Chinese settlers in villages and
towns (*see* Han Yang), and who had recently murdered the magistrate of Yang-
shuo.

While military authorities considered
the assembling of tens of thousands of
men from several provinces for a protracted and costly campaign against the
tribesmen, Mao persuaded Ying Chia to
grant him full authority to carry out his
own plan, which involved only the five
thousand men stationed in that area. He
called his scheme tiao-chiao 鵰勦 (eagle
strike), which called for a well-planned
thrust aimed at a quick and decisive vic-

tory, as compared to a large scale expedition, ta-cheng 大征. For the execution of his tactic he first picked only the fittest men to undergo strict training, assigning the rest either to guard or to service duties. He then took steps to split the tribal leaders, announcing that he wanted only those who had taken part in killing the magistrate, and would spare the rest if they held their peace. Some who came to declare their innocence were given rewards. By sending teams of spies to tribal areas and specialists to draw accurate maps in invisible ink, he learned enough about the tribesmen's strength and distribution to construct a model in relief of the area and to make detailed plans for the campaign. His objective was to take the seventeen rebel strongholds east of the river, but he first stationed a force of about a thousand men on the west bank, partly to mislead the enemy and partly to cut off tribal communications. Meanwhile he deployed seven detachments at distances of about twenty to thirty miles from the rebels. When he ascertained that they had set a date for the uprising, he sent secret orders to his detachments to march. On the night of November 12, 1552, each suddenly converged on its object of attack, and in one day's fighting they crushed all seventeen tribal strongholds according to plan. Such a complete victory at no extra cost to the government, or to anyone but the marauders, won Mao the approbation of the people. In their gratitude they erected a monument on the river bank, the inscription of which, written by Wang Tsung-mu (q.v.), was entitled "Yang-shuo chi-shih pei" 紀事碑. Mao in 1568 gave his own account of the campaign entitled *Fu-chiang chi-shih*. Both are included in his collected works.

As a reward for his success, Mao was raised two grades (from 5A to 4A) and late in 1553 promoted to surveillance vice commissioner of Honan serving as intendant of military affairs of the Ta-ming 大名 circuit, southern Pei-Chihli. It happens that, beginning in 1550, the Ta-ming intendant had been given the additional duty of guarding a section of the Great Wall about ninety miles southwest of Peking. Mao contributed his own funds for the manufacture of three hundred carts and trained three thousand men in their use for transportation and for protection when attacked. His superiors highly praised him, but in 1554 he was dismissed on the charge that while in Kwangsi he reported as his own certain achievements which should have been credited to others. Again he attributed his downfall to the machinations of Hsü Chieh. All writers about Mao seem to agree with him in this matter. On examining Mao's literary remains, however, one finds that the real cause of his downfall in 1554 was not Hsü's dislike, nor even anything Mao did in Kwangsi as officially charged. A long letter in his collected works submitted (about March, 1554) to the powerful head of the Embroidered-uniform Guard, Lu Ping (q.v.), praises Lu for exposing Ch'iu Luan (q.v.), and compares him to Huo Kuang (d. 68 B.C.), who crushed a group of plotters and gained control of the court for a period of twenty years (87-68 B.C.). In this letter Mao indiscreetly declared himself a faithful follower of Lu even unto death. Apparently Lu did not take kindly to such a declaration of devotion, which might lead to serious trouble for himself. So he probably discussed the matter with the high officials and perhaps even with the emperor, and conceivably they decided to have Mao discharged for some minor reason, but with the understanding that he was not to be reinstated.

When Mao returned home to Chekiang in 1554, he found his friend Hu Tsung-hsien serving as censor-inspector of that province and trying to cope with the defense of the coast against the pirates. Mao became a consultant to Hu throughout the latter's service in Chekiang and was said to have advised Hu on military matters. Reportedly Hu rewarded

Mao with title to some government land belonging to the Hangchow Guard. Meanwhile Hu paved the way for the eventual defeat of the pirates by his use of guile and trickery to eliminate their leaders: Hsü Hai (*see* Chao Wen-hua) in 1556 and Wang Chih 王直 (*q.v.*) a year later. In June, 1562, Hu's sponsor at court, Yen Sung (*q.v.*), lost his high office and five months later Hu himself was placed under arrest on ten charges, three of which were his once close relationship with the pirate Wang Chih, his squandering of military funds with the help of some members of his staff, such as Mao K'un, and assigning to Mao a public building in Hangchow as his private residence. The emperor, however, soon ordered the case dropped and had Hu released, possibly after reading an anonymous report of Hu's exploits in the capture of Wang Chih. This account was probably written in 1562, but was printed in the series *Chin-sheng yü-chen chi* under the title *Hai-k'ou hou-pien* (*see* Yüan Chiung), with a forged colophon dated in January, 1560. When Hu was arrested for the second time in 1565, another acount of his dealings with the pirates was inserted in the same series, as a supplement to the *Hai-k'ou hou-pien*, but with Mao K'un's name as author. It was obviously offered, like its predecessor, as part of the defense of Hu, this time stressing his success in dealing with the other pirate leader, as shown in its alternate title *Chi-chiao Hsü Hai pen-mo* 紀勦徐海本末. By comparing the style and sequence of the two reports, one is compelled to draw the conclusion that both were written by the same author. Although both have been cited as authoritative sources, at least one late Ming writer, Hsü Fu-tso (*q.v.*), after studying many documents on the pirates, expressed serious doubts as to Mao's credibility. Later Huang Tsung-hsi (ECCP) also criticized some of them as unreliable. Neither those who approved of the two accounts nor those who questioned them seemed to realize that each was written as a polit-

ical tract aimed at influencing the outcome of Hu Tsung-hsien's case at a particular time; they were not intended as unbiased reporting.

Early in 1566 the censor-inspector of Chekiang, P'ang Shang-p'eng (*q.v.*), accused several retired officials of that province of abusing their privileges by maltreating the people of their communities. In March four of these officials, Mao K'un among them, were stripped of all ranks, and reduced to commoner status. In Mao's case one reads that his eldest son, Mao Weng-chi 翁積 (T. 稚延, H. 同川, b. 1542), was talented but self-indulgent, and had committed serious offenses with the help of several unprincipled servants. P'ang punished (executed ?) the latter severely, and put Mao Weng-chi in prison where he died. Mao K'un again used his writing to place the blame on others, and once more tried to confuse the issue with an involved story. Reduced to its simplest form the story relates that when his elder brother, Mao Ch'ien 乾 (T. 健甫, H. 少溪, 1506–84), was serving as an acting magistrate in Kwangtung he cleared a man of a murder charge brought up by none other than P'ang Shang-p'eng, and so the latter now took revenge by hurting the Mao family. Even if true, the story does not explain why P'ang brought charges against several other families at the same time, and all these charges were also substantiated.

Mao K'un expressed his frustration over his unsuccessful official career by naming his residence San-ch'o-t'ang 三黜堂 (the hall of the thrice rejected), and in 1567 wrote an account of his three reverses: when he was sent out as a magistrate in 1540, when he was forced out of the ministry of Personnel in 1546, and finally when he was summarily cashiered in 1554. Blaming each failure on someone in power, he unwittingly revealed the real cause of his failure, namely, his excessive eagerness to display his talents, and his partiality towards his fellow provincials. In retirement he sought to recover his self-esteem by rendering service to Hu Tsung-hsien. When that failed too and Hu was twice imprisoned, Mao made strong pleas on behalf of the commander by writing letters appealing to those in power and by publishing the two accounts of the pirates in Hu's defense. These tracts enumerated not only Hu's exploits but hinted also at Mao's own part as an adviser. Meanwhile he turned his attention to the acquisition of property, in which respect he was apparently very successful until the debacle of 1566, when he was deprived of his official rank and influence. From that time until he died, Mao K'un occupied himself with the writing of essays and the making of anthologies. Here too he was a success and won national acclaim. He became especially known as the editor of an anthology of the works of eight great prose writers (Han Yü, 768-824; Liu Tsung-yüan, 773-819; Ou-yang Hsiu, 1007-72; Su Hsün, 1009-66; Su Shih, 1037-1101; Su Che, 1039-1112; Tseng Kung, 1019-83; and Wang An-shih, 1021-86), entitled *T'ang Sung pa-ta-chia wen-ch'ao* 唐宋八大家文鈔, 144 *ch.*, printed in 1579.

An admirer of Ssu-ma Ch'ien (fl. 135-93 B.C.) and Ou-yang Hsiu, Mao made selections from their historical writings. He edited the former's work as *Shih-chi ch'ao* 史記鈔, 91 *ch.*, printed 1575; and the latter's as *Ou-yang kung shih* 歐陽公史 *ch'ao*, consisting of *Hsin-T'ang-shu* 新唐書 *ch'ao*, 2 *ch.*, and *Wu-tai* 五代 *shih ch'ao*, 20 *ch.* In some editions of the *T'ang Sung pa-ta-chia wen-ch'ao*, the *Wu-tai-shih ch'ao* is appended, bringing the anthology to a total of 164 *ch.* Mao also edited a *Han* 漢-*shu ch'ao*, 93 *ch.*, printed in 1589. His editions of *Mo-tzu* 墨子, 6 *ch.*, and *Huai-nan hung-lieh chieh* 淮南鴻烈解, 21 *ch.*, were both reprinted in Japan, the former in 1757 and the latter in 1664. About 1573 he edited a work on the establishment of a sub-prefecture for the township of Wu-chen 烏鎮, which included the southeast corner of Kuei-an, under the title *Che-chih fen-shu chi-shih pen-mo* 浙 直分署紀事本末, 6 *ch.* His own home was situated north of Wu-chen, in a village called Hua-hsi 花溪, where his enormous collection of books was housed. His grandson, Mao Yüan-i (*q.v.*), compiled a catalogue of it entitled *Pai-hua-lou shu-mu* 白華樓書目. Later the grandson transported the books to his house in Nanking, where he compiled the *Wu-pei chih.*

As an editor Mao K'un has been sharply criticized as lacking in insight and precision and as negligent in the verification of his facts. In connection with advocating the ku-wen style of prose writing he had to yield precedence to Kuei Yu-kuang (*q.v.*) and in the promotion of the eight great T'ang and Sung masters he was preceded by Chu Yu 朱右 (T. 伯賢, H. 序賢, 1314-76) and T'ang Shun-chih (*q.v.*). Yet his anthology was so popular that in the minds of its readers his name usually comes first in association with the term T'ang Sung Pa-ta-chia. This popularity stems from the belief that his analysis of a model essay shows the steps for the development of an idea as an aid in the speedy composition of the papers required in civil examinations. By learning this construction, a student might readily compose a readable essay on any subject. The weakness of Mao's own historical writings is that he tended to be dramatic so as to impress the reader, and convince him with an account that could not stand close scrutiny, especially with regard to chronological sequence. He thought he had achieved the level of Ssu-ma Ch'ien in his historical accounts, but his writings show that he was primarily a man of letters, a storyteller, or an essayist, for he often failed to indicate the time when an event took place, a vital element in the historian's craft.

The first collection of the writings of Mao K'un began to be printed in 1564 under the title *Pai-hua-lou ts'ang-kao* 藏稿, 11 *ch.*, which was supplemented in 1584 with a *hsü* 續 *kao*, 15 *ch.*, and a *yin* 吟 *kao* (poems only), 10 *ch.* (A complete set is in the Library of Congress.) In 1588 he printed his later writings in the collection *Yü-chih shan-fang* 玉芝山房 *kao*, 22 *ch.* The writings of his last years were published as the *Mao-nien lu* 耄年錄, 7 *ch.* After he died, a complete edition of his prose was brought out under the title *Mao Lu-men hsien-sheng wen-chi* 先生文集, 36 *ch.* Selections of his prose also appear in various anthologies, two of which are the *Huang Ming shih-ta-chia wen-hsüan* 十大家 文選, edited by Lu Hung-tso 陸弘祚 (early 17th century), and the *Ming pa-ta-chia wen-chi*, edited by Chang Ju-hu 張汝湖 in 1682.

It is interesting to note that when Mao K'un's sons edited his collected works they did not include his poems. As one critic commented, Mao K'un's poetry was not a success, but this lack was made up for by his youngest son, Mao Wei (*q.v.*), who excelled in that form of expression. Mao K'un's second son, Mao Kuo-chin (*see* Mao Yüan-i), served as magistrate of Chang-ch'iu 章丘, Shantung (1583-89), as a censor (1589), as magistrate of Hsi-ch'uan 淅川, Honan (1592-95), and as a secretary in the ministry of Works in Nanking (1599-1601), and later in Peking (1605-6). His last post was as a bureau director in charge of the Grand Canal in southern Shantung, where he died in office. He was responsible for the abridged editions of two histories, *Chin-shih shan* 晉史刪, 40 *ch.*, and *Nan* 南*-shih shan*, 31 *ch.*, both of which may be found in the Naikaku Bunko collection. Mao K'un's grandson, Mao Yüan-i, became a celebrated writer on military matters, as did a grandnephew, Mao Jui-cheng (*q.v.*), grandson of Mao Ken 艮 (T. 靜甫, H. 雙泉). During the last year of the war against the Japanese in Korea, the officer in command of the three thousand Chekiang troops was a Mao Kuo-ch'i 國器, who took part in the battles of Wisan 蔚山 (January 1598) and Sach'ŏn 泗川 (October, 1598). He was probably one of Mao K'un's close relatives. According to Chang Li-hsiang (ECCP),

the Mao family lost its wealth and influence after the Ch'ing take-over, and in their village one could find only poor relatives living among ruins of once splendid mansions. Chang said that other wealthy families of Kuei-an brought on their own ruin through misconduct, but the Mao family, which had been circumspect, was impoverished by the excessive demands of tax collectors. What Chang refrained from saying explicitly is that the properties of the patriotic Mao family were ruined during the Manchu conquest in 1645. Mao K'un's branch suffered further persecution when one of his grandsons, Mao Yüan-ming 元銘 (T. 鼎升), was executed in 1663 for having taken part in the writing of a history of the Ming dynasty (*see* Chuang T'ing-lung, ECCP).

Bibliography

1/287/12b, 227/1a, 317/15b; 5/51/100a, 82/6a; 22/9/15a; 40/42/24a, 54/23b, 71/1b; *Huang Ming ts'ung-hsin-lu* 從信錄, 38/15b, 20a, 26b; Ch'ien Ch'ien-i, *Lieh-ch'ao shih-chi*, IV: 3/40a; *Hu-chou-fu chih* 湖州府志 (1874), 58/20a, 30b, 33b, 36a, 60/5b, 94/32a; Lu Hsin-yüan (ECCP), *Kuei-an-hsien chih* (1882), 6/1b, 5a, 36/20b; *Ming-wen hai* (microfilm), 7/4/17, 19/3/20; MSL (1965), Shih-tsung, 5857, 8460, 8930; *Ts'ang-wu tsung-tu chün-men chih* 蒼梧總督軍門志 (NCL microfilm), 28/21a; SK (1930), 64/8a; Hsü Fu-tso, *Hua-tang-ko ts'ung-t'an*, 8/16a; *Chuang-shih shih-an* 莊氏史案 in *T'ung-shih* 痛史 (1912); *Mao Lu-men wen-chi* (NLP microfilm, no. 884), *ch.* 29, 30; Huang Tsung-hsi (ECCP), *Huang Li-chou wen-chi*(1959), 62; Ma Huan, *Ying-yai sheng-lan*, "The overall survey of the ocean's shores," tr. and ed. by J. V. G. Mills (Cambridge, 1970), 238.

Chaoying Fang and Else Glahn

MAO Po-wen 毛伯溫 (T. 汝厲), July 21, 1482–July 9, 1544, official, was a native of Chi-shui 吉水, Kiangsi. A *chin-shih* of 1508, he became prefectural judge of Shao-hsing, Chekiang. He was with the Censorate from 1511 to 1522 and served successively as regional inspector of Fukien, Honan (1516), and Hukuang (1518), and as an assistant minister of the

Grand Court of Revision from 1522 until 1527. In May, 1527, he was appointed governor of Ning-hsia but was replaced in October when accused of some mistakes while serving in the court. Five years later (March, 1533), when recalled to service, he received appointment as vice-censor-in-chief. Again he remained in office for only a few months, as he was impeached by Chu Yu-liang 朱祐椋, a member of the imperial clan, and was cashiered (July, 1533). In November, 1536, Hsia Yen (q.v.), minister of Rites, memorialized that Annam had for twenty years failed to send tribute to the court and urged the despatch of a punitive expedition. Mao was summoned to serve as censor-in-chief of the right and to work with Ch'iu Luan (q.v.), marquis of Hsienning, in the training of troops for the expedition. Mao begged leave to decline, pleading his father's recent death, but his request was refused and he reluctantly took up his duties at the capital in 1537.

The Annam problem became acute when in March of the same year a mission from Annam sent by the ruler, Lê Ninh 黎寧 (r. 1533-48), arrived asking help from the Ming court to expel the usurper Mac Dang-dung (q.v.). The emperor, skeptical of the envoy's veracity, ordered a slow mobilization of forces and commissioned imperial representatives stationed in the southern provinces to investigate the matter. During the winter, Mao was transferred to the post of minister of Works, and in that capacity devised a vehicle with eight wheels for the transportation of heavy stone columns to be used in the construction of the imperial mausoleum north of Peking.

Meanwhile Mac Dang-dung, made aware of the consequences of a punitive expedition, despatched an emissary to present an offer of submission. Mac Dang-dung's usurpation being confirmed, opinions at the court vacillated between war and peace. Officials like Wang Wensheng 汪文盛 (T. 希周, cs 1511, d. 1543),

governor of Yünnan, and Mu Ch'ao-fu 沐朝輔 (Pth. 恭禧), duke of Ch'ien-kuo 黔國, argued that, since Mac Dang-dung had admitted his guilt and offered to surrender, there was no need to dispatch an expedition. While the court decision was in the making, however, events took a sharp turn for the worse, and made for a change in opinion. Lê Ninh, the deposed ruler, fearing that the Ming court might accept Mac's bid for recognition and thus invalidate his own claim, sent in a petition with a full description of Mac's usurpation, and openly invited Chinese intervention. In the end the emperor took the side of the pro-war faction in the ministry of War and authorized the expedition. It remained the desire of the emperor, however, to overawe the usurper by a display of force without having to resort to arms.

On April 26, 1538, Mao Po-wen was installed as minister of War and appointed civilian head of the expeditionary force, assisting Ch'iu Luan. At this time opinions on the Annam problem were still divided, and, in spite of the earlier decision, the punitive order was not enforced. Meanwhile, in February, 1539, Mao was temporarily transferred to Shansi to supervise the defense of the northern frontiers in order to ward off the raids of the Mongols. He was credited, together with Liang Chen (q.v.), with completing the construction in three months of the five forts in the Tatung region. For this achievement he was favored with the title of junior guardian of the heir apparent. On September 8, the expedition was finally launched. Mao and Ch'iu led the troops into Annam, and their show of force successfully brought Mac Dang-dung into the fold on terms satisfactory to the Chinese. On April 28, 1541, an imperial proclamation was issued investing Mac as commander of the newly established territory of Annam. Thus, "without the shooting of a single arrow," Annam was once more returned to tributary status. As a reward for the success of his mission, Mao was given the higher title of grand guardian of the heir apparent.

Mao returned to the capital on January 23, 1542, which was the eighth day of the first month by the lunar calendar. Although regular court sessions were suspended during the New Year's holidays (from the 1st to the 15th), the emperor held a special court at the Wu-men 午門 (Meridian Gate) to receive him. Thereafter he served as head of the Censorate for almost a year and early in 1543 he became minister of War, succeeding Chang Tsan (*see* Yang Po) who had died the previous month. During the eight years of Chang Tsan's incumbency, the defense posture of the country had sunk alarmingly. Mao presided over sweeping reforms of the military establishment involving the removal of much surplus personnel. Although the emperor was pleased with his work, several men close to the throne whose personal interests were affected by the reforms were understandably unhappy.

In October, 1544, Mao ill-advisedly, upon the request of a local commander, withdrew from the northern frontier some temporary troops stationed there to ward off Mongol raids. The following month the invaders swept down in force and threatened the capital itself. In a rage the emperor struck Mao's name from the registry of officials. Soon after his return home Mao passed away. His reputation was restored in 1567 on the ascent to the throne of Chu Tsai-hou (*q.v.*), who honored him for his service to the state. At the beginning of the T'ien-ch'i period, he was given the posthumous name of Hsiang-mao 襄懋.

Mao's memorials are collected in *Tung-t'ang hsien-sheng tsou-i* 東塘先生奏義 (also known as *Mao Hsiang-mao tsou-i*), 20 *ch.*, printed in 1566. Eighteen of his memorials are included also in the *Huang Ming ching-shih wen-pien* of Ch'en Tzu-lung (ECCP). His writings are in *Mao Hsiang-mao chi* 集 (also known as *Tung-t'ang chi*) containing 10 *chüan* of

poetry and 8 *chüan* of prose. It includes a *nien-p'u* of Mao Po-wen by his son, Mao Tung 毛棟.

Bibliography

1/198/16a, 321/25b; 3/174/11b; 5/39/42a; 40/33/3b; 86/10/19a; SK (1930), 56/3a, 176/9a; MSL(1940), Chia-ching 257/2b: KC(1958), 3542, 3545, 3582, 3585, 3663; *Chi-shui-hsien chih* (1875), 33/6b; Ku Ying-t'ai (ECCP), *Ming ch'ao chi-shih pen-mo*, 22/27b; Chang Hsüan, *Hsi-yüan wen-chien lu*, 68/22b; Yamamoto Tatsuro, *Annan-shi no kenkyū*, Vol. 1: W. Franke, *Sources*, 5. 5. 23.

Benjamin E. Wallacker

MAO Qara, *see* **MAO Chung**

MAO Sheng 毛勝 (T. 用欽), 1401-September 21, 1458, military officer, was one of the several commanders of Mongol descent ennobled during the early years of the Ming dynasty for distinguished service. Mao was first known by his Chinese personal name Fu-shou 福壽; it was only after he became an earl that he adopted the one by which he came to be known. Mao's family, which did not assume the Chinese surname until his generation, reportedly held noble titles under the Yüan while living in the territory of modern Peking. The *Ming shih-lu* asserts that they belonged to the same clan as Aruγtai (*q.v.*), the powerful Mongol prince. Mao's uncle Na-hai 那海 (Noqai) seems to have been the first in the family to serve the Chinese. He distinguished himself under Chu Ti (*q.v.*) during his rebellion and became a vice regional commander. Noqai having died without sons, Mao's father, An-t'ai 安太, inherited his brother's position and soon became a commander in the Yü-lin 羽林 imperial bodyguard. An-t'ai's son, known as Mao Chi 濟 the first in the family to use the Chinese surname, inherited the rank, but he too died early without heirs, so that Mao Fu-shou succeeded to the title in 1431.

Sometime after this, for unknown

reasons, Mao Fu-shou deserted to the Mongols but soon returned to China. He then served in the Embroidered-uniform Guard at Peking, advancing to the rank of commander. Early in 1441 he took part in the campaign led by Wang Chi (q.v.), the minister of War, against the rebellious Shan tribesmen at Lu-ch'uan, Yunnan (see Ssu Jen-fa). He distinguished himself in battle and, returning to the capital, he was promoted to be an assistant commissioner-in-chief in June, 1442. Two months later the court again sent him back to Lu-ch'uan at the head of a unit of soldiers of Mongol ancestry. Having successfully completed his mission he returned to the north. In June, 1443, following the resurgence of the rebels, Mao received another summons to go back to the south. He remained in Yunnan for the next few years in charge of the suppression of the tribesmen, eventually advancing to the rank of vice commissioner-in-chief.

In July, 1449, as the Oirat were preparing an all-out assault on the Chinese, Mao was sent back to the north in charge of the defense of Tatung. Immediately after the T'u-mu debacle, Mao, lately promoted to commissioner-in-chief, was entrusted by the new court of Chu Ch'i-yü (q.v.) with the supervision of the training of army corps (see Yü Ch'ien). About this time trouble again flared among the tribesmen of Yunnan and Kweichow, apparently provoked by poor discipline in the army and maladministration. Because of his past experience, Mao received orders to lead an expedition to the south. Before he departed, Esen (q.v.), who had held Emperor Chu Ch'i-chen (q.v.) captive, threatened Peking with his armies (November); whereupon Mao was summoned to participate in the defense of the capital. A month later, Esen withdrew his forces and the emergency was over. When reports reached the court that tribal unrest was still endemic in Kweichow and Hukuang, Mao received a summons to head an expeditionary force of Mongol

soldiers recruited from the garrisons of Shantung and to join the command of Wang Chi in crushing the rebellion. At this juncture, a secretary of the ministry of Revenue, Ch'en Ju-yen (see Keng Chiu-ch'ou), voicing the general suspicion about the loyalty of the Mongol army officers as a consequence of the T'u-mu disaster, submitted a memorial (February, 1450) expressing his doubt about the advisability of sending Mao on such an important mission. The ministry of War, acting on Ch'en's memorial, sent a dispatch to Wang Chi, exhorting him to be more cautious with foreign soldiers under his command. It turned out, however, that Mao executed his mission with vigor and skill; the tribal rebels, hard pressed, extradited their own leader and surrendered in May, 1451. Then in April, 1452, Mao was sent to command the garrisons on the southwestern border of Yunnan.

In recognition of his meritorious performance (January, 1453), Emperor Chu Ch'i-yü appointed Mao earl of Nan-ning 南寧伯, with an annual stipend of 1,000 piculs of rice. It is obvious that this title was chosen because of his long and outstanding service in the south. All this time he was known as Fu-shou; in March, 1455, he requested that his name be changed to Sheng, which seemed more fitting for a seasoned campaigner. In his subsequent administration on the Sino-Burmese border, however, Mao had some difficulty in maintaining order, and was criticized by his Chinese colleagues for incompetence. A censor of Yunnan, Mou Feng 牟俸 (cs 1451, d. 1479), accused him (October, 1455) of greed and cruelty and several illegal acts. He maintained that Mao, being a "barbarian," was cunning and difficult to control, and that he had even been in touch with the enemy across the border, implying that Mao was plotting against the Chinese authorities. The emperor ordered an investigation, but for unknown reasons the matter was soon dropped.

Mao died at the age of fifty-seven.

As a tribute to his service, the reinstated emperor, Chu Ch'i-chen, promoted him posthumously to the rank of marquis and gave him the canonized name Chuang-i 壯毅 (strong and courageous). Late in December, 1459, the emperor appointed his son, Mao Jung 榮, to inherit the hereditary earldom. Early in 1464 Mao Jung became involved in the case of Ch'ien P'u (*see* Han Yung), who was punished for communicating with a eunuch in the hope of gaining a high official appointment, and was sentenced to exile in Kwangsi. Following his pardon in 1466 Mao became the commander-in-chief of Kweichow, and there he died on February 6, 1470. His descendants successively inherited the title to the end of the dynasty.

Bibliography

1/156/8a, 107/16a; 5/9/54a; MSL (1963), Ying-tsung, *ch.* 92-294, Hsien-tsung (1964), 1439; Chang Hung-hsiang 張鴻翔, "*Ming-shih* chüan i-wu-liu chu-ch'en shih-hsi piao" 明史卷一五六諸臣世系表, *Fu-jen hsüeh-chih* 輔仁學誌, 5: 1-2 (1936), 23; Henry Serruys, "Mongols Ennobled during the Early Ming," HJAS, 22 (1959), 237.
Hok-lam Chan

MAO Wei 茅維 (T. 孝若, H. 僧曇), February, 1575-1640?, fourth and youngest son of Mao K'un (*q. v.*), of Kuei-an, Chekiang, was a historian, poet, and dramatist. In his youth he became known, along with Tsang Mou-hsün (*see* Ch'en Pang-chan), as one of the four noted writers of his native prefecture. In poetry he was considered to be superior to his father and elder brother, Mao Kuo-chin (*see* Mao Yüan-i), but in the civil examinations he failed. When he began to take the provincial examination in 1597, he apparently was quite sure of himself for he purchased the title of a student of the National Unversity in order to compete in Peking, since there was a slightly greater prestige for one who became a *chü-jen* in the capital. He did not pass in that year, nor in the next session (1600).

In 1603 he stayed home mourning the death of his father. Then he failed seven more times in succession. In 1615 he placed on the auxiliary list (fu-pang 副榜), thus becoming a kung-sheng 貢生 or regular student of the National University, which was a little better than the purchased title.

During these years he came to know many scholars and officials of that day, including Nan Chü-i, Yeh Hsiang-kao, and Ts'ao Hsüeh-ch'üan (*qq. v.*). In 1619 he made a trip to Fukien, where he stayed with Yeh and Ts'ao as their guest. In 1624, after the ninth failure in the provincial examination in Peking, he was recommended to serve as a chief clerk of the Hanlin Academy to take part in a national history project. This did not materialize and he returned home. Meanwhile his sponsors, Yeh Hsiang-kao and Chu Kuo-chen (ECCP), were forced out of office by the eunuch party. During the persecution of the Tung-lin associates (*see* Kao P'an-lung), Mao Wei was not seriously involved but had to appear at a court to be interrogated, and this prevented him from taking the examination in 1627. After hearing of the collapse of the eunuch party later that year, he wrote several poems to celebrate the occasion.

Under the new emperor, Chu Yu-chien (ECCP), most officials victimized by the eunuchs were rehabilitated. In March, 1629, after the birth of the emperor's eldest son, the edict celebrating that occasion proclaimed an amnesty and called for the induction of talented commoners. Mao Wei, then approaching sixty years, went to Peking in the vague hope of winning imperial notice by submitting a proposal on current affairs. He arrived in October armed with the draft of a memorial on the raising of funds to meet military expenses. Early in 1630, when Peking was under attack by the Manchus, he wrote another memorial. While he waited for an official to volunteer to submit these to the throne for him, he was strongly denounced by his nephew, Mao Yüan-i, who, then in Peking as an unassigned military officer of high rank, regarded the uncle as a lunatic adventurer. Meanwhile a former neighbor of Mao Wei brought up charges against him for having illegally occupied the neighbor's properties. The accusation somehow came to the attention of the emperor, who ordered an investigation. Instead of answering the charges in Peking, Mao Wei fled south and went into hiding. Late in 1630 he was placed under arrest and during the following year was detained in the prison of the Hangchow guard awaiting trial. It seems that his case was settled in March, 1632, but he was reduced to the status of a commoner.

Meanwhile Mao Wei kept up the feud with Mao Yüan-i. Late that year there was a meeting at their ancestral temple to decide which of the recently deceased relatives were worthy to be commemorated therein. Over some small matters the two clashed and after the meeting exchanged some unpleasant correspondence. In 1634, because Mao Yüan-i sold his house without consulting Mao Wei, the latter reported the matter to the ancestral temple in a prayer, saying that the house was built in 1592 on his, Mao Wei's, land and with funds from his share of the inheritance, and that the debt had not been fully repaid; he added that he did not mind the expense, but resented the slight. The dispute seems to have continued for several years, for early in 1637 Mao Yüan-i wrote a nasty letter to the uncle accusing him of meddling in the sale of the house, to which Mao Wei replied that he was not to be intimidated and was holding his ground. He also published the promissory note, which Mao Kuo-chin (Mao Yüan-i's father) had written (on the schedule of repayment of his debt on the house), as evidence that the debt had not been fully paid.

Later in 1637 Mao Wei again offered his service to the emperor. He sold some of his properties to finance a trip to Peking and distributed a public letter among his acquaintances asking to be recommended to the throne as a military strategist. Apparently it again came to naught. Ch'ien Ch'ien-i (ECCP) recorded in his collected poems that Mao Wei paid him several visits in 1639, and apparently stayed on in the neighborhood (Soochow ?), for, a year later, on the seventh day of the seventh moon, he took a concubine. In the poem Ch'ien explicitly mentions her as a young virgin.

Mao Wei excelled in various styles of poetry. Some of his long poems on historical events, such as his observation of the movement of troops on their way to Liaotung in 1621, are noteworthy. He named his earlier collected works *Shih-lai-t'ang chi* 十賚堂集, of which the first collection, *Chia* 甲 *chi* (poems, 5 *ch.*, prose, 12 *ch.*), and the second, *I* 乙 *chi* (poems, 18 *ch.*), were printed about 1618. The third collection, *Ping* 丙 *chi* (poems, 12 *ch.*), was printed in 1628. He is said to have made several more collections, entitled *Ku-yüan chi* 孤園集, *P'ei-hsi ts'ao* 佩觽草, *Min-yu ts'ao* 閩遊草, etc. His later collection seems to be the one entitled *Mao Chieh-hsi chi* 潔溪集 (24 *ch.*?), printed during 1632 to 1640. It includes the following items: "Huan-shan san-t'i shih" 還山三體詩, 4 *ch.* (1632); "Tung-kuan 多館 shih" (1632); "Yüan-hsia shang-ko" 轘下商歌, 3 *ch.* (1636); "Yü-t'an" 迂談, essays written in 1634; accounts of his feud with Mao Yüan-i written in 1632, 1634, and 1637; "Hsü 續 shang-ko," poems of 1637 to 1640, in which he mentions the titles of two song-dramas, written in 1638, "Mei-nai-ho" 沒奈河 (What can you do?) and "I-i-hu" 已矣乎 (Give up); "Hua-shih" 花史, on some flowers in his garden, written in 1633; "Mei-kuei, mu-tan" 梅桂牡丹 (On plum, cassia, and peony, 1633); and two dramas, "Ch'un-ming tsu-chang" 春明祖帳 and "Yün-ho hsün-meng" 雲壑尋盟, apparently about some personal experiences. The engraving of his later works after 1636 (to which he gave a collective title, *Ling-hsia-ko hsin-chu* 凌霞閣新著) seems to have been done in the printing establishment of Mao Chin (ECCP). All these works are available on microfilm. Six of his dramatic works were included in the *Sheng Ming tsa-chü* 盛明雜劇, 3d series (reproduced in 1941): 1) *Su-yüan-weng* 蘇園翁, on a talented man who preferred tending his garden to serving in the government, even at a time of crisis; 2) *Ch'in-t'ing ch'iung* 秦廷筑, on Ching K'o (d. 227 B. C.), the unsuccessful assassin; 3) *Chin-men chi* 金門戟, about the Han emperor Wu (157-87 B. C.) on an indiscreet excursion; 4) *Tsui Hsin-feng* 醉新豐, on the eighteen early T'ang ministers; 5) *Nao men-shen* 鬧門神, a satire; 6) *Shuang ho-huan* 雙合歡, a comedy. According to the *Ming-shih*, he is credited with a historical work, *Chia-ching ta cheng-chi* 嘉靖大政記, 2 *ch.*, and three anthologies, *Lun-heng* 論衡, 6 *ch.*, *Piao -heng* 表-heng, 6 *ch.*, and *Ts'e-heng* 策-heng, 26 *ch.* As the titles indicate, he compiled these to serve as models for writing expositions and memorials in congratulatory and advisory styles. The last, known also as *Huang Ming ts'e-heng*, was listed for destruction in the 1780s. Fortunately a copy printed in 1605 is preserved in the Naikaku Bunko, Tokyo. He is said to have compiled a list of paintings entitled *Nan Yang ming-hua piao* 南陽名畫表.

Bibliography

1/99/27a, 287/7b; 3/268/11a; 24/4/97a; 40/71/1b; 43/6/2a; 64/庚30下/6a; *Kuei-an-hsien chih* (1881), 21/6a, 22/6b, 36/24b; Chou I-po 周貽白, *Ming-jen tsa-chü hsüan-chu* 明人雜劇選註 (Peking, 1958), 459; Ch'ien Ch'ien-i, *Lieh-ch'ao shih-chi*, IV: 15/74b; *id.*, *Mu-chai ch'u-hsüeh chi* (SPTK ed.), 15/14a, 16/13a, 17/10b; TSCC (1885-88), XVII: 763/6a.

T. Pokora and Chaoying Fang

MAO Yüan-i 茅元儀 (T. 止生, H. 石民), 1594-*ca.* 1641, a scholar and author, was a native of Kuei-an 歸安, Chekiang. His father, Mao Kuo-chin 國縉 (T. 薦卿, H.

二岑, 1555-1607, cs 1583), was an official of substance and a writer. Little is known of Mao Yüan-i's early education. It is entirely possible, as some scholars have suggested, that a major influence on him in his youth was his grandfather, Mao K'un (*q. v.*), who had participated in the suppression of pirates and had written substantially on military matters. His collection of books, which his grandson inherited, was rich and in all likelihood contained charts and other illustrative matter which Mao Yüan-i later put to use. In any event, from an early age two characteristics persisted and continued throughout his life. One was his predilection for direct action in the face of critical situations; the other was his intense interest in military matters. He read widely in military history, and reports have it that he was able to recount all the important military stratagems of the past, describe the strategical geography of many localities, and illustrate his accounts with charts as easily as if he had all the information in the palm of his hand. When pressure from the Manchus became critical, he was eager to make his own contributions for the defense of the country.

The opportunity came in 1621 when Sun Ch'eng-tsung (ECCP) was appointed commander of the army defending the northeastern frontier. Sun invited Mao to be an advisor, often discussed military tactics with him, and benefited from his knowledge and advice. His position in Sun's army ended soon after Sun's resignation. In 1628, on the accession to the throne of Chu Yu-chien (ECCP), Mao presented his treatise on military preparedness, *Wu-pei chih* 武備志, a work of 240 *chüan*, with his own preface dated 1621. At the same time he memorialized on the general problems of national defense, including the situations on the eastern frontier (Liaotung) and the coastal areas of Fukien and Kwangtung, as well as plans for the provisioning of the armed forces. As a result the emperor ordered that Mao be made a tai-chao 待詔 of the Hanlin Academy. Unfavorable comments from officials opposed to Mao at court, however, led to the withdrawal of this appointment.

In December, 1629, when Sun Ch'eng-tsung was summoned to take command of an army stationed at T'ung-chou 通州 to meet with a new threat from the Manchus, he recalled Mao to service. Mao joined Sun's force promptly and with enthusiasm. After a succession of Chinese victories, Mao was appointed regional vice commander and placed in charge of the defense of Chüeh-hua Island覺華島, a major provisioning center some twelve li off the coast in the Gulf of Chihli. Again his opportunity for service turned out to be short-lived; a troop mutiny led to his dismissal and imprisonment, followed by exile to the coastal city of Chang-p'u 漳浦 in southern Fukien. The Manchu threat increased, and Mao petitioned for permission to recruit volunteer "suicide squads" to help defend the Ming dynasty. His petition, however, was blocked by powerful courtiers unfriendly to him. Left without a means to express his desire for action at a time when the dynasty was in dire straits, Mao took to excessive drinking, and soon died a frustrated and unhappy man.

Mao left voluminous writings, both prose and poetry. One critic of his poems remarked that his phrasing was not mellow and refined enough. His close friend Ch'ien Ch'ien-i (ECCP) recorded that Mao took himself to be a man of unusual talent, and seldom bothered to cultivate friendships with persons he considered ordinary or uncongenial. It was Mao's habit to write at high speed, his poetry and prose bursting with power. His major lifelong concern, as expressed in his writings, was the quest for a way to strengthen the defenses of the country. The Hu-chou-fu chih 湖州府志 lists thirty-four titles under Mao's name. Twenty-two of these, including Wu-pei chih, are listed in the Index Expurgatorius of the 18th century. The Wu-pei chih is a work of primary importance and has been quoted and utilized by many scholars. The work was reprinted in Japan in 1664 and several parts were copied in the 1720s into the T'u-shu chi-ch'eng. No one concerned with military organization, arms, armor, explosive weapons, ships, maps of the northern frontier, and the routes from the Yangtze delta to lands rimmed by the Indian Ocean, can afford to neglect it. His collected poems, entitled Shih-min shih-chi 石民詩集, 52 ch., were arranged under six titles. His collected prose, which he gathered together when he was approaching his fortieth year, is entitled Shih-min ssu-shih chi四十集, 148 ch., and the pieces he wrote during his military service were collected in a separate edition known as Shih-min wei-ch'u chi 未出集, 20 ch.

Bibliography

40/70/1b; 64/辛 26/10a;84/丁 13 下/29a;86/19/29a; Hu-chou-fu chih (1872), 59/23b; Kuei-an-hsien chih (1881), 36/20b, 23b; SK (1930), 54/5a, 90/4b, 128/8a, 143/11a, 197/9b; Ch'ing-tai chin-shu tsung-mu ssu-chung 清代禁書總目四種 (1930); Sun Tien-ch'i (1957), 15, 22, 51, 67, 88, 90, 172, 188, 196; Ts'ang-shu chi-shih shih 藏書紀事詩 (1958), 3/118; W. Franke, Sources, 7.2.7; J.J.L. Duyvendak, Ma Huan Reexamined (1933), 19; Joseph Needham and Wang Ling, Science and Civilization in China, III (1959), 559; Tenney L. Davis and James R. Ware: "Early Chinese Military Pyrotechnics," Jo. of Chemical Education, Vol. 24 (1947), 522; Ma Huan, Ying-yai sheng-lan, "The Overall Survey of the Ocean's Shores," tr. and ed. by J. V. G. Mills (Cambridge, 1970), 238.

E-tu Zen Sun

MAR-KÖRGIS 麻兒可兒 was a Mongol qaɣan who reigned from 1454 to 1466. For no other individual is there so much confusion and uncertainty in Mongol and in Chinese sources as there are for both his name and his chronology. His father, strangely enough, is known to Chinese historians under a Mongol name, Toɣtobuqa (*see* Esen), and in Mongol sources under a Chinese name, Tayisung (Chinese T'ai-tsung 太宗). Theoretically he was great-qaγan of Mongolia, but in fact he was no more than a figurehead and a tool in the hands of his "lieutenant" (the Oirat Esen) who was not a member of the imperial family. In the long run an open conflict could not be averted. Esen, confident that nobody would dare resist him, decided to assume the supreme dignity of qaγan. Defeated by Esen, Toγto-buqa was murdered as he fled from the scene of battle. The Mongol chronicler Saγang-sečen puts Toγto-buqa's death in the year jen-shen: 1452. According to the *Ming shih-lu*, however, his death occurred at the very end of the year hsin-wei (1451), which overlaps into the following Western year: January 19, 1452. According to the Mongol historian, Toγto-buqa's younger brother was qaγan for a very short while, only to be eliminated by Esen, who then proclaimed himself qaγan. The Chinese historians record nothing of this interim succession, relating only that Esen made himself qaγan immediately after his victory over Toγto-buqa, and that he so notified the Ming court.

Chinese and Mongol sources are agreed that after Esen's death (1454) a son of Toγto-buqa was made qaγan. According to the Chinese he was the youngest son. In Mongol histories his name appears as Mar-körgis, or Maqa-körgis 馬可古兒吉斯; the Chinese write his name in a variety of ways, Ma-er-k'o-er, Ma-ma-k'o-er-chi-ssu 麻馬可兒吉斯, Ma-k'o-ku 古 -er-chi-ssu, Ma-er-k'u-er-chi-ssu, 麥 Mai -er-k'u-er-chi-ssu, etc. Only one form can be correct: Mar-körgis. Saγang-sečen adds that he became known as Ükegtü qaγan, *i.e.*, the qaγan "with the box" because his mother immediately after Esen's death took the seven-year-old boy in a box with her on horseback to assume the lead in a military campaign and retake the throne for him. Besides the fact that Saγang-sečen is mistaken in putting Esen's death in 1452, he also states that Mar-körgis reigned

less than one year and was murdered "in the year of the cock" (1453). According to the *Altan-tobči* (*nova*), he occupied the throne for eight years and died "in the year of the cock" (1453 or 1465?). According to Saγang-sečen, Mar-körgis was succeeded by an elder brother named Molon 摩倫 or Molan, who reigned from 1453 to 1454, when he too was murdered at the age of eighteen.

The compilers of the *Ming-shih* admit that Mongolia during this period was so disturbed by civil wars and that the qaγans, or the "Little kings," as the Chinese called them, succeeded each other so rapidly that it became impossible to follow the events closely and to keep track of them. Thus, according to the *Ming-shih*, after Esen's death, a son of Toγto-buqa, Ma-er-k'o-er, was made qaγan; but he was murdered in 1462 by the man who had been his main support in 1455. In 1462, Ma-er-k'o-er was succeeded by one Ma-ku-k'o-er-chi-ssu, who was murdered in 1466, again by the same man who had put to death his alleged predecessor Ma-er-k'o-er. It is evident that Ma-er-k'o-er and Ma-ku-k'o-er-chi-ssu are one and the same person, and that both names are corrupt.

In the *Ming shih-lu* too Mar-Körgis' name appears in various transcriptions, first in May, 1455, when he presented his initial tribute to the Ming court. It is interesting that at this time his principal envoy was one Pir-Muhammad (*see* Esen) who for more than a decade came to Peking almost every year to present the tribute for Toγto-buqa and Esen. Between 1455 and 1466, the qaγan offered tribute on several occasions, and although the name of the qaγan is not always written with the same characters, there is no mention of a succession of qaγans during those years. It seems certain that there was only one who reigned from 1455 to 1466 (or perhaps early in 1467) when the Chinese court learned that he had been murdered by the same individual who in the narrative of the *Ming-shih* had murdered both "Ma-er-k'o-er" and "Ma-ku-k'o-er-chi-ssu." Apart from his name and his yearly tribute presentation, nothing else is known about this Markörgis. The *Ming shih-lu* mentions a successor but does not record his name, which is another proof of the lack of information about events in Mongolia.

Some Chinese sources state that Esen was succeeded by one of his sons; and when he died, an "elder brother" or an "elder cousin" of the Little King by the name of T'o-ssu 脫思 succeeded him. This T'o-ssu is not mentioned either in the *Ming shih-lu* or in the *Ming-shih*; moreover, the name T'o-ssu recalls nothing known in Mongol, and it is impossible to identify him.

Mar-Körgis is a Christian name, derived from the Syriac: Mar, *i.e.*, Venerable, George. During the Yung-lo period another Mongol prince had borne a name of Syriac origin: Mar-haza (Mar-hasia). But if Mar-Körgis bore a Christian name, his elder brother and successor (according to Mongol sources) is known by a Buddhist name: Molon or Molan (Skr. Maudgalyayana),

Bibliography

1/327/9b; MSL (1963), Ying-tsung, 5241, 5249; KC (1958), 1917, 1975; Ch'ü Chiu-ssu 瞿九思, *Wan-li wu-kung lu* 武功錄 (1612), *Kuo-hsüeh wen-k'u* ed. (1936), *chüan* 7; Cheng Hsiao, *Huang Ming pei-lu k'ao, Kuo-hsüeh wen-k'u* ed. (1937), Vol. 45; Saγang-sečen, *Erdeni-yin tobči, Scripta Mongolica*, II, Cambridge, Mass., 1956; C. R. Bawden, *The Mongol Chronicle Altan Tobči* (Wiesbaden, 1955), 174; bLo-bsaṅ bsTaṅ-' jin, *Altan Tobči (nova), Scripta Mongolica*, I, Cambridge, Mass., 1952; D. Pokotilov, *History of the Eastern Mongols during the Ming Dynasty from 1368 to 1634*, tr. by R. Loewenthal, *Studia Serica*, ser. A, no. 1 (Chengtu, 1947), pt. 1, 60; W. Franke, "Addenda and Corrigenda," *ibid.*, no. 3 (1949), pt. 2, 44; H. Serruys, "Notes on a Few Mongolian Rulers of the 15th Century," JAOS, 76 (1956), 85; Tamura Jitsuzō 田村實造, *Mindai Mammō shiryō, Min jitsuroko-shō, Mōko hen* 明代滿蒙史料, 明實錄抄, 蒙古篇, Vols. 4–5 (1956); L. Hambis, *Documents sur l'histoire des Mongols à l'époque des Ming* (Paris, 1969), 32, 34, 36.

Henry Serruys

MEI Ch'ing 梅清 (T. 淵公, 潤公, H. 瞿仙) 1623–97, artist and writer, was a native of Hsüan-ch'eng宣城 (Anhwei), the great-grandson of Mei Ting-tso (*q.v.*). On the collapse of the Ming, his family who owned a large estate became impoverished, and, perhaps to avoid marauders, he escaped into the countryside where he lived for several years frugally and in a depressed state of mind. Eventually, possibly to protect what remained of his family's property as well as to increase his income, he decided to sit for the state examination and seek office under the new dynasty. He achieved the *chü-jen* in 1654, but failed repeatedly in his attempts to qualify for the advanced degree. It is said that he tried ten times, which would place the last time he journeyed to Peking for the metropolitan examination in 1682, *i.e.*, when he was sixty years of age by the Chinese way of counting. During these years he traveled widely, north and south, meeting many friends of like interests and at the same time making sketches and writing melancholy poetry.

Around the year 1662, Mei befriended Tao-chi (*q.v.*), some eighteen years his junior, and for years they were in close contact. Tao-chi visited him in Hsüan-ch'eng frequently during the decade following, and once they traveled together to the famous mountain, Huang-shan黄山, nearby. Here they both found inspiration and executed many paintings. Mei is said to have filled several albums with scenes of Huang-shan, of which a collector recorded in 1939 that he had seen more than twenty. From 1919 to 1939 at least four of the albums were reproduced; one entitled "Huang-shan shih-chiu-ching ts'e" 十九景冊 consists of nineteen scenes on twenty-four leaves, and was painted at the age of seventy-one. The Ch'ing critic, his younger contemporary, Wang

Shih-chen (ECCP), wrote enthusiastically of his landscapes and pine trees. Although Tao-chi was younger, some critics hold that Mei learned much from him; nevertheless Mei had his own personal style and both seem to have held each other in high regard. One of Mei's special interests was the plum blossom; hence one of the names he gave himself: Mei-ch'ih 梅癡 (befooled by the plum). An example of one such painting is a short hand scroll on paper "Fang P'o-hsien pi-i 倣坡仙筆意 (dated 1692) in the Academy of Arts in Honolulu. He used a flat board-like brush to achieve his unusually fanciful and original effect. He was not one to accept conventional rules. His total composition usually was simple: a few dynamic features leaving much open space. Even in his most crowded pictures, there is still an airy and lyrical atmosphere. He painted as though he were writing a poem.

His poetry has been gathered together in several collections: *T'ien-yen-ko shan-hou shih* 天延閣刪後詩, 16 *ch.*, and *T'ien-yen-ko shih hou-chi* 後集, 13 *ch.* (plus 4 additional *chüan*). A later edition known as *Ch'ü-shan shih lüeh* 瞿山詩略, 33 *ch.*, includes three additional *chüan* of poems. The *ts'ung-shu*, *Huang Ch'ing po-ming-chia shih* 皇清百名家詩, includes the *Mei Ch'ü-shan shih* in one *chüan*. He also published the *Mei-shih shih-lüeh* 氏詩畧, 16 *ch.*, an anthology of selections of the writings of one hundred eight poets of the past thousand years, T'ang through Ming.

Mei Ch'ing had several talented cousins. In addition to Mei Keng 庚 (T. 耦長, cj 1681), also a painter, who served as magistrate of T'ai-shun 泰順, -hsien Wenchou 溫州 prefecture, Chekiang, from 1710 to 1718, there were Mei Ch'ung 冲 (T. 羽中, 抱村), who wrote the *Chuang-tzu pen-i* 本義, and the mathematician, Mei Wen-ting (ECCP).

Bibliography
Yin-te 9: 489/25a; *Hsüan-ch'eng-hsien chih* (1889), 13/36a, 18/24a, 27b; SK (1930), 182/2a; *T'ai-shun fen-chiang lu* 分疆錄 (1880), 4/3b; Ch'in Tsu-yung 秦祖永(1825–84), *T'ung-yin lun-hua* 桐陰論畫；Teng Chih-ch'eng 鄧之誠, *Ch'ing-shih chi-shih ch'u-pien* 清詩紀事初編 (1965), 583; *Wan-ya* 宛雅 (3d series), 8/9a, 13/1a; *Mei Ch'ü-shan hua-chi*, Shanghai, 1960 (46 plates); *Huang-shan sheng-chi t'u ts'e* 勝蹟圖冊 (1936); *Huang-shan t'u ts'e* (1935); *Mo-pi shan-shui ts'e*(1934); *Huang-shan shih-chiu ching ts'e* (1934); *Huang-shan ch'üan-ching ching-p'in* 全景精品 (in the collection of the Chou family studio, Chin-chüeh-an 今覺庵, 1939); O. Sirén, *Chinese Painting*, (New York 1956–58), Vol. V, 142, Vol. VII, 385; E. J. Laing, *Chinese Paintings in Chinese Publications, 1956–1968* (Ann Arbor, 1969), 275; V. Contag and C. C. Wang, *Seals of Chinese Painters and Collectors of the Ming and Ch'ing Periods* (Hong Kong, 1966), 306, 682; James Cahill, *Fantastics and Eccentrics in Chinese Painting* (New York, 1967), 53.

                                    Yu-ho Tseng Ecke

MEI Ting-tso 梅鼎祚 (T. 禹金, H. 叔子, 太一生, 勝樂道人), 1549-1618, scholar, poet, dramatist, and bibliophile, was a native of Hsüan-ch'eng 宣城, Nan-Chihli. His father, Mei Shou-te 守德 (T. 純甫, H. 宛溪先生, 1510-January 17, 1578, cs 1541), officiated both in Peking and in the provinces (Chekiang, Shantung, and Yunnan). After serving as left administration vice commissioner of Yunnan, he retired in 1557, returned home to be with his mother, and to devote his time to studies. In 1564, under the sponsorship of Keng Ting-hsiang (*q.v.*), then commissioner of education at Nanking, and Lo Ju-fang (*q.v.*), the prefect of Ning-kuo 寧國, within whose jurisdiction Hsüan-cheng was situated, the academy, Chih-hsüeh shu-yüan 志學書院, was founded. Mei Shou-te and another native scholar Shen Ch'ung (*see* Shen Yu-jung) were invited to be co-directors. The academy became an influential center of learning, attracted many visitors and scholars, as well as artists, poets, Buddhist monks, and Taoist priests. Mei Shou-te participated in the editing of two gazetteers, the *Hsü-chou chih* 徐州志, 12 *ch.*, and the *Ning-kuo-fu chih* 寧國府志, 10 *ch.* Among other remains are his collected literary works, entitled *Ts'ang-chou kao* 滄州稿.

Mei Ting-tso's mother, née Kuo 郭 (1514-81), also a native of Hsüan-ch'eng, married his father in 1528, and gave birth to one daughter and three sons. An unusually wide gap separated the three older children and the youngest, Ting-tso. When he was nine years old both his brothers died on the same day. They had already been married and achieved the *hsiu-ts'ai*. The father, overcome with sorrow, blamed the death of his sons on over-concentration on their studies. He therefore became indulgent toward the remaining son. For three years Mei Ting-tso did not attend school. Only on his mother's insistence did he resume his schooling. It was also due to his mother that he stopped rebelling against punishments meted out by his teacher. Perhaps this also resulted in his distaste for the strict regulations of the examination system, causing him to abandon the pursuit of higher degrees soon after he had successfully passed the district examination in 1564.

In 1589, already known in literary circles, he was selected to be a *kung-sheng* and entered the National University in Peking. At this time Grand Secretaries Shen Shih-hsing, Wang Hsi-chüeh (*qq.v.*), and Hsü Kuo (*see* Ku Hsien-ch'eng) all agreed to offer him a position in the Hanlin Academy, having in mind Wen Cheng-ming (*q.v.*) as precedent, but he declined and preferred retirement. At home, enjoying his garden, the Shu-tai-yüan 書帶園, and his library, the T'ien-i-ko 天逸閣, he spent his time collecting books, making comprehensive compilations, and writing poetry, prose, dramas, and some other pieces of lighter literature. The *Ssu-k'u* catalogue records nineteen titles of his authorship, thirteen being copied into the Imperial Library.

Of those included in the latter, eleven constitute a series of prose compilations (文紀) dating from ancient times down to the Sui dynasty (590-618), one *Shih wen-chi* 釋文紀, a prose compilation

of 45 *chüan*, all written by Buddhist monks, of which the Commercial Press made a photolithographic copy in 1934-35, and included in the *Ssu-k'u ch'üan-shu chen-pen*, first series 珍本初集, and one a compilation of ancient poetry, the *Ku-yüeh-yüan* 古樂苑. The prose compilations later served as one of the primary sources for Yen K'o-chün (ECCP) in his assemblage of material for the gigantic work, the title of which may be rendered "Complete Collection of Prose Literature from Remote Antiquity through the Ch'in and Han Dynasties, the Three Kingdoms, and the Six Dynasties." As to poetry, besides the *Ku-yüeh-yüan*, Mei compiled the *Han Wei shih-sheng* 漢魏詩乘 and the *Liu-ch'ao* 六朝 *shih-sheng*, which together were known also as the *Pa-tai* 八代 *shih-sheng*. There is also his *Wan-ya* 宛雅, a collection of poetry by ninety-two authors of his native place, who lived between the T'ang dynasty and his own time.

A few decades previously, a Shantung scholar, Feng Wei-no, the grandfather of Feng Ch'i (*q.v.*) and younger brother of Feng Wei-min (*q.v.*), the dramatist, had compiled the *Ku-shih chi* 古詩紀, 156 ch., a collection of poems written from ancient times through the 6th century A.D. Feng's work was first printed in Shensi, so it was rare in the Yangtze area. This fact moved Mei to make his own compilations first of poetry and then of prose. As a matter of fact Feng's work not only inspired Mei Ting-tso, but also several other similar endeavors, such as *Ku-shih-so* 所 of Tsang Mou-hsün (*see* Ch'en Pang-chan) and *Ku-shih lei-yüan* 類苑 of Chang Chih-hsiang 張之象 (T. 玄超, 月鹿, H. 王屋山人, 1507-87). According to the *Ssu-k'u* editors all the later compilers founded themselves more or less on Feng's work, but none surpassed it. Ming scholars, particularly in the 16th and 17th centuries, set the trend toward issuing large compilations and collections (*ts'ung-shu*), which undoubtedly led to the preservation of many writings.

Mei's own collected literary work, the

Lu-ch'iu shih-shih chi 鹿裘石室集, 65 *ch.*, first printed in 1623, contains 25 *chüan* of poetry, 25 of prose, and 15 of correspondence. Although banned in the 18th century, it has survived. On a less serious level he wrote the *Ch'ing-ni lien-hua chi* 青泥蓮花記, biographical sketches of prostitutes known for certain virtues, and the *San-ts'ai ling-chi* 三才靈記, anecdotes about talented immortals and spirits (才幻記), talented deities (才神記), and talented ghosts (才鬼記). He confessed that since childhood he had been fond of jest and humor, so he made a collection of witty stories entitled *I-hsü lu-chih* 囈噓臚志.

The three lyrical dramatic works that he composed are the *K'un-lun-nu chien-hsia ch'eng-hsien* 崑崙奴劍俠成仙, (better known in its abbreviated form as *K'un-lun-nu*), the *Yü-ho chi* 玉合記, and the *Ch'ang-ming-lü chi* 長命縷記. The plot of the first is based on the T'ang story of the loyalty and superhuman feats of a Negro slave; the latest reprint of this appeared in 1958 in the *Sheng Ming tsa-chü* 盛明雜劇. The plots of both the second and the third dramas have to do with the romance of the T'ang poet Han Hung (fl. middle of 8th century). Han's famous poem, which begins with the line "Chang-t'ai liu" 章臺柳 and the poetic response made by Liu-shih 柳氏, provides the substance for dramatic and imaginative use.

Bibliography

40/62/21b; 64/庚 8/13b; 84/丁下/49b; TSCC (1885–88), XI: 769/21b, XXIII: 113/15a; SK (1930), 144/6a, 11b, 180/5b, 189/5a, 189/8b, 193/11b; Chi Yu-kung 計有功, *T'ang-shih chi-shih* 唐詩紀事 (Shang-hai, 1965), 470; Mei Ch'ing, *Mei-shih shih-lüeh* (preface 1691), 5/1a, Fu Hsi-hua 傅惜華, *Ming-tai ch'uan-ch'i ch'üan-mu* 明代傳奇全目 (Peking, 1959), 55; *Ming-tai tsa-chü ch'üan-mu*, (Peking, 1958), 131; Sun Tien-ch'i (1957), 143; L. of C. *Catalogue of Rare Books*, 954; Chang Hsing-lang, "The Importation of Negro Slaves to China under the T'ang Dynasty (A. D. 618–907)," *Bulletin No. 7 of the Catholic University of Peking* (December, 1930), 46.

Lienche Tu Fang

MEI Tsu 梅鷟 (T. 鳴岐, H. 致齋, 平埜) cj 1513, historian, was a native of Ching-te 旌德 (Anhwei). Beyond the fact that he was senior instructor in the National University in Nanking (1543–44), was promoted to assistant prefect of Ch'ang-chou-fu 常州府 (1544–?), and later served as an inspector of the salt works in Yun-nan, few details of his life are recorded. His family was isolated and of modest means; books were scarce, and access to them was mainly through borrowing and copying. An older brother, Mei O 鶚 (T. 百一 H. 鳧山, cs of 1517), received wide acclaim as a writer but died in his forty-fifth year before he could begin his official career. He did, however, leave a literary collection entitled *Fu-shan chi* 鳧山集, 4 *ch.*

The recognition to which Mei Tsu himself can lay claim rests almost entirely on his being the first historical critic to assert energetically and adduce imposing evidence to show that the so-called ku-wen 古文 (ancient text) of the *Shu-ching* 書經 or *Shang-shu* 尚書 (Classic of History) was a forgery, apparently of the third or early fourth century A. D. His book supporting this conclusion, entitled *Shang-shu k'ao-i* 考異 (Discrepancies in the *Shang-shu*), was probably completed about 1543. There does not seem to be any record of a printed edition of it in the Ming period. Even the great bibliophile Chiao Hung (ECCP), who knew about the book and managed to give a summary of Mei's ideas, was unable to consult the book himself. In the early 18th century Chu I-tsun (ECCP) mentioned it in his bibliography, *Ching-i-k'ao*, but listed it as in one *chüan* and made a mistake in the title. In the late 18th century the compilers of the *Ssu-k'u* manuscript library edited a five *chüan* edition of the *Shang-shu k'ao-i* based on a manuscript copy in one *chüan* from the T'ien-i ko Library (*see* Fan Ch'in, ECCP, p. 230). In 1814 there appeared the first printed edition in 6 *chüan*, edited by Sun Hsing-yen (ECCP) with the assistance of Ku

Kuang-ch'i (ECCP). It was included in Sun's collection, *P'ing-ching kuan ts'ung-shu*. In his preface to it Ku remarked that, although scholars of the Ch'ing period such as Yen Jo-chü and Hui Tung (both in ECCP) had produced works proving conclusively that the *Shu-ching* in the "ancient text" was spurious, Mei's work was still worth printing not only because it was the first work to identify the sources from which the forger derived his style and his ideas, but also because some of Mei's findings were not cited in Yen's work.

It took courage for Mei to attack the ancient text of the *Shu-ching* because what he tried to prove as spurious actually formed a large part of the official text that had received imperial sanction since the fourth century, and was utilized in the civil examinations from the seventh century until the termination of the examination system in 1905. It was also the text translated by James Legge and printed in 1865 in two volumes entitled *Shoo King*. A version consisting of twenty-nine sections of this classic, supposed to embody ancient documents edited by Confucius, survived the burning of books in 213 B. C. The script was later converted from the ancient to the more readable script of the second century B. C., and hence acquired the designation *chin-wen* 今文, or modern text. Early in the first century B. C. there suddenly appeared, it was said, a broken set of the Confucian classic written in the ancient script on bamboo slips. Among them was a copy of the *Shu-ching* consisting of 16 additional sections. The claim that this version was in the old style script won it the designation ku-wen, or ancient text, implying greater authenticity. Further credence was given to it when a descendant of Confucius, K'ung An-kuo (fl. 100 B. C.), was credited with converting it to the contemporary reading and supplying a commentary to it. However this may be, K'ung An-kuo's ancient text of the *Shu-ching* did not survive unless it be in a few fragmentary

quotations. In the early fourth century, however, a governor, Mei Tse (fl. 317) submitted to the throne a copy of the *Shu-ching* in 29 sections which included the chin-wen text, intermingled, however, with sub-sections containing what was asserted to be the ku-wen text. This composite work, together with a preface attributed to K'ung An-kuo, gained imperial sanction, and after the seventh century became the official text of the *Shu-ching*.

Five hundred years later, in the twelfth century, the scholars Wu Yü (cs 1124) and Chu Hsi (1130–1200) expressed doubts about the authenticity of the ancient text, and characterized K'ung's preface as spurious. But it was Mei Tsu who four hundred years later traced the ideological or textual origin of some three hundred fifty passages of the *Shu-ching* to many works of later Chou and early Han authorship such as *Meng-tzu*, *Lao-tzu*, *Hsün-tzu*, and *Shih-chi*. Furthermore he judged some geographical names to be anachronistic and some moral sentiments not to have been current in antiquity when these documents were supposed to have been produced.

Mei Tsu probably worked for more than thirty years on the *Shang-shu k'ao-i*, which was more or less completed about 1543. In any case, in that year he took part in the editing of the history of the National University at Nanking—a history entitled *Nan-yung-chih* printed in 1544 (*see* Huang Tso). He contributed to it *chüan* 17 and 18 which constitute a section called "Ching-chi k'ao" 經籍考—a descriptive catalogue of books and printing blocks in the library of the institution. By using this official compilation as a platform to announce his findings concerning the spurious nature of the ancient text of the *Shu-ching*, he made his conclusions known to the scholastic world in briefer form. He provoked some scholars, such as Ch'en Ti (*q.v.*), to refute him; apparently he also succeeded in winning more to his side for in 1589, during the *chin-shih* examination, the one who received the highest honors was the afore-mentioned Chiao Hung who wrote an essay advocating the elimination of the ancient text of the *Shu-ching* from the Classics. It seems, however, that the matter received no further attention. Not until the 17th/18th century were Mei's theories seconded by Yen Jo-chü, Hui Tung, and other scholars, and especially praised by the editors of the imperial manuscript library, the *Ssu-k'u ch'üan-shu*. Even so, the ancient text of the *Shu-ching* continued in use as part of the official text for the civil examinations.

The importance of the *Ching-chi-k'ao* (embedded, as stated, in the *Nan-yung-chih*) as a source for the bibliographical history of the Ming period was recognized by Yeh Te-hui (BDRC) who had it printed as a monograph in 1902. It may also be found in the *Nan-yung-chih* which was reproduced in 1931 from a print of 1621 in the possession of the Kuo-hsüeh Library at Nanking.

In addition to the *Shang-shu k'ao-i* and the *Nan-yung-chih ching-chi-k'ao* Mei Tsu left two minor works (both receiving notices in the *Ssu-k'u* catalogue): another work on the *Shu-ching*, entitled *Shang-shu p'u* 尚書譜 and a work on the Book of Changes, *Ku-i k'ao-yüan* 古易考原, 3*ch*. The latter is included in the Taoist library, the *Hsü Tao-tsang* 續道藏.

Bibliography

Ching-te-hsien chih (1808), 8/16a; TSCC (1885–88), XXI: 116/6/7b; Chu I-tsun, *Ching-i-k'ao* (SPTK ed.), 89/6b; Chang Hsin-ch'eng 張心澂, *Wei-shu t'ung-k'ao* 僞書通考 (1954), 126; Tai Chün-jen 戴君仁, "*Ku-wen shang-shu* tso-che yen-chiu" 古文尚書作者研究, in *K'ung Meng hsüeh-pao*, 1961, no. 1, 35; Chiao Hung, *Chiao-shih pi-sheng, chüan* 1; Mao Ch'i-ling (ECCP), *Hai-ho wen-chi, ch.* 5–7; Wang Hsien-ch'ien (BDRC), *Shang-shu K'ung-chuan ts'an-cheng*, 36 *ch.* (Changsha, 1904); Chu Chün-sheng 朱駿聲 (1788–1858), *Shang-shu ku-chu pien-tu* 尚書古注便讀 4 *ch.* (Chengtu, 1935); SK (1930), 7/5b, 12/4a, 13/4a.

Arthur W. Hummel and Chaoying Fang

MEI YIN, *see* **NING-KUO Kung-chu**

MEI Ying-tso 梅膺祚 (T. 誕生), fl. 1570–1615, was a native of Hsüan-ch'eng 宣城 (Anhwei). He served in the directorate of the Court of Imperial Entertainments as a steward (rank 8b), but apart from this, and the fact that his death made it necessary for his sons to oversee the completion, final checking, and printing of his dictionary, the *Tzu-hui* 字彙, nothing else is known of his career and other writings, which were, however, still spoken of as being extensive as late as 1691.

The *Tzu-hui*, in twelve parts plus a prefatory and a concluding chapter, is the major lexicographical compilation of the Ming period, and the source to which the later Ch'ing lexica were most deeply in debt both for content and for organization. It has 33,179 character entries, arranged according to the graphic structure of the characters under 214 pu 部 (keys or radicals), essentially the same as the system of graphic indexing which the *K'ang-hsi tzu-tien* 康熙字典 of 1716 later made standard and which remains today the principal means for indexing Chinese language dictionaries and other reference works. As a rationalization and simplification of the considerably more complex systems previously in use and ultimately going back to the *Shuo-wen chieh-tzu* (*see* Tuan Yü-ts'ai, ECCP), Mei's scheme of character indexing was an important achievement, and marked the first time any Chinese lexical source had been arranged so as to permit easy, rapid use. He also included for the first time several kinds of lists of difficult-to-locate or otherwise troublesome characters, which are still popular with the users of Chinese dictionaries.

Mei drew his materials in part from the *Hung-wu cheng-yün* 洪武正韻 (completed 1375), an important Ming phonological work. The compilers, Yüeh Shao-feng,

Sung Lien (*q.q.v.*), *et al.*, represented a wide variety of dialects, who drew also from earlier lexical and phonological sources.

For each entry Mei gives first the pronunciation by means of fan-ch'ieh 反切 (the combining of the initial of one character and the final of a second one), then one or more semantic glosses, and where possible also an epigraphic etymology generally derived from the *Shuo-wen chieh-tzu*. Mei was clearly as interested in phonology as in lexicography, and the *Tzu-hui* in its original Ming version includes two phonological excursuses of considerable interest; both are Mei's version of works by other authors. One is a complete syllabary by tones, initials, and finals, using a special symbol to indicate positions in the syllabary for which a syllable existed but for which there was no character in use; it also includes a description of the four tones illustrated with what are probably the originals of the drawings of a human hand as a mnemonic device for correlating initials with tones and finals which were to become favorites with the Ch'ing lexicographers. Mei obtained the anonymous original on which he based his first phonological excursus in 1612. The second is Mei's reworking of a phonological treatise by Li Chia-shao 李嘉紹 (T. 世澤, fl. 1614), a tabular syllabary arrangement of the early seventh-century Ch'ieh-yün phonology (*see* Ch'en Li, ECCP).

The *Tzu-hui* was the chief source from which the Ming scholar Chang Tzu-lieh 張自烈 (T. 爾公, fl. 1627) put together his *Cheng-tzu-t'ung* 正字通, which the Ch'ing scholar Liao Wen-ying 廖文英 (T. 百子) printed with his preface of 1670 and attempted to pass off as his own. Chang asserted that his work corrected errors and rectified other failings in Mei's dictionary, but in reality his version of Mei's work, which gained general acceptance, was simply the most successful of a large number of vulgate versions of the *Tzu-hui* which circulated widely in late Ming and early Ch'ing times, and which dominated

both popular and professional Chinese lexicography until the *K'ang-hsi tzu-tien* became available. Among the more important of these vulgate versions of the *Tzu-hui* was that of Wu Jen-ch'en (ECCP); best known and most widely circulated was that of Ch'en Ch'i-tzu 陳淇子, popularly known under the title *Yü-t'ang tzu-hui* 玉堂, printed in 1676. All the vulgate versions of the *Tzu-hui* are unfaithful to the Ming text in one respect or another, which fact helps to explain the criticisms of inaccuracy and carelessness levied against the work by Ch'ing bibliographers. Insofar as these criticisms are valid with respect to the original Ming text of the *Tzu-hui*, they are indicative of the level to which lexicography in particular and philology in general had come in the first decades of the 17th century; the Ch'ing bibliophile Chu I-tsun (ECCP) wrote with considerable feeling of the sorrows of the age, when "philology languishes and vulgar studies flourish, while the village ancients clasp the *Tzu-hui* of Mei and the *Cheng-tzu-t'ung* of Chang to their bosoms as their *vade mecum* in all matters, referring all problems of unfamiliar characters to these books." Still, the K'ang-hsi lexicographers did not scruple to take over both the plan and organization of the *Tzu-hui* virtually intact and many entries as well.

The *Tzu-hui* was first printed in Japan in 1671, and here too vulgate versions by several hands appeared. Two Japanese Buddhist priests, Eiryū 叡龍 (fl. 1688-1703) and Musō 無相 (1700-63), wrote on Mei's phonological treatises; the second studied (1754) evidence in Mei's work for confusion in the Ming of the distinction between the apical and palatal sibilant and nasal initials as a group on the one hand and the apical, palatal, and retroflex sibilant initials as a group on the other, as well as the evidence found there for the interchange of the glottal stop initial with the voiceless glottal spirant.

Bibliography

1/96/22b; *Tzu-hui*, Ming ed. (1615 preface of Mei Ting-tso) in Columbia University Library; Mei Ch'ing, *Mei-shih shih-lüeh* (preface 1691), 4/18b; Li Shih-tse 李世澤, *Ch'ieh-yün she-piao* 切韻射標 (preface 1614), in *Shuo-fu hsü* 說郛續, no. 32; SK (1933), 0874, 0929; Tai Liu-ling 戴鎦齡, "Tzu-tien chien-lun" 字典簡論, *Wen-hua t'u-shu-kuan-hsüeh chuan-k'o hsüeh-hsiao chi-k'an* 文華圖書館學專科學校季刊 7:1 (March, 1935), 5; *ibid.*, 7.2 (June, 1935), 169; Liu Hsieh-ch'iu 劉叶秋, *Chung-kuo ti tzu-tien* 中國的字典 (Peking, 1960), 29; Katsura Gojūrō 桂五十郎, *Kanseki kaidai* 漢籍解題(Tokyo, 1905), 695; "Mindai no insho" 明代の韻書, 97, in Tōdō Akiyasu 藤堂明保, *Chūgokugo on'inron* 中國語音韻論, Tokyo, 1957; Kondō Moku 近藤杢, *Chūgoku gakugei daijiten* 中國學藝大辭典 (rev. ed., Tokyo, 1959), 435.

[Editors' notes: (1) The story that Liao Wen-ying appropriated as his own the *Cheng-tzu-t'ung* by Chang Tzu-lieh needs further examination. According to the Imperial Catalogue it was first told in a collection of anecdotes, *Ku-sheng* 觚賸, by Niu Hsiu 鈕琇 (T. 玉樵, d. 1704), who in 1698 went to Kao-ming 高明, west of Canton, as magistrate and wrote a post-face to the book in 1700 while in the magistrate's residence. As Niu relates it, the *Cheng-tzu-t'ung* was compiled by Chang Tzu-lieh but was purchased at a high price by Liao, the prefect at Nan-k'ang, who printed it as his own. There is, however, another version of the story told by a certain Wu Yüan-ch'i 吳原起 in the preface of his edition of the *Cheng-tzu-t'ung* (*see* Hsieh Ch'i-k'un [ECCP], *Hsiao-hsüeh-k'ao*, 27/1a). According to Wu, Liao took the printing blocks from Nan-k'ang to his home in Lien-chou 連州, Kwangtung, where they were stored and after he died sold to creditors. Wu then purchased the blocks and learned from the local scholars that Liao had paid a high price for Chang's manuscripts, which Liao edited while serving as associate prefect at Heng-chou 衡州, Hukuang, and later printed in Nan-k'ang. When Wu published his edition of the dictionary, he credited Chang with the authorship and made Liao the editor and publisher. It seems that Niu based his story on Wu's preface. In any case, Chang's authorship of the *Cheng-tzu-t'ung* has been accepted by all bibliographers.

In Liao's original edition there are five prefaces dated in 1670 and 1671. One was written by the director of education of Kiangsi. All praised Liao for his labor on the dictionary. Throughout the book Chang's name is not mentioned. We know that Liao and Chang were acquainted, for while the latter headed the Po-lu-tung 白鹿洞Academy in Nan-k'ang, Liao was an official there, first as prefectural judge (about 1660) and from 1668 as prefect. It is said that after Chang died Liao led the local officials and gentry in conducting the funeral. In the dictionary, after the five prefaces, there are lists of sponsors, collaborators, or assistants. These are followed by a list of teachers and students of the academy, including the name of Chang Tzu-hsün 張自勳, Tzu-lieh's younger brother. The list is categorized as Po-lu-tung shou-yeh hsing-shih 受業姓氏, or names of disciples of the academy; this seems to indicate a relationship with Chang Tzu-lieh rather than with Liao. Hence it appears that if indeed Liao did purchase Chang's dictionary, it was with the understanding of everybody concerned that Liao was to publish it as his own. It suggests either a business deal or a friendly transaction.

The editors of the *Yüan-chou* 袁州-*fu chih* of 1874, after enumerating Chang's works in his biography and again in the bibliographical section, do not give even a hint of any connection he might have had with the *Cheng-tzu-t'ung*. Only at the end of the gazetteer, among anecdotes and gossipy items, there is a story about Liao plagiarizing Chang's dictionary; the story is given in a quotation without comment, as if to say that the editors were aware of such a legend but could not find conclusive evidence to substantiate it.

(2) The relationship between Mei

Ting-tso and Mei Ying-tso throws some light on the date of the latter's birth. Mei Ting-tso in his *Lu-ch'iu shih-shih ch'üan-chi*, 6/17a (NLP microfilm no. 783), dedicated a poem to Ying-tso on his becoming a district school student referring to him as wu-ts'ung-ti 五從弟 and describing him as shao to-ts'ai 少多才. This indicates that Ying-tso was much younger than Ting-tso (b. 1553), that they were of common ancestry, perhaps sixth cousins, and that Ying-tso apparently passed the district examination before he reached the age of twenty. In Ting-tso's preface to the *Tzu-hui* written in 1615, Ying-tso is described as ch'iang-nien 彊年, or between forty and fifty, having just registered as a student in the National University. It thus may be inferred that Ying-tso was born about 1570, became a district school student before 1590, and, after taking the provincial examinations without success over a twenty-five-year period, entered officialdom by purchase some time after 1615. This career as conjectured is rather typical of the life among literati of that day.]

Roy Andrew Miller

MENG Ch'eng-shun 孟稱舜 (T. 子若, 子適, 子塞), fl. 1629–49, poet and dramatist, was a native of K'uai-chi 會稽, Chekiang. Little is known of his life except that he lived in the middle of the 17th century and graduated as a senior licentiate in 1649. He was a close friend of Ch'en Hung-shou (ECCP), Ma Ch'üan-ch'i 馬權奇 (T. 撰倩, cs 1643), Cho Jen-yüeh 卓人月 (T. 珂月), and other men of letters from his native place. He named his country villa the Hua-hsü pieh-yeh 花嶼別業 (Floral hillock). It may be inferred that he led a life of leisure and perhaps even maintained a troupe of actresses at his home as did some other dramatists of that day.

His tsa-chü 雜劇, or lyrical dramas of the Northern style, received some acclaim in the 1620s, three of them being included among the thirty dramas in the first series of the collection *Sheng Ming tsa-chü* 盛明, published in 1629 by Shen T'ai 沈泰 (T. 林宗, H, 福次居主人) of Hangchow. This was an elegantly printed work, illustrated with two excellent woodcuts for each drama, in a format established by Tsang Mou-hsün (*see* Ch'en Pang-chan) for the collection *Yüan-ch'ü hsüan* 元曲選, printed in 1616. The three items by Meng in the *Sheng Ming tsa-chü* are: *T'ao-hua jen-mien* 桃花人面, based on a poem by Ts'ui Hu 崔護 (late 8th century); *Ssu-li t'ao-sheng* 死裏逃生, based on a case of kidnaping two women in a Buddhist monastery; and *Hua-fang yüan* 花舫緣, based on a romantic adventure attributed to T'ang Yin (*q.v.*). The last one, however, did not follow Meng's original text as circulated under the title, *Hua-ch'ien i-hsiao* 花前一笑, but was a version revised by Cho Jen-yüeh. The reason for the revision has some social implications. According to the traditional story, T'ang sold himself as a bond servant in order to approach a slave girl, but Meng changed the characterization of T'ang to that of one with the higher status of a clerk for hire, and of the girl to that of an adopted daughter. Cho considered such changes erroneous, for in his view a great artist like T'ang was impervious to such matters as social status. It seems that Meng disagreed and made his own version available as well.

In 1633 Meng issued a collection of fifty-six tsa-chü, selected by himself under the title *Ku-chin ming-chü ho-hsüan* 古今名劇合選, printed also in the expensive style set by Tsang Mou-hsün and Shen T'ai. Grouping the selections under the two categories, romantic affairs and heroism, Meng called the former group of twenty-six plays *Liu-chih chi* 柳枝集, and the latter group of thirty *Lai-chiang chi* 酹江集. In the preface he criticized the dramatic work of Shen Ching (*q.v.*) for its stress on the musical effect on stage and that of T'ang Hsien-tsu (ECCP) as less suitable for the stage but of greater interest to a reader for its lyrics. Meng insists that his selection was based on quality in both respects. The fact that he included four of his own works among the fifty-six indicates the kind of confidence he had in his own craftsmanship. The four plays are: *T'ao-yüan san-fang* 桃源三訪 (a slightly different version of the *T'ao-hua jen-mien*), *Hua-ch'ien i-hsiao*, *Yen-er-mei* 眼兒媚, and *Ts'an T'ang tsai-ch'uang* 殘唐再創. He is said to have written another tsa-chü which seems to be no longer extant.

Soon after the publication of the *Ku-chin ming-chü ho-hsüan* it became extremely scarce, and only odd volumes seem to be occasionally recorded. In 1933, three hundred years after its publication, the scholar Cheng Chen-to (BDRC) acquired a complete copy. This set later became the property of the Shanghai Library and was reproduced in 1958 in the *Ku-pen hsi-ch'ü ts'ung-k'an* 古本戲曲叢刊, 4th series.

In the Southern style of lyrical dramas (ch'uan-ch'i 傳奇) Meng wrote the following: *Chiao-hung chi* 嬌紅記 (or *Yüan-yang chung* 鴛鴦塚) and *Chen-wen chi* 貞文記, both included in the collection *Ku-pen hsi-ch'ü ts'ung-k'an*, series 2; and *Er-hsü chi* 二胥記, included in the same collection, series 3. Other dramas by Meng do not seem to be extant.

When Meng printed the *Ku-chin ming-chü ho-hsüan* in 1633, he also issued the first printed edition of the *Lu-kuei-pu* 錄鬼簿, a repertory of authors of song and dramatic pieces, originally written by Chung Ssu-ch'eng 鍾嗣成 in 1330, but expanded by later editors. This important source on early dramatists had existed for over two hundred years only in manuscript. It seems that each manuscript differs somewhat from any of the others. The one on which Meng based his edition was probably one of the earliest versions. Another early version (from a 1584 copy of a manuscript dated 1398) was the one printed about 1713 by Ts'ao Yin (ECCP). The most complete version is the manuscript copy in the Peking Library that once belonged to T'ien-i ko 天一閣 of the Fan family (*see* Fan Mou-chu, ECCP). This T'ien-i ko copy, as reproduced in two volumes in 1960, includes Chung's list of 147 names, comments on most of them by Chia Chung-ming 賈仲明 (H. 雲水散人, *ca.* 1343-*ca.* 1422), and a supplement, *hsü-pien* 續編, by an anonymous editor of the middle of the 15th century. All these editions, duly collated, may be found in the collection *Lu-kuei-pu* (*wai ssu-chung* 外四種), Peking, 1957.

According to the editors of the *Ssu-k'u* catalogue, Meng was also the author of a book of historical criticism, entitled *Shih-fa* 史發 or *Meng-shu-tzu shih-fa*. His preface to this work is dated 1631.

Bibliography

43/8/7b; SK (1930), 90/5a; *Shao-hsing-fu chih* 紹興府志 (1792), 34/48b; Fu Hsi-hua 傅惜華, *Ming-tai tsa-chü ch'üan-mu* 全目 (Peking, 1958), 215; *id.*, *Ming-tai ch'uan-ch'i ch'üan-mu* (Peking, 1959), 339; Ch'i Piao-chia (ECCP), *Yüan-shan-t'ang Ming ch'ü-p'in chü-p'in chiao-lu* 遠山堂明曲品劇品校錄 (Shanghai, 1955), 184, 191; *Ku-pen hsi-ch'ü ts'ung-k'an*, ser. 2 (Shanghai, 1955), nos. 64, 65, ser. 4 (Shanghai, 1958); Shen T'ai, *Sheng Ming tsa-chü* (1958), *ch.* 17, 18, 23; Chang Ch'üan-kung 張全恭, "Ming-tai te nan 南 tsa-chü," *Ling-nan hsüeh-pao* 嶺南學報, 6:1 (1937), 64, 69; Cheng Chen-to, *Chung-kuo wen-hsüeh yen-chiu* 中國文學研究 (1957), 628, 1319.

Ching-hwa Ho Jen and Chaoying Fang

MENGGETIMUR (Meng-ko-t'ieh-mu-er 猛哥帖木兒 or Meng-t'e-mu 孟特穆), died November 30, 1433, Jurchen chieftain of the Odoli 斡朶里 tribe, one of the three tribes which originated in the area of I-lan 依蘭 in the lower Sungari valley in what came to be known as northeast Manchuria. In the 1380s the tribe moved southward and came to the lower valley of the T'u-men 圖們 River and finally settled down around Wo-mu-ho 斡木河, the present Hoeryong 會寧, in north

Korea. In 1395 Menggetimur visited the Korean court and presented tribute for the first time, and in 1404 he was appointed to an honorary military position (rank 3A). In these days the Ming court frequently sent envoys in order to pacify local chieftains in the area, but Menggetimur did not respond. This pleased the king of Korea, and Menggetimur was nominated early in 1405 to be an actual military commander, or myriarch. In April the Ming eunuch envoy Wang Chiao-hua-ti 王教化的 (probably a Jurchen) came to Korea with imperial edicts to persuade the king of Korea and Menggetimur to enter into tributary relations. The king ordered Menggetimur not to let the Chinese seduce him. The latter at first pretended to obey the king's order, but soon capitulated and in September of the same year he visited Nanking and was appointed regional commissioner.

In the following years Jurchen tribes, including the followers of Menggetimur in the T'u-men valley, frequently made trouble, and the Koreans fought against them. Finding themselves insecure in Korean territory, Menggetimur and his followers fled westward and settled in May, 1411, in the area of Feng-chou 鳳州 in the valley of the Hui-fa 輝發 River, an affluent of the Sungari, the region where the Chien-chou guard (建州衞) under Li Hsien-chung (father of Li Man-chu, *q.v.*) was located. Here the Ming government established the Left Chien-chou (guard) apart from the Chien-chou guard, and Menggetimur became regional commissioner of the new guard, although the date of its establishment is uncertain. At this time Emperor Chu Ti (*q.v.*) frequently sent expeditionary forces against the Mongols, and Menggetimur joined the one in 1422. Being menaced by retaliatory invasions of the Mongols, on one hand, and because of the dominance of Li Man-chu on the other, Menggetimur and his followers, numbering more than six thousand, were obliged to leave Feng-chou, and returned to their old place Wo-

mu-ho in 1423.

After his return Menggetimur realized that the best policy of self-preservation was to serve both the Ming and Korea. In 1426 he visited Peking and was promoted to assistant commissioner-in-chief. In 1432 his half-brother Fanca 凡察 (d. 1451), assistant commander, presented tribute to the emperor and was promoted to assistant commissioner. In 1433 Menggetimur again visited Peking and was made associate commissioner-in-chief while Fanca was promoted to regional commissioner. Meanwhile, beginning in 1427, Menggetimur sent his eldest son A-ku 阿谷 (alias Ch'üan-tou 權豆), and others to the Korean court several times, and A-ku even hoped that he might become a royal bodyguard in Korea.

On November 30, 1433, Menggetimur and A-ku were killed in a riot led by Yang Mu-ta-wu-ta 楊木荅兀荅 of another Jurchen tribe. Yang Mu-ta-wu had been a battalion commander in the area of K'ai-yüan 開原 and followed Menggetimur when the latter returned to Wo-mu-ho from Feng-chou. When Menggetimur died, his second son Tung-shan 董山 (alias T'ung-ts'ang 童倉, 1419?-67) was still too young, so Fanca became the actual leader of the troubled Left Chien-chou tribe. Since the official seal of the commission was lost during the riot of Yang Mu-ta-wu-ta, Fanca received a new official seal, and was promoted to assistant commissioner-in-chief.

The Left Chien-chou tribe pretended to be content with Korea's policy of peaceful relations, and Tung-shan expressed the desire that he might get a position in Korea and marry a Korean girl; the tribe, however, finally decided to move westward and join the Chien-chou under Li Man-chu who was hostile toward Korea. In 1440 Fanca and Tung-shan with their tribesmen managed to escape from Korea and unite with Li Man-chu, settling down in the upper valley of the Su-tzu 蘇子 River near Chiu-lao-ch'eng 舊老城. Tung-shan, who had recovered the old official seal, now rose to be a tribal chieftain, and started to contend with Fanca for leadership. In 1442 the Ming court decided to split the commission in two, calling them the Left and the Right Chien-chou. Tung-shan was appointed vice commissioner-in-chief of the former and Fanca of the latter. The two commissions lasted, with some vicissitudes, until the Ming rule north of the Wall collapsed. Nurhaci (ECCP) claimed descent from Menggetimur.

Bibliography

MSL (1963), T'ai-tsung, Hsüan-tsung, and Ying-tsung; Hsü Chung-shu, "Ming-ch'u Chien-chou Ju-chen chü-ti ch'ien-hsi k'ao," CYYY, 6:2 (1936); Sonoda Kazukame 園田一龜, *Mindai Kenshū Jochokushi kenkyū* 明代建州女直史研究 (Studies on the history of the Chien-chou tribe of the Jurchen people under the Ming), 2 vols. (Tokyo, 1948 and 1953); id., "Kenshū san-i no ichini tsuite" 建州三衞の位置について (On the localities of the three Chien-chou tribes in the Ming period), *Shigaku zasshi* 史學雜誌, 60:4 (Tokyo, 1951); Wada Kiyoshi 和田清, "Minshono Manshū keiryaku" 明初の滿州經畧, *Man-Sen chiri rekishi kenkyū hōkoku* 滿鮮地理歷史研究報告, 15 (Tokyo, 1937); Oshibuchi Hajimu 鴛淵一, "Kenshū saino senjūchini tsuite" 建州左衞の遷住地について, *Kuwabara hakushi kanreki kinen tōyōshi ronsō* 桑原博士還曆紀念東洋史論叢 (Tokyo, 1930); id., "Kenshū saino setsuritsu nendaini tsuite" 建州左衞の設立年代について, Rekishito chiri 歷史と地理, 26 (Tokyo, 1930); Ikeuchi Hiroshi 池內宏, "Senshono Tōhokukyōto Joshintono kankei" 鮮初の東北境と女眞との關係, ibid, 2, 4, 5, and 7 (1916, 1917, 1918, and 1920); Inaba Iwakichi 稻葉岩吉, "Kenshū Jochokuno genjūchi oyobi senjūchi" 建州女直の原住地及々遷住地, *Manshu rekishi-chiri* 滿州歷史地理, 2 (Tokyo, 1913); Henry Serruys, *Sino-jürčed Relations during the Yung-lo Period (1403–1424)* (Wiesbaden, 1955), 39, 51.

Chun Hae-jong

MIAO Ch'ang-ch'i 繆昌期 (T. 當時, H. 西溪), August 15, 1562–1626, scholar-official, was a native of Chiang-yin 江陰, north of Soochow. Little is known of his family background. His mother bore four sons and a daughter, but he was the only son

to survive an epidemic of smallpox. In 1578 he obtained the *hsiu-ts'ai* degree on his second attempt. Twenty-two years were to pass before he became a *chü-jen* (1600). The intervening years were devoted to study and tutoring in his home district. He married in 1581 and became the father of five sons. During this period he occasionally visited the great scholar Ku Hsien-ch'eng (*q.v.*), later head of the Tung-lin party. After traveling five times to the capital for the metropolitan examination, he eventually became a *chin-shih* in 1613 and was selected a Hanlin bachelor. One of the examiners, Yeh Hsiang-kao (*q.v.*), was impressed by his showing in this test and came to regard him as his protégé.

His first year in Peking, 1614, was uneventful, but trouble was brewing. In the summer of the following year there occurred the first of the famous "three great cases" (*see* Kao P'an-lung). This was the "club case." An unidentified man armed with a club, entered the palace of the heir apparent and was arrested. At the trial certain censors wished to dismiss the matter as a simple case of insanity, while another group of officials demanded a full investigation. Miao sided with the latter group and publicly criticized the position taken by the former. When his views became known to the censors, one of them angrily demanded that Miao concern himself henceforth with affairs of the history bureau and stop meddling in judicial matters which did not concern him. This made him a marked man and his enemies waited for an opportunity to impeach him.

While intrigues were going on at a lower level, Miao won promotion. In the summer of 1616 he was recommended for the position of corrector in the Hanlin. He waited some time for the imperial command permitting him to take office, but none was forthcoming. Meanwhile his enemies continued their criticisms. Feeling that the best course of action was to leave the city for a while on the ground of illness, he asked a Hanlin member, Liu I-ching (*see* Chou Chia-mu), to protect his interests in the capital. When an appointment finally came from the palace, he had already left Peking. Annoyed by his promotion, his enemies among the censors openly attacked him in a memorial.

For the next four years he remained at home in Chiang-yin. His enemies had not forgotten him, however, and during the official evaluation proceedings in 1617, they made further charges. His friend, Liu I-ching, supported him and he escaped censure. At this time he occasionally visited Ch'ien Ch'ien-i (ECCP) at his home in Ch'ang-shu, situated between Chiang-yin and Soochow.

In 1620 the tide turned in favor of those who were associated ideologically or politically with the Tung-lin party. Miao went back to Peking early in 1621 and resumed his old position as corrector. A rumor was then circulating that Liu I-ching, now one of the grand secretaries, had attempted to prevent Yeh Hsiang-kao from returning, for Yeh would then become the senior member of the Grand Secretariat. On his arrival Yeh became extremely displeased with Liu. The eunuch, Wei Chung-hsien (ECCP), took this opportunity to impeach Liu. Hearing the news, Miao visited Yeh and obtained a pardon for his friend. In the same year (1621), Miao went to Wuchang to serve as a director of the *chü-jen* examination for Hukuang. The answers in certain papers contained some uncomplimentary remarks about Wei Chung-hsien and about eunuchs in general. When this news reached Wei, he was angry, but, out of deference to the esteemed position in which Miao was held in the eyes of his contemporaries, he took no action. This was the second time that Miao had come into conflict with the eunuch leader in the same year.

While various factions were struggling for power in the capital, the empire was being attacked from the northeast by the Manchus. Defense at the front was in the hands of two men, Wang Hua-

chen and Hsiung T'ing-pi (both in ECCP), but they differed on the question of strategy. The majority of officials, including Yeh Hsiang-kao, favored the more militant policy of Wang. Miao was one of the few who favored the containment measures proposed by Hsiung. The soundness of Hsiung's position was vindicated by the disastrous defeat of Wang Hua-chen, but the incident unhappily seems to have brought about a temporary rift in the good relations between Yeh and himself. In the following year he was given charge of composing imperial edicts and performing other duties of a Hanlin official. Meanwhile Wei Chung-hsien was attending to the matter of his tomb in the hills west of Peking. He sent a messenger to ask Miao to write an inscription for it. The latter declined, saying that he disliked writing flattering epitaphs, when a eunuch was involved. This open insult sealed his fate. Late in the year Miao was given another promotion. At this time Tsou Yüan-piao and Feng Ts'ung-wu (*qq. v.*) set up an academy in Peking intended as a center for conferences and discussions (*see* Tsou Yüan-piao). Miao had opposed the idea at its inception and his foresight proved correct. Before the end of the year both founders were forced to leave the capital and the academy was closed. At the end of 1622 Miao was sent to Honan to perform the enfeoffing ceremonies of an imperial prince, and afterwards he received permission to return home, where he spent the following year. He went back to Peking early in 1624 and received further promotions. Wei was now in charge of the Eastern Depot, a part of the imperial secret service. His power and arrogance were growing daily. Men such as Yang Lien and Tso Kuang-tou (*qq. v.*) came to realize that something would have to be done to curb his power. A group of them, including Miao, met to discuss what action should be taken. At the meeting held at Miao's residence it was decided that Yang should submit a memorial attacking Wei. This was the famous "twenty-four crimes" memorial. Realizing that they faced a powerful enemy, they sent Miao to visit Yeh Hsiang-kao to enlist his support. The grand secretary, however, was evasive and refused to collaborate on the ground that it would be difficult to displace Wei. Later Yeh changed his mind and did submit a memorial asking the emperor to allow the eunuch to resign. Far from bringing about the eunuch's resignation, the memorial resulted in the purge of Tung-lin men from government in 1624. Yang Lien, Kao P'an-lung, and Chao Nan-hsing (q.v.) were among those immediately removed. Then a rumor started that Miao had drafted the memorial for Yang Lien. He further offended Wei Chung-hsien by accompanying the deposed officials to the gates when they left the capital. By this time most of his friends had been removed from office, and he felt that it would be impossible to remain in the city. He memorialized asking for leave. Simultaneously Wei attacked him in a memorial and he was forced to quit, returning home at the end of the year. Meanwhile the purge continued. Wei was not content with removing his enemies from office. He also wanted them removed from the official rolls, and in some cases executed. Using a forged confession which stated that a number of officials including Miao had accepted bribes, Wei had them purged. Miao's name was among those stricken from the official rolls.

Wei's vengeance, however, was not yet complete. Early in 1626 he had Miao arrested at his home on the ground that he still wore official garb, despite the fact that he was no longer in office. When he reached the capital, however. Miao was tried on the score that he had accepted bribes. Refusing to confess any crime, he was tortured and died in prison on or about May 24, 1626. Only two years later he was exonerated and given the posthumous title of supervisor of imperial instruction and accorded an official burial. His collected works, entitled *Ts'ung-yeh-t'ang ts'un-kao* 從野堂存稿, 8 *ch.*, were first published in 1637.

Although he did not play a leading role in the major historical events of his day, Miao was an honest bureaucrat, who based his political beliefs on what he felt was best for the country. The events of his life show that neither friendship, nor patronage, nor official opinion swayed his decisions on major political issues. He has always been celebrated among the upright and righteous officials of the late Ming period, and as one of the twenty-one who lost their lives in the political strife against the eunuch party. He is also remembered as one of the six martyrs, whose writings while in prison were brought together in the work entitled *Pi-hsüeh lu*, 2 *ch.*, edited by Huang Yü (ECCP, p. 893).

Bibliography

1/245/3a; 8/82/4a; 30/3/20a; 31/x/12a; 39/4/1a; 52/x/10a; 61/109/15a; *Chiang-yin-hsien chih* (1878), 16/32a; *Huang Ming wen-hai* (microfilm), 8/5/9; W. Franke, *Sources*, 3. 7. 6.

Edward Kelly

MING Yü-chen 明玉珍, 1331–66, founder of the Hsia 夏 state in Szechwan, was a native of Sui-chou 隨州 (about two hundred miles northwest of Wuchang). His original name seems to have been Min Jui 旻瑞, *tzu* Yü-chen; it has been suggested that he changed his surname out of a desire to show his belief in Manicheism (Ming-chiao 明教). When the Red Turban rebellions broke out in 1351 and 1352, Ming was serving as a local police chief, a category of compulsory labor service incumbent upon certain peasant families during the Yüan period. In spite of his youth, he became the organizer and leader of a group of some one thousand peasants and stationed himself with them in the hills south of Sui-chou in order to protect his home area from the riots and disorder the rebellions had set off. Around 1352, Ming and his men were approached by a rebel leader under the T'ien-wan emperor Hsü Shou-hui (*q. v.*) who ordered them either to join the T'ien-wan movement or suffer annihilation. Ming joined at once, and was posted to Mien-yang 沔陽, about sixty miles west of Wuchang, with the title "Grand Commander who leads troops to conquer the barbarians" (統兵破虜大元帥).

Around 1357, when Mien-yang fell short of rations, Ming was sent up the Yangtze to K'uei-chou 夔州, Szechwan, to load his boats there. It was while thus engaged in taking on supplies that Ming chanced to encounter a group of mutinied militiamen who had come down from the interior of Szechwan. The militiamen, who had been helping the Yüan imperial forces quell the rampaging Green Turban (青巾) rebels of Li Hsi-hsi (*see* Han Lin-er), told Ming that Öljeitü 完者都, the chief Yüan provincial official in Szechwan, had murdered their commander Yang Han 楊漢 with a view to incorporating them all into his own forces. They said further that, since the city of Chungking was not adequately provisioned or guarded, and since Öljeitü and his chief officer were not on good terms with each other, Szechwan could be easily taken. After consulting with his aides, Ming decided they had nothing to lose by trying to seize the province. In January, 1358, he captured Chungking with little difficulty, forbidding any looting by his troops. Upon receiving a report of the victory, Hsü Shou-hui appointed Ming governor (with title yu-ch'eng 右丞) of Lung-Shu 隴蜀 (*i. e.*, Shensi and Szechwan). By 1359, Chengtu and Chia-ting 嘉定 were taken, and most of the rest of Szechwan surrendered soon after.

When Ch'en Yu-liang (*q. v.*) assassinated Hsü Shou-hui in June, 1360, Ming Yü-chen not only refused to aid Ch'en in his attack on the capital of Chu Yüan-chang but even posted a contingent of troops at Ch'ü-t'ang 瞿塘 Gorge to block off Ch'en completely. Soon afterwards, probably in the same year, Ming declared his independence by assuming the title "prince of Lung-Shu." He set up a shrine in Chungking in honor of the murdered T'ien-wan emperor, and ordered seasonal sacrifices carried out. In the edict he issued upon becoming Prince Ming gave the same kind of explanation for his rise that Chu Yüan-chang did for his: he was originally a village peasant; when the disorders occurred, he was pushed into leadership by others so that all might protect themselves; then in obedience to Heaven he cleared Szechwan of the Green Turbans because there was no one else around to do it. Ming was careful to stress that he took Szechwan away from the Green Turbans and not the Yüan authorities, yet he did try to enhance his acceptability to the people by asking them to rejoice in the disappearance of the "vile practices" of the Mongols and the return of the "transforming influences of Chinese civilization." Two years later, urged by his advisers who were hopeful of eventually conquering all of China and eager for some means to stop the troops from deserting and returning to their homeland in the east, Ming Yü-chen assumed imperial authority on March 28 or 29, 1362. The dynasty was called the Hsia after the first of the three dynasties of antiquity, and the reign title chosen was T'ien-t'ung 天統, meaning "controlled by Heaven."

The Hsia governmental structure, set up by Liu Chen 劉楨 (T. 維周, d. 1369), a Yüan *chin-shih* and former official who was living in retirement in Szechwan when Ming engaged him, borrowed some of its forms and nomenclature from pre-Ch'in institutions, as if to emphasize its authentic Chinese character. Thus Tai Shou 戴壽 as prime minister was known by the archaic title of Chung-tsai 冢宰, one of the six ministers of Chou times. Also established were a Hanlin Academy, an academy for Sons of State (Kuo-tzu-chien), plus a system of schools (t'i-chü-ssu chiao-shou-so 提舉司教授所) for commoners in the cities of Szechwan and southern Shensi.

Palace examinations for the *chin-shih* degree were held at least twice: one in 1363 graduated eight men, and another in 1369, six. A tithe system of taxation was imposed; close attention was paid to Confucian sacrifices and ceremonies and, while Buddhism and Taoism were proscribed, a special hall was set aside for the worship of the Maitreya Buddha. Apparently the archaizing aspects of the administration led to some confusion, because in 1365 the six minister system was abolished and replaced by the more familiar Yüan organization and terminology.

For the purpose of conquering all of China, military preparations were made on three fronts. Besides his base at Chungking, Ming established military headquarters in Hsing-yüan 興元 (Nan-cheng 南鄭), Shensi, and at I-ling 夷陵. In 1364 he sent three separate columns of troops to attack Yunnan. The first column, led by his top general, Wan Sheng 萬勝 (also known as Ming San 明三), arrived first and reduced the provincial capital of Chung-ch'ing 中慶 (Kunming). When the other two columns proceeding through Tibetan tribal territory failed to arrive, the Yunnan defenders under the Yüan Prince Bolod (*see* Kökö Temür) drove out Wan Sheng and recovered the capital. Other skirmishes carried out about the same time in Shensi apparently met with indifferent success. Ming's territory at its greatest extent reached north as far as Hsing-yüan and south as far as northern Kweichow.

In the spring of 1366, Ming Yü-chen died at the age of thirty-five. There is a rumor that he was assassinated by his younger brother, who was in turn murdered by the empress, née P'eng 彭, who then put Ming Yü-chen's son, Ming Sheng 明昇, on the throne as the rightful successor. Ming Yü-chen, who had received the posthumous title T'ai-tsu Wen-wu Chih-sheng Huang-ti 太祖文武至聖皇帝, is said to have left a will in which, taking account of the recent reverses he had suffered in Shensi and in Yunnan, he admitted that it was not Heaven's intention after all that the Hsia should reunite China, and enjoined his successors to observe a strictly defensive policy, specifically warning them not to start incidents with neighboring states (*i. e.*, with Chu Yüan-chang). Although this injunction was adhered to, the Hsia empire began to weaken internally upon Ming Sheng's accession. Known as the "lesser Lord of Radiance" (小明主), an epithet similar to the Manichean title "Lesser Prince of Radiance," assumed by the rebel Sung emperor Han Lin-er, Ming Sheng was only a boy when he ascended the throne under the title K'ai-hsi 開熙 (beginning of brilliance), his mother ruling as regent. The ensuing factionalism at the Hsia court made it necessary for some of the generals posted in the cities outside to act in their own interest. After Wan Sheng was murdered by court enemies, Wu Yu-jen 吳友仁, serving in Pao-ning 保寧 (Lang-chung, Szechwan), moved into Chungking and had the party responsible for the murder executed. Wu thereafter played a leading role in the affairs of the Hsia state.

Regular diplomatic relations between Ming Yü-chen and Chu Yüan-chang appear to have begun shortly after the fall of Wuchang and the capture of Ch'en Li (*see* Ch'en Yu-liang) in the autumn of 1363. It seems that Ming first made approaches to Chu; Chu then sent an emissary with a letter for Ming in which he proposed a joint attack on the Central Plains, after which each would retire to his respective territory and continue friendly relations. Ming's reply was polite but noncommittal. Later on Chu chided Ming for his failure in Yunnan, but at the same time invited him to speak up if he had any criticism of Chu's own actions. Ming Yü-chen's death and the accession of Ming Sheng were reported to Chu by Hsia envoys, and Chu reciprocated with embassies of condolence for the first and congratulations for the second. These missions actually had espionage as their primary aim; besides sizing up the adversary, Chu's envoy was careful to prepare maps of the Szechwan terrain for later military purposes. When Chu began his attack on the north in 1367, he had one of Ming Sheng's ambassadors accompany Hsü Ta (*q.v.*) as an observer. Chu hopefully assumed that the envoy on his return to the Hsia court would be impressed with the strength of his army and would counsel the Hsia to surrender without resistance.

In this Chu's assumption failed him. The Hsia court was alarmed at the rapidity of Chu's successes on the Central Plains and in Shensi, but Wu Yu-jen pointed out that Szechwan was more easily defended than north China, and his argument that defenses should be bolstered, at the same time that friendly missions continued to be exchanged with Chu, carried the day. Elaborate bulwarks were set up at the Ch'ü-t'ang Gorge; an iron chain was stretched across the Yangtze at that point in order to hold back attacking boats, and a "flying bridge" over the river, consisting of rope overlaid with planks, served as an aerial platform from which the enemy ships could be bombarded. Chu sent off a barrage of letters to the Hsia urging them to surrender, but the Hsia court stood firm. Then Chu seized upon a number of supposed provocations to justify his intended attack on Szechwan: the Hsia had refused to respond to a demand for large timbers, they had refused to allow his army a right-of-way through their territory for the purpose of an attack on Yunnan, and worst of all, Wu Yu-jen had committed the unforgivable act of attempting to regain Hsing-yüan in the summer of 1370 after having lost it to imperial forces.

Chu's conquest of Szechwan occupied most of the year 1371. An assault on land from the north was led by Fu Yu-te (*q.v.*), a former Green Turban follower of Li Hsi-hsi who was presumably familiar with the terrain, at the same time that T'ang Ho (*q.v.*) attacked with his fleet proceeding

westward up the Yangtze. Fu reached Chengtu at about the same time that T'ang's forces, after some difficulty, breached the Ch'ü-t'ang defenses and surrounded Chungking. Ming Sheng surrendered on August 3, 1371, and was transported to Nanking. There he was given the title Kuei-i hou 歸義侯 (Marquis who turns to righteousness) and, like Ch'en Li, was given a residence in the capital. Wu Yu-jen's stronghold at Pao-ning fell in the autumn of 1371, and Wu was executed. Most of the Hsia military commanders, however, were put on garrison duty in Hsü-chou 徐州.

In 1372 both Ch'en Li, aged twenty-one, and Ming Sheng, aged seventeen, were deported. They were said to be unhappy in Nanking and constantly complaining. Chu Yüan-chang, afraid that they might become a rallying point for disaffected elements, wrote the Korean king a letter saying that there was no place for "the Emperor Ch'en and the Hsia emperor" in China, and requested permission for them to live in Korea. Since Ch'en and Ming and their entourage were sent without waiting for the Korean king's reply, Chu told the king to send the two ex-emperors back if he could not accept them. The king decided to let them live in Korea. In March, 1373, Ming Sheng married the daughter of Yun Hŭi-chong 尹熙宗, a Korean official. By order of Chu Yüan-chang, Ming Sheng and his family were to be given farm land but exempted from taxation and corvée service. These privileges were confirmed by Yi Sŏng-gye (*q. v.*) by issuing a patent, after the founding of the Yi dynasty in 1392. By 1636, however, Ming Sheng's descendants in Pyongyang and Yŏnju 延州 lost the patent during the Manchu invasion, and local officials raised questions about the privileges. Although reconfirmed by royal order in the same year, they were finally withdrawn in 1655.

The Hsia regime was ended but not forgotten. An uprising led by one Shih Ch'üan-chou 石全州, a self-styled descendant of Ming Yü-chen, broke out among the Miao aborigines of Kweichow in 1475.

Bibliography

1/123/15b; 3/158/1a; 5/119/13a; MSL(1963), T'ai-tsu, 1068, 1167, 1256; Yang Hsüeh-k'o 楊學可, *Ming-shih shih-lu* 明氏實錄; Huang Piao 黃標, *P'ing Hsia lu* 平夏錄; Wu Han 吳晗, "Ming-chiao yü Ta-Ming-ti-kuo" 明敎與大明帝國 in *Tu-shih cha-chi* 讀史劄記 (Peking, 1957); *Chosŏn wangjo sillok*, 34/467, 36/30; *Koryo-sa*, I, 648.

John Dardess

MO Shih-lung 莫是龍 (T. 雲卿, 廷韓, H. 秋水, 後明, etc.), fl. 1552-87, painter and author, was a native of Hua-t'ing 華亭, prefecture of Sung-chiang 松江 southwest of Shanghai, long a center of scholars and artists. Mo Shih-lung's great-grand-father, Mo Sheng 勝 (T. 景剛), a tribute student in the National University in 1441, was known for his calligraphy and paintings of fish; his father, Mo Ju-chung 如忠 (T. 子良, H. 中江, 1509-89, cs 1538) who served in provincial posts for a number of years, was a minor poet and calligrapher; and his younger brother Mo Shih-yüan是元 (cj 1597) left a name as a writer. Mo Shih-lung showed his talent at an early age, becoming a *hsiu-ts'ai* at the age of fourteen (according to one account), but never went beyond the first degree. He studied for a short while in the National University, but for the most part it appears that he remained at home in comfortable surroundings, basking in the company of his father and friends, both of his father and himself. They included such men as Huang-fu Fang, Wang Shih-chen (*qq.v.*), and his contemporaries Ch'en Chi-ju and Tung Ch'i-ch'ang (both in ECCP). The latter was also his student.

Mo Shih-lung's paintings are known in a number of collections. Osvald Sirén lists eleven, John C. Ferguson eighteen, and V. Contag and C. C. Wang ten (approximately). A well-known example is a landscape in the Dubois Morris collec-

tion, Princeton University. Sirén records the earliest as painted in 1567 and the last in 1601. Although highly regarded as a painter in his time, it is by his writings that Mo is best remembered. They include *Pi chu* 筆塵, 1 *ch.*, a short miscellany on painting and calligraphy, Buddhism, literary composition, horticulture, and gardening, the preface of which is dated 1582. A better known piece is his discursus on painting, *Hua shuo* 畫說, 1 *ch.*, first published by Ch'en Chi-ju, which is given a notice by the editors of the Imperial Catalogue but not copied into the *Ssu-k'u chüan-shu*. Mo seems to have been the first, as the editors remark, to divide T'ang painters into northern and southern schools. He was the author too of the *Shih-hsiu-chai chi* 石秀齋集, 10 *ch.*, a copy of which (printed 1604) is in the National Central Library, Taipei. These three works, together with a collection of his prose and verse, entitled *Mo Shao-chiang chi* 少江集, have all been included in various collectanea. The Naikaku Bunko reports in addition a copy of his *Mo T'ing-han i-kao* 廷韓遺稿, 16 *ch.*, edited by Ch'en Chi-ju, and printed during the last decades of the Ming.

Bibliography

1/288/12a; TSCC (1885-88), XIV: 526/9a; SK (1930), 114/5a; Mo Shih-lung, *Pi chu*; id., *Hua Shuo*; *Hua-t'ing-hsien chih* (1879), 12/10b, 14/36b, 15/3b; Ferguson, *Index of Artists* (Nanking, 1934), 286b; V. Contag and C. C. Wang, *Seals of Chinese Painters and Collectors* (Hong Kong, 1966), 314, 690; V. Contag, "Tung Ch'i-chang's Hua Ch'an Shih Sui Pi . . . und das Hua Shuo des Mo Shih-lung." OZ 19 (1933), 83, 174; O. Sirén, *Chinese Painting* (New York 1958), V: 219, VII: 10; Nelson I. Wu, "Tung Ch'i-ch'ang (1555-1636): Apathy in Government and Fervor in Art," *Confucian Personalities*, ed. by A. F. Wright and D. Twitchett (Stanford, Calif. 1967), 270.

L. Carrington Goodrich

MORALES, Juan Bautista de (Li Yü-fan 黎玉範), 1597-September 17, 1664, missionary to China, was born at Ecija, Spain, where be became a Dominican in 1614. In 1620 he joined the Holy Rosary province, and, still a deacon, left Cádiz for Mexico with Angelo Cocchi (*q.v.*). They were both ordained as priests in Mexico and left Acapulco on March 25, 1621, for Manila, which they reached in the middle of the following year after a terrifying voyage. Morales was appointed to Binondo (1623) and then made vicar of the Parian of the Chinese (Sangleys) in Manila, where he undertook the study of the "Chincheo" and Tagalog languages. Forcing the hand of his superiors, he was sent in 1628 with four confreres to Cambodia in the suite of Spanish shipbilders hired by King Poñā To. Upon arrival in January, 1629, the missionaries found that the king (who had invited them) had died. The new king, Poñā Non, welcomed them and allowed them to preach and open a temporary chapel a few days later. Soon Morales was obliged to accompany the shipbuilders back to Manila. On his return to Cambodia he found that the king had changed his mind and forbade the missionaries to proselytize his people; Morales then decided to return to Manila.

In March, 1633, in answer to an appeal for help from Cocchi, Morales and a Franciscan, Antonio Caballero (*q. v.*), left Cavite and met Cocchi in Fu-an 福安, where they resumed their study of the Chinese language. Cocchi died in November of that year, so Morales asked Caballero to help him care for the new missions and to help finish the construction of the church at Ting-t'ou 頂頭, which Cocchi had begun. But when the Dominican, Francisco Díez (*see* Caballero), and the Franciscan, Francisco Bermúdez, joined them in Fu-an in 1634, they all agreed that the Dominicans should care for Fu-an and the Franciscans for Ting-t'ou.

At this time Morales learned of certain rites being performed by Chinese converts to honor Confucius, the city gods, and their ancestors. When he be-

came convinced that they were religious in nature, he forbade them. In an effort to establish a uniform pastoral method in China, Morales went to Foochow to interview the Jesuit vice-provincial, Francisco Furtado (*q.v.*). The negative result of the meeting caused the friars to examine the question in juridical form in December, 1635, and again in January, 1636; they finally submitted a report and thirteen questions to the archbishop of Manila, who in turn referred them to Rome. In 1637 the Dominican province sent Juan García (*see* Caballero) and Pedro Chaves and three Franciscans to Ting-t'ou. Leaving Díez and García at Fu-an, Morales and Chaves went to Tz'uch'i 慈谿 and Hangchow in Chekiang to open new mission stations. Fearing an outbreak of persecution (after the capture of two Franciscans in Fukien), Morales and his companion returned in haste to Ting-t'ou, but then had to flee to the hills. From there they went to Foochow to preach in the streets. When an edict condemning Giulio Aleni and Manuel Dias (*qq.v.*) was issued in the city, they seized the occasion to denounce it and to continue their preaching. The governor, before whom the Domincans were taken, disciplined instead one of the three men who had molested them, and invited the friars to spend the night at his residence. In February, 1638, another edict was displayed at Fu-an. Díez preached against it and attempted to tear it down. He was apprehended, sent to the prefect of Funing, flogged, forced to wear a cangue, and sent to the governor at Foochow, who expelled him to Macao. When Díez passed through Hsing-hua 興化, Fukien, a Chinese Catholic took his place, and pretending to have been mistaken for Díez, asked the magistrate to release him. The following day a new magistrate believed the story and let him go. As if these warnings were not enough, Morales and Díez went to Chekiang in March and preached in the streets with crucifix in hand, but when they moved to Wen-chou

溫州 they were reported to the governor and exiled. At Sui-an 邃安 they found a sympathetic magistrate who asked them to address the crowd. When they reentered Fukien, however, the Fu-ning prefect had them flogged, cangued, and imprisoned. On their way to Macao they had to pass before some twenty other tribunals. At Hsiang-shan 香山 they ended a two-month ordeal by escaping on horseback to Macao, and took passage to Manila with Joachin Kuo, who helped Díez compile a Chinese reader and a Chinese-Spanish dictionary.

In May, 1640, Morales left Manila for Rome, reaching there in February, 1643, after a journey fraught with danger. He immediately submitted his report and the questions relating to the Chinese cults on which the missionaries needed rulings. Impressed by Morales' personality and achievements, Pope Urban VIII named him notary, judge, and prefect apostolic to China in March, 1644, and in June he received replies to the questions favorable to his point of view. In September the new pope, Innocent X, issued a decree condemning certain Chinese rites as superstitious. Morales obtained permission and support for a mission band of twenty-seven; they reached Manila in July, 1648. In August he presented the papal decree of 1645 and answers to twelve of the seventeen questions to the cathedral chapter at Manila, and notified it of the appointment of the archbishop as patron of the churches of China and Japan; in this way the churches were taken away from Portuguese patronage. Morales declined the offer of a bishopric, but asked for an extension of his jurisdiction over the Chinese in Dominican care.

As he waited for a chance to reenter China, Morales taught Mandarin Chinese to his confreres. At the request of the Dominican provincial, Governor Diego Fajardo Chacón granted permission to send missionaries to China and offered the Franciscans the same opportunity. So in July, 1649, four Dominicans, including

Morales, together with Caballero and three other Franciscans, sailed from Pasig in a Chinese boat, carrying a letter of introduction to the corsair, Cheng Chih-lung (ECCP). They landed on August 3 at a port three miles south of An-hai 安海, Fukien, where they were met by Lo Wen-tsao (see Wu-Li, ECCP, p. 876); he informed them of the war between the Chinese and Manchus, the suicide of Governor Liu Chung-tsao (see Chu I-hai, ECCP), who had been sympathetic to the Catholic missions, the beheading of a scholar, known as John Mieu (see Caballero), and of Admiral Joachin Kuo, and the persecution of Garcia, who had gone into hiding. Waiting to move on to Fu-an, then occupied by the Manchu forces, the friars were guests in the residence of the local chief, Cheng Chih-lung, then held in custody in the capital (see Caballero). The missionaries were given various assignments but later gathered with Morales at Fu-an to prevent the threatened destruction of their mission stations. He took this opportunity to notify the flock assembled there of the 1645 decisions and decree and sent copies to the Jesuit vice-provincial, Dias. Meanwhile, Garcia, aided by confreres and converts, was completing a church at Ting-t'ou that was blessed in April, 1651. One day in November, however, 300 sailing boats carrying marines in the service of Emperor Chu Yu-lang (ECCP), landed at Ting-t'ou; six marines went ashore the next day and set fire to the church. This put an end to the mission station, but the the missionaries continued to spread their gospel and build simpler edifices at Che-yang 柘洋, Hsi-yin 西音, Lo-chia-chiang 羅家港, as well as at Ting-t'ou.

At this time China was divided between the Manchus, who controlled most of the country, and the Ming loyalists, who were struggling to hold the southern provinces, including part of Fukien which was actually ruled by Cheng Ch'eng-kung, better known as Koxinga (ECCP). In July, 1655, the Dominicans received reinforcements, but Morales and another Dominican decided to leave the disturbed province of Fukien and open new mission stations in Chekiang; they had to hasten the execution of their plan when, in November, 1656, eighteen of Koxinga's boats sailed along the coast near Amoy to plunder and destroy. The missionaries left in haste for Pai-shih-chien 白石尖 and then Lan-ch'i 蘭谿, Chekiang, where a prominent convert helped them buy a house for a residence and church; this became the center of missionary activity. Meanwhile, Koxinga's armada of 3,000 boats entered (December 10) the inlets of Fu-an, pillaging and killing the Chinese subjects of the Manchus, while Chinese mountaineers also looted. The Lo-chia mission was sacked. The armada returned to Amoy in the middle of 1657 and Fu-an enjoyed a respite. In June, 1658, however, Koxinga again embarked on a campaign of several years to recover China from the Manchus.

During this time most of the Dominicans in China were working in Chekiang under the guidance of Morales. Dissatisfied with a decree of 1656 which interpreted certain rites according to the explanation submitted by the Jesuit, Martino Martini (1614-61), the Dominicans held a meeting at Lan-ch'i where they discussed at length all the pastoral problems of the day, and compiled a comprehensive essay on Confucius, city gods, and ancestor worship. On April 20, 1661, they made a rule for the practical solution of cases arising in their own ministry, pending a definitive resolution by the Holy See. To enlighten their converts on the subject, Morales wrote a booklet explaining the Christian way of filial piety. A few weeks later the group drew from this essay a "Relation and petition" (Relatio et libellus supplex) with twenty-two questions to be submitted to Rome; later they added another "Petition" (Libellus supplex), which was subsequently submitted. In November, probably because of overwork, Morales suffered a stroke which paralyzed his left side. He moved in 1662 to the warmer climate of Fu-ning and opened a church. He spent the following year writing a treatise in three volumes on ritual problems. He continued his writing and guidance of his converts practically to the end. Morales passed away at Fu-ning, where Cocchi had founded the first Dominican mission in China.

He wrote a number of books, papers, reports, and letters, most of which are as yet unpublished. Of particular interest to the student of Chinese is his Chinese-Spanish dictionary ("Vocabulario Chino-Español alphabetico" with Chinese characters arranged in alphabetical order of their romanization. It is a manuscript of 326 pages, preserved at the Biblioteca Apostolica Vaticana (Fondo Borgiano Cinese 503), and supplemented by his *Sheng-chiao hsiao-ch'in chieh* 聖教孝親解 (Explanation of Catholic filial piety), 8 folios, bearing the Chinese name of Morales.

Bibliography

José Maria González, *Historia de las Misiones Dominicanas de China 1632-1700*, Vol. I (Madrid, 1964), 71, 233, 634, 681, 684, 686; K. S. Latourette, *A History of Christian Missions in China* (New York, 1929), 108, 136; Benno M. Biermann, *Die Anfänge der neueren Dominkanermission in China* (Münster in W., 1927), 27; Antonio Sisto Rosso, *Apostolic Legations to China of the Eighteenth Century* (South Pasadena, 1948), 104; Pablo Fernández, *Dóminicos donde nace el sol* (Barcelona, 1958), 106, 151; Henri Cordier, *Bibliotheca Sinica* (2d ed. Paris, 1922-24), col. 3910.

Antonio Sisto Rosso

MU Tseng 木增 (T. 長卿, H. 華岳, 生白, native name A-chai a-ssu 阿宅阿寺, known in the local patois as Muan-ssä-hä), September 19, 1587-September 9, 1646, held the hereditary Na-khi chieftainship with the rank of native prefect of Li-chiang chün-min fu 麗江軍民府 in northwestern Yunnan from 1598 to 1623. Possibly the most celebrated of the Na-khi rulers, he was a descendant in the 19th generation of the legendary founder of the chieftainship, who, known as Ye-ye 爺爺, was recorded in the family records as a Mongol from the Western Regions arriving at the Li-chiang area in the 12th century. (From the sequence of events and ethnological evidence it seems that the Na-khi derived from the nomads of the Ch'iang 羌 region on the northwestern border of Szechwan. There is the possibility that they migrated south at the time of the Mongol conquest of Ta-li 大理 (1253) when the Mongol army followed the course of the Ta-chin-ch'uan 大金川 south from Kansu, passing through the Ch'iang area. In any case it seems that the Na-khi authority in the Li-chiang area began with the award of chieftainship by the Mongols in the 13th century.)

When the Ming army advanced to Ta-li in Yunnan in 1382 (*see* Fu Yu-te), Mu Tseng's ancestor, the then chief, joined the new dynasty and, for his military contributions, was awarded the Chinese name Mu Te 得 (T. 自然, H. 恒忠, 1311-90), and in 1384, for his military services, the rank of native hereditary prefect of Li-chiang (*see* Yang Shen). Mu Tseng, the thirteenth prefect after Mu Te, succeeded his father Mu Ch'ing 青 (H. 松鶴, 1569-97) when the latter lost his life in a campaign to suppress a local revolt.

Mu Tseng's life story is a succession of similar campaigns in which he was uniformly successful. In his first year as chieftain a brigand named A-chang-la-mao 阿文刺毛 failed in an attempt to put him out of the way, and in the following year Mu was victorious against other rebels. In 1600 the ministry of Personnel confirmed the youth in office, and in ensuing years he justified his appointment by suppressing every uprising as it showed its head. As a result the same ministry conferred on both his father and himself (1606) the honorary titles of 4th grade officials. During the following decade his exploits continued, and in 1618 it is recorded

that he sent envoys to Peking with gifts of horses and local products as tribute to the emperor, and to celebrate the emperor's birthday. In return the court presented him and his wife Lu Fan 祿蘩 with gifts of hemp, silk, colored satin, gauze, socks, and boots. Because of the defeat that same year in Manchuria (*see* Nurhaci, ECCP), Mu made a donation of ten thousand taels of silver to the ministry of Revenue to meet military expenses. This so pleased the court that it published a report of it for the information of officials throughout the empire, and Mu in turn received the decorations of a 3d grade official. Two years later he made another donation (1,200 taels of silver) to the government for the purpose of purchasing mounts for the army. His reward for this was the imperial designation of chung-i 忠義 (loyal and righteous).

In 1620 he received orders to suppress the effort of a certain Kao Lan 高蘭 to usurp the magistracy of Pei-sheng-chou 北勝州. He succeeded in taking Kao and many others prisoner and was awarded a medal and other gifts. When, in July, 1622, the tribal chief She Ch'ung-ming 奢崇明, a Lolo and hereditary pacification officer of Yung-ning 永寧, Szechwan, headed a revolt, Mu Tseng sent funds to help meet the expense of the government soldiers in their campaign against him. The revolt was put down in March, 1623. Meanwhile Mu had dispatched a ten point memorial to the throne on the subject of awards and had contributed another thousand taels of silver to be used on behalf of the families of those slain in the war or for those who had demonstrated their loyalty. For this the ministry of Personnel appointed him administration vice commissioner of Yunnan. The following year (1624) he resigned in favor of his eldest son, Mu I 懿 (T. 琨瑜, H. 台美, also known as 阿春, 1608-92), but this step seems hardly to have made a significant change in his manner of life. He continued to make cash donations for the soldiery and the families of the bereaved, and he requested permission to sacrifice to two heroes lauded for their loyalty, Chang Ch'üan (ECCP) and Ho T'ing-k'uei 何廷魁 (T. 汝謙, cs 1601), both of whom lost their lives in 1621 in the defense of the city of Liao-yang 遼陽 against the Manchus. The government in its turn conferred on him ever higher (but empty) titles. Mu Tseng also provided corvée labor, and received permission (1627) to build an arch in memory of his mother, née Lo 羅. In ensuing years he continued his military successes against rebellious leaders, helped both the court and provincial governors with funds, and assisted in rebuilding certain villages and bridges. He likewise dispatched laborers to work on the imperial tombs (near Peking), as a result of which he was accorded the title of administration commissioner of Szechwan and given the right to build an arch in his own honor in Yunnan-fu. Instead of erecting it, however, he contributed the money thus saved for the expenses of the imperial troops (1644). In 1642 four Hsi-fan and Lolo tribes surrendered to him, and in 1643, on orders again, he took captive Li Yung-chen 李永鎮 and his brothers, who had murdered the magistrate of Chien-ch'uan 劍川, a city south of Li-chiang. In spite of the loss of north China to the Manchus during the year following, he and his family continued their support of the Ming, and received appropriate recognition from the Hung-kuang emperor (Chu Yu-sung, ECCP) in Nanking (1645). He died a year later.

Mu Tseng appears to have left an almost unblemished reputation among his followers, who came to call him Mu T'ien-wang 天王 (the celestial king). And in modern times, a western scholar—in recognition of Mu's prowess—has even named one of the province's loftiest peaks after him: A-ssu or Mu Tseng shan, an eminence of some 19,000 feet. Mu was a loyal Buddhist, and welcomed the Karma-pa lamas who established

lamaseries in his district. A portrait of him, clad in Buddhist robes, and holding a rosary, with an image of Amitābha depicted above his head, is reproduced by Joseph Rock. Mu was responsible for printing a number of Tibetan Buddhist works, and encouraged their use among his people. He himself was literate and maintained a library of ten thousand *chüan* 萬卷樓; whatever writings, both prose and poetry, he himself composed, however, seem to have disappeared during the Musllm outbreaks of the 19th century; his calligraphy is represented by two scrolls, also pictured by Rock. Several temples too are the result of his largesse, notably the Hua-yen ssu 華嚴寺, situated on a mountain northeast of Er-hai 洱海, the Hsi-t'an 悉檀 ssu, and a lamasery known either as Fu-kuo 福國 ssu or as Chieh-t'o-lin 解脫林. The last is the only one which has survived fairly intact down to modern times. He saw to it that each religious seat received a copy of the Tibetan canon, which he either contributed or sought from the imperial court.

Mu Tseng married three times. His eldest son and heir was born to the second wife, A-shih-hui 阿室揮. His third wife, A-shih-ko 哥 (or jung 榮), became the mother of three more sons. When he died in 1646, most of China had already been invaded by the Manchus. He lived through the period of turmoil at the end of the Ming but at his death he was in contact with the Ming courts in south China. It was during his son's chieftainship in 1659 that the surrender to the new Manchu dynasty took place. In 1723 the office of hereditary prefect of Li-chiang was abolished and the office of prefect became appointive by the provincial government with confirmation by the central government. The Mu family, however, retained the title of hereditary assistant prefect but was deprived of administrative power. There is a report that the last head of the house, probably the one in the 33d generation, born in 1929, was executed in the 1950s.

Bibliography

1/314/8b; MSL (1940), Hsi-tsung, 29/7b; KC (1958), 5206, 5216, 5274; *Tien-hsi* 滇繫, 8/9/14b, 11/16a: Chang Tan 張紞 (d. 1402), *Yün-nan chi-wu ch'ao-huang* 雲南機務鈔黃, 1/13b; *Ta Ch'ing i-t'ung-chih* 大清一統志 (1790), 382/4a; *Yün-nan t'ung-chih* (1736), 21/37b, 22/63b, 24/25b, 26/24a: E. Chavannes, "Documents historiques et géographiques relatifs à Li-kiang," TP, 13 (1912), 574, 629; Joseph F. Rock, *The Ancient Na-khi Kingdom of Southwest China* (Cambridge, Mass., 1947), 125, pl. 29, 30, 44, 64, 89; *id., The Life and Culture of the Na-khi Tribe of the China-Tibet Borderland* (1963), 9, 23.

Chaoying Fang and
L. Carrington Goodrich

MU Ying 沐英 (T. 文英), 1345–June 7, 1392, military leader and first chief of the garrison defense command 鎮 established by the Ming in Yunnan, was a native of Ting-yüan 定遠 (Anhwei). Orphaned at the age of seven, he came to the attention of Chu Yüan-chang in the early 1350s and, along with a number of other orphaned boys, was adopted by the future founder of the Ming dynasty. Mu grew up in Chu's household and used the name Chu Wen-ying 朱文英, given him by his foster father; according to all accounts, he was unaware that he was not Chu's son. The foster parents were particularly fond of this boy; he shared the living quarters of their own eldest son, Chu Piao (*q.v.*), and eminent scholars tutored them together. Later one could discern in both individuals the influence of the humane personality of the Empress Ma (*q.v.*) as well as the respect for learning which they acquired in those years. As a boy Mu is described as having been extremely quick of mind, mature in manner, and unfailingly diligent and respectful, qualities that probably are not mere biographer's clichés since Chu Yüan-chang made a point of calling attention to the shortcomings of those about him, even in his own children and grandchildren. The records contain no mention of anything but his praise for the young Mu Ying.

Mu also possessed qualities that complemented his gentler side. From the age of eighteen he received military training and experience in the field as Chu Yüan-chang's personal aide, and as junior officer on the staffs of leading generals. Before he was twenty he was given military assignments carrying considerable responsibility, *e.g.*, for some years he was garrison commander at the important bastion of Chinkiang, and in 1368 he achieved conspicuous merit for leadership in battle during the campaign against the Fukien warlord Ch'en Yu-ting (*see* Fang Kuo-chen). It was only after that series of engagements that Chu Yüan-chang told Mu he was an orphan, and recounted the circumstances. He also instructed Mu, as he at that time instructed all his other adopted sons, to resume his original surname. But he continued to regard Mu Ying with special favor, arousing the speculation, discussed but generally discredited by serious historians later on, that Mu may have been his own son, the offspring of some irregular alliance that he did not wish to acknowledge.

In the early years of the Hung-wu reign, after working briefly in Fukien garrison assignments, Mu served in the chief military commission in Nanking, first as an assistant commissioner-in-chief and then as vice commissioner-in-chief. In 1377 he was named vice commander to Generalissimo Teng Yü (*q.v.*) in an expedition that went far out into the Kokonor region and the Tibetan uplands on the western borders of Szechwan. On the conclusion of that campaign, he was awarded in November the title marquis of Hsi-p'ing 西平侯 and an annual stipend of 2,500 *shih* with rights of inheritance. During the following four years he was continuously active as a field commander in the north and northwest.

Mu Ying's special place in history stems from his role in the conquest of Yunnan and its integration into the empire as a new province. When military action against Yunnan was decided upon in 1381, Fu Yu-te (*q.v.*) was named generalissimo of the expeditionary forces, with Lan Yü (*q.v.*) and Mu Ying as vice commanders. The military action, commencing with the battle for Ch'ü-ching 曲靖 in the northeast corner of the province in January of 1382, followed by the capture of Kunming and Ta-li 大理 in the following months, produced a series of major victories without conclusive results (*see* Fu Yu-te). By 1383 the emperor had decided that a continuing military presence of special size and nature would be needed to bring the region under permanent control; he informed his field command there that Mu Ying should remain behind with the major portion of the expeditionary force after the completion of the conquest, and that Fu and his staff were to withdraw.

There were three aspects to the military problem in Yunnan. First, and perhaps of greatest initial importance to the Ming court, was to eradicate the Mongol princely line established there by Qubilai Khan following his conquest of the Nan-chao state in 1254. Called by the Chinese the Liang 梁 princedom, this remnant of Mongol power seemed capable of establishing alliances with other Mongol bases on the west and north of China, and therefore was intolerable. The Liang princedom was eliminated with comparative ease with the capture of Kunming, its capital, in the summer of 1382, and the suicide of the prince and members of his family and court. Second, there was the old Ta-li kingdom, ruled over by the Tuan family (*see* Lan Yü), originally from north China, who in the Sung dynasty established their suzerainty over the tribal groupings making up the Nan-chao confederation. Although Qubilai had executed the head of the family, the reigning "king," he had found it expedient to continue to use the family and their network of connections throughout the tribal structure. Their power remained great, and was not eliminated when Mu Ying captured their

Ta-li stronghold. Third, there was the base level of tribal power structure, comprising the greatest part of the population. Most important were the speakers of Tibeto-Burman languages, loosely called Lolo by the Chinese; they were the dominant group, and the descendants of the tribes that had created the Nan-chao state six centuries earlier. But there were also important clusters of Thai-related peoples such as the Shan 撣 and the Pai-i 百夷 who probably had been increasing in numbers and importance there since the 12th century. All of these peoples lived in agricultural villages and were similar enough to the Chinese of the southwest so that they could be readily absorbed into Chinese-type society. but they were fiercely independent and capable of stubborn military resistance. The Shan state in particular was in a period of resurgence in the late 14th century; its king, Ssu Lun-fa (*see* Ssu Jen-fa), gave Mu Ying his most serious continuing problems as military governor of the region in the decade that followed, and pacification of the Shan remained unsuccessful for a century.

Mu Ying faced all these problems with effective military strategy and, more significantly in the long range, with intelligent encouragement of civil government. Local leaders were sent to Nanking on many occasions for audiences at the court, their sons were given educational privileges, and on some occasions the emperor bestowed Chinese surnames on tribal leaders who had not previously acquired them. Mu Ying was particularly attentive to developing educational facilities within the province. He also concerned himself with irrigation and drainage, and other technological improvements to agriculture. Throughout all the efforts to transform the region according to Chinese standards, a very broad-minded spirit of accommodation to local custom is evident. Mu was a humane and patient governor.

To attend to the military problem of that border area, the court decided to

confirm Mu and his descendants in hereditary tenure as chiefs of a special defense
command in the region, to exist side by
side with the usual structure of provincial
civil government. Also on April 13, 1385,
Nanking issued orders that all military officials serving under Mu in Yunnan, down
to the level of company commanders, were
to be promoted one rank and confirmed
in hereditary tenure there. Since this in
effect retained the troops serving under
them, it transformed the major portion
of the original expeditionary force, said
to have numbered 300,000, mostly recruited in the Nanking region, into a permanent garrison for Yunnan. Major cities
in the region already had possessed Chinese inhabitants; they were in fact cities
in the Chinese form. But the influx of
these military families, mostly added to
the urban population, did a great deal to
strengthen the Chinese character of the
leading centers, as well as to establish
their links with the rest of the country.
The oft-noted similarity of Yunnanese
Mandarin to that of some Yangtze valley
areas may well be evidence of the cultural impact which Mu Ying's garrison
forces had on the region.

In November, 1389, Mu Ying was called
back to Nanking for a court banquet
in his honor and other rewards including
lavish gifts of gold, silver, and currency.
The emperor reportedly patted him fondly
on the shoulder and said: "Knowing that
you are there, I can sleep soundly with
no worries about the southwest." Mu
returned to Yunnan after this short visit,
and in the next year or two faced repeated outbreaks of rebellious tribal leaders,
but broke all military resistance and had
the satisfaction of seeing all of Yunnan
at peace by 1392. Chu Piao died on May
17, 1392, and, on July 7, within a day or
two of hearing the news, Mu also passed
away apparently due to grief, according
to contemporary accounts. The emperor
ordered that Mu's body be returned to
Nanking for burial in a mausoleum near
the imperial tombs, then under construc-

tion. He was posthumously elevated to
prince of Ch'ien-ning 黔寧王, and granted
the honorific Chao-ching 昭靖. Shrines
were erected to his memory in Yunnan,
and his spirit tablet was included with
those to which imperial sacrifices were
offered in the imperial ancestral shrine
(T'ai-miao 太廟).

Mu Ying was survived by his widow,
née Keng 耿, born the same year as her
husband; she lived until 1431, residing in
Nanking where the family maintained its
principal residence for several generations.
Five sons are mentioned. The eldest, Mu
Ch'un 春 (T. 景春, Pth. 惠襄, 1363–98),
was confirmed in the succession to the
marquisate and in the hereditary tenure
of the office of chief of the special defense command for Yunnan on November
6, 1392. He served in that capacity until
some illness brought about his premature
death. His achievements include striking
successes in both the military and the
civil fields. Mu Ch'un had no son; he was
succeeded in the title and the Yunnan
defense command post by his younger
brother, Mu Ying's second son, Mu Sheng
晟 (T. 景成, 1368–1439, posthumously
elevated to prince of Ting-yüan with
honorific 忠敬). Mu Sheng was confirmed
in the succession in January, 1399, shortly
after Chu Yün-wen (q.v.) came to the
throne, but the civil war did not affect
either Mu Sheng or the Mu family. His
forty-year tenure in the office was marked
by further administrative successes and
some military ones, but he is a somewhat controversial figure. Although he
held military posts from his youth onward, and as a young man won the
warm approval of Chu Yüan-chang, he
appears to have lacked his father's and
his older brother's sincerity, integrity, and
common touch, and earned an unflattering reputation for self-aggrandizement
through exploiting his contacts within the
official elite. As the general responsible
for military affairs in a province bordering on Annam, Mu Sheng was repeatedly
ordered to lead armies from Yunnan and

the southwest into that country from 1406 onward. In the first campaign in 1406–7, they pursued the enemy all the way to the Cham border and, according to the Chinese accounts, "captured 48 commanderies and 186 hsien with a population of 3,125,900 households (see Chang Fu and Huang Fu); also elephants, horses, herds, and military equipment beyond counting ...." Mu Sheng returned in triumph to Yunnan, and in the spring of 1408 was called to the court to be rewarded by Emperor Chu Ti (q.v.) with the title duke of Ch'ien-kuo 黔國公, an annual stipend of 3,000 shih, and lavish material gifts. But Mu was unsuccessful on the subsequent occasions in which he had to help with military action in Annam, and even within his own province. As a field commander he was incompetent and cautious to the point of cowardice. In 1427 he was impeached at the court for his inept conduct of a campaign, but the emperor refused to heed the charges, and the matter was closed. During his last campaign against Ssu Jen-fa in 1438–39, he suffered serious defeats and retreated ignominiously to his base at Ch'u-hsiung 楚雄 so shaken that he either died of illness induced by his mental state, or took poison. Yet the Mu family had acquired such a reputation for infallibility in Yunnan that the court at Peking felt it important to have a son of Mu Ying in charge there, even though a somewhat incompetent one; so it always continued to support Mu Sheng. Certain Muslim authorities assert that he belonged to their faith, but this is not officially confirmed.

In the Annàmite campaigns and in other military tasks, Mu Sheng was aided by his brother (Mu Ying's third son), Mu Ang 昂 (T. 景高, posthumously elevated to earl of Ting-pien 定邊伯, with honorific 武襄, 1445). He acted temporarily as regent for the family in their Yunnan responsibilities after Mu Sheng's death, and appears to have been an able and vigorous military commander. The emperor in 1440 had confirmed Mu Sheng's son,

originally named Mu Yen 儼, in the succession, and awarded him the new name Mu Pin 斌 (T. 文輝, Pth. 容康, 1397–1450). He continued to live in Nanking and to hold a minor post at court until the death of his uncle, Mu Ang, after which he went to Yunnan to take up the headship of the family there, assuming the hereditary rank of duke of Ch'ien-kuo, and the military responsibilities that went with it.

Nothing is known about the fourth son of Mu Ying. A fifth, Mu Hsin 昕, became the husband of the imperial princess Ch'ang-ning 常寧 (1420–41), the youngest of Emperor Chu Ti's five daughters. Counting from Mu Sheng as the first duke of Ch'ien-kuo, the fourth duke, Mu K'un 崑 (T. 元中, H. 玉岡, 1482–1519, enf. 1497, Pth. 莊襄), was a great-great-grandson of Mu Ang, whose line continued to the end of the Ming dynasty. The last one, the thirteenth duke, Mu T'ien-po 天波 (T. 星海, enf. 1628, d. 1661), served under the southern Ming emperor, Chu Yu-lang (ECCP), and accompanied the latter in the retreat to Burma in 1659; two years later he was murdered by the Burmese.

Although Mu Ying and later inheritors of the dukedom were granted state funerals and burial in mausolea in the Nanking suburbs, and the principal residence of the family continued to be in Nanking, they referred to themselves as natives of Ting-yüan, where they also acquired family property. Yet they had extensive holdings in Yunnan too; one account states that they possessed 365 estates, farms, or other productive properties there, "one to sustain them for each day of the year." Mu Ying is said also to have had a great fondness for horses and owned a notable stable in Yunnan. The family retained its hereditary responsibilities in Yunnan through the Ming dynasty, and gradually shifted its roots to that province, where it continued to be prominent until recent times. It is the unique example in Ming history of a family possessing continuing regional or local responsibilities, almost feudal in nature, one which reflects the special circumstances of Yunnan society, and the Ming government's way of dealing with that region.

Bibliography

1/126/17a; 5/5/19a; 61/92/17a; 63/3/36a; MSL (1962), T'ai-tsu; KC (1958), 350, 359, 555, 605, 730, 734, etc.; Ho Ch'iao-yüan, *Ming-shan-ts'ang*, "Ch'en-lin-chi," 1; Chin T'ien-chu 金天柱, *Ch'ing-chen shih-i pu chi* 清眞釋疑補輯 (preface 1738), 101; Fu T'ung-hsien 傅統先, *Chung-kuo hui-chiao shih* 回教史 (Shanghai, 1940), 102; Cha Chi-tso (ECCP), *Tsui-wei-lu*, "Chuan" 傳八上 8-a, 41a; Ku Ying-t'ai (ECCP), *Ming-ch'ao chi-shih pen-mo*, ch. 12, 22; Ch'en Tan 陳紝, *Yün-nan chi-wu ch'ao-huang* 雲南機務鈔黃(in *Shen Chieh-fu, Chi-lu hui-pien*, ch. 45); *Yunnan t'ung-chih* (1736), 16/52a, 17/6b; Jung-pang Lo, "Policy Formulation and Decision-making on Issues Respecting Peace and War" in C. O. Hucker, ed., *Chinese Government in Ming Times: Seven Studies* (1969), 55; Camille Sainson, *Nan-tchao ye-che* (Paris, 1904), 146, 222; R. A. D. Forrest, *The Chinese Language* (London, 1948), 204.

F. W. Mote

NAγAČU 納哈出 (died August 31, 1388), a powerful Mongol chieftain who surrendered to Chu Yüan-chang shortly before his death, was for twenty years the overlord of Liaotung and a formidable foe of the Ming. The origin and early years of Naγaču are rather obscure. The *shih-lu* asserts that he was a descendant of Muqali (Mu-hua-li 1170-1223), a distinguished general under Jenghiz khan. Naγaču joined the Mongol army, outshone his fellows in battle, and rose to become a battalion commander. He saw action in T'ai-p'ing太平 (Anhwei) when Chu Yüan-chang attacked the city in July, 1355. He was captured but soon released on order of the rebel chief and sent back to the north. Apparently Chu hoped that his generous treatment of Naγaču might induce other Mongol leaders to submit. Naγaču, however, rejoined the Yüan forces

and was assigned to Liaotung. By 1362 he is reported to have held the rank of assistant governor in Liao-yang 遼陽. On his flight from Ta-tu to Shang-tu in September, 1368, the powerful Mongol chieftain Toγon Temür (*q.v.*) appointed Naγaču the senior governor with the title of grand commandant (太尉). Thereafter Naγaču set up his quarters in Chin-shan 金山, about seventy miles north of Shen-yang 瀋陽, and steadily expanded his power in the Sungari River area, then the center of the Jürchen settlement.

Between these years, Naγaču made several attempts to expand his authority across the border at the expense of the Koreans. Early in 1362, taking advantage of the raids of the Red Turban rebels into Korea, and guided by a band of native renegades, he led an army across the Yalu River and raided the northern border. The Koreans suffered several setbacks, but in August, under the command of King Kongmin (Wang Chŏn, *see* Kwŏn Kün) and General Yi Sŏng-gye (*q.v.*), they defeated Naγaču in the plain of Hamju 咸興 (modern Hamhŭng). Naγaču then sued for peace and in subsequent years sent several tribute-bearing embassies to the Korean court to maintain friendly relations.

Early in 1368, on the impending collapse of the Yüan house and the threat of the rebel forces to Liaotung, Naγaču sent a delegation to negotiate with the Korean king for a joint defense agreement against the Chinese. To offset the possible alliance between the two, Chu Yüan-chang dispatched an envoy, in June, 1369, to persuade King Kongmin to sever ties with Naγaču and to take over the Ming calendar. The Korean king, eager to free himself from the Mongol yoke, readily accepted the emperor's demand. In the following months, presumably with Chinese backing, King Kongmin launched a series of campaigns aimed at recovering their territories from the Northern Yüan. Late in 1370, under the command of Yi Sŏnggye, the Koreans invaded Liaotung and captured Liao-yang from the Mongols, but soon retreated owing to cold weather and shortage of provisions. Avoiding a confrontation, Naγaču continued to send tribute to the Korean court.

Between the time of the initial campaign and the crossing of the Yalu, Chu Yüan-chang sent a special envoy, in June 1370, to Chin-shan to persuade Naγaču to surrender, but received a negative response. In July of the following year, the Ming emperor dispatched another representative to convey a similar message. This time Naγaču was outraged; he detained the envoy, and later reportedly had him executed. These actions, however, brought no immediate reprisal from Chu Yüan-chang. During the next two years, taking advantage of the inaction of the Ming court, Naγaču steadily built up his power and expanded his domain across the Chinese boundaries. In December, 1372, he overran a Chinese grain depot at Niu-chia-chuang 牛家莊 in Liaotung, burning over one hundred thousand bushels of grain, and killing over five thousand soldiers; this dealt a severe blow to the Chinese supply line in the northeastern region. Two years later Naγaču made a surprise attack on Liao-yang, but was driven back by the Ming forces. Another delay followed and then in January, 1376, he launched a large-scale offensive against Liaotung. After being repulsed at Kai-chou 蓋州, he turned to Chin-chou 金州, where he also encountered stiff resistance. He lost this battle, during which his able lieutenant, Nayira'u 乃剌兀, was wounded and captured by the Chinese. Naγaču then abandoned his adventure and turned north, narrowly surviving an ambush set by pursuers on his return journey. In the following years Naγaču waged few offensives; he was presumably busy regrouping his forces while the Ming continued to stay on the defensive. Chu Yüan-chang made another effort to persuade Naγaču to surrender (September, 1378), but the Mongol chieftain remained adamant.

Finally Chu decided to use force. In January, 1387, he appointed General Feng Sheng (*q.v.*) as commander-in-chief, with Fu Yu-te and Lan Yü (*qq.v.*) as deputies, to head an expedition against Naγaču. Starting in April with an army of about two hundred thousand men, including contingents of Mongol soldiers under the command of Nayira'u, Feng and others crossed the Liao River in July and made contact with the enemy. It is said that Feng sent Nayira'u ahead of the troops with a message for Naγaču to surrender. The presence of the Ming forces apparently convinced Naγaču of the futility of continued resistance; so he finally agreed to submit. A few days later Lan Yü arrived in Chin-shan to receive his surrender. In consequence, over two hundred thousand of his men went over to the Chinese side; they, together with countless sheep, horses, camels, and supplies formed a line which reportedly stretched for over a hundred *li*. The rest of Naγaču's forces in the Sungari valley, shocked by the surrender of their chieftain, disintegrated. When the news reached Nanking, Chu Yüan-chang gave orders to send lavish gifts to Naγaču and his followers.

In October Naγaču and his retinue arrived at the capital and were received in audience. Delighted over his submission, the emperor bestowed on him the title of marquis of Hai-hsi 海西侯 with an annual stipend of 2,000 bushels of rice to be drawn from the public fields in Kiangsi, and additional gifts. His followers also received titles and rewards. All these favors were apparently intended to keep him satisfied; Naγaču had lost all power, however, and he remained in Nanking. His troops were subsequently incorporated into the Chinese army and assigned to garrisons in Jehol, the Peiping area, Shantung, Nanking, and also in the deep south.

Naγaču, who was given to excessive use of liquor, was not in good health. In July of the following year, however, he received a summons to join General Fu Yu-te in his expedition against the rebel-

lious tribesmen in Yunnan. By this time
he had become very sick and was under
the care of a court physician; nevertheless
he was forced to comply with the imperial order. As the expeditionary forces
included many of his former troops, Naγačn's presence in the campaign would
seem desirable to guarantee their loyalty.
While the expedition was on its way to
Yunnan, Naγačn died at the end of August aboard ship near Wuchang. His remains were brought back and buried outside of one of the southern gates of
Nanking.

According to report, Naγačn's knowledge of Chinese was rather poor. The
Yijo sillok 李朝實錄 (T'aejo 太祖), records
that one day in 1388 a Korean envoy to
China tried to address the emperor in
Chinese. Chu Yüan-chang, however, was
unable to understand the Korean, and
jokingly remarked that he spoke Chinese
like Naγačn.

Naγačn was survived by a son named
Ch'a-han 察罕 (Čaγan) who inherited the
marquisate from his father, but on September 12, 1388, the title was changed
from Hai-hsi to Shen-yang. Two years later (April, 1390) the emperor sent Ch'a-han
to Tung-ch'ang 東昌 -fu Shantung, to be
in charge of the drilling of troops, and later rewarded him with a string of
400 cash. In 1393 he became involved in
the alleged conspiracy of Lan Yü, and
was executed on May 18 of that year.

Bibliography

1/1/4a, 3/6a, 105/33a, 132/5b, 327/3b; MSL (1962),
T'ai-tsu, ch. 3-193, 3009, 3040; Liu Chi 劉佶,
Pei-hsün ssu-chi 北巡私記 (1937), 3; KC (1958),
671, 675, 689; Ku Ying-t'ai (ECCP), *Ming-ch'ao
chi-shih pen-mo*, ch. 15; *Yijo sillok* (1953-56),
ch. 1; Chong In-chi 鄭麟趾, *Koryŏ-sa* 高麗史
(1908), ch. 40-44; Henry Serruys, *Sino-Jürčed
Relations during the Yung-lo Period (1403-1424)*,
(Wiesbaden, 1955), 68; *id.*, *The Mongols in China
during the Hung-wu Period (1368-1398)*, Brussels,
1959; *id.*, "Mongols Ennobled during the Early
Ming," HJAS, 22 (1959), 212; H. B. Hulbert,
History of Korea, ed. by C.N. Weems, I, (1962),
251; Louis Hambis, *Documents sur l'histoire des
Mongols à l'époque des Ming* (Paris, 1969), 13.

Hok-lam Chan

NAN Chü-i 南居益 (T. 思受, H. 損齋), *ca.*
1565-1643, governor of Fukien who forced
the Dutch to vacate the Pescadore Islands
(P'eng-hu 澎湖) in 1624, was a native
of Wei-nan 渭南, Shensi. He came from
a family of military registry which nevertheless was famous for producing ten
civil *chin-shih* in five generations, from
Nan Chao 釗 in 1460 to Nan Chü-jen 居
仁 in 1622.

Nan Chü-i's great-grandfather, Nan
Feng-chi 逢吉 (T. 元眞, H. 姜泉, *cs* 1538),
served (*ca.* 1553) as intendant of the
Yen-men 雁門 circuit, Shansi, and was a
disciple of Wang Shou-jen (*q.v.*). His
grandfather Nan Hsüan 軒 (T. 叔後, H.
陽谷, *ca.* 1515-*ca.* 1596, *cs* 1547), served
(*ca.* 1565-*ca.* 1575) as an intendant in
Szechwan, Hukuang, and Shantung. His
father, Nan Hsien-chung 憲仲 (*ca.* 1545-
ca. 1580, *cs* 1574), died in office while
magistrate of Tsao-ch'iang 棗强, in Pei-
Chihli.

Nan Chü-i himself became a *chü-jen*
in 1591 and a *chin-shih* in 1601. After a
term as novice in the ministry of Revenue he was appointed a secretary in the
ministry of Justice, rising to the directorship of a bureau. Then he became
prefect of Kuang-p'ing-fu 廣平府, Pei-
Chihli, director of education of Shansi province, and then for four years
(1616-1619?) intendant of the Yen-men
circuit with headquarters at Tai-chou 代
州, where his great-grandfather had once
held office. Later he served as surveillance commissioner and as an administration commissioner. His next appointment
was to the Court of the Imperial Stud
(October 23, 1621) which kept him in
Peking for over a year.

On March 18, 1623, Nan Chü-i was named
governor of Fukien to deal with the critical
situation there caused by the Dutch occupation of the Pescadores in July of the
previous year. It was late in the 16th
century, after the defeat of the Spanish

Armada (1588), that the English, and
later the Dutch, contended seriously with
the Spaniards and the Portuguese for the
lucrative China trade. The Dutch tried to
break the Portuguese monopoly at Macao
by force but failed repeatedly(1601, 1603,
and 1607). Then they sought, and in 1609
obtained, permission from the Japanese
to trade with Chinese smugglers at Hirado,
and later at Nagasaki. In 1622 they again
tried to open direct trade with China and
attacked Macao with eight hundred men
and thirteen ships under the command of
Cornelis Reijersen. On June 24 the Dutch
landing party suffered a crushing defeat
by the Portuguese defenders, losing hundreds of men and most of the officers
(*see* Giacomo Rho). They proceeded
next to the Fukien coast. As base of
operation they occupied the Pescadores
on July 5, 1622, and tried to negotiate
with the local Chinese authorities at
Amoy. Early in 1623 Shang Chou-tso
(*see* Ch'i Ch'eng-han), then governor of
Fukien, reported to Peking that the Dutch
had been in the Pescadores for over six
months trying to obtain the rights to
trade at a Fukien port; that they once
sent five ships in an attempt to land at
Liu-ao 六敖 (south of Chang-p'u 漳浦) but
lost a ship together with several sailors
who were captured; that they then cruised
farther along the coast without success;
and that they finally decided to re-open
negotiations. Shang said that he told the
Dutch to return to Yao-liu-pa (咬嚼吧,
i.e. Batavia) to await the Chinese traders
as before, but if they left the Pescadores
at once and kept away from any place
patrolled by the Chinese, they would be
permitted to stay at any of the nearby
non-Chinese ports. Shang did not mention
Formosa by name, although he apparently
meant it to be the place that the Dutch
might occupy. At that time Formosa
was a rendezvous for the smugglers from
China to trade with the Japanese. It was
referred to as Ta-wan (Tai-wan) 大灣,
the Big Bay, which was probably the
bay sheltered by the then An-p'ing

安平 Isthmus.

Shang's handling of the Dutch apparently did not satisfy the Peking government and Nan Chü-i was appointed his
successor. Before Nan's arrival, Shang
made two more reports, the first in April
saying that he had the promise of the
Dutch to leave the Pescadores and the
second, two months later, remarking bitterly that the Dutch had received reinforcements and were not leaving; further,
that if another warning from him failed
to impress them the use of force would
be inevitable, with its concomitant additional military expenses.

Late in July, 1623, Nan Chü-i arrived
at Foochow. He reported that the six
Dutch ships in the Pescadores had been
reinforced by five more, and that they
had captured over six hundred Chinese
sailors and traders who were being forced
to work on strengthening the fortress at
their base. He then requested men and
funds to prepare for war on the Dutch
and was granted a free hand. He at
once conducted preparations for a military offensive, and it was rumored that
the Portuguese of Macao had made some
contributions to finance his campaign.

In October, 1623, when a Dutch fleet
of four ships under Christian Francs put
in at Amoy harbor, the Chinese staged a
successful resistance. One ship was burned
and Francs himself captured. Other engagements along the coast were also reported. Nan Chü-i was determined to force
the Dutch to leave the China coast and
in February, 1624, began to send warships
to the Pescadores and land troops to
build a fort. Preparations for war were
carried on for several months. Meanwhile
both sides sought the help as intermediary
of the Chinese merchant at Hirado, Li
Tan (*q.v.*), the Dutch requesting him to
negotiate for permission to trade at a
Chinese port, while the Chinese, who
thought the Japanese might come to the
aid of the Dutch, wanted him to make
sure that no Japanese would do so. Late
in July Nan ordered the Chinese troops

to advance on the Dutch fort. On August 3, 1624, the Dutch asked for peace and agreed to destroy their fort and evacuate their Pescadores base, which they did in ten days. They then occupied An-p'ing, Formosa, and remained there for thirty-eight years until their final dislodgement by Cheng Ch'eng-kung (ECCP) in 1662. The acquiescence of the Dutch was brought about partly by Nan's determined military preparations and partly by the Dutch realization that they would never obtain trade with China by hostile action. This regret was expressed eloquently by Martinus Sonck, Reijersen's successor, in his report to Batavia on the surrender of the Pescadores: "Now we must needs first atone for all these and many other wrongs, consigning them to oblivion as best we may, before ever the Company will be able to enjoy the long coveted fruits of the magnificent China trade."

Nan Chü-i's report of his success in dealing with the Dutch must have reached Peking in September. In it he said that the "red-haired barbarians" had been forced to leave Chinese territory and had sailed away. He also delivered to Peking the twelve Dutch prisoners of war; they were received by the emperor, it is said, at a celebration of the victory. Nan also submitted in 1625 a ten-point plan on coastal defense of Fukien to prepare against a repetition of similar aggression. His plans were probably shelved, for at that time the war on the northeastern frontier required the full attention of Peking.

It is said that Nan did not mention in his report any word in praise of the then all-powerful eunuch Wei Chung-hsien (ECCP), and so was given no reward for his achievement. In May, 1625, he was made a vice minister of Works in charge of the Grand Canal. The people of Fukien, however, considered Nan's success magnificent. They knew that he had succeeded in forcing the enemy to leave without actually resorting to a protracted conflict which might have proved disastrous for the local people. In gratitude they voluntarily

built shrines in his honor at four places. Nan was also remembered in three other shrines where he held office, in Kuang-p'ing, Taiyüan, and Tai-chou. Wei Chung-hsien, however, thought otherwise and soon (1625?) had Nan cashiered and deprived of all honors. He returned home and lived there quietly for several years. About 1620 he built a country house for himself in the foothills south of his home town which he called P'u-yüan 瀑園 (Waterfalls Garden), but he had had no opportunity to live there. Hence he must have appreciated the privileges of an enforced retirement.

In 1627, after the new emperor had brought about removal of Wei Chung-hsien, officials harmed by that powerful eunuch had their privileges restored. Nan was recalled and appointed vice-minister of Revenue in charge of the granaries. He was then sent to inspect the grain transportation on the Grand Canal. Just at that time the Manchus invaded the Peking area and Nan was ordered to supervise the military defense of T'ung-chou 通州. After the Manchus retreated, Nan was credited with the successful defense of that city. Meanwhile he was also belatedly credited with the Pescadores victory of 1624, and in January, 1630, was promoted to minister of Works, only to be dismissed six months later on the charge that the new cannon manufactured by his ministry had broken to pieces at a trial firing. This time he went home for good. He was then about seventy sui. As a reward for his T'ung-chou defense, his rank and titles were soon restored. This was the time when many rebels were on the rampage in Shensi and neighboring provinces. Nan helped in the defense of his native city, and in 1640 contributed heavily to the relief of a famine.

In November, 1643, after the bandit leader, Li Tzu-ch'eng (ECCP), captured Sian, he had Nan brought before him. Nan refused to join the bandits and was tortured while being held for ransom. It is said that he suffered from burning with a hot iron before he died. A number of other members of the Nan family also lost their lives in the same year. It seems that no one from that family rose to prominence during the Ch'ing period. Thus the Nan family of Wei-nan may be said to have risen and fallen with the fortunes of the house of Ming.

Bibliography

1/264/3a; 3/251/2b; 30/6/31a; 41/1/26a; 55/2/17a; 64/ 辛乙 /9b; Li Yin-tu 李因篤 (1631-1692), *Hsü Shou-ch'i-t'ang wen-chi* 續受祺堂文集, 1/1a; MSL (1966), Hsi-tsung, 1535, 1681, 1828, 1927, 1929; KC (1958), 5215, 5302; Shen Kuo-yüan, *Liang-ch'ao ts'ung-hsin-lu*, 19/11a, 23/38a, 26/1a; *Wei-nan-hsien chih* (1892), 2/又42a, 49a, 3/14b, 8/18b, 11/7a; *Shan-hsi t'ung-chih* 山西通志 (1892), 12/45a; *Ming Ch'ing shih-liao* 乙編, 7/624a; *Pa-ta-wei-ya ch'eng jih-chi* 巴達維亞城日記 (Chinese translation of a Japanese translation of selected chapters from the *Dagh-Register gehouden int Casteel Batavia vant passerende daer ter plaetse als over geheel Nederlandt India, 1624-1682* [Batavia, 1896-1931], Taipei, 1970; Bank of Taiwan 臺灣銀行 ed., *Ming-chi Ho-lan jen ch'in-chü P'eng-hu ts'an tang* 明季荷蘭人侵據澎湖殘檔 (1962); C. R. Boxer, *Fidalgos in the Far East* (1948), 72.

Chaoying Fang

NI Ch'ien 倪謙 (T. 克讓, H. 靜存), December 31, 1415-April 9, 1479, scholar, official, was a native of Shang-yüan 上元, one of the two districts comprising the city of Nanking. His ancestors during the troubled days of the 12th century had fled from north China to Hangchow, where they apparently became prosperous. In 1366 the forces of Chu Yüan-chang conquered Hangchow. Shortly thereafter he ordered the resettlement of its wealthy families of various trades in his capital (Nanking) in order to build up the city and to supply money, labor, and materials to his budding administration. Ni Ch'ien's great-grand-father was registered in Nanking among the artisans, apparently as an ironworker, for his residence was situated in the street known as T'ieh-tso-fang 鐵作坊 (iron foundries). Ni Ch'ien was a bright child and went to school. In 1438 he became a *chü-jen* and a year later passed first in the metropolitan examination and was third on the *chin-shih* list; he received an appointment as a compiler in the Hanlin Academy. In 1444 a drought affected a large part of China. On May 11 of that year Ni Ch'ien was named among the sixteen officials dispatched from Peking, each to pray for rain at one of the shrines to the sacred mountains, rivers, and seas. Ni was sent north to the one called pei-yüeh 北岳 (*i. e.*, Heng-shan 恒山 in Shansi). It happened that on that very day his first son was born. So he named him Ni Yüeh (*q. v.*) and gave him the courtesy name Shun-tzu 舜咨 (*see* Legge, *Shoo-King* 1/3/11, 12).

In March, 1449, Ni Ch'ien was promoted to a sub-expositor. Half a year later, after the Oirat captured Emperor Chu Ch'i-chen (*q. v.*), his half-brother Chu Ch'i-yü (*q. v.*) ascended the throne. Late that year Ni was appointed chief envoy to Korea to bear the new emperor's proclamations to that country. He arrived in Seoul in February, 1450. During his stay of half a month he composed a number of poems which, together with those presented to him by the Koreans, were printed in 4 *chüan* under the title. *Liao-hai-pien* 遼海編. A shorter version, *Feng-shih Chao-hsien ch'ang-ho shih* 奉使朝鮮倡和詩, also circulated. There is also an account of the journey, *Chao-hsien chi-shih* 紀事. These works greatly enhanced his fame. While he was in Korea his first wife (1419-50) died in Nanking. After his return to Peking he married a descendant of Kuo Ying (*q. v.*), the first marquis of Wu-ting 武定. Meanwhile Ni was chosen to tutor in the palace a group of selected young eunuchs. These connections indicate his rise on the political stage. In 1452 he became a lecturer on the Classics to the emperor and, it is said, was ordered to continue in service and forego the three-year mourning period on the death of a parent. When the emperor's own son was proclaimed heir apparent (*see* Chu Ch'i-yü) Ni became one of the minor functionaries in the supervisorate of instruction. In 1454 he was named to the editorial board to compile a gazetteer of the empire. When the work was completed in June, 1456, and printed under the title *Huan-yü t'ung-chih* (*see* Shang Lu), he was rewarded with promotion to grand secretary of the directory of instruction (右春坊大學士, not a participant in the grand secretariat).

On the restoration of Emperor Chu Ch'i-chen early in 1457, Ni seems to have weathered the change unscathed. He was appointed an assistant to the transmission commissioner, still retaining his Hanlin post, and then sent on a mission to the princedoms of Liao 遼, Ching 荆, and Ch'u 楚, all in Hukuang. On his return in January, 1458, he was promoted to chancellor of the Hanlin Academy. Later he became a tutor to the heir apparent, Chu Chien-shen (*q. v.*). In September, 1459, he served as associate director of the provincial examination held in Peking. Soon afterwards a disgruntled candidate, blaming his own failure on the examiner, accused Ni of accepting gifts from one of the deposed princes of the Liao princedom. It happened that this one-time prince's mother was also a descendant of Kuo Ying and so closely related to Ni's second wife. Perhaps some innocent transactions among relatives were misrepresented as evidence of a political intrigue. Ni was tried at the imperial court of the Embroidered-uniform Guard, then controlled by the notorious investigator Men Ta (*see* P'eng Shih), found guilty, and sentenced in May, 1460, to exile in Hsüan-fu, north of Peking, as a common soldier.

For four years he remained there until, on Chu Chien-shen's succession to the throne (1464), a general amnesty gave him release. Ni then returned home as a commoner. The emperor apparently remembered him as a tutor, for he was impressively stout, his belt having been described as large enough to encircle four average persons. His former students among the eunuchs also remembered him and helped to have him reinstated. In May, 1465, after retrieving his title as Hanlin chancellor, he retired. Four months later his son, Ni Yüeh, became a Hanlin compiler.

Ni Ch'ien, obviously seeking rehabilitation, came to Peking in July, 1466, on the excuse of offering thanks to the emperor. He was given an office in the East Hall 東閣 which meant his return as an active member of the Hanlin Academy. This created the unusual occurrence of a father and son holding office in the academy at the same time. It is said that both also served together as editors of the *Ying-tsung shih-lu* (*see* Li Hsien; the official list of editors gives only the son's name). This flouted the rules against nepotism and aroused strong objections from the censors. As a result, on July 28 his appointment was changed to Hanlin chancellor at Nanking. This did not please him and apparently he worked with friends at court to give him a new office. On August 9 he was named junior vice minister of Rites in Peking. This time the censors submitted a joint memorial of protest and so did the supervising secretaries. Three days later the emperor was forced to withdraw the appointment and sent Ni back to retirement.

Seven years later, in June, 1473, Ni was again reinstated, this time as a vice minister of Rites in Nanking. Again protests came but the emperor stood firm. After three years of service, Ni went to Peking as representative of the Nanking officials attending the emperor's thirtieth birthday celebration (which fell on November 18, 1476). On December 16, by direct imperial order, by-passing the ministry of Personnel, Ni was promoted to minister of Rites at Nanking. His age and excessive weight now told and in May, 1477, shortly after he returned to Nanking, he suffered a stroke. Five months later he was permitted to retire.

When he died two years after this, he was granted a state funeral and the posthumous name Wen-hsi 文僖.

During his last years in Nanking Ni Ch'ien edited his own works in several collections totalling 170 *chüan*. Some of these were lost during a fire. From what remained Ni Yüeh edited a collection in 32 *chüan* and printed it in 1493 under the title *Ni Wen-hsi kung chi* 公集. This was copied into the *Ssu-k'u* library in the late 18th century and reprinted in 1900 by Ting Ping (ECCP) in the collection of Hangchow authors. This edition includes a woodcut of his likeness, showing features of excessive corpulence. It is said that he had eyes which shone like lightning and was born with four nipples. Besides Ni Yüeh, he had another son, Ni Fu 阜 (T. 舜董, cs 1487), who also entered the Hanlin Academy; he later rose to be administration commissioner of Szechwan.

There is a story of social interest connected with Ni Ch'ien. Being an official of ministerial rank in Nanking, the common people were supposed to stand up whenever he passed by. On his own street, however, the residents and workers were all neighbors of several generations. So he told them to continue whatever they were doing and not to get up in his presence. After his death another official took this behavior as a personal insult and this strange custom among the blacksmiths had to be explained to him. The son, Ni Yüeh, later moved to Ch'ung-li chieh 崇禮街, a fashionable street southwest of the imperial palace. Also Ni Yüeh's registry was changed to Kuan-chi 官籍, or a household in high government service.

Bibliography

5/36/12a; 32/11/16a; 40/20/10a; Ch'ien Chien-i (ECCP), *Lieh-ch'ao shih-chi*, 丙 3/3b; *Huang Ming ming-ch'en mu-ming* 皇明名臣墓銘 (1969), 485; P'eng Hua 彭華, *P'eng wen-ssu-kung wen-chi* 文思公文集 (NCL microfilm), 5/6b; KC (1958), 1758, 1926, 1958, 2060, 2103, 2190, 2213, 2329, 2413; MSL (1964), Hsien-tsung, 0631, 2253, 3355; W. Franke, *Sources*, 7. 9. 1.

Chaoying Fang

NI Tsan 倪瓚 (T. 元鎮, H. 雲林子), February 26, 1301?-December 14, 1374, painter and poet, was a native of Wu-hsi, northwest of Soochow. The dates are based on his epitaph written by his friend Chou Nan-lao 周南老 (1301-83), and have been generally accepted. Another epitaph, however, gives April 1, 1302-November 9, 1385. Furthermore, because of some uncertainty in the epitaph written by Chou, and some other sources, there is a possibility that he was born in 1306, a date supported by two recent writers. Ni Tsan came from a wealthy family and was the youngest of three sons. His father died when he was very young, so he was brought up by his eldest brother Ni Ts'an 璨 (T. 昭奎, H. 文光), who, besides managing the family estate, served as a Taoist official for some time, probably as a way to protect the family fortune. Ni Ts'an died in 1328, and the second brother, who was mentally retarded, also died young. As a consequence, Ni Tsan became head of the family, handling its wealth and responsibilities. He is said to have demonstrated his intelligence at an early age, and to have become well-schooled in the Classics and literature. Beginning in 1328, with the family fortune at his disposal, he spent a considerable amount in developing a famous garden in Wu-hsi with sumptuous pavilions and beautiful trees and flowers. So well known did it become that it attracted the attention not only of local people but also of visitors from abroad. It boasted several buildings of note, the most unusual being without doubt the Ch'ing-pi-ko 清閟閣, which reportedly housed a library of several thousand volumes, many paintings and calligraphic pieces, ancient bronze vessels, musical instruments, and other antique objects. Living on this estate during his middle years, he led a life of leisure, devoting his time to poetry and painting, to visiting scenic places nearby, and to entertaining close friends in literary gatherings.

Ni is said to have been on one hand proud and uncompromising and on the other generous and helpful. He sometimes refused requests for his paintings from the rich and well placed, but gave away large sums of money to close friends and relatives. Perhaps the best-known side of his personality was his fastidious urge for cleanliness, which became almost an obsession. His dwellings and pavilions and even a wu-t'ung 梧桐 tree in his garden were washed and cleaned meticulously several times a day. He upset a number of his acqaintances by his insistence on ridding food and other objects of impurities. He also took a special delight in fragrant incense. Everywhere he went, he would have it burned around him. As a result, people could always locate him by the tell-tale aroma. A portrait of Ni Tsan, showing him seated on a dais, holding a brush in one hand and a piece of paper in the other, with a screen depicting a landscape behind him, and with two attendants standing on either side, is now in the Palace Museum, Taipei. To the left of his portrait is an inscription by Chang Yü (q. v.), a close friend to whom he is said to have once given a large sum of money. A number of copies of his paintings are known, including one attributed to Ch'iu Ying (q.v.).

During these years Ni seems to have followed his eldest brother's example by associating with Taoists. As one of the richest persons of his day, he may well have been the target for taxes by government officials, and for extortion by others in positions of power. Largely because he wanted to dodge these annoyances, he began (1350) to lead a wandering life. This phase lasted almost to the end of his days. He lived with his family on a houseboat, traveling around Lake T'ai and the surrounding districts. By 1354, he had probably given away, mostly to his relatives and close friends, almost all his possessions, such as land and houses, and to have led a leisurely life, sometimes visiting friends and other literati, sometimes staying in Taoist and Buddhist temples. One he especially favored was the K'ai-yüan Ch'an monastery 開元禪寺 in Soochow, which reputedly was built with money he donated because its abbot, Fang-yai 方厓, a painter of bamboos, was a special friend. Among other acquaintances he visited were two of the richest literati of his time, Ku Chung-ying 顧仲瑛 (1310-69) of K'un-shan 崑山 and Ts'ao Chih-po (see Wang Mien) of Sung-chiang, both painters and poets who shared many of his own tastes. He also often participated in some of the well-known literary parties; an example is the gathering in 1365 in the T'ing-yü-lou 聽雨樓 of Soochow. Here the host was Lu Shih-heng 盧士恆, who had as his guests famous painters and poets, such as Wang Meng, Kao Ch'i, and Chang Yü (qq.v.), all Ni's friends. Indeed, hardly a poet or painter of his time who lived in Wu-hsi and the region of his wanderings but could be counted as a friend or acquaintance.

After Chang Shih-ch'eng (q.v.) had made Soochow his power base, a group of intellectuals in that city gradually became involved in serving his government. Many of Ni's close friends, such as Ch'en Ju-yen, Chou Chih (qq.v.), Kao Ch'i, and Chang Yü accepted positions, but Ni declined. On one occasion, Ni even refused a request by the brother of Chang Shih-ch'eng for one of his paintings. This reflected his attitude toward Chang's regime. Later, the brother took revenge by humiliating him in front of a number of his literary friends on a boating party. After Chu Yüan-chang had come to the throne, Ni had to continue his wandering life to avoid facing all the demands for taxes imposed by the new officials. At one time he was caught and imprisoned, but was released later. Eventually, in 1374, he returned to Wu-hsi to stay with a relative, but soon fell ill and died.

Because of his extraordinary life and eccentricity, Ni Tsan became a legend in his lifetime. Stories about him continued to grow in the Ming period, as evidenced by many of the informal writings of various authors of the Soochow area. Later on these stories were collected in a book, Yün-lin i-shih 雲林遺事, by Ku Yüan-ch'ing (see Hsü Chen-ch'ing). During the last years of the Ming, he also came to be regarded as one of the "Four Masters of the Yüan," ranking with Huang Kung-wang (1269-1354), Wu Chen (1280-1354), and Wang Meng. In particular, he became the foremost example of the artists of the i-p'in 逸品 (untrammeled class). It is said that leading families in the area regarded possession of a Ni painting as a mark of their taste.

A few of the paintings and examples of calligraphy in Ni's collection are recorded in the Ch'ing-ho shu-hua-fang 清河書畫舫. His poems and other writings were collected during his own time, but the earliest edition seems to be the Ni Yün-lin hsien-sheng shih-chi 雲林先生詩集, first printed in 1460. Later, this was expanded several times to include other materials, and published as the Ch'ing-pi-ko ch'üan-chi 全集, the standard edition being the 1713 one. It was reproduced in Taiwan in 1970. There is a 1917 edition of his poems, Ch'ing-pi-ko shih 詩-chi, 6 ch., with two appendices: a collection of poems by twenty-one of his descendants, entitled Ch'ing-pi-ko fu 附 chi, 2 ch., and a collection of writings about his life and his art, entitled Ch'ing-pi-ko chih 志, 10 ch. As a poet he composed in a more direct, more natural, and freer style, and insisted that poetry was for the expression of inner feeling.

Extant paintings attributed to him number more than one hundred. Opinions concerning the genuineness of these paintings range widely. Jung Keng 容庚, after an extensive study based on painting records of the Ming and Ch'ing, made during early 1940, listed 162 as possibly his. More recently, Wang Chi-ch'ien, in an article

published in 1967, accepted only 42. Other scholars agree on far fewer. In an article entitled "Chinese Painting: A Statement of Method," Wen Fong shows why only one painting, the "Jung-hsi studio" 容膝齋 of 1372, now in the Palace Museum, Taipei, is considered genuine. The problem of authenticity of Ni's works is so complicated that there is as yet no definitive study of his oeuvre.

His painting generally falls into two categories: landscapes and bamboos. The former usually depict an open lake or river scene, with a kiosk and a few trees in the foreground and some mountains in the distance. This composition, with many variations, was almost the standard formula. His bamboo paintings include both rocks and bamboos, but sometimes show only one branch of bamboo in an extremely simple arrangement. Paintings taken more seriously are: "Ch'iu-t'ing yeh-hsing" 秋亭野興 (Enjoying the wilderness in an autumnal grove), dated 1339, perhaps most reliable of several versions of the same painting recorded by various catalogues, now in the John M. Crawford collection, New York. There are "Sung-lin t'ing-tzu" 松林亭子 (A pavilion among pines), dated 1354, Palace Museum, Taipei; "Yang Chu-hsi hsiang" 楊竹西像 (Portrait of Yang Chu-hsi), the portrait by Wang I and pine and rocks by Ni Tsan, dated 1363, Palace Museum, Peking; "Jung-hsi chai" dated 1372, Palace Museum, Taipei; "Shih-tzu lin" 獅子林 (The lion grove), done in collaboration with Chao Yüan (q.v.), dated 1373, former Manchu household collection; "An-ch'u chai" 安處齋 (An-ch'u studio), undated, Palace Museum, Taipei; "Ch'un-yü hsin-huang" 春雨新篁 (Bamboos in the rain), dated 1374, Palace Museum, Taipei.

Other works taken seriously but presenting special problems include: "Liu-chün-tzu" 六君子 (The six gentlemen), dated 1345, Shanghai Museum; "Yü-chuang ch'iu chi" 漁庄秋霽 (A place for fishing after rain in autumn), dated 1355, Shanghai Museum; "Chiang-an wang-shan" 江

岸望山 (Looking at mountains from a river bank), dated 1363; "Chu-shu yeh-shih" 竹樹野石 (Rock, tree, and bamboo), dated 1363; "Yü-hou k'ung lin" 雨後空林 (A grove after rain), dated 1368; "Tzu-chih shan-fang" 紫芝山房 (The Tzu-chih studio), the last four being in the Palace Museum, Taipei. Although few of Ni Tsan's early paintings are extant, Ming critics generally traced the sources of his art to that of the first great masters of landscape in the Five Dynasties and early decades of the Northern Sung. What distinguished him was that he was able to transform their characteristics into a new style in tune with his own personality and taste. In his works, these characteristics are usually quite evident: a sparing use of ink reflecting his fastidious taste for cleanliness, the use of oblique brush, structural composition, simplification of details, a feeling for austere and even chaste quality, and an expression of his love of seclusion. All of them seem to show his insistence on individuality and eccentricity. It was this quality, in a period when Chinese intellectuals, under the strong pressure of the Mongols, tried to preserve their identity by demonstrating their own individuality, that distinguished him from his many contemporaries and became a clear mark of Yüan art. In the Ming, his strong influence may be seen in the works of the following major artists: Wang Fu, Shen Chou, Li Liu-fang, Wen Cheng-ming, Lu Chih (qq.v.), Tung Ch'i-ch'ang (ECCP), and members of the so-called "Hsin-an School" 新安派 (of Anhwei), which included such artists as Hsiao Yün-ts'ung (ECCP, p. 87), Cha Shih-piao, and Hung-jen (qq.v.).

[Editors' note: Wang Chi-ch'ien, in his article, "The paintings of Ni Yün-lin," records forty-two he had studied and considered to be authentic. Of these, seven are noted as housed in Wang's own studio, the Pao-wu-t'ang 寶武堂. The first twenty-eight bear dates of execution and are listed chronologically, thus offering clues to help place the undated ones in proper order. Each painting is described by citing former colophons and adding Wang's own comments. Twenty-four are reproduced. There are also quotations from twenty-seven commentators on Ni's art in general.]

Bibliography

Yin-te, 35: 22/238/11a; 23/36/32a; 25/91 下 /11b; 29/初辛; *Yin-te*, 24: 1/298/2a; 5/115/26a; 22/1/36a; 32/27/7a; 61/14a/10a; 84/甲前/17a; 85/2/3; 88/10/30a; Ni Tsan, *Ni Yün-lin hsien-sheng shih-chi* (SPTK ed.); Ku Yüan-ch'ing, *Yün-lin i-shih*, in *Ch'ing-pi-ko ch'üan-chi*, Vol. 11; Jung Keng, "Ni Tsan hua chih chu-lu chi ch'i wei tso," *Ling-nan Jo.* 嶺南學報, VIII: 2 (1948), 29; Wang Chi-ch'ien 王季遷, "The life and writings of Ni Yün-lin," *National Palace Museum Q.*, 1:2 (October, 1966), 29; *id.*, "The paintings of Ni Yün-lin," *ibid.*, III (1967), 1, pl. 5, 6, 9, 11, 15, 21; Lee Jun-woon 李潤桓, "Ni Tsan: a study of the life of a Yüan poet-artist," unpublished M. A. thesis, Univ. of Hong Kong, 1971; Yü Ta-ch'eng 于大成, "Ni Yün-lin yü 與 Ch'ing-pi-ko," *Chun-wen-hsüeh* 純文學, 9: 3 (September, 1971), 58; Chang Ch'ou, *Ch'ing-ho shu-hua-fang*, Vol. 11, 50; *T'u-hui pao-chien hsü-tsuan* 圖繪寶鑑續纂 (*Hua-shih 畫史 ts'ung-shu*, Shanghai, 1962), 1/10; Ch'in Tsu-yung 秦祖永, *T'ung-yin lun-hua* 桐陰論畫, 上 /2a; *Ku-kung shu-hua lu* 故宮書畫錄 (增訂本, 1965 ed.), 6/83; *Ku-kung ming-hua* 名畫, VI (Taipei, 1966), pl. 12, 13; Shen Hsiu-liang 沈修良, *Ni Kao-shih nien-p'u* 高士年譜, 1909; Huang Miao-tzu 黃苗子, "Tu Ni Yün-lin chuan cha-chi" 讀倪雲林傳札記, *Chung-hua wen-shih lun-ts'ung* 中華文史論叢, III (Shanghai, 1963), 247; Cheng Ping-shan 鄭秉珊, *Ni Yün-lin* (Shanghai, 1958); A. Watanabe 渡邊明義, "A chronological account of the life and deeds of Ni Yün-lin," *Kokka*, 829 (April, 1961), 147, 830 (May, 1961), 219; Laurence Sickman (ed.), *Chinese Calligraphy and Painting in the Collection of John M. Crawford, Jr.* (New York, 1962), 111; Wen Fong, "Chinese Painting: A Statement of Method," *Oriental Art*, n. s. IX: 2 (1963), 2; Osvald Sirén, *Chinese Painting*, IV (London, 1956), 79, pl. 94, VII (1958), 125; E. J. Laing, *Chinese Paintings in Chinese Publications, 1956–1968* (Ann Arbor, 1969), 129.

Chu-tsing Li

NI Wei-te 倪維德 (T. 仲賢, H. 敕山老人), 1313-July 25, 1377, medical author and practitioner, was a native of Soochow. Both his grandfather and father being doctors, Ni Wei-te followed in the family tradition. He soon became a practitioner of wide fame and enjoyed the reputation of being efficient and benevolent, not caring whether his patients were rich or poor. He was also a considerable bibliophile who used to place standing orders with the local booksellers so that he might obtain any new publications when they came out. His library consisted of more than five thousand *chüan* for which he had to build an extra room.

Although Ni's fame as a medical man did not reach that of his contemporary Chu Chen-heng (1281-1358), either as an author or as a practitioner, he is important as one of the first to write a treatise on ophthalmology, the *Yüan-chi ch'i-wei* 原機啓微 (Investigation of therapies and explanation of subtleties) in 2 *chüan*. This book is a mixture of theoretical speculations on the basis of the Yin-yang school of quotations from ancient authorities and of therapeutic recipes. It was incorporated into the medical collection *Hsüeh-shih i-an* 薛氏醫按 by Hsüeh Chi 薛己 (T. 立齋, fl. *ca.* 1520-30) who added a chapter of his own, and two centuries later into the encyclopedia *T'u-shu chi-ch'eng*. Ni was married to a lady from the Chang 章 family, and had one son Ni Ch'i 起 who inherited his father's practice.

Bibliography

1/299/4a; 3/281/4a; 5/78/96a; Sung Lien, *Sung Hsüeh-shih wen-chi* (SPTK), 49/15a; TSCC (1885-88), XVII: 160/1a; L. of C. *Catalogue of Rare Books*, 501.

Herbert Franke

NI Yüeh 倪岳 (T. 舜咨, H. 青谿), May 11, 1444-November 19, 1501, scholar-official, was a native of Nanking, the eldest son of Ni Ch'ien (*q.v.*). Unusually intelligent and diligent, Ni Yüeh demonstrated an interest in studying both the Classics and actual administrative works. Once a group of clerks from the ministry of Personnel tested him on a certain lawsuit and found his judgment comparable to that of an experienced clerk. His years as a youth were not smooth, however. When he was six years of age his mother died. Ni Yüeh accompanied his father, exiled to Hsüan-fu, and registered at the local school there. In 1462 he achieved the *chü-jen* in Peking. Two years later at the age of twenty he became a *chin-shih* and was selected a bachelor in the Hanlin. Appointed a compiler in 1465, he was assigned to help in the compilation of the *Ying-tsung shih-lu* (*see* Li Hsien). When the *shih-lu* was completed he received a promotion in rank.

In 1465 his father was restored to his position. Two years later he was made junior vice minister of Rites in Nanking. The new rank aroused the bureaucrats because it was not based on merit or routine but was the result of patronage by some powerful eunuchs whom Ni Ch'ien had tutored during the Ching-t'ai period. Ni Ch'ien was allowed to retire in 1468. Ni Yüeh then took leave on the pretext of looking after his father, and remained at home until 1474, except for one excursion to the family tombs at Hangchow.

His father was again recalled (1473), and the following year Ni Yüeh also resumed his duties, submitting at this time a well-known memorial on military affairs, which may have accounted for his later assignment to the ministry of War. In 1475, as a routine procedure, he was promoted to reader-in-waiting in the Hanlin, and a year later served as expounder of the Classics. At this point his father became minister of Rites in Nanking, presumably with the help of some eunuchs who had aided him earlier; but he retired in less than a year. Not surprisingly Ni Yüeh declined the offer of a higher office, and took another leave to wait on his father. This time his leave was a long one, for after two years his father died and he went into mourning.

During his years at home he did not neglect his studies and, on his resumption of official duties late in 1481, the chief grand secretary recommended him as compiler of the *Wen-hua ta-shun* 文華大訓, 28 *ch.*, a work designed for the instruction of the prince: on the inculcation of learning, the cultivation of virtue, the promotion of proper relationships, and the manifestation of good government. Unhappily this book no longer exists. There is a truncated version in 3 *chüan*, however, edited by Wu Tao-nan (*see* Ch'en Yü-pi), which is listed in the Imperial Catalogue. With this task completed in January, 1483, Ni was made chancellor of the Hanlin and ordered to take charge of the *chü-jen* examinations in Shun-t'ien (Peking). In the following year the emperor appointed him tutor of the heir apparent. Whenever he lectured he always used the Classics to illustrate current affairs and exhorted the heir apparent to do what was right. His teaching impressed the youth. In 1486 he was promoted to junior vice minister of Rites but was ordered to continue his tutoring tasks. When Chu Yu-t'ang (*q.v.*) ascended the throne, Ni received the appointment of senior vice minister in January, 1489, and minister in August, 1493, serving in this high office until May, 1496. Rewarded with the title of junior guardian of the heir apparent, Ni was posted to Nanking as minister of Personnel.

It was during these later assignments in the Hung-chih era that he submitted most of his famous memorials, won decision-making power at court conferences, and had a number of his valuable ideas put into practice. He was considered by his contemporaries a statesman with talent and ability in both civil and military matters. He was, above all, a true Confucian scholar because of his preference for nonviolent moral reform in state and society, and his respect for history. A few incidents in his career may serve to illustrate these generalizations. Early in the reign, when the court took the initiative to eliminate "immoral shrines" 淫祠, Chang Chiu-kung 張九功 (T. 敘之, cs 1478) and Ch'eng Min-cheng (*q. v.*) both suggested the removal of images of Confucius' seventy-two disciples and of Han Confucianists from the K'ung miao 孔廟. Ni opposed the idea, contending that the Han Confucianists, though not without faults in their personal lives, had contributed to the preservation and transmission of the Classics, and as the names of the disciples had been recorded in history for more than a thousand years, there was no ground for eliminating them. Because of his opposition, the proposal collapsed.

Working in the ministry of Personnel, Ni based his recommendations for promotion and appointment on an official's own merits rather than on his personal likes or dislikes. His decisions were regarded as fair and objective. Among his colleagues, he particularly admired Ma Wen-sheng (*q.v.*), but he did not hesitate to attack the latter's opinion if he believed it unsuitable. Once Ma suggested an increase in the land tax of the Soochow-Sung-chiang area to meet the increased expenses of government. Ni vehemently opposed the idea, arguing that the people there were already burdened with heavy taxes and a further increase would force them to rebel. The issue was then dropped. His views on economic affairs also reflected Confucian tradition. He advised the emperor to practice frugality—limiting the number of princes, cutting down on unnecessary construction, and doing away with superfluous offices and needless expenses—as the best way to redress the government's financial situation. As a consequence he was strongly against the idea of increasing taxes. When he learned that the ministry of Revenue had sent representatives to supervise the local customs offices and to add to the imposts on commodities, the rate of which rose sharply and caused alarm among the merchants, he attacked the ministry for violating the precedents established by the founders of the Ming house, and requested the emperor to remove the charges on new items and to return to former arrangements. He also asked the emperor to empower the governors and surveillance commissioners to supervise the customs officials so that the latter would abide by the regulations.

In September, 1499, Ni was reassigned to be minister of War in Nanking. According to his biographer, Wu K'uan (*q. v.*), of the six boards in Nanking that position bore the heaviest responsibility after the capital was moved. During his stay the imperial guards were well equipped and disciplined, and the city was maintained in orderly fashion. Though a minister now, he continued to live at his ancestral home in the T'ieh-tso fang, behaving himself as a member, observing the proper decorum required in a Confucian household. Once he remarked that during the time that a child revealed his aptitude for learning, entered school, and gained degrees to become an official, his neighbors and relatives all shared a youth's experiences and happiness; in these long years no one mentioned the financial aid rendered him. What kind of a man was he if this individual, now an official, should become stingy and harsh toward them?

His final office was that of minister of Personnel in Peking in 1500, and there he died some sixteen months later. The court honored him with the posthumous name Wen-i 文毅 (literary and resolute), and appointed his adopted son, Ni Lin 霖, drafter of the central drafting office through the yin privilege. A collection of Ni Yüeh's papers, *chüan* 11-14 including his memorials, entitled *Ch'ing-ch'i man kao* 青谿漫稿, 24 + 1 *ch.*, has come down to us, both in the original and as copied into the *Ssu-k'u ch'üan-shu*; Ting Ping (ECCP) reprinted it in 1900.

It is interesting to note that both his father and he had held some of the same offices. Ni Yüeh is described as stout, like his father, and somewhat taller, but the woodcut representation of him in the 1900 edition of his collected works makes him less corpulent.

Bibliography

1/183/14a; 5/24/81a; MSL (1964), Hsien-tsung, 0940, 2676, 3992, 4795, Hsiao-tsung, 0264, 0370, 0491, 1495, 2038, 2712, 3318; KC (1958), 2089, 2777; SK (1930), 96/2a, 170/12a; *Shang Chiang liang-hsien chih* 兩縣志 (1876), 22/10a, 34上/20a; TSCC (1885-88), XI: 302/4/1b, XIV: 102/6b; *Ming-shih i-wen-chih, pu-pien, fu-pien* 補編附編 (Peking, 1959), 66, 786; *Hsü wen-hsien t'ung-k'ao, ch.* 18, 2933; Wan Piao, *Huang Ming ching-chi wen-lu* (Ming ed.), 6/17a; Cheng Hsiao, *Ming-ch'en chi* (Ming ed.), 16/10b; *id., Huang Ming ming-ch'en yen-hsiang-lu* (Ming ed.), 7/5b; W. Franke, *Sources*, 5. 4. 14.

Angela Hsi and L. Carrington Goodrich

NIEH Pao 聶豹 (T. 文蔚, H. 雙江), February 6, 1487-November 19, 1563, official and thinker, was a native of Yung-feng 永豐, Kiangsi. His ancestral home had been in this locale since the Tsin (A. D. 265-420), first situated near a rock pond, then near two creeks, from which Nieh Pao took his *hao* shuang-chiang. He achieved the *chü-jen* in 1516 and *chin-shih* in 1517. He became magistrate of Hua-t'ing 華亭 (prefectural city of Sung-chiang) in 1520, staying on for five years. In this capacity he was active in rooting out administrative abuses and corruption, and busied himself with water conservancy projects, eventually returning 3,223 families to self-support in the area. In 1525 he received the appointment of investigating censor and soon sent in a memorial on the evil deeds of the eunuch director of ceremonial, Chang Tso 張佐. While touring as a censor in Fukien, he memorialized the throne urging the dismissal of the eunuch grand defender, Chao Ch'eng 趙誠, and also proposed the abolition of the maritime trading superintendency, achieving for himself a reputation as an able remonstrator. In 1530 he became prefect of Soochow. A year later he retired to mourn the death of his father, and in 1534 his mother passed away.

Nieh Pao did not return to official life until 1541, when he became prefect of P'ing-yang 平陽 in Shansi, a region much threatened by incursions from the northwest. There he urged the rich to contribute and the criminally suspect to ransom themselves, thus collecting about 20,000 taels to fortify the strategic passes of Kuo-chia kou 郭家溝, Leng-ch'üan 冷泉, and Ling-shih靈石. He also personally supervised the training of six thousand able-bodied men, whose presence deterred the invading bands in 1542. News of his success reached the court. On the recommendation of Grand Secretary Yen Sung (q.v.), Nieh was appointed surveillance vice commissioner for Shensi and told to fortify T'ung-kuan 潼關 (1543), the pass at the bend of the Yellow River.

As Nieh Pao came more into the public eye his enemies grew in number. Various critics built up a case accusing him of graft during his days as prefect of P'ing-yang. Grand Secretary Hsia Yen (q.v.) particularly detested him. Arrest and imprisonment followed. Not until 1549 was he cleared, but he had lost his rank and office, and returned home.

When Altan-qaγan (q.v.) threatened the capital in 1550, the minister of Rites, Hsü Chieh (q.v.), a protégé of Nieh Pao from Hua-t'ing, seized the opportunity to recommend his former mentor. In 1551, when Nieh Pao became vice minister of War, Ch'iu Luan (q.v.), being in charge of troop training in the capital, asked to have the troops at Hsüan-ta 宣大 transferred to the capital guards. The northern marches were threatened. Nieh opposed his plan, saying that Hsüan-ta must be defended, that the security of that post meant the security of Peking. Ch'iu was angered but could not prevail against Nieh. In 1552 Nieh became minister of war. The next year saw Nieh

memorializing on defense matters, pleading for the construction of an outer wall north of Peking to ward off invasions. During the autumn Altan-qaγan moved in force into Shansi, overwhelmed the army of Li Lai 李淶 (T. 減甫, H. 養愚, cs 1571), and looted for twenty days before withdrawing. Despite the success of the raid and consequent plunder, the governor-general, Su Yu 蘇祐 (T. 允吉, 舜澤, cs 1526), reported signal victories. This inconsistency was reported by the investigating censor, Mao P'eng 毛鵬 (T. 汝南, cs 1547). An imperial order came to the ministry of War asking for details. Nieh Pao, who seems to have become inflexible and insensitive to the state of affairs by this time, answered by saying that, even though the enemy had gained some, Chinese armies had also scored notable successes. He invoked divine providence and imperial grace with his argument that China actually scored in this encounter. He requested the throne, furthermore, to give thanks to the gods and to reward the troops. So, by saying favorable things, Nieh achieved the title of junior guardian of the heir apparent. When the wall near Peking was completed, he became junior tutor. Repeated reports of victories, in spite of increasing incursions on both land and maritime frontiers (the latter from the wo-k'ou), flowed through Nieh Pao to the throne. To these reports he added notations of divine protection and imperial grace, and again recommended thanks to the spirits and rewards for the troops. The throne continued to favor him by giving him the lofty title of grand guardian of the heir apparent.

Finally, despite the intervening influence of his trusted friends, Yen Sung from his home area and Hsü Chieh his former protégé, Nieh's shortcomings were revealed to the emperor as the threats of invasions increased. Nieh could offer no effective plans and his memorials became mere formal literary displays. Such officials as Chao Wen-hua (q.v.) and Chu Lung-hsi

朱隆禧 (cs 1529) all made suggestions; the latter even proposed that a plenipotentiary official be sent to supervise Fukien and that the harbors and maritime trading centers be reopened. Nieh ignored them all. The emperor, now enraged by Nieh's lack of action, severely rebuked him and lowered his rank and salary two grades. Finally, in 1556, when he was sixty-nine years of age, Nieh was dismissed altogether and replaced by Yang Po (*q.v.*). In 1567, four years after his death, Nieh Pao's title of junior guardian, was posthumously restored and he was given the name Chen-hsiang 貞襄.

Nieh, though ending his official career ingloriously, is also remembered as a post-Wang Yang-ming thinker (*see* Wang Shou-jen). In 1526, when he was censor for Fukien, he crossed the Ch'ien-t'ang River to meet Wang at Shao-hsing. In 1528, upon hearing of the death of the master, Nieh wept and called himself a student of the Wang school. While serving as prefect of Soochow (1531), he invited Ch'ien Te-hung and Wang Chi (*qq.v.*), both of whom were close followers of Wang Shou-jen, to witness a solemn ceremony of sacrifices to Wang during which he formally declared himself a disciple.

Nieh Pao's thought, stemming from Wang's doctrine of attaining intuition, revolves around the concept of chi 寂. He seems to have conceived this "contemplative solitude" as the key to intuition while he was in prison between 1544 and 1549. His composure and imperturbable bearing amidst the hardships of these years impressed even his major enemy Hsia Yen. This meditative power won him also the persistent admiration of Lo Hung-hsien (*q.v.*), who agreed with Nieh on the role of inner solitude in discovering one's intuition. Only through this method, Nieh believed, could intuition be realized and knowledge of self and the external world be united in full awareness. When intuitive power was thus achieved, one would be able to face the changes

and demands of the world without spoiling one's nature. This concept of chi is actually the same as that of ching 靜, upon which the Sung thinkers Chou Tun-i (1017–73) and Ch'eng Hao (1032–85) had often dwelt. Thus Nieh was in opposition to Wang Chi, who, as one of the favored disciples of the master, had always treated intuition as innate, thus requiring no effort for its discovery. Nieh believed that there ought to be effort, but his effort is not the same as the "action" in Wang Yang-ming's theory of the unity of knowledge and action. Rather, this effort must be total contemplation in solitude. Nieh's system remains within the wide scope of Wang Yang-ming's idealistic, subjective, moral philosophy.

Nieh Pao recorded his famous *K'un-pien lu* 困辨錄, 8 *ch.*, while in jail. Here is found much of his philosophical thought. Lo Hung-hsien annotated it. The work is incorporated in the *Shuang-chiang wen-chi* 文集, 14 *ch.*, compiled by his nephew Nieh Ching 靜 (T. 子安, cs 1535).

Bibliography

1/202/12b; 3/184/14b; 5/39/99a; 83/17/8b; Jung Chao-tsu 容肇祖, *Ming-tai ssu-hsiang shih* 明代思想史, 127; SK (1930), 96/3a, 176/14a.

D. W. Y. Kwok

NIEN Fu 年富(T. 大有, H. 謙齋), January 17, 1396-May 21, 1464, official, was a native of Huai-yüan 懷遠 in the prefecture of Feng-yang 鳳陽, Nan-Chihli. It is said that his family name had originally been Yen 嚴 and that his great-grand-father served during the Mongol period as a military officer (commander of a corps of Chinese volunteers?) stationed at Ch'üan-chiao 全椒, Yang-chou 揚州-lu, Honan province. Apparently after the Mongols were defeated, this officer went into hiding in Huai-yüan under the assumed name of Nien which the family adopted.

Nien Fu entered the district school at the age of eleven and graduated as *chü-jen* in 1417. A year later he received an appointment as assistant instructor in the local school of Te-p'ing 德平 in the prefecture of Tsinan, Shantung, where he stayed for over a decade. Because of his record Nien was promoted in March, 1428, to be a supervising secretary of the office of scrutiny in Peking. He served in this capacity for eight years, during which he made a name for himself as a critic of state affairs. One of his far-sighted observations, made in 1435, was on the large number of Mongols holding military rank in the Peking area, which he considered a threat to national security. Early in 1436 he was sent to Shensi as an administration vice commissioner in charge of military supplies. He stayed there for two years, during which he reduced the military expenses by eliminating sinecure offices and official corruption, and stabilized the prices of commodities by introducing stringent rules against speculation. In June, 1444, he was accused by a subordinate of torturing an army officer to death for minor offenses. The emperor exonerated him but ordered his stipend suspended for three months. Two months later, he was appointed administration commissioner of Honan. There he promoted the general welfare of the population and, in 1447, under the direction of the governor, Yü Ch'ien (q. v.), introduced measures to rehabilitate the refugees from the Oirat raids who were streaming into Honan from the neighboring provinces. Following the defeat of the government forces by the Mongol tribes in the battle of T'u-mu (see Chu Ch'i-chen), Yü Ch'ien, then minister of War, relied on Nien to look after the delivery of military supplies. As a reward for his performance, Nien was promoted in April, 1451, to be governor of Tatung, and in December he was also entrusted with the supervision of the military farm in that area. In the next few years Nien devoted himself to solving the financial difficulties of the Tatung region. He memorialized the throne suggesting a temporary suspension of taxes, and dealt harshly

with those who appropriated the government supplies for their own use, impeaching a number of military officials, including the powerful Shih Heng (q. v.), the regional commander of Tatung, and his nephew, General Shih Piao (see Shih Heng); the emperor, however, took no action. Embittered by his trenchant criticism, Nien's enemies responded with countercharges, but Yü Ch'ien supported him. In November, 1452, for example, Lin Hou 林厚 (cs 1421), the junior administration vice commissioner of Shansi, accused Nien of illegally punishing his junior staff. After careful inquiry his superiors found Lin guilty of falsifying the record, and he was penalized accordingly, while Nien was once more cleared of a false allegation.

In March, 1457, shortly after Chu Ch'i-chen regained the throne, there followed a screening of officers to root out those who had supported Yü Ch'ien; scores of officials, including Nien Fu, were involved. In the following month, taking the occasion of Nien's ebbing fortunes, Shih Piao accused him of breaking the law during his administration in Tatung. Nien was arrested and sent to the capital for trial. Fortunately for Nien, the influential Hanlin chancellor, Li Hsien (q. v.), intervened; the emperor ordered a thorough investigation and, finding that Shih had falsified his report, acquitted Nien of the charges, but still ordered him to go into retirement. Before long, however, some officials memorialized the court in praise of Nien's integrity. In February, 1458, the emperor recalled him to serve as the junior vice minister of War in Nanking. During the next two years Nien moved rapidly from one office to another. On May 22 he was transferred to the ministry of Revenue; three days later he was appointed governor of Shantung; then in July he became a vice censor-in-chief. When the office of the minister of Revenue became vacant in March, 1460, through the recommendation of Li Hsien the emperor appointed Nien to fill the post despite strong criticism for his overbearing disposition. In April, 1462, he left office to mourn his father, but returned to his post in due course. Early in 1464, pleading advanced age, Nien begged to retire, but the emperor declined his request. A few months later a malignancy developed on his forehead, and he died shortly afterwards while still in office. Two years later (October, 1466), acting on the recommendation of the assistant minister of Rites, Yeh Sheng (*q. v.*), Emperor Chu Chien-shen (*q. v.*) ordered the authorities to look for Nien Fu's descendants with a view to offering them official appointments.

Nien, who was one of the few officials of his rank without a *chin-shih* degree, had a successful career and enjoyed the support of several officials of the highest rank. Due to his mettlesome personality, he incurred the enmity of many officials, however, both civil and military, which accounted for several setbacks. According to Yeh Sheng, Nien disliked officials with *chin-shih* degrees, probably owing to an inferiority complex.

Bibliography

1/177/4b; 5/28/35a; 9/ 后 3/2a; 61/122/10b; MSL (1963), Hsüan-tsung, 918, 1892, 1955, 2321, Ying-tsung, *ch.* 4–338; KC (1958), 1496, 1896, 2037, 2170, 2239; Li Hsien, *T'ien-shun jih-lu*, in *Chi-lu hui-pien*, ed. by Shen Chieh-fu, 22/5a, 23b; Yeh Sheng, *Shui-tung jih-chi*, 27/9a; *Huai-yüan-hsien chih* (1819), 18/31b; H. Serruys, "Were the Ming Against the Mongols' Settling in North China?" OE, 6:2(1959), 148; C. O. Hucker, *The Censorial System of Ming China* (Stanford, 1966), 133, 247.

Hok-lam Chan

NING-KUO Kung-chu 寧國公主, 1364-September 3, 1434, was the second daughter of Chu Yüan-chang, reportedly by his chief consort who became Empress Ma (*q.v.*). After his succession the emperor gave her the designation princess of Ning-kuo. In 1378 she was married to Mei Yin 梅殷 (T. 伯殷, d. 1405), a native of Hsia-i 夏邑, Honan, who was well read and proficient in military skills. He was the nephew of Mei Ssu-tsu 思祖 (d. 1382) who, for his help in the founding of the Ming, was created marquis of Ju-nan 汝南 in 1370. He was punished posthumously for his connections with Hu Wei-yung (*q.v.*); however, the nephew escaped involvement. As most of Chu Yüan-chang's sons-in-law lived through the tumultuous years of the struggle for the throne by Chu Ti (*q.v.*), some of them were unavoidably implicated and took the consequences. Of these Mei Yin was one. Because the *shih-lu* of the Hung-wu and Yung-lo periods suffered both deletions and falisifications, it is difficult to ascertain what really happened. Mei Yin, for example, may have played a more important role than can be pieced together from surviving documents.

The year after the marriage Mei Yin was given an annual stipend of 600 *tan* of grain. In 1383, because of his literary accomplishments, he was sent to Shantung as provincial superintendent of schools, a rare appointment for an imperial relative. As one of a group of consorts, he was dispatched the following year to Honan and Peiping to administer flood relief, and in 1395 he led a mission to review the troops and their registrations in Chung-tu 中都 (Lin-hao 臨濠), the emperor's native place. Some later authors recount that during the last moments of the first emperor's life, both Chu Yün-wen (*q.v.*) and Mei Yin (said to be his favorite son-in-law) were present at his side. With his eyes on his grandson, the monarch asked the son-in-law to look after the future emperor and to beware of the prince of Yen. Early in 1402 Mei Yin was sent to head a military force to guard the strategic area of Huai-an 淮安 in the Huai River valley. When Chu Ti attempted to cross the Huai later in the same year and found the region strongly defended, he communicated with Mei Yin, asking for safe passage on the pretext that he wished to pay respects to his deceased imperial father. Mei refused, stating that the first emperor had prohibited this kind of rite. Chu Ti then crossed upstream, headed for Yangchow, crossed the Yangtze, and took Nanking. Mei Yin reportedly commanded an army of some four hundred thousand men, but was hopelessly outflanked.

Chu Ti, after ascending the throne, asked his sister to call her husband back to Nanking. The sister, who seems not to have approved of her brother's rebellion, complied by writing to her husband with blood from her finger. Mei Yin, deeply moved, returned to the capital, but the feeling between the couple and the new emperor was not friendly. In 1404 a censor made certain charges against Mei Yin. In October, 1405, two military officers murdered Mei Yin under a bridge while he was on his way to court, and left the body in the water as though he had drowned himself. When the culprits were brought to book, according to some unofficial accounts, they asserted that they were merely carrying out the emperor's orders. The emperor in a rage had their teeth smashed before sentencing them to death. When this news reached the princess, she is said to have gone to the emperor, wept aloud, clung to his garment, and accused him of killing her husband. Early in 1406 the princess found herself elevated to imperial grand princess, and her two sons, Mei Shun-ch'ang 順昌 and Mei Ching-fu 景福, received higher ranks and handsome stipends. Mei Yin was buried with honors and posthumously entitled Jung-ting 榮定. Thus another phase of the life and death struggle in the imperial family came to an end. The Mei family, however, was later represented by a great-grandson of the princess, Mei Ch'un 純, who became a chin-shih in 1481.

According to official records, Chu Yüan-chang had sixteen daughters; the tenth and thirteenth died in childhood; the others grew up and married. The first, Lin-an 臨安 kung-chu (1360-1421), married Li Ch'i, the eldest son of Li Shan-ch'ang (q.v.), in 1376. The third, Ch'ung-ning 崇寧 kung-chu, married Niu Ch'eng 牛誠 (城) in 1384, but died soon afterwards. The fourth, An-ch'ing 安慶 kung-chu, became the wife of Ou-yang Lun 歐陽倫 in 1381, who, for his illegal smuggling of tea for export, died by imperial order in 1397. The fifth, Ju-ning 汝寧 kung-chu, in 1382 married Lu Hsien 陸賢, a son of Lu Chung-heng 仲亨 (d. 1390; made marquis of Chi-an 吉安 in 1370. The Ming-shih, 121/5a, errs in using the character 賈 for 賢). The sixth, Huai-ch'ing懷慶 kung-chu, married Wang Ning 王寧 in the same year. Wang for some political reason was imprisoned in Nanking during the Chien-wen period, made marquis of Yung-ch'un 永春 early in the Yung-lo years, but lodged in prison again and died October 5, 1411. (One of his sons, Wang Chen-ch'ing 王貞慶 [T. 善甫] achived some note as a poet.) Also in the same year the seventh, Ta-ming 大名 kung-chu (d. 1426), married Li Chien 李堅, who became marquis of Lüan-ch'eng 灤城 early in the Chien-wen period, took part in an expedition against the prince of Yen, was wounded in battle, captured, and died on the way to Peiping. The eighth, Fu-ch'ing福清 kung-chu (d. 1417), in 1385 married Chang Lin 張麟, son of Chang Lung 龍 (d. 1397, created marquis of Feng-hsiang 鳳翔 in 1379). The ninth, Shou-ch'un 壽春 kung-chu (d. 1388), became in 1386 the wife of Fu Chung, a son of Fu Yu-te (q.v.). The eleventh, Nan-k'ang 南康 kung-chu (1373-November 19, 1438) in 1388 married Hu Kuan 胡觀, whose father was Hu Hai 海 (alt. ming 海洋, 1329-91, made marquis of Tung-ch'uan 東川 in 1384). As an aide to Li Ching-lung (see Li Wen-chung), Hu Kuan went on a northern expedition against the prince of Yen in 1400 and was taken prisoner. Early in the Yung-lo period, after repeated accusations were made against him, he committed suicide. The twelfth daughter, Yung-chia 永嘉 kung-chu (d. 1455), married in 1389 Kuo

Chen, a son of Kuo Ying (*q.v.*), marquis of Wu-ting. The fourteenth, Han-shan 含山 kung-chu (1381-1462), married Yin Ch'ing 尹清 in 1394, and lived to the age of eighty-one. The fifteenth, Ju-yang 汝陽 kung-chu, in the same year became the wife of Hsieh Ta 謝達 (d. 1404), son of Hsieh Yen 彥 (T. 子超, 1332-1400), a commander highly regarded by the founding emperor. The sixteenth and youngest, Pao-ch'ing寶慶 kung-chu (1396-1433), was only seven in 1403 when Chu Ti ascended the throne, and is said to have been brought up by Empress Hsü (*q.v.*). In 1413 the emperor selected a handsome guard officer, Chao Hui 趙輝 (1389-1478) to be her husband.

Of the sixteen imperial princesses, the first and sixth were sisters, both born to Imperial Consort Ch'eng-mu, née Sun (*see* Chu Su). The second and fourth were sisters, both probably daughters of Empress Ma. The mother of the eighth was Imperial Consort An, née Cheng安妃鄭氏. The mother of the twelfth was Imperial Consort Hui, née Kuo, and the mother of the fourteenth was the daughter of a Korean, née Han (for both *see* Chu Yuan-chang).

Imperial princesses were ranked in three categories: kung-chu (imperial princess), chang 長-kung-chu (grand imperial princess), and Ta 大 -chang-kung-chu (great-grand imperial princess). Not until 1424 did these designations become precise and automatic. In the short reign of Chu Kao-chih (*q.v.*), the designations were definitely established: kung-chu for the daughters of the emperor, chang-kung-chu for the sisters of the emperor, and ta-chang-kung-chu for the aunts of the emperor. Late in 1424 all eight of the emperor's living aunts, namely, Ning-kuo, Huai-ch'ing, Ta-ming, Nan-k'ang, Yung-chia, Han-shan, Ju-yang, and Pao-ch'ing, were elevated to ta-chang-kung-chu with increased stipends.

In the *Pi-li tsa-ts'un* 碧里雜存 by Tung Ku 董轂 (T. 碩甫, H. 碧里山樵, 漢陽歸叟, cj 1516), there is a note about Mei-shao 梅梢, or Mei the boatman, which reports that, during a battle on Poyang Lake against Ch'en Yu-liang (*q.v.*), the boatman saved Chu Yüan-chang by quickly pulling away his seat. As Chu fell, an arrow whizzed over his body. After Chu became emperor, Mei-shao, at first forgotten, was later rewarded handsomely, and his grandson given an imperial daughter in marriage. This could be just one of the many stories involving the first Ming emperor, but it is an interesting one.

Bibliography

1/105/8a, 20a, 26a, 30b, 41a, 106/21a, 121/1b; 5/4/6a; *Huang Ming wen-hai* (microfilm), 20/5/3; Li Chih, *Hsü ts'ang-shu* (1959), 90; MSL (1962), T'ai-tsu, 1944, 1955, 1973, 2345, 2348, 2552, 3443, T'ai-tsung (1963), 0717, 0720, 0737; KC (1958), *ch*. 6-9, 11, 13, 17, 22, 24.

Lienche Tu Fang

OU-YANG Te 歐陽德 (T. 崇一, H. 南野), 1496-April 24, 1554, a native of T'ai-ho 泰和, Kiangsi, is best known as a dedicated disciple of Wang Shou-jen (*q.v.*). From a historical perspective, however, one may say that Ou-yang Te was instrumental in spreading among scholar-officials in the Ming bureaucracy Wang's fame as one of the most creative teachers in the Confucian tradition. Although his contribution to the development of the master's philosophical thinking was not as profound as that of Wang Chi (*q.v.*), and his achievement in formulating a balanced interpretation of Wang's teaching was not as great as that of Ch'ien Te-hung (*q.v.*), his success in delivering Wang's message of the "learning of the body and mind" 身心之學 to the educated elite of his times, especially scholar-officials at the court, was unsurpassed among the first generation of Wang Shou-jen's followers. Had he lived longer, as some of his fellow students contended, he might have established Wang's approach to teaching as an integral part of the educational program for the heir apparent.

As soon as Ou-yang Te acquired the *chü-jen* (1516), he traveled to southern Kiangsi, to receive instructions from Wang Shou-jen, whose lectures on the organismic unity of mind 心 as subjectivity, and principle 理 as ontological reality, had generated much controversy at the time. Through experiential verification as well as intellectual evaluation, Ou-yang concluded that Wang Shou-jen's attempt to transcend any fixed method of pedagogy and to confront the inner demands of the student in a specific situation was in perfect accord with the "true learning" 正學 of Confucianism. He thus completely ignored the accusation made by many of his contemporaries that Wang's teaching was in essence a variation of Ch'an Buddhism. Indeed, he was so impressed by Wang's perception that he twice decided not to take part in the metropolitan examination in order to develop an experiential understanding of Wang's thinking. After seven years' delay, Ou-yang Te obtained the *chin-shih* in 1523. His success was considered an important triumph for Wang Shou-jen and his loyal disciples; for the ts'e-wen 策問 portion of the examination in that year actually contained questions intended to be a critique of Wang Shou-jen's philosophical position (*see* Lü Nan). Caught in such a dilemma, some of Wang's students simply walked out of the examination hall. Ou-yang and others chose to voice their unreserved support for Wang's teaching in their answers. His unexpected advancement to the highest degree provided him a great opportunity to put into practice the ideas he shared with his master.

Thereupon he was appointed magistrate of Liu-an 六安 (Anhwei). In his first tenure as a scholar-official he distinguished himself in areas such as supporting relief efforts, improving irrigation systems, simplifying legal procedures, and, most important, promoting education. There he founded an academy called Lung-chin shu-yüan 龍津書院. In 1526 he was appointed a vice director

of a bureau in the ministry of Justice, but was soon transferred to be a compiler of the Hanlin Academy. His pertinent comments on the general interpretation and concrete application of a variety of rituals in the court won him the reputation of being a perceptive scholar of li 禮. Five years later he was promoted to be director of studies in the National University in Nanking. His main concern at the time was to orient his students to appreciate the intrinsic value of moral self-cultivation. To introduce what may be called an ethico-religious dimension into his teaching, he had a lecture pavilion 講亭 built and invited scholars from all parts of the country to lead discussion sessions there. He also made himself available to students for daily conversations. If a question were put to him, he would first ask the student to relate it to areas of concern such as classical instructions, daily affairs, human feelings, and current events. The intention was to help the student understand his problem through self-knowledge. His personalized style of teaching was said to have attracted many followers.

Unlike many of his fellow students, Ou-yang Te's great influence as a teacher was closely linked with his brilliant career as a scholar-official. The range of his experience in the bureaucracy was quite impressive: he had served successively as director of the seal office in Nanking (1535), vice director of the Court of the Imperial Stud (1536), director of the Court of State Ceremonial in Nanking (1542), a director of the Court of Imperial Sacrifices in Nanking (1547), vice minister of Personnel, and director of the supervisorate of imperial instruction (1550). In this year he was appointed chief officer in charge of the metropolitan examination, but soon left office to mourn the death of his mother. His official career reached a peak in April, 1552, when he was promoted to be minister of Rites, while simultaneously holding the chancellorship of the Hanlin Academy.

His insistence upon observing the court ritual of designating the heir apparent at an early date, despite the emperor's superstition about such matters (*see* T'ao Chung-wen), greatly enhanced his prestige as a courageous and upright minister. He died two years later and was awarded the posthumous rank of junior guardian of the heir apparent and the canonized name Wen-chuang 文莊. Late in 1570 the court approved the request of the officials of Kiangsi to offer annual sacrifices to his shrine erected in his native place.

It can be maintained, however, that Ou-yang's vocation was teaching 講學 rather than political participation. Indeed, it was in teaching that his ultimate commitment really lay. As one of the most prominent scholars in the country he was able to shape the direction of intellectual atmosphere in his times. Together with Nieh Pao, Tsou Shou-i, and Lo Hung-hsien (*qq.v.*), he made liang-chih 良知 (intuitive knowledge), the central precept of Wang Shou-jen's mature philosophy, a household word in educational circles. In 1554 Ou-yang and a few of his friends organized a meeting 會 in Peking. According to one account, as many as five thousand people were attracted to the great occasion. Historians agree that it was a rare phenomenon, especially at a time when the court was not at all in sympathy with intellectual activities of this kind.

As Wang Chi pointed out, Ou-yang Te's teaching evolves out of the precept of "solitary knowing" 獨知. This seems to have anticipated Liu Tsung-chou (EC-CP) especially in terms of his single-minded dedication to the notion of "self examination" 慎獨 in the Great Learning. It is misleading, however, to interpret Ou-yang's precept of solitary knowing as a form of subjective idealism. It is actually predicated on a continuous process of self-rectification through the efforts of ko-wu 格物. Solitary knowing depends upon purity of the mind which is only attainable when selfish desires have been extirpated. Since selfish desires can only be eliminated by rectifying daily affairs, Ou-yang's solitary knowing is not obtainable by the method of "quiet sitting" 靜坐. Ou-yang seems to contend that although liang-chih as intuitive knowledge of the good is both self-sufficient and self-creating, it must constantly be manifested in daily affairs. Huang Tsung-hsi (ECCP) has pointed cut that, unlike Nieh Pao's notion of "returning to tranquillity" 歸寂, Ou-yang's approach to self-cultivation is the rectification of human affairs. In his response to Lo Hung-hsien (*q.v*), Ou-yang makes it clear that although his solitary knowing is qualitatively different from knowledge acquired by sensory perceptions 聞見之知, it is fundamentally inseparable from that type of knowledge.

Two years after his death his collected works, *Ou-yang Nan-yeh hsien-sheng wen-chi* 南野先生文集, 30 *ch.*, were edited and published (1556) at Nanchang by the Kiangsi provincial government. The editor was his disciple, Wang Tsung-mu (*q.v.*), who was then the administrative commissioner. The book was reprinted two years later in Shansi by another disciple, Liang Ju-k'uei 梁汝魁 (cj 1543).

Bibliography

1/283/15a, 274/5a; 3/265/6b; 5/34/15a; 8/54/12a; 16/16/25b, 40/46, 133/17b, 157/6b, 159/49a; 22/7/39a; 32/67/3a; 40/39/9a; 83/17/1a; MSL (1965), 12/18a, 17/23a.

Tu Wei-ming

PA-TA shan-jen, *see* CHU Ta

PAI Kuei 白圭 (T. 宗玉), May 23, 1419-January 27, 1475, minister of War from 1467 to 1475, was a native of Nan-kung 南宮 in the prefecture of Chen-ting 眞定 Pei-Chihli. The Pai family originally came from Tz'u-chou磁州 on the Honan border and his grandfather, Pai Chin-chung 進忠 (d. 1401+), is said to have been a battalion commander in the Mongol army. At one time the family lived in Lung-ch'ing 隆慶 (subprefectural and guard city, the name of which was changed in 1567 to Yen 延 -ch'ing, situated about fifty miles northwest of Peking). As this was the place where persons sentenced to exile were often sent, it may be assumed that that was the reason why the Pai family lived there for some time. Apparently after being pardoned they settled in Nan-kung.

A brilliant student, Pai Kuei became a *chin-shih* in 1442, the same year as Yao K'uei, Hsiang Chung, and Han Yung (*qq. v.*). In July, 1443, he was appointed a censor. Early in the following year, he served as supervisor of the expeditionary force commanded by Chu Yung (*see* Hsiang Chung) to drive out from Urianghai the Mongols who had been raiding Liaotung. The government forces scored a few victories over the enemy and concluded their operation in April; Pai then returned to his post in Peking.

In 1447 Pai Kuei received an assignment to Shansi to investigate the judicial procedures; he settled a number of unresolved cases, discharging his duties with dispatch. In the autumn of 1449 he served on the ill-fated expedition against the Oirat led by Emperor Chu Ch'i-chen (*q.v.*), and is said to have been one of only two censors who survived the disaster. Upon his return he supervised the training of troops in Pei-Chihli in preparation for renewed Oirat hostilities. In December of this year he received promotion to be the surveillance commissioner of Shensi, where he won a reputation as a competent judge and enlightened administrator. Pai stayed in this office to the end of 1452, when he was appointed junior administrative commissioner of Chekiang. He routed the remnants of the bandits of Yeh Tsung-liu (*q.v.*), pronounced fair sentences on criminals, and when the province was struck by drought, devised a scheme to relieve the inhabitants by seeing to it that the wealthy merchants

contributed surplus grain.

Pai became vice censor-in-chief in May, 1458, and served under Fang Ying 方瑛 (1415-59), marquis of Nan-ho 南和, (Pth. 忠襄) as supervisor of military affairs in the suppression of the rebellious Miao 苗 tribesmen in eastern Kweichow. The government forces successfully crushed the uprising with the capture of the chieftain in August, 1459. In November while still in the field Pai was promoted to be governor of Hukuang. He held this post until his promotion to assistant secretary of War in October, 1460. Early in the following year the Mongol chieftain Bolai 孛來, (fl. 1451-65) launched an attack on northern Shensi and broke through the Chinese defenses; the court then sent Pai and the censor-in-chief Wang Hung (*see* Han Yung) to lead an army to Ku-yüan 固原 to resist the invaders. In February, 1462, the Chinese forces reported a victory over the enemy near Ku-yüan. Pai was recalled to Peking in April; a year later he became minister of Works, but continued to act in a military capacity.

In February, 1466, Pai Kuei was appointed supervisor of military affairs to accompany Chu Yung in crushing an uprising in what was later known as the Ching-Hsiang 荊襄 area, a vast expanse of rugged, mountainous territory on the borders of Hukuang, Honan, Shensi, and Szechwan. Here a band of illegal immigrants, outlaws, and tax-evaders, under the leadership of a strong man, Liu T'ung (*see* Hsiang Chung), had defied government orders and staged an open rebellion. The punitive forces succeeded in defeating the rebels, capturing their ringleader, and killing several tens of thousands of his followers, but left the problem unresolved as to how to settle the illegal residents. Pai returned to Peking in June; in August he learned of the death of his father and asked permission to leave to fulfill his mourning duties, but the emperor overruled his request. In February of the following year he received the rank of junior guardian of the heir apparent. As a means of preventing renewed trouble in the Ching-Hsiang territory, Pai proposed the setting up of additional chiliarch commanderies and police stations in strategic areas. These security measures, however, proved ineffective; another uprising developed in 1470, and a new solution had to be sought (*see* Hsiang Chung).

Pai Kuei became minister of War in May, 1467, and received an imperial order to join the ranks of General Kuo Teng 郭登 (earl of Ting-hsiang 定襄, d. June 6, 1472, Pth. 忠武), the eunuch Liu Yung-ch'eng (*q.v.*), and several other high officials for training the newly reorganized army corps, known as Shih-er-t'uan-ying (*see* Chu Chien-shen). Meanwhile Pai occupied himself with plans to cope with unrest in various parts of the country: the tribal uprising in Szechwan, the Mongol incursions on the northern frontier, and the renewed rebellion in Hukuang and Kweichow. The main threat, however, came from the Mongols; the latter, under the leadership of their new chieftain Ma'aliqai 毛 (or 卯) 里孩, 摩里海 (d. *ca.* 1472), had lately made repeated raids into Yen-sui 延綏 and Yü-lin 榆林 in northern Shensi. In March, 1472, Pai Kuei, echoing the views of many of his colleagues that peace on the border could not be obtained as long as the Mongols lingered in the Ordos region, proposed the dispatch of a huge expeditionary force to rout the enemy. In preparation for the expedition Pai requested contributions of grain and fodder from the inhabitants of Honan, Shansi, and Shensi, and when they failed to respond he demanded an advance of a year's revenue from them. This created an uproar and invited criticism from the opponents of his policy, but the emperor supported his scheme. In June the court appointed Chao Fu (*see* Han Yung) and Wang Yüeh (*q.v.*) to organize the expedition, but in October they submitted a memorial, pointing out the impossible task of dealing with the highly mobile nomads

with meager resources, and requested an army totaling a hundred fifty thousand. Their proposal was rejected on financial grounds. In December the court appointed Liu Chü (*see* Liu Yung-ch'eng) to replace Chao Fu, but the expedition that materialized in the following spring yielded few substantial gains. The plan of expelling the Mongols from the Ordos region thus doomed to failure, the Chinese reverted to the policy of defensive tactics.

As minister of War Pai Kuei was critical of the performance of the field commanders, and does not seem to have worked satisfactorily with most of them. The cause of disagreement possibly lay in the gap between planning and performance, but Pai's strong views may also have contributed to strained relations with his colleagues. He was concerned about the accuracy of their reports and sometimes expressed his doubts openly. The first occurence was in June, 1472, when he memorialized on some discrepancies in figures given in Hsiang Chung's reports of his victory over the rebels in the Ching-Hsiang area in 1471, and asked for a formal investigation. Another took place in October, 1473, when he suggested that there were inconsistencies in the figures given in the dispatch of Han Yung on his campaign against the bandits in Kwangsi that year, and again proposed an inquiry. The emperor, however, rejected both requests.

In September, 1473, Pai left office to mourn his stepmother, but returned shortly afterwards. Early in the following year he fell ill; then in September, after news came that the Mongols had invaded the defense area north of Peking, he received orders to undertake an inspection tour. The rugged journey to the frontier must have further impaired his health, for he died in November, shortly after his return, at the age of fifty-five. As a tribute to his service, the emperor granted him the posthumous name Kung-min 恭敏, and awarded him the hereditary rank of a centurion in the Embroidered-uniform Guard, which was inherited by his eldest son Pai Pin 鑌 His second son, Pai Yüeh (*see* Huang-fu Fang), the secondus among the *chin-shih* of 1484, served as minister of Rites (1508 -10) under Emperor Chu Hou-chao (*q.v.*).

A selection of Pai Kuei's memorials, entitled *Pai Kung-min tsou-shu* 奏疏, is preserved in the *Ming ching-shih wen-pien* by Ch'en Tzu-lung (ECCP).

Bibliography

1/172/16a; 5/38/58a; MSL (1963), Ying-tsung, *ch.* 82–350, Hsien-tsung (1964), *ch.* 1–136; KC (1958), 2349; *Nan-kung-hsien chih* (1936), 23/10a, 14a; Shang Lo, *Shang Wen-i kung chi* (NLP microfilm, no. 987), 27/5a; D. Pokotilov, *History of the Eastern Mongols during the Ming Dynasty from 1368 to 1634*, tr. by Rudolf Loewenthal, *Studia Serica Mon.*, ser. A, no. 1 (Chengtu, 1947), pt. 1, 61; Louis Hambis, *Documents sur l'histoire des Mongols à l'époque des Ming* (Paris, 1969), 33, 39.

Hok-lam Chan

P'AN Chi-hsün 潘季馴 (T. 時良, 惟良, H. 印川), 1521-May 20, 1595, a native of Wu-ch'eng 烏程, Chekiang, was the foremost hydraulic engineer of Ming times. Upon earning his *chin-shih* in 1550, he served a term as prefectural judge of Kiukiang, for which he received high praise; and in 1554 he became a censor. In 1557, after the main halls of the palace were burned down, lumber of unusual size had to be assembled; on this task P'an served as an inspector. During the ensuing nine years he held the posts of inspecting censor in Kwangtung, education intendant of Pei-Chihli, and vice minister of the Grand Court of Revision. In 1561, when P'an relinquished his office in Kwangtung, he submitted a memorial requesting that the chün-p'ing 均平 system, an earlier form of the single-whip (*see* P'ang Shang-p'eng), which he had devised, be enforced in that province. In 1565 he received an appointment as imperial commissioner for the restoration of the bed of the Yellow River, which had broken one of its dikes. The break took place near P'ei-hsien 沛縣, resulting in loss of life and property. What concerned the government most was the effect on the main artery of the empire because this section of the river constituted part of the Grand Canal on which all grain ships proceeded to the capital. In this area where the borders of Shantung, Honan, and Nan-Chihli converge, the river bed was already so high that any added embankment only increased the potential danger. To divert the current to the north was impractical. To channel it to the south might upset the drainage system near the tombs of the emperor's ancestors. How to harness the Yellow River in this region became a matter under endless debate for more than a century. Taxing the talents of the water control specialists of the empire, the issue also caused the rise and fall of P'an's career.

P'an's authority over the project was by no means complete. As an assistant censor-in-chief, he was outranked by Chu Heng 朱衡 (T. 士南, 惟平, H. 鎮山, 1512- 84, cs 1532), who, with the title of minister of Works and vice censor-in-chief, had been appointed commissioner in charge of the Grand Canal three months earlier. In the winter of 1565–66 the two commissioners had their first clash of opinion. Chu, in the belief that the P'ei-hsien section of the Yellow River had already been silted beyond hope of reclamation, wanted to dig a new channel curving slightly to the north. He pointed out that the scheme, once attempted by Sheng Ying-ch'i 盛應期 (T. 思徵, H. 值庵, 1474–1535, cs 1493) in 1527, but left unfinished, was from an engineering point of view sound. P'an argued that the proposed route ran into difficult terrain where the water table was too high, and that the artificial channel could never be made sufficiently wide and deep to serve as the natural bed of the river. With the dispute unresolved, the court dispatched a supervising secretary to make a field inspection; his report favored Chu's proposal. Chu then constructed the new channel with all speed and reported its completion in the autumn of 1566. P'an was not completely defeated, however. Following his persistent pleas the court also permitted him to work on the old channel, apparently with less funds and less manpower. Unfortunately, before the end of the year, he was forced to leave his post because of the death of one of his parents.

While Chu Heng concentrated on the reopening of the grain traffic, he paid less attention to the flood problem. His new channel, indeed, was constructed under serious physical difficulties; but, as P'an predicted, it did not have the capacity to accommodate the incoming water. In 1569 and 1570 dikes broke on the river bend, the new channel overflowed, and the whole region adjacent to it was inundated. Chu had already left the scene; on September 1, 1570, P'an was once again made commissioner in charge of the Yellow River, this time with the title of right vice censor-in-chief, and also invested with the authority to give orders to the local military commanders.

Soon after P'an's arrival the Yellow River in the troubled area further divided into a dozen or so branches; for seventy miles downstream from Hsü-chou 徐州 the main channel became silted. Many officials, eager to restore water transportation to Peking, envisioned another new channel to the east, running northward from Su-ch'ien 宿遷 to Chao-yang 昭陽 Lake, thus detouring the grain ships from the Hsü-chou region altogether. P'an admitted the merit of the proposal, but objected to its taking priority over the restoration of the Yellow River system. He calculated that the new channel, later designated as Chia Ho 泇河, would take years to complete, and at the moment funds and manpower under his administration would not allow simultaneous execution of both projects. In his opinion the

restoration of the main course of the river should first be accomplished; otherwise any artificial channel connected to it would be a waste. He deepened the river bed, strengthened existing dikes, and constructed new ones. Above all he rerouted all branch streams into the main course. Unlike other water control specialists in his time who wished to divide the stream to reduce the current, he held that the Yellow River needed to maintain its strong current to prevent the sixty or even eighty percent of silt, which it carried, from being deposited along its course. [Editors' note: P'an's statement, if somewhat exaggerated, may not be far from the truth. Matteo Ricci (q. v.), who traveled on the Yellow River in 1598, casually noted in his journal that the stream was no less than one third silt. Prior to World War II, Chinese engineers sampled the water in three major branches of the river and discovered that the silt content ranged from 42.9 to 63 percent.] For sixteen months P'an persisted in his effort in spite of protests. After again making the river navigable, however, he was impeached. In the winter of 1571/72 a number of grain ships capsized in the main channel. Seizing this opportunity, a supervising secretary charged P'an with not coordinating his construction with the movement of ships. He was summarily dismissed and replaced by Chu Heng.

As the problem of the Yellow River seemed to be unending, officials in Peking busied themselves with prolonged disputation over its solution. Opinions were abundant, constructive ideas few. Nevertheless during that decade suggestions were made to revive the sea traffic (see Liang Meng-lung) and to construct a new canal cutting across the Shantung peninsula. In 1573 and 1574 the Huai River also overflowed, breaking the dikes to its east and flooding Kao-yu 高郵 and Pao-ying 寶應. Some officials believed that the Yellow River was taking over the Huai's opening to the sea and forcing the latter to find a new outlet elsewhere. They therefore urged the diversion of the Huai into the Yangtze. Wu Kuei-fang 吳桂芳 (T. 子實, H. 自湖, 1521–78, cs 1544), who became commissioner of the Grand Canal in 1575, had a strong conviction that the whole problem of the Yellow River lay in its inadequate outlet. His proposal was to deepen and widen the estuary. When, in 1577, the river dike broke at Ts'ui-chen 崔鎮 on the north bank between Hsü-chou and Huai-an 淮安, he attempted to leave the break open to form an extra approach to the sea. The commissioner of water control of the Yellow River, Fu Hsi-chih 傅希摯 (H. 後川, cs 1556), however, wanted to seal the gap as soon as possible. The disagreement prompted the court to remove Fu and put Wu in charge of the conservancy of both the Yellow River and the Grand Canal. But Wu died immediately after he had won the argument. His combined assignment fell to P'an Chi-hsün. In March, 1578, he became commissioner for the third time, with the rank of right censor-in-chief and concurrently a vice minister of War.

For the next two years P'an enjoyed undisputed authority in his work. Dismissing Wu Kuei-fang's suggestions altogether, he closed the gap at Ts'ui-chen. Firm in his belief that the silt-laden Yellow River had to be constantly washed by the clear current of the Huai, he was determined to restrict both channels and maintain their converging point west of Huai-an. Instead of allowing the latter stream to reach the sea by another outlet, he reinforced the Kao-chia 高家 dike, which separated the drainage systems between east and west, thus enabling the Huai to reach the confluence in full volume. In March, 1580, the project was completed. P'an was awarded the high ranks of grand preceptor of the heir apparent and minister of Works.

In executing these projects P'an had the support of Chang Chü-cheng (q. v.), who, though wholly convinced of P'an's competence, had reservations about his proposals. The ten letters written to P'an, found in Chang's collected works, disclose that the grand secretary questioned the wisdom of closing the gap at Ts'ui-chen. He also asked P'an to write him confidentially so that he would be better prepared in case the censorial officials should raise questions about the water control project. When this was near completion, he let the commissioner know beforehand what awards and promotions were awaiting him. A contemporary writer suggests that the cordial relationship between the two officials later came to an end when P'an failed to construct the Chia Ho as Chang had suggested. The story can be neither confirmed nor denied. In one of Chang Chü-cheng's letters, however, he did urge P'an to consider the suggested channel. [Editors' note: Chang Chü-cheng's proposal for the Chia Ho was vindicated by its construction in 1604 (see Li Hua-lung) and its integration with the Grand Canal for two and a half centuries. Chang often qualified his opinion on the problem of control of the Yellow River at the junction with the Grand Canal by saying that he had never visited the area and so could not have full confidence in the correctness of his own judgment. The soundness of his idea is thus another indication of his foresight.]

In August, 1580, P'an became minister of War in Nanking. He was ordered to Peking in January, 1583, to take over the ministry of Justice, in time to be involved in the controversy over the posthumous condemnation of Chang Chü-cheng. In the summer of 1584 he petitioned Emperor Chu I-chün (q. v.) asking leniency for Chang's mother, then over eighty. As a result she was released and allowed to retain one and a half acres of land for her subsistence. But when P'an besought the emperor to be merciful toward Chang's other relatives, he met his downfall. On August 20 of that year he was labeled as Chang's henchman and dismissed from his ministerial position, even having his name removed from the civil service register. Four years later, however, he emerged again as commissioner of the Yellow River system.

P'an's many ups and downs reflected in part the lack of a persistent policy by the Ming court. Administrative specialists seldom held office long enough to put their programs into realization. Often they were criticized by amateurs. When a new formula failed at any time to achieve the expected results, there was pressure and agitation to return to the old method. P'an once complained that it was easier to tame the Yellow River than to face the criticisms of the court. During his fourth term as commissioner he achieved little. He had planned to reconstruct another section of the Yellow River, but because of the shortage of funds his ambition was not realized. In 1589 and 1590 he twice controlled the flood situation near Hsü-chou, but inundation followed almost on the heels of his emergency measures. The seeping of water in the ceremonial hall next to the imperial tombs in the autumn of 1591 made him again the object of censure. Already in poor health, he turned in his resignation which was accepted by the emperor with no gesture of regret; he retired early in 1592.

P'an left this famous motto on water control: 建堤束水, 借水攻沙 (Build dikes to restrict the water; utilize the current to move the silt), which is referred to by specialists as the "self-scour method" and channel contraction theory. (The effectiveness of this approach, however, has not been entirely confirmed by modern laboratory experiments.) For construction of dikes P'an specially recommended a second line which he designated as "distant dikes," usually a mile or so from the river. His reasoning was that when a flood reaches such a distance its intensity is greatly reduced and the dikes can check it more effectively. He further emphasized that dikes should never be planned as an unbroken bulwark to check the water. At places they should be constructed in depth; at other places outlet

must be provided as safety valves. Thus while advocating the channel contraction theory he had not overlooked the usefulness of the retention basins. (Present day engineers tend to believe that the two methods contradict each other.) For stopping breaks in dikes in emergencies he relied on a device called liu-kun 柳輥 (willow rolls), fascine bundles of twigs filled with grass and compacted soil. Wang Shih-chen (q. v.), a close friend of P'an, described the largest ones that he made as twenty feet in diameter.

Several works by P'an deal with water control in general and the taming of the Yellow River in particular. The earlier titles are *Liang-ho kuan-chien* 兩河管見, 3 *ch.*, *Liang-ho ching-lüeh* 經畧, 4 *ch.*, and *Se-chüeh-liang-ho ta-kung lu* 塞決兩河大工錄, 10 *ch.*, some editions having slightly varied topics and numbers. In his later years he published his *Ho-fang i-lan* 河防一覽, 14 *ch.*, which incorporates most of the contents of his previous works. Reprinted in 1748 and 1936 it contains maps, geographical and historical studies of the Yellow River, his essays on water control in the form of dialogues, and related official documents. The 1936 edition contains several appendices including memorials found in his earlier publications but not in the original issue of this work, biographies of P'an, and Chang Chü-cheng's correspondence with him. Several editions of his memorials are in circulation, variously edited in six or twenty *ch.* Columbia University has a facsimile of such a collection, entitled *Hsing-pu tsou-shu* 刑部奏疏, 2 *ch.*, which contains exclusively those memorials submitted by him while he was minister of Justice. Included in the volumes are his petitions on behalf of Chang Chü-cheng's family. Other papers in this work indicate that he commuted punishments to fines and fought against abuses such as interference with justice by nonjudicial agencies, notably the secret police. His poetry and belles lettres appear in the *Liu-yü-t'ang chi* 留餘堂集, 4 *ch.*

Bibliography

1/83/27b, 84/5a, 223/7b; 5/59/95a; MSL (1965), Shih-tsung, 8181, 8885, 8936, 9057, Mu-tsung (1940), 48/1b, 64/13a, Shen-tsung 72/8b, 96/11b, 101/5b, 132/11b, 149/8a, 151/6a, 197/12a, 244/3a, 247/4a; *Hu-chou* 湖州-*fu chih* (1874), 58/22b, 69/17b; *T'ien-hsia chün-kuo-li-ping-shu* (SPTK), 11/31a, 13/22b, 25b, 32a, 18/42b; Wang Shih-chen, *Yen-chou-shan-jen ssu-pu kao* (1577), 59/1a; Shen Shih-hsing, *Tz'u-hsien-t'ang chi* 賜閒堂集 (NLP microfilm roll no. 865), 18/6a; Li Wei-chen 李維楨 (1547–1626), *Ta-pi shan-fang chi* 大泌山房集 (NLP microfilm roll no. 888), 27/26 a; SK (1930), 55/9a, 75/3a, 178/3a; Ts'en Chungmien 岑仲勉, *Huang-ho pien-ch'ien shih* 黃河變遷史 (Peking, 1957), 466, 513; Sung Hsi-shang 宋希尚, *Chung-kuo ho-ch'uan chih*, 中國河川誌, I (Taipei, 1954), 42; Cheng Chao-ching 鄭肇經, *Chung-kuo shui-li-shih* 中國水利史 (Changsha, 1939), 49; *Ho-fang i-lan*, Shanghai, 1936; *Hsing-pu tsou-shu*; Pasquale M. d'Elia, *Fonti Ricciane*, II (Rome, 1949), 18; Joseph Needham, *Science and Civilization in China*, IV, pt. 3 (1971), 229, 237, 325, 344.

Ray Huang

PAṆḌITA 班的達 (written also 板的達, 班迪達),   the honorific title of Saha jaśrī 薩曷拶室哩 (variant 撒哈咱失哩, translated into Chinese as Chü-sheng-chi-hsiang 具生吉祥), died June 16, 1381, was the leader of a twelve-member Indian Buddhist mission to China, a translator, and a monk-official in the Ming court.   He was born into a Kṣatriya (warrior) family, at Kapilavastu, the holy place of pilgrimage of Buddhists, located on the Indo-Nepalese border,   but in his youth left his   native place for Kashmir, renounced his family, and received ordination in the Buddhist order at the So-lo-sa (Śūrasena ?) monastery.   Subsequently he studied the Five Subjects according to Indian tradition (wu-ming 五明), the Buddhist canon, and its commentaries. His performance in religious discussion is said to have been brilliant, surpassing even many of the eminent and experienced Buddhist teachers of Kashmir. Finally he realized that discourses and debates are not the Ultimate Truth and began to practice Buddhist meditation, remaining strictly confined with-

in the monastery for more than a decade.

During these years he heard that in China a mountain existed which rose in five terraces (Wu-t'ai) and was called Ch'ing-liang-shan 清凉山 (Pure and Cool Mountain), where Mañjuśrī miraculously manifested himself. Considering the place worthy of pilgrimage, he left Kashmir with a few disciples for China via Central Asia, crossed the Indus River and passed through the kingdoms of the T'u-ch'üeh 突厥 (Turks), Ch'ü-chih 屈支 (Kucha), and Kao-ch'ang 高昌 (Turfan) on his way. Wherever he went rulers and nobles are reported to have accepted the precepts which he expounded. After four years of travel he arrived at the Chinese frontier.

When the Yüan emperor Toɣon Temür (*q.v.*) learned of his arrival, he deputed a messenger to welcome him. Paṇḍita, summoned to the capital (Ta-tu) in 1364, was asked to reside at the Chi-hsiang-fa-yün 吉祥法雲 monastery. Many followers came to sit at his feet. On occasion the Yüan emperor consulted him on affairs of state; although he was treated ceremoniously, his conversations with the Yüan ruler were "never cordial." Some time later he left the capital for Ch'ing-liang Mountain to fulfill his vow of pilgrimage.

In 1371, after the collapse of the Yüan dynasty, Paṇḍita, together with his disciples, went to Nanking and was granted an audience by the first Ming emperor, who honored him with the title Shan-shih ch'an-shih 善世禪師. Concurrently a silver decoration was bestowed on him, and he was assigned to the office supervising the Buddhist affairs of the empire. The emperor ordered the ministry of Rites to permit anyone who so wished to request instruction from him. On the mountain known as Chung-shan 鍾山, near Nanking, Paṇḍita constructed a temple and there established his residence. Whenever his Majesty visited the mountain, he paid the monk a visit; their conversations sometimes continued for hours. The emperor dedicated at least three poems to Paṇḍita, gave him presents, and showed him other courtesies. Meanwhile Paṇḍita was given permission to undertake a pilgrimage to the holy places in the eastern and central provinces of China. Starting from Nanking in the autumn of 1376, he visited P'u-t'o 普陀 Island, climbed the Shih-tzu yen 獅子巖 (Lion Cliff) on T'ien-mu 天目 Mountain sailed across Poyang Lake, traveled to Lu-shan 廬山, north of the river Huai, and paid homage to the reliquary pagodas of the fourth and fifth patriarchs of the Ch'an school of Buddhism (i. e., Tao-hsin, 580-651, and Hung-jen, 602-75).

When he returned to Nanking from this pilgrimage, he was received by the emperor at an audience in the Hua-kai 華蓋 palace and liberally rewarded. Those who were ordained in the Order under his administration reportedly numbered eighty thousand. The treasures donated to him by the public were numerous. He distributed the entire amount either to the poor or to the repair of Buddhist establishments. He said that he needed no money for himself.

Later Paṇḍita suffered from an ailment in his legs and was unable to walk. Though he was ministered to by the imperial physicians, their treatment was ineffective. Before his demise, he instructed his disciples to uphold the Law of Buddha. He also asked his Indian disciple Kumaraśrī (Ku-ma-lo-shih-li 孤麻囉室哩, variant Ko-ma-la-shih-li 嘅瑪拉實哩), to scatter his ashes over Wu-t'ai Mountain. He passed away in 1381. Following the cremation, however, his ashes were collected and a pagoda erected on a spot outside the Chü-pao 聚寶 Gate of Nanking. A memorial temple was also built, which was named by the emperor the Hsi-t'ien 西天 monastery, the name indicating that his birthplace was India in the west.

At court the main contribution of Paṇḍita was that he served as a model for other monks, particularly when they had to respond to government policies dealing with Buddhists. As a foreigner,

his status and privileges placed him in a position to soften the autocratic temper of the emperor. His appearance in China was considered by certain Buddhist writers as a symbol of the revival of religious contacts between China and India, which had once been a dominant factor in the spread of Buddhism in China. He left two works entitled Shih-chung yü 示眾語 (Instructions to Buddhists) in 3 chüan, and Pa-chih-chieh pen 八支戒本 (The first eight commandments). Another work attributed to him, the Ssu-chung-titzu P'u-sa-chieh 四眾弟子菩薩戒, was translated by his disciple Chih-kuang 智光 (H. 無隱, family name Wang 王, d. 1435); but the latter compilation, it seems, is identical with the Pa-chih-chieh pen. None of them, however, is at present extant.

According to certain later records, such as Ti-ching ching-wu lüeh by Liu T'ung (q.v,) and Jih-hsia chiu-wen k'ao by Chu I-tsun (ECCP), Paṇḍita arrived at the Ming court during the early years of the Yung-lo period. These sources also connect him with the construction of the Chen-chüeh 眞覺 monastery, popularly known as the Five Pagoda Temple, to the west of Peking. This tradition was subsequently repeated in an inscription on the above-mentioned monastery erected by the Ch'ien-lung emperor in 1761, and has also been voiced by Tokiwa Daijō 常盤大定 and Sekino Tei 關野貞, Shan Shih-yüan 單士元 and Wang Pi-wen 王璧文, and Lo Che-wen 羅哲文. The tradition is, however, based on later sources and is not authentic; earlier documents clearly refute it. After his death, two of his Indian disciples, Kumaraśrī and Sa-mu-tan-shih-li 薩木丹實哩 (Samudraśrī ?), requested the emperor's permission to return to India. In the ninth month of 1381, they received it from the ministry of Rites along with a written document, and then left China to return home. Another disciple named Ti-wa-ta-ssu 底哇答思 (Devadas) remained and died in China.

The most eminent disciple of Paṇḍita was the monk Chih-kuang, the leader of a solitary party of Chinese Buddhist pilgrims who visited India and Nepal during the Ming period. Chih-kuang served at court, holding the offices of Seng-lu Yu-ch'an-chiao 僧錄右闡教 and Yu-shan-shih 右善世, and was honored with a long title usually abbreviated as Yüan-yung ta-kuo-shih 圓融大國師.

Bibliography

61/160/6a; Ko Yin-liang 葛寅亮, *Chin-ling fan-ch'a chih* 金陵梵利志 (*ca.* 1607), 37/1a; Ming-ho 明河, *Pu-hsü kao-seng chuan* 補續高僧傳 in *Hsü-tsang-ching* 續藏經 (1928), IIB vii/1/27d; *Li-pu chih kao* 禮部志稿, 92/41a; Tokiwa Daijō and Sekino Tei, *Shina bukkyō shiseki hyōkai* 支那佛教史蹟詳解 (Tokyo, 1928), V/230–233; Shan Shih-yüan and Wang Pi-wen, *Ming-tai chien-chu ta-shih nien-piao* 明代建築大事年表 (Peiping, 1937), part VI/79; Lo Che-wen, *Wu-t'a-ssu* 五塔寺 (Peking, 1957), 1.

Jan Yün-hua

P'ANG Shang-p'eng 龐尚鵬 (T. 少南), *ca.* 1524–*ca.* 1581, official noted for his integrity and courage in championing the interest of the common people and one of the pioneers in the practice of i-t'iao pien-fa 一條鞭法 (single whip system of taxation), was a native of Nan-hai 南海, Kwangtung. A *chin-shih* of 1553, he received an appointment as magistrate of Lo-p'ing 樂平, Kiangsi, and was later promoted to the position of censor. In 1559, along with supervising secretary Lo Chia-pin 羅嘉賓 (T. 興賓, H. 一山, cs 1553), he was sent to the southern capital and Chekiang to audit the accounts of the military in their operations against the coastal pirates. While there the two were ordered to check the correctness of the accusations lodged against Hu Tsung-hsien (*q.v.*) and his officers for submitting false reports. In their joint memorial to the emperor, P'ang and Lo were critical of such military leaders as the local commander, Ch'i Chi-kuang (*q.v.*), for their failure to crush the pirates; they went further, impeaching the supreme com-

mander Hu Tsung-hsien and his immediate subordinates for flagrant violation of military regulations and gross misappropriation of military funds. They even had some unkind words for the chief grand secretary, Yen Sung (*q.v.*), who was still influential in the government. The emperor paid no heed to their comments about Yen, but he did issue a warning to Hu and authorized punishment for his subordinate officers. In the light of this affair, it is safe to infer that P'ang was partial to the second grand secretary, Hsü Chieh (*q.v.*), then a keen rival of Yen Sung. Meanwhile Lo and P'ang conducted the auditing of the accounts mentioned above. A year later (1560) they reported their findings, accusing Hu and other commanders of irregularities and unauthorized expenditures, for which almost all the ones named were punished, even the descendants of those already deceased (*see* Chao Wen-hua). Only Hu, on the advice of Yen Sung and others, for the sake of expediency, was spared at this time. After his return to the capital, P'ang repeated his criticisms and proposed measures on how to deal with the problem of piracy.

P'ang was next sent to the province of Honan in the capacity of regional inspector. While there (1562) the governor, Ts'ai Ju-nan 蔡汝楠 (T. 子木, H. 白石, 1514?–65, cs 1532), obtained a white deer and wanted P'ang to join him in presenting the rare animal, a token of heavenly blessing, to the emperor, but P'ang refused. While serving as regional inspector in Chekiang (*ca.* 1565), P'ang learned that the people of the province had suffered from the burden of corvée services. To relieve their plight—for he remarked also the disparity in taxation between households which had adult males but no cultivated fields and those which had large land holdings but few adult males— P'ang experimented in one or two prefectures with the single whip system. In this all corvée fees and extra levies were grouped together in terms of a lump sum of money which was then equitably distributed according to a fair ratio between adult males and cultivated land. With the money thus acquired the local governments could hire people for needed services. Now every adult male or householder knew how much he had to pay and there was no room for corrupt officials and petty clerks to make exactions. The system proved so convenient that it was extended throughout the province. The people of Chekiang expressed their gratitude by erecting a shrine in P'ang's honor while he was still alive. Another of his acts was to accuse some retired officials, such as Mao K'un (*q.v.*), of letting members of their families act overbearingly in their own districts; he succeeded in having a number of them downgraded to the status of commoner. In the case of Mao K'un who had served on the staff of Hu Tsung-hsien, it may safely be conjectured that P'ang's action was motivated by his partisanship, since he seems to have supported Hsü Chieh on several occasions (*see* Yen Sung and Hsü Chieh). His next assignment was as censor having to do with educational affairs in the Peking metropolitan area. The editors of the Ming History record that P'ang was a man of integrity and above partisanship, and that wherever he went he assailed the unjust actions of the influential and powerful to such a degree that both officials and people dreaded him.

In 1567 P'ang submitted a memorial advising the emperor to attend court regularly, to receive the high-ranking officials in audience, and to restore to honor posthumously those officials who in their memorials had offended the deceased emperor (Chu Hou-ts'ung, *q.v.*) and as a result had lost their lives. One of those named by P'ang was Ma Ts'ung-ch'ien 馬從謙 (T. 益之, 1495-December 24, 1552, cs 1535) who had accused a eunuch of embezzlement but whom the latter falsely charged with slandering the emperor. In Ma's case, however, no ac-

tion was taken. P'ang also became involved in the power struggle between Hsü Chieh and his two rivals, Kao Kung (*see* Chang Chü-cheng) and Kuo P'u 郭朴 (T. 質夫, H. 東野, 1511-93, cs 1535). When supervising secretary Hu Ying-chia 胡應嘉 (T. 祁禮, H. 杞泉, cs 1556) was punished for having impeached Grand Secretary Kao Kung, P'ang went to Hu's rescue. P'ang also submitted a memorial attacking Kuo P'u for the latter's improper conduct; this resulted in Kuo's abrupt departure from the government (October 24, 1567) and P'ang's promotion to the post of junior assistant minister of the Grand Court of Revision.

In the spring of 1568 the government became interested in reforming the salt and military farm administration in the nine garrisoned frontier areas, and P'ang was made junior assistant censor-in-chief to share the task with the vice censors-in-chief, Tsou Ying-lung (*see* Lin Jun) and T'ang Chi-lu 唐繼祿 (T. 子廉, cs 1553). While in Ch'ang-p'ing 昌平 (Peking), P'ang impeached the eunuch Chang En 張恩 for carrying out an execution without authorization and the gabelle censor for the two Huai regions, Sun I-jen 孫以仁 (cs 1562), for corruption; both were punished. In the autumn of the same year, after the recall of Tsou and T'ang, P'ang was left in sole charge. In this capacity he was eager to carry out reforms in the salt administration which had long been overdue. He inspected all the frontier areas personally and made a number of proposals. Unfortunately the deterioration in the administration was of long standing, and P'ang's measures went unheeded. Certain censors resented his intrusion into areas under their jurisdiction; one of them, Kao Yung-ch'un 郜永春 (cs 1565), assailed him for his management of affairs. According to the *Ming-shih* the then minister of Personnel, Yang Po (*q. v.*), recommended P'ang's retention, but since the eunuchs disliked Yang they persuaded the emperor to dismiss both him and P'ang (January 22, 1570). From then on, no official with the title of censor-in-chief was sent to manage the salt administration. It is interesting to note that only five days later Kao Kung, the man P'ang had antagonized earlier, was restored to power. This also most probably explains why (not long afterwards) he was downgraded to the status of a commoner on the retroactive charge that, while serving as regional inspector in Chekiang, he had allowed silver of poor quality to be delivered to the palace treasury.

Upon the accession to the throne of Chu I-chün (*q.v.*), a number of censors recommended P'ang for reappointment, and the governor of Paoting, Sung Hsün (*see* Chu I-chün), also memorialized protesting P'ang's innocence. Yang Po's recall to government service came promptly (April 17, 1571), but it was not until November 12, 1576, that P'ang was restored to his former official title and ordered to serve as governor of Fukien. While there, he canceled the provincial taxes in arrears up to a total of half a million taels and impeached the regional commander, Hu Shou-jen (*see* Lin Feng), which resulted in the latter's dismissal from office. Here too, as in Chekiang, he put into effect, with imperial approval, the single whip system to the satisfaction of the local population. His success in these two provinces encouraged its extension and probably contributed to the government adoption of the system throughout the empire in 1581.

In February, 1578, P'ang received a promotion to the rank of senior vice-censor-in-chief. In the same year, however, a great controversy arose over whether chief Grand Secretary Chang Chü-cheng (*q. v.*) should remain in his official position since he was conventionally required to observe the mourning regulations for his father. A number of officials who dared to speak out against Chang's by-passing the traditional rules (or against Chang's ambition to hold on to the office of premier) were severely punished. P'ang memorialized the throne appealing their

case and hence antagonized Chang. It so happened that P'ang had committed the error of counting the period between his dismissal and reappointment towards his tenure and had also used an improper seal in stamping his official documents. Taking note of these blunders, Chang instructed chief supervising secretary of Personnel, Ch'en San-mu 陳三謨 (T. 汝明 H. 錦江, cs 1565), to impeach him. The end result was P'ang's dismissal in July of the same year.

Upon his return to his native district, he found his mother seriously ill, and fate enabled him to attend her until her death. Four years after he had left office, P'ang died, aged fifty-seven. In commemoration of his service in relieving the corvée burden, the people enshrined him in Chekiang, Fukien, and even in Kwangtung, the province of his birth. During the T'ien-ch'i period, he received the posthumous title of Hui-min 惠敏.

P'ang left one work entitled *Pai-k'o-t'ing chai kao* 百可亭摘稿 in 9 *chüan*. This contains memorials he wrote when serving as a censor and as governor of Fukien (4 *ch.*,) miscellaneous prose (3 *ch.*), and poetry (2 *ch.*). A rare copy is in the Tōyō Bunko. The editors of the *Ssu-k'u* catalogue list it but did not include it in the Imperial Library. Another of his literary remains is the *P'ang-shih chia-hsün* 氏家訓, 1 *ch.*, which is preserved in at least two collections. [Editors' note: Among the rare books of the National Library of Peking, there is one (microfilm roll no. 723) which includes a proclamation on eight double leaves printed in the 5th month, 5th year of Wan-li (June, 1577) by order of P'ang Shang-p'eng, then governor of Fukien. The document may be given the title "Regulations on fire fighting for Foochow and other cities of Fukien"; it consists of six articles on fire fighting as proposed jointly by the intendant of Foochow and the regional military commissioner, preceded by an endorsement from the governor ordering the officials of all urban areas to observe these regulations.]

Bibliography

1/227/1b; 5/55/40a; MSL(1965), Mu-tsung, 0340, 0992, Shen-tsung (1966), 1641; KC(1958), 3927, 3943, 4300, 4337; *Kwangtung t'ung-chih* 通志 (1602), 25/30b (1934 ed.), 4851; *Chekiang t'ung-chih* (1934 ed.), 2639; SK (1930), 178/4b; *Honan t'ung-chih* (1914), 31/3b; *Yüeh-tung shih-hai* 粵東詩海, ed. by Wen Ch'ien-shan 溫謙山, 28; Hsü Wei, *Hsü Wen-ch'ang wen-chi* (*Hai-shan hsien-kuan* 海山仙館 *ts'ung-shu* ed.), 25/8b; Huo Yü-hsia 霍與瑕 (cs 1559), *Huo Mien-chai chi* 勉齋集, 11/86b; Liang Fang-chung 梁方仲, "Ming-tai i-t'iao-pien-fa nien-piao" 明代一條鞭法年表, *Lingnan Jo.*, 12:1 (1952), 15 (tr. into English by Wang Yü-ch'üan as *The Single-Whip Method of Taxation in China* (Cambridge, Mass., 1956).

Kwan-wai So

PANTOJA, Diego de (Diogo, Didace de, 龐迪我 T. 順陽), 1571–1618, a Christian missionary, was born in Valdemoro, near Seville, in Spain. He entered the Society of Jesus in 1589 and in 1596 sailed from Lisbon to begin a missionary career in the Far East. He reached Macao on July 20, 1597, and spent the next three years there completing his theological studies, expecting to be assigned to Japan. In 1600, however, Alessandro Valignano (*q.v.*) ordered him to join Matteo Ricci (*q.v.*) who was in Nanking planning his second attempt to establish himself in Peking. Pantoja arrived in Nanking in March of the same year, and in May left with Ricci and the Jesuit brother, Chung Ming-jen (*see* Lazzaro Cattaneo) for the imperial capital. They arrived in Peking on January 24, 1601, after being detained six months, first at Lin-ch'ing 臨清 (Shantung) and then at Tientsin, by the notorious eunuch, Ma T'ang (*see* Matteo Ricci), a tax collector at Lin-ch'ing.

Pantoja spent his entire missionary career in the imperial capital. While most of Ricci's time was taken up with the intellectual apostolate, Pantoja devoted his major energies to catechetical work in and about Peking. By 1608 Ricci was able to report that there were two thousand converts in Peking, many of them undoubtedly the result of Pantoja's efforts. He also assisted in the less directly evangelical aspects of the work. It was Pantoja who shortly after their arrival entered the palace area every day for a month to give lessons to four eunuchs assigned by the court to learn to play the spinet, one of the presents which Ricci had brought with him for the emperor. When in 1612 the Jesuits were commissioned to reform the Chinese calendar, a commission soon withdrawn (*see* Sabatino de Ursis), Pantoja, as a preliminary project, calculated the latitude of all major Chinese cities from Canton to Peking.

Upon the death of Ricci on May 11, 1610, Pantoja, assisted by Li Chih-tsao (ECCP), composed a memorial to the Wan-li emperor (Chu I-chun, *q.v.*) requesting a worthy burial site for the deceased founder of the Christian mission. The Chinese text of this memorial, with Italian translation, is published in *Fonti Ricciane*. The request, endorsed by the ministry of Rites, was granted. An imperial rescript gave the Jesuits title to a plot of land near the Fu-ch'eng gate 阜成門 in the western wall of the city.

Following the imperial edict of February 14, 1617, calling for the banishment of Christian missionaries from the empire (*see* Alfonso Vagnoni), Pantoja, whose name was mentioned, was exiled to Macao where he died in January of the following year.

Pantoja left at least seven writings in Chinese, one of which, *Ch'i k'o ta ch'üan* 七克大全 (Seven victories won over seven capital sins), published in Peking in 1614, was honored with a notice in the *Ssu-k'u* catalogue one and a half centuries later. (A copy of this, dated 1798, is in the Cambridge University Library.) This work had a profound effect on the scholar Wang Cheng (ECCP), leading him to seek out Pantoja and converse with him on numerous occasions. In the end Wang wrote a short work

entitled *Wei-t'ien ai-jen chi-lun* 畏天愛人極
論, 1 *ch.*, preserved in manuscript in the
Bibliothèque Nationale, Paris, which
sharply criticized the Buddhist-influenced
scholars of his day. Further, it demonstrates how Chinese intellectuals, converted
to Christianity, made their peace with the
Chinese texts of antiquity.

Pantoja is known also for four maps,
one of each part of the world, which he
painted for the emperor, and on which
he included simple comments on the geography, history, government, and natural
products of every country.

Bibliography

1/326/19a; SK (1930), 125/8b; Fang Hao 方豪,
Chung-kuo t'ien-chu-chiao shih jen-wu chuan 中國
天主教史人物傳 (Hong Kong, 1967), 139; Dan-
iello Bartoli, *Dell'istoria della Compagnia di Gésu.
La Cina. Terza parte dell'Asia*, 4 vols. (Ancona
ed., 1843); Henri Barnard, *Le père Matthieu
Ricci et la société chinoise de son temps (1552–
1610)*, I (Tientsin, 1937), 371; George H.
Dunne, *Generation of Giants* (Notre Dame,
1962), 74, 79, 104, 115, 136; Pfister (1932), 69;
Pasquale M. d'Elia, *Fonti Ricciane* (Rome, 1942–
49), I: 333, 385, II: 91, III: 3; *Roman Archives
of the Society of Jesus* (*ARSI*, Jap-Sin); H.
A. Giles, *A Catalogue of the Wade Collection of
Chinese and Manchu Books in the Library of
the University of Cambridge* (Cambridge, 1898),
124; Jacques Gernet, "A propos des contacts
entre la Chine et l'Europe aux XVIIe et
XVIIIe siècles," *Acta Asiatica*, 23 (Tokyo,
1972), 88.

George H. Dunne

P'ENG Nien 彭年 (T. 孔嘉, H. 隆池),
1505–66, poet and calligrapher, was a native of Ch'ang-chou 長洲 (Soochow). His
family, registered in the military category,
came from Ch'ing-chiang 清江, Kiangsi,
but later settled in the Soochow area. His
father, P'eng Fang 昉 (T. 寅之, cs 1511),
served (1520–21) as magistrate of Hsin-
hui 新會, Kwangtung, but because, according to report, he never flattered superiors, he held office for only a few
months. The family was not rich, but had
sufficient means to permit P'eng Nien, a

youth of unusual aptitude, to spend his
time in extensive reading and study; it is
said, however, that he disliked writing
pa-ku essays in preparation for the civil
service examinations. He wrote other
kinds of essays with rapidity, however,
these often running into thousands of
characters. Thanks to the support of the
prefect of Soochow, Wang T'ing 王廷 (T.
子正, H. 南岷, cs 1532), who recommended him as a subsidized *hsiu-ts'ai* (*lin-
sheng* 廩生) to sit for the *chü-jen* examination, P'eng Nien was able to journey
to Nanking. He enjoyed the excursion but
took no part in the tests. After his return
to Soochow, he declined to accept the
hsiu-ts'ai subsidy. He spent all his time
studying arts and literature under Wen
Cheng-ming (*q.v.*). For years he labored
to acquire his teacher's competence. Although of limited resources, he never solicited any gift from a person who was not
his friend in literature or in art. He had a
wide circle of acquaintances, which included a number of the prominent people
of the day, and was fond of drinking
and sojourning in the beautiful hills
of Soochow. One son and one daughter
survived him, the latter becoming the
wife of Wen Fei 騑, a grandson of Wen
Cheng-ming.

A story is told that P'eng Nien usually
enjoyed good health. As years went on and
it declined, he ordered the members of
his family to prepare for his funeral. On
the last day he asked them to ignite one
stick of incense. As the incense was about
to be consumed, he requested another
stick. When this had burned to the halfway point, he said: "This is as it should
be," and peacefully breathed his last.

His poetry follows the style of Tu Fu
(712–70) and Po Chü-i (772–846). In
calligraphy he imitated Yen Chen-ch'ing
(709–85), Ou-yang Hsün (557–641), and
Su Shih (1037–1101). According to Wang
Shih-chen (*q.v.*), P'eng's small characters
were his best. Chu I-tsun (ECCP) later
remarked: "P'eng Nien's poetry is quite
inferior to that of Wen Cheng-ming. His

fine personality and noble aims, however, are almost equal to his master's." Actually, as a calligrapher, his fame is sometimes favorably compared with that of Wen Cheng-ming.

A collection of his writings entitled *Lung-ch'ih shan-ch'iao-chi* 隆池山樵集 2 *ch.*, is listed by title only in the *Ssu-k'u* catalogue. It is not a complete compilation, only poetry being included. Most of his literary pieces have been lost since his death. His sketchbook known as *Yen-shui-lu* 烟水錄, 1 *ch.*, is included in *Kuang pai-ch'uan hsüeh-hai* 廣百川學海, compiled by Feng K'o-pin 馮可賓 (cs 1622), and fortunately still exists.

Bibliography

1/287/3b; 3/268/2b; 22/9/12a; 32/24/29a; 40/50/1b; 84/丁中/5b; 86/14/34a; *Hsin-hui-hsien chih* (1966 repr. of 1841 ed.), 128; *Soochow-fu chih* (1881), 86/31a, 70/18b; Wang Shih-chen, *Yen-chou-shan-jen ssu-pu kao*, 115/50a, 132/10a, 154/14a; SK (1930), 178/12a; *Chung-kuo ts'ung-shu tsung-lu* 中國叢書綜錄, 總目/7.

Liu Lin-sheng

P'ENG Shao 彭韶 (T. 鳳儀, H. 從吾), 1430-February 5, 1495, scholar and official, was a native of P'u-t'ien 莆田, Fukien. A *chin-shih* of 1457, he was appointed a secretary in the ministry of Justice, later rising to vice director of the Kwangtung bureau. Late in 1466 he sent a memorial to the throne asserting that Chang Ch'i 張岐 (T. 來鳳, 1425-74, cs 1454) was not qualified to be an assistant censor-in-chief. For making this charge, P'eng was imprisoned, awaiting investigation. After payment of a fine, he was reinstated, and later promoted to be a director of a bureau. In 1469 he memorialized again, accusing certain relatives of the emperor with seizing the people's property, and once more was sent to jail.

Having twice suffered imprisonment, he gained, like Ho Ch'iao-hsin (*q.v.*), a wide reputation for courage and integrity. Released again, he was promoted in 1470 to be a surveillance vice commissioner of Szechwan and three years later made a full commissioner. In 1478, probably because of his acquaintance with affairs in Kwangtung, he received a transfer to that province as an administration commissioner. Among his noteworthy services there was the support he gave (1482-83) to the Confucian scholar Ch'en Hsien-chang (*q.v.*). He also lodged several memorials complaining about the excesses of the eunuchs sent out by the emperor as supervisor and pearl collector. When he attacked a cousin of the emperor's favorite eunuch, Liang Fang (*q.v.*), however, he was transferred to Kweichow to serve in the same capacity (1483). Nine months later he was promoted to be governor of Nan-Chihli. In 1485 he became governor of Pei-Chihli.

After the enthronement of Chu Yu-t'ang (*q.v.*) in 1487, P'eng was made a vice minister of Justice. Ordered to look into an insurrection in Chekiang, he succeeded in suppressing it. Then he was given the responsibility of introducing reforms in the salt administration of that province. He returned to the capital after about one year. The following year (1489) he received an appointment as vice minister of Personnel under the minister Wang Shu (*q.v.*). After becoming minister of Justice in October, 1491, he began to charge some members of the nobility and certain eunuchs and high officials with wrongdoing. As the emperor did not accept his advice, he begged leave to retire, and returned home in 1493.

P'eng was acclaimed in all the provinces where he saw service, and respected at the court for his impartiality. He, Wang Shu, and Ho Ch'iao-hsin became known as the san ta-lao 三大老 (three elders). After his death he received the posthumous name Hui-an 惠安, which was considered inadequate. An attempt to change it, however, was unsuccessful. He left a collection entitled *P'eng Hui-an kung wen-chi*, 8 *ch.*, available on microfilm. The *Ssu-k'u ch'üan-shu* includes this work in 11 *chüan*, it has recently been reproduced in the *Ssu-k'u chen-pen* 珍本, series 3.

Bibliography

1/183/6b; 5/44/56a; MSL (1964), Hsien-tsung, 1396; KC (1958), 2669; SK (1930), 170/10a, 175/13a; Cheng Hsiao, *Wu-hsüeh-pien*, 22/1a; *Fukien t'ung-chih* (1922), 4250; *Kweichow t'ung-chih* (1909), 19/16b; *Chekiang t'ung-chih* (1934), 2631; *Szechwan t'ung-chih* (1816), 6/21a; *P'u-t'ien-hsien chih* (1880), 17/34a; Ho Ch'iao-hsin, *Chiao-ch'iu wen-chi* (NCL microfilm, 1523 ed.), 28/11a; Wang Shu, *Wang Tuan-i kung wen-chi* (NCL microfilm, 1553 ed.), 1/9a; P'eng *Hui-an kung wen-chi* (NLP microfilm, roll 978).

Liu Chia-chu

P'ENG Shih 彭時 (T. 純道), 1416-April 27, 1475, a native of An-fu 安福, Kiangsi, served as a grand secretary from 1457 to 1475. His ancestors had been local officials and members of the gentry in An-fu since late in the 11th century. He passed his youth in the calm of his father's library where he is said soon to have acquired a passion for study, and where he achieved a name for his literary ability. After having succeeded in placing first in the *chin-shih* examination of 1448, he entered the Hanlin Academy as compiler. The following year he was called into the Grand Secretariat, and soon rose to become a reader; because of mourning for his stepmother, however, he resigned in February, 1450. On regaining office in 1452 he was awarded the rank of vice minister of the Court of Imperial Sacrifices and in 1456 the rank of a grand secretary after completion of the gazetteer of the empire, *Huan-yü t'ung-chih* (*see* Shang Lu). Upon the restoration to the throne of Chu Ch'i-chen (*q.v.*), he was recalled (September 21, 1457) to the Grand Secretariat. Although the emperor generally preferred northerners, he held P'eng in high esteem. P'eng was also liked by the then leading official Li Hsien (*q.v.*), but had many arguments with him

nonetheless; he considered Li (a native of Honan) to be a champion of the northern bureaucrats and, since he was not a Hanlin Academician, to be unfamiliar with the proper procedure of the "inner court." When a colonel of the Embroidered-uniform Guard, Men Ta 門達, tried to oust Li Hsien, P'eng came to the latter's support. He did so because he seems to have felt a responsibility to uphold a Grand Secretariat tradition instituted by his fellow provincial Yang Shih-ch'i (*q.v.*). After the death of Chu Ch'i-chen (*q.v.*), P'eng was among those who strongly urged a ritual ranking of the former empress with the title Tz'u-i huang t'ai-hou (*see* Chu Chien-shen) above that of the mother of the new emperor.

The last argument P'eng managed to win was that against the Nanking minister of War, Ch'eng Hsin (*see* Kunjilai), over the proper handling of the high command fighting the west China rebels. P'eng insisted on leaving it to Hsiang Chung (*q.v.*), while the courtiers wanted to send a "commissar" of the Embroidered-uniform Guard to the front. The sources indicate that after Wan An (*see* Chiao Fang) rose to power in the early 1470s, the Secretariat's influence dwindled. P'eng, after several unsuccessful requests to be sent home because of illness, died in office at the age of fifty-nine, after eighteen years of service in the Grand Secretariat; he received the posthumous title of Wen-hsien 文憲. His literary achievement is not as conspicuous as that of some other grand secretaries, for it seems that he worked more for the archives in an attempt to preserve the tradition of the Secretariat. He was editor-in-chief of the *Ying-tsung shih-lu*, 361 *ch.*, annals covering the years 1435 to 1464, completed in 1467, and was second only to Li Hsien on the editorial staff of the *Ta Ming i-tung-chih*, 90 *ch.*, completed in 1461. He also left a collection of miscellaneous notes, *P'eng Wen-hsien kung pi-chi* 公筆記 or *P'eng kung pi-chi*, 1 *ch.*, which comments on some contemporary events in a simple matter-of-fact style. A dedication given on the renovation of an academy is contained in the *Ming wen-tsai* 明文在 (*chüan* 57); it shows him to be a *chuang-yüan* in style and a neo-Confucian in thought. Another collection of his prose, *P'eng Wen-hsien chi* 集, 4 *ch.*, is listed by the editors of the Imperial Catalogue, but seems to have disappeared.

Bibliography

1/176/10b; 3/159/9b; 5/13/19a; 8/29/1a; 61/125/2497; 63/11/14a; MSL (1963), Ying-tsung, 6050, 6107, Hsien-tsung, 0636, 0781, 2604; KC (1958), 2007; *Ming-shan-ts'ang* (*ch'en lin-chi* 臣林記), 10/1a; Cheng Hsiao, *Wu-hsüeh pien*, 36/9a; *Tien-ko tz'u-lin chi*, 3/22b; Ch'en Tzu-lung (ECCP), *Huang Ming ching-shih wen-pien, ch.*37; SK (1930), 143/4a, 175/11a; L. Carrington Goodrich, "Geographical Additions of the XIV and XV Centuries," MS, 15 (1956), 203; W. Franke, *Sources*, 4. 5. 5.

Tilemann Grimm

PIEN Kung 邊貢 (T. 庭實, H. 華泉), September, 1476-March 1532, scholar, was a native of Li-ch'eng 歷城, Shantung. It is said that his ancestors for three generations assumed the name Wang 王. It was not until the time of his grandfather, Pien Ning 寧 (cj 1459), that the family resumed its original name. Pien Ning became a vice prefect of Ying-t'ien 應天 (Nanking), *ca.* 1470, and his son, Pien Chieh 節 (T. 時中, H. 介菴, cj 1486, 1450-1511), Pien Kung's father, served as sub-prefect of Tai-chou 代州, Shansi (1506-8).

After gaining his *chü-jen* in 1495 and his *chin-shih* in the following year, Pien Kung served as an erudite in the Court of Imperial Sacrifices. On the death of Emperor Chu Yu-t'ang (*q.v.*) in June, 1505, he joined in the criticism of the court physicians for their misuse of medicine. In the following month he received an appointment as supervising secretary of the office of scrutiny for War and showed himself to be a well-informed, outspoken, and unreserved critic of cur-

rent affairs. In September, shortly after the succession of Emperor Chu Hou-chao (*q.v.*), he became an assistant minister of the Court of Imperial Sacrifices. Because of his opposition to the powerful eunuch, Liu Chin (*q.v.*), Pien was transferred to be the prefect (1509) of Wei-hui 衞輝, Honan, then (1510) of Ching-chou 荆州, Hukuang, where he helped to suppress the uprising of Lan T'ing-jui 藍廷瑞 (fl. 1509-11) and his band. A year later he became education intendant in Shansi but soon left office upon his father's death. The mourning period over, he was appointed to a similar position in Honan. In this capacity he devoted himself to organizing the school system and promoting Confucian studies in that area. In 1514 his mother died, and once more he had to retire.

Shortly after Emperor Chu Hou-ts'ung (*q.v.*) ascended the throne in 1521, Pien Kung received an appointment as vice minister, then chief minister of the Court of Imperial Sacrifices of Nanking in 1524. In May, 1527, he became chief minister of the same Court and overseer of the College of Translators (*see* Cheng Ho). At that time several foreign languages required the attention of the College but there was a shortage of qualified instructors. Pien then solicited the services of former interpreters and with their help standardized the transcription of a number of languages to aid in foreign intercourse. In December he became an assistant vice minister of Justice in Nanking, and in the following year received a promotion to be minister of Revenue, also in Nanking. Two years later he relinquished this position. The *shih-lu* states that the emperor, acting on the charges of a censor who happened to be Pien's enemy, dismissed him for indulgence in liquor and negligence of his duties. The author of his tomb inscription, however, avers that he retired on the grounds of ill health, possibly a face-saving excuse for his disgrace.

Pien was a great lover of literature

and possessed a fine library. He is said to have squandered his fortune purchasing books to the point that he left his family in poverty. Unfortunately in 1532, a year after his retirement, a fire destroyed his precious collection. He never recovered from this shock, which further impaired his health, and died shortly afterwards, at the age of fifty-six.

According to contemporaries, Pien Kung had a charming personality. He was talented, loved conversation, enjoyed visitors, and was always eager to help those in need, even after only the slightest acquaintance. Pien owed his fame to his literary virtuosity. In the history of literature, he is acclaimed one of the "seven early masters" (*see* Li Meng-yang) of the middle years of the Ming who advocated a return to the style of T'ang and pre-T'ang in poetry and Han or pre-Han in prose. He is also known as one of the "four outstanding poets" (四傑) of his time, following in the footsteps of Li Meng-yang, Ho Ching-ming, and Hsü Chen-ch'ing (*qq.v.*). His poetry, superb in five-character verse, is distinguished by its natural and elegant style and occasional outbursts of wit.

Pien Kung's collection of prose entitled *Pien Hua-ch'üan chi kao* 華泉集稿, 6 *ch.*, and his collected poems, *Pien Hua-ch'üan chi*, 8 *ch.*, were engraved in 1538. An incomplete copy of the original edition of the prose collection containing the first three *chüan*, with a subtitle *Hua-ch'üan hsien-sheng wen-chi* 先生文集, is preserved in the rare book library of Keiō University, Tokyo. The Library of Congress has a copy of *Pien Hua-ch'üan chi* with prefaces of 1538 and 1544. A collated edition of the two known as *Ch'üan-chi* 全集 was printed in 1705, and reprinted with revisions in 1805 and 1912. A selection of his poetry, 4 *ch.*, was printed in 1700 by Wang Shih-chen (EC CP), a great admirer of Pien Kung, in his *Yü-yang san-shih-liu chung* 漁洋三十六種, which includes also the work of Pien's youngest son, Pien Hsi 習 (T. 仲子),

called *Shui-tsu-hsüan* 睡足軒, or *Pien Chung-tzu shih* 仲子詩, 1 *ch.*

Bibliography

1/286/18a; 5/31/71a; 40/31/11b; 84/ 丙 /65b; MSL (1965), Shih-tsung, 1676, 1849, 2482, 2871, 2987; SK (1930), 171/7b, 176/3a; Ho Ch'iao-yüan, *Ming-shan ts'ang*, 81/16b; *Li-ch'eng-hsien chih* (1773), 17/38a, 21/2a, 29/12a, 17a, 18b, 37/20a, 40/13a; *Pien Hua-ch'üan chi* (1538), NCL microfilm; Li Meng-yang, *Li Kung-t'ung chi* 44/15b; Ho Liang-chün, *Ssu-yu-chai ts'ung-shuo*, 26/2, 3; Chang Hsüan, *Hsi-yüan wen-chien lu*, 23/5b; Wang Shih-chen, *Yü-yang san-shih-liu chung* (1700), Bk. 69; *Keio gijuku toshokan zō wakan sho zenhon kaidai* 慶應義塾藏和漢書善本解題 (1958), 167; Ping-ti Ho, *The Ladder of Success in Imperial China* (New York, 1962), 146.

Hok-lam Chan

PIEN Wen-chin 邊文進 (T. Ching-chao 景昭), *ca.* 1356-1428 +, a man of learning, a poet, but best remembered as a painter of flowers, fruit, birds, and animals, was a native of Sha-hsien 沙縣, Fukien. A good deal of uncertainty surrounds both his name and place of origin. Certain authorities give his *ming* as Ching-chao and his *tzu* as Wen-chin; they also record his birthplace as Lung-hsi 隴西, Kansu; actually, however, his family had moved south before he was born. In the period of Yung-lo he began to serve as an artist (待詔) in the Wu-ying-tien 武英殿. When Chu Chan-chi (*q.v.*) came to the throne (1426), Pien, in response to the emperor's request for talented men, recommended Lu Yüeh 陸悅 and Liu Kuei 劉珪. But a censor reported that they had police records, and that they had bribed Pien to forward their names to the throne. This terminated Pien's official service (January 10, 1427). He was reduced to a commoner but not further punished, the emperor taking pity on him as he had passed the age of seventy *sui*.

H. A. Giles, translating a passage from the *Ch'ang-chou chih* 常州志, writes that "the human figures of Chiang Tzu-ch'eng 蔣子成, the tigers of Chao Lien 趙

廉, and the plumage of Pien Wen-chin were collectively known as the three wonders of the age." Han Ang in his supplement (1519) to the *T'u-hui pao-chien* of Hsia Wen-yen (for both *see* Lan Ying), makes this comment: "In his brushwork, Pien achieved mastery in his portrayal of his subjects, whether they were the pleasing smile of a flower, the flight of a bird in song, or the light and shade of leaves. His use of color, moreover, was exactly right."

Pien's paintings, generally in color, are known in China, Japan, and in the West. The Hermitage (Leningrad) boasts the possession of a realistic painting on silk in color, showing two geese and a flowering tree in the foreground and a pheasant in the background. Another of his paintings in color, entitled "Ch'un-hua san-hsi" 春花三喜 (Spring blossoms and three magpies), preserved in the Palace Museum, shows two magpies, fighting amid some rocks on a slope, their feathers flying, each trying to seize the other's bill with its claws. Green bamboo trees, tender bamboo shoots, and red azaleas among the rocks dominate the background. A third magpie, perched on one of the branches, screams at the two fighters. It is lifelike and full of vigor.

Pien had two sons, Pien Ch'u-hsiang (or fang) 楚祥 (芳) and Pien Ch'u-shan 善; also a son-in-law, Chang K'o-hsin 張克信, and a nephew, Yü Ts'un-sheng 俞存勝, all of whom were painters.

Bibliography

65/6/2b; MSL (1963), Hsüan-tsung, 0618; *Yen-p'ing-fu chih* 延平府志 (1873), 31/26a; Han Ang, *T'u-hui pao-chien, hsü-tsuan* 續纂; Huang Hsi-fan 黃錫蕃 (Ch'ing dynasty), *Min-chung shu-hua lu* 閩中書畫錄, 4/14a; *Ku-kung yüeh-k'an* 故宮月刊, 7 (March 1939), pl. 11; Sun T'a-kung 孫豀公, *Chung-kuo hua-chia jen-ming ta tz'u-tien* 中國畫家人名大辭典 (1962), 720; TSCC (1885–88), XVII: 183/17/18a; H. A. Giles, *History of Chinese Pictorial Art* (Shanghai, 1918), 177; O. Sirén, *Chinese Painting*, VII (New York, 1956–58), 221; E. J. Laing, *Chinese Paintings in Chinese Publications, 1956–1958* (Ann Arbor, 1969), 182; H. Vanderstappen, "Painters at the early Ming court," MS, 15 (1956), 297.

L. Carrington Goodrich and Lee Hwa-chou

PIEN Wen-yü 卞文瑜 (T. 潤甫, H. 浮白, 花龕老人), a painter from Ch'ang-chou 長洲, near Soochow. It has been suggested that his name may originally have been Hsü 徐, but was changed to Pien for some reason. Pien Wen-yü seems to have had a very long career, active from 1616 to 1654. He studied with, or rather learned from, Tung Ch'i-ch'ang (ECCP), and his landscape motifs such as trees, rock, and mountains are a weak image of the great master's work.

Pien Wen-yü was considered by Wang Chieh 王節 (T. 貞明, 1599-1660) as one who could capture the true spirit of all the Sung and Yüan masters, thus rivaling Shen Chou (*q.v.*) in his art. Wang also reported that Pien painted ever more diligently toward the end of his life before he died in his eighties. According to Wang, Pien stayed with Wang Shih-min (ECCP) for a period of time, and while there benefited from Wang's collection of ancient paintings, making great improvements in his own art. Wang Chieh's death in 1660 makes the work attributed to Pien, but dated later than 1660, at least problematical. Pien lived to participate in the last phase of the Southern School 南宗 movement, when a few limited landscape forms were maneuvered within equally limited compositional devices (*see* Ku Cheng-i). Because of his industrious study of the Sung and Yüan masters, he was able to increase his repertoire. For this he received much praise. One other reason for his popularity is the fact that Wu Wei-yeh (ECCP), in his famous "Hua-chung-chiu-yu ko" 畫中九友歌 (Song of nine friends in the art of painting), included Pien Wen-yü along with Tung Ch'i-ch'ang, Wang Shih-min, Ch'eng Chia-sui, Wang Chien, Yang Wen-ts'ung (all in ECCP), Li Liu-fang, Shao

Mi (*qq.v.*), and Chang Hsüeh-tseng 張學增 (T. 爾唯, H. 約庵).

The National Palace Museum at Taipei has two of his albums, "Mo ku shan-shui ts'e" 摹古山水册 and "Su t'ai shih ching ts'e" 蘇臺十景册. The former, dated 1653, is a collection of twenty leaves painted in the styles of various ancient masters, and the latter, dated 1654, has ten leaves depicting scenes in and around his native Soochow.

Bibliography

Ming-hua-lu (1962), V/65; Sun T'a-kung 孫礊公, *Chung-kuo hua-chia jen-ming ta-tz'u-tien* 中國畫家人名大辭典(1962), 13 (this work quotes 藝芳書畫錄 as the source on Pien's original name); *T'u-hui-pao-chien hsü-tsuan* 圖繪寶鑑續纂 (1962), 1/10; Ch'in Tsu-yung 秦祖永, *T'ung-yin lun-hua* 桐陰論畫, 上/2a; *Ku-kung shu-hua-lu (tseng-ting-pen)* 故宮書畫錄 (增訂本), VI/83.

Nelson Wu

PIRES, Tomé, *ca.* 1468-*ca.* May, 1524, (known in Chinese records as Chia-pi-tan-mo 加必丹末 = capitão mor, and even as Huo-che Ya-san 火者亞三), first Portuguese envoy to China, born either in Leira or in Lisbon, was the son of the apothecary to João II (r. 1481-95), who became an apothecary himself in the service of Prince Afonso (1475-91). Manuel I (r. 1495-1521) arranged for him to proceed to India, commending him to Afonso de Albuquerque, then "governor" of the Indies, as a possible director of a vacant trading post. In 1511 Pires left Portugal in an armada commanded by Garcia de Noronha, hoping that he might open a drug shop somewhere. On his arrival in India, Albuquerque sent him on to Malacca as clerk of a trading post and as controller of the apothecary stores. During these years (1512-16), Pires visited some of the neighboring islands to study various species of native plants, acquiring in Java, for example, a supply of cloves. In a letter which he wrote in 1516 to King Manuel he reported on his examina-tion of medicinal herbs—a report which was later to inspire the Portuguese physician Garcia de Orta (d. 1570), author of a treatise on the drugs of India, published in Goa in 1563, who followed him to the East. In these same years he wrote the *Suma Oriental*, called by its translator "surely the most important and complete account of the East produced in the first half of the sixteenth century." It includes, writes J. M. Braga, "the earliest description of China . . . after the book of Marco Polo." Among interesting points about Southeast Asia, Pires tells of a heavy demand in Cochin China in his day for sulphur and saltpetre imports. This helps to explain the developing use of explosive powder in southeast Asia.

In 1516 Lopo Soares de Albergaria, successor to Albuquerque, appointed Pires ambassador to China. João de Barros, writing a few decades later on this choice, has this to say (as translated by A. Corte-são): "Although he was not a man of very much quality, being an apothecary, and serving in India to choose the drugs which should come to this kingdom, he was most skilled for it; for besides his distinction and natural inclination to letters, according to his ability, and his liberality and tact in negotiation, he was very curious in enquiring and knowing things, and he had a lively mind for everything." In June of the following year Pires joined a small flotilla of eight vessels (three of them junks), all armed and carrying Chinese pilots, commanded by Fernão Peres de Andrade. In reached Canton in September. When Andrade returned to Malacca the following year, he left Pires behind. Two years later (January 23, 1520) Pires and his staff started the long journey to Peking in three galleys. At the Mei-ling Pass 梅嶺關, on the border between Kwangtung and Kiangsi, they left the boats and proceeded in litters, on horseback, or on foot. They reached Nanking in May, having lost one of their party, Duarte Fernandez, en route. It so happens that Emperor Chu Hou-chao (*q.v.*) was currently in Nanking. When he heard that Pires wished to see him, he agreed to an audience in Peking on his return. Pires probably reached the capital, presumably via the Grand Canal, in July of the same year, and was lodged in the Hui-t'ung-kuan 會同館 (hostelry for foreign envoys). In the meantime the emperor was in no hurry to go back to the capital; he re-entered Peking on January 18, 1521, a sick man, and was to die within three months. At once all foreign envoys (the *shih-lu* specifies tribute-bearers from Hami, Turfan, and Fo-lang-chi 佛朗機) were ordered to return home. So Pires and his party were forced to leave (either April 22 or May 22, 1521, and arrived in Canton three months later.

During their approximately ten months in Peking they were apparently confined to quarters, and had little or no chance to plead their cause. Officials at court, however, were active in building up a case against the Portuguese. They discovered a major discrepancy between a sealed letter from King Manuel and letters written by Chinese interpreters for Peres de Andrade. Information came too from Canton and Malacca, relating Portuguese seizure of the latter, and describing their improprieties and mischief in the former. While the emperor, if he had lived, might have tolerated their presence and been willing to receive the embassy —one member of the mission (Christovão Vieyra) later reported that the emperor responded to the above charges: "These people do not know our customs; gradually they will get to know them"—, following his death the officials had their way and carried it out with the utmost dispatch.

On their arrival in Canton they were housed in various prisons, the items of "tribute" meant for the throne being kept under Pires' control. According again to Vieyra, the captors "treated us like free people." They may even have been permitted female companionship, for the same authority writes of "the women of the interpreters and also those of Tomé Pires." After a month or so they and certain Malays were summoned to the provincial court, ordered to kneel, and informed that the emperor required Pires to see that the Portuguese withdrew from Malacca. Pires replied that he knew nothing of what was happening in Malacca and could not discuss the question. The interrogation lasted four hours; when finally released, they were led to their places of confinement. On August 14, 1522, with chains on their wrists and irons on their feet Pires and his associates were paraded through the city to the provincial surveillance office. There the fetters were removed to be replaced by still stronger ones. Overcome by this punishment, one of Pires' companions, Antonio d'Almeida, died. That same evening Pires was once more chained and conducted barefoot and bareheaded to the provincial prison to inspect the "tribute" which had to be inventoried. That done, his fetters and those of his staff were removed but they were still held in prison. Two years later Pires died. (Damião Góis writes that he may have been poisoned.) Vieyra is authority for the statement that, of the original embassy of thirteen persons, only three remained: himself, "a Persian from Ormuz, and a lad of mine from Goa." There is a dispute both as to the date of Pires' death and his (second) name in Chinese. Paul Pelliot, after reviewing all the evidence, came to the conclusion that he died probably in May, 1524, and that the name Huo-che Ya-san, which he suggests is a Chinese attempt to render Ḫōja Asan (given in the *Ming-shih* as the name of the Portuguese ambassador), is actually the name of a subordinate envoy from Malacca (*see* Chu Hou-chao). A. Cortesão, however, who wrote before Pelliot's article appeared, believed that Pires was banished from Canton about the end of 1523 and died shortly before 1540. Chang T'ien-tse, in his rebuttal of Pelliot, holding that Pires' Chinese name at some point had been changed to Hou-che Ya-san, maintains that he died not later than 1523.

Five documents written by Pires are known: 1) a letter written from Malacca on November 7, 1512, to his brother João Fernand, a belt and saddle maker by profession, then residing in Lisbon; 2) a letter written from Malacca on January 10, 1513; 3) a letter of the same date addressed to Albuquerque; 4) the *Suma Oriental* written in Malacca and in India in the years 1512 to 1515; and 5) a letter written from Cochin on January 27, 1516, to King Manuel on certain drugs and other matters of the Orient.

Bibliography

1/325/19a; MSL (1965), Wu-tsung, 2911, 3603, 3630, 3682, Shih-tsung, 0086, 0208; KC (1958), 3631; Ku Ying-hsiang, quoted in Mao Yüan-i, *Wu-pei chih*, 122/7b; Chang Wei-hua 張維華, "P'u-t'ao-ya ti-i-tz'u lai-Hua...." 葡萄牙第一次來華..., *Shih-hsüeh nien-pao* 史學年報, 5 (1933), 103; *id.*, *Ming-shih fo-lang-chi lü-sung...chu-shih* 明史佛朗機呂宋...注釋, YCHP mon. series #7, Peiping, 1934; Chang T'ien-tse, *Sino-Portuguese Trade from 1514 to 1644* (Leyden, 1934), 38; *id.*, "Malacca and the Failure of the First Portuguese Embassy to Peking," JSAH, 3 (September, 1962), 45; Paul Pelliot, "Le Ḫōja et le Sayyid Ḥusain de l'histoire des Ming," TP, 38 (1947), 81; Armando Cortesão, tr. ed., *The Suma Oriental of Tomé Pires*, 2 vols., London, 1944; *id.*, "A propósito do illustre Boticário Quinhentista Tomé Pires," *Revista Portuguesa de Farmácia*, Vol. XIII, no. 3 (September, 1963), 298; João de Barros and Deogo do Couto, *Asia* (new ed., Lisbon 1777-88, 24 vols.), II, chap. VII, 217; Damião Góis, *Crónica do Felicissimo Rei Dom Manuel* (Coimbra, 1924), pt. 4, 59; Donald Ferguson, *Letters from Portuguese Captives in Canton Written in 1534 and 1536*, Bombay, 1902; C. R. Boxer, *South China in the Sixteenth Century* (London, 1953), xx; *Grand Enciclopedia Portuguesa e Brasileira*, Vol. 21, 948; Diogo Barbosa Machado, *Bibliotheca Lusitana*, Vol. 3 (Coimbra, 1966), 760; J. M. Braga, "A Portuguese Account of East Asia in 1514," THM, 9:1 (August, 1939), 378.

Albert Chan and L. Carrington Goodrich

QONINČI, fl. *ca.* 1376-*ca.* 1394, a Mongol born in China and familiar with the Chinese language and script, was appointed Mongolian compiler in the Hanlin Academy on April 18, 1376. By 1382 he was an expositor in the Academy, and had sinicized his Mongolian name to Huo Yüan-chieh 火源潔 (also written 火原潔 and 火你亦); earlier he appears also to have used another sinicized name, Huo Chuang 霍莊. On January 20, 1382, he and a certain Mašāīḥ Muḥammad or Ma Šaīḥ Muḥammad (Ma-sha-i-hei Ma-ha-ma 馬沙亦黑馬哈馬, with a sinicized surname), *et al.* were ordered by the first emperor to compile a Sino-Mongolian bilingual text; this was the *Hua-i i-yü* 華夷譯語, which was completed in 1388 and printed the following year with a preface dated November 3, 1389, by the celebrated literatus Liu San-wu (*q.v.*). The completed *Hua-i i-yü* makes no mention of Qoninči's Muslim collaborator who was also a Hanlin compiler, though in what language is not clear; perhaps he died before its publication, and his role in the preparation of this Sino-Mongolian bilingual document is obscure at best.

The *Hua-i i-yü* of 1389 consists of three parts: 1) a Chinese-Mongolian lexicon, giving Mongolian equivalents for Chinese terms arranged under seventeen traditional semantic categories (astronomy, geography, the seasons, botany, zoology, etc.), with the Mongolian transcribed phonetically into Chinese script; 2) the Mongolian texts, transcribed phonetically into Chinese script and furnished with interlinear word-for-word and smooth line-by-line Chinese translations, of five documents from the Chinese court and Chinese officials to the Mongols; and 3) the Mongolian texts, similarly transcribed, of seven documents from Mongols to Chinese officials, with word-for-word interlinear Chinese translations only. One of these documents is dated (November 6, 1388); one of the others can be shown by internal evidence to date from before November, 1384, the remainder from early November, 1388, through August, 1389. All the Mongolian in the *Hua-i i-yü* is transcribed in Chinese characters, with no use of the Uighur or other non-Chinese scripts. The transcription is similar to that employed in the Chinese recension of the *Mongγol-un Ni'uča Tobča'an* as the *Yüan-ch'ao pi-shih* 元朝秘史 (The secret history of the Mongols) with which work both Qoninči and Mašāīḫ Muḥammad were also associated.

In the *Hua-i i-yü* transcription, which uses some 436 different graphs, the Chinese script is used in an impressively precise fashion. The Chinese unaspirated and aspirated voiceless initials are regularly used for the Mongolian voiced and voiceless initials, respectively; an attempt is made to indicate Mongolian vowel harmony, if only in those few cases where the syllabic structure of the fourteenth century Chinese permitted; and most significantly of all, a small number of Chinese graphs are used with considerable rigor as diacritics to indicate non-Chinese sounds or sounds found in Chinese but occurring in Mongolian in positions in the syllable where they did not appear in Chinese. The Chinese characters used as diacritics are printed smaller than the rest of the text and to the right or left and below the character to which they refer, thus 丁安 for Mongol *al, i. e.,* Chinese *an* with a small diacritic 丁 to indicate the non-Chinese final-*l*, 舌羅 for *ra,* Chinese *la* plus a diacritic for initial *r-,* and 中合 for back-velar *qa.* Thus, 中忽舌魯溫 = *quru'un* 'finger', with small diacritic 中 for the back-velar initial, small 舌 for *-r-* instead of *-l-,* and 魯 for *-l/ru*-rather than *-l/rü-,* which would have been 呂; again, 斡莎勒丹 = *osoldan,* the *converbum modale* of *osalda-*'be lazy', with 莎 for *-so-* and small 勒 for *-l-,* against 雪你 = *söni* 'night'. By these methods the Chinese script was made into a very useful medium for recording Mongolian, one far more efficient than the Uighur script with its many ambiguities. The Chinese transcriptions in the *Hua-i i-yü* have fewer instances than those in the *Secret History* where the choice of transcription characters was clearly influenced by semantic considerations, as if the author were attempting to render not only the sound but also the sense of the foreign original; this has been used in the past to argue for dating the Chinese version of the *Secret History* after the *Hua-i i-yü,* but is now generally thought to be a more effective argument for the reverse relationship. The two texts stand in a complex relationship with each other, one considerably obscured by lack of information concerning earlier texts and drafts, now lost, from which they both probably represent later descent.

The compilation of the *Hua-i i-yü* of 1389 shows the importance which the first Ming emperor placed on a command of the Mongolian language, and how significant Mongolian was in his time for dealings with the then still recently deposed Mongol power. Its authorship also is a significant comment on the membership of the Hanlin Academy at the time, since both Qoninči and Mašāīḫ Muḥammad were occupying posts normally reserved for Chinese degree holders. (The Ssu-i kuan 四夷館 [College of translators] was established under the Hanlin Academy several years later [*see* Cheng Ho]; even after its reassignment to the Court of Imperial Sacrifices in 1496 it remained under Hanlin supervision.)

Qoninči was also probably a compiler of another, purely Chinese-language work, the *Huan-yü t'ung-ch'ü* 寰宇通衢, completed in 1394, dealing with stagestops and distances from the capital to various parts of the Empire. Later his sinicized name Huo Yüan-chieh became virtually a byword for all Sino-foreign vocabularies, and several subsequent *Hua-i i-yü* type works dealing with languages other than Mongolian were ascribed to him, though geographical and chronological considerations rule out any actual connection.

Because of its extensive data and the precision of its transcriptions the *Hua-i i-yü* of 1389 is a priceless linguistic source for Middle Mongolian, and as such has been extensively laid under contribution by all modern Mongolists, notably F. Cleaves, A. Mostaert, P. Pelliot, and N. Poppe, while E. Haenisch and M. Lewicki have both made it the subject of extensive monographs.

Bibliography

Hua-i i-yü Ming Palace edition of 1389 reproduced with 1918 postface by SunYü-hsiu 孫毓修 in *Han-fen-lou pi-chi* 涵芬樓秘笈, coll. 4; SK (1930), 43/3b; M. Lewicki, "La langue mongole des transcriptions chinoises du XIVᵉ siècle. Le Houa-yi yi-yu de 1389, édition critique précédée des observations philologiques et accompagné de la reproduction phototypique du texte" (Wroclaw, 1949); *id.*, "La langue mongole des transcriptions chinoises du XIVᵉ siècle, Le Houa-yi yi-yu de 1389, II, Vocabulaire-index" (Wroclaw, 1959); E. Haenisch, "Sino-mongolische Dokumente vom Ende des 14, Jahrhunderts," *Abhandlungen der Deutschen Akademie der Wissenschaften zu Berlin, Klasse für Sprachen, Literatur und Kunst* (Jahrgang, 1950) Nr. 4 (published 1952; contains [p. 6ff.] translations of the 1389 preface by Liu San-wu and the 1918 postface by SunYü-hsiu; *id.*, "Sino-mongolische Glossare, I, Das Hua-I ih-yü," *ibid.* (Jahrgang, 1956) Nr. 5; P. Pelliot, "Le Sseu-yi-kouan et le Houei-t'ong-kouan," = Appendice III to "Le Ḫōja et le Sayyid Ḥusain de l'Histoire des Ming," TP, 38 (1948), 207; W. Hung, "The Transmission of the Book Known as *The Secret History of the Mongols*," HJAS, 14 (1951), 433; H. Serruys, "The Dates of the Mongolian Documents in the *Hua-yi i-yü*," HJAS, 17 (1954), 419; *id.*, "The Mongols in China during the Hung-wu Period," MCB, 11 (1959), 1; Murayama Shichirō, "On the chronological relation between the *Yüan ch'ao pi-shih* and the *Hua-i i-yü* (in Japanese), *Tōhōgaku*, 22 (1961), 130 (*sic*); R. A. Miller, "Qoninči, Compiler of the *Hua-i i-yü* of 1389," *Ural-Altaische Jahrbücher*, 38 (1966), 112.   *Roy Andrew Miller*

QORγOČIN 火里火眞, 1349-September 23, 1409, a Mongol officer who surrendered to the Ming court at the beginning of the dynasty, was a distinguished military commander in the service of the future emperor, Chu Ti (*q.v.*). The early years of Qorγočin are obscure. He is reported to have hailed from a place near K'ai-p'ing 開平, the Shangtu cf the Mongol emperors, and to have joined the Yüan army in his early youth. The area from which Qorγočin came was settled by Chinese farmers and opened to Chinese influence at an early stage. It may be assumed, therefore, that he acquired some knowledge of the Chinese language and an understanding of Chinese life. After September, 1368, Qorγočin withdrew with the retreating Mongol armies into southern Mongolia, and, since K'ai-p'ing after this date came under Ming control, he must have fled to some place much farther to the north. On August 9, 1381, according to the *shih-lu*, Qorγočin, leading a sizable group of his people, arrived in Peiping to surrender; they received a handsome reward and were ordered to settle in the area. In subsequent records, Qorγočin's name is generally reduced to two characters, Huo Chen 火眞; the first one being improperly considered his surname, and the second his personal name.

After his surrender, Qorγočin received an appointment as battalion commander in the central protective guard of Yen-shan 燕山中護衞, one of the military garrisons of Peiping under the command of Chu Ti, then prince of Yen. The guard was made up of the surrendered Mongol households. In July, 1399, when Chu Ti launched his campaign aimed at displacing his nephew, Chu Yün-wen (*q.v.*), Qorγočin sided with the prince and took active part in the military operations. He commanded an independent unit and was credited with twice defeating (in September) the government forces under Keng Ping-wen (*q.v.*) at the battle of Chen-ting 眞定, south of Peiping. He also accompanied Chu Ti when in November the latter marched north to occupy the strategic town of Ta-ning 大寧 in present-day Jehol. In these campaigns Qorγočin commanded the Mongol cavalry, breaking through the enemy ranks recklessly, and was acclaimed for his bravery and determination. On October 3, 1402, he was appointed to the hereditary rank of marquis of T'ung-an 同安, with an annual stipend of 1,500 *shih* of rice.

Some time after 1402 Qorγočin, together with Wang Ts'ung 王聰 (1356–1409; ennobled as marquis of Wu-ch'eng 武城 in 1402), was sent to Hsüan-fu in charge of the defense of the northern frontier to prepare against possible Mongol intrusion. The *shih-lu* mentions them several times, always together, not so much for direct military action as for defense measures which they undertook against the Mongol threat. Although no major clashes occurred during these days, the relations between China and Mongolia remained strained; the fact that Qorγočin, a Mongol officer recently surrendered, was given such great responsibility, indicates the trust the emperor placed in him.

In 1409 Qorγočin became involved in a major operation against the Mongols in the heart of their own domain. This occurred after news reached Peiping in July that the Mongol chieftain Bunyaširi (*see* Aruγtai) had killed the envoys whom the emperor had sent to the Mongol camp for the improvement of relations. In consternation, Chu Ti in August commanded Ch'iu Fu 丘福 (ennobled the duke of Ch'i 淇 in October, 1402) to head an expeditionary force of a hundred thousand men against Bunyaširi; four generals, including Qorγočin and Wang Ts'ung, served under him. The Chinese vanguard rapidly advanced without much opposition and soon reached the Kerülen River in upper Mongolia, to which the Mongols had retreated steadily, seemingly reluctant to engage in battle. The generals continued to warn Ch'iu Fu against falling into a trap; they favored building a camp and keeping on the defensive until the main body of the army arrived. Ch'iu nevertheless refused to stop the advance, and even ordered Qorγočin forward, on the pretext that he was an envoy begging for peace. Qorγočin hesi-

tated, but Ch'iu threatened to execute anyone who did not obey his orders. On September 23 the Chinese met an ambush and were annihilated by the Mongol cavalry. Ch'iu Fu and the other generals, including Qorγočin, were captured and put to death. Qorγočin was then sixty years of age. As scapegoats, Ch'iu Fu and Qorγočin were posthumously disgraced. Qorγočin was stripped of the title of marquis, though he had served the Ming faithfully.

Qorγočin's descendants received appointments to the hereditary rank of battalion commander in the Kuan-hai 觀海 guard on the coast of northern Chekiang. One of his grandsons, Huo Pin 斌 (T. 德光), served as a commander under Yü Ta-yü (*q.v.*) in the suppression of the *wo-k'ou* on the Chekiang coast during the Chia-ching period. He was killed in an encounter with the enemy on P'u-to Island 普陀山 off the coast of Ting-hai 定海, on May 1, 1554. Acting on the petition of an elder brother, also a military commander, the local authorities erected a shrine to the memory of Huo Pin and one other officer who died with him; it was called Chung-yung tz'u 忠勇祠 (Shrine for the loyal and brave).

Bibliography

1/145/13a; 3/134/13a; 61/140/13b; MSL (1962), T'ai-tsu, 2178, T'ai-tsung (1963), ch. 5–95, Shih-tsung (1965), 7130; KC (1958), 1026; Cheng Jo-tseng, *Ch'ou-hai t'u-pien*, 9/3b; *Tz'u-ch'i-hsien chih* 慈谿縣志 (1890), 28/44a;. Chang Hung-hsiang 張鴻翔, "Ming wai-tsu tz'u-hsing k'ao" 明外族賜姓考, *Fu-jen hsüeh-chih* 輔仁學誌, Vol. 3, no. 2 (1932), 22; Henry Serruys, *The Mongols in China during the Hung-wu Period (1368–1398)*, (Brussels, 1959), 247; L. Hambis, *Documents sur l'histoire des Mongols à l'époque des Ming* (Paris, 1969), 21.

Hok-lam Chan

QUTUγTAI 虎禿大-sečen qung-tayiji was a grandson of the jinong Gün-bilig-mergen 袞必里克墨爾根(濟農). According to the chronicle written by his famous descendant Saγang-sečen, he was born in

1540 and died in 1586. This latter date is confirmed by Chinese records which always refer to him as Ch'ieh-chin huang-t'ai-chi 切盡黃台吉, i. e., Sečen (Čečen) qung-tayiji. His youth of course prevented him from taking part, or playing an important role, in many border invasions. At any rate he is mentioned much less frequently than either the jinong Gün-bilig-mergen and Altan-qaγan (q.v.), or the latter's son, Sengge-dügüreng qung-tayiji (see Altan-qaγan), although otherwise he seems to have been no less active than any of the other princes of the Ordos. Saγang-sečen records campaigns conducted by him against the Oirat and other nations of central Asia in 1562, 1572, and 1574; also in northern Tibet in 1566. [Editors' note: According to Wada Sei 和田清 the exploits of Qutuγtai-sečen qung-tayiji in central Asia included a raid on the Turghud土爾扈特 tribe (1562) near Ili. Half a century later the Turghud were forced by neighboring tribes to migrate to the lower Volga valley where they were visited by Tulišen (EC CP) in 1714 and whence they returned to the Ili region in 1771. Their sufferings from the long journey and the attacks by the Cossacks on the way inspired Thomas De Quincey (1785–1859) to compose his essay, "Revolt of the Tartars, the Flight of the Kalmuck Khan."]

When relations between Altan-qaγan and the Ming were being regularized in 1570 and 1571, Qutuγtai-sečen was sent by his uncle the jinong Noyandara 那言大兒 (1522–72) to the headquarters of Altan-qaγan to arrange with the governor-general of Tatung, Wang Ch'ung-ku (q.v.) for tribute relations for the Ordos as well. The governor-general of the three military districts of Shensi was of the opinion that the Ordos Mongols could not be accepted immediately as tribute barbarians until they had proved themselves by abstaining from all border raids for at least one year. Wang Ch'ung-ku, however, argued that such a delay would only complicate matters unnecessarily and

perhaps make a final settlement impossible; it would have to be the Ordos and the Tümed together or none at all. Wang thought that if the Ordos were left out of the arrangement they would continue their border raids while at the same time trying to pass for Tümed Mongols taking part in border trade; and on the other hand, the Tümed, while to all external appearances at peace with China, would still be able to take part in border raids organized by the Ordos. Wang's views prevailed, and in 1571, only a few days after the Tümed princess had been granted honorary rank, forty-nine outstanding princes of the Ordos were also given similar ranks with the right to present a yearly tribute and to trade in several border markets. Qutuγtai-sečen was given the rank of a chih-hui ch'ien-shih 指揮僉事 (assistant commander of a guard), a rank far too low to please him. Shortly afterwards, in July, 1572, at the request of Wang Ch'ung-ku. he was promoted to vice commander. Some time later Qutuγtai-sečen expressed the desire to be made a marquis or an earl, no doubt because Altan-qaγan had been made a prince 王 in 1571, but this dignity was never bestowed upon him. Around 1577, Altan-qaγan requested for him the title of tu-tu 都督 (commissioner-in-chief), but this was never granted either. In 1579 and 1580 Qutuγtai-sečen, at the time of the tribute presentation, called himself a general of the dragon and tiger (lung-hu chiang-chün 龍虎將軍); indeed around that time, or shortly thereafter, he was granted that title. Saγang-sečen relates that the Chinese had gone back on their promise to make him a lung-hu chiang-chün and that Qutuγtai-sečen, angry over the refusal, plundered a number of Chinese towns in 1580. Chinese records mention no such large scale raid for 1580, and Saγang-sečen must be in error both for the raid and the year, but it is certain that for a number of years Qutuγtai-sečen had been trying to secure a higher title from the Ming. That he should have violated the borders in order to force the hand of the Chinese, however, is highly improbable. Chinese records are full of praise for his diligence in enforcing the agreements of 1571; not that all occasions of friction or incidents could be entirely avoided. He earnestly tried, however, to prevent his own subjects and his fellow princes from harming the Chinese population, especially on their frequent trips through Kansu territory when going to or coming from Köke-nuur. On more than one occasion Qutuɣtai-sečen was granted special rewards for maintaining order at the horse fairs.

Qutuɣtai-sečen never became jinong or supreme ruler of the Ordos tribes, yet he was perhaps the most influential man in the Ordos during his lifetime. Most of his prestige was due no doubt to his friendship with Altan-qaɣan of the Tümed and later to his role in reviving Lamaism in Mongolia and inviting (1577–78) the Dalai-lama of Lhasa to visit Mongolia. Chinese records describe him as "intelligent, skilled in letters, and versed in Buddhist doctrine." He is also noted for his deep devotion to Buddhism.

When Altan-qaɣan presented his first tribute in July, 1571, the vassal letter (piao 表) accompanying the tribute had been composed by Qutuɣtai-sečen. This document, certainly written in Mongol, had to be rewritten because "it was full of Buddhist terms," and also because a Chinese version had to be forwarded to the court in a style approved for this sort of document. Qutuɣtai-sečen seems to have gained some knowledge of Tibetan and Chinese through reading sūtras, but it is very doubtful that he was able to write Chinese. At any rate, the Ming court decreed special rewards to him for composing the piao.

No sooner had peaceful relations with China been established than, like Altan qaɣan, he repeatedly requested sūtras, Buddhist rosaries, and other objects for the cult from the Chinese. Officials were much impressed with his devotion to Lamaism and tended to encourage it in the hope that it would make for continued peaceful contacts. According to Saɣang-sečen, it was Qutuɣtai-sečen who first suggested to Altan-qaɣan in 1577 that he invite the Dalai-lama to Mongolia. This is confirmed in a way by Chinese sources which state that Qutuɣtai-sečen had waged several unsuccessful wars against Tibetan tribes; he had tried to obtain the cooperation of Altan-qaɣan, but the latter, who was getting on in years and weary of the strain of such expeditions, had consistently refused until Qutuɣtai-sečen persuaded him to go along with his men to meet the Dalai-lama in Köke-nuur. How much of this version is true; how much of a warlike design lay behind the trip is difficult to make out; but the fact that no military action ensued was due, according to Chinese historians, to the exhortations of the Dalai-lama. It seems to have been Bingtü 兵 (or 丙) 兔 who took advantage of the presence of Altan-qaɣan in Köke-nuur to raid Tibetan tribes; Qutuɣtai-sečen was not involved, and Altan-qaɣan tried to enforce order.

The Dalai-lama declared Qutuɣtai-secen to be a reincarnation of the early protector of Buddhism and king of Magadha, gZugs-čan sñiṅ-po (in Mongol: čoɣčas-un jirüken: "essence, or heart, of the aggregations of matter") and as such he has always been the object of a cult by the Mongols of the Ordos until recent times.

To Qutuɣtai-sečen is ascribed a revised edition of a work *Arban buyan-tu nom-un čaɣan teüke* (White history of the doctrine of the ten meritorious works), traditionally believed to have been written by Qubilai Khan. His interest in Buddhist literature is also attested by Chinese sources which inform us about a monk by the name of Wan-ch'ung 宛沖 from a monastery called Kuei-hua 歸華, versed in Tatar, Uighur, and Tibetan script, who made translations of Buddhist sūtras for Qutuɣtai-sečen qung-tayiji.

Bibliography

Saɣang-sečen, *Erdeni-yin tobči;* 1/327/25a; Tamura Jetsuzō, *Mindai Mammō shiryō, Min-Jitsuroku-shō,* Mōkohen, Vols. 7, 8; Ch'ü Chiu-ssu 瞿九思 (cj 1573), *Wan-li wu-kung lu, ch.* 7, 14; Wada Sei, *Toa-shi ronsō* 東亞史論藪 (1942), 341; Louis Hambis, *Documents sur l'histoire des Mongols à l'époque des Ming* (Paris, 1969), 224; Henry Serruys, *Sino-Mongol Relations during the Ming,* MCB, XIV (Brussels, 1967), 24, 193, 285, 464; Paul Pelliot, *Notes Critiques d'Histoire Kalmouke* (Paris, 1960), 25, 33; Wolfgang Franke, "Addenda and Corrigenda" to Pokotilov's *History of the Eastern Mongols during the Ming Dynasty from 1368 to 1634, Studia Serica,* ser. A, pt. 2 (Chengtu, 1949), 57.

Henry Serruys

RADA, Martín de, July 20, 1533-June, 1578, scientist and Augustinian friar in Mexico and the Philippines, who visited Fukien in 1575, was born into a noble family of Pamplona, capital of Navarra, Spain. In the autumn of 1544 he went to the University of Paris, where he showed extraordinary aptitude for mathematics, geography, astronomy, and languages. In 1552 war between Henry II of France and Charles V of Spain forced him to return home and enroll at the University of Salamanca, where in August, 1553, he entered the Augustinian novitiate, professing his vows a year later. He continued his theological studies at the university, and after priestly ordination was assigned to the convent of San Esteban at Toledo where he made preparations for the Mexican mission. The opportunity came in September, 1559, when Philip II, at the suggestion of Luis de Velasco, viceroy of Mexico, issued a dispatch ordering him to proceed to Mexico. Rada left Spain, while still listed as a member of San Esteban's community, early in 1560, reaching Mexico in May. Once there he was assigned to work among the highland Otomi Indians, whose difficult language he learned with such rapidity that within five months he could preach and later write *Sermones* and *Arte* in Otomi.

Meanwhile the king had invited Andrés de Urdaneta, famous mariner and cosmographer, to make an exploration of the Philippines and find a return route to Mexico. On May 28, 1560, Urdaneta signified his acceptance of the king's request, but stated his belief that the Philippine island of Mindanao lay clearly within the Portuguese demarcation set by the Saragossa treaty of 1529. On February 9, 1564, Rada and four other Augustinians, selected by Urdaneta, were given by their superiors the patent to join the expedition to the Islas del Poniente (West Islands). The fleet left Navidad on November 21 (the tenth anniversary of Rada's profession), without one of their number who had died in port. It comprised the flagship *San Pedro* carrying Commander Miguel López de Legazpi, Navigator Urdaneta, and the friars Rada and Andrés de Aguirre, the galleon *San Pablo* carrying Diego de Herrera and Pedro de Gamboa, and the tenders *San Juan* and *San Lucas.* After sailing one hundred leagues on a southwesterly course, Legazpi opened the secret instructions from the Audiencia which had taken over the direction of the expedition on the death of Viceroy Velasco in July. His instructions were for him to proceed straight to the Philippines. On Urdaneta's urging Rada took along a medium-sized instrument he had invented and produced in Mexico; he expected to determine the longitude from the meridian of Toledo and help Urdaneta check his course and draw accurate sea charts.

The fleet reached Cebu on April 27, 1565. In June Urdaneta took the *San Pedro* back to Mexico, making his way far to the north and swinging south along the California coast and so to Navidad, thus finding the return route. Meanwhile Rada began to learn the Visaya language by his direct method and to catechize the Visaya of Cebu. Soon he opened schools for them and did much charitable work even among the famished Spanish soldiers. Beginning in 1566, he made excursions to Panay, opening stations at Dumangas and Oton. Eager to prepare himself for China, in 1567 he engaged a Chinese servant in order to learn the language. In 1568 a Portuguese squadron led by Gonzalo Pereyra, which was sent by the viceroy of India to oust the Spaniards from Cebu, anchored there. In his exchanges with Pereyra, Governor Legazpi, assisted by Rada, implied that Cebu lay within Portuguese boundaries, but diplomatically endeavored to gain time if not the argument. Indeed, pinched by shortage of food and uncertain of his own government's support, Pereyra eventually withdrew. Free from extraneous cares, Rada (1569) continued his teaching, preaching, studying, and writing. Among other works he compiled an *Arte* and an extensive *Vocabulario* of the Visaya language as an aid to newcomers. Just then a group of Augustinian recruits arrived to join forces with Rada and Herrera. Taking stock of the situation, the friars decided to elect Herrera minister of a prospective Augustinian Philippine province. In this capacity Herrera went to Mexico to seek permission to establish a separate province, to send an appeal for new missionaries also from other religious orders, and to carry various dispatches. Rada entrusted him with a report dated July 8, 1569, to Viceroy Martín Enríquez wherein he explained conditions in Cebu, requested protection for the natives from colonial oppression, and outlined a plan for the temporal and spiritual conquest of China, though he knew little about that country.

In June, 1570, Herrera brought back from Mexico royal and viceregal instructions for the annexation and settlement of the Islands, as well as authorization to set up an Augustinian Philippine province. In a letter dated from Panay July 21, 1570, Rada informed the viceroy that Governor Legazpi had summoned a meeting of captains and missionaries to peruse and implement the instructions, and

once more requested protective measures for the oppressed natives. Back in Cebu he carried to completion his plan for building a new town, the inauguration in November being presided over by Legazpi. Rada did not attend the inauguration of Manila in May, 1571, but was there for the first Augustinian chapter which elected him minister provincial a year later. Better informed on China by a Chinese named Canco (Kuan Kao?) and other Sangleys (ch'ang-lai 常來, travelers), he asked the vicerory on August 10 for permission to send two friars to China. In his letter of the following day, Legazpi told the viceroy that he, too, would send them in one of the returning junks hoping that they might arrange a treaty of peace and friendship with China; the Chinese captains, however, refused to take them without a license from the Fukien provincial authorities. From their explanations made evident by a south China map which they drew in his presence, Legazpi realized that it was a journey of some 10 days and 150 leagues sailing, but his policy was not to disturb the Fukien authorities and endanger the promising China trade. Ten days later the worthy Legazpi, attended by Rada, died of a heart attack and was mourned by the entire colony.

Supported by the new governor, Guido de Lavezares, Rada fostered his mission work through the Island. His eagerness to open China to Christianity was heightened by a block-printed Ming atlas he had secured and described in *Relación de una pintura de molde que trujeron los Chinos este año de 1573*, copies of which he later forwarded to Alonso de Veracruz and the viceroy of Mexico (letters of June 30, 1574). [Editors' note: This map might well have been the *Ch'ou-hai t'u-pien* of Cheng Jo-tseng (*q.v.*), published in 1562.] On his part, in order to make Philip II appreciate the east Asian situation, Lavezares informed him about the growth of the Fukien junk-trade with Luzon despite active piracy (letters of July 16 and 17,

1574), and on July 30 sent him a dispatch with three enclosures: an outline map of Luzon and the China coast, the above-mentioned Chinese atlas, and Rada's *Relación* about the latter, along with useful information on Japan and the Liu-ch'iu Islands. Seven months later the Chinese pirate Lin Feng (*q.v.*) attacked Manila with a seventy-ship armada, setting the town on fire; the conflagration destroyed also some of Rada's books and manuscripts. Rada took an active part in the defense of the city and in the subsequent expedition against the pirate's stronghold on the hills of Pangasinan Bay where Camp-master Juan de Salcedo's forces burned forty pirate ships and set up a blockade (1575). The bottling up of the pirate's forces had lasted only a few weeks when the coast guard junk of Garrison Commander Wang Wang-kao 王望高, who had been ordered by the governor of Fukien to track down Lin Feng, appeared off Pangasinan. Pleased with the encounter, Salcedo invited Wang and Sinsay 信師 (Master Hsin?) a Chinese merchant acting as interpreter, to proceed to Manila and meet with the authorities. The governor gave Wang a cordial welcome and promised him full cooperation in the capture of Lin. In return Wang agreed to take envoys from Manila to the officials in Fukien. Just at that time Rada had finished his term as provincial and had been appointed prior (April, 1575) of the convent of Oton; he was thus available for the China venture. Thereupon Lavezares chose Rada and Jerónimo Marín as envoys to be assisted by officers Miguel de Loarca and Pedro Sarmiento and a staff of fifteen others, who were to return to Manila with the news of the embassy if the Chinese allowed the two friars to remain. The governor instructed Rada to negotiate a trade agreement with China and rights to a trading post such as Macao for the Portuguese, to gather precise information about the Chinese people and their country, to secure permission to preach, and to submit a letter to the emperor.

The embassy left Manila aboard Wang's ship on June 12, 1575, and entered the port of Chung-tso-so 中左所 (old name for Amoy) on July 5, under escort of a whole garrison alerted by the provincial authorities. After complying with local protocol, Rada and party were escorted (July 7) in style to T'ung-an 同安 (Rada's Tangua), where they were met by a representative of the magistrate and the same evening were granted a travel patent issued by the Hsing-ch'üan intendant 興泉道 (Rada's Inzuanto, the intendant of Hsing-hua 化 and Ch'üan-chou 州). On the 8th, after thanking the magistrate for provisions and gifts, the embassy, escorted by a battalion of the intendant, proceeded to Ch'üan-chou (Rada's Chinchiu), where they arrived on the evening of the 9th. There they called on the intendant, made the required prostrations (kowtow) before him, and handed him their credentials and a list of presents. On the following day the intendant sent for the presents and summoned officers Loarca and Sarmiento, a Spanish orderly, and a Sangley as interpreter, and questioned them about Lin Feng, whose capture and doom seemed to be a matter of time. On the 11th the intendant entertained the party at a sumptuous banquet and directed them to call on the governor, Liu Yao-hui 劉堯誨 (T. 君納, 1522–85, cs 1553), at the provincial capital. Accordingly on the 12th Rada and staff were escorted to Hsing-hua and Foochow, where they arrived on the evening of the 17th. The following day they visited the governor and handed him their letter. On the 19th Liu sent for his presents and gave the envoys an elaborate banquet. On the 20th Rada sent him a message asking permission to stay, to learn the language and customs, and to preach. The governor replied that he had to submit the request to the emperor and await his decision, and proceeded to ask many questions about western usages, inventions, and religion.

While the envoys were the guests of

Governor Liu in Foochow, on the night of August 2 Lin Feng broke the blockade and escaped with a makeshift armada of thirty-seven ships built in the Pangasinan woods. Before this bad news reached Fukien, the governor summoned his council and decided to send the envoys back to Manila pending an imperial rescript. Accordingly on August 22 the envoys, accompanied by General Shao Yüeh 邵岳 (Rada's Siahoya Oxiaoguac [Xiaoguac], seemingly two approximate transliterations of the same surname and name; in Fukienese Siao Gak), and Commander Wang Wang-kao left Foochow for Amoy and ultimately Manila. When Rada and party left Amoy in a Chinese squadron of ten war-junks under Wang Wang-kao in the beginning of September, 1575, they were shown the Wu-hsü islet 梧嶼 at the southern entrance of the harbor as one among the likely places for a trading-post, which could be given the Spaniards if Lin Feng were eliminated. But on September 14, while sailing past the Pescadores, the fleet entered the mouth of a river, probably the Cho-shui-ch'i 濁水溪 on Taiwan's west coast, where, according to some fishermen, Lin Feng with eleven of his ships had anchored farther up stream. Therupon Commander Wang summoned a meeting of his officers to decide whether to go back and inform the Chinese authorities about it or to pursue and fight Lin. General Shao Yüeh overruled both propositions, saying that his orders called for returning the envoys to Luzon. Leaving the Pescadores at midnight on October 11, the fleet was caught in a storm in which two ships, Wang's flagship with the envoys aboard and a smaller one, parted company and reached Manila ahead of the others on October 17. On his arrival Rada felt doubly discouraged by the replacement of Governor Lavezares by Dr. Francisco de Sande and by the confirmation of Lin's escape. At any rate Rada brought back a collection of invaluable notes and over one hundred Chinese books covering a comprehensive range of subjects on the geography, history, government, administration, philosophy, religion, sciences, arts, crafts, products, and customs of China. That he was able to gather this precious and complex source material in but two months' stay in Fukien and then organize it into a masterful *Relación* concerning his embassy, together with a penetrating description of China, gives a measure of his versatility.

Owing to Lin's escape, Rada's chances of returning to China grew very slim and soon (Spring, 1576) were ruined by the rude behavior of Governor Sande toward the Chinese captains. Surely that was no fit preparation for Rada's second mission to China which the governor sponsored. In his letters of May 1 and 4, 1576, to Philip II and to Viceroy Enríquez respectively, Rada expressed critcism of Sande and forebodings about his mission. Despite such ill omens, on May 7 Rada and his companion Augustín de Albuquerque embarked on the returning Chinese fleet, the captains of which, however, once at sea made every effort to dissuade the friars from undertaking the crossing to Fukien, arguing that the authorities would not allow them to land and might even kill them. The captains lost patience with the undaunted friars and two weeks later put them ashore in a region inhabited by Zambales headhunters whence they were rescued unharmed by a Spanish patrol and brought back to Manila at the end of May. Writing to Veracruz on June 3, Rada reported the failure of his second expedition to China and, answering his friend's questions, he listed and briefly described the books and papers he had written or had begun, grieving over those he had lost at sea. Though appointed prior by royal order of the convent of Calumpit, Bucalan province, in December, 1576, he resumed his scientific studies and writings at Cebu, his ordinary residence, and at Manila.

Over his protest he was taken away from his studies in January, 1578, when King Sirela of Brunei, dethroned by his own brother, went to Manila for help and made Governor Sande dispatch an armada under Rada's direction to dislodge the usurper and restore order. The operation was partly successful through Rada's prestige and tact, but because of the insalubrious climate and the resulting mortality among the soldiers, Rada had the expedition recalled. During the return journey in mid-June, 1578, Rada died at the age of forty-five and was buried at sea. Thus ended the life of one of the great scholar-missionaries of all time.

Martín de Rada produced a number of books and essays on religion, geography, ethnology, history, languages, and mathematics, some of which were lost while he was still alive, and the remainder preserved at the time of his death in the convent at Cebu, as appears from Albuquerque's letter to Philip II (Manila, June 22, 1578). Some of the works then extant may yet lie unidentified in certain monastic or public collections. Those that particularly concern China are the following: 1. "Arte y Vocabulario de la lengua China," praised by contemporary Juan González de Mendoça in his celebrated *Historia de las cosas más notables, ritos, y costumbres del gran reyno de la China* (Rome, 1585), but as yet unidentified; 2. "Relación de una pintura impresa de molde que trujeron los Chinos este año de 1573," a manuscript review of a block-printed edition of a Ming atlas; 3. "Relación verdadera de las cosas del reyno del Taibin, por otro nombre China, y del viage que a él hizo el muy reverendo padre fray Martín de Rada, provincial que fuè del orden de St. Augustín, que lo vio y anduvo, en la provincia de Hocquien año de 1575 hecha por el mismo 1577" (actually written between November, 1575 and May, 1576), published serially in *Revista Agustiniana*, Vol. 8 (Valladolid, 1884), pp. 51–53, 112–122, 293–300, and Vol. 9 (1885), pp. 231–237; and 4. "De lo que les sucedio à los Padres Fray Martín de Rada, y Fray Geronimo Marin en su embaxada de China

hasta que bolvieron à Manila con los Capitanes españoles que los accompañaron," in *Conquistas de las Islas Filipinas*. (Two of these, with a competent introduction, have heen rendered into English by C. R. Boxer, namely, the "Narrative of Rada's Mission to Fukien [June-October 1575]," and his "Relation of the Things of China, Which Is Properly Called Taybin." Among the numerous comments of interest which Rada makes one may be especially noted. It was he, as Boxer remarks, who "was the first modern European to identify China correctly and convincingly with Marco Polo's Cathay." Rada's writings were known to Juan González de Mendoça, whose own work on China, published in 1585, made them widely known in Europe.) Rada's correspondence comprises letters, reports, and opinions sent to the authorities and to Veracruz, in which he lost no occasion to champion the cause of the natives against the vexatious behavior of the colonists. Noteworthy is a letter to Philip II (Manila, May 1, 1576), probably accompanying the "Relación verdadera" and confirmed by the above cited letter to Veracruz.

Bibliography

1/323/11a; 64/己11/5a; MSL (1966), Shen-tsung, 1264; KC (1958), 4276, 4299; Chang Wei-hua張維華, *Ming-shih Fo-lang-chi Lü-sung Ho-lan I-ta li-ya ssu ch'uan chu-shih* 明史佛郎機呂宋和蘭意大里亞四傳注釋 (Pei-p'ing, 1934), 73; Wu Ching-hung吳景宏, "Hsi-pan-ya shih-tai ti-i chieh-tuan chung kuan-hsi chih shan-t'ao" 西班牙時代第一階段中關係之探討, *Ta-lu tsa-chih* 大陸雜誌, 36: 8 and 9 (Taipei, Ma 15, 1968), 1; C.R. Boxer, *South China in the Sixteenth Century* (London, 1953), xlv-xlix, lxvii-xci, 241, 345; Juan de Medina, O. S. A., *Historia de la Orden de S. Agustín de estas Islas Filipinas* (written in 1630, but pubished in Manila, 1893); Gaspar de San Agustín, O. S. A., *Conquistas de las Islas Filipinas* (Madrid, 1698), 56, 305; Gregorio de Santiago Vela, O. S. A.; *Ensayo de una Biblioteca Ibero-Americana de la Orden de San Agustín*, Vol. 3 (Madrid, 1917), 226, and Vol. 6 (Madrid, 1922), 444; Pedro Martínez Vélez, "El Agustino Fray Martín de Rada insigne misionero moderno,"

Archivo Agustiniano, Vol. 19 (1932), 340; Edward J. McCarthy, O. S. A., *Spanish Beginnings in the Philippines, 1564–1572* (Washington, 1943), 22, 100; Manuel Merino, O. S. A., "Semblanzas misioneras: Fr. Martín de Rada, Agustino," *Missionalia Hispanica*, Vol. 1 (Madrid, 1944), 167; *id.*, "La Provincia Agustina del Santisimo Nombre de Jesús de Filipinas," *Archivo Agustiniano*, Vol. 56 (1962), 303 and Vol. 58 (1964), 153; Donald F. Lach, *Asia in the Making of Europe*, 2 vols. (Chicago, 1965), 298, 746, 752, 778, 789; Ch'en Ching-ho, *The Overseas Chinese in the Philippines during the Sixteenth Century* (Hong Kong, 1963), 31.

Antonio Sisto Rosso

RHO, Giacomo 羅雅谷 (T. 味韻 Jacques), 1593 (1590, 1592)-April 26, 1638, Catholic missionary and mathematician, was the son of a scholar and member of a noble family of Milan. Mediocre in most of his studies, he turned out to be brilliant in mathematics. Entering the Society of Jesus in 1614 (1616?) he was ordained in 1617. He volunteered for the China mission and left Italy in 1618 in the company of several other missionary scientists, such as Johann Terrenz and Johann Adam Schall von Bell (*qq. v.*), for whose services there had been insistent demands (*see* Nicolo Longobardi). After spending several years in Goa to complete his theological training, he arrived in Macao in 1622.

Shortly after his arrival the port was blockaded by thirteen Dutch and two English ships, Cornelis Reijersen (*see* Li Tan) commanding, bent on supplanting the Portuguese on the Peninsula, and on taking over the lucrative trade in Chinese silk with Japan, the Philippine Islands, and indeed the world market. On the 24th of June, instead of attempting a landing in the well-defended harbor, a Dutch force of eight hundred men, including some Japanese, Bandanese, and Malays, but no English, disembarked on the east side of the peninsula. This tactic caught the defenders largely unprepared, and was on the point of success when

Rho, assisted by the Italian Bruno (whose original name was Burro), superior of the Jesuit College, and Schall, opened fire with four outmoded cannon set up on a low eminence near the college (where the ruin of the cathedral now stands). One of the cannon balls luckily hit a powder cask, which exploded among the advancing invaders with disastrous effect. The Dutch halted and turned towards another hill, only to be checked again by a body of Macaonese and black (Madagascar?) recruits. With their powder near exhaustion and with fresh defenders arriving from the city, the Dutch beat a retreat, leaving behind several hundred dead and wounded, among them a Dutch captain who was taken captive by Schall.

In 1624 Rho accompanied Alfonso Vagnoni (*q.v.*) to Shansi, settling down for the next five or six years in Chiangchou 絳州; there in spite of bodily afflictions he gave himself to language study and to preaching. His scientific work began when, in 1630, orders came to proceed to Peking to join Schall in an effort to improve the calendar under the direction first of Hsü Kuang-ch'i (ECCP) and then (1634) of Li T'ien-ching (ECCP). Their work involved as well calculating the distances from the earth of the stars, their positions, etc. They had repeatedly to make reports to the throne, fashion instruments of precision, and answer objections raised by high officials jealous of their authority. By 1635 they had printed and presented to the emperor the last of several installments of a work on all branches of European astronomy and mathematics entitled *Ch'ung-chen li shu* in 137 *chüan* (*see* Li T'ien-ching), later copied in reduced form (100 chüan) into the *Ssu-k'u ch'üan-shu*. About the same time (the end of 1634) they also presented to the emperor a telescope and in 1635 two other instruments.

Three years later, on April 26, Rho passed away. Longobardi (*q.v.*) had planned a quiet funeral, but this was not to be. The church adherents, together with eunuchs, palace women, and officials, poured out to pay their homage to this faithful, hard-working, and able man. His body was laid to rest at Cha-la-er near the grave of Matteo Ricci (*q.v.*), but the headstone erected at the time no longer stands. Only a fragment of it was buried in one of the walls of the little church at the site.

Among his religious writings one may be singled out, the *Ai-chin hsing-ch'üan* 哀矜行詮, 3 *chüan* (1633); it includes seven contributions on distress both spiritual and physical, of which he seems to have had his full share. This work was put to use by a contemporary scholar, Han Lin (EC CP), who doubtless became acquainted with Rho in his Chiang-chou years. Like Terrenz he wrote a book on the human body, the *Jen-shen t'u-shuo* 人身圖說 but this is known only in manuscript. He was responsible as well for a dozen works on astronomy and mathematics. While consciously beholden to Copernicus and Galileo, he did not accept the heliocentric system, preferring to consider the assertions of these masters unproved. Possibly his hesitation was due to tactical consideration—not to disturb either ideas held by the Chinese or the official doctrines of the church.

Bibliography

SK (1930), 106/5b; Pfister (1932), 188; P. M. d'Elia, *Fonti Ricciane*, II (Rome, 1949), 251 n.; *id.*, *Galileo in China*, tr. by R. Suter and M. Sciascia, Cambridge, Mass., 1960; J. M. Planchet, *Le cimitière et les oeuvres Catholiques de Chala, 1610-1927* (Peking, 1928), 132, 167; George H. Dunne. *Generation of Giants* (Notre Dame, 1962), 184; C. R. Boxer, *Fidalgos in the Far East, 1550-1770* (The Hague, 1948), 79; P. Pelliot, "Livres reçus," TP, 27 (1930), 436; Joseph Needham, with the collaboration of Wang Ling, *Science and Civilization in China*, III (Cambridge, England, 1959), 447; George H. C. Wong, "China's Opposition to Western Science during late Ming and Early Ch'ing," *Isis*, 54 (1963), 154.

L. Carrington Goodrich

RICCI, Matteo (Li Ma-tou 利馬竇, T. 西泰), October 6, 1552-May 11, 1610, Jesuit missionary, was born at Macerata, Italy, went to Rome to study law in 1568, and entered his novitiate there on August 15, 1571. He left for Portugal May 18, 1577, and thence for Goa, where he arrived in the autumn of 1578. After finishing his studies he was ordained on July 26, 1580. Two years later he was dispatched to Macao and started at once to learn Chinese. Up to this point Jesuit and other Catholic missionaries were able to remain for only two or three days, or at most for some weeks, in interior China. In 1583 the Jesuits finally received permission of the governor-general of Kwangtung and Kwangsi, Kuo Ying-p'ing 郭應聘 (T. 君賓, 華溪, 1529-86, cs 1550), to establish themselves at Chao-ch'ing 肇慶, west of Canton, where the viceroy's residence was at that time. Ricci and another Jesuit, Michele Ruggieri (*q.v.*), went to Chao-ch'ing on September 10, 1583. Through the assistance of the prefect, Wang P'an 王泮 (T. 宗魯, b. 1539, cs 1574), they soon acquired a piece of land outside the city, where they built a house with a chapel, the first mission station in China. The prefect presented the establishment with two plaques, one reading Hsien-hua ssu 僊花寺 (Fairy Flower Monastery), the other Hsi-lai ching-t'u 西來淨土 (Pure Land from the West), both indicating that the Chinese at that time thought of the missionaries as Buddhists. The first reference to the Christian God as T'ien-chu 天主 dates from this period. Through their exemplary way of living and their devotion to scholarship, and at the same time through their careful avoidance of any obtrusive act in promulgating the Christian faith, the missionaries gradually succeeded in becoming respected and in making friends with a few educated Chinese. The sympathy manifested in public by the prefect greatly enhanced their prestige. Nevertheless they were also the target of xenophobia and jealousy and of calumnies of all sorts. Ricci, once wrongly indicted, was able to prove his innocence and the calumniator was punished. In his residence Ricci displayed a world map which aroused the interest of some of his visitors. At their suggestion he copied the map, translating the names into Chinese. This became the first edition of Ricci's famous world map *Yü-ti shan-hai ch'üan-t'u* 興地山海全圖, printed late in 1584. No copies of this edition are extant, but the outlines are reproduced in the *T'u-shu pien* by Chang Huang (*q.v.*), who later became a friend of Ricci. The efforts of Ruggieri and Ricci to pave the way for further Jesuits to come to China and to penetrate other provinces, as well as the embarrassment caused by one of the few Christian converts who proved to be an impostor, increased the difficulties they met from certain officials and from the populace. Ricci, however, becoming more and more familiar in dealing with the Chinese, managed to stay on for some time. The display of western clocks, prisms, and other things unknown in China attracted many visitors of the official and educated class; also by the gentle and cultivated way he entertained his guests Ricci formed a number of friendships among them and gained much respect from those who made his acquaintance. None of these overtures, however, could definitely guarantee favorable status for them; nor could his friends protect Ricci when their superior, the newly appointed governor-general, Liu Chi-wen 劉繼文 (T. 永謨, H. 簡齋, cs 1562, d. 1592), in 1589 ordered their expulsion. In August of that year the Jesuits had to abandon their residence at Chao-ch'ing. But due to his adroitness in conversation with the viceroy, Ricci managed to get permission to settle at another place in the province. Instead of returning to Macao, as originally ordered, Ricci went to Shao-chou 韶州 in the northern part of Kwangtung with letters from Liu commending him to the local authorities.

At Shao-chou Ricci, now more experienced with Chinese social conventions, found a more friendly atmosphere than at Chao-ch'ing. He soon received permission to acquire a piece of land and to build a house and a church. He established amicable relations with the officials and with members of the educated elite in and near Shao-chou. The local prefect granted particular protection to the mission; as a result mistreatment of the foreigners could be nipped in the bud. Attracted by the rumor that the foreign priests were experts in alchemy, Ch'ü Ju-k'uei (*see* Ch'ü Shih-ssu, ECCP, p. 199) of the well-known Ch'ü family of Ch'ang-shu, asked Ricci if he might study under him. Ricci instructed him especially in mathematics and astronomy as well as in the Christian religion. Ch'ü became a devoted student and later a Christian. Western science was at that time in some respects ahead of the Chinese, and Ch'ü spread the fame of the extraordinary scholarship of Ricci and thus induced not a few like-minded people to call on him. Up to this time the Jesuits in China had adopted an attire similar to that of the Buddhist priests, and like them were referred to as seng 僧, or ho-shang 和尚. Ricci gradually became aware, however, that the social status of monks was considered inferior to that of the literati who held official degrees. He therefore requested permission of his superiors to wear the attire of the Chinese scholar class, to grow his beard and his hair as they did, and to discontinue the designation of seng or ho-shang. He first chose the name tao-jen 道人; the terms shen-fu 神父 and ssu-to 司鐸 were adopted several years later. In so doing he disassociated the Jesuit priests from the Buddhist clergy and stressed their relationship with the Confucian literati. At Shao-chou Ricci was probably already speaking Chinese fluently, but he continued to study, to read, and to write the classical language. A result of these studies was the first translation of the Four Books into Latin which he completed during his stay at Shao-chou. In addition he elaborated the first system of romanization of Chinese. These two achievements justify crediting Ricci with originating western sinology.

In the spring of 1595 Ricci seized the opportunity to travel north. He crossed the Mei-ling 梅嶺 pass into Kiangsi and proceeded by boat on the Kan 贛 River from Nan-an 南安 (Ta-yü 大庾) through Kan-chou 贛州 and Chi-an 吉安 to Nan-chang, and farther via Poyang Lake and the Yangtze to Nanking, where he arrived at the end of May. Although Ricci had recommendations to several officials in Nanking, he did not yet have permission to stay and had to leave after two weeks and return to Nanchang. Through the good offices of a friend Ricci was received by the governor of Kiangsi, Lu Wan-kai 陸萬垓 (T. 天溥, 仲鶴, cs 1568), and at once received the required permit. Two imperial princes residing at Nanchang also welcomed him. On this occasion he wrote his first book in Chinese, *Chiao-yu lun* 交友論 (Treatise on making friends), 1 *ch.*, a discussion based on the maxims of famous westerners, and presented a handwritten copy to Chu To-chieh 朱多𤏺, prince of Chien-an 建安王 (enfeoffed 1573, d. 1601). At this time Ricci became acquainted also with Chang Huang. In 1596 Ricci rewrote the catechism, entitling it *T'ien-chu shih-i* 實義, 2 *ch.*, using the new terminology; this superseded the earlier *T'ien-chu shih-lu* 錄 written by Ruggieri.

In 1598 the Nanking minister of Rites, Wang Hung-hui (*see* Lazzaro Cattaneo), expressed willingness to escort Ricci and Cattaneo to Peking. He thought he might introduce the missionaries to the court in order to put their knowledge of mathematical and astronomical methods to use in correcting the calendar. Ricci himself was most eager to make the trip to obtain permission to establish the church in China. He took with him some presents for the emperor, hoping thereby to attract the latter's interest. The Japanese invasion of Korea and the subsequent involvement of China in the war, however, had made the officials at Nanking and Peking suspicious of all foreigners, for fear that they might be spies. In spite of their sponsorship the missionaries were unable to stay at Nanking and had to remain on their boat; if they did go ashore, they could travel only by closed sedan chair. Ricci nevertheless made the acquaintance of the governor, Chao K'o-huai 趙可懷 (T. 德仲, cs 1565, d. November, 1604), who was friendly towards Ricci and kept him at his house for several days. In addition he provided him with funds for the trip, but warned him at the same time of the difficulties he would encounter at Peking. The party traveled on the Grand Canal to T'ung-chou 通州 and arrived at Peking on September 7, 1598. There they were able to stay in the house of Wang Hung-hui, but owing to the Korean war people were reluctant to meet them. It soon became evident that there was no hope for them to reach their objective, and Wang Hung-hui advised them to return to Nanking. They first hesitated, but eventually left after a sojourn of nearly two months, traveling again by boat on the Grand Canal and arriving at Lin-ch'ing 臨清, Shantung, early in December. Due to the winter cold Ricci had to continue his trip overland. He first went to Soochow and stayed there with his friend Ch'ü Ju-k'uei for a few weeks. In February, 1599, he proceeded to Nanking. Because of the death of the Japanese leader, Hideyoshi (*see* Konishi) in the autumn of 1598, the situation for the Chinese in Korea had greatly improved, and the atmosphere at Nanking was much more favorable. Wang Hung-hui invited Ricci to settle in the southern capital. At this time Ricci had become well known, and not a few of the highest officials at Nanking were eager to make his acquaintance. His knowledge of the newest achievements in western mathematical and astronomical science in particular attracted the scholar class. Following the sug-

gestion of one of his friends Ricci published in 1600 a revised edition of his
mappa mundi, now with the slightly modified title *Shan-hai Yü-ti ch'üan-t'u.*

Among the people Ricci met at Nanking were leading officials such as the
ministers of the six Nanking ministries,
the grand commandant at Nanking, Li
Huan 李環 (d. 1601), descendant of Li Pin
(*see* Lê Lọ'i), whose title he inherited
in 1573, the eunuch Feng Pao (*q.v.*), and
eminent scholars such as Chu Shih-lu (*see*
Ch'eng Ta-yüeh) Wang K'en-t'ang 王肯堂
(T. 宇泰, b. 1553, cs 1589), Li Chih (*q.v.*),
and Chiao Hung (ECCP). Ricci was often
invited to large banquets, where scientific
and religious questions were discussed.
Now as well versed in the Chinese Classics as his interlocutors, Ricci proved to
be able in argumentation. In a letter to
a friend Li Chih gave the following characterization of Ricci:

"... Ricci lived nearly twenty years at
Chao-ch'ing in Nan-hai and has read the
whole literature of our country. He asked
scholars to read and explain to him [the
meaning of the texts] and requested
those understanding the doctrine of human nature and of reason (hsing-li 性理)
in the Four Books to explain the main
principles therein. He furthermore asked
those familiar with the interpretation of
the six Canonical Writings to pass on
their explanations. Now he can speak
our language fluently, write our script,
and act according to our rules of conduct.
He is an extremely impressive man,—a
person of inner refinement, outwardly
most straightforward. In an assembly of
many people, all talking in confusion
with each holding to his own point of
view, Ricci keeps his silence and cannot
be provoked to interfere or to become
involved. Amongst the people of my
acquaintance no one is comparable to
him. All those who are either too overbearing or too flattering, or those who
parade their cleverness or are narrow-
minded and lacking in intelligence are
inferior to him ...."

Notwithstanding his first failure Ricci
steadily pursued his plan to return to
Peking and to try to obtain the sanction
he had sought earlier. Again he hoped
that his gifts might attract attention and
win him an imperial audience. The presents—among them beautifully fashioned
clocks, a clavichord, a statue of the
Madonna, crucifixes, triangular glass
prisms, etc.—had been shown to high
officials and occasionally exhibited in Ricci's
residence at Nanking, in order to spread the
knowledge of their extraordinary quality
and so arouse the curiosity of the dignitaries
at court and perhaps of the emperor
himself. After consultation with his
friends in the spring of 1600, Ricci considered conditions sufficiently favorable to
make another attempt. He left Nanking
by boat together with Diego de Pantoja
(*q.v.*) and two Chinese lay brothers, and
once more proceeded via the Grand
Canal. At Chi-ning 濟寧 Ricci again met
Li Chih who introduced him to his host,
the supreme commander of grain transportation on the Grand Canal, Liu Tung-
hsing 劉東星 (T. 子明, H. 晉川, 1538-1601,
cs 1568). Liu was particularly friendly
and helpful. The Jesuits continued their
trip unmolested as far as Lin-ch'ing.
There they were stopped by orders of
the director of the tax administration of
Lin-ch'ing and Tientsin, the powerful and
greedy, much feared eunuch Ma T'ang 馬
堂. Ma confiscated part of their belong-
ings and some of the presents destined
for the emperor and kept the party under
custody at Tientsin for almost half a year.
Certain friends whose help they sought
could do nothing and they were in despair. Eventually, however, an order arrived
from Peking telling the missionaries to
come at once and bring their presents
to the emperor. Since the time was
winter and the Canal frozen, they traveled
overland as guests of the government
and arrived at the capital on January 24,
1601. The emperor took delight in the
presents and ordered the missionaries to
stay in the palace to instruct the eunuchs

in the care of the clocks and other objects, and teach them how to play the clavichord. Their treatment was respectful and correct, but eunuchs of Ma T'ang's clique guarded them constantly and almost completely prevented them from getting in touch with any of the officials, lest they should pass on information about Ma T'ang's machinations.

Outside the palace, however, the director of the bureau of receptions in the ministry of Rites, Ts'ai Hsien-ch'en 蔡獻臣 (T. 體國, cs 1589), in charge of foreign ambassadors, considered it an encroachment on the jurisdiction of his bureau that the foreigners had been introduced to the court by Ma T'ang and his eunuch henchmen. The resulting dispute about jurisdiction put Ricci and Pantoja in a very unpleasant position. Eventually, much to their relief, they went under the protection of the bureau and were lodged in the residence for foreign envoys. Here they met people coming from central Asia, and basing himself on their accounts Ricci concluded correctly (as had Martín de Rada, q.v., before him) that Cathay was but another name for China, and Khanbalik another for Peking. He wrote to Europe advising scholars there to correct the maps which placed Cathay north of China. This identification was later convincingly proved by Bento de Góis (q.v.).

The sojourn in the residence for foreign envoys as guests of the government was nevertheless a kind of detention preventing the foreigners from freely moving about the city. Finally with the help of the courageous supervising secretary of the office of scrutiny for Personnel, Ts'ao Yü-pien (see Wen T'i-jen), who had become their friend, they were discharged from the residence and permitted to rent a house in the city. Soon afterward this permission was confirmed by the emperor and at the same time a monthly stipend granted. As soon as their status was satisfactorily adjusted officials and scholars in the capital no longer hesi-tated to associate with Ricci, and he became acquainted with such high officials as Grand Secretary Shen I-kuan, ministers of war Hsiao Ta-heng, of Rites Feng Ch'i, and of Personnel Li Tai (qq.v.), and many others. [Editors' note: Among the nine men with whom Ricci held dialogues, as recorded in Chi-jen shih-p'ien (printed 1608), seven are known, namely, Li Tai, Feng Ch'i, Hsü Kuang-ch'i, Ts'ao Yü-pien, Li Chih-tsao (ECCP), Wu Chung-ming 吳中明 (T. 左海, cs 1586), and Kung Tao-li 龔道立 (T. 應身, cs 1586)].

A few of Ricci's new friends took a serious interest in the Christian religion. Most outstanding among them were the learned scholar-officials Feng Ying-ching 馮應京 (T. 可大, H. 慕岡, 1555-1606, cs 1592, Pth. 恭節), editor of the great encyclopedia Huang Ming ching-shih shih-yung pien 皇明經世實用編, 28 ch., who was prevented only by his untimely death from being baptized, and Li Chih-tsao. The latter became one of the closest collaborators of the Jesuits in their scientific and religious activities. With Li's assistance Ricci published in 1602 and in 1603 the third and fourth editions of his world map, now with the title K'un-yü wan-kuo 坤輿萬國 ch'üan-t'u. In addition Li reprinted Ricci's catechism and his Chiao-yu lun. Because of efforts to make a synthesis of Confucian and Christian teaching, to the exclusion of Buddhism and Taoism, Ricci met much opposition from the Buddhist clergy and from officials with strong Buddhist or Taoist sympathies. Therefore a kind of purge in 1607 against heretics at the imperial court and among the officials, in which Ricci's former friend Li Chih had previously fallen victim, was as such welcomed by Ricci.

His success in China was, of course, much appreciated by the authorities of the Jesuit order and in 1604 the China mission ceased to be subordinate to the Jesuit College of Macao and became independent with Ricci in charge. Nevertheless Ricci's missionary policy met consid-

erable oppostion both within and without
the Jesuit order. Ricci considered the
accommodation of the practice of the
Christian religion—not of its contents—to
the particular Chinese conditions as an
absolute necessity. In view of his obvious
achievements Ricci succeeded in overcoming opposition at least among other Jesuits, and his *modus operandi* was soon accepted as basic for the conduct of the
Jesuit mission in China. Widespread disapproval of Jesuit practices continued, however, and resulted finally in the so-called
Rites Controversy and in the eventual
suppression of the Jesuit mission by the
authorities in Rome. Only some three
hundred years later, in 1939, were Ricci's
views and the Jesuit mission policy sanc-
tioned by the Roman authorities.

By the publication of the world map
and of the *Chiao-yu lun*, Ricci became
famous as an author among Chinese scholars. Being aware of the particular importance and the efficacy of the written
word to promote new ideas among the
Chinese literary class, Ricci continued to
study Chinese literature in Peking and to
practice writing in Chinese. In 1604 he
published a collection of short notes on
Christian ethics, *Er-shih-wu yen* 二十五言
(Twenty-five sayings), and a new edition of the catechism, *T'ien-chu shih-i*; in
1608 he brought out a book on philosophical and ethical questions in the form
of ten short dialogues, *Chi-jen shih-p'ien*
畸人十篇 (Ten chapters by a non-confor-
mer), 1 *ch*. Besides Li Chih-tsao, Ricci
found that year another close friend
and influential collaborator in the person
of Hsü Kuang-ch'i (ECCP), whom he
had already met briefly at Nanking in
1600. Hsü took a deep interest in the
Christian religion and was baptized at
Nanking in 1603. In the following year he
came to Peking where he passed the metropolitan examination and was subsequently appointed to the Hanlin Academy. In
1606/7 Ricci together with Hsü prepared
a Chinese translation of the first six chapters of Euclid's *Elements*, initially published

probably in 1607 with the title *Chi-ho
yüan-pen* 幾何原本 (Elements of geometry),
6 *ch*. Further scientific works in the
preparation of which Ricci took a major
or minor part (some of them published
only after his death) were the *Ch'ien-k'un
t'i-i* 乾坤體義, 2 (or 3) *chüan*, a treatise
on the celestial bodies, *Ts'e-liang fa-i*,
測量法義, 1 *chüan*, a work on trigonometry
dictated by Ricci and written by Hsü
Kuang-ch'i, *Yüan-jung chiao-i* 圜容較義, 1
chüan, a treatise on geometry, and *T'ung-
wen suan-chih* 同文算指, 11 *ch*., a work
on arithmetic, dictated by Ricci and written by Li Chih-tsao.

During the first few years Ricci and
other missionaries had occupied rented
houses in Peking and had moved several
times. Only in 1605 did they manage to
buy a compound of their own in the
western central section of the city, just
inside Hsüan-wu Gate 宣武門, later (after
a church building was erected) known as
Nan-t'ang (*see* Schall). The new residence
was opened on August 27 of that year,
and was still in the possession of the
Catholic church in the early 1950s, but
since has been taken over by the government; the original buildings are, however,
no longer standing. Here Ricci and his
fellow-clergy were busy receiving visitors
from all over the country who had read some
of Ricci's publications and were eager to
see him in person. This was the case in
particular in 1607 and 1610, when the
metropolitan examinations were held and
scholars from every province in China
assembled at the capital. One of the
visitors was Ai T'ien 艾田 (T. 計伯, b. 1546,
cj 1573), a member of the Jewish community at Kaifeng. Through him the first
information of the existence of this community, as well as of the earlier penetration of Nestorian Christians, came to
the West.

During all these years Ricci and the
other Jesuits were at intervals ordered to
the imperial palace, particularly to take
care of the foreign clocks and other instruments. Ricci had hesitated to present

his world map to the emperor for fear that the representation of China as only one part of the world, and not according to the usual Chinese concept as the world's center occupying the major part of the earth, might arouse the emperor's resentment. The latter, however, learned about the map and became quite interested in it. As a result Ricci was asked (1608) to prepare a special copy for imperial use. This further enhanced Ricci's and the mission's prestige.

The number of Ricci's friends among the scholar-officials constantly increased. Not a few of them became converted to the Christian faith and eventually were baptized. The high favor Ricci enjoyed at the capital had its effect throughout the empire and the Jesuit missions at other places, in particular at Nanking, were able to expand their activities. Difficulties encountered occasionally could be overcome with the help of Ricci's influential friends. There was actually considerable opposition to the foreign priests and their doctrine on the popular as well as on the educated level. Sometimes this opposition found its expression in written broadsides. Thus in 1609 Ricci published a short treatise *Pien-hsüeh i-tu* 辨學遺牘, 1 *chüan*, arguing against the Buddhist polemics of Yü Ch'un-hsi (*see* Ku Hsien-ch'eng), and of the monk Chu-hung (*q. v.*).

On May 3, 1610, Ricci fell seriously ill and foresaw his approaching end. A number of the most famous physicians called in for consultation were of no help. Stress and overwork had ruined his physique. He died calmly and peacefully on May 11 at the age of fifty-seven. After the funeral mass, one of the Christian officials suggested that the emperor be asked to grant a burial place for Ricci. Whereupon Pantoja drew up a memorial, with the help of Li Chih-tsao, which through Li's good offices was presented to the throne. On June 18 the request was granted. Among several places offered, the Jesuits selected a villa outside the western city gate, Fou-ch'eng men 阜城門, which had been confiscated from a eunuch sentenced to death. In spite of the opposition of some eunuchs the place was eventually handed over to the mission; it was spacious enough for a cemetery, a chapel, and a residence. On November 1, 1611, Ricci was laid to rest there, and after him a number of other Jesuits who died at Peking. The place, known as Cha-la-er 柵欄兒, was in the 19th century transferred to the congregation of the Marist brothers. During the Boxer uprising in 1900 it was almost completely destroyed but later restored. In 1966 it was once more desecrated.

Looking back with our present understanding of Chinese civilization of the late Ming period, we find it almost incredible that a foreigner—however well educated and intelligent he might be—without any previous knowledge of the Chinese language and civilization was able within less than twenty years to take up residence in the capital, be accepted by a very different, highly sophisticated, sinocentric, anti-foreign and exclusive society, become a prominent member of this society, make friends with a number of the most eminent scholar-officials of the time, and even convert some of them to his Christian faith, and receive a regular allowance from the emperor during his lifetime and a burial place after his death. Only Ricci's particular intellectual and personal qualities made such an achievement possible. Ricci had become aware at an early date that for the beginning there was no need to make as many Christian converts as possible; it was of basic importance instead to secure for the foreign missionaries a solid and respected position within Chinese society, and that such a position could be gained only by way of a complete accommodation to the leading Chinese scholar-official class. This accommodation included a thorough Chinese literary education in order to carry on discussions with Chinese scholars and to talk to them on the achievements of European science and development of thought in their own terms. Ricci himself was particularly able to master a highly sophisticated form of accommodation, and was therefore accepted by the Chinese scholar-officials as one of their own. This becomes evident by such statements as the one by Li Chih quoted above. Another scholar, Kuo Tzu-chang (*q. v.*), at that time governor of Kweichow, even stated that in accordance with other examples from Chinese history Ricci must be treated as a Chinese and not as a "barbarian." Shen Te-fu (*q. v.*), author of the *Yeh-hu-pien*, wrote:

"... When I previously lived in the capital, Peking, Ricci was my neighbor. He is indeed an unusal man.... Ricci had vowed to use all his efforts to convert the Chinese to his doctrine. In particular did he oppose the Buddhists.... When I did not agree with him, he did not on this account become obstinate. He is very generous, and readily helps those in need. People also feel his sincere kindness and do not attempt to default on what they owe... One of his followers is P'ang Shun-yang with the personal name Ti-wo [Pantoja], another Jesuit who practices his doctrine together with him and had lived before in southern China. But he is far from being equal to Ricci."

The last remark shows how the Chinese considered Ricci much superior to other Europeans. Ricci's ingenious, gentle, and kindly nature conformed to the highest Chinese standards. This natural talent inclined him to appreciate and value the essence of Chinese culture. Thus it was probably more the unique personality of Ricci which appealed to many Chinese than the religious doctrine practiced by him. All in all Ricci may be considered as the most outstanding cultural mediator between China and the West of all time.

A striking portrait of Ricci painted after his death by Yu Wen-hui 游文輝, a Chinese artist from Macao (known as Brother Manoel Pereira, 1575-1628 +) who saw him on his deathbed, appears as a frontispiece in *Fonti Ricciane*.

Bibliography

1/326/17b; MSL (1940), Shen-tsung, 354 /1a, 470/11a; KC (1958), 4865, 5020; Shen Te-fu, *Wan-li yeh-hu-pien* (Shanghai, 1959), 783; Li Chih, *Fen-shu* (Peking, 1961), 249; *id.*, *Hsü fen-shu* (Peking, 1959), 36; Ku Ch'i-yüan, *K'o-tso chui-yü* (*Chin-ling* 金陵 *ts'ung-shu* ed.), 6/18b; Chu I-tsun (ECCP), *Jih-hsia chiu-wen k'ao*, 96/14b; SK (1930), 106/4a, 107/6a, 125/7b; Juan Yüan (ECCP), *Ch'ou-jen chuan* (Shanghai, 1935), 563; Ai Ju-lüeh (Giulio Aleni), *Li Ma-tou hsing-shih*, Peking, 1620, repr. 1919; Lo Kuang 羅光, *Li Ma-tou chuan*, T'ai-chung, 1960; Fang Hao 方豪, *Li Chih-tsao yen-chiu* 李之藻研究, Taipei, 1966; *id.*, *Chung-kuo T'ien-chu chiao shih jen-wu chuan* 中國天主教史人物傳, I (Hong Kong and Taipei, 1967), 72; *id.*, "Notes on Matteo Ricci's *De Amicitia*," MS XIV (1949-55), 574; Nakayama Kushirō 中山久四郎, "Ri Matō den," *Rekishi chiri*, 26 (1915), nos. 3 & 4, 29 (1917), nos. 3 & 5 (Chinese tr. by Chou I-liang 周一良, "Li Ma-tou shih-chieh ti-t'u chuan-hao" 世界地圖專號, *Yü-kung* 5 (1936), nos. 3 & 4; Pietro Tacchi-Venturi, S. J. (ed.), *Opere storiche del P. Matteo Ricci, S.J.*, 2 vols., Macerata, 1911-13; Pasquale M. d'Elia, S. J. (ed.), *Fonti Ricciane*, 3 vols., Rome, 1942, 1949; *id.*, "Presentazione della prima traduzione Cinese di Euclide," MS XV (1956), 161, and "Further Notes on Matteo Ricci's *de Amicitia*," 356; Pfister (1932), 22; Henri Bernard, S. J., *Matteo Ricci's Scientific Contribution to China*, Peiping, 1935; *id.*, *Le père Matthieu Ricci et la société Chinoise de son temps (1552-1610)*, Tientsin, 1937; *id.*, "Il Trattato sull'Amicizia, primo libro scritto in cinese da Matteo Ricci, S. J. (1595)," *Studia Missionalia*, VII (1952), 425; *id.*, "Sunto poetico-ritmico di 'I Dieci Paradossi' di Matteo Ricci, S. I.," R.S.O., XXVII (1952), 111; *id.*, "Musica e canti italiani a Pechino, marzo-aprile 1601," *ibid.* XXX (1955), 131; George L. Harris, "The mission of Matteo Ricci, S. J.," MS, XXV (1966), 1.

Wolfgang Franke

ROCHA, João da (羅如望, T. 懷中), 1565-March 23 (or July 21), 1623, a native of Braga, Portugal, was a missionary in the Jesuit order. He joined the society at Coimbra (1583) and in 1586, following his novitiate, left Lisbon with a group of thirty other missionaries and Japanese ambassadors (*see* Lazzaro Cattaneo) for Goa. Here he studied philosophy for three years (1587–90) before going on to Macao, where he spent four more years pursuing courses in theology and in the Chinese language. His first assignments were to the centers at Shao-chou 韶州, Kwangtung (1597–98), Nanchang (1598–1600), and Nanking (1600), where he joined Cattaneo at the time that Matteo Ricci (*q.v.*) left on his second trip to Peking. It was in the southern capital that Rocha cultivated the acquaintance, among others, of two rising scholars, Hsü Kuang-ch'i (ECCP) and Ch'ü Ju-k'uei (*see* Ch'ü Shih-ssu, ECCP, p. 199), the first of whom he baptized as Paul in 1603, and the second as Ignatius in 1605. Four years later he returned to Nanchang as superior of the mission, but withdrew in 1616 on the eve of the first anti-Christian persecution. His first place of refuge was Chien-ch'ang 建昌, a town situated southeast of Nanchang in the same province. Here he and two other missionaries carried on their evangelizing efforts without hindrance in spite of the proscriptions farther north. From Kiangsi he proceeded south to Chang-chou 漳州 in Fukien, then north again to Chia-ting 嘉定 in the Yangtze delta, where he and Cattaneo built the first churh, but were constrained shortly afterwards to seek the protection of Yang T'ing-yün (ECCP) in Hangchow. At this hospitable center he and his host and Hsü Kuang-ch'i worked on a memorial to defend themselves against the assaults of Shen Ch'üeh (*q.v.*), a document which Hsü planned to present to the emperor. But it proved unnecessary. Shen fell from favor in 1622.

Rocha was nominated about this time to be vice-provincial of the mission, but he died before word of the appointment reached him. Hsü took charge of the funeral, burying him outside the walls of Hangchow where later Cattaneo and several other fellow missionaries were laid to rest.

Rocha is known for two works, one a translation of a catechism in the form of a dialógue written in 1561 by another Portuguese Jesuit, Marco Jorge, the title of which Rocha rendered as *T'ien-chu sheng-chiao ch'i-meng* 天主聖教啓蒙 (1619), the second known as the method of the rosary, entitled *Nien-chu kuei-ch'eng* 念珠規程 (*ca.* 1620). The latter is illustrated with fifteen woodblock prints, Tung Ch'i-ch'ang (ECCP), or someone of his school, is said to have been responsible for adapting the pictures, made originally by Girolamo Nadal in 1595, for Rocha's book. The latter is extremely rare but a copy, probably an original, is preserved in the Vatican library, Pasquale M. d'Elia in 1939 reproduced all fifteen illustrations, together with Nadal's on facing pages.

Bibliography

Pfister (1932), 67; P. M. d'Elia, *Fonti Ricciane*, I (1942), 383, n. 6; *id.*, *Le origini dell' arte cristiana cinese* (Rome, 1939), 68, Jos. Jennes, "L'art chrétien en Chine au début du XVIIe siècle," TP, XXXIII (1937), 129; Fang Hao 方豪, *Chung-kuo T'ien-chu-chiao shih jen-wu chuan* 中國天主教史人物傳, I (Hong Kong, 1967), 176.

L. Carrington Goodrich

RODRÍGUES, João (Lu Jo-han 陸若漢), 1561–1634, missionary and scholar, was a native of Sernancelhe in the diocese of Lamego, Portugal. It is not known when he set out for the East, but by 1576, when he was only fifteen, he was already in Japan in the service of the celebrated Ōtomo Yoshishige, daimyō of Bungo. At first he took part in military expeditions, then in December, 1580, he entered the Jesuit novitiate at Funai in Bungo, where he later studied Latin and philosophy and taught grammar. He was also able to keep up his study of the language, literature, and philosophy of Japan, thus laying the foundation for his later proficiency as a preacher, writer, and interpreter. In 1588, before his ordination to the priesthood, he had started to preach in Japanese. Earlier still he had acted as interpreter, first for Alessandro Valignano (*q.v.*), visitor of the Jesuit Order in the Orient, and later for Gaspar Coelho, the local vice provincial around the years 1581 to 1590. In July, 1590, he accompanied Valignano on a visit to Toyotomi Hideyoshi (*see* Konishi), regent and *de facto* ruler of Japan. Hideyoshi was so impressed by Rodrígues that he kept him in his court as his personal interpreter, a distinction which won him the appellation Tcuzzu (Tsuji 通事). This name probably served to distinguish him from his colleague and fellow-scholar of Japanese—João Rodrígues Girão (1558-1633). He completed his theological studies at Nagasaki in 1593 and was ordained at Macao in 1594. Two years later he returned to Japan and to his work as procurator of the Japan mission, an office to which he was appointed in 1591 and which he was to hold until the year 1626. Some days before Hideyoshi's death (September 16, 1598) Rodrígues paid a visit to the dying man and tried unsuccessfully to convert him.

Under Tokugawa Ieyasu (*see* Konishi), shōgun after Hideyoshi, Rodrígues remained *persona grata* at the shōgunate court down to 1612. It was owing to his influence that the Jesuits and their converts were permitted to live and work unmolested at Nagasaki, Kyoto, and Osaka. His popularity soon aroused jealousy and suspicion in many quarters and repeated efforts were made to get rid of him. Even Ieyasu on several occasions tried to catch him in some misdemeanor but had to admit that his suspicions were unfounded. Ultimately Rodrígues' enemies succeeded in having him expelled from Japan on an accusation of involvement in a commercial scandal. From Japan Rodrígues went to Macao and after a short stay there transferred to the China Mission. Following a first assignment at Chinkiang, near Nanking, he traveled widely in the interior, where he sought out traces of Nestorian Christianity and wrote a description

of the eighth-century Nestorian tablet unearthed in Sian-fu in 1625. He also participated in discussions on Chinese rites, dealing especially with the Chinese term for God, being one of the first to oppose the interpretation of Matteo Ricci (*q.v.*).

Despite his many activities in China, Rodrígues was able to find time for his Japanese studies. While still in Japan he had written a Japanese grammar entitled *Arte da Lingoa de Japam*, in three parts, published at Nagasaki in the years 1604-8, a copy of which is in the Bodleian Library, Oxford. This is one of the first Japanese grammars, the best perhaps up to that period. It is no mere dry sketch but contains a good deal of information on Japan—imperial dynasties, commercial information, lists of coins, weights, and measures, etc. Doi Tadao 土井忠生 in 1955 made a complete translation of this into Japanese. In 1620 his *Arte Breve da Lingoa Iapoa* was published at Macao. In this work, which is quite different from the *Arte Grande* (*i.e.*, the *Arte da Lingoa de Japam*), he formulated, clearly and concisely, the principal grammatical rules and syntactical constructions of Japanese. A copy may be found in the Marsden collection at the School of Oriental and African Studies, London, and another in the Ajuda Library, Lisbon. Still a third, found in manuscript in the Bibliothèque du Roi, Paris, was translated into French by M. C. Landresse under the title, *Elémens de la Grammaire japonaise*, Paris, 1825, with a supplement published 1826.

Rodrígues also wrote the *Historia da Igreja de Japão*, a monumental work on the history of Japan which he apparently intended as a supplement to the unfinished works of Valignano and Luis Fróes. From the plan of this history it is clear that the work would have been very large had he had the time to complete it. His manuscript was discovered about 1900 by Joseph M. Cros, S.J., in the Ajuda Library. In 1953-55 two volumes were printed in Tokyo as T. XIII of the *Colecção, noticias de Macau*, and they cover only pages

1-181 of the manuscript. Rodrígues worked also on a detailed treatise on the Chinese Buddhist sects, with special reference to their links with Japanese Buddhism. In addition he wrote a voluminous geographical description of China after the style of Abraham Ortelius' *Theatrum Orbis Terrarum*. Only fragments of two of these works have survived.

When the Manchus invaded China toward the end of the Wan-li period, several of the Chinese ministers saw the advantage of using the more effective European firearms. Two of these, Hsü Kuang-ch'i and Li Chih-tsao (both in ECCP), strongly recommended inviting Portuguese soldiers from Macao to train Chinese soldiers in their use. In 1623 a group of Portuguese artillerymen arrived in Peking with Rodrígues as interpreter. Unfortunately the cannon exploded at a demonstration, killing a Portuguese and three Chinese (*see* Manuel Dias). Shortly afterwards the expedition returned to Macao.

Six years later (1629) a second Portuguese expedition left for Peking and again Rodrígues served as interpreter. He was by then a man of sixty-eight, but still vigorous and alert. The group arrived in Cho-chou 涿州, Pei-Chihli, on January 5, 1630. After some delay they eventually reached the capital, but owing to the jealousy and suspicion of some of the Chinese ministers they were not welcomed but dispatched to Teng-chou, Shantung, where they served under the governor, Sun Yüan-hua (ECCP). In the following year (1631) a mutiny broke out among the soldiers of K'ung Yu-te (ECCP). The mutineers laid siege to Teng-chou on February 11, 1632, and within less than a fortnight the city fell. Twelve of the Portuguese soldiers are reported to have perished in a desperate fight with the enemy while fifteen others saved their lives, although seriously wounded. Rodrígues made a hazardous escape by jumping from the city wall into the sea, and eventually made his way to Peking. He was sent back to Macao in 1633 after receiving an imperial decree extolling his services. The *Kung-sha hsiao-chung chi* 公沙効忠紀, an account of the Portuguese captain Gonçalo Teixeiro who sacrificed his life in defense of Teng-chou, was one of his last works. The old padre did not survive very long; in a letter sent by the visitor to Rome, dated March 20, 1634, his death is announced. A memorial to the throne, drawn up in 1639 by Francesco Sambiasi (*q.v.*), states that Rodrígues' remains had not yet been properly buried. His colleagues therefore petitioned for a plot of land beside the São Paolo church in order to establish a graveyard. The emperor consented. His remains were later interred, however, within the church edifice.

Bibliography

Daniello Bartoli, *Dell'Istoria della Compagnia di Gesù: II Giappone* (Turin, 1825), XI, Lib. 2, 164, 326; C. R. Boxer, *The Christian Century in Japan, 1549–1650* (Los Angeles, 1951), 179, 195, 218, 244; id., "Padre João Rodrígues Tçuzu, S. J. and his Japanese Grammars of 1604 and 1620," *Miscelanea de Filologia, Literatura, e Historia Cultural* (Lisbon, 1950); De Charlevoix, *Histoire de Japon* (Paris, 1754), Tome 3e, Lib. 8e, 362, 379, Tome 4e, Lib. 2e, 11, 97, 118, Tome 6e, 341; Fang Hao 方豪, *Chung-kuo T'ien-chu-chiao shih jen-wu chuan* 中國天主教史人物傳 (Hong Kong, 1970), 34; *Hsü Kuang-ch'i chi* (Shanghai, 1963), I, 300; Huang Pai-lu 黃伯祿, *Cheng-chiao feng pao* (Shanghai, 1904), 15b, 17a; Pfister (1932) Vol. 2, Addenda et Corrigenda, 23; Georg Schurhammer, S.J., "P. Johann Rodríguez Tçuzzu als Geschichtschreiber Japans," *Archivum Historicum Societatis Jesu* (Rome, 1932), I, 23; Johannes Laures, *Kirishitan Bunko* (Tokyo, 1957), 3d ed., 27, 28, 35, 684, 687, 1399; Doi Tadao, *Nippon dai bunten* 日本大文典 (Tokyo, 1955); P. Pelliot, "Un ouvrage sur les premiers temps de Macao," TP 31 (1935), 87.

Albert Chan

RUDOMINA, Andrzej (Lu An-te 盧安德, T. 盤石), 1594–September 5, 1632, scholar and missionary to China, was born into a Polish family of ancient lineage in the duchy of Lithuania. He entered the Society of Jesus at Wilno in Lithuania in 1618 and continued his higher education at Wilno College, completing his studies in philosophy and theology at the Collegio Romano. Being accepted for the China mission, he took ship from Lisbon and reached Macao, after a brief stay in Goa, in 1626. It is said that the poet laureate M. Sarbiewski had celebrated his departure at the Papal Court in a classical ode. His life in China was a short one. He had suffered much during his passage to the East and was plagued by illness throughout his remaining six years. His assignment was to work with Giulio Aleni (*q.v.*), who had just begun his missionary labors in the province of Fukien. Besides preaching and other evangelical activities, mostly in Foochow, he joined with Aleni in composing a book entitled *K'ou to jih ch'ao* 口鐸日抄, 8 *ch.* (published in Foochow 1630, reprinted 1872 and 1922 in 4 *ch.*, in Shanghai), giving answers to various questions posed by Chinese scholars. These involved not only religious matters, but also European scientific knowledge. One of the three who wrote prefaces for the book, and who doubtless paid as well for the expense of publication, was Chang Keng (*see* Aleni), who, on a visit to Sian in 1625, seems to have been the first Chinese Christian to appreciate the importance of the newly discovered Nestorian monument erected in 781. Rudomina wrote also two manuscripts in Chinese, *Shih-pa fu hsin t'u* 十八幅心圖 (18 illustrations of virtues and vices, frequently reproduced), and *Shih fu ch'in tai t'u* 十幅勤怠圖 (ten pictures of man both industrious and lazy). Rudomina was no stranger to authorship. Before leaving Europe he had already written in Polish and in Latin a work on political science (published respectively in Wilno and in Cracow in 1652, and reprinted in Polish in 1738 in Wilno under a new title).

He died in Foochow and his body was laid to rest outside the city in the same spot where Aleni later was buried.

Bibliography

Pfister (1932), 191; P. Ribadeneira, *Bibliotheca scriptorum Societatis Jesu* (Rome, 1676), 56; S. Zaleski, *Jezuici w Polsce* (Lwów, 1900–6), I, 191, II, 588, 592, IV, 919; R. Streit, *Bibliotheca missionum* (Aachen, 1916), X, 153; J. C. Cordara, *Historiae Societatis Jesu* (Rome, 1859), II, 323, 413, 670; J. Krzyszkowski, "Andrzej Rudomina," *Misje katolickie*, 1933, Hos. 7–8, 329; H. Cordier, *L'imprimerie Sino-Européenne en Chine* (Paris, 1901), 4, 42; Bento de Mattos, *Historia vitae et mortis R. P. Andreae Rudomina, S. J.*, published in Polish translation by K. Druzbicki in Wilno, 1652, and in Metz, 1858, ed. by A. Kurowski; *id.*, *Essai d'une bibliographie des ouvrages publiés en Chine* (Paris, 1883), 499, 528; D. Bartoli, *Dell'historia della Compagnia di Gesù-La Cina* (Rome, 1663), 976; A. W. Kojalowicz, *Miscelanea rerum ad status ecclesiae in M. Lithucaniae Ducatu* (Wilno, 1650), 18; K. Niesiecki, *Herbarz polski* (Leipzig, 1839–46), VIII, 182; Sommervogel, VIII, 287.

Boleslaw B. Szczesniak

RUGGIERI, Michele (**Michel**, 羅明堅 [or 鑒]), 1543–May 11, 1607, was a Christian missionary, born in Spinazzola in Puglia, Italy. He held a doctorate in law and served as a civil lawyer before entering the Society of Jesus at the age of twenty-nine, after holding government posts under Philip II, King of Naples. His given name was Pompilio, but upon entering the Jesuit order he adopted the name Michele. Assigned to the missions in the East, he arrived in Goa on September 13, 1578, on the same ship as Matteo Ricci (*q. v.*). In July of the following year he was sent to Macao to implement the new and, in the context of the times, revolutionary missiological policy inaugurated by Alessandro Valignano (*q. v.*).

For several years Ruggieri applied himself to Chinese studies in Macao. During this time he succeeded in establishing sympathetic contacts with several Chinese officials in the province of Kwangtung. In 1583, through Wang P'an, the prefect of Chao-ch'ing, he requested a small piece of land and permission to build a church and residence; his request was granted by the governor-general, Kuo Ying-p'ing (for both *see* Ricci).

Ruggieri, accompanied by Ricci, arrived in Chao-ch'ing in September, 1583. This is his chief title to fame, that he established the first post-medieval Christian mission in China and that he introduced to China Matteo Ricci, who, during the ensuing twenty-seven years, laid the foundations of a remarkable evangelical enterprise.

Ruggieri himself did not remain long in the empire. In 1588 he was sent by Valignano to Rome in the hope of organizing a papal embassy to the emperor of China to request imperial sanction for full freedom to preach the Christian Gospel. The death of four popes in rapid succession made it impossible to accomplish anything in Rome. Meanwhile, Ricci, having come to a better understanding of the realities in China, persuaded Valignano that the embassy project was not wisely conceived. Ruggieri, who had struggled with poor health in China, remained in Italy until his death at Salerno in 1607.

There are many unedited, and scarcely legible letters of Ruggieri in the Jesuit archives in Rome. He also wrote (1584) a catechism which was translated into Chinese under the title *T'ien-chu shih-lu*. 天主實錄, 1 *ch*. It was published in China, Japan, and Korea. Ruggieri also collaborated with Ricci in compiling a Portuguese-Chinese dictionary.

Bibliography

Daniello Bartoli, *Dell'istoria della Compagnia di Gésù. La Cina. Terza parte dell'Asia*, 4 vols. (Ancona ed., 1843); Henri Bernard, *Aux portes de la Chine* (Tientsin, 1933), 139; *id.*, *Le Père Matthieu Ricci et la société chinoise de son temps* (1552-1610), I (Tientsin, 1937), 33, 47, 59, 78, 88, 95, 127; George H. Dunne, *Generation of Giants* (Notre Dame, 1962), 18, 28, 48; Pfister (1932), 15; Pasquale d'Elia, *Fonti Ricciane*, I (Rome, 1942), 147, 174, 177, 264; *Roman archives of the Society of Jesus* (*ARSI*, Jap-Sin.).

George H. Dunne

RYŌAN Keigo 了菴桂悟 (H. 鉢袋子, 三浦桂悟, 伊川桂悟), 1425-1514, was a Japanese, birthplace unknown, who had a profound knowledge of neo-Confucianism. At an early age he became a priest of Shinjo-ji 眞如寺 at Kyoto, and studied under Daigi 大疑, who appreciated his worth and later gave him an appointment. In the early years of the Bunmei period 文明 (1469-87) he moved to Anyō-ji 安養寺 at Ise 伊勢 and then went to Tōfuku-ji 東福寺 in Kyoto to become the one hundred seventy-first abbot of the temple.

Emperor Gotsuchi 後土御門天皇 (r. 1465-1500), learning of Keigo's reputation, invited him to an audience and put some questions to him about Buddhism. As his responses pleased the emperor, he conferred on him the name Ryōan. In 1486 the latter retired to live at Daiji-in 大慈院 where he spent his days in literary activity. In 1506 Shōgun Yoshizumi 將軍義澄 (r. 1494-1511) appointed him the chief envoy to China, but four years passed before his mission was ready to embark. Before the departure the Shōgunate conferred on him the honorary title of Butsunichi Zenji 佛日禪師 (perhaps, as Wang Yi-t'ung remarks, to impress the Chinese). The embassy finally left Yamaguchi (1510) but it was not until the following year that it arrived in Ningpo. Since the purpose of the mission was trade, Ryōan became angry when the Ming court offered to buy his Japanese swords for a mere three hundred coins each, following the example of 1510, when another mission, headed by Sung Su-ch'ing (*q. v.*) came to China and sold swords at that price. Ryōan wrote a letter of protest and threatened the possible revival of Japanese piracy if the Chinese made no concessions in the interests of trade. Nothing further is known about this dispute. While negotiations were going on Emperor Chu Hou-chao (*q. v.*) invited Ryōan to stay at Kuang-li ssu 廣利寺 on Mt. Yü-wang 育王山 near Ningpo. On the day that Ryōan arrived at the temple, an imperial messenger presented him with a gold embroidered surplice, and Huang Hsiang黄相 (T. 國佐, cs 1517) also celebrated his arrival. From then on several priests and scholars came to visit him at the monastery.

In 1513 Ryōan returned to Japan. At the time of his departure from China, a number of scholars are said to have seen him off, among them Wang Shou-jen (*q. v.*) who presented a letter in which he expressed his regret at parting. Ryōan then lived in a studio known as Taiun-ken 堆雲軒 which he had built at Daiji-in for his residence before starting for China. But soon Emperor Gokashiwabara 後柏原 天皇 (r. 1501-26) asked him to live at Nanzen-ji 南禪寺 in Kyoto. During his stay at Nanzen-ji he reconstructed the main gate of the temple with his own funds; shortly afterwards he returned to Taiun-ken, where he died at the age of eighty-nine.

Ryōan wrote two books. One entitled *Goroku* 語錄, containing his discourses, was published after his death. It has a preface written by a certain Huang Lung 黃隆. There are a few copies of this book, one being preserved in the Japanese ministry library. The other entitled *Jinshin nyūmin ki* 壬申入明記 describes his experiences in China. This is preserved at Saga Myōchi-in 嵯峨妙智院 in Kyoto,

Bibliography

MSL (1965), Wu-tsung, 1817; Akiyama Kenzō 秋山謙藏, "Nichimin Kankei" 日明關係, *Iwanami kōza* 岩波講座; *Nihonshi* 日本史, 8 (Tokyo, 1933), 59; Kitamura Sawakichi 北村澤吉, *Gozanbungaku shi-kō* 五山文學史稿 (Tokyo, 1941), 699; Nishimura Tokihiko 西村時彦, *Nihon sōgaku shi* 日本宋學史 (Tokyo, 1909), 130; Uemura Kanko 上村觀光, "Gozan shisō den" 五山詩僧傳, *Gozanbungaku zenshū* 全集 (Tokyo, 1936), 609; Wang Yi-t'ung, *Official Relations Between China and Japan, 1368-1549* (Cambridge, Mass., 1953), 75.

Toyoko Y. Chen

RYŪKI Ingen, *see* LUNG-CH'I

SAMBIASI, Francesco (Chinese name: Pi Fang-chi 畢方濟, T. 今梁), 1582-January, 1649, Christian missionary, was born at Cosenza, near Naples. After entering the Society of Jesus (October, 1602) and completing his studies, he left for the East in 1609, and arrived in Macao in 1610. Besides studying Chinese he taught mathematics for a year, and was then (1613) dispatched to Peking. When the persecution against the Catholics broke out in 1616 and 1617 (*see* Shen Ch'üeh), he first sought refuge, along with Nicolo Longobardi (*q.v.*), in the home of Hsü Kuang-ch'i (ECCP) and next in Hangchow in the residence of Yang T'ing-yün (ECCP). In the meantime, with raids across the boundaries of both China and Korea becoming more serious, Hsü made the proposal (1619) to the throne that he be sent as envoy to Korea to strengthen the hands of the Koreans in their efforts to repel the Manchus, and further suggested to Sambiasi that he accompany him and work towards the conversion of the king and his court. Although the proposal seems at first to have been favorably received, and all preparations made for departure, it was eventually disallowed on the ground that Hsü's services could ill be spared.

In 1621, instead of returning to Macao as he had planned, Sambiasi accepted the invitation of Sun Yüan-hua (ECCP), a native of Chia-ting 嘉定 (near Shanghai), to take up his residence there in a commodious establishment which Sun turned over to him. Here he was able to instruct a number of pupils undisturbed by the disruptive events going on in Nanking and elsewhere. This too became the center of Chinese studies of certain new members of the mission (*see* Lazzaro Cattaneo). After a few years, possibly due to overwork and refusal to take care of himself, Sambiasi fell gravely ill in 1628, and his associates thought that the end had come. He rallied, however, and was sent inland bound for Shensi. En route he stopped at Kaifeng at the home of a merchant who had been converted, and remained to establish a church. Among the friends he made there was the prince of Fu, Chu Ch'ang-hsün (*see* Cheng Kuei-fei). His next post (1634) was in Nanking, a center made difficult by the deep-rooted antagonism of Shen Ch'üeh and his supporters. It was Hsü Kuang-ch'i, eager to reestablish the church in Nanking, who conceived the idea of sending him there on imperial business—it was one of his last acts, as he died at the end of 1633. By appointing Sambiasi to serve as a member of the astronomical bureau, Hsü hoped that he would be protected from official interference. Sambiasi was assigned such tasks as the observation of the eclipses and improvement of the calendar. At the end of 1639 he presented to the emperor, Chu Yu-chien (ECCP), Hsing p'ing 星屏 (Map of the stars) and Yü 輿 p'ing (Geographical map), together with a number of other gifts including a clock which sounded the hours, a convex lens for concentrating solar rays, a clepsydra, and a telescope. In spite of official involvements he found time to continue evangelistic work over a wide area in the lower Yangtze valley.

On the collapse of the Ming in north China (1644), Prince Chu Yu-sung (EC-CP), who became "administrator of the realm" and then emperor in Nanking, and who had become acquainted with the Jesuit in Kaifeng, invited Sambiasi to serve as his representative in securing help from the Portuguese in Macao. No objection being raised by the authorities, both civil and religious, to such an appointment, the missionary left in March for Canton, accompanied by a considerable entourage of officials, scholars, and soldiers. Although the prince was taken captive in June while the embassy was still on its way, the latter continued on its course, and was received in Macao with appropriate honors. Sambiasi bided his time, however, before presenting his cause, awaiting orders from Chu Yu-sung's successor, Chu Yu-chien, who

proclaimed himself emperor in Foochow in August, 1645. This prince, who had become acquainted with Sambiasi some twenty years earlier, when he was living in Ch'ang-shu 常熟 (near Soochow) as a guest of Ch'ü Shih-ssu (ECCP), confirmed him in his powers, and sent him a very friendly letter (dated February 19, 1646) inviting him to serve not only as ambassador but also as adviser. Sambiasi agreed to the first, but refused to become his minister. Instead he received permission to establish a church and residence in Canton. With the help of the eunuch P'ang T'ien-shou (ECCP, p. 195), this was accomplished just before the seizure of the city by the Manchus (January 20, 1647). He nearly lost his life at the time but was saved by a servant. For two more years he lived on, laboring in the nearby villages. On his death he was buried outside the north gate of the city with unusual pomp, ordered by the then reigning Ming sovereign, Chu Yu-lang (ECCP).

Sambiasi left several works, most of them in Chinese. It is said that one of them, *Ling-yen li shuo* 靈言蠡勺, 2 *ch.*, a treatise on the human soul, printed in 1624, which he dictated to Hsü Kuangch'i, brought about the conversion a century later of Surgiyen (*see* Sunu, ECCP), a member of the Manchu imperial clan. He also composed two short colloquies on sleep and allegorical pictures, *Shui hua er ta* 睡畫二答 (1629), which contains a preface by Li Chih-tsao (ECCP); it deals with the laws of perspective.

Bibliography

Fang Hao 方豪, *Chung-kuo T'ien-chu-chiao shih jen-wu chuan*中國天主教史人物傳, I (Hong Kong, 1967), 198; Pfister (1932), 136; George H. Dunne, *Generation of Giants*, Notre Dame, 1962; Sommervogel VII (1896), col. 502; Pasquale M. d'Elia, *Galileo in China*, tr. by R. Suter and M. Sciascia (Cambridge, Mass., 1960), 49; *id.*, *Fonti Ricciane*, II (Rome, 1949), 566, n. 3; Alexander Wylie, *Notes on Chinese Literature* (repr. Shanghai, 1922), 175.

L. Carrington Goodrich

SAYYID Ḥusain 寫亦虎仙, died 1521, Muslim government official, was an intimate of Chu Hou-chao (*q.v.*).

The key city of Hami (Qamil, Qomul) presented the Chinese with many problems in their continuing attempts to exercise suzerainty in that portion of Central Asia, not the least of which were the difficulties caused by its multiracial population. Near the end of the 15th century the Chinese made an attempt to bring order out of the near anarchy which then obtained among the different ethnic groups in that region by putting a local prince in charge of the city and the surrounding area (*see* Aḥmad). They appointed a distant heir to the Yüan line to this post, probably in 1491, and named as his assistants important figures representing each of the chief racial communities in the area, who were to serve as overseers with the title tu-tu 都督. Later, in July, 1494, Sayyid Ḥusain became the Muslim overseer. Somewhat before this appointment, which is evidence for his important position in the Hami Muslim community, he had taken refuge in Chinese territory from an invasion of Hami by Turfan, and his private intrigues with Turfan elements, probably with the aim of one day establishing himself as prince of Hami under the hegemony of Turfan, date from this period. These intrigues were one of the factors which eventually led to his execution, but only after several additional years of colorful activity in high places.

In 1516 he was accused of treason by a commission of inquiry in Kansu, and was sent to the capital in chains, but once there he was able to bribe the emperor's favorite general Ch'ien Ning 錢寧 (d. June 25, 1521), who arranged to have the affair whitewashed, and who provided him with entrée to the debauched coterie then surrounding the Cheng-te emperor.

Ch'ien Ning was related to the eunuch, Ch'ien Neng (*see* Chu Hou-chao). He more than anyone encouraged the emperor's libertine excesses and organized and built the Pao-fang 豹房 (Leopard House). This infamous institution was partly devoted to occult Lamaist cult practices of the tantric variety, and partly to indulging the emperor's increasingly bizarre sexual tastes. Ch'ien had the Leopard House constructed in 1507; it was here that Chu Hou-chao died. Its attached Lamaist temple was built in 1512. The clergy were mainly Tibetans. The Chinese officials objected as much to their presence within the palace enclosures and to their growing familiarity with the emperor as they did to the activities of the Leopard House; the Tibetans, for their part, appear to have been equally faithful in their attendance upon the activities of both institutions. But official remonstrances were of no avail in the face of the emperor's tastes, which included a great fondness for foreigners and even for dabbling in foreign languages. His infatuation with Tibetan Buddhism reached its peak in his dispatch of a mission in 1516 to invite a Living Buddha to China, but the Tibetans interpreted the mission as an invasion and harassed it severely. By the time its surviving stragglers were able to return to China, still without their Living Buddha, Chu Hou-chao had died.

Ch'ien Ning's intrigues with the rebellious prince of Ning were eventually discovered; he was executed in 1521, but not before his association with the throne had resulted in the emperor's honoring him and his two adopted sons with the imperial surname Chu 朱. His execution took place two weeks before that of the equally infamous Chiang Pin (*q.v.*), one of his great rivals for the imperial favor.

After Ch'ien had arranged to Sayyid have and his sons presented to the throne, Sayyid soon became an intimate of the emperor and his companion in the activities of the Leopard House. Like Ch'ien, Sayyid and his sons were honored by receiving the imperial surname. They accompanied the emperor on his punitive expedition to the south to direct the supression of Chu Ch'en-hao (*see* Wang Shou-jen). They left the capital on September 15, 1519. After a sojourn in Nanking and their return to Peking, followed by the death of the emperor, Sayyid was immediately denounced by Yang T'ing-ho (*q.v.*), and was executed in 1521. The charges against him included his earlier treasonous intrigues with Turfan, his bribery of and other associations with the disgraced Ch'ien Ning, and his association with the outlawed Leopard House. One of his sons met his end in 1523, the other in 1524.

Bibliography

1/*ch.* 307, 329; KC (1958), 2659, 2665, 3103, 3121, 3274; Chang Hung-hsiang 張鴻翔, "Ming wai-tsu tz'u-hsing k'ao 明外族賜姓考," *Fu-jen hsüeh-chih* 輔仁學誌, 3:2 (July, 1932), 20; Satō Hisashi 佐藤長, "Min no Buso nō 'katsubutsu' keisei ni tsuite," 明の武宗の(活佛)迎請について," *Tsukamoto hakuse sōju kinen bukkyo shigaku ronshū* 塚本博士頌壽記念佛教史學論集 (Kyoto, 1961), 351; Paul Pelliot, "Le Ḥōja et le Sayyid Ḥusain de l'Histoire des Ming," TP, 38 (1948), 81, 129; D. Pokotilov, *History of the Eastern Mongols during the Ming Dynasty from 1368 to 1634*, tr. by R. Loewenthal, *Studia Serica* mon., ser. A, no. 1 (Chengtu, 1947), 94; W. Franke, "Addenda and Corrigenda," *ibid.*, no. 2 (1949), 52; Arlington & Lewisohn, *In Search of Old Peking* (Peking, 1935), 311.

Roy Andrew Miller

SCHALL von Bell, Johann Adam (湯若望, T. 道未), May 1, 1592-August 15, 1666, missionary and astronomer, originated from an old noble family at Cologne, Germany. In 1608, after preparatory studies at Cologne, he traveled to Rome to study for the Catholic priesthood at the renowned Roman College, and in 1611 entered the Society of Jesus. When in 1614 Niklaas Trigault (*q. v.*) returned to Rome to recruit new men for the China mission, Schall volunteered and, after extensive studies of theology and mathematics and his ordination to the priesthood, he sailed (April 16, 1618) for the East via Lisbon and Goa, arriving at Macao on July 15, 1619. Owing to a temporary persecution of foreign missionaries (*see* Shen Ch'üeh), Schall was retained at Macao for over two years, during which he took part in the repulse of the invading Dutch (*see* Giacomo Rho). By January 25, 1623, Schall was in Peking where Hsü Kuang-ch'i (ECCP) promptly sought his help in the reform of the Chinese calendar. In the same year Schall calculated for Hsü the three eclipses of the moon (which occurred as he predicted) and composed a small illustrated work on lunar eclipses which Ch'iu Liang-ping 邱良稟 put into literary Chinese and which Hsü Kuang-ch'i presented to the ministry of Rites. But for the next few years Schall's foremost concern was the intensive study of the Chinese language. In the autumn of 1627 he was ordered by his Jesuit superiors to do missionary work in Shensi and stayed for nearly two years in Sian. There Schall kept in friendly contact with the Christian literatus Wang Cheng (ECCP) whom he had met in Peking, With his assistance Schall not only erected a new church in Sian, but also translated a booklet on famous Christian saints for which Wang wrote a preface and published under the title *Ch'ung-i-t'ang jih-chi sui-pi* 崇一堂日記隨筆, 1 *ch.*—the *ch'ung-i* referring to the first words of the Ten Commandments. During the last days of Johann Terrenz (*q. v.*), Schall was hurriedly recalled to Peking (Spring, 1630) and charged with the work in the calendrical bureau. Under Hsü Kuang-ch'i, official head of the bureau, Schall worked together with Rho and a team of Chinese assistants in translating or composing a large number of basic works on astronomy and mathematics which on several occasions were presented in manuscript form to the emperor, and as a collection are known as the *Ch'ung-chen li-shu* 崇禎曆書. At the same time Schall was also engaged in supervising the construction of the most important astronomical instruments. On February 28, 1634, the first calendar according to the new European method was presented to the throne and promptly approved. Throughout these years, however, in spite of imperial sanction, considerable opposition, both open and secret, was developing amongst Chinese and Muslim authorities in astronomy and the calendar. In 1631 Wei Wen-k'uei 魏文魁 published under the name of his son, Wei Hsiang-ch'ien 魏象乾, two critical volumes, *Li yüan* 曆元 and *Li ts'e* 曆測; these Schall considered of sufficient importance to write a refutation entitled *Hsüeh-li hsiao-pien* 學曆小辯, 1 *ch.* His knowledge of astronomy and mathematics gained him the reputation of being expert also in other fields, and thus he was commanded to cast cannon to be used against the Manchu invaders. He not only succeeded in his task, but also composed a book on the methods of making and firing cannon, the *Huo-kung ch'ieh-yao* 火攻挈要, 3 *ch.*, (1643). To help the Ming government in its financial plight, he submitted (July 20, 1640) through Li T'ien-ching (ECCP), then head of the calendrical bureau, the *K'un-yü ko-chih* 坤輿格致, 4 *ch.*, a translation of a well-known European work on mining: Agricola's *De re metallica*, which had appeared in Basel in 1556. For these various services Schall was repeatedly honored by the emperor; in 1639 he received the tablet with the inscription Ch'in-pao t'ien-hsüeh 欽褒天學, which literally means "Imperially approved astronomical studies," but which could be interpreted as an allusion to Catholicism. Besides his work for the imperial court Schall prudently advanced the cause of Christianity, making converts not only in Peking and its neighborhood, but even within the precincts of the palace, where, with the assistance of the eunuch P'ang T'ien-shou (ECCP, p. 195), he had a Christian congregation. During the last years of the Ming, Schall also published several religious books for the benefit of his Christian followers and prospective converts, namely, the *Chu-chih ch'ün-cheng* 主制羣徵 (On divine providence), 2 *ch.*

(*ca.* 1629), the *Chen-fu hsün-ch'üan* 眞福訓詮 (About the eight beatitudes), 1 *ch.* (Peking, 1634), and the *Chu-chiao yüan-ch'i* 主敎緣起 (On the origin of Christianity), 4 *ch.* (Peking, 1643).

When in 1644 Peking fell first to Li Tzu-ch'eng (ECCP) and then to the Manchus, Schall stayed behind in the ruined city to help the poor. Before long Prince Dorgon (ECCP) recognized Schall's ability and entrusted him with the calendar of the new dynasty. After a spectacular test in which he proved his superior knowledge, he was put, on September 1, 1644, at the head of the astronomical bureau with the title Ch'in-t'ien-chien cheng 欽天監正. Now Schall had a position of influence. In 1645 the collection of astronomical books was published in 100 *chüan* with the title *Hsi-yang hsin-fa li-shu* 西洋新法曆書. Gradually Schall reorganized the bureau according to European standards, doing away with all Muslim participation. His influence increased when after 1651 he enjoyed the confidence of the youthful emperor, Fu-lin (ECCP), who affectionately called him Ma-fa (Grandpa), and of other members of the imperial family. Schall received successively several honorary titles, including those of vice minister (1646), minister of the Court of Imperial Sacrifices (1651), and transmission commissioner (1657). In 1658 he was given the title Kuang-lu tai-fu 光祿大夫 (High dignitary) which, though honorary only, made him an official of the first rank. At this time Schall held a position at the court which probably no other European in China ever held. Because of this Schall became the influential protector of Christian missions in all China. With imperial permission he had built in 1650 a new mission compound and a public church near the Hsüan-wu-men 宣武門, known at that time as Hsi-t'ang 西堂 (later as Nan-t'ang南堂). By 1656 he was powerful enough to frustrate the efforts of the Dutch embassy in Peking defending Portuguese interests. In 1662 his intervention helped to save the city of Macao from contemplated destruction. After 1657, however, when Fu-lin became more interested in Ch'an Buddhism than in the Christian religion, opposition to Schall increased. The disgruntled Muslim astronomers especially worked against him. One of them, Wu Ming-hsüan 吳明炫, accused him (1657) of making false astronomical predictions. Failing in this, he collaborated with Yang Kuang-hsien (ECCP), an arch enemy of Christian missionaries, to discredit Schall personally, his astronomical ideas, and his Christian religion. In 1660 Yang Kuang-hsien published his *P'i-hsieh-lun* 闢邪論, a bitter invective against Christianity. Li Tsu-po (ECCP, p. 890), a Christian official of the calendrical bureau, replied with the *T'ien-hsüeh ch'uan-kai* 天學傳概 (Summary of the spread of the heavenly doctrine), using arguments furnished by Ludovico Buglio (利類思, T. 再可, 1606-82) and Gabriel de Magalães (*see* F. Furtado). This book, which asserted that mankind had originated in Judea and that a branch had migrated to China in the time of the mythical emperor Fu-hsi, enraged Yang Kuang-hsien anew, and he countered it with his *Pu-te-i* 不得已, in which he makes charges against and slanders Christianity. Buglio in turn refuted this work in 1665 with the publication *Pu-te-i-pien* 辯 (Disputing the *Pu-te-i*). As long as Fu-lin lived, however, Schall and his friends remained unharmed, but under the four regents his position became insecure. On April 20, 1664, he became partially paralyzed and this impeded his movements and speech. Five months later Yang Kuang-hsien launched a formal accusation to the ministry of Rites charging Schall and his collaborators with treason, with spreading a heterodox religion, and with teaching false astronomy. A long state trial ensued which Yang's party won. Schall was condemned to death, first to decapitation, later even to dismemberment. But, as was commonly believed, Heaven itself stepped in. An earthquake on April 16, 1665, and a fire in the imperial palace thirteen days later frightened the

judges. Schall and the other missionaries were set free. Schall died that summer in deep humiliation. Two years later, however, when the young K'ang-hsi emperor, Hsüan-yeh (ECCP), took over the government, Ferdinand Verbiest (南懷仁, T. 敦伯, 1623-88) sent in a petition, and a new investigation showed that Yang Kuang-hsien had calumniated Schall and his work. Thereupon Schall's name was rehabilitated and his former ranks and titles restored. He was honored with an official burial and his remains, which had been secretly buried outside the Jesuit cemetery, were then laid to rest in a handsome grave at Cha-la-er (*see* Matteo Ricci). A portrait of Schall, thought to have been painted about 1660 by Johann Grueber, S. J. (1623-80), hangs in the Jesuit house, Villa S. Ignacio, Florence, Italy. Another appears in Athanasius Kircher, S. J., *China... Illustrata* (Amsterdam, 1667). Still others may be found in the work by Alfons Väth, together with an illustration of a statue which up to World War II stood in front of the Wallraf-Richartz Museum in Cologne. Väth has also reproduced a photograph of Schall's tombstone, taken before its destruction in 1900.

As to Schall's writings, he left many others besides the works mentioned above. Several have not as yet been examined sufficiently. Schall's largest work in a European language is his unfinished volume of Memoirs which with additions was published as *Historica Narratio de Initio et Progressu missionis Societatis Jesu apud Sinenses* (Vienna, 1665) and as *Historica Relatio de Ortu et Progressu Fidei orthodoxae in regno Chinensi* (Regensburg, 1672). A modern edition with critical notes and a French translation by Paul Bornet was published under the title *Relation Historique* (Tientsin, 1942).

Other Chinese works which may be mentioned include: 1) *Yüan-ching shuo* 遠鏡說 (On the telescope), illustrated, 1 *ch.*, preface of 1626, first printed in Peking in 1630 (Li Tsu-po put this into Chinese at Schall's dictation), 2) *Hsin-fa-*

li-yin 新法曆引 (Introduction to the new calendar), 1 *ch.*, composed about 1634; 3) *Hsin-fa piao-i* 表異 (Divergences of the new calendar), 2 *ch.*, composed about 1634 and similar to the preceding; 4) *Hun-t'ien-i shuo* 渾天儀說 (Construction and use of celestial and terrestrial spheres), illustrated, 5 *ch.*, revised by Nicolo Longobardi (*q. v.*), Rho, and others (Peking, 1634); 5) *Heng-hsing piao* 恒星表 (Tables for calculating the fixed stars), 2 *ch.*, revised by Longobardi, Rho, and others, with considerable changes in later editions; 6) *Heng-hsing li-chih* 曆指 (Theory of the fixed stars), 4 *chüan*, first version before 1644, revised by Rho; 7) *Chiao-shih li-chih* 交食曆指 (Theory of solar and lunar eclipses), 7 *ch.*, composed before 1644, revised by Rho; 8) *Chiao-shih piao* 表 (Tables of eclipses), 9 *ch.*, written before 1644, revised by Rho; 9) *Ts'e-shih shuo* 測食說 or *Hsi-yang ts'e-lüeh* 西洋測略 (Method of calculating eclipses), illustrated, 2 *ch.*; 10) *Heng-hsing ch'u-mo piao* 出沒表 (Table of rising and setting of fixed stars), 2 *ch.*, revised by Rho; 11) *Ku-chin chiao-shih k'ao* 古今交食考 (Examination of ancient and modern eclipses), 1 *ch.*, revised by Rho (Peking, 1633); 12) *Li-fa hsi-ch'uan* 曆法西傳 (story of Western astronomy), 2 *ch.*, These works and the *Hsüeh-li hsiao-pien* are included in the *Hsi-yang hsin-fa li-shu*. Also under Schall's name were these works in Chinese: *Hsi-yang ts'e-jih-li* 西洋測日曆 (European method of compiling the calendar), 1 *ch.* ; *Ch'ih-tao nan-pei liang tung-hsing-t'u* 赤道南北兩動星圖 (Two general maps of the stars south and north of the equator, Peking, 1634); *Hsin-li hsiao-huo* 新曆曉惑 (Questions and answers on the new calendar), 1 *ch.* (Peking, 1645); *Min-li pu-chu chieh-huo* 民曆補註解惑 (Meaning of calendrical prediction), 1 *ch.*, composed 1661–62, published by Verbiest in 1683. There must be mentioned in addition the annual calendars, a number of important letters, and many memorials both in Chinese and European languages. [Editors' note: In ending his review of

Väth's book Paul Pelliot concludes with remarks which may be rendered in English as follows: "It remains to add that Schall is one of the two or three Europeans who, after Ricci and before Verbiest, played a role in the modern history of China. He was acquainted with all the science of his time, and did much to propagate it. At the same time his numerous writings, both European and Chinese, show the practical clarity of his mind. Man of the church, man of science, man of action, a plain man as capable of irony as of passion, this multi-faceted figure attracts and intrigues; Schall made his mark everywhere."]

Bibliography

Alfons Väth, *Johann Adam Schall von Bell, Missionar in China, Kaiserlicher Astronom und Ratgeber am Hofe von Peking, 1592–1666* (Cologne, 1933) [An English adaptation by Rachel Attwater: *Adam Schall, a Jesuit at the Court of China*(London, 1963); Chinese translation by Yang Ping-ch'en 楊丙辰, entitled *T'ang Jo-wang chuan* 湯若望傳 (Shanghai, 1949)]; P. Pelliot, Rev. of Väth in TP, 31 (1935), 178; Henri Bernard, "L'Encyclopédie astronomique du Père Schall: *Ch'ung-chen li-shu* (1629) *et Hsi-yang hsin-fa li-shu* (1645): La réforme du calendrier chinois sous l'influence de Clavius, de Galilée et de Kepler," MS, 3 (Peiping, 1938), 35, 441; id. (ed.), *Lettres et mémoires d'Adam Schall, S. J.: Relation Historique*, Latin text with French translation of Paul Bornet, Tientsin, 1942; Pfister (1932), 162; Ch'en Yüan (BDRC), *T'ang Jo-wang yü mu Ch'en-wen* 湯若望與木陳忞 (1938), 1 (unfinished German translation by D. W. Yang in MS, 5, 1940, 316); Fang Hao 方豪, *Chung-kuo T'ien-chu-chiao shih jen-wu chuan* 中國天主教史人物傳 (Hong Kong, 1970), 1; Pasquale d'Elia, *Galileo in China. Relazioni attraverso il Collegio Romano tra Galileo e i Gesuiti scienziati missionari in China (1610–1640)*, Rome, 1947 [English translation by Rufus Suter and Matthew Sciascia: *Galileo in China* (Cambridge, 1960)]; id., "The Double Steller Hemisphere of Johann Schall von Bell, " MS, 18 (1959), 328; Joseph Needham, *Science and Civilization in China*, Vols. III–IV, London, 1959 –65; George H. Dunne, *Generation of Giants* (Notre Dame, 1962), 350; J. M. Planchet, *Le cimitière et les oeuvres catholiques de Chala*, 1610–1927 (Peking, 1928), 17, pl. 2; Fu Lo-shu, *A*

Documentary Chronicle of Sino-Western Relations
(*1644-1820*), (Tucson, 1966), 3, 10, 12, 35, 44.
B. H. Willeke

SEMEDO, Álvarō (Chinese name: Tseng
Te-chao 曾德照, T. 繼元), 1585-1658, missionary and scholar, was born in Villa de
Nisa, a small Portuguese town, then under
the spiritual jurisdiction of the priory of
Crato of the Order of Malta. At the age
of seventeen he entered the Jesuit novitiate at Evora. While studying philosophy
he expressed an ardent wish to go to a
foreign mission in the East; he was therefore sent to India, arriving at Goa in
1608. Five years later he completed his
studies and asked to be transferred to
the China mission in which he was
greatly interested. Arriving at Macao in
1613, he was promptly sent to Nanking to
study Chinese. There he became an almost inseparable companion of Alfonso
Vagnoni (*q.v.*), an Italian Jesuit and an
accomplished Chinese scholar. Semedo
initially took Hsieh Wu-lu 謝務祿 as his
Chinese name.

Shen Ch'üeh (*q.v.*), who was appointed vice minister of Rites in 1615, disliked
Christianity, mainly, we are told, because
of the personal embarrassment he had
suffered on various occasions when he
engaged in discussions on religious beliefs.
It has also been asserted that the Buddhist monks of Nanking, jealous of the
achievements of the missionaries, had
approached Shen with an offer of ten
thousand taels of silver, asking for their
expulsion. Whatever may have been the
cause, in 1616 Shen submitted a memorial
to the throne petitioning that the missionaries be expelled on the ground that
they had entered China secretly, that they
had meddled with the Chinese calendar,
and that they had led the people astray by
their teaching. Despite the intercession of
Hsü Kuang-ch'i (ECCP) and a number of
other officials who had been converted to
Christianity, edicts were issued on August
20, 1616, and subsequent dates, ordering

that they be first imprisoned and then
sent home. Accordingly, Semedo, Vagnoni,
and others in Nanking were thrown into
prison and their properties confiscated.
Semedo was spared a beating due to illness, but he and his companions underwent great humiliation. In his history of
China he gives an account of their sufferings: "They kicked us and slapped us on
the face.... Some spat on our cheeks, others
pulled our hair.... However, the prisoners
took everything in good spirit and none
of them tried to defend himself." The
court records describe Semedo as having
a ruddy complexion, deep set eyes, sharp
nose, and a flaxen beard.

It was Shen Ch'üeh's intention that
capital sentence be passed on the missionaries, but the tribunal, adhering strictly
to the instructions from Peking, ordered
only their expulsion from China. On April
30, 1617, Semedo and Vagnoni were put
in two small narrow cages and conducted by soldiers to Canton and thence to
Macao, a journey of thirty days. At
Macao, Semedo kept up his study of Chinese and waited for a chance to return
to the mission field. This came in 1620,
when he took up a new post in Chekiang
with the help of Yang T'ing-yün (ECCP).
To avoid suspicion he changed his name
to Tseng Te-chao. For several years he
worked in that province, spending most
of his time in Hangchow, paying a visit
to Kiangsi, and for a period also working
in Chia-ting 嘉定 and Shanghai.

There is some uncertainty about the
date of Semedo's arrival in Shensi, but he
was there by 1625, when the Nestorian
monument was discovered in the Sian
area, and was the first European to inspect it. He sent a description and an
inked squeeze to his colleagues in Peking
and made a rough translation of the
Chinese text. Remaining in Shensi until
1630, he was transferred again to Kiangsi.
In 1636, as procurator of the vice-province
of China, he was ordered to return to
Lisbon and Rome to explain the problems
facing the mission and to recruit new

members in Europe. Leaving Macao in 1637, Semedo arrived in Goa the following year, where he completed his book *Relação da propagação da fé no reyno da China e outros adjacentes*. His arrival in Portugal in 1640 was followed by a large number of applications for the China mission, especially in Coïmbra and Evora, where more than ninety volunteered. He reached Rome in 1642.

Setting out for China in 1644 at the head of a small group of recruits, he eventually reached Macao to find that the Manchus had displaced the Ming in north China. In south China, however, several of the Ming princes were still trying to hold their own against the invaders. For some years Semedo acted as vice-provincial of the China mission. In 1649 he went to Canton to fill the vacancy left by Francesco Sambiasi (*q.v.*) who had died earlier that year. He and Andreas Koffler (*q.v.*) visited the court of Chu Yu-lang (ECCP) in Chao-ch'ing 肇慶 (Kwangtung). Having appointed Michāl Boym (*q.v.*), then newly arrived in China, as his substitute, Semedo returned to Canton. A year later (1650) the Manchus recaptured Canton and he became their prisoner. His life was in danger, but fortunately a Christian eunuch recognized him as one of the companions of Johann Adam Schall von Bell (*q.v.*), and released him. He remained working in Canton till his death in 1658. His remains were removed later to Macao for burial. Authorities differ regarding the date of his death, putting it anywhere from May 6 to August 2, 1658.

Semedo left many writings; some of these were later published; others are still unedited. While in Portugal in 1640 he made arrangements for the publication of his *Relação propagação da fé no reyno da China e outros adjacentes* and he may have published an extract, the *Breve Recopilação* of 1642. Faria i Sousa, having a complete copy of the manuscript, changed the order of subject matter and the style, and translated it into Spanish, publishing it

under the title *Imperio de la China* (1642). Several other editions were printed, besides translations into French, Italian, English, and other languages. (The manuscript for the Italian version, published in Rome in 1643, is preserved in the Wason Collection, Cornell University.) A retranslation from the Italian into Portuguese was printed at Macao in 1956. It bears the title *Relação de Grande Monarquia da China*. This book, besides the description of China in Semedo's time, contains also his views on the rites and term controversies. He backed the opinion of Matteo Ricci (*q.v.*) and opposed the interpretations of Francesco Pasio (1554-1612), Nicolo Longobardi, João Rodrigues, and Sabatino de Ursis (*qq.v.*), thus speaking for many of his colleagues in China.

The *Tzu-k'ao* 字考, a Chinese-Portuguese and Portuguese-Chinese dictionary in two volumes compiled by Semedo, was kept for a long time in the Seminario de San José, Macao, but was sent to the Biblioteca de Lisboa in 1870 by Antonio Luis de Carvalho. It is still in manuscript (codex F. G. 3306). Carlos Sommervogel and Henri Cordier mention a book compiled from Semedo's letters printed in Paris, 1619: *Narré veritable de la persécution excitée contre les Chrestiens au Royaume de la Chine*. Sommervogel says that letters by Semedo may be seen at Brussels and Montpellier. Pelliot reports that the reedition, printed in Bordeaux in 1620 under the title *Histoire veritable de la persécution excitée contre les Chrétiens au royaume de la Chine*, is not the same. Semedo's *Breve Recopilação dos principios continuação e estado da Christandade da China*, Lisbon 1642, is a short work in twelve pages, and still exists; a French translation appeared in Rouen in 1643, entitled *Recueil des commence, progrez et estat moderne de la Christienté de la Chine*. For a portrait of Semedo see the English translation of his *Imperio de la China*, entitled *The History of that Great and Renowned Monarchy of China* (London,

1655), or *T'ien Hsia Monthly* 7 (1938), opp. p. 32.

Bibliography

Hsü Ch'ang-chih 徐昌治, ed., *P'o-hsieh chi* 破邪集 (1855 Mito reprint of 1639 ed.), 1/20b; Philipp de Alegambe, *Bibliotheca Scriptorum Societatis Iesu* (Rome, 1676), 44; Daniello Bartoli, *Dell'Historia della Compagnia di Giesu: La China*, Rome, 1633; Antonio Franco, *Imagen da virtude em o Noviciado de Evora* (Lisbon, 1714), 85; Antonio de Gouveia, *Asia Extrema*, Book 6, cap. 3 (Ms. codex, Ajuda Library, Lisbon, 49-V-1 and 49-V-2); Barbosa Machado, *Biblioteca Lusitana* (Lisbon, 1741; new ed. 1930), I, 111; Álvaro Semedo, *Relação da Grande Monarquia da China*, tr. from the Italian by Luis G. Gomes, Macao, 1956; Faria e Sousa, *Asia Portuguesa* (Lisbon, 1666-75), Par. 3, Cap. 12, n. 29, Cap. 14, n. 13; Henri Cordier, *Bibliotheca Sinica*, I (1904), cols. 23-26, II (1905-6), 813; Sommervogel, Vol. 7, 1114; Paul Pelliot, TP, XXXI (1935), 79; *Grande Enciclopédia Portuguesa e Brasileira* (Lisbon, 1935-58), XXVIII, 213.

Albert Chan

SESSHŪ Tōyō 雪舟等揚, 1420–August 26, 1506, the Zen priest and artist who assumed the sobriquet Sesshū about 1460 and came to be known by that name in the world of art, was born in Akahama 赤濱, Bitchū (near Soja-shi 總社市, Okayama), Japan. The younger son of a family named Oda 小田, he was sent in his youth to a local monastery to become a novice. About the year 1440, now a Buddhist priest, he went to Shōkoku-ji 相國寺, the most prosperous Zen temple in Kyoto of that day. There he studied Zen under Shunrin Shūtō 春林周藤 (d. 1463) and painting under Tenshō Shūbun 天章周文 (fl. 1423-63); in time he rose to be a shika 知客 (a monk in charge of public relations).

Around 1460 he moved to western Honshū and lived in a temple named Unkoku-ji 雲谷 (in Yamaguchi-shi) where he painted under the patronage of the Ōuchi 大內 feudal lords, then in control of western Japan and its maritime activities. By being commissioned as a sort of purchasing agent to the Ōuchi, he was able to join the official embassy from Japan to China in 1468. The three ships carried armor, swords, spears, folding screens, and ten thousand pounds of sulphur. They landed at Ningpo, visited various famous Ch'an temples there, such as the T'ien-t'ung 天童 ssu and the A-yü-wang 阿育王 ssu (also called Yü-wang ssu), and then started their journey to Peking. En route the party made stops at Hangchow (Sesshū later painted West Lake), Soochow, Chinkiang (visiting particularly the Chin-shan 金山 ssu), and then took the Grand Canal northward, reaching Peking in December, 1468. The Japanese delegation represented one of many countries granted audience on the occasion of the New Year celebrations.

[Editors' note: The experience of the Japanese trade mission of 1468-69, which afforded Sesshū the opportunity to visit China, makes an interesting study of Chinese-Korean-Japanese relations in the middle years of the 15th century. It was the twelfth Japanese mission to China since 1401 and the second sent by the Shōgun, Ashikaga Yoshimasa 足利義政 (1435-90). His first mission returned to Kyoto in 1454. Four years later he planned to send another mission ahead of schedule, and so asked the Korean king to transmit his request to the Chinese emperor. He actually received a favorable reply from Peking by way of Seoul. The mission was a joint enterprise of the Shōgun and two daimyō, Hosokawa Katsumoto 細川勝元 (1430-73) and Ōuchi Masahiro 大內政弘 (? -1954). Ōuchi's was the third ship, Tera Maru 寺丸, and Sesshū traveled on this in his official capacity. According to the *Ming shih-lu*, the mission's arrival at Peking was announced the eleventh month 甲戌 (December 2, 1468). Eight days later a Japanese was accused of manslaughter while drunk; the case was settled by requiring him to pay a fine of ten taels of silver and entrusting the culprit to the head of the mission for punishment after returning to Japan. When the New Year's celebrations were over and it was time to settle the accounts, the ministry of Rites reported that the Japanese demanded more for their goods than the ministry's offer of thirty-eight thousand taels. The matter was somehow resolved and a farewell feast for the Japanese took place at court in the first month 辛巳 (February 21, 1469). After most of the mission had left, however, the Ōuchi group remained in Peking to plead for more compensation. It seems that during a storm their ship had lost part of its freight, and so they received payment only for what was left of their lord's original consignment. Without additional allowance from the Chinese government they were afraid to go back and run the risk of punishment. The ministry of Rites, on reporting this case, suggested that their request be refused, but the emperor ordered a supplementary gift of one hundred rolls of silk and ten double-lengths of satin. To their further plea for five thousand thousand-units of copper coins, only a tenth was granted. The interpreter of the mission, a Chinese originally from Feng-hua 奉化, Chekiang, by the name of Yen Tsung-ta 閻宗達, was charged with being a troublemaker by the ministry which also proposed a punishment. The emperor, however, permitted Yen to return to Japan with the mission and warned him that should he cause any more mischief his relatives in his native place would be made to suffer. The mission of 1468 took place during the Ōnin 應仁 rebellion (1467-77), and the shōgun and the other lords who sponsored this mission were all involved in the fighting and in financial difficulties. This may partly explain the unseemly bargaining. On the other hand, this episode may serve as an illustration of the true nature of such missions called in Chinese chronicles "tributary embassies."]

During his residence in China, Sesshū sought out well-known Chinese teachers of ink painting. About four years after his return, he wrote about one of his own works:

"I journeyed to China and while there saw famous paintings. Many [painters] used Kao Yen-ching 高彦敬 (T. of Kao K'o-kung 克恭, H. 房山, known for his landscapes and bamboos, 1248-1310) as a model. Therefore I also followed this popular style and in painting landscapes imitated him...."

Eight years after his return Ryōshin 良心, a fellow traveler, wrote:

The minister, Yao K'uei (*q. v.*) ordered the venerable Sesshū to paint on the [walls of the] central room of the ministry of Rites, Peking. He said: "Nowadays, although tribute comes to China from about thirty distant countries which use strange languages, I have seen no painting like Sesshū's. Furthermore, as this place is headquarters for those directing the examinations, all men of note in China will come to this hall. And when they do, they will call the candidates together and will point to the wall and say, 'This is the excellent painting of the honorable Japanese priest, Yo 楊 Sesshū. If outside barbarians possess such rare skill as to reach this level, why do not you study more diligently at your tasks?'"

Whether Sesshū actually painted on the walls of the ministry of Rites or not, the fact that he had been educated to admire the idealistic landscape painting of the Southern Sung masters means that what he saw in Peking in 1469 must have been disappointing to him, because at that time a new style in art had developed in the Yangtze estu ary, bringing more interest in realistic light and shade and greater play of ink contrasts. He had no way of knowing the rising artists of Soochow.

The Japanese artist's friend, Genryū 彦龍, later wrote that Sesshū had said: "In the great country of China there are no painting masters. That is not to say that there are no paintings, but no painting teachers except as there are mountains... and as there are rivers... strange plants, trees, birds, and beasts, different men and their manners and customs. Such are the real paintings of China [to be studied...].”

The Japanese delegation returned in 1469. Sesshū did not go to the Japanese capital, where the Ōnin rebellion was still raging, but stayed in Unkoku-ji, Yamaguchi. Hence, he is sometimes referred to as Unkoku-ken 軒. He had a studio, named Tenkaizukarō 天開圖畫樓, where his disciples studied with him. He painted several landscapes showing Chinese temple layouts. Some of his paintings include a signature which may be rendered: “Painted by Sesshū, Occupant of the First Seat at T’ien-t’ung,” so he must have been proud of the honors that he received at this Ch’an temple fifteen miles from Ningpo.

His most famous painting is a horizontal landscape scroll, over fifty-seven feet long, showing the terrain of southern China, which he painted in his sixty-seventh year. In fact, his vigorous brush strokes, with their emphasis on angularity portray the igneous rock of China rather than that of Japan. Since he had many followers in landscape painting over several subsequent centuries, the scenery of China was painted by a number of Japanese artists who had never visited there. This scroll was reproduced in 1959 with introduction and notes by Reiko Chiba.

[Editors’ note: There are several versions of the place and year of Sesshū’s death, one of which holds that he died in 1502 at the temple Daiki-an 大喜庵 (in Masuda-shi 益田市, Shimane). The year 1506, however, has been generally accepted and in 1956, in honor of the four hundred fiftieth anniversary of his death, there were several exhibitions and many publications. One of these publications is a folio volume entitled *Hsüeh-chou* 雪舟, published (August, 1956) in Peking, containing an appreciation of the artist by Fu Pao-shih 傅抱石 (the editor), a preface by Kuo Mo-jo (BDRC), and some fifty illustrations, mostly reproductions of Sesshū’s paintings. This is probably one of the few times in the

history of Chinese publishing that a non-Chinese has been so honored.]

Bibliography

MSL (1963); Hsien-tsung, 1228, 1231, 1259, 1268, 1275, 1280, 1347; *Chosŏn wangjo sillok* 朝鮮王朝實錄 (Sejo, 1955–63), 298, 320, 323, 330; *Zenrin kokuhō-ki* 善隣國寶記; *Boshi nyūmin-ki* 戊子入明記; Fu Pao-shih(ed.), *Hsüeh-chou* (Peking, 1956); *Sesshū, 450-nen kinen-ten zuroku*, 450 年記念展圖錄; Jon Carter Covell, *Under the Seal of Sesshū* (New York, 1941); *Nakamura Tanio, Sesshū Tōyō, 1420–1506*, English text by Elise Grilli, Tokyo and Rutland, Vt., 1957.

Jon Carter Covell

SHANG Lu 商輅 (T. 弘載，H. 素庵), March 16, 1414–August 17, 1486, a native of Ch’un-an 淳安, Chekiang, served as senior grand secretary from 1475 to 1477. Shang was a prominent man at the start of his career, for he placed first in all three literary examinations: the provincial in 1435, and the metropolitan and the palace examinations in 1445, and became known as a “triple primus” 三元, the only one in the Ming dynasty. Together with another “optimus,” P’eng Shih (*q. v.*), he was immediately destined for one career, that of Hanlin academician to serve in the Grand Secretariat. When the imperial army was defeated at T’u-mu 土木 in 1449, and Chu Ch’i-yü (*q. v.*) ascended the throne, the two holders of first place in 1445 and 1448, Shang and P’eng Shih, were called to enter the secretariat and advise on matters of state. Shang remained in office until the *coup d’état* of Chu Ch’i-chen (*q. v.*) in 1457 when he was tried as a member of the clique of Yü Ch’ien (*q. v.*). He was sentenced to be beheaded, but the order was changed by the newly restored emperor to that of retirement as a commoner to his native place. The next emperor, Chu Chien-shen (*q. v.*), recalled him and he served long enough to become senior grand secretary, which office he held for two years before resigning for political reasons in 1477. Wan An (*see* Chiao Fang) succeeded him.

A career in the Grand Secretariat (*see* Yang Shih-ch'i) had by now become rather conventionalized: one rose from a low Hanlin grade through various Hanlin and Chan-shih-fu 詹事府 offices to the rank of a Hanlin chancellor, a grand secretary, and finally the senior grand secretary; meanwhile the promotion in rank was indicated by concurrent titles in the six ministries. Title and rank, however, did not necessarily indicate any real power. Since the autocrat emperor, institutionalised by the founder of the dynasty, had to rely on someone who was not involved in other official duties, such an individual as a grand secretary, a eunuch, or some other person, whom the emperor thought he could trust, would enter the scene. As it developed, a eunuch had more opportunities to be close to the Son of Heaven, and so power and influence were often on his side. The fame of Shang, it turned out, was not so much founded on his literary brilliance, as one might surmise, as on his personal courage. He seems to have been more than just a drafter of edicts and recorder of state history. It is said that, after Chu Ch'i-chen had reascended the throne, Shang was urged by the military dictator Shih Heng (*q. v.*) to annul all edicts and rescripts of that year bearing the Ching-t'ai style; he stoutly refused. After he became senior in the Grand Secretariat in 1475, he was in a position to facilitate the rehabilitation of Chu Ch'i-yü. When the eunuch Wang Chih 汪直 (*q. v.*) started to dominate the government by means of his Western Depot 西廠 special police in the late 1470s, Shang led the opposition. To his first démarche the emperor angrily retorted that the appointment of a minor eunuch would not endanger the empire. Under threat of punishment Shang upheld his protest. Every court official, he said, who had committed a fault, was subject to

investigation, but "that man" confiscated property at will from the high metropolitan officials and seized whomever he wished. The strongholds along the Great Wall north of Peking, the protest continued, could not be left unprotected for a single day, but "that man" had seized and beaten several of the commanding officers within a given day. Nanking was the holy ground of the imperial ancestor and yet "that man" cared not one whit and imprisoned its leading officials at his own discretion. Furthermore, he willfully altered assignments of the officials close to the emperor. If Wang Chih were not dismissed, the protest ended, surely the state would be in peril. At last the emperor gave in. But other officials did not stand their ground as firmly; so Shang resigned in 1477 and went into retirement. He died ten years later, at the age of seventy-two and was canonized as Wen-i 文毅.

A contemporary, Ma Wen-sheng (*q. v.*), is said to have ranked Shang at the top of the great ministers of the time, neither Yang Shih-ch'i nor Li Hsien (*q. v.*) possessing his caliber. The collected writings of Shang Lu have been assembled under the title *Shang Wen-i kung chi* 公集, one edition in 30 ch., another in 10 ch. The first includes twenty of his memorials, the second eighteen. Others are included in *Shang Wen-i shu-kao lüeh* 疏稿略. Certain jottings on historical subjects are in his *Che-shan pi-chu* 蔗山筆塵, 1 ch. The last two were copied into the *Ssu-k'u*. He took part in the editing of the continuation of the general history of China, known as the *Hsü Tzu-chih t'ung-chien kang-mu* 續資治通鑑綱目, 27 ch., and the great geography of the empire and the other lands of Asia entitled *Huan-yü t'ung-chih* 寰宇通志, 119 ch. The first of these was also copied into the Imperial Library of the 18th century. The latter, superseded almost at its inception (1456) by the *Ta Ming i-t'ung-chih* 一統志 of 1461, became rather obscure until a copy was reproduced in 1947 in the *Hsüan-lan t'ang ts'ung-shu* 玄覽堂叢書, 2d series, of Cheng Chen-to (BDRC).

Bibliography

1/176/15a; 3/159/14b; 5/13/23a; 8/29/7a; 40/20/14a; 61/121/2425 (TsSCC ed.); 63/11/10a; Cheng Hsiao, *Wu-hsüeh pien*, 36/5b; Liao Tao-nan, *Tien-ko tz'u-lin chi*, 2/3b; L. Carrington Goodrich, "Geographical Additions of the XIV and XV Centuries," *MS* 15 (1956), 203; W. Franke, *Sources*, 5.3.3, 8.1.1, 2.

Tilemann Grimm

SHAO-CH'I 紹琦 (T. 楚山, H. 幻叟, 荆璧), 1404-April. 11, 1473, master of the Ch'an sect (Lin-chi 臨濟 branch), was born into the Lei 雷 family of Chiang-yüan 江源, Szechwan. Even as a little boy he is said to have been unusually serious as well as an apt student. At the age of eight, following the death of his father, he left home to become a novice in a monastery of the Ch'an sect. Later, in an interview with Wu-chi 無際 (*ming* 了悟, fl. 1436-49), he demonstrated some understanding of Ch'an beliefs and obtained a seal. One day in 1443, on a second visit with Wu-chi, he showed a still deeper comprehension. One recorded passage of their dialogue may be rendered as follows:

Wu-chi: During all these years where have you stayed?

Shao-ch'i: In no fixed place.

Wu-chi: Have you acquired anything?

Shao-ch'i: There is nothing to lose; what is there to be gained?

Wu-chi: That is something you have obtained through learning.

Shao-ch'i: Not even a Dharma exists; where does learning come from?

Wu-chi: Are you falling into the void?

Shao-ch'i: Even I am not I; who is falling into whose void?

In the evening Wu-chi summoned him again and said, "See if you can tell me all that I have elucidated every day." Shao-ch'i responded according to what he had learned. Wu-chi replied, "Give me the meaning of the word wu 無." Shao-ch'i answered with a verse, the last line of which runs: "From his fussiness only doubt arises." "What is that which you do not doubt?" asked Wu-chi. "Blue mountain, green water, swallows' talk, orioles' song, everything is so clear; what else is there to be doubted?" was his response. "You have not yet hit the point," said Wu-chi. "My head supports the void, my feet tread the firm earth," replied Shao-ch'i.

Well satisfied with this, Wu-chi ordered his disciples to sound the temple bell to summon the monks to a ceremony. In this he gave Shao-ch'i a duster and a monk's robe, thus making him a Ch'an master in the twenty-seventh generation after the sixth Ch'an patriarch, Hui-neng (638-713).

In 1452 Shao-ch'i paid a visit to I-shan monastery 翼善寺, southeast of Nan-king. While there, in response to their questions, he gave to the assembled monks his replies in poetic form. For example, when they asked him, "What is T'ien chu ching 天柱境?" (region of the heavenly pillar), he answered with this couplet:

To the wide valley the clouds return late;

Behind the high mountain the sun emerges slowly.

In 1455 Shao-ch'i transferred to Shu-chou 舒州 (Anking), where an early Ch'an master of note, Ts'ung-shen 從諗 (778-897*sic*), had once stayed. From here he traveled to Kiangsi, and then in 1457 returned to his native province where he became the abbot of Yün-feng monastery 雲峯寺 at Fang-shan 方山, west of Lu-chou 瀘州. He was known for teaching his disciples to be patient in meditation. He left no written work; a short piece, however, recording his teachings and two letters about Ch'an Buddhism are preserved in *Huang Ming ming-seng chi-lüeh* 名僧輯略. He is chiefly remembered for his witty repartee. It is said that once while at a vegetable garden noticing a big winter melon he asked the gardener:

This winter melon has no mouth,

why has it grown so big?

Because I have never been lazy for a single moment, answered the gardener.

Has the owner ever put in any effort?

It is all because of his effort; said the gardener.

Please come to see this old monk.

The gardener made his obeisance.

That is still like slave and servant, said the master.

When the gardener returned, bringing some bamboo sticks to support the melon, the master laughed heartily. He looked around at his attendants and said, "There are worms in the vegetable garden." This dialogue has remained as an interesting example of Ch'an discourse.

It seems that Shao-ch'i lived the last part of his life in the T'ien-ch'eng monastery 天成寺 to the southwest of Chengtu, and it is there that he passed away. A pagoda with the same name was erected in his honor.

Bibliography

Hsü teng cheng-t'ung 續燈正統, 28/406a, in *Taishō zokuzōkyō* 大正續藏經, 乙套, case 17, vol.5; *Hsü teng ts'un-kao* 存稿, 9/105a, 106a, 108a, *ibid.*, case 18, vol. 1; *Huang Ming ming-seng chi-lüeh*, 2/2b, *ibid.*, case 17, vol. 3; *An hei-tou chi* 揞黑豆集, 3/439b, *ibid.*, case 18, vol. 5; *Wu-teng hui-yüan hsü-lüeh* 五燈會元續畧, 6/489b, *ibid.*, case 11, vol. 5; *Pu hsü kao-seng chuan* 補續高僧傳, 15/136b, *ibid.*, case 7, vol. 2; *Shih chien ch'i ku-lüeh hsü-chi* 釋鑑稽古略續集, 3/136b, *ibid.*, case 6, vol. 2; *Wu-teng yen-t'ung* 嚴統, 23/497b, *ibid.*, case 12, vol. 5; *Szechwan t'ung-chih* (1810), 168/12a; *An-hui t'ung-chih*(1877), 24/3b; *Dai Nihon Bukkyō zensho* 大日本佛教全書 (Tokyo, 1912), 73, 481; *Dai Nihon zokuzōkyō* 大日本續藏經 (1912), case 17, vol. 5.

Yang Chin-yi

SHAO Ching-pang 邵經邦 (T. 仲德, H. 弘齋, 弘毅先生), 1491-1565, poet, writer, and literary commentator, whose official career ended in exile, was born in Jen-ho 仁和, Hangchow. According to his own account, his family was one of modest means, both his father and grandfather earning their living as private tutors. After failing the metropolitan civil service examinations in 1518, he attended the National University at Nanking. No sooner was he enrolled than he submitted a long memorial to Emperor Chu Hou-chao (*q.v.*), urging the latter to refrain from indulgence in personal pleasures, but the paper never reached its destination. In 1521, after obtaining the *chin-shih*, Shao eventually received an appointment as secretary in the ministry of Works, and was dispatched to Ching-chou 荊州, Hukuang, to manage the office of levies on produce. In three months the proceeds from the waterfront levy exceeded the office's annual quota; so Shao suspended the collection for the rest of the year, and allowed ships to pass the inland port free of duty. The buildings of his office were in disrepair, but his sense of frugality would not permit him to refurbish them. Yet he built public pavilions in the city's suburbs. Such eccentricities were overlooked by his contemporaries. In 1526 he was promoted to be a vice director, but his mother's death that year caused him to withdraw from office. After the mourning period he returned to Peking (1529) and was transferred to the ministry of Justice. Barely three months later he suffered imprisonment.

Chang Fu-ching and Kuei O (*qq.v.*), grand secretaries who had endeared themselves to Emperor Chu Hou-ts'ung (*q.v.*), were unpopular at court. Shao Ching-pang, along with the majority of his colleagues, regarded Chang and Kuei as improper advisers. In the autumn of 1529 the emperor abruptly dismissed his two favorites. Before their case was closed, however, he reversed himself and recalled them both. At this point Shao asked permission to intervene. Seizing the opportunity given by an eclipse predicted for November 1, he submitted his memorial the day before. An eclipse, he argued, should never occur on such a day (the first day of the tenth lunar month) unless it portended an admonition to the throne. He cited the Book of Odes, and laid on Chang Fu-ching most of the responsibility for the omen. The memorial implied that even the emperor's position in his family tree might be considered as not permanently settled; it might be reopened for discussion. When Chu Hou-ts'ung read the petition on November 5, he personally directed that the memorialist be arrested and flogged, and on November 22 exiled Shao to Chen-hai-wei 鎮海衞, south of Amoy. There he died some thirty-six years later.

Shao's writings attest that his life in exile was not all bad. The commanding officers of the military colony treated him more as a guest than as a prisoner. There were other scholar-officials in exile too, such as Feng Hsi (*q.v.*). They visited each other, played chess, discussed philosophy, and befriended local magistrates. One undated poem by Shao indicates that he watched "captured fo-lang (Portuguese) soldiers" parade in the street. [Editors' note: Could this possibly refer to the incident of 1549 recorded in the biography of Lu T'ang in which Lu captured certain Chinese and Portuguese in a raid on a pirate stronghold? According to the account of Gaspar da Cruz, four of the Portuguese were dressed up to represent the Kings of Malacca and paraded through many towns in the region.] In his memorial of 1529 he declared that, at thirty-nine *sui*, he had yet to have a male offspring. But his tombstone inscription which he himself wrote, when he was about seventy, names five sons born of three concubines. He never ceased to hope that the emperor would forgive him. In 1537 the ministry of Justice recommended a general order of pardon that would release one hundred forty-two former officials in exile on various charges; the emperor approved the amnesty but deleted eight names from the recommended list, Shao's among them. Only on March 1, 1573, was his former official title posthumously restored.

Shao was a diligent scholar, but also unusually egotistic and self-assertive. He did not hesitate to claim for himself many virtues, among them loyalty, filial piety, straightforwardness, and thrift. He bragged that he had worn one hat for twenty years. The publication of one of his works, *Hung-chien lu* 弘簡錄 (254 *ch.*), cost him one thousand taels of silver, which, he emphasized, he had saved through thirty years of simple living. Regarding himself as a brilliant historian, he also considered himself an outstanding interpreter of Confucian orthodoxy. Unabashedly he declared that his own writing "clarified what hundreds of sages had failed to clarify," and could "enable the blind to see and the deaf to hear." In exile he was not especially bitter. His self-pity, which is occasionally revealed in his writings, seems to have been modified by his spirit of independence.

With his *Hung-tao* 道 *lu* (56 *ch.*) Shao attempted to reaffirm Confucian ethics through historical study. The work consists of five major parts in accordance with five traditional virtues: benevolence, righteousness, propriety, wisdom, and sincerity. Each part has five subtitles to correspond to the emperor-subject, father-son, husband-wife, brother-brother, and friend-friend relationships. Passages quoted from the Confucian Classics and dynastic histories constitute the main entries of the book, interlaced with the author's comments. In spite of this neatly laid-out plan, the work falls short of a topical analysis. Shao fails to give each virtue a clear-cut definition. Even though he develops his themes, the writer equally fails to evaluate the virtues with any historical insight. On many occasions he confuses administrative efficiency with ethical value. Inasmuch as the compiler regards history as immutable, Confucian virtues constant and self-evident, the writing does not lead the reader in any direction. The *Hung-chien lu* was probably at first projected as part of a larger work under the title, *Hsüeh-shih hui t'ung-lu* 學史會同錄. In its present form it is a condensation of the dynastic histories which covers the years from 618 to 1279. The author indicates that he has corrected numerous errors and inadequacies found in the original works. He revised the contents not only "to preserve historical continuity," but also to suit his own personal historical perspective, which he considers as "correct." The whole book is a gigantic collection of historical biography, omitting the tables and topical essays characteristic of dynastic histories. He regards the T'ang and Sung as orthodox dynasties, calling their emperors T'ien wang 天王 "heavenly kings." The Five Dynasties, together with the Liao and Chin, are grouped under the subtitle tsai-chi 載記. His great-grandson, Shao Yüan-p'ing (ECCP, p. 851), continued his work a century later, entitling his contribution *Yüan-shih lei-pien* (42 *ch.*) which is also known as the *Hsü* 續 *hung-chien lu*. The *Hung-i* 藝 *lu* (32 *ch.*), basically a collection of poems and belles lettres, is also a work which helps a reader to become familiar with the author. It seems to have been issued for the first time in 1525, while Shao was at Ching-chou. The current edition is based on the second and enlarged edition published by Shao Yüan-p'ing in or about 1685. Included in the work are his autobiography, tombstone inscription composed by himself, three memorials, and a number of miscellaneous papers, with editorial notes added.

Ironically, while in his lifetime Shao never considered poetry his particular metier, he came to be best known in later days as a poet. His own feeling about the art was that a poet must constantly search for the unexpected and strive for originality. Talent was essential; even so, a gifted writer must seek new experiences and exercise his gifts daily. His own poetic vocabulary is simple, his expression direct; though he experimented with a variety of forms, his verses are not elaborate or ornamental. Of particular interest are those poems recording contemporary events which throw light on the social and political conditions of his time.

Bibliography

1/196/84a, 206/24b; 64/戊 14/20b; MSL (1965), Shih-tsung, 2501, 4155, Shen-tsung (1966), 0338; *Hang-chou-fu chih* (1895), 124/14b; SK (1930), 176/17a; *Hung-tao lu* in *Tao-tsang* 道藏 (1926), Vols. 1067-80; *Hung-chien lu* and *Hung-i lu* in *Wu-lin wang-che i-chu* 武林往哲遺著 (1897), Vols. 49-53; C. R. Boxer, *South China in the Sixteenth Century* (London, 1953), 195.

Ray Huang

SHAO Mi 邵彌 (T. 僧彌 瓜疇, etc.), fl. 1626-1660, probably originally named Shao Kao 高 (T. 彌高), was a native of Wu 吳-hsien (Soochow). Noted primarily as an artist, Shao Mi was also known as a poet and calligrapher. His father was a physician and the family lived at a place known as Lu-mu 陸墓, located to the west of Shih-hu 石湖 (Stone Lake). He was a sickly child and consequently did not undergo the strenuous preparations for the civil service examinations. He developed certain pecularities such as a mania for cleanliness and order; much to the despair of his wife and servants, he constantly brushed and adjusted his garments or dusted and rearranged his ink-stones and desk top. When guests arrived, he conversed with them but never invited them inside while he leisurely prepared to go out with them. At parties he drank only half a cup of wine and then drifted off to sleep regardless of the company present. Probably due to his ill health, as well as to his easy-going disposition (and the lack of pressure to study), he was described as being "as thin as a yellow crane and as free as a sea gull." He followed his personal inclinations and, in addition to practicing the arts of poetry, calligraphy, and painting, collected curios and antiquities. He owned, for instance, a painting by T'ang Yin (*q. v.*) which he once showed to the connoisseur, Chang Ch'ou (*q. v.*). Shao named his house I-t'ang 頤堂 (Contentment hall), and there he delighted in his treasures.

In his middle years Shao contracted a lung disease (or, according to some sources, a kidney disease) and began to delve into pharmaceutical books, seeking prescriptions of medicine which might relieve his affliction, but in vain. As he grew increasingly uncomfortable, he became more eccentric and introverted. After his death, his writings, paintings, and possessions were scattered and lost as his family suffered impoverishment. He had two sons, the elder, Shao Yü 豫, drowned sometime before 1672; the younger son, Shao Kuan 觀, who was lame, became a monk at Mt. Hsüan-mu 女墓, southwest of Wu-hsien.

Although Shao had no degree, he and the literati had common interests, and thus Wen Chen-meng (*q. v.*) and other leading members of the intelligentsia of Soochow were his friends and companions. In this respect, Shao Mi is interesting because, even as a talented and appreciated individual, he never achieved true prominence, but remained in the shadow of the illustrious and the wealthy. Wu Wei-yeh (EC-CP) not only wrote Shao's epitaph, but also, elsewhere, reveals that Shao enjoyed conversing about Soochow's luminaries of bygone days. He was reputed to be an avid admirer of plum blossoms; he is mentioned in this connection by Yao Hsi-meng (*see* Ch'ien Shih-sheng). In 1628 Shao Mi and Ch'ien Ch'ien-i (ECCP), who also was acquainted with Shao's father, went out to enjoy the plum blossoms. In his writing Ch'ien several times refers to Shao and his appreciation of these blooms; Shao often painted scrolls depicting them.

In 1637, while at the Ch'ing-yin hall 清蔭堂 of the Fa-shui monastery 法水寺 (one of his haunts), Shao painted the farewell scene "I-hao chi-shu t'u"貽鶴寄書圖 (Sending a crane to deliver a message) for a poet-friend, Ch'u Chuan 褚篆 (T. 蒼書, 1580-1676 or 1607-1700). Shao also had numerous acquaintants among the Buddhist clergy, such as the poet Pen-ch'eng 本成 (T. 在久) who lived at the Hui-ch'ing 慧慶 monastery and Chih-hsü (*q. v.*) who resided at Ling-feng 靈峯. One of Shao's pupils, the monk Tzu-chiung 自扃 (T. 道開, 1601-52), gained some

fame as a calligrapher and was one of Shao's more intimate friends. Although Wu Wei-yeh included Shao Mi as one of the "Nine friends of painting," there appears, however, to have been little direct social communication between them and Shao.

Shao's paintings display great virtuosity. A long handscroll entitled "Yün-shan p'ing-yüan 雲山平遠 t'u" (Cloudy mountains and level distance), dated 1640, and now in the Abe collection of the Osaka Municipal Museum, reveals the artist's consummate ability in interpreting the styles of Sung and Yüan dynasty masters. Many works by Shao were influenced by the artistic style of T'ang Yin, while still others are more individualized, such as the album including the poem "Ling-ching hsien so pi meng ts'eng lai tz'u p'in"靈境仙所閟夢曾來此頻(Dream journey to Ling-ching), dated 1638. Most of Shao's paintings depict landscapes or plum blossoms, but sometimes bamboo; a painting of a goose, another of a dragon, as well as a few figure paintings, are also among those signed by or assigned to Shao Mi. Two portraits of Shao have been published. One, painted by Tseng Ching 曾鯨 (T. 波臣, 1568-1650), depicts Shao seated in a chrysanthemum garden. The other portrait, executed in 1657 by Hsü T'ai 徐泰 (T. 階平) and Lan Ying (*q. v.*), shows Shao seated on the gnarled roots of a slanting tree.

Bibliography

Chang Ch'ou, *Chen-chi jih-lu* (1918), 3/12b; Chang Keng 張庚, *Kuo-ch'ao hua-cheng lu* 國朝畫徵錄 (*Hua-shih* 畫史 *ts'ung-shu* ed.), 1/7; Hsü Ch'in 徐沁, *Ming hua lu* 明畫錄 (*ibid.*), 5/68; Chiang Shao-shu 姜紹書, *Wu-sheng shih-shih* 無聲詩史 *ibid.*, 7/129; Ch'ien Ch'ien-i, *Ch'u-hsüeh chi* (SPTK ed.), 4/8a, 5/1a, 2b, 3b; *id.*, *Yu-hsüeh chi* 有學集(SPTK ed.), 48/11a; Ch'in Tsu-yung 秦祖永, *T'ung-yin lun-hua* 桐蔭論畫 (1929), I, 上 /1b; Chou Liang-kung (ECCP), *Tu-hua lu*, 1/13; Hsü Pang ta, *Li-tai. . . shu-hua. . . nien-piao* (Shanghai, 1963), 135; *Shih-ch'ü pao-chi hsü-pien* 石渠寶笈續編 (1888), 6/143a; Lu

Shih-hua 陸時化 (1714-79), *Wu Yüeh so-chien shu-hua lu* 吳越所見書畫錄 (1910), 5/72a; Wu Wei-yeh, *Mei-ts'un chia-ts'ang kao* (SPTK ed.), 11/4a, 30/5a; *id., Wu Mei-ts'un wen-chi* (SPTK ed.), 14/13b; Yao Hsi-meng, *Ch'iu-min chi* 秋旻集, 9/8a, in *Yao Hsi-meng ch'üan-chi* 全集 (late Ming ed.), Cheng Chen-to (BDRC), *Yün-hui chai ts'ang T'ang Sung i-lai ming-hua chi*, Vol. 2 (Shanghai, 1947), pl. 98; *Sōraikan kinshō* 爽籟館欣賞, Part I, Vol. 2 (Osaka, 1930-39), no. 42; E. J. Laing, "'Riverside' by Liu Yüan-ch'i and 'The Waterfall on Mt. K'uang-Lu' by Shao Mi," The University of Michigan Museum of Art *Bulletin*, Vol. V, n. s. (1970-71); 1; *id., Chinese Paintings in Chinese Publications, 1956-1968* (Ann Arbor, 1969), 183; Osvald Sirén, *Chinese Painting* (New York, 1956-1958), Vol. V, 32, Vol. VI, pl. 284, 320, Vol. VII, 222; *id., A History of Later Chinese Painting* (London, 1938), Vol. 2, pl. 142; *Kokka*, no. 593, pls. 4-6; John C. Ferguson, *Index of Artists* (Nanking, 1934), 181a; François Fourcade, *Art Treasures of the Peking Museum*, tr. Norbert Guterman (New York, 1965), pl. 29.

E. J. Laing

SHAO Ts'an 邵璨 (T. 文明, H. 弘治?), fl. 1470, author of the drama *Hsiang-nang chi* 香囊記, was a native of I-hsing 宜興, east of Nanking. In biographical data which are often scanty and erroneous, he is referred to by various names and titles. The 1590 edition of the gazetteer, *I-hsing-hsien chih*, contains the only brief sketch of his life that may be deemed authentic. In it he is grouped among the yin-i 隱逸 (men who preferred staying at home to serving as officials), which is generally a more polite way of speaking of those who gave up after failing in civil examinations. The sketch describes Shao Ts'an as a well-read scholar who in his youth took part in the examinations but abandoned this course to devote himself to poetry, leaving a collection of poems, *Lo-shan chi* 樂善集, apparently never published; he was also noted as a student of music and a player of Chinese draughts. The local history does not mention his authorship of the *Hsiang-nang chi*, probably because drama was considered frivolous and vulgar. In a later edition the sketch is condensed to just a few words attached to the end of another clansman's biography.

Both editions of the local history give much more space to Shao Kuei 邵珪 (T. 文敬, H. 半江, cj 1468, cs 1469, prefect in 1481 of Yen-chou 嚴州, Chekiang), whose name and *tzu* indicate that he and Shao Ts'an were brothers (or cousins). In the *chin-shih* roster Shao Kuei listed his family as belonging to the military registry which usually implies ownership of land and the privileges of a hereditary officer's rank. Perhaps an affluent family background explains why Shao Ts'an could afford a life of expensive diversion. In the first half of the 15th century, the art of the theater was continued chiefly in the palaces of certain princes (*see* Chu Su and Chu Ch'üan), probably as a result of the prohibition of dramatic performances in 1389. It seems that although the ban was lifted in these years only the wealthy could afford its enjoyment. In any case, for a man to be as well-versed in theatrical art as Shao, it was probably necessary to maintain a private troupe at home for a long period of time. A story relates that while he was writing his drama, he was baffled at one point; here his brother offered him a suggestion. This so pleased Shao that he yielded to him title to a tract of land over which the two had been contending. This story, if true, serves to confirm the possession of land by the Shao family.

After Shao failed the provincial examination he was probably chagrined to see his kinsman pass it with ease in 1468 and become a *chin-shih* a few months later. He then turned his back on the examination system just as many other talented men in the Ming dynasty did (*see* Hsiang Yüan-pien and Ho Liang-chün). By devoting themselves to various pursuits these men contributed much to the arts, philosophy, and literature of the day. Shao chose music and drama and wrote the *Hsiang-nang chi*. If indeed these were the circumstances under which the drama was composed, it should have been completed about 1470. Conceivably the author was then about thirty or forty years of age.

Perhaps following the example of Ch'iu Chün (*q. v.*), who called his drama *Wu-lun ch'üan-pei chung-hsiao chi*, Shao named his the *Wu-lun chuan* 傳 *hsiang-nang chi*. Its story is set in the late Northern Sung period (early 12th century); the involved plot centers around a young scholar who, after being detained by the northern invaders, manages to escape to China and become reunited with his family and friends, thus fulfilling the duties of a man's five relationships, wu-lun. The drama is also entitled *Tzu* 紫 *hsiang-nang* signifying a purple perfume pouch which plays an important part in the plot and serves as the means of recognition and reunion. The early version of the story is included in the collection *Feng-yüeh chin-nang* 風月錦囊 of which a unique copy is preserved in Spain. Probably basing his drama on this simpler version, Shao developed the play into forty-two scenes and this became his *magnum opus*. The earliest edition extant has the imprint of Shih-te-t'ang 世德堂 which is known to have published books around the year 1530. There is also a Chi-ku ko edition (*see* Mao Chin, ECCP).

Shao wrote the *Hsiang-nang chi* in the form of a Southern drama or ch'uan-ch'i 傳奇 (*see* Kao Ming), but employed a highly refined literary style replete with allusion and parallelisms. For this he was accused by Hsü Wei (*q. v.*) of introducing the eight-legged essay style of the examination hall into the writing of drama. Hsü also criticized Shao for starting a pedantic trend in dramatic composition, for Hsü was an advocate of the Northern or tsa-chü 雜劇 style of play which followed stricter rules in music and plot—usually in four acts; its language is colloquial rather than literary, and the presentation follows a strict pattern for the stage. Shao's work, however, was intended for a different kind of audience, the more sophisticated and better-read urbanites. In this

sense it occupies an important position in the development of playwriting in China, for it is one of the early examples of the ch'uan-ch'i, a form which was to include thousands of titles written in the next four centuries.

Bibliography

I-hsing-hsien chih (NLP microfilm no. 381), 8/46a, 56a; *I-hsing-hsien chih* (1882), 8A/95a, 8B/38a; Chiao Chou 焦周 (fl. 1573-1620), *Shuo-k'u* 說楛 (1593); Hsü Wei, *Nan-tz'u hsü-lu;* Aoki Masaru, *Shina kinsei gikyoku shi* 支那近世戲曲史 (Chinese version by Wang Ku-lu 王古魯 1st ed. , Shanghai, 1931; revised ed., Peking, 1958). James J. Y. Liu 劉若愚, "The Feng-yüeh chin-nang: a Ming Collection of Yüan and Ming Plays and Lyrics Preserved in the Royal Library of San Lorenzo, Escorial, Spain, " JOS (Hong Kong, 1957-58) IV, 79; Fu Hsi-hua 傅惜華 *Ming-tai ch'uan-ch'i ch'üan-mu* 明代傳奇全目 Peking, 1959; *Yen-chou-fu chih* (1883), 10/37a; Chou I-pai 周貽白, *Chung-kuo hsi-chü shih* 中國戲劇史 (Shanghai, 1953), 351.

James J. Y. Liu and Chaoying Fang

SHAO Yüan-chieh 邵元節 (H. 雪崖, 太和子, a style given him by the emperor), July 26, 1459-Aprll 2, 1539, Taoist priest, was a native of Hsing-an 興安, Kiangsi. An orphan at the age of thirteen, he entered the Taoist temple Shang-ch'ing kung 上清宮 on Mt. Lung-hu 龍虎山 in the neigboring district of Kuei-hsi 貴溪 (*see* Chang Cheng-ch'ang). This temple, which belonged to the Cheng-i 正一 sect, dated from the 11th century and had a high reputation. Here he sat at the feet of a number of masters. It is said that he refused an invitation from Prince Chu Ch'en-hao (*see* Wang Shou-jen), and so avoided being involved in the latter's unsuccessful rebellion in 1519. In 1524 the succeeding emperor, Chu Hou-ts'ung (*q. v.*), summoned him to Peking. By March 13, 1526, he had so established himself as a favorite through his prayers and use of magic that the emperor gave him the title of Chen-jen (*see* Chang Cheng-ch'ang), four seals made of gold, silver, jade, and ivory, made him patriarch of Taoism of the state, and placed him in charge of three Taoist sanctuaries at the capital: Ch'ao-t'ien kung 朝天宮, Ling-chi 靈濟 kung, and Hsien-ling 顯靈 kung (the seat of the patriarch). A year later the emperor granted him leave to return to Kiangsi, but Shao was soon back at the capital. In 1530 the emperor bestowed honorific titles on his parents, made his grandson, Shao Ch'i-nan 啓南, an assistant minister of the Court of Imperial Sacrifices, and his grandnephew, Wei Shih-yung 魏時雍, an erudite. Envious of the rewards showered on Shao, Chang Yen-pien 張彥頨 (d. 1561), the 48th Celestial Master holding the hereditary post at Mt. Lung-hu, sent some of his disciples to Szechwan and Yunnan in search of drugs, scriptural texts, and sacrificial vessels for presentation to the court. The emperor, though gratified, did not swerve from his attachment to Shao. When, in September, 1530, a supervising secretary in the War ministry, Kao Chin 高金 (T. 汝良, H. 孟門, cs 1526), criticized the throne for the excessive privileges meted out to Shao, the emperor had Kao turned over to the Embroidered-uniform Guard, who saw to his imprisonment and torture. Meanwhile the rewards continued. In 1532 the emperor had a mansion built for Shao. As his annual stipend Shao received 100 empiculs of grain, 30 *ch'ing* (over 400 acres) of farm land on the outskirts of the capital (the produce from which was exempt from taxation), and forty men from the Embroidered-uniform Guard to wait on him. In addition, eunuch emissaries were dispatched to Kuei-hsi to arrange for the erection of another Taoist shrine, called Hsien-yüan 仙源 kung, to serve as his residence. In 1534, while en route home, Shao sent a memorial to the emperor to report that on his way he had been humiliated by a bureau director of the Nanking ministry of Works, Li Wen 李旼 (cj 1522), a younger brother of senior Grand Secretary Li Shih (*q.v.*). In a rage the emperor imprisoned Li Wen and forced

Li Shih to apologize to Shao. On the latter's return via the Grand Canal the emperor sent eunuchs to meet his boat at the T'ung-chou 通州 terminus. Again he was the recipient of imperial gifts including a jade seal and a ceremonial robe embroidered with four-clawed dragons. It happened that after September, 1533, the emperor began to be blessed with male children, and he attributed this to the prayer meetings at which Shao presided. As a reward on January 22, 1537, Shao was given the rank of minister of Rites, an unusual appointment which gave him even greater prestige and added to the privileges of his relatives and followers. In March, 1539, when the emperor embarked on his journey to visit his father's tomb in Hukuang, Shao regretted that owing to illness he could not be in the entourage and recommended that T'ao Chung-wen (*q.v.*) go in his place. Shao passed away a month later and was buried with extraordinary honors—those accorded an earl. The emperor made him junior preceptor, granted him the posthumous title Wen-k'ang jung-ching 文康榮靖, and ordered Grand Secretary Hsia Yen and Minister of Personnel Hsü Tsan (*qq.v.*) to prepare eulogistic compositions. On the accession of Emperor Chu Tsaihou (*q.v.*), however, these honors were withdrawn.

The *Ming-shih* records one book by Shao: *Shao Yüan-chieh chi* 集, 4 *ch.*, but this seems no longer extant. He is described as tall in stature, possessed of luminous eyes, a round face, and a handsome beard, and very circumspect in conduct.

Bibliography

1/307/21a; 3/285/19b; 5/118/143a; 61/160/20a; *Ming-shih* (Taipei ed.), 119, 124, 1090, 2350, 2406, 2424, 3474, 3480; MSL (1965), Shih-tsung, 1427, 2766, 3391, 4135, 4626; KC (1958), 3574; *Kuei-hsi-hsien chih* (1871), 10/1/20b.

Liu Ts'un-yan

SHEN Chieh-fu 沈節甫 (T. 以安, H. 錦宇, 耐庵居士, 太樸主人, Pth. 端靖), 1533-1601, official and bibliophile, was a native of Wu-ch'eng 烏程, Chekiang. His grandfather, Shen Tuan 端 (T. 光伯, H. 雨川, cj 1519), and his father, Shen Su 塾 (T. 子居, H. 巽洲, d. 1593), were both scholars but held no official positions. A chü-jen of 1558, Shen Chieh-fu became a chin-shih the following year. He first served as a secretary in the bureau of ceremonies and then advanced to director of the bureau of sacrifices in the ministry of Rites. It seems that he and Grand Secretary Kao Kung (see Chang Chü-cheng) had little regard for each other. His opposition to permitting Taoist priests to serve in court was not in accord with the grand secretary's wishes; so he retired from his post in 1567, under the pretext of illness. When recalled to be assistant minister of the Court of Imperial Entertainments in 1570, he declined the appointment as Kao was again grand secretary. After Kao's ouster in 1572, Shen resumed his official career in the seal office, first as assistant, then as minister. Transferred to head the Nanking seal office in 1577, he again retired in 1578, refusing to take part in the great to-do in connection with the trip to Peking of Chang Chü-cheng's mother. Soon after Chang's death (1582), Shen went back to Nanking to be assistant administration commissioner of the office of transmission and then right vice minister of Justice. In 1592 he received appointment as left vice minister of Works in Peking. In the latter capacity he pled for restraint in imperial demands for various articles of luxury (porcelain, silk, etc.), and memorialized on the reduction of nonessential conservancy work on the Yellow River. Upon his father's death in 1593, he returned home to observe the mourning period and from then on remained in retirement until the end of his days.

Shen Chieh-fu left a catalogue of his own library, the Wan-I-lou shu-mu 玩易樓書目, 2 ch., and two collectanea or ts'ung-shu, the (Kuo-ch'ao) Chi-lu hui-pien

[國朝] 紀錄彙編, and the (Hsien-cheng) Yu-ch'un lu [先正] 由醇錄. The first ts'ung-shu, in 216 chüan made up of 127 titles, mainly sources on contemporary history by some seventy Ming authors, including the writings of three emperors, was first printed in 1617 by Ch'en Yü-t'ing 陳于廷 (T. 孟諤, Pth. 恭定, cs 1601) in Kiangsi. While a few items may be regarded as trivial and irrelevant, on the whole it is a useful collection for the study of Ming history. In 1938 it was reprinted photolithographically by the Commercial Press as one of ten reproductions of Yüan and Ming rare editions. The second is a much smaller work consisting of 12 titles by Sung, Yüan, and Ming authors on ethics and morality governing personal, family, and community conduct. One work compiled by Shen himself and included in the Yu-ch'un lu is entitled Jen-shu hsü-pien 忍書續編, 3 ch.; it promotes the virtue of forbearance and serves as a supplement to the Jen-shu by a Yüan author; another item in the same collection (a Wan-li edition of the Yu-ch'un lu) is in the National Library of Peking. The Wu-ch'eng-hsien chih lists five other titles attributed to Shen, including 15 chüan of literary works, T'ai-p'u chu-jen chi 太樸主人集.

Shen Chieh-fu, according to report, was quiet and undemanding, dutiful both to his parents and to his emperor. For his clan he set aside land for its welfare, established free schooling, provided funds for the support of the senior members and emergency needs of others. His three sons all became officials. The eldest, Shen Tsung 淙 (T. 伯聲, H. 祖洲, cj 1585), was made sub-prefectural magistrate of T'ai-ts'ang 太倉, Nan-Chihli; the second, Shen Ch'üeh (q.v.), rose to become grand secretary; and the third, Shen Yen 演 (T. 叔敷, H. 何山, d. 1638), served as minister of Justice in Nanking (1631–32?). Although the family produced more degree holders, misfortune beset the descendants of Shen Chieh-fu during the transitional years of the Ming and Ch'ing dynasties. Because of their activities in the Ming resistance movement, Shen Jung 榮 (T. 仁叔, 塵外, original surname Yen 嚴, d. 1659), an adopted son of Shen Yen, was beheaded, and Shen Ch'ung-hsi 重熙 (cj 1651), a grandnephew of Shen Yen, died in prison about the same time. From 1657 to 1666, the affluent family was blackmailed and involved in crippling law suits resulting in the exhaustion of their wealth.

Bibliography

1/218/20b; 5/51/73a; SK (1930), 134/2b; TSCC (1885-88), XI/332/12a, 16a, XIV/449/15a; *Wu-ch'eng-hsien chih* (1881), 14/15a, 17a, 28a, 15/2a, 19b, 28a, 34/7b, 23b; Cheng Yüan-ch'ing 鄭元慶, *Wu-hsing ts'ang-shu lu* 吳興藏書錄 (*Fan Sheng-shan tsa-chu* 范聲山雜著), 1930; Yeh Ch'ang-ch'ih (BDRC), *Ts'ang-shu chi-shih shih* 藏書紀事詩 (Shanghai, 1958), 144; *Yu-ch'un lu* (NLP microfilm, no. 530).

Lienche Tu Fang

SHEN Ching 沈璟 (T. 伯英, 聃和, H. 寧庵, 詞隱), March 8, 1553-January 30, 1610, dramatist, was a native of Wu-chiang 吳江, situated south of Soochow. He was born into a wealthy family which began to flourish in the time of his great-grandfather, Shen Han 漢 (T. 宗海, H. 水西, 1480-1547, cs 1521), who, as a supervising secretary, was cashiered in 1527 for opposing Kuei O (*q.v.*) in the case of Li Fu-ta (*see* Chang Fu-ching). One of his uncles, Shen Wei 位 (T. 道立, H. 虹台, 1529-72, cs 1568), became a Hanlin bachelor. The prosperity of the Shen family reached its peak during Shen Ching's generation. He received the *chin-shih* in 1574; then his brother and three of his cousins successively achieved the same degree. Beyond this show of talent it is interesting to note that a collection of poems entitled *Wu-chiang Shen-shih shih-lu* 沈氏詩錄 (prefaces of 1740 and 1867), contains the effusions of 91 members of the Shen family, including 21 women, who flourished from the 16th to the 18th centuries. It gives some hint as to the cultural and material background of the

Shen clan during this stretch of two hundred years. After graduating, Shen Ching was assigned to the ministry of War as an apprentice, and then was formally appointed secretary in its bureau of operations, retiring for personal and family reasons the following year. Recalled in 1579 as a secretary in the ministry of Rites, he was soon promoted to be vice director of a bureau. Two years later he received a transfer to the ministry of Personnel as vice director in the bureau of records (1581), then in the bureau of evaluations (1582), and finally in the bureau of honors (also 1582). In March, 1586, Shen Ching and Chiang Ying-lin (*see* Li-shih), a supervising secretary, each sent a memorial raising objections to the imperial order which elevated the rank of the imperial consort Cheng Kuei-fei (*q.v.*). For this both were punished, Shen being demoted to be an official in the messenger office.

In September, 1588, Shen Ching served as one of the eighteen assistant examiners in the provincial examination of Shun-t'ien (Peking), and shortly thereafter was promoted to assistant minister in the Court of Imperial Entertainments. In the following year, however, a secretary of the ministry of Rites, Kao Kuei 高桂 (cs 1577), pointed out the defects in the papers of eight men who passed the previous provincial examination at the capital and suggested that they be reexamined. Kao also remarked that Wang Heng, who passed first on the list, happened to be the son of Grand Secretary Wang Hsi-chüeh (*qq.v.*) and so should also be reexamined to allay any suspicion of favoritism. The reexamination showed all nine to be qualified and Kao was punished by a fine, but mischief was done; it caused the ruin of several careers and contributed to the heightening of the factional strife of that time (*see* Wang Hsi-chüeh). Shen Ching, who was responsible for passing four of the candidates mentioned in Kao's memorial, one of whom was Li Hung 李鴻 son-in-law of another grand secretary,

Shen Shih-hsing (*q.v.*), was cleared of any wrongdoing. Later, finding his position in Peking untenable, he retired. He spent the rest of his life at home.

Shen and another dramatist, who lived in Wu-chiang, Ku Ta-tien 顧大典 (T. 道行, H. 衡寅, cs 1568), came at this time into close association. Both men retained singers and actors in their residences, and enjoyed themselves by writing plays and songs. It is said that Shen was so obsessed by his work on pieces for the stage that he left his sons' education to his younger brother, Shen Tsan 瓚 (T. 孝通, 子勺, H. 定庵, 1558-1612, cs 1586), author ·of *Chin-shih ts'ung-ts'an* 近事叢殘, 4 *ch.*, printed in 1794.

Shen Ching wrote in all seventeen plays, known by the general title *Shu-yü-t'ang shih-ch'i chung* 屬玉堂十七種. Reportedly they were tried out first in his own theater. Recently the *Ku-pen hsi-ch'ü ts'ung-k'an* 古本戲曲叢刊 published, in its volumes 1 and 3, seven of them, namely the *Mai chien chi* 埋劍記, *Shuang yü* 雙魚 *chi*, *I-hsia* 義俠 *chi*, *T'ao-fu* 桃符 *chi*, *I-chung ch'ing* 一種情, *Po hsiao* 博笑 *chi*, and *Hung-ch'ü* 紅蕖 *chi*. It is said also that he rewrote the *Huan-hun* 還魂 *chi* (otherwise known as *Mu-tan t'ing* by T'ang Hsien-tsu [ECCP]), to make it suitable for singing in the Wu dialect. Shen's san-ch'ü 散曲 (songs) may be found scattered through the *T'ai-hsia hsin-tsou* 太霞新奏, *Wu-sao ho-pien* 吳騷合編, *Ts'ai-pi ch'ing-tz'u* 彩筆情詞, and *Nan-tz'u hsin-p'u* 南詞新譜. The *Nan kung shih-san-tiao ch'ü-p'u* 南宮十三調曲譜, 21 *ch.*, was originally written by Chiang Hsiao 蔣孝 (T. 維忠, cs 1544). Shen revised and greatly supplemented it. The present form of the work was again edited by his nephew, Shen Tzu-chin 自晉 (T. 伯明, H. 西來, 鞠通生, 1583-1665), and published under the title *Nan-tz'u hsin-p'u*, which became one of the basic sources in the field of southern ch'ü.

Bibliography

1/206/6b; 40/52/23a; KC (1958),4527, 4595; MSL (1966), Shen-tsung, 3787, 3874, 3889, 3891; *Wu-chiang Shen-shih shih-lu* (1867), 2/12b, 3/1a, 16b, 20a, 4/1a; Ling Ching-yen 凌敬言, "Tz'u-yin hsien-sheng nien-p'u chi ch'i chu-shu" 詞隱先生年譜及其著述, *Wen-hsüeh nien-pao* 5 (1939), 1; *id.*, "Yü-yang 漁陽 hsien-sheng ni'en-p'u," *ibid.*, 7 (1941), 101; Fu Hsi-hua 傅惜華, *Ming-tai ch'uan-ch'i ch'üan-mu* 明代傳奇全目 (Peking 1959), 70, 82; Hsü Fu-ming 徐扶明, "Kuan-yü Shen Ching chi ch'i chü-tso te p'ing-chia," 關於沈璟及其劇作的評價, *Wen-hsüeh i-ch'an tseng k'an*, 7 (Peking, 1959), 244; Chou Shao-liang 周紹良, "Wu-chiang Shen-shih shih-chia 世家," *ibid.*, 12 (1963), 48; Yao Hsin-nung, "The rise and fall of the K'un Ch'ü" *THM*, 2 (1936), 74; Chao Ching-shen 趙景深, *Hsi-ch'ü pi-t'an* 戲曲筆談 (1962), 73; Ku Chieh-kang, "A Study of Literary Persecution during the Ming," tr. by L. Carrington Goodrich, HJAS, III (1938), 290.

Mingshui Hung

SHEN Chou 沈周 (T. 啓南, H. 石田, 白石翁, etc.), December 9, 1427–September 4, 1509, was a painter, calligrapher, and poet who, more than any other artist of his time, made Soochow a leading center for great art. Traditional critics have called him the founder of a type of painting and the initiator of artistic ideals which came to be called the Wu-p'ai 吳派 (Wu school). Shen Chou never entered offical service, giving the highly acceptable excuse that he must care for his aging mother, widowed in 1477. (Unless we can postulate a long illness, this is a rather late rationale since Shen Chou was already fifty at this time.) The stories of his devotion to filial duty and other virtues tend to portray him as an ideal exemplar of Confucian conduct and learning, the cultivated, independent scholar-gentleman.

Shen Chou was born on the ancestral estate in the town of Hsiang-ch'eng 相城, about ten miles north of Soochow city. It seems that his great-great-grandfather founded the family fortune in land during the Yüan period, and from about the year 1368 the head of the family had been designated one of the local liang-chang 糧長 (tax collector); this indicates that the family was among the most affluent in the district. About 1441 Shen Chou, then only fourteen, was for some reason delegated by his father to take charge of the delivery of tax grain from his district to the granary at Nanking. There is a story about his winning praise at this time from a high official at Nanking who tested him on his ability to write poetry, but the plausibility of the story is shaken by its identification of the high official as Ts'ui Kung 崔恭 (T. 懋仁, H. 岱屏, 1409-79, cs 1439, Pth. 莊敏), who did not become governor of Soochow and Nanking until 1458. Chou Ch'en (*see* Chang Hung), however, served as governor there from 1430 to 1451 and so, if the rest of the story is true, he must have been the high official in question. Shen Chou represented the fourth generation of a family of artists, his great-grandfather, grandfather, uncle, and father all being known as poets and painters.

It is not clear whether he or any of his ancestors had ever taken the competitive civil examinations, but since they are grouped in the local gazetteer among scholar-officials some of them at one time or another may perhaps have entered the district school. There is the anecdote that Shen was once summoned by a prefect to decorate the walls of a new building, a task from which he could have been exempted if only he were to ask one of his influential friends to intervene or even to hire someone to act in his place; he went himself, however, saying that it was his duty as a commoner to perform the service. This may be interpreted to mean that he, like Ch'iu Ying (*q. v.*), was registered as a professional painter and never as a student of the district school. On the other hand, people highly respected him, his friends including such local scholar-officials as Wu K'uan, Tu Mu, Wang Ao (*qq. v.*), and Wen Lin, the father of Wen Cheng-ming (*q. v.*), and his admirers including Grand Secretary Li Tung-yang and Wang Shu (*qq.v.*), the governor of Soochow from 1479 to 1484. The anecdote about the prefect summoning Shen to decorate a wall, like the earlier story about his being tested on his skill as a poet, seems to be a fabrication, for the surname of the prefect is given as Ts'ao 曹, which could have referred only to Ts'ao Feng 鳳, prefect of Soochow from 1497 to 1499; by that time no prefect, however new to the scene, could have been ignorant of an artist of Shen's stature.

These stories, although shown to include anachronisms, indicate that honored as Shen is known to have been he was still socially classed as merely a commoner painter. Only with such a realization may one gain a true picture of him through the euphemistic expressions used by his biographers. Take for example the term hsing-wo 行窩 which they used for his retreat in the suburbs of Soochow. By it the scholar-official writers tried to suggest that Shen, living in lordly style in his well-furnished home, Yu-chu-chü 有竹居 (Abode among the bamboos) in Hsiang-ch'eng, occasionally went to a studio in the outskirts of the city, where he spent at most only the daytime hours on each visit, and where, as soon as he arrived, the news spread and customers flocked with their orders.

The figures most often mentioned in connection with Shen's early life and training were closely linked to the scholarly-artistic world. Ch'en K'uan was his teacher, and Ch'en in turn was the son of Ch'en Chi (for both *see* Ch'en Ju-yen), who had been the teacher of Shen's father and uncle, and who was the grandson of Ch'en Ju-yen, a known painter of the mid-fourteenth century whose work still survives. The Ch'en family came from the area of the famed Kiangsi mountain, Lu-shan 廬山, and the whole sense of Shen's relation to his teacher has been caught by the large hanging scroll Shen painted for him in 1467, "Lu shan kao" 高 (Towering Mt. Lu, now in the National

Palace Museum, Taipei). With this symbol the artist quite literally extols Ch'en K'uan as a lofty figure of learning.

Others certainly important in his early training were his father and uncle, who both had talents similar to those Shen Chou was to develop to such a high degree. The well-known early Ming scholar-painter, Tu Ch'iung (*q. v.*) is also said to have taught Shen. Later Shen gratefully wrote a chronological biography of his teacher entitled *Tu Tung-yüan hsien-sheng nien-p'u* 杜東原先生年譜. Finally, the gifted painter Liu Chüeh 劉珏 (T. 廷美, H. 完菴, 1410-72) was close to the younger artist. Two of his finest paintings are intimately connected with Shen Chou or his family. "Ch'ing-pai-hsien" 青白軒, Liu Chüeh's painting of his house in 1458, carries colophons by Shen Chou's grandfather and father; while a swift sketch of 1471, "Lin-an shan se t'u" 臨安山色圖(Mountain Scene, Freer Gallery of Art, Washington, D. C.), was painted during a trip to Hangchow on which Shen Chou was one of Liu Chüeh's companions.

We have thus the clear picture of a young painter deeply immersed in the scholarly aristocratic life of fifteenth-century Soochow. As an artist he developed out of the early Ming which for the scholar class was linked closely to the late Yüan. There were only fifty-two years between the death of Wang Meng (*q. v.*) in 1385 and Shen Chou's birth. Wang Meng is said to have been a friend of Shen's grandfather. Shen Chou, according to Wen Cheng-ming, brushed only small paintings until he was forty. This in itself is an indication of Shen's dependence on the rather intimate personal vision of the Yüan. Huang Kung-wang (1269-1354) and Wang Meng were a particularly strong influence on the developing painter. At present the earliest known dated painting by Shen Chou is called "Yu-chü t'u" 幽居圖 (Retreat) now housed in the Osaka Municipal Museum. Painted in 1464, it is symptomatic of the artist's early skills, both in its subject and in its delicate sensitive style.

The year 1471 is of special significance in Shen's outwardly rather uneventful life. This was the year he completed his own home, the Yu-chu-chü. Although the actual location in not certain, it was still within the Hsiang-ch'eng area of the family estates. The move was heralded by a series of poems written by friends and relatives, among them Shen Chen-chi 沈貞吉 (T. 南齋), Liu Chüeh, and Wu K'uan. Thus the stage was set for his own independent pursuit of a life he had idealized in his painting of seven years before. Old friends were soon to leave him. Liu Chüeh died in 1472; Tu Ch'iung in 1474. His father passed away in 1477 and his younger and only brother, Shen Chao 召 (T. 繼南), in 1472. "In my life brothers are few," Shen Chou wrote, "there is only Chao and Chou."

Among Shen Chou's acqaintances who had written poems on the occasion of the building of the "Abode among the bamboos" was the famous statesman Wu K'uan. Evidence of their friendship runs through the lives of both men. They seem to have been particularly close when Wu returned to Soochow for the period of mourning upon the death of his own father. We know from recorded poems that Shen stayed at Wu K'uan's residence in 1478. On another occasion they were together at Shen's dwelling viewing a painting of the tenth-century painter Li Ch'eng, and examining an old Shang dynasty bronze. Together they went on an excursion to Yü-shan 虞山. When Wu K'uan was to return to Peking in 1479, Shen Chou painted a long handscroll for him, now in the Kadogawa collection in Tokyo. It was both a leave-taking present and a gift in return for Wu K'uan's having written the memorial inscription for the tomb of Shen's father. Besides being a painter, Shen was famous as poet and calligrapher. In literature he was especially versed. His poetry is said to have been strongly influenced by Po Chü-i (772-846), Su Shih (1037-1101), and Lu Yu (1125-1210). The most important early model for his calligraphy was Huang T'ing-chien (1045-1105).

His paintings are often specific recordings of the scenery of the Soochow area, for he was a figure completely absorbed in his own locale. Of these a long, free yet strongly executed handscroll. "Su-chou shan-shui ch'üan-t'u" 蘇州山水全圖 (A complete painting of the Soochow landscape; National Palace Museum), is apparently one of the most important. In 1488 he painted "Ku Su shih ching" 姑蘇十景 (Ten views of Soochow; present whereabouts unknown). There is an album "Liang chiang ming-sheng ts'e" 兩江名勝冊 (Famous views of two rivers; formerly in China), and another entitled "Hu-ch'iu 虎丘 ts'e" (Twelve views of Tiger Hill; in the Cleveland Museum). A journey to I-hsing 宜興 in 1499 and a visit to a famous stalactite grotto there has been preserved in two versions, one in the collection of Mr. H. C. Weng in New York. Finally it is known that he painted "San kuei 三檜 t'u" (Historic ancient junipers of Ch'ang-shu 常熟) presumably as the result of a trip there.

As an artist, Shen certainly emerges by the 1480s as a strong individual personality. He is no longer dependent upon the past, the accomplishments of the late Yüan and early Ming. The whole course of his development has been given a near contemporary analysis by Wen Cheng-ming on an original colophon of 1516, "Shen shih-t'ien Wen Cheng-chung shan-shui ho-chüan" 文徵仲山水合卷 (Five-leaf album; Nelson Gallery, Kansas City). He succinctly describes his teacher's greatness as what "no artist-craftsman could attain. In his early years the master studied Wang Meng and Huang Kung-wang and then went on to work in the style of Tung Yüan and Chü Jan [both 10th century]. The more he did, the deeper he went; and one could not distinguish the point of origin." The more intimate touch of his earlier painting may be seen in such rather modest but sensitive dated works as the "Retreat" of 1464 already

mentioned, a scroll, "Ch'iu hsi yü yin 秋溪漁隱 t'u" (Fishermen in a landscape [1471]; Honolulu Academy of Arts), and a delicate landscape revealing an excursion to Tiger Hill in 1476 (National Palace Museum, Taipei). His style changes as he is now well into his fifties. He becomes far more deliberately strong in his expression, blocking out exact compositions, and defining forms with thick blunt strokes of the brush. Yet withal he retains a sense of ease and the importance of personal and individual expression that have made him such a central figure in the whole history of scholarly painting in China.

Thus in 1494, after a famous series of album-leaves, he describes the circumstances of their origin: "I brushed this album for fun, painting things as they looked just to go with my leisurely and well-fed delight...." (National Palace Museum). Several paintings might be cited as examples of his characteristic strong style: "Shih-ssu yeh yüeh 十四夜月 t'u" (Watching the mid autumn moon), painted when Shen was about sixty (Museum of Fine Arts, Boston); the Five-leaf Album, the colophon of which has been cited; the album also mentioned above, Twelve views of Tiger Hill, Soochow; "Chiang ts'un yü lo 江村漁樂 t'u" (River village and the joy of fishing; Freer Gallery of Art); "Ts'e chang 策杖 t'u" (The staff-bearing wanderer; National Palace Museum). While this type of painting appears to continue to the end of Shen's life, his later works may show greater looseness and freedom. Sometimes these latter are associated with the style of the great Yüan master Wu Chen (1280-1354).

Much subsequent painting in Soochow owed a debt to Shen Chou but, aside from Wen Cheng-ming, painters are seldom listed as his direct pupils. Thus Hsieh Shih-ch'en (q. v.) was influenced by his style, and artists like Ch'en Tao-fu and Ch'ien Ku (qq. v.) reflect his influence through their immediate master, Wen Cheng-ming. Shen died aged eighty-two,

outliving by several years his son, Shen
Yün-hung 雲鴻, who lived in the neighboring hsien, K'un-shan 崑山. The burial
rites were thus carried out by a concubine's son, Shen Fu 復 and a grandson,
Shen Lü 履.

Shen is the author of several books,
among them K'o-tso hsin-wen 客座新聞,
1 ch., Shih-t'ien chi 集, 9 ch., Shih-t'ien tsa-
chi 雜記, 1 ch., Shih-t'ien shih-hsüan 詩選,
10 ch., and (with others) Chiang-nan ch'un
tz'u 江南春詞, 1 ch., all of which are
extant, except possibly the last. Of these,
only the fourth, a collection of his poetry,
found a place in the Imperial Library.
Among the more interesting is his brief
Shih-t'ien tsa-chi, which includes his recipes for varnishing, cooking, certain medi-
cines, wine, vinegar, and the like. His
portrait has been reproduced in the frontispiece of The Field of Stones.

Bibliography

1/298/7a; Cheng Ping-shan 鄭秉珊, Shen Shih-
t'ien, Shanghai, 1958; Shen Chou tso Ku-su shih-
ching 作姑蘇十景, Tokyo, 1914; Shen Shih-t'ien
Chang-kung tung chüan 張公洞卷, Shanghai,
1931; Shih-t'ien hsien-sheng chi 先生集, comp. by
Ch'en Jen-hsi, ed. by Ch'ien Yün-chih 錢允治
(b. 1541), 1615(Shanghai ed., 1914); Ch'ü Shih-
ssu (ECCP), Shih-t'ien hsien-sheng shih ch'ao 詩
鈔, 1644; Shih-t'ien hsien-sheng shih-wen chi 詩文集,
intro. by Wu K'uan, Li Tung-yang, and Ch'ien
Ch'ien-i (ECCP), Shanghai, 1915; Chiang Shao-
shu 姜紹書 (17th cent.), Wu sheng shih shih
無聲詩史 (Shanghai, 1962), 2/24b, SK (1930),
143/4b, 170/11b, 175/12b, 191/9b; Ku-kung
shu-hua lu 故宮書畫錄 (Taipei, 1958), 1/95,
4/155, 5/295, 6/32; Shih-t'ien chi; "A Landscape
by Shih-t'ien," Kokka, no. 545 (1936), 133, pls.
III-IV; Cleveland Museum Bulletin, January, 1966;
Gustav Ecke, Chinese Painting in Hawaii, 3 vols.
(Honolulu, 1964), pl. XLIV; Richard Edwards,
The Field of Stones, Washington, D. C., 1962;
id., "Shen Chou and the Scholarly Tradition,"
The Journal of Aesthetics and Art Criticism,
XXXIV/1, Fall (1965), 45; Osvald Sirén, Chinese
Painting (London, 1956-58), Vol. IV, 148, Vol. VI,
pls. 170-93, Vol. VII, 223; Tseng Hsien-chi and
Richard Edwards, "Shen Chou at the Boston
Museum," Archives of the Chinese Art Society
of America, 8 (1954), 31; K. Tomita and A. K.
Chiu, "An Album of Landscapes and Poems by
Shen Chou (1427-1509)," Bulletin of the Museum
of Fine Arts, 46 (Boston, 1948), 55; E. J.
Laing, Chinese Paintings in Chinese Publications,
1956-1968 (Ann Arbor, 1969), 183.

Richard Edwards

SHEN Ch'üeh 沈㴶 (T. 銘縝, H. 仲雨, Pth.
文定), died June 26, 1624, a native of
Wu-ch'eng 烏程, Chekiang, was the second
son of Shen Chieh-fu (q. v.), and rose
to be grand secretary in 1621-22. He and
his younger brother, Shen Yen (see Shen
Chieh-fu), both became chü-jen with high
honors in 1591, and in the following year
they became chin-shih. Selected as Hanlin
bachelor, Shen Ch'üeh entered the academy which had long been regarded as a
preparatory stage for future grand secretaries. While there he was assigned to
teach in the school for eunuchs, the Nei-
shu-t'ang 內書堂. Among his pupils were
Li Chin-chung, who later changed his
name to Wei Chung-hsien (ECCP), one
of the most powerful and notorious eunuchs of the Ming dynasty, and Liu Ch'ao
劉潮, another aggressive and domineering
individual of this group. This relationship,
while it doubtless contributed to the rise
of Shen Ch'üeh, also most certainly
brought on the unfavorable opinion of him
held by his contemporaries and by posterity.

In 1615 Shen received appointment as
vice minister of Rites in Nanking, where
he launched strong attacks against the
Christian missionaries. During the preceding decade under the leadership of Al-
phonso Vagnoni (q. v.), Christianity had
spread and prospered in Nanking and a
church had been erected there in 1611.
Naturally Vagnoni became the prime
target of Shen's attacks. In rapid succession, Shen presented three memorials in
June and September, 1616, and in January, 1617, advising the throne to forbid
the spread of this foreign religion and
to punish and deport the foreign missionaries. Among the things he found objectionable were their use of the terms

Ta-hsi-yang 大西洋 and T'ien-chu-chiao 天
主教, which he held as belittling China
and the Chinese emperor, the foreigners'
unorthodox ways of calculating the calendar, their preaching against ancestor worship, their acquisition of real property in
the vicinity of the mausoleum of the founding emperor, and their use of material
wealth to attract followers (giving three
taels of silver to each new convert). He
also mentioned their construction of the
beamless hall 無樑殿 (the church?) as
overstepping proper bounds and showing
disrespect. He insinuated that not only
did the uneducated believe in this foreign
religion, but so also did certain gentry
and high officials. To answer his insinua-
tions and to support the Jesuits, such Christian officials as Hsü Kuang-ch'i, Li Chih-
tsao, Sun Yüan-hua, and Yang T'ing-yün
(all in ECCP), rebutted his arguments
in memorials to the throne. Shen in the
end emerged victorious, although the
measures adopted were not as harsh as
those he proposed. As a result Vagnoni,
Álvarō de Semedo (q.v.), and a number
of Chinese Christians were arrested and
thrown into prison. Finally on April 30,
1617, the two missionaries were sealed in
their cages, and dispatched to Canton
from which, after seven months, they
were escorted to Macao to await depor-
tation. The buildings they had erected
were all demolished.

Shen Ch'üeh's three memorials, known
by the collective title Nan-kung shu-tu 南
宮書牘, as well as another memorial submitted in June, 1617, reporting the conclusion of the case, may be found in the P'o-
hsieh chi 破邪集. This work in 8 chüan is
a compilation of anti-Christian documents
of late Ming years, collected by Hsü
Ch'ang-chih 徐昌治, first printed in 1639,
and reprinted in Japan and in Cochin
China. An original edition used to be in
the Zikawei Library, Shanghai, and another in the Songeigaku, Tokyo. Certain missionary sources report that Shen received
bribes amounting to ten thousand taels
from Buddhist monks in Nanking. While

this accusation does not seem to appear
in Chinese documents, the Buddhists
certainly had a hand in the anti-Christian
activties. In the P'o-hsieh chi we may
notice that fourteen pieces writtten by
seven Buddhist monks are included.

In 1619 Fang Ts'ung-che (ECCP, p.
176) recommended Shen Ch'üeh to
Emperor Chu I-chün (q.v.) for a grand
secretaryship. Shen was then (1620) summoned to Peking to be minister of Rites
and grand secretary of the Tung-ko 東閣.
He did not arrive at the capital to assume
the new office, however, until the summer
of the following year. In the meantime,
the short reign of Chu Ch'ang-lo (ECCP)
had come and gone, and the succession
of Chu Yu-chiao (ECCP) had taken
place. Shen Ch'üeh received the honor
of becoming grand guardian to the heir
apparent and was advanced before long to
be grand secretary of the Wen-yüan-ko
文淵閣. Another promotion followed,
which made him minister of Revenue,
junior guardian, and grand secretary of
the Wu-ying-tien 武英殿. Not only did his
close relationship with Wei Chung-hsien
and Liu Ch'ao arouse criticism, but also his
advocacy of a plan to raise an army to be
trained inside the imperial palace gave rise
to numerous accusations. Even with the
emperor on his side he became increasingly the center of denunciations, and he
began to feel uneasy. Finally he asked to
be retired. When his request was granted
(August 23, 1622), more honors were
bestowed on him. The records give no
clear indication as to whether he originated the proposal to train troops in the
palace grounds, or whether he was simply
carrying out the wish of the eunuchs; it
is evident, however, that the proposal
brought an end to his official career.

Bibliography

1/218/20b; MSL (1966), Hsi-tsung, 1182, 2632;
KC (1958), 5209, 5280; TSCC (1885-88), XIV:
449/17a; Chekiang t'ung-chih (1934), 2346, 2468;
Wu-ch'eng-hsien chih (1881), 31/12b, 34/7b; P'o-
hsieh chi (1855 Japanese ed.); Pfister (1932),

84, 86, 122, 138; George A. Dunne, *Generation of Giants* (Notre Dame, 1962), 130, 146; W. Franke, *Sources*, 5. 7. 33.

Lienche Tu Fang

SHEN FU 沈富 (T. 仲榮), also known as Shen Wan-san 萬三 and Shen Hsiu 秀, fl. 1360s, was one of the wealthiest men of his day. His family had moved from Wu-hsing 吳興, Chekiang, to Ch'ang-chou 長洲 (Soochow) in his grandfather's time. It seems that Shen Fu had accumulated his wealth through business enterprises which might have included foreign trade, although one dissenting source mentions that the family had grown prosperous by applying itself diligently to agriculture. It is very likely that, starting out with vast land holdings, he was able to increase his property spectacularly during the period of turmoil, possibly under the protective wing of Chang Shih-ch'eng (*q.v.*). What appears to be certain is the fact that when the first Ming emperor Chu Yüan-chang was building his capital at Nan-king, Shen was allowed (or forced) to contribute to the enlargement of the city wall, paying, it is said, one-third of the cost. Legend has it that the new South Gate was renamed at that time Chü-pao-men 聚寶門 because Shen's magical treasure-accumulating vessel was buried underneath the site by the emperor's order; it supposedly not only corrected a chronic flooding problem at that spot, but also provided that henceforth no subject in the empire would be able to grow so rich as to rival the imperial house in wealth. It is interesting to speculate how such a myth came to be generated: the gate in question opens on a view of Chü-pao-shan 山, the name of this hill being current long before the rise of the Ming. Perhaps in the popular mind the story was preserved for its symbolic significance.

After helping to build the city wall, Shen offered (or was ordered) to present gifts to the army. At this juncture he incurred the wrath of the emperor, who wanted to have him executed. Only the intervention of Empress Ma (*q.v.*) saved Shen's life, but his properties were confiscated and he himself exiled to Yunnan, where he passed into oblivion.

Shen Fu's younger brother Shen Kuei 貴 survived the early Ming difficulties, prospered, and had a great-grandson Shen Chieh 玠 who entered the bureaucracy by recommendation. While he was glad to accept the title and rank, Shen Chieh, in a tactfully worded memorial, declined the official salary that was due him. Even after three generations, therefore, a note of caution still prevailed in the relations between the Shen family and the house of Ming.

Bibliography

1/113/4b, 3/106/4a; *Chiang-ning-fu chih* 江寧府志 (1668), 1/23b, 24b; Chu Kuo-chen (ECCP), *K'ai-kuo ch'en chuan* 開國臣傳 (1632), 10/40b; Ho Ch'iao-yüan, "Huo-chih chi" 貨殖記, la, in *Ming-shan ts'ang* (Ch'ung-chen ed.); Wang Hsiao-t'ung 王孝通, *Chung-kuo shang-yeh shih* 中國商業史 (1936), 172; Wu Han 吳晗, *Chu Yüan-chang chuan* 傳 (1949), 252.

E-tu Zen Sun

SHEN I-kuan 沈一貫 (T. 肩吾, H. 蛟門), 1531-February 26, 1615, a grand secretary for thirteen years, was a native of Yin-hsien 鄞縣, Chekiang. After qualifying for the *chü-jen* in 1561 and the *chin-shih* in 1568, he became a Hanlin bachelor. Later he was promoted to be corrector. During these years he helped in the preparation of both the *Shih-tsung* and (after 1572) the *Mu-tsung shih-lu* (*see* Chang Chü-cheng). At the beginning of the Wan-li period, he was made lecturer in the palace. One day when he was giving a lesson in the Classics and dealing with the paragraph, "How government had to be carried on during the three years of silent mourning by Emperor Kao-tsung [of the Shang dynasty]," (*see Lun-yü, ch.* 14), he said respectfully to the young emperor, Chu I-chün (*q.v.*), that it would be better for a new ruler to direct affairs himself rather than to follow strictly the classical precedence of entrusting power to a prime minister, for the latter might not prove entirely reliable. Assuming that these words alluded to him, the chief grand secretary Chang Chü-cheng conceived an instant dislike for Shen.

After the death of Chang in 1582, Shen received several promotions and late in 1584 was appointed a vice minister of Personnel. In 1594 he was made minister of Rites in Nanking and later in the same year he and Ch'en Yü-pi (*q.v.*) both became grand secretaries.

At this time the war against the Japanese invaders in Korea had already been going on for two years and had bogged down inconclusively. Consequently, as soon as he was made grand secretary, Shen saw to the cessation of trade relations with Japan. (As a native of the Ningpo area, which was one of the chief centers of Sino-Japanese trade, he may have had some personal intererest in the matter.) In 1595 the official title of junior guardian of the heir apparent was conferred on him, and two years later he was elevated still more. At this time many people at court were exercised over the succession problem and frequently asked the emperor to appoint his first son, Chu Ch'ang-lo (EC CP), as heir apparent. By 1599, when the prince was eighteen *sui*, these entreaties became more frequent and more forcefully put. In the face of this situation, the emperor ordered the ministry of Revenue to grant him twenty-four million taels in silver for the estimated expenditure for ceremonies connected with the appointment of his sons, as heir apparent, prince, and so on. Obviously the emperor wanted to cause his ministers trouble by means of this order because such a large sum of money was impossible to collect in a short time. Government finances at this stage were at a particularly low ebb, due partly to the long war in Korea, also to the misuse of funds by eunuchs and others, to the expense of the campaign of 1592 in Ninghsia, and to the extensive repair of the imperial palace structures damaged by fire in 1596 and 1597. This added substantially to the people's already heavy burden. Although Shen remonstrated, the emperor paid no attention to him.

Shen I-kuan continued to press the emperor to make Chu Ch'ang-lo heir apparent. On October 13, 1601, he finally agreed and issued a decree to that effect. When this was received by the Grand Secretariat, however, the emperor regretted his action and tried to postpone the appointment. This time Shen was firm in his refusal. As a consequence, on November 9 of that year (1601), the monarch bestowed on the prince the title of heir apparent, and accorded princely rank and domains to his four half-brothers—Chu Ch'ang-hsün, Chu Ch'ang-hao (*see* Cheng Kuei-fei), Chu Ch'ang-jun, and Chu Ch'ang-ying (*see* Chu I-chün).

Shen had been elevated in 1600 to titular minister of Personnel and concurrently grand secretary with the title of junior guardian. When, on October 8, 1601, another grand secretary, Chao Chih-kao 趙志皋 (T. 汝萬, H. 瀔陽, 1524-October 8, 1601, cs 1568 Pth. 文懿), died, Shen became chief grand secretary. During Chao's illness Shen repeatedly asked the emperor to increase the number of grand secretaries because there were then only two, himself and Chao. Since the emperor distrusted those ministers who were likely to form cliques in their own interest, he had in mind selecting certain retired officials who lived remote from the capital. Whereupon he appointed Shen Li (*see* Hsüan Ni) and Chu Keng 朱賡 (T. 少欽, H. 金庭, Pth. 文懿, cs 1568, 1535-January 4, 1609) as grand secretaries in October, 1601. In 1603 Shen I-kuan's rank was raised to that of grand secretary with the titles of Left Pillar of State and junior tutor of the emperor. In 1605 he was promoted to the rank of junior preceptor of the emperor and concurrent grand preceptor of the heir apparent.

When Shen entered the Grand Secretariat in 1594, the court had already been suffering from several years of misrule and the situation continued to deteriorate. Eunuch emissaries who collected taxes on mines went throughout the country seriously disturbing the people; officials generally received no response to their memorials submitted to the throne, many of them being punished and detained in jail owing to the outspokenness of their remonstrances; nor did the emperor attend court, almost no one, except the eunuchs, having an opportunity to see him. Even when Shen became chief grand secretary he found it extremely difficult to arrange for an audience. Under such circumstances, Shen could do little for the country; he made it his practice to flatter the emperor; his popularity declined as a result.

On March 9, 1602, the emperor suddenly fell ill; the grand secretaries and a number of ministers were summoned to the palace. Later that day the emperor invited Shen to his presence. Thinking himself dying, he instructed Shen to draw up an edict abrogating the tax on mines, withdrawing the orders to the imperial weaving and dyeing factories in Soochow and Hangchow and the imperial kilns in Kiangsi, recalling the eunuchs assigned to these missions, and releasing the officials detained in jail for their remonstrances. Late that same night the grand secretaries and minsters, who had remained on duty, received from the eunuchs the imperial decree practically as it was drafted. They were deeply gratified. On the next day, however, the emperor's health took a turn for the better and he regretted having issued the decree. He bade his eunuch emissaries go to the Grand Secretariat to see to its recall. At first Shen turned a deaf ear to their appeals. But they knelt at his feet and pled with him insistently. Shen eventually relented. This action elicited sharp criticism, as others thought that he should have kept the decree and carried out its provisions immediately. Now all high officials, one after another, implored the emperor to abolish the taxes on mines, but he refused.

Shen I-kuan found it difficult to work harmoniously with his junior colleague Shen Li. In like vein the latter, thinking that he owed his appointment as grand secretary solely to the emperor, refused to be condescending to Shen I-kuan. So the relations between these two became strained. At this time the right vice minister of Rites, Kuo Cheng-yü (q.v.), known for his learning and moral courage, was one whom Shen Li valued highly; while the censor-in-chief, Wen Ch'un 溫純 (T. 景文, H. 一齋 or 亦齋, cs 1565, 1539-1607), and left vice minister of Personnel, Yang Shih-ch'iao 楊時喬 (T. 宜遷, H. 止菴, cs 1565, d. 1609), were among those whom Shen I-kuan disliked. In August, 1603, Kuo Cheng-yü wished to withdraw the posthumous title of Lü Pen 呂本 (T. 汝立, cs 1532), who had served as grand secretary from 1549 to 1561. Shen I-kuan and Chu Keng, however, refused their consent, as Lü Pen was their fellow provincial. Kuo's suggestion was accordingly blocked, and Shen I-kuan came to dislike Kuo as well. His attitude towards Shen Li, Wen Ch'un, and Yang Shih-ch'iao also worsened. Party strife thus became more intense, and those officials who hailed from Chekiang province became further alienated from other regional cliques.

Late in 1603, when Kuo Cheng-yü was forced out of office, leaving for home by boat, an anonymous poster "Hsü Yu-wei-hung-i" concerning the imperial succession (see Cheng Kuei-fei) came to light. It is said that because of his hatred of both Shen Li and Kuo Cheng-yü, Shen I-kuan bade the Embroidered-uniform Guard make a careful search of Shen Li's house in Peking, and at the same time stop Kuo's boat and make a search there too. Nothing relating to the authorship of the poster was found, however. In 1604 the court conducted a special evaluation of the officials of the metropolitan area for which Wen Ch'un and vice minister of Personnel Yang Shih-ch'iao were responsible. In this evaluation some followers of Shen I-kuan were put on the list for demotion. Aroused over this Shen lodged a complaint with the emperor. Accordingly, the report of the evaluation, together with the names of the people listed for demotion, was pigeonholed within the palace for several months. Instead an imperial edict was unexpectedly issued at the beginning of 1605 announcing that all censors and supervising secretaries listed for demotion this time might remain in office, and that Wen Ch'un's resignation was approved. Many who objected memorialized the emperor to reconsider, pointing out that in the past two hundred years no report of a special evaluation of officials had ever been ignored by the throne. Finally, in August, 1605, the report was authorized and promulgated.

Shen I-kuan was now subjected to more and more criticism, and various officials frequently denounced him, accusing him of wrongdoing and cupidity. Shen begged to be retired and on August 19, 1606, he was allowed to leave; on the same day Shen Li was removed from office. While living in retirement in his native place, Shen I-kuan was still the object of attack by critics; his fellow provincials who served at court were similarly treated. He died about ten years after leaving the Grand secretariat. The court posthumously gave him the official title of grand preceptor of the emperor and canonized him as Wen-kung 文恭.

Shen I-kuan was the author of a number of books, three of which are noticed in the Ssu-k'u catalogue, namely, I-hsüeh 易學, 12 ch., Han-lin kuan-k'o ching-shih hung-tz'u 翰林館課經世宏辭, 15 ch. (also known as Ching-shih hung-tz'u), a compilation of essays by Hanlin members, and Hui-ming shih-chi 喙鳴詩集, 18 ch., his collected poems. The latter two, however, together with his collection of works in prose, Hui-ming wen 文 chi, 21 ch., were listed for destruction in the

1770s. Fortunately all three may be found in libraries in Japan. Also preserved in Japan are the following titles listed under Shen's authorship: Ching-shih ts'ao 敬事草, 19 ch., collected memorials; Lao-tzu t'ung 老子遛, 2 ch.; Tu-Lao kai-pien 讀老概辨, 1 ch.; Chuang 莊-tzu t'ung, 10 ch.; Tu-Chuang kai-pien, 1 ch.; Kuo-ch'ao ming-ju wen-hsüan po-chia p'ing-lin 國朝名儒文選百家評林, 12 ch. (printed 1586, also known as Po-chia p'ing-lin); Kuo-ch'ao li-k'o 歷科 Han-lin wen-hsüan ching-chi hung-yu 經濟宏猷, 16 ch. (apparently a later edition of the above mentioned Ching-shih hung-tz'u); and T'ai-kuan hung-chang 臺館鴻章, 19 ch., a collection of works in prose and verse by Ming censors and Hanlin members, published in 1594. Some of these titles may also be found in Taiwan. In 1607 Shen wrote the preface to a new edition of Ming chuang-yüan t'u-k'ao 明狀元圖考, 5 ch., illustrated anecdotes about the optimi of Ming chin-shih examinations, by Ku Ting-ch'en 顧鼎臣 (original ming T'ung 仝, T. 九和, H. 未齋, 1473-November 4, 1540, cs 1505). An incomplete copy of parts of the first and last chüan of a mid-seventeenth century edition is in the Columbia Universty Library. The Library of Congress has an imperfect copy of the Chuang-tzu t'ung.

Bibliography

1/217/6b, 218/4b, 9a, 219/6b, 11a, 220/18a, 224/21a, 226/17b; 3/172/17b, 202/1a; 84/丁中/68b; KC (1958), 5079; Ku Ying-t'ai (ECCP), Ming-ch'ao chi-shih pen-mo, ch. 65-67; Chao I (ECCP), Nien-er shih cha-chi, ch. 35; Yin-hsien chih (1877), 37/1a, 55/30a, 57/5a; SK (1930), 7/10a, 56/6b, 192/13a; Naikaku Bunko Catalogue, 157, 317, 356, 397; NCL Catalogue, 310; L. ofC. Catalogue of Rare Books, 799; Sun Tien-ch'i (1957), 159, 173; P. M. d'Elia, Fonti Ricciane, II (Rome, 1949), 154.

Chou Tao-chi

SHEN Lien 沈鍊 (T. 純甫, or 純父, H. 青霞山人, 1507-October 5, 1557), scholar, patriot, and martyr, was a native of K'uai-chi 會稽, Chekiang. A chü-jen of

1531, he became a *chin-shih* in 1538. He was three times a magistrate, first of Li-yang 溧陽 (Nan-Chihli), 1540-42, then of Shih-p'ing 茌平 (Shantung), 1542-43, and finally, after the observance of the mourning period on the death of his father, he went back to Shantung and became magistrate of Ch'ing-feng 清豐, 1547-49.

In 1549, at the invitation of Lu Ping (*q.v.*), the powerful commander of the Embroidered-uniform Guard, he accepted the office of registrar of the Guard and went to Peking. Realizing his moderate resources, Lu Ping ordered a house built for his family by the government. This was the first time that a registrar of the Embroidered-uniform Guard had an official residence, and Shen Lien wrote an account to record this memorable occasion.

In Peking, however, Shen Lien found the affairs of the central government oppressive and likely to be injurious to the empire, particularly because of the conduct and influence of Yen Shih-fan and his father, Yen Sung (*q.v.*). Then in the summer of 1550 the Mongols, under Altan-qaγan (*q.v.*), again invaded China, sweeping over the Great Wall with little difficulty, and came within 20 *li* of the capital. The court was shaken, and the safety of Peking threatened. The officers in command (*see* Ch'iu Luan) revealed their incompetence, and the highest civil officials seemed powerless. This situation greatly angered Shen Lien. In an urgent conference called to draft an answer to Altan qaγan's demand for trade, Shen Lien boldly seconded the proposal of Chao Chen-chi (*q.v.*) to adopt a strong posture against the invaders. Being in a low official position, he was blamed for speaking out of order and accused of creating a scene at the conference. Acting under the guidance of Hsü Chieh (*q.v.*), the conference refused the Mongol demand. In the meantime the invaders fortunately turned away without attacking the capital. But Shen Lien was so incensed by the events that soon after he submitted a memorial asking to be

given the authority to commandeer a large force to guard the imperial mausolea northwest of Peking, and another army of equal size to protect the transportation line of supply from T'ung-chou 通州 to the capital. He advocated the combining of the forces from the provinces and the launching of an offensive. The memorial was acknowledged but apparently pigeon-holed.

At this time Yen Sung, who never took a strong position in this matter, basked in imperial favor and was all-powerful. Early in 1551 Shen Lien decided to take another daring step by impeaching Yen Sung. He submitted a second memorial accusing Yen of ten unforgivable crimes which were leading the empire to disorder and ruin. The emperor promptly ordered Shen's arrest. He was flogged and sentenced to exile in Pao-an 保安, beyond the Great Wall.

In Pao-an Shen Lien and his family found the people honest and hospitable. Since it was a rare occasion to have a scholar of his caliber living among them, it was not long before many young men gathered around him as his students. Shen Lien's patriotic fervor did not subside, however, and his detestation of Yen Sung and his son persisted, possibly even increased. He repeatedly told his new acquaintances about their harmful affect upon the empire and upon the people. He tried to help the border inhabitants in self-defense in the event of another Mongol invasion. Among other things he led the young people in practicing archery; as targets he set up three effigies, naming them Li Lin-fu (d. 753) of T'ang, Ch'in K'uei (1090-1155) of Sung, and Yen Sung, traitors one and all in Shen Lien's opinion.

Before long Shen Lien's activities came to the ears of the Yen faction in Peking, and they naturally sought means to destroy him. By 1557 the opportunity for his liquidation seemed imminent as the supreme commander of Hsüan-hua (宣化) and Tatung and the regional inspector of the area were both henchmen of the two Yen. When the case, which involved a group of White Lotus (白蓮教) followers who had established connections with the Mongols, broke, Shen Lien was falsely implicated. Accused of sedition, he was executed in October, 1557, in the market place of Hsüan-hua.

With him in exile was his wife, née Hsü 徐, and their three younger sons, Shen Kun衮, Shen Pao褒, and Shen Chih 褺. Shen Kun and Shen Pao were put to death after their father, but Shen Chih escaped the same fate because of his extreme youth. The eldest son Shen Hsiang 襄 (H. 小霞), who was already a *hsiu-ts'ai* at this time, remained at home in K'uai-chi. As expected, an order for his arrest was issued. While his life was in danger for several years, through a series of strange coincidences, he managed to survive. Following the downfall of the two Yen in 1562 he was no longer pursued.

At the start of the new reign of Lung-ch'ing (1567), Shen Lien's name was cleared and he was given posthumous honors. Later in1621 the posthumous title of Chung-min 忠愍 was also bestowed on him. In both his native placé and in Ch'ing-feng, Shantung, where he once served as magistrate, the townsfolk erected shrines in his memory.

Shen Lien left two collections of literary works, the *Ming-chien chi* 鳴劍集, 12 *ch.*, and the *Ch'ing-hsia chi* 青霞集, 11 *ch.*, with a *nien-p'u* 年譜, 1 *ch.* (not consulted). (The Imperial Catalogue lists the latter only). An abridged edition of the *Ch'ing-hsia chi* in four *chüan* was reprinted in 1848 in the *Ch'ien-k'un cheng-ch'i chi* 乾坤正氣集.

Shen Lien was a very competent writer, lucid and fluent in both poetry and prose. His patriotic spirit and deep concern for the national welfare stand out in many of his essays and letters. Perhaps it was for this reason that he developed a strong interest in military matters and regarded himself as something of an expert. He left a short work of 81 articles of instruction on military tactics. He was also very candid about his belief in Taoism, both religious and philosophical. Of the immortals he said that he had believed in them since childhood. He argued that people should not refuse to credit certain things simply because they had not seen them.

The relationship between Shen Lien and Lu Ping may have been closer than records show. Even in exile Lu Ping corresponded with him confidentially, and Shen sent Lu some poems filled with Taoist imagery. Here we may venture a new theory, which past historians either did not care to mention, or never considered. Lu Ping enjoyed the favor of the emperor, Chu Hou-ts'ung (*q.v.*), who was an ardent devotee of Taoist rituals and the adepts' practices. For days on end Taoist rites were performed in the palaces, the emperor demanding that his favorite high officials participate and submit compositions in the peculiar literary form known as Ch'ing-tz'u青詞, for sacrificial purposes. Lu Ping, after all, was not a literary man by training; probably in order to maintain his standing on such occasions, he needed help. Shen Lien being a scholar, accomplished in literature, and a Taoist believer, would be an excellent choice to fill this need. This is, however, only a conjecture.

The story bearing the title "Shen Hsiao-hsia hsiang-hui ch'u shih piao" 沈小霞相會出師表, included in one of the famous collections of Ming short stories, the *Yü-shih ming-yen* 喻世明言 (later also included in *Chin-ku ch'i-kuan* 今古奇觀), recounts the story of Shen Lien and his eldest son Shen Hsiang. The part about Shen Lien, strange as it may seem, is very close to the biographical sources in nonfictional materials. As for the part about Shen Hsiang, although they differ, the supposedly factual account is not any less strange than that which appears in fiction. This hints strongly at the importance of Ming fiction in the study of Ming history.

Bibliography

1/209/18a; 5/81/38a; 42/92/10a; 63/23/37a; 84/丁中/30b; MSL (1965), Shih-tsung, ch. 356-451; KC (1958), 3898; *Huang Ming wen-hai* (microfilm), 18/2/1, 2, 3, 4; SK (1930), 172/6b; "Shen Hsiao-hsia hsiang-hui ch'u-shih piao" in *Yü-shih ming-yen* or *Chin-ku ch'i-kuan*; "The Persecution of Shen Lien," tr. by E. B. Howell in *The China Journal of Science and Arts*, Vol. 2 (1924), 311, 412, 503, Vol. 3 (1925), 10; L. of C. *Catalogue of Rare Books*, 946.

Lienche Tu Fang

SHEN Pang 沈榜 (T. 子登), fl. 1550-96, official and author of the first gazetteer of Wan-p'ing 宛平 (western half of Peking and its suburbs), was a native of Lin-hsiang 臨湘, northeast of Yo-yang 岳陽, Hukuang. Apparently he came from a wealthy family, for it is recorded in the local history that in 1518 his granduncle and grandfather contributed money and grain for public works and famine relief, and a few decades later his father, an avid reader, gave a collection of ten thousand *chüan* of books to the district school. Shen Pang's cousin, Shen Chih 植, a *chü-jen* of 1546, served as an assistant surveillance commissioner in Kwangtung in 1579. Shen Pang himself passed the provincial examination in 1567. After failing several times in the higher examination, he qualified for a magistracy and was appointed to Nei-hsiang 內鄉, Honan, where he served with distinction from 1581 to about 1584, and then was transferred to Tung-ming 東明, Pei-Chihli.

About 1587 there followed promotion to head the Nanking district of Shang-yüan 上元 and in 1590 a transfer to Wan-p'ing. These offices had the designation ching-hsien 京縣, or national capital magistracies. There were four: Ta-hsing 大興 and Wan-p'ing in Peking and Chiang-ning 江寧 and Shang-yüan 上元 in Nanking, and the administrators were selected from more than a thousand magistrates and raised two grades in rank (7 A to 6A). The holder of such an office was subjected to the supervision of many central government officials and had to deal with the most influential people of the empire. In Peking especially he could ill afford to incur the displeasure of the emperor and his relatives, not to mention the thousands of eunuchs and security police. Apparently Shen performed his duties to satisfaction, for in 1593 he was shifted to the ministry of Revenue as chu-shih 主事 (secretary 6A), which amounted to a promotion in prestige if not in grade.

Just at the time that Shen assumed his new post in May a political upheaval shook the court; Chao Nan-hsing (*q.v.*), the director of the bureau of appointments in the ministry of Personnel, after conducting a strictly fair and just evaluation of the central officials, at this moment became the target of attack by unscrupulous courtiers, and was denounced in an imperial edict and sent home a commoner. As usually happens in such cases Chao was shunned by friends and foes alike. Shen, however, pointedly went to see Chao off. When Shen received his first three months' pay in his new office, he sent the whole amount in the originally sealed envelope to Chao with a letter saying that he felt he did not deserve any salary while an upright and honorable person like Chao was denied it. Chao recorded the action in his miscellaneous notes, *Hsien-chü tse-yen*, with the comment that he accepted Shen's gift but had not yet found a way of repayment. It was a symbolic gesture, for the money involved was insignificant, but it showed Shen's disapproval of the political situation.

As a secretary in the ministry of Revenue Shen Pang was delegated, in May, 1596, expediter of tax collections in Shantung for that year. It was the fourth year of the war against the Japanese in Korea when the ministry, having exhausted the reserves of the treasury and several times without success requested contributions from the emperor's privy purse, now tried to collect as much as possible from the more affluent provinces, Chekiang, Kiangsi, Hukuang, Nan-Chihli, and Shantung. To each province it dispatched a secretary as expediter. Each was armed with a commission paper including the imperial instruction that he was not to return without the full quota of taxes for that year, even if he had to make it up by borrowing temporarily from the provincial treasury. Whether Shen Pang fulfilled his quota is unrecorded. Little is known about his life after that and he would have been ignored as of no consequence had he not written a remarkable account of the Wan-p'ing district under the title *Wan-shu tsa-chi* 宛署雜記, 20 *chüan*, printed in 1593. It was as much a fully documented gazetteer of Wan-p'ing as a personal account of his experiences while its magistrate at the very center of the imperial power structure during its period of decline. As told in his book, when he assumed office in August, 1590, he found its treasury almost empty, with only fifty-two taels on hand and a deficit of over four thousand. He almost resigned in despair; instead he attacked the problem directly, exposing the counterfeiters of deeds, imposing fines on tax delinquents, and tightening the control of all records. The immediate result was an increase in receipts several times the average of preceding years—thousands of taels rather than hundreds. So did he cope with this first emergency.

The first part of his book deals with this and similar aspects of the administration. Each section contains documents and statistics and usually concludes with some pertinent criticisms and suggestion for improvement. The book includes such information as the price of hundreds of commodities, the rate of pay of various kinds of labor, and the requisitions for supplies or services by the imperial palace and central government offices. The last five *chüan* forming the second part of *Wan-shu tsa-chi* consist of articles on customs, festivals, colloquialisms, religious establishments; also documents, essays, poems, anecdotes, and some inscriptions taken from ancient monuments. One of the anecdotes tells of a group of families which supplied women to shoulder sedan chairs serving the ladies of the imperial palace. These families, originally conscripted from Fukien, were apparently Hakka, whose women never bind their feet. At the end of the book Shen even recorded eight names, each a champion of his art in sixteenth-century Peking; these included a drummer, a flutist, a dart thrower, and the master players of two different stringed instruments, a kind of football, and two varieties of chess.

Shen's book, being an invaluable source on Peking and representing the best in Chinese historiography, was strangely ignored by the readers of his day. In the early 17th century it received only passing mention in the bibliography of Ming literature of Chiao Hung (ECCP), the guidebook to Peking of Liu T'ung (*q. v.*), and one or two local histories. By the latter part of the 17th century it was no longer available even to the compilers of the Wan-p'ing gazetteer of 1683.

In the *Ch'ien-ch'ing-t'ang shu-mu* of Huang Yü-chi (ECCP), it appears with the author's name given as Shen Piao 標 instead of Shen Pang.

It was thus practically lost in China for three hundred years until about 1940, when Fu Yün-tzu 傅芸子 discovered a copy, perhaps the only one extant, preserved in Marquis Maeda's Sonkeikaku 尊經閣 Library in Tokyo. Fu wrote two articles about the discovery, published in *Chung-ho yüeh-k'an* 中和月刊 of February, 1941, and May, 1942. In 1961 the Academia Sinica in Peking, utilizing a microfilm of the Sonkeikaku copy, published a punctuated edition of the work. This time it was received with enthusiasm.

It happens that Shen Pang and a contemporary of the same name led remarkably similar careers. The two even became *chü-jen* in the same year (1567). The coincidence goes even further, for both held offices of the same grade, 6A. The first one received an appointment in 1593 in Peking and the other, four years later, the office of assistant prefect of Jao-chou-fu 饒州府 in Kiangsi, a lucrative post involving control over the porcelain factories of Ching-te-chen 景德鎮. In 1599 the second Shen Pang achieved national notoriety, being censored for corruption (keeping for himself twenty percent of all funds paid out through his office), irregularity (selling government porcelain in personally owned stores), and immoral conduct (including incest and murder); then surprisingly, after notice of removal from office had been posted by the ministry of Personnel, an imperial order reinstated him on the recommendation of the eunuch, Su Hsiang 蘇相. Li Tai (*q.v.*), the minister of Personnel, and Feng Ch'i (*q. v.*), the vice minister, each submitted a memorial protesting the eunuch's interference with ministerial affairs. The second Shen Pang himself submitted in 1600 a memorial begging to be permitted to leave office. The difference between the two men becomes clear only when one finds in the *Jao-chou-fu chih* that the second Shen Pang was a native of Jen-ho 仁和 (Hangchow), not of Lin-hsiang, Hukuang. The lives of the two men may be compared in the following table:

SHEN PANG

I

Native of Lin-hsiang, Hukuang
1567   *Chü-jen*
1581–93 Served as district magistrate
1593   Appointed *chu-shih* (6A)
           Published *Wan-shu tsa-chi*
ca. 1596 Expediter of tax collections in Shantung

II

Native of Hangchow, Chekiang
1567   *Chü-jen*
1597   Appointed assistant prefect (6A)
1599   Removed from office
1600   Submitted memorial

From this, one may readily discern, that, if it were not for the difference in birth-

place, the two careers might easily have been taken as one. Even during their lifetimes this confusion may have occurred with the possible result that, when the wrongdoings of Shen Pang II were revealed in 1599, bibliophiles mistook him for the author of the *Wan-shu tsa-chi* and rejected the book for that association. This theory, though unsubstantiated, seems to be a plausible explanation as to why such an informative and readable book all but suffered the fate of oblivion.

Bibliography

MSL (1966), Shen-tsung, 5536, 6328, 6356, 6436; *Wan-shu tsa-chi*, Peking, 1961; *Hunan t'ung-chih* (1934), 1095, 5847; *Lin-hsiang-hsien chih* (1872), 10/4b, 22a, 11/3a, 13/16a; *Nan-yang-fu chih* 南陽府志, 4/70a; *Tung-ming-hsien chih* (1756), 4/6a; Wang Shih-chen (ECCP), *Ch'ih-pei ou-t'an*, 7/8a; Fu Yün-tzu, *Chung-ho yüeh-k'an*, II (1941), 2, III (1942), 5. For Shen Pang II: 1/242/6a; *Hang-chou-fu chih* (1965 reprint of 1579 ed.), 57/23b; *Jao-chou-fu chih* (1872), 9/17b; Tung Ch'i-ch'ang (ECCP), ed. *Wan-li liu-chung tsou-shu hui-yao*, 4/11b; Feng Ch'i, *Tsung-po chi*, 52/16b.

Chaoying Fang

SHEN Shih-hsing 申時行 (T. 汝默, H. 瑤泉, 休休居士), 1535-August 23, 1614, official and scholar, was a native of Ch'ang-chou 長洲 in Soochow prefecture. In the provincial examinations of 1561 he placed third, but in the palace examinations the following year he placed first and was forthwith made a compiler of the Hanlin Academy. His ancestral name was Shen but since his grandfather's time the family had used the surname Hsü 徐. It is as Hsü Shih-hsing that his name appears in the *chü-jen* and *chin-shih* lists, and also as the author of one of his books: *Ch'ün-shu tsuan-ts'ui* 羣書纂粹, 8 *ch.* He did not change his name to Shen until after 1567. In the decade and a half to follow he received a succession of promotions: junior supervisor of instruction and acting head of the Hanlin Academy (1574), grand supervisor of instruction (January, 1577), and later in the same year right vice minister of Rites, then an equivalent office in the ministry of Personnel. One of the tasks which particularly engaged his attention from 1576 on was the revision of the *Ta Ming hui-tien* (*see* Hsü P'u), the contents of which were brought down to the year 1585 (from 1549), completed two years later (March 24) in 228 *chüan*, and subsequently printed in the palace. Several copies of the original edition survive, and the work has recently (1963) been reprinted in Taiwan. His name is associated too with the preparation of the *Shih-tsung* and *Mu-tsung shih-lu*, completed respectively in the years 1577 and 1574 under the general editorship of the grand secretary, Chang Chü-cheng (*q.v.*). The latter was not slow to remark Shen's talents and, when he was about to return home to bury his father in 1578, Chang recommended Shen's appointment as left vice minister of Personnel and grand secretary. Thus did Shen begin his participation at the center of the administration. At the end of 1579 he became minister of Rites and concurrently grand secretary. Three years later he was given the noble titles of junior guardian of the emperor and grand guardian of the heir apparent as part of the celebration of the birth of Chu Ch'ang-lo (ECCP), the emperor's first son.

In the first decade of the Wan-li reign, Chang Chü-cheng served as chief grand secretary. Because he found it difficult to tolerate anyone whose views differed from his own, almost all of the officials who were opposed to him were dismissed. When he died in July, 1582, the responsibility of composing imperial orders fell largely on Grand Secretaries Chang Ssu-wei (*q.v.*) and Shen. Many officials who had opposed Chang Chü-cheng were restored to their posts. This action put Chang Ssu-wei and Shen in good repute. In May, 1583, when Chang Ssu-wei was obliged to return home to mourn the death of his father, the duties of the chief grand secretary fell to Shen Shih-

hsing. On October 31 of the same year he was given the titular rank of minister of Personnel with the titles of junior tutor (of the emperor) and grand tutor of the heir apparent. A year later the titles of junior preceptor and grand preceptor of the heir apparent followed. Since Chang Chü-cheng's death, the censors and other critics had become outspoken and often attacked the administration sharply. In the spring of 1584 the censor Chang Wen-hsi 張文熙 (cs 1577) memorialized the emperor asking him to rescind four practices in order to prevent the governmental authority from becoming too concentrated in the Grand Secretariat, especially in the hands of a single chief grand secretary. In essence Chang remarked: 1) the personnel reports and records of the six ministries and the Censorate should not be submitted to the Grand Secretariat for reevaluation; 2) the appointments and dismissals of the officials of the ministries of Personnel and War should not, one and all, be left to the discretion of the Grand Secretariat; 3) concerning public affairs, supreme commanders, governors, regional inspectors, and so on should not secretly and directly report to the Grand Secretariat and request instruction; and 4) when one grand secretary drafts a suggested rescript for the emperor, he should discuss the matter with all other members of the Grand Secretariat. On Shen's advice the emperor completely rejected Chang's proposals. Later in the year, the right vice minister of Rites, Kao Ch'i-yü 高啓愚 (cs 1565), accused of a supposed affront to the throne by Censor Ting Tz'u-lü 丁此呂 (T. 右武, cs 1577) was cashiered. Shen, however, sharply rebuked Ting for the accusation and in consquence the latter was reduced to the post of prefectural judge of Lu-an 潞安, Shansi. Subsequently Censors Li Chih 李植 (T. 汝培, cs 1577) and Chiang Tung-chih 江東之 (T. 長信, cs 1577) sought other pretexts to attack Shen directly and in their turn were downgraded (1585) and transferred to distant provinces. From that time on, although the critics were frequently punished for their outspokenness, they continued their attacks on the administration even more energetically.

Hoping to win popularity, Shen in 1586 requested the emperor to annul the special regulations for the examination of official merits established by Chang Chü-cheng; this the emperor promptly accepted. Afterwards, among other things, he successively asked the emperor to reduce the amount of silk and cloth annually presented to the palace; to reply to the various memorials submitted by the bureaucracy as soon as possible; and to experiment with rice planting near Peking. Generally speaking, however, he tended to flatter the emperor, and his record in office was undistinguished. During this time, laxity in discipline was setting in, and the laws became less and less respected.

At the beginning of 1590, Lo Yü-jen 雒于仁 (T. 少經, cs 1583), one of the commentators in the Grand Court of Revision, submitted to the emperor a memorial which included warnings against drinking (酒箴), lust (色箴), greed (財箴), and loss of temper (氣箴). When he read this, the emperor was incensed. He ordered Shen to quash the memorial and wanted to punish Lo severely. A few days later, however, Shen, with the emperor's concurrence, did not directly reply to Lo's memorial but gave him a hint that he had better resign. In consequence Lo fortunately escaped the emperor's wrath; from that time on the officials generally received no response to their memorials.

It had been customary for lectures to be given in the palace for the emperor. At that time, however, these lectures were canceled because the emperor had no interest in them. In the face of this situation, Shen suggested early in 1590 that the papers be submitted to the emperor. In the year 1586, when the emperor's first son, Chu Ch'ang-lo, had reached the age of four, a son named Chu Ch'ang-hsün was born to the emperor's favorite, Cheng Kuei-fei (q.v.). Because Chu

Ch'ang-lo had not been appointed heir apparent, and the imperial consort was reported as conniving to have her own son so recognized, many officials remonstrated with the emperor and requested that Chu Ch'ang-lo receive the appointment at once. This angered the emperor, so Shen proposed that he issue an order that all suggestions offered to the throne by various officials should be within the limits of their responsibilites and be first submitted to their superiors for review. This order was soon issued, to the annoyance of most of the court.

One day in 1590, the emperor gave audience to his sons, Chu Ch'ang-lo and Chu Ch'ang-hsün, at Yü-te palace 毓德宮, summoning Shen as well to his presence. At this time Shen begged the emperor to make a decision on the succession problem. After pondering for some time, the emperor replied that if for a year no one memorialized on the matter he would appoint Chu Ch'ang-lo heir apparent. Shen promptly passed the word along, urging his colleagues not to irritate the emperor. For this he was repeatedly attacked. When someone deliberately memorialized on the question of the heir apparent before the year was up, Shen could no longer ask the emperor to keep his word. He then begged to retire. Early in 1591 the title of t'ai-fu 太傅 (grand tutor) was conferred on him, and on October 28 of the same year he was allowed to resign from office. It was a decade later that Chu Ch'ang-lo was finally declared heir apparent.

After Shen's death at the age of eighty sui, he was posthumously given the official title of grand preceptor and canonized as Wen-ting 文定. A fanciful portrait of his mother dreaming of his success in the palace examinations appears in the Ming chuang-yüan t'u k'ao 明狀元圖考. He had three sons and two daughters. The first son died early; the second, Shen Yung-mou 用懋 (T. 敬中, H. 元渚, 1560-1638), a chin-shih of 1583, served as minister of War for a month at the close of 1629; and the third, Shen Yung-chia 用嘉, a *chü-jen* of 1582, became an administration vice commissioner of Kwangsi province. One of his grandsons, Shen Shao-fang 紹芳, a *chin-shih* of 1616, after several promotions rose to be·a vice minister of Revenue.

Shen Shih-hsing was the author *inter alia* of *Tz'u-hsien-t'ang chi* 賜閒堂集, 40 *ch.*, the *Lun-fei chien-tu* 綸扉簡牘, 10 *ch.*, the *Lun-fei tsou-ts'ao* 奏草, 4 *ch,*, and the *Lun-fei ssu-ts'ao* 笥草, 4 *ch.*, all of which have survived. Copies of the *Tz'u-hsien-t'ang chi*, printed in 1616, are still extant. The Hosa Bunko in Nagoya has a copy of his complete works, *Shen Wen-ting kung ch'üan-chi* 全集, 68 *ch.* Of Shen and the first named work, which is a collection of fu 賦 and shih 詩 in 6 *chüan*, essays and miscellaneous comments in 34 *chüan*, the editors of the *Ssu-k'u* catalogue have this to say: "When he was chief minister he committed no faults, nor was he responsible for any good acts either; his poetry and prose are of the same character." One poem in the second *chüan* drew the criticism of the Ch'ien-lung officials (*ca.* 1780) and was ordered expunged. It had to do with a picture of someone passing beyond the frontier on a fine autumn day.

Bibliography

1/218/1a, 229/18a, 234/10a, 236/1a, 6b; 3/201/4b; 5/17/144a, 81a; 18/13/5a; 40/44/20b; 61/133/22a; 64/已14/1a; 84/丁中/63b; *Tz'u-hsien-t'ang chi* (NLP microfilm, rolls 865-66), 7/19a, 10/1a; *Wu-hsien chih* 吳縣志 (1933), 12/10b, 66上/28b; *Su-chou-fu chih* (1877), 60/22b, 61/40b, 80/24a, 32a; MSL (1965), Mu-tsung, 0215, 1210, Shen-tsung (1966), *ch.* 9-240; KC (1958), 5074; *Huang Ming wen-hai* (microfilm), 2/3/1-3; SK (1930), 13/5b, 53/9b, 137/11b, 178/6b; Sun Tien-ch'i (1957), 212; W. Franke, *Sources*, 5. 7. 36, 6. 1. 2; Shen I-kuan *et al.*, *Ming chuang-yüan t'u k'ao* (1875), 下/45a

Chou Tao-chi

SHEN Te-fu 沈德符 (T. 虎臣, 景倩), 1578 -1642, was a native of Hsiu-shui 秀水, Chia-hsing 嘉興 -fu, Chekiang, where his family had been established for several generations. His great-grandfather, grandfather, and father all qualified for the *chin-shih*, and were drawn into government service. Shen Mi 謐 (T. 靖夫, H. 石雲, 石山, cs 1529) became a follower of Wang Shou-jen (*q.v.*), Shen Ch'i-yüan 啓原, or 源 (T. 道初, 道卿, H. 霓川, 1526-91, cs 1559) was known for his large collection of books, and Shen Tzu-pin 自邠 (T. 茂仁, H. 几軒, 1554-89, cs 1577) helped to prepare the *Ta Ming hui-tien* (*see* Shen Shih-hsing). Shen Te-fu spent much of his time in Peking and had ample means to pursue a life of scholarship. He became a *chü-jen* in 1618, but never succeeded in obtaining the *chin-shih* degree. He is now best known and perhaps will ever be remembered as the author of the *Wan-li yeh-hu-pien* 萬曆野獲編, 30 *ch.*, with preface of 1606 and *pu-i* 補遺, 4 *ch.*, preface of 1619. In 1700 Ch'ien Fang 錢枋 rearranged the book under 46 headings in 30 *chüan*. A supplement of 4 *chüan* was added to this edition by the author's descendant Shen Chen 振 in 1713. During the Ch'ien-lung period it fell under the ban; as a consequence the complete text was printed only in 1827 and reprinted in 1869. In 1959 the Chung-hua shu-chü published in Peking a new edition in three volumes.

Shen Te-fu was truly historically minded; he did his work conscientiously and recorded facts without partisanship; he tried to seek out hidden motives and causes. He disclosed the seamy side of life and portrayed also the human and personal elements in the seemingly grandiose political sphere. He gives us, for instance, detailed descriptions of the relationship and rivalry among Yen Sung, Hsia Yen, and Hsü Chieh (*qq.v.*). He informs us also that even the powerful minister Chang Chü-cheng (*q.v.*) had to league himself with the eunuch Feng Pao (*see* Chang Chü-cheng); this and other articles on the eunuchs tell much about the eunuch system under the Ming. Shen supplies, incidentally, interesting and valuable information about the novel *Chin P'ing Mei* (*see* Wang Shih-chen), holding that it was written by a famous figure of the Chia-ching period to attack certain contemporary political figures and expose their machinations. The title of Shen's book may be rendered "The private gleanings in the reign of Wan-li," but it includes data on persons, events, and institutions from the beginning of the dynasty to his own time. As Chu I-tsun (ECCP) remarks, "It is the best private historical work written in and about the Ming dynasty." It is indispensable for a full understanding of Ming history. An index to the work is included in the *Chūkoku zuihitsu zatsucho sakuin* 中國隨筆雜著索引.

Shen seems to have been too circumspect and cautious a writer, however, to present all the facts available to him. For instance, 1) he mentions the various imperial concubines of foreign race of the Ming house but refrains from mentioning Kung-fei 碩妃, the consort of the founder of the dynasty; still less does he discuss the mystery surrounding her; 2) although writing more than two hundred years after the rebellion of Chu Ti (*q.v.*), he repeats without qualification all the incriminating epithets and innuendoes applied to the defeated party and its members; 3) he is also reticent about Yü Ch'ien (*q.v.*).

Shen's collected works entitled *Ch'ing-ch'üan-t'ang chi* 清權堂集, in 22 *chüan*, printed during the years ending in 1642, receive no mention in the Imperial Catalogue, but an original copy is known to be extant in the Naikaku Bunko, Tokyo. The Catalogue does, however, record four other works by Shen, all originally parts of the *Yeh-hu-pien*, but only one of these was copied into the Imperial Library, the *Ku-ch'ü tsa-yen* 顧曲雜言, 1 *chüan*, which sketches the history of song writing in north and south China. All four have been reprinted separately in various collectanea.

Bibliography

40/61/10a; 64/庚 23/15b; 84/丁下/75; *Wan-li yeh-hu-pien*; SK (1930), 83/6a, 130/2b, 199/10a; Ts SCC, nos. 1540, 1559, 2684, 2943; Sun Tien-ch'i (1957), 154; *Chia-hsing-fu chih* (1877), 52/12b, 19b, 26a; Sheng Feng 盛楓, *Chia-ho cheng-hsien lu* 嘉禾徵獻錄, 2/7a; L. Carrington Goodrich, *Literary Inquisition of Ch'ien-lung* (Baltimore, 1935), 153, 253; W. Franke, *Sources*, 4. 1. 5.

Tsung-han Yang

SHEN Tu 沈度 (T. 民則, H. 自樂), 1357–1434, official and calligrapher, was a native of Hua-t'ing 華亭, Sung-chiang 松江 prefecture. He and his younger brother, Shen Ts'an 粲 (T. 民望, H. 簡菴, 1379–1453), were both known for their calligraphy, as well as for their prose and poetry. Sometime about 1590 Shen Tu became implicated in a lawsuit and was banished to Yunnan where he served on the staff of instruction of Chu P'ien (*see* Chu Su). Around 1398, when a military commander named Ch'ü Neng 瞿能 (T. 世賢, d. 1400) made an official trip to Nanking, he was taken along as an assistant. Shortly after Chu Ti (*q.v.*) had been enthroned in 1402, when the court was looking for qualified calligraphers to join the Hanlin Academy, Shen was recommended by Yang P'u (*see* Yang Shih-ch'i) to enter the service as a recorder. Although there were other good calligraphers such as Hsieh Chin and Hu Kuang (*qq.v.*) at court, the emperor admired Shen's writing most. Official copies of many important rescripts and documents of this period were penned by him. Soon his son, Shen Tsao 藻 (T. 凝清), and his brother Shen Ts'an joined him. Shen Tu was then promoted to senior expositor, Shen Ts'an to reader, and Shen Tsao to drafter in the central drafting office. Shen Tu was allowed to wear the official apparel of the second rank. The two brothers accompanied the emperor on his trips between Peking and Nanking on several occasions and were showered with tokens of the imperial esteem.

After Chu Chan-chi (*q.v.*) came to

the throne (1426), Shen Tu became chancellor of the Hanlin Academy. When he reached the age of seventy-two, he petitioned the emperor for retirement, but this was denied. In due course, however, through an imperial rescript he received his salary, but was absolved from official duties.

Shen Tu was an expert in various styles of calligraphy, although his seal script was considered as most refined and classical, following that of the Han dynasty. His contemporary Yang Shih-ch'i once remarked: "Shen Tu's seal script is the best of his time and Hu Kuang's running hand is unexcelled," Wang Wen-chih (ECCP), a calligrapher of the 18th century, thought that the Shen brothers' writing was the harbinger of the so-called Hanlin style in Chinese calligraphy. Emperor Chu Yu-t'ang (q.v.), who fancied himself a calligrapher, admired Shen Tu's handwriting so much that he sought out his descendants. He found a great-grandson, named Shen Shih-lung 世隆, and appointed him a drafter in the central drafting office. It was unusual for calligraphers like the Shen brothers to receive so much favor from successive emperors. They were nicknamed "elder academician" and "younger academician." Wang Shih-chen (q.v.), a connoisseur, recorded (ca. 1580) that examples of Shen Ts'an's handwriting had a lower market value than that of contemporary young calligraphers, and lamented the unpredictability of the national taste.

Bibliography

1/286/4b; 5/20/31a; Yang Shih-ch'i, *Tung-li wen-chi*, 9/9a, 16/3a; Wang Shih-chen, *Yen-chou ssu-pu kao*, 131/11a; Cha Chi-tso (ECCP), *Tsui-wei lu*, 27/3a; Weng Fang-kang (ECCP), *Fu-ch'u-chai wen-chi*, 9/10a, 31/1a; TSCC (1885-88), XXIII: 95/83/5a, XXIV: 118/24/6a; *San-hsi-t'ang fa-t'ieh* 三希堂法帖 (1894), Vol. 27; Ma Tsung-huo 馬宗霍, *Shu-lin tsao-chien* 書林藻鑑 (Shanghai 1935), 11/296a; Li Chin-hua 李晉華, *Ming shih tsuan-hsiu k'ao* 纂修考 (1933), 105.

Liu Lin-sheng

SHEN Yu-jung 沈有容 (T. 士弘, H. 寧海), January 22, 1557-June/July, 1627, soldier, was a native of Hsüan-ch'eng 宣城, south of Nanking. He came from a family of literary tradition. His grandfather, Shen Ch'ung 寵 (T. 思畏, H. 古林, cj 1537, d. 1571), one-time assistant administration commissioner of Kwangsi, was a disciple of Wang Chi (q.v.) of the Wang Yang-ming school. His father, Shen Mao-ching 懋敬, entered officialdom by purchase and served as a vice-magistrate of P'u-chou 蒲州, Shansi. His uncle, Shen Mao-hsüeh 懋學 (T. 君典, H. 少林, 白雲山樵, 1539-82), attained the distinction of being chosen *chuang-yüan* in the *chin-shih* examination of 1577. Energetic and outspoken, Shen Mao-hsüeh offended the powerful grand secretary, Chang Chü-cheng (q. v.), and discreetly left Peking on leave. It is said that in the last few years of his life he received instructions from the Taoist priestess, Wang Tao-chen (q. v.), and was devoted to the attainment of supernatural powers.

Shen Yu-jung, able-bodied and vigorous, preferred horsemanship and swordsmanship to literary studies and passed the military examinations of 1579. He then served as a junior officer in the garrisons north of Peking where in one border raid in 1584 he sustained two arrow wounds but returned with six enemy heads. A year later he was transferred to Liaotung as firearms officer under the governor, Ku Yang-ch'ien 顧養謙 (T. 益卿, cs 1565, 1537-1604). Shen distinguished himself in the attack on the Yehe fortresses in 1588 (*see* Narimbulu, ECCP), receiving a wound and losing two horses from under him. He was rewarded with a minor hereditary rank in the Kuang-ning chung-wei 廣寧中衞 and given the command of a fort. It is said that he served under Sung Ying-ch'ang (*see* Li Ju-sung) for some time and then (1595?) retired to his home in Hsüan-ch'eng where he made good returns from farming.

In 1597, for the defense of the southern Fukien coast against Japanese raiders, the governor of Fukien, Chin Hsüeh-

tseng 金學曾 (T. 子魯, cs 1568), invited
Shen to come out of retirement and serve
as a naval officer on the island Hai-t'an
海壇, east of Foochow. It happened that
his elder brother, Shen Yu-yen 有嚴 (T.
士莊, cj 1579), was then an assistant prefect of Foochow in charge of coastal
defense. Together they built up a well-
disciplined force. By surprising a pirate ship
preying on merchant vessels, Shen Yu-
jung gained his first naval victory. About
this time the provincial authorities planned
to send him on a secret mission to Japan
and appropriated a thousand taels for the
purpose. He took no part in the financial
arrangements and so was not involved
when the mission was called off and
the money had to be refunded. For this
his superiors admired him and promoted
him to be Wu-yü pa tsung 浯嶼把總,
commander of the naval forces in south
Fukien with headquarters on Amoy
Island. In 1602 the command post was
removed to Shih-hu 石湖, a fishing
village on the estuary of the Chin-chiang
晉江. He supervised the construction of
a large fort, including even a building
for literary activities where such scholars as
T'u Lung, Ch'en Ti, and Ho Ch'iao-yüan
(qq. v.) stayed as his guests.

Late in that year (1602) Shen was
informed of the presence of a Japanese
pirate fleet of seven ships off the Taiwan
coast. He made preparations to fight and,
early in 1603, when his men were expected
to prepare for the New Year festivals, he
ordered them to embark on twenty-one
ships at Liao-lo 料羅 (on Quemoy Island).
A storm dispersed the fleet while it was
sailing past the Pescadores. With fourteen
ships that reached Taiwan he attacked
the pirates, sinking six ships and recovering more than three hundred men, women,
and children taken into captivity by the
pirates. Ch'en Ti, who accompanied Shen
on the expedition, wrote a report of his
observations on Taiwan; it is the first
reliable Chinese account of the aborigines
(see Ch'en Ti). The victory was also celebrated by other writers, including the

grand secretary, then in retirement, Yeh
Hsiang-kao (q. v.).

When the Dutch admiral, Wijbrand
van Waerwijck (韋麻郎, or 麻韋郎, 1569-
1615?, sent out by the Dutch in 1602 to
join the East India Company), arrived at
the Pescadores with a fleet of three ships
in 1604, he dispatched Li Chin 李錦, a
Fukienese merchant at Pattani on the east
Malay coast, to Foochow to negotiate
with the eunuch, Kao Ts'ai 高寀, then in
charge of customs and taxes of Fukien.
The understanding was that, after the re-
ceipt of a certain sum of money, Kao was
to report favorably to the throne on the
desirability of granting the Dutch the
privilege of trading at the Pescadores.
The new governor, Hsü Hsüeh-chü (q.v.),
was opposed to this arrangement and sent
Shen with a fleet of fifty ships to the
island to deal with the Dutch. With prom-
ises to send Chinese merchants to trade
at Pattani, Shen persuaded the Dutch to
leave without concluding any transactions
with the eunuch. This achievement further
enhanced Shen's prestige as a naval commander and strategist, but the eunuch resented his interference. Instead of a substantial reward Shen was transferred to
Chekiang as an assistant regional military
commissioner (autumn of 1606).

Shen served eight years in Chekiang,
holding successively the posts of major in
command of the Ch'ang Kuo 昌國 garrison and lieutenant colonel in charge of
the coastal defense of southeastern Chekiang. About 1612 he submitted an intelligence report on the Japanese activities,
referring to the Satsuma subjugation of
Liu-ch'iu (Ryūkyū) in 1609 and the thriving trade at Pusan in Korea. The report,
transmitted to the Korean government,
evoked a long explanation from the
Korean king, who asserted that the Japanese in Pusan were under control. In
1614, for some reason, Shen left his post
and returned home. Three years later,
when the Fukien coast was again menaced by pirates, the then governor, Huang
Ch'eng-hsüan 黃承玄 (T. 履常, cs 1586),

invited Shen to resume command of coastal defense. In June, shortly after he arrived at Foochow, he led a fleet in an attack on some Japanese pirates on the Tung-sha 東沙 Islands and returned with sixty-nine prisoners, a number of Fukienese fishermen, and several sailors of the Chekiang navy who had been held in captivity by the Japanese. Although Shen accomplished this by a ruse, the exploit was memorialized to the throne as a military victory and the senior members of the provincial government were all handsomely rewarded. Hence, when Shen's commission from Peking arrived merely confirming his new appointment with his former rank of lieutenant colonel, he offered his resignation and prepared to leave. Shortly thereafter, however, he also received a reward, the promotion to colonel in command of southern Fukien coastal defense (Nan-Chang fu-tsung-ping 南漳副總兵). In that capacity he succeeded in pacifying large pirate bands on the coast, enlisting some of their members under his command and sending the rest to their homes.

This was the time when the rebellion of the Jurchen chief, Nurhaci (ECCP), turned the attention of the Peking court to the front in Liaotung. Both for the defense of Shantung and for the maintenance of the supply route to Liaotung by sea, the northern Shantung port of Teng-chou 登州 gained increasing importance. In 1620 Shen Yu-jung, as one of the few experienced naval officers, was made commander-in-chief of Shantung with headquarters at Teng-chou (Teng-Lai tsung ping-kuan 登萊總兵官), a post he held for four years. He was then in his late sixties, but was energetic enough to lead naval raids on the Liaotung coast, winning several engagements. He also helped thousands of refugees to cross the sea from Liaotung to Shantung. His relations with Mao Wenlung (ECCP), the general occupying the Korean island of P'i-tao 皮島 (i. e. Chiatao 椵島), however, were strained, probably because he thought that Mao was

self-aggrandizing and could not be fully trusted. In the conduct of this campaign he differed with the policy makers in Peking who counted on Mao for offensive action against the Manchus. Even Yeh Hsiang-kao, then first grand secretary, who had known Shen for forty years, upheld Mao in the dispute, as is revealed in his letters to Shen. In the end (1624) the government granted Shen's plea for resignation. After living three years in retirement he died of heart failure.

In 1628, one year after his death, one of his eight sons, Shen Shou-ch'ung 壽崇 (H. 旭海, d. 1645), became a military chin-shih; after serving in the army for fifteen years, he was killed in action defending Hsing-tu 興都 (An-lu 安陸 in Hukuang) against the rebels under Li Tzu-ch'eng (ECCP). Another son, Shen Shou-ch'iao 嶠, succeeded to the hereditary rank of a chiliarch of the Kuang-ning Guard. Still a third son, Shen Shou-min 民, fought against the Manchus in 1645.

Shen Yu-jung was commemorated in temples or by monuments every place in which he served as commanding officer, Amoy, P'eng-hu(Pescadores), Ch'üan-chou, Teng-chou, etc. He preserved in an album the writings and eulogies presented to him. About a year after his death, his sons printed the collection in 6 chüan, under the title Min-hai tseng-yen 閩海贈言. Although it includes chiefly prose and poetry about his exploits in Fukien, there are also a few items dating from later years, including an elegy by Ho Ch'iao-yüan. The book, fortunately preserved in the library of Tokyo University, was printed in 1959 as No. 56 in the series T'ai-wan wen-hsien ts'ung-k'an 臺灣文獻叢刊 with a preface by Fang Hao 方豪.

Bibliography

1/270/4a, 6a, 325/24a; 3/249/14a; MSL (1966), Shen-tsung, 10557; KC (1958), 5109; Min-hai tseng-yen; Hsüan-ch'eng-hsien chih (1888), 15/15b, 17/9b, 18/4a, 19/29b; Ch'en Jen-hsi, Wu-meng-yüan chi (1633) 駐 2/65a; Wang Tsai-chin (ECCP), San Ch'ao Liao-shih shih-lu (1931), 2/30b,

3/28b, 5/27b, 6/27b, 13/10b; Yeh Hsiang-kao, *Hsü Lun-fei ch'ih-tu*; *Chia-hsing* 嘉興 *-fu chih* (1878), 52/30a; *Dai Nihon shiryō* 大日本史料, vol. 12, pt. 16 (1926), 899; *Kwanghaegun ilgi* (Chŏngjoksan copy, *see* Yi Hon), 66/11b (32/172); W. P. Groeneveldt, *De Nederlanders in China* ('s-Gravenhage, 1900-5), 11.

Chaoying Fang

SHENG Mao-yeh 盛茂燁 (T. 念庵, H. 研菴, 硯菴, 與華), fl. 1620-40, artist, was a native of Ch'ang-chou 長洲 (Soochow). Nothing is known of his life; the authors of his biographical notices discuss his painting only. They state that he produced landscapes in color depicting misty groves and wide plains with slanted and intertwined trees and lofty mountains, and that his figures were refined and skillfully done. They add that his paintings, although lacking the influence of Sung and Yüan dynasty styles, were exceedingly good when compared with those of the late Wu 吳 school; the "scholarly" spirit of his paintings also receives praise.

Many of Sheng's landscapes are quite somber in effect, displaying a marked preference for sparse groves of spindly or tortured pines or thickets of blunt-branched leafless trees. This is explained partly by the artist's penchant for illustrating poetry and for frequently selecting precisely those couplets, most often conceived by T'ang dynasty poets, which refer to chill and wintry scenes. Stylistically, Sheng's landscape forms are produced not so much by outlines, as by built-up layers of soft dabs and strokes of wash. Contrasted with this are the harshly rendered forms of branches and trees. Often the stunted or bare branches are done with brusque, blunted strokes of stark, dark ink, while tree trunks are presented as folded and twisted angular patterns rather than as rounded forms.

Sheng, whose style was influenced by that of Li Shih-ta (*q. v.*), peopled his landscapes with scholar-figures of a distinctive type. They tend to be of ample proportion and to wear heavy, full garments which increase their rotundity. Their rather portly physiques are further emphasized by the artist's inclination to ignore the interior folds of garments and instead to concentrate upon defining the overlapping folds of cuffs, collars, and hems with wide, wavering lines. (Examples of Sheng's paintings are reproduced by Osvald Sirén.)

Sheng was apparently the leading figure in a family of landscape painters which included his son, Sheng Nien 年(T. 大有). This youth painted plum blossoms and bamboo as well as landscapes, but had an uncontrollable mania for chess, in which he excelled, and so had little time to devote to painting. Further, according to Yeh Te-hui (BDRC), two landscape artists from Soochow, Sheng Mao-chün 焌 and Sheng Mao-ying 穎, were Sheng Mao-yeh's brothers. None of Sheng Nien's works seems to have survived, and only one landscape, a fan dated 1626, by Sheng Mao-chün is known to exist (unpublished, listed by Kuo Wei-ch'ü 郭味蕖). A handscroll entited "Ma-ch'i yen-yü t'u" 馬嶜烟雨圖 (The Ma-ch'i temple in misty rain), painted in 1633, is signed "Sheng Ying" and may be the work of Sheng Mao-ying (reproduced in *Liao-ning-sheng po-wu-kuan ts'ang-hua chi* 遼寧省博物館藏畫集). Both the *Liaoning* catalogue and the *Shih-ch'ü pao-chi*, the catalogue of the Ch'ien-lung emperor's collection (to which this painting once belonged), assign it to the otherwise unknown artist, Sheng Ying. Hsü Pang-ta (*see* Lu Chih), however, considers it to have been the work of Sheng Mao-ying. If this assumption be correct, a seal following the artist's signature gives his *hao* as T'ao-an chu-jen 陶菴主人.

Bibliography

Chiang Shao-shu 姜紹書, *Wu-sheng shih-shih* 無聲詩史 (*Hua-shih* 畫史 *ts'ung-shu* ed.), 4/70; Hsü Ch'in 徐沁, *Ming hua lu* 明畫錄, *ibid.*, 8/111; Hsü Pang-ta, *Li-tai … shu-hua … nien-piao* (Shanghai, 1963), 118, 347; Kuo Wei-ch'ü, *Sung Yüan Ming Ch'ing shu-hua-chia nien-piao* 宋元明清書畫家年表

(Peking, 1962), 210; *Liao-ning-sheng po-wu-kuan ts'ang-hua chi*, Vol. 2 (Peking, 1962), 55; Lan Ying 藍英 and Hsieh Pin 謝彬, *T'u-hui pao-chien hsü-tsuan* 圖繪寶鑑續纂 (*Hua-shih ts'ung-shu* ed.), 1/6, 2/23; *Shih-ch'ü pao-chi hsü-pien* 石渠寶笈續編 (1888), Chung-hua kung 重華宮, 7/162b; Yeh Te-hui, *Hsi-yüan hsiao-hsia pai-i shih* (1908), 上 7a; Osvald Sirén, *Chinese Painting* (New York, 1956-58), Vol. 5, 28, Vol. 6, 278, 279, Vol. 7, 230; E. J. Laing, *Chinese Paintings in Chinese Publications, 1956-1968* (Ann Arbor, 1969), 187; John C. Ferguson, *Index of Artists* (Nanking, 1934), 323a.

E. J. Laing

SHENG Yung 盛庸, died October (?), 1403, was a military officer, reportedly a native of Shensi, but data concerning his origins are lacking. He achieved his greatest prominence as a general commanding the imperial field armies during the civil war of 1399-1402, which led to the usurpation of Chu Ti (*q.v.*). Sheng served initially under Hsü Ta, Ch'ang Yü-ch'un, and Fu Yu-te (*qq.v.*) in the military campaigns of the early years of the Hung-wu era, by the end of which he received the appointment of regional military commissioner. He was thus one of the higher-ranking and more experienced generals available to the government when, on August 25, 1399, an expeditionary force, nominally numbering over 300,000, but actually having only about 130,000 men, was formed to take the field against the prince of Yen. Sheng was assigned to the staff of Keng Ping-wen (*q.v.*), named generalissimo for the conquest of the north. Keng's forces took up positions at Chen-ting 眞定, Ho-chien 河間, and other points in central Pei-Chihli, and throughout September engaged in skirmishes and probing operations against the relatively small but well-led units of Chu Ti, based on Peiping. A small engagement led to the rout of Keng's inexperienced junior officers and perhaps undisciplined men; on September 24 he was forced to fall back on Chen-ting, with heavy losses in men and horses. On the 30th, recalled to court,

he was replaced by Li Ching-lung (*see* Li Wen-chung), a distant cousin of the emperor, probably on the advice of Huang Tzu-ch'eng (*see* Lien Tzu-ning). Li subsequently took over the main field army left by Keng, plus additions, perhaps totaling half a million men. Sheng Yung came under his command at this time.

When Chu Ti forced Li to retreat to Te-chou 德州, and then to Tsinan (May 31, 1400), after the battle of Pai-kou River (*see* Chu Ti), T'ieh Hsüan (*q.v.*) and Sheng Yung swore to defend the city to the death. The initiative they assumed and their success in raiding attacks on Chu Ti's forces kept the city from surrendering during the siege, which lasted from June 6 to September 4. With the recall of Li on September 28, the court appointed Sheng Yung commander-in-chief in the north with the title P'ing Yen chiang-chün 平燕將軍 (General for the pacification of Yen) and concurrently regional commander. He was also awarded the title of marquis of Li-ch'eng 歷城侯. A new phase in the military operations now commenced.

Under Sheng Yung the conduct of the war was at first considerably more succesful. The greatest victories over the rebellious forces occurred during the winter of 1400-1. Sheng Yung is remembered most prominently for his massive victory at Tung-ch'ang 東昌 (modern Liao-ch'eng 聊城, Shantung) on January 9, 1401. Tung-ch'ang was a prefectural city lying west of the Grand Canal and southwest of Tsinan on the principal overland route to the south from Pei-Chihli. Chu Ti's consistent strategy seems to have been to avoid main strongholds on the Grand Canal supply route unless the enemy was in retreat and disorder; otherwise he employed guerrilla tactics, diversionary attacks and feints, and sought routes to the south that would avoid major obstacles. He personally led his principal army in such operations in southwest Pei-Chihli throughout December, and Sheng Yung was able to confront him at Tung-ch'ang under favorable conditions. At midpoint in the battle P'ing An (*see* Chu Ti) arrived with his fearsome cavalry, and the decimation of Chu Ti's army followed: Several leading rebel generals were captured and beheaded on the battlefield. This is often referred to as the low point in Chu Ti's fortunes. It should have been followed by a general attack, coordinating the efforts of all the garrisons at Chen-ting, Ts'ang 滄 -chou, Te-chou, and other points. But commanders at those points failed to heed the call for such a movement, and the opportunity was lost. Throughout the remainder of January Chu Ti was remarkably successful in regaining the initiative in several places, retaking important bastions in central Pei-Chihli, and blunting the aggressive operations of P'ing An and others. But on January 31 the court at Nanking announced the victory of Tung-ch'ang in a triumphant mood, called Huang Tzu-ch'eng and Ch'i T'ai (*q.v.*) back to office, and bestowed promotions and rewards on the generals.

Although an aggressive follow-up of the Tung-ch'ang victory had not immediately materialized, Sheng Yung was able to mount a general offensive by March; several crucial engagements took place in the last days of the month and through April, 1401, north from Te-chou along the main routes to Peiping. On April 5 Sheng personally led a raid that captured several prominent officers, and the mood of his commanders may have grown overconfident. On the following day, on a field north of the Hu-t'o 滹沱 River, the main armies confronted each other. The accounts say that the battle seesawed throughout the day. Sheng Yung held his ground, facing the northeast, awaiting the arrival of other forces. In mid-afternoon a gale began to blow from the northeast, carrying heavy dust, blinding and confusing his soldiers, while Chu Ti's men, with their backs to the wind, were at an advantage. Several loyalist generals died fighting, the soldiers broke and fled, and Sheng Yung was forced to retreat in

disorder, having lost "over one hundred thousand troops." He fell back upon Te-chou, only to learn that the tardy relief force expected during the battle had learned of his defeat and retreated to Chen-ting. On April 8 at Shan-chia-ch'iao 單家橋, and again on April 23 at Kao-ch'eng 藁城, P'ing An was seriously defeated with heavy cavalry losses. All of southern Pei-Chihli fell to Chu Ti. The court again dismissed Huang Tzu-ch'eng and Ch'i T'ai, and assumed a mood of gloom. The aggressive phase of Sheng Yung's field command had been brought to an unsuccessful conclusion.

During July and August, 1401, Chu Ti succeeded in bypassing Te-chou and Tsinan, and putting out of commission warehouses and supply vessels on the Grand Canal. Sheng Yung's offensive capacity was thus temporarily reduced, and he was obliged to fall back to defend the Huai River line farther south. In 1402 Chu Ti ordered one column to outflank Sheng by moving south of the Huai from a point in Shantung, ready to prevent any disengagement from the Huai defense system and rapid move to the southwest, where Chu Ti was attempting to approach the Yangtze. He reached there at last at the end of June. By this time, Sheng was able to make a dash to the Yangtze, and prepare a joint land and naval defense. The imperial forces repulsed Chu Ti at P'u-tzu-k'ou 浦子口 in the last days of July. This was a dark moment for him, with victory almost in sight. In the nick of time, however, his son Chu Kao-hsü (*q.v.*) arrived with reinforcements, and permitted him to seize the initiative once more and cross the river. He entered Nanking on July 13. Sheng Yung was not involved in any of the events that occurred immediately afterwards.

Like most of the field commanders and important military officers throughout the realm, Sheng Yung acquiesced in the *fait accompli*, and acknowledged the legitimacy of the usurpation, shortly after Nanking had fallen and the new reign was proclaimed. Chu Ti made a show of treating his most able opponents in the field generously. Sheng Yung was first returned to the command of the garrison at Huai-an 淮安 and shortly thereafter named governor of Shantung, charged to lead in the rehabilitation of the region following the destruction of war. There may have been a calculated irony in this since the previous governor had been T'ieh Hsüan, Sheng's ardent colleague in the aggressive counterattacks of 1400, who remained an uncompromising loyalist to the end and had just been executed as an enemy of the new regime. After a very short term as governor, in 1403 Sheng reached the retirement age and went home. Early in October of that same year, Censor-in-chief Ch'en Ying impeached him for harboring seditious thoughts (see Ju Ch'ang); he was subsequently deprived of his noble title, and later committed suicide.

Nothing seems to be known about Sheng Yung's heirs, and other facts about his life are curiously missing. The late Ming historian Wang Shih-chen (q.v.) made the comment, "[Sheng] Yung achieved the rank of regional military commissioner in the Hung-wu period, but had achieved no particular fame by reason of merit in battle. The histories record only that his daughter was the consort 妃 of the prince of the second degree of the Chou 周 line, [Chu] Yu-k'uang 有爌; it would seem that the historians must have suppressed facts." Chu Yu-k'uang was born in 1400, the eighth son of Chu Su (q.v.), the first prince of Chou, at his place of temporary exile in Yunnan. He was enfoeffed during the Yung-lo reign as prince of Chen-p'ing 鎮平, and lived until 1472, having achieved some reputation for scholarly pursuits. His marriage to Sheng Yung's daughter must have taken place fifteen years, more or less, after Sheng Yung's suicide. It is difficult to say whether the "suppressed facts" which Wang Shih-chen suspects concerned the troubled career of Chu Su and his children, or Sheng Yung's own history. A recent scholar has located a poem written for Sheng by a friend on the occasion of his appointment to the governorship of Shantung. It conveys some sense of the incongruity of the final years of the great old general's career, and strongly suggests that he must have been tortured by his own sense of guilt and by the reproaches of his contemporaries. But no other information about his final years or about his descendants seems to exist.

Bibliography

1/144/1a; MSL (1963), T'ai-tsung, 0075, 0425; KC (1958), ch. 11-12; Cheng Hsiao, Wu-hsüeh pien, 18/58a, 55/6b; Wang Ch'ung-wu 王崇武, Ming ching-nan shih-shih k'ao-cheng kao 明靖難史事考證稿 (1948); id., Feng-t'ien ching-nan chi chu 奉天靖難記注 (1948), 200.

F. W. Mote

SHIH Chin-ch'ing 施進卿, died ca. 1421, Ming pacification commissioner of Palembang, Sumatra, was a native of Kwangtung. At the time of his birth in the latter part of the 14th century the empire of Majapahit in Java had annexed Srī Vijaya (or Sambodja), and at the end of the century, when its power declined, it still claimed suzerainty over this ancient state in southern Sumatra. Actual control of Palembang, former capital of Srī Vijaya, called Chiu-kang 舊港 (the old port) by the Chinese, had fallen into hands of the local leaders, among whom were the Chinese. One of the first to rise to prominence and to exercise authority over the region was Liang Tao-ming 梁道明, a native of Nan-hai 南海 in Kwangtung province, who, with several thousand families of soldiers and traders from Kwangtung and Fukien, had settled at Palembang and had been chosen chief. Shih Chin-ch'ing at the same time was made assistant chief.

At the beginning of the Yung-lo period a guard commander, Sun Hsüan 孫鉉, sent to southeast Asia on a diplomatic mission, met Liang's son, Liang Er-nu

二奴, and persuaded the latter to return with him for a visit to the imperial capital. As a consequence of Liang Er-nu's visit, the Ming court in February, 1405, sent a messenger, T'an Sheng-shou 譚勝受, with a chiliarch commander, Yang Hsin 楊信, to Palembang to establish relations with Liang Tao-ming. The mission returned in December with Liang Tao-ming and another leader, Cheng Po-k'o 鄭伯可. While he was away, Liang left the administration of the Chinese community at Palembang to Shih Chin-ch'ing.

Liang returned home with gifts of brocades, lustring, and paper money from the emperor. In August of the following year another embassy from Palembang arrived at Nanking, but, instead of Liang Tao-ming, Ming chronicles give the name of Ch'en Tsu-i 陳祖義 (d. 1407) as the chief of Chiu-kang. This suggests that during his absence, or shortly after his return, other Chinese had come to challenge Liang's position and that he had lost control during the struggle for power. The *shih-lu* states that Ch'en Tsu-i sent his son, Ch'en Shih-liang 士良, and Liang Tao-ming sent his nephew, Liang Kuan-cheng 觀政, to China. After this there is no further mention of Liang Tao-ming. Instead, there are accounts of a conflict between Ch'en Tsu-i and Shih Chin-ch'ing.

By going in person or by sending close relatives as envoys to the Ming imperial court, the Chinese leaders of Palembang had sought to enhance their authority and bolster their positions, but the Ming government did not become involved in the affairs of the Chinese in Palembang until 1407 when Cheng Ho (*q.v.*) touched at the seaport on his return from India with his ships laden with merchandise and treasures. Under a date equivalent to October 1, 1407, the *shih-lu* states:

"The grand eunuch Cheng Ho returned from his mission to the countries of the Western Ocean bringing as prisoners the pirate Ch'en Tsu-i and others. Previously, when [Cheng] Ho arrived at Chiu-kang he sent messengers to summon [Ch'en] Tsu-i. Tsu-i and others pretended to submit but secretly planned to waylay the government fleet. Ho and others learned about this and, having marshaled their forces, were ready. When Tsu-i led his men to attack, Ho, in command of his troops, fought and defeated them, killing over five thousand pirates, setting fire to ten pirate ships, capturing seven ships, and seizing two unauthorized brass seals. [He also] took as prisoners Tsu-i and two others [who], upon arrival at the capital, were immediately ordered to be executed."

This passage, if the facts are correct, reveals the scale of the engagement. According to a modern historian, Pao Tsun-p'eng 包遵彭, Cheng Ho had under his command, during his first voyage, 62 treasure ships, 255 smaller vessels, and nearly 28,000 men. The attackers lost 5,000 men and 17 ships; so their forces too must have been originally quite strong. Since contemporary accounts describe the people of Palembang as being skilled in naval warfare, predatory, and feared by their neighbors, it is possible that the attackers were not just Chinese pirates but Sumatrans as well.

As for Ch'en Tsu-i, who was labeled a pirate chief, there is the statement of Ma Huan (*q.v.*) that Ch'en Tsu-i was a Cantonese who had fled to Palembang during the Hung-wu period and who, as chief of the Chinese settlement there, was overbearing and oppressive, and had plundered merchant ships. These charges were repeated in contemporaneous Chinese accounts. Piracy was rampant in the South Seas at this time, and it is quite possible that Ch'en Tsu-i was a freebooter who had fled from China when the imperial coast guard intensified its campaign to suppress piracy. When Chu Ti (*q.v.*) sent naval expeditions to the South China Sea and the Indian Ocean, they were entrusted with two main missions: one, to proclaim the might of China, and the other, to make the sea routes safe. Cheng Ho's defeat and arrest of Ch'en Tsu-i was thus in line with his orders.

Beyond the officially published versions of the event there are other aspects that should be taken into account. The Ming government was seeking to monopolize foreign trade in its effort to strengthen its tributary system, and Cheng Ho was one of the chief agents of this policy. The extensive private trade of the Chinese merchants had to be brought under control and limited, and those who did not comply would be treated as outlaws. Ch'en Tsu-i could have been one of them. Then, too, Ma Huan reveals that it was Shih Chin-ch'ing who informed Cheng Ho about Ch'en Tsu-i's lawless activities and his plan to attack the imperial fleet. Shih, according to a modern scholar, Tan Yeok Seong, was a Chinese Muslim and it is likely that Cheng Ho, also a Chinese Muslim, would lend a ready ear to his words, and that Ma Huan, of the same faith, would side with him.

Six days after the reception of Cheng Ho at the Ming court and the presentation of the captives, Shih Chin-ch'ing's son-in-law and emissary, Ch'iu Yen-ch'eng 丘彦誠, was granted an audience at court. The emperor issued a decree proclaiming the establishment of an office of pacification at Palembang and the appointment of Shih Chin-ch'ing as the commissioner. Ch'iu received the robes, sash, and seal of office to take back to Shih. This is the only occasion in history when the Chinese government had an overseas agency to take charge of Chinese settlers. But neither its authority over Shih nor Shih's control over his domain was very strong. Concerning Shih Chin-ch'ing, the *Ming-shih* states: "Although he accepted the decrees of the imperial court he was also a vassal of Java. His territory was a small strip and cannot be compared with Srī Vijaya of the past." Still the Ming court regarded Java as a vassal, and in 1413 it intervened when the Majapahit ruler of Java protested against claims of Malacca to Palembang. With the port of Palembang in friendly hands and

the sultanate of Malacca having the status of a Chinese protectorate and a base for the Ming fleet to assemble and to refit, the Chinese were able to dominate the sea lanes of southeast Asia.

Shih Chin-ch'ing carried on diplomatic and commercial relations with other countries in addition to those with the Ming empire in China and the Majapahit empire in Java. A Japanese record (discovered in 1932) reveals that in July, 1408 (15th year of Ōei), a "southern barbarian" (namban) ship sent by "the king named Arya [Shih] Chin-ch'ing" 帝王御名亞烈 [施] 進卿 carrying gifts to the "king" of Japan was wrecked off the coast of Kyushu. The rescued crew was sent home in another vessel. Ya-lieh (aretsu in Japanese) is the Malay term arya for a nobleman, and Chinese envoys in the service of the rulers of states in southeast Asia often bore this title.

Since the *shih-lu* mentions a mission from the Chiu-kang office of the pacification commissioner in November, 1416, it may be presumed that Shih Chin-ch'ing was then still alive. The *Li-tai pao-an* 歷代 寶案, a collection of the official documents of Liu-ch'iu (Ryūkyū), contains a letter dated November, 1428, from the chief minister of Liu-ch'iu to the administrator of Chiu-kang 舊港管事官, which refers to an embassy headed by Teng Tzu-ch'ang 鄧子昌 sent by the arya Shih Chih-sun of Chiu-kang 舊港施主(亞)烈智孫 in 1421. This may indicate that Shih Chin-ch'ing had died and his title had passed on to his son.

In February, 1424, this Shih Chih-sun (written as Shih Chi-sun 濟孫 in the *shih-lu* and *Ming-shih*) sent his brother-in-law, Ch'iu Yen-ch'eng, as his envoy to the Ming court to request the emperor to confer on him his father's title as the pacification commissioner of Palembang and to grant him a new seal of office to replace the old one, which had been destroyed by fire. Both requests were approved and Cheng Ho was ordered to proceed to Palembang to invest Shih Chi-sun with the office. Whether Cheng Ho followed this order is open to serious doubt. Emperor Chu Ti died in August, 1424, and his successor, Chu Kao-chih (*q.v.*), canceled further expeditions to the South Seas. In the six months between February and August there was scarcely sufficient time to equip a fleet, and furthermore, there is no mention of such a mission in the inscriptions recording Cheng's voyages. In August, 1425, following the death of Chu Kao-chih and the accession of Chu Chan-chi (*q. v.*), an embassy from the pacification commissioner of Chiu-kang, Java [sic], headed by the arya Chang-fo-na-ma 張佛那馬, arrived to present tribute, and again asked for a new seal of office to replace the one which had been destroyed by fire. The request granted, Chang-fo-na-ma was given one to take back with him.

The *shih-lu* does not mention the name of the ruler of Palembang who sent Chang-fo-na-ma and there is no further mention of Shih Chi-sun. The *Li-tai-pao-an* contains two letters from the chief minister of Liu-ch'iu both bearing the same date (November 3, 1430) but each listing a different set of gifts. One was addressed to Seng ya-la Wu 僧亞剌吳 of Chiu-kang and the other to the pen-mu-niang 本目娘 of Palembang. While Seng ya-la Wu cannot be identified, the fact that there were two letters may indicate that there were two rulers at the time. [Editors' note: Kobata Atsushi and Matsuda Mitsugu suggest (p. 137, n. 3) that "Seng-a-la-wu may have denoted a sultan."] In reply there were two letters to the chief minister of Liu-ch'iu on March 16, 1431, both with the same date but recording different sets of gifts. One was from the pen-t'ou-niang 本頭娘 of Palembang and the other from "the Humble Woman of Palembang, the pinatih, the Elder Mistress Shih" 寶林邦愚婦俾那智施氏大娘仔, in which the writer added pointedly, "I have taken temporary charge of the major affairs of this state" 權掌當朝之大事. Pen-mu-niang and pen-t'ou-niang may

be contractions for pen t'ou-mu niang— "the head lady"—and some scholars conjecture that she and the Elder Mistress Shih may be one and the same person. However, after his visit to Palembang in 1432, Ma Huan wrote that when Shih Chin-ch'ing died "the position was not inherited by his son but by his daughter, Shih Er-chieh 施二姐 (Second Mistress Shih), who became the ruler. All rewards and punishments, dismissals, and promotions were at her command." Thus it would seem that the "head lady" may be the Second Mistress Shih and that she may have shared her authority with her sister, the Elder Mistress Shih. The *Li-tai pao-an* also includes two letters to the chief minister of Liu-ch'iu in 1438: one from the administrator of Chiu-kang and the other from the Elder Mistress Shih, and also two letters in 1440: one from the pen-t'ou-niang and the other from the Elder Mistress Shih.

There was also a Niai Gede Pinatih who, in the beginning of the 15th century, became the shahbandar (chief of port) of Gresik in Java, and who had a part in the introduction of Islam to the island. One scholar (Tan Yeok Seong) suggests that she was Chinese, had come from Palembang, and could be the Elder Mistress Shih and the daughter of Shih Chin-ch'ing.

Bibliography

1/324/26b; MSL (1963), T'ai-tsung, 38/4b, 48/3b, 56/7b, 71/1a, 5a, 89/8a, 267/3a, Hsüan-tsung, 5/7b, 6/9a, 7/5a, 9a; Ma Huan, *Ying-yai sheng-lan*; Fei Hsin, *Hsing-ch'a sheng lan* in *Ying-yai sheng-lan chiao-chu* 校注 (1953), 16, and *Hsing-ch'a sheng-lan chiao-chu* annotated by Feng Ch'eng-chün 馮承鈞 (1937), 18; KC (1958), 948, 962, 994, 1208; Pao Tsun-p'eng, *Cheng Ho hsia Hsi-yang chih pao ch'uan k'ao* 鄭和下西洋之寶船考 (Taipei, 1961), 15; O. W. Wolters, *The Fall of Srivijaya in Malay History* (Cornell University Press, 1970), 60; Kobata Atsushi and Matsuda Mitsugu, *Ryukyuan Relations with Korea and South Seas Countries* (Kyoto, 1969), 131, pl. 143-49, 152; Kobata Atsushi 小葉田淳, "Kyokō oyobi sono Nichi-Ryū ryōkoku tono kōshō ni tsuite" 舊港及其日琉兩國との交渉こついて, *Shirin* 史林,

XX: 3 (July, 1935), 590; Takayanagi Mitsuhisa 高柳光壽, "Ōei nenkan ni okeru nanbansen raikō no monjo ni tsuite" 應永年間における南蠻船來航の文書について, *Shigaku zasshi* 史學雜誌, XLIII: 8 (1932), 1058; Tan Yeok Seong, "Chinese Elements in the Islamization of South East Asia—A Study of the Strange Story of Njai Gede Pinatih, the Grand Lady of Gresik, " *Proc. of the Second Biennial Conference of the International Association of Historians of Asia* (Taipei, 1962), 399.

Lo Jung-pang

SHIH Heng 石亨 , died March 8, 1460, was a soldier and military leader. He inherited from an uncle the position of an assistant commander of K'uan-ho wei 寬河衞, outside Hsi-feng-k'ou 喜峯口. [Editors' note: The K'uan-ho used to be one of the Ta-ning 大寧 guards set up in 1387 in eastern Mongolia (about 150 miles north of Hsi-feng-k'ou) after the conquest of that region (*see* Feng Sheng). During the following fifteen years it changed its name twice. As one of the princely bodyguards of Chu Ch'üan (*q.v.*), its name was Ying-chou chung hu-wei 營州中護衞. Later it became the K'uan-ho wei, apparently after it was stationed for a time at the place by that name (now K'uan-ch'eng 寬城), some thirty miles north of Hsi-feng-k'ou. But in 1403 or thereabouts, when all the Ta-ning guards were withdrawn from Mongolia, it was stationed in Peking and became one of the thirty-three guards in the northern capital. Hence Shih Heng apparently began his service in Peking.] His original home was in Wei-nan 渭南, Shensi. Well-trained and proficient in such military arts as horseback riding, archery, and swordsmanship, he distinguished himself in several battles and received promotion in 1436 to the rank of assistant regional commissioner at Tatung, and in 1438 to the rank of vice commissioner and subsequently of left assistant commander in the defense of the Tatung border region. Later Shih became regional commissioner, in 1447 assistant commissioner-in-chief, and on July 12, 1449, vice commissioner-in-chief. Three weeks thereafter, on August 3, just the day before the emperor set out on his ill-fated campaign, an Oirat force crushed the Chinese troops at Yang-ho-k'ou 陽和口 in the Tatung area, killing several commanders and scattering the rest of the garrison. Shih managed to reach Tatung on August 19. The court charged him with the defeat and demoted him, but permitted him to rehabilitate himself by recruiting and training new soldiers. This ruling was made on September 7, six days after the debacle at T'u-mu (*see* Chu Ch'i-chen).

Soon after Yü Ch'ien (*q.v.*) became minister of war he recommended that Shih be assigned to a leading position in the military preparations for the defense of the capital against an expected attack by the Oirat. Shih, now a close collaborator of Yü, distinguished himself late in October, 1449, in several engagements with the enemy in the suburbs of Peking. For his success he received the title Wu-ch'ing po 武清伯 (earl of Wu-ch'ing), and later hou 侯 (marquis). In 1452 Shih was appointed grand preceptor of the heir apparent. He participated in the army reorganization carried out by Yü and became regional commander.

Eventually, however, Shih and Yü began to find cooperation difficult. Yü learned of Shih's tolerance towards his subordinates engaging in various kinds of corruption. Probably with the intention of silencing Yü Ch'ien, Shih soon afterwards recommended the promotion of Yü's son, Yü Mien (*see* Yü Ch'ien), to the rank of vice commander of a battalion. Yü opposed this promotion, bluntly hinting at Shih's ulterior motive in making such a recommendation. In spite of Yü's several protests the emperor agreed to Shih's proposal and ordered the promotion. After this incident Shih several times offered to resign but the emperor ignored his request. Once, in the spring of 1454, Shih tendered his resignation simultaneously with the commissioner-in-chief of the metropolitan garrison, Chang Yüeh (*see* Chu Ch'i-yü), a man with whom he was to collaborate closely in the *coup d'état* of 1457. Shih's offers to resign were apparently due to his conflict with Yü, which originated not later than 1451 and which grew in intensity. When, at the end of 1452, Yü tendered his resignation from his position as supreme commander of military affairs, he referred to the problems of competence arising between himself (a civil official) and the military commanders. In this connection Yü mentioned Shih's name expressly. The emperor in refusing to approve the resignation stated that Yü and Shih collaborated effectively in the most critical days of the Ming empire, and he expressed the hope that both would continue to cooperate under the more favorable conditions prevailing.

Shih was ambitious and greedy, and thirsted for power, eager for a chance to permit a large clique of relatives and friends to enrich themselves through corrupt practices. Most notorious among them was his nephew Shih Piao 彪, residing at Tatung, likewise an able military man, who rose to the rank of assistant commissioner-in-chief. Several censors charged Shih Piao with misappropriating the property of local peasants, but the emperor took no action. The responsible and strict Yü Ch'ien was apparently in the way of Shih Heng and his clique in their nefarious practices.

Shih, together with Hsü Yu-chen (*q.v.*), Chang Yüeh, and Ts'ao Chi-hsiang (*q.v.*), instigated the plot for the reinstallation of Chu Ch'i-chen as emperor, hoping thereby to get rid of Yü and be free to follow his own devices. Only by relying on Shih's military power were the conspirators able to succeed in their plot, and to put the one-time ruler again on the throne. As a consequence the emperor rewarded Shih with the noble rank of Chungkuo kung 忠國公. Several thousands of Shih's relatives and friends received rewards, mostly without any justification, for their participation in the *coup*. Shih thus became the most powerful and influential man at court. He and his collaborators were responsible for unfounded accusations lodged against Yü and others and for his execution. Shih, not politically minded, had no particular aims beyond wealth and prestige. Almost every day he saw the emperor who tolerated him because Shih had been so responsible for his regaining the throne. Shih erected a splendid residence on an estate east of the imperial palace on a street which bore his name, Shih ta-jen hu-t'ung 石大人胡同, until it was changed after 1912 to Wai-chiao-pu chieh 外交部街. The residence had the dimensions and the luxury which was the due only of palaces of imperial princes, and was not permitted for the residences of even the highest officials. The emperor knew about this, but raised no objection.

By his overbearing and extravagant behavior, however, Shih gradually forfeited the imperial favor and his position. First in 1459 some unlawful actions by Shih Piao, who had become Ting-yüan hou 定遠侯 (marquis of Ting-yüan), became notorious and incensed the emperor. Shih Piao was imprisoned, the case investigated, and Shih Heng's implication became evident. The emperor wavered before taking action against Shih Heng, merely ordering him to retire from office (November 15, 1459). The investigations continued and further accusations were lodged for more serious crimes. Eventually, on February 17, 1460, Shih Heng was committed for trial. Subsequently his property, including his rural estates at Wei-nan and Tatung, was confiscated. He died in prison of cold and starvation on March 8, 1460. Shih Piao and Shih Heng's grand-nephew, Shih Hou 後 (cs 1457), were executed. All the relatives and friends who had been rewarded for their alleged support at the restoration were degraded and punished. Only Shih Heng's youngest son, Shih Chin 溍 (born in 1457 or later), was considered too young to be implicated. He is reported to have been still living in Peking during the Cheng-te period.

Bibliography

1/173/7a; 3/155/6b; 5/10/21a; 61/154/3039; 63/13/262; KC (1958), 1773, 1781, 2093; MSL (1940), Ying-tsung, 205/11b, 206/3a, 223/11b, 238/14b, 312/5b; Yü Ch'ien, *Yü-kung tsou-i*, 5/12a; Yang Hsüan, *Fu-p'i lu* (*Chi-lu hui-pien* ed.); Ku Ying-t'ai (ECCP), *Ming-ch'ao chi-shih pen-mo*, chüan 36; Lin Ch'uan-chia 林傳甲 (ed.), *Ching-shih chieh-hsiang chi* 京師街巷記 (Peking, 1919), 4/2; Chu I-hsin 朱一新 , *Ching-shih fang-hsiang chih* 坊巷志 (Peking, 1918); Wolfgang Franke, "Yü Ch'ien Staatsmann und Kriegsminister, 1398-1457, " MS, XI (1946), 87.

Wolfgang Franke

SHIH Nai-an 施耐菴 , fl. 14th century, is the writer to whom has been attributed the initial version of the present text of the picaresque tale, *Shui-hu-chuan* 水滸傳 (Water margin). Like the romances involving Robin Hood and his band, it is a story of outlawry justified as a struggle against injustice. Though it is difficult to prove, Shih may well have been the first to assemble the various tales, folklore, and storytellers' prompt-books of the 12th and 13th centuries (chiefly in the Southern Sung capital of Hangchow), and the dramatic works issued during the ensuing Yüan dynasty (1260-1367). Since the 1930s a story has circulated telling of the discovery of a clan register and a tomb inscription, recording Shih's acquisition of the *chin-shih* about the year 1330 and his service as magistrate of Ch'ien-t'ang 錢塘 (Hangchow). As not a shred of corroborative evidence, however, has come to light, this is now believed to be a forgery. One is forced to conclude then that we know nothing of the man.

The *Shui-hu-chuan*, widely regarded as prime among all the fictional works of the Ming, has been subjected to more scholarly critical attention—Chinese, Japanese, and western—than any other. See, *inter alia*, the bibliography of Tien-yi Li and the writings of Irwin, Demiéville, and Liu. This attention has to do not just with the filiation of texts, dating from the Chia-ching period, in one hundred, one hundred fifteen, one hundred twenty, and seventy sessions, or hui 回, and other matter, but also with the speech of north China and the Hangchow region in the Ming dynasty. Because of the inflamatory nature of numerous episodes, one Chinese scholar has asserted that the *Shui-hu-chuan* influenced the spread of banditry at the end of the Ming and beginning of the Ch'ing. Certainly the Manchus were to find it objectionable. In 1652 Asitan (ECCP) recommended that its translation into Manchu be forbidden, the K'ang-hsi emperor on January 10, 1684, promulgated an edict ordering the burning of books of this class, and this was followed up by edicts of his grandson dated January 1, 1753, and December 11, 1774, and in the Ch'ing code of 1808. In spite of these prohibitions, in which woodblocks as well as texts suffered equally, publishers continued to reprint the work, and it must have had a vast under-cover sale. Translations of single or multiple episodes have appeared in many languages, including Japanese, Latin, French, Italian, German, and English; and complete or nearly complete renderings have been made in Korean, Japanese, English, and Russian. Its vogue in Japan had a special influence on Takizawa Bakin (*see* Wu Ch'eng-en), author of the famous fictional work *Nansō Satomi hakkenden* 南總里見八犬傳.

Bibliography

An-t'ai安泰, *Ch'in-ting hsüan tse li shu* 欽定選擇 曆書 (1684/85) 題稿, 2b; Cheng Chen-to (BDRC), *Chung-kuo wen-hsüeh yen-chiu* (Peking, 1957), 101; Sun K'ai-ti孫楷第, *Chung-kuo t'ung-su hsiao-shuo shu-mu* 通俗小說書目 (Peking, 1957), 181; *id.*, *Jih-pen tung-ching so chien hsiao-shuo* 日本東京所見小說 *shu-mu*, Peking, 1958; Liu Ts'un-yan, "On the Authenticity of Lo Kuanchung's historical romances," (1970) in ms. ; Ogawa Tamaki, "The author of the *Shui-hu chuan*," MS, 17 (1958), 312; Richard G. Irwin, *The Evolution of a Chinese Novel: Shui-hu-chuan*, Cambridge, Mass., 1953; *id.*, "Water Margin Revisited," TP, 48 (1960), 393; B. Karlgren, "New Excursions in Chinese Grammar," BMFEA, 24 (1952), 52; P. Demiéville, "Au bord de l'eau," TP, 44 (1956), 242; Lu Hsün, *A Brief History of Chinese Fiction*, tr. by Yang Hsin-yi and Gladys Yang (Peking, 1959), 185, 423; Leon M. Zolbrod, "Tigers, Boars, and Severed Heads: parallel series of episodes in Eight '*Dogs*' and *Men of the Marshes*," *The Chung Chi Jo.* (Hong Kong), VII: 1 (November, 1967), 30; Pearl Buck, *All Men Are Brothers*, New York, 1933; J. H. Jackson, *The Water Margin*, Shanghai, 1937; A. P. Rogachev, *Rechnye Zavody*, Moscow, 1955; C. T. Hsia, *The Classic Chinese Novel* (New York, 1968), 75; Tien-yi Li, *Chinese Fiction* (New Haven, 1968), 140.

L. Carrington Goodrich

SMOGULECKI, Jan Mikołaj (Smogolenski 穆尼閣, T, 如德), 1611-September 17, 1656, missionary, was born on the family estate of Smogulec in Poland. Educated in a Jesuit college at Krakow and in the Collegio Romano, he demonstrated an interest mainly in the sciences. Joining the Society of Jesus in 1636, he left for the China field in 1644, together with six other Jesuits, At first Smogulecki labored in Nan-Chihli; then in the years from 1647 to 1649 he served under Giulio Aleni (*q.v.*) in Fukien. Next, with Simon da Cunha (瞿西滿, 1590-September, 1660), he went to Chien-ning-fu 建寧府, whence they moved to Chien-yang 建陽 (both in Fukien). Here Smogulecki taught mathematics. During the local persecutions of missionaries, however, his astronomical instruments were lost. Smogulecki now transferred to Nanking, but in 1653 the newly established Manchu government summoned him to Peking to serve in the astronomical bureau. Two years later he left for Kwangtung and lived briefly in Hainan. His final move was to Chao-ch'ing 肇慶-fu, in the same province, where he died suddenly in the following year.

While in Nanking Smogulecki taught higher mathematics and astronomy. There Hsüeh Feng-tso (ECCP, p. 571) collaborated with him in writing twenty works on astronomy, the calender, and mathematics, collectively known as *Li-hsüeh hui-t'ung* 歷學會通 or *T'ien* 天*-hsüeh hui-t'ung*. They are said to have introduced spherical trigonometry and logarithms to China, although Giacomo Rho (*q.v.*) may have priority in this. The Polish missionary was also the author of *T'ien-pu chen-yüan* 天步眞原, a treatise on the calculation of the eclipses, according to European astronomical practice. In the work *Li-hsüeh hui-t'ung* he attempted to bring about the unification of the Chinese and European astronomical calculations of eclipses through the use of centesimal calculus instead of the hexagesimal. These works are confirmed as the writings of Smogulecki by Juan Yüan (ECCP) in his *Ch'ou-jen chuan*, *chüan* 45, published in 1799. For his eclipptical calculations he prepared a map of eclipses which is preserved in manuscript in the Bibliothèque Nationale in Paris (No. Xy. C. 1656, G. 214).

Smogulecki is sometimes confused with his father, Maciej Smogulecki, who, as a widower, entered the Jesuit Society in 1619; he was also a man of fine education and a poet. To Jan Mikołaj Smogulecki is erroneously ascribed *Quinque odae in laudem Sigismundi III regis Poloniae* (Rome, 1629), which, most probably, belongs to his father. Jan M. Smogulecki recognized the astronomy of Nicolas Copernicus (Mikołaj Kopernik); however, he rejected it as not following what the Scripture says about the "movement of the sun." Smogulecki was one of the most prominent Western scientists among the 17th century missionaries in China.

Bibliography

Pfister (1932), 199; T. Dunin Szpot, *Chinarum historia*, a ms. in the Roman Curia of the Society, Volumes of 1647-57 *Epistolae missionariorum*, S.J., mss. nos. 4169-71 and 49, Bibliothèque Royale de Belgique; Yoshio Mikami, *The Development of Mathematics in China and Japan* (Leipzig, 1913), 115; B. Szczesniak, "Notes on Kepler's *Tabulae rudolphinae*," *Isis* (1950), 344; *id.*, "Notes on the Copernican Theory in

China," JRAS (1945), 30; A. Wylie, *Notes on Chinese Literature* (Shanghai, 1922), 89, 106; *Relation du voyage du P. Joseph Tissanier* (Paris, 1663), 73; Sommervogel, VII, 1328.

Boleslaw Szczesniak

SOERIO, João 蘇如望 (or 漢, T. 瞻淸, Giovanni, Jean), 1566-August (or October 2), 1607, missionary, was born at Monte-môr-o-velho, Portugal. In 1584 he entered the Jesuit order at Coimbra, and on April 13, 1586, along with thirty other missionaries and members of a Japanese embassy returning from Rome (*see* L. Cattaneo), left Lisbon for Goa where he completed his studies. He reached Macao in 1591 and four years later was assigned to Nanchang, arriving on December 4, 1595. There, besides evangelical work, he devoted himself to improving his knowledge of Chinese, studying *inter alia* the Four Books and one of the Five Classics 四書五經. Among his neophytes were members of the princely family of Chu 朱 whom he baptized (1605) as Joseph, Melchior, Gaspard, and Balthazar. (Could these be descendants of the prince of Ning 寧王 [*see* Chu Ch'üan] whose fief was Nanchang?) Another was a man named Lin 林 whose concubine was also of imperial descent. While he refused to part from her, Lin presented for baptism their three children.

In August, 1607, the Jesuits purchased a new "residence-college." An outburst of anti-church animosity, which lasted a year, resulted, brought about by the "bachelors" of the city. It was at the start of this unpleasantness that Soerio, never a well man in his later years, passed away. He was the author of a compendium of Catholicism, *T'ien-chu sheng-chiao yüeh yen* 天主聖教約言, which has been frequently reprinted.

Bibliography

Pfister (1932), 56; P. M. d'Elia, *Fonti Ricciane*, I (Rome, 1942), 373, n. 2; George H. Dunne, *Generation of Giants* (Notre Dame, 1962), 49, 70; Walter Simon, "The *China Illustrata* romanization of João Soeiro's *Sanctae Legis Compendium...*," *Studia Serica Bernhard Karlgren Dedicata* (Copenhagen, 1959), 265.

L. Carrington Goodrich

SOUSA, Leonel de fl. 1546-71, son of Ruy and brother of Vicente de Sousa of Tavira in the Portuguese province of Algarve, and cousin of Don Pedro, future viceroy of India, was, as captain-major, the one mainly responsible for reaching an understanding with the Chinese over the use of the region of Hao-ching 壕鏡, *i.e.*, Ao-men 澳門 (called by the Portuguese O-mun, Amacao, Macao), as a base for trade in Kwangtung. Little is known of his early life. We do know, however, that his brother was a "fidalgo" (gentleman or petty noble) of the royal house who served for a time as captain at Tangier. This may have awakened in him a desire to venture abroad himself. Reportedly King João III (r. 1521-57) twice granted him permission to embark on a ship of state to the Indies, but this was denied by the governors of India. He finally sailed on a merchant vessel, arriving in 1547, and settling in Chaul (later known as Rewadanda) on the west coast of India. He married a lady of the area, a daughter of Antonio Pessoa, then inspector of estates of India, and began to trade in a boat (or boats) which he owned.

At this time the Portuguese had for some years been engaging in a more or less illicit trade with the Chinese (landing at various points as far up the coast as the prefecture of Ningpo), and also with the people of the Liu-ch'iu Islands and Japan. About 1550 there developed a practice of exchanging goods with the Chinese at Shang-ch'uan-tao 上川島 (Sancien, São João, St. John's), an island some fifty miles southwest of Macao. This was the place, for example, where Francisco Xavier (1506-52) spent his last days bemoaning his inability to reach the mainland. The Portuguese were eager, however, to gain official permission to use a more protected harbor and one closer to the great mart at Canton. The Chinese with mercantile interests, such as the influential figure Lin Hsi-yüan (*q.v.*), were also moving towards accommodation with them and towards a relaxation of the decree against maritime trade with the Fo-lang-chi (*see* Tomé Pires) and others.

In 1552/53 Sousa, aware of the fortunes to be made in commerce with the Chinese and Japanese, set out to do business in China, but found all ports closed to him. In 1554 he returned and, according to both his own report of January 15, 1556, to Prince Luis (younger brother of João III), written from Cochin on the western coast of India, and to the *Tractado das Cousas da China* by the Dominican Gaspar da Cruz, who was in Canton in 1556, he succeeded that year in obtaining verbal permission from the Chinese for Portuguese merchants to land and trade at Lang-po-kao 浪白滘, a large island thirty miles west of Ao-men. The *Kuang-tung t'ung-chih* 通志 and the *Ao-men chi-lüeh* 記略 both record that the Chinese negotiator was Wang Po 汪柏 (T. 廷節, cs 1538), then the hai-tao fu-shih 海道副使 (intendant of Kuang-chou Circuit) stationed at Canton. The first source reports that Wang was bribed, but if money passed hands it was probably an accepted practice of that day, like payment for service rendered. In any case Wang was shortly to receive a promotion to become administration vice-commissioner of Chekiang.

From this time on Portuguese and others were free to settle at Lang-po-kao, a strand which later disappeared, and to trade with merchants in Canton and elsewhere, and the name Lambacão or its equivalent begins to appear in Portuguese documents. By the year 1560 there are said to have been five or six hundred Portuguese living there, housed in mat sheds. This must have been inconvenient or uncomfortable for, during the years

1557 to 1565, they, together with thousand of others of diverse nationalities (Malay, Indian, and African), were gradually making Macao their main base. The story that Sousa took Luis de Camões (1524-79), Portugal's best-known poet, to Macao where he wrote part of *Os Lusíadas*, seems to have no foundation whatever. Sousa was responsible, however, for escorting the first Jesuit missionary, Melchior Nunes Barreto (1520-August 10, 1571), to the mainland of China. He picked up Barreto in Malacca, and put him ashore on Shang-ch'uan Island. By August 3, 1555, Barreto was in Lang-po-kao, whence he made two excursions of a month each to Canton. In 1555 and 1558 he wrote letters to his Order about Lang-po-kao and the city of Canton.

It is worth noting that the authors of the *Ming-shih* record that beginning in 1565 the Portuguese started to call themselves P'u-tu-li-chia 蒲都麗家. This was a suggestion Sousa himself had made to Prince Luis in 1556. He declared that they should deny that they were Franks as Franks were not allowed to enter Chinese harbors. The editors of the *shih-lu*, under date of May 16, 1565, record the Chinese view of this attempt at subterfuge more fully. "A foreigner calling himself Ya-jo-li-kuei 啞喏唎歸 (possibly Gil de Goes, appointed head of a Portuguese embassy to China in 1563)," they write, "arrived by sea and asked permission to present tribute. He initially asserted that he was from the country of Malacca but later maintained that he represented P'u-li-tu-chia (*sic*). The civil and military officials of the two Kwang reported this. Whereupon the ministry of Rites memorialized: 'There is no such place as P'u-li-tu-chia among the foreign countries in the south. Presumably it is a name assumed by the Fo-lang-chi. We propose that the above-mentioned officials be told to make a thorough investigation. If it is determined that the name is an assumed one, he [the foreigner] should be politely refused. If any Chinese is discovered to have been in illicit contact with him, he should be punished according to law.' The memorial was approved."

We hear little of Sousa's movements following his conversations with Wang Po. He was back in India in 1556 and two years later sailed to Hirado, Japan. On the return voyage he suffered shipwreck on the south China coast after leaving Lang-po-kao. He survived, however, to reach India eventually, where he served as captain of the galley *Monserrate* in the expedition to Jafnapatam in northern Ceylon (1560-61) and in the siege of Chaul (1570-71), when he was in command of the Portuguese ships defending the area.

Sousa's best-known writing is his report to Prince Luis. This was discovered in the archives in Lisbon and first published by Jordão de Freitas in 1910, and reproduced by J. M. Braga in 1930 (with annotations) and again in Appendix D of *The Western Pioneers.* Braga has also published a letter Sousa wrote to the queen dowager of Portugal, dated December 11, 1563, asking her to provide for his wife in the event of his death, because of the service both her father and he had rendered to the crown.

Bibliography

1/325/21b; MSL (1965), Shih-tsung, 8803; *Kuang-tung t'ung-chih* (1602), 69/72a; *Ao-men chi-lüeh* (1751, repr. 1956), 13b; *Jao-chou-fu chih* 饒州府志 (1872), 14/50b, 22/12a; *Chekiang t'ung-chih* (1934), 2095; Chang Wei-hua 張維華, *Ming-shih fo-lang-chi ... chu-shih* 注釋, YCHP, mon. ser. #7 (Peiping, 1934), 57; Yü Ta-yu, *Cheng-ch'i-t'ang chi*, 15/24a, 40b; José Maria Braga, *The Western Pioneers and the Discovery of Macao* (Macao, 1949), 81, 202; *Archivo Historico Portuguez*, VIII (Lisbon, 1910), 209, 216; T'ien-tse Chang, *Sino-Portuguese Trade from 1514 to 1644* (Leyden, 1934), 88; Paul Pelliot, "Un ouvrage sur les premiers temps de Macao," TP, 31 (1935), 67, 74; Albert Kammerer, *La Découverte de la Chine par les Portugais au XVIème Siècle et la Cartographie des Portulans* (Leiden, 1944), 96; C. R. Boxer, "Macao, Three Hundred Years Ago," THM, 6 (1938), 286; *id.,* "Was Camoens Ever in Macau?" *ibid.,* 10 (1940), 324; *id., Fidalgos in the Far East, 1550-1770* (The Hague, 1948), 31, 34; *id., The Great Ship from Amacon* (Lisbon, 1963), 23; Frederick Charles Danvers, *The Portuguese in India*, I (London, 1894), 569; Joseph Wicki (ed.), *Documenta Indica*, III (Rome, 1954), 353, n. 44; Pfister (1932), 8; Donald Ferguson, *Letters from Portuguese Captives in Canton* (Bombay, 1902), 34.

Earl H. Pritchard and
L. Carrington Goodrich

SSU Jen-fa 思任發, or 思任法, is the Chinese name of Thonganbwa, fl. 1400-1445, a Maw Shan 木撣 chieftain. (The Chinese character 發 corresponds to the Shan word "bwa" which means king. In some Chinese sources this character is omitted and his name appears as Ssu-jen.) His life story and family history highlight the tripartite struggle among the Shan people, the Burmese, and the Chinese in the western Yunnan-northern Burma region that continued throughout almost the entire Ming period.

The Shan people gained dominance in this region during the 13th century. After the fall of Pagan in 1287 they established many tribal states in the region stretching from the Brahmaputra to the Mekong. Even the petty kingdom which had its capital set up at Ava after 1364 was continuously ruled by Shan kings, though some of them found it politic to call themselves Burmese.

Ava-Burma, known to the Chinese as Mien-tien 緬甸, always had an eye on Lu-ch'uan 麓川, or the upper Shweli 龍川江 valley and the adjacent mountains, and Meng-yang 孟養, the region around the present city of Mohnyin in Burma. It is likely that the ancestors of the Ava-Burmese kings, as Shan chieftains, at one time or another had controlled these two territories. But by the mid-fourteenth century Lu-ch'uan also rose as a state to reckon with. Ssu Jen-fa's great-grandfather, Ssu K'o 可, was recognized as a native chief 土官 of Lu-ch'uan under the

Yüan. Beginning in 1348 Ssu K'o started to enlarge his domains in defiance of the Mongol emperor's orders. After repelling a Yüan army sent to chastise him, however, he dispatched his son, Man San 滿散, to Ta-tu to apologize. The Mongols could do no more than accept his apology.

In the early years of the Ming period Man San's son, Ssu Lun-fa 倫發, then ruling chieftain, made Lu-ch'uan powerful enough to invade Yunnan. Only after the Ming armies moved into the province did he pledge his allegiance to the new Chinese dynasty. In 1384 he presented his tribute to Emperor Chu Yüan-chang. On September 14 of that year the emperor recommissioned him as the native chieftain with the title Lun-ch'uan p'ing Mien hsüan-wei-shih 平緬宣慰使. But Ssu Lun-fa did not long remain submissive. Already in control of Meng-yang, he drove eastward in the winter of 1385–86 with hordes of warriors boasting, it is said, a total strength of three hundred thouusand men, crossed the Mekong, and defeated a Chinese army, killing its commanding officer. The situation was so grave that Chu Yüan-chang instructed his generals in Yunnan to strengthen their positions and avoid giving battle. In 1387 the imperial forces under Mu Ying (q.v.), by using firearms to turn back the invader's elephant phalanx, handed the tribesmen a great defeat. Yet the Chinese army was still unable to dislodge the rebel leader. In 1389 Ssu Lun-fa broke the deadlock by declaring that he had no intention of offending the emperor, the rebellion being the idea of his evil subordinates. The emperor wrote a personal letter to the chieftain, accepting the excuse. Thereafter Ssu Lun-fa presented his tribute triennially to the Ming court. His expansion scheme was by no means completely abandoned, however; he simply turned his attention to the south. In time he acquired the service of a Chinese deserter who manufactured firearms for his army. Ava-Burma then became the chief target of his aggression. But internal dissension interrupted his empire building.

Scores of tribal leaders under him rebelled in 1396 and Ssu Lun-fa had to flee to Kunming. Escorted to Nanking, he was well received by the emperor. Eager to make the Shan chieftain feel obligated to him, Chu Yüan-chang directed his generals to put down the tribal uprising. Ssu Lun-fa then returned to Lu-ch'uan in the summer of 1398 under Chinese protection. His territory was the same except that both Meng-yang and Mu-pang 木邦 (Mong-kawng, around the present Hsenwi in Burma) were now detached from his domain. He was also saddled with an annual payment to the imperial government of 24,900 taels of silver known as ch'ai-fa-yin 差發銀, or money in lieu of labor (reduced to 6,900 taels in 1404), though the amount seems never to have been met in full.

Ssu Lun-fa died either late in 1399 or early in 1400. His son, Ssu Hsing-fa 行發, appears in history as an inconspicuous figure. While he was overburdened with the payment of commissary money, the tribal leaders under him remained autonomous. Both Ava-Burma and Mu-pang encroached upon his territory. The creation of local chieftainships at Meng-yang and Mu-pang by Emperor Chu Ti (q.v.) in 1403 further weakened his position, since these two rival states now gained imperial recognition. In 1413 he retired and his brother, Ssu Jen-fa, took over.

Shrewd and ambitious, Ssu Jen-fa was determined to resume the expansion program left by his father. Having consolidated his position, in 1422 he annexed the domains of the neighboring tribes, first gingerly and slowly. Then he raided the nearby towns and cities and massacred the population. In 1428 his marauding became so flagrant that the commander-in-chief of the imperial forces in Yunnan, Mu Sheng (see Mu Ying), recommended to Emperor Chu Chan-chi (q.v.) that he be suppressed. The emperor, upon hearing that the campaign would involve fifty thousand men, decided that the operation would be too heavy a financial burden to the nation at a time when the affairs in Annam had not yet been settled (see Lê Lợi). Instead the Ming court for almost another decade carried on a policy of appeasement interspersed with military threats.

In 1436 the Shan tribesmen appeared on the eastern bank of the Shweli and threatened Chin-ch'ih 金齒 (later Yung-ch'ang-fu 永昌府, present Pao-shan 保山), even when Peking was undecided on the question of war or peace. The court instructed Mu Sheng to exercise discretion in dealing with Ssu Jen-fa. By 1438 it became evident that the problem could not be solved without resorting to force. Ssu Jen-fa had already constructed three hundred ships, signaling a broad offense to the east of the Salween. At the end of the year Emperor Chu Ch'i-chen (q.v.) ordered Mu Sheng to chastise the rebel. Troops to augment the Yunnan command, as well as military provisions, came from Hukuang and Kweichow. The native chieftain of Mu-pang was induced to take part in the campaign with his tribeamen. The battles which took place in the summer of 1439 seem to have been fierce but indecisive. Contemporary sources fail to designate the positions of the opposing armies and other details. Only a court order issued at the end of August that year, giving awards to 8,364 officers and men as having "achieved merit in killing and capturing the savage bandit Ssu Jen-fa's soldiers and elephants," suggests the intensity of the engagement.

While the war dragged on, peace negotiations continued. Ssu Jen-fa repeatedly declared that he was willing to surrender; the emperor and Chinese officials in their turn assured him that he would be treated leniently if he would lay down his arms. On August 3, 1440, Ssu Jen-fa's tributary mission to the emperor arrived in Peking and was generously rewarded by the monarch. On the following day a report on the heavy fighting in Yunnan also received His Majesty's attention. An official suggested that the rebel's tributary mission, if given an imperial reception at all,

should not be allowed as much courtesy as under normal circumstances. This the emperor would not permit.

The tribesmen clearly gained an upper hand on the battlefield that summer. A court order dated August 22, 1440, acknowledged the loss of the right military commissioner-in-chief, Fang Cheng 方政. Fang, unhappy over the indecision of the government, had crossed the Salween without authorization. Surrounded by the Shan warriors northeast of T'eng-ch'ung 騰衝, his command, consisting probably of no fewer than ten thousand men, was wiped out. The defeat spurred Peking to prosecute the war with ever more vigor. The remaining force in Yunnan, having a strength of forty-six thousand, was once more reinforced by some fifty thousand fresh troops hailing from Hukuang, Kweichow, and Szechwan. On February 8, 1441, Wang Chi 王驥 (q.v.), minister of War, became supreme commander for the expedition. Not all officials at court agreed with the war policy. An expositor-in-waiting, Liu Ch'iu (see Wang Chen), subsequently died in jail mainly because of his persistent argument against the military action. Many critics of the expedition charged that the whole campaign was decided by the eunuch in power, Wang Chen (q.v.).

Wang Chi's campaign of 1441/42 appears in Ming annals as a brilliant success. According to his own report, the two engagements east of T'eng-ch'ung between November 14 and 23 resulted in the decapitation of fifty thousand Shan tribesmen, and at the battle of Shan-mu-lung 杉木籠 (Hotha) on January 24, 1442, his soldiers beheaded another 2,390. On January 26 he declared his mission accomplished. He had captured the rebels' headquarters, a city of seven gates, but Ssu Jen-fa and his family had succeeded in slipping through the lines. Recognizing his military merit, the emperor made Wang Chi an earl, the first civil official of the dynasty so honored. The enemy's casualty rate reported by Wang was undoubtedly exaggerated; circumstances also lent support to the charge that the Chinese soldiers indiscriminately massacred natives in reprisal. Nevertheless the campaign remains one of the bloodiest struggles in Ming history. Immediately after the victory the supreme commander, in submitting a memorial to the emperor suggesting the punishment of one of his subordinates, reveals that this officer alone had lost eighteen hundred men in battle.

Soon the Ming court learned that Ssu Jen-fa was taking refuge in Ava. His son, Ssu Chi-fa 機發, reentered Lu-ch'uan in an attempt to establish himself as the next chieftain. In the summer of 1442 Wang Chi, already back in Peking, once more rushed to the Yunnan frontier. The so-called second expedition to Lu-ch'uan involved not so much military action as diplomatic manoeuvers. Ava-Burma, acknowledging that Ssu Jen-fa was in its hands, demanded the territory of Meng-yang as the price for surrendering the rebel leader to Chinese authorities. And Mu-pang, which held that it had contributed fifty thousand men in the first campaign, asked for Lu-ch'uan as its reward. (The rulers of these two states were bound by family relations and trade agreement.) They based their demands on a previous promise by the emperor that whoever destroyed Ssu would receive his domain. But now the rebel's son held both territories. The two tribal states then insisted that the Chinese must first eliminate Ssu Chi-fa lest he take vengeance on them. While these negotiations were proceeding, Ssu Chi-fa sent his brother, Ssu Chao-sai 招賽, to deliver tribute to the emperor, apparently in the hope that the imperial government would recognize him as his father's successor. He arrived in Peking early in 1443. The emperor rewarded him but prevented his return to the Shan mountains.

Wang Chi's bargaining with Ava-Burma and Mu-pang brought forth no results. In the winter of 1443/44 he deployed his troops to menace Ava (the capital), while the latter mobilized a larger army to accept the challenge. Forward units of the opposing forces clashed on the eastern bank of the Irrawaddy, both claiming victories. Probably the Ava-Burmese fared slightly better than the Chinese, but the outcome of the skirmishes was indecisive. Ssu Chi-fa fled westward as the Chinese army reappeared, yet his tribesmen still controlled the mountains. In the spring of 1444 Wang Chi returned to the imperial capital empty-handed. The emperor then delivered an ultimatum to the native chieftain (king) of Ava-Burma, threatening that "your cities will be razed and your people annihilated," if Ssu Jen-fa is not promptly delivered. Late in 1445 Ava finally yielded. Chinese sources assert that the sudden darkness of the sky over Ava caused its ruler, Pu-la-lang Ma-ha-sheng I-su-la 卜剌浪馬哈省以速剌 (according to a modern Chinese historian a combination of the names of two Ava-Burmese kings, Minrekyawswa, r. 1440-43, and Narapati, r. 1443-69), to lose his will to fight; but Burmese sources indicate that King Narapati gave in under Chinese military pressure. The *shih-lu* enters Ssu Jen-fa's death under the date of January 14, 1446, which agrees with the Burmese records. But the Chinese chronicles state that by the time the imperial army detachment took over custody of Ssu Jen-fa and his thirty-two family members and followers, the rebel leader had refused food for several days and was on the point of death. The Chinese officer decapitated him in an unnamed Burmese city on the Irrawaddy and subsequently delivered his head to Peking. Burmese writers, however, point out that Thonganbwa (*i.e.* Ssu) had committed suicide before the take-over, so that it was his body which was handed to the Chinese.

At the time of the rebel leader's death his son, Ssu Chi-fa, still held Meng-yang and continued to send tributary emissaries to the Ming court, one mission arriving early in 1446, another a year later; in charge of one such mission was Ssu Chi-fa's son. The Chinese government detained them and ordered Ssu Chi-fa to present himself in Peking, but the latter refused. He wrote humble messages and sent gifts to the authorities in Yunnan, which failed, however, to move the officials. Ava now pressed for a joint attack on Ssu Chi-fa and the emperor authorized Wang Chi's third expedition. Wang resumed the title of supreme commander in the spring of 1448. He reported that his forces totaling one hundred thirty thousand men started from T'eng-ch'ung on March 12, 1449, and made a rendezvous on the Irrawaddy with one hundred thusand troops from Mu-pang and Ava-Burma. "The imperial army then ran out of food," his report reads; "I therefore authorized a forage for three days during which my men collected four hundred thousand piculs of grain." Ava provided two hundred ships to form a pontoon bridge across the Irrawaddy. West of the river on Kuei-k'u-shan 鬼哭山 (Kaukkwei mountain ?), a savage battle took place. Once again Wang Chi's victory was sweeping and complete. In his own words, "the number of beheaded and captured is beyond calculation." But he admitted that Ssu Chi-fa and his younger brother, Ssu Pu-fa 卜發, had managed to escape.

Wang Chi's alleged victory was later thoroughly discredited by a memorial to the emperor submitted by Chan Ying 詹英, a local Confucian instructor. The writer, maintaining that he was an eyewitness, described the supreme commander as corrupt and barbarous. He further asserted that Wang's operation lacked sound planning and that the supreme commande rfalsely reported battle results, making defeats appear as victories. After the battle, the instructor charged, Wang's soldiers rounded up innocent fishermen as captives. This memorial, still extant, is supposed to have been read by Wang Chi's sponsor at court, Wang Chen. The eunuch never bothered to investigate the case; instead he ordered the memor-

ialist to report to Wang Chi's army.

Events following the battle of Kuei-k'u-shan appear in Chinese sources in various versions. The *shih-lu* indicates that Wang was immediately recalled. In the same year he was charged with suppression of a Miao 苗 rebellion in Hukuang and Kweichow. The territory of Meng-yang was placed "under the administration of Mien-tien." For a while both Ssu Chi-fa and Ssu Pu-fa were held prisoners in Ava. But for some unknown reason the Ava-Burmese released Ssu Pu-fa (allowed him to escape?); the latter, therefore, reestablished himself as the ruler of Meng-yang. At the same time Ava-Burma played its previous game with the Ming court: it refused to hand Ssu Chi-fa over to the Chinese until they delivered promised territory. Another version asserts that before his recall Wang Chi actually occupied Meng-yang. He had by then marched his troops "one thousand *li* west of T'eng-ch'ung" and reached the shores of a large lake (the Indawgi?). Another son of Ssu Jen-fa, Ssu Lu 祿, nevertheless, was able to hold out in the mountains. Fearful that his army would be exposed in the remote region for too long Wang permitted Ssu Lu to remain in Meng-yang; but he erected stone tablets (or a stone tablet) on the bank of the Irrawaddy, forbidding the Shan leader ever to cross the river. To such terms Ssu Lu agreed.

Ssu Chi-fa was finally delivered to the Chinese on April 26, 1454, by his captors and later executed in Peking. Ava-Burma and Mu-pang received some minor territorial concessions from the Chinese, probably at the expense of Meng-yang. Ssu Pu-fa's name appears once more in the *shih-lu*. In 1456 his tributary mission arrived in Peking. Emperor Chu Ch'i-yü (*q.v.*) rewarded him with some fifty rolls of silk. Without granting him an official title, the imperial government by carrying on the tributary relationship with him nevertheless recognized him as *de facto* headman of Meng-yang. Ssu

Pu-fa's heirs remained masters west of the Irrawaddy down to the 16th century. Their tributary missions continued to arrive in Peking, where they were always well received. When the tribal wars broke out in 1474 in the Shan states and dragged on over several decades, the officials in Yunnan sought help from Meng-yang, Ssu Lu 陸, (or 六), descendant of Ssu Jen-fa, answered the call and dispatched several thousand soldiers in 1494. (Some historians consider this Ssu Lu to be the same Ssu Lu as the one who made an agreement with Wang Chi in 1449, but this seems most unlikely.) Once across the Irrawaddy, these troops intended to occupy the eastern bank permanently. Only in 1503 did Ssu Lu reluctantly recall them. He had expected the Ming court to confer on him an important title, but when the imperial government showed itself willing to grant him only a minor one, he declined the offer. Another explanation for his withdrawal was his discovery that a weakness was developing in Ava-Burma where he could use his troops more profitably. From this point on he drove southward, bent on revenging his ancestor Ssu Jen-fa's death. Ssu Lu's son, Ssu Lun 倫 (Sawlon), carried on the southward expansion. In 1524 he took and looted the city of Ava. In 1527 he killed the king of Ava-Burma, Mang Chi-sui 莽紀歲 (Shwenankyswshin), and divided the latter's territory with Mu-pang. His son, Ssu Hung-fa 洪發 (Thohanbwa), not to be confused with one of his ancestors of the same name who delivered tribute to Peking in 1465, became the king of Ava-Burma and ruled until 1543. A brutal tyrant, Thohanbwa is said to have burned Buddhist sūtras and massacred monks. All Shan chieftains took orders from him and his influence extended to lower Burma. At Prome he met his final defeat in 1542 and was murdered a year later.

The death of Thohanbwa ended an era. Burma was once again unified and the Shan chieftains fell into oblivion. The new Burmese leader, Tabinshwehti (r.

1531-50, appearing in Chinese works as Jui-t'i 瑞體, Mang 莽 Jui-t'i, or Ta-la 噠喇 Jui-t'i), founder of the Toungoo dynasty, established his capital at Pegu in 1539. In quick succession he devoured the petty kingdoms in lower Burma and proceeded to conquer the tribal states in the north. His career was followed by that of his brother-in-law, Bayinaung (known in western chronicles as Braginoco, r. 1551-81, confused by Ming writers with Tabinshwehti), and the latter's son, Manda Bayin (r. 1581-99, known to the Chinese as Ying-li 應裏 or Ying-li La-wei 喇鮪). These rulers, aided by Portuguese adventurers, had no difficulty in subduing the Shan tribesmen. The days of Ssu Jen-fa and mounted elephant attacks were over. The Maw Shan people, if they had acquired the knowledge of gunpowder at all, seem never to have mastered its use. Their favorite weapons were catapults and poisoned arrows. They had developed a written language of their own; but its lack of sophistication may be observed from the fact that on important matters they wrote in Burmese. Their taxation and conscription systems, as well as their field networks for transmitting messages, seem to have been reasonably adequate; but they could never shake off their mountain hunters' tradition which involved them in incessant petty tribal wars. Facing Bayinaung's onslaught they were helpless. Meng-yang, the last Shan state in northern Burma, long controlled by Ssu Jen-fa's descendants and for a time with Chinese assistance, fell in 1579.

In the 1570s the combined forces of Burmese and Shan tribesmen frequently clashed with Chinese troops on the western Yunnan frontier. In 1583-84 they were defeated by a Ming general, Liu T'ing (q.v.). But they were able to regroup their troops and harass the borderland again. In 1593 Ch'en Yung-pin (q.v.) became governor of Yunnan, and did much to settle the situation. The mountain passes west of the Shweli valley, which had been designated as Lung-ch'uan

龍川 or 隴川 after Ssu Jen-fa's rebellion, were fortified in 1594. The walled city of Lu-ch'uan was constructed in 1596 and Chinese colonists were encouraged to settle in the region. Again in 1594 Ch'en dispatched Huang Kung 黃龔 to Siam, to arrange a joint attack on Burma. Subsequently, in the winter of 1599/1600, the Siamese and Arakan troops entered the Burmese capital, Pegu, burning and depopulating it. The Chinese considered that their actions had now eliminated the threat of Burma. In the early 17th century several states in northern Burma once again delivered tribute to Peking, signifying the decline of influence of the Toungoo dynasty.

Bibliography

1/10/3b, 8a, 20/6b, 11a, 171/1a, 172/3a, 272/4a, 314/20a, 315/1b, 15a, 22a; 5/9/37a; MSL (1962), T'ai-tsu, 2534-3723, T'ai-tsung (1963), 0311-1489, Hsüan-tsung, 1015-25, Ying-tsung, 0476-5667, Hsien-tsung (1964), 0327, 2385, 3873, Hsiao-tsung, 1727, 2608, 3591, Shih-tsung (1965), 2167, Shen-tsung (1966), ch. 10-153; Yunnan t'ung-chih (1894), 291/28a; Shih Fan 師範, Tien-hsi 滇繫 (1887), 3/1/16b, 5/1/63b, 2/22b, 8/1/50b, map preceding chüan 9, 9/2/23a, 40b; T'ien-hsia chün-kuo-li-ping-shu (SPTK), 44/61a, 45/3a, 4a, 5a, 8a, 17a, 25a, 34a; Ch'en Yü-k'o 陳玉科, Yunnan pien-ti-wen-t'i yen-chiu 雲南邊地問題研究, Kun-ming, 1933; Donald F. Lach, Asia in the Making of Europe (Chicago, 1965), Vol. 1, bk. 2, 539; Godfrey Eric Harvey, History of Burma from the Earliest Time to 10 March 1824, London, 1925; id., History of Burma, tr. into Chinese by Yao Nan 姚楠, Shanghai, 1947-48, 3 vols.; J. G. Scott and J. P. Hurdeman, Gazetteer of Upper Burma and the Shan States (Rangoon, 1900--1), part 1, Vol. 1, 198, 270, part 2, vol. 1, 192, vol. 2, 346; Sao Saimong Mangrai, The Shan States and the British Annexation (Cornell, 1966), 49; L. Carrington Goodrich and Feng Chia-sheng, "The Early Development of Firearms in China," Isis, XXXVI, pt. 2 (1946), 121.

Ray Huang

SU Po-heng 蘇伯衡 (T. 平仲), born 1329, a prose-writer, was a native of Chin-hua 金華, Chekiang. He claimed descent in the ninth generation from the famous Sung writer Su Ch'e (1039-1112), a younger brother of the even more famous Su Shih (1037-1101). Su Ch'e's eldest son Su Ch'ih (d. 1155), as prefect of Wu-chou 婺州 (Chin-hua), established his family there, this branch of the clan remaining in the prefecture. The Chin-hua family remained conscious of their illustrious ancestors, and Su Po-heng in his works refers to himself as a man of Mei-shan 眉山 (the original home of the Su clan in Szechwan).

Su Po-heng as boy and young man accompanied his father, Su Yu-lung 友龍 (T. 伯夔, H. 栗齋, 1296-1378), through the latter's series of official posts in the southeast (the modern provinces of Kwang-tung, Fukien, and Chekiang), from 1335, when he began in a minor local post at Lan-ch'i 蘭溪, near Chin-hua. The last posts held by Su Yu-lung seem to have been 1) as a chief clerk in the provincial office of Chiang-che 江浙, in Hangchow, where he took part in fighting the Red Turban invaders in 1352; 2) as assistant magistrate of Hsiao-shan 蕭山, east of Hangchow; 3) as records clerk of the Chekiang military commissioner's office at Ch'u-chou 處州 (1357-60?); and 4) for a time also as an adviser to Shih-mo I-sun (see Chang I). He then lived in retirement. Su Po-heng passed the chü-jen examination in 1362, the father accompanying his son to Ta-tu, the Yüan capital. Wang Wei (q. v.) in his biographical account of Su Yu-lung, saw an historical parallel to the earlier occasion when Su Hsün (1009-66) went to the Sung capital for the examination with his sons, Su Shih and Su Ch'e.

In 1363 Su Po-heng responded to Chu Yüan-chang's invitation to Confucian scholars to gather at his rebel court in Nanking, and he was included with Hsia Yü 夏煜 (T. 允中), T'ao An, Liu Chi, Chang I, and Sung Lien (qq. v.) in the institution of the Li-hsien kuan 禮賢館 on June 16 in that year. Su Po-heng was fifteen to twenty years younger than the other scholars so honored, and this would seem to indicate that he enjoyed high esteem among Chu Yüan-chang's advisers.

On August 10, 1366, Su Po-heng was appointed a junior instructor in the National University, and a year later was promoted to senior instructor. About this time his father was accused of having a son serving Ch'en Yu-ting (*see* Fang Kuo-chen) in Fukien, and was sentenced to exile, but the sentence seems not to have been carried out. Meanwhile Su Po-heng remained in the university until the end of July, 1370. Then he received appointment as a compiler in the history office. He himself states that he declined the appointment because of impaired hearing, but it is clear from a number of his poems and references elsewhere in his works that he stayed for some time in the history office, undertaking editorial work on the *Yüan-shih*. It was probably not until 1371 that he returned home.

For the next fourteen years he lived in retirement. Much of his surviving work dates from this period; he was then in great demand as a writer of inscriptions for the studies and halls of the living and the tombs of the dead, both in his home district and in the region of the coastal city of Wen 溫-chou, which he visited a number of times in the later part of this period. When Sung Lien resigned from the Hanlin at the end of 1377, he proposed Su as his successor, but once again Su refused the appointment. In the next year, in May, his father died and he requested Sung Lien to compose the tomb inscription. Around this time Su made the acquaintance of a young disciple of Sung, Fang Hsiao-ju (*q. v.*), whose outstanding literary gifts he appraised as greater than his own. Fang, on his side, showed a great respect and affection for the older man, and in a preface which he wrote for Su's works he praised him for having truly comprehended the ideas of Su Shih. Su also wrote a biography of Fang's father.

In 1385, after this long absence from the public scene, Su Po-heng responded to a summons to the capital to be an examiner for the metropolitan examination. Afterwards he went north to Shensi as an examiner, and then, probably by 1387, became instructor for the prefecture of Ch'u-chou in his home province of Chekiang. In 1388 he served as examiner in the provincial examination at Nanking. Of the rest of his life it is known only that he gave offense by a memorial, was arrested, and died in prison. The date of his death was unknown to the compilers of the *Ming-shih*, but, if the latest date which appears in his works has been correctly transmitted, it must have occurred some time after March 6, 1392. His two sons, Su T'ien 恬 and Su I 怡, who were probably still comparatively young men, since their father is said not to have married before his fortieth year, perished in an attempt to save his life.

Su himself made collections of his writings during his lifetime; there are surviving prefaces by Liu Chi, dated 1371, and by Sung Lien, dated 1380 (the preface by Fang Hsiao-ju probably also dates from 1380). A collection in 16 *chüan* was made and printed, perhaps after Su's death, by Lin Yü-chih 林與直 (T. 敬伯) of Wen-chou, a friend of Su's later years, whose name appears several times in his writings. Lin's edition was restored and reprinted by Li Liang 黎諒, prefectural judge of Ch'u-chou, in 1442, and this *Su P'ing-chung chi* 平仲集, copied into the *Ssu-k'u chüan-shu*, is the edition of the *Ssu-pu ts'ung-k'an*. There are 14 *chüan* of prose and only one of verse; the final *chüan* is one giving his ideas in a "philosopher" style, and is sometimes printed separately as *K'ung-t'ung tzu ku-shuo* 空同子贅說 (Stupid discourses of Master K'ung-t'ung), 1 ch., for which there is a postface by Hu Han (*see* Wang Wei), dated 1375.

Bibliography

1/285/4b; 3/266/4a; 61/145/9b; 64/甲 13/5b; MSL (1962), T'ai-tsu, 0153, 0239, 0291, 0384; SK (1930), 124/4a, 169/5b; *Chin-hua-hsien chih* (1915), 4/36b, 6/15a, 9/70b; Sung Lien, *Sung hsüeh-shih wen-chi*, 54/1a; Wang Wei, *Wang Chung-wen kung*

chi, 18; *Ming kung-chü k'ao-lüeh* 明貢舉考略, 1/3a;
Ku Chieh-kang (BDRC), "A Study of Literary
Persecution during the Ming," tr. by L. Car-
rington Goodrich, HJAS, III (1938), 257, 263.

A. R. Davis

SUN Fen 孫蕡 (T. 仲衍, H. 西菴), 1335–
90 or 1338–93, official, poet, scholar, was
a native of Shun-te 順德, Kwangtung. About
the year 1363, he was one of the scholars
enlisted as a staff officer by the local
leader, Ho Chen (*q. v.*), at Tung-kuan 東
莞. In 1368, when the Ming expeditionary forces under General Liao Yung-chung
(*q. v.*) entered Kwangtung from Fukien,
Sun assisted Ho in drafting the memorandum of surrender, facilitating Liao's occupation of the province without a fight.
Liao then made him head of the prefectural school, and in 1370, in the first provincial examination under the Ming dynasty, Sun became a *chü-jen*. His first
appointment in the bureaucracy was as
commissioner of the bureau of textiles in
the ministry of Works, after which he
was transferred to Hung 虹-hsien (Anhwei), as a registrar. As this district had
suffered much during the recent war, he
did what he could to ease the situation,
and to encourage the people to return to
their former occupations. After a year he
was recalled and made a librarian in the
Hanlin Academy, where he participated in
the compilation of the phonetic dictionary,
the *Hung-wu cheng yün* (*see* Sung Lien).

In 1376 he was dispatched to Szechwan as a supervisor of sacrifices (to the
imperial tombs of former dynasties?). His
next post was in P'ing-yüan 平原, Shantung, again as an assistant magistrate. Found
guilty of some infraction, he was punished
by being sent to Nanking to help in the
construction of the city wall around the
Wang-tu gate 望都門. Once as he worked
on the job, he sang a song in Cantonese,
and this brought him before the court
again. The emperor, however, could find
no hint of disloyalty in the words of the

song, and released him (1378?). In 1382
he was recalled and appointed head secretary to the prefect of Soochow, but in
1389 for some reason he was banished to
Liaoyang 遼陽 to serve with the frontier
guards. In the year 1393 the authorities
were determined to root out all associates
of Lan Yü (*q. v.*). As Sun had written
verses on some paintings belonging to
Lan, he was one of those who received
the death penalty. His one-time student, a
fellow poet and scholar, Li Chen 黎貞
(T. 彥晦, H. 陶生, d. 1394 or later, *ae.* 59
sui), who was also serving a sentence in
the frontier guards, was allowed to gather
up his remains and give them burial at
An-shan 安山 (the 鞍山 south of Liao-
yang?).

[Editors' note: Most sources seem to
indicate that Sun's execution took place
about 1390, in which event he would
have been involved perhaps in the case
of Li Shan-ch'ang (*q. v.*). If we accept
the statement that he was executed because of his friendship for Lan Yü, then
the year must be 1393. His age at death
being 56 *sui*, the year of his birth would
accordingly be 1338.]

Sun was a highly respected scholar
and left several works in such fields as
history, canonical criticism, and neo-Confucian ethics; but these seem largely to
have disappeared. Those which remain
include collections of his writings entitled
Hsi-an chi 西菴集, 9 *ch.*; his poems may
be found in the anthology *Lieh-ch'ao shih-
chi* (甲21/1a) and in the collection *Kuang-
chung wu hsien-sheng shih* 廣中五先生詩,
the other four poets being Wang Tso
王佐 (T. 彥舉, d. 1375), Chao Chieh 趙介
(T. 伯貞, d. 1389), Li Te 李德 (T. 仲修),
and Huang Che 黃哲 (T. 庸之, d. 1375).
His biographers report that he was able
to toss off brilliant impromptu compositions both in verse and in prose.

Bibliography

1/129/11b, 130/21b, 132/5a, and 285/23b; 5/22/
55a, 115/4a; SK (1930), 42/6a, 165/10b; *Kuang-*

tung t'ung-chih (1934), 4708; TSCC (1885-88), XIV: 149/2a, XXIII: 92/19b.

W. Pachow

SUN Lou 孫樓 (T. 子虛, H. 百川), September 21, 1515-January 18, 1584, bibliophile, official, and man of letters, came from a cultured and wealthy family of Ch'ang-shu 常熟, Soochow. From the time of his great-grandfather, Sun Ai 艾 (T. 世節, H. 西川居士, 端陽子, 1452-after 1526), this branch of the Sun clan established and kept up a tradition of book collecting for several generations. Sun Ai had two sons, Sun Lei 耒 and Sun Chou 舟 (a *chin-shih* of 1517), who between them had eight sons, whom the grandfather named by number, I-yüan 一元, Er-i 二儀, San-ts'ai 三才, Ssu-hsiang 四象, Wu-ch'ang 五常, Liu-i 六藝, Ch'i-cheng 七政, and Pa-shih 八士. Of the eight, Sun Ch'i-cheng (T. 齊之, H. 滄浪生), became best known; he had literary accomplishments, and left a collection of works entitled *Sung-yün-t'ang chi* 松韻堂集, 12 *ch.*, which received a notice in the *Ssu-k'u* Imperial Catalogue.

Sun Lou was Sun I-yüan's son and Sun Chou's grandson. His father died when Sun Lou was only five *sui*. The boy was precocious and devoted to his mother (née Miao 繆, d. 1582) throughout her long life. Participating in the provincial examinations conducted in Nanking in 1546, he emerged with the *chü-jen* degree. Like his uncle, Sun Ch'i-cheng, however, he was frustrated in the metropolitan competition. Over a period of twenty years, after seven tries, he finally gave up, and decided to take an official position in the provinces. In 1568 he received an appointment as a prefectural judge of Hu-chou 湖州, Chekiang, a lucrative post. He seems to have proved himself a conscientious administrator, and served several times as acting magistrate to fill in the temporary vacancies in that prefecture. His ability as a writer enhanced his prestige as an official. At this time both Li P'an-lung and Wang Shih-chen (*qq. v.*), leading poets of that era, officiating in Chekiang, made special acknowledgement of his literary ability. Around 1573 he was ordered transferred to Han-chung 漢中, Shensi. Taking it as a sign of demotion, Sun Lou resigned and retired. About his lack of success in the examinations and his official career he wrote the essays "Chi-ch'u" 紀黜 and "Hou 後 Chi-ch'u." At home he pursued his long cherished bibliographical interests and expanded his library.

As early as 1550 he had already amassed a collection of some ten thousand *chüan* of books and drafted a classified catalogue, the *Po-ya-t'ang ts'ang-shu mu-lu* 博雅堂藏書目錄 (possibly never printed), divided into twenty categories. In 1565 he built his library Chi-ts'e kuei 亣冊庋 and wrote a short account about it. From his preface to the catalogue, which is included in his collected works, we learn that his family library was destroyed three times before 1550. Refusing to be discouraged, he continued collecting. Whenever the book boats (書船) arrived, he reported, he always got on before others, and stayed on and on until even the book dealers considered him a nuisance. In traveling to Nanking or Peking at examination times, he always visited the book shops. If he chanced to obtain some rare items, he would treasure them, not minding any overpayment. He further tells us that neither winter cold nor summer heat prevented him from reading his books. Usually some member of his family had to call him to dinner, or announce to him that it was time to retire. His concern over the future of his library also seems to have been more liberal than that of some contemporary bibliophiles. He declared that after him, if his direct descendants could not read the books, he would not mind their giving them to relatives or friends who could, or placing them in government schools, or somewhere in the mountains to wait for people who later would be able to read them.

Fortunately, he had worthy descendants to carry on the book-loving tradition. A grandson, Sun Yin-chia 胤伽 (T. 唐卿, 伏生), and a great-great-grandson, Sun Chiang 江 (T. 岷自, d. *ca.* 1664), were both known as ranking bibliophiles of their time.

Sun Lou is said to have been witty and jovial, and to have had a good knowledge of music. His collected literary works are entitled *Po-ch'uan chi* 百川集, 12 *ch.*, first printed in 1620. He also left a small dictionary of unusual words in the Soochow dialect, giving pronunciation and meaning, entitled *Wu-yin ch'i-tzu* 吳音奇字.

Sun Ch'i-cheng's branch of the family continued the scholarly tradition for several generations. Sun Ch'i-cheng's sons were known for their poetic abilities, and one of them, Sun Sen 森, was a *chü-jen* of 1606. His grandson, Sun Ch'ao-su 朝肅 (T. 恭甫, or 功父), was a *chin-shih* of 1616, and another Sun Ch'ao-jang 讓 (T. 光甫), was a *chin-shih* of 1631. His two great-grandsons, Sun Hsiao-jo 孝若 (known by his *tzu*, *ming* unknown) and Sun Fan 藩 (T. 孝雅), both left bibliographic notes in some of the books they had read.

Sun Lou's father, Sun I-yüan, had a name identical with that of the poet, Sun I-yüan 孫一元 (T. 太初, H. 太白山人, 1484–1520), whose collection of literary writings, entitled *T'ai-po shan-jen man-kao* 太白山人漫稿, was copied into the *Ssu-k'u* Library. There is also an element of mystery concerning this second Sun I-yüan's background, because of a confusion in the records about his origin. In some accounts it is indicated that he called himself a native of Shensi, but in others it is intimated that he may have been a descendant of the imperial family from the branch of the rebel prince of An-hua, Chu Chih-fan (*see* Yang T'ing-ho); still others consider that he may have been an illegitimate son of a prince of Ch'in 秦 by a mother of ill-repute.

Bibliography

5/85/59a; 40/48/17b; 64/己20/10b; 84/丁上/47a; Sun Lou, *Po-ch'uan chi* (Wan-li ed.), NLP microfilm, no. 869, 1/14a, 3/4b; TSCC (1885-88 ed.), XXIII: 104/12a, 14a; *Soochow-fu chih* (1862), 61/54a, 99/1a, 22a; Shao Sung-nien 邵松年, comp., *Hai-yü wen-cheng* 海虞文徵 (Shanghai, 1905), 16/15a, 37b; Yeh Ch'ang-ch'ih (BDRC), *Ts'ang-shu chi-shih-shih* (Shanghai, 1958), 127; SK (1930), 171/10b, 177/11b, 178/6b.

Lienche Tu Fang

SUN P'ei-yang 孫丕揚 (T. 叔孝, H. 立山), 1532-September 14, 1614, official, was born into a family of the military category of Fu-p'ing 富平, prefecture of Sian, Shensi. His father, Sun Wei-ch'ien 惟謙 (T. 幼撝, H. 前川), a student of the National University, was made in 1547 magistrate of Pao-ti 寶坻, south of Peking, left an honorable record, and was commemorated by the local people in a shrine. After achieving the *chü-jen* in 1552 and *chin-shih* in 1556, Sun P'ei-yang received an appointment in the messenger office. In 1561 he took part in escorting the prince of Ching (*see* Chu Hou-ts'ung) during his three-month voyage from Peking to his princedom in Hukuang. On the Grand Canal Sun managed to prevent some of the eunuchs from making illegal demands on local officials. In July, 1562, he was promoted to censor, in which capacity he served as inspector of the Peking metropolitan area in 1564, as supervisor of the confiscation of the Kiangsi properties of Yen Shih-fan (*see* Yen Sung) in 1565, and as inspector of the Yangchow area in 1566. A year later he retired on sick leave. He returned to Peking as a censor in 1570 but in the following year, just after promotion to assistant minister of the Grand Court of Revision, he was dismissed. Reportedly this happened because he had once attacked the grand secretary, Kao Kung (*see* Chang Chü-cheng) in a memorial, and one of Kao's henchmen brought charges against him. After Kao himself was forced out of office (1572), Sun was reinstated and in February, 1573, became assistant censor-in-chief and concurrently governor of Paoting and other prefectures in Pei-Chihli. In this capacity he served for four years, during which he was particularly active in strengthening the defenses of the region. For this he was rewarded with promotion to titular vice censor-in-chief. Early in 1577 he again retired on the plea of illness. It is said that he left his office because he became apprehensive after refusing to build a memorial arch in honor of the eunuch, Feng Pao (*see* Chang Chü-cheng), as suggested to him by Grand Secretary Chang Chü-cheng. In any case he stayed home for eight years. During this time he received a demerit and was marked for a Nanking appointment at reinstatement. Meanwhile his father died, and he had to observe the mourning period. It was probably during this period of enforced idleness that he worked with Liu Tui 劉兌 on the local history, *Fu-p'ing-hsien chih*, 10 *ch.*, published in 1584, a copy of which is in the Library of Congress.

When he applied for an appointment in 1585, he was sent late in that year to Nanking as governor of Ying-t'ien and other prefectures. In May, 1586, he was summoned to Peking as chief minister of the Grand Court of Revision, and the next year rose to be junior vice minister of Revenue. Just at this time there was a severe famine in Sun's home area, where, according to Sun, the destitute were so stricken that they were reduced to eating bark, grass, and earth. He presented samples to the emperor and told him that the entire country was in need of relief from extra levies and taxes. He suggested that the throne put an end to such levies and nonessential expenses, and practice frugality. The emperor, it is said, was deeply moved by his memorial and granted some reduction in taxes. In August, 1589, Sun was promoted to senior vice minister of Revenue, but three months later he was sent to Nanking as censor-in-chief. In

mid-1590 he again pleaded illness and went home.

On his resumption of duty in February, 1592, he was named minister of Justice. In this capacity, he instituted reforms to speed up trials and made suggestions looking towards the reduction of criminal cases. In December, 1593, he was appointed head of the Censorate. Barely a month later he was ordered to join the minister of Personnel in making a judgment on the case of Kao P'an-lung (*q. v.*), who had submitted a memorial attacking the grand secretaries, particularly the senior one, Wang Hsi-chüeh (*q. v.*), as being responsible for the dismissal of certain upright officials. When Wang declared that the grand secretaries had nothing to do with the matter except to compose the edicts according to the emperor's instructions, the emperor evaded the issue and chose an irrelevant matter in Kao's memorial for questioning. The minister of Personnel tried to beg off from the case. Sun scolded him, saying that if everyone evaded his duty the emperor would be left without any help. Thus Sun, following the emperor's wish, adjudged Kao guilty of failure to verify his facts in a memorial, and had him sentenced to demotion. For such loyalty Sun was rewarded with the extraordinary favor of having his deceased parents honored with official burial and sacrifices in the emperor's name. Meanwhile Sun made some suggestions for the reform of the civil administration, the emphasis being on promotion of honest and incorruptible officials.

In September, 1594, he was assigned to head the ministry of Personnel, a position which he was to hold on and off until his eventual retirement in 1612. Early in this responsible post Sun became known for his objectivity and fairness in handling official assignments. In particular in June, 1595, he devised a system, ch'e-ch'ien 掣籤, by means of which vacancies in lower local offices in the provinces could be filled by drawing lots. The system was designed to tackle the problem of favoritism, created by unscrupulous persons in power. Sometimes it was a grand secretary, such as Yen Sung from 1542 to 1562, and sometimes a eunuch, such as Feng Pao from 1572 to 1582. At this time, however, it was the emperor himself (Chu I-chün) who was trying to extend his control of official appointments to the lower provincial offices, a category hitherto left to the director of the bureau of appointments and supervised by the minister and senior vice minister of Personnel. By introducing the method of drawing lots to fill such vacancies, Sun made it impossible for the usual practices of corruption to function. For this he was criticized by some pedants as failing to observe the tradition of selecting the right man for the right post according to talent and merit. On the other hand, the method was at once almost universally acclaimed as just and honest, and its feasibility may be proved by the fact that it was followed continuously for three hundred years until the end of the Ch'ing dynasty.

Later in 1595 Sun was criticized on two counts. The first one involved a subordinate accused of accepting bribes. Sun, without first verifying the facts, tried to protect the man in a memorial and as a result received a resounding reprimand from the throne. In the second case, Sun had a dispute at court with the vice minister of War, Shen Ssu-hsiao (one-time governor of Shensi; *see* Yao Shih-lin and Ku Hsien-ch'eng), over the dismissal of the administration vice commissioner of Chekiang, Ting Tz'u-lü (*see* Shen Shih-hsing). Shen Ssu-hsiao held the dismissal unjustified. Sun then submitted to the throne a memorial on the case, enclosed with, as evidence, fourteen memoranda, accusing Ting of corruption and other misdeeds. (Such a memorandum, known as fang-tan 訪單, or inquiry sheet, contains information submitted to the minister of Personnel by the officials in Peking concerning the conduct of provincial offi-

cials. Primarily it constituted information on those serving in one's home province. Hence it was imperative for the ministry of Personnel to keep it confidential so as to protect the informer and his family at home from possible retaliation and at the same time to ensure future sources of information.) When Sun, perhaps in anger, revealed these inquiry sheets to the throne, it must have been a great shock to those informed on. Fortunately the emperor did not make public any of the names. Sun thus was generally considered to have committed an act of indiscretion. He sought leniency for Ting Tz'u-lü, but the emperor refused and had Ting sentenced to exile at a frontier post. Because of Sun's integrity, however, few held it against him, but he became apprehensive and asked for permission to retire. Apparently he did it half-heartedly to test the political climate. When Grand Secretary Chang Wei (*see* Ch'en Yü-pi) expressed himself as agreeable to his resignation, Sun was outraged and accused Chang of taking a partisan stand in connection with Ting and Shen. When two other grand secretaries, Ch'en Yü-pi and Shen I-kuan (*q. v.*), came to Chang's defense, the emperor remonstrated with Sun for intolerance and lack of tact, and in less than a month dismissed him from office (1596).

Early in 1601 Sun was recalled to be minister of Personnel in Nanking, but he retired at the end of the year on the pretext of ill health, perhaps because he considered the post not high enough. From then until his recall in October, 1608, he is known to have become actively involved with the Tung-lin Academy (*see* Ku Hsien-ch'eng). At this time the main opponents of the Tung-lin were the Chekiang party headed by Shen I-kuan. They attacked Shen for various faults and managed to force his retirement (1606). The next year, when Yeh Hsiang-kao (*q. v.*), who was in general sympathetic to the Tung-lin party, became a grand secretary, Sun was recalled to be the minister of

Personnel (November, 1608), but did not take office until May 19, 1609. During his administration of this post, factional struggles between Tung-lin and opposition parties (*see* Ku Hsien-ch'eng) broke out into the open. It is small wonder that Sun, as the one in control of the great merit evaluations of the capital officials which took place in 1611, favored the Tung-lin, and saw to the demotion and dismissal of its opponents, a decision agreed to by Yeh Hsiang-kao and reluctantly approved by the emperor. Sun in turn was subjected to vehement attacks by his opponents and other officials. His recommendation to reappoint a number of former dismissed officials, many of them members of the Tung-lin, was ignored by the emperor. For both reasons he decided to withdraw from the scene, and ended his career in March, 1612, without waiting for the emperor's approval. At his death he was granted the title of grand guardian of the heir apparent. In January, 1621, he was honored with the posthumous name Kung-chieh 恭介 (reverent and resolute).

Besides helping to compile the above mentioned gazetteer he was the author of two short books on Confucian thought, both of which are listed in the Imperial Catalogue, but were not considered worthy of inclusion in the *Ssu-k'u ch'üan-shu* and do not seem to be extant.

Bibliography

1/224/14a; 3/208/12b; 8/71/9a; 21/17/51b; 32/104/52b; 39/15/9a; MSL (1966), Shen-tsung, 0335, 4545, 5309, 5340, 8516, 8620, 9266, 9846; KC (1958), *ch.* 74-82; SK (1930), 96/5b; TSCC (1885-88), XI: 304/6/12b, 16/12b, XIV: 150/6/3a; *Fu-p'ing-hsien chih* (1887), 2/45b, 3/12a, 30a, 33b, 5/9a, 35b, 6/61a, 7/3a; *Pao-ti-hsien chih* (1917 repr. of 1745 ed.), 8/3a, 11/7b, 18/47b; *Wan-li ti-ch'ao* (*see* Chu I-chün), 901, 907, 970; W. Franke, *Sources*, 282; C. O. Hucker, "The Tung-lin Movement of the Late Ming Period," *Chinese Thought and Institutions*. ed. by J. K. Fairbank (Chicago, 1957), 132.

Angela Hsi and Chaoying Fang

SUNG Hsü 宋旭 (T. 初暘, H. 石門), 1523-1602?, painter and calligrapher, was a native of Chia-hsing 嘉興, Chekiang. Shih-men 石門, the *hao* he adopted, was the name of the region in Chia-hsing where he made his home. [Editors' note: Sung Hsü's dates have been variously given as: 1523-1605, 1525-1605, and 1523-1602; the last offered by Chiang Liang-fu, basing himself on a literary source, agrees with *Ming-hua lu* 明畫錄 in that Sung died at the age of eighty. Paintings attributed to Sung Hsü, bearing dates of 1603-5, have led some scholars to think that Sung had lived longer than the reported eighty years; this is not to be taken as conclusive, however. Hsü Pang-ta (*see* Lu Chih) reports 22 works by Sung Hsü dated between 1566 and 1605.] Whether or not he joined a monastic order in his later years is not clear. At any rate, to this last period of his life three other names, all Buddhist in flavor, have been attributed to him: 祖玄, 天池髮僧, and 景西居士.

As a painter, unlike so many others of a generation later, Sung Hsü specialized in both landscape and figures. In calligraphy, he favored the archaic pa-fen 八分 style which he often employed in writing his colophons and signing his names on his paintings. When Sung began his career, the world of painting was dominated by the influence of Shen Chou (*q. v.*). He studied Shen Chou's works and they made a deep impression on him. He produced powerful and large compositions with details of mountains and trees that were authoritative and strong but also had an air of studied artful awkwardess 古拙. Later, toward the last quarter of the 16th century, when the Yüan dynasty masters became the models to copy as a result of the Southern School movement promoted by three Hua-t'ing 華亭 painters, Ku Cheng-i, Mo Shih-lung (*qq.v.*), and Tung Ch'i-ch'ang (ECCP), Sung Hsü seems to have changed to working in the Yüan landscape style. In this regard Mo Shih-lung as a friend and a fellow painter from a neighboring town could have had a role in influencing him. He was much more than just a versatile technician in painting, however. A knowledgeable student of the history of Chinese painting, he once made a judicious evaluation of the works of three most important ancient masters: Li Ch'eng, Kuan T'ung, and Fan K'uan of the 10th and 11th centuries. He forcefully pointed out that the works of these giants in painting were like the Confucian Classics, while the followers and latter day innovators could produce paintings that were only like commentaries, elaborating on what had already been stated in the Classics. The text of this statement is preserved in the *Wu-sheng-shih shih* 無聲詩史 by Chiang Shao-shu 姜紹書 (17th c.).

Sung Hsü may be regarded as one of the last painters in the late Ming era to have made a sincere and relatively successful effort to imitate the past. Later the Southern School painters were to emulate the ancients, and to turn the table on the Classics, so that this time it would be the Classics that would serve to comment on their own paintings 六經注我, if one may paraphrase the neo-Confucian philosopher Lu Chiu-yüan (1139-92). The situation during the late Ming was indeed rich in both neo-Confucian and Ch'an overtones.

Sung Hsü was an influential artist in another way. He was the teacher of Chao Tso 趙左 (T. 文度) and Sung Mou-chin 宋懋晉 (T. 明之), both natives of Sung-chiang 松江 and both prominent in the Sung-chiang (Hua-t'ing) school of painting. As the number of schools proliferated, Chao Tso was considered the founder of yet another one, known as the Soochow Sung-chiang school. These two famous students of Sung Hsü were of two rather different temperaments. Chao Tso was studious and cautious in his design and execution; Sung Mou-chin, on the other hand, produced his work effortlessly while enjoying himself. Still another painter from Hua-t'ing, Shen Shih-ch'ung 沈士充 (T. 子居), active a decade or so later than the other two, studied with both of them, prolonging the

influence of the Hua-t'ing tradition beyond the 1630s.

It is interesting to note that, while the literati Southern School movement had as its central figures Ku Cheng-i, Mo Shih-lung, and Tung Ch'i-ch'ang, all from the gentry class, Sung Hsü and his followers were commoners. None had any title nor did they pass any government examinations. Unlike the literati, this group did not leave elaborate personal data nor volumes of writings. Chao Tso, however, associated himself with Tung Ch'i-ch'ang and expressed a concern for the artistic issues involved. An essay written by him commenting on the importance of the dynamic potentials in landscape composition has been preserved in *Wu-sheng-shih shih*.

Sung Mou-chin, on the other hand, exuded native talent. He came from a gentry family, but was not interested in study for the examinations. It is reported that, when he was young, he painted a child riding a water buffalo on a wall and captured the lively spirit of the scene. Later he studied painting with Sung Hsü and established himself as a landscapist and was particularly good in painting pine trees. From his brush there frequently came charming and elegant colophons.

Chao Tso, Shen Shih-ch'ung, and Wu I 吳易 (originally 吳翹, T. 素友, 楚侯)— the last a native of Shanghai where Tung Ch'i-ch'ang was born—all in one way or another were overshadowed by Tung, the overwhelming master artist, scholar, and critic. Frequently works attributed to Tung Ch'i-ch'ang would turn out to be from these men's hands, either done deliberately or even on commission to pass as Tung Ch'i-ch'ang's work, or made to serve the same purpose by unscrupulous dealers or collectors at a later date. The situation eventually deteriorated to such a confusing state that a collector would congratulate himself for having purchased a Chao Tso or a Shen Shih-ch'ung while going after a Tung Ch'i-ch'ang; for he could have done much worse and collected a fake by one of the many inferior imitators. Wu I, on the other hand, while a painter in his own right, is said to have been in Tung Ch'i-ch'ang's employ. At times, even Tung himself, according to report, could not tell Wu's imitation from his own work.

Bibliography

Sung-chiang-fu chih (1819), 61/18a, 24b; Hsü Ch'in 徐沁, *Ming-hua lu* (*Hua-shih* 畫史 *ts'nng-shu* (Shanghai, 1962), 4/53; *T'u-hui pao-chien hsü-tsuan* 圖繪寶鑑續纂 (*same ed.*), 1/4, 10, 2/15; Chou Liang-kung (ECCP), *Tu-hua lu* 讀畫錄 (same ed.); Chiang Shao-shu, *Wu-sheng-shih shih* (same ed.), 3/22a, 4/61, 69; *id.*, *Yün-shih-chai pi-t'an* 韻石齋筆談, 下/15b.

Nelson Wu

SUNG K'o 宋克 (T. 仲溫, H. 南宮生), 1327-87, poet, calligrapher, painter, and official, was a native of Ch'ang-chou 長洲 in Soochow prefecture. As a youth he behaved in a non-conformist and unrestrained manner. Tall in stature, he was fond of riding, fencing, and shooting with a crossbow. At the same time, however, he read widely in history and literature. His family was wealthy, but he squandered his fortune in entertaining his friends, with whom he drank and gambled.

When he reached maturity, he disassociated himself from his boon companions and studied military strategy. Then he traveled north and apparently served on the staff of some frontier commander. Kao Ch'i (*q.v.*), in his biography of Sung, entitled *Nan-kung-sheng chuan* 傳 (which is the principal source of information about Sung and to which later biographical notes have added little), says vaguely that, after having mastered the *Feng Hou wo-ch'i chen fa* 風后握奇陳法 (also known as *Wo-ch'i ching* 經, a book on strategy purporting to have been written by Feng Hou, a minister of the mythical Yellow Emperor, but probably a

forgery of the Sung period), and as he was about to go north and join other men of like mind and discuss plans for action, Sung found no one with whom he could cooperate. In one of Kao's poems, however, he addresses him as "Military adviser Sung" and refers explicitly to the latter's having served a general in Yen 燕 and helped guard the border. The title of the poem is "Ch'ou Sung chün-tzu chien-chi" 酬宋軍咨見寄 (In reply to military adviser Sung who has sent me a poem), and the lines in question read in translation, "When he completed his studies he served a Yen general, and guarded the Three Passes on the remote frontier" (業成事燕將, 遠戍三關營). It seems that in the biography Kao was being deliberately vague so as to cover up the fact that Sung had served under the Yüan, whereas in the poem addressed to Sung himself there was of course no reason to be circumspect. Sung's brief military career is further confirmed by a line from one of his own poems, "Serving in the army is also unsatisfactory" (從軍事亦非). But we have no information as to whom he served under or for how long. Subsequently Sung traveled to Chekiang and other places before returning to Soochow, probably sometime before 1356. There he became one of the famous Ten Friends of the North Wall (*see* Hsü Pen), the group of talented young men centered around Kao Ch'i. Sung also associated with many others of both high and low social standing. He was frank and argumentative, and often admonished his friends. Once he subdued two bullying generals by a quiet demonstration of strength.

When Chang Shih-ch'eng (*q.v.*) rebelled against the Yüan, Sung privately predicted the outcome of Chang's military operations, and most of his predictions came true. Chang wished to recruit Sung to his own staff, but the latter declined. This annoyed Chang who tried to frame him, but Sung saved himself by clever maneuvering. Kao is again vague about the circumstances surrounding this episode, but it seems that Sung became impoverished as a result, although he continued to behave in an expansive and hospitable manner to friends and strangers alike. Later he grew tired of social activities and shut himself in a room full of antiques and books, amusing himself with writing poetry and practicing calligraphy.

At the beginning of the Ming, Sung was summoned to court to be a calligrapher-in-waiting at the Hanlin Academy. Then he served as deputy prefect of Feng-hsiang 鳳翔 in Shensi. According to the *Ming-shih*, he died at his post, but the *Ming-shu* states that he gave up his post before his death.

Sung was a well-known poet but his poetry was scarce even at the beginning of the Ch'ing period, when Chu I-tsun (ECCP) compiled the *Ming-shih tsung*. The two poems, both entitled "Thinking of my brothers on an autumn day," included in the *Lieh-ch'ao shih-chi* by Ch'ien Ch'ien-i (ECCP), seem to be the only ones still extant. These are written in a simple and direct style reminiscent of the early T'ang. As a calligrapher, Sung practiced various styles, but excelled particularly in the chang-ts'ao 章草, which had not been in vogue for a long time and which he brought back into fashion. He and another calligrapher, Sung Kuang 宋廣 (T. 昌裔), were often referred to as the Two Sung. Chu Yün-ming (*q.v.*) writes of Sung K'o's calligraphy: "Seeing it is like viewing ancient ritual bronzes; it must be the result of natural talent rather than human effort." An example of his calligraphy, "Kung yen shih" 公燕詩 (Poem on an official banquet) by Liu Chen (d. 217), is now in the Palace Museum in Taiwan. Another is in the collection of John M. Crawford, Jr., New York. As a painter, Sung confined himself to bamboos and is credited with having initiated the technique of painting them in vermilion. A handscroll by him entitled Wan-chu t'u 萬竹圖 (A myriad of bamboos), an ink painting on paper, dated 1369, is now in the Freer Gallery, Washington, D. C.

Bibliography

1/285/23a; 3/266/16b; 5/115/29a; 32/18/22b; 34/13/1a; 40/10/2b; 61/151/1b; 64/甲 8/7b; 65/7/1b; 84/甲前 11/17a, 24b; 86/3/19b; 88/10/3a; Kao Ch'i, *Ch'ing-ch'iu shih-chi* (SPPY), 3/20a, 4/1a; 6/12b; *id.*, *Fu-tsao chi* (SPPY), 4/1a; Chang Ch'ang 張昶, *Wu-chung jen-wu chih* 吳中人物志 (mid-16th cent.), NLP microfilm, no. 290; Chang Te-fu 張德夫 and Huang-fu Fang, *Ch'ang-chou-hsien chih* (1598); *Chung-hua mei-shu t'u-chi* 中華美術圖集 (NCL Taipei, 1955) 書 3; *Su-chou-fu chih* (1748), 55/15b; *Ku-kung shu-hua lu* 故宮書畫錄 (Taipei, 1956), 2/4; Hsü Pang-ta, *Li-tai shu-hua⋯nien-piao*, 39; Osvald Sirén, *Chinese Painting*, (New York, 1956-58), Vol. 6, pl. 56; F. W. Mote, *The Poet Kao Ch'i* (Princeton, 1962), 102; J. J. Y. Liu, *The Chinese Knight Errant* (Chicago, 1967), 51; Harrie Vanderstappen, "Painters at the Early Ming Court (1368-1435)," MS, 15 (1956), 299; Tseng Yu-ho Ecke, *Chinese Calligraphy* (Philadelphia, 1971), no. 37.

James J. Y. Liu

SUNG Li 宋禮 (T. 大本), died 1422, official and canal builder, was a native of Yung-ning 永寧, Honan. After studying at the National University, he was appointed an assistant surveillance commissioner in Shansi. Later he was demoted to be a secretary in the ministry of Revenue, but at the beginning of the Chien-wen reign was restored to his former rank and sent to Shensi. Again he was demoted to be a vice director in the ministry of Justice. Shortly after Chu Ti (*q.v.*) came to the throne, Sung served first as vice minister of Rites, then in January, 1405, as minister of Works. In 1406 (and again several times up to 1421) he was ordered to go to the mountains in Szechwan to find timber for building the palaces in Peking. When his mother died in 1409, he was commanded by imperial decree to oberve the mourning period in office owing to the importance of his duties. It was during this time that he achieved fame as an untiring worker. Early in 1411 he was ordered to deepen the northern section of the Grand Canal or Hui-t'ung-ho 會通河.

The Hui-t'ung-ho, long in building,

had been completed in 1325. Because of its shallow depth it could not accommodate large vessels. Grain transport to Peking under the Yüan and at the beginning of the Ming, therefore, relied largely on the sea route. The canal, moreover, by 1391 became partly choked with silt, so much so that portage had to be established at eight points. Meanwhile, the sea route was hazardous due to occasional storms and to piracy. When Sung Li was ordered to restore the Canal in 1411, he first mobilized one hundred sixty-five thousand laborers to deepen its bed from Chi-ning 濟寧 to Lin-ch'ing 臨清, a distance of about one hundred fifty miles. Relying partly on the suggestion of a local inhabitant named Pai Ying 白英, Sung designed and supervised the construction of two dikes, several reservoirs, and a series of thirty-eight locks. He completed this assignment in July of that year. Sung was then sent to help restore the old waterways of the Yellow River in Honan and bring the river back into its former channel. When he returned to Nanking in August-September of the same year he received high honors and awards. With the completion of the southern section in 1415 (*see* Ch'en Hsüan), the Grand Canal was in operation all the way from Hangchow to Peking.

Sung Li served eighteen years as minister of Works. In these years, besides conservancy activities he also acted as a judge in Kiangsi in 1418, as builder of sea-going ships in 1419, and as supervisor of the land and population register in 1421. He returned to the capital in that year, then went back to Szechwan for the last time a few months later, dying there shortly afterwards. His death was reported to the throne on August 7, 1422. During his own day, possibly because of certain unspecified faults and strictness in administration, he was not fully appreciated. Not until the end of the century was a shrine built at Chi-ning in memory of his contribution to the construction of the locks on the Grand Canal, and not until a

century and a half after his death (1572) was he honored with the title grand guardian of the heir apparent.

Bibliography

1/153/1a; 3/142/1a; 5/50/3a; 6/1/29a; 44/18a; 42/43/3a; 63/9/12a; MSL (1963), T'ai-tsung, 0635, 1482, 2336; *Shantung t'ung-chih* (1911), 118, 124, 126; Wu Chi-hua 吳緝華, *Ming-tai hai-yün chi yün-ho ti yen-chiu* (A study on transportation by sea and the Grand Canal in the Ming dynasty, Taipei, 1961), 69; Chu Hsieh 朱偰, *Chung-kuo yün-ho shih-liao hsüan-chi* 中國運河史料選輯 (1962), 71; *Chi-ning Chih-li-chou chih* 濟寧直隸州志 (1858), 6/39.

Lee Hwa-chou

SUNG Lien 宋濂 (T. 景濂, H. 潛溪), November 4, 1310-June 12, 1381, eminent scholar-official and literary figure, was born in the ancestral home in Chin-hua 金華-fu, Chekiang. As his birthday happened to be the same as his grandfather's, he was given the name Shou 壽 (longevity) but changed it to Lien at an early age. Although his lineage was distinguished, by the early 14th century his family was obscure and poor, barely clinging to its scholarly traditions. Sung Lien later recollected that he often had to borrow books from wealthy neighbors, copy or memorize them, and return them in order to borrow others. Prosperous neighbors and books were plentiful in that region and the boy, whose aptitude for learning was displayed very early, read extensively. His prodigious memory and his skill in composing poetry at the age of twelve or thirteen attracted much attention; at fourteen he was taken as a private student by the prefectural director of studies, Wen-jen Meng-chi 聞人夢吉 (1293-1362). Later, when he respectfully visited eminent scholars of the region in the hope of being accepted as a student, they would defer to him as an equal. Among them may be mentioned such great names in scholarship and literary pursuits as Wu Lai (1297-1340), Huang Chin (1277-1357), and Ou-yang Hsüan (1283–1357). Sometime before 1340 Sung went to P'u-chiang 浦江, a neighboring district, to study under Wu Lai who was then teaching at the private school of the famous Cheng 鄭 clan, known as I-men 義門 (the righteous clan), who had for seven generations (since the early 12th century) lived there as a unit. About 1343, after succeeding Wu as teacher in the Cheng school, Sung moved his home to P'u-chiang and changed his registry to the government school of that district. Meanwhile, he participated in the provincial examinations but failed to place. As a writer, however, he became widely acclaimed and his commemorative essays, mortuary inscriptions, prefaces, and the like were in great demand.

In 1349 some friends in the Yüan capital obtained for Sung an appointment as compiler in the historiography office of the Hanlin Academy. Apparently he accepted the honor but requested permission to stay at home to be near his aging parents. In 1356 he went into seclusion in the nearby Lung-men mountains 龍門山, where he wrote a work of Taoist-Confucian syncretic philosophy called the *Lung-men-tzu ning-tao chi* 子凝道記. Meanwhile he wrote some commentaries on the Classics, thus gaining a reputation also as the leading exponent in his time of the long flourishing Chin-hua tradition in neo-Confucian studies. This tradition, in so far as it is identifiable, was rather narrowly orthodox, considered to be directly in the line from Chu Hsi (1130–1200) and Lü Tsu-ch'ien (1137–81) through an important intermediary figure, Hsü Ch'ien (1270–1337). Yet it was characterized by unusual breadth of intellectual concern, as well as literary refinement. These qualities in particular are features of Sung Lien himself. A product of this rich and comprehensive intellectual milieu, Sung not only investigated variant Confucian traditions, but also went far beyond Confucian studies and became deeply concerned with the thinkers of

ancient times as well as with Taoist and Buddhist learning, Wu Lai exerting a special influence on his thought.

In the winter of 1358/59, after Chu Yüan-chang had conquered Chin-hua, he commanded that a prefectural school of Confucian studies be established, gave an interview to Sung Lien, and later ordered the new prefect to invite Sung to become erudite of the Five Classics, or senior scholar at the Academy. Although Sung at first politely refused, he eventually accepted the appointment. Thus commenced the nineteen-year period of his service under Chu Yüan-chang.

Chu sent an emissary in April, 1360, with gifts and honors to invite Sung, along with three other eminent scholars of the region, Liu Chi, Chang I (*qq.v.*), and Yeh Ch'en (*see* Chang I) to come to his capital Ying-t'ien 應天 (Nanking) to serve in the rebel government. Being under great pressure to accept, they did. Sung was subsequently appointed provincial director of Confucian studies for an area administered from Ying-t'ien, and later in that year became tutor to Chu Yüan-chang's eldest son, Chu Piao (*q.v.*). He lectured to Chu and his staff in September, 1362, on the Spring and Autumn Annals. Two years later, after Chu had taken the title prince of Wu and reorganized his court accordingly, Sung was named diarist 起居注. The future emperor in these years of growing ambition and matching success repeatedly consulted Sung about passages in the Classics and the Histories and their meaning for contemporary situations. Sung's explications were always praised and rewarded. In April, 1365, Sung requested leave to return home to recuperate from an illness; leave was granted and both Chu Yüan-chang and Chu Piao, gave him rewards and testimonials to his valued service. From P'u-chiang he sent a letter of thanks to the heir apparent, exhorting him to study diligently. This greatly pleased the emperor. Shortly after arriving home, Sung lost his father, and went into the required period of mourning through 1368, the first year of the newly proclaimed Ming dynasty. During this period, however, he sometimes composed imperial rescripts and other writings for the court. Early in the following year he received an imperial command to return to Nanking and his old duties. On March 9 he and Wang Wei (*q.v.*) were named associate directors of the bureau established to compose the Yüan history. Sixteen persons of scholarly reputation were recruited to assist them, and six months later, on September 12, the manuscript was submitted to the throne, complete except for the last reign, for which materials were not available. With the arrival at Nanking of archives sent from Ta-tu (Peking), the Yüan history bureau was reopened in March of 1370, again headed by Sung and Wang but with some changes among the assistants; the extended and completed *Yüan-shih* was submitted on July 23, 1370. At the beginning of that year, between the two phases of the work, Sung was named chancellor of the Hanlin (with rank 3A), under the early Ming system, prior to the reorganization of 1381. The emperor frequently called upon him, in addition to his regular duties, to prepare background documents relevant to pending issues. Sung prepared a study of the history of noble titles and ranks and other honors for meritorious officials, used as the basis for the emperor's system of honors for his dynasty. Shortly after submitting the *Yüan-shih*, Sung Lien failed to appear at court according to regulations; he was demoted to Hanlin compiler (rank 8A) in punishment. He then served as an examiner in the provincial examinations in the autumn and in the metropolitan of 1371. [Editors' note: It is not without interest that, besides the Chinese who competed in the provincial examination of 1370, there were students from Korea, Annam, and Champa who apparently came as in the days of Mongol rule. One hundred twenty of them passed. Three Koreans also succeeded in passing the metropolitan test the following year, but only one, Kim To 金濤, became a *chin-shih* and received an appointment as a deputy magistrate. He was, however, sent back to Korea because of his inability to speak Chinese.]

Early in 1371 he was promoted to director of studies (5A) in the National University, but in September, due to a minor mishap, he was demoted to magistrate (7A) of An-yüan 安遠, Kiangsi. In March of the following year he was recalled to serve as a secretary of the ministry of Rites (6A), and resumed his close relationship with the emperor. Once the emperor asked Sung's advice as to a book most essential to clarify the tasks of ruling. He suggested that the extensive commentary on the *Ta-hsüeh* 大學 (Great Learning), called the *Ta-hsüeh yen-i* 衍義 by the Sung scholar Chen Te-hsiu (1178-1235), was the quintessential distillation of governmental wisdom. The emperor examined and admired the book and had long excerpts from it copied on the walls of palace passage ways. Thereafter senior courtiers were occasionally assembled before the inscriptions where, under the emperor's direction, Sung Lien was commanded to discourse on the texts. Chen Te-hsiu's work combined Chu Hsi's orthodox teaching with elements of practical statesmanship; it was an admirable choice for the situation in which scholar-officials were struggling to make the holder of power susceptible to their humanistic views and yet not irritate him by appearing to be impractically idealistic.

Sung Lien (who had served as the heir apparent's senior tutor since 1360) was formally installed in January, 1373, in Chu Piao's newly-established household staff; his title (T'ai-tzu tsan-shan, feng-yi ta-fu 太子贊善, 奉議大夫) and position were not as high or as significant as that of guidance officials, but his personal influence on Chu Piao was undoubtedly strongest. In August he was promoted to expositor-in-waiting in the Hanlin Academy (rank 4A), held concurrently with his other positions. His special assignments included a commission to compile a daily record, the *Ta Ming jih-li* 大明日曆 (Great Ming calendar), 100 *ch.*, in June, 1374. At the same time he was put in charge of preparing a compendium on mourning rites; this was known as *Hsiao-tz'u lu* 孝慈錄, completed in December (*see* Chu Su). Next (1375) he submitted a work entitled *Hung-wu sheng-cheng chi* 洪武聖政記 (Emperor's sage-like governing), a descriptive account of the early Ming governmental measures which he had been commanded to compile. Then he was made chief examiner at the triennial metropolitan examinations of 1376. It was in this year that the young Fang Hsiao-ju (*q.v.*) presented himself at Nanking to Sung and asked to become his pupil. In July Sung was again appointed chancellor of the Hanlin Academy; he had worked his way back to the position and rank (3A) from which he had been demoted six years earlier. At this time three generations— Sung Lien, his second son, Sung Sui 璲 (T. 仲珩, 1344-80), and his grandson, Sung Shen 慎 (T. 子畏, 1354-December 24, 1380), by his elder son, Sung Tsan 瓚 (T. 仲珪, d. 1386, —were officials at the court together.

Just before the lunar New Year (February, 1377), Sung Lien requested permission to retire on account of age. This well-prepared request was approved, the emperor granting him new honors and gifts, and personally composing the rescript permitting his retirement. Sung returned to P'u-chiang, but remained very active as a writer. Requests for his work continued to come from the court, from the scholar elite, and from abroad. Ambassadors from Korea, Japan, the Liu-ch'iu, and Annam inquired about his health as if he were one of the symbols of China's cultural suzerainty. Sung also taught; Fang Hsiao-ju went to live at P'u-chiang so that he could continue as Sung's student, and he remained for more than three years. The emperor had requested that Sung return to the court once a year to be among those congratulating him on the imperial birthday. When Sung went back on these occasions, he was again greeted with honors and gifts, and detained for a month or two to turn out requested essays and other writings. In 1379 Fang Hsiao-ju accompanied him (now almost seventy) to assist with the heavy burdens of this court appearance, During the following year, Sung's wife, née Chia 賈, died, and he failed to appear for the emperor's birthday. On February 8 a chief minister, Hu Wei-yung (*q.v.*), had been executed on the trumped-up charge of plotting the overthrow of the emperor, and a terrible purge followed. Thousands of persons, on the basis of any kind of contact or connection with Hu, were implicated and executed along with their families. Sung's grandson, Sung Shen, was among them. He was put to death along with all his family including his parents and uncle, Sung Sui. Sung Lien's biographers say that he too was to have been executed for his grandson's guilt, but Empress Ma (*q.v.*) and Chu Piao intervened on his behalf, gaining for him a reduction of sentence to banishment. Whether for this reason or for some other, Sung Lien and the surviving members of his household (including three grandsons) set out for the point of exile, Mao-chou 茂州, a frontier post in northwest Szechwan. Leaving in the middle of winter to travel upriver, by May of 1381 he had reached K'uei-chou夔州, just inside the eastern boundary of the province, where he stopped at a Buddhist monastery to rest from the exertions of travel. There he died in June, 1381, and there he was given temporary burial.

Historians, however, differ in their opinion on Sung Lien's death. A recent study by Hsü Dau-lin 徐道鄰 offers evidence that Sung Shen's implication in the Hu Wei-yung case was not responsible for his exile and death; he believes that Sung did not die a natural death as all of the standard accounts say, but that he committed suicide at K'uei-chou. According to this view, Sung Lien himself aroused the Ming founder's unreasoning anger and jealousy. In 1379, when Sung went to Nanking to attend the emperor's birthday festivities, the emperor had taken him for a walk through some palace buildings and had observed Sung stumble and fall on a stairway; noting his physical condition the emperor told Sung that he need not come the following year, but by the next year Chu had forgotten that. When Sung failed to appear, he sent spies to P'u-chiang to see whether the old man might be ill. The spies reported that he was well, at ease, and enjoying the company of friends on the very day of the emperor's birthday. Chu Yüan-chang was infuriated by what he regarded as an intentional slight. He would have had Sung executed immediately, but for the empress and heir apparent. According to the same reconstruction of events, Sung despondently discussed his life and fate with a learned monk at K'uei-chou, complaining that he thought he had done nothing in his life to earn disgrace and exile. The monk asked him: "What office did you hold under the previous dynasty?" Sung replied: "Hanlin compiler." The monk had nothing further to say, indicating that Sung's trouble stemmed from the fact that he had served two dynasties in the same capacity. That night Sung hanged himself. This account is plausible, but somewhat unflattering; the reason why the other version of his death has been preferred is perhaps to better preserve Sung's dignity in history.

Sung has been described as small of stature, plump, and of pleasant appearance, and to the end of his life able to read with ease the smallest of characters. He said that he had never spent a day without reading. He was notably unable to drink, had no vices, and indulged in no excesses. He was a cautious, yet an open and frank person. On first meeting Chu Yüan-chang and being asked how one should conquer the empire, he replied: "By avoiding killing people." Throughout

nineteen years of intimate service to one of history's most dangerously unpredictable personalities, he seems always to have spoken forthrightly of Confucian and humanistic values and never to have compromised them. The suspicious emperor frequently had his spies check on innocent details of the man's private life and then question him to see whether he would report the same accurately; he never caught Sung in any dishonesty and seems genuinely to have trusted him. In 1375 the emperor issued a command that he be consulted on matters of importance to the state, intending to involve him prominently in administration. Sung cautiously but firmly declined, saying that he could express opinions about past governmental actions recorded in history, but that he had no talent for practical affairs of the present. His honesty and his preference for a peripheral position, rather than one of real authority, formed the basis for his success, a fact which increased the emperor's confidence in him. Most Ming and later historians have bestowed high praise on Sung as one of the constructive influences on the early years of the dynasty. An exception is the late Ming scholar and eccentric, Li Chih (*q. v.*), who offers a harsh judgment of Sung in a biography he appended to his history of the Ming dynasty, the *Hsü ts'ang-shu*; he regarded Sung as a typically pompous and hypocritical Confucian literatus.

Sung Lien's writings include belles-lettres, scholarly studies of classical texts, and historical works. Some were published in the last years of the Yüan, and others during his lifetime; various versions of his collected works were repeatedly published thereafter. Ch'ien Mu (BDRC), who has published a study of his collected works, finds the 1810 edition, entitled *Sung Wen-hsien-kung chi* 宋文憲公集, 50 *ch.* (reprinted in *Ssu-pu pei-yao*), the most nearly complete. Five works credited to Sung were copied into the Imperial Library: 1) *Hung-wu cheng-yün*, 16 *ch.*, preface dated 1374 (*see* Chu Yüan-chang), is a

phonological dictionary compiled on imperial command by a commission nominally headed by Sung Lien and not significantly representative of his own scholarship (*see* Mei Ying-tso). 2) The *Yüan-shih*,
210 *ch.*, completed in 1370; often cited
as the poorest of the dynastic histories,
this work and its two supervising editors
have been severely criticized almost since
it appeared. One may say that Sung Lien
is perhaps more to be praised for organizing and completing the vast task in an
incredibly short time than to be blamed
for its shortcomings. 3) *P'u-yang jen-wu
chi* 浦陽人物記, 2 *ch.*, *ca.* 1350. This consists of biographical studies of twenty-nine
noteworthy personages from his native
region; it has been highly praised as a
fair-minded work of both literary and historical value, in the tradition of Ou-yang
Hsiu (1007-72). 4) *Sung hsüeh-shih ch'üan-
chi* 宋學士全集, 36 *ch.* [Editors' note: This
collection in 33 *ch.* (erroneously described
in the Imperial Catalogue as 36 *ch.*) was
printed in 1551 by Han Shu-yang 韓叔陽
(T. 進甫, cs 1547), the magistrate of P'u-
chiang, who also built a shrine to Sung's
memory. It was then the largest collection
of Sung's works, for it made use of the
1457 Chengtu edition in 18 *ch.*, the 1514
edition by Chang Chin 張縉 (cs 1469),
75 *ch.* (reproduced in *Ssu-pu ts'ung-k'an*),
and the 1536 edition by Hsü Sung 徐嵩
(T. 中望, cs 1521), 8 *ch.* The Library of
Congress has two copies of the 1551 edition
and the National Central Library three.]
5) *Sung Ching-lien wei-k'o chi* 景濂未刻集,
2 *ch.*, the second *chüan* consisting of "previously unpublished" items by Sung Lien,
intended to complement the former. Taken
together, they do not represent the best
collection of Sung's literary works. The
Ssu-k'u catalogue also lists by name but
rejects three works by Sung Lien: 1)
P'ien-hai lei-pien 篇海類編, a dictionary
credited to Sung Lien and the late Ming
scholar T'u Lung (*q.v.*) but clearly having
nothing to do with either man; 2) *Lung-
men-tzu ning-tao chi*, 2 *ch.*; and 3) *Hung-
wu sheng-cheng chi*, 2 *ch.* Still others include works imperially commissioned but
only nominally by Sung, and a few conventional and unimportant didactic works
on classical texts. One of the latter, a
brief introduction to the philosophical writings of antiquity called *Chu-tzu-pien* 諸子
辨, preface dated 1358, was punctuated
and republished in 1936 by Ku Chieh-kang
(BDRC). In 1911 a scholar from Chekiang, Sun Ch'iang 孫鏘, printed a collection of biographical and bibliographical
material on Sung Lien entitled *Ch'ien-hsi
chi* 潛溪集, 6 *ch.*; five years later, he and
another scholar published a *nien-p'u* of
Sung. Two short items of passing interest
are Sung's brief account of the embassy
to the Jurchen of T'eng Mao-shih 滕茂實
(cs 1118), entitled *Sung T'eng Chung-chieh
kung shih Chin pen-mo* 宋滕忠節公使金本
末, 1 *ch.* (reprinted 1935), and an essay
on the five-wheeled sand clock, which has
been translated by Needham, Wang, and
Price in their study of clockwork in China.
Sung also wrote for a Japanese Buddhist
priest, Bunkei 文珪, an account of
the building of a revolving bookcase in a
monastery in Kyoto, but there seems to
be no record of it in Japanese sources.

As to Sung Lien's two sons, Sung
Tsan and Sung Sui, the latter was both
an official and a well-known calligrapher,
and was executed in 1380 along with his
nephew, Sung Shen, the two having been
implicated in the Hu Wei-yung treason
plot. Sung Tsan's second and third sons
had died before their exile, but a second
wife and two daughters accompanied him
in attendance on Sung Lien into Szechwan, and a fourth son was born there
in 1386. Three younger sons of Sung Sui
also went to Szechwan, and appear to
have made that province their home thereafter. The eldest surviving son (after
Sung Shen) was Sung I 懌, who later was
patronized by the literary-minded Chu
Ch'un, the eleventh son of Chu Yüan-
chang who took up his residence at
Chengtu in 1391. Sung I was named to a
minor Hanlin post by Emperor Chu Yün-
wen (*q.v.*) about 1400. The second, Sung

Wen 慍, was a minor official who was implicated (July, 1412) in criminal proceedings against another person, but was pardoned by the emperor in recognition of
his grandfather's service to the throne.
The youngest, Sung Ch'üeh 恪, remained
to tend Sung Lien's grave in Szechwan.
In 1413 Chu Ch'un, professing himself an
admirer of Sung Lien, made a grant of
land to Sung Ch'üeh at Chengtu, the income
from which was to be used to maintain
the grave and shrine, transferred with
his assistance to Chengtu at that time. In
March, 1496, through the petition of the
governor of Szechwan, the authorities
recommended regular sacrificial offering
to Sung Lien; then in January, 1514, the
court awarded him the posthumous title
Wen-hsien 文憲.

Bibliography

1/12/8b; 70/3b; 5/20/1a; 61/144/1a; 63/2/19a; MSL
(1962), T'ai-tsu, *ch.* 8-111, T'ai-tsung (1963),
1599, Hsiao-tsung (1964), 2002, Wu-tsung(1965),
2193; Ch'ien Chi-po 錢基博, *Ming-tai wen-hsüeh*
明代文學 (1964 ed.), 4; Wang Ao 王鏊, *Shou-hsi
pi-chi* (*Chi-lu hui-pien* ed.), 124/1a; KC (1958),
284, 287, 313, 419, 535, 602; SK (1930), 46/6b,
52/8a, 58/1b, 147/10b, 169/1a, 192/7b; Cha Chi-
tso (ECCP), *Tsui-wei lu*, "Chuan"傳, 8 中/16a;
Ho Ch'iao-yüan, *Ming-shan-ts'ang, Ch'en-lin chi* 臣
林記, 4; Sun Ch'iang *et al., Sung Wen-hsien-kung
nien-p'u* 年譜, 2 *ch.* (1916); *id., Ch'ien-hsi chi*
(1912); Ch'ien Mu, "Tu Ming-ch'u k'ai-kuo
chu ch'en shih-wen-chi" 讀明初開國諸臣詩文集,
The New Asia Journal, VI: 2 (August, 1964),
245; Hsü Tao-lin (Hsü Dau-lin), "Sung Lien
yü Hsü Ta chih ssu" 宋濂與徐達之死 in *Tung-
fang tsa-chih* 東方雜誌, I: 4 (October, 1967),
56; Kuo Shao-yü 郭紹虞, *Chung-kuo wen-hsüeh
p'i-p'ing shih* 中國文學批評史 (1964), 280; *An-
yüan-hsien chih* (1872), 6/3/36b; Fang Hsiao-ju,
Hsün-chih-chai chi (SPTK ed.), 18/13a, 22/58a; J.
Needham, L. Wang, D. Price, *Heavenly Clockwork*
(Cambridge, England, 1960), 158.

F. W. Mote

SUNG Su-ch'ing 宋素卿, fl. 1496–1523, originally known as Chu Kao 朱縞 (T. 素卿),
a native of Yin 鄞-hsien (Ningpo), who
emigrated to Japan at the end of the 15th
century, served as Japanese envoy to the
Ming court in 1510 and 1523. The accounts of how Chu Kao went to Japan do
not completely agree. According to one
of them, Chu's father made lacquer ware,
and had frequent dealings with the Japanese merchants who ventured to Ningpo
for trade. Once, having accepted a deposit
for merchandise from a Japanese trader,
but failing to keep his agreement, he
delivered his son, then a young lad, to
settle his debt. Chu Kao then went (*ca.*
1496) to Japan in the company of a
home-bound Japanese tributary mission.
Intelligent, gifted in poetry and singing,
he soon won the favor of Hosokawa Ta-
kakuni 細川高國, a rival of the Ōuchi 大
內 family dominant in the late years of
the kangō 勘合 (tally) trade with China.
To offset the advantage enjoyed by his
rival, Hosokawa appointed Chu to head a
mission to China. He took the route
around southern Kyushu, while the envoy
of the Ōuchi family was still in Japan. It
was then that Chu changed his name to
Sung Su-ch'ing, pronounced in Japanese
Sō Sokyō. He arrived in Ningpo in March,
1510, nearly twenty months ahead of
the legitimate Ōuchi mission led by a
famous Buddhist monk, Ryōan Keigo (*q.
v.*). Sung's identity was subsequently revealed and as a Chinese, who had defied
the prohibition not to travel overseas, he
was liable for punishment. In view of
his position as head of a foreign tributary
mission, however, Sung was exonerated.
Instead; according to the *shih-lu*, because
of a bribe of a thousand ounces of gold
made to the eunuch Liu Chin (*q. v.*),
Sung was well treated in Peking where
Emperor Chu Hou-chao (*q. v.*) feted him
and gave him presents.

When Ryōan Keigo finally reached
Ningpo in October, 1511, he was in for
serious trouble. From the local viewpoint,
the Chinese had already received one
Japanese mission, thus leaving little legal
ground for still another so soon afterward. Furthermore, Ryōan Keigo brought

with him far more tribute than was allowable by the regulation of 1496, and he requested that all his staff—two hundred ninety-two persons—be permitted to proceed to Peking, although the Ming court as a rule accepted only fifty persons for each mission. The Ryōan mission was obviously not nearly so successful as that of Sung Su-ch'ing.

Encouraged by Sung's adventure, Hosokawa asked him to head another mission in 1523. This time, however, an Ōuchi mission, led by Shūsetsu Gendō 宗設謙道, arrived in Ningpo in May, a few days ahead of Sung. Possibly because of Sung's past connection with the Ningpo authorities—he was after all a native son—and as he reportedly bribed a eunuch in charge of maritime trade, he was able to have his ships examined and cleared before those of Ōuchi, and at a feast was given a seat of higher honor than the one accorded the latter's envoy. A quarrel between the two diplomats erupted during the banquet, which soon flared into a tumultuous melee. In the course of the riot, the Ōuchi group killed Sung's vice-envoy and pillaged Ningpo. Sung himself was drummed out of Ningpo by the victorious Ōuchi embassy, which then sailed home without even conducting the kangō business. The local Chinese officials, on their part, imprisoned Sung and confiscated his merchandise. Sung was subsequently condemned to death, but it is not certain when the execution took place. One source avers that he died as late as 1544.

In response to a Chinese reprimand, the Japanese shōgun submitted a memorial in 1527, apologizing for the incident, emphasized the illegality of the Ōuchi embassy, and requested that Sung Su-ch'ing be returned to Japan by way of the Liu-ch'iu (Ryūkyū). As a result of this unhappy incident, Chinese-Japanese relations were discontinued during the next seventeen years, and the Japanese missions of 1540 and 1548 were received with apprehension and suspicion (see Chu Wan). The continual struggle between the Hosokawa and Ōuchi families further weakened Japan's position as an effective tributary nation in conducting the kangō trade, which finally came to an end in 1549. The Japanese shōgun, unaware of Sung Su-ch'ing's fate, made repeated requests to the Ming court for Sung's return, together with the confiscated goods. He transmitted these messages through his delegate, Koshin Sekitei 湖心碩鼎 (1481-1564), head of the Japanese mission of 1540. The court ignored his pleas, however, without mentioning whether Sung was still alive.

Sung Su-ch'ing is said to have had ten sons. One of them, known as Sung I 宋一 (Sō Ichi in Japanese), followed his father in the kangō trade. The envoy of the last Japanese mission, Sakugen Shūryō (see Chu Wan), reported to the Ming court (July 1549) that seventy-five out of ninety tallies of the Hung-chih period granted the Japanese had been stolen by Sung I, and asked for new tallies in their place. The court rejected his request and instead commanded the shōgun to chastise Sung I and recover the stolen tallies.

Bibliography

1/322/8b; 3/301/7a; MSL (1965), Wu-tsung, 1321, Shih-tsung, 0773, 0779, 1255, 4796, 6155, 6322; Hsüeh Chün 薛俊 (1474-1524), *Jih-pen k'ao-lüeh* 日本考略 (TsSCC ed.), 9; Hsü Tsung-lu 徐宗魯(?), *Sung Su-ch'ing chuan*傳, in Cheng Chen-to (BDRC), ed., *Hsüan-lan-t'ang ts'ung-shu hsü-pien*, ts'e 15 (1941); Cheng Jo-tseng, *Ch'ou-hai t'u-pien*, 2/18a; Yen Ts'ung-chien 嚴從簡, *Shu-yü chou-chih lu* 殊域周知錄 (1930 ed.), 2/11a; Sanjonishi Sanetaka 三條西實隆 (1455-1537), *Sanetakakō ki* 公記, Vol. 3 (Tokyo, 1931), 558; Keijo Shūrin 景徐周鱗 (d. 1518), *Kanrin koro shū* 翰林葫蘆集 in *Gosan bungaku zen sho* 五山文學全書, Vol. 6 (1937), 362; Kimiya Yasuhiko 木宮泰彥, *Nisshi kōtsū-shi*日支交通史, Vol. 2 (Tokyo, 1928), 325, 332; Mikata Tairyō牧田諦亮, *Sakugen Shūryō nyūmin ki no kenkyū* 入明記の研究, Vol. 1 (1959), 128, 370; Obata Atsushi 小葉田淳, *Chūsei Nisshi tsūkō boeki shi no kenkyū* 中世日支通交貿易の研究 (1930), ch. 4; R. Tsunoda and L. Carrington Goodrich, *Japan in the Chinese Dynastic Histories* (So. Pasadena, 1951), 120, 127; Wang Yi-t'ung, *Official Relations between*

China and Japan, 1368-1549 (Cambridge, Mass., 1953), 76, 87.

Yi-t'ung Wang and Hok-lam Chan

TA-YEN-HAN, *See* **BATU Möngke**

TAI Chin 戴進 (or 璡, T. 文進, H. 靜菴, 玉泉山人), 1388-1462, painter of landscapes, figures, flowers, grapes, and birds, was a native of Hangchow. His name and records of his work appear in numerous writings of his time and later, but his life is obscure. It appears that some time during the Hsüan-te reign he went to Peking in the hope of receiving an appointment. After he had resided there for several years, Emperor Chu Chan-chi (*q. v.*) invited him and a number of others to a viewing of paintings, at which Tai exhibited his "Ch'iu-chiang tu-tiao t'u" 秋江獨釣圖 (A lone fisherman on an autumn river). Although only Tai among those present knew how to make the difficult application of the color of red in the manner of the ancients, this proved to be his undoing. Another painter present, Hsieh Huan (*see* Wang Chih 王直), informed the emperor that Tai had transgressed the rules of etiquette by coloring the coat of the fisherman red—a hue reserved for the attire of officials. The emperor agreed, and Tai left the court for home. Subsequently he moved (for reasons of safety?) to Yunnan, then under the control of Mu Sheng (*see* Mu Ying), the duke of Ch'ien-kuo, where he reportedly made his living by selling paintings of guardians and doorpost divinities. But he must have lived for most of his life in Hangchow, for that is where he made his reputation as the leading artist of the Che 浙 school. Grand Secretary Yang Shih-ch'i and minister of Personnel Wang Ao 翺 (*qq. v.*) became two of his sponsors. Poems describing Tai's paintings are by such a contemporary as Yeh Sheng (*q. v.*); and the Palace Museum, Peking, boasts another with his signature, which includes poems by four others of his contemporaries. Besides, one of Tai's firm friends was Hsia Ch'ang (*q. v.*), not to mention the above named sponsors. All those referred to hailed either from the lower Yangtze valley or from Pei-Chihli.

The paintings left by Tai have received varying evaluations. Critics such as Lu Shen and Lang Ying (*qq. v.*), who lived in the early decades of the Ming, placed him first among all the painters of the dynasty. Then, with the rise of the Wu school and its leader, Shen Chou (*q. v.*), this judgment came to be qualified. Wu K'uan (*q. v.*), for example, asserted that Tai Chin could not be listed above the skillful (or professional) if one compares him with Shen Chou; and Ho Liang-chün (*q. v.*), in comparing him with Wen Cheng-ming (*q. v.*), held that, whereas Wen combined aspects of skill as well as the power to inspire, Tai could claim skill only. However relevant these judgments may be, one may regard Tai Chin as an artist who had the talent to imitate almost any of the painters of the past, and do it supremely well. Li K'ai-hsien (*q. v.*), in listing some of the great names Tai followed, added: "Tai Chin is superior to the Yüan masters but does not equal the Sung painters."

Tai Chin's paintings transform the academic traditions of the Sung and Yüan. Nature and the activities of men are painted in sharp and crisp lines and bold ink forms. His compositions resemble Sung paintings but under his impact the focus of interest changes from large spatial unity to the lively contrasts of local interest and genre. Whether Tai copies a painting or paints a scene the effect is one of an immediate experience. Fortunately many of his paintings have survived and may be seen in numerous collections of both East and West. Osvald Sirén gives a list of forty-two known works and Ellen Laing adds another sixteen. The earliest one now known (it used to belong to the collection of the late Robert van Gulik) is dated 1426. The latest comes from the Ching-t'ai years. Lang Ying is authority for the allegation that Tai Chin died in poverty, but this is unlikely, for one of Tai's contemporaries, Tu Ch'iung (*q. v.*), contradicts him on this point.

Bibliography

65/2/10b; Ho Ch'iao-yüan, *Ming-shan ts'ang* (Taipei ed.), 5868; Hsia Wen-yen 夏文彦 (fl. 1365) and Han Ang (fl. 1519), *T'u-hui pao-chien* 圖繪寶鑑, 6/159; Chiang Shao-shu 姜紹書 (fl. 1640), *Wu-sheng shih-shih* 無聲詩史, 1/14; TSCC (1885-88), XIV: 474/10b, XVII: 784/18/4b; Ho Liang-chün, *Ssu-yu-chai ts'ung-shuo* (Ts SCC), Vol. 5, 336; Kei Suzuki 鈴木敬, *Mintai kaiga-shi kenkyū* 明代繪畫史研究, Tokyo, 1968; Ferguson, *Index of Artists*, 448; O. Sirén, *Later Chinese Painting* (London, 1938), I, 231; *id.*, *Chinese Paintings*, V, 36, VI, pl. 144-151, VII, 235; *Peintures chinoises, Ming et Ts'ing*, Cernuschi Museum (Paris, 1967), 1; H. A. Vanderstappen, "Painters at the Early Ming Court," MS 15 (1956), 259; *id.*, MS 16 (1957), 333; V. Contag and C. C. Wang, *Seals of Chinese Painters and Collectors*, rev. ed. (Hong Kong, 1966), 483, 720; E. J. Laing, *Chinese Paintings in Chinese Publications, 1956-1968* (Ann Arbor, 1969), 190; Robert van Gulik, *Chinese Pictorial Art* (Rome, 1958), pl. 60; H. A. Giles, *History of Chinese Pictorial Art* (Shanghai, 1918), 177; Gustav Ecke, "Two Landscapes of the Che School," MS III, 2 (1938), 565, pl. XXV.

H. A. Vanderstappen

TAI Liang 戴良 (T. 叔能, H. 九靈山人, 雲林先生, 囂囂生), June 22, 1317-May 19, 1383, prose stylist and poet of some note, who remained a Yüan loyalist, was a native of P'u-chiang 浦江-hsien, Chin-hua 金華 prefecture, Chekiang. The Tai family migrated to Chin-hua from Ch'ang-an during the ninth century. His ancestor, Tai Chao (825-82), was appointed imperial commissioner in eastern Chekiang, and Tai Chao's son, Tai T'ang 堂, set up permanent residence in P'u-chiang, at the foot of Chiu-ling shan 九靈山. Tai Liang's father, Tai Hsüan 暄 (T. 景和, 1284-

1350), was a man of moderate means and an acquaintance of the brilliant belle-lettrist and important Yüan official and fellow-townsman, Liu Kuan (1270-1342). Tai Liang studied under Liu, who became the major influence in his life. Two other famous Chin-hua prose masters, Huang Chin (1277-1357) and Wu Lai (1297-1340), also influenced him.

At the age of twenty Tai was appointed master 山長 of the Yüeh-ch'üan Academy 月泉書院 in P'u-chiang. His subsequent loyalist behavior is perhaps explainable by the influence of the Sung loyalist exemplars whose heroism was undoubtedly the subject of much admiration in P'u-chiang during the early years of Yüan control. [Editors' note: There appears to be a difference between the loyalty to Sung in the early years of the Yüan and the loyalty of men like Tai of the early Ming towards the Yüan dynasty; in the latter case the element of nationalism is suppressed, ignored, or rationalized. Both types, however, were "compulsory" rather than "voluntary" with respect to men who had served the preceding dynasty.] Tai's masters, Wu Lai and Liu Kuan, died when Tai was at the age of twenty-one and twenty-five respectively. On the latter's death, Tai dropped everything and spent the next three years of his life looking after Liu's household. The two men had been especially close.

Another major influence on Tai's life pattern was the famous Tangut martyr for the Yüan cause, Yü Ch'üeh (1303-58). Yü passed through Chin-hua as a Yüan official in the summer of 1350. When he was told about Tai Liang's outstanding literary talents, he made a point of establishing an acquaintance with him. Tai and Yü became fast friends and reportedly held one another's poetic talents in high regard. In 1358 Yü lost his life in the defense of Anking at the time of the attack of Ch'en Yu-liang (*q.v.*), and instantly became a Yüan hero. That Tai fondly remembered him is attested to by a colophon written on the occasion of his having discovered a sample of Yü's calligraphy sometime near the end of the Yüan. Tai called himself Yü's disciple, and praised Yü for his patriotic self-sacrifice. Tai's feeling for Yü Ch'üeh also indicates a significant but not (for his time) unusual characteristic of Tai's personality. He was open-minded about the achievement in Chinese literature of some of the non-Han ethnic peoples then in China. One such individual, who later became a close friend and fellow recluse during the Hung-wu period, was the Muslim poet Ting Ho-nien (*q.v.*). In a preface to Ting's early collection of verse Tai writes from a Chinese point of view, but is able to see the uniqueness of the Yüan period in its ability to produce poetic figures like Yü Ch'üeh, Sa-tu-la (T. 天錫, 1308–88 cs 1327), a Danishmand, and Ma Tsu-ch'ang (1279–1388), an Öngüt. Tai wrote: "The three gentlemen are all natives of remote kingdoms in the northwest. Who knows how many myriad *li* they are even beyond Pin 豳 and Ch'in 秦 [the western extremities of ancient China of the Chou]? And yet their poetry has the stylistic legacy of the writers of the Middle Kingdom of antiquity. This fact is sufficient to demonstrate our dynasty's great realization of the 'kingly transformation' 王化 and the significant changes among popular customs. Not even the Chou at its height under King Ch'eng 成王 [traditional dates of r. 1115–1070 B. C.] could match it." Tai also had nothing but praise for the sinicized Mai-li-ku-ssu 邁里古思 (adopted Chinese name: Wu Shan-ch'ing 吳善卿, cs 1354), the darugachi who lost his life following his unsuccessful defense of the city of Shao-hsing when Fang Kuo-chen (*q.v.*) attacked in 1358. Tai notes that Mai-li-ku-ssu had been well received by Chinese intellectuals in southeast China who rallied to his support to help staff his civil administration as well as to use his patronage to advance their own professional aspirations.

In 1357 Tai moved into the hills around P'u-chiang in order to get away from the flames of war that had reached the city. The following year Chu Yüan-chang's troops took Chin-hua prefecture. Around the end of 1358 the future emperor sought to attract Tai Liang, Hu Han (*see* Wang Wei), Sung Lien (*q.v.*), and other Chin-hua intellectuals, about a dozen men altogether, to join him and his new government. He persuaded Tai a month or so later (1359) to serve as instructor in the prefectural school at Chin-hua (then known as Ning-yüeh 寧越-fu). How long this appointment lasted is not indicated, but it is evident that Tai soon parted company with Chu Yüan-chang, and resumed his loyalty to the Yüan. Tai and Sung thus went their separate ways, and yet no evidence of enmity between them exists. The two scholars seem to have remained on friendly terms throughout their lives.

Tai continued living in the hills of Chin-hua until 1361 when he was granted, on the basis of recommendation, the post of director of schools in the branch central secretariat of Huai-nan 淮南, Chiang-pei 江北. This was territory under the control of Chang Shih-ch'eng (*q.v.*). Due to military operations in Chekiang, Tai waited some time and then went instead to Soochow, where Chang's capital was located. The year 1362 was also the year when Kökö Temür (*q.v.*) took over the Mongol military command in north China.

Chang Shih-ch'eng revolted again in 1363, proclaiming himself prince of Wu. Tai remained at Soochow nevertheless for four more years, until it appeared obvious that Chang's days were numbered. In 1366 he made a quick trip home, and then went to Yin 鄞 (Ningpo) and spent approximately half a year readying for a sea trip to Shantung to try to attach himself in some way to Kökö Temür's camp. It is not known precisely why he made the trip. Huang Tsung-hsi (ECCP) speculates in *Sung Yüan hsüeh-an* that he went to seek military assistance for Chang. Other sources say that he had given up on Chang, however. At that time Kökö may have seemed the only possible source of pro-Yüan strength anywhere. In any case, his attempt to reach the general's camp was unsuccessful. With his elder brother's son, Tai Wen 溫 (or Ssu-wen 思溫), he stayed in Shantung's Ch'ang-lo 昌樂-hsien for about a year as the guest of a member of the local gentry. In the autumn of 1367 he returned south to Yin. In that year Chang Shih-ch'eng died, Kökö was deprived of his post by the Yüan court, and Chu Yüan-chang took Shantung.

Tai stayed with friends in Yin and carried on the life of a respected literatus. He also lived at Buddhist temples in the Ssu-ming hills 四明山 of Chekiang. Late in 1368 he wrote a piece called *Pai-yüan t'u chi* 百猿圖記 which was noticed by the Ch'ing authors of Tai's chronological biography and considered a veiled lament on the passing of the Yüan. The piece was composed upon seeing a painting of one hundred gibbons, and points out that the gibbon is civilized and human, in contrast to the hou 猴 (ape). The homophonous pun of yüan = Yüan was deliberate, say the *nien-p'u* authors. (This piece is dated ping-wu 丙午 [1366-67], but, as the *nien-p'u* authors have shown, it was written in 1368, after the Yüan had fallen.) At Ssu-ming Shan Tai carried on as a Yüan loyalist, writing poetry and drinking wine with others of like mind. Among them was the poet Ting Ho-nien. As a Yüan loyalist and one of the few Chin-hua people of any note who flatly refused to have anything to do with the newly enthroned Ming emperor, Tai became rather famous. In 1383 Chu Yüan-chang extended courtesies to Tai, presenting gifts in an attempt to have him accept office in Nanking. Tai went to Nanking and was well provided for; yet he refused the emperor's offer of a position in the hostelry for foreign envoys, thereby antagonizing the emperor. What happened after this is a matter of conjecture. Tai's relative, Chao Yu-t'ung 趙友同 (1364-

1418), author of his funerary inscription, writes that Tai died of old age while sitting erect in his study after having settled outstanding affairs. Tai's son had tried to persuade him apparently to return voluntarily to P'u-chiang, but failed. No contemporary or nearly contemporary accounts indicate that Tai committed suicide. Yet Ch'ien Ch'ien-i (ECCP) wrote that Tai "most likely took his own life." This hypothesis was widely circulated and flatly accepted by Huang Tsung-hsi and Tai's own descendants, but it was rightly doubted by Ch'üan Tsu-wang (ECCP) in a note in *Sung Yüan hsüeh-an.*

Tai Liang was broadly learned in a spectrum of subjects including medicine, divination, Taoism, Buddhism, astronomy, classical Confucianism, and Sung philosophy. His knowledge of medicine was extensive. In fact, the entire Tai family was closely connected with medical studies through acquaintance with the great physician from I-Wu 義烏-hsien (Chin-hua prefecture), Chu Chen-heng (1281-1358), whose *Tan-hsi hsin-fa* 丹溪心法 was reprinted in Shanghai in 1959. When Tai's mother became ill and other physicians proved unsuccessful in treating her, the family called in Chu, who was able to give the woman considerable relief. Her death was unavoidable, however, and inspired Tai's elder brother Tai Shih-shih 士世 (T. 仲積, 1307-49) to study medicine under Chu. Tai Shih-shih's sons, Tai Yüan-li 原 (元) 禮 (*ming* 思恭, sometimes given as 恭, 1324-1405) and Tai Wen 溫, both studied medicine under Chu. Tai Liang treated his two nephews as his own sons after Tai Shih-shih's death. Tai Yüan-li became a physician in his own right. He served the first emperor as imperial physician 御醫, and the second emperor as commissioner in the Imperial Academy of Medicine 太醫院使. When Chu Ti (*q.v.*) usurped the throne, Tai Yüan-li discreetly retired. Tai Liang's younger son, Tai Lo 樂, served P'u-chiang as assistant instructor in medicine 醫學訓科 (his elder son Tai Li 禮 was assistant instructor in Confucian schools also in P'u-chiang). Tai Liang himself may have engaged in medical studies with Chu, since his writings display a considerable grasp of the field. No records, however, attest to this directly. Tai Liang wrote comments on Chu's life and work in a biography that is an important source for information on medical practice in Yüan times. Tai also devoted attention to other physicians, including Hsiang Hsin 項昕 (both a practitioner and an author of the Yüan period), Lü Fu 呂復 (another considerable Yüan author on medicine), who hanged himself when Ming troops descended on Foochow early in January, 1368, and Chou Chen 周貞 (1274–August, 1356), who starved himself to death when Chang Shih-ch'eng attacked Soochow.

Aside from his extensive familiarity with the medical field, Tai was learned in Ch'un-ch'iu studies. Unfortunately his 32 *chüan* work, *Ch'un-ch'iu ching-chuan k'ao* 春秋經傳考, was never published and is now lost. The preface (in Tai's works) indicates that it was an eclectic compendium comparing and contrasting the three commentaries to the Spring and Autumn Annals. Another title, *Ch'un-ch'iu san-chuan tsuan-hsüan* 三傳纂玄, is probably the same work, according to Hu Tsung-mou 胡宗楙; Kao Po-ho 高伯和, however, thinks they are separate books. Tai's works under the name *Chiu-ling shan-fang chi* 房集, 30 *ch.* are divided into four separate collections. The first, *Shan-chü kao* 山居稿, contains his earliest compositions written while living in the mountains of his native prefecture. The second, *Wu-yu* 吳游 *kao* (Wanderings in Wu), contains those pertaining to his years as an official under Chang Shih-ch'eng. The final two, *Yin-yu* 鄞游 *kao* (Wanderings in Yin) and *Yüeh-yu* 越游 *kao* (Wanderings in the Shao-hsing area), contain his later writings.

Tai Liang in his early years was an activist who felt that society needed positive effort by talented men if it was to be improved. He did not approve of "voluntary eremitism," whereby frus-

trated scholars justified withdrawal from society. Instead he argued in his writings that it would be better for the world if men of talent did whatever they could to improve the situation. He realized that the Yüan rule had its drawbacks, but did not submit to the argument that this justified reproof of it through eremitism. Yet in his later years Tai was not prevented from subscribing himself to that of the "compulsory" type. In the early years of the Ming, Tai never gave in to pressure to accept or endorse the new regime through actions that would have compromised his strong commitment to the narrow concept of loyalty to one dynasty that is developed in *Chung ching* 忠經 (Classic of loyalty).

Bibliography

Yin-te #35: 22/238/7b; 23/36/23b; 25/91下/13b; 29/二辛; *Yin-te* #24: 1/285/5b; 3/266/5a; 84/甲前/7a; MSL (1962) Tai-tsu, 0075, 0080; Huang Tsunghsi, *Sung Yüan hsüeh-an*, 82/1583; Wang Tzu-ts'ai 王梓材 and Feng Yün-hao 馮雲濠, *Sung Yüan hsüeh-an pu-i* 補遺, 82/352a; *Chin-hua-fu chih* (1578, repr. of 1964), 1157; *Ningpo-fu chih* (1733, repr. of 1957), 2260; Huang Pin 黃彬 and Chu Yen 朱琰, comp., *Chin-hua shih lu* 夏蘇 詩錄 (1773), 18/a; Tai Tien-ssu 殿泗 and Tai Tien-chiang 江, *Tai Chiu-ling hsien-sheng nien-p'u* 年譜; Chao Yu-t'ung, *Ku Chiu-ling hsien-sheng Tai-kung mu-chih-ming* (1411, TsSCC ed.), 428; Sung Lien, *Sung hsüeh-shih ch'üan-chi* (TsSCC ed.), 785; SK (1930), 168/8a, 174/19a; Hu Tsung-mou, *Chin-hua ching-chi chih* 經籍志 (1926, repr. of 1970); Kao Po-ho, *P'u-yang i-wen k'ao* 藝 文考 (Taipei, 1968); Ch'ien Mu (BDRC), "Tu Ming-ch'u k'ai-kuo chu-ch'en shih-wen chi" 讀 明初開國諸臣詩文集, *New Asia Jo.*, 6:2 (August 1964), 245; Chao I (ECCP), "Ming-ch'u wen-jen to pu shih" 明初文人多不仕, *Nien-er shih cha-chi* (Taipei, 1956 repr.), 466; Chu I-tsun (ECCP), *P'u-shu-t'ing ch i* (1714), 997; Cheng Po, *Chin-hua hsien-ta chuan* 賢達傳 (in *Hsü* 續 *Chin-hua ts'ung-shu*); Ch'en Yüan (BDRC), *Yüan hsi-yü-jen hua-hua k'ao*, tr. and annot. by Ch'ien Hsing-hai and L. Carrington Goodrich as *Western and Central Asians in China under the Mongols* (Los Angeles, 1966), 98, 158, 293; F. W. Mote, "Confucian Eremitism in the Yüan Period," *The Confucian Persuasion*, ed. by Arthur F. Wright (Stanford, 1960), 202.

John D. Langlois, Jr.

TAI Shan 戴珊 (T. 廷珍, H. 松厓), 1437–
January 16, 1506, an outstanding censor
under Emperor Chu Yu-t'ang (*q.v.*), was
born into a family of scholar-officials
which settled in Fou-liang 浮梁, Kiangsi,
during the Sung dynasty. His father, Tai
Han 唅 (T. 士儀, H. 訥菴. 退叟, 1399–
1466, cj 1420), served as an instructor in
the prefectural school of Chia-hsing 嘉興,
Chekiang, and earned a name as a dedicated teacher and upright official. A *chü-
jen* of 1462, Tai Shan achieved his *chin-
shih* in 1464, in the sme year as his
distinguished colleague, Liu Ta-hsia (*q.v.*).
Two years later Tai received an appointment as a censor, but did not assume
office until he had completed the required
mourning for his father who had died
some months earlier. In 1472 he was appointed supervisor of schools in Nan-Chihli,
where he spent six years. He was transferred (1478) to Shensi with the higher
rank of an assistant surveillance commissioner, where he performed his duties as
successfully as in Nan-Chihli. In 1484 he
was again transferred to be the surveillance commissoner of Chekiang, and three
years later became the administration commissioner of Fukien. In the last two posts
he made an effort to improve the administration, solve the financial problems, and
govern the area with justice.

Through the recommendation of Wang
Shu (*q.v.*), then minister of Personnel, Tai
received a promotion (June, 1489) to vice
censor-in-chief, and served as governor
of Yün-yang 鄖陽 in the northwestern
corner of Hukuang bordering on Honan,
Shensi, and Szechwan. This prefecture,
established in 1476 (*see* Hsiang Chung),
and its adjacent area had become the
haven of refugees and outlaws who
exploited the unclaimed land and evaded
tax payments. Invoking stringent measures,
Tai restrained the lawbreakers, made the
tax delinquents pay their debts, and
drilled the inhabitants on how to guard
against the raids of the bandits. Early in the
following year, a band from Szechwan,
led by Yeh-wang-kang 野王剛, crossed into

Hukuang and Shensi, inflicting considerable damage. Tai then proposed that the
court order the authorities of these two
provinces to launch a joint expedition
against the outlaws. They complied and
crushed the bandits in December. From
March, 1491, to May, 1496, Tai served as
an assistant minister of Justice, first
under Ho Ch'iao-hsin and then under
P'eng Shao (*qq.v.*).

During these years Tai was put in
charge of a number of litigations, including two cases involving imperial kinsmen,
and executed his duty competently. In
June, 1492, he was sent to review the
case of Chu Chien-su 朱見溮, the third
prince of Ching 荊 (appointed 1464, d.
1494), who was indicted for killing his
brother and for other offenses. Then in
1495 he performed a similar task when
Chu Chung-ping 鍾鈈, the third prince of
Ning-hua 寧化 (appointed 1472, d. 1508),
was charged with committing acts of extreme cruelty and other misdeeds. Acting
on the evidence gathered by Tai and his
associates, the emperor punished the two
princes by demoting them to be commoners, the former in January, 1493, and
the latter in December, 1495.

Tai received a promotion (May, 1496)
to be the minister of Justice in Nanking,
with the concurrent title of junior supervisor of instruction; here he built up an
impressive record during his years in
office. In July, 1500, he was transferred
to Peking to become the senior censor-in
-chief, and held this post until his death.
During these years Tai helped the ministry of Personnel evaluate the record of
officials. It is said that he often upset
precedents by reassessing the officials on
the basis of their performance rather
than on recommendations submitted by
the inspecting censors. This caused some
uneasiness among his colleagues, but it
served to improve the administration.
When the emperor occasionally presided
over the trial of serious cases of offense,
Tai was present to watch the proceedings
and answer the questions of the monarch.

He was reportedly one of the few officials whom the emperor sometimes consulted privately. Another so privileged was his friend Liu Ta-hsia. Tai's insistence that justice prevail, however, displeased the less scrupulous officials and they sought to slander him for their own protection. Thus in 1504 two junior officials, one from the ministry of Personnel and the other from Revenue, submitted separate memorials accusing Tai of allowing his wife and concubine to accept stolen goods from a certain racketeer. Whereupon Tai submitted (in August) a request to retire on the pretext of illness; but the emperor, finding his service indispensable, ignored his appeal. When, in September, the emperor ordered an investigation, it turned up little evidence in support of the allegation; Tai's name was cleared, and the slanderers subsequently cashiered. Probably due to health reasons, his desire to retire persisted. Early in 1505 he pleaded with Liu Ta-hsia, now minister of War, to put his request before the emperor; the latter again talked with him and asked him to stay. So Tai reluctantly continued his service into the next reign. He died early in the following year before he had a chance to submit a similar request to the new emperor, Chu Hou-chao (q.v.). He was then sixty-eight years of age. In March of this year, acting on the memorial presented jointly by his former students, headed by Censor Yang I 楊儀 (T. 宗德, cs 1493), Chu Hou-chao honored him with the posthumous name Kung-chien 恭簡 and the title of grand guardian of the heir apparent. His son Tai Ch'ing 晴 later entered the National University through the yin privilege.

Tai reportedly left a collection of memorials which does not seem to have survived. A portrait of him and a specimen of his handwriting are reproduced in the scroll "Chia-shen shih t'ung-nien t'u chüan" (see Li Tung-yang).

Bibliography

1/183/19a; 5/54/62a; 8/32/31a; 61/127/1a; 63/17/ 24a; MSL (1964), Hsiao-tsung 585, 981, 1802, 1940, 2044, 2603, 2942, 4038, 4043, 4060, 4148, Wu-tsung (1965), 253, 310; KC (1958), 2630, 2825, 2849; Jao-chou-fu chih 饒州府志 (1872), 20/ 38a, 21/5a, 26/20b, 31/23a; Ho Liang-chün, Ssu-yu-chai ts'ung-shuo (Peking, 1959), 78.

Hok-lam Chan

T'AN Ch'ien 談遷 (T. 孺木, H. 觀若, original name I-hsün 以訓, H. 射父), November 23, 1594-January 14, 1658, historian, came from a scholarly but not wealthy family of Hai-ning 海寧, Chekiang. A student of the district school, he failed in the competitive examinations and, except during the last few years of his life, does not seem to have traveled beyond the Hangchow-Nanking area. Apparently he made a living by serving as teacher in affluent families or as secretary to an official. About 1621, while reading various histories of the Ming dynasty, he found none completely satisfactory and so began to compile a chronological history to which he gave the title Kuo-ch'üeh 國榷 (An evaluation of the events of our dynasty). The first draft was completed about 1626 but he continued to enlarge and revise it during the following years. Around 1642 he was engaged in Nanking as a private secretary-adviser by the minister of Revenue, Chang Shen-yen 張慎言 (T. 金銘, H. 藐山, 1577-1645), and probably continued in the latter's service until 1644. After the fall of Peking in April, Nanking for a while became capital of the empire. T'an was then employed by Grand Secretary Kao Hung-t'u 高弘圖 (T. 研文, d. 1645, cs 1610). Chang proposed to recommend him for the position of an office manager 司務 (9B) in the ministry of Rites; and Kao later suggested the post of a drafter 中書 (7B) in the Grand Secretariat. He declined both offers for he still hoped for a regular degree by taking the civil examinations. Then Kao planned the establishment of an office for the compilation of the national history and wished to recommend T'an as an historiographer. This time T'an begged off emphatically. In any case the new emperor (Chu Yu-sung, ECCP) proved to be unworthy, indulging in dissolute practices; as a consequence, both Kao and Chang left the court after a few months' service. In 1645 T'an accompanied Kao to Shao-hsing, Chekiang, where the latter, on hearing of the approach of the Manchu troops, committed suicide.

For several years thereafter T'an lived in or near his home and applied himself seriously to the compilation of the chronicles of the dynasty. Heretofore he had been writing simply as an historian, but now, as a surviving subject of a defunct dynasty, he assumed the mission of compiling a reliable history of that house while living under alien rule. By this time he was making his sixth revision of the *Kuo-ch'üeh*. It seems that the writing of Ming history was then in vogue and that someone coveted T'an's manuscripts. One night in 1647, it is said, the manuscript of *Kuo-ch'üeh* was stolen. It is not recorded whether all his notes and earlier versions were also lost.

Refusing to be discouraged, T'an started at once to compile a new version which was probably a better one because of his one-time association with high officials, his maturity in scholarship, and especially his freedom to write as he pleased as a result of the dynastic change. Furthermore, at this time the Manchu court had not begun to censor books on Ming history, and so he was unhampered in his writing especially with respect to references to the Manchus. He seems, moreover, to have had access to more private libraries than before, because he records that for the new compilation he made use of three different manuscript copies of the *Ming shih-lu*, belonging to the T'ang 唐 family of Kuei-an 歸安 (the library formed by T'ang Shu 樞, T. 惟中, H. 一庵, 1497-1574, cs 1526), the Shen 沈 family of Chia-hsing 嘉興 (the Shang-po chai 尚白齋 of Shen Fu-hsien 孚先?), and the

library of his friend Ch'ien Shih-sheng (*q.v.*), who had served as a grand secretary (1634-36).

In 1653 T'an had the good fortune to go to Peking for the first time in his life. It happened that a fellow provincial, Chu Chih-hsi 朱之錫 (T. 孟九, 1623-64, cs 1646) of I-wu 義烏, was returning to Peking and engaged T'an as secretary. The two traveled together on the Grand Canal, arriving at Peking the day before T'an's sixtieth birthday. Apparently he had by this time become reconciled to life under Manchu rule, styling himself Chiang-tso i-min 江左遺民 (Left-over Ming subject from east of the Great River), and even dating a preface by the Shun-chih reign-title. His sentiments may be seen in the last two lines of a poem written about this time: 殘編催白髮, 猶事數行書, "The incomplete compilations hurry the graying of my hair, yet I continue to work on these few lines." As a matter of fact he wrote more than just a few lines. By the time he left Peking in March, 1656, he proudly took with him several thousand sheets of notes recording chiefly what he had learned about the last decades of the Ming dynasty from documents, memoirs, and personal interviews. He received help from several scholars then living in Peking who were also interested in the writing of Ming history, including Huo Ta 霍達 (T. 魯齋, cs 1631), Ts'ao Jung, and Wu Wei-yeh (both in ECCP). These bibliophiles opened their libraries to him. He also consulted persons who had served at court, including eunuchs and high officials, and recorded their words. As a result, his account of the years from 1627 to 1645 in his *Kuo-ch'üeh* contains more information on that period than any other historical work. In the 1958 edition of *Kuo-ch'üeh* these 18 years occupy 833 pages, at an average of 46.3 pages to a year as compared to 5,384 pages for the 260 years from 1368 to 1627, averaging 20.7 per year. In contrast, in the 1940 edition of the *Ming shih-lu*, the Ch'ung-chen period (17 years) accounts for only three volumes (0.18 volumes per year) as compared to 497 volumes for the other 260 years (1.5 volumes per year).

In 1657 T'an was engaged by a fellow townsman, Shen Chen-heng 沈貞亨 (T. 仲嘉, H. 靜園, cs 1652), to serve as a secretary in his office of prefectural judge of P'ing-yang-fu 平陽府, at Lin-fen 臨汾, Shansi. In the spring of that year he and another secretary engaged by Shen, a younger man named Ch'ien Ch'ao-wei 錢朝瑋 (T. 大球), journeyed together from Chekiang to Shansi. Their association was a short one, for T'an died several months later during the winter. The younger man, impressed by his honesty and directness and overwhelmed by his erudition, wrote a biographical sketch of him. Thus the last year of T'an's life is vividly recorded. According to Ch'ien, while they were traveling outside of Tung-ch'ang in Shantung, they met two highwaymen who "charged us on horseback with drawn swords; on being told by Mr. T'an that we had no money, only books and writings, and after verifying this by a search they saluted us with raised hands, saying, 'Sorry to have disturbed you,' and galloped away." From this we may infer that, while on a thousand mile journey at sixty-three years of age, T'an still had his manuscripts with him. While working in Shen's office he continued to make revisions of the Kuo-ch'üeh, copying twelve sheets a day regularly. He enjoyed good health until the end when he fell ill and died of botulism.

T'an probably completed the final version of the Kuo-ch'üeh except for some minor revision or supplementation. There is the report of a man who saw the original manuscript, describing it as consisting of over twenty thousand leaves, with many of them full of notes and changes and some having added slips pasted in. But this copy seems to have been lost. Fortunately a number of manuscript copies are extant, and in 1955 a scholar, Chang Tsung-hsiang (BDRC), produced a collated copy from which the edition of a thousand copies was printed in 1958 in Shanghai, on 6,217 pages in six volumes. This great work on Ming history, besides its fuller treatise on the last 18 years of the dynasty, frequently differs from the Ming shih-lu in the accounts of the earlier periods too, especially the first three reigns (1368-1424) and the Wan-li period. The book, moreover, is interspersed with comments on the events, quoted from more than three hundred sources in addition to T'an's own. It was probably because of the editing and interspersed critical remarks that T'an chose for the title the character ch'üeh 榷, meaning originally the stopping of freighters for tax assessment; hence, evaluation or comment.

Besides the Kuo-ch'üeh, T'an Ch'ien compiled a collection of miscellaneous notes, Tsao-lin tsa-tsu 棗林雜俎, 8 ch. It is described in the 1782 official list of books to be partially banned, as containing fourteen passages of objectionable matter. The book in its entirety was printed from a defective manuscript copy in 1911 in the Chang-shih Shih-yüan ts'ung-shu ch'u-chi 張氏適園叢書初集. One item in the Tsao-lin tsa-tsu, entitled Chin-ling tui-ch'i lu 金陵對泣錄, is his recording of an eyewitness report of the fall of Peking. Another item, which dealt with men of literature and poetry, was abridged and printed in the Hsüeh-hai lei-pien (see Ts'ao Jung) under the title Tsao-lin i-k'uei 藝簣. His complete collection of essays and poems probably no longer exists, but a collection of his poems in 3 chüan was printed in 1914 in the Ku-hsüeh hui-k'an 古學彙刊 under the title Tsao-lin shih-chi 詩集 to which is appended the above-mentioned biographical sketch by Ch'ien Ch'ao-wei. Several other works by T'an exist only in manuscript, including the history of his native place, Hai-ch'ang wai-chih 海昌外志, and a second collection of notes, Tsao-lin wai-so 外索, completed in 1654. He left two accounts of travels during his last two years. One entitled Pei-yu lu 北游錄 contains his writings in Peking from 1653 to 1656; this work was printed about 1959 in Peking from a manuscript (reproduced, without original imprint, in Hong Kong in 1969). The other, entitled *Hsi* 西 *-yu lu* of 1657, which may be the *Chin* 晉 *-yu lu* in some records, seems to be no longer extant.

The term "Tsao-lin," appearing in so many titles of T'an's works, signifies a place on the seacoast in Hai-ning where there used to be jujube orchards but which had long been lost to the sea. The T'an family, which had come to Hangchow from Kaifeng, Honan, at the end of the Northern Sung dynasty early in the 12th century, was forced to move at the end of the Southern Sung (about 1276) to a place near Tsao-lin. T'an said at the end of the Ming dynasty that he was determined not to move again and so chose Tsao-lin for some of his titles.

It is remarkable that the *Kuo-ch'üeh* remained hundreds of years only in manuscript form, surviving the hazards of several devastating wars and the strict censorship of the 18th century; today it has become an indispensable reference work on the history of the Ming dynasty. In 1644, when T'an refused to take part in the government bureau of history, he recorded his reason, namely, that as a commoner without a degree, he would have been outranked by other participants. Apparently, he thought too much of his scholarship to place himself in such a position. There is no question of his confidence, however, in his own standing. This may be seen from the fact that in, or shortly after, 1644 he changed his name from T'an I-hsün to T'an Ch'ien, thus combining in his new name the characters for the given names of the foremost of China's historians, Ssu-ma T'an (d. 110 B.C.) and his son, Ssu-ma Ch'ien (*ca*. 135-*ca*. 93 B.C.).

Bibliography

1/97/3a; *Hai-ning-chou chih kao* 海寧州志稿, 12/5/1a; Huang Tsung-hsi (ECCP), *Huang Li-chou wen-chi* (1959), 117; Ch'ien Ch'ao-wei, biography of T'an Ch'ien in *Ku-hsüeh hui-k'an*, no. 12; WMSCK, 1/12b; Wu Han 吳 (BDRC) *Teng-hsia chi* (1962), 169, 195; Sun Tien-ch'i (1957), 168; Biography by Chu I-shih 朱一是 (cj 1642) in *Kuo-ch'ao wen-hui* 國朝文滙, 甲集, 9/16b.

Chaoying Fang

T'AN Hsi-ssu 譚希思 (T. 子誠, H. 嶽南), 1542-1610, official and historian, was a native of Ch'a-ling-hsien 茶陵縣, Hukuang. His family, a cultured one, came originally from T'ai-ho 太和, Fukien. T'an's initial posts, after graduating as *chin-shih* in 1574, were as magistrate first of Wan-an 萬安 (1575-77) and then of Yung-feng 永豐, both in the prefecture of Chi-an 吉安, Kiangsi. Here he became a much respected man, emphasizing justice and promoting education. While in Wan-an he purchased land, the income from which was to be used for the schooling of the poor. (Many years later at his death the people of both areas held sacrifices in his honor.) Next he received an appointment as censor in Nanking. In this capacity T'an sent memorials to the throne which in part proposed the curtailing of the power of the eunuchs and of the relatives of the consorts and mother of the emperor (Chu I-chün, *q. v.*). This did not amuse the emperor, who demoted him to a provincial post. A year later, however, he was back at the capital serving successively as secretary of a bureau, director, vice administrator of the seal office (1592), vice administrator of the Grand Court of Revision, vice governor of Nanking, and finally, in 1593, vice governor of the Shun-t'ien prefecture (Peking). He reached the peak of his official career as assistant censor-in-chief and concurrently governor of Szechwan (beginning March 2, 1594).

This was at the time that the central government was having increasing difficulties with the "uncivilized" Miao tribesmen of Po-chou, led by Yang Ying-lung (*q. v.*). Yang had dealt the Szechwan army a crushing blow just prior to his arrival; so it fell to T'an to conserve what was left, build up the provincial defense forces, and await the decision of Peking —now heavily engaged in the war against the Japanese in Korea—as to what policy to follow next. T'an early proposed pacification of the tribespeople by cultural means, but was eventually overruled. Meanwhile he made a study of the tribes of Szechwan, entitled *Ssu-ch'uan t'u-i k'ao* 四川土夷考, 4 *ch.*, published in 1598. The notice of this work, which the editors of the *Ssu-k'u* inserted in the catalogue, indicates that it included 78 maps, the first one general, the rest showing the boundaries of each individual tribe—more useful for military purposes, the editors write, than for geographical information. The fragment which has survived (the 3d *chüan*) contains 16 maps only. While the province was at peace, T'an enjoyed traveling over the countryside, visiting scenic spots, and entering into amicable relations with the local literati. With the recurrent attacks of Yang Ying-lung, however, his policy became discredited, he was transferred to the south (March 4, 1597), and a few months later (September 15) dismissed.

A much larger work than his study of the tribes, the *Ming ta-cheng tsuan-yao* 明大政纂要, 60 *ch.* (printing of 1895, made from a manuscript copy and edited by the Mongol bannerman Chung Lin 鍾麟, cs 1903, in 63 *ch.*), is a compilation of significant governmental affairs for the years from 1382 to 1572, chronologically arranged; this was revised in 1619, and bears the preface of Han Ching 韓敬 (T. 敬求, *chuang-yüan* of 1610). At the conclusion of materials supplied for each reign, T'an wrote down his judgment of that era. Chung Lin considers the book superior to similar works by Chu Kuo-chen (ECCP) and Lei Li (*q.v.*). The editors of the *Ssu-k'u* catalogue mention both books, but did not include them in the Imperial Library. T'an wrote other works, several in harmony with the neo-Confucian school of thought, but they seem to have disappeared.

Bibliography

1/221/1b; 3/207/1b; MSL (1966), Shen-tsung, 4998, 5138, 5159, 5731, 6118, 6253; KC (1958), 4760; *Ch'a-ling-chou chih* (1871), 17/7a, 8b, 18/8a, 20/8b; *Chi-an-fu chih* (1875), 12/43b, 14/39b; *Wan-an-hsien chih* (1873), 9/13b; *Shun-t'ien-fu chih* (1965), 4967; *Hunan t'ung-chih* (1934), 3299; *Szu-ch'uan t'ung-chih* (1816), 100/3b; SK (1930), 48/5a, 78/5b; *Szu-ch'uan t'u-i k'ao* (NLP microfilm); *Ming ta-cheng tsuan-yao*; Chao Shih-hsien 趙世顯 (cs 1583), *Chih-yüan wen kao* 芝園文稿 (NCL microfilm), ch. 4, no. 9; Liu Jih-sheng 劉日升 (1546-1617), *Shen-hsiu-t'ang chi* 慎修堂集 (NCL microfilm), 20/1a; W. Franke, *Sources*, 1. 3. 5.

Yang Chin-yi and L. Carrington Goodrich

T'AN Lun 譚綸 (T. 子理, H. 二華), August 4, 1520-April 20, 1577, official and military administrator, was a native of I-huang 宜黃, Kiangsi. He was the second son of T'an Hao 鎬 (T. 宗周, H. 東吾, d. 1561), a scholar who served as instructor in the Kuei-an歸安, Chekiang, district school (*ca.* 1537) and later in the home of a prince. T'an Lun became a *chü-jen* in 1543 and a *chin-shih* the following year. After appointments as a secretary in the ministry of Rites in Nanking (1545-49) and in the ministry of War in Peking (1552) he was transferred to the southern capital as an acting department director of the ministry of War. This was the time when Japanese and other pirates, known as *wo-k'ou*, were on the rampage along the coast, especially in the wealthy Nan-Chihli and Chekiang areas; T'an's post gave him the opportunity to become acquainted with the military situation and to take part in the defense of Nanking in 1555 when a band of the pirates ventured near that city. Later in 1555 he was sent as prefect to T'ai-chou 台州, Chekiang, where he undertook the training of a thousand local troops. In 1557 and 1558 he led his men against the marauders and won several victories, for which he was promoted in the middle of 1558 to surveillance vice-commissioner of Chekiang with headquarters at Ningpo. He often accompanied his men on forced marches to the front and bravely took part in the fighting with his sword. He also cooperated closely with General Ch'i Chi-kuang (*q.v.*) in fighting off the brigands along the Chekiang coast, especially during the series of battles in the T'ai-chou area in 1559. The pirates were later forced to shift south to Fukien and Kwangtung. In 1561 T'an Lun's father died and he retired to his home in I-huang for the mourning period. After T'an left, the people of Ting-hai 定海 erected a monument in gratitude to him for his successes over the pirates. The inscription on the monument was written by Feng Fang (*q.v.*).

Back in I-huang T'an found the place in a turmoil, for just then some roaming bandits from Kwangtung and Fukien were ravaging eastern and southern Kiangsi. T'an helped the government troops in their suppression of them. He was appointed an administration vice commissioner of Fukien in 1562 but begged to be permitted to complete the mourning period at home. Late in 1562 the *wo-k'ou* took the prefectural city of Hsing-hua 興化, south of Foochow, and a special imperial order came to T'an early in 1563 to hurry to the front in Fukien, his full title being assiststant censor-in-chief, director of Fukien military affairs, and governor. At this time Generals Liu Hsien (*see* Chang Lien) and Yü Ta-yu (*q.v.*) were both camped near Hsing-hua while Ch'i Chi-kuang was on his way south from Chekiang. On T'an's order, the first two generals held their position to await the arrival of himself and Ch'i. After consolidating their strength at the village of Chu-lin 渚林, about twenty miles east of Hsing-hua, they fought the pirates, gaining a signal victory over them. The pirates soon lost most of their positions on the Fukien coast. At T'an's recommendation Ch'i was made regional commander of Fukien. His other recommendations included restoration of some naval bases, training of local troops, and repeal of the law forbidding foreign trade which he blamed as the chief cause of piracy. In June, 1564, he again returned to I-huang.

As soon as the twice interrupted mourning period was over in October, 1565, T'an was named governor of Shensi. When he received the order, he wrote a letter to the minister of Personnel, Chang Chü-cheng (*q.v.*), whom he styled as "a friend with real understanding whom he had not yet met" (不識面之知己), for he was told that Chang was the one who sponsored him. While he was on his way a new order was received changing his appointment to Szechwan where the soldiers at a minor post west of Chungking had mutinied. Before he arrived in that province he found that the mutiny had already been suppressed. Later the uprising of a native chieftain of Wu-ting 武定, Yunnan, Feng Chi-tsu 鳳繼祖, was disturbing the peace on the Szechwan border region at Hui-li 會理. A strong force composed of the provincial troops from Szechwan and Yunnan, together with the warriors of several native chieftainships, encircled the rebels. The assassination of Feng put an end to the uprising. The commander who contributed most to the success of the campaign was the widow, née Feng 鳳, of An Chung 安忠, a chieftain under the Chien-ch'ang guard (建昌衞). She was permitted to continue as chief for life.

Late in 1566 T'an was promoted to be governor-general of Kwangtung and Kwangsi with his headquarters at Chao-ch'ing 肇慶 where he served for over a year. A year later he was summoned to Peking and in April, 1568, appointed senior vice-minister of War and supreme commander of Chi-liao 薊遼, the frontier region north and northeast of Peking, with his headquarters at Mi-yün 密雲, where he served for over three years. In that short time he was able to organize an effective defense along the seven hundred miles of the Great Wall at its eastern end. Under his command, Ch'i Chi-kuang, who had been transferred from Fukien, undertook the training of about thirty thousand troops to form a corps specializing in the use of carts set up to form a fortress-like square. These carts, equipped with firearms of various sizes, from hand guns to mounted cannon, thus gave protection to foot soldiers defending themselves against the swift thrusts of the Mongol horsemen. T'an also built over a thousand parapets at strategic points on top of the Great Wall to house and protect the guards. The parapets were constructed by the troops themselves in their spare time at less than one tenth the usual cost of such government fortifications. Yet various rumors unfavorable to the work were rampant in Peking, probably started by persons connected with the ministry of Works and the eunuchs, who used to profit from such undertakings. T'an submitted a strong memorial to protest these rumors, describing the construction by the soldiers as substantial, and welcomed any investigation by the government. The rumors subsided. Late in 1570 he was given the additional duty of associate director of the training divisions of Peking and in 1571 promoted to be minister of War. Towards the end of that year he suffered a stroke of paralysis and resigned from office. He soon recovered and in August of 1572 was recalled to Peking. This was the time when Chang Chü-cheng was in full power and a program of reform was taking place. T'an, a stanch supporter of Chang, was summoned as a member of the inner circle and again appointed minister of War. In a letter to his friend Ling Yün-i (see Ch'en Lin), T'an wrote that he came out of retirement because he thought that, at this unusual juncture when the purpose of both ruler and minister coincided, there was a chance for great plans to be realized, and that he did not want to miss such an opportunity. He declared that the intention of his group was to make the government as good as that which obtained under the ancient sage-kings. These conscientious statesmen did achieve much towards the revival and prosperity of the Ming empire (see Chang Chü-cheng). In

military affairs, for which T'an was responsible until he died in office in 1577, successful campaigns were carried out against non-Chinese tribesmen in Hui-chou 惠州 (1573), in Huai-yüan 懷遠, Kwangsi (1574), and in Hsü-chou 敍州 prefecture, Szechwan (1573). All along the northern frontiers a century of Mongol raids came to an end. The peace of 1571 (see Altan-qaɣan) accounted only for the northwestern parts of the front. It was the strengthening of the defenses north of Peking under T'an Lun and Ch'i Ch'i-kuang that deterred the Mongols from further raids in the northern and northeastern areas. When T'an died Ming military prestige was higher than it had been since the mid-fifteenth century. He was given special honors at burial, granted the posthumous name of Hsiang-min 襄敏, and accorded a minor hereditary rank (centurion ?) in the Embroidered-uniform Guard, which went to his son, T'an Ho-t'u 河圖.

According to the *Ming-shih*, T'an Lun served for thirty years in connection with military matters and was credited with over twenty-one thousand five hundred heads (of rebels and pirates killed in his campaigns). T'an Ch'ien (*q.v.*), the historian, described T'an Lun as follows: "Although T'an Lun liked women and money, was known for possessing a kind of magic libidinous power, and favored Chang Chü-cheng, he nevertheless was clearheaded, experienced, and clever, and his talents were noteworthy." The third of the derogatory remarks is obviously prejudiced and the first two based on hearsay. Only the words of praise, begrudgingly given, seem to be fitting. As to T'an Lun's ability as a commander, this may be seen from the fact that many of his former subordinates became famous generals, such as Ch'i Chi-kuang, Yü Ta-yu, and Liu Hsien, or effective administrators, such as Wang Tao-k'un (*q.v.*) and Ling Yün-i. On their part they all had high praise for T'an's leadership. Perhaps the most extraordinary eulogy T'an received was the edict inscribed on a monument set up inside the main gate of the palace in Peking, in which the emperor, then a lad of fourteen, stated emotionally that he wept and could not sleep on learning of T'an's death and was at a loss to find another minister so devoted. The inscription was dated August 18, 1577, four months after T'an's death. The monument was probably destroyed six or seven years later after Chang Chü-cheng was posthumously discredited.

T'an Lun wrote hundreds of memorials but only 104 of them, selected from those written from 1563 to *ca.* 1569, appeared in a collection edited by his descendants and admirers and engraved in 1600 by Ku So-yu 顧所有 (T. 謙叔, H. 潁泉), then magistrate of I-huang, under the title *T'an Hsiang-min kung tsou-i* 公奏議, 10 *ch.*, in which a likeness of T'an may be found. A copy of this work, with the collector's seals of K'o Feng-shih 柯逢時 (cs 1883, governor of Kiangsi, 1902-3), is in the Columbia University library; it was printed after 1645 because the characters 夷 and 虜 have been removed and left blank. A new engraving of the collected memorials appeared in 1704. In the latter part of the 18th century this collection was listed among the banned books because it contained certain objectionable words. An apparently revised version of the work was copied into the Imperial Library *Ssu-k'u ch'üan-shu*, and given a rather laudable review in the catalogue. The *Ming-shih* lists a work on military regulations by T'an Lun, entitled *Chün-cheng t'iao-li lei-k'ao* 軍政條例類考, 7 *ch.*, probably compiled when he was minister of War. His literary works were edited by Huang Hsi-yüan 黃錫褒 (T. 仲佩, H. 定軒, cs 1802) and engraved in 1819 under the title, *T'an Hsiang-min i-wen hui-chi* 遺文彙集, 3 *ch.*

Bibliography

1/97/13a, 222/1a; 3/205/1a; 5/39/120; 32/61/51b; *I-huang-hsien chih* (1824), 29/12b; Ou-yang Tsu-ching 歐陽祖經, *T'an Hsiang-min kung nien-p'u kao* 年譜稿 (Nanchang, 1936); SK (1930), 55/8b; Sun Tien-ch'i (1957), 241, and *Wai-pien*, 71.

Chaoying Fang

T'AN-YANG-TZU, *see* **WANG Tao-chen**

T'AN Yüan-ch'un 譚元春 (T. 友夏). *ca.* 1585-1637, essayist and literary critic, was a native of Ching-ling 景陵, Hukuang. About 1600 he became interested in writing poetry, probably because his special Classic for the civil examination was the Book of Odes. Five years later he met Chung Hsing (*q.v.*), a fellow townsman who had recently passed the provincial examination. Although Chung was ten years or more his senior, the two at once struck up a lifelong friendship. In a letter to Ts'ai Fu-i 蔡復一 (T. 敬夫, Pth. 清憲, d. 1625, cs 1595) written in 1610 Chung recommended the young poet as ten times better than himself. At this time Chung had already felt a keen dissatisfaction with the current trend in poetry which stressed free and lucid expression of natural feeling and inspiration (hsing-ling 性靈, *see* Yüan Hung-tao) to the neglect sometimes of refinement in style. In this T'an concurred. The two friends decided to select from T'ang and pre-T'ang poetry what they considered to be models of style for study and imitation. By offering their anthology to the public they hoped to rectify the trend which they considered aberrant. Pursuing their task in earnest in 1614 and 1615 they produced an anthology printed in 1617 under the collective title, *Shih-kuei* 詩歸 (Aim of poetry), consisting of *Ku shih-kuei* and *T'ang shih-kuei* (*see* Chung Hsing).

The anthology immediately gained recognition not only among the youth but also among such older poets as Ts'ai Fu-i. It won for the joint editors too an enviable fame as founders of a new school of poetry, called Ching-ling t'i 竟陵體, after the ancient name of their home town. Chung was at once acclaimed as the arbiter of the art of poetry, and publishers began to use his name on title pages to promote the sale not only of anthologies but also of books on a variety of subjects: drama, history, and even fiction and jokes.

This phenomenon, typical of the late Ming period, may be explained by the fact that it was the time when literati, frustrated politically by the ineptitude of the emperor, the insolence of the eunuchs, the defeats on the frontiers, and the ineffectiveness of their protests, were ready to welcome the promise of a change and a chance at smashing some idols. Meanwhile the prosperity of the urban areas in the lower Yangtze valley created a market for objets d'art and for books, which made publishing a profitable enterprise. The name of any editor who had entered the temple of fame was exploited for the promotion of sales. Chung Hsing's was one such name, along with those of Li Chih, Feng Meng-lung, T'u Lung (qq.v.), Yüan Hung-tao, Ch'en Chi-ju (ECCP), et al., seized upon by publishers for this purpose.

Though a student only of a local school, T'an Yüan-ch'un suddenly became nationally famous, sharing recognition with Chung Hsing but always as a junior partner. In 1623 he was selected as a tribute scholar to study in the National University in Peking. Four years later he passed the chü-jen examination with first honors, but thereafter failed to gain the chin-chih degree. On his way back to take the metropolitan examination he died in an inn ten miles from Peking (1637). He left several collections; these were brought together in 1633 under the title T'an Yu hsia ho-chi 譚友夏合集, 23 ch., printed in Soochow by an admirer, Chang Tse 張澤. It consists of three parts, namely, Yüeh-kuei-t'ang hsin-shih 嶽歸堂新詩, chüan 1-5 (poems written after about 1621); Ku-wan wen-ts'ao 鵠灣文草, chüan 6-14 (essays); and Yüeh-kuei-t'ang i-k'o shih-hsüan 巳刻詩選, chüan 15-22 (poems selected by Chang Tse from T'an's earlier publications, the prefaces to which constitute chüan 23). None of T'an's writings after 1633 seems to have survived; perhaps that was why one source (the anthology of Hukuang poets, Ch'u-feng pu 楚風補, 50 ch., 1749) stated erroneously that he died in that year. Appended to the T'an Yu-hsia ho-chi is a collection of poems by Chang Tse himself, entitled Chih-chai shih-ts'ao 旨齋詩草. There are at least two other Ming editions of T'an's works, the Yüeh-kuei-t'ang ho-chi 合集 and T'an-tzu 譚子 shih-kuei, each in 10 chüan.

As in the case of Chung Hsing, but to a lesser degree, T'an's name was exploited by book publishers. A case in point is the T'ung-chi chieh-lan 通紀捷覽 mentioned in the Index Expurgatorius Wei ai shu-mu 違碍書目. It is apparently an annalistic treatment of the Ming dynasty, a type of book which forgers in the early Ch'ing period usually assigned to Chung Hsing; in this case, however, T'an's name was used.

A drama entitled Wan-ch'un yüan 綰春園 (Garden of late spring), attributed to a Shen Fu-chung 沈孚中 and printed at the end of the Ming dynasty, indicates that both Chung and T'an furnished comments. Another drama, the Hsiang-tang-jan 想當然 (The way it must have happened), attributed to Lu Nan (q.v.), even includes a preface in Lu's name and another in T'an's name identifying Lu as its author. According to Chou Liang-kung (ECCP), however, the drama was actually written by one of his students, Wang Kuang-lu 王光魯 (T. 漢恭), who faked the authorship by audaciously inventing the Lu preface. Presumably the T'an preface was forged to substantiate the fraud. Judging from the facsimile reprint of 1930, the Hsiang-tang-jan is beautifully printed and has sixteen woodblock illustrations of excellent quality, which suggests that the forgery of the authorship was not for monetary gain but probably motivated by the author's fear of ostracism by orthodox Confucianists. This drama was included in the first series of the collection, Ku-pen hsi-ch'ü ts'ung-k'an 古本戲曲叢刊 (1954), as was the Wan-ch'un yüan in its second series

(1954–55).

Most literary critics seem to recognize Chung and T'an for their achievement as anthologists; some, however, think that, in trying to give illustrations of selections which emphasize profundity and detachment (shen-yu ku ch'iao 深幽孤峭), they tended to go out of their way to avoid lucidity and freedom of expression and to seek for hidden meaning in unfamiliar utterances and uncommon words. Their own poems fared much worse. Ch'ien Ch'ien-i (ECCP) even described the Chung-T'an style as ghostly and suggestive of a battlefield, thus symbolizing the last days of a dynasty. Ch'ien's ridicule, however, was directed chiefly at the writings by T'an, whom he judged to be deficient in talent and limited in learning, often mistaking vulgarity for naturalness and unintelligibility for profundity. Ch'ien also ranked the Ching-ling style of poetry, the western religion (Christianity), and the Ch'an Buddhism of the Three Peaks (San-feng ch'an 三峯禪, i. e., the teachings of Fa-tsang 法藏, 1573–1635) as the three heresies of his day. In this connection it is interesting to note here the last two lines of T'an's poem on his visit to the tomb of Matteo Ricci (q.v.), who introduced Christianity to China: 行盡松楸中國大不敎奇骨任荒寒. This may be interpreted to mean: After passing by so many burial grounds, he found that the greatness of China lay in the fact that it does not abandon to wild and cold this unusual man's bones. This poem is not mentioned in P. M. d'Elia's *Fonti Ricciane*.

Bibliography

T'an Yu-hsia ho-chi (1935), 13, 57, 79, 142, 147, 382; *Ch'u-feng pu*, 25/14a, 29/10b, 31/21a; Ch'ien Ch'ien-i, *Lieh-ch'ao shih-chi*, 丁12/71a; SK (1930), 180/6b, 193/6a; Sun Tien-ch'i (1957), 240; Wade Library *Catalogue*, University of Cambridge (1898), 99; Gest Oriental Library *Catalogue*, D68.

Chaoying Fang

T'ANG Ho 湯和 (T. 鼎臣), 1326–August 22, 1395, a native of Feng-yang 鳳陽 (Anhwei), was one of the closest associates and principal lieutenants of Chu Yüan-chang. He came from the same village as Chu and joined Kuo Tzu-hsing (q.v.) at the time of the latter's original uprising (March, 1352), receiving promotions in rank and responsibility as Kuo's fortunes rose. Early in 1354 he was selected by Chu Yüan-chang, then Kuo's protégé, to be one of twenty-four men to serve as the core of his personal command, and, after Chu's capture of Ch'u-chou 滁州 in April, he received the rank of battalion commander (管軍總督). when Chu's authority was contested by the other generals at Ho-chou 和州 in 1355, T'ang strongly supported him. Later that year he participated in the crossing of the Yangtze to attack the government troops and other rebel rivals, and was wounded by an arrow in the storming of T'ai-p'ing 太平. Serving under Hsü Ta (q.v.), T'ang took part in the campaigns leading to the capture of Chin-ling (Nanking) in 1356 and the subsequent consolidation of Chu Yüan-chang's authority to the east and south of the city. Following these successes, he was promoted to wing commander (統軍元帥), and after the fall of Ch'ang-chou 常州 (April, 1357), was placed in command there with the rank of deputy assistant chief of the bureau of military affairs.

Ch'ang-chou was the most important of the several walled cities in Chu Yüan-chang's hands which constituted the line of defense against the regime of Chang Shih-ch'eng (q.v.). T'ang Ho and the large garrison under his command had both to defend the city and to act as a mobile reserve when other cities in the region were theatened. T'ang beat off one attack in February, 1358, and in May, 1359, ambushed the attackers, capturing, it is said, over one thousand men and forty ships. The threat that Chang might attack again required the continued presence of large garrisons in the lower Yangtze valley. Because of this T'ang did not participate

in the struggle against Ch'en Yu-liang (*q.
v.*); his activities were confined to occasional brief counterattacks against Chang
Shih-ch'eng's territories. In February,
1363, he received a promotion to junior
administrator of the secretariat and then
in April, 1364, became chief administrator.

The fall of Ch'en and the return of
Chu's main army to Nanking permitted the
use of T'ang's troops in other areas. In
December, 1364, he defeated Chang Shih-
hsin (*see* Chang Shih-ch'eng) and relieved
the siege of Ch'ang-hsing 長興 in a hard-
fought battle in which he reportedly captured eight thousand prisoners. The following year he fought under the command
of Ch'ang Yü-ch'un (*q. v.*), taking Yung-
hsin 永新 in Kiangsi. He then returned
to Ch'ang-chou, and in the following year
(1366) took part under the command of
Hsü Ta in the final campaign against
Chang Shih-ch'eng. His fleet first destroyed
the enemy on Lake T'ai and then sailed
to Wu-chiang 吳江, south of Soochow.
After capturing that city, T'ang's ships
rejoined the main force besieging Soochow itself; they were placed opposite the
Ch'ang 閶 gate, where T'ang was once
more wounded. He returned to Nanking
to convalesce, but was back in time for
the fall of Soochow in October, 1367. In
November he was appointed a left censor-
in-chief, and was given the nominal title
of instructor to the heir apparent in
February of the following year.

After the collapse of their last great
enemy in the Yangtze valley, the victorious armies erupted in all directions at
once. T'ang was commissioned general in
charge of the southern expedition with
Wu Chen 吳禎 (first *ming* 國寶, T. 幹臣,
1328-79) as his deputy, and ordered to
lead the former garrisons of Ch'ang-chou,
Ch'ang-hsing, and Chiang-yin 江陰 to suppress Fang Kuo-chen (*q.v.*) in Chekiang.
The fleet sailed from the mouth of the
Yangtze to Ningpo. That city fell at the
end of November, but Fang escaped to
the sea with the loss of only a few units.
Chu Yüan-chang ordered Liao Yung-

chung (*q.v.*) to go to T'ang's assistance
with his own ships. The combined fleets
pursued Fang, who surrendered his four
hundred vessels and twenty-four thousand
men at the end of December.

At the same time that Hsü Ta pressed
forward to the conquest of north China,
Chu's armies under Hu T'ing-jui (*see* Teng
Yü) were invading Fukien overland from
the west. In support, the fleet of T'ang Ho
and Liao Yung-chung sailed in January
from Ningpo to Foochow. That port fell
after a short siege, and this led the coastal
cities of Hsing-hua 興化, Chang-chou
漳州, and Ch'üan-chou 泉州 to surrender
soon afterward. The expeditionary force
then pushed up the Min 閩 River and
captured Yen-p'ing 延平, taking the pro-
Yüan warlord Ch'en Yu-ting (*see* Fang
Kuo-chen) alive. This completed the
coastal campaign, probably T'ang's greatest
military achievement. In March he
received orders to return to Ningpo to
organize, presumably in collaboration with
Fang Kuo-chen's former staff, the transportation of grain by sea to the north. Liao
Yung-chung remained in command of the
fleet, and took it south to Canton.

T'ang accompanied the emperor to
Kaifeng in August, 1368. There he was
assigned the task of assisting Feng Sheng
(*q. v.*) in reducing the cities of northern
Honan and southern Shansi. After fulfilling his mission he led his forces to join
the main Ming army under Hsü Ta, and
together they entered Shensi early in 1369.
The campaign ended in September, and in
the following month both Hsü Ta and T'ang
Ho were recalled to Nanking. They were
among the scores of officers to receive
rewards from the emperor in January,
1370, but because T'ang's part in the Fukien
campaign seemed less then satisfactory to
the emperor he received a smaller reward
than the principals. A few weeks later
T'ang became Hsü Ta's assistant deputy
commander for the northern campaign,
and was present at the great victory over
Kökö Temür (*q.v.*) at Ting-hsi 定西, Kansu;
afterwards his division was detached

and sent north. He captured Ning-hsia and then penetrated the Ordos region, taking several tens of thousands of horses, cattle, and sheep. His army continued to operate in the upper bend of the Yellow River until the end of the year, when he and the other senior generals were recalled to Nanking to participate in a ceremony at which the emperor awarded noble titles. This time T'ang was made marquis of Chung-shan 中山侯 with an annual stipend of 1,500 *shih*; he was seventh in precedence among the Ming nobles and first among the marquises of that day.

In February, 1371, two armies, one by land and the other by water, were sent to conquer the independent state of Hsia 夏 in Szechwan (*see* Ming Yü-chen). T'ang was given over-all command of the fleet on the Yangtze River, his task being to pass through the gorges to Chungking, with Liao Yung-chung and Chou Te-hsing 周德興 (d. 1392) as deputies. Fu Yu-te (*q.v.*), assisted by Ku Shih 顧時 (T. 時學, 1334-79, Pth. 襄靖), had command of an army marching south from Shensi in the direction of Chengtu. Fu's operations were successful, but the fleet could not fight its way past the Yangtze gorges. T'ang lost heart; eventually Liao Yung-chung, whose entire career had been on the water, was able to break through with his squadron of the fleet and continue upstream. T'ang followed in his wake. Chungking fell early in August, while Chengtu also surrendered to Fu's army later in the same month. When they returned to the capital in November, the emperor judged T'ang's performance insufficient; the rewards for the campaign went to Fu Yu-te and Liao Yung-chung.

In 1372 T'ang commanded one of the armies sent against the Mongols in the north. On August 10 at Tuan-t'ou-shan 斷頭山 (north of Kuei-sui 歸綏 ?), he suffered a severe defeat. Coming only two months after Hsü Ta's setback at the hands of Kökö Temür, it provided a factor in the emperor's decision to settle down to a defensive posture in the north. T'ang him-

self was not punished for this loss, and in April of the following year he once again commanded one of the armies on the northern frontier. During the next two years he supervised the training of troops, the founding of military colonies, and the repair of the walls of Peiping and Chang-te 彰德. At the end of 1374 he and Teng Yü were summoned back to Nanking briefly, but in February, 1375, they returned to the northen border, where T'ang founded military colonies in Shensi. The death of Kökö Temür in that year reduced the danger from the Mongols, but Bayan 伯顏 Temür took his place as the leader of the Mongols raiding Shensi. At the beginning of 1376 T'ang, with the aid of Fu Yu-te, Lan Yü (*q. v.*), and others had the task of fortifying Yen-an 延安, Shensi, and resisting Mongol incursions. He remained on the frontier for almost two years, until Bayan Temür's armies left the area.

In February, 1378, T'ang was made duke of Hsin 信國公 and his annual stipend was raised to 3,000 *shih*. In March of the following year he led a group of other officers training troops at Lin-ch'ing 臨清 (Shantung); this and similar assignments occupied him for the next two years. At the beginning of 1381 he was one of Hsü Ta's two deputies in the successful campaign against the Mongols in the northwest, and he remained in that region for the following year. In 1383 he was sent to command the army in the troubled area of Yung-ning 永寧 in Szechwan, and the next year he toured Fukien and Chekiang inspecting the military organization in order to improve the coastal defenses against the Japanese pirates. These duties occupied him through 1384.

When the aboriginal inhabitants of Kweichow revolted in 1385, the emperor sent (October) his sixth son, the prince of Ch'u 楚王, Chu Chen (*see* Chu Yüanchang), with an army to suppress them; T'ang, who held the title of general in charge of the pacification of the aborigines, was sent out as nominal adviser to the prince and actual commander-in-chief. In the course of a hard-fought campaign he reportedly captured forty thousand rebels and pacified the province in the following month. After returning to the capital in February, 1386, T'ang requested the emperor's permission to retire. Chu Yüan-chang, though impressed by his plea, thought he was still vigorous and assigned him to lighter duty in Chekiang to inspect and improve the coastal defenses. In July, 1388, T'ang again submitted a request for retirement, which the emperor approved, sending him off with lavish rewards. In March of the following year T'ang received a summons to supervise the defense of Feng-yang with Chou Te-hsing, but apparently to hold this post for only a year. Following a court appearance on New Year's Day (1390), T'ang suffered a stroke, involving the loss of his voice; the emperor allowed him to retire and he made only rare public appearances thereafter. He died at the age of sixty-nine, and was posthumously enfeoffed as prince of Tung-ou 東甌王, and given the name Hsiang-wu 襄武. Though adjudged a mediocre commander by many of his contemporaries, T'ang manged to retain the emperor's favor to the end. He was an example of the class of peasant solder who rose to fame and power during the end of the Yüan and the founding of the Ming dynasty. Chu Yüan-chang's trust in him was based on boyhood friendship and on the steady support he gave him during his rise to eminence, especially in the crisis at Ho-chou in 1355; this trust continued after 1380 because of T'ang's willingness to relinquish his command at a time when the emperor was striving to consolidate the military power in his own hands.

T'ang Ho had five sons, but only the youngest, T'ang Li 醴, who later reached the rank of vice commissioner-in-chief, survived him, and the dukedom was terminated. It was not until 1492, when Emperor Chu Yu-t'ang (*q.v.*) appointed T'ang Shao-tsung 紹宗 (d. 1535), T'ang's descendant in the sixth generation, to the rank of guard commander of the Embroidered-uniform Guard in Nanking, that one of T'ang Ho's lineage received a hereditary title. In 1532 Emperor Chu Hou-ts'ung (*q.v.*) honored T'ang Shao-tsung with the title of marquis of Ling-pi 靈璧, and with an annual stipend of 1,000 *shih*, which was inherited to the end of the dynasty. T'ang Ho was also blessed with five daughters. The eldest became the concubine of the prince of Lu, Chu T'an, tenth son of Chu Yüan-chang, and after her death one of her sisters (d. April, 1433) took her place in August, 1387.

Bibliography

1/105/7a, 126/12a; 5/5/100a; 9/2/13a; 61/92/12a; 88/1/36a; MSL(1962), T'ai-tsu, *ch.* 3-240, Hsuan-tsung (1963), 2250; KC (1958), 264, 347, 351, 355, 458, 661, 700, 759; Chu Yüan-chang, *Ming T'ai-tsu yü-chih wen-chi* (Taipei, 1965), 3/3b, 9/4b; Wang Shih-chen, *Yen-chou shan-jen hsü-kao* (NCL microfilm), 82/1a.

Edward L. Dreyer

T'ANG Jo-wang, *see* **SCHALL Von Bell**

T'ANG Sai-er 唐賽兒 (fl. 1420), woman leader of the Shantung insurrection of 1420, was a native of P'u-t'ai 蒲臺, Shantung. Her husband Lin San 林三, who died early, was from the same district. Little about her family background, or her personal life, is revealed in the various sources, but most agree that she was a believer in Buddhism and able to read the scriptures. Some imply that she even became a Buddhist nun after her husband's death. When she assumed the rebel leadership, she called herself Fo-mu 佛母, or Buddha mother. Regarding her acquisition of supernatural power, the story goes that one day, when returning from a visit to her husband's grave, she passed a cliff where she noticed a stone box under the rocks. In the box she discovered a divine book on military tactics. Other versions indicate that she also obtained a magic sword there. By studying this book, she gained powers which enabled her to tell past events and predict future happenings. She was said to know how to cut paper figures and turn them into real soldiers and horses, an accomplishment often attributed to the White Lotus sect.

The report of the insurrection T'ang Sai-er initiated reached Peking on March 24, 1420. At that time she was leading a gang of some five hundred men who held a stockade by the name of Hsieh-shih-cha chai 卸石栅寨 in the district of I-tu 益都, and engaged in raiding the surrounding villages. Meanwhile, about a dozen of her followers, heading groups of various sizes, roamed about the areas to the south and east. When they killed a local garrison commander who tried to subdue them, their insurrection was reported to Peking. The central government first offered amnesty to the insurgents if they would surrender. After this offer was refused, Liu Sheng (see Lê Lợi), the marquis of An-yüan 安遠侯, was appointed commander-in-chief on April 10, to lead a force into Shantung.

Liu Sheng bungled the attempt to take the stockade, however, the rebels successfully eluding his men and slipping away. Simultaneously two of T'ang Sai-er's followers attacked and raided An-ch'iu 安丘 and Chü-chou 莒州. Only the timely aid of the assistant commissioner of Shantung, Wei Ch'ing 衛青 (T. 明德), saved the situation. By the end of April the insurrection was suppressed and most of the rebel leaders captured and taken to Peking for execution; T'ang Sai-er was not among them. This annoyed the emperor, Chu Ti (q.v.); so he ordered all Buddhist nuns and female Taoists of the Peking metropolitan area, as well as of the province of Shantung, to be brought to the capital for questioning. This naturally caused considerable turmoil, but T'ang Sai-er was never found. Perhaps it was for this reason that certain myths as to her magic powers developed.

Hsü Hsüeh-chü (q.v.) in the Kuo-ch'ao tien-hui and the shih-lu both state that

T'ang Sai-er was captured, but as the sword could not hurt her at the execution and the implements of punishment fell away from her body, she made her escape and disappeared. This same story appears again in Ku Ying-t'ai's (ECCP) topical history of the Ming dynasty, the Ming-ch'ao chi-shih pen-mo.

By the early 18th century, T'ang Sai-er had become the heroine of a tale, the Nü-hsien wai-shih 女仙外史, by Lü Hsiung 呂熊 (T. 文兆, H. 古稀逸田叟), who elevated her from a rebel to the status of an immortal. Lü felt deeply resentful of Chu Ti's usurpation of the throne of his nephew, Chu Yün-wen (q.v.). To express his view he attempted in fictional form to right the wrong by presenting T'ang Sai-er's rebellious force as a righteous army on the side of the nephew. As Chu Ti eliminated the reign title of Chien-wen, so Lü Hsiung eliminated the reign title of Yung-lo; in this way he extended the reign of Chien-wen to the twenty-sixth year. Since Shantung offered the strongest resistance to Chu Ti's forces during his campaigns to gain the throne, one need not be surprised that a creative writer would make it the locale of his story. In actual fact, however, the uprising in Shantung led by T'ang Sai-er occurred over two decades later and had no connection with Chu Yün-wen.

Bibliography

1/154/17b, 175/1a; MSL (1963), T'ai-tsung, 2193-2238; KC (1958), 1167; Ch'en Chien and Shen Kuo-yüan 沈國元, Huang Ming ts'ung-hsin lu 皇明從信錄 (1620), 15/1a; Lei Li, Huang Ming ta-cheng chi 皇明大政紀 (1602), 8/38a; Teng Ch'iu 鄧球, Huang Ming yung-hua lei-pien 皇明泳化類編 (1965?), 8/57; Chu Kuo-chen (ECCP), Huang Ming ta-shih chi (1632), 17/3b; Hsü Hsüeh-chü, Kuo-ch'ao tien-hui (1963), 1869; Ku Ying-t'ai (ECCP), Ming-ch'ao chi-shih pen-mo, chüan 23.

Lienche Tu Fang

T'ANG Shun-chih 唐順之 (T. 應德, H. 荆川, 義修), November 9, 1507-April 25, 1560, has long been recognized in Chinese learned circles primarily as an essayist, his prose style being widely praised and admired. His many other adventures and pursuits, however, have failed to win such approval. T'ang came from a celebrated scholar-official family in Wu-chin 武進, Nan-Chihli. His ancestors for six generations were all civil service degree holders or recipients of imperial honors. Upon his qualification for the *chin-shih* in 1529 he was nominated to enter the Hanlin Academy along with twenty-two other successful candidates. But at this time Emperor Chu Hou-ts'ung (*q. v.*) decided that at least for the time being no new bachelors should be appointed. T'ang received an assignment instead as a secretary in the ministry of War. A year later he left office on sick leave. After his return to Peking in 1532 he was posted to the ministry of Personnel and in August, 1533, transferred to the Hanlin as a compiler. About eighteen months later he again requested leave of absence on account of illness. The emperor ordered (March, 1535) that he be retired and never again employed for governmental service.

While his health was indisputably poor, his repeated requests for leave were, according to his biographers, designed to dissociate himself from Grand Secretary Chang Fu-ching (*q. v.*) whom he detested, though the latter appreciated his talent and tried to patronize him. Angered by T'ang's ingratitude, Chang drafted the harsh rescript for the emperor. Exactly four years later the situation changed. In March, 1539, Chang died and the installation of the heir apparent took place. On a single day the emperor appointed some forty officials as his tutors and advisers, T'ang among them. Resuming his title of Hanlin compiler, he became a junior adviser to the prince. But once more he scuttled his own career. Early in 1541 he and his close friend, Lo Hung-hsien (*q. v.*), submitted two separate memorials to the throne intimating that, as long as the emperor did not maintain the tradition of

giving daily audiences, the heir apparent might appropriately act on his behalf. The petitions resulted in the dismissal of both memorialists and the removal of their names from the civil service register. Lo retired for good but the high point of T'ang's governmental service still lay ahead.

While in Peking T'ang studied the ideas of Wang Shou-jen (*q. v.*) under Wang Chi (*q. v.*). Out of official employ, he befriended Buddhist and Taoist scholars and practiced meditation. A strain of neo-Confucian thought, obviously under strong Buddhist influence, may be traced in T'ang's writing, especially on occasions when he discusses the oneness of the universe, the perfection of the original mind, and the vital importance of spontaneity. But in spite of all this he denounced the principle of instant and effortless enlightenment. In the main he was too much involved in practical matters and had too wide a range of interests to be concerned with philosophical consistency. He became a serious student of geometry, astronomy, weaponry, and military strategy. The decade subsequent to his second banishment from the court probably constituted the best years of his life. He himself stated that at the age of forty he experienced an important turning point. He traveled extensively, studied mathematics under Ku Ying-hsiang (*q.v.*), and took a cottage in the hills of I-hsing 宜興 not far away from his home, where he read, wrote, and played host to his friends. His *Ching-ch'uan wen-chi* 荊川文集, 12 *ch.*, was published in 1549 and reprinted in 1553; most of his other works were also produced about this time. Above all, in these years he developed his own literary style. Previously, following the trend of the time represented by scholars like Li Tung-yang (*q. v.*), he acted in the belief that prose had been perfected in the Ch'in and Han and poetry in the T'ang. Therefore he tended to imitate earlier writers, often word for word and phrase for phrase. But after the age of forty he abandoned the stereotyped

structure and endeavored to make his
own expressions more fluent and powerful. Along with Kuei Yu-kuang and Wang
Shen-chung (*qq. v.*) he was credited by
his contemporaries with giving Ming literature new life. Under their influence
later writers became more creative and
less imitative. T'ang tried to illustrate his
principles in the writing of prose by compiling the anthology, *Ching-ch'uan wen-pien*
編, of various earlier authors including
those of the Sung dynasty.

Despite his seeming unconcern about
advancement in an official career, T'ang
maintained a genuine desire to serve the
state and the people. Whether this derived
from a sense of devotion or from personal
vanity is a matter of opinion. Otherwise
he is known to have been a man of few
worldly wants. His asceticism is almost a
legend. He could sleep on a hard-surfaced
board without adequate bedding, be content to wear a plain cloth robe, and travel
on foot for long distances. His vegetarian
diet is understandable, considering the in-
testinal disorder and spleen ailment about
which he often complained. He must too
have had considerable will power to sur-
mount his physical weakness. In spite of
his chronic illness, he loved to ride horseback and indulge in swordplay. Yet criticism of T'ang for certain eccentricities is
not without some justification; an account,
written by a devoted friend, indicates that
"for twenty years he never washed his
feet." His temperamental disposition was
such that, when he encountered a person
whom he judged to be lacking in moral
character or merely not to his liking, he
did not hide his displeasure. If possible
he avoided the man. In a letter to Wang
Ch'ung-ku (*q. v.*), he wrote assuring the
latter that he did not deliberately evade
him; but his explanation is so phrased
that it indicates the opposite. His later
associations with Chao Wen-hua, Yen
Sung, and Yen Shih-fan (*qq. v.*) seem to
be, to say the least, contrary to his usual
practice.

In 1555, when Chao Wen-hua arrived in

Nan-Chihli to inspect the operation against
the *wo-k'ou*, T'ang met and discussed
the military situation with him. Soon
afterwards Chao recommended to Emperor Chu Hou-ts'ung that T'ang be recalled to governmental service. Offered a
secretaryship in the Nanking office of the
ministry of War, T'ang hesitated. Only
the urging of Lo Hung-hsien brought him
around. But his father's death at this
juncture delayed his reporting to duty.
Finally, in 1558, he received appointment as
a director of a bureau in the war ministry
in Peking and as such inspected the army
command at Chi-chou 薊州 under Wang
Yü (*see* Wang Shih-chen). His close contact with Yen Sung seems then to have
been established. Upon returning from the
inspectioo trip he reported that not only
was the command under strength, but
also that training was grossly neglected.
The report resulted in Wang's demotion.
Before the end of the year T'ang received
orders to proceed to Chekiang. His assignment, ambiguously phrased, called for him
to observe the campaign against the pirates and to assist Governor-general Hu
Tsung-hsien (*q. v.*). T'ang, however, took
his assignment seriously. Not satisfied
with the inactive role of an imperial observer, he went to the front and stayed
with the troops. By an informal arrangement with Hu Tsung-hsien he became
virtually the governor-general's forward
echelon commander. Soon he was administering military supplies and directing field
operations. In battle he wore armor, went
about on horseback, and supervised the
attack at close range. More than once,
when the generals hesitated, he dismounted
and threatened to attack the pirates himself. Arguing that they should be dealt
with either at sea or on the offshore
islands, he sailed to Chou-shan 舟山 and
Ch'ung-ming 崇明, and often remained
for long stretches at his command post
on a warship. His exploits were not always successful. His own papers acknowledge his setbacks and frustrations for
which the inadequate army supply, un-

trained troops, and poor generalship were largely responsible. But even his vigorous leadership earned only a few favorable comments. The editors of the *Ssu-k'u* catalogue, on balance, ridicule him for meddling in military affairs. The *Shih-tsung shih-lu* has no kind word for him. In describing his performance as a tactician it remains thoroughly scornful, charging him not solely for blundering but also for irresponsibility. Only his biography in the *Ming-shih* treats him with sympathy. Even there the writer blames T'ang for diminishing his own reputation in later years because of his association with Chao Wen-hua and Yen Sung.

The critics are undoubtedly correct in holding that T'ang owed the last span of his official career to Yen. Included in his *wen-chi* is his letter to Yen thanking the grand secretary for his patronage. He and Yen also exchanged poems. Other correspondence between the two, however is largely impersonal, having to do with state affairs such as transportation, taxation, and frontier defense. Apparently he hoped that the grand secretary would use his influence to put his ideas   (T'ang's) into practice.

With the support from the inner court and recommendations by Hu Tsung-hsien, T'ang received two titular promotions in 1559. First he became vice minister of the Court of the Imperial Stud, and about a month later was further elevated to be right vice transmission commissioner. Early in 1560 he received the post of governor of Feng-yang 鳳陽. He immediately proceeded to reorganize the defense of his territory in anticipation of another wave of invasion by the pirates. Already seriously ill, on his journey to the south he died aboard a ship near the confluence of the Grand Canal and the Yangtze. Some seventy years later he was accorded the posthumous name Hsiang-wen 襄文.

T'ang's biographers list his publications under six headings entitled *Tso-pien* 左編, *Yu* 右-*pien*, *Wen* 文-*pien*, *Wu* 武-*pien*, *Ju* 儒-*pien* and *Pai* 稗-*pien*. But neither is the list inclusive nor do all the titles exactly correspond to those appearing on the book covers. Notably the *Ching-ch'uan wen-chi* and *wai-chi* 外集 are omitted. The *Ssu-k'u* catalogue lists twelve works written or compiled by him. The complete title of *Tso-pien* is *Shih-tsuan* 史纂, *tso-pien*, 124 *ch.* A book dealing with historical events, it also includes sections on hermits, nonconformists, jugglers, Buddhist and Taoist priests. In the preface the author acknowledges the influence of the Han historian Ssu-ma Ch'ien. The *Yu-pien* is alternatively designated as *Tu-shih* 讀史 *yu-pien*, 40 *ch.* The work which is a collection of historical documents was not completed in T'ang's lifetime. The manuscript fell into the hands of Chiao Hung (ECCP) who brought it to completion with the editorial help of Chu Kuo-chen (*q. v.*). The *Wen-pien*, 64 *ch.*, which is not to be confused with T'ang's own *wen-chi*, is a collection of prose written by literary figures from the Chou to the Sung, arranged according to the style of writing. The current edition of *Wu-pien* is known as *Ching-ch'uan wu-pien*, 12 *ch.* It is divided into two parts.   The first   (6 *ch.*) deals with military technology and equipment. In *chüan* 6, there are several interesting illustrations of weapons including western firearms (西洋砲). The second part deals with military strategy. A copy of this work is available at the Library of Congress. The *Ju-pien* is a shortened designation of the *Chu-ju yü-yao* 諸儒語要, 20 *ch.*, a collection of essays and dialogues of twelve philosophers starting with Chou Tun-i (1017-73) and ending with Wang Shou-jen. The Library of Congress has another edition of this work in 14 *chüan* under the title *Ching-ch'uan ching-hsüan p'i-tien yü lu* 精選批點語錄, printed in 1571. The *Ching-ch'uan pai-pien*, 120 *ch.*, published by one of his disciples, was intended to be an encyclopedia, but it also includes passages of essays and poems. Critics point out that there are numerous errors in it. Rare copies (printed 1581) are in both the Library of Congress and the Harvard University library. The former has in all twelve works listed under Tang's authorship.

Although T'ang is not considered an outstanding historian, he published two volumes of historical commentaries, *Liang Han chieh-i* 兩漢解疑, 2 *ch.*, and *Liang Chin* 晉 *chieh-i*, 1 *ch.* In addition, two works dealing with contemporary events carry his name as author. The *Kuang-yu chan-kung lu* 廣右戰功錄, 1 *ch.*, describes the military operations conducted against the native tribes in Kwangsi by one of the generals of Wang Shou-jen. The *Nan-pei feng-shih chi* 南北奉使集, 2 *ch.*, is a collection of his memorials, memoranda, and poems connected with his official assignments to Chi-chou and Chekiang, apparently published posthumously. Aside from all of these, several other minor works are credited to his authorship, though of doubtful authenticity. Most of T'ang's works are extant, several of them being included in different collectanea. One of them, the *Shao-wei t'ung chien* 少微通鑑, 20 *ch.*, was proscribed in the 18th century, but it too has survived,

He included in his *wen-chi* several articles on mathematics, such as a discourse on the Pythagorean theorem and its applications, another on circle measurements, and one on simple simultaneous equations and common multiples. Even this elementary achievement won some acclamation for him because in the Ming dynasty mathematical studies, which had developed to a high point in the early 14th century, were no longer actively pursued (*see* Ch'eng Ta-wei, ECCP).

Bibliography

1/205/20b; 5/63/103a; 63/26/1a; MSL(1965), Shih-tsung, 2365, 3464, 3741, 4593, 4916, 7828, 7850, 7906, 7918, 7924, 7932, 8017, 8060; *Ch'ang-chou* 常州-*fu chih* (1884), 23/53a; SK (1930), 53/7a, 56/11a, 65/3b, 90/1b, 96/4b, 99/5a, 107/5b, 136/1b, 172/5a, 177/6b, 189/4b; *Ching-ch'uan hsien-sheng wen-chi, wai-chi* (SPTK); *Ching-shih wen-pien* (1964), 2735; *Chung-kuo wen-hsüeh-shih* 中國文學史 (Peking, 1959), III, 191; Ch'iu K'ai-ming 裘開明, CHHP, n. s. II: 2 (June, 1961), 97; Sun Tien-ch'i (1958), 38; Ping-ti Ho, *Studies on the Population of China*, 1368-1953(1959), 103; Joseph Needham, *Science and Civilization in China*, III (Cambridge, 1959), 51, 105; L. of C. *Catalogue of Rare Books*, 91, 192, 282, 453, 468, 710, 944, 1084, 1094; W. Franke, *Sources*, 6. 6. 6, 7. 5. 5.

Ray Huang

T'ANG Yin 唐寅 (T. 伯虎, H. 子畏, 六如), April 6, 1470–January 7, 1524, painter and poet, was a native of Soochow, the son of a restaurateur. He showed two outstanding traits in his personality early in life. First, he was unusually bright and versatile. Second, he led a carefree life, drinking excessively. In his youth he and his neighbor and good friend, Chang Ling 張靈 (T. 夢晉), who later also became a painter, were known for their profligacy. Fortunately, perhaps because of his intelligence, he came under the guidance of a well-known scholar in Soochow, Wen Lin, father of the great artist, Wen Cheng-ming (*q.v.*). Through Wen Lin the literary world of Soochow seems to have opened up for him. Chu Yün-ming (*q.v.*) became a close friend and remained so throughout his life. He also became acquainted with some of the influential men of the city, such as Shen Chou, Wu K'uan (*qq.v.*), and the prefect Ts'ao Feng (*see* Shen Chou). All these connections assured him apparently a bright future.

A series of misfortunes befell him when he was around the age of twenty-four. During the year 1493/94, his father, mother, wife, and sister died one after the other, leaving only himself and a younger brother. His father does not seem to have left much for the two sons. After this family tragedy, T'ang Yin changed his ways. Admonished by his friend Chu Yün-ming, he shut himself up for a whole year to concentrate on his studies. When the mourning period was over, he participated in the provincial examination of 1498 and won first place.

Prior to the metropolitan tests in 1499, T'ang Yin came to know Hsü

Ching 徐經 (d. 1519), a rich man's son, who was also heading for the capital for the same purpose. In Peking, because of his penury, T'ang depended on Hsü for high living. Hsü, who does not seem to have had much confidence in his own ability to place, is said to have bribed the servant of one of the two chief examiners, Ch'eng Min-cheng (q.v.), to get hold of the questions, and then to have shared them with T'ang. Actually Ch'eng had already received reports about T'ang from the official examiner in Nanking, Liang Ch'u (q.v.). Before long the matter came to light and was reported to the emperor. As a result, T'ang Yin and Hsü Ching were thrown into jail, and the examiner Ch'eng likewise (May 31). For T'ang, who was regarded as a leading figure among the hopefuls in the examination, this was a shattering blow, for it meant the end of any official career. Although after release he was offered a petty position in Chekiang, he declined and returned to Soochow.

According to Chu Yün-ming who wrote T'ang's epitaph, the latter traveled extensively in this period, south to Fukien and west to Szechwan, as a way to forget his troubles. This has been disputed recently by Chiang Chao-shen 江兆申, however, who thinks that this was Chu's way of disguising his friend's depression after the disaster, for T'ang actually would not have had the means to take such lengthy journeys. In disgrace and frustration, T'ang found little outlet for his talents, and gave himself entirely to drinking and the bohemian life. He divorced his second wife, and became quite cynical, sometimes using in his poetry extremely colloquial expressions as a means to shock the public. When Wen Cheng-ming reproached him for his ways, he retorted rudely, almost breaking up their friendship. Still he needed to support himself. It was probably about this time, around 1500, that he began to study painting under Chou Ch'en (q.v.), thinking of using this art to earn his livelihood.

Soon his fame in this medium rose to such an extent that reportedly Chou Ch'en was asked to paint for him in order to fill his commissions. Later, around 1505, he seems to have done so well that he was able to build a villa on the Peach Blossom Embankment in Soochow.

In 1514 Chu Ch'en-hao, the prince of Ning (see Wang Shou-jen), an ambitious man who was planning to rebel, after hearing about T'ang's talents invited him to join his staff in Nanchang. Glad to have this opportunity, T'ang accepted the position, and enjoyed himself with visits to some of the famous mountains and lakes in Kiangsi, such as Mt. Lu 廬山. When, however, he discovered the prince's real intentions, he tried to disengage himself. He feigned madness, drinking heavily and causing all kinds of embarassments. Eventually, deciding that T'ang was too unruly to be of any use to him, the prince let him go.

In his later years, back in Soochow, he became quite famous. Many more of the leading men of the area, both scholars and artists, were numbered among his acquaintances. His daughter married the son of Wang Ch'ung (q.v.), also a poet and painter. On the other hand, his indulgence in wine and women, often with Chu Yün-ming as companion, became excessive. Many anecdotes about his brawls, his escapades with prostitutes, his mischievous tricks on friends and prominent literati, were the talk of the town. As a result, T'ang gradually became known in the popular media as a colorful, frivolous, and comic hero involved in a whole series of romantic attachments. The most famous story about him is the "San hsiao yin yüan" 三笑因緣 (Romance of the three smiles), the theme of which developed into a drama, T'an-tz'u 彈詞, and short stories. Later scholars have shown that T'ang's name was substituted in the story for that of a character in a play which originated during the Yüan. In spite of this, the legend spread his fame in later Chinese literature.

Toward the end of his life, to lament his own fate, he carved a seal for himself with the characters "Chiang-nan ti-i feng-liu ts'ai-tzu" 江南第一風流才子 (The foremost rake south of the Yangtze River). He also turned to Buddhism, and took the pseudonym Liu-ju 六如 (Six likes), a term borrowed from the *Diamond Sūtra*. Because of his reckless life, his health suffered and he died at the age of nearly fifty-four. T'ang is known as a poet, calligrapher, and painter. As a poet, his name came to be bracketed with those of Chu Yün-ming, Wen Cheng-ming, and Hsü Chen-ch'ing (*q.v.*) as one of the "Four Talents of Wu" 吳中四子. A translation of one of his poems appears in *The Penguin Book of Chinese Verse*. His poems and essays were assembled in one volume, *T'ang Po-hu ch'üan chi* 伯虎全集, first brought together in 1534, not long after his death. Additions were made in 1592, 1607, 1614, and finally in 1801. The last edition includes his poems, essays, and other writings, and also some of the biographical accounts and other episodes in Ming and Ch'ing informal writings, as well as the book on painting which he is supposed to have edited. Among his best-known writings are three letters which he addressed to his friend Wen Cheng-ming, lamenting his fate.

T'ang's greatest claim to fame undoubtedly lies in his painting. He is generally regarded as one of the "Four Masters of the Ming," together with Shen Chou, Wen Cheng-ming, and Ch'iu Ying (*q. v.*), each with his own distinctive style. As a professional painter, T'ang was generally quite eclectic. Wang Shih-chen (*q. v.*) writes about his painting: "Po-hu has very high ability. From Li Ch'eng, Fan K'uan, Li T'ang, Ma Yüan, and Hsia Kuei of the Sung to such masters as Chao Meng-fu, Wang Meng (*q.v.*), Huang (Kung-wang) of the last dynasty [Yüan], he studied them and understood them all. His handling of the brush is elegant and rich as well as cautious and precise, but full of consonance at the same time." T'ang's painting, typical of the Ming approach, does not have so much direct contact with nature as that of the artists of Sung and Yüan. His work reflects his knowledge of the past and his blending of various elements from the earlier masters into one. In scope, his works range from the more eclectic paintings, which must have derived from those of Chou Ch'en, to the more literati works close to those of Shen Chou and Wen Cheng-ming.

Among some two hundred extant works attributed to T'ang's hand, the most interesting are those scattered in various museums, such as the Palace Museum, Taipei, and others in mainland China. The outstanding piece in sheer skill among his early works is "Chiang-nan nung-shih t'u" 江南農事圖 (Farming in Chiang-nan) in the Palace Museum. It is characterized by its exquisite, minute brushwork on paper, a unique piece. Typical of his middle period under the strong influence of Chou Ch'en is a group of hanging scrolls now on the mainland and published in the *T'ang Liu-ju hua chi* 畫集, reprinted by Chiang Chao-shen. They include "Mao-wu feng-ch'ing 茅屋風清 t'u" (Thatched cottage in clear wind), "Kao-shan ch'i-shu 高山奇樹 t'u" (Lofty mountains and rare trees), "Hsüeh-shan hsing-lü 雪山行旅 t'u" (Traveling in snowy mountains), "K'an-ch'üan t'ing-feng 看泉聽風 t'u" (Looking at the waterfall and listening to the wind), and "Pao-ch'in kuei-lai 抱琴歸來 t'u" (Returning home with lute). The "Han kuan hsüeh-chi chou" 函關雪霽軸 (Clearing after snow in a mountain pass) in the Palace Museum also belongs to this group. A more mature style is shown in the following paintings, probably belonging to the period when he was forty years of age: "Lo hsia ku-wu 落霞孤鶩 t'u" (Pavilion of the prince of T'eng) on the mainland, and "Shan-lu sung-sheng 山路松聲 t'u" (Whispering pines on a mountain path), and "Hsi-chou hua-chiu 西洲話舊 t'u" (Exchanging reminiscences in Hsi-chou), both in the Palace Museum. While the group of works printed when he was between thirty and forty are characterized by their eclecticism in modeling after the pattern of both Northern and Southern Sung, but with more stylized rocks and trees, the later works show some of the same tendencies, but are more relaxed in brushwork and in treatment. In his last years, however, his best works are those exhibiting a more literati approach, such as "Chen-tse yen-shu 震澤烟樹 chou" (Trees in the mists of Lake T'ai), "Ts'ai lien 採蓮 t'u" (Gathering lotus), dated 1520, and "Kao-shih 高士 t'u" (A scholar), all in the Palace Museum. The last was modeled after Liang K'ai (fl. 1204), in which the very free and sketchy brushwork of the painter is imitated.

T'ang was also known for his portrayal of courtly ladies, a tradition that goes back to such eighth-century artists as Chou Fang and Chang Hsüan. Several paintings in the Palace Museum illustrate this: "T'ao Ku tseng-tz'u 陶穀贈詞 t'u" (T'ao Ku presents a poem), "Fang T'ang-jen shih-nü" 倣唐人仕女 (Figures in the T'ang style), and "Pan-chi 班姬 t'uan-shan 團扇 t'u" (Lady Pan holds the autumn fan).

As indicated above T'ang Yin is also known to have compiled a book on painting, called *Liu-ju chü-shih hua p'u* 居士畫譜, with treatises on painting from T'ang, Sung, and Yüan writers. Sometimes it appears as one of his collected works, such as the one mentioned above, but sometimes it is printed either as a separate volume or as a part of books of treatises on painting. It is, however, now generally considered to be by another hand.

Bibliography

1/286/16b; 5/115/48a; 64/乙11/14a, 丁11/17b; 84/丙/48b; MSL (1964), Hsiao-tsung, 147/9b, 148/2a, 149/9b, 151/1a; Han Ang 韓昂, *T'u-hui pao chien* 圖繪寶鑑 (*Hua-shih ts'ung-shu* ed.), 6/167; Chiang Shao-shu, *Wu-sheng shih shih* 無聲詩史, *ibid.*, 2/30; Wang Chih-teng, *Wu-chün tan-ch'ing chih*, *ibid.*, 2; Ho Liang-chün, *Ssu-yu-chai ts'ung shuo*, 29; Wang Shih-chen, *I-yüan fu-yen*, 2/48b; *id.*, *Ming shih-p'ing* (*Chi-lu hui-pien* ed.), 2/27b; Yen Hsiu-ch'ing 閻秀卿, *Wu-chün er-k'o chih* 吳郡二科志,

ibid., 6b; Wang Ao 王鏊, *Chen-tse ch'ang yü*, *ibid.*, 27a; Ch'en Chi-ju (ECCP), *T'ai-p'ing ch'ing hua*, 2/6a; Ts'ao Ch'en 曹臣, *She hua lu* 舌華錄 (*Li-tai hsiao-shuo pi-chi hsüan*, Ming), 157; Li Jih-hua, *Tzu-t'ao-hsüan yu cho*, 3/12b; *id.*, *Liu-yen-chai er-pi*, 1/30a; Wang K'en-t'ang, *Yü kang-chai pi-ch'en*, 2/15b; Shen Te-fu, *Wan-li yeh-hu-pien*, 23/1; Lang Feng 閬風, "T'ang Liu-ju p'ing-chuan, "*Ch'ing-hua chou-k'an* 清華週刊, 38:4, 1; Yang Ching-an, 楊靜盦, *T'ang Yin nien-p'u* 年譜, Shanghai, 1947; Wen Chao-t'ung 溫肇桐, *Ming-tai ssu ta hua-chia* 明代四大畫家, Hong Kong, 1960; Chao Ching-shen 趙景深, *T'an-tz'u k'ao-cheng* 彈詞考證, Taipei, 1967; *Min Shitaika Gafu* 明四大家畫譜, Osaka, 1924; Werner Speiser, "T'ang Yin, "OZ, 1935; Osvald Sirén, *Chinese Painting: Leading Masters and Principles*, IV (1956-58), 193; Tseng Yu-ho, "Notes on T'ang Yin," *Oriental Art*, II, 3 (Autumn, 1956), 103; E. J. Laing, *Chinese Paintings in Chinese Publications, 1956-1968* (Ann Arbor, 1969), 191; Chiang Chao-shen, *Studies on T'ang Yin*, in four parts （關於唐寅的研究）, *Palace Museum Quarterly* 故宮季刊, II:4 (April, 1968), 15, III:1 (July, 1968), 33, III:2(October, 1968), 31, III: 3 (January, 1969), 35; James Cahill, "T'ang Yin or Chou Ch'en," *ibid.*, IV: 1 (July, 1969), 23; Chiang Chao-shen, "Additional Comments on a Work by T'ang Yin," *ibid.*, 27; Ku Chieh-kang, "A Study of Literary Inquisition during the Ming," tr. by L. Carrington Goodrich, HJAS, III (1938), 282; A. R. Davis (ed.), *The Penguin Book of Chinese Verse* (Baltimore, 1962), 58.

Chu-tsing Li

TAO-CHI 道濟 (T. 石濤, H. 苦瓜和尙, 枝下叟, 淸湘老人, 大滌子, 瞎尊者, 靖江後人, etc.), died *ca.* 1719, a monk-painter of the early Ch'ing period, was born into a family of high degree. His original name was Chu Jo-chi 朱若極. As a descendant in the twelfth generation of the brother of the founder of the Ming imperial line, he became heir to the Ching-chiang 靖江 princedom and was enfeoffed in Kweilin, Kwangsi. A year after the dynasty came to a close, Tao-chi's ambitious father, Chu Heng-chia (*see* ECCP, p. 200), declared a regency, thereby involving himself in a futile struggle against the prince of T'ang, Chu Yü-chien(ECCP), the reigning prince. At the final debacle, Chu Heng-chia was captured (1646), and died in disgrace. Thus dispossessed, Tao-chi (then between five and ten *sui*), was forced to flee in the company of a faithful servant. They made their way to the neighboring district of Ch'üan-chou 全州, where presumably he had to live incognito, especially after the Ch'ing army reoccupied that area in 1650 (*see* Li Ch'eng-tung, K'ung Yu-te, ECCP). Meanwhile the adolescent Tao-chi developed an interest in art and in Buddhism, two forces that were to mould his life. Before the age of twenty, he had become so well versed in painting, calligraphy, and poetry that he achieved a measure of renown. Partly due to an otherworldly inclination and perhaps also for his personal safety, he became a Buddhist neophyte. About 1662, on arriving at Sung-chiang 松江, near Soochow, he took a new master in the person of Pen-yüeh 本月 (H. 旅庵, d. 1676) under whose guidance he became a devotee of the Ch'an sect. Thereafter he stayed for some time (1666-80) in a monastery on Ching-t'ing-shan 敬亭山 in Hsüan-ch'eng 宣城 (Anhwei), seven years in Nanking (1680-87), and over a decade at Yangchow (1687-97), interrupted by visits to Peking (1689-92) and neighboring provinces, such as Kiangsi and Chekiang. In sum, Tao-chi spent a period of more than thirty years in various places, during which he came again into contact with the world at large, assuming the dual role of monk-painter, for which he is best remembered. Throughout these decades his coterie grew to include a select group of secular associates, whose friendship he dearly cherished. Among the notable figures in his life, the best known and perhaps the most influetial was Mei Ch'ing (*q. v.*) whose death coincided with Tao-chi's fateful break with the sangha. A gifted poet and painter, Mei came to share many of his tendencies and predilections in the creative realm with the younger man, emulating and being emulated in turn. On the other hand, Ch'ü Ta-chün (ECCP) found a community of interest with Tao-chi on the basis of a similar background and views. A third confidant and benefactor, Po-er-tu 博爾都 (fl. 1700), was surpisingly enough a Manchu; his presence loomed large during Tao-chi's sojourn in Peking. It was he who came to Tao-chi's rescue in those years when the latter was faced with financial crisis, after he had emerged from the monastic discipline. Conversely, aloof and inaccessible though Tao-chi was on occasion, harboring a tenacious will and a mocking contempt for the conventional values, he nonetheless won his way into Confucian circles by a disarming ebullience and candor and, in even greater measure, by his achievement in the arts, which reached maturity about this time. During this phase, Tao-chi maintained a delicate balance between monkish duties and artistic pursuits, intermingled with frequent outings and excursions that in themselves were the occasion for so many of his works. Trips to Huang-shan 黃山 were particularly fruitful. With this scenic mountain for his inspiration, Tao-chi ventured in his own way to evoke the natural wonder, simulating, as he is known to have said, the palpitation of "T'ai-chi's quintessence," which had given Huang-shan its sublime form. Of the several versions of his studies of Huang-shan extant today, the album in the Sumitomo collection is perhaps the most famous. Painted sometime between 1667 and 1674, when the master was roaming about its thirty-six peaks, his sense impressions were rendered with such vivid freshness that the album virtually assured him a place in the history of art. Another work, a handscroll in the same collection dated 1699, however, presents a different overtone; this Tao-chi painted when, after a prolonged absence, he conjured up Huang-shan's visual semblance from the depth of tangled memories, suffusing the whole with a lingering scent of nostalgia. To a lesser extent, the picturesque environs of Nanking and Yangchow also drew his attention and gave rise to a number of significant works, now mainly preserved in later copies.

These thirty years, however, were not without dramatic incidents. Among them his encounters with the K'ang-hsi emperor, during the latter's tour of the lower Yangtze valley, were of foremost importance even if they tend to cast Tao-chi in an unfavorable light. Little is known of his first audience with the monarch, which took place at Nanking in 1684. But in the Yangchow sequel of 1689, when meeting the Ch'ing emperor for the second time, the former scion of the Ming house presented himself as a loyal subject, thus shattering the popular myth that portrayed him as a Ming patriot.

Only less important was Tao-chi's meeting with his nemesis, Wang Yüan-ch'i (ECCP), which climaxed his visit to the north. The youngest of the four Wang, Wang Yüan-ch'i was then at the height of his career, radiating his influence and stamping his own impressions on contemporary trends in art; by contrast, the rustic monk was much less known at the capital. Through the efforts of Po-er-tu, these two painters were brought together in 1691 and collaborated in an ink rendering of bamboo and orchid, which may still be seen in a version at the Palace Museum. This courteous gesture, however, could scarcely veil the differences that stemmed from their antithical views on art. For some time Wang Yüan-ch'i had been prone to dismiss the painters of the Yangchow and Nanking regions, branding their freely individualistic as "aberrant manners," and comparing them to the then disgraced Northern School. For his part, the visiting monk also remained adamant in his stand against tendencies toward imitation, which from the days of Tung Ch'i-ch'ang (ECCP) had become orthodox. Where painting assumed the guise of fang 仿, literally "in style of," it tended to foster a reliance on past models and conventions, and, in the process, stifle original expression. As existing evidences show, Tao-chi, while in the north, was openly critical of the prevailing orthodoxy, and attempted to instill an individ-

ualistic spirit into those he came to know. Under the circumstances the meeting with Wang Yüan-ch'i did not end in any meaningful rapport. It did, however, intensify his opposition to the orthodox school, and thereby led him to clarify his own thoughts on art. Out of this came his *Hua-yü lu* 畫語錄, a work of great originality and force, which demonstrates his emergence from mere polemic against the contemporary modes to a new awareness of painting's profound import.

By the time that the *Hua-yü lu* was written, however (*ca.* 1700), Tao-chi was no longer a member of the Buddhist monk-hood. Irked by the unproductivity of Ch'an life, and weary of its rituals, *e.g.*, "waving the duster, wielding the priestly staff, shouting and crying to men and devas···," Tao-chi in 1697 withdrew from the monks' community, bringing to a close several decades of involvement. In lieu of a sacred shrine, the one-time monk substituted a humble dwelling, a ts'ao-t'ang 草堂 (thatched cottage), to give him shelter during his remaining years. By naming it Ta-ti 大滌 and himself Ta-ti-tzu, Tao-chi had in mind the shedding of his clerical past, and by implication the onset of a new life.

Hereafter, in his last phase, Tao-chi appeared in the city of Yangchow as a painting master, garbed in a monk's cap and Confucian robe. For an indigent ex-priest otherwise unequipped to cope with mundane exigencies, it was his art that provided him with a means of subsistence. In art he discerned a purposiveness, a positive value, to which perhaps inspired by Pen Yüeh he gave vent under the concept of I-hua 一畫 (the primordial line). By this is meant, in a teleological vein, the organic order of becoming or the archetype of growth and maturation, *i.e.*, the innate urge for things to evolve in a self-defining and independent way, conceived as a series of release and fulfillment of the latent resources under their command. According to the master, painting, itself a concrete manifestation of

I-hua, should, on one hand, demonstrate the very same process that occurs in nature and display it in visual terms, and, on the other, exert a refining influence upon one's inner being. On the whole, with his emphasis on active realization and its individualistic premises, Tao-chi struck a chord in harmony with the teachings of the resurgent neo-Confucianism.

By this time, the aging master felt with increasing acuteness the impact of the early trauma, which had changed his life. An embittered Tao-chi began openly to lament his woes, unleashing in his later poems years of pent-up emotion, charging the verses with a surging intensity and grief. Anxious to revive his link to the remote past, the master began to sign his works with such signatures and epithets as Tsan's tenth generation descendant 贊之十世孫, referring to Chu Tsan-i 贊儀 (grandnephew of Chu Yüan-chang, enf. 1400, d. 1408), being the second of the Ching-chiang princes, but the first in line to receive his name from the Ming founder. Indeed, the emperor had, by force of edict, charted the genealogical course for the offshoots of each branch of the Chu clan by laying down a verse of twenty characters, to be employed in the names of successive generations of which Tsan is a typical example. In sum, as if in penitence for his betrayal of the 1680s, Tao-chi in the post 1700 era intently and valiantly resumed his rightful heritage, however illusory it had become. He lived on into his seventies in Yangchow and died about 1719.

Of Tao-chi's paintings in existence, only a few may safely be attributed to him, the rest being copies and pastiches occasioned largely by his posthumous rise to fame, i.e., from the 19th century onward. Among them the majority are album leaves, lending weight to a critical appraisal that adjudged the master as considerably more at ease with smaller pieces than with large, monumental compositions. In general, Tao-chi's works shun not only the "sweet ripeness" of an artisan, but also the quality of "bland placidity" that has long been acclaimed as the summit of scholar-painting. Instead Tao-chi favored a "raw and pungent" undertone, with a penchant for discordant effect. His early paintings revealed a refined touch, using brush strokes sparingly to sustain a measured tempo and a faint, austere mood. This is exemplified by the aforementioned Huang-shan album, when Tao-chi was indubitably at his lyrical height. But over the years the master evolved a more forceful and tortuous vision, where a quivering surface and a darkened luminosity were in order, assisted by tensed lineal passages, dense moisture, and atonal modulation. His range also broadened; a perpetual innovator, Tao-chi came to encompass a kaleidoscopic variety of moods and expressions, unsurpassed by any contemporary painter. The last years at Yangchow saw the master producing prolifically, when his own financial needs and the demands made upon him by local collectors kept him working at an unprecedented pace.

Second only to his painting, Tao-chi's calligraphy also earned him a measure of renown. His formal spectrum, in this case, shows a free mixture of the li 隷 script with the "running" and "cursive," ranging from the restrained archaism of his early phase to the bold and seemingly careless style of mature years. An occasional carver of seals, the versatile Tao-chi is still better known for his rockery or garden design, two examples of which are recorded to have been at Yangchow.

Besides the Hua-yü lu, Tao-chi's extant writings consist chiefly of colophons and inscriptions that at one time accompanied (or may still accompany) his paintings. Several collections of such colophons were made during the course of two centuries after his death: the earliest being Ta-ti-tzu t'i-hua shih pa 大滌子題畫詩跋 by Wang I-ch'en 汪繹辰 (T. 陳也, H. 勺亭), a little-known amateur painter and collector of the 1730s and an admirer of the master. Similar collections were made by other editors in later years. To Wang I-ch'en we also owe a manuscript of the *Hua-yü lu* dated to 1731, now in the Nanking Library. The printing of the art treatise, however, did not start until some sixty years later, when the compiler of the *Chih-pu-tsu-chai ts'ung-shu* (*see* Pao Ting-po, ECCP) included it in the miscellany of 1779-80. Another fifty years had to pass before the editors of *Chao-tai* 昭代 *ts'ung-shu* took pains to collate the text, and append to it a series of critical and historical references to Tao-chi, including the "Hsia-tsun-che chuan" 瞎尊者傳, a contemporary impression of the monk-painter, written by Ch'en Ting 陳鼎 (T. 定九, b. 1651) toward the end of his Nanking stay. Several other editions have since followed suit. In 1936 Osvald Sirén attempted a partial—and far from accurate—translation in his *Chinese on the Art of Painting* which remains intact in the 1963 reissue, but did undergo some changes in Sirén's other publications. A German rendition is available in Victoria Contag's *Die Beiden Steine* (1950) and *Zwei Meister Chinesischer Landschafamalerei* (1955); it likewise falls short of critical standard. Recently, Pierre Ryckmans has provided a French translation of *Hua-yü lu* which appeared in *Arts Asiatiques* XIV (1966). Modern annotative efforts include those by Yü Chien-hua 俞劍華 in *Shih-t'ao hua-yü lu* (1962); Chu Chi-hai 朱季海 in *Hua-p'u* of the same year; Huang Lan-p'o 黃蘭波 in *Shih-t'ao hua-yü lu i-chieh* 譯解 (1963); and a full length monograph by Chiang I-han 姜一涵 entitled *K'u-kua ho-shang hua-yü lu yen-chiu* 苦瓜和尚畫語錄研究 (1965) provides us with the most intensive of Tao-chi's art theory so far.

Bibliography

Fu Pao-shih 傅抱石, *Shih-t'ao shang-jen nien-p'u* 上人年譜, Shanghai, 1948; Wen Fong, "A Letter from Shih-t'ao to Pa-ta-shan-jen and the Problem of Shih-t'ao's Chronology," ACASA, XIII (1959), 22; Cheng Wei 鄭爲, "Lun Shih-t'ao sheng-huo hsing-ching ssu-hsiang ni-pien chi i-shu ch'eng-chiu" 論石濤生活行徑思想逆變及藝術成就, WW (1962), 12: 43; Cheng Cho-lu 鄭拙廬, *Shih-t'ao yen-chiu* 研究, Peking, 1961; Kobara Hironobu 古原宏伸, "Shih-t'ao *Hua-yü lu* no ihon ni tsuite," の異本について, *Kokka*, no. 876, March, 1965; Osvald Sirén, *Chinese Painting* (New York, 1956-58), VI, pl. 388-99, VII, 405-12; Victoria Contag and C. C. Wang, *Seals of Chinese Painters and Collectors* (Hong Kong, 1966), 348 and 348a.

[Editors' note: After this was written there appeared an illustrated catalogue of an exhibition of the paintings of Tao-chi, held at the Museum of Art, University of Michigan, August 13-September 17, 1967, entitled *The Painting of Tao-chi, 1641-ca. 1720*, with contributions by Charles H. Sawyer (foreword), Richard Edwards (Tao-chi, the Painter), Jonathan D. Spence (Tao-chi, an Historical Introduction), Wu T'ung (Tao-chi, a Chronology), Sazaki Kozo (Tao-chi, Seals), and Chou Ju-hsi (Tao-chi, a Note on His Writings.]

Ju-hsi Chou

T'AO An 陶安 (T. 主敬), 1312?-October 17, 1368, scholar and early supporter of Chu Yüan-chang, was a native of Tang-t'u 當塗, the seat of T'ai-p'ing 太平 prefecture (Anhwei). He was notable as the first Ming chancellor of the Hanlin Academy and as the principal designer of early Ming court ceremonials. During his childhood, T'ao's family was in difficult circumstances. At the age of five he lost his father and his paternal grandfather died three years after that. He was able, nevertheless, to pursue a literary education. One of his first teachers was the venerable Li Hsi 李習 (d. 1357), who later joined him in the service of Chu Yüan-chang. In 1344 he passed the provincial examination but failed in the metropolitan competition at Peking in 1345 and 1348. Meanwhile he interested himself in governmental affairs and apparently it was his comments on current matters that came to the attention of provincial officials; through their recommendation he was appointed a teaching official. In the autumn of 1348 he taught briefly at Tang-t'u and in the winter of the same year he began a three-year term in the Ming-tao 明道 Academy (Nanking). He kept his widowed mother with him during this period, the better to care for her, aud in 1351 brought her back again to Tang-t'u where he resumed his teaching in the local academy.

The disorders of the great anti-Yüan rebellion spread to T'ai-p'ing in 1352 and a state of emergency was declared in the prefecture. For three years longer, T'ao remained loyal to the Mongol regime. He composed several accounts of military preparations and of victories over the invading rebel forces. Late in 1353 he accepted a new teaching appointment near Shao-hsing, but found that there, too, the local militia were being mobilized. As the end of 1354 he concluded that the rebels could not be suppressed and he finally quit his post and went home.

In July, 1355, Chu Yüan-chang crossed to the east back of the Yangtze and turned south to attack T'ai-p'ing. The city's defenses where overcome and loyalist officials either retreated to continue their resistance or committed suicide. Despite the misconduct of many of his troops, Chu made a good impression on the inhabitants by posting orders against looting and by publicly executing a soldier who had violated his command. Presently, T'ao An and Li Hsi led a group of local dignitaries to greet the victor in his camp. T'ao was allegedly so impressed by the appearance of the future emperor that he said to his companions, "He is no ordinary man; we have found our true lord." In a subsquent conversation he praised Chu for having forsworn the rapacious behavior of other militarists, and encouraged him in his ambition to conquer Nanking (then known as Chi-ch'ing 集慶 and referred to as Chin-ling 金陵), and make it his capital. He pointed out that it had a glorious history as a seat of dynasties and was so situated as to dominate the Yangtze. Chu then appointed Li Hsi prefect of T'ai-p'ing and gave lesser offices to T'ao An, Wang Kuang-yang (q.v.), P'an T'ing-chien 潘庭堅, T'ao's protégé, and Wang K'ai (see

Hu Ta-hai). All except Wang Kuang-yang had served the Yüan at T'ai-p'ing as teaching officials or as minor administrators.

Nanking fell to Chu Yüan-chang in April, 1356, and on July 28 he was acclaimed duke of Wu. T'ao was then given a modest appointment in the new branch secretariat and was soon entrusted with a diplomatic mission, probably to deliver an offer of some kind to Chang Shih-ch'eng (q.v.), then ominously extending his control over the region east and south of Nanking. T'ao's mother died while he was away. On his return, he buried her in T'ai-p'ing, moved his wife and children into Nanking for their safety, and began his three years' mourning. He subsequently held office in the capital from 1358 to 1364. It does not appear that he played an important role in the government there, but he did at least serve Chu Yüan-chang as a kind of court poet, composing occasional pieces celebrating his travels and his victories and lamenting the death in battle of some of his officers. He even went to war occasionally with Chu's army and witnessed the battle of Poyang Lake in the autumn of 1363. His wife died in 1362 and he promptly remarried.

From 1364 to 1367 T'ao held office in several local governments. The collapse of the state of Han (see Ch'en Yu-liang) in the winter of 1363/64 brought many new districts under Chu's authority, and created a sudden demand for additional qualified administrators. T'ao An and Wang Kuang-yang were sent early in 1364 to Kiangsi, where T'ao was prefect of Huang-chou 黃州. At the same time P'an T'ing-chien and Wang K'ai were sent to Chekiang. Tao reportedly won the affection of the people of Huang-chou by his benevolent rule. In the latter part of 1364 he was demoted to serve as magistrate of T'ung-ch'eng 桐城 because of some supposed wrongdoing (salt smuggling by members of his household, according to one account). In February of the following year he was promoted again to prefect of Jao-chou 饒州, leaving a vacancy at T'ung-ch'eng to be filled by Chu Yüan-chang's ill-fated nephew, Chu Wen-cheng (*see* Chu Yüan-chang). At Jao-chou, T'ao persuaded some of the inhabitants to help provide for the defense of the city against an attack by bandits. On this occasion Chu Yüan-chang composed a poem to praise him for having prevented the army officers from executing peasants who had collaborated with the enemy. In 1366 Chu granted him an audience in Nanking. On his return to his post, T'ao was allowed to suspend a local military tax with the result that many Jao-chou people who had moved away now returned to their homes.

In 1367 Chu Yüan-chang anticipated his enthronement by setting his scholars the task of creating the laws, ceremonials, and music for the new regime. In June he re-established the Hanlin Academy under the direction of T'ao An and T'ao's old T'ai-p'ing associate, P'an T'ing-chien. It is said that the new emperor awarded T'ao two parallel phrases as decoration for his gate, reading: "Kuo-ch'ao mo-lüeh wu-shuang shih, Han-yüan wen-chang ti-i chia" 國朝謀畧無雙士，翰苑文章第一家 (without equal as adviser of this dynasty; the first one in essay writing in the Hanlin Academy). Soon afterward, learned officials of the academy and other central government agencies were organized in several specialist groups under the over-all authority of Li Shan-ch'ang (*q.v.*). T'ao was the effective head of the group working on ceremonial, and was specifically responsible for the "great sacrifices." These were the sacrifices to Heaven, Earth, Ancestors, Morning Sun, Evening Moon, and First Farmer, *i.e.* Shen Nung. (Later, the last three were dropped to the second rank of sacrifices.) The *Ming-shih* succinctly describes the method employed by the commission on ceremonial: "In each case, they were able to adduce classical principles as the basis and to consult traditional standards and later refinements... Where compromises were made, the decisions conformed to the emperor's will."

The classical text used was the *Chou-li* (Rites of Chou). Later ceremonial practice was then studied dynasty by dynasty. A reasonable middle way was found to solve the problems raised by contradictory precedents. The work of the commission was presented in the form of several compilations. The first two were undertaken during T'ao's service in the Hanlin Academy. One was the *Chiao-she tsung-miao yen-ko* 郊社宗廟沿革 (Continuity and change in the altars of heaven and earth, soil and grain, and the ancestral temple). This work, in one *chüan*, is summarized in the *shih-lu*, ch. 30. The emperor, in his anxiety about ritual error, was not satisfied, and ordered another and much larger compilation, the *Ts'un-hsin lu* 存心錄 (Record of the constant heart), fragments of which survive in the *Ming-ch'ao k'ai-kuo wen-hsien*. This work was probably completed after T'ao had left the capital, and was presented by a colleague.

T'ao's commission found that the Rites of Chou enjoined sacrifices to Heaven and Earth on altars on the south and north (yang and yin) sides of the city. They also found, however, that, beginning with Wang Mang (d. A. D. 23), the usual practice had been to make a joint sacrifice to both Heaven and Earth on the southern altar. During the Sung dynasty, an effort was made to reinstitute the separate sacrifices, but this ended with the court's move to Hangchow. Chu Yüan-chang was now advised to return to the ancient practice, and altars were constructed according to Han dynasty specifications east of the Nanking city walls. Like many other early plans, this one was soon altered. The emperor decided that Heaven and Earth were analogous to father and mother, and that it was therefore unnatural that they should be served in different places. In 1377 he ordered construction of the Ta-ssu tien 大祀殿 (Great sacrifice hall, usually called the Nan-chiao 南郊, South suburban altar) on the site of the original Altar of Heaven. Here, until the end of his reign, he offered joint sacrifices to Heaven and Earth. A separate altar for the Earth spirit was built north of the outer wall of Peking in 1530 and the joint sacrifice was finally abandoned.

The establishment of sacrifices to the spirits of Soil and Grain proved especially difficult. The first time the rites were performed under the Ming regime on February 25, 1368, the participants were drenched by a heavy rain, and the emperor very nearly executed the ceremonial officials whom he believed responsible for producing this inauspicious result (*see* Chang I). The emperor then embarrassed his advisers by proposing that a roof be constructed over the altars in order to protect them. It fell to T'ao An to expalin to him that, to retain their efficacy, the altars had to be exposed to the forces of nature, and that the Soil and Grain altars of defeated enemies were roofed over for precisely this reason. He suggested instead that the emperor offer the sacrifice in the nearby Hall of Abstinence, Chai Kung 齋宮, in the event of bad weather. T'ao's last contribution to Ming ceremonial may have been in March, when he submitted a memorial in which he argued for the ancient precedent that the emperor should wear five different hats for different sacrificial rites. Chu decided, however, that two hats would be quite enough.

T'ao's service in the capital ended in May, 1368. In that month, the Kiangsi administration vice-commissioner, Wang Kuang-yang, was transferred to Shantung, and T'ao, despite his polite first refusal, was ordered to fill the vacancy. Why T'ao should have been selected is not clear, but it seems possible that the emperor was not altogether satisfied with the performance of the ceremonial experts. T'ao was accused by a censor of certain crimes. Pressed to reveal his source of information, the censor admitted that he was repeating what he had heard "in the streets." The emperor then accused him of engaging in slander and ordered him dismissed from the Censorate. T'ao's acquittal came none too soon; he died at

his post in October. He was posthumously invested with the title duke of Ku-shu prefecture 姑孰郡公. This mark of imperial favor was not enough, however, to protect his sons from being executed at some later date on grounds of corruption. T'ao's collected works survive in the *T'ao hsüeh-shih hsien-sheng wen-chi* 學士先生文集, which was included in the Imperial Library.

Bibliography

1/136/1a; 5/6/48a; 8/9/1a; MSL (1962), T'ai-tsu, *ch.* 3-35; KC (1958), 373; SK (1930), 169/2a; Hsia Hsin 夏炘, *T'ao Chu-ching nien-p'u* 主敬年譜; T'ao An, *T'ao hsüeh-shih hsien-sheng wen-chi*; Hsia Hsieh 夏燮, *Ming t'ung-chien* 明通鑑 (1959), 180, 202.

Romeyn Taylor

T'AO Chung-wen 陶仲文 (original surname P'an 潘; another *ming* 典眞), *ca.* 1481-December 11, 1560, Taoist priest, was a native of Huang-kang 黃岡, Hukuang. He probably started his career as a yamen clerk. Learning about charms and talismans from a fellow provincial, Wan Yü-shan 萬玉山 (original *ming* 福敦), he later made the acquaintance of the Taoist patriarch Shao Yüan-chieh (*q.v.*). During his middle years T'ao appears to have served as a minor official first in Hukuang and then in Liao-yang 遼陽 under the Liaotung regional military commission. On the completion of his nine-year tour of duty in the north he had to report to the capital. Here he stayed with Shao, then wrestling with the problem of exorcizing an evil spirit that had allegedly invaded the palace precincts. Shao gladly turned the reponsibility over to T'ao, who is said to have succeeded with his own charms and holy water. Beginning with this feat T'ao gradually insinuated himself into the confidence of Emperor Chu Hou-ts'ung (*q.v.*), and before long assumed the duties of Shao Yüan-chieh. For example, it is reported that T'ao foretold early in 1539 that the emperor was soon to have a nearly fatal accident. One actually did occur in March when, at a stop in Honan on his way to pay a visit to his father's tomb in Hukuang, a fire broke out in the imperial quarters. The emperor's life was saved by Lu Ping (*q. v.*). There may have been a plot behind this near catastrophe, but the emperor chose instead to recall T'ao's prescience. Meanwhile Shao died and his position passed on to T'ao. In October the emperor titled T'ao an immortal, made him patriarch of Taoism of the state and chief director of the affairs of the central Taoist registry in Peking, and gave honors to his parents and his wife. Again, in the following year, when the young heir apparent, Chu Tsai-jui (*see* Chu Hou-ts'ung) nearly succumbed to smallpox, the emperor credited the prayers of T'ao and other Taoist medical advice with saving his life. In December, 1540, the emperor made T'ao a supernumerary minister of Rites and a junior guardian, and promoted his wife to lady of the first rank.

To remain in the good graces of the throne, T'ao began his frequent donations of cash and cotton cloth (200 bales at a time) to the soldiers on the frontier. He also cultivated the acquaintance of an alchemist named Tuan Ch'ao-yung (*see* Kuo Hsün) who asserted that he could turn base metals into gold and silver; actually he presented several dozen fine gold and silver vessels to the emperor in 1540. T'ao was at this time initiating a plan to flatter the emperor by setting up altars throughout the land where sacrifices might be offered to the god of thunder, for Chu Hou-ts'ung associated himself with this deity. T'ao counted on Tuan to finance the building of the altars, but eventually thought better of the association, and warned the emperor against him. Not long after, Tuan became implicated in a murder, suffered imprisonment, and died in jail (March 29, 1543) without a word on his behalf from T'ao. Tuan's removal from the scene did not end the construction of the altars. As the emperor's one-time principality was at An-lu in Hukuang, and the fact that this was hardly more than

one hundred miles northwest of T'ao's birthplace near Huang-kang, he approved the idea of erecting the grand altar there. In addition, the local shrine of the tutelary god was repaired and later converted into the Wei-ling temple 威靈宮. A year after Tuan's death (August, 1544) the emperor made T'ao junior tutor—a rank which he held concurrently with that of junior guardian. A few months after this (November), following the capture of some Mongol spies, the emperor in gratitude made T'ao junior preceptor, this sign of favor coming as a result of T'ao's erection of an altar in the palace area, invoking the suppression of barbarian invaders (鎮虜 法壇). T'ao now held concurrently, unlike any other figure in the whole history of the Ming, all three titles known as the san ku 三孤 (the three solitaries). The altar was dismantled in the summer of 1551, when relations between the Chinese and the Mongols seemed to have quieted down. It was immediately reerected, however, on word of another invasion by Altan-qaγan (*q.v.*). Meanwhile T'ao was the recipient of still higher honors, possibly because, among other things, he had arranged in 1542 for the construction of a hall of the "thunder-god who protectes the state and enriches the people" (祐國康民雷殿) in the secluded park in the Forbidden City where the emperor chose to reside in 1543; and four years later he received imperial permission to initiate 24,000 followers as Taoist priests. Whatever the reason, the emperor, on September 4, 1547, made him a great officer of the Court of Imperial Entertainments and Pillar of the State, entitled to receive a salary equal to that of a grand secretary. And in May 1550, T'ao became the earl of Kung-ch'eng 恭誠伯, with an annual stipend of 1,200 piculs of grain.

During all these years T'ao and Grand Secretary Yen Sung (*q.v.*) were cementing their alliance. Though they were often accused by certain officials of collusion, the emperor discredited the reports. When in 1542 Hsia Yen (*q.v.*), then senior grand secretary, became vexed over the loss of the emperor's favor, he unwisely took Yen Sung into his confidence, unaware that the latter had plotted with T'ao to ruin him. After Yen succeeded Hsia at the end of 1548 and following the death of the heir apparent (1549), he and T'ao worked to effect the removal of the two surviving princes from the palace, Chu Tsai-ch'uan (*see* Chu Hou-ts'ung) and Chu Tsai-hou (*q.v.*). T'ao advised the emperor that "two dragons (the reigning emperor and his heir the potential ruler) should not see each other." In other words, it would be inappropriate to appoint another heir, for then there would be only one ruler, and the spirits would not keep a jealous eye on the future monarch. This theory suited the emperor very well. He did not like to be reminded of his own poor health by designating a successor when still in middle-age;nor did he especially favor his older son. The scheme of Yen Sung and T'ao finally worked; both princes were obliged to leave the Forbidden City in February, 1553. If the emperor felt any remorse, he must have been gratified when, later in the year, T'ao memorialized that, during the construction of a bridge in Ch'i-ho-hsien 齊河縣, Shantung, a huge dragon bone, several tens of feet in length and weighing a thousand catties, was dredged from the river. T'ao took this to be a sign of heaven's favor, and proposed donating 15,000 taels of silver towards the building of the bridge. The emperor showed his pleasure by ordering a grant from the privy purse, and praised T'ao for his loyalty.

Through all of his twenty odd years as Taoist adviser to the throne T'ao generally remained in the capital. He was well aware of the value of the emperor's protection, although on occasion he went on missions to various Taoist centers of importance. Besides catering to the emperor's Taoist interests, he also ministered to his sexual appetite. T'ao was responsible not only for procuring and compounding the best and most expensive aphrodisiacs, but

also with helping to select (in December, 1552 and September 1555) very young virgins—300 the first time, 160 the second —from whom would be extracted the ingredients necessary for the prescription T'ao demanded. These, together with other potions, may well have been responsible in part for the emperor's weakened condition and eventual demise.

In 1559 T'ao retired to his home in Huang-kang because of failing health, leaving one of his sons, T'ao Shih-en 世恩, to carry on his services at the court. He died a year later, at the age of nearly eighty. Before his death he memorialized his master in the humblest terms, and returned to him the articles fashioned in jade, the embroidered dragon robes, a golden dharma-crown for the patriarch, many vessels of gold, and 10,000 taels of silver, all of which the emperor had given him. At his death the throne accorded him the same honors as had been granted to Shao Yüan-chieh, and awarded him the posthumous title Jung-k'ang-hui-su 榮康惠肅. These were all cancelled on the accession of the new emperor in 1567.

Bibliography

1/307/22a; 3/285/21a; 5/10/70a, 118/148a; 61/160/22a; MSL (1966), Shih-tsung, 4736, 4900, 5343, 5561, 5594, 5731, 5874, 6029, 8160; KC (1958), 3748, 3950; Ku Ying-t'ai (ECCP), *Ming-ch'ao chi-shih pen-mo*, 52/1a, 54/1a; Ch'en Hao 陳鶴 (1757-1811) *Ming chi* 明紀, *ch.* 28-38; Shen Te-fu, *Yeh-hu pien*, 27/30b, *pu-i* 補遺, 1/24b; Hsü Hsüeh-chü, *Kuo-ch'ao tien-hui* (Taipei, 1965), 3/1637; Shen Chieh-fu, *Chi-lu hui-pien* (Shanghai, 1938), 190/13a; TSCC (1885-88), XVIII: 287/5/16a; *Tao-tsang* 道藏, 1065, 8/14b, 26; Wang Shih-chen, *Yen-shan-t'ang pieh-chi* (Taipei, 1965), 6/15a, 7/4b, 10/2b, 11/6a, 14/13b, 15/10a, 41/13a.

Liu Ts'un-yan

T'AO Tsung-i 陶宗儀 (T. 九成, H. 南村, 泗濱老人), 14th century historian and poet, was born into a scholarly family of Huang-yen 黃巖, Chiang-che, but lived most of his life in Sung-chiang松江, near Shanghai. His father, T'ao Yü 煜 (T. 明元, H. 逍奥山人, 白雲漫士, 1286-1358), was employed by the Chiang-che provincial government as a commoner clerk (掾史) in Lan-ch'i 蘭溪, Chiang-yin 江陰, and Sung-chiang (1341 ?), and later served as a head clerk (典史) in Hangchow (*ca.* 1345-52), Kuei-an 歸安 (*ca.* 1352-56), and Shang-yü 上虞 (1356-58). T'ao Tsung-i's mother, Chao Te-chen 趙德眞 (d. 1346), was the daughter of Chao Meng-pen 孟本, a descendant of the founder of the Sung dynasty in the tenth generation.

The birth and death dates of T'ao Tsung-i can only be approximated. It is known that when he was about twenty he took the provincial examination at Hangchow, most likely the one held in 1335, and that he was still living in mid-year 1402. Hence his dates may be given tentatively as *ca.* 1316-*ca.* 1402. The conjecture by Paul Pelliot that he was born about 1320 cannot be ruled out, however.

At the provincial examination T'ao wrote some sharp criticisms of the Mongol regime which caused him to be rejected by the offended authorities. According to some sources he refused from then on to take any more civil examinations and devoted the rest of his life to studying and teaching. This is the kind of description often resorted to by biographers as one way of saying that the biographee failed to pass, or was barred from taking examinations. It seems therefore that if T'ao did refrain from sitting for the examinations it could not have been voluntary. He did not waver in his loyalty to the Yüan emperor, at least not until the fall of the dynasty in 1368. He maintained his interest in writing essays in the examination style for which he was famous as a teacher. Both of his brothers served in the Yüan government; one, T'ao Tsung-ch'uan 傳, as an assistant magistrate and the other, T'ao Tsung-ju 儒 (T. 漢生) as a head clerk (tu-shih 都事, 7A) in the branch court for military affairs of Fukien-Kiangsi province (*ca.* 1365-67).

From the few sketches about Ta'o Tsung-i and from the casual remarks about himself found in his writings, we may piece together these facts and surmises regarding his life. For some twenty years after 1335 he seems to have lived with his father. About 1341, when in Sung-chiang (where his father was temporarily employed) he married a local girl, Fei Yüan-chen 費元珍, the daughter of a wealthy general in charge of the transport of grain by sea. Her mother was the second daughter of the great artist Chao Meng-fu (1254-1322), another descendant in the tenth generation of the first Sung emperor. Thus both T'ao Tsung-i and his wife were descended from Sung T'ai-tsu (Chao K'uang-yin) on the maternal side.

Sometime in 1351 T'ao Tsung-i was recommended for office first by T'ai-pu-hua 泰不華 (Tai Buqa, 1304-52, cs 1321) and then by Ch'ou-lü 丑閭 (cs 1333, d. 1352). It is said that he declined the offers but what may have happened was that both sponsors died before the recommendations went through. When the rebellions that started in 1348 in his native place (*see* Fang Kuo-chen) forced him to look for greater safety, he chose Sung-chiang where the influence of his wife's family afforded some protection. In 1356, after the city was ransacked first by rebels and then by government troops, T'ao moved to Ssu-ching 泗涇, a town halfway between Sung-chiang and Shanghai. Here his students contributed on his behalf to the purchase of a house which became known as the Nan-ts'un ts'ao-t'ang 南村草堂. By the middle of 1356 the area fell under the control of the troops of Chang Shih-ch'eng (*q.v.*) and a period of comparative peacefulness prevailed. A number of refugee artists and men of letters congregated there, and together with T'ao formed a small group called the Chen-shuai hui 眞率會 (Club of candid directness). They enjoyed a season of cultural activities celebrated in their poems, essays, paintings, and books—a body of material that has not yet been fully explored.

At one point a general under Chang Shih-ch'eng summoned T'ao Tsung-i to serve as an adviser, but he declined and was allowed to continue his life of teaching and study. In this way he was spared the fate of many who, as Chang's active supporters, suffered greatly when Chu Yüan-chang took over the country. In subsequent years, T'ao went at least twice to Chu's capital at Nanking. On the recommendation of local officials, T'ao, summoned to appear at court (1373), succeeded in persuading the emperor that he was ill and so obtained exemption from service. During this period his brother, T'ao Tsung-ju, was serving as a secretary in the ministry of Personnel. The second occasion occurred in 1396 when each teacher was required to accompany his students to the capital; there they were examined on their ability to recite the emperor's exhortations on observance of his law presented in the *Ta-kao.* The surmise that he once held some kind of official post between these two visits to Nanking seems plausible but cannot be substantiated. A poem in his collection, the *Nan-ts'un shih-chi* 詩集, 4 *ch.*, bears the date: 29th day, 10th month, *hsin-ssu* year (December 4, 1401). There is also a poem on the floods of the summer of 1402. He probably died soon after that.

The most important work left by T'ao is the collection of miscellaneous notes and essays completed in 1366 under the title *Ch'o-keng lu* 輟耕錄, or *Nan-ts'un ch'o-keng lu*, 30 *ch.* It includes his study notes on art, literature, science, etc., as well as his recording of current events and modes of life; these have proved to be indispensable sources for knowledge and understanding of the late Yüan period, as shown in such works as *Chinese Pictorial Art* by R. H. van Gulik and *Mediaeval Researches* by E. Bretschneider. Records of that time may also be found in his collected poems, *Nan-ts'un shih-chi* and *Ts'ang-lang cho-ko* 滄浪櫂歌, 1 *ch.*, and in his anthology *Yu-chih hsü-pien* 遊志續編, which he compiled about 1376, modeled after a work with a preface dated 1243. Most of the authors of these accounts of tours and excursions were his contemporaries, some acquaintances among them. T'ao himself was a member of one jaunt to the hills east of Nanking, according to a record left by Sun Tso 孫作 (T. 大雅, 次知) in 1373. A manuscript copied by the artist Ch'ien Ku (*q.v.*) in 1561 was reproduced in facsimile by T'ao Hsiang (*see* Ch'eng Ta-yüeh) in 1925.

T'ao culled the materials of interest to him from an extensive number of books in his own and his friends' libraries. He was a noted calligrapher too and compiled a work on famous men who excelled in that art, entitled *Shu-shih hui-yao* 書史會要, 9 *ch.*, printed in 1376. Later he himself added one *chüan* of addenda, and the prince from Nanchang, Chu Mou-yin 朱謀垔 (T. 隱之, H. 厭原山人, fl. 1631), included another supplement. T'ao interested himself also in ancient inscriptions on stone, making a collection of seventy-one items. By giving the full text of each, he thus preserved a number of important documents and biographical data. There are several editions of this collection known by the title *Ku-k'o ts'ung-ch'ao* 古刻叢鈔, of which the original manuscript seems to be still extant. All of these works by T'ao were copied into the 18th century Imperial Library, *Ssu-k'u ch'üan-shu.* T'ao likewise left a collection of exempla, *Ts'ao-mang ssu-ch'eng* 草莽私乘, which preserves some important biographical materials on the two martyrs of the 13th century, Wen T'ien-hsiang (1236-83) and Lu Hsiu-fu (1238-79). This work is accorded a notice in the *Ssu-k'u* catalogue.

Another compilation credited to T'ao is the famous *ts'ung-shu*, *Shuo-fu* 說郛, 100 *ch.*, which includes excerpts from over a thousand books. Some of these books and early editions of others, no longer extant, are represented only by his selections. Unfortunately, by the latter part of the 15th century only some 70 *chüan* of his manuscripts for the *Shuo-fu* remained. About 1481 this imperfect copy came into the possession of a native of Shanghai, Yü Wen-po 郁文博 (cs 1454), who, after adding over one hundred fifty titles taken from various collections, had a number of manuscript copies, each in 100 *chüan*, made for sale. Later, when a movable type edition of the 13th century work, *Pai-ch'uan hsüeh-hai* (*see* Hua Sui), appeared, it became evident that Yü had extracted many items from that earlier work to make up his edition of the *Shuo-fu*. Thereupon he wrote a preface with the date of 1495, in which he told the unlikely story that it was his clerical help who had copied from the *Pai-ch'uan hsüeh-hai* without his knowledge. The assertion that Yü's edition was printed at that time cannot be substantiated even by one printed leaf. On the contrary, the only known copies are all in manuscript made in the 16th century. In 1927, when Chang Tsung-hsiang (BDRC) of the Shanghai Commerical Press published the 100 *chüan* edition of the *Shuo-fu*, consisting of 725 items, he could find no printed edition and consulted six manuscript copies only. When Wang Ch'i (*q.v.*) published his *Pai-shih hui-pien* (1607), he stated plainly that up to that year the *Shuo-fu* had not been printed. It now appears that, among the rare books and manuscripts of the Chinese library at the University of Hong Kong, there is a Ming manuscript copy of the *Shuo-fu* in 69 *chüan*, unknown to Chang Tsung-hsiang, which once belonged to Shen Han 沈瀚 (T. 原約, H. 夷齋, cs 1535). Professor Jao Tsung-i 饒宗頤, who has subjected it to a careful examination, believes that it is a true representation of the original work of T'ao Tsung-i, lacking only a single *chüan*.

Sometime between 1607 and 1620, a bookdealer in Hangchow made printing blocks for the first edition of the *Shuo-fu* containing some twelve hundred items in 120 *chüan*, with a supplement *Shuo-fu hsü* 續, 46 *ch.*, the latter edited by T'ao T'ing 陶珽 (T. 紫闐, H. 不退, cj 1591, cs 1610). It seems that after the two conflagrations of 1621 in Hangchow, the printing blocks, or what remained of them, were sold to several publishers, each printing what he owned under a different collective title. Among such collections of the 1620s may be mentioned *Kuang Han-Wei ts'ung-shu* 廣漢魏叢書, *I-yu pei-lan* 藝游備覽, *Hsi-ch'ao lo-shih* 熙朝樂事, *Pai-ch'uan hsüeh-hai* (*ca.* 1625 ed.), *Hsü pai-ch'uan hsüeh-hai* (Wu Yung 吳永 ed.), and *Kuang* 廣 *pai-ch'uan hsüeh-hai*. A decade or so later someone reassembled these printing blocks and, after readjusting the identifying marks, and adding some new titles, produced another edition of *Shuo-fu*, still 120 *chüan* but listing 1,360 titles, with a *Shuo-fu hsü* of 44 *chüan* and 544 items. Then there appeared another set listing 1,364 items in the *Shuo-fu* and 542 in the *Hsü shuo-fu*. The sets printed after 1644 frequently varied also in the number of titles. The *Shuo-fu* which contains only excerpts and leaves out all prefaces and colophons, demonstrates the most undesirable way of editing a *ts'ung-shu*, which, unfortunately was followed by a number of publishers of later centuries. On this matter, however, T'ao Tsung-i may be excused for he may have made the excerpts only for personal reference. In any case it was probably the 15th century editor Yü Wen-po who was responsible for the format of the *Shuo-fu*. Even less to be excused than Yü were those editors who extracted short pieces from the *Ch'o-keng lu* and printed them as separate works by T'ao. There are twelve such works but they are at least T'ao's own. The following two, however, are attributed to him spuriously: *Hsin-shang-pien* 欣賞編 and *Ch'in-chien t'u-shih* 琴箋圖式.

Bibliography

1/285/17b; 3/266/13a; 5/115/14a; Ch'ien Ch'ien-i (ECCP), *Lieh-ch'ao shih-chi*, 16/27b; *Huang-yen-hsien chih*, *Huang-yen chi* (1877), 2/1a, 3/5a, 5/6b, 9/9b, 13/26a, 21/25b; Ch'ang Pi-te 昌彼得, *Shuo-fu k'ao*考, *Bulletin, China Council for East Asian Studies* (1962), 1-276; *id.*, "T'ao Nan-ts'un nien-p'u ch'u-kao" 年譜初稿, *T'u-shu-kuan hsüeh-pao* 圖書舘學報 (T'ai-chung, 1965?), nos. 7 & 8; *id.*, "T'ao Tsung-i sheng-nien k'ao" 生年考, *Ta-lu tsa-chih*, June, 1963; *Shih-ku t'ang shu-hua hui-*

k'ao (*see* Pien Yung-yü in ECCP), *shu* 21; P. Pelliot in *TP*, XXIII (1924), 163; Yeh Kung-ch'o (BDRC), *T'ao Nan-ts'un shou-hsieh* 手寫 *Ku-k'o ts'ung-ch'ao pa*," *Peiping Library Bulletin*, IV (1930); Wang Ch'i, preface to *Pai-shih hui-pien* (1607 ed.); Sun Tien-ch'i (1957), 249; R. H. van Gulik, *Chinese Pictorial Art* (Rome, 1958), 224, 231; E. Bretschneider, *Mediaeval Researches from Eastern Asiatic Sources* (London, 1888), 669, Nieh Ch'ung-ch'i (comp.), *Index du Tcho Keng-Lou*, Peking, 1950; Jao Tsung-i, "Un inédit du *Chouo-fou*: Le manuscrit de Chen Han, de la période *kia-tsing* (1522-1566),"*Mélanges de Sinologie offerts à Monsieur Paul Demiéville*, I (Paris, 1966), 87.

Peter Chang and Chaoying Fang

TE-CH'ING 德清 (T. 澄印, H. 憨山), November 5, 1546–November 3, 1623, one of the great Buddhist masters of late Ming, was born into an obscure family by the name of Ts'ai 蔡 in Ch'üan-chiao 全椒, some thirty miles west of Nanking. His mother, a devout Buddhist, played an important role in his early education. She believed in the usefulness of Confucian instruction and exercised strict discipline combined with almost evangelical zeal, urging him to aim at a religious vocation. At eleven he left home over the objection of his father, and went to live in the Pao-en monastery 報恩寺 south of the city of Nanking. The abbot, Yung-ning 永寧 (H. 西林, 1483-1565), did not admit him into the order right away but had him continue his literary studies with a lay teacher. For several years Te-ch'ing resided in the monastery and studied a few sūtras; otherwise he lived almost like the Confucian candidates of his district with whom he enjoyed a comradery spiced with literary contests. When he was sixteen, he left school as the result of poor health and difficulties with an uncongenial inspector of schools. The next year, however, Te-ch'ing was tempted by the successess other members of his literary club scored at the local examination. As he wavered he met the priest, Fa-hui 法會 (H. 雲谷, 1500-79)who dispelled his doubts and brought him back to the Buddhist fold. Thereupon he received the tonsure.

His training in the next several years was characteristic of the late Ming ecumenical practice—a mixture of the Pure Land and Meditation (Ch'an) teachings. In 1567 a free school was established in his monastery and he was appointed the teacher. At T'ien-chieh 天界 monastery he made the acqaintance of Fu-teng (*q.v.*), his fast friend throughout his life. Te-ch'ing taught until he was twenty-six, when he decided to travel. His wanderings eventually took him to Peking, where he was befriended by several members of the literati. In 1573 he made his first visit to the sacred mountain, Wu-t'ai in Shansi where he so admired the peak called Han 憨 -shan that he thought some day he might take the name as his sobriquet. Two years later he revisited Wu-t'ai and found the snowy peaks there so much to his liking that he settled down in a hut at Lung-men 龍門, a secluded point near the northern summit. When spring arrived he was no longer at ease, for the strong winds and the thundering torrents dashing from the peaks made the place unbearably noisy. He consulted his friend, Fu-teng, and was told that consciousness of environment came not from outside but arose from the mind. Following instruction, he chose a footbridge over a brook and sat or stood on it every day. As he relates in his autobiography, he at first heard the sound of the water clearly. After a while he reached the point when the sound would become audible only when his mind was not yet subdued. One day as he sat on the bridge he suddenly forgot his own person and the water seemed to be completely mute. From that time on he was no longer bothered by any noise.

Later in the same year he achieved enlightenment. One day after a meal of rice porridge he took a stroll. All of a sudden he stopped and was not aware of his body or mind; there was only something huge and bright, something perfect, full, and silent like a gigantic round mirror, with mountains, rivers, and the great earth reflected in it. After regaining consciousness, he felt relieved of his former doubts and confusions.

The following year he decided to seek confirmation of his experience with enlightenment by reading the *Shou leng-yen ching* 首楞嚴經 (the Śūraṅgama sūtra), a text he had found puzzling. After eight months of sustained effort he came to understand the book entirely. This must have laid the foundation for the several exegetical works he was to write on the sūtra. In the spring of that year the great Buddhist master, Chu-hung (*q.v.*), visited him and remained for ten days. For the next several years Te-ch'ing returned to his secluded retreat from time to time, but it seems that he resided mainly in the T'a-yüan 塔院 monastery, which was situated in a more accessible part of Mount Wu-t'ai.

As Te-ch'ing's fame gradually spread to the rest of the country his name came to the attention of the empress-dowager, Li-shih (*q.v.*), who was a pious Buddhist. In 1577 she selected him as one of the Buddhist monks commissioned by the court to recite sūtras for the benefit of the country. Two years later she sent three thousand craftsmen to rebuild the T'a-yüan temple. Te-ch'ing's fame as a great preacher reached its zenith in the spring of 1582, when his lectures on the *Hua-yen* 華嚴 *ching* (Avataṁsaka sūtra) drew a daily audience numbering more than ten thousand. After he completed the series he left Wu-t'ai in search of a new retreat. In the year following he found in the Chi-mo 即墨 district of Shantung province a secluded and scenic spot between Lao 勞 Mountain and the sea, where he believed he might escape completely from all wordly involvements. It was then that he changed his sobriquet to Han-shan. For several months he camped under a tree until a local lay Buddhist built a hut for him.

The empress-dowager, however, continued to bestow favors on Te-ch'ing. When the emperor in 1586 decided to distribute fifteen sets of the newly enlarged *Tripiṭaka* to various great Buddhist centers, she persuaded him to send one of the sets to Te-ch'ing. To house the scriptures as well as to honor Te-ch'ing, she and her ladies-in-waiting donated money to have a monastery built near his hut on the site of a dilapidated Taoist temple, and later named it Hai-yin ssu 海印寺. Within a year the sanctuary was enlarged and admirers of Te-ch'ing, both lay and secular, began to flock to the new center.

As a result of the favors bestowed on him by the empress-dowager, Te-ch'ing now became more and more entangled in one of the major controversies of the Wan-li period. His involvement had begun in 1581 when he was commissioned by the empress-dowager to pray for the birth of an heir to the emperor. The following year a son was born to a lady-in-waiting (*see* Chu I-chün), but shortly afterwords the emperor became the father of several more sons by other court ladies. The empress-dowager favored the eldest prince; her cause was supported by Te-ch'ing and his friend, the Buddhist master Chen-k'o (*q.v.*), as well as by people at court. The emperor, however, preferred the son born to his favorite, Cheng Kuei-fei (*q.v.*). As years went on and the emperor continued to avoid making a clear choice as to which son should be made heir apparent, the dispute became increasingly acrimonious; several high officials who remonstrated with the emperor were punished. The Cheng faction apparently desired to have Te-ch'ing punished as well. Early in 1595 a eunuch, disguised as a Taoist priest, denounced Te-ch'ing to the emperor, charging him with appropriating a Taoist temple and falsifying the religious register in 1586 so as to receive a set of the *Tripiṭaka* from the emperor. Te-ch'ing was brought to the capital for trial. After spending eight months in jail, he was defrocked and sent to serve as a soldier in the garrison at Lei-chou 雷州, Kwangtung.

The punishment seems to have solidified Te-ch'ing's alliance with the leading neo-Confucianists of his day, and the journey to the south appeared more like a triumphal march. He made many stops either to receive well-wishers or to meet prominent officials, such as Tsou Yüan-piao and Chou Ju-teng (q.q.v.). When he arrived at his destination he found the commanding officers lenient and even respectful. Consequently, in spite of his sentence, he was free to continue writing, lecturing, and traveling about the south. In 1600 he was invited to stay in the Nan-hua 南華 ssu at Ch'ü-chiang 曲江, about 120 miles north of Canton. That monastery, once headed by the sixth patriarch of Ch'an Buddhism, is also known as Ts'ao-hsi 曹溪, the famous site of the Ts'ao-tung 洞 sect. Te-ch'ing introduced many reforms there. When in 1603 the heir apparent controversy flared up again resulting in the imprisonment and death of Chen-k'o, Te-ch'ing, though not implicated, was ordered to return to Lei-chou. In 1605 the birth of a son to the heir apparent, who had formally been granted the title in 1601, occasioned a general amnesty, which restored Te-ch'ing to civilian status. He returned to Ts'ao-hsi to continue with the renovation of the monastery. In 1611, when he was sixty-five years of age, he received a full pardon.

Old age diminished neither his power as a preacher, nor his productivity as an exegetist; his wanderlust too continued. Universally revered, he was constantly surrounded by admirers wherever he traveled. In the last several years of his life he completed the commentaries on the Shou-leng-yen ching, the Ch'i-hsin lun 起信論 (The awakening of faith), and the Hua-yen ching. Early in 1623 he returned to Ts'ao-hsi. He wrote his autobiography before he began a series of lectures on basic Buddhist scriptures. He also wrote a biography of his old friend, the great monkish architect, Fu-teng. Taken ill late in the autumn, he refused medication but prepared himself for the end.

In many ways Te-ch'ing exemplifies the contemporary intellectual climate in general and late Ming Buddhism in particular. True to the spirit of syncretism, he not only wrote commentaries on the sūtras associated with different Buddhist schools but also extended his exegetical efforts to such Confucian and Taoist texts as the Ta hsüeh, the Tso chuan, the Tao-te ching, and the Chuang-tzu. In monastic discipline he emphasizes equally the nien-fo 念佛 (chanting the Buddha's name) of the Pure Land school and the meditation of the Ch'an school. It was no accident that his friends ranged from the leading Buddhists of his day to prominent Confucianists like Kao P'an-lung (q.v.), Tsou Yüan-piao, and Ch'ien Ch'ien-i (ECCP). The last indited an inscription (塔銘) for him and was instrumental in bringing out his collected works in 1657, the Han-shan lao-jen meng yu chi 老人夢遊集, containing his letters, poems, and most of his prose pieces, 55 ch. His two studies on the Śūraṅgama-sūtra, probably his most important religious contribution, were reprinted together under the title Ta fo-ting shou-leng-yen ching t'ung-i 大佛頂首楞嚴經通義 (Shanghai, 1894). His autobiography, written in the form of a chronological record, was first published in 1651 with annotations and a supplement prepared by his disciple Fu-cheng 福徵. A slightly different version is included in the collected works under the title, Han-shan lao-jen tzu-hsü nien-p'u shih-lu 老人自敘年譜實錄. The first Chinese Buddhist monk to have written such an autobiography, Te-ch'ing made innovations in the nien-p'u form by giving detailed attention to childhood, by arranging events in such a way that a pattern of gradual conversion emerges, and by recording his intensely personal spiritual experience.

Bibliography

MSL (1966), Shen-tsung, 5291; Ku Ying-t'ai (ECCP), Ming-ch'ao chi-shih pen-mo, ch. 67; Han-shan ta-shih 大師 nien-p'u su-chu 疏注, Taipei, 1967; Chi Wen-fu 嵇文甫, Wan-Ming ssu-hsiang *shih lun* 晚明思想史論 (Chungking, 1944), 90.

Wu Pei-yi

TENG Mao-ch'i 鄧茂七 (original *ming* 雲),
died April 9, 1449, was the ring leader
of an insurrection that ravaged a large part
of Fukien from 1448 to 1449. Teng's origin
is not clear. Official records state that he
was a native of Sha 沙-hsien, Fukien,
that he and his brother Teng Mao-pa 八
were tenant peasants who later served as
chiefs of the local security force. Other
accounts hold that he was originally from
Chien-ch'ang 建昌, Kiangsi, that he fled
to Ning-hua 寧化, Fukien, after committing
a criminal offense, and that he changed
his name. There are also reports that he,
like his notorious contemporary Yeh
Tsung-liu (*q. v.*), was at one time involved
in the illicit exploitation of the government silver mines. The fact that the Teng
brothers had served in the local security
force was important to the uprising in its
initial stage. These forces were created
in 1446 in many districts of Fukien upon
the recommendation of Censor Liu Hua
柳華 (T. 彥輝, cs 1430) as a means to
ensure order. Members of the team were
recruited from among the peasants and
were trained in the use of weapons. That
the Teng brothers rose from the security
force meant that they had easy access to
the arsenal and possessed an intimate
knowledge of the local conditions at the
time of their uprising.

The brothers were known for their
rash and rebellious nature. According to
custom, tenant peasants were obliged to
send seasonal gifts to the landlord in
addition to regular rent payment in grain,
but they refused to comply and incited
their fellow villagers to follow their example. The landowners, alarmed, brought
the case before the local magistrate who
immediately ordered their arrest. The ten-
ants refused to give in and, taking the
arms supplied them, clashed with the
security force and killed a number of
government soldiers.

In March, 1448, shortly after the
incident, Teng rallied around him a band
of disaffected villagers. After swearing a
blood-smearing oath, he proclaimed himself
the king of Min (閩王), known as Ch'an-
p'ing wang 剗平王 (king of extermination),
created an official hierarchy, and staged
an uprising. In time he attracted tens
of thousands of peasants and miners, who
came out openly as organized outlaws. The
information about Teng's area of operation
varies. Official records state that the trouble
initially flared up in Sha-hsien and later
extended to neighboring districts. Other
sources aver that it started from Ning-
hua, then spread northeast to Sha-hsien,
after looting several districts on the way.
In September the bandits ravaged Yen-
p'ing 延平, inflicting heavy casualties on
the government forces, then continued
their pillaging into the neighboring districts. The local authorities, however,
succeeded in keeping the population from
siding with the rebels by acceding to
their request for a three-year exemption
from corvée labor.

In September, 1448, alarmed at the
insurgency, the court ordered Chang K'ai
張楷 (T. 正之, 1398–1460, cs 1424), associate censor-in-chief, to head a punitive
expedition against the bandits. Chang,
however, proved to be a mediocre commander, timid, and afraid of responsibility.
Mobilizing his forces from Kiangsi, he
was blocked from entry into Fukien on
the border of Ch'ien-shan 鉛山 by the
band of Yeh Tsung-liu, who was reportedly communicating with Teng and his
men. At this point Han Yung (*q. v.*), then
a censor in Kiangsi, urged Chang to take
immediate action against them. After
much vacillation and indecision, Chang
dispatched a division to meet the challenge
and succeeded in quelling them. He failed,
however, to confront Teng Mao-ch'i. Instead of pursuing the insurgents, Chang
dallied in Chien-ning 建寧 -fu, indulging
in merrymaking, and imposing unlawful
exactions on the population. In December,

despairing of Chang's inaction, the court ordered Earl Ch'en Mou (*see* Esen Tügel), to head a punitive force of fifty thousand men recruited from Chekiang and Kiangsi.

Before the reinforcements arrived, the local authorities had made substantial gains in the field. In January, 1449, they succeeded in stopping Teng's band near Chien-yang 建陽, inflicting heavy losses on them. At this point the censor of Fukien, Ting Hsüan 丁瑄 (d. *ca.* 1550), secured the defection of a headman; with his assistance, Ting set a trap for the outlaws in Yen-p'ing. At the end of February, Teng and his fellow leaders were captured in an ambush; they were subsequently sent to Peking for public execution (April 9). The insurgents, however, were not completely crushed; under their new leader, Teng Po-sun 鄧伯孫, remnants of them remained active in several districts. Jealous of the success of the local authorities, Chang K'ai hurried to Yen-p'ing, and forced his subordinates to change the content of the report to show that it was he who devised the strategy and should have the credit for the suppression. Disgruntled, Ting later referred the case to the court.

In the meantime, the forces of Ch'en Mou arrived and steps were taken to suppress Teng Po-sun and his band, who by then had retreated into the mountains near Sha-hsien. Utilizing similar tactics, the commander adopted a policy of pacification and successfully induced the surrender of several headmen, whose defection further weakened the rebels. Early in May the government forces raided their quarters in Sha-hsien and captured Teng Po-sun alive, along with other bandit leaders. The remaining rebels, however, continued to harass the province and were not completely crushed until the following year.

Because of his inept performance, Chang K'ai became a target of attack. In November, upon his return to the capital, Chang was charged by the censors with falsifying the report so as to assume the credit for the successful operation, and was subsequently stripped of his title by Emperor Chu Ch'i-yü (*q. v.*). When Emperor Chu Ch'i-chen regained the throne in 1457, however, he forgave Chang and restored his title. To save face Chang later composed a chronicle of the expedition called *Chien-chün li-lüeh* 監軍曆略, in which he sought to excuse his failure by conjuring up a different picture of the incident. This account is included in *Huang Ming ching-chi wen-lu* by Wan Piao (*q. v.*) and other Ming collections; because of his biased treatment, it should be consulted with caution as a source for study of the insurrection.

The uprising appears to have been the product of rural unrest due to social inequities and economic hardship compounded by official corruption, and the discontent of the miners under the existing regulation of quota fulfillment, while the agitation of the criminal elements goaded them into action. The disregard for the plight of the population, the laxity of local security, coupled with the ineptness of such leaders as Chang K'ai charged with suppression, account for the prolonged duration of the rebellion. In determining the causes, oddly enough, the censors found fault with Liu Hua for having set up the local security force which supplied arms for the rebels. Liu, who by then had passed away, escaped being made a scapegoat, but his descendants were punished for the blunder of their ancestors.

In an effort to rehabilitate the displaced population, the court ordered a temporary cessation of tax collection and corvée labor in these areas, as well as reduction of the output quota imposed on the miners (*see* Yeh Tsung-liu). In addition, the court turned its attention to the corruption of local administrators, and ordered that henceforth all land illegally seized by the wealthy families should be returned to the owners. The inequities which had burdened the tenant farmers to open revolt nonetheless stood uncorrected in the ensuing years.

Bibliography

61/161/13a; MSL (1963), Ying-tsung, ch. 169-193; KC (1958), 1744, 1763; Chou Ting 周鼎 (1401-87), *T'u-chü chi* 土苴集, *fu-lu* 附錄, 5a (in *Han-fen-lou pi-chi* 涵芬樓秘笈, vol. 7); Huang Yü (*see* Huang Tso), *Shuang-huai sui-ch'ao*, 6/11b; Chang Hsüan, *Hsi-yüan wen-chien lu*, 36/18b, 98/15a; Wan Piao, *Huang Ming ching-chi wen-lu*, ch. 21; Cha Chi-tso(ECCP), *Tsui-wei lu* (SPTK, 3d ser.), *lieh-chuan* 列傳, 31/10a; Ku Ying-t'ai (ECCP), *Ming-ch'ao chi-shih pen-mo* (preface 1658), 31/1b; Hsü T'ien-tai 徐天胎, "Ming-tai Fu-chien Teng Mao-ch'i chih luan" 明代福建鄧茂七之亂, *Fu-chien wen-hua chi-k'an* 福建文化季刊, 1:4 (1941), 11; Li Lung-ch'ien 李龍潛, "Ming Cheng-t'ung chien Yeh Tsung-liu Teng Mao-ch'i ch'i-i ti ching-kuo chi t'e-tien" 明正統間葉宗留鄧茂七起義的經過及特點, *Li-shih chiao-hsüeh* 歷史教學 (1957), no. 3, 11; Tanaka Masatoshi 田中正俊, "On the Historical Records Concerning the Rebellion of Teng Mao-ch'i" (in Japanese), in *Studies on the Ming Period Presented to the Late Taiji Shimizu* (Tokyo, 1962), 637; Ku Chieh-kang, "A Study of Literary Persecution during the Ming," tr. by L. Carrington Goodrich, HJAS III (1938), 308.

Hok-lam Chan

TENG Yü 鄧愈 (original name: Yu-te 友德), March 17, 1337-December 9, 1377, a native of Hung 虹-hsien, Ssu-chou 泗州 (Anhwei), was one of the leading generals under Chu Yüan-chang. His father, Teng Shun-hsing 順興, was one of the minor rebels who joined Kuo Tzu-hsing (*q.v.*) in occupying Hao-chou 濠州 early in 1352, but was soon killed in action, and the leadership of his band passed on to Teng Yü, then fifteen years of age. He held it together by his courage in battle, but was not successful in developing an independent power. His movements over the next three years are not clear.

Early in 1355 Kuo Tzu-hsing died and his leading subordinates fell out. Teng Yü, realizing that he could not stand alone and preferring to deal with the strongest (Chu Yüan-chang, based on Ch'u 滁-chou), marched south from Hsü-i 盱眙 to join him, and was given the rank of kuan-chün tsung-kuan 管軍總管, perhaps indicating that he commanded about one thousand men. In this capacity he proved his mettle in the crossing of the Yangtze River and in the campaigns of 1355 and 1356. After the collapse of Kuang-te 廣德 (July, 1356), subsequently renamed Kuang-hsing 興-fu, he was appointed commander of the newly installed local military command. Having successfully defended this city against the attack of Yüan troops (December), he was ordered south, overrunning Chi-ch'i 績溪. He then joined forces with Hu Ta-hai (*q.v.*) and took Hui 徽-chou, where he was given command of the city with the rank of assistant magistrate of a branch of a chief military commission.

A month previously, while Hu Ta-hai was still in the vicinity, Hui-chou had been besieged by Yang Wan-che (*see* Chang Shihch'eng), the Miao general who had for so long been the main support of the Yüan regime in Chekiang. Teng defended the city until the arrival of the reinforcements of Hu Ta-hai, and succeeded in routing the enemy. In February, 1358, Teng took Wu-yüan 婺源, whereupon the southwestern segment of Nan-Chihli came under Chu Yüan-chang's control. After this Teng was ordered to join the forces of Hu Ta-hai and Li Wen-chung (*q.v.*) to invade Chekiang. They did not go by the obvious route (directly downstream from Hui-chou) but instead marched over the mountain passes, capturing Sui-an 遂安 and Ch'un-an 淳安, finally arriving in Chien-te 建德 (April) to find that the Yüan defenders had abandoned the city. In June Yang Wan-che counter-attacked but was again repulsed with heavy losses. For this performance Teng was promoted to be an assistant commissioner of the chief military commission (October). Early in 1359 Teng led his troops to raid the cities west of Hangchow. Hu besieged and captured Wu 婺-chou (modern Chin-hua 金華) in central Chekiang. After Chu Yüan-chang's victory in 1360 over Ch'en Yu-liang (*q.v.*) in the region of Nanking, the latter's subordinates holding cities east of Poyang Lake began to look for a chance to change sides. In August two of them tried to surrender Fou-liang 浮梁 -hsien to Chu but were defeated and forced to flee the city. On February 26, 1361, Teng Yü was given the civil rank of administration vice commissioner of the secretariat while retaining his military rank. Teng took Fou-liang on September 5, opening the campaign to wrest Kiangsi from Ch'en.

On September 11 Chu Yüan-chang left Nanking with his fleet. His voyage upstream met weak opposition and city after city surrendered. After Chu reached Poyang Lake, Wu Hung 吳宏, Ch'en Yu-liang's commander at Jao 饒-chou, surrendered (September 29). To test his new loyalty, Wu was ordered to join forces with Teng Yü to take Fu 撫-chou farther south. Since Wu Heng had surrendered voluntarily, Chu Yüan-chang had given him his previous rank of chief administratrator; he therefore nominally commanded the joint forces. Teng K'o-ming 鄧克明, the leader holding Fu-chou, responded favorably to the demand that he surrender, but Teng Yü felt that he was merely stalling for time. Marching swiftly with his troops, Teng Yü arrived at Fu-chou at dawn and simultaneously stormed the north, east, and west gates of the city. Teng K'o-ming fled through the south gate, but was caught by Teng Yü's horsemen and surrendered (December 9).

Ch'en's commander at Lung-hsing lu 龍興路 (Nanchang), Hu T'ing-jui 胡廷瑞 (later changed his name to Hu Mei 美, d. 1383; appointed the marquis of Yü-chang 豫章 in 1370, and then marquis of Lin-ch'uan 臨川 in 1380), surrendered early in 1362. Chu Yüan-chang brought his main body there February 9 and entered the city the following day. He assessed the situation, appointed officials, and changed the name of the city from Lung-hsing lu to Hung-tu 洪都-fu. Teng Yü's appointment as administration vice commissioner brought about his transfer from the secretariat to the newly created Kiangsi province

(March 11), and he was placed in civil and miltary control. Chu Yüan-chang then returned to Nanking.

Ch'en Yu-liang himself had fled upstream to the powerfully fortified city of Wuchang. Hsü Ta (*q.v.*) had been sent after him, but his fleet was insufficient to seize or even properly blockade the city. To reinforce it Chu Yüan-chang ordered two of Hu T'ing-jui's generals, Chu Tsung 祝宗 and K'ang T'ai 康泰, to go to his assistance. Finding themselves alone on the Yangtze far from any force loyal to Chü Yüan-chang, they reversed course. They arrived back at Hung-tu on April 12 shortly after sunset, used cannon to storm the Hsin-ch'eng 新城 gate from the river, took the guards by surprise, and spread through the city killing and looting. Teng Yü was evidently at dinner at the time, and no one reported the attack to him; when he heard the noise of the battle, he assembled a few of his guards and rode about the city trying to find enough loyal soldiers to restore order. Three horses were killed under him that night; finally he gave up and escaped out the Fu-chou gate, returning overland to Nanking to report. Chu Yüan-chang himself had just learned from Hu T'ing-jui that Chu Tsung and K'ang T'ai had held out longest against surrendering; he did not blame Teng Yü for a mishap which was largely the result of his own carelessness. This left the problem of re-establishing his authority in Kiangsi. Since the army of the reserve at Nanking had been sent into Chekiang to suppress the revolts which had broken out there, Hsü Ta's fleet anchored near Wuchang was the only force available for this task. Hsü Ta recaptured Hung-tu on April 13 against disorganized resistance; meanwhile Ch'en Yu-liang was freed from surveillance.

Teng Yü returned to Hung-tu in his old capacity, but Chu now (June) ordered his nephew, Chu Wen-cheng (*see* Chu Yüan-chang), the supreme commander, to make his headquarters in Hung-tu. The wall of the city was ordered moved thirty

paces back from the river bank, so that
it could no longer be scaled from the
stern of a ship. Chu's position in Kiangsi
was still insecure when Ch'en came
downstream with an armada and laid
siege to Hung-tu (June 5, 1363). The
changes in the city wall prevented him
from capturing the city in the first assault
as Hsü Ta had done the year before. Chu
Wen-cheng prepared for a long siege and
divided sections of the wall among his
chief sudordinates, Teng Yü commanding
the southeastern sector including the Fu-
chou gate. On June 9 Ch'en in person
led an assault on that gate. His troops
knocked down a long section of the wall
and Teng Yü led the defenders in impro-
vising a temporary defense with wooden
palisades. Chu Wen-cheng threw in the
reserves, and his troops fought all through
the night, rebuilding the wall as they
fought, so that it was finished by morning. During the rest of the siege, Ch'en
confined his assaults to the northern and
western sides of the city.

Chu Yüan-chang at Nanking had been
occupied with a campaign against Chang
Shih-ch'eng in the east and it was not
until August 15 that he was able to lead
his fleet westward. Ch'en took most of
his ships into Poyang Lake to oppose
him, and the siege of Hung-tu was lifted
by the arrival after an overland march of
the Kuang-hsin 廣信 army commanded by
Hu Te-chi, adopted son and sole surviving
heir of Hu Ta-hai. In October, along with
Li Shan-ch'ang (q.v.), Teng was ordered
to take charge of the defense of Nanking.
In the following year he participated in
the campaigns which wiped out Ch'en Yu-
liang's former subordinates in central and
southern Kiangsi, and was promoted to
be the junior administrator of the branch
secretariat of Kiangsi (February, 1365).
Three months later he was promoted
to be the associate administrator of the
Hukuang branch secretariat and sent to
command this area. Chu's victory of 1363
had alarmed the northern warlords, and the
greatest of them, Kökö Temür (q.v.), had

assembled an army in southern Honan and
was trying to get his jealous colleagues
to agree to concerted action. Chu
Yüan-chang planned to deal with Chang
Shih-ch'eng before turning north. Any
sign of weakness in the Han River valley
would have invited the northern armies
to march south across the undefended
border into Hukuang. This was the last
possible opportunity to put together a
coalition strong enough to defeat Chu.
Teng Yü, carrying out his detailed instructions, supervised the demobilization of
certain of Ch'en's former troops, the
establishment of military farms, and the
return of land to cultivation. The crisis
passed and Chu's authority remained
strong in northern Hukuang; later in the
year (1365) Chu was able to issue orders
for the elimination of Chang Shih-cheng.
Teng Yü did not participate in the campaign against Chang or in the northern
expedition of 1367. In November of this
year he was appointed a right censor-in-
chief and became instructor of the heir
apparent in February of the following year.
His military commission, awarded in the
same month, involved the task of destroying the Yüan forces in southern Honan,
an undertaking which he accomplished
with dispatch. In 1369 he conducted several
operations against hill forts in Honan and
Shansi. His outstanding performance earned
him a place in the Kung-ch'en miao 功臣
廟 (temple of meritorious ministers),
erected in July.

Early in 1370 a great expedition was
ordered against the main remaining Mongol army under Kökö Temür. Hsü Ta was
in over-all command with Teng Yü as
one of his four principal subordinates
(the others being Li Wen-chung, Feng
Sheng, and T'ang Ho, qq.v.). At this time
Teng held the title of a deputy vice general in charge of the pacification of the
Mongols. The main army went west;
late in April they encountered the enemy
entrenched near Ting-hsi 定西 (in modern
Kansu). Teng Yü distinguished himself in
the frontal assault which won the battle,

and Kökö Temür fled across the desert, leaving, it is said, some eighty-four thousand of his men prisoners of the Ming army. Hsü Ta then released Teng Yü to establish Ming authority along the upper stretches of the Yellow River. In June Teng marched from Lin-t'ao 臨洮 (Kansu) via Ho-chou 河州 into northern Tibet, where he accepted the submission of the local rulers who had previously been vassals of the Yüan. When the generals returned to Nanking in December, the emperor awarded them noble titles; Teng Yü, as duke of Wei 衞國公, became sixth in order of precedence with a hereditary annual stipend of three thousand *shih*. The following year he was sent back to Hsiang-yang 襄陽 (Honan) to train replacements and superintend the grain supply for the army of T'ang Ho engaged in conquering Szechwan.

Early in 1372 he was in chief command of the armies sent into Hukuang and Kwangsi to suppress the aboriginal inhabitants who were resisting the extension of Ming administration. After the successful conclusion of these campaigns at the end of the year, he was given a commission to conquer Tibet (February, 1373), but at the beginning of the following year, because of the defeats which Hsü Ta and T'ang Ho had suffered at Mongol hands, the Ming went over to a defensive posture, and Teng Yü became simply one of the deputies to Hsü Ta in maintaining the defense of the northern border. He and T'ang Ho were summoned back to the capital late in 1374, and the following February sent to establish military farms in Shensi.

The last campaign was in 1377. In May, with Mu Ying (*q.v.*) to assist him, he was sent to subdue a ruler in Tibet who had defied the Ming court. Teng Yü pursued the enemy as far as the K'un-lun 崑崙 range, and is said to have taken ten thousand heads and captured "over one hundred thousand" horses, cattle, and sheep. On the way back he died in Shou-ch'un 壽春 (Anhwei), aged only forty.

He was given the posthumous title of prince of Ning-ho 寧河王, and the canonized name Wu-shun 武順.

Teng was survived by five sons, two of whom are worthy of notice. His eldest, Teng Chen 鎮, a military officer, was made the duke of Shen-kuo 申國公 in 1380, but was executed in 1390, at the age of twenty-two, on a trumped-up charge as a member of the clique of Li Shan-ch'ang. The title was then inherited by his adopted heir, Teng Yüan 源, son of his brother Teng Ming 銘; after Teng Yüan's death during the reign of Chu Ti (*q.v.*), it passed on to his son Teng T'ing 梃 but the dukedom was soon abolished. Teng Ming was appointed an assistant commander of the Sian right escort guard in 1379. In 1492 Teng T'ing's son, Teng Ping 炳, received the hereditary rank of a commander of the Embroidered-uniform Guard in Nanking. In 1532 Emperor Chu Hou-ts'ung (*q.v.*) bestowed upon Teng Ping's son, Teng Chi-k'un 繼坤, the hereditary title of the marquis of Ting-yüan 定遠. The last to become marquis, Teng Wen-ming 文明 (T. 見龍, Pth. 節愍), also a military officer, perished in the fall of Peking in 1644.

Bibliography

1/126/8b; 5/5/95a; 9/2/7b; 88/1/32a; MSL (1962), T'ai-tsu, *ch.* 3-195, Shih-tsung (1965), 3226; KC (1958), 556; *Ssu-Hung ho-chih* 泗虹合志 (1888), 11/6a, 25b, 16/11b, 48b; Chu Yüan-chang, *Ming T'ai-tsu yü-chih wen-chi* (Taipei, 1965), 5/7b, 10a, 19/9b; Wang Shih-chen, *Yen-chou shan-jen hsü-kao* (NCL microfilm), 81/17a; P'an Ch'eng-chang 潘檉章, *Kuo-shih k'ao-i* 國史考異 (TsSCC), 12; Huang Chang-chien 黃彰健, "*Ming-shih tsuan-wu*" 纂誤, 31, CYYY (1960), 323; L. Carrington Goodrich and Feng Chia-sheng, "The Early Development of Firearms in China," *Isis*, 36 (1946), 114.

Edward L. Dreyer and Hok-lam Chan

TENG Yüan-hsi 鄧元錫 (T. 汝極, H. 潛谷), April 6, 1529 -August 10, 1593, man of letters, was a native of Hsin-ch'eng 新城, Kiangsi. His great-great-grandfather, Teng I 義 (T. 直方, H. 栢崖, cs 1411), held various posts in the bureaucracy, including those of censor and assistant surveillance commissioner of Kwangsi, and died in the fullness of years, aged eighty-seven. An able and perspicacious student, Teng Yüan-hsi, then only sixteen, made a proposal that part of the harvest in his district be conserved in public granaries against the onset of hard times and for the relief of the indigent. In his youth he traveled and studied with his older contemporary and fellow townsman, Lo Ju-fang (q.v.), and also spent some time (after 1549) in the neighboring prefecture of Chi-an 吉安 sitting at the feet of other scholars of note. After successfully qualifying for the chü-jen (1555), he continued his studies under other literati of Chi-an such as Tsou Shou-i (q.v.) and Liu Pang-ts'ai 劉邦采 (T. 君亮, cj 1528), both disciples of Wang Shou-jen (q.v.). Failing three times in the metropolitan examinations (in 1562, 1565, and 1568), he entered the National University, completed his course of studies, and became qualified for an appointment. Owing to illness, however, he spent the rest of his years at home writing on canonical and historical subjects. His friends tried to persuade him to take part in public affairs, but he resisted their blandishments until 1593 when, on the recommendation of Chao Yung-hsien (q.v.), he received an appointment as an adviser of the Hanlin Academy, an honored post but of low rank (9B). He breathed his last just as he started on his way to the capital. His friends privately conferred on him the title Wen-t'ung hsien-sheng 文統先生 (master of literature). Although brought up in the school of Wang Shou-jen, he did not accept without question all of Wang's theories. He did, however, stanchly support their reasonableness and credibility.

All five of Teng's principal works (eight are listed in the local history) receive notices in the Imperial Catalogue, but not one found its way into the Ssu-k'u collection. Three of them also were considered objectionable during the Ch'ien-lung era but have survived. These are his Ch'ien-hsüeh kao 潛學稿, 12 ch., printed in 1639, the Huang Ming shu 皇明書, 45 ch., preface of 1606 (Columbia University has an original edition), and the Han shih 函史, 81 plus 21 ch., preface of 1573. (An original edition is in the Library of Congress; according to its Catalogue the number of chüan of the first 上 part is 82). Of these perhaps the most valuable is the second; it is essentially a biographical dictionary of people who lived from the beginning of the Ming into the Chia-ching period whom the author considered worthy of treatment. The order of these biographies is of interest, as it departs from the norm: sovereigns (10 ch.), empresses and concubines (1 ch.), members of imperial consort families (1 ch.), eunuchs (1 ch.), ministers of state (5 ch.), noted officials (9 ch.), upright government clerks (2 ch.), able subordinates (1 ch.), men of loyalty (2 ch.), military commanders (1 ch.), noted generals (1 ch.), neo-Confucians 理學 (3 ch.), men of letters (2 ch.), magnanimous people and their conduct (1 ch.), men known for their filial righteousness, business acumen, and knowledge of divination (1 ch.), Wang Shou-jen and his followers 心學 (3 ch.), and women (1 ch.). The editors of the Ssu-k'u catalogue criticized this order, holding that the biographies of palace ladies and of eunuchs should have been put last as of least importance. An interesting feature of the work is the distinction Teng makes between the followers of Chu Hsi (1130–1200) and those of Wang Shou-jen, to whom, incidentally, he devotes an entire chüan. The Huang Ming shu, doubtless because of its rarity, escaped the notice of the Harvard-Yenching Institute indexers, and seems to have been rarely consulted by recent writers on Ming biography. Including the notices of ten emperors, it deals altogether with some five hundred individuals.

TERRENZ, Johann [1282]

Bibliography

1/283/29b; 3/265/17b; 5/114/79a; *Nan-ch'eng-hsien chih* 南城縣志 (1873), 9/3/3a; *Hsin-ch'eng-hsien chih* (1871), 8/5b, 10/名臣 3b, 理學 4a, 11/書目 2b, 書序 6a, 文徵 23b; *Huang Ming shu*; SK (1930), 25/2b, 34/2a, 50/11a, 178/5b; Sun Tien-ch'i (1957), 96, 123, 205; L. of C. *Catalogue of Rare Books*, 22, 134; 798; Wolfgang Franke, *Sources* 2. 1. 2, 6. 6. 6.

L. Carrington Goodrich

TERRENZ (originally Schreck), Johann (鄧玉函, T. 涵璞), 1576–1630, missionary and scientist of note, was born of Suebian origin at Constance in southern Germany. He received an excellent education and became versed not only in Latin, Greek, and Chaldean, but also in the natural sciences, especially medicine and chemistry. He studied medicine at the then renowned University of Altdorf near Nuremberg where his father, Sebastian Schreck, a lawyer by profession, is said to have taught jurisprudence for some years. Even as a young man Terrenz was a physician of repute and met on his extended travels in Germany and Italy some of the outstanding scholars of his time. In 1603 he enrolled at the University of Padua and began at this time his close acquaintance with Galileo Galilei (1564–1642). By 1611 his scholarly reputation had grown to such a height that, on May 3, 1611, eight days after Galileo, he was received into the small and exclusive circle of the academy of the Lincei (i.e., the lynxes, the "sharp sighted"), founded at Rome by Prince Federico Cesi. It was presumably then that he adopted the Latinized name Terrentius (Terentius). Terrenz, in collaboration with his pharmacist friend, Johann Faber, prepared for Prince Cesi a Latin edition of Francisco Hernandez' three volume Natural History of Mexico as condensed by Nardo Antonio Recchi, to which he added numerous scholarly comments and explanations. The work which began to appear in 1611, was, after several revisions, fully printed only in 1630 in Rome, bearing the title *Thesaurus Rerum Medicarum Novae Hispaniae, seu Plantarum, Animalium, Mineralium, Mexicanorum Historia*. It was in this same year, on November, 1611, that Terrenz gave up his promising worldly career and entered religious life in the Society of Jesus. In 1614, while still pursuing his theological studies in Rome, he encountered Niklaas Trigault (*q.v.*) who had returned from China to seek help for the mission, and was won over to his plan to promote the Christian cause in China through scholarly achievements. In 1616 he traveled widely with Trigault in western Europe, collecting funds and equipment and buying books and scientific instruments for China. Here Terrenz acted as Trigault's expert adviser and used his knowledge and his acquaintance with scholars and princes to arouse interest for his scientific projects. Among the many gifts they received was a valuable telescope donated by Cardinal Frederico Borromeo of Milan, the first such instrument to reach China. Of the books assembled at this time a good many used to be preserved in the Peitang Library of Peking. In 1618 Terrenz joined Trigault's new expedition composed of twenty-two recruits for missions in the East. Traveling by way of Goa, Bengal, Malacca, Sumatra, and Indochina, he was indefatigable in observing and gathering information on strange plants, stones, animals, fishes, reptiles, and insects, and planned a book similar to the one on Mexico that was to bear the title *Plinius Indicus*. Though he continued to work on the book when he was in China, the two volumes in folio remained unfinished. Giulio Aleni (*q.v.*) is authority for the statement that Terrenz discovered more than five hundred species of plants he had not seen before. Preserved for years in the archives of the Roman College, the manuscript of these volumes unfortunately has disappeared. Arrived in Macao, Terrenz was prevented from entering China for two years because of a persecution of European missionaries. Without delay, however, he began to study Chinese. When he finally reached Hangchow on June 26, 1621, and Peking late in 1623, he continued his language studies with the view to translating scientific books into Chinese. In Peking Terrenz worked together with the Christian official Wang Cheng (EC CP), to whom he gave much curious information on mechanical instruments and principles which Wang published in 1627 under the title *Yüan-Hsi ch'i-ch'i t'u-shuo lu-tsui* 遠西奇器圖說錄最.

Both are said to have composed a book defending the missionaries against the charge of disloyalty to the government. The discovery of the Nestorian monument aroused Terrenz' interest (*see* Manuel Dias); a letter in which he discusses the Syriac names of the bishops and priests named on the stone still survives. Other extant letters attest to his continuing contact with his scholarly friends in Europe. Repeatedly he addreseed himself to Galileo requesting tables for the calculation of eclipses, but Galileo after the censure by church authorities refused to answer. Johann Kepler, however, not only published a letter from China, adding his own comment, but sent him charts and books.

The eclipse of the sun of June 21, 1629, gave the missionaries in Peking a chance to assist in the correction of the Chinese calendar. While the calculations of the Chinese and Muslim astronomers proved faulty, the prediction made by Terrenz and Nicolo Longobardi (*q.v.*) was correct. On September 1, 1629, an imperial edict commanded the reform of the calendar according to European methods and appointed Hsü Kuang-ch'i (ECCP) director of the work. Hsü entrusted the practical execution of the plan to Terrenz and the aged Longobardi, who worked with a team of Chinese assistants. Terrenz prepared a vast translation program of technical books on arithmetic, geometry, hydraulics, music, optics, and astronomy as well as the construction of six big quadrants, three devices for measuring angles, three armillary spheres, an instrument for representing eclipses, a celestial sphere, a terrestrial globe, three ordinary quadrants, three other quadrants for measuring sidereal time, three clocks, three telescopes in copper, iron, and wood—a program which Hsü Kuang-ch'i presented to the emperor on September 13, 1629. Terrenz set himself to work on planned translations and to procure instruments, but unfortunately fell sick and died on May 13, 1630. Johann Adam Schall von Bell and Giacomo Rho (*qq.v.*) were called to continue the work.

Besides the books already mentioned Terrenz left a number of Chinese works which were instrumental in bringing European science to China. His *Ts'e t'ien yüeh shuo* 測天約說 (Abridged theory of the measures of the sky), 2 *ch.*, was finished in 1628. The first part deals with static astronomy: of the equator and the horizon; the second with dynamic astronomy: with the ecliptic, orbit of the stars, daily motion, the sun, the moon, and the fixed stars. The manuscript was later revised and published by Schall. This work contains a full description of the telescope invented by Galileo as well as an account of the sun spots which at that time appeared as a new discovery though they had been known in China for over a millennium. The *Huang-ch'ih cheng-ch'iu* 黃赤正球 in two parts deals with the ecliptic, the equator, and the sphere. The first part entitled *Huang-ch'ih-tao chü-tu piao* 黃赤通距度表, which before publication was revised by Longobardi, contains tables of the differences between the ecliptic and the equator; the second called *Cheng-ch'iu sheng-tu piao* 正球升度表, revised and prepared for publication by Schall, contains tables of the grades of the sphere. The *Ta ts'e* 大測, 2 *ch.*, is an illustrated work by Terrenz on trigonometry which Schall also revised before publication. A fourth work is the *Pa-hsien piao* 八線表 on the sines, the tangents, and the secants, with revisions before publication by Schall and Rho. All four works were inserted in the *Ch'ung-chen li-shu* 崇禎曆書 and its later printed editions. In earlier years, before 1624, when he was studying Chinese at Hangchow, Terrenz had composed, perhaps with the help of Li Chih-tsao (ECCP), a book of medical interest, the *T'ai-hsi jen-shen-shuo kai* 泰西人身說概 (European theories on the human body), 2 *ch.*, of which the first deals with bones, nerves, fats, veins, skin, flesh, and the blood; the second with sensation, sight, hearing, smell, touch, motion, and speech. The book was printed only in 1643 after Pi Kung-ch'en (ECCP) had borrowed the manuscript and put it into acceptable Chinese. Terrenz' work has sometimes been confused by Chinese writers with a similar work on the human body by Rho entitled *Jen-shen t'u shuo* 人身圖說. A number of letters which Terrenz wrote to friends in Europe are still extant and were published by Kepler and later by Giuseppe Gabrieli.

Bibliography

1/326/21a; Fang Hao 方豪, *Chung-kuo T'ien-chu-chiao shih jen-wu chuan* 中國天主教史人物傳 (Hong Kong, 1967), 216; Hsü Tsung-tse 徐宗澤, *Ming Ch'ing-chien yeh-su hui-shih i-chu t'i-yao* 明清間耶穌會士譯著提要 (rev. ed., Taipei, 1958), 36a; Pfister (1932), 153; Giuseppe Gabrieli, "Giovanni Schreck, Linceo Gesuita e Missionario in Cina e le sue Lettere dall' Asia, "Reale Academia Nazionale dei Lencei: *Rendiconti della classe di scienze morali, storiche e filologiche*, Ser. VI: Vol. XII (Rome, 1936), 462; *id.*, "I Lincei e la Cina," *ibid.* 240; Henri Bernard, "L'encyclopédie astronomique du Père Schall," MS 3 (1938), 35, 441; *id.*, "A Father of Botany," *Yenching Jo. of Social Studies*, III (1941), 225; Pasquale d'Elia, *Galileo in China (1610-1640)*, tr. from the Italian by Rufus Suter and Matthew Sciascia (Cambridge, Mass., 1960); Joseph Needham, *Science and Civilization in China*, Vol. III (1959), 182, 444; Edmond Lamalle, "La propagande du P. Nicolas Trigault en faveur des missions de Chine (1616), " *Archivum Historicum Societatis Jesu*, 9 (Rome, 1940), 49-120; Johannes Beckman, "Die Heimat des Chinamissionars P. Johannes Terrentius (Schreck) SJ,"

Neue Zeitschrift für Missionswissenschaft, 23 (Schröneck, 1967), 143.

Bernard H. Willeke

THONGANBWA, *see* SSU Jen-Fa

T'IEH Hsüan 鐵鉉 (T. 鼎石), 1366-November 12, 1402, who was a victim in the struggle for the throne by Chu Ti (*q.v.*), came from a Se-mu 色目 family in Teng-chou 鄧州, Honan, where his grandfather had settled around the middle of the 13th century. After graduating from the National University, T'ieh Hsüan served as a supervising secretary in the ministry of Rites, then became a judge (tuan-shih kuan 斷事官) in the five chief military commissions. Because of T'ieh's judgment and competence, Emperor Chu Yüan-chang took him into his confidence, granted him an honorific *tzu*, Ting-shih 鼎石 (tripod and stone), and assigned him to the work of settling doubtful judicial cases.

Shortly after the accession of Chu Yün-wen (*q.v.*), T'ieh Hsüan received an appointment in June, 1399, as administration vice commissioner of Shantung. Two months later, Chu Ti, then prince of Yen, started his rebellion, and the court hastily organized an expeditionary army against him. When Li Ching-lung (*see* Li Wen-chung) with headquarters in Te-chou 德州, Shantung, took over command of the force, T'ieh was assigned the task of provisioning it. In the ensuing months, Li suffered a series of setbacks, and abandoned Te-chou in June, 1400, for Tsinan, where T'ieh, together with Sheng Yung (*q.v.*), had been organizing the defense against enemy raids. During his retreat, Li again suffered defeat, and hurriedly fled to the south, leaving his subordinates to defend Tsinan. T'ieh is said to have devised an ingenious plot to lure Chu Ti into a trap by feigning surrender, but, unfortunately for the imperial cause, Chu escaped unhurt. After laying siege to the city for two months, the rebels finally abandoned their attempt in August; meanwhile, Sheng Yung's army recaptured Te-chou. Informed of his superior performance, the emperor summoned T'ieh to the capital, rewarded him lavishly, and appointed him first administration commissioner of Shantung, and then, minister of War (December 1400/January 1401).

At this juncture, a counselor by the name of Sung 宋 proposed to T'ieh that he take advantage of Chu Ti's absence from Peiping to launch a counter offensive against the enemy headquarters, arguing this as a tactical move to turn the rebels back to the north. (Sung is generally not identified, but T'an Ch'ien [q.v.] in Kuo-ch'üeh refers to him as Sung Cheng 徵, who served as a registrar in the imperial clan office. When Chu Yün-wen came to the throne, Sung advised the emperor to strip the imperial princes of their registered households. He was later executed by Chu Ti.) Though impressed by Sung's proposal, T'ieh dismissed it as impractical, as the army, he held, was short of supplies. Historians in later times have deplored this rebuff, maintaining that T'ieh Hsüan missed an opportunity to nullify Chu Ti's advance. In the meantime, T'ieh concentrated his attention on the defense of Shantung, with a view to stop the enemy from penetrating the Huai River valley.

It was T'ieh Hsüan's aim to defend the key cities, while Sheng Yung maintained mobile units operating out of Tsinan. While they were thus occupied, Chu Ti, following his setback at Tsinan, was reassembling and reequipping an army in the Peiping area. At the end of 1401 he carried his campaign farther west in an attempt to break the imperial offensive. T'ieh Hsüan, however, was on the alert. In this same month, having taken over the defense of Tung-ch'ang 東昌, Shantung, he frustrated Chu Ti's attempt to seize the city. Subsequently he moved with his forces to the north of the Huai

region. In May of the following year he again confronted Chu Ti in Hsiao-ho 小河, northern Hukuang, inflicting heavy casualties. In pursuit of his victory, T'ieh was about to round up the rebel forces south of the Huai River when he learned that Chu Ti had made the strategic move down to and across the Yangtze and captured Nanking (July). Undaunted, T'ieh continued to hold his forces in the Huai region in the forlorn hope of eventually crushing the rebellion. In November, however, he was captured and taken into the presence of Chu Ti. Being unswervingly loyal to Chu Yün-wen, T'ieh refused to surrender and courageously denounced the prince for his usurpation. Outraged, Chu Ti gave him probably one of the most cruel punishments ever recorded. It is said that he had T'ieh sliced to death, and his body thrown into a vat of boiling oil and completely obliterated. T'ieh Hsüan was then thirty-six years of age.

Chu Ti also meted out severe punishment to members of T'ieh's family. T'ieh Hsüan's father, then over eighty, and his mother were exiled to Hainan Island; his eldest son, T'ieh Fu-an 福安, eleven years of age, was sent to the Ho-ch'ih 河池 guard, Kwangsi, as a conscript; his youngest son, T'ieh K'ang 康-an, only six years, was made an artisan in a government bureau. Later, both suffered violent death. His wife and two daughters were sent to the office of music as slaves. The former later had a mental collapse and died, and the two daughters refused to allow themselves to be violated. Informed of the chastity of T'ieh's daughters, Chu Ti was moved and ordered their release; they were allowed to marry scholar-officials. In January, 1645, when Emperor Chu Yu-chien (ECCP) of the short-lived Southern Ming court conferred posthumous honors on a number of illustrious officials of the early reigns, T'ieh Hsüan received the title of grand guardian and the canonized name Chung-hsiang 忠襄 (loyal and helpful).

T'ieh Hsüan's gallantry and tragic

death later received dramatic treatment in popular literature. The story of his stanch loyalty to Chu Yün-wen and his defense of Tsinan were made into a play called *Mang shu-sheng* 莽書生 (The rude scholar), so named because it involved a university student who courageously attempted to stop Chu Ti by presenting him with a persuasive petition. The chastity of T'ieh's daughters likewise inspired the Ch'ing dramatist Lai Chi-chih 來集之 (d. 1682) to make them heroines in a play called *T'ieh-shih nü* 氏女 (The daughters of Mister T'ieh), also known as *Hsia-nü hsin-sheng* 俠女新聲 (New song for chivalrous ladies). Both works are preserved in Ming and Ch'ing drama collections.

Bibliography

1/142/1b; 5/38/13a; 9/11/13a; 61/102/21b; KC (1958), 809, 817, 821, 885; TSCC (1885-88): XI/736/30b, XIV/524/2a; Lang Ying, *Ch'i-hsiu lei-kao, hsü-kao*, 5/818; T'u Shu-fang, *Chien-wen ch'ao-yeh hui-pien*, 8/31a; Chi Liu-ch'i 計六奇, *Ming-chi nan-lüeh* 明季南略 (1936 ed.), 5/109; *Honan t'ung-chih* (1735), 63/40a; *Teng-chou chih* (1755), 16/19b; Huang Wen-yang 黃文暘, *Ch'ü-hai tsung-mu t'i-yao* 曲海總目提要 (Peking, 1957), 9/22b, 43/17a; Wang Ch'ung-wu 王崇武, *Ming ching-nan shih-shih k'ao-cheng kao* 明靖難史事考證稿 (1948), 74.

Hok-lam Chan

T'IEN Ju-ch'eng 田汝成 (T. 叔禾, H. 藥洲 ?, cs 1526), scholar-official, was a native of Hangchow. He lived probably from 1500 to 1563+. When serving as a secretary in the Nanking ministry of Justice, he boldly memorialized the throne (in January, 1532) suggesting that, since Heaven had not yet favored the emperor with an heir apparent, His Majesty should release from prison the less serious offenders and banish them to outlying regions of the empire. His reward for this memorial was a sharp reprimand. The following year (1533) he was dispatched to Kwangtung as assistant surveillance commissioner, and in 1534 served as assistant educational commissioner. While in Kwangtung he published a collection of his prose under the title *Yao-chou hsien-sheng chi* 藥洲先生集, 6 *ch.*, Possibly printed at the same time was a collection of his poems: *Yao-chou hsien-sheng shih* 詩 *chi*. Later, transferred to the ministry of Rites, he received a promotion to the post of director of the bureau of sacrifices and then became right assistant administration commissioner of Kwangsi province. Here he received credit for suppressing a rebellion of certain tribesmen of the southwest. His final office was as vice commissioner of education in Fukien. At this point he was permitted to retire, and spent the rest of his days in his native city writing.

It is through his published work, both poetry and prose, that T'ien is best remembered. The *Ming-shih tsung* of Chu I-tsun (ECCP) includes five of his poems, and the *Ming-shih chi-shih* 明詩紀事 of Ch'en T'ien 陳田 (cs 1886) includes four. There are four critical appraisals of his poetry, only one of them enthusiastic. It is rather his prose which is of genuine worth. His *Kuei-lin hsing* 桂林行, written in 1538, and included later in his collected works, gives an interesting account of a trip he made from Hangchow to Kuei-lin, which lasted sixty-four days. Historically of more value, perhaps, is a work published under two titles, the first being *Yen-chiao chi-wen* 炎徼紀聞, 4 *ch.* (preface by the author, 1560), and the second *Hsing-pien* 行邊 *chi-wen*, 1 *ch.* (preface by Ku Ming-ju 顧名儒, 1557). It consists of fourteen reports on the aboriginal tribes in Kwangsi, Kweichow, and Yunnan of his day, his dealings with them, and the mishandling of them by previous administrators. More detailed than the *Ming-shih* account, it serves as an important supplement to it. T'ien is sharply critical of Wang Shou-jen (*q.v.*), but the editors of the *Ssu-k'u* catalogue, who included it in the Imperial Library, pass over his strictures against Wang, agreeing only with his criticism of the tactics followed by Wang and other officials sent to the area. A modern editor of a photolithographic edition of the book (1936), Hsieh Kuo-chen 謝國禎, also comes to Wang's defense, and holds that T'ien's charges of appeasement and false reporting on the part of Wang Shou-jen are simply not true.   The controversy points to the fact that T'ien and Wang were at opposite ends of the political spectrum, one believing in a policy of suppression, the other in pacification by milder means if possible.

T'ien's largest works, also copied into the Imperial Library, are the *Hsi-hu yu-lan chih* 西湖遊覽志, 24 *ch.*, and *Hsi-hu yu-lan chih-yü* 餘 (his own preface, 1547, published 1584), 26 *ch.*, which deal with the West Lake and Hangchow. Both books in original editions are in the Library of Congress. The editors of the *Ssu-k'u* catalogue write concerning the first: "It chiefly concerns the Lake during the time of the Southern Sung [1127-1279], discoursing on everything connected with the scenic spots; it is in part a local history and in part a miscellaneous one." The second, on the other hand, deals principally with Hangchow, relating anecdotes and descriptions of court life and politics in the same century and a half. One of his pieces of gossip, for example, is that the last emperor of the Yüan dynasty, Toγon-temür (*q.v.*), was the son of Chao Hsien, one of the last emperors of the Sung. While the Ch'ing editors justly criticize the author for his failure to cite his sources, and Chu I-tsun berates him for failing to consult others, the books remain possibly T'ien's most enduring monument, because of their charm and the information they contain.

T'ien's collected writings are variously titled: *T'ien Shu-ho chi* 集, *Yü-yang* 豫陽 *chi*, and *Yang-yüan* 楊園 *chi*, 12 *ch.*, which were brought together late in his life, and edited by his son. This collection, together with the two books about the West Lake, was reprinted by the late Ch'ing bibliophile, Ting Ping (ECCP) of Chekiang, in his collectanea dealing with Hangchow, the

Wu-lin wang-che i-chu and the *Wu-lin chang-ku ts'ung-pien*. A final work, which the *Ssu-k'u* editors think unworthy of serious regard, is a slight treatise on Liaotung border problems from 1369 to 1537, entitled *Liao chi* 遼紀, 1 *ch.*

The son, T'ien I-heng 藝蘅 (T. 子藝), 1524-74?, only less well known than the father, was also a writer. Though precocious as a youth, and an omniverous reader with wide-ranging interests, he never succeeded in getting beyond the *kung-sheng* degree in the state examinations. He did, however, serve for a while as an educational official in Hsiu-ning 休寧 and Hui-chou 徽州 (Anhwei), and rose to be sub-director of studies in Nanking. In 1557, when the *wo-k'ou* were threatening the Chekiang coast, he assisted in leading a volunteer corps of a thousand men to repel the invasions. A decade later the local authorities asked him to collect materials to be presented to Peking for the compilation of the *Shih-tsung shih-lu*. Although the author of a number of works, several of them published in such collectanea as the *Shuo-fu hsü* (*see* T'ao Tsung-i) and the *Ts'ung-shu chi-ch'eng*, his best known is possibly the *Liu-ch'ing jih-cha* 留青日札 (Daily jottings), 39 *ch.*, which has two prefaces dated 1573. This includes a collection of aphorisms, random reflections on felicitous and unfelicitous lines in poetry, thoughts on how to enjoy wine, games people play at literary parties (some clever, some obscene), fables, short stories, a treatise on spring water and on tea, etc.), altogether over six hundred essays or short sketches. T'ien gives *inter alia* one of the earliest notices of maize (introduced to China about mid-16th century), and makes authoritative comments on the porcelain of his day. An index of an abridged edition of 4 *chüan*, included in the *Chi-lu hui-pien* (*see* Shen Chieh-fu), appears in the *Chūkoku zuihitsu satsucho sakuin* 中國隨筆雜著索引 (Kyoto, 1960).

Like his father, T'ien I-heng also wrote on the West Lake—*Hsi-hu chih-yü* 餘, 26 *ch.*

In addition he produced an account of the outpourings of poetesses from the earliest times to his own day—*Shih-nü shih* 詩女史, 14. *ch.*, and compiled a dictionary arranged according to the sounds of characters—*Ta Ming t'ung-wen-chi chü-yao* 同文集舉要 (prefaces of 1582), 50 *ch.*, an original edition of which is in the Library of Congress. His portrait appears in the original edition of the *Liu-ch'ing jih-cha*.

Bibliography

1/287/10b; 3/268/8a; 40/40/13a, 62/10b; 64/戊16/13b, 庚 28/3a; 84/丁上/18b, 丁中/28a; Wang Sen (EC CP, p. 184), *Yüeh-hsi ts'ung-tsai* 粵西叢載, 3/7b; MSL (1965), Shih-tsung, 3154; SK (1930), 43/6b, 49/2b, 53/6b, 116/6b, 128/2a, 177/5a, 178/13a, 192/13b; *Kuang-tung t'ung-chih* (1934), 368; *Kuo-li Pei-p'ing t'u-shu-kuan shan-pen ts'ung-shu ti-i chi*, Peking, 1936; NLP, microfilm no. 624; L. of C. *Catalogue of Rare Books*, 70, 361; W. Franke, *Sources*, 7. 5. 9; W. T. Swingle, *Report of the Librarian of Congress* (Washington, 1934), 8; P. David in *Transactions of the Oriental Ceramic Soc.* (1936-37), 34.

Wolfgang Franke and
L.Carrington Goodrich

TING Ho-nien. 丁鶴年 (T. 行原), 1335-1424, a poet of central Asian origin, was brought up in Wuchang, spent his middle years in the lower Yangtze valley until he was forced to flee because of troubled conditions there, and ended his days in Wuchang. He is an interesting example of a Muslim turned Confucian, who became a Buddhist, possibly because of political expediency. Nevertheless, his poems indicate that he knew Ch'an Buddhism well and believed in it.

Ting's great-grandfather was A-lao-ting 阿老丁 ('A lā-'d-Dīn?), who, together with a younger brother Wu-ma-er 烏馬兒 (Umar, 'Omar?), came to China as a merchant in the days of Qubilai, late in the 13th century. In the ensuing decades Wu-ma-er served as an official in a number of localities, ending his career as deputy prefect (tsung-kuan 總管) of Hu-chou 湖洲, *ca.* 1330. Ting's grandfather, Chan-ssu-ting 苫思丁 ('Sams-'d-Din), was for a time prefect (daruγači) of Lin-chiang 臨江 in Kiangsi. Ting was the youngest of five sons of Chih-ma-lu-ting 職馬祿丁 (Ĵamal al-Dīn, d. 1346), one-time magistrate of Wuchang; his mother, née Feng 馮, was a concubine. At his father's death, following traditional Chinese custom, Ting Ho-nien, then a boy of only eleven, is said to have spent the next three years in mourning, refusing even to accept the property that was rightly his by inheritance, passing it on to his brothers. Again, following Confucian practice, as did his brothers, he studied the canon industriously, mastering the Odes, History, and Rites by the age of sixteen. One of his early teachers was his sister Ting Yüeh-o 月娥, who committed suicide rather than suffer indignities from the soldiery (in T'ai-p'ing 太平 in 1350?), and was later celebrated as the first biographee in the *Ming-shih* chapter on women. Another of his teachers was a certain Chou Huai-hsiao 周懷孝 of Nanchang, a Confucian scholar then living in Wuchang. His estimation of Ting Ho-nien was so high that he wished to arrange a marriage between his daughter and the youth.

When in 1352 Wuchang became the base of operations of the anti-Yüan rebel Hsü Shou-hui (*q.v.*), Ting decided to flee. In the turmoil he and his mother became separated, but he escaped with his father's principal wife, to whom he referred as "mother," and made his way slowly eastward. They seem to have suffered much hardship, reaching Chinkiang only after a journey of three months. Frequently in need of food and water, Ting was compelled to do odd jobs as peddler or watchman. When his "mother" died, he is said to have abstained from salt and lao 酪 (a milk product) for five years. In 1356, after Chinkiang fell to the forces under Chu Yüan-chang, it appears that Ting fled eastward to Ssu-ming (Ningpo) where Fang Kuo-chen (*q. v.*) was in control. From then until about 1367 Ting lived chiefly in eastern Chekiang as a Yüan loyalist. He probably did not approve of Fang who, though technically a Yüan appointee, had sent submissive epistles to Chu Yüan-chang. It is known that he stayed for a time with one of his cousins, Chi-ya-mo-ting 吉雅謨丁 (cs 1357, mistakenly confused with Ma Yüan-te 馬元德, cs 1362, who preceded him in office), who served as a Yüan magistrate of Feng-hua 奉化 (1364) and Ch'ang-kuo 昌國; when Chi-ya-mo-ting was later transferred to Kiangsi, Ting had the courage to be his companion, slipping through enemy lines.

About 1366 Ting was once more living in the Ming-chou 明州 (Ningpo) area, teaching children or selling medicine for a living. It was in that year that his friend Tai Liang (q.v.) wrote a preface to his poems. Shortly thereafter Tai also wrote a biography of Ting, praising him as a "highminded scholar" (高士) who held official positions in low esteem, and who had refused to have anything to do with the Yüan general Fang Kuo-chen when the latter was in power in eastern Chekiang. It is quite possible that this biography was written as a testimonial on Ting's behalf after Fang's defeat and the occupation of Chekiang by the troops of Chu Yüan-chang at the end of 1367. In any event it was with very real concern for his own safety that Ting found refuge in a monastery of the Ch'an sect, probably even becoming a Buddhist monk. He named his studio T'ao-ch'an-shih 逃禪室 (Dhyana refuge), and his poems indicate that the priesthood was to him a means of livelihood.

Early in the summer of 1379 Ting obtained permission to return to Wuchang for the proper burial of his own mother. Originally she had been laid to rest without benefit of coffin, as was the Muslim custom, and probably without marker. For six months he searched to no avail; not until a dream gave him a clue was he able to uncover a skeleton which he assumed to be the remains of her body. This was now placed in a coffin, a tablet put over the grave, and sacrifices made of meat and wine. For this act of filial piety he received the sobriquet of Ting hsiao-tzu 丁孝子 (dutiful son Ting).

He was a man possessed of an unusually retentive mind; reading a passage once was enough for him to commit it to memory. His poems, collected under the title Ting Ho-nien chi 集, in 4 chüan, simulated those of the T'ang; many of them were indited to his monkish friends, thirty-one of them in all. Appended to Ting's poems were a few by his cousins, Chi-ya-mo-ting, Ai-li-sha 愛理沙 (T. 允中), and Wu Wei-shan 吳惟善. He died at the age of eighty-nine and was laid to rest in the Muslim cemetery in Hangchow.

Bibliography

1/285/6b, 301/3a; 3/266/14b; 84/甲前 9b; Ch'en Yüan (BDRC), Ch'ung-k'o Yüan Hsi-yü hua-hua k'ao (1934), 41a, 65a, 104a, 122a; Kansu hsin t'ung-chih 甘肅新通志 (1909), 66/16a; Wu-ch'ang hsien-chih (1885), 11/11b; Chekiang t'ung-chih (1934), 2068, 2700; Feng-hua hsien-chih (1908), 16/21b, 18/6b; Fang Hao 方豪, Chung-hsi chiao-t'ung shih 中西交通史, III (1953); 125; SK (1930), 168/5b; Ting Ho-nien chi (Lin-lang mi-shih ts'ung-shu 琳琅秘室叢書 ed.); Ch'en Yüan, Western and Central Asians in China under the Mongols, tr. and annot. by Ch'ien Hsing-hai and L. Carrington Goodrich (Los Angeles, 1966), 98, 154.

L. Carrington Goodrich

TING Yün-p'eng 丁雲鵬 (T. 南羽, H. 聖華居士), fl. 1584-1618, painter, was a native of Hsiu-ning 休寧, prefecture of Hui-chou 徽州 (Anhwei). From Sung times on his family had been medical practitioners, but his father Ting Tsan 瓚 (T. 汝器) broke the tradition by becoming a (professional?) calligrapher and painter. (The latter is not to be confused with another of the same name, a native of Tan-t'u 丹徒 in the prefecture of Chinkiang, cs 1517, who rose in office to become a provincial surveillance vice commissioner.) Little is known of Ting Yün-p'eng's life. He must have become widely known, however, for he counted among his admirers such famous contemporaries as Ch'en Chi-ju and Tung Ch'i-ch'ang (both in ECCP). The former describes his brushwork as having the consistency of silk thread, capturing the quality of human expression, while the latter in admiration presented him a seal for his studio carved with the sentiment 毫生館 ("where every hair of the brush conveys life"). When Ch'eng Ta-yüeh (*q.v.*) of the same prefecture needed someone to illustrate his famous catalogue of ink-tablets, *Ch'eng-shih mo-yüan*, he turned to Ting, who furnished the majority of the five hundred illustrations. Ting was also one of the contributors of the literary pieces included in the catalogue along with Tung Ch'i-ch'ang, Matteo Ricci (*q.v.*), *et al.*

Ting is remembered for his landscapes, which show the influence of the Wu school (*see* Shen Chou), and for his figures, especially his Buddhist subjects. A famous example of the latter is the handscroll, painted with gold ink on blue sūtra paper, known as 十八羅漢 (Eighteen arhats), now in the collection of the Academy of Arts, Honolulu. Other arhats he painted are done in an angular archaistic style said to reflect that of Kuan-hsiu 貫休 of the 10th century and of his own contemporary, Wu Pin (*q.v.*); an example of this type is in the collection of the National Palace Museum, Taipei. Besides Buddhists he also depicted Taoists. In the Cheng Te-k'un collection (Cambridge, England) is a scroll showing Taoist figures in a mountain landscape. He is known too, perhaps more than anyone else in his age, for his ink sketches in the pai-miao 白描 (plain drawing) style, a tradition reaching back to Li Kung-lin (1049–1106) and Chao Meng-fu (1254–1322). Yu Ch'iu (active 1572–82), the son-in-law of Ch'iu Ying (*q.v.*) was especially noted for pai-miao painting; he seems to have had a direct influence on Ting Yün-p'eng.

Ting's writing, assembled in a collection called *Ting Nan-yü chi* 南羽集, is extremely rare, and, indeed, may not be extant.

Bibliography

Hui-chou-fu chih (1827), 14/2/6b; TSCC (1885-88), XVII: 532/9/11a; *T'an-t'u-hsien chih* (1880), 22/16b; Hsü Ch'in 徐沁 (fl. 1694), *Ming hua lu* 明畫錄 (*Hua-shih* 畫史 *ts'ung-shu* ed.), 1/4; Chiang Shao-shu 姜紹書, *Wu-sheng shih shih* 無聲詩史 (same ed.), 4/67; *T'u-hui pao-chien hsü tsuan* 圖繪寶鑑續纂 (same ed.), 1/4; P'eng Yün-ts'an 彭蘊璨, *Hua-shih hui chuan* 彙傳 (1882), 34/13b; Chuang Shen, "Ming Antiquarianism, an Aesthetic Approach to Archaeology," *Jo. of Or. Stud.* 8 (1970), 77; K. T. Wu, "Ming Printing and Printers," HJAS, VII (1942-43), 204; O. Sirén, *Chinese Painting* (New York, 1956-58), V, 59, VII, 241; E. J. Laing, *Chinese Paintings in Chinese Publications, 1956-58* (Ann Arbor, 1969), 194; V. Contag and C. C. Wang, *Seals of Chinese Painters and Collectors of the Ming and Ch'ing Periods* (Hong Kong, 1966), 1.

Yu-ho Tseng Ecke

TOγON Temür 妥懽貼睦爾 (Temple name: Shun-ti 順帝, Mongol title: Uqaγatu Qaγan), May 25, 1320-May 23, 1370, was the last emperor of the Mongol Yüan dynasty. He was a son of Emperor Kušala (Ming-tsung, 1300-29) who ruled for a few months only in 1329, and of Mai-lai-ti 邁來迪, daughter of the Qarluq Turk, T'ieh-mu-tieh-er 帖木迭兒 (Temüder). Kušala had met Mai-lai-ti during his exile in central Asia, a fact which made this union appear illegitimate in the eyes of some court factions and of the historiographers who did not list Mai-lai-ti among the empresses in *chüan* 106 of the *Yüan-shih*. Toγon Temür was enthroned July 19, 1333, after a particularly long and involved series of political intrigues at the Mongol court. He had a claim to the throne as son of Kušala but Emperor Togh Temür (Wen-tsung, 1304-32) who was, it seems, responsible for the former's premature death, had a son of his own. The court was divided into two factions, one of which favored Kušala's sons and heirs whereas the other, led by the powerful Qipčaq

Turk noble, El Temür (Yen T'ieh-mu-er 燕鐵木兒) of the Baya'ut tribe, wished to appoint Togh Temür's son, El Tegüs (Yen T'ieh-ku-ssu 燕帖古思). When Emperor Togh Temür died September 2, 1332, El Temür failed to achieve his aim and Irinjinbal (I-lin-chen-pan 亦璘眞班), a son of Kušala, aged six, was put on the throne October 23, but died, unnaturally perhaps, a few weeks later (December 14). Again El Temür tried to persuade Togh Temür's widow to enthrone El Tegüs but she insisted that Irinjinbal's half-brother, Toγon Temür, should succeed to the throne. Her surprising attitude of preferring the succession of Toγon to that of her own son, El Tegüs, may, as some sources suggest, be explained by the remorse which she and her late husband felt over the murder of Kušala. At that time Toγon Temür did not live in the capital, as he had been banished to a distant place on El Temür's advice. He had first been interned in 1330 on the island of Taech'ong-do (off the west coast of northern Korea) and later sent to Ching-chiang 靜江 (modern Kweilin, Kwangsi).

Toγon Temür thus found himself an emperor at the age of thirteen much to his own and many other people's surprise. He occupied the throne for thirty-seven years, and was emperor over China for thirty-five of them. His reign is the longest of all Yüan emperors, exceeding even that of Qubilai (thirty-four years). It is out of place to describe here even summarily the political, social, and economic events and changes which occurred under his rule. An outline of his personal biography and a tentative description of his character is more appropriate. This is difficult, as practically all sources about him are written *post eventum* and tainted by the trite age-old historiographical ideas relating to a "bad last ruler." It appears, however, that he was of a kindly and genial disposition, though weak and given to sensual pleasures. He had received a modicum of Chinese education when he was banished to Kwangsi, where he was entrusted to the care of a Buddhist monk named

Ch'iu-chiang 秋江, abbot of the Ta-yüan 大圓 monastery. Under this monk he studied such texts as the *Lun-yü* and *Hsiao-ching*. But he was at the same time a playful child, and some charming anecdotes are told about the time when he lived in the south. Even after his enthronement he continued to show a certain interest in Chinese education and certainly was not one of those Mongols who were fundamentally hostile to Chinese civilization. He was fond of Chinese calligraphy and liked to display his skill in this art.

After his enthronement Toγon Temür was clearly no more than a figurehead for the empire; the actual power lay then as later in the hands of Mongol grandees. At the beginning of his reign the leading figure was El Temür, who tried to win over the young emperor by marrying him to his daughter, Danаširi (Ta-na-shih-li 苔納失里), a Buddhist name derived from Sanskrit Dānаšrī. She was haughty and harsh if we are to believe the sources. In 1335, after her brother, Tangkis (T'ang Ch'i-shih 唐其勢), was involved in a plot, Danаširi became a victim of the subsequent purge of the El Temür faction. She was murdered in Shang-tu on July 22, 1335. El Temür's successor *de facto* ruler of the empire was a Mongol by the name of Bayan 伯顔 who had been responsible for the elimination of the El Temür clique and for the murder of the empress. Bayan was definitely anti-Chinese and so came into conflict with the young emperor, who tended to favor those Mongol officials showing some concern for Chinese tradition.

In 1337 Toγon Temür remarried, this time a girl from the Qonggirad tribe from which the Yüan emperors traditionally chose their spouses. She was a daughter of Bolod Temür (*see* Kökö Temür). Her enthronement as empress took place on April 18, 1337, when she was thirteen years of age. Her Mongol name is given as Bayan Quduq (Pai-yen Hu-tu 伯顔忽都). It seems that she was a plain person of simple and economising habits, preferring to lead a retired life, perhaps because the emperor showed her little attention. She died childless September 8, 1365. The woman, however, who fascinated the emperor throughout his whole life was a Korean concubine, née Ki 奇. She had received a good Chinese and Korean education and was as clever as she was attractive. This remarkable woman succeeded in remaining the emperor's favorite from 1334 or even earlier and gave birth to the heir apparent Ayuširidara (*q.v.*) in 1339. Her Mongol name was Öljei Quduq (Wan-che Hu-tu 完者忽都); her Korean or Chinese name has not been recorded. Within an inordinately short time after the demise of the Qonggirat empress, the emperor made the Lady Ki his legal consort (December 13, 1365) and had her family name changed to Sulangqa or Solongqa 蕭良合, the Mongol name for the Koreans.

After the much-hated Bayan had been ousted from office in 1340, Toγon Temür relied more and more on Toγto (1313-55), a Mongol who represented the pro-Chinese elements among the ruling minority of his time. In 1340 the classical examinations, which had been abolished under Bayan's influence in 1335, were reintroduced, and several Chinese literati rose to important offices at the Mongol court. It is not clear to what extent this development was due to Toγto's influence, but the emperor at least seems to have sympathized with this particular aspect of Toγto's policy. Generally Toγon Temür kept aloof from politics, even after the dangerous Red Turban rebellions broke out in 1351. He left all measures against these and other rebellions to his generals, even when they failed disastrously, and never tried to lead his armies in battle. Instead he occupied himself with rather unorthodox activities. In 1353 Qama (Ha-ma 哈麻), a Qangli Turk, introduced Tibetan monks at court who managed to win the emperor over to Shaktist Buddhism. The Chinese admittedly biased sources describe the Buddhist rites in which the emperor and his circle of friends (Mong. *inaγ*, "companions") took part, as mere sexual mass orgies. It is true that in Tibetan lamaism sexual intercourse with an initiated woman was considered to be one way of attaining religious merit. What shocked the Chinese of that time most was the openness of these activities and the fact that even wives and daughters of noble families participated. In 1358 the heir apparent too was admitted to these cults. Other activities of the emperor were less subject to criticism. He was a lover of mechanical gadgets and liked to build. It is even recorded that he constructed with his own hands a small model for a palace hall, a hobby which brought him the nickname of Lu Pan t'ien-tzu 魯班天子 (carpenter emperor). He seems also to have been interested in astronomy and astrology.

It cannot be said that it was solely the emperor's fault that finally the Ming rebels became victorious. He may have been an incompetent and inactive ruler, but he also never took any decisive steps himself and therefore can be held only partly responsible for the failures of his government. If there is one personal characteristic which may have contributed to the downfall of the dynasty it is his lack of confidence and distrust of his ministers from which even an eminent and loyal servant of the throne like Toγto had to suffer temporarily. When finally Toγon Temür was forced to flee from his capital Ta-tu, site of modern Peking, on September 10, 1368, he withdrew to the steppes of Mongolia with his empress and a host of faithful followers. He died of dysentery in Ying-ch'ang 應昌, northwest of Jehol, in 1370, as an exile but at the same time as a ruler whose successors still regarded themselves as the legitimate heirs to the Chinese empire. The subsequent wars of the Ming emperors against the Mongols are the outcome of this unbroken feeling of legitimacy.

A curious legend concerning the birth of Toγon Temür arose even during the 14th century. It was widely believed that he was not the son of Kušala but of the duke of Ying 瀛國公, *i.e.*, the Sung emperor (Chao Hsien) who was taken prisoner by Qubilai in 1276 as a six-year old boy, and who became a Buddhist monk in 1288. This legend may be due to a tendency to link the two last unsuccessful rulers of the Sung and Yüan dynasties respectively, and also to the fact that the marriage of Toγon Temür's father was considered by some to be illegal. An equally unfounded tradition makes him the father of Chu Ti (*q.v.*). It is reflected not only in Chinese but also in Mongol sources. Mongol tradition agrees with Chinese historiography in several characteristics regarding the last Yüan emperor, at least insofar as his indulgence in sensual enjoyments is concerned. Several Mongol chronicles ascribe to him a long moving poem in which he mourns the loss of his beloved capital when he had to flee before the victorious Ming armies.

Bibliography

Yüan-shih, ch. 38-47, 114/7b, 9a; *Hsin Yüan-shih*, *ch.* 23-26; Ch'üan Heng 權衡 (fl. 1369), *Keng-shen wai-shih* 庚申外史 (TsSCC ed.); T'ao Tsung-i, *Cho-keng lu* (TsSCC ed.); Yang Yü 楊瑀, *Shan-chü hsin-yü* 山居新語 (*Wu-lin Wang-che i-chu* ed.); Liu Chi 劉佶 (14th century), *Pei-hsün ssu-chi* 北巡私記 (*Yün-ch'uang ts'ung-k'o* ed.); Wan Ssu-t'ung (ECCP), *Keng-shen chün i-shih* 庚申君遺事 (*Chao-tai ts'ung-shu* ed.); Wang Kuo-wei (BDRC), *Kuan-t'ang chi-lin* 觀堂集林 (Taipei, 1956), 17/29b; Saγang Sečen, *Erdeni-yin tobči*, tr. by I. J. Schmidt, *Geschichte der Ost-mongolen und ihres Fürstenhauses* (St. Petersburg-Leipzig, 1829), 123; *Koryŏ-sa* 高麗史 (1955), 35/31a, 36/4a, 10a, 37/11a, 39/2b, 91/13b; Charles R. Bawden, *The Mongol Chronicle Altan Tobči* (Wiesbaden, 1955), 149; Otto Franke, *Geschichte des chinesischen Reiches*, Vol. IV (Berlin, 1948), 518, Vol. V (Berlin, 1952), 257; Helmut Schulte-Uffelage, *Das Keng-shen wai-shih, eine Quelle zur späten Mongolenzeit* (Berlin, 1963); Louis Hambis-Paul Pelliot, *Le Chapitre CVII du Yuan Che* (Leiden, 1945), 140; *id.*, *Le Chapitre CVIII du Yuan Che* (Leiden, 1954), 170; Herbert Franke, "Some Remarks on the Interpretation of Chinese Dynastic Histories," *Oriens* 3 (1950), 113; *id.*, "Could the Mongol Emperors Read and Write Chinese?" *AM*, n. s. 3 (1952), 28; *id.*, *Beiträge zur Kulturgeschichte Chinas unter der Mongolenherrschaft-Das Shan-kü sin-hua des Yang Yü*, Wiesbaden, 1956; D. Pokotilov, *History of the Eastern Mongols during the Ming Dynasty from 1368 to 1634*, tr. by R. Loewenthal, *Studia Serica*, Ser. A, no. 1 (Chengtu, 1947), 5; Wolfgang Franke, *Addenda and Corrigenda* to D. Pokotilov, *Studia Serica*, Ser. A, no. 3 (Chengtu and Peiping, 1949), 5; S. J. Shaw, "Historical Significance of the Curious Theory of the Mongol Blood in the Veins of the Ming Emperors," *Chinese Social and Political Science Review*, XX, 4 (1937), 492; Erich Haenisch, *Zum Untergang zweier Reiche: Berichte von Augenzeugen aus den Jahren 1232-33 und 1368-70*, Wiesbaden, 1969.

Herbert Franke

TOγUS Temür 脫古(忽)思帖木兒, 1342-1388/89 (referred to as 豆仇叱帖木兒 in Korean records), emperor, was the younger brother of Ayuširidara (*q.v.*), and succeeded to the leadership of those Mongols who remained loyal to the Yüan dynasty. At the time of his accession in the summer of 1378 he received a diplomatic mission from Chu Yüan-chang offering condolences on his father's death, but declined to accept the authority of the Ming emperor. He changed the Yüan reign title to T'ien-yüan 天元.

The reign of Toγus Temür saw further decline of Mongol power. Late in April, 1380, the Ming general, Mu Ying (*q.v.*), made a surprise attack on the Mongol forces massed near Qaraqorum, and defeated them, capturing Toγoči 脫火赤 and another of Toγus Temür's principal supporters with all their men. Later (December 16) Öljei-buqa 完者不花 and Nair-buqa (*see* Chu Ti), invading Ming territories at Yung-p'ing 永平, were defeated and Öljei-buqa was captured. In 1381 Hsü Ta (*q.v.*) was sent on another expedition against the Mongols, and on May 9 defeated Nair-buqa and scattered his forces. With Kökö Temür (*q.v.*) long dead, the principal remaining Mongol leader was Naγaču (*q.v.*) commanding an estimated two hundred thousand Mongols in the

region north of Peiping. In the same year
Fu Yu-te (*q.v.*) achieved the conquest of
Yünnan, whose ruler, Basalawarmi, the
prince of Liang (*see* Fu Yu-te), had remained loyal to the Yüan since 1368.

The Ming northern frontier remained
relatively calm for several years thereafter.
Following Hsü Ta's death in 1385, Feng
Sheng (*q.v.*) succeeded as commander-in-
chief at Peiping assisted by Fu Yu-te and
Lan Yü (*q.v.*). Ming policy remained
confined to passive defense and the establishment of military colonies until late
January, 1387, when Feng and his colleagues were ordered to conquer Naɣaču. In
the ensuing campaign Lan Yü won a small
success and Naɣaču finally surrendered in
July. Soon afterwards Lan Yü replaced
Feng Sheng as commander-in-chief, and
on November 11, 1387, he led an expeditionary force into an area north of the Gobi
desert. After a brilliant forced march, his
men attacked the Mongol encampment at
Lake Büyür 捕魚兒海 by surprise on May
18, 1388, and completely defeated the Mongols. Toɣus Temür and his eldest son T'ien-
pao-nu 天保奴 were fortunately mounted
when the Ming soldiers threatened, and
made good their escape, but a younger
son, Ti-pao-nu (*see* Kuo Ying), and
other princes were captured, along with
Toɣus Temür's harem, an estimated three
thousand officials, seventy-seven thousand
ordinary Mongols of both sexes, and one
hundred fifty thousand domestic animals.

This defeat broke the power of the
Yüan remnants for a score of years. Toɣus
Temür survived as a refugee until the
winter of 1388/89, when he and T'ien-
pao-nu were set upon and murdered in
the vicinity of Qaraqorum by a distant
relative named Yesüder 也速迭兒. The
Yüan imperial family then entered upon
a period of short reigns by weak rulers
who were merely puppets in the hands of
rival leaders. Toɣus Temür was posthumously canonized as Usaqal Qaɣan 烏薩哈
爾汗.

Bibliography

1/327/2b; MSL, (1962), T'ai-tsu, 2060, 2074, 2128,
2137, 2162, 2721, 2750, 2783, 2865, 2978; K'o
Shao-min (BDRC), *Hsin Yüan-shih*, 26/18b, 27/
55b; Huang Chang-chien 黃彰健, "Lun Ming-
ch'u Pei Yüan chün-chu shih-hsi" 論明初北
元君主世系, CYYY 37, pt. 1 (1967), 314; *Koryŏ-sa* 高麗史, Vol. 3 (1908), 696; Henry H.
Howorth, *History of the Mongols* (London, 1876),
part 1, 345; Henry Serruys, *The Mongols
in China during the Hung-wu Period (1368-1398)*,
MCB, 11 (1959), 42, 51, 80, 185, 289; Louis
Hambis, *Documents sur l'histoire des Mongols à
l'époque des Ming* (Paris, 1969), 12.

Edward L. Dreyer

TŌYŌ, *see* **Sesshū Tōyō**

TRIGAULT, Niklaas (Nicolas Nicola
金尼閣, T. 四表), March 3 (or 13),1577-
November 14, 1628, a Belgian missionary,
was born in Douai, studied in a Jesuit
school in the same city, and entered the
Society of Jesus at Tournai on November
9 (or 22), 1594. He moved next to Lille
and thence to Ghent where for eight
years he taught rhetoric while continuing
his education in languages, geography, astronomy, mathematics, and medicine. After
a further course in theology he received
permission (1606) to leave for the East,
embarking from Coimbra in 1607. Following two years and more in Goa and the
vicinity he proceeded to Macao (1610)
and thence overland to Nanking (March,
1611), where he studied Chinese briefly
under the direction of Alfonso Vagnoni
and Lazzaro Cattaneo (*qq.v.*). Nicolo
Longobardi (*q.v.*), the new superior of the
mission in China, next ordered him to
Hangchow (May 8, 1611), where the
father of Li Chih-tsao (ECCP) had just
passed away, and thence to Peking and
Nanking (August, 1611) to continue his
work on the language. On all his travels,
we read, he determined the latitude and
longitude of each place.

At this juncture Longobardi had his mind set (apparently independent of higher authority) on securing certain concessions from the Pope, to enlist recruits, and financial aid, and to build up the collections of European books in Peking and elsewhere. As his envoy he selected Trigault. The latter probably left Macao on February 9, 1613. His journey back to Rome was no ordinary one, for—traveling by an Arab vessel out of Goa—he touched down at Hormuz, and proceeded overland via Basra, Baghdad, Mosul, and Aleppo, and thence by ship across the Mediterranean, reaching Rome at the end of 1614. An account of his travels has been preserved in manuscript in Brussels and in Vienna. During the next three and a half years he busied himself in Rome, where he successfully discharged his mission with Pope Paul V and published (1615; see below) his version of the memoirs of Matteo Ricci (q.v.), to which he added two final chapters telling of the death and funeral of his forerunner. He also traveled to many of the most important centers in Europe, where he persuaded people of substance and rank to make donations of books, clocks, astronomical and mathematical instruments, and items of special quality (such as tapestries from Flanders, the gift of Marie de Medici of France, church ornaments and paintings, given by Isabel of Spain, and a reliquary from the archbishop of Trêves), besides coin of the realm, all to advance the cause of the church in China. By February, 1618, he was again in Lisbon, where twenty-two recruits were assembled to accompany him to China, among them Johann Terrenz Giacomo Rho, and Johann Adam Schall von Bell (qq.v.). The party set sail on April 16, after he had obtained permission from King Philippe III for the departure of several Spanish Jesuits and a donation sufficient to found fifteen residences in China. On board, until illness struck, the missionaries went through a regular regimen of study, on alternate days Trigault teaching

Chinese, and Terrenz mathematics, every day being given over to astronomy. Disease unhappily took a heavy toll, Trigault's own brother (Élie or Philippe) being among the casualties, Niklaas himself barely surviving. He finally reached Macao on July 22, 1619, where the report of his meeting with the pope and news of fresh funds and rich gifts received were welcomed with unfeigned delight.

During the next nine years he served in a number of places in interior China. From Hangchow in 1622 he left for Kaifeng in 1623, thence (1624) to Chiang-chou 絳州 in Shansi, from there to Sian (where he was the first European to see the Nestorian monument of 781; see Manuel Dias, the younger), and back (1625) to Hangchow. In spite of his years abroad he seems to have acquired a superior knowledge of the language, both written and spoken, for he spent much of his time writing and publishing works of utility both for Chinese and for European readers. In Chiang-chou and in Sian he instituted establishments for printing in Chinese and in Latin. Though he did not neglect pastoral and administrative duties (he served for a time as procurator for Nan-Chihli, Kiangsi, and Kwangtung), it is probably by his published work and his signal services in Europe that he is best remembered. He passed away in Hangchow, and was buried alongside several of his confrères at Fang-ching 方井. A portrait by Rubens of a Jesuit missionary in Chinese dress, dating from 1617, is said to depict Trigault; it is preserved in the National Museum in Stockholm. Another (?) copy is in the Musée de Douai.

Among his publications in Chinese one may cite his calendar (written also in Latin and Syriac) composed for Chinese Christians, giving the times of fasts and festivals according to both European and Chinese calendrical systems, T'ui-ting li-nien chan-li jih-tan 推定曆年瞻禮日單, Hangchow, 1625 (Matteo Ricci had initiated this enterprise but Trigault completed it); his key to the pronunciation of Chinese characters, *Hsi-ju er-mu tzu* 西儒耳目資, Hangchow, 1626 (a work edited by Wang Cheng [ECCP] , which was to influence Fang I-chih [ECCP] , and to receive critical attention in the *Ssu-k'u* catalogue); and his translation of Aesop's fables, *K'uang-i* 況義, Sian, 1625 (later enlarged and reprinted in Hong Kong, 1840). In western languages his outstanding work was entitled *De Christiana Expeditione apud Sinas ab societate Iesu suscepta. Ex P. Matthaei Ricci jeiusdem societatis commentarijs* (Rome, 1615). This is not the original work of Ricci who had left in manuscript an account of China and his mission, written in Italian, supplemented after his death by Gaspar Ferreira (*q.v.*), Longobardi, and Cattaneo. Rather it is an amplification, with some omissions and misreadings, written in Latin. Attracting almost immediate attention, it was translated successively into French, German, Spanish, Italian, and (partly) into English. In 1910 the learned Jesuit Pietro Tacchi Venturi prepared a critical edition of Ricci's original manuscript, together with his letters, bringing them out in two volumes, *Opere storiche*. His lack of knowledge of Chinese, however, made it necessary for Pasquale M. d'Elia, S. J., to produce an edition in three volumes with full critical apparatus, entitled *Fonti Ricciane*. In spite of these superb editions, it is still probably Trigault's rendering which has received the widest attention, at least among the English reading public. In 1942 Louis J. Gallagher, S. J., published *The China that Was*, based on the first volume of Trigault's work, and in 1953 *China in the Sixteenth Century: The Journals of Matthew Ricci: 1583-1610*, which is based on all five.

The books which Trigault brought to China in 1619 are among the most precious relics of the Jesuit mission of three and a half centuries ago (*see* Longobardi). Reportedly seven thousand in all (though the number is in question), they included 534 works in 457 volumes from the Pontifical library, which Trigault thus describes (in the English rendering of H. Verhaeren, C. M.): "As to the variety of the works contained, besides literature, philosophy and theology, the Fathers and other kinds of works usually to be found in our libraries, this Library contains many authors on medicine, Ecclesiastical law, civil law, and music; and as for mathematics, I collected with hardly a single exception all that exist. As to the splendour of the volumes, they are all bound in red skin, with the Papal arms and the titles in letters of gold. I also tried to get volumes of a big size." A large number of these have survived the buffetings of time and (at least until 1949) were the proud possessions of the Pei-t'ang Library in Peking.

Bibliography

Pfister, 111; Sommervogel, Vol. 8, cols. 237-244; Pasquale M. d'Elia, *Galileo in China*, tr. by R. Suter and M. Sciascia (Cambridge, Mass., 1960), 23, 29, 94; *Fonti Ricciane*, I (Rome, 1924), clxxi; H. Verhaeren, *Catalogue of the Pei-t'ang Library* (Peking, 1949), vii-xi; George H. Dunne, *Generation of Giants* (Notre Dame, 1962), chap. 10; H. Havret, *La stèle chrétienne de Si-ngan-fou* (Shanghai, 1895), 69; H. Cordier, *Bibliotheca Sinica* (2d ed., Paris, 1904-8), cols. 773, 809-11, 814, 1097-98, 3565; SK (1930), 44/5b; Fortunato Margiotti, *Il cattolicismo nello Shansi dalle origini al 1738* (Rome, 1958), 85; Fang Hao 方豪, *Ming-chi hsi-shu ch'i ch'ien-pu liu-ju Chung-kuo k'ao* 明季西書七千部流入中國考, in *Wen-shih tsachih* 文史雜誌 (1945), Vol. 3, nos. 1-2.

L. Carrington Goodrich

TS'AI Ching, *see* **CHANG Ching** 張經

TS'AO Chao 曹昭 (T. 明中, H. 寶古生), fl. 1387-99, antiquarian, was a native of Sung-chiang 松江 in the lower Yangtze valley, then a center of some affluence. He grew up in a well-to-do family of collectors and men of letters, who had originally come from Shanghai. Ts'ao Chao himself vouchsafes that his father was a collector and a connoisseur of the arts; so too apparently was his elder brother, Ts'ao Ti 迪 (T. 簡伯, H. 古村), as one of his studios bore the name Pao-ku-chai 寶古齋 (studio of appreciation of antiquities), from which Ts'ao Chao took his own literary name. We learn also from another fellow-townsman, Ku Ch'ing 顧清 (T. 士廉, H. 東江, 1460–1528, cs 1493), that Ts'ao Chao and Ts'ao Ti were friends of such literati as Yang Wei-chen (q.v.) and Ch'ien Wei-shan 錢惟善 (T. 思復, H. 心白道人). This seems to be the extent of information that can be gleaned about Ts'ao Chao and his family, except, of course, that he was the author of a famous book entitled Ko-ku yao-lun 格古要論, 3 ch., which Sir Percival David has translated and elegantly produced. (Actually Sir Percival never lived to see his book between covers; it was published posthumously through the efforts of Basil Grey and others.)

The Ko-ku yao-lun originally appeared in Nanking in 1387 or 1388, in 3 chüan. During the following decade the author revised and enlarged it to 5 chüan, of which a certain Shu Min 舒敏 (T. 志學), a contemporary otherwise unknown, seems to have made some rearrangement and added a few words to Ts'ao Chao's text. Besides these two 14th century editions there are at least five more issued before the end of the Ming dynasty. The most important is the one published (posthumously?) in 1462, which Wang Tso 王佐 (T. 功載, H. 竹齋, cs 1427), who served as prefect of Hangchow in 1457–59 [not to be confused with the minister of Revenue of the same name who died in 1449], augmented to 13 chüan in 1459, and published under the new title Hsin-tseng 新增 ko-ku yao-lun. Among the others may be mentioned an abridged version published in 1596 in 5 chüan by Hu Wen-huan 胡文煥, a bookseller of Hangchow, who changed the title to Ko-ku lun-yao; a revised edition in 13 chüan made by Cheng P'u 鄭

朴, ca. 1600; and the editions brought out by Huang Kung 黃琪 and Huang Cheng-wei 正位, both of Hsin-tu 新都 (i. e., Hui-chou 徽州, Anhwei, not in Szechwan as Basil Gray assumes in the introduction to David's translation).

In 1940 the Commercial Press in Shanghai reprinted a ts'ung-shu entitled I-men kuang-tu 夷門廣牘, compiled by Chou Lü-ching 周履靖 (T. 逸之, H. 梅顛道人, 螺冠子, fl. 1582-96) in 1596, which included a facsimile of the 3 chüan edition of 1387/88. Though this has a number of misprints, it has made Ts'ao's original book widely available. The same edition was copied into the Ssu-k'u ch'üan-shu.

The Ko-ku yao-lun is a pioneer work on Chinese art and archaeology. It deals with calligraphy, paintings, zithers, stones, jades, bronzes, ink-slabs, ceramics, and lacquer; also with certain imported items, such as carpets, rare woods and stones. Wang Tso, who lived during the years following the great expeditions of Cheng Ho, Ch'en Ch'eng (qq.v.), et al., was able to expand this area somewhat, as he did in certain new subjects—imperial seals, iron tallies, official costumes of the Sung and Yüan dynasties, and palaces of the Five Dynasties, Sung, and Yüan. One omission, noted long ago, is a general discussion of seals, possibly because both Ts'ao and Wang saw no need to add to the existing literature on this subject. Perhaps the most significant contributions are the descriptions of porcelain and lacquer. At the beginning of this century Stephen W. Bushell gave a translation in full of the latter in his book Chinese Art, and David himself several decades ago made use of the part on the former in his discussion of Ju 汝 ware.

Bibliography

Ts'ao Chao, Ko-ku yao-lun, I-men kuang-tu edition (Shanghai, 1940); Sung-chiang-fu chih (1819), 72/22a; Chi-an-fu chih 吉安府志 (1875), 28/40a; SK (1930), 123/1b; Chang T'ieh-hsüan 張鐵弦, "Ming-tai te wen-wu chien-shang shu Ko-ku yao-lun" 明代的文物鑒賞書‥‥, Wen-wu 文物

(1962), 1: 43; Chuang Shen, "Ming Antiquarianism, an Aesthetic Approach to Archaeology," *Jo. of Or. Studies*, 8 (1970), 64, 69; Berthold Laufer, "Arabic and Chinese Trade in Walrus and Narwhal Ivory," TP, 14 (1913), 325; Paul Pelliot, "Bibliographie," *ibid.*, 25(1928), 102; *id.*, "Le prétendu album de porcelaines de Hiang Yuan-pien," *ibid.*, 32 (1936), 50, 53, 55; S. W. Bushell, *Chinese Art*, Vol. 1 (1904, repr. of 1924), 111; Schuyler Cammann, "The Story of Hornbill Ivory," *Bull. of the Univ. Museum*, 15: 4 (Philadelphia, December, 1950), 26; Sir Percival David, "Commentary on Ju Ware," *Transactions of the Oriental Ceramic Society*, 14 (1936-37), 29; *id.*, *Chinese Connoisseurship, the Ko Ku Yao Lun*, London, 1971.

L. Carrington Goodrich

TS'AO Chi-hsiang 曹吉祥, died August 10, 1461, eunuch, a native of Luan-chou 灤州 (Pei-Chihli), who was executed for his *coup d'état* against Emperor Chu Ch'i-chen (*q.v.*), rose during the Cheng-t'ung period as a protégé of the grand eunuch Wang Chen (*q.v.*). In the campaigns (1438–43) against Ssu Jen-fa (*q.v.*) of Lu-ch'uan (Yunnan), Ts'ao served as supervisor of the armed forces, and in the campaign against the Uriyangqad Mongols early in 1444 he commanded a division of the army. In a subsequent campaign against the rebel Teng Mao-ch'i (*q.v.*) of Fukien (1448-49) Ts'ao was in charge of the firearm units. In these engagements he distinguished himself by his military ability, and built up a following among the officers.

Ts'ao was in the capital when the Ming army was almost liquidated in the T'u-mu battle (1449) by the Oirat leader, Esen (*q.v.*), and he and his close colleague Shih Heng (*q.v.*) threw their support behind minister of War Yü Ch'ien (*q.v.*), who insisted that the court remain in Peking and defend it at all costs. Shih was made earl and then marquis of Wu-ch'ing for this, and in 1453 Yü Ch'ien, Shih, Ts'ao, and the eunuch Liu Yung-ch'eng (*q.v.*) jointly assumed charge of the integrated divisions called t'uan-ying, a novel organization to which the combat-ready troops in Peking were assigned.

When Emperor Chu Ch'i-yü (*q.v.*) fell ill early in 1457, Ts'ao Chi-hsiang and Shih Heng were the key military figures behind the restoration of his elder brother, the ex-emperor Chu Ch'i-chen, who was released from captivity by Esen late in 1450. Together Shih and Ts'ao engineered an extensive purge of the main supporters of Emperor Chu Ch'i-yü, headed by Yü Ch'ien, who were either executed or banished. Shih was rewarded with the noble title of duke, while Ts'ao was promoted to director of Ceremonial (though he was illiterate), which gave him control over the palace staff, and commander-in-chief of the Three Garrisons 三大營 in Peking. Ts'ao's adopted son and heir Ts'ao Ch'in 欽 and his nephews were made military commissioners-in-chief; late in this year Ts'ao Ch'in was made earl of Chao-wu 昭武. Shih and Ts'ao thus dominated the court and government, and initiated further purges to cosolidate their power. Among their victims were Hsü Yu-chen and Li Hsien (*qq.v.*). Shih and Ts'ao's domination, however, aroused bitter opposition.

In the meanwhile Yang Hsüan 瑄 (*q.v.*), then censor, had learned that the families of both Shih Heng and Ts'ao had been responsible for misappropriating a great deal of arable land in Pei-Chihli from the local people; on June 14 he issued a memorial accusing them of gross malfeasance. Several members of the Censorate joined Yang in his complaint, and things looked black for Shih and Ts'ao, as the emperor had ordered an inquiry. But they were forehanded, and lodged counter accusations. The upshot was that Yang Hsüan, his fellow censors, and two high officials were all sentenced to prison, and Yang nearly lost his life. Both Shih and Ts'ao escaped punishment, remaining for a time at least in the good graces of the emperor. On February 17, 1460, however, nettled by further charges, the emperor had Shih Heng sent to prison, where he eventually died. After this Ts'ao began to fear for his position, especially since the commander of the Embroidered-uniform Guard, Lu Kao 逯杲, did not belong to his party. As their power declined, Ts'ao Chi-hsiang, his nephews, and Ts'ao Ch'in, allegedly inspired by the historical example of Ts'ao Ts'ao (adopted son of a eunuch family who had succeeded in founding an imperial dynasty), plotted rebellion.

Ts'ao had arranged for Ts'ao Ch'in and his nephews to lead an armed rising in the capital in the pre-dawn darkness on August 7, 1461. The plot was betrayed the night before to Sun T'ang (see Chu Chien-shen) and Wu Chin 吳瑾 (T. 廷璋, 1413-61, made marquis of Kung-shun恭順 in 1449, d. August 7, 1461, Pth. 忠壯), two generals not of Ts'ao's party (the latter was a Mongol), who were then in Peking organizing an army to suppress a rebellion which had broken out in Kansu. Sun and Wu managed to gain access to the emperor, who had Ts'ao Chi-hsiang placed under arrest in the palace. Ts'ao Ch'in, hearing of this, led his troops into the city, killed Lu Kao, and attempted to storm the gates of the Imperial City. Wu Chin was killed in the fighting, and Ts'ao Ch'in's troops succeeded in burning down the Tung-an Gate 東安門, but the heat of the resulting conflagration was so intense that they were unable to enter the Imperial City. By dawn troops loyal to the emperor had gained the upper hand. Ts'ao Ch'in fled and barricaded himself in his mansion; when the imperial troops broke in, he committed suicide by jumping in a well. Three days later Ts'ao Chi-hsiang was executed by being torn to pieces by chariots; his nephews and his civil and military supporters were also put to death. His property, which was enormous, was confiscated and returned to the proper owners.

Ts'ao Chi-hsiang's coup against the throne gives another illustration, after the fall of Wang Chen, of the tremendous power enjoyed by the eunuchs and the political consequences of their domination. His case was repeatedly cited in later periods by scholar-officials who implored the throne to curb their power, but the emperors failed to appreciate the historical lessons, and the great use of these imperial favorites eventually sapped the strength of the dynasty.

Bibliography

1/10/3b, 116b, 12/1a, 106/31b, 304/10a; 5/117/52a; 61/158/9b; MSL (1963), Ying-tsung, 2257, 3303, 5787, 5961, 5968, 6099, 6777, 6783; KC (1958), 2124; Yang Hsüan, *Fu-p'i lu* in *Chi-lu hui-pien* ed. by Shen Chieh-fu, 21/5a; Li Hsien, *T'ien shun jih-lu, ibid.,* 22/3b; Lu Jung 陸容, *Shu-yüan tsa-chi* 菽園雜記, *ibid.,* 183/6b; Wang Shih-chen, "Chung-kuan k'ao 中官考," *Yen-shan-t'ang pien-chi,* 90/16a, 91/21b; Ting I 丁易, *Ming-tai t'e-wu cheng-chih* 明代特務政治 (1950), 60, 87, 345, 418, 521; R. B. Crawford, "Eunuch Power in the Ming Dynasty," TP, 49 (1961), 146, n. 1.

Edward L. Dreyer

TS'AO Hsüeh-ch'üan 曹學佺 (T. 能始, H. 雁澤, 雁峯), 1574-1646, scholar and official, was a native of Hou-kuan 侯官 (Foochow). After obtaining the *chin-shih* in 1595 he was appointed secretary in the ministry of Revenue, and rose, following a succession of posts in Nanking and Szechwan, to become intendant of Kuei-p'ing circuit 桂平道, Kwangsi (1624). One incident in his career at this time demonstrates his forthrightness and courage. At the trial of the "club case" in 1615 (see Chu I-chün), the defendant was pronounced insane and the case dismissed; but Ts'ao disagreed with the findings of the court and wrote a book on the affair entitled *Yeh-shih chi-lüeh* 野史紀略. When it came to the attention of the eunuch faction of Wei Chung-hsien (ECCP), he was accused of distorting the facts in the case. Dismissal from office followed, along with complete suppression of the book. The authorities in Kwangsi, believing that Wei intended to do away with Ts'ao, kept him in protective custody, but being unable to verify Wei's designs, later let him go.

About 1628 Ts'ao was restored to his former rank and invited to return to office but declined and for nearly twenty years spent most of his time at home studying and writing. In 1645 when the prince of T'ang (Chu Yü-chien, ECCP) fled to Fukien and set up his court at Foochow, Ts'ao was appointed chief minister of the Court of Imperial Sacrifices. Subsequently he was promoted to be first vice minister and later minister of Rites with the additional title of grand guardian of the heir apparent.

A conscientious official, Ts'ao was always eager to relieve the sufferings of the people and they appreciated his concern for them. For some time he was given the task of supervising army provisions and relief work. As a scholar he was considered one of the most learned men of his time and was frequently consulted on details of ritual. His colleagues respected his integrity. Although Ts'ao himself knew that the political situation was desperate, he resolved to do what he could to help resist the invader. In 1645 there was talk of forming a Fukien fleet to recover Nanking from the Manchus. Ts'ao was one of the most enthusiastic supporters of this plan, holding that the employment of such a force might be a turning point in Ming fortunes. The plan never was carried out despite Ts'ao's sacrifice of his own property and his efforts to scrape together ten thousand silver taels. It is said that the military leader in power, Cheng Chih-lung (ECCP), did not support it.

In the summer of that same year Ts'ao was appointed chief compiler of the *shih-lu* of the Ch'ung-chen period and the court set aside a special building, naming it Lan-t'ai kuan 蘭臺館, for him. By this time the situation in Fukien had deteriorated. Cheng Chih-lung's complete control of the province had caused dissatisfaction among the other officials; the Manchus were approaching from Chekiang; and the Ming adherents were short of both

soldiers and provisions. In moments of despair Ts'ao could only sigh and say to his colleagues that he was not a soldier but that if Fukien were saved from the enemy he would carry through the compilation of the *shih-lu;* if all failed he was determined never to surrender. Early in 1646 the prince of T'ang, tired of the domination of Cheng Chih-lung, accepted the invitation of Ho T'eng-chiao (ECCP) to move his court to Changsha, Hukuang. Months later, while on his way, he was taken prisoner at T'ing-chou 汀州 (October 6). Meanwhile another of the Ch'ing detachments had marched against Foochow, where Cheng Chih-lung surrendered. Ts'ao retired to a Buddhist monastery and is said to have become a monk.

Some of the loyal adherents of the Ming attempted an uprising. Teng T'ing-ts'ai 鄧廷寀 in his book *Tung-nan chi-shih* 東南紀事 identifies three of them as: Ch'i Hsün 齊巽, student of the National University, Chang Pin 張份, a drafter in the Grand Secretariat, and Pu-k'ung 不空, a physician and Buddhist monk. They approached Ts'ao and told him that, since the families of means in the city had all fled, he was the only one on whom they could rely for help. They implored him therefore to leave the monastery and join them in resisting the Manchus. The hopelessness of the project was all too clear to Ts'ao, yet he was moved by their sincerity and agreed to take up arms. Three days later (October 24, 1646) the Manchu prince Bolo (ECCP) marched into the city with a large army. Ts'ao, seeing that all was over, hanged himself in his own home. The members of his family were all imprisoned by the conquerors and his property confiscated. Not till the fifth day after his death were they able to bury his body. The posthumous title Chung-chieh 忠節 was conferred on him in 1776.

Ts'ao was a prolific writer and is known for literary work of various genres. The poet Wang Shih-chen 王士禎 (ECCP) remarked that, for the last fifty years of the Ming, Ts'ao was the only poet who could be said to have caught the spirit of the poetry of the Six Dynasties and the T'ang. Wang went on to say that Ts'ao was the only poet of his time besides T'ang Hsien-tsu (ECCP) whom Ch'ien Ch'ien-i (ECCP) admired.

As a bibliophile Ts'ao accumulated a large number of books and filled them with annotations marked with ink of different colors. Eight of his own writings totaling 87 *chüan*, were studies of the canon. His fellow townsmen Hsü Po and Hsieh Chao-che (*qq. v.*) too were noted bibliophiles. It is said that in cooperation with his friends he labored on a collection of works in the Confucian field, to be called *Ju tsang* 儒藏, which would parallel the *Tao tsang* of the Taoists and the *Tripiṭaka* of the Buddhists, but the project was never brought to completion. (*See also* Huang Yü-chi and Chou Yung-nien in ECCP.) Because of his stay in Szechwan Ts'ao also devoted a great deal of time to writings on aspects there which caught his fancy: biographies of famous men, accounts of deified genii and Buddhist abbots, records of gardens and writers, reviews of poems, and notes on learned Buddhists, local customs, local products, and famous places. The last, entitled *Shu-chung kuang-chi* 蜀中廣記, 108 *ch.*, was included in the 18th century imperial manuscript library; in 1935 a copy was reproduced in the *Ssu-k'u chüan-shu chen-pen ch'u-chi* 珍本初集. The first part of this work, however, had been printed in 1618 under the title *Shu-chung ming-sheng chi* 名勝記, 30 *ch.* Famous places seem to have fascinated him, for he wrote as well on various sites, all included in a general work for the whole of China, *Ta Ming i-t'ung* 大明一統 *ming-sheng chih*, 208 *ch.*, printed in 1631 in Foochow. A copy of this work is preserved in the Columbia University Library. Ts'ao likewise produced a number of other pieces, both prose and poetry. A collection of these, usually entitled *Shih-ts'ang ch'üan-chi* 石倉全集, in 100 *chüan*, with over 30 subtitles, was

prohibited over a century later by the commissioners of Ch'ien-lung. Several copies are in the Naikaku Bunko. His anthology of the poetry dating from the earliest days down to the middle Ming period, an immense work numbering 506 *chüan*, entitled *Shih-ts'ang li-tai shih-hsüan* 歷代詩選, was printed in 1632. It was apparently added to from time to time, with the result that the total number of *chüan* as reported by collectors varies greatly. Chao-lien (ECCP) notes that his copy of this book numbered 1,743 *chüan*. It is also known by the title *Shih-ts'ang shih-er-tai* 十二代 *shih-hsüan*.

Ts'ao was interested in public works in his native community. Besides concern with dredging of rivers and construction of reservoirs, he took part in rebuilding the famous pagoda, Lo-hsing t'a 羅星塔, and in erecting several bridges, at one of which, the Hung-shan ch'iao 洪山橋, a shrine was put up in his memory.

Bibliography

1/288/15a; 3/269/11b; 36/2/21b; 40/74/10a; 41/10/54b, 13/4b; 59/26/1a; 64/辛1/11a; 84/丁下/32a; 86/21/4a; SK (1930), 72/2b, 189/7b; *Nan-Ming yeh-shih* 南明野史 (Shanghai, 1933) B. 7b, 69a; *Ssu-wen ta-chi* 思文大紀 (T'ung-shih 痛史 edition), 1/11a, 3/2a, 2/8a, 9a, 8/12ab; Cha Chi-tso (ECCP), *Tung-shan kuo-yü* (SPTK 3rd ser.), *Min-yü* 閩語, 2/66b; Chang Tai (ECCP), *Shih-kuei-shu hou-chi* (Shanghai, 1959), 330; Chao-lien, *Hsiao-t'ing tsa-lu* (Shanghai, 1880?), 8/12a; Chou Liang-kung (ECCP), *Min hsiao-chi* (Shanghai, 1936), 34, 46; Fa-shih-shan (ECCP), *T'ao-lu tsa lu* (Shanghai, 1959), 3/94; Huang Yü-chi (ECCP), *Ch'ien-ch'ing-t'ang shu-mu*; *Naikaku bunko kanseki bunrui mokuroku* 內閣文庫漢籍分類目錄 (Tokyo, 1956); Teng T'ing-ts'ai, *Tung-nan chi-shih* (Shanghai, 1940), 1/155, 4/211; Sun Tien-ch'i (1957), 52, 251; Yeh Ch'ang-chih (BDRC), *Ts'ang-shu chi-shih-shih* (Shanghai, 1958), 3/159; Sa Shih-wu 薩士武, "Ts'ao Hsüeh-ch'üan sheng-tsu nien-sui k'ao-cheng," 生卒年歲考正, *Ta-kung pao shih-ti chou-k'an* 大公報史地周刊, no. 137 (Shanghai, May 21, 1937); Kuo Po-ts'ang 郭柏蒼, *Ch'üan Min Ming-shih chuan* 全閩明詩傳, 34/1a; Chang Hsi-hu 張錫祜, "On Fukien literature and writers of the Ming" (in Chinese), *Fu-chien wen-hua* 福建文化, V (November 26, 1937), 70.

Albert Chan

TS'AO Tuan 曹端 (T. 正夫, H. 月川), 1376-July 7, 1434, thinker and teacher, was a native of Mien-ch'ih 澠池, Honan. His forebears came from Shansi, and belonged originally to the Yang 楊 clan. One of his ancestors took the name Ts'ao, as an adopted son of a maternal uncle. Ts'ao Tuan's father was the first to move to Mien-ch'ih. Ts'ao Tuan was reportedly a serious-minded youth, and a good student. In 1408 he acquired the *chü-jen* and the following year, as he failed to qualify as a *chin-shih*, but was placed on the secondary list, he was appointed instructor in Huo-chou 霍州, Shansi. He stayed there nearly nine years, till the death of his parents obliged him to return to his native place and observe the traditional mourning. This lasted nearly five years. Many of his students came from Huo-chou to be near him, continuing to study under him. At the termination of the mourning period (1422), he was transferred to be instructor in P'u-chou 蒲州, Shansi. He remained there until 1425, when, on the occasion of the government's review of officials, the students, both from Huo-chou and from P'u-chou, separately petitioned the court to allow Ts'ao to be sent to them. Since the petition from Huo-chou arrived first, Ts'ao was sent there. He was to remain in Huo-chou another nine years till he died on duty in 1434, aged fifty-eight. The news of his death was reportedly an occasion of genuine sorrow for the local people of the town, who stopped marketing and wept openly in the streets. He was buried in Huo-chou where his two sons, Ts'ao Yü 瑜 and Ts'ao Shen 深, after observing mourning at their father's grave, continued to reside until their deaths. Both Huo-chou and P'u-chou built shrines in Ts'ao Tuan's honor. In 1621 he received the posthumous name Ching-hsiu 靖修.

Ts'ao Tuan, it is alleged, was so studious as a youth that he made hollows with his feet in the floor bricks under his desk. But he did not take instruction from any renowned teacher of philosophy.

As Liu Tsung-chou (ECCP) has pointed out, his learning came from his personal reading of ancient texts, upon which he carefully meditated. Liu compares Ts'ao Tuan to Chou Tun-i (1017-73), and reports how Ts'ao himself had said that, till the age of forty, he had found the quest for Tao very difficult; but that, ten years afterwards, he was awakened (wu 悟) to the knowledge of nature (hsing 性) as that which comprehends all in the universe and that which permeates it. Thus Ts'ao is said to have continued the transmission of Confucian learning interrupted after the death of Fang Hsiao-ju (*q. v.*), in 1402 and he was much esteemed by both Hsüeh Hsüan and Hu Chü-jen (*qq.v.*). Ts'ao Tuan placed some emphasis on the mind and heart, through which man attains the dignity of being one of the "Three Powers," on nearly equal standing with Heaven and Earth. He therefore regards the cultivation of the mind and heart as the principal task of the follower of Confucius.

Ts'ao Tuan is also known for his uncompromising attitude toward Taoist and Buddhist practices. He was determined to have nothing to do with considerations of saṁsāra, nor with practices of sorcery and geomancy (feng-shui 風水), which were so current at the time. He even succeeded in persuading his own father to adopt his views in this regard. He objected to his fellow officials paying reverence to the Taoist deity, Wen-ch'ang chün 文昌君, as the patron of learning, for he regarded Confucius in this light. He also criticized the practice of inviting Buddhist monks to pray for the deliverance from suffering of one's deceased parents, saying that this implied a son's disbelief in his parents' virtue.

Ts'ao Tuan left very few writings that are extant. The editors of the *Ssu-k'u* Catalogue report the existence of three small works. The first is the *T'ai-chi-t'u shu-chieh* 太極圖述解, 1 *ch.* (which gives his view of Chou Tun-i's "Ultimate"); at the end is attached the Pien-li 辨戾, an investigation into the differences between those parts of the commentaries and the recorded dialogues of Chu Hsi (1130-1200) which concern the T'ai-chi and the yin-yang. It carries his own preface, dated 1428. There are also the *T'ung-shu* 通書 *shu-chieh*, 1 *ch.* (explanations of Chou Tun-i's other work), with a preface by Sun Ch'i-feng (ECCP), and the *Hsi-ming* 西銘 *shu-chieh*, 1 *ch.* (a commentary on a work by Chang Tsai, 1020-77). These three works have been published in the same collection. So far as is known they appear only in the *Ssu-k'u ch'üan-shu.* Ts'ao wrote a short treatise, entitled *Yeh-hsing chu* 夜行燭, for the instruction of his father, who had shown more than usual interest in non-Confucian practices. It contains simple, practical quotations from the Classics and their commentaries. Other short works are the *Yüeh-ch'uan yü-lu* 月川語錄, 1 *ch.*, which contains his recorded sayings, the *Li-hsüeh yao-lan* 理學要覽, 1 *ch.*, the *Hsing-ch'ing lun* 性情論, 1 *ch.*, the *Ju-chia tsung-t'ung p'u* 儒家宗統譜, and the *Ts'un-i lu* 存疑錄. One extant collection of Ts'ao's writings is the *Ts'ao Yüeh-ch'uan chi* 集, 1 *ch.*, compiled by Chang Po-hsing (ECCP). It contains the *Yeh-hsing chu, Chia-kuei chi-lüeh* 家規輯畧, *yü-lu, Lu-ts'ui* 錄粹, seven of his prefaces, and fifteen poems. Attached to this collection are certain comments, given by various Confucian scholars, as well as a chronological biography, compiled by Chang Hsin-min 張信民. This collection is preserved in the *Kuang li-hsüeh pei-k'ao* 廣理學備考, compiled by Fan Hao-ting 范鄗鼎 and published in 1825. The Japanese libraries, both the Naikaku and the Seikado, report the existence of hand-written copies of *Ts'ao Yüeh-ch'uan hsien-sheng* 先生 *chi*. It is not known whether this is similar to the version compiled by Chang Po-hsing.

Ts'ao Tuan is often spoken of together with Hsüeh Hsüan and Hu Chü-jen, both of whom are said to have resembled him in character and temperament. Whereas Hsüeh Hsüan's and Hu

Chü-jen's writings are readily available, Ts'ao's are rare. Compared to Hsüeh especially, Ts'ao's prose and poetry appear even less polished. What he left to posterity is especially the exemplary life of a dedicated teacher and earnest follower of the Confucian Way.

Bibliography

1/282/17a; 3/263/5b; 4/6/2a ; 5/97/128a; 32/90/61b; 42/72/1b; 61/111/15b; 83/44/1a, *Shih-shuo* 師說/7a; KC (1958), 1474, 5184; SK (1930), 92/1a, 95/9a, 10b, 170/7a; Feng Shih-k'o 馮時可 (cs 1571), *Ts'ao po-shih* 博士 *Tuan hsiao chuan* 小傳, *Huang Ming wen-hai* (microfilm), 18. 7. 8; Wang I-wu 王以悟, *Yüeh-ch'uan hsien-sheng nien-p'u hsü* 序, in *Wang Hsing-so* 惺所 *hsien-sheng chi*, preface 1623 (NCL microfilm), 1/1a; id., *Yüeh-ch'uan hsien-sheng lu ts'ui hsü*, in *Wang Hsing-so hsien-sheng chi*, 1/6a; id., *Yeh* 謁 *Ts'ao Yüeh-ch'uan hsien-sheng tz'u* 祠, in *Wang Hsing-so hsien-sheng chi*, 10/8a; *Huo-chou chih* (1826), 20/3a; *P'ing-yang-fu chih* (1736), 20/65a, 23/38b, 60a; *P'u-chou-fu chih* (1754), 7/25b; Wing-tsit Chan, "The Ch'eng-Chu School of Early Ming," in W. T. de Bary (ed.), *Self and Society in Ming Thought* (New York, 1970), 33.

Julia Ching

TSENG Ch'i-hsin, *see* HAN-SHIH

TSENG Hsien 曾銑 (T. 子重, H. 石塘), 1499-April 25, 1548, an official, born into a family of the military category, who urged the recovery of the Ordos from the Mongols, was a native of Chiang-tu 江都, prefecture of Yangchow. A bright youth, he qualified for the *chü-jen* in 1528 and the *chin-shih* the following year. His first assignment was as magistrate of Ch'ang-lo 長樂, Fukien, after which he was made (January, 1534) a censor and regional inspector of Liaotung. In April, 1535, while in Chin-chou 金州 on the Liaotung peninsula, he received an urgent report of a mutiny by soldiers of Liao-yang 遼陽 who had expelled their tormentor, the governor of Liaotung, Lü Ching 呂經 (T. 道夫, H. 九川, 1476-1544, cs 1508). Tseng Hsien at once ordered (May) the regional vice commander, Li Chien 李鑑, to take charge. Later they succeeded in seizing and executing the ringleaders, and putting down the mutiny. This won Tseng the name of an expert on military affairs. Late in this year he became director of the Grand Court of Revision, then moved up to the post of left assistant censor-in-chief and governor of Shantung in 1541.

Altan-qaγan (q.v.) was just at this point beginning his frequent raids into Chinese territory. In 1542 Tseng, acting on the recommendation of the local military commander, proposed construction of an outer rampart for the city of Lin-ch'ing 臨清 on the Grand Canal. Having obtained access to the writings of Ch'iu Chün (q.v.), he set about erecting an elaborate affair, some seven miles in length, which encircled the city and bestrode the two streams which meet there: the Wen 汶 and the Wei 衛, which form part of the Grand Canal system. It had two gates on both the east and the west sides, and a single gate on each of the other sides, as well as three water gates, besides towers and stations for the guards. It came to be popularly known as Yü-tai ch'eng 玉帶城 (Jade girdle wall). This done, he advanced to vice censor-in-chief (September, 1543) after which he was made governor of Shansi (February, 1544) as well as defender of Yen-men 雁門 and other passes in the Great Wall. For a time, it is said, the Mongols ceased making mischief. Early in 1546 Tseng rose to the rank of a vice minister of War and on May 8 he received the appointment of supreme commander of Shansi. Altan-qaγan was now on the rampage. Having been rebuffed by the court in the matter of trade arrangements, he sent one large army of horsemen into Shensi via Yen-an 延安 and Ch'ing-yang 慶陽. Tseng, on his part, dispatched a local commander, Li Chen 李珍, to attack the rear of the Mongol force by a circuitous route where the older men, the women, and the children were encamped. He himself, with the main army, met the invaders head on, and after slaying over a hundred compelled their retreat. In January, 1547, Tseng proposed that the emperor reverse the defensive policy and recover the whole region within the bend of the Yellow River. Grand Secretary Hsia Yen (q.v.) supported his proposal. Accordingly the emperor asked Tseng to submit a detailed report on how this could be done. Tseng, on January 10, 1548, presented a memorial containing eighteen points, together with eight maps and diagrams. A number of his points are about what one might expect: rebuilding of frontier walls, selection of men of military ability and of those capable of training others, addition of good horses and mules, preparation of boats and wheeled vehicles, procuring an abundance of explosive weapons, and a clear statement as to rewards and punishments. But he also explained how valuable the region was in pasture land and salt lakes, how for years it had served the Mongols for their attacks on Hsüan-fu and Tatung, and how important it had been in the opinions of previous monarchs. He suggested that each spring and summer a detachment of soldiers be given him, with supplies for fifty days, to defend the region and keep the Mongols at bay. For this purpose he calculated that he would require sixty thousand men, plus two thousand from Shantung equipped with firearms. Several other officials, including Weng Wan-ta (see Wang Chiu-ssu), then supreme commander, suggested instead an increase in the fortifications of the frontier. For a time the emperor seemed favorably disposed towards Tseng's proposal, and had given him some financial support; but Yen Sung (q.v.) and Minister of War Wang I-ch'i 王以旂 (T. 士招, H. 石岡, cs 1511, d. April 13, 1553, Pth. 襄敏), considering the enormity of the funds required, were not. Furthermore, Ch'iu Luan (q.v.)—then regional commander of Kansu, whom Tseng had found insubordinate and sent to Peking into the tender care of the Embroidered-uniform Guard—in turn filed an accusation against Tseng. This spelled the end for the two principal advocates of an offensive policy: Hsia Yen and Tseng. Tseng was accused *inter alia* of recommending an unrealistic military policy which would squander government resources; his opponents also charged him with intimidating his dissenters. Both men were condemned to death and executed. Tseng was then forty-nine years of age. His wife and son, Tseng Ch'un 淳, who was admitted to the National University in 1546, suffered exile to a point almost seven hundred miles away. When word of this sentence was noised abroad, people grieved, considering it too harsh. Early in the Lung-ch'ing period (1567) the supervising secretary, Hsin Tzu-hsiu (*see* Ku Hsien-ch'eng) and the censor Wang Hao-wen 王好問 (T. 裕卿, H. 西塘, 1517-82, cs 1550) demanded that justice be done in Tseng's case. Thereupon the court granted him posthumously the name Hsiang-min 襄愍, and the rank of minister of War. In the following reign a petition was presented requesting the erection of a shrine in Shensi in Tseng's honor.

The inquiry into the proposal of Tseng Hsien came to be recorded in a document dating from the year 1548, entitled *Ping-pu wen* 兵部問 *Ning-hsia an* 案, which Cheng Chen-to (BDRC) recently reproduced.

Tseng was the author of a single book entitled *Tseng Hsiang-min kung fu T'ao i* 公復套議, 1 *ch.*, printed in the Wan-li period, which also deals with his proposal to recover the Ordos; it is available in microfilm from a copy once housed in the National Library of Peiping.

Bibliography

1/204/8b; 5/58/15a; 16/121/21a, 126/50a; MSL (1965), Shih-tsung, 3564, 3821, 3850, 5413, 5494, 5824, 5901, 5924, 6087, 6122, Mu-tsung (1965), 263, 277; KC (1958), 3709, 3711, 3715; SK (1930), 56/4a; *Yang-chou-fu chih* (1810), 39/19b, 40/7b, 47/35b; *Lin-ch'ing-hsien chih* (1934), 3冊/3a, 11冊/16a; *Ping-pu wen Ning-hsia an* (*Hsüan-lan-t'ang ts'ung-shu* #83, ed. by Cheng Chen-to); *Tseng Hsiang-min kung fu T'ao i* (NLP microfilm 39); I Chih 伊志, "Ming-tai 'ch'i-T'ao' shih-mo" 明代「棄套」始末, *Ming-tai pien-fang* 邊防 (Taipei, 1968), 197; *Shantung t'ung-chih* (1934), 1708, 2307; *Ku-yüan-chou chih* 固原州志 (1967), 2/54a; TSCC (1885-88), XI: 581/33/9a; L. Hambis, *Documents sur l'histoire des Mongols à l'époque des Ming* (Paris, 1969), 54; D. Pokotilov, *History of the Eastern Mongols during the Ming Dynasty from 1368-1634*, tr. by R. Loewenthal (Chengtu, 1947), 110; W. Franke, *Sources*, 7. 3. 11.

L. Carrington Goodrich

TSENG Te-chao, *see* SEMEDO, Álvarō

TSO Kuang-tou 左光斗 (T. 共之, 遺直, H. 浮丘, 滄嶼), October 12, 1575-August 26, 1625, an official, was one of the "six Tung-lin party heroes" who died by order of the eunuch dictator Wei Chung-hsien (ECCP; also *see* Kao P'an-lung). He was the fifth of nine sons in a long-established, reputable farming family of T'ung-ch'eng 桐城, Anking prefecture. Because he showed aptitude in his childhood, his parents gave him special schooling; and in his young manhood he was patronized by the rich and influential Tai 戴 family of the district. He passed the provincial examination in 1600 after one failure and the metropolitan examination in 1607 after two failures.

Tso was a paragon of Confucian morality and a bold and imaginative official. His career in office was short but spectacular. In 1607 he received the appointment of drafter in the central drafting office. He became favorably disposed toward the so-called "good elements" at court who were associated directly or indirectly with the Tung-lin Academy (*see* Ku Hsien-ch'eng), and for his private use he began making lists of worthy men deserving of responsible employment. In 1613 he was promoted to be an investigating censor, but Emperor Chu I-chün (*q.v.*) in this period consistently refused to confirm official appointments, and Tso had to wait at home until 1619 before being called to actual service. He then submitted eight successive memorials urging the emperor to attend audience with the court officials (a great rarity for almost thirty years). In four years of service as an investigating censor he made a name for himself by reducing corruption in the administration of the capital city (on ward-inspecting assignment), by promoting water control programs and introducing paddy rice crops in the Peking-Tientsin region (on agricultural-colony assignment), and by reinvigorating military schools and reviving military studies in Confucian schools (on education-intendant assignment in Pei-Chihli).

Tso quickly emerged as one of the principal leaders of the Tung-lin partisans at court (*see* Kao P'an-lung). In close association with Yang Lien (ECCP) Tso in 1619 devised political schemes by which Wang Wen-yen (*see* Ku Hsien-ch'eng) was able to break up the coalition of opposing factions at court and thus pave the way for the recall in 1620 of long-ousted Tung-lin men. Yang Lien and Tso proved their leadership qualities during the stormy controversies of that year, when Chu I-chün and his successor Chu Ch'ang-lo (ECCP) died a month apart. Tso was particularly influential in what came to be known as "the case of the removal from the palace," in which Tso and others repeatedly insisted upon getting the young new emperor Chu Yu-chiao (ECCP) freed from dominance by one of his father's more ambitious concubines, Madame Li (*see* Kao P'ang-lung). Tso brashly snubbed Madame Li and her eunuch aides, Wei Chung-hsien among them; and at one time he became so aroused about the delicate situation at court that he spat angrily in the face of his friend Yang Lien.

Tso was responsible for resolving the difficult, unprecedented calendrical problems that grew out of deaths in quick succession of the two above mentioned emperors. Some proposed that the whole year (1620) be redesignated the inaugural year of Chu Ch'ang-lo's era, called T'ai-ch'ang, even though it was already established as the 48th year of Chu I-chün's era, Wan-li. Others proposed that, in normal fashion, 1621 be considered the inaugural year of the T'ai-ch'ang era, even though the beginning of Chu Yu-chiao's era, T'ien-ch'i, would thus have to be postponed unreasonably to 1622. Tso's compromise proposal was finally agreed upon: the first seven months of 1620 were considered a truncated 48th year of Wan-li, the last five months of 1620 were considered a truncated inaugural year of T'ai-ch'ang, and the new T'ien-ch'i period began in normal fashion with 1621.

In 1623 Tso was promoted to be assistant minister and then vice minister of the Grand Court of Revision, and in 1624 he became assistant censor-in-chief. His promotion to this latter post antagonized some officials of greater seniority. Juan Ta-ch'eng (ECCP), a fellow townsman who eventually fell into total disrepute because of his flagrant partisanship at the end of the dynasty, blamed Tso for conniving with the minister of Personnel to put Wei Ta-chung (*see* ECCP, p. 893) into the influential post of chief supervising secretary of the office of scrutiny for Personnel, a post that Juan coveted for himself. In mid-1624 Tso helped Yang Lien, now vice censor-in-chief, to draft his famous exposure of "the 24 great crimes" of Wei Chung-hsien; and then he helped the censor-in-chief demote the investigating censor Ts'ui Ch'eng-hsiu (*see* Kao P'an-lung), who promptly sought support from Wei Chung-hsien and precipitated the Tung-lin disaster. Enemies soon persuaded the supervising secretary Fu K'uei 傅櫆 (cs 1613), an intimate crony of palace eunuchs, to attack Wei Ta-chung and bring about his demotion. Tso responded by repeatedly impeaching Fu K'uei, and openly slandering Wei Chung-hsien in the process. He was drafting his own public denunciation of the newly emergent eunuch dictator when, on December 8, he was silenced by an imperial order stripping both Yang Lien and himself of their civil service status, on the pretext that they had wrongfully submitted nominations for vacancies in the Grand Secretariat.

Tso and Yang Lien left Peking together to return to their homes in the south. Early in 1625 Yang wrote a letter to Tso intimating that he might commit suicide rather than wait for a disgraceful fate at eunuch hands, but Tso wrote in return that dying under arrest, if need be, would be a more worthy end. On April 24 an imperial order was issued for the arrest and imprisonment of Tso, Yang, Wei Ta-chung, and three other Tung-lin leaders (see Kao P'an-lung). Wang Wen-yen had already died in prison, and his confession (apparently either forged or elicited under torture) indicated that all these men had taken bribes to protect the military leader Hsiung T'ing-pi (ECCP), discredited by the ruling clique. A sum of 20,000 taels was to be recovered from Tso.

When imperial guardsmen arrived to arrest Tso, there were popular demonstrations of protest at T'ung-ch'eng, and all along the route by which they escorted him northward. In parting from his family, Tso exhorted his younger brothers to care for his parents and his children. "One who is a loyal minister," he lamented, "cannot also be a filial son." On July 27 he was incarcerated at Peking in the prison maintained by the imperial bodyguard, under instructions that he be tortured every fifth day until he confessed. In a series of notes to his sons from prison, he wrote, "I have now endured a hundred kinds of torture. I can neither live nor die.... By now my pain and distress are extreme. I can no longer even walk a step.... By now I am thoroughly done in. My thirst is agonizing, and day and night my blood flows out like a stream.... My pain and suffering are beyond description. My body has been transformed into an inhuman lump without any whole flesh.... Every bone in my body seems broken, and my flesh is blood-logged.... My misery is extreme, my filth is extreme, my disgrace is extreme, my pain is extreme. There is nothing left for me to do but cry out to Heaven. Crying out to Heaven and getting no answer, I can only submit to Heaven. How can I any longer cling to these dregs of my life?" A month later he died in prison, simultaneously with Yang Lien and Wei Ta-chung.

Local authorities were now forced to press Tso's relatives for payment of the money demanded. His brother Tso Kuang-chi 霽 was put to death. His eighty-year-old father, Tso Ch'u-ying 出穎 (T. 逢時, H. 碧衢, 1545–1628), fell ill of anxiety and became almost wholly paralyzed, and his mother grieved herself to death. His brothers and sons, one second cousin, eleven nephews, and one grand nephew were all imprisoned at one time or another until, through confiscations of property, the fine was fully paid. Of the total required, Tso's own property upon confiscation realized less than 1,000 taels. Throughout his life he had turned over all his official income to his father.

After Tso's death, a young concubine took care of his parents and four sons and eventually became renowned as a virtuous widow, dying in 1670 at the age of seventy-one. A younger brother, Tso Kuang-hsien 先, became a provincial graduate in 1624 and later an investigating censor. After the fall of Peking to the Manchus in 1644, he took service in the Ming loyalist cause in south China and argued against the rise to influence of his brother's old enemy, Juan Ta-ch'eng. Juan had him arrested, but he escaped from his captors and survived.

One of Tso Kuang-tou's principal protégés was Shih K'o-fa (ECCP), whom Tso met while serving as education intendant in Pei-Chihli. Tso encouraged Shih and even took him into his own home to study alongside his own sons and nephews. Shih later slipped in disguise into the prison to visit Tso before his death;

and he eventually became a famous martyr of the Ming loyalist cause.

After the end of Chu Yu-chiao's reign in 1627, Tso Kuang-tou was posthumously promoted to be junior guardian of the heir apparent and was canonized Chung-i 忠毅. His collected writings, *Tso Chung-i-kung wen-chi* 公文集, in 3 *chüan*, exist in several editions: one of 1662, reprinted in 1775; another of 1673, reprinted in 1846; and a third of 1739 reported in the libraries of Columbia and Fukien Christian University. The work was proscribed in the 1780s, but has been made generally available in the collection entitled *Ch'ien-k'un cheng-ch'i chi* 乾坤正氣集 printed 1848. Another version in 5 *chüan* with a 1-*chüan* supplement which includes his letters is in the rare *ts'ung-shu*, *Tso-shih shuang-chung chi* 左氏雙忠集. A late Ming publication of over fifty of Tso's memorials written between 1620 and 1624, *Shao-pao Tso-kung tsou-shu* 奏疏, is preserved in the Sonkeikaku Bunko, Tokyo. A biography compiled by Tso's great-grandson Tso Tsai 宰 in 1739, in 2 *chüan*, is appended to the Ch'ing edition of the *wen-chi* and is preserved in another rare collection, *Lung-mien* 龍眠 *ts'ung-shu*; and a biography by the modern T'ung-ch'eng historian Ma Ch'i-ch'ang (ECCP, p. 235) is included in the *Chi-hsü ts'ao-t'ang* 集虛草堂 *ts'ung-shu* and *Ma-shih chia-k'o chi* 馬氏家刻集.

Bibliography

1/244/11a; Tso Tsai, *Tso Chung-i-kung nien-p'u*; Tsou I 鄒漪, *Ch'i-Chen yeh-sheng* 啓禎野乘 (pref. 1677), 5/10; SK (1930), 60/9b; MSL (1940), Kuang-tsung, 1/1a, 1/36b; Hsi-tsung, 2/39a, 45a, 21/21a, 32/2a, 14b, 41/6b, 9b, 43/8a, 47/6b, 52/37b, 55/29a, 56/17a, 65/20a; Sun Tien-ch'i (1957), 50; C. O. Hucker, *The Censorial System of Ming China* (Stanford, 1966), 165, 281; W. Franke, *Sources*, 5. 8. 38.

Charles O. Hucker

TSONG-KHA-PA (Tsung-k'o-pa 宗喀巴), 1357-1419, founder of the Yellow Hat Sect of Tibetan Buddhism, repeatedly rejected the entreaties of Chu Ti (*q. v.*) to visit the Chinese court and thus never set foot on Chinese soil. He nonetheless influenced the course of Sino-Tibetan relations in the early years of the Ming. According to a perhaps spurious legend he took the vow of a Buddhist layman (upāsaka) at the age of three. It is certain, however, that his father entrusted him to the care of a monk at an early age. His monk-teacher introduced him to the Tantras when he was barely seven years old. After almost a decade of study Tsong-kha-pa started to travel from one monastery to another in central Tibet, seeking training in the monastic curriculum of non-Tantric Buddhism. He was apparently a brilliant student and soon gained renown. Students flocked to him and sought instruction. Before accepting students, he decided to become a monk. In 1380 he passed the examinations and was ordained at Rnam-rgyal in the Yar-luṅ district.

Tsong-kha-pa's ordination marked the beginning of his career as a teacher of non-Tantric Buddhist treatises. During the next twelve years, he not only wrote such works but also continued to study with eminent teachers of the Tantras. In this period he produced his *Gser-hphren*, a preliminary outline of his views. Besides completing several other works, he divided his time between teaching and solitary meditation. His success may be measured by the growing number of his disciples and by the frequency of his visions. In 1392 he finally had the confidence to start his new school, later known as the Gelugpa. Accompanied by eight disciples, he set forth to preach his doctrine to the Hol-kha family, an influential group in central Tibet who now became his patrons. This new support permitted him to expound his views freely. He insisted on rigorous discipline for the monks in his sect. A candidate, with the assistance of his guru, had to train his mind (blo sbyon) in the common path, that is, the path shared by the non-Tantric and the Tantric Buddhists. Tsong-kha-pa also demanded that monks remain celibate, wear yellow robes, and pursue a prescribed course of ritual and meditation. By the early years of the 15th century, his fame had spread to China. In 1407 Chu Ti, who had already induced the Tibetan Buddhist Halima (*q. v.*) to appear at a court audience and to perform "miracles," and had awarded him a rarely bestowed title and presented him with elaborate gifts, extended an invitation to Tsong-kha-pa to visit China. The Chinese emperor no doubt conceived such a visit of the greatest living Tibetan monk as a boost to his prestige. Tsong-kha-pa saw no advantages for himself and declined. He pleaded ill health as an excuse for his refusal. In 1413 the emperor sent him a second invitation. Tsong-kha-pa found it prudent to comply with his request and dispatched one of his leading disciples to represent him. Neither of these invitations is recorded in the Chinese historical records, presumably because Tsong-kha-pa's negative responses might have damaged the emperor's standing among his own people.

From the start of the 15th century to his death in 1419, Tsong-kha-pa produced several of his most important works. In 1407 he wrote the *Legs-bsad-snin-po*, a treatise discriminating between the "provisional meaning" (neyartha) and the "final meaning" (nitartha) of the sūtras. In 1410 he issued his commentary on the *Pañcakrama* called the *Rab-tu-gsal-bahi sgron-me* and in succeeding years he offered commentaries on Candrakirti's *Pradīpodyotana* and *Madhyamakāvatāra* and on *Cakrasaṃvara*. According to one account, on an autumn day in 1419 he crossed his legs, held his two hands in samapatti-mudra (level at the chest), and exactly at sunrise ceased to breathe.

Tsong-kha-pa was followed by one of his disciples, dGe-'dun-grub (*q. v.*), who became known some time after his death as the first Dalai-lama. Under his leadership

the Yellow Church, as it came to be known, increased its influence, spiritual and economic, but took no part in politics. His successor, dGe-'dun-rgya-mts'o (*q.v.*), likewise did not assume temporal power, but undoubtedly his prestige increased during his later years (*ca.* 1524-42). The third Dalai-lama, bSod-nams-rgya-mts'o (*q. v.*), characterized by H. E. Richardson as a brilliant scholar and zealous missionary, paid a visit to Mongolia where, in 1578, he succeeded in converting Altan-qaγan (*q. v.*), to his faith. This constituted a turning point in the political fortunes of the church. It became involved in disputes with the ruling Karmapas at the time of the fifth Dalai-lama, Nag-dbaṅ-blo-bzaṅ-rgya-mts'o (October 22, 1617-*ca.* April 3, 1682), but in 1642 an Oirat prince, Gusri (or Gushi) Khan (ECCP, p. 265), and other followers of the sect invaded Tibet, dispossessed the Karmapas, and established him as the country's religious head.

Bibliography

Mkhas-grub-rje, Rje-btsun bla-ma Tsoṅ-kha-pa chen-pohi rnam-parthar-pa yons-su-brjod-pahi-gtam-du bya-ba dad-pahi-hjug-nogs zes bya-ba (Lhasa ed.); *Akya Blo-bzan-bstan-pahi-rgyal-mtshan Dpal-bzan po, Rje thams-cad-mkhyen-pa Tsoṅ-kha-pa chen-pohi rnam-thar gyi bsdus-don cun-zad brjod-pa* (Peking ed.); Alexandra David-Neel, *Textes tibétains inédits, traduits et présentés* (Paris, 1952), 39; Li Tieh tseng, *Tibet: Today and Yesterday* (New York, 1960), 26; Yü Tao-ch'üan 于道泉, "I chu Ming Ch'eng-tsu ch'ien shih chao Tsung-k'o-pa chi shih chi Tsung-k'o-pa fu Ch'eng-tsu shu" 譯註明成祖遣使召宗喀巴紀事及宗喀巴復成祖書 *"Ts'ai Yüan-p'ei hsien-sheng liu-shih-wu sui lun wen-chi* 蔡元培先生六十五歲論文集 (Peiping, 1935), II, 939; Yang Ho-chin, *The Annals of Kokonor* (Bloomington, 1969), 33; Rudolf Kaschewsky, *Das Leben des Lamaistischen Heiligen Tsongkhapa Blo Bzaṅ-Grags-Pa (1357-1419), dargestellt und erläutert anhand seiner Biographie "Quellenort allen Glücks"* (Wiesbaden, 1971); H. E. Richardson, *Tibet and its history* (London, 1962), 40; L. Petech, "The Dalai-Lamas and Regents of Tibet, a Chronological Study," TP, 47 (1959), 370.

Alex Wayman and Morris Rossabi

TSOU Shou-i 鄒守益 (T. 謙之, H. 東廓, 文莊), 1491–1562, thinker and official, was a native of An-fu 安福, Kiangsi. He spent part of his childhood in Nanking, where his father, Tsou Hsien 賢 (T. 恢才, 1454–1516, cs 1496), served in the Grand Court of Revision, and where the boy himself attracted the notice of the scholar Lo Ch'in-shun (*q. v.*). Tsou Hsien later rose to be assistant surveillance commissioner in Fukien. Tsou Shou-i early distinguished himself, acquiring the *chü-jen* at the age of sixteen. In 1511 he went to the capital for the *chin-shih* examinations. His answers attracted the attention of the assistant examiner, Wang Shou-jen (*q. v.*), who helped to rank him first in the metropolitan tests. Subsequently, he came out third in the palace examinations. Tsou was then appointed a Hanlin compiler, but was obliged to return home after one year on account of his mother's death. He remained in Kiangsi for nine years. After Wang Shou-jen became governor of southern Kiangsi in 1517, Tsou came to study under him, discussing with him the meaning of the "investigation of things" (ko-wu 格物) of the Great Learning and of "vigilance in solitude" (shen-tu 愼獨) of the Doctrine of the Mean. In 1519 Tsou Shou-i assisted Wang in the campaign against the rebel, Prince Chu Ch'en-hao (*see* Wang Shou-jen). After the accession to the throne (1521) of Chu Hou-ts'ung (*q. v.*), Tsou was summoned back to the capital to resume his official duties. He did so after another visit with Wang Shou-jen, who was then living in retirement in Shao-hsing, Chekiang. In 1524 Tsou Shou-i offended the emperor by his memorials, in which he counseled Chu Hou-ts'ung not to confer additional posthumous honors on his deceased father. For this he suffered imprisonment; he was beaten, and subsequently demoted to be assistant magistrate in Kuang-te 廣德 (Anhwei). There he established the Fu-ch'u 復初 Academy, for the purpose of promoting Confucian learning, and invited his fellow disciple, Wang Ken (*q. v.*), to

give lectures. In 1527 he received a promotion to be director of the bureau of receptions in the ministry of Rites in Nanking. It was there that the news of Wang Shou-jen's death reached him, early in 1529. He went to Shao-hsing for Wang's funeral, mourned for him as a disciple, and arranged, with other fellow disciples, to have regular meetings and lectures at the T'ien-chen 天眞 Academy outside Hangchow, to honor the memory of their master. Several years later (1538) he was transferred to the ministry of Personnel, as director of the bureau of evaluations; then, in the following year, he was recalled to Peking, to assist in the education of the heir apparent, as librarian and reader-in-waiting. He had thus the occasion to be in touch with such scholars as Hsü Chieh, Lo Hung-hsien, and T'ang Shun-chih (*qq.v.*). Later he and Huo T'ao (*q.v.*), then supervisor of imperial instruction, jointly drew up a set of thirteen pictures, entitled the *Sheng-kung t'u* 聖功圖, representing various exemplary emperors, beginning with the legendary Yao. The work was done to help the young prince understand the importance of good government. But it provoked the displeasure of Chu Hou-ts'ung. Fortunately, the emperor listened to the explanations of Huo T'ao and did not pursue the matter. In 1540 Tsou was promoted to be chief minister of the Court of Imperial Sacrifices, and reader-in-waiting, in charge of the Hanlin Academy in Nanking. According to some sources, this appointment was arranged by Hsia Yen (*q. v.*) for the purpose of keeping Tsou away from Peking. A year later, Tsou became chancellor of the National University, Nanking. Then, after fire had broken out in the imperial ancestral temple in Peking, Tsou submitted a memorial urging the emperor to reform his manner of government. Instead of bringing about the desired effect, it angered Chu Hou-ts'ung, prompting Tsou to resign from his official duties, and spend the next twenty odd years in his native place, teaching disciples who flocked

to him from everywhere. He died in
October, 1562, at the age of seventy-one.
In 1567 the court awarded him the posthumous title of vice-minister of Rites,
and the canonization Wen-chuang 文莊.

In the history of philosophy by Huang
Tsung-hsi (ECCP), Tsou Shou-i heads the
list of Kiangsi scholars who were disciples
of Wang Shou-jen. According to Huang,
they alone have preserved the true
thought of Wang who, after all, spent
his best teaching years in the region of
Kiangsi. As Wang's faithful disciple and
good friend, who had been singled out
for special praise during the master's
lifetime, Tsou Shou-i continued to teach
the doctrine of the unity of all things,
advocating the practice of moral cultivation for the development of the Confucian
virtues of loyalty and filial piety. In his
expositions of Wang Shou-jen's idea of
the extension of liang-chih, Tsou laid
special emphasis on the ideas given in
the Doctrine of the Mean, particularly on
the need to maintain an inner disposition
of reverence and caution, and of vigilance in solitude. In so doing, he manifested his attachment to the Sung thinkers,
Chou Tun-i (1017-73) and Ch'eng Hao
(1032-85). He also sought to correct the
abuses of the extremists of the T'ai-chou
branch of the school of Wang Shou-jen,
whose unilateral emphasis on inner enlightenment tended to destroy the whole
teaching of moral cultivation. Tsou Shou-
i's efforts, together with those of his
fellow disciples, Ou-yang Te (q. v.), who
taught especially the investigation of
things, Nieh Pao (q. v.) and Lo Hung-
hsien, who advocated tranquillity in meditation, contributed to the restoration of a
true understanding of Wang Shou-jen's
thought, and prepared the way for the
gradual rise of the teachings of Liu
Tsung-chou (ECCP) and Huang Tsung-hsi,
as well as of the great masters of the
Tung-lin Academy (see Ku Hsien-ch'eng).

There are various collections of the
writings of Tsou Shou-i. The *Tung-kuo
hsien-sheng wen-chi* 東廓先生文集, 9 *ch.*,
with a preface dated 1538, exists in the
Peiping National Library collection as
well as in the Naikaku Bunko, but it is
obviously incomplete. So too, according to
the *Ssu-k'u* catalogue (where it is listed
only) is the *Tung-kuo Tsou hsien-sheng
wen-chi* (1572), 12 *ch.*, which may be
found in the Naikaku Bunko. *Chüan* 3 of
this work includes five of Tsou's memorials. There is another collection, entitled
Tung-kuo Tsou hsien-sheng i-kao 遺稿, 13
ch., published during the Wan-li period, a
copy of which is preserved in the Sonkeikaku Library, Tokyo. The Japanese catalogues also report the existence of Tsou's
collected writings, in 10 *chüan*, and of his
collected poems, *Shih-chi* 詩集, 9 *ch.*

Tsou Shou-i's family produced several
scholars. His son, Tsou Shan 善 (H. 穎泉,
cs 1556), became an assistant education
commissioner in Shantung, and his three
grandsons, Tsou Te-han 德涵 (T. 汝海,
H. 泉所, 1538-81, cs 1571), Tsou Te-p'u 溥
(T. 汝光, H. 四山, cs 1583), and Tsou Te-
yung 泳 (T. 汝臣, cs 1586), all had careers
worthy of note. The eldest served as director of a bureau in the ministry of Justice
and as assistant surveillance commissioner
in Hunan. As a friend of Keng Ting-li
(*see* Keng Ting-hsiang), Tsou Te-han was
admittedly influenced by Ch'an Buddhist
thought, and laid more emphasis on the role
of inner illumination in the development
of one's learning. He left a collection of
writings, *Tsou Chü-so wen-chi* 聚所文集, 6
ch., and *wai-chi* 外集, 1 *ch.* The younger,
Tsou Te-p'u, acted also as librarian for
the heir apparent, and left a treatise on
the Book of Changes, the *I-hui* 易會, 8
ch., giving his own insights, and another
work, the *Ch'un-ch'iu k'uang-chieh* 春秋匡
解, 6 *ch.*, allegedly giving explanations of
the Spring and Autumn Annals, but actually resembling an examination manual.
The editors of the *Ssu-k'u* catalogue express doubt regarding its authorship. The
third, Tsou Te-yung, cousin of the other
two, rose to be a censor. He adhered to
Wang Shou-jen's teaching of the extension
of liang-chih, and developed his own

ideas especially on the investigation of things.

Bibliography

1/283/8a; 3/162/13b; 4/9/26a; 5/74/11a; 16/22/8b; 32/67/23b; 42/76/6b; 61/114/14b; 63/22/11a; 83/16/3a; MSL (1965) Shih-tsung, 4812, 4897; SK (1930), 30/5a, 176/10a, 179/4a; Huang Wan, *Shih-lung chi* (Ming ed.), 3/14b; Keng Ting-hsiang, *Keng T'ien-t'ai hsien-sheng wen-chi* (1589 ed., Taipei reprint, 1970), 14/10a; Tsou Shou-i, *Tung-kuo hsien-sheng wen-chi* (preface of 1538), NLP microfilm no. 1005; id., *Tung-kuo Tsou hsien-sheng wen-chi* (1572), Naikaku Bunko copy; Wang Chi, *Wang Lung-hsi ch'üan-chi*, 14/17a; Wang Shou-jen, *Wang Wen-ch'eng kung ch'üan-shu* (SPTK 1st series, double-page lithograph ed.); *An-fu-hsien chih* 安福縣志 (1872), 11/1a; Okada Takehiko 岡田武彦, *Ō Yōmei to Minmatsu no Jugaku* 王陽明と明末の儒學 (Tokyo, 1970), 166; W. Franke, *Sources*, 5. 5. 28.

Julia Ching

TSOU Yüan-piao 鄒元標 (T. 爾瞻, H. 南皋), 1551–1624, an official and philosopher who was prominent in court controversies of the 1570s, 1580s, and early 1620s, was a native of the prosperous intellectual center Chi-shui 吉水, Kiangsi. He is said to have been a precocious child devoted to study, and in his young manhood he was greatly influenced by Hu Chih (*q.v.*), a highly subjective and Ch'an-influenced follower of Wang Shou-jen (*q.v.*).

Tsou won his metropolitan degree in 1577 and was assigned to probationary duty as an observer in the ministry of Justice. This happened to be the heyday of the powerful grand secretary Chang Chü-cheng (*q.v.*), and the very year in which Chang suffered numerous attacks for not observing traditional mourning rites. After witnessing in court public beatings of four officials who criticized Chang, Tsou brashly presented a bitingly critical memorial of his own to the palace, evading the warnings of eunuch attendants by pretending that his memorial was merely a request for leave of absence. The young emperor, Chu I-chün (*q.v.*), is reported to have flown into a rage. Tsou thereupon was given eighty blows publicly and sent away in disgrace to serve as a common soldier in the Tu-yün 都匀 guard among the southwestern aborigines of Kweichow.

During the six years of this demeaning but apparently not arduous service, Tsou devoted himself to neo-Confucian studies of the Wang Yang-ming variety, no doubt keeping in mind that Wang had endured similar exile in Kweichow seventy years before and had there gained his most important philosophical insights.

In 1583, after Chang Chü-cheng's death, Tsou was recalled to court as a supervising secretary of the office of scrutiny for Personnel. He immediately got into new trouble, partly by submitting moralistic preachments to the increasingly irritable emperor, and partly by driving out of office men favored by the current senior grand secretary Shen Shih-hsing (*q.v.*); he was consequently demoted in 1584 to be recorder in the Nanking ministry of Justice.

In 1585 Tsou was successively transferred to be secretary of the bureau of operations in the Nanking ministry of War, secretary of the bureau of honors in the ministry of Personnel at Peking, and vice director of the bureau of records in the same ministry. After being transferred to the bureau of honors again in 1586, he was given sick leave. The court recalled him to duty in 1589 and in 1590 transferred him to the Kwangtung bureau of the ministry of Justice. He apparently went home ill once more in 1593, and thereafter did not serve the Wan-li emperor, although in 1598 he was offered promotion to the directorship of the same bureau.

For some twenty-seven years, until 1620, Tsou remained at home studying and teaching. The empire's private academies had been closed by Chang Chü-cheng in 1579. Tsou played a part in reopening the famous Sung dynasty academy, Pai-lu-tung 白鹿洞, in Hsing-tzu 星子, Kiangsi; and he opened an academy of his own in Chi-shui, called Jen-wen 仁文 [not to be confused with an academy of the same name in Chia-hsing 嘉興, Chekiang, sponsored by Yüeh Yüan-sheng (see Chang Huang)]. He acquired a national reputation as a moderate expounder of Wang Yang-ming's doctrines and attracted hundreds of students. His thinking, like that of other members of the Kiangsi school, emphasized perception of "the substance of the mind" as the goal of moral cultivation. He had contacts, at least in correspondence, with the Jesuit missionary Matteo Ricci (q.v.), to whom he wrote in friendly fashion that he had investigated Christianity and found much in common between it and the Chinese tradition. Ch'ing scholars thought Tsou would have been classified as a Buddhist were it not for his resoluteness in political action. His eclectic, idealistic, subjective philosophical position was no doubt close to the "left wing" ideas that Tung-lin academicians deplored, and Tsou seems never to have taken a direct part in the scholarly assemblies at the Tung-lin Academy not far away in Wu-hsi (near Soochow). But Tsou was a devoted friend and correspondent of the Tung-lin founders, Ku Hsienchʻeng and Kao Pʻan-lung (qq.v.), and even wrote Ku's epitaph. It was inevitable that his enemies at court considered him a member of the Tung-lin.

After the emperor's death in 1620, Tsou was one of the many old-time "good elements" quickly called back to service. He was appointed chief minister of the Grand Court of Revision, but even before he arrived in Peking to assume that post in 1621 was promoted to be vice minister of Justice. In the course of the same year he received a transfer to the ministry of Personnel and then a promotion to be censor-in-chief. In order to make suitable posts available to the large number of other officials who had left government service in the previous reign, he persuaded the young emperor, Chu Yu-chiao (ECCP), to authorize supernumerary appointments in several court agencies; and he was largely responsible for the recall to Peking of Kao P'an-lung, Chao Nanhsing, (q.v.), Liu Tsung-chou (ECCP), and others.

Whereas Tsou had earlier been considered arrogant and combative, he now advocated tolerance and harmony. When questioned about this change, he explained that one style was suited to a young censorial official, but something else was expected of a senior statesman. Thus, although he took part in some of the acrimonious debates about the "three great cases" that agitated the court (see Kao P'an-lung), he argued against the vengeful partisanship of such Tung-lin stalwarts as Chao Nan-hsing. Tsou nevertheless soon found himself once again at the very center of a great partisan controversy, championed by the Tung-lin "good elements" who were to suffer mass humiliation and worse from 1624 to 1626 at the hands of the dictator eunuch Wei Chunghsien (ECCP).

Tsou found a congenial companion in the vice censor-in-chief, Feng Ts'ung-wu (q.v.), despite the fact that Feng was a stanch supporter of orthodox neo-Confucianism. In 1622 they joined in opening the Shou-shan 首善 Academy right in Peking, inviting all interested scholars to participate in philosophical discussions there, but warning that the academy should not be used for Tung-lin style political discussions. Immediately Tsou and Feng were attacked for unacceptably flagrant partisanship—and Tsou for teaching Buddhism as well—by the supervising secretaries Chu T'ung-meng 朱童蒙 (cs 1610), Kuo Hsing-chih 郭興治 (cs 1610), and Kuo Yün-hou 郭允厚 (cs 1607); and their academy was closed by imperial order. Tsou and Feng had no choice but to ask permission to retire, and their requests were granted. The Shou-shan Academy grounds were transformed into an imperial astronomical observatory, and Jesuit missionaries, who soon began service there, eventually established a church on the property known in later times as the Nan-t'ang (*see* Schall von Bell).

Tsou left Peking late in 1622, consoled with a promotion to the honorific rank of junior guardian of the heir apparent. He died at home two years later. The following year, when Wei Chung-hsien was endeavoring to eliminate all Tung-lin men, Tsou's name was posthumously erased from the civil service roster; but in the subsequent reign of Chu Yu-chien (EC CP), he was made grand guardian of the heir apparent and concurrently minister of Personnel, and canonized Chung-Chieh 忠介.

Tsou's teachings seem not to have been influential very long after his time, and most of his published writings exist only in Ming editions. Collected writings called *Tsou-tzu yüan-hsüeh chi* 鄒子願學集 were published in 6 *chüan* in 1619, reprinted in 8 *chüan* in the Ch'ung-chen period, and included over a century later in the *Ssu-k'u ch'üan-shu* (also 8 *ch.*). The Library of Congress has a copy of the the first edition, and the National Central Library, Taiwan, has a copy of the second. Other extant writings in Ming edition include *Tsou Nan-kao chi-hsüan* 集選, 7 *ch.* (copies in the Gest Collection, Princeton, National Central Library, and the Sonkeikaku Bunko, Tokyo, and also in the uncommon collection *Kuang li-hsüeh pei k'ao* 廣理學備考); *Tsou Chung-chieh tsou-shu* 奏疏, 5 *ch.* (copies in the Sonkeikaku Bunko, the Naikaku Bunko, and the Cambridge University Library, ed. of 1641); *Tsou Nan-kao yü-i ho-pien* 語義合編, 4 *ch.* (Sonkeikaku Bunko); and *Tsou tzu ts'un-chen chi* 存眞集, 12 *ch.* (Naikaku Bunko). References may also be found to *Tsou Chung-chieh ch'üan-chi* 全集, 16 *ch.*, *T'ai-p'ing shan-fang hsü-chi* 太平山房續集, 12 *ch.*, and *T'ai-i shan-fang shu-ts'ao* 太乙山房疏草, 1 *ch.*, but these writings seem to have been lost. Several of Tsou's books were ordered proscribed in the 18th century; hence their rarity.

Bibliography

1/243/5b; 3/227/5a; 39/13/1a; 83/23/1a; MSL (1966), Shen-tsung, 1485, 2710, Hsi-tsung (1940), 16/18a, 21/11b, 22/14a; KC (1958), 4324, 4466, 5197, 5205, 5209, 5211; Tsou I 鄒漪, *Ch'i-Chen yeh-sheng* 啓禎野乘 (preface of 1679, repr. 1936), 3/17b; SK (1930), 96/8a, 172/14a; SunTien-ch'i (1957), 189; L. Carrington Goodrich, *Literary Inquisition of Ch'ien-lung* (Baltimore, 1935), 255.

Charles O. Hucker

TSU-SHAN 祖闡 (T. 仲猷, H. 雪軒翁), fl. 1360–73, Buddhist monk, who served as chief envoy of a mission to Japan in 1372, was descended from a well-to-do family surnamed Ch'en 陳 in Tz'u-ch'i 慈谿, Chekiang. Entering the Buddhist order in his youth at Yung-lo ssu 永樂寺, Tz'u-ch'i, Tsu-shan became a disciple of Yüan-sou (*see* Fan Ch'i) the Ch'an patriarch of the Lin-chi 臨濟 sect, and later adopted the title Chiu-feng 鷲峯. After several years of study in the Buddhist teachings, he was invited to lecture in Chiang-shan 蔣山 ssu (renamed Ling-ku 靈谷 ssu in 1381) in Nanking in the early 1360s and attracted a considerable number of converts. At the start of the rebel uprisings against the Yüan, he returned to his native place and took refuge in his former monastery. Later, he was appointed abbot, first of Hsiang 香-shan ssu in Tz'u-ch'i, and then of T'ien-ning 天寧 ssu in Yin 鄞-hsien (Ningpo). It was while serving in the latter post that he came into frequent contact with visiting Japanese monks and merchants, and acquired a good knowledge of things Japanese. In 1371 Tsu-shan returned to Nanking, the capital, as one of the religious celebrities who responded to the summons of Chu Yüan-chang. He then received an appointment as deputy patriarch (闡教, 6b) of the central Buddhist registry, and concurrently abbot of T'ien-chieh 天界 ssu in Nanking.

In October, 1371, Tsu-shan received an order from Chu Yüan-chang to head a special mission to Japan, the third of its kind following the inauguration of the Ming dynasty. Before this, the emperor had sent two embassies (March, 1369 and April, 1370), to announce his enthronement and to open relations with his neighboring kingdom, aiming primarily at persuading the ruler to restrain the piratical activities of his countrymen on the China coast. Tsu-shan's appointment followed the arrival (September, 1371) of the first Japanese embassy, headed by the monk Sorai 祖來, in response to the Chinese initiatives. The decision to entrust Tsu-shan with such an important mission was probably because the emperor, having discerned the priestly character of the Japanese embassy, thought that his Buddhist servants might play a useful role in fostering Chinese-Japanese accord. During these years Japan was divided between the Ashikaga 足利 shogunate and other adherents of the "Northern" court at Kyoto, and the supporters of the "Southern" court at Yoshino 吉野. The mission led by Sorai was sent by Prince Kanenaga 懷良, chief representative of the "Southern" court in western Japan with headquarters in northern Kyūshu; hence Chu Yüan-chang was dealing only with the "Southern" court. Around this time, however, Chu happened to learn from the Japanese monk Chintai Kaiju 椿庭海壽 (1322–1401), who had come to China to study, of the existence of a rival ruler in Japan, the Ashikaga shogun. Accordingly he instructed Tsu-shan to present himself to Kanenaga and to explore avenues of communication with him. The mission turned out to be a success, largely due to the defeat of Kanenaga and the occupation of Kyūshu by Ashikaga, thereby inaugurating a new phase in Chinese-Japanese relations.

Chu Yüan-chang appointed in addition another monk, K'o-ch'in 克勤 (T. 無逸), as deputy envoy, and six others to the mission, including Chintai Kaiju and one other Japanese monk who had resided in China as interpreters, with the instruction that they accompany Sorai on his homebound journey. Before their departure in March, 1372, the emperor ordered a big Panca-parishad (P'u-tu-hui 普渡會) to be held in the T'ien-chieh monastery, and appointed ten master monks of the three popular Buddhist sects to conduct the ceremony. Chu Yüan-chang took part in this gathering, which lasted three days; it was attended by one thousand monks and conducted on such an imposing scale that it was never surpassed by any other Buddhist gathering during his reign. Sorai and his companions, who were still in China, probably also witnessed the ceremonies. It may have been part of the imperial scheme to impress the Japanese envoys by a display of such magnificence. As the delegates departed, the emperor led the religious celebrities and court officials in seeing them off; he and monk Tsunglo (q.v.) each composed a farewell poem, and other dignitaries made similar addresses.

On June 21 Tsu-shan and his party left Ningpo for Japan by way of the Goto 五島 archipelago west of Kyūshu, arriving in Hakata 博多 in northern Kyūshu ten days later. Almost immediately upon their arrival, they were caught in the civil war between the "Northern" and the "Southern" courts, and were confined on the spot by their hosts. According to their own accounts, it seems that they were detained because the officials of the Ashikaga shogunate, who had gained control of Kyūshu earlier this same year after defeating Kanenaga, thought they had come to Japan with a mission to help their rival. After three months' confinement, K'o-ch'in, a convert of the T'ien-t'ai 天台 sect, achieved a breakthrough by writing to the Tendai patriarch, then held by a prince representing the "Northern" court, explaining to him their intention to establish contacts with the Ashikaga shogunate. It was not until June of the following year that the prince, after a thorough investigation, relayed the message of the Chinese envoys to his master in Kyoto. Astonished by the news, the shōgun immediately dispatched an emissary to make arrangements for their journey.

On July 19 Tsu-shan and his party arrived in Kyoto and were housed in a shrine at Saga 嵯峨, a few miles west of the capital; they were the first Chinese delegation to reach the Ashikaga shogunate. The shōgun, Ashikaga Yoshimitsu (*see* Chang Hung 張洪) was surprised to learn that the Ming emperor had sent three delegations to Japan and that they had all been stopped in Kyūshu by the representatives of the "Southern" court. Tsu-shan's presence in Kyoto not only stirred the officials, but also excited the Zen monks who were favorably disposed towards Chinese literature. He and K'o-ch'in were soon befriended by such leading religious figures as Zekkai Chū-shin (*q.v.*) and Gidō Shushin 義堂周信 (1325–88), who expressed much admir-ation for their poetry. Under the influ-ence of the Zen monks, the shōgun in-vited Tsu-shan to become abbot of the Tenryūji 天龍寺, a famous Zen monastery near Kyoto, and asked K'o-ch'in to return to China alone, but neither complied. Tsu-shan stated that he had come to Japan to open official relations, not to preach Buddhism; hence he could not accept the offer without prior approval of the Chinese emperor. He did, however, agree to conduct lectures and preside at gatherings in the Tenryūji. Finally, on September 16, the Chinese envoys were permitted to leave Kyoto in the company of a Japanese delegation headed by three Zen monks, including Chintai Kaiju as interpreter, who were to pay homage to the Ming court. They went by way of Kyūshu to collect native products as tribute and repatriate one hundred nine Chinese and Koreans taken captive by the Japanese pirates. They also picked up Chao Chih 趙秩, who had headed the mission to the court of Kanenaga in 1370, and had been detained in Kyūshu ever since. They did not embark, however, until the following spring as they had missed the sailing sea-son, and arrived in Nanking in June, 1374. (Several Ming accounts suggest that they were delayed because Tsu-shan and his party called on the representative of the "Southern" court and were de-tained in reprisal for their earlier visit to the "Northern" court. Japanese scholars, such as Obata Atushi 小葉田淳 and others, however, dispute the story with evidence from the writings of the contemporary Zen monks, and assert that they did not make such a visit.)

Upon their return, Tsu-shan and K'o-ch'in were received in audience by the emperor on July 9 to present their report, and on the following day the Japanese delegates, headed by the monk Sembunkei 宣聞溪, were also granted an imperial audience. Tsu-shan and K'o-ch'in were complimented not only on their efforts in establishing contacts with the Ashikaga shogunate, but also on their success in persuading the Japanese lord to repatriate the Chinese and Korean captives. Each of them received one hundred taels of gold and other rewards. The Japanese envoys, however, were snubbed, as the emperor refused their tribute on the ground that their accompanying letter was addressed not to him but to the central secretariat. This seems somewhat strange in view of the emperor's desire to establish relations with the Ashikaga shogunate; it may be inferred, however, that he intended it as an act of reprisal against their improper treatment of his own emissaries. In any event, while Chu Yüan-chang received the representatives of Ashikaga, he con-tinued and preferred to deal with Kane-naga as the legitimate ruler, until definite proof pointed to the contrary; this came belatedly towards the end of his reign.

Little is known of Tsu-shan's later years. He returned to his native place and built a lodge by the side of his former monastery, Yung-lo ssu, for his domicile. He called it Kuei-an 歸庵 (the shrine of retreat), from which he came to be known as the monk Kuei-an, and lived there to the end of his life.

Besides being known as a poet, Tsu-shan was also a skillful lute player. He had composed a song extolling the orchid, entitled "I-lan p'ei-lan" 猗蘭佩蘭, and named his studio "er-lan" 二蘭. One of his disciples was his townsman, Wu Ssu-tao 烏斯道 (T. 繼善), a noted belle-lettrist of the early 14th century, who had written an essay for his studio entitled "Er-lan-chai chi" 齋記. Tsu-shan is known to have compiled a collection of Ch'an sayings on the elimination of evils obstructing the path to enlightenment, entitled *Ch'an-tsung tsa-tu hai* 禪宗雜毒海, 10 *ch.*, with a preface by the monk Wu-yün 無慍 (1309-86), dated 1384. It receives a notice in the *Dai Nihon zokuzōkyō* 大日本續藏經 series 2, vol. 19, but the text is not included.

K'o-ch'in, who served as Tsu-shan's deputy on his mission to Japan, was a native of Hsiao-shan 蕭山, Shao-hsing fu. K'o-ch'in's lay name was Hua 華. As a member of the T'ien-t'ai sect, he became proficient in both the Buddhist and Confucian canon. In the early 1360s he was appointed an instructor in the Wa-kuan 瓦官 monastery in Nanking, and was later summoned to serve Chu Yüan-chang. During his mission to Japan in 1372-74, he rendered a valuable service in establishing contacts with the Ashikaga shogunate, and impressed the Japanese monks with his knowledge of Buddhism and his literary skill. Following his return, the emperor, besides giving him a rich reward, ordered him to resume his original name and return to the capital for an official appointment after he had visited his family. The monarch also awarded his father Hua I 毅 a cap and sash to qualify him for official services. Upon his departure, the Hanlin scholar Sung Lien (*q.v.*) composed a laudatory essay in his honor, giving a good account of his early years as well as his mission to Japan.

Returning to Nanking in July, 1376, under his original name, Hua K'o-ch'in received an appointment as director of the bureau of evaluations. Four months later (October 24), he was promoted to be an administration commissioner of Shansi, where he officiated for several years. The official records contain several documents about his administration. The emperor, for example, wrote two special orders exhorting him to follow his command in the execution of the unscrupulous officials condemned to death. He is also known to have proposed, according to a memorial dated March, 1379, the abrogation of the practice of making the local people manufacture uniforms for the military guards in the Tatung and neighboring regions, because they often failed to produce the right sizes. Instead, he recommended that the authorities provide the soldiers with materials and make them manufacture the uniforms themselves. The emperor accepted his suggestion and the new ruling came to be applied to the frontier commanderies extending from Shansi to Peiping.

It is not known how long Hua K'o-ch'in remained in this post, but the gazetteer of Shao-hsing (1673) asserts that he ended his career as administration commissioner of Shansi, which probably occurred *ca.* 1381. A skillful poet, Hua K'o-ch'in left several poems in contemporary anthologies; those he composed in honor of Sung Lien have been preserved in the appendices to Sung's collected works.

Bibliography:

1/322/2b; MSL (1962), T'ai-tsu, 1282, 1578, 1777, 1803, 1983; *Tz'u-ch'i-hsien chih* (1899), 40/14a, 42/11a; *Shansi t'ung-chih* (1892), 12/1a, 103/1b; Chu Yüan-chang, *Kao huang-ti yü-chih wen-chi*, 2/4b, 7/8a; Sung Lien, *Sung hsüeh-shih wen-chi* (SPTK), 27/1a, 28/12b, 29/2a; Wu Ssu-tao, *Ch'un-ts'ao-chai chi* 春草齋集 (*Ssu-ming* 四明 *ts'ung-shu* ed., 1934), 6/46a, 8/14a; Yen Ts'ung-chien 嚴從簡, *Shu-yü chou-tzu lu* 殊域周咨錄 (1930 ed.), 2/2b; Hsü Hsiang-mei 徐象梅, *Liang-Che ming-hsien lu* 兩浙名賢錄 (preface 1621), 62/20b; Lü Hai-huan (ECCP, p. 312), *Feng-shih chin-chien* 奉使金鑑 (1905), 57/22a, 58/39b; Huang Tsun-hsien (ECCP), *Jih-pen-kuo chih* (1898), 5/9a; Li Kuang-ming 黎光明, "Ming T'ai-tsu ch'ien seng shih Jih-pen k'ao" 明太祖遣僧使日本考, CYYY, VII: 2 (1936), 255; Gidō Shunsei, *Kūka ki* 空華集, in *Gozan bungaku zenshu* 五山

文學全書, vol. 4 (1937), 906, 927; Hayashi Shunsai 林春齋 (1618-80), *Zoku Honchō tsūgan* 續本朝通鑑 (1919 ed.), vol. 12, 4112, 4114; Nakajima Shō 中島疎, comp. (*Shintei*) *Zenrin kokuhō ki* (新訂) 善鄰國寶記 (1932 ed.), ch. 1; *Dai Nihon shoryō* 史料 (1961), ser. 6, vol. 33, 9; Miyajima Sadasuke 宮島貞亮, "Ashikaga jidai no nichimin kōtsū" 時代の日明交通, *Shigaku* 史學 3: 3 (1924), 94; Obata Atsushi, *Chusei nisshi tsūkō boeki shi no kenkyū* 中世日支通交貿易史の研究 (Tokyo, 1930), *ch.* 1; Wang Yi-t'ung, *Official Relations between China and Japan (1368-1549)* (Cambridge, Mass., 1953), 12.

Hok-lam Chan

TSUNG Ch'en 宗臣 (T. 子相, H. 方城山人), 1525-March 12, 1560, writer and official, was a native of Hsing-hua 興化 in the prefecture of Yangchow. His father, Tsung Chou 周 (T. 維翰, H. 理庵, cj 1531), who once served as prefect of Ma-hu-fu 馬湖府, Szechwan, and taught the Confucian Classics, was the author of several books, one of which, the *Chiu-cheng lu Li-chi hui-yao* 就正錄禮記會要 , 6 ch., on the Book of Rites, was to receive a notice in the *Ssu-k'u* catalogue. Tsung Ch'en, following in his father's footsteps in the study of the Rites, achieved the *chü-jen* in 1549 and the *chin-shih* the following year, along with Wu Kuo-lun (*q. v.*), Liang Yu-yü (*see* Huang Tso), and Hsü Chung-hsing (*q.v.*). All four became known in Peking as talented in composing poetry and were later among those called the "Seven Later Masters," the other three being Wang Shih-chen, Li P'an-lung (*qq.v.*), and Hsieh Chen (*see* Hsü Chung-hsing). Tsung's first appointment was as secretary in the Kwangsi office of the ministry of Justice. Because of his literary talent, the minister of Personnel, Li Mo (*see* Chao Wen-hua), recruited him for the bureau of evaluations in his ministry. While at the capital Tsung often met and discussed literary problems with Wang Shih-chen, Li P'an-lung, and others. At the end of 1551, following the fall of Li Mo who had clashed with Yen Sung (*q.v.*), Tsung asked permission to retire

as he appeared to be suffering from tuberculosis. He erected a house in Po-hua chou 百花洲, a tiny island less than a mile to the south of Hsing-hua, where he lived the life of a scholar and enjoyed occasional visits with literary friends.

In the autumn of 1553, his old post restored, Li Mo returned to court (January 2, 1554), and invited Tsung Ch'en to resume his former duties. Three months later Tsung was promoted to a post in the bureau of appointments in the same ministry. Here he served for one year, then was transferred to the bureau of records as vice director. In March, 1556, Li Mo suffered imprisonment because of the machinations of Yen Sung. With his sponsor's removal, and also as a consequence of his support of Yang Chi-sheng (*q.v.*), Tsung received a demotion (spring, 1557) to be assistant administration commissioner in Fukien. Here, in the following summer, he made a name for himself in the part he played in the defense of Foochow, then under attack from the *Wok'ou*. He allowed inhabitants living outside to enter the walled city, and protected them from enemy action, while, in contrast to his actions, the governor of Fukien Juan 0 (*see* Cheng Hsiao), who was responsible for military affairs in the province, was trying to buy off the pirates with government property, which included six large vessels. (Juan was eventually taken to Peking to face a court of inquiry.) Tsung, who guarded the west gate, and Hu T'ing-lan 胡廷蘭 (cs 1550), who guarded the east gate, together with other leaders, saved the city. As a result Tsung was promoted to be vice surveillance commissioner and put in charge of educational affairs in Fukien (1559). In this position he gave a creditable performance, helping those who were indigent and winning the respect of the students for his ability as a teacher. In spite of poor health he kept on writing. He died of tuberculosis while still in office.

It is said that three poems, entitled "Chüeh-ming shih" 絕命詩 (Farewell to life), preserved in both the local history of Hsing-hua and in one of his anthologies, were composed just before he passed away.

In them he conceived of himself as originally a fairy who, being exiled to the world of man for thirty-six years, was about to return to the world of the immortals. He asked to be buried in Nanking, but his father, recalling his son's fondness for Po-hua-chou where his studio was located, buried him on the island. Wang Shih-chen composed his epitaph, and a few days after his death his tablet was set up in the shrine honoring worthy officials in Fukien. Sixteen years later, on the recommendation of Hsü Chung-hsing, then administration vice commissioner in the same province, a shrine was built in his memory at Wu-shih-shan 烏石山, a mountain near Foochow, where Tsung and Hsü had spent many happy hours together. Again it was Wang Shih-chen who wrote Tsung's eulogy on the stone tablet at the shrine.

An anthology of Tsung's poems and essays, entitled *Tsung Tzu-hsiang chi* 宗子相集 (or *Fang-ch'eng chi* 方城集), 15 *ch.*, appeared after his death. The editors of the *Ssu-k'u* accepted it for inclusion in the Imperial Library, averring that his poetry achieved a certain elegance, and his writings on the defense of the country against the marauding Japanese were meaningful. This anthology was published in several editions, with variant number of *chüan*, and is widely available. The copy in the Library of Congress is in 25 *chüan* and may well be the most nearly complete. Besides his own contributions it includes biographical data on him. His essays and poems deal with his acquaintance with literary friends, especially with members of the "Seven Later Masters," descriptions of his excursions to places of interest, and his love of nature. One short piece, a "letter on the secret of getting along," a satire on the politics of the day, has been rendered into English by Lin Yutang. He admired many of his predecessors, but refused to imitate any of them. Every author should be creative, he thought. Besides the anthology mentioned above, the editors of the *Ssu-k'u* catalogue drew attention to another, known as *Tzu-hsiang wen-hsün* 子相文選, 5 *ch.* (4 of essays, 1 of poems), but they excluded it from the *Ssu-k'u ch'üan-shu;* fortunately the National Central Library boasts a copy. Still a third, in 1 *chüan*, *Tsung Tzu-hsiang chi*, is included in the *Sheng Ming pai-chia shih* 盛明百家詩, *ch'ien-pien*, of Yü Hsien (*see* Feng Wei-min).

Bibliography

1/205/13b, 287/16a; 3/268/13a; 5/90/71a; 14/5/10b; 64/己 2/9b; 84/丁上/56a; 86/13/40a; *Tsung Tzu-hsiang chi* (NLP microfilm); *Hsing-hua-hsien chih* (1852), 1/2a, 7/13b, 8/6b, 9a, 9/2a, 14a; KC (1958), 3934; SK (1930), 24/1b, 172/9b, 178/3b; MSL (1965), Shih-tsung, 7729; L. of C. *Catalogue of Rare Books*, 956; Lin Yutang, *Translations from the Chinese* (Cleveland, 1963), 402.

                                    Yang Chin-yi

TSUNG-LO 宗泐 (T. 季潭, H. 全室), 1318-October 12, 1391, a Buddhist monk, was born into the Chou 周 family of Lin-hai 臨海, Chekiang. At the age of eight *sui* (1325) he was sent to the Chung T'ien-chu ssu 中天竺寺 in Hangchow where he became a pupil of the Ch'an master Ta-hsin 大訢 (H. 笑隱, 1284-1344). His teacher was not only a famous Buddhist cleric but also a literary figure of some reputation and a favorite of the Mongol emperor Togh Temür (1304-32). Tsung-lo became a novice in 1331 and was ordained in 1337. In Hangchow he moved in literary circles, enjoying the company of such well-known literati as Huang Chin (1277-1357), Chang Ch'i-yen (1285-1353), and Yü Chi (1272-1348). He rose to become abbot of the Chung T'ien-chu ssu but soon after 1368 took up residence in the T'ien chieh ssu 天界寺 (Temple of Devagati [Realm of the Gods]), Nanking. This temple had been built in the

1320s as a residence for the heir apparent, Prince Togh Temür, then was converted into a Buddhist monastery after he ascended the throne. The name Lung hsiang ssu 龍翔 (Temple of the Soaring Dragon) was changed in 1357 to T'ien-chieh ssu. It was the largest and most magnificent temple in Nanking, situated in the northern part of the city. For some time it housed the learned committee which compiled the *Yüan-shih* (*see* Sung Lien).

In 1369, Tsung-lo was introduced to the Ming emperor, Chu Yüan-chang, who immediately favored him and even proposed that he give up monastic life and accept a civilian office. The monk, however, declined; he nevertheless maintained close relations with the emperor, whose strong Buddhist affiliations are well known and who seems, for some time at least, to have favored Buddhism as the ideology influencing his rule. The emperor on this occasion wrote for Tsung-lo a dissertation entitled *Mien-kuan shuo* 免官說 (On exemption from offices). On imperial command, in 1372 or 1373, Tsung-lo organized a Buddhist disputation in Nanking. Some years later, in 1377, he and Ju-ch'i 如玘 (T. 具庵, H. 太璞 or 樸, 1320-December 19, 1385) were commissioned to provide a new commentary for those sūtras which the emperor considered as basic texts: the *Vajracchedikaprajñāpāramitā-sūtra* (*Chin-kang p'an-jo-po-lo-mi ching* 金剛般若波羅密經), the *Prajñāpāramitāhṛdaya-sūtra* (Hsin-ching心經), and the *Laṅkavatāraratnasūtra* (*Leng-chia-a-po-to-lo-pao ching* 楞伽阿跋多羅寶經). This work was finished in 1378 and the commentaries printed in 1379 after the emperor had approved the manuscript. Sung Lien wrote a preface to the new *Vajracchedika* edition and a postface to the *Laṅkavatāra-sūtra*, whereas an imperial preface precedes the *Hsin-ching* (Heart Sūtra). For the *Vajracchedika* Tsung-lo and his fellow author used the Kumārajīva (344-413?) version (*Taishō Issaikyō*, no. 235), for the *Laṅkavatāra-sūtra* the Gunabhadra (394-468) version (*T. I.*, no. 670), and for the Heart Sūtra the Hsüan-

tsang (602-64) version (*T. I.*, no. 251). The three commentaries by Tsung-lo and Ju-ch'i have been incorporated into the Buddhist canon in China and are among the last important Chinese contribution to the exegesis of Buddhist scriptures.

At the end of 1378, soon after completion of the commentaries, the emperor sent Tsung-lo on a mission to the Western Regions (Hsi-yü 西域). This is another instance of the first Ming emperor's using Buddhist monks for diplomatic and political purposes. Tsung-lo returned three years later, arriving in Nanking on December 20, 1381. Although no details of his mission are available, it is certain from circumstantial evidence that he went to Tibet and returned with some holy scriptures. [Editors'note: Tsung-lo's travels from 1378 to 1381 can only be guessed at. He mentions in several of his poems, included in the anthology *Lieh-ch'ao shih-chi* (*see* Ch'ien Ch'ien-i, ECCP), such place names as Ling-chiu-shan 靈鷲山 (the Chinese name for Mt. Gṛdhrakūṭa or Vulture Peak near Patna) and an I-pa--li 宜八里 kingdom where men wear turbans and (women?) mark their foreheads, and where the palm leaves are as large as mats. This would indicate that Tsung-lo must have traveled to India. It is uncertain whether he went by way of Tibet or Yunnan. Since the above was written (1966), Mr. Kazuo Enoki has made an interesting contribution on Tsung-lo in *Oriens Extremus* (1972). His statement that Tsung-lo traveled by way of I-pa-li (which he equates with Nepal) to northeast India confirms our own hypothesis. He adds that on Tsung-lo's way home he traveled be way of central Tibet, his embassy involving some thirty people.]

One source alleges that he was sentenced to death in a case involving irregularity in the issuance of patents, but was pardoned and sent on. His embassy was apparently regarded as a success because soon after his return Tsung-lo was made Yu-shan shih 右善世 (Right Buddhist Patriarch) and therefore head of the recently established Seng-lu-ssu 僧錄司 (Central Buddhist Registry) which exercised supervision over Buddhist monks and nuns throughout the whole empire (*see* Paṇḍita) His close associate, Ju-ch'i, became Left Buddhist Patriarch at about the same time (1383). Tsung-lo took part in the funeral rites for Empress Ma (*q.v.*) in 1382, an occasion at which he improvised a gatha in eulogy of the deceased. He was also responsible for introducing Tao-yen (Yao Kuang-hsiao, *q.v.*) to the emperor. Later he was accused of involvement in the case of Hu Wei-yung (*q.v.*) and sentenced to building a monastery in Feng-yang 鳳陽 (Anhwei). In 1386 he resumed his office as abbot of T'ien-chieh ssu. Two years later this temple was destroyed by a fire and he petitoned to have it rebuilt on a site south of the Chü-pao 聚寶 gate of Nanking. By 1390 the old structure had been repaired and Tsung-lo again took up residence there. When he was on his way back to Feng-yang the following year, he died in a monastery situated on the northern bank of the Yangtze River, and his ashes were interred in the T'ien-chieh ssu.

Tsung-lo was one of the leading figures in Chinese Buddhism during his time and, like many other monks, well versed in literature and the Confucian classics. Among his friends Sung Lien and Kao Ch'i (*q.v.*) should be mentioned. His poems have been collected and printed in 10 *chüan* under the title *Ch'üan-shih wai-chi* 全室外集 in the *Ch'ih-ch'eng i-shu hui-k'an* 赤城遺書彙刊 (1915). For a translation into Italian of one of his poems on contemplating the source of the Yellow River, see Emilio Bottazzi, "Una poesia di epoch Ming sulle sorgenti del Fiume Gialla."

Bibliography

40/90/4b; 61/160/3a (TsSCC ed., 3152-53); 84/閏/9b (Shanghai ed., 1957, 666); 85/2/54; MSL (1963) T'ai-tsu, 1966, 2209; Sung Lien, *Sung hsüeh-shih wen-chi* (SPTK ed.), 47/10b, 62/8b; *Taishō Daizōkyō*, nos. 1703, 1714, 1789; *Shih-shih chi-ku lüeh hsü-chi* 釋氏稽古略續集, *ibid.*, Vol. 49, 928c, 933c, 937a; *Ta Ming Kao-seng chuan* 大明高僧傳, *ibid.*, Vol. 50, 909b, c; *Chin-ling fan-ch'a chih* 金陵梵刹志 (1936 ed.), 16/22b; *Bukkyō Daijiten*, Vol. 8, 117, 212; F. W. Mote, *The Poet Kao Ch'i* (Princeton, 1962), 201; Heinz Friese, "Der Mönch Yao Kuang-hsiao (1335–1418) und seine Zeit," OE, Vol. 7 (1960), 173; Emilio Bottazzi, *Annali dell' Instituto Orientale di Napoli*, XXX: 4 (1970), 559; Enoki Kazuo, "Tsung-lo's Mission to the Western Regions in 1378-1382," OE, 19 (1972), 47.

Herbert Franke

TU Ch'iung 杜瓊 (T. 用嘉, H, 王塢山人, 東原耕者, 鹿冠道人), January 4, 1397-December 5, 1474, scholar and minor painter, was born into a wealthy family of the T'ai-p'ing quarter 太平坊 in Soochow. Only one month after his birth, his father Tu Yü 玉 died in Nanking where he had been compelled to stay on account of an imperial edict promulgated in 1391 which required certain wealthy persons to reside at the capital. It was not until 1419 that Tu Ch'iung obtained his father's books and antiques that had been left there. He began to attend school at the age of seven; later he became the pupil of Ch'en Chi (*see* Ch'en Ju-yen). A brilliant student, he was chosen by Ch'en to teach the other pupils in 1411 when Ch'en was summoned to an official post. Obliged by a requirement for all early Ming teachers, he accompanied his students in 1420 to the capital (now Peking) so that they might be examined on their ability to recite the first emperor's exhortation on observance of the law presented in *Ta-kao* (*see* Chu Yüan-chang). This was the only journey to the north that he ever made.

From 1434 onward, he declined successively the recommendations of local officials to enter the civil service. In 1437, when again recommended, he refused once more, but, in compliance with his own request, his mother received honors as a noteworthy example of motherhood and widowhood by imperial edict in 1439, eleven years before her death. In addition to this, his family was exempted from land tax and in 1441 registered as Ju-chi 儒籍 (Confucianist) in Soochow following two precedents, those accorded to Yü Chen-mu 俞貞木 (1331-1401) and Ch'en Chi. Although he declined official posts, he was asked to participate in collecting local materials for the compilation of both the *T'ai-tsung shih-lu* (1425) and the *Hsüan-tsung shih-lu* (1435). In 1454 he was again charged with collecting local information for the geography of the empire. In the early part of 1474, the year of his death, he was still engaged in revising the local history of Soochow compiled by others.

Apparently Tu's wealth increased as the years went by, for it is recorded several times that he built new quarters, opened a new garden, or acquired more land. From 1459 on, repeated invitations came to him to take part in the ancient rite of village wine drinking reinstituted at the beginning of the Ming; it was under the sponsorship of local educational officials and designed to permit the respected elders of the local community to meet together. This was considered a great honor for the local gentry at that time.

The year following his death, several thousand men, among whom were numerous people of influence, attended his burial ceremony. He was posthumously given an official rank in 1494 when his second son, Tu Ch'i 啓 (T. 子開, b. 1452, cj 1474) was serving as magistrate of Ch'ang-yüan 長垣, Pei-Chihli. Four years later his name was entered in the local temple of worthies.

To sum up, his principal career was no more than that of a local teacher. His renown derived from the fact that Soochow was the cultural center south of the Yangtze where many scholars of note became his students. These included, among others, Wu K'uan and Shen Chou (*qq.v.*), authors of his epitaph and his chronological biography.

Neither Wu nor Shen mentions his pictorial art, but he became known also as a painter. Eight of his extant paintings are listed in Oswald Sirén's great corpus. Since he had absolutely no impression of his father, it is said that he asked other people about his father's appearance and then painted a portrait to serve as an object of worship when he grew up.

As to his literary output, *Tung-yüan chi* 東原集, 7 *ch.*, and *Chi-shan lu* 紀善錄 (an attempt at a book of exempla), 1 *ch.*, are both noticed by the editors of the *Ssu-k'u* catalogue. The *Tung-yüan chi*, included in the *T'ien-ch'ih-lou ts'ung-ch'ao* 天尺樓叢鈔, represents only one *chüan* of prose and one *chüan* of poetry. An example of his poetry in English translation is given by Susan Bush; it concerns the development of landscape painting.

Bibliography

5/111/28a; 21/12/42b; 32/24/41a; 64/乙6/16a; 84/乙/48a; SK (1930), 61/7b, 176/18a; *Ta Ming hui-tien* 大明會典, 19/2/a; Wu K'uan, *Pao-weng chia-tsang chi*, 72/1 (SPTK, 1st series); Shen Chou, *Tu Tung-yüan hsien-sheng nien-p'u* (in *Hsüeh-t'ang ts'ung-k'o* 雪堂叢刻); Chang Ch'ang 張昶, *Wu-chung jen-wu chih* 吳中人物志, 9/24; Ho Ch'iao-yüan, *Ming-shan ts'ang*, 96/2; Wen Chen-meng, *Ku-su ming-hsien hsiao-chi*, 上/17下; Chiang Chao-shu 姜紹書, *Wu-sheng shih-shih* 無聲詩史, 2/1; Wang Chih-teng, *Tan-ch'ing chih*, 1/1; Oswald Sirén, *Chinese Painting*, VII (New York 1958), 246, E. J. Laing, *Chinese Paintings in Chinese Publications, 1956-1968* (Ann Arbor, 1969), 196; S. Bush, *The Chinese Literati on Painting* (Cambridge, Mass., 1971), 163.

T. W. Weng

TU Mu 都穆 (T. 玄敬, H. 虎邱山人, 南濠居士), 1459-October 8, 1525, author and art critic of Wu 吳-hsien (Soochow). His father Tu Ang 卬 (T. 維明, H. 豫軒, 1426-1508) was the author of *San-yü chui-pi* 三餘贅筆, which was copied into the *Ssu-k'u ch'üan-shu*. The appendix of this book includes a birthday essay (壽序) written by Wang Shou-jen (*q.v.*) in 1505, which runs in part as follows: "I visited Soochow in the winter of 1503 where I met my fellow *chin-shih*, Tu Mu, who accompanied me on a visit to Hsüan-mu shan 玄墓山, T'ien-p'ing 天平 shan, and Hu-ch'iu 虎邱 (Tigers' Mount), then all snow covered. I had a pleasant time with him for fifteen days and found that he is really a well informed scholar. Upon our return I had the honor of meeting his father, Tu Ang, who is eighty *sui* this year. Tu Mu is now a secretary in the ministry of Works. As the emperor (Chu Yu-t'ang, *q.v.*) has granted special favors to all officials this year, Tu Ang received the same title as his son." Tu Mu was appointed a secretary in the ministry of Works; later came promotion to director of a bureau in the ministry of Rites. When he retired in 1512, he was granted the title of vice minister of the Court of the Imperial Stud.

Besides intensive study of books on a variety of subjects, Tu Mu was fond of traveling, and investigated whatever interested him on his journey. When sent on an official mission, he would visit the scenic spots and search for historical relics. He delighted in collecting rubbings of stone and metal inscriptions. In 1513, following an official tour to Ninghsia, he wrote an account of the trip called *Hsi-shih chi* 西使記, 1 *ch.* (or *Shih-hsi jih-chi* 使西日記, as listed in the *Ssu-k'u* catalogue). The full account of his study of rubbings was published as *Chin-hsieh lin-lang* 金薤琳瑯, 20 *ch.* It was written in imitation of, and as a supplement to, *Li shih* 隸釋 by Hung K'ua (1117-84). This may be considered his *magnum opus*.

In spite of a fairly successful official life, Tu Mu was not well off. Oftentimes when his family was short of food, he would simply smile and remark: "The world would not let Tu Mu die of hunger." One incident may have discredited Tu Mu. He and T'ang Yin (*q.v.*) were friends of long standing. When T'ang was unfortunately involved in a bribery case, someone reported that it was Tu who had spread the story. For this reason T'ang made up his mind never to meet Tu again. Tu Mu was filled with regret that he had been responsible and remained remorseful to

the end of his life.

It is said that Tu Mu wrote in all twenty books; his literary style, however, as remarked both by Ch'ien Ch'ien-i (ECCP) and the *Ssu-k'u* editors, was rather commonplace. The *Ssu-k'u* catalogue lists seven publications. Others that are extant today are: *Nan-hao-chü-shih wen-pa* 南濠居士文跋, 4 *ch.*, *Nan-hao shih-hua* 詩話, 1 *ch.*, *Yu ming-shan chi* 遊名山記, 4 *ch.*, and *Yü-hu ping* 玉壺氷, 1 *ch.* In regard to *T'ieh-wang shan-hu* 鐵網珊瑚, 20 *ch.*, the *Ssu-k'u* editors comment that the book is an admixture of *Yü-i pien* 寓意編, 1 *ch.*, and some materials from other works. Lu Wen-ch'ao (ECCP), who wrote the preface to *Chin-hsieh lin-lang* in 1776, concurred in this opinion. In this connection a book bearing a similar title, *Shan-hu mu-nan*, compiled by Chu Ts'un-li (*q.v.*), is sometime confused with the above. As to *Yü-i pien*, it was written in imitation of *Shu-hua shih* by Mi Fu (1051-1107) and has been reprinted several times. Tu also left a collection of anecdotes entitled *T'an-tsuan* 談纂, 2 *ch.*, later edited by Lu Ts'ai 陸采 (T. 子玄, H. 天池山人, 1497-1537), his son-in-law. Lu Ts'ai made a name for himself by writing a drama called *Ming-chu chi* 明珠記 at the age of nineteen *sui*. *T'an-tsuan* came to be known as *Tu-kung* 都公 *t'an-tsuan*; it has been reprinted in the *Ts'ung-shu chi-ch'eng*. In addition Tu left a list of persons ennobled in 1402, entitled *Jen-wu kung-ch'en chüeh-shang lu* 壬午功臣爵賞錄 (with a supplement, *pieh-lu* 別錄), of which a Ming edition is available on microfilm.

Bibliography

3/267/13a; 5/72/41a; 22/9/9a; 32/22/36b; 40/27下/ 19a; 64/丁8/5a; 84/丙53a, 丁/22a; Wang Shou-jen, *Wang Wen-ch'eng kung ch'üan-chi*, 29/3a; Lu Ts'ai, *Tu-kung t'an-tsuan*, 2/54a; SK(1930), 53/4a, 64/2b, 86/7a, 113/1b, 127/4a, 130/1b, 144/3a, 197 /6a; *Soochow-fu chih* (1881), 80/3b, 136/15a; Pien Yung-yü (ECCP), *Shih-ku-t'ang shu-hua hui-k'ao*, 26/2b; Li Yü-sun (ECCP, p. 457), *Chin-shih hsüeh-lu*, 2/4a; NLP microfilm, no. 166.

Liu Lin-sheng

T'U Lung 屠隆 (T. 長卿, 緯眞, H. 赤水,
由拳山人, 鴻苞居士), 1542-1605, poet and
dramatist, came from a clan that had
settled in Yin 鄞-hsien (Ningpo), Chekiang, beginning in the 12th century. During
the Ming period several of his clansmen,
such as T'u Yung 滽 (T. 朝宗, H. 丹山,
1440-1512, cs 1466, minister of Personnel
1496-1500, censor-in-chief 1507-9), T'u
Chiao 僑 (T. 安卿, H. 東洲, 1480-1555, cs
1511, censor-in-chief 1547-55), and T'u
Ta-shan 大山 (T. 國望, H. 竹墟, 1500-79,
cs 1523, governor of Nanking area 1554)
rose to high positions in the government.
T'u Lung's ancestors, however, were rather
undistinguished. His father, T'u Chün 濬
(T. 朝文, 1497-1566), spent his youth on
such unproductive skills as shooting with
the bow and crossbow. At about the age
of sixty he gambled his fortune on an
adventurous sea voyage; the wreck of his
ship (on the way to Japan?) bankrupted
him. His debtors, all clansmen, showed no
mercy and he landed in jail. Dispossessed,
he moved with his family to live in improvised shelters on unclaimed tideland,
and became a boatman, but he kept up
his spirits by planting chrysanthemums.
One night he lay in wait for the thief
who had been stealing his flowers, caught
cold, and died. His elder sons continued for
some time as boatmen. T'u Lung, youngest of five brothers, somehow continued
his studies, becoming a student in the
district school in 1561. It is said that he
owed his name as a promising writer to
two elder fellow townsmen: the above
mentioned T'u Ta-shan, and the one-time
minister of War, Chang Shih-ch'e (*see*
Feng Fang). When T'u Lung became a
chin-shih in 1577 he was already well
known in Peking as were some of his
classmates, including Shen Mao-hsüeh (*see*
Shen Yu-jung), Feng Meng-chen (*see* Chu
Lu), Feng Ch'i, Wang Shih-hsing, and
Tsou Yüan-piao (*qq.v.*). Late in 1577 he
received an appointment as magistrate of
Ying-shang 潁上, about 170 miles northwest
of Nanking. There he found a section of
the dike that protected the city from river

floods urgently in need of repair. For
lack of sufficient funds his predecessors
had been unwilling to embark on the
project. T'u went ahead with the work
anyhow, and by personally taking part
led the conscripted laborers to finish the
job swiftly, and at low cost. In gratitude
the people erected a pavilion on the dike
in his honor. This feat earned him a
transfer to the much more populous district of Ch'ing-p'u 青浦, east of Soochow,
where he served for four years (1578-82).
Here his problem was to conduct a
new land survey (*see* Chang Chü-cheng).
Because of the concentration of land
ownership in influential families who
had devious ways of avoiding payment of
their share of the tax quota, he found
that any increase in tax resulting from
his survey would add only to the burden
of the common people. So he arranged
his report in such a way that the added
acreage (probably described as non-produc-
tive surplus land) did not make any
significant increase in the total tax quota.
It happened that the most influential of
the landowners in Ch'ing-p'u was Hsü
Chieh (*q.v.*), then living in retirement in
a neighboring district. As soon as T'u
took office he wrote a letter to Hsü, trying to persuade him to contribute to a
fund to finance the opening of some
waste land to cultivation by the landless
poor, but received an indirect warning
not to do anything to offend the retired
grand secretary who still had connections
throughout the empire.

For the first time in his life T'u now
had command of a sufficient expense
account; he used it during his office at
Ch'ing-p'u to maintain a troupe of players and to entertain such friends as Feng
Meng-chen and Shen Mou-hsüeh. Among
the famous men of letters who lived nearby were Wang Shih-chen and Wang
Hsi-chüeh (*qq.v.*), both his close friends.
He joined the former in becoming a
disciple of the latter's Taoist daughter
(Wang Tao-chen, *q.v.*). About this time
his first collection, entitled *Yu-ch'üan chi*

由拳集, 23 *ch.*, was printed by Feng Meng-chen. It helped to increase his popularity as a poet, far transcending that of any magistrate, although even in that capacity he performed so well that he was promoted late in 1582 to secretary in the ministry of Rites in Peking.

While in the capital in 1583 he enjoyed for a few months practically the status of an arbiter of poetry and drama. It was a time when several of his friends whom Chang Chü-cheng had sent into exile had just been recalled. Thus politically too T'u became a man to be watched. Among his admirers was Sung Shih-en 宋世恩 (d. 1597), the eleventh marquis of Hsi-ning 西寧侯. (The first marquis, Sung Sheng 晟 [T. 景陽], served as military commander on the Kansu frontier for over twenty years [1379–91 and 1398–1407] and was created a marquis in 1405, two years before his death.) On Sung Shih-en's insistence, T'u became his sworn brother, and during a feast in Sung's home met his wife (ordinarily an unheard-of thing at such a function). At this time Yü Hsien-ch'ing 俞顯卿 (T. 子如, H. 適軒, cs 1583), a native of Shanghai who held a grudge against T'u because he had slighted Yü's poetry, was appointed a secretary in the ministry of Justice. By embroidering on the story of the feast, Yü accused T'u and Sung of having an improper gathering. They protested their innocence, but the emperor strangely had both T'u and Yü cashiered and Sung fined half a year's stipend.

Expelled from the government after a service of only six years, T'u left Peking practically penniless. He could not foresee that he was to spend the rest of his life in penury, often depending on the generosity of his friends. Dressed in Taoist garb, he stopped at Ch'ing-p'u on his way home, and received a warm welcome from some of the local people who offered to purchase a tract of land for him if he would settle among them. He politely refused the offer and returned to Ningpo.

In the following decades he paid frequent visits to his friends, probably as a practicing Taoist priest. About this time (1590) he published his second collection, *Ch'i-chen-kuan chi* 栖眞館集, 31 *ch.* During these years the main source of his income seems to have been from writing tomb inscriptions and commemorative pieces. Once when he passed by Soochow in a boat he had to send a letter to a friend inside the city begging for some rice to stave off hunger. Yet he never lost his self-respect and in 1587 even wrote a work on his philosophy in the style of *Chuang-tzu*, entitled *Ming-liao-tzu chi-yu* 冥寥子記遊, 2 *ch.*

In 1598 he published a song-drama, *T'an-hua chi* 曇花記, 2 *ch.*, which in 55 scenes tells the story of a nobleman who abandoned his family and possessions to search for immortality. Guided by a Taoist priest and a Buddhist monk, the hero visited hell and both the Taoist and Buddhist heavens. Then he returned home as a lay immortal to resume normal relationships with his wife and children. If anything, the drama reflects the desire of certain of the wealthy and powerful of that day to find some magical formulae for the prolongation of life and enjoyment of mundane pleasures. Apparently T'u himself believed in this kind of Taoist theory, for in his letters he mentions that he was under the spell of first one Taoist priest and then another. At this time he probably gained some wealthy patrons too. In 1600 a Hui-chou friend sponsored the printing of his third collection, *Po-yü chi* 白榆集, 8 *chüan* of poems and 20 *chüan* of prose. In the same year he wrote some one hundred thirty proverbs in parallel sentences, entitled *Po-lo-kuan ch'ing-yen* 婆羅館清言, 2 *ch.* In his own preface he remarked that he had a profound work on philosophy which a friend advised him not to publish; so he wrote these proverbs instead. The work apparently was well accepted, for some time later he added a supplement of sixty-six proverbs.

According to Ch'ien Ch'ien-i (ECCP), in 1603 T'u went to Fukien, where he resided for some time on the scenic hill, Wu-shih-shan 烏石山, near Foochow; there Ts'ao Hsüeh-ch'üan (*q.v.*) gave a reception in his honor and also in honor of Juan Tzu-hua 阮自華 (T. 堅之, cs 1598), then prefectural judge of Foochow. The occasion was immortalized in a number of poems. We learn that about seventy local celebrities gathered at a pavilion where at the end of the theatrical event T'u took over the drum and gave an expert demonstration of his art. Returning north, he stayed almost a year in the Soochow area. He died soon after reaching home. According to report, he believed to the end in the pursuit of immortality taught by Taoist magicians, for even on his deathbed he expected a fairy band to come and welcome him as one of the latter had promised.

T'u is known to have had two sons and a daughter. The elder son, T'u Ta-ch'un 大諄 (T. 國敎, H. 西昇), who married Shen T'ien-sun 沈天孫 (T. 七襄, daughter of Shen Mou-hsüeh), died at the age of twenty-one. The daughter, T'u Yao-se 瑤瑟 (T. 湘靈, wife of Huang Chen-ku 黃振古) died at the age of twenty-seven. T'u Lung lamented their deaths by printing a joint collection of their poems entitled *Liu-hsiang ts'ao* 留香草 (Poetry preserving fragrance), which seems to be no longer extant. He also composed a song-drama about the brother and sister, entitled *Hsiu-wen chi* 修文記, 2 *ch.*, which tells a story based on Taoist belief that their early death in this world was the result of their talents being needed by the gods in heaven. T'u's second son, according to the genealogy of their clan compiled about 1747, had descendants, but by the mid-18th century was represented by only one male child.

T'u Lung had a fourth collection, *Hung-pao chi* 鴻苞集, 49 *ch.*, of which the Hōsō Bunko in Nagoya seems to have the only copy recorded in a library. All the other three collections already mentioned may be found in libraries in Japan and Taiwan, and on microfilm. Among other works under T'u's name as author or editor may be mentioned these smaller collections, each in 2 *chüan: Heng-t'ang chi* 橫塘集, *Nan-yu chi* 南遊集, *Ts'ai-chen chi* 采眞集, and *Po-lo-kuan i-kao* 逸稿. There is a selection of his works, also in 2 *chüan*, entitled *T'u Ch'ih-shui hsien-sheng hsiao-p'in* 赤水先生小品, being the first one of a series of selections from sixteen late Ming authors, the *Ts'ui-yü ko p'ing-hsüan, shih-liu chia* 翠娛閣評選十六家 *hsiao-p'in, ca.* 1640, compiled by Lu Yün-lung 陸雲龍. T'u Lung is credited with the printing of two sixth-century collections, the *Hsü Hsiao-mu chi* 徐孝穆集 by Hsü Ling (507-83) and *Yü Tzu-shan chi* 庾子山集 by Yü Hsin (513-81). T'u's edition of these two works was reproduced in 1929. Another work attributed to T'u is the *Huang-cheng k'ao* 荒政考 on famine relief. He also left a third song-drama, *Ts'ai-hao chi* 彩毫記, 2 *ch.*, on the life of the T'ang poet, Li Po (699-762). There is a work on high living and on the collection of art objects attributed to T'u Lung, entitled *K'ao-p'an yü-shih* 考槃餘事, 17 chapters in 4 *chüan*. Judging from the expensiveness and rarity of most of the articles mentioned in the book, it seems unlikely that T'u could have had the means to afford them, the patience to evaluate them, or the temperament to describe them. It may well be the work of a collector, affluent and devoted, someone like Hsiang Yüan-pien (*q. v.*). In fact Hsiang did have a similar work attributed to him, entitled *Chiao-ch'uang chiu-lu*. The fact that almost all the Hsiang text is exactly the same as that in the *K'ao-p'an yü-shih* has led some scholars to the opinion that a publisher took excerpts from T'u's work and passed them off as Hsiang's. Actually if one has to choose between the two, Hsiang seems the more likely author. In any case, the *K'ao-p'an yü-shih* is one of the most readable and informative works on Chinese objets d'art. Several of its topics have been rendered into western languages, such as the ones on goldfish, the hanging of scrolls, and procelain.

Bibliography

1/288/4a; 3/269/3a; 40/47/23b; 43/4/6b; 64/丁上/68b, 閩中 /38; 84/己 6/4b; 86/14/4b; SK (19 30), 43/3b, 125/3b, 130/2a, 138/3a, 179/15a, 193/1b; *Ying-shang-hsien chih* (1878), 6/12b, 8/8a; *Yin chih kao* 稿(1935), 14/20a; *Ch'ing-p'u-hsien chih* (1879), 13/2a, 14/2a; Yao Chin-yüan (1957), 27, 34, 補 301; Jen Wei-k'un 任維焜, "Chung-lang shih-yu k'ao" 中郎師友考, *Shih-ta kuo-hsüeh ts'ung-k'an* 師大國學叢刊, 2 (1931); Fu Hsi-hua 傅惜華, *Ming-tai ch'uan-ch'i ch'üan-mu* (1956), 57; A. C. Moule, TP, 39 (1950), 15; R. H. van Gulik, THM, 12 (1941), 37; Paul Pelliot, TP, 22 (1923), 53, n. 1; Sir Percival David, *Trans. of the Or. Cer. Soc.* (1936-37), 42.

Chaoying Fang

T'U Shu-fang 屠叔方 (T. 宗直, H. 瞻山), fl. 1564-98, scholar-official, came from a branch of the T'u clan that had settled in P'ing-hu 平湖, Chekiang, beginning in the 12th century. The other branch settled at the same time in Yin 鄞-hsien to the south, later producing the famous dramatist and poet T'u Lung (*q. v.*). T'u Shu-fang's grandfather, T'u Hsün 勳 (T. 元勳, H. 東湖, Pth. 康僖, 1446-1516, cs 1469), served for a long time in the ministry of Justice, advancing to the rank of minister (1507-8). His father, T'u Ying-chün 應埈 (T. 文升, H. 漸山, 1502-46, cs 1526), a Hanlin bachelor, held office in various posts, retiring as senior instructor of the heir apparent. Both were men of letters and left collections of their writings. Graduating as *chü-jen* in 1564, T'u Shu-fang belatedly achieved the *chin-shih* in 1577. Following this he received an appointment as magistrate of Su-sung 宿松 (Anhwei), and served in this post for the next two years. During his administration, he conducted in 1578 a land survey of the district on the orders of Grand Secretary Chang Chü-cheng (*q. v.*). According to the local gazetteer, T'u completed his survey in one year, showing a larger area of cultivated land, which meant an increase in taxes, to the dismay of the local people. The court, on the other hand, commended him for his results and for swiftly completing his work. He was rewarded in 1579 with a transfer to the more populous, strategic district of P'o-yang 鄱陽, Kiangsi. In his new position T'u was credited with the construction of two embankments and four reservoirs to regulate the flow of water and to guard against flooding along the Yangtze. It was also during this time that he came to the attention of several families whose ancestors, serving as scholar-officials unde Emperor Chu Yün-wen (*q. v.*), had been condemned to exile by the order of Chu Ti (*q.v.*); they still suffered as a result of the nearly two-centuries-old decree. Out of his sympathy for these innocent individuals he later submitted a memorial pleading for their pardon; this aroused his interest in the historical records of the Chien-wen period. In September, 1583, T'u received promotion to be a censor in the Kwangtung office of the Censorate.

Early in April of the following year T'u Shu-fang submitted his famous memorial requesting the emperor to pardon the Chien-wen martyrs and their descendants. In his petition he cited the example of Hu Jun 胡閨 (T. 松板, *hsiu-ts'ai* of 1371, Pth. 忠烈), a native of P'o-yang who perished in the fall of Nanking in 1402; nevertheless, members of his family, friends, and associates several generations later still suffered in spite of repeated official pronouncements to spare people like them. Acting on his memorial the emperor ordered the local authorities to search for the surviving members of these condemned families in their places of exile, grant them immunity, and provide them with proper means of rehabilitation in their native localities. Strangely, however, he did not grant this privilege to members of the families of either Ch'i T'ai (*q. v.*) or Huang Tzu-ch'eng (*see* Lien Tzu-ning).

T'u left office (1587) upon the death of his mother, a granddaughter of Hsiang Chung (*q.v.*); after observing the mourning requirement in December, 1589, he returned to the Censorate. In September of the following year he was promoted to be the surveillance vice commissioner of Shantung. Six months later, however, he was charged with negligence and his salary reduced. One source states that he received a demotion for connivance in a corruption case; he was soon reinstated, but apparently stayed in his last post for only a short period.

After leaving office T'u returned home, where in the following years he devoted himself to compiling a record of the events of the reign of Chien-wen. He started this project in 1595, at a time the court was considering the compilation of an official history of the dynasty (see Ch'en Yü-pi), and he anticipated presenting this work as a contribution to the history. His opus, entitled *Chien-wen ch'ao-yeh hui-pien* 建文朝野彙編, 20 *ch.*, was completed in 1598. The original Wan-li edition includes T'u's own preface in which he calls himself a "censor at the Kwangtung office," and also an undated preface by Ch'en Chi-ju (ECCP), a distinguished contemporary belle-lettrist. The first 6 *chüan* in annalistic form cover the period from the appointment of Chu Yün-wen as heir apparent to the year 1402; the next 12 *chüan* are devoted to the biographies of personalities who were victims of the rebellion of Chu Ti, and the last two contain a collection of varying accounts of the fate of Chu Yün-wen as well as official documents on the events leading to the restoration of the reign-title of the dethroned emperor. It is not a critical nor definitive study, yet it brings together materials from a wide range of sources, some of them no longer extant, and is therefore an indispensible work for the study of the reign of Chu Yün-wen, matched only by the *Chien-wen shu-fa ni* by Chu Lu (*q. v.*) that appeared twenty years later. The editors of the Imperial Catalogue gave it a notice, but did not include it in the *Ssu-k'u ch'üan-shu*.

T'u Shu-fang married the granddaughter of Chao Wen-hua (*q.v.*), who had been accused of misappropriating government funds. When the court ordered members of Chao's family to refund this money, T'u is said to have been required to pay off an amount of over 30,000 taels. He was survived by a son named T'u Hung-yin 弘胤, a *chü-jen* of 1642, who gained a reputation for scholarship.

Bibliography

21/19/42a; MSL (1966) Shen-tsung, 2613, 2727, 4053, 4200, 4296; *P'ing-hu-hsien chih* (1886), 15/44a; *P'o-yang-hsien chih*(1871), 5/3a; *Su-sung-hsien chih* (1921), 12/19b, 15 下/5a; Sheng Feng (*see* Hsiang Chung), *Chia-ho cheng-hsien lu*, in *T sui-li* 檇李 *ts'ung-shu* (1936), Vol. 2, *ch.* 8; SK (1930), 54/1b; Ku Hsien-ch'eng, *Ku Tuan-wen kung chi* (NPL microfilm, no. 811), 7/1a; T'u Ying-chün, *T'u Ch'ien-shan chi* 漸山集 (NCL microfilm), *fu-lu* 附錄; T'u Shu-fang, *Chien-wen ch'ao-yeh hui-pien* (NCL microfilm); W. Franke, *Sources*, 2.4.4.

Hok-lam Chan

T'U Tse-min 塗澤民 (T. 志伊), died 1569, official, was a native of Han-chou 漢州, Szechwan. A *chin-shih* of 1544, he was appointed (1547) magistrate of Neihuang 內黃, Honan. During the following year he served in various other official capacities until he was made assistant censor-in-chief to the right (July 3, 1566) and delegated to Fukien as governor. In 1567 the pirate Tseng I-pen (*see* Lin Tao-ch'ien) pillaged various coastal districts in Fukien and Kwangtung. T'u Tse-min suggested to the throne the uniting of the troops of Fukien and Kwangtung in order to attack successfully Tseng I-pen's stronghold at Chao-an 詔安 in the border region between the two provinces. Before the reinforcements from Kwangtung arrived, T'u, together with the local commanders Yü Ta-yu and Ch'i Chi-kuang (*qq. v.*), succeeded in annihilating Tseng I-pen and his band in July, 1569. For this he was raised to the rank of vice censor-in-chief. T'u remained governor of Fukien until 1569 when he died in office. Shortly before his death he was accused by the supervising censor Lo Wen-li 駱問禮 (T. 纘亭, cs 1565) of being derelict in his duties. The ministry of Personnel, however, emphasized that he discharged them satisfactorily and succeeded in maintaining him in office. T'u was followed by Ho K'uan 何寬 (native of Lin-hai 臨海, Chekiang, cs 1550) late in 1569. Because of T'u's merits, one son of his was given hereditary civil service status.

Although T'u Tse-min has not been found important enough to be given an official biography, he nevertheless greatly influenced the military and political situation of his time. He not only managed to suppress coastal piracy by military means but above all he clearly saw the interdependence between piracy and illegal private trade with countries overseas. As early as 1567 he memorialized the throne, proposing that it renounce the traditional policy of maritime prohibition, observing that in Fukien particularly the coastal populace depended on ocean trade for maintenance. His recommendation to liberalize private seafaring to countries in the eastern and western oceans with the exception of Japan was followed, modifying somewhat the anti-maritime policy which had stood for some two hundred years. His initiative not only immediately reduced coastal piracy by giving the necessary legal security to overseas merchants but it also opened the way for a valuable Chinese trade abroad which could be taxed, and could be employed in supplying the country and the court with foreign goods.

T'u is said to have written a work on the Book of Odes, Shuo Shih i-te 說詩意得. He is known to have left a collection of writings entitled *T'u chung-ch'eng chün-wu chi* 塗中丞軍務集. The original edition does not seem to be extant, but selections from this work, in 3 *chüan*, are preserved in the *Huang Ming ching-shih wen-pien* (*see* Ch'en Tzu-lung in ECCP).

Bibliography

Fu-chien t'ung-chih (1868), 96/2a; *Ssu-ch'uan t'ung-chih* (1816), 124/29a, 145/21a; *Ho-nan t'ung-chih* (1902), 34/1a; *Ch'eng-tu-fu chih* (ed. T'ien-ch'i), 13/67a, 20/16b; Chang Hsieh, *Tung-hsi-yang k'ao* (ed. *Hsi-yin-hsien ts'ung-shu* 惜陰軒叢書, 1896), 7/1b; Ku Yen-wu (ECCP), *T'ien-hsia chün-kuo li-ping shu* (SPTK 3d series), 16/86b; *Kuo-ch'ao lieh-ch'ing chi* 國朝列卿記, 106/4b; MSL (1940) Mu-tsung, 8/6b, 15/6b, 36/5b, 37/1a, Shen-tsung, 316/5a; KC (1958), 4114; *Ming-shih* (Taiwan ed.), 2497.

Bodo Wiethoff

TUNG Ssu-chang 董斯張 (or 嗣暲, T. 然明 H. 遐周, 借庵), 1586-1628, scholar and poet, was a native of Wu-ch'eng 烏程, Hu-chou prefecture 湖州府, Chekiang, the descendant of a long line of ancestors reaching back thirteen generations in the same district. His grandfather, Tung Pin 份 (T. 用均, 體化, H. 潯陽山人, 1510-April 14, 1595, cs 1541), left several works of note, including the *Pi-yüan chi* 泌園集, 37 ch., printed 1606 (available on microfilm), and *Hsün-yang wen-hsüan* 潯陽文選, 2 ch. He served briefly in 1565 as minister of Rites and chancellor of the Hanlin Academy. The Tung family in those years was among the most eminent and prosperous in the lower Yangtze valley, having enormous land holdings and numerous servants and slaves. For a time it furnished the world of gossip with several murder stories, legends, and scandals, but by the 17th century, when its fortunes declined, the family produced several noteworthy men of letters. Tung Ssu-chang's father. Tung Tao-ch'un 道醇 (T. 子儒, cs 1583), and mother, a daughter of Mao K'un (*q. v.*), had six sons, four of whom achieved distinction. Tung Tao-ch'un himself rose to be a supervising secretary in Nanking; his eldest son, Tung Ssu-ch'eng 嗣成 (T. 伯念, H. 青芝, 1560-95, cs 1580), vice director of a bureau in the ministry of Rites; his third, Tung Ssu-chao 昭 (T. 叔弢, H. 中條, cs 1595), an observer in the ministry of Rites; and the fourth, Tung Ssu-hsin 昕 (T. 季爽), became known for his ability in calligraphy and painting.

Tung Ssu-chang, the sixth son, although schooled in the Confucian canon, took a special interest in Buddhism and Taoism as well as in all things literary, and was on terms of easy friendship with some of the poets of his day, such as his maternal uncle, Mao Wei (*q.v.*), and Chou Yung-nien 周永年 (T. 安期, 1582-1674).

Though his life was short, forty-two years, and his last years were plagued by illness, Tung Ssu-chang's productivity was considerable. Principal among his writings are the following: 1) *Ching-hsiao-chai i-wen* 靜歗齋遺文, 4 *ch.*, a collection of his verse which was condemned in the 18th century. A copy of the original edition of 1629 survives in Taipei; reprinted in 1924 it was included in the *Wu-hsing* 吳興 *ts'ung-shu*. 2) The *Wu-hsing pei-chih* 備志, 32 *ch*. A collection of facts and anecdotes about Hu-chou, it was given high praise by the editors of the *Ssu-k'u* catalogue, who had it copied into the Imperial Library. It too survives in the *Wu-hsing ts'ung-shu*. Five friends joined Tung in compiling this work for which they plumbed all available sources to make extensive quotations. It was designed to serve as a supplement to the *Chang ku chi* 掌故集, 17 *ch.*, by Hsü Hsien-chung 徐獻忠 (T. 伯臣, H. 長谷, cj 1525), published in 1560 and 1564; fortunately it is still extant. 3) *Wu-hsing i-wen pu* 藝文補, 70 *ch.*, printed 1633, is a bibliography of writings by Hu-chou authors in the compilation of which Tung collaborated with two other scholars. A copy is in the Library of Congress. 4) The *Kuang po-wu chih* 廣博物志, 50 *ch.* (printed 1607) is an enlargement of the *Po-wu chih* of Chang Hua (232-300), which has come down only in occasional quotations. Tung made use of a wide range of material, which he put under 22 headings and 168 subdivisions. The book is of genuine value as it preserves much that might otherwise have been lost, but is marred by Tung's inclusion of some matter which is of little or no relevance to the subject involved. The book is uncommon, but both the Harvard Library and the National Central Library, Taipei, have copies of the original edition; the Columbia Library owns a copy of the edition of 1761, and the *Ssu-k'u* editors entered it into the Imperial Library.

Tung Ssu-chang seems to have resented the fact that he never became a monk. His son, Tung Yüeh 說 (T. 若雨, H. 西庵, 鵾鶋生, , 1620-86), who inherited some of the father's characteristics, actually succeeded in taking the tonsure. He too was a poet and scholar and even wrote a supplement to the *Hsi-yu chi* (*see* Wu Ch'eng-en), entitled *Hsi-yu pu* 補, 16 *ch.*, which, like its predecessor, is a fantastic tale. Tung Yüeh made excursions into astronomy and geography, but his favorite subjects of study were Buddhism and Taoism. Because of his talents literary acquaintances were his in considerable number, and he is known to have had contacts with the semi-political society known as the Fu-she (*see* Chang P'u, ECCP). But again, like his father, he never became an official; in fact, he urged his six sons to avoid bureauratic connections, and gave them such names as woodcutter (樵), shepherd (牧), plow (耒), boat (舫), fisherman (漁), and village (村). From childhood on he read Buddhist sūtras and associated with several monks. The Manchu conquest of 1644/45 probably accelerated his decision to forsake the life of a layman. First a recluse, living in a straw hut, in the autumn of 1656 he took monastic vows in Ling-yen ssu 靈巖寺, a monastery in Lo-ch'ing hsien 樂清縣, Chekiang, were he changed his name to Nan-ch'ien 南潛 (T. 月涵, 月嚴, etc.). Actually he took many names, seemingly to show his contempt for them, for he wrote in one of his poems, "A name is no name," and he carried a seal bearing the characters: yü wu ming 余無名 (I have no name). As a monk he traveled much, frequently by boat on the Hsiang River 湘江 (Hukuang) and other streams. When his mother died in 1684 he settled down. His end came two years later.

Like his father, Tung Yüeh wrote incessantly. A biography by Liu Fu (BDRC) written in 1955 lists 112 items. Most of these, however, are either short or pieces he never brought to completion. Today few remain as he destroyed some in 1643, others in 1646; the rest simply disappeared. The editors of the *Ssu-k'u* mention five of them and had one copied into the Imperial Library, the *Ch'i kuo k'ao* 七國考 a study of the systems of government of the seven states, Ch'in, Ch'i, Ch'u, Chao, Han, Wei, and Yen, which flourished in the fourth and third centuries B.C. A copy of the original edition (Ch'ung-chen era) is in the library of Columbia University. Two the editors failed to list are a collection of his poetry and prose, *Tung Jo-yü shih-wen chi* 若雨詩文集, 24 (or 27) *ch.*, and the aforementioned *Hsi-yu pu* which Liu Fu republished in 1955. The former happens to include Tung's *Feng-ts'ao-an shih chi* 豐草菴詩集, 11 *ch.*, which was placed on the Index Expurgatorius of the 18th century. Fortunately it still survives; copies are in the National Library of Peiping and the Toyo Bunko, and it was reprinted in 1914.

Bibliography

40/65/21b, 81 上/14b; 60/4/12a; 64/辛 28/10a; 84/丁下/77a; 86/18/24b, 22/41a; KC (1958), 3913, 3939, 3944, 4739, 4747; Ch'ien Ch'ien-i (ECCP), *Lieh-ch'ao shih-chi* 丁16/45a; *Wu-ch'eng-hsien chih* (1881), 14/22a, 15/9b, 31/5a, 6a, 7a, 11b, 14a; *Nan-hsün chih* 南潯志 (1922), 18/4b, 8a, 9a, 14a, 23b, 47/27a, 49/2a, 51/21b, 54/8b; *Chekiang t'ung-chih* (1934), 3127; SK (1930), 8/11b, 68/10a, 81/5a, 105/8b, 107/11a, 136/4b, 193/13a, 14b; Sun Tien-ch'i (1957), 187, 220; Liu Fu, *Hsi-yu pu tso-che Tung Jo-yü chuan* 作者董若雨傳 (Peking, 1955); Ch'iu K'ai-ming 裘開明, CHHP n. s. II: 2 (1961), 100; Teng Chih-ch'eng 鄧之誠, *Ch'ing-shih chi-shih ch'u-pien* 清詩紀事初編 (1965), 266; Chou Ch'ing-yün 周慶雲, *Hsün-hsi shih-cheng* 潯溪詩徵 (1917); *id.*, *Hsün-hsi wen* 文 *cheng* (1924); NCL *Catalogue of Rare Books* (1968), 273, 642, 1071, 1109, 1114; *Naikaku Bunko Catalogue*, 288, 424; L. of C. *Catalogue of Rare Books*, 1114; Chu Shih-chia 朱士嘉, *Catalogue of Chinese Local Histories in the Library of Congress* (1942), 61; Robert E. Hegel, Monkey Meets Mackerel, a Study of the Chinese Novel Hsi-yu pu (in ms., 1967); C. T. Hsia and T. A. Hsia, "New Perspectives on Two Ming Novels: *Hsi-yu chi* and *Hsi-yu pu*," *Wen Lin* (ed. by Chow Tse-tsung, 1968), 239.

Yang Chin-yi and
L. Carrington Goodrich

URSIS, Sabatino de (Sabbathin, 熊三扰, T. 有網), 1575-May 3, 1620, missionary, was born into a well-known family in the kingdom of Lecce, Naples. After studying philosophy in Rome he entered the Society of Jesus in 1597. Following a brief sojourn at Coimbra, he left for Goa (1602) with fifty-nine other missionaries, and arrived (1603) in Macao where he completed his theological studies while awaiting assignment to Japan. Because his talents in mathematics and architecture might prove useful, however, in the intellectual apostolate which Matteo Ricci (*q.v.*) was developing in Peking, Alessandro Valignano (*q.v.*), shortly before his death in January, 1606, wrote a memorandum transferring Ursis to the China mission. He joined Ricci in the imperial capital early the following year.

Ricci saw in him an assistant of great promise and took special pains in directing his Chinese studies. Although Diego de Pantoja (*q.v.*) had been with him seven years longer, it was Ursis whom Ricci appointed on his deathbed to take charge of the Peking mission. Ursis wrote, in Portuguese, the first biography of Ricci, basing it upon a diary which he found among the effects of the deceased founder of the mission. It was not published until 1910, the tercentenary year of Ricci's death.

On December 15, 1610, the imperial bureau of astronomy miscalculated an eclipse, the incident being reported in the *Shih-lu* and later in the *Ming-shih*. Chou Tzu-yü 周子愚, secretary of the calendrical office of the bureau, called the attention of the court to the mathematical skills of Ursis and Pantoja. Weng Cheng-ch'un (*see* Ch'eng Ta-yüeh), a vice minister of

Rites, supported by others, recalled that in the early years of the dynasty, a Muslim school had been made a part of the bureau of astronomy. He recommended that this example be imitated in the case of the Jesuits. These initiatives met with success. The emperor issued an edict commissioning the Jesuits to undertake a reform of the calendar. Ursis, assisted by Hsü Kuang-ch'i and Li Chih-tsao (both in ECCP), translated into Chinese a treatise on planetary theory. He also calculated the longitude of Peking. Pantoja worked out the latitude of all the principal cities from Canton to Peking.

As a result of pressures generated by jealous mathematicians attached to the bureau of astronomy, the order for the commission was rescinded and the reform project abandoned. Ursis then turned his attention to the design and construction of hydraulic machines, which excited great interest in official and intellectual circles. He wrote a six *chüan* treatise on hydraulics, *T'ai-hsi shui-fa* 泰西水法 (Peking, 1612) which Hsü Kuang-ch'i put into elegant literary style. Hsü also wrote a preface to the work, as did the metropolitan censor, Ts'ao Yü-pien (*see* Wen Ti-jen). Hsü later included this work in his own sixty *chüan* treatise on agriculture, *Nung-cheng ch'üan-shu*. Besides the above-mentioned work on hydraulics, Ursis left two other slight books on astronomy: *Chien-p'ing-i shuo* 簡平儀說, 1 *ch.*, which describes an instrument providing the orthographic projection of the sky—according to the Ptolemaic theory—and *Piao tu shuo* 表度說, 1 *ch.*, which explains the gnomon. All three of these works were copied into the Imperial Library, the *Ssu-k'u ch'üan-shu*, and are available in microfilm.

In 1617, as a consequence of the imperial edict banishing all missionaries (*see* Alfonso Vagnoni), Ursis was obliged to leave China. He and Pantoja left Peking under escort on Palm Sunday, March 18. Ursis died in exile in Macao.

Bibliography
1/326/19a; SK (1930), 102/3a, 106/4b; MSL (1966), Shen-tsung, 9001; KC (1958), 5026; SK (1930), 102/3a, 106/4b; Daniello Bartoli, *Dell'istoria della Compagnia di Gêsù La Cina. Terza parte dell'Asia*, 4 vols. (Ancona ed., 1843); Henri Bernard, *Le père Matthieu Ricci et la société chinoise de son temps* (1552-1610), II (Tientsin, 1937), 370; George H. Dunne, *Generation of Giants* (Notre Dame, 1962), 105; Pfister (1932), 103; Pasquale M. d'Elia, *Fonti Ricciane*, II (Rome, 1949), 133, 387, 615; *id., Galileo in China* (tr. by R. Suter and M. Sciascia, Cambridge, Mass. 1960), 61.

George H. Dunne

VAGNONI, **Alfonso** (Alphonse, first known as 王豐肅 T. 一元泰穩, then as 高一志 T. 則聖), 1566-1640, was a missionary. The former Chinese name is that by which he is identified in the *Ming-shih*, and was the name by which he was known during the first phase of his China career. Upon reentering China after banishment, he adopted the second name. He was born into a noble family of Trofarello in Turin, Italy, entered the Society of Jesus in 1584, and for five years taught humanities and rhetoric, followed by three years of philosophy at Milan. In 1603 he left for the East and landed at Macao in 1604, In February or March of 1605 he was sent to Nanking. A year and a half later, Matteo Ricci (*q.v.*) reported to the superior general of the order that Vagnoni was "studying Chinese letters with great diligence and considerable success." In 1609 he succeeded João da Rocha (*q.v.*) as superior of the Nanking mission.

During the years immediately following, this mission was the most flourishing in the empire. Vagnoni built a new church which he officially opened on May 3, 1611, in the presence of a large crowd and with considerable ceremony, the Christians carrying the furnishings from the old chapel in solemn procession.

Hitherto the Jesuits had avoided conspicuous and public demonstrations of their faith, certain to irritate adherents of

Sung neo-Confucian orthodoxy and Buddhist monks and to arouse the fears of a sensitive officialdom always suspicious of large gatherings. Vagnoni, carried forward on a wave of optimism induced by the fervor and charity of Nanking Christians which seemed to him to recapture the spirit of the primitive church, thought the days when such caution was needed had passed. Events proved him mistaken. In 1615 Shen Ch'üeh (*q.v.*) arrived in Nanking to assume the post of vice minister of Rites. Encouraged by a group of *hsiu-ts'ai*, who demanded that the foreigners be expelled from the realm for threatening the state and public good, Shen memorialized the throne in June, 1616, urging that the missionaries and their converts be put to death. Hsü Kuang-ch'i, Yang T'ing-yün, Li Chih-tsao (all in ECCP), and others rallied to the defense of the missionaries and of Christianity. Shen Ch'ueh, however, had the support of other officials of his ministry. The *Ming-shih* mentions several of these men by name: Hsü Ju-k'o 徐如珂 (T. 季鳴, 1562–1626, cs 1595), Yen Wen-hui 晏文輝 (cs 1598), and Yü Mou-tzu 余懋孳 (T. 舜仲, cs 1604). The accusations described in the *Ming-shih* are vague: that they were deceiving the people by heretical teachings, that they had recruited no fewer than ten thousand followers, and, a charge which sounds oddly familiar to twentieth-century ears, that they spread *tso-tao* 左道 (leftist doctrines). The accusers referred too to the fact that the Christians met together both morning and night and a comparison was made to the Pai-lien chiao 白蓮教, the notorious White Lotus Society. The persistent efforts of Shen Ch'üeh finally brought results. An imperial edict of February 14, 1617, ordered Vagnoni, mentioned by name, and other missionaries out of the country.

Shen had not waited for the imperial order before taking punitive measures. Some months earlier he had imprisoned Vagnoni, together with his colleague Álvarō Semedo (*q.v.*) and a number of Chinese Christians. He now subjected them to further investigation, had them severely beaten, and sent them under guard to Canton with orders that they be returned to Europe. The prefect of Canton was of a different mind. He released them from prison a month after their arrival, provided them with board and lodging in a temple, and seven months later had them honorably conducted to Macao.

The emperor, Chu I-chün (*q.v.*), died in 1620. With the fall from favor of Shen Ch'üeh in 1622 and his death in 1624, the suppression of missionary activities ended, and the 1617 edict calling for the banishment of the missionaries became a dead issue. In 1624 the Jesuits were officially invited to reestablish themselves in Peking. The same year Vagnoni returned to interior China from Macao. He did not go to Nanking, but established a residence in Chiang-chou 絳州, Shansi. For the next sixteen years he labored indefatigably in this province. In 1634 Francisco Furtado (*q.v.*), after visiting all twelve Jesuit residences in the empire, observed in a letter to the superior general of the order in Rome: "I derived the greatest consolation from Father Vagnoni, in the province of Shansi, and Father Nicolo Longobardi (*q.v.*) in the imperial province of Peking. Both are well advanced in age, having passed their seventieth year, and both labor in this vineyard of the Lord as if they were but thirty years old."

When Vagnoni entered Shansi in 1624 there were no more than two dozen Christians in the province. When he died on April 9, 1640, he left some eight thousand in one hundred two Christian communities. Of these over two hundred were graduates in letters, and some were important officials. Two thousand Christians walked in his funeral procession. The head of a branch of the imperial family paid his respects. Han K'uang (*q.v.*), a one-time grand secretary in Peking, sent two members of his family from his home in P'u-chou 蒲州 to represent him. He also wrote a eulogy of Vagnoni which he caused to be read before the latter's coffin in the presence of the leading citizens of Chiang-chou, many of whom wrote similar eulogies.

There is a report by Longobardi in the Jesuit archives in Rome which suggests that in the first phase of his career in China Vagnoni sometimes made enemies as a consequence of a quick temper and a certain asperity of manner. Perhaps this contributed to the difficulties in Nanking. The record of his later years in China, however (the second phase), fully supports the judgment of Daniello Bartoli that, next to Ricci, there was no man in the mission so universally esteemed by Christian and non-Christian alike. Vagnoni was also, next to Ricci, the most accomplished sinologist among the early Jesuits. In the long debate among the Jesuits about the use of certain Chinese words to express Christian concepts, he was the most formidable spokesman for the majority opinion against the minority position defended among others by Longobardi.

A list of Vagnoni's many Chinese works is found in Louis Pfister's *Notices*. The best account of his experiences at the hands of Shen Ch'üeh is his own unpublished story to be found in the Jesuit archives in Rome. Another account was written twenty years later by his colleague, Álvarō Semedo. Shen's side of the story is told in the official documents he published at the conclusion of affair. They appear in a work by Hsü Ch'ang-chih (*see* Shen Ch'üeh), extracts from which are translated in Auguste Colombel's history.

Bibliography

1/326/19b; Daniello Bartoli, *Dell'istoria della Compagnia di Gésù. La Cina. Terza parte dell' Asia,* 4 vols. (Ancona ed., 1843); George H. Dunne, *Generation of Giants* (Notre Dame, 1962), 92, 121, 193, 215, 284, 303; Fortunato Margiotti, *Il cattolicismo nello Shansi dalle origini al 1738* (Rome, 1958); Pfister (1932), 85; Pasquale M. d'Elia, *Fonti Ricciane,* II (Rome, 1949), 277; Álvarō Semedo, *Histoire universelle de la Chine* (Lyons, 1667); Hsü Ch'ang-chih, *P'o-hsieh chi* 破邪集, *chüan* 1 and 2; Auguste Colombel, *Histoire de la Mission du Kiangnan,* I (Shanghai, 1895-1905), 204; *Roman Archives of the Society of Jesus* (*ARSI,* Jap. Sin).

George H. Dunne

VALIGNANO, Alessandro (Alexandre Valignani, 范禮安, T. 立山), February, 1539–January 6 or 20, 1606, superior of all Jesuit missionary enterprises in India and the Far East, was a scion of a noble family of Chieti in Abruzzi, Italy. He became a doctor of civil law before entering the Society of Jesus in 1566 at the age of twenty-seven. In 1573 the head of the order appointed him superior, with the title of visitor, of the Jesuit missions in the East Indies, a geographical expression which included China and Japan as well as India. He sailed from Lisbon on March 21, 1574, together with forty other Jesuits assigned to the foreign missions. Except for a four-year interval, 1583–87, when he held the office of provincial of the Jesuit province of India, he remained in over-all command as visitor of India until 1596 and of China and Japan until his death.

Valignano was regarded by Matteo Ricci (*q.v.*), himself the great pioneer, as the founder of the China mission because, although he never set foot upon the mainland beyond Macao, as superior he initiated the policy of cultural accommodation which for the first time opened Ming China to Christian evangelization. Prior to his arrival in Macao in October, 1577, repeated efforts by missionaries of several orders, during the twenty-five years which had followed the death of Francesco Xavier on the island of Sancian 上川, had accomplished nothing. Valignano was quick to analyze the cause of these failures and to give new direction to the Christian enterprise. "The only possible way to penetration," he wrote to the superior general of his order in Rome, "will be utterly different from that which has been adopted up to now in all the other missions in these countries."

The policy to which he referred, and which he repudiated, showed scant respect for and little interest in the indigenous culture, and tended to identify Christianity with European cultural forms. In Macao, as in Goa, converts were obliged to take Portuguese names, wear Portuguese clothes, learn the Portuguese language, and adopt Portuguese customs. Valignano ordered an end to this. He directed those who would be missionaries in China to "sinicize" themselves, instead of "Portugalizing" their converts. Because the old Jesuit hands at Macao, deeply imbued with Europeanism, were not psychologically predisposed to carry out his orders, he sent to India for a new man to implement his policy. The new man was Michele Ruggieri (q.v.), who settled down in Macao under Valignano's orders to learn "to read, write, and speak Chinese," something his predecessors had not thought relevant to their missionary objectives.

Valignano brooked no interference with the policy which he had established. When, upon returning from a visit to Japan in 1582, he found that the local Jesuit superior in Macao had been interfering with Ruggieri's Chinese studies by assigning him to ministerial tasks, he promptly removed him from office and transferred him to Japan. That same year he ordered Matteo Ricci to come on from India, where he had already given evidence of being in full accord with Valignano's own missiological views. Because he was convinced that an understanding of Chinese civilization was an essential preliminary to an effective apostolate, he directed Ricci to prepare, in conjunction with his Chinese studies, a summary description of the people, customs, institutions, and government of China.

These initiatives led to the successful establishment, on September 10, 1583, of the first Christian mission in China since the demise of the thirteenth-century Franciscan enterprise. Until his death in Macao, Valignano gave full support to the methods of cultural adaptation developed by Ricci which distinguished the Jesuit endeavor in China and accounted for its success.

More than two hundred sixty of his letters, mostly unedited, are in the Jesuit archives in Rome. His other writings, published and unpublished, are listed by P. M. d'Elia in *Fonti Ricciane*.

Bibliography

Daniello Bartoli, *Dell'istoria della Compagnia di Gésù. La China. Terza parte dell' Asia*, 4 vols. (Ancona ed., 1843); George H. Dunne, *Generation of Giants* (Notre Dame, 1962), 17, 24, 30, 48, 102; Pfister (1932), 13; P. M. d'Elia, *Fonti Ricciane* (Rome, 1942-49), I: lxxxvi, 143, 146, II: 552, 637; Franz Josef Schütte, *Valignanos Missionsgründsätse für Japan*, 3 vols. (Rome, 1951-58); J. M. Braga, "The Panegyric of Alexander Valignano, S. J.," (*Monumenta Nipponica* V: 2 (1942), 237; *Roman Archives of the Society of Jesus* (*ARSI, Jap-Sin*).

George H. Dunne

WAN Kuei-fei 萬貴妃 (Pth. 恭肅), 1430-February 3, 1487, favorite consort of Chu Chien-shen (q.v.), was a native of Chuch'eng 諸城, Shantung. Her father, Wan Kuei 貴 (d. 1475), was a yamen clerk who for some offense was shifted to Pachou 霸州, south of Peking. When his daughter was a child of only three, she was chosen to enter the palace to serve the Empress Sun (*see* Chu Chienshen). As she grew up she became the empress' favorite and was assigned to the retinue of her grandson, Chu Chien-shen, born in 1447, hence seventeen years the girl's junior. When he ascended the throne in 1464, she had already been his favorite consort for some time. This aroused the jealousy of the newly installed Empress Wu 吳 (a native of Peking, d. 1506), who had the Lady Wan flogged. In this encounter Empress Wu was bested, losing her title after only thirty-two days (August 23-September 23), and being replaced by Empress Wang 王 (a native of Nanking, daughter of Wang Chen 鎮, Pth. 孝貞, d. 1518); the latter, by resigning herself to the situation, restored peace and maintained her position.

After this victory Lady Wan assumed unchallenged power inside the palace for over a decade. In 1466 she gave birth to a son and was awarded the title of Huang 皇 Kuei-fei, a rank immediately below that of the empress. Even after the boy died a year later she continued to hold sway as *de facto* empress. It is said that she sometimes wore military garb, indicating a masculinity which probably explains her dominance over the emperor and the eunuchs. In any case, during the first twelve years of his reign, the emperor might be found most of the time in her chambers, the Chao-te-kung 昭德宮. (It is said that she later moved to the An-hsi-kung 安喜宮.) In 1468 the emperor's exclusive attention to her became the subject of several memorials by courtiers who admonished and exhorted him to pay attention to other women in order to provide his ancestors with a male heir. It is recorded that for ten years Lady Wan took measures to make sure that any pregnancy in the palace would result in a miscarriage. In two cases, however, she was unsuccessful. One was that of the birth of a boy in 1469 who was proclaimed heir apparent late in 1471, but soon died. The second case occurred on July 30, 1470, when an attendant woman presumably named Chi 紀 (a native of Kwangsi, brought in as a captive in 1467, Pth. Empress Hsiao-mu 孝穆, d. 1475), gave birth to a male child who was at once secreted by some eunuchs in the quarters occupied by the deposed Empress Wu. Five years later (June, 1475), when the emperor felt depressed by the want of an heir, a eunuch broke the news to him. He visited the boy at once and brought him to Lady Wan's palace where he was living. Lady Chi was installed in another palace, where she died a month later under suspicious circumstances. Towards the end of 1475, the boy, Chu Yu-t'ang (*q.v.*), was proclaimed heir apparent. Meanwhile Lady Wan's father died. These events seem to have lessened her influence over the emperor, for beginning with 1476 the record of births of children of the emperor and his consorts shows a total of eleven boys and six girls in eleven years.

About this time Lady Wan's attention apparently turned to business activities, such as trading in pearls and other treasures, transactions in the salt monopoly, sale of patents for the Taoist and Buddhist priesthood, and the improper award of minor official ranks directly by imperial order. The eunuch office (Yü-yung-chien), headed by Liang Fang (*q.v.*), was under her control and served as a kind of holding company, supervising a store in Peking and agents in the provinces. When apprised of the illicit and harmful doings of Liang Fang, Wang Chih 汪直 (*q.v.*) who controlled the secret service of Peking from 1476 to 1480, and other eunuchs, the emperor generally ignored the accusations and once in a while punished the accusers, but seldom the eunuchs. Possibly the emperor himself connived with Lady Wan in raising funds to meet the expenses of the palace, for the government was then in financial straits. As early as 1466 there had been a reduction in the salaries of the officials in Peking. Conceivably a large part of the money exacted by the eunuchs throughout the empire helped to meet the emperor's needs. As a matter of course Lady Wan and her own family profited by the transactions. Her brothers became hereditary officers in the Embroidered-uniform Guard; one of them, Wan T'ung 通 (d. April, 1482), who held the rank of an assistant regional military commissioner, is said to have accepted bribes from officials seeking favor, and made his wife his go-between on her visits to the palace. At his death he was buried west of Peking. When his tomb was excavated in 1969 it yielded, among other finds, a gold cup and saucer set, a gold wine pot with engraved dragon design, and two gold buckles, all inlaid with precious stones. They are described as matching in elegance the articles found in the tomb of Chu I-chün (*q.v.*).

The death of Lady Wan in 1487 preceded that of the emperor by only eight months. Soon after Chu Yu-t'ang succeeded to the throne in September, two censors brought various charges against Liang Fang and other eunuchs serving Lady Wan, and also against officials who obtained promotion or appointment through them. Certain ones were swiftly convicted, some being sent into exile, and others either cashiered or reduced in rank. Her brothers were degraded. Later they were ordered to return to the state the land and gifts acquired during her heyday. The emperor, however, would not approve of any investigation into the death of his own mother, the lady Chi, thus sparing the Wan family further persecution.

In the Musée Cernuschi, Paris, there is a bronze incense burner with designs inlaid with silver and with four Sanskrit characters in gold. On the base inlaid with silver is the inscription "Ta Ming Ch'eng-hua nien Wan-chia tsao" 大明成化年萬家造. Only Wan Kuei-fei's family, it seems, could have been sufficiently affluent and influential to aspire to such a treasure.

Bibliography

1/113/21b, 300/15b; 5/109/2a; MSL(1964), Hsientsung, 2650, 3869, 4830, Hsiao-tsung, 0026; Mao Ch'i-ling (ECCP), *Sheng-ch'ao t'ung-shih shih-i chi* in *Hsi-ho ho-chi*, 3/3b; *K'ao-ku* 考古 (Peking, 1972), 40; *The Arts of the Ming Dynasty* (an exhibition, London 1958), no. 285, 76, pl. 77.

Chaoying Fang

WAN Piao 萬表 (T. 民望, H. 鹿園, 九沙山人), September 6, 1498-March 4, 1556, army officer, philosopher, and poet, a native of Yin-hsien 鄞縣, Ningpo, Chekiang, was born into a family with a military tradition which extended throughout the Ming dynasty. As early as 1354, his ancestor, Wan Pin 斌 (original name 萬國珍), became a follower of Chu Yüan-chang, who, gave him the name by which he is generally known. When Chu ascended the throne as emperor (1368), Wan Pin was made a chiliarch commander of Ch'uchou 滁州 (Anhwei). Later he died in action fighting the Mongols in the north. Wan Pin's son, Wan Chung 鍾, inherited his father's rank in 1376. To strengthen the defense against the Japanese, the emperor promoted Wan Chung to be assistant commander of the guard in Ningpo in 1384. For his achievements he was given a residence in Ningpo and his post made hereditary. His two sons were Wan Wu 武, who died in service in Cochinchina, and Wan Wen 文, who died in a typhoon in 1418 while leading a fleet against the Japanese. Three generations later, the hereditary military post came to Wan Wen's great-grandson Wan Lingch'un 齡椿 (T. 有年, H. 愼庵, d. 1514), the father of Wan Piao. It seems that Wan Ling-ch'un was the first of the family to show definite interest in scholarly pursuits and who was also a Buddhist adherent.

Wan Piao succeeded his father as assistant commander of the guard in Ningpo at the early age of seventeen *sui*. Perhaps because he had an education superior to that of most of his forebears, and possessed more ambition, he was not satisfied with the hereditary post, and tried his luck in the military examinations. In 1519 he passed the military provincial examinations (wu 武 *chü-jen*), and in 1520 he was successful again, becoming a wu *chin-shih*. Later in the same year, he received appointment as a company commander of the Chekiang defense area. In the following year he was promoted to acting regional assistant commander, supervising the transportation of tribute grain, an official duty that occupied him altogether for almost ten years (1521-25, 1533-36, 1554-55). He performed his duties well, and made suggestions for improvements in the administration as well as in river conservancy; some of his writings on these subjects have been consulted by later officials and scholars. By 1546 he rose to the rank of commissioner and commander of grain transportation. Four times he was given a post at Nanking, in 1529 as commandant of the training camp, in 1536 as an officer in the Embroidered-uniform Guard, in 1550 and again in 1554 as assistant commander in the central military commission.

From the early years of the Ming dynasty China's coastal region from Manchuria to Kwangtung was periodically troubled by marauders, commonly known as *wo-k'ou*. By the Chia-ching period disturbances along the coast from Shantung to Fukien reached a serious and alarming pass. As a patriotic military man and a native of an area most seriously affected, Wan was greatly concerned. He contributed his family wealth to recruit a private force including some Shao-lin 少林 Buddhist monks, who were recognized for their fighting skill. In a running battle near Soochow (1552), Wan was shot by an arrow. Later he wrote his sons that, in the light of the family's tradition of giving their lives for the country, he would regard his scar as an honor. He also left a treatise, the *Hai-k'ou-i* 海寇議, on the trouble caused by the marauders in the Ningpo area, its history, cause, and how to deal with it. It is said that later Hu Tsung-hsien (*q.v.*), who successfully stopped the piratical activities in Chekiang, did adopt some of Wan's suggestions. When Yüan Chi'ung (*q.v.*) compiled his collection of short works by Ming authors, the *Chin-sheng yü-chen chi*, he included the *Hai-k'ou-i* among his selections, but unfortunately wrote Wan Piao's name as Fan 范 Piao, an error later pointed out by editors of the *Ssu-k'u* catalogue. In the

19th century, when Chang Hai-p'eng (ECCP) compiled the *Chieh-yüeh shan-fang hui-ch'ao*, he entered the *Hai-k'ou-i* in the eleventh series, and corrected the error.

Wan Piao's career was frequently interrupted by illness and periods of convalescence, as in 1527, 1531, 1532, 1542, 1543, and 1550. Finally he requested retirement, his wish being granted in 1555, but he never regained his health and died the following year. Perhaps it was because of his own physical condition that he paid special attention to medicine. He edited a work on prescriptions, the *Wan-shih chia-ch'ao chi-shih liang-fang* 萬氏家鈔濟世良方, later enlarged by his grandson. His health might also have been responsible for his interest in both Taoism and Buddhism and his friendship with followers of both religions.

Wan Piao had two sons, Wan Ch'ien-fu 謙甫, born to a concubine, and Wan Ta-fu 達甫, born to his wife née Fang 方. As a consequence it was the younger son who inherited the assistant commandership of the Ningpo guard. The hereditary post next went to Wan Ta-fu's son, Wan Pang-fu 邦孚 (T. 汝永, H. 瑞巖, 1544-1628), who like his grandfather took charge of the transportation of tribute grain. He also participated in the defense of Korea in 1598. By 1608 he rose to be assistant commissioner and area commander of Fukien and retired from active duty in 1609.

In the uninterrupted history of the Wan family we notice a tendency to shift from military to civil careers. Beginning with Wan Piao's father, members of the clan began to show increasing interest in scholarly pursuits, mixing their military activities with literary achievements. Wan Pang-ta, although he performed his duties as a military officer, had already taken part in the civil examinations, for he was a *hsiu-ts'ai* when he came to his inherited post. His son, Wan T'ai (ECCP), went a step further becoming a *chü-jen* in 1636 and never succeeding to the hereditary post. In the following generation we find eight brothers, all scholars and accomplished men of letters (*see* Wan Ssu-t'ung and brothers in ECCP). Later the Wan family produced more scholars and civil officials, but no more military men. In this case, however, we must also take into consideration the change of dynasties, which might have both facilitated and necessitated the break.

Of Wan Piao's writings the principal work he left is the *Wan-lu-t'ing kao* 玩鹿亭稿, 8 *ch.*, first printed in the late 1550's, reprinted about 1600, and recently again in 1940 in the seventh series of the *Ssu-ming ts'ung-shu* 四明叢書. (This series contains another work by Wan, entitled *Shao-ai chi* 灼艾集, 8 *ch.*, which is not presently available.) Of the 8 *chüan*, *ch.* 1-2 include poetry, *ch.* 3 essays, *ch.* 4 correspondence, *ch.* 5 the *Chiu-sha ts'ao-t'ang tsa-yen* 九沙草堂雜言, miscellaneous prose, of which one item is the *Hai-k'ou-i* already mentioned above, *ch.* 6 memorials, *ch.* 7 official papers, and *ch.* 8 the *Tao-ching chui-yen* 道經贅言, annotations of the *Lao-tzu*. The last is a little-known and rarely mentioned work on the *Tao-te-ching*. It covers only the first 37 chapters of the 81 chapter edition of the Classic, however. Whether Wan Piao left it as an unfinished work, or the last part was lost, is not clear. Appended to the *Wan-lu-t'ing kao* are also a number of letters and poems addressed to Wan Piao by his friends, such as Lo Hung-hsien, T'ang Shun-chih, Wang Chi 畿, Wu Ch'eng-en (*qq. v.*), *et al.*, and two biographies, one by Wang Chi, and one by Chiao Hung (EC CP).

Wan Piao also compiled a collection of Ming memorials entitled *Huang Ming ching-chi wen-lu* 皇明經濟文錄 in 41 *chüan*, printed in 1554 in Hangchow. According to his own preface, four earlier collections of the same nature formed the nucleus of this work which he further supplemented. This book was prohibited in the 18th century, and is now quite rare. *Chüan* 34-36 dealing with the northern borders were reprinted in Peking in 1934.

As a philosopher, Wan is placed among the Chekiang followers of Wang Shou-jen (*q.v.*) in the *Ming-ju hsüeh-an* by Huang Tsung-hsi (ECCP). While he was closely associated with several of Wang's important disciples, such as Wang Chi, Ch'ien Te-hung (*q.v.*), and Lo Hung-hsien, he never knew Wang personally. Furthermore, according to the long and intimate biography written by Wang Chi, Wan had reservations about the doctrine of liang-chih 良知 (innate knowledge). He advocated the investigation of things, emphasizing the investigation of matters of the mind (格心之物). Wan also had little enthusiasm for large lecture gatherings and seldom attended any. For both Taoism and Buddhism he had great respect, but he detested most of the religious practices of the time, refrained from discussions of fate (性命), and did not believe in immortality.

It is said that he had a very distinguished appearance, and from his youth on was an admirer of Chu-ko Liang (181-234), the able minister of Shu-Han in the time of the Three Kingdoms. In the latter part of his life, while hiking one early morning in the mountains, wearing a Buddhist monk's robe, as he saw the rising sun, he suddenly received "enlightenment" (悟). It is also said that, because of his fondness for a special kind of plum (楊梅), he planted over a hundred plum trees on his own premises and, as far as he could manage, always tried to feast on the fruit when it became ripe.

Bibliography

5/107/79a; 61/141/14a; 64/己18/5b; 83/15/1a; SK (1930), 100/4a, 105/6a, 176/16a; Wang Chi, *Wan-lu-ting kao* (microfilm), appendix; *Huang Ming wen-hai* (microfilm), 17/4/6; Huang Tsung-hsi, *Huang Li-chou wen-chi* 黃梨洲文集 (Peking, 1959), 94: Sun Tien-ch'i (1957), 127; W. Franke, *Sources*, 5. 1. 3, 7. 8. 3.

Lienche Tu Fang

WANG Ao 王翱 (T. 九皋), March 4, 1384-December 2, 1467, minister of Personnel from 1453 to 1467, was a native of Yen-shan 鹽山 in the prefecture of Ho-chien 河間, Pei-Chihli. Wang's father, Wang Te-lin 得林 (T. 三老, 1341-1419), a peasant from Luan-chou 灤州, Pei-Chihli, took his family to Yen-shan in the 1360s to seek refuge from the rebel uprisings. He raised five children, among whom Wang Ao was the fourth.

A precocious and hard-working student, Wang graduated as *chü-jen* in 1411 and as *chin-shih* in 1415, achieving a high rank in both examinations. This was the first *chin-shih* examination held in Peking and Emperor Chu Ti (*q.v.*), pleased to find Wang Ao (a native of that area) placing fourth, named him a Hanlin bachelor. In 1424, after a prolonged apprenticeship in the Hanlin Academy, Wang became an assistant minister in the Grand Court of Revision, and was known as an impartial judge. A year later, owing to a slight mistake, he was demoted to a post in the messenger office. In April, 1426, through the recommendation of Grand Secretary Yang Shih-ch'i (*q.v.*), Wang received a promotion to censor. In 1431 he served a term as inspecting censor in Szechwan, where in June he submitted a five-point memorandum aimed chiefly at ending the chaos in the Sung-p'an 松藩 guard (in northwestern Szechwan) resulting from the insurrection of the Ch'iang 羌 (Tibetan?) tribesmen. Wang pointed out that the uprising was in part caused by the absence of a responsible official; hence, he urged the court to order the regional commander, Ch'en Huai 陳懷 (appointed earl of P'ing-hsiang 平鄉 in 1444, d. 1449, Pth. 忠毅), then stationed in Chengtu some eight hundred *li* away, to transfer to the rebellious area. He also proposed an alternate procedure to insure the safe delivery of rations to the guard garrisons. On long-term reforms he suggested the establishment of schools, and enforcement of the law that local people qualifying as yamen clerks, on completion of

a term in the province, were to be sent to Peking for assignment; further, they were not to be permitted to remain at home where they might use their knowledge of legal procedure to disturb the *status quo*. He also made the suggestion that convicts held for minor offenses should be allowed to redeem themselves by delivering grain to the silver mines at the Hui-ch'uan 會川 guard (about 90 miles north of Kunming and 250 miles south of Chengtu), thus saving the provincial government the cost of transportation. All of his suggestions were adopted.

In February, 1435, Wang was promoted to be an assistant censor-in-chief, and sent with a general to Kiangsi—both to serve as joint grand defenders. During his term in office he was once dispatched to Hukuang (May, 1435) as governor (acting?). In September, 1437, he returned to the Censorate in Peking. In December of the following year he became involved in the case of Chu Kuei-ch'ia 朱貴焓 (the second prince of Liao 遼, d. 1449), who had been indicted for torturing his stepmother, for licentious conduct, and for other violations of the law. Certain officials, accused of concealing the crimes of the prince, were brought before the Censorate for trial. A verdict was pronounced, but a supervising secretary charged that it was biased in favor of the culprit; consequently several senior officials, including Wang, were clapped into prison by the Embroidered-uniform Guard. Before long, however, the emperor pardoned Wang and his colleagues, and punished Chu Kuei-ch'ia simply by demoting him to be a commoner (April, 1439). Following this incident, Wang was sent back to Kiangsi to help in the pacification of the bandits from Chekiang who had crossed the border; he returned to the capital in September.

Towards the end of this year, the Ch'iang tribesmen again rebelled. In January, 1440, the court appointed Li An 李安 as the regional commander to lead an expeditionary army of twenty thousand men, with Wang (as associate in military affairs) in charge of supplies. While in Sung-p'an, Wang discovered that the incident was triggered by the angry tribesmen over the treachery of the regional commissioner who, having lured their chieftain Shang-pa 商巴 into a trap, robbed him of his property and made a false report against him. Wang then ordered the punishment of the culprit, released the chieftain from prison, and invited the rebels to surrender. Executing a carrot-and-stick policy, he persuaded the dissident tribesmen once more to submit to the government. This accomplished, Wang returned to the capital, and in February, 1441, received promotion to be the grand defender of Shensi. During his administration, one of his memorable acts was to request the rescinding of the debts of those who had received loans from the government in earlier years and could not afford repayment. In December, 1442, he was named the superintendent of military affairs of Liaotung.

From the beginning of the dynasty, Liaotung was an important outpost of defense against the intrusion of Mongol tribes (such as the Oirat and the eastern branch, collectively known as the Uriyang-qad after the name of their settlement). By this time, owing to the incompetence of the military officers, Liaotung fell prey to constant pillaging by Mongols from the north and by Jurchen from the east. In cooperation with the regional commander, Ts'ao I 曹義 (T. 敬方, 1390–1460, enf. as earl of Feng-jun 豐潤 in 1457, Pth. 莊武), Wang overhauled the military establishment, invoked emergency regulations to maintain order, made frequent visits to the border, and bolstered the reserves by allowing convicts to redeem themselves with grain. Early in 1443, following an inspection tour to the Kuang-ning 廣寧 guard, Wang became aware of the value of constructing a more permanent defense wall against the invaders. Already, in April, 1437, the assistant commander of the Ting-liao 定遼 frontier guard, Pi Kung 畢恭 (T. 以謙), had memorialized

the court recommending such an undertaking, and even before that had erected a barrier of willow palisades. Under Wang's supervision, a defense wall was constructed as an extension of the Great Wall, with a length of seven hundred li, running between the mountains and the Liao River from Shan-hai-kuan 山海關 to K'ai-yüan 開原 district in the northeast. Along this section of the wall, a station (pao 堡) was built every five li, and a village (t'un 屯) every ten li, with numerous barricades, ditches, beacon-fire towers, and other facilities. When completed, this, though far from impregnable, at least provided a partial deterrent to the tribesmen. In December of the same year Wang received promotion to deputy censor-in-chief. Except for occasional trips to the capital for consultation, he remained in Liaotung until his recall in 1452.

In May, 1447, Wang became censor-in-chief. Two years later, after the Oirat overwhelmed the Ming army at T'u-mu (see Chu Ch'i-yü), the eastern wing of the Mongols, under its chieftain Toɤto Buqa (see Esen), invaded the border posts of Liaotung, and inflicted considerable damage. In another surprise attack on the Kuang-ning guard (October, 1449), according to the shih-lu, they destroyed eighty walled post-stations and villages, captured more than thirteen thousand men and women in the military colonies, seized over six thousand horses, twenty thousand cattle and sheep, and two thousand helmets and coats of mail. Wang Ao and Ts'ao I, who were held responsible for the debacle, were punished by a deduction of half a year's stipend. Almost at the same, Liaotung faced a threat from the Jurchen of the Chien-chou 建州 guard, whose shrewd, ambitious chieftain, Li Man-chu (q.v.), exploiting the chaotic situation and in collusion with the Mongols, seized livestock and supplies from the Chinese in the border towns. Having been alerted to the impending uprising, Wang proposed to the court in July, 1450, that measures be taken at the outer perimeter of Chien-chou to insure the security of Liaotung. Approving Wang's proposal in March, 1451, the court recommended cautious actions against the Jurchen consonant with the situation; before Wang initiated any maneuver, however, Li had reportedly fled to the upper valley of the Fu-er 富爾, an affluent of the Yalu River. In March, 1452, probably displeased with his performance, the court decided that Wang had stayed at his post too long and recalled him to the capital, replacing him by the deputy censor-in-chief K'ou Shen 寇深 (T. 文淵, 1393–1461, Pth. 莊愍).

Following this Wang resumed his duties as censor-in-chief. In May, 1452, he was among the score of officials who, under pressure, endorsed the proposal to replace the heir apparent, Chu Chien-shen (q.v.), by Chu Chien-chi, son of the then emperor (see Chu Ch'i-yü). For this he received the title of junior guardian of the heir apparent. In August, on the recommendation of the minister of War, Yü Ch'ien (q.v.), he was appointed supreme commander and governor of Kwangsi and Kwangtung, the first of such important posts ever established. His mission was to coordinate the military commands of the two provinces, a task which he executed with merit.

In April, 1453, Wang was recalled to the capital; three months later he was appointed co-minister in the ministry of Personnel with Wang Chih 王直 (q.v.), and assumed full responsibility when the latter retired in February, 1457. After the *coup d'état* (see Chu Ch'i-chen), Wang submitted a request for retirement. He gave as an excuse his age (he was then seventy-three), but he acted probably out of apprehension over his part in the displacement of the heir apparent. It is said that Shih Heng (q.v.), the notorious general who gained power owing to his part in the restoration movement, wanted Li Hsien (q.v.), then Hanlin chancellor in the Grand Secretariat, to receive the appointment as Personnel minister in place of Wang Ao. Li, a northerner who had lately gained imperial favor, preferred to stay in the Secretariat to build up his influence, with Wang's cooperation; so he persuaded Wang to withdraw his request. Jointly they carried out the policy of giving preference to the northerners in government. This seems to have been in accord with the emperor's wish.

Over these years Wang gained a reputation as a scrupulous and competent minister, and was respected for his integrity and judgment. During his administration scores of highly qualified individuals, including many southerners, were appointed to key government posts. He earned the confidence of the emperor who, because of Wang's seniority, used to address him as "Wang the elder" (老王) instead of of calling him by his full name. As a gesture of appreciation, the emperor appointed his son, Wang Chu 竚, a vice battalion commander of the Embroidered-uniform Guard, who retired as assistant commander in 1498, and died September 12, 1501. Wang Ao, however, was not without enemies. As a leader of the northern group, Wang was often criticized by some southerners. Probably because of this, Wang again requested permission to retire (September, 1464), but the young emperor, Chu Chien-shen, asked him to remain in office. In April of the next year, the emperor honored him with the title of grand guardian of the heir apparent. In June, when the censor-in-chief Li Ping (see Han Wen) charged Wang and several of his colleagues with concealing the case of a disqualified official seeking to gain new appointment through bribery, Wang once more sought to retire, but the emperor ignored his request and kept him in office.

In September, 1467, Wang fell seriously ill; this time the emperor allowed him to withdraw and sent a physician to visit him. He died three months later at the advanced age of eighty-three, less than a year after Li Hsien. He was subsequently awarded the canonized name

Chung-su 忠肅, and his son's rank in the Embroidered-uniform Guard made hereditary in March, 1468.

Wang was not a man of letters and so left no literary works. A collection of his memorials, entitled *Wang Chung-su kung tsou-su* 公奏疏, is presumably lost, but two fragments survive in the *Ming ching-shih wen-pien* by Ch'en Tzu-lung (ECCP).

Bibliography

1/177/1a; 5/24/3a; 9/后 9/1a; MSL (1963), T'ai-tsung, 1839, Hsüan-tsung, 401, 1830, 1841, Ying-tsung (1964), ch. 1-230, Hsien-tsung (1964), *ch.* 8-51, Hsiao-tsung (1964), 3267; KC (1958), 2241; *Yen-shan hsin-chih* 新志 (1916), 26/14a; *Kwangsi t'ung-chih* (1800), 190/24a; Hu Yen, *Hu Chi-chiu wen-chi* (NCL microfilm), no. 993, 23/5b; Wang Ao 王鏊, *Chen-tse chi-wen* in *Chi-lu hui-pien*, 124/15a; Li Hsien, *T'ien-shun jih-lu*, in *Chi-lu hui pien*, 22/2b, 31b; Yao K'uei, *Yao Wen-min kung i-kao*, 9/1a; Yeh Sheng, *Shui-tung jih-chi*, 5/1a; Li Fu 李輔 (cs 1559), *Ch'üan Liao chih* 全遼志 (1931-34 ed.), 4/6b, 5/9b; *Chosŏn wangjo sillok* 朝鮮王朝實錄 (1963), Sejong 世宗, 125/8a, 11a, Munjong 文宗, 5/51a; Ch'en Lun-hsü 陳綸緒 (Albert Chan), "Chi Ming T'ien-shun Ch'eng-hua chien ta ch'en nan-pei chih cheng" 記明天順成化間大臣南北之爭, *Sinological Researches* 中國學誌, no. 1 (Tokyo, 1964), 96; Sonoda Kazuki 園田一龜, *Mindai Kenshū jochoku-shi kenkyū* 明代建州女直史研究 (Tokyo, 1948), 184, 200; W. Franke, "Addenda and Corrigenda" to Pokotilov's *History of the Eastern Mongols during the Ming Dynasty from* 1368 *to* 1634, *Studia Serica*, Ser. A, 3 (Chengtu, 1949), 40.

Hok-lam Chan

WANG Ao 王鏊 (T. 濟之, H. 守溪, 拙叟), September 12, 1450-April 14, 1524, man of letters and grand secretary (1506-9), was born into a peasant family which had settled south of Soochow in a village that came to be known as Wang-hsiang 巷. It was situated on the east shore of Lake T'ai on the peninsula Tung Tung-t'ing shan 東洞庭山. In 1439 it was such an unsophisticated rural area that, when the officials came to solicit students to study in the district school, all the young men went into hiding. The only one who volunteered happened to be Wang Ao's father, Wang Ch'ao-yung 朝用 (H. 靜樂, 1419-1503), then twenty years old and commonly regarded as not overly bright. He worked hard, though, and after repeatedly failing in the provincial examination attended the National Universty as a student. Later he served a term as magistrate of Kuang-hua 光化 in northwestern Hukuang (*ca.* 1473-76) where in 1476 he accompanied Yüan Chieh (*see* Hsiang Chung) to survey the mountainous region for the registration of the settlers. He then retired.

A precocious and serious child, Wang Ao became a student in the district school, and in 1467, at the age of seventeen, went to Peking to be with his father, then studying in the National University. Duly impressed by the youth's promise, Yeh Sheng (*q. v.*), the minister of Rites, recommended him to study under Ch'en Yin 陳音 (T. 師召, H. 愧齋, 1436-94, cs 1464), an erudite Hanlin scholar. In 1474 he passed first on the *chü-jen* list, and a year later achieved third place in the *chin-shih* examination. He was immediately appointed to the Hanlin Academy as compiler. In April, 1488, when the new emperor, Chu Yu-t'ang (*q. v.*), appointed the ching-yen 經筵 commission in charge of his regular classical studies, Wang Ao was at first named one of the eight leaf-turners (chan-shu kuan 展書官), but later he was raised to be an expositor 侍講, then senior expositor. On numerous occasions he exhorted the emperor to be frugal, to extricate himself from the influence of eunuchs (alluding to Li Kuang [*q. v.*] in particular), and to attend to state affairs. His candor and earnestness made a marked impression on the emperor.

In February, 1488, Wang took part in the compilation of the veritable records of Emperor Chu Chien-shen (*q. v.*), the *Hsien-tsung shih-lu*, completed in 1491. Thereafter he advanced steadily in the Hanlin Academy and participated in the compilation of the *Ta Ming hui-tien* (April, 1497; never published, *see* Shen Shih-hsing). In August, 1500, he became an assistant minister of Personnel and developed a reputation as a thoughtful and outspoken critic of current affairs.

Early in 1500 the Mongol tribesmen, under the leadership of their chieftains, Hsiao-wang-tzu (*see* Batu Möngke) and Qošai 火師, having recovered from their earlier defeats by the Chinese on the northern frontier (*see* Wang Yüeh), renewed their depredations in Tatung and neighboring regions. The Chinese commanders, first Ch'en Jui (*see* Liu Ta-hsia), and then Chu Hui (*see* Batu Möngke), both failed to halt the enemy. In February, 1501, the emperor summoned a court conference to deliberate on strategy; Wang participated, and followed up with an eight-point memorandum in which he pointed out the diffusion of authority and frequent quarrels among the eunuch in charge, the censor-in-chief, and the military commander; he also proposed the appointment of a supreme general to coordinate the command, recommending an experienced official, Ch'in Hung (*see* Wang Chih 汪直). Ch'in was duly given the post in October, 1501, following a Mongol setback of Chu Hui and his deputies in the Ordos region in August. The continual reliance on inept commanders, despite their repeated failures, however, further weakened the Chinese position on the northern frontier. In April, 1503, Wang left office to observe the mourning period for his father who had died some months earlier, and he did not return to public life until the ensuing reign.

In December, 1505, through the recommendation of his disciple, Liu Jui 劉瑞 (T. 德符, H. 五清, cs 1496, Pth. 文肅), a corrector in the Hanlin Academy, Wang was reinstalled as vice minister of Rites under the new emperor, Chu Hou-chao (*q. v.*). In the following month he served as associate director-in-chief of the compilation of the veritable records of Chu Yu-t'ang, the *Hsiao-tsung shih-lu*,

and received promotion to senior assistant minister in May, 1506. During this time the young emperor fell under the influence of a group of junior eunuchs led by Liu Chin (*q. v.*). In October, after Grand Secretaries Liu Chien and Hsieh Ch'ien (*qq. v.*) lost out in their contest for power against the eunuchs and were forced to retire, Liu Chin gained the emperor's full confidence and became head of the directorate of ceremonial. To bolster his influence, Liu maneuvered to appoint his protégé, Chiao Fang (*q. v.*), then minister of Personnel, to fill the vacancy in the Grand Secretariat, but court opinion strongly favored Wang Ao. In November, as a gesture of compromise, the emperor appointed both Chiao and Wang to the Secretariat. With the eunuchs in control, Wang Ao was rather reluctant to assume the charge, and submitted three separate memorials declining the appointment, but the emperor ignored them. In September, 1507, when the emperor honored him with the title of junior tutor, grand tutor to the heir apparent, and concurrently grand secretary of the Wu-ying-tien, he again begged to resign, but received a similar rebuff. In March of the following year he was put in charge of the supervisorate of imperial instruction. He and his senior, Li Tung-yang (*q. v.*), were now the only officials in a position to restrain the excessive misdeeds of the eunuchs and protect their fellow colleagues from becoming their victims. Aware of his precarious situation, Wang pleaded failing health and again submitted three successive memorials begging for retirement; his request finally gained approval in May, 1509. The emperor granted him a monthly stipend of five *shih* of rice, and eight attendants. Thereupon Wang went to his native village and devoted himself to study and writing.

After the fall of Liu Chin in 1510, many officials, recalling Wang's record, wished him to return to public life, but Wang declined. Early in 1522, probably as a prelude to summoning him to serve, the new emperor, Chu Hou-ts'ung (*q. v.*), sent a special messenger to inquire after his health. In return, Wang submitted in December a letter expressing gratitude, together with two chapters of lectures, one entitled "Chiang-hsüeh" 講學 (the importance of learning) and the other "Ch'in-cheng" 親政 (attention to state affairs), at the same time expressing his wish to stay out of office. In his first lecture, Wang urged the emperor to reinstitute the advisory council 弘文館 (College of literature), which functioned briefly under the first emperor (1370-76), but was dissolved after a few months of revival in 1425. This council, to be headed by a grand secretary, he proposed, should draw upon a small group of men of outstanding learning and literary attainment who could readily provide advice to the emperor on state affairs and other important matters. Wang apparently felt that the presence of such an advisory corps would help to influence the emperor and serve as a possible deterrent to domination by the eunuchs, as had been the case during the previous reign. His recommendation, however, does not seem to have impressed the emperor. Wang died in April, 1524, at the age of seventy-four. (The *shih-lu*, however, records his death on June 6, which is probably the date the court conferred posthumous honors on him.) The emperor gave him the posthumous title of grand tutor and the canonized name Wen-ko 文恪 (cultured and faithful).

Wang Ao was an outstanding official of his time; he was known for his integrity and outspoken comments on state affairs. Unlike many of his colleagues, however, Wang enjoyed a relatively stable career in spite of the chaotic political situation which obtained during his years in office. One reason was in part his perspicacity and his readiness to relinquish office to avoid confrontation with his enemies. The other reason, which is probably more important, was his relation with the maternal side of the imperial family through his marriage to a member of the Chang 張 family. It appears that Wang's second wife was either a younger sister of Empress Chang or a daughter of Chang Ho-ling (*q. v.*). This special relationship must in some ways have contributed to the stability of his career.

Wang was also an accomplished scholar and belle-lettrist. Being an orthodox Confucianist, he favored the commentaries on the canon by the Han scholars, which he considered closer to the original, over the metaphysical speculations of the Sung neo-Confucianists. He wrote very little on the Classics, preferring to expound his views on concrete cases and in practical situations, especially during his presentation of lectures to the emperor. Some of his comments on the Four Books have been collected in the *Ming wen-ch'ao* 明文鈔, compiled by Kao T'ang 高嵣 (1786). His piece on human nature elicited the admiration of Wang Shou-jen (*q. v.*), who composed a biography of him in 1527. As a writer, Wang Ao was well known for his prose essays and miscellaneous jottings. He excelled also in poetry and calligraphy. A sample of the latter is reproduced in *Shodō zenshu* 書道全集, another in Tseng Yu-ho Ecke, *Chinese Calligraphy*.

Four out of six titles of Wang Ao's writings listed in the *Ssu-k'u* catalogue survive. His collected works, *Chen-tse hsien-sheng chi* (Chen-tse 震澤 being his style adopted from the ancient name of Lake T'ai), 36 *ch.*, was first printed in 1536, with a preface by Huo T'ao (*q. v.*). This was reprinted early in the 17th century under the title *Wang Wen-k'o kung chi*, by his great-grandson, Wang Yü-sheng 禹聲 (T. 邁考, H. 聞 [文] 溪, cs 1589), who added three appendices entitled *Ming-kung pi-chi* 名公筆記, a random sampling of contemporary opinion on Wang Ao, *Chüan-yin* 鵑音, and *Pai-she shih-ts'ao* 白社詩草, 1 *ch.* each, the last two being the poetry of Wang Yü-sheng himself. Wang Ao's well-known miscellanies, *Chen-tse ch'ang-yü* 長語, 2 *ch.*, and *Chen-tse chi-wen* 紀聞 (a slightly different version entitled *Shou-ch'i* 守溪 *pi-chi* in some collectanea), 1 *ch.*, are collections of notes on the institutions, political events, and personalities in Ming times. They include interesting information on topics such as the compilation of the veritable records, the government organizations of the middle-Ming period, the education of palace attendants, the vaults for the preservation of gold in the palace, the career of Liu Chin, and the special mission sent to Champa in 1441, with an excerpt from the diary of the envoy (*see* Wu Hui). These two titles were later incorporated in the *Chen-tse hsien-sheng pieh-chi* 別集, 6 *ts'e*, edited by Wang Yü-sheng, together with *Hsü* 續 *Chen-tse chi-wen*, a supplement to the previous title by Wang Ao, and *Ying-shih chi-lüeh* 郢事紀略, an account written by Wang Yü-sheng on the Wuchang uprising of April, 1601, against the alleged atrocity of the notorious tax-collector Ch'en Feng (*q. v.*). A late Wan-li edition of this work, which is rare, is in the Naikaku Bunko. A short story by Wang Ao entitled *Lü-mu chuan* 慺母傳 is included in *Hsiang-yen* 香艷 *ts'ung-shu* (1909–11 ed.), volume 9.

In addition, Wang edited two important local gazetteers. The first, *Ku-su chih* 姑蘇志, 60 *ch.*, which he compiled from the draft of Wu K'uan (*q. v.*), was the most comprehensive gazetteer of the Soochow prefecture in Ming times. It has a preface of 1506 and was reprinted in Taipei (1965) in two volumes. The other, *Chen-tse pien* 編, 8 *ch.*, is about the history and geography of the Lake T'ai region. It contains two parts; the first, dealing with the island Hsi 西 Tung-t'ing shan, the work of Ts'ai Sheng 蔡昇 (T. 景東) of early Ming; the other, concerning Tung Tung-t'ing, was Wang's own contribution. The original edition, with a preface of 1505 by Yang Hsün-chi (*q.v.*), is available on microfilm.

Wang had four sons; one son by his second wife, and three sons by a later marriage. The eldest, Wang Yen-che 延喆 (T. 子貞, 1483–1541), was brought up in Peking and apparently learned from members of his mother's family how to use influence in acquiring properties and gaining advantages in trade, for about 1502 he returned to Soochow and in a few years became one of the wealthiest men in the empire. It is said that he built a large house in the western suburbs of Soochow where in the front part he kept musicians and actors and in the rear beautiful women. It is said that he later tired of his excesses and decided to conform to the rules of society. Through favors granted his father he became a student in the National University, then a drafter, and later a deputy chief justice in the Grand Court of Revision. In 1527 he published a reproduction of a Sung edition of the *Shih-chi* 史記. It took two years to engrave and became a treasured item among bibliophiles.

The other three sons were Wang Yen-su 素 (T. 子儀, H. 雲屋, 1492–1562), magistrate of Ssu-nan 思南, Kweichow; Wang Yen-ling 陵 (T. 子永, H. 少溪), and Wang Yen-chao 昭. His eldest daughter, Wang I 儀 (1476–1517), the only child by his first wife, née Wu 吳, married Hsü Chin 徐縉 (T. 子容, H. 崦西, 1479–1545, cs 1505), an assistant minister of Personnel.

Bibliography

1/181/21a; 5/14/62a, 103/78a; 34/5/1a; 40/25/1b; 43/2/4b; 61/128/2b; 64/丙7/2a; 84/丙/31b; MSL (1964), Hsiao-tsung, *ch.* 86-199, Wu-tsung(1965), *ch.* 7-49, Shih-tsung (1965), *ch.* 20, 39; KC (1958), 2352, 2621, 2871, 2944, 3297; SK (1930), 68/8b, 76/1b, 122/5b, 171/3a, 191/10b; Wu K'uan, *P'ao-weng chia-ts'ang chi* (SPTK ed.), 64/11b; Shao Pao 邵寶 (1460-1527), *Jung-ch'un-t'ang hsü-chi* 容春堂續集 (NLP microfilm, no. 952), 16/1a (with mistake in date of birth); Wen Cheng-ming, *Fu-t'ien chi*, 28/1a; Wang Shou-jen, *Wang Wen-ch'eng kung ch'üan-shu*, 25/719; Li Shao-wen 李紹文, *Huang Ming shih-shuo hsin-yü* 皇明世說新語 (NLP microfilm, no. 247), 2/17a, 3/34b, 4/4b; Wang Ao, *Chen-tse pien* (NLP microfilm, no. 457); *Ming-wen-hai* (Tokyo microfilm), 1/6/7, 3/10/28, 8/8/14; Wang Shih-chen (ECCP), *Ch'ih-pei ou-t'an* 池北偶談 (1700), 22/14b; Yeh Ch'ang-chih (BDRC), *Ts'ang-shu chi-shih shih* (Shanghai, 1958), 86; Lo Chi-tsu 羅繼祖, *Ming tsai-*

hsiang shih-ch'en chuan 明宰相世臣傳 (1936), 1/1a;
Wu Chi-hua 吳緝華, "Ming-tai chih hung-wen
kuan chi hung-wen ko," 明代之弘文館及弘文
閣, CYYY, Vol. 40, pt. 1 (1968), 387; *Shodō
zenshu* (Tokyo, 1930-32), Vol. 23, 157; D. Pokotilov, *History of the Eastern Mongols during the
Ming Dynasty from 1368 to 1634*, tr. by Rudolf
Loewenthal, *Studia Serica*, ser. A, no. 1 (Chengtu,
1947), pt. 1, 84; W. Franke, "Addenda and
Corrigenda," *ibid.* (1949), pt. 2, 50; *id., Sources*,
4.4.1, 5.10, 5.4.16; Ping-ti Ho, *The Ladder of
Success in Imperial China* (New York, 1962),
144; Tseng Yu-ho Ecke, *Chinese Calligraphy*
(Philadelphia, 1971), 44.

Hok-lam Chan

WANG Chen 王振, died 1449, was a eunuch from Yü-chou 蔚州 in northern Shansi.
He was castrated and entered the palace
service at an early age during the Yung-
lo period. He belonged to one of the first
groups of youthful eunuchs selected to
receive a thorough Confucian training in
the palace school, Nei-shu-t'ang 內書堂,
established in 1426. [Editors' note: Yen
Ts'ung-chien 嚴從簡 (cs 1559) records in
his *Shu-yü chou-tzu lu* 殊域周咨錄, 17/16b,
that Emperor Chu Ti (*q.v.*) persuaded
several Confucian instructors, who already
had male offspring, to let themselves
suffer castration, so that they might teach
the women of the palace. Wang Chen,
was one of this group, and naturally made
his mark.] The first Ming emperor had
issued an order strictly forbidding the
education of eunuchs but his descendants
discarded this policy. Wang was assigned
to the heir apparent, Chu Ch'i-chen
(*q.v.*), and obtained his complete confidence. Thus, when in 1435 the prince became emperor, he relied much upon Wang
Chen, and in spite of his youth Wang
became one of the three head officials of
the directorate of ceremonial, the most
influential of the various eunuch agencies. This directorate controlled the whole
eunuch staff and its head officials were
thus very powerful. With his ingenuity
and ambition, together with his institu-

tional power, Wang had every opportunity to influence the emperor's decisions
in personnel and political matters or even
to intercept communications sent by high
officials to him. Because of the emperor's minority, however, the empress-
dowager, née Chang (*see* Chu Chan-chi),
widow of the fourth emperor, Chu Kao-
chih (*q.v.*), and grandmother of Chu
Ch'i-chen, retained considerable influence
over her grandson and the making of
government decisions. She seems to have
been an energetic woman and had the
respect of all within the palace. Becoming
suspicious of the activities of Wang Chen,
she admonished her grandson to follow
solely the advice of the elder statesmen
surviving his father's reign, and considered
ordering Wang Chen to commit suicide.
At this point the young emperor implored
the empress-dowager on his knees to
spare Wang's life, and the high officials
present joined in his supplication. Thus
Wang's life was saved, and he restrained
himself, acting more cautiously until her
death on November 20, 1442.

From this time on Wang Chen was
able to exercise a far-reaching influence
over the emperor and gradually built up
among the higher officials a group of
people indebted to him for their promotions or who, for other reasons, closely
cooperated with him; men such as Hsü
Hsi 徐晞 (T. 孟初, minister of War, 1442–
45, d. 1446), Wang Yu 王佑 (vice minister of Works, 1441–43, d. 1443), Ma Shun
馬順 (commander of the Embroidered-
uniform Guard, d. 1449), and Wang's
nephew, Wang Shan 山, who became a
vice commander of the same guard in
1442. Since the Embroidered-uniform
Guard functioned as the personal bodyguard
of the emperor and had police and judicial authority, it was of crucial importance
for Wang to control the guard through
persons associated directly with him. He
saw to the removal of the big iron tablet,
suspended by order of the founder of the
Ming dynasty at a conspicuous place on one
of the gates within the imperial palace, on

which was the order prohibiting eunuchs from participating in politics. In 1443/44 he built a large temple for his personal residence. The emperor granted it the name Chih-hua ssu 智化寺 and supplied a stone inscription. This Buddhist temple was still standing in the 1940s at the northeastern corner of Lu-mi ts'ang 祿米倉, close to the eastern city wall. The previously influential grand secretaries, in particular Yang Shih-ch'i, Yang Jung, and Yang P'u (qq.v.), had either died or retired, leaving no one with sufficient authority to check Wang's activities. He managed to have several officials, who ventured to defy him, either liquidated or ousted from their positions. Wang advocated the huge campaigns of 1441 and 1443/44 against Lu-ch'uan in the Yunnan-Burma border region (see Ssu Jen-fa). The Chinese forces were under the command of Wang Chi (q.v.), who apparently enjoyed Wang Chen's confidence. These campaigns, however, drained off manpower and other resources badly needed for the protection of the northern border. In 1443 the Hanlin expositor, Liu Ch'iu 劉球 (T. 廷振, 求樂, from An-fu 安福, Kiangsi, 1392-1443, cs 1421) presented a long memorial wherein he covertly protested against Wang's influence, warning the emperor not to delegate power, but to decide measures himself with the help of loyal officials, and to distinguish between good and evil advisers. He opposed the Lu-ch'uan campaign advocating better defense of the northern frontier. Thereupon Wang Chen succeeded in having Liu Ch'iu indicted and done to death in the prison of the Embroidered-uniform Guard (June 30, 1443). Late in 1449 Liu Ch'iu was posthumously rehabilitated and given the honorary title Chung-min 忠愍. Many stories are related telling how Wang managed to imprison, humiliate, or cause the death of such officials as Hsüeh Hsüan (q. v.). The emperor, however, continued to rely on him, giving him and the other eunuchs rewards in 1446 and bestowing upon his nephew, Wang Lin 林, the hereditary rank of assistant commander in the Embroidered-uniform Guard.

In the autumn of 1449 Wang Chen, in the face of strong opposition, including a stern warning from the director of the astronomical bureau, P'eng Te-ch'ing 彭德清, persuaded the emperor to embark personally on a campaign against the Oirat chieftain Esen (q.v.). One of his purposes is said to have been to persuade the emperor to visit his native district near Tatung. Wang and other eunuchs. who had no understanding of military organization, directed the operation. Thus it was badly organized and in disorder almost from the beginning. The imperial convoy had hardly reached Tatung when the fighting superiority of the Mongols and the imminent danger for the imperial expedition became evident. An immediate retreat was ordered. On September 1, 1449, the Mongols made a sudden assault against the imperial convoy at T'u-mu 土木, near Huai-lai 懷來, just beyond the Great Wall northwest of Peking. The emperor was taken prisoner; the majority of the Chinese army and of the emperor's retinue, including Wang Chen and many high officials, were killed. [Editors' note: For a plot against his life in mid-August see Li Hsien.]

On September 9 the censor-in-chief, seconded by numerous high officials, presented a bill of indictment to the regent (Chu Ch'i-yü, q.v.), accusing Wang Chen of usurpation of power and of terrorizing officials and fellow eunuchs. Wang's crimes and atrocities were enumerated item by item—including the killing of Liu Ch'iu. He was held responsible for the imperial campaign and for its disastrous end. The indictment asked for the confiscation of Wang's property and for the execution of the members of his clan and of his clique. After some initial hesitation the regent eventually agreed. A conflict arising immediately afterwards within the palace between adherents of Wang and their enraged opponents resulted in the death of several people, among them the commander of the Embroidered-uniform Guard,

Ma Shun. Subsequently Wang's nephews, Wang Shan and Wang Lin, and many others were put to death. In the course of the confiscation of Wang Chen's property inside and outside the capital, enormous quantities of gold and other treasures as well as several tens of thousands of horses, are said to have been seized by the government.

Chu Ch'i-chen, however, retained his affection for Wang Chen. After his restoration as emperor in 1457, he ordered (October 24) Wang's rehabilitation, a funeral sacrifice, and the setting up of an ancestral hall, named Ching-chung tz'u 旌忠祠 containing a memorial inscription and Wang's image, in the Chih-hua ssu. Throughout the next two centuries this hall was maintained by Buddhist monks and incense burned in honor of Wang Chen. In 1742 the Ch'ien-lung emperor, following the advice of Shen T'ing-fang (ECCP), ordered the destruction of the ancestral hall and Wang's image; Wang Chen's name was erased, moreover, from the three stone inscriptions. By a strange mischance the eunuch's portrait on a fourth tablet, dated 1459, which was dumped into a privy, escaped destruction.

Practically all Chinese historical sources have been written or edited by members of the scholar-official class who affected to despise and to disparage the eunuchs, in particular those playing a role in politics. Thus all sources tend to emphasize the evil done by eunuchs and to minimize the responsibility of the emperor and the high civil officials in permitting eunuchs to act in administrative and political matters. It is difficult, therefore, to decide to what degree Wang Chen was responsible for the atrocities and malpractices attributed to him. The affection shown by Emperor Chu Ch'i-chen, in spite of the fact that the disastrous campaign, allegedly promoted by Wang Chen alone, had made him a prisoner and deprived him for a time of the imperial dignity, may perhaps indicate that Wang was not entirely the monster which the historical records portray.

Bibliography

1/304/7b; 3/283/8a; 5/117/47a; 61/158/3112; MSL (1963), Ying-tsung, 2124, 2720, 3492, 3520, 6074; KC (1958), 1488, 1633, 1647, 1695, 1783, 2056; Ku Ying-t'ai (ECCP), *Ming-ch'ao chi-shih pen-mo*, 29; Shen Te-fu, *Wan-li yeh-hu pien* (1959), 822; Chu I-tsun (ECCP), *Jih-hsia chiu-wen k'ao* (1774), 48/20b; Liu Tun-chen 劉敦楨, "Pei-p'ing Chih-hua ssu Ju-lai tien tiao-ch'a chi" 北平智化寺如來殿調查記, in *Chung-kuo ying-tsao hsüeh-she hui-k'an* 中國營造學社彙刊, 3: 3 (1932) 1; *Shih-liao hsün-k'an* 史料旬刊, no. 12, leaf 420; Gustav Ecke, "The Institute for Research in Chinese Architecure," MS 2 (1936-37), 468.

Wolfgang Franke

WANG Chi 王驥 (T. 尚德, Pth. 忠毅), 1378-May 30, 1460, a native of Shu-lu 束鹿, Pei-Chihli, and *chin-shih* of 1406, set an early example in Ming governmental employ by shifting from civil to military service. He also helped to advance the power of eunuchs at court through his connection with Wang Chen (*q.v.*).

Wang Chi is described as tall and well built, agile and full of life. A skilled archer and a superb horseman, he also demonstrated physical courage and military talent. He enjoyed indulging in good food and musical entertainment. His love for creature comforts was such that even on the battle field his personal luggage was carried by several hundred men. His field tents were made of various materials to suit any climate.

Wang began as a supervising secretary for War, then vice surveillance commissioner of Shansi and prefect (1425) of Shun-t'ien (Peking) before his elevation to be right vice minister of War (June 1, 1427). He remained in the latter position for almost seven years, the last year and a half acting as minister. He made a number of inspection trips in the provinces and redistributed the army units under the territorial commands. In 1433, on orders from Emperor Chu Chan-chi (*q.v.*), he assembled six thousand boys from the hereditary military families and placed the special youth corps thus organized under the command of the heir apparent, then six years old. Aimed at educating him in military affairs, this arrangement in the long run paved the way for Wang Chen's ascent to power. Wang Chen had already endeared himself to the young prince, the future emperor Chu Ch'i-chen (*q.v.*). After the latter's succession to the throne (February 7, 1435), Wang Chen arranged numerous parades and military reviews to please him. On such occasions he influenced the youth into granting impromptu promotions to army officers, thus establishing himself as an adviser on state affairs and setting the stage for his own ascendancy.

Historians have not yet been able to ascertain how Wang Chi at first made connections with Wang Chen. Events in the 1430s suggest, however, that, while serving a minor on the throne, Wang Chi might have felt compelled to look to the latter for security. Wang Chi was formally promoted to minister of War on April 3, 1434, barely nine months before the imperial succession. Early in 1437 the emperor put him in prison for failing to report the military situation on the northwest frontier as promptly as the boy monarch wished. Sometime after his release that year, however, he was (June 4) ordered to proceed to Kansu to take complete charge of military operations. These capricious actions of the emperor clearly evidence the precariousness of Wang Chi's position and help to explain why he had to seek the support of someone close to the throne.

Wang's campaign on the Kansu frontier (winter of 1437 38) involved a series of punitive expeditions against A-t'ai (*see* Aruɤtai) and To-er-chih-po 朶兒只伯 (Dorjibeg), Mongol leaders who controlled the remnants of Aruɤtai's tribes. Upon arriving in the field, Wang reorganized the army command, executed a general

accused of failure in a previous campaign, and personally directed the attack. His report places the fighting in the Alashan desert between Yü-hai 魚海 (Kara-nōr) and Ch'ang-ning Lake 昌 (or 常) 甯湖. He claimed a complete victory reporting that the Mongols were decimated, the two tribal leaders had barely escaped, and their chief lieutenants had been captured. When he returned to Peking to resume his ministerial duties (Spring 1438), Wang was made concurrently chief minister of the Grand Court of Revision.

Not all historians agree as to the three successive campaigns which Wang Chi carried out in the years from 1441 to 1449 in the west Yunnan-north Burma region (*see* Ssu Jen-fa). It is clear nevertheless that his ties with Wang Chen during this decade were very close. In his reports of victory Wang Chi never failed to cite the several eunuch inspectors attached to his command before he mentioned his generals. His triumph in turn enhanced the prestige of his sponsor at court. On June 20, 1442, he was enfeoffed as earl of Ching-yüan 靖遠伯; only then did he relinquish his office in the War ministry.

Directly after his third tour of duty in Yunnan, in the summer of 1449, Wang Chi again received the designation of commander-in-chief, this time to suppress a Miao 苗 rebellion in Kweichow and Hukuang. The field assignment enabled him to escape the consequence of an accusation made in Peking late that year of having been an associate of Wang Chen. It is said also that Emperor Chu Ch'i-yü (*q.v.*) honored him as an elder statesman who, aside from his military merits, had faithfully served four preceding emperors. By order of the emperor he was made supreme commander at Nanking late in 1450 with the rank of minister of War.

Wang Chi maintained this post until 1452. In that year he returned to Peking and retired from active service. After Chu

Ch'i-chen's restoration in 1457 he once again became minister of War serving from March 13 through June 29. Then approaching the age of eighty, he was still energetic and active. Asserting that he had participated in the coup that made the restoration possible, Wang petitioned that his earldom be made hereditary; the emperor consented. After he died his rank was posthumously raised to that of marquis (Ching-yüan hou 侯). Eight of Wang's descendants were to inherit the earldom and stipend before the fall of the dynasty. Several became army generals, though none served with as much distinction as their colorful ancestor. With the single exception of Wang Shou-jen (q.v.), no other holder of a *chin-shih* degree in Ming times received such high awards. Twelve memorials submitted by Wang Chi dealing with his frontier operations and matters on army administration are preserved in the *Huang Ming ching-shih wen-pien* (*see* Ch'en Tzu-lung, ECCP).

Bibliography

1/171/1a, 327/8b; 63/13/1a; MSL (1963), Hsüantsung, 0726, 2233, 2271, 2456, Ying-tsung, 0499, 0591, 0611, 0656, 0689, 0701, 0759, 0764, 0790, 0800, 1861, 3827, 3956, 4130, 4142, 4258, 5971, 5974; *Chi-fu t'ung-chih* (1934), 6270, 7717; *Huang Ming ching-shih wen-pien*, I, 203.

Ray Huang

WANG Chi 王畿 (T. 汝中, H. 龍谿), May 26, 1498-July 25, 1583, thinker and official, native of Shan-yin 山陰 in the prefecture of Shao-hsing, Chekiang, traced his descent from the same ancestor as his teacher, Wang Shou-jen (q.v.). His grandfather, Wang Li 理, was a district magistrate. His father, Wang Ching 經, served as surveillance vice commissioner in Kweichow. Wang Chi's elder brother, Wang Pang 邦, was an invalid whom Wang Chi in later life looked after attentively. A good student, Wang Chi obtained the *chü-jen* at the age of twenty-one (1519). In 1521 Wang Shou-jen returned to Yü-yao and started to teach the doctrine of chih liang-chih 致良知 (extending the knowledge of the good), arousing thereby much criticism and opposition. Wang Chi and his friend, Ch'ien Te-hung (q.v.), were among the first to become Wang Shou-jen's disciples. Wang Chi failed to pass the *chin-shih* examinations held in 1523; so he returned to Yü-yao to study under Wang. After about a year, he was able to comprehend the meaning of the master's teachings. Together with Ch'ien Te-hung he was given the charge of assisting him in the instruction of new disciples. In 1526 Wang Shou-jen urged Wang Chi and Ch'ien to go once more to Peking for the examinations. They did so. Disappointed, however, by the mediocre calibre of the officials of the time, and angered by veiled attacks made on their master's teachings, Wang Chi and Ch'ien Te-hung both returned to Yü-yao without taking the final palace examinations. Three years later, when the two friends went again to Peking for the same tests, word of their master's death obliged them to return south prematurely. Both mourned for Wang Shou-jen as for a deceased father.

Besides taking care of the master's family affairs, they also established the T'ien-chen 天眞 Academy outside Hangchow where they displayed a portrait of him. This provided an assembly place for fellow disciples and scholars, who gathered there twice a year to offer sacrifice to Wang Shou-jen and hold lecture meetings. Thus it was not until 1532 that Wang Chi and Ch'ien Te-hung finally acquired their *chin-shih* degrees. Wang Chi's talents were recognized by the Grand Secretary, Chang Fu-ching (q.v.), who appointed him secretary of the bureau of operations in the ministry of War, Nanking. Sickness, however, soon obliged him to take home leave. After his recovery, Wang Chi was approached by a messenger from the new Grand Secretary,

Hsia Yen (*q.v.*), regarding the possibility of his filling a vacancy as adviser in the household of the heir apparent. Wang declined the offer, thus provoking Hsia. He was sent back to Nanking, and rose later to become a director of the personnel bureau in the ministry of War. When fires in the palace precincts caused the emperor, Chu Hou-ts'ung (*q.v.*), to invite counsel (1541), many officials, including the supervising secretary, Ch'i Hsien 戚賢 (T. 秀夫, H. 南山, 1492-1553, cs 1526), recommended Wang Chi for higher office. Hsia Yen then rebuked Wang Chi for teaching "false doctrines," and demoted Ch'i Hsien to the provincial administration office in Shantung. Wang Chi immediately begged leave to resign. He was not dismissed until a year later, however, following unfavorable evaluation given by Hsüeh Ying-ch'i (*q.v.*) for the bureau of investigations of the ministry of Personnel. Huang Tsung-hsi (ECCP) notes that Hsüeh, himself a follower of the school of Wang Shou-jen, did so for the purpose of "correcting" the course of "learning." In any case, Wang Chi returned home, and for the next forty-odd years devoted himself exclusively to teaching philosophy. Although his friends, the scholars Ou-yang Te and T'ang Shun-chih (*qq.v.*) wished to recommend him once more for government service, Wang advised them against doing so. In spite of his ever-rising reputation, therefore, Wang Chi remained in retirement. He spent his time traveling widely between Peking and Nanking, in the provinces south of the Yangtze, and in Fukien and Kwangtung, giving lectures in the numerous lecture halls (chiang-she 講舍) established by himself and other disciples of Wang Shou-jen. His ease of manner, gentleness, and eloquence drew large audiences. Such activity went on even after he had passed the age of eighty. He died at the age of eighty-five.

Wang Chi was very devoted to his wife, but she bore him no children. She gave him a concubine so that he might produce an heir. After her husband put into practice certain sexual techniques related to Taoist cultivation, which he learned from some individual possessing esoteric knowledge (i-jen異人), he achieved success. His wife had received some instruction in the Confucian Classics but became a fervent Buddhist in middle life, devoted to Kuan-yin, and reciting the Diamond Sūtra daily. To her, Wang Chi explained that the extension of liang-chih was the same as the Buddhist notion of preparing oneself for inner illumination. He greatly mourned her death, which occurred many years before his.

Wang Chi's eldest son, Wang Ying-chen 應禎, died relatively young. The second, Wang Ying-pin 斌, passed the military examinations and served as assistant commissioner of a regional military commission. The youngest, Wang Ying-chi 吉, became a *chü-jen* in 1579.

As a thinker, Wang Chi's interpretation of Wang Shou-jen's "Four Maxims" (*see* Wang Shou-jen and Ch'ien Te-hung) shows the depth of his penetration into the master's teaching, while it also inaugurates a period of controversy regarding the mind-in-itself (hsin chih t'i 心之體) being beyond good and evil (wu-shan wu-o 無善無惡). Besides, inferring from this principle, Wang Chi also asserted that intentions (i 意), knowledge (chih 知), and things, or rather "acts" (wu 物) are all, in a sense, beyond good and evil. In other words, he taught a complete "transcendance" of the ethical categories of good and evil which occurs with the recognition in oneself that the mind (hsin) is, fundamentally speaking, independent of moral judgments while being at the same time the source of such judgments. The sage, for example, is so in tune with ultimate reality—the "highest good" which is beyond good and evil—that he can follow all the dictates of his mind and heart without fear of making any moral transgression. This interpretation has often been described as the theory of the "Four Negatives" (ssu-wu 四無). Wang

Shou-jen himself expressed approval of it when he said that the man of superior spiritual perception was capable of penetrating at once into the meaning of the mind-in-itself, and of uniting the internal and external in his efforts towards self-cultivation. But he also warned that few men in the world would be so spiritually perceptive as not to need to make efforts to do good and avoid evil; he could not merely meditate upon the mind-in-itself; this, indeed, was a practice that might lead into "emptiness and the void." He therefore cautioned Wang Chi personally to emulate his fellow disciple, Ch'ien Te-hung, who held a differing interpretation of the maxims, in his concern for self-cultivation (kung-fu 工夫), while at the same time he counseled Ch'ien to seek to follow Wang Chi in his insights into the fundamental nature of things (pen-t'i 本體).

Wang Chi's insistence upon the negative character of the mind-in-itself stemmed from his concern for the very absoluteness of this mind-in-itself, or of liang-chih. He sometimes referred to it also as sheng-chi 生機 (the springs of life). The experience of enlightenment, therefore, lies in recapturing the hidden springs of life in oneself, and in allowing this to flow freely and operate naturally. Later on, Wang Chi would develop his insight into the mind-in-itself as being beyond good and evil to a teaching which has been called liang-chih hsien-ch'eng lun 良知現成論 (the doctrine of the ready-made liang-chih). He taught that the seed of sagehood, liang-chih, universally present in all men, is, in a sense, already "developed" (hsien-ch'eng) in all. One need merely to awake to its full meaning and power to become a sage. And, according to Wang Chi, this awakening could best be attained through faith (hsin 信) in liang-chih. This constant reiteration of having "faith" in liang-chih gave Wang Chi's philosophy a strong religious orientation, suggesting his personal discovery of the absolute within himself, and his desire to share this discovery of the absolute within himself, and

his desire to share this discovery with others. But he offers no method of verifying the attainment, through faith, of one's real liang-chih. And his nearly exclusive encouragement of inner enlightenment in preference to careful self-cultivation, tended to obscure the difference between the real sage and the potential one or even the hypocrite, between liang-chih in its purity and perfection and liang-chih as it lies hidden, not fully purified and activated. Thus the danger was that the absolute might become hidden and forgotten, as moral life and the pursuit of goodness shifted its basis to the relative principle of everyman's liang-chih, and away from the conventional standards, drawn from classical injunctions as well as personal insights discovered through careful cultivation, accompanied by occasional moments of sudden illumination.

Wang Chi's emphasis on inner enlightenment caused him to treat the subject in greater detail. He described three kinds of enlightenment or illumination (wu 悟): that which comes from the understanding of words, chieh 解-wu, is the lowest; that which is "confirmed" by meditation, cheng 證-wu, is superior to the former; while that which comes from confrontation with life "penetrating enlightenment" (ch'e 徹-wu) is the best and highest form. This shows certainly his regard for constant attentiveness, a kind of "cultivation akin to non-cultivation." While such practice was natural and spontaneous to the men of keen spiritual perception, it was nevertheless open to misinterpretation by those less gifted, even among his own disciples.

Wang Chi was virtually uninhibited in his overt efforts to promote an amalgamation of Confucian teaching with Buddhist and Taoist insights. He described the doctrine of liang-chih as the focus of integration for the "Three Teachings," and identified it with the Buddhist concept of wu (nothingness) and the Taoist notion of hsü 虛 (emptiness). He continued to regard himself, however, as a Confucian, and criticized the Buddhist and Taoist tendency to fall into empty abstraction, and to withdraw the individual from his family and social involvements. Wang Chi made free use of Buddhist and Taoist terminology, but he did so mainly to illustrate the oneness of truth itself, and the foolishness of seeking any monopoly for it in any arbitrary fashion. He also gave a real importance to using certain techniques of Taoist cultivation, particularly with reference to breath circulation.

These teachings provoked much debate and criticism, first among Wang Chi's fellow disciples, especially Nieh Pao and Lo Hung-hsien (*qq.v.*), who took him severely to task, and Tsou Shou-i (*q.v.*), and Ou-yang Te, who sought to remedy the defects of his teaching. This controversy even continued long after his lifetime, and became the occasion for various attempts aimed at turning the tide toward an increasingly individualist and subjectivist tendency in moral and social behavior. It led to the gradual development of many "branches" in the school of Wang Shou-jen, with the followers of Wang Chi himself and of Wang Ken (*q.v.*) as the promoters of a mass movement of social protest marked by eccentric individual action, and with the best critics of this movement emerging especially from the scholars of the Tung-lin Academy (*see* Ku Hsien-ch'eng), who formed a distinct group as thinkers in themselves, but show unquestioned influences deriving from the school of Wang Shou-jen.

Wang Chi had many disciples. These included some who were formally known as Wang Shou-jen's or Wang Ken's disciples, but who came under Wang Chi's influence at one time or another—for example, Wang Ken's own son, Wang Pi (*see* Wang Ken), T'ang Shun-chih, Lo Ju-fang, and Chou Ju-teng (*qq.v.*). Of his own immediate followers, his favorites seem to have been three lesser known men, Chou Meng-hsiu 周夢秀 (T. 繼實),

a cousin of Chou Ju-teng, Ting Pin 丁賓 (T. 禮原, H. 改亭, cs 1571, d. 1633), and Lu Kuang-chai 陸光宅 (T.　與中). The *Ming-shih* adds that later scholars, who were "superficial and eccentric," frequently called themselves Wang Chi's disciples. Without endorsing this statement, one can safely say that Wang Chi's influence diffused itself during his own lifetime and after.

Together with Wang Ken, Wang Chi has been praised and blamed, during his own day and after, by those persons who either favored or disapproved of their free and individual interpretations of the Confucian Classics and of Wang Shou-jen's teachings. Wang Ken's plebeian origins have, in our own time, given occasion for more applause among certain historians of Chinese thought, while Wang Chi has been celebrated less. He was, nevertheless, the most original thinker among all of Wang Shou-jen's disciples, more daring than the faithful Ch'ien Te-hung and more learned than Wang Ken.

Openly and without inhibition he made frequent use of Ch'an Buddhist and Taoist illusions and devices in his teachings. Although a native of Shan-yin, he was to be recognized, together with Wang Ken, as the spiritual founder of the T'ai-chou branch of the school of Wang Shou-jen. Huang Tsung-hsi has compared the achievements of Wang Chi, as Wang Shou-jen's spiritual heir, to those of Yang Chien (1149-1225), the disciple of Lu Chiu-yüan (1139-92). Wang Chi and Yang Chien both developed further the Buddhistic implications in their masters' doctrines, thus stimulating intellectual controversy and ferment. Criticized in their own day for having done so, both thinkers deserve reassessment for their personal and creative contributions to the development of the "School of the Mind" (hsin-hsüeh 心學), that branch of the neo-Confucian movement which made such an impact especially on Ming and post-Ming thought.

Of Wang Chi's writings, a collection entitled *Wang Lung-hsi ch'üan-chi* 全集, 20

ch., consisting of his recorded dialogues, prose works, poems, and epitaphs, was compiled first by his sons, Wang Ying-pin and Wang Ying-chi, and published by his disciple, Hsiao Liang-kan 蕭良幹 (T. 以寧, H. 拙齋, cs 1571, 1534-1602). This was later republished in 1822, and reprinted in Taipei in 1970. The same collection, with the addition of Wang Chi's short treatise, *Ta-hsiang i-shu* 大象義述, 2 *ch.*, which purports to explain certain parts of the Book of Changes, and of biographical accounts of him by Hsü Chieh (*q.v.*) and Chao Chin 趙錦 (T. 元樸, H. 麟陽, cs 1544, 1516-91), published by Ting Pin in 1615. This may be found in the National Central Library, Taipei, and in the Naikaku Bunko, Tokyo. There exists also a collection, *Lung-hsi yü-lu* 語錄, 8 *ch.*, Wang Chi's recorded dialogues and essays, published during the Wan-li period, with a preface by Li Chih (*q.v.*). A copy of this is in the Seikado Bunko, Tokyo, which holds a second collection, entitled *Lung-hsi Wang hsien-sheng yü-lu ch'ao* 鈔, 9 *ch.* Another work by Wang Chi, entitled *Chung-chien lu* 中鑒錄, 7 *ch.*, is not included in the "Complete Works" and may be no longer extant.

Bibliography

3/185/13b; 4/10/2a; 32/51/20b; 40/41/31b; 42/76/8a; 61/114/10a; 83/12/22b; *Shih-shuo* 師說/15b; *Ming-shih* (Taiwan ed.), 17/123, 283/3185; KC (1958), 3611; SK (1930), 177/10a; *Che-chiang t'ung-chih* (1934), 3140; *Shao-hsing-fu chih* (1792), 52/16b; Chou Ju-teng, *Sheng hsüeh tsung-chuan*, 14/19a; Wang Chi, *Wang Lung-hsi ch'üan-chi* (1822 ed., Taipei reprint, 1970); *id.*, *Lung-hsi Wang hsien-sheng ch'üan-chi* (1615 ed.), microfilm copy; Wang Shou-jen, *Wang Wen-ch'eng kung ch'üan-shu* (SPTK, 1st series, double-page lithograph ed.); Liu Ts'un-yan, "The Penetration of Taoism into the Ming Neo-Confucian Elite, " TP, LVII (1971), 88; Okada Takehiko 岡田武彦, *Ō Yōmei to Minmatsu no jugaku* 王陽明と明末の儒學 (Tokyo, 1970), 125; *id.*, "Wang Chi and the Rise of Existentialism, " in W. T. de Bary, ed., *Self and Society in Ming Thought* (1970), 121.

Julia Ching

WANG Ch'i 王圻 (T. 元翰, H. 洪洲), fl. 1565-1614, official and author, was a native of Shanghai, and the son of Wang I 熠 (H. 怡樸), a student of medicine. [Editors' note: The *Shang-hai-hsien chih* gives Wang Ch'i's age at death as eighty-five *sui* and various sources indicate that he died before 1620. Supposing he was eighty in 1614 when he compiled the work on salt administration, his year of birth would be about 1535.] A *chin-shih* of 1565, Wang's official career was hampered at critical junctures by a combination of two factors: he appears to have been a strong-willed individualist, and was not allied with any of the powerful factions in the central government. He first received appointment as magistrate of Ch'ing-chiang 清江, Kiangsi (1565-67). After serving in the same capacity at Wan-an 萬安, Kiangsi (1567-69), he was promoted to be a censor at the capital. At this point he became involved in court politics and in 1570, after serving as a censor for less than a year, he was sent away from the capital to be assistant surveillance commissioner of Fukien in charge of educational affairs. In November, 1570, at a special examination of the censors (*see* Chao Chen-chi), he was one of twenty-seven cashiered or demoted. As one of the ten receiving less severe censure, viz., for incompetency (才力不及), he was demoted to assistant department magistrate of Ch'iung-chou 邛州, Szechwan. Afterwards he served as magistrate of Chin-hsien 進賢, Kiangsi (1573-75), and of Ts'ao 曹, Shantung (1575-76), and as department magistrate of K'ai-chou 開州, Pei-Chihli (1576-78), and as prefect of Ch'ing-chou-fu 青州府, Shantung (1578-81). Late in 1581 he was promoted to be assistant surveillance commissioner of Hukuang, serving first as an intendant and then as director of educational affairs. Ultimately he was named assistant administration commissioner of Shensi, but by now he had decided that he had served long enough in the bureaucracy. Pleading that he was needed at home to care for his aged parents, he asked to be relieved of all official duties and returned to his native district.

Here on the banks of the Wu-sung River 吳淞江, near the western border of Shanghai, he built an estate which he called Mei-hua-yüan 梅花源 (Plum Blossom Stream); and here among the myriad Chinese plum trees that he planted was his studio, where he spent the rest of his life studying and writing books. Most of his published works deal with history and problems of public administration, with economic affairs occupying a significant portion of his attention. The best known is the *Hsü Wen-hsien t'ung-k'ao* 續文獻通考, 254 *ch.* (one of two works with the same title, the other one being compiled in the 18th century [see Ch'i Shao-nan, ECCP], which was intended as a sequel to a compilation of major events and documents made by Ma Tuan-lin (1223-89), the *Wen-hsien t'ung-k'ao* (published 1319-24). But Wang's work also includes six sections that are not in the compilation of Ma Tuan-lin, together with several new items. It is particularly valuable for its treatment of the Ming period down to *ca.* 1586 when it was brought to a close. Printed about 1603 it brought him wide acclaim. (The Harvard-Yenching Library reports also another addition to this work entitled *Hsü Wen-hsien t'ung-k'ao tsuan* 纂, 12 *ch.*, written by Wang Ch'i, and edited by Lang Hsing 郎星 *et al*, printed in the Ch'ung-chen era.) Another frequently consulted encyclopedic work he compiled, supplemented by his son, Wang Ssu-i 思義, is the *San-ts'ai t'u-hui* 三才圖會, 106 *ch.*, completed in 1609. Containing a number of maps and illustrations, it too stresses the Ming period. The illustrations, however, are sometimes imaginary rather than factual. A Japanese edition differs in certain details to meet the demands of its readers; it is entitled *Wakan* 和漢 *sansai zue*, 105 *ch.*, and edited by Terajima Ryōan 寺島良安, who published it in 1714. A third of Wang's compilations on a large scale is the *Pai-shih hui-pien* 稗

史彙編, 175 *ch.*, a collection of anecdotes. In addition he served as chief compiler of the gazetteer *Ch'ing-p'u* 青浦-*hsien chih* of 1597, 8 *ch.*, and the revised edition of the records of the Chekiang salt gabelle, *Liang Che ts'o chih* 兩浙鹺志, 24 *ch.*, completed about 1614. He is also credited with a work on the *Chou-li*, entitled *Chou-li ch'üan-ching chi-chu* 周禮全經集注, 14 *ch.*, a treatise on the textbook of military science, *Wu-hsüeh ching chuan chü-chieh* 武學經傳句解, and an annotated text of the work on forensic medicine, *Hsi-yüan chi-lan* 洗寃集覽. In all he compiled works totaling more than six hundred *chüan* on various subjects. The editors of the Imperial Library of the 18th century, while giving notices of seven of his works, found minor faults with all of them and allowed none to be copied into the Library. Today, however, both the *Hsü Wen-hsien t'ung-k'ao* and the *San-ts'ai t'u-hui* are regarded as valuable reference works on the Ming period.

As a bureaucrat Wang Ch'i was honored in several shrines for celebrated officials. Especially in Ts'ao and K'ai-chou, because he held office during the years of tax reform (*see* Chang Chü-cheng), was he remembered for the new tax regulations which he instituted. It is said that in K'ai-chou a shrine with his statue was erected soon after he left and, according to legend, some twenty years later, when a minor repair was made on the statue, it was found that a sore at the same spot on Wang's body healed at once.

Wang Ch'i's other works are: *Shih-fa t'ung-k'ao* 謚法通考, 18 *ch.* (*ca.* 1596); *Hai-fang chih* 海防志; *Tung-wu shui-li* 東吳水利 *k'ao*, 10 ch.; and a collection of his essays and poems entitled *Hung-chou lei-kao* 洪州類稿, 4 *ch.*

Bibliography

1/286/21b; 2/268/18b; 40/44/32b; 64/巳15/7a; 86/13/17b; SK (1930), 138/1a; L. of C. *Catalogue of Rare Books*, 408, 725, 1172; *Shang-hai-hsien chih* (1871), 19/11a.

                                      E-tu Zen Sun

WANG Chih 汪直, fl. 1476-*ca.* 1481, a eunuch, was originally a member of the Yao 猺 minority group from Ta-t'eng-hsia 大藤峽, Kwangsi. He began his palace career while young, serving at first as an attendant in the Chao-te Palace 昭德宮. Noticed for his superior intelligence, he was promoted to be in charge of the imperial stables. He evidently remained in the imperial favor, and began to exercise some measure of influence in court affairs even before the attainment of high power.

In 1476 the palace guard caught, and subsequently executed, one Li Tzu-lung 李子龍, said to be a sorcerer, who was found guilty of gaining illegal entrance into the imperial palace through the connivance of certain palace attendants. This untoward happening within his own gates prompted the emperor (Chu Chien-shen, *q.v.*) to seek more information about the world outside. To this end he ordered in 1477 the setting up of the Western Depot 西廠, an intelligence agency to which Wang was appointed as the officer in charge. The functions of this agency were similar to those of the Eastern Depot 東廠, another eunuch agency, but from the start the Western Depot was more powerful than its older counterpart.

Before long an event occurred which further enhanced Wang Chih's position at court: T'an Li-p'eng 覃力朋, a eunuch stationed at Nanking, was found smuggling one hundred boatloads of illegal salt while on his return trip south after escorting a tribute mission to Peking; in addition, T'an also was heaping demands on the local population all along his route of travel. When a local official at Wu-ch'eng 武城 (Shantung) remonstrated, T'an and his followers resorted to force, which resulted in one official being wounded and another person killed. When Wang Chih heard of this case, he had T'an arrested and asked for the death penalty, which, however, was not carried out. Nevertheless, Wang's exertion in this case greatly impressed the emperor, who henceforth regarded Wang as an efficient eradicator of evil. He was given the rank of a centurion of the Embroidered-uniform Guard. From now on the Western Depot became the organ that was free to carry out a large number of persecutions accompanied by extremely harsh torture, and Wang became the most feared man in Peking. When he went abroad with his train of numerous followers, it is recorded that all the high ministers and noblemen who happened to encounter him always yielded the right of way.

This state of affairs generated a certain amount of protest, and the Western Depot was temporarily abolished as a result of memorials, submitted by a number of high metropolitan officials, denouncing Wang's conduct. The memorials, however, did not succeed in impairing the emperor's trust in Wang Chih, and soon the entire machinery of the Western Depot was revived. The outcome of this interlude was the further ascendancy of Wang, who apparently learned his lesson quickly and began to bring his associates into important government posts. Hsiang Chung (*q.v.*), the minister of War who was one of those to impeach him, now was dismissed (July 18, 1477) and divested of all official ranks and honors. Meanwhile Wang Chih's collaborators, Wang Yüeh (*q.v.*) and Ch'en Yüeh 陳鉞 (T. 廷威, cs 1457), were entrusted with important commands, with Wang Yüeh in the capital and the northwest and Ch'en Yüeh on the northeastern frontier. These two men enhanced Wang Chih's standing, each in his own way.

These developments marked a new turn in Wang Chih's career. Heretofore he had been chiefly concerned with internal politics, but now he embarked on a period of military service on the northern frontier, during which he intended to cut as domineering a figure as he did in court politics, and which he was to use as an additional factor in furthering his own power. In this he was temporarily successful. In 1479 he was ordered by the emperor to inspect the frontiers, a mission he carried out with gusto: dashing across the territories at the head of a troop of horsemen, he sometimes covered several hundred *li* a day, and along the route the censors, the secretaries, and other provincial officials paid homage in front of his mount. Their servility was at least in part due to the fear Wang inspired among the officials of the inspected areas. It was known that he had uncovered a case of extreme corruption and cupidity in one of the provincial censors, and the man had been sent into exile. One exception among the officials was Ch'in Hung 秦紘 (T. 世緙, 1426-1505, cs 1451, Pth. 襄毅), then governor of Honan. Ch'in contested Wang Chih's assumption of precedence during his tour of Ch'in's territory and later dispatched a memorial to the throne reporting on Wang's highhanded conduct. Upon his return to the capital, however, Wang adroitly brushed aside Ch'in's charges and remained securely in power. Another official who refused to do homage to him, the vice minister of War, Ma Wen-sheng (*q.v.*), was dismissed on trumped-up charges on May 27, 1479, and sent into exile. Even reports of malfeasance by Wang Yüeh and Ch'en Yüeh did not immediately shake Wang Chih's position as the most trusted servant of the emperor.

When finally a blow did fall to undermine Wang's position, it came from a fellow eunuch and a rival from the Eastern Depot, Shang Ming 尚銘. Shang had just led a successful campaign against Mongol border intruders and was heavily rewarded, but his accomplishments were not reported by Wang Chih to the emperor out of jealousy and chagrin. Infuriated, Shang memorialized on the malfeasance of Wang Yüeh, and on the fact that Wang Chih revealed confidential palace affairs to unauthorized persons.

Shang Ming's action brought about a change in the emperor's attitude toward Wang Chih. In 1481 Wang Chih and Wang Yüeh were ordered to direct the defense of Hsüan-fu. After the invaders were repulsed, the emperor ordered these two to remain indefinitely on border posts, while other military officers were recalled to the more favored positions at court. This marked the beginning of Wang Chih's fall. Subsequently the Western Depot was abolished, and the officials who had belonged to Wang Chih's faction were dismissed or punished. Finally Wang Chih's own career reached the end of a full cycle: divested of all ranks, he was made once more a plain eunuch, and was transferred to work in the imperial stables at Nanking. His life was spared, however, despite suggestions that he be given the death penalty for his misdeeds.

Bibliography

1/304/13b, 178/1a, 182/14a; 3/283/13b; 5/117/66a; 6/46/37b; 42/25/12a; 61/158/15a; MSL (1940), Hsien-tsung, 167/2, 173/7; KC (1958), 2383.
                                    E-tu Zen Sun

WANG Chih 王直 (T. 行儉, 抑菴), 1379-October 15, 1462, a scholar-official who served for over thirty years in the Hanlin Academy and fourteen years as minister of Personnel, was a native of T'ai-ho 泰和, Kiangsi. His father, Wang Po-chen 伯貞 (*ming* 泰, H. 止菴, 1342-1416), at a special examination held in Nanking in 1382 was accorded the top place among some five hundred men. In the next few years he served first as intendant at Lei-chou 雷州, Kwangtung, and then as a secretary in the ministry of Revenue. About 1390, for a minor offense, he was exiled to Anking where he lived some nine years. He was then pardoned and sent to Hainan Island as prefect of Ch'iung-chou 瓊州, a post he held for about fourteen years. Reportedly he died in Peking in 1416 just after receiving a new assignment. His name was long treasured in Kwangtung as one the worthy administrators of that province.

Wang Chih himself became a *chin-shih* in 1404, was selected a Hanlin member, and as such served during the next thirty-four years in a literary capacity, especially on the editorial board of the first four *shih-lu*. Meanwhile he rose in rank until he became a vice minister of Rites in 1438. About this time he was in line for membership in the Grand Secretariat, but was instead appointed minister of Personnel in February, 1443, an office he administered creditably until he retired in 1457. It has been recorded that he was barred from being made a grand secretary because his fellow townsman and relation, the powerful grand secretary, Yang Shih-ch'i (*q. v.*), held a grudge aginst him. According to a rumor, Wang learned of a misdeamenor committed by Yang's son. As a concerned neighbor and friend , he reported it to Yang. On being questioned, the son refused to admit his fault. Consequently Yang began to distrust his old friend. This story may be authentic but it does not follow that it resulted in Wang's being denied a place in the Secretariat. Actually it seems that the designation of Wang to head the ministry of Personnel in 1443 was one of the wisest moves which Yang made. By relying on Wang's integrity the government was able to resist to some degree the rising influence of the eunuchs and to strengthen the administration. During the critical years that followed, Wang Chih, in his position as doyen of the ministers and through his appointment of the right persons to provincial posts, helped to save the country. All this seems to demonstrate Yang's judgment of character, and if he indeed ever held any grudge against Wang, it shows his statesmanship and magnanimity.

In the ministry of Personnel Wang's work was characterized not only by competence but also by a rigorous sense of justice. Wang was diligent and strict in the performance of his duties. For example, he made it a practice to test all those receiving censorial offices, and graded them, so that he might be guided later in their promotion or demotion. He took care that no charge of nepotism might be laid against himself. In the case of his own son, Wang Tzu 稽 (T. 希稷), then a lecturer in the National University in Nanking, a certain director of a bureau in his ministry proposed that the young man be transferred to the University in Peking, the better to look after his father. Wang Chih blocked the transfer. His first years in office (1443–49) were at a time when the iufluence of the eunuch Wang Chen (*q. v.*) was paramount, and injustice at the capital rampant. Local governments, however, were generally well ruled, as Wang had chosen superior men to administer them.

In 1446 Li Heng 李亨 (cs 1443), a vice minister of Revenue, taking advantage of his connections with Wang Chen, made a false charge against a director of a bureau, named Chao Min 趙敏 (T. 子聰). When Wang Chih and two junior colleagues became involved in the case, all four, including Li Heng, were thrown into prison. On September 24 the emperor released Wang and one of his colleagues, but Li and Wang's other colleague received punishments of three and two months' loss of pay respectively.

The year 1449 was a critical one in the Ming dynasty. When Wang Chen learned of the invasion of Esen (*q. v.*) in the northwest, he urged the emperor to organize and take personal leadership of an expedition against the Oirat leader. On July 20 Wang Chih issued a forthright memorial strongly protesting any such action. The emperor stubbornly brushed it aside and took off not long after, ordering Wang to remain behind. A calamitous defeat followed. Back in Peking, in the distraught days which ensued, while Yü Ch'ien (*q. v.*), first as acting minister of War, then as minister (September 7), set about stabilizing the situation, Wang Chih as head of the ministers rendered full cooperation. That his help at this juncture was appreciated is indicated by the award, on September 13, of the title of grand guardian of the heir apparent.

In the next nine months one of the most vexing questions that arose at court was whether or not to accept Esen's offer of peace and permit him to return his imperial prisoner, Chu Ch'i-chen (*q. v.*). Wang Chih took the lead (July 9, 1450) in proposing that Esen's overtures be accepted. The new emperor, Chu Ch'i-yü (*q. v.*), did not relish this idea; it might lead to the loss of his throne. Wang joined others in contending that the emperor should at least send an envoy to Esen. The upshot was that on August 8 three envoys were dispatched. On their return the emperor still hesitated to comply with the suggestion, repeatedly urged by Wang and others, that his half-brother be welcomed back to the capital. But Esen did not wait for compliance. He returned his prisoner on September 20. It was a cool welcome, however, which the emperor gave him at the Tung-an Gate 東安門. Not surprisingly, later historians were to criticize both the emperor for his lack of fraternal piety and the ministers, including Wang Chih, for failing to be more urgent in their pressures on Chu Ch'i-yü. In April of the ensuing year, when the Oirat sent an embassy to the court asking for one in reply, and the emperor once more paid no heed, Wang Chih and others remonstrated, holding that at the very least courtesies should be maintained. But the emperor stubbornly refused. So Wang in a memorial submitted in June importuned him to pay attention to the defense of the frontier and to the reorganization of the army, which had become demoralized. To this the emperor gave his assent.

By this time Wang Chih was seventy-two years of age. The emperor, while sympathizing with his desire for retirement, did not wish to lose his counsel. So he relieved Wang of his administrative duties (but not his office) and appointed a co-minister, first Ho Wen-yüan (*see* Ho Ch'iao-hsin), then Wang Ao 翱 (*q. v.*), at the same time according him additional honors. Meanwhile another problem was developing—that of dynastic succession. There was already an heir apparent in residence; his nephew Chu Chien-shen (*q. v.*). But the emperor had other intentions. Acting on a memorial from a sycophantic hereditary official in Kwangsi, Huang Hung (*see* Chu Ch'i-yü), the emperor proposed the substitution of his own son. The high officials at court, Wang Chih among them, were astounded. Softened by bribes, however, they finally agreed. Wang reportedly stamped his feet in dismay over his own weakness in signing the document signifying approval.

A few days after the *coup d'état* of Chu Ch'i-chen, Wang was permitted to retire. The new regime treated the elderly courtier well, loading him with gifts and ordering him conveyed home by imperial post horses and barges. For the next five years he lived quietly, surrounded by members of his family and friends, and indulging his taste for poetry and prose and calligraphy of which he was a master. He passed away at the age of eighty-three, the court honoring him with more high sounding titles aud the posthumous name Wen-tuan 文端.

Wang's writings, collected under the title *I-an chi* 抑菴集, 13 *ch.*, *Hou* 後 *chi*, 37 *ch.*, edited and published after his death by two of his sons, were copied two centuries later into the *Ssu-k'u ch'üan-shu*. Another collection in 40 *chüan*, entitled *Ch'ung-pien* 重編 *Wang Wen-tuan kung wen* 文 *chi*, with preface of 1563, was printed in the Lung-ch'ing period, and reprinted in 1867. While active in Peking during his years in the Hanlin Academy Wang was well known for his literary attainments, and was responsible for many of the state papers of his day. A slight work (illustrated) bearing the general title *Er yüan chi* 二園集 (Two garden assemblies), 2 *ch.*, a copy of which is in the Library of Congress, gives some indication of his associations and of his station in polite society. The first volume tells of a meeting on April 6, 1437, in the Apricot Garden 杏園 in Peking of nine men: the three Yang (see Yang Shih-ch'i), Wang Ying (see Li Ch'ang-chi), Wang Chih, Li Shih-mien (q. v.), and three others of consequence at court. Each man contributed a poem, and these are recorded in the volume along with the depiction of the scene, contributed by Hsieh Huan 謝環 (T. 廷循), a favorite landscapist of the emperor Chu Chan-chi (q. v.). Some of Wang Chih's writings were probably commissioned by powerful eunuchs, as in the case of the dedication of the Buddhist temple Fa-hai ssu 法海寺 in 1443. The temple, situated about fifteen miles west of Peking, was rebuilt by the senior eunuch, Li T'ung 李童. Wang Chih is also known to have compiled a textbook for young girls, entitled Nü-chiao hsü-pien 女教續編, as a supplement to similar works by Chu Hsi (1130–1200) and others.

Bibliography

1/169/5a; 3/139/9b; 5/24/25a; 6/2/23b, etc.; 8/19/4a; 9/ 后 2/3b; 11/1/67a; 12/7/1a; 14/3/29a; 40/18 上/7b; 42/46/1a; 43/2/2a; 44/2/14a; 61/120/2b; 64/乙 8/7a; 74/×/3b; 84/乙/13a; 86/6/20b; MSL (1964), Hsüan-tsung and Ying-tsung; KC (1958), 1382, 1389, 1511, 1703, 1705, 1771, 1857, 1862, 1866, 1875, 1948, 2140; I-an chi (NLP, microfilm nos. 993–4), 3/23a, 6/14a, 9/2b; Shen Chieh-fu, Chi-lu hui-pien, 127/3b, 131/12b, 140/12a, 152/3b, 179/7a; Lung Wen-pin 龍文彬 (1821–93), Ming hui yao 明會要, 14/1b; Huang-fu Lu 皇甫錄 (1470–1540), Huang Ming chi-lüeh, 16b; TSCC (1885–88), XXIV:119/25/11a; SK (1930), 170/6b; Yamane Yukio 山根幸夫 and Ogawa Hisashi 小川尚, Ming-jen wen-chi mu-lu 明人文集目錄 (Tokyo, 1966), 16; Arthur W. Hummel, Report of the Librarian of Congress (June 30, 1940), 163.

George Wong

WANG Chih-teng 王穉登 (T. 伯穀, 百穀, 伯固, H. 長生館主), 1535–1612, poet and calligrapher, was a native of Ch'ang-chou 長州 (Soochow). He demonstrated his gifts at a tender age. After becoming a hsiu-ts'ai, he visited Peking in 1564. Here he became the house guest of Yüan Wei (see Liang Meng-lung), a grand secretary. One day Yüan gave a written test to Hanlin bachelors, asking each to compose a verse on the purple peony. None met his approval; but when Wang wrote one, it, in Yüan's opinion, surpassed the others. As a consequence, Yüan employed him as a private secretary and recommended him to be an editor in the Imperial Library. Unfortunately his patron soon passed away, and Wang returned home. In 1567 he revisited Peking. By this time Hsü Chieh (q.v.), who had never liked Yüan Wei, had become grand secretary. So his friends advised Wang Chih-teng not to let his old relations with Yüan become known, but he retorted: "Why shouldn't I? Friendship is friendship. It is everlasting," and he proceeded to publish two poetical works: Yen-shih chi 燕市集 and K'o-yüeh chi 客越集, both reflecting on his association with Yüan.

Following the death of Wen Cheng-ming (q.v.), Wang Chih-teng played a leading role among the literary circles of Soochow for some thirty years. Another cultural leader in the area was Wang Shih-chen (q.v.). According to Ch'ien Ch'ien-i (ECCP), there were three significant poets without official distinction at this time, namely: Shen Ming-ch'en 沈明臣 (T. 嘉則), a distant relative of Shen I-kuan (q.v.), Wang Shu-ch'eng 王叔承 (T. 承父, H. 子幻), and Wang Chih-teng. Of these, Wang Chih-teng was preeminent. Shen Shih-hsing (q.v.), now living in retirement in Soochow, highly appreciated Wang Chih-teng's talents, and frequently met with him to compose poems. Wang Shih-chen was also a friend, but their views on literature were divergent. Wang Shih-chen listed Wang Chih-teng as only one of the forty literati of his time. After the former's death, his second son Wang Shih-su (see Wang Shih-chen) suffered imprisonment. Wang Chih-teng did everything

possible to effect his release. His
behavior made him greatly esteemed. He
was fond of conversing with friends,
often chatting until midnight. People gathered around him, listening to his stories
with untiring interest. In Soochow only
Shen Shih-hsing's house was as crowded
as Wang Chih-teng's. As he was a well-
known calligrapher, tourists coming from
distant parts usually paid him a courtesy
call and treasured his writings as a
souvenir.

In the reign of Emperor Chu I-chün
(q.v.), Grand Secretary Chao Chih-kao
(see Shen I-kuan) recommended Wang
Chih-teng's participation in the compilation of the national history, but the suggestion was not carried out. According
to Chang Hsüan (q. v.), Wang Chih-teng
declined the offer. He spent the rest of
his life at home, pursuing his literary
work. When he was sixty-nine years of
age, he met his former paramour, Ma
Hsiang-lan 馬湘蘭 (original name 馬守眞
T. 玄覺, 玄兒, H. 月嬌, 1548–1604), a
courtesan in Nanking. She had made a
name for herself by painting orchids and
bamboos and writing poems. In former
days Ma Hsiang-lan once expressed a
wish to marry him, but Wang Chih-teng
declined. Now she was fifty-six. In honor
of Wang's birthday, she arranged a big
celebration in Fei-hsü yüan 飛絮園 (Garden
of willow catkins), where drinking, writing, and revelry lasted almost a whole
month. The story came to be described
in an opera entitled Pai-lien ch'ün 白練裙,
written by Cheng Chih-wen 鄭之文 (T.
豹先). The main theme, however, related
the romance of T'u Lung (q.v.) and a
courtesan named K'ou Ssu-er 寇四兒
(original name 寇文華). Both T'u Lung
and Wang Chih-teng were old friends,
then sojourning in Nanking. In the same
year Ma Hsiang-lan breathed her last
quietly and serenely after a long prayer.
She was a devout Buddhist. Her poetical
works were printed in 2 chüan with a
preface by Wang Chih-teng, who also
wrote 12 stanzas as an elegy. Ma Hsiang-

lan wrote one opera as well. Neither of
these is extant.

Wang Chih-teng was survived by
several sons, his youngest Wang Liu 留
(T. 亦房) was a poet. His daughter was
wedded to Wen Yüan-shan 文元善 (T. 子
長, H. 虎丘, 1554–89), son of Wen Chia
(see Wen Cheng-ming). Wang Chih-teng
wrote this epigram on the tomb of Wen
Yüan-shan: "His painting is of the first
quality, and so also is his poetry." Ch'ien
Ch'ien-i, in penning the short biographical sketch of Wang Chih-teng, wrote:
"When I reached thirty sui, I was informed that Mr. Wang was still in good
health. We were acquainted with each
other, but never met. I regret now that I
missed his fine companionship." In his
Ming anthology, Ch'ien Ch'ien-i selected
203 poems from Wang Chih-teng's works.
But Chu I-tsun (ECCP) thought the selection too generous. He remarked: "Wang
Chih-teng's poems are bred in the flesh
rather than in the bones." In any case
his poetical writings are voluminous, being
published under various titles, such as
Chin-ling chi 晉陵集, 2 ch., Chin-ch'ang 金
昌 chi, 4 ch., Yü-hang chi 雨航集, 1 ch.,
etc., running to 15 titles. His complete
works were known as Wang Pai-ku chi 伯
穀集, 24 ch. (Another edition is in 38
chüan.) In the 18th century, this was
ordered burned, but some copies are still
preserved today in China and Japan. The
copy in the Library of Congress is incomplete.

Wang Chih-teng's letters were printed
under the title Mou-yeh 謀野 chi, 10 ch.
(The copy in the Library of Congress is
in 4 chüan.) The sketchbooks, bearing
various titles and describing travel, hob-
bies, etc., have been reprinted in many
collectanea. Wu-she pien 吳社編, 1 ch., gives
account of religious customs in Soochow.
Wu-chün tan-ch'ing chih 吳郡丹青志, 1 ch.,
comments on the famous painters of
Soochow, with Shen Chou (q.v.) topping
the list. I-shih 奕史, 1 ch., is a short history of the game of chess. These three
the editors listed in the Ssu-k'u catalogue,

but failed to include in the Imperial Library.

During this golden age of K'un-ch'ü 崑曲, when T'ang Hsien-tsu (ECCP) and Liang Ch'en-yü (*q.v.*) were making great strides in their art, Wang Chih-teng also wrote one opera known as *Ch'üan-te chi* 全德記, and in collaboration with Chang Ch'i 張琦 (T. 楚叔, H. 騷隱居士) compiled an anthology of san-ch'ü 散曲 (dramatic lyrics), entitled *Wu-sao chi* 吳騷集, 1 *ch.* Later Chang Ch'i and his younger brother, Chang Hsü-ch'u 旭初, expanded the book to 4 *chüan*, and called it *Wu-sao ho-pien.* Another opera by the name of *Ts'ai-p'ao chi* 彩袍記 carries the name of Wang Chih-teng as the author, but there is no proof of this attribution.

In calligraphy Wang Chih-teng's writing was chiefly influenced by Wen Cheng-ming. It is noted for its harmony. His fame as a calligrapher was equal to that of Chou T'ien-ch'iu 周天球 (T. 公瑕, H. 幼海, 1514-95), a close disciple of Wen Cheng-ming. Chou T'ien-ch'iu, however, was asked to write more stone inscriptions than Wang Chih-teng. They were firm friends, although sometimes they made fun of each other. While Chou T'ien-ch'iu compared Wang Chih-teng's handwriting to a praying mantis extending its feelers, Wang Chih-teng retorted that Chou's writing looked like an earthworm groveling in the mud. The well-known art critic and author, Liang Chang-chü (ECCP), once kept two examples of calligraphy, known as Lin lan-t'ing chou 臨蘭亭軸 (imitation of the Lan-t'ing scroll), one by Wang Chih-teng written at the age of seventy-seven *sui*, and the other by Chou T'ien-ch'iu written at the age of sixty-seven *sui*. The handwriting on both scrolls, commented Liang Chang-chü, was forceful and exquisite, showing no sign of senility. It appears that both were competing also for calligraphic honors.

Bibliography

1/288/4b; 3/269/2a; 40/50/24a, 98/3; 64/已16/3b; 84/丁中/10a; 86/14/41b, 23/55; SK (1930), 114/4a/ 10a, 143/8a; Ch'ien Ch'ien-i, *Lieh-ch'ao shih-chi*, 丁8/23, 丁9/16b; Chang Hsüan, *Hsi-yüan wen-chien lu*, 22/18; Shen Te-fu, *Ku-ch'ü tsa-yen*, 15; Hsü Ch'in 徐沁 (fl. 1694), *Ming-hua lu* 明畫錄, 6/70; Liang Chang-chü, *T'ui-an t'i-pa*, 8/23a; Shih Yün-yü (ECCP), *Tu-hsüeh-lu kao*, 二稿中/26; Ch'en Cho 陳焯, *Hsiang-kuan-chai yü-shang-pien* 湘管齋寓賞編, 4/125; Sun Tien-ch'i (1957), 26; *Naikaku Bunko Catalogue*, 356; *Sho-en* 書苑, 10/3; Fu Hsi-hua 傅惜華, *Ming-tai ch'uan-ch'i ch'üan-mu* 明代傳奇全目, 87.

Liu Lin-sheng

WANG Chin 王瑾 (T. 潤德), died 1451, original name Ch'en Wu 陳蕪, a native of Chiao-chih (Annam), was one of the most favored eunuchs in the early years of the Ming dynasty. On his return from military service in Chiao-chih, presumably in 1408, the duke of Ying-kuo, Chang Fu (*q.v.*), brought with him several boys of presentable appearance to Nanking, made them eunuchs, and sent them to the palace as a gift to the emperor, Chu Ti (*q.v.*). This group included, besides Ch'en Wu, Fan Hung 范弘 (original *ming* 安), Juan An, and Juan Lang (*qq.v.*), all of whom were to become well known in government circles. Fan Hung, who acquired a superior education, rose to be charged with the directorate of ceremonial (a eunuch agency) in the period of Cheng-t'ung and died in the T'u-mu disaster (*see* Wang Chen); Juan An, a functionary in the ministry of Works, was responsible in the same years and later for much of the rebuilding of Peking; and Juan Lang served in the treasury.

Ch'en Wu's initial assignment was to serve in the residence of the heir apparent, Chu Chan-chi (*q.v.*). Some time after the latter ascended the throne (1426), Ch'en's name was changed to Wang Chin, and in due course he was given charge of the directorate of ceremonial, a post of considerable power. When the emperor found it necessary to take the field against his uncle, Chu Kao-hsü (*q.v.*) Wang Chin accompanied him. The monarch apparently appreciated his counsel on military matters, consulted him frequently throughout his reign, and gave him several military assignments. In July, 1429, Wang joined the expeditionary army of General Shih Chao 史昭 (d. February, 1444) against the rebellious Uighur chieftain of the Ch'ü-hsien 曲先 Guard (southwest of Su-chou 肅州 in modern Kansu), who was accused of robbing the envoys from the Western regions and blocking their passage. In 1432, in addition to other monetary gifts, the emperor presented Wang with four golden seals, one of which carried the inscription "Chung-kan i-tan" 忠肝義膽 (loyal and faithful). He also awarded him two palace girls as maids, and offered an appointment to his adopted son Ch'en Lin 陳琳, who then assumed the new name Wang Ch'un 春 (椿). By this time Wang Chin must have also acquired considerable property, for when the court ordered him and five other high officials to surrender the land they illegally appropriated in Kansu and turn it over for military farming in June, 1437, they were reported to own more than six hundred ch'ing (almost 10,000 acres).

Wang Chin continued to serve the next emperor Chu Ch'i-chen (q.v.). When the latter decided to abandon the costly expeditions of Cheng Ho (q.v.) shortly after his accession, he dispatched Wang Chin to T'ai-ts'ang 太倉, near Soochow, to take charge of the ocean-going vessels. In December, 1448, when a punitive army was sent to Fukien to suppress the rebellion of Teng Mao-ch'i (q.v.), Wang Chin and another eunuch, Ts'ao Chi-hsiang (q. v.), were appointed to supervise the firearms units.

Wang Chin lived into the reign of the succeeding emperor, Chu Ch'i-yü (q. v.), and enjoyed his confidence. When Wang died, the emperor, in addition to giving him an elaborate burial, is said to have awarded his family some five hundred thousand strings of cash. The reason for such a lavish gift, according to the

Shui-tung jih-chi of Yeh Sheng (q.v.), who based himself on the authority of Ch'en Hsün (see Lü Yüan), was in recompense for Wang Chin's "protection of the heir apparent"; this seems to suggest that Wang supported him in his designation of Chu Chien-chi (see Chu Ch'i-yü) as the heir to the throne. The favors granted to the Wang family did not continue, however; immediately following his death Wang Chin's residence in Nanking was converted into a monastery known as Ch'eng-en ssu 承恩寺, and in March, 1457, the reinstated emperor, Chu Ch'i-chen, ordered the transfer of Wang Chin's land and that of several other eunuchs to his new favorite, Ts'ao Chi-hsiang, apparently as a reward for the part he took in the restoration of his throne.

Bibliography

1/304/5b, 7a; 3/283/7b; 42/25/6b; 61/158/3b; MSL (1963), Hsüan-tsung, 542, 1697, Ying-tsung, 599, 5860; TSCC (1885-88), XIV: 274/22/17a; Yeh Sheng, Shui-tung jih-chi (Taipei, 1965), 34/1b; Wang Shih-chen, "Chung-kuan k'ao," 中官考, in Yen-shan-t'ang pieh-chi (Taipei, 1965), 90/14b, 16b; Shen Te-fu, Wan-li yeh-hu pien (1959), 156; Ko Yin-liang 葛寅亮 (cs 1601), Chin-ling fan-ch'a chih 金陵梵剎志 (1936 ed.), 23/1b.

L. Carrington Goodrich and
Hok-lam Chan

WANG Ching-hung 王景弘 (or 宏), died ca. 1434, a eunuch and contemporary of Cheng Ho (q.v.), was second in command on several of the admiral's voyages. His name first appears in the records on July 11, 1405, when he joined the first of the great expeditions to the South Seas. This one lasted until September 21, 1407, having been dispatched ostensibly to carry imperial edicts to the rulers of countries to be visited, and to present them with gold embroidered silk appropriate to their rank, but actually to demand tribute and, according to some legends, to make a search for the vanished Emperor Chu Yün-wen (*q.v.*). The fleet included sixty-two (or sixty-three) large and 255 smaller vessels, and touched at Champa, Java, Sumudra, Lambri, Ceylon, and Calicut. Wang went too on the second and third voyages of 1407-9 and 1409-11, on which the fleets (now somewhat reduced in size) revisited some of the same countries and made additional stops on the coast of India and at Hormuz. In Ceylon, on the third expedition, the Chinese encountered opposition, suppressed it, seized the king and queen and their children, and took them captive to Nanking. On this occasion the Chinese erected at Galle a tablet bearing a date equivalent to February 15, 1409; apparently prepared in advance in Nanking, it carries a trilingual inscription (Chinese, Persian, and Tamil). This inscription reports that the principal envoys were Cheng Ho and Wang Kuei-t'ung 貴通 or Wang Ch'ing-lien 清濂. This is puzzling, as other sources relate that the envoys who accompanied Cheng were Wang Ching-hung, Hou Hsien (*q.v.*), Li Hsing 李興 (fl. 1403-30), Chu Liang 朱良 (fl. 1409-30), Chou Man 周滿 (fl. 1409-22), Hung Pao (*see* Cheng Ho), Yang Chen 楊眞 (fl. 1409-30), Chang Ta 張達, and Wu Chung 吳忠—all grand eunuchs; also the regional military commissioner Chu Chen 朱眞, Fei Hsin, and Ma Huan (*qq.v.*), the religious leader 掌教 Ha-san 哈三 (Ḥasan), and P'u Ho-jih 蒲和日 (fl. 1409-1417).

The name of Wang Ching-hung appears again at the beginning of 1425 when the new emperor, Chu Kao-chih (*q.v.*), ordered Cheng Ho to assure the safety of the southern capital (Nanking) by employing the troops who had gone among the "barbarians," and proposed that he should take counsel from Wang Ching-hung and others. These eunuchs were commanded as well to repair the palace buildings of Nanking and buy gold leaf for their beautification. Five years later Emperor Chu Chan-chi (*q.v.*) decided to dispatch a seventh expedition, and again named Cheng Ho and Wang Ching-hung as his

chief agents. This time they visited some twenty kingdoms, including the Maldive Islands and Arabia, and such places on the eastern coast of Africa as Mogadishu, Brava, and Juba. Their main fleet, starting out in February, 1431, reached Hormuz in January, 1433, and returned in July of the same year. On the way one or more vessels stopped over in Taiwan, at Ch'ih-ch'ien 赤嵌, where Wang is credited with curing certain aborigines of an ailment by adding a potion to the water and making them bathe in it.

In 1434 Wang, this time in command, was sent on an expedition to Sumatra to tender the sympathy of the imperial court to the king, whose younger brother, Ha-li-chih-han 哈利之漢, had died in Peking. Reportedly Wang lost his life in a shipwreck off the coast of Java while on this mission. He must have left a deep impression, for his name is still remembered there as Wang San-pao 三寶 (the three jewels or Triratna)—an epithet applied in this age to certain important eunuchs. A grotto in a temple at Semarang is named San-pao tung 洞, and a cult among the Chinese residents kept his memory green for four centuries and is still alive. Pictures of the grotto and of the tablet honoring him are reproduced in the *T'oung Pao* of 1898.

Bibliography

1/304/2b; MSL (1963), Yung-lo, 0685, Hung-hsi, 0280, 2232, Hsüan-te, 0219; Lu Jung 陸容 (1436 -94), *Shu-yüan tsa-chi* 菽園雜記 (TsSCC), 23; Hsü Yü-hu 徐玉虎, *Ta-lu tsa-chih* 大陸雜誌, Vol. 13 (July 15, 1956), 21, Vol. 16 (January 15, 1958), 19 (April 30), 14 (May 15), 22; T. Yamamoto 山本達郎: "Cheng Ho's Expeditions to the West" 鄭和の西征, TG 21 (1934), 528; W. P. Groeneveldt, *Notes on the Malay archipelago and Malacca compiled from Chinese sources* (1880, repr. Jakarta, 1960), 42, 90; Fang Hao 方豪 in *Tung-fang tsa-chih* 東方雜志, Vol. 1, no. 2 (August 1, 1967), 45; Liang Chia-pin 梁嘉彬, "Hsiao Liu-ch'iu k'ao" 小琉球考, *Taiwan wen-hsien*, v. 19, no. 1 (March 27, 1968), 164; I. W. Young, "Sam Po Tong.... la grotto de Sam Po," TP (A) IX (1898), 93; W. W. Rockhill, "Notes on the Relations and Trade of China--

during the Fourteenth Century," TP XVI (1915), 92; P. Pelliot, "Pāpīyān—Po-siun," TP, XXX (1933), 91; id., "Les grands voyages maritimes chinnois au début du XVᵉ siècle," ibid. 239, 267, 273, 283; id., "Notes additionelles sur Tcheng Houo et sur ses voyages," TP, XXXI (1935), 293, 310; J. J. L. Duyvendak, "The True Dates of the Chinese Maritime Expeditions in the Early Fifteenth Century," TP, XXXIV (1938), 343, 389, 391.

Lee Hwa-chou and
L. Carrington Goodrich

WANG Chiu-ssu 王九思 (T. 敬夫, H. 渼陂, 紫閣山人), 1468-1551, famous as writer of san-ch'ü (song poems) and as one of the "seven early masters" of the classical prose style (ku-wen-tz'u, *see* Li Meng-yang), was a native of Hu 鄠-hsien, Shensi, close to the home districts of his good friend K'ang Hai and the eunuch Liu Chin (qq.v.). His grandfather served as a magistrate in Shansi and Shantung, and his father, Wang Ju 儒 (T. 友宗, 1438-1512), rose to be director of studies in the Nan-yang 南陽 prefecture in Honan. Wang Chiu-ssu won a high position in the metropolitan and palace examinations of 1496, was taken into the Hanlin Academy, and later promoted to the position of director of a bureau in the ministry of Personnel. In this position he became more involved in Liu Chin's political actions than his younger friend K'ang Hai, since the ministry played a key role if any attempt were to be made to revise the personnel of the imperial government. In building up a faction, Liu also preferred his fellow provincials from Shensi to the central officials of predominantly southern origin. After Liu's downfall, Wang was demoted to become assistant sub-prefect in Shou-chou 壽州 (Anhwei) and then cashiered like K'ang Hai. Coming from "the same area, the same office, and receiving the same demotion after Liu Chin's downfall," as the *Ming-shih* narrates, both prose and poetry writers from China's northwest were destined for a life in common.

Wang also wrote a one-act drama on the Chung-shan lang 中山狼 (Wolf of Central Mountain) theme (like two other dramatists of the time). His magnum opus, however, was the drama on Tu Fu's sentimental springtime journey, entitled *Tu Tzu-mei ku-chiu yu-ch'un chi* 杜子美沽酒遊春記, also called *Ch'ü-chiang ch'un* 曲江春 (*Sheng Ming tsa-chü* 盛明雜劇 edition, with a preface of K'ang Hai dated 1519). It is said that his account of the wicked T'ang minister Li Lin-fu (d. 753) is a covert attack on Li Tung-yang (q.v.), a bureaucrat and master of bureaucratic literature. Wang died after more than forty years at home, aged eighty-three.

Besides editing his home district's gazetteer, the *Hu-hsien chih*, Wang left a collection of literary works: the *Mei-p'o chi* 渼陂集, 16 ch., to which was later added a supplementary collection, *hsü-chi* 續集, 3 ch., edited by Wang Hsien 王獻 (T. 惟從 H. 南澧, 木石子, 1487-1547, cs 1523) and Weng Wan-ta 翁萬達 (T. 仁夫, H. 東涯, 1498-November 30, 1552, cs 1526, Pth. 襄毅). These writings were well received in Ming times and went through several editions. There is also a complete collection of his song poetry, entitled *Pi shan yüeh-fu* 碧山樂府, 8 ch., printed in 1640 as an appendix to the *Mei p'o ch'üan* 全 -chi, an enlarged edition of the *Mei-p'o chi*.

K'ang Hai and Wang Chiu-ssu at first belonged to the inner circle of Ming China's bureaucratic elite, namely the Hanlin Academy, which stood in close proximity to the Grand Secretariat. Usually the best writers among the palace examination degree holders were selected for it to prepare for literary duties and possibly a higher service in the central bureaucracy. Wang and K'ang unfortunately became involved in court politics which interrupted their careers in the government. Being northerners and active promoters of a new style of writing, they got into trouble with the bureaucracy then dominated by southerners. Their downfall may well have been caused by the literary

and political antagonism which characterized many a dispute in the northern capital.
As masters of the Chinese language, however, they helped to bridge the gap between the conservative ancient style and
language more like the southern by writing song poems of a new kind; in this
style they came to be acclaimed by later
critics of the present century, such as Jen
Chung-min (see Feng Wei-min) and Cheng
Ch'ien (see Chao Nan-hsing) as two of
China's greatest masters. In this respect
they have a secure place among the best
writers of Ming China.

Bibliography

1/286/13a; 5/22/25a; *Ming-shan ts'ang Wen-yüan-chi*
名山藏文苑記, 81/25; SK (1930), 176/2b, 200/8a;
Ch'ung-hsiu 重修 *Hu-hsien chih* (1967), 4/3b,
5/6b; Cheng Ch'ien, "Wang Chiu-ssu *Pi-shan
yüeh-fu* shou-lü chü-li" 守律擧例, in *Ts'ung shih
tao ch'ü* 從詩到曲 (Taipei, 1961), 213, 217.

                                    Tilemann Grimm

WANG Ch'iung 王瓊 (T. 德華, H. 晉溪),
October 3, 1459-August 20 (or 22), 1532,
official, was a native of Taiyuan, Shansi.
A precocious child, he could write at four
sui and four years later had read the
Book of History. A *chin-shih* of 1484, he
was assigned to the ministry of Works
and appointed a year later a secretary in
that ministry. From 1493 to 1496 he
served as director of one of the three
sections of the Grand Canal and compiled
a handbook about the canal as a whole
(*Ts'ao-ho t'u-chih* 漕河圖志, 8 *ch.*, printed
in 1496) which, according to the comments of his successors, was accurate even
in minute details. In 1496 he was transferred to the ministry of Revenue, where
for three years he was in charge of the
department responsible for the rations
and salaries for the offices in Peking and
for the men stationed along the northern
frontiers. He thus became familiar with the
organization and supplies of the frontier
armies. He next served as an intendant

in Shantung (1499-1501) and in Honan
(1503-5), as one of the administrative
commissioners of Honan (1505-6), as a
vice-minister of Revenue (1506-8, 1512-13)
in Peking, and as a vice-minister of Personnel in Nanking (1508-9). After that he
held the exalted offices of minister of
Revenue (1513-15), of War (1515-20),
and of Personnel (1520-21).

This was the notorious Cheng-te period
when a high official had difficulty in maintaining his dignity and integrity or even
in carrying out his proper duties. Emperor
Chu Hou-chao (*q.v.*) abandoned himself to
pleasure seeking and entrusted the imperial duties at first to the eunuch, Liu
Chin (*q.v.*), and later to a group of
unscrupulous figures (see Chiang Pin).
Several times the emperor, accompanied
by his favorites, left Peking on extended
trips while rebellions and local uprisings
broke out in the empire. As minister of
War, Wang Ch'iung maintained order in
the capital and appointed men of talent
to strategic posts. Especially during the
rebellion of the prince of Ning, Chu
Ch'en-hao (see Wang Shou-jen), in 1519,
a great deal of the credit for the speedy
suppression of the Nanchang uprisings
was due to Wang Ch'iung for first placing
competent commanders in the east and
south and then, when the fighting started,
for directing the campaign efficiently and
quietly. In order to perform his own
duties he had to placate the emperor's
favorites to a degree. For some reason,
however, he was detested by certain of
the censors and was not on friendly terms
with Grand Secretary Yang T'ing-ho (*q.
v.*).

After the Chia-ching emperor succeeded to the throne in 1521, the former
emperor's favorites were executed. Grand
Secretary Yang, for his part in enthron-
ing the new emperor, retained his power.
Wang Ch'iung, accused of certain misdeeds, was first imprisoned and then exiled
to Sui-te in northern Shensi, where he
remained for five years.

In 1524 Yang left the court and a

new group of favorites of the emperor came to power. Led by Kuei O and Chang Fu-ching (*qq.v.*), the group tried to enlist all who had opposed Yang. Three years later they recommended Wang for pardon, and in March, 1528, he was given the title of minister of War and sent to Ku-yüan 固原 as supreme commander of the Shensi and Kansu frontier area. By this time approaching seventy yet still energetic, he served meritoriously for three and a half years. During his term of office he advocated peace with Turfan but pursued a stern and relentless policy towards the Mongol and Tibetan invaders. When recall came late in 1531, the northwestern border was at peace and the local people regretted seeing him leave.

On his return to Peking he was named minister of Personnel. At once some censors, calling him an old rascal of the former reign, tried to have him removed. Nevertheless, he held his post until his death six months later. He was posthumously granted the title of grand preceptor, and given the name Kung-hsiang 恭襄. Undoubtedly an able administrator, Wang Ch'iung was particularly suited to the ministries of Revenue and War. It is said that he knew all the details about the granaries and provisions on the frontier posts and could tell at once whether a commander's request for supplies was justified. Huo T'ao (*q.v.*), who had never met him in person, became his admirer when Huo examined his documents in the archives of the ministry of War. Huo later wrote the eulogy inscribed on Wang's tombstone in which he went out of his way to clear Wang of the charges made against him in 1521. Li Chih (*q.v.*) also supported Wang against detractors who had accused him of accepting bribes.

In addition to *Ts'ao-ho t'u-chih*, Wang left two collections of memorials: one, known as *Hu-pu tsou-i* 戶部奏議, 2 *ch.*, covers the period from 1513 to 1515 when he was minister of Revenue; the other, known as *Chin-ch'i tsou-i* 晉溪奏議

(also known as *Pen-ping fu-tsou* 本兵敷奏), 14 *ch.*, covers the years from 1515 to 1521 when he was minister of War. *Huang Ming ching-shih wen-pien* (*see* Ch'en Tzu-lung, ECCP) includes thirty-seven of his memorials. His remaining writings include biographical sketches of Ming officials who rose from sub-official yamen clerks to high positions, *Yüan-ts'ao ming-ch'en lu* 掾曹名臣錄, and supplement, *hsü-lu* 續錄 each in 1 *chüan*; two accounts, each in 1 *chüan*, relating his encounters with Tatars and Tibetans during the period from 1521 to 1531, known as *Pei-lu (pien) shih-chi* 北虜(邊)事蹟 and *Hsi-fan shih-chi* 西番事蹟 respectively; and finally a collection of random jottings on court affairs in 1 *chüan*, known as *Shuang-ch'i tsa-chi* 雙溪雜記.

Bibliography

1/198/8a; 3/146/12b; 5/24/106a; 63/17/363; MSL (1965), Wu-tsung 3610, 3641, Shih-tsung, 3158, 3276; Kao Ming-feng 高鳴鳳, ed., *Chin-hsien hui-yen* 今獻彙言 (Shanghai, 1937), bk. 6; Yüan Ch'iung 袁裘, ed., *Chin-sheng Yü-chen chi* (Peking, 1959), bks. 11–12; KC (1958), 3207 3211, 3457, 3467; SK (1930), 56/3a; 61/4b; 75/1b; 100/3b.

Benjamin E. Wallacker

WANG Ch'ung 王寵 (T. 履仁, 履吉, H. 雅宜山人), 1494–1533, poet and calligrapher, was a native of Wu 吳-hsien (Soochow). His father, born in Wu-chiang 吳江, south of Soochow, was originally surnamed Chang 章 but was adopted by the Wang family of Soochow. In his youth Wang Ch'ung studied under Ts'ai Yü (*see* Lu Chih). Wen Cheng-ming, T'ang Yin (*qq.v.*), and other literati of the locality regarded Wang Ch'ung highly as a promising young poet. After Wang became a *hsiu-ts'ai*, Hu Tsuan-tsung (*see* Chiao Fang), then prefect of Soochow, recommended him for study at the National University. He took part in the provincial examination eight times without success, despite his extensive knowledge and wide acquaintance with the Classics. In the end he gave himself up to reading, writing, and visiting famous mountains and lakes. According to the tombstone inscription written by Wen Cheng-ming, Wang Ch'ung was a tall, handsome man, loving tranquillity and repose, never speaking a vulgar word, and never flaunting his literary talent. He made a name for himself even though he passed away at an early age.

His elder brother, Wang Shou 守 (T. 履約, cs 1526), rose to be governor of Yün-yang 郧陽 (1543-44). The daughter of T'ang Yin married one of Wang Ch'ung's sons.

In calligraphy Wang Ch'ung is sometimes ranked next to Wen Cheng-ming and Chu Yün-ming (*q.v.*). Many commentators, including Ho Liang-chün (*q.v.*), considered that Wang Ch'ung's refined handwriting was a reflection of his unblemished character. He wrote more verse than prose. Ku Lin (*see* Yüan Chiung), a contemporary poet in Nanking, records that Wang Ch'ung set a high standard for poets. He seldom painted, but the few examples of his art that are known show a lofty style.

Wang's literary works were gathered together under the title *Ya-i-shan-jen chi* 雅宜山人集, 10 *ch.*, 8 *chüan* of verse and 2 of prose. Published in the Chia-ching period this book was reproduced in 1968, and is also available on microfilm. Yü Hsien (*see* Feng Wei-min), who spent most of his days compiling an anthology of Ming poetry, entitled *Sheng-Ming pai-chia shih* 盛明百家詩, published one *chüan* of Wang Ch'ung's poems; the title is given as *Wang Lü-chi chi* 履吉集. This anthology, containing the output of 160 poets and 17,600 of their poems, is known only in a Ming edition; it was copied in the 18th century, however, into the *Ssu-k'u ch'üan-shu* and so exists in manuscript as well.

[Editors' note: Ho Liang-chün, after a visit to Wang Ch'ung, left the following vivid sketch of him: "At that time Ya-i (Wang's *hao*), though an invalid, always stood up to talk to us. He did not like to speak in his dialect but always preferred the official speech. Our conversation concentrated on his recollections of great men of the past, which he related one after another like a string of pearls. Brilliantly eloquent speaking in a voice deep and musical, he gave an impression of dignity and intelligence.... a pity he died before forty. Today I can't see anyone of his stature." By official speech, kuan-hua 官話, Ho apparently meant the Peking dialect which most southerners, aspiring to high office in the imperial court, learned as a necessary accomplishment.

As Wang failed to pass the civil examination he was barred from officialdom and came to be known as a poet only. Yet, as Ch'ien Ch'ien-i (ECCP) cynically remarked, Wang Shou, who did rise to be a governor, is remembered merely as the brother of Wang Ch'ung.]

Bibliography

5/115/86a; Wang Shih-chen, *Yen-chou ssu-pu kao*, 132/10a; Weng Fang-kang (ECCP), *Fu-ch'u-chai wen-chi*, 9/10a, 31/15b, 32/10a; *Wu-hsien chih* (1933), 66 上 /22a; *Su-chou-fu chih* (1881), 7/17a, 50/37a, 80/11a; SK (1930), 176/18b, 192/8a; TSCC (1885-88), XVII: 786/20/8b, XXIII: 102/90/6b, XXIV: 121/27/17b; *Shang-hai po-wu-kuan ts'ang li-tai fa-shu hsüan-chi* 上海博物舘藏歷代法書選集 (Shanghai, 1964), 17; *Shodo zenshu* 書道全集, Vol. 20 (1931), 20/8, 40; *Sho-en* 書苑 (1939), 3/5/26; *Seikado Catalogue* 725.

Liu Lin-sheng

WANG Ch'ung-ku 王崇古 (T. 學甫, H. 鑑川, Pth. 襄毅), May 4, 1515-January 3, 1589, a native of P'u-chou 蒲州, Shansi, was the governor-general who negotiated the peace settlement with Altan-qaɣan (*q. v.*) in the winter of 1570/71. After becoming a *chin-shih* in 1541, Wang served successively as a secretary and a director in the ministry of Justice, prefect of An-ch'ing 安慶, Nan-Chihli, and of Ju-ning 汝寧, Honan, before his appointment in 1555 to the newly created office of intendant of Ch'ang-chou and Chinkiang circuit in Nan-Chihli and charged to combat the pirates (see Chang Ching). Always active on the front line, on occasion he accompanied the troops to sea. In 1559 he was transferred to northern Shensi where three years later he became the provincial surveillance commissioner. In 1564 he was advanced to be right administration commissioner of Honan but barely four months later another court order elevated him to the governorship of Ninghsia and concurrently right assistant censor-in-chief.

The frontier defense during the reign of Chu Hou-ts'ung (q. v.) was grossly mismanaged. The emperor, while paying no genuine attention to state affairs, exercised his power arbitrarily and trusted compliant favorites (see Yen Sung and Ch'iu Luan) who constantly fed him false reports. When something went awry the monarch directed his rage toward some hapless officials and punished them. His despotic rule allowed little possibility for reform. The army was undermanned, yet the rising military budget caused an annual deficit in the state treasury. Military supplies were delivered behind schedule; commanding officers were under stringent orders to keep their units intact. Those who suffered battle losses were deemed as lacking in generalship, regardless of the military situation. In the meanwhile the Mongol hordes under Altan-qaγan were growing powerful enough to make incursions along the entire frontier from Liaotung to Ninghsia. Advised by a party of Chinese fugitives who, for one reason or another, had fled to the north to render service to the nomadic chieftain, Altan-qaγan began to penetrate deep into Ninghsia, Shansi, and Pei-Chihli, several times threatening Peking. In the 1550s and 1560s his plundering of the northern provinces was almost a routine annual event. The imperial army, after suffering a long series of defeats, was seriously demoralized. Generals did not hesitate to bribe the Mongols for temporary respite in their respective territories, or,

even worse, to make arrangements with the enemy, accept his bribes, and allow him free passage at strategic points. Only when the invaders were heading home with their loot would they give chase. Upon recovering a few civilians captured by the Mongols, they unabashedly reported these actions as victories. Those who refused to do so and stood firm against the nomadic warriors were often outnumbered and annihilated by the tribesmen. Wang Ch'ung-ku, upon arrival in Ninghsia, disclosed that Chinese troops stationed at the forward posts dared not venture outside their encampments and had to pay the nomads for safe conduct while fetching drinking water and gathering grass and dry wood for fuel.

Wang's administration in Ninghsia was short of a miracle; through his vigorous leadership, however, he restored confidence and disciplined the officer corps. Frequently shifting his battle formations along the border lands, he impressed the Mongol tribesmen so much that they seldom attempted to probe his territory. At times his patrols fought the nomads outside the Great Wall, probably on equal terms. The engagements seem to have been indecisive, as the damage he declared inflicted on the enemy was never spectacular. That he was able, nonetheless, to take the offensive at a time when all other territorial commands could not even hold their defense lines indicated a significant turning point in the offing. His merit was recognized. In 1567 Wang was promoted to be governor-general of Shensi with the rank of right vice minister of War, the Ninghsia front remaining under his jurisdiction.

The accession to the throne of Chu Tsai-hou (q. v.) in 1566 and the appointment to grand secretaryships of Kao Kung and Chang Chü-cheng (q.v.) also marked a change in central leadership. Both grand secretaries took a keen interest in frontier defense. Their personal hand in state affairs was effected, in accordance with the usage of these days, largely through informal but quite elaborate letters to the provincial governors. Their discussion by correspondence with Wang on a variety of subjects enabled the latter to gain support in the inner court before his formal memorials to the throne were submitted. In the next few years the governor-general took full advantage of this channel of communication. Subsequently he memorialized the emperor to keep the military budget of his command intact, pointing out that any budgetary reduction must start with the pay and allowances of the supernumerary personnel at the capital. He recommended that the escapees from the Mongol prison camps should be well treated and rewarded, not indiscriminately detained and executed as traitors. Above all, he petitioned that the frontier governors-general should have sufficient freedom in formulating their war schemes and not be interfered with by the censorial officials who criticized their strategy without seeing the terrain, knowing the weather, appraising the morale of the army, and studying the enemy disposition. Most of such recommendations met with imperial approval. As an army commander, Wang stressed the importance of military intelligence. He himself had an intimate knowledge of the various Mongol leaders. His reports detailed their personalities, named the Chinese advisers at their service, and circumstantially related their family and command relations. Later such knowledge proved to be an enormous asset during his confrontation with Altan-qaγan.

Wang's transfer from Shensi to Shansi early in 1570 was most opportune, as nine months later Baγa-ači (d. 1583), Altan-qaγan's favorite grandson, turned up in the latter territory and surrendered himself. The youth had deserted his grandfather after a family quarrel. He did not realize that his action would play into Wang's hands. Working closely with Fang Feng-shih (*see* Liang Meng-lung), governor of Tatung, Wang kept the news within his command for a fortnight before reporting it to Peking. Once that was done, lengthy discussion by correspondence between the governor-general and the two grand secretaries ensued. It is difficult to ascertain who originally outlined the strategy, but apparently all three agreed upon the scheme. It called for liberal treatment of Baγa-ači. Should Altan-qaγan ask for the grandson's safe return, the chieftain must change his warlike posture and petition the emperor. To demonstrate his sincerity he must first surrender his Chinese advisers to the governor-general. Should Altan-qaγan use the incident to start a new war, the governor-general would execute Baγa-ači to answer the challenge. The officials were convinced that not all the Mongols were enthusiastic over revenging the death of the latter, who, in their eyes, had deserted their tribe. In case Altan-qaγan should neither humble himself nor attack, then the imperial government would proceed to groom Baγa-ači as a Mongol leader to attract his tribesmen.

As it turned out, Altan-qaγan needed little persuasion to come to terms, He had advanced toward Tatung with twenty thousand mounts. Realizing that his grandson's life was at stake, he toned down his demand, withdrew his forces, pledged that never again would he invade Chinese territory, and delivered to Wang the nine advisers whom the Chinese wanted most. The emperor was pleased. Baγa-ači was returned to his grandfather as agreed upon. Wang, still governor-general' received the rank of minister of War. But the case was by no means closed; more difficulties lay ahead.

The emperor's acceptance of Altan-qaγan's submission implied recognition of him as the head of a border state, and as such, entitled to tributary relations with the empire. Some noble title had to be granted, and similar honors bestowed on lesser chieftains. Another corollary was that once relations with the Mongols were normalized, trading privileges would have to be extended to the tribesmen at

large. Contemporary writers emphasize
that, in his preliminary negotiations with
Altan-qaɣan, Wang never committed himself to such terms; he merely promised
that if the Mongol leader would follow
his advice, he would in turn plead on his
behalf. It suffices to say that a tacit
understanding had been reached. From a
practical point of view the opening of
trade was also inevitable under the
circumstances, for, if the tribesmen should
be denied access to their necessities
from the Chinese market, they would
necessarily resort to plunder again.

To maneuver the court into accepting
these terms, however, involved more
difficulty than pacifying the tribesmen.
With the support of Chang Chü-cheng
and Kao Kung, Wang submitted his eight-
point memorial to the emperor that winter, outlining the aforementioned settlement. The document spells out every con-
ceivable detail with regard to the opening
of trade, specifying even the kind of
cooking pots (which could not be easily
recast into weapons by the tribesmen)
that would be permitted in the market.
In his petition Wang emphasized that,
with a peaceful settlement, the imperial
government could purchase time to
strengthen its frontier defense. Despite its
cautious approach, the proposal nevertheless stirred up a storm of criticism in
Peking. Some officials pointed out that
under the reign of Chu Hou-ts'ung the
Mongols were granted trading privileges
in 1551 which ended only in the renewal
of hostilities the following year, and, after
the incident, the emperor was supposed
to have issued a standing order making
any further suggestion of trade with the
Mongols a crime punishable by death.
Others cited the parallel between Wang's
proposal and submissions to the nomads
in earlier times. Still others wanted Wang
to guarantee that the Mongols would not
breach the proposed settlement in a hundred years. When the emperor brushed
aside such objections and reservations,
one censor brought an impeachment act-

ion against Chang Ssu-wei (*q. v.*), Wang
Ch'ung-ku's nephew then serving as a vice
minister of Personnel. In his arraignment
the official accused Chang's father, a salt
merchant, of making profit by violating
imperial laws regulating the gabelle, and
insisted that Wang, as a relative of Chang,
must also be held responsible. Wang
in turn charged his critic with corruption.
Then all the investigating censors representing the thirteen circuits signed a joint
impeachment against Wang, accusing him
of silencing criticism. Annoyed, the emperor, after giving each side a sharp reprimand, ignored the charges and countercharges.

Wang's eight-point memorial was referred to the ministry of War for comment.
The minister, Kuo Ch'ien 郭乾 (T. 一泉.
cs 1538), unwilling to assume the responsibility, suggested that the issue was of
such importance that opinions must be
obtained from a joint conference of the
ranking officials from the military and
civil bureaucracy. The ensuing meeting
seems to have been attended by all military commissioners-in-chief, vice ministers
and above, and representatives from the
censorate, altogether no fewer than forty
officials. The deliberation resulted in
twenty-two voices for the proposal, seventeen against, and five approving the tributary relations but not the opening of the
market. The emperor was dissatisfied
with the result and ordered the ministry
of War to undertake further deliberation.
The issue hung over the court throughout
the winter. Only after prodding by Chang
Chü-cheng and Kao Kung did the monarch
accept the proposal. Altan-qaɣan was
enfeoffed as the prince of Shun-i and
sixty-three chieftains under him received
imperial commissions ranging from lieu-
tenant-general to captain. A formal agreement with the prince was reached in
June, 1571, or more than half a year
after Baɣa-ači's defection. Containing
thirteen articles, this agreement, still extant, resembles a treaty to the extent that
it includes provisions for repatriation of

fugitives and punishment for killing and plundering. But in the preamble it specifies that the Mongols had to take an oath facing the sky, pledging that they and their posterity would never again invade China, and that any chieftain violating this rule was punishable by the disbandment of his tribe. The agreement was renewed and amended in 1577, 1587, and 1603. Wang remained as governor-general in Shansi until 1573, when, in the autumn, he was recalled to Peking and put in charge of the capital garrison. Two years later he became minister of Justice. In the spring of 1577 he was transferred to head the ministry of War.

His peace settlement was a success inasmuch as the Mongols never again appeared as a major menace to the Ming empire. The tributary trade, as well as the subsequent opening of the market, did result in some extra expenses to the government which were met out of army funds. But the diversion of this money, involving only a negligible fraction of the military budget, in no significant way weakened the frontier defense. Evaluating Wang's statesmanship, Ming writers tended to commend his resourcefulness in dealing with the tribesmen; what they overlooked is that it required more courage and steadfastness on his part to win on the home front. Undoubtedly he would not have succeeded without the support of Chang Chü-cheng. After the settlement of 1571, the two officials became much attached to each other. But this friendship did not last long. According to the composers of Wang's tombstone inscriptions, as minister of Justice (1575-77) Wang defended one of Chang's critics, Fu Ying-chen 傅應楨 (T. 公善, cs 1571), and exposed the disobedience of Ch'i Chi-kuang (q. v.) against Chang's orders. This strained the relationship between minister and grand secretary, eventually leading to Wang's retirement, after serving a few months as minister of war in 1577. No such explanation appears in the official annals. What does appear is a record of

Fu Ying-chen's memorial (of January, 1576) to Emperor Chu I-chün (q. v.), in which he insinuated that Chang Chücheng was like Wang An-shih (1021-86), together with a notice dated November 13, 1577, of Wang Ch'ung-ku's retirement within the forty-nine day mourning period granted Chang by the emperor upon the death of his father. Preceding his retirement, Wang was impeached by several censorial officials mainly because at this time Altan-qaγan was requesting permission to make a trip to the western steppe land and asking that tea be included in the frontier trade. They considered such demands excessive and requested that Wang, Altan-qaγan's patron in their eyes, be censured.

Wang seems to have been responsible for a number of publications but all that have survived are twenty of his memorials, preserved in the *Huang Ming ching-shih wen-pien*, edited by Ch'en Tzu-lung (ECCP), and others in a collection entitled *Shao-pao chien-ch'uan Wang-kung tu-fu tsou-i* 少保鑑川王公督府奏議, 15 ch., published early in the Wan-li period. [Editors' note: In the *Kuo-ch'üeh* by T'an Ch'ien (q. v.) another man of the same period is erroneously recorded as Wang Ch'ung-ku. This man's name is Wang Ch'ung 王崇 (T. 仲德, H. 麓泉, a native of Yung-k'ang 永康, Chekiang, cs 1529); he served as provincial examiner of Shensi (1531), governor of Shansi (1553-56), and supreme commander in west Hukuang, east Kweichow, and Szechwan against the Miao (1557-59). Reference to him in *Kuo-ch'üeh* is given once as Wang Ch'ung-yeh 業 and at least six times as Wang Ch'ung-ku but never by his correct name of Wang Ch'ung.]

Bibliography

1/222/5b, 327/24b; 5/39/113a; 64/戊21/6a; MSL (1940), Mu-tsung, 13/7b, 41/11b, 13b, 50/5b, 8a, 51/5a, 52/1b, 7b, 9b, 54/12a, 55/24b, 26b, 34b, 56/37b, Shen-tsung, 67/5a, 68/2a; *Shansi t'ung-chih* (1892), 130/9b; KC (1958), 3424, 3445, 3841,

3843, 3891, 3903, 3919; Wang Shih-ch'i (*see* Wang Tsung-mu), *San-yün ch'ou-tsu-k'ao*, 2/11b, 20a; *Yung-k'ang-hsien chih* (1893), 7/17b; Chang Chü-cheng, *Chang-t'ai-yüeh wen-chi* (1612), 21/20b-33/22b; Kao Kung, *Fu-jung chih-shih* (in *Chi-lu-hui-pien*), 53/1a; Wang Hsi-chüeh, *Wang-wen-su-kung wen-chi* (NLP, microfilm roll no. 886), 7/1a; Shen Shih-hsing, *Tz'u-hsien-t'ang chi* (NLP microfilm roll no. 866), 19/10a; *Ming ching-shih wen-pien* (1964), 3343; Chu Tung-yün, *Chang Chü-cheng ta-chuan* (Shanghai, 1945), 101; Henry Serruys, *Genealogical Tables of the Descendants of Dayan-Qan* ('s Gravenhage, 1958), 72, 102; D. Pokotilov, *History of the Eastern Mongols during the Ming Dynasty from 1368 to 1634*, tr. by R. Loewenthal (Chengtu, 1947), 125; W. Franke, *Sources*, 5.6.21.

Ray Huang

WANG Fu 王紱 (T. 孟端, H. 友石, 友石生, 九龍山人, etc.), June 1362-March 5, 1416, painter, calligrapher, and poet, was a native of Wu-hsi, Nan-Chihli. Little is known about Wang's early life beyond the fact that he had already shown some promise as a painter and poet in his early youth, and that he became a first degree licentiate in 1376. Possibly because of some misconduct on his part, he soon retired to Mt. Chiu-lung 九龍 and was married there. Two years later, in response to the government's call for unemployed licentiates, he went to Nanking, the capital, to seek employment. A great deal of mystery surrounds the subsequent twenty years of his life. Either because he was implicated in the case of Hu Wei-yung (*q.v.*), or involved in some misadventure, he was banished to the frontier near Tatung, Shansi, in 1380. It seems that his wife and two young sons also accompanied him. Their life there was marked by extreme hardship, and he as a frontier guard hardly had time to paint. In these years, he probably executed no more than seven paintings. One, a landscape in ink, the "Ts'eng-luan tieh-chang" 層巒疊嶂 (Layered mountains with overlapping peaks), dated 1393, in the Yamamoto collection

in Tokyo, was one of the few. When his wife died, Wang managed to send his children back to Wu-hsi. In 1399 (according to another source, 1400), after the enthronement of Chu Yün-wen (*q.v.*), Wang saw an opportunity to return home. Succeeding in persuading his adopted son, a native of Shansi, to take his place, he left Tatung and went to live on Mt. Chiu-lung. For the next three or four years, he painted and gave lectures.

In 1403, after Chu Ti (*q.v.*) came to the throne, someone recommended him for employment in the Wen-yüan Hall 文淵閣 because of his skill in calligraphy. It was a rather unimportant position. Once, during the nine years he held this office, he accompanied a certain imperial son-in-law on a journey to Szechwan. In March, 1412, he became a drafter in the central drafting office, a more satisfactory position. On the emperor's trips to Peking in 1413 and 1414, Wang was in his retinue. It was on his second journey there that he painted the "Pei-ching pa-ching" 北京八景 (Eight scenes of Peking), a handscroll in eight sections. It appears that Wang remained in Peking after that. He died two years later after a brief illness.

Wang Fu was an eccentric. It is said that whenever he became intoxicated, he would put on a yellow cap and robe. With a haughty and dignified look, he would then spread out some paper, roll up his sleeves, and immediately start to paint. To those he liked and respected, he would give his paintings freely and generously; but to those of whom he thought lightly, he would give nothing. One account has this to say: "When living in Nanking he once, on a moonlight night, heard a man next door playing the flute. Inspired by the music, he painted bamboos on a scroll and presented it to the flutist the following morning. It developed that the man was a wealthy merchant. Overjoyed by the unexpected gift, he presented Wang with two rolls of flannel and two of silk, and asked Wang to do another picture so as to make a pair. This angered Wang. He returned the expensive gifts, took his picture back and tore it to pieces. "

Judging from a fair number of his preserved paintings, Wang was a versatile artist. He could paint landscapes on a grand scale, or a bamboo spray on a small album leaf. The range of his composition was broad, though he is best remembered for his landscapes and bamboos. The former, mainly in ink, show clearly his indebtedness to Ni Tsan and possibly also to Wang Meng (qq.v.). The "Hushan shu-wu" 湖山書屋 (A studio on a lake shore at the foot of a mountain), dated 1410, in the collection of the Palace Museum, Peking, and the "Chiang shan yü-lo" 江山漁樂 (The joy of fishermen in mountain and stream), undated, a handscroll of nine or ten sections, are the two most famous ones. Both Wen Cheng-ming and Shen Chou (qq.v.) praised them highly. His "Ch'iu-lin yin-chü" 秋林隱居 (Hermitage in a forest in autumn), dated April 3, 1401, in the Yamamoto collection, is less renowned but more representative of his works. In the painting he depicts the retreat of a friend whom he visited in 1401. The setting is autumn; a broad river runs diagonally across the composition. In the foreground are an unoccupied pavilion and two bare trees which stand on a low promontory. Farther away in the background are three hilly islands. The whole painting suggests the desolate emptiness of the open view. The pavilion and the trees in the foreground, which stand out from the rocks and water about them, accentuate rather than relieve the mood of loneliness. The painting is distinguished for its refined simplicity and structural strength, and is reminiscent of Ni Tsan's quiet and deserted views. In one of his bamboo paintings, the "Wan-chu ch'iu-shen" 萬竹秋深 (Ten thousand bamboos in late autumn), undated, a long handscroll consisting of several sections, in the collection of the Freer Gallery, Washington, the leaves unfold with the greatest freedom and are replete with living beauty, as Osvald Sirén writes. Another bamboo painting, the "Hsiu-chu ch'iao-k'o" 修竹喬柯 (Thin bamboos and a tall tree), dated autumn, 1409, in the Yamamoto collection, shows two bamboo trees with long slender leaves, one in dark ink and one in light ink, swaying gracefully in the wind. Next to them is a tall old tree with big dot-like leaves, rising high above the bamboos. In the background is a level slope with rocks, tiny ponds, and moss. It is in the best tradition of the literati school of painting. A third, the "Shuang-ch'ing" 雙清 (Two unexcelled ones), depicting bamboos and cranes, undated, in color, in the collection of the Palace Museum, was executed jointly by Pien Wen-chin (q.v.) and Wang Fu. Pien was responsible for the two cranes, while Wang painted the bamboo grove.

Wang was also known for his poetry and calligraphy. A collection of the former, *Wang She-jen shih-chi* 王舍人詩集, 5 ch., published by his elder son after his death, is included in the *Ssu-k'u* library. In calligraphy he is remembered for his k'ai-shu of small size.

Bibliography

1/286/3a; 3/267/3a; 5/82/4a; 32/27/14a; 40/17/22a; 61/151/17b; 64/乙6/1a; 65/7/2b; 85/1/7; 86/6/15a; Ho Ch'iao-yüan, *Ming-shan ts'ang*, 99/2a; Chiang Shao-shu 姜紹書 (fl. 1640), *Wu-sheng shih-shih* 無聲詩史, 1/9; Hsia Wen-yen 夏文彥 (fl. 1365) and Han Ang 韓昂 (fl. 1519), *T'u-hui pao-chien* 圖繪寶鑑, 6/158; Pien Yung-yü 卞永譽, *Shih-ku-t'ang shu-hua hui-k'ao, hua-chuan* 式古堂書畫彙考, 畫卷 (Taipei, 1958), 26/428; *Wu-hsi-hsien chih* (repr. of 1968), 353; Chu Hsiang-ch'u 儲祥, *Chung-kuo hua-chia jen-ming ta tz'u-tien* 中國畫家人名大辭典 (1962), 37; Yü Chien-hua 俞劍華, *Wang Fu*, Shanghai, 1961; *Nihon genzai shina meiga mokuroku* 日本現在支那名畫目錄 (Tokyo, 1938), 127; O. Sirén, *Chinese Painting*, VII (New York, 1956-58), 252; *id.*, *A History of Later Chinese Painting*, I (London, 1938), 31; E. J. Laing, *Chinese Paintings in Chinese Publications, 1956-1968* (Ann Arbor, 1969), 198.

Lee Hwa-chou

WANG Hsi-chüeh 王錫爵 (T. 元馭, H. 荆石), August 30, 1534-February 11, 1611, official and grand secretary during the years 1585 to 1594, was a native of T'ai-ts'ang 太倉, Nan-Chihli. In the 16th and 17th centuries, there were two prominent Wang families in T'ai-ts'ang: one, that of Wang Shih-chen (*q.v.*), which traced its origin to Lang-ya 瑯琊, Shantung, and the other, that of Wang Hsi-chüeh, which claimed Taiyuan, Shansi, as its ancestral home. As a matter of fact, the prominence of the Taiyuan Wang family lasted through the 19th century, and produced not only degree holders and officials, but also artists and scholars. Wang Hsi-chüeh's grandson, Wang Shih-min (ECCP), and Wang Shih-min's grandson, Wang Yüan-ch'i (ECCP), were both celebrated painters, and one of Wang Shih-min's sons, Wang Shan (ECCP), rose to be grand secretary (1712-23) in the K'ang-hsi period. The whole clan has been described as prosperous, but Wang Hsi-chüeh's branch was especially so, as a result of the business acumen of his grandfather, Wang Yung 王湧 (H. 友荆, d. 1558), who was known as a landowner and had pawnshops and probably conducted other commercial activities as well. Following the usual pattern of social mobility, Hsi-chüeh's father Wang Meng-hsiang 王夢祥 (H. 愛荆, 1515-82), who was a *hsiu-ts'ai* and a student in the Nanking National University, began the attempt to break into officialdom. His mother, née Wu 吳 (1514-95), also came from a well-to-do family, and had been trained in childhood in the management of fiscal affairs. By the following generation both Wang Hsi-chüeh and his younger brother, Wang Ting 鼎-chüeh (T. 家馭, 1536-85, cs 1568), vice commissioner of education of Honan province, 1580), achieved important positions in the bureaucracy.

Wang Hsi-chüeh became a *chü-jen* in 1558, and a *chin-shih* four years later. As the winner of the second highest place in the palace examinations, he was appointed compiler in the Hanlin Academy. Except for a brief period in 1570 as director of studies in the National University in Nanking, he served in the capital with regular promotions. In 1574 he was named chancellor of the National University in Peking, and in 1577 became grand superviser of instruction and concurrently reader-in-waiting in the Hanlin. He also particpated in the compilation of the *Mu-tsung shih-lu* (the Veritable Records of the Lung-ch'ing era) and in the revision of the *Shih-tsung shih-lu* of the previous era, as well as acting as a supervisor of the local and metropolitan examinations. Up to this point his duties and activities were mainly literary and educational; he was yet to be involved in court politics.

As a rule, after the death of a parent, an official had to observe a period of mourning by retiring, nominally for three years, but actually for twenty-seven months. The practice of recalling an official from mourning before the prescribed time, a rarely employed device, was known as to-ch'ing 奪情, implying that the bereaved son is forced back into official service by an imperial command of some urgency. When the father of Chang Chü-cheng (*q.v.*) died in 1577, this powerful grand secretary had no intention of staying away from his position for long; so he applied to himself the to-ch'ing provision in the name of the boy emperor. His opponents seized the opportunity to try to discredit him politically, and probably a few honest Confucianists did protest his failure to be filial. The government was in a furor. In the lead to impeach Chang were Chao Yung-hsien (*q. v.*) and Wu Chung-hsing (*see* Chao Yung-hsien) both colleagues of Wang Hsi-chüeh in the Hanlin Academy. Chang was incensed, and had Chao and Wu sentenced to be punished by flogging. Hearing of this, Wang with a group of his other colleagues went to Chang Chü-cheng's residence to speak on behalf of the two men. Chang refused to let them off. Finally Wang visited him alone, but again failed to sway Chang, and the punish-

ment was carried out. Wang felt deeply
depressed. After Chang left for Hukuang
for the interment of his father, Wang
received promotion to the office of vice
minister of Rites. To please Chang Chü-
cheng, the heads of various ministries
memorialized begging the throne to recall
Chang at the earliest possible date. To
this memorial Wang refused to affix his
signature; this made him an enemy of the
all-powerful minister. About the time
that Chang returned to Peking in the
middle of 1578, Wang resigned from
office, went home, and remained there
for over six years.

Chang Chü-cheng died in 1582 and
was posthumously stripped of his honors
the following year. By this time the political atmosphere had changed, so early in
1585 Wang was brought back to the capital
as minister of Rites and grand secretary.
Another new appointee to the grand
secretaryship was Wang Chia-p'ing 王家屏
(T. 忠伯, H. 對南, January 13, 1537-January
22, 1604, cs 1568). At this time the senior
grand secretary was Shen Shih-hsing (*q.
v.*), also a *chin-shih* of 1562 and the optimus of that year, while Wang Hsi-chüeh
was secundus. Second in rank among the
four grand secretaries was Hsü Kuo (*see*
Ku Hsien-ch'eng). The four were on
good terms. Some of Chang Chü-cheng's
one-time enemies sought to avenge themselves for indignities suffered, but Wang
Hsi-chüeh headed them off and succeeded
in according Chang the merit he deserved.
This did not add to his popularity with
certain factions at court.

During this time one of the foremost
concerns was the problem of imperial
succession, the reluctance of Chu I-chün
(*q.v*) to name his eldest son Chu Ch'ang-
lo (ECCP) officially as heir apparent. The
more the grand secretaries insisted, the
more obstinate the emperor became, and
the problem remained in a state of suspension. Feeling frustrated, Wang begged
to resign. Not until August, 1591, however, did he obtain leave to go home,
giving as pretext the necessity of caring

for his aging mother. While he was
absent from Peking during the following
year and a half the other three grand
secretaries also resigned one after another.
Then Wang received a call to return
as senior grand secretary. In the meantime the emperor had issued an edict
declaring that the designation ceremony
would take place around the spring of
1593. Accordingly, when Wang Hsi-chüeh
returned to the Grand Secretariat, he
asked the emperor to carry out the procedure. By this time, however, the emperor
had changed his mind and bade certain
eunuchs give Wang a new edict, in which
he declared that he wished only to appoint Chu Ch'ang-lo, as well as his two
brothers, Chu Ch'ang-hsün and Chu Ch'ang-
hao (for both *see* Cheng Kuei-fei) princes;
as for the heir apparent, he preferred
waiting to see whether his empress Hsiao-
tuan, 孝端, née Wang (*see* Chu I-chün),
would give birth to a son; if so, he would
make the latter heir apparent. Under
orders from the sovereign, Wang drafted
the required rescript; at the same time,
however, to show his regard for public
opinion, he drafted another which ran:
"In ancient times, there were a number
of empresses who adopted consorts' or
concubines' sons as their own. Now I
beg Your Majesty to let the empress
adopt Chu Ch'ang-lo and then appoint
him heir apparent." Both rescripts were
submitted to the emperor simultaneously,
but the other grand secretaries, Chao
Chih-kao (*see* Shen I-kuan) and
Chang Wei (*see* Ch'en Yü-pi) were not
informed of their contents. A few days
later, the emperor approved the first
rescript, which, however, he was eventually
forced by public clamor to rescind. Meanwhile Wang was violently criticized by
both censors and others.

December 11, 1593, being the birthday
of his mother, the emperor received the
congratulations of his courtiers. Directly
after that he summoned Wang to his
presence. Seizing the opportunity thus
given, the latter entreated the emperor

to appoint Chu Ch'ang-lo immediately. His words and obvious sincerity impressed the emperor. Later, on March 25, 1594, Chu Ch'ang-lo was ordered to begin his imperial education, every detail of which was of the kind due an heir apparent. This measure was welcomed though not considered completely satisfactory.

After promotions both in rank and in honor, Wang by 1594 was minister of Personnel, grand secretary, and junior tutor and grand guardian to the heir apparent. In the course of the years in which he served in the Grand Secretariat Wang Hsi-chüeh advised the emperor to discontinue support of certain imperial factories in Soochow and Hangchow; to lessen the burden laid on the imperial kilns at Ching-te-chen 景德鎮 in Kiangsi; to decrease the amount of taxes of Yunnan; and to appropriate a sum of money from the palace to relieve the famine occasioned by both drought and flood in Honan. The emperor treated him well; nevertheless he seldom accepted his advice. For example, Wang voiced strong opposition to the sentence of punishment by flogging of Li I (see Chang Ching 黥), who had brought an accusation against the eunuch, Chang Ching, head of the Eastern Depot, but his protests had no effect on the court, the sentence being carried out at the beginning of 1589. By February, 1593, his popularity declined when it became known that he did not dare reject the emperor's command to draft the rescript proposing the identical designations of the emperor's three sons to the status of princes. Not long afterwards, the director of the bureau of evaluations in the ministry of Personnel, Chao Nan-hsing (q.v.), and several others were demoted or cashiered because of their criticism of the government. Surmising that these officials were being punished as a result of Wang's maneuvers, the public generally put the blame on him. In spite of his repeated memorializing of the throne in an effort to exonerate himself, even to speaking up on behalf of the

above mentioned men, he had to endure further criticism. Later he begged frequently to be retired, but was ordered to remain at his post; permission finally came in July, 1594.

After a lapse of more than seven years, Chu Ch'ang-lo was finally appointed heir apparent (November 9, 1601). Soon thereafter, the emperor sent off messengers to tender his compliments as well as gifts to Wang Hsi-chüeh. In 1607 the emperor selected a new group of men for the Grand Secretariat, among them Wang Hsi-chüeh, but he declined. By 1611 Wang was dead. He received posthumous honors and the title of Wen-su 文肅.

Wang's only son, Wang Heng 王衡 (T. 辰玉, H. 緱山, 1561–1609), was a chü-jen of 1588, and a chin-shih of 1601. Like his father, he emerged from the palace examinations second in rank, and was made a Hanlin compiler. In the earlier examination, however, when he headed the list in Shun-t'ien fu 順天府 (Peking), along with some relatives of other influential officials of the time, certain critics made an accusation of nepotism. As he was genuinely talented, his father was outraged. After a reexamination, the son proved his ability. It was for this reason that he never participated in the metropolitan examinations during all the years that his father served as grand secretary. Wang Heng left a collection of literary works entitled Kou-shan hsien-sheng chi 緱山先生集, 27 ch., printed in 1616, which was condemned to be partially censored a century and a half later. He also wrote a play, the Yü-lun-p'ao 鬱輪袍, which may be found in the second series of the Sung-fen-shih ts'ung-k'an 誦芬室叢刊 (1917). The hero of the play is Wang Wei (701–61?), the great poet and painter of the T'ang dynasty, but actually it is believed to have an autobiographical background, the author voicing his grievance over the accusation of 1588. Besides the son, Wang Hsi-chüeh had three daughters, the second being the mysterious and controversial figure Wang Tao-chen (*q.v.*), widely known by her religious appellation, T'an-yang-tzu.

Wang Hsi-chüeh's collected literary works, the *Wang Wen-su kung wen-chi*, 55 *ch.*, were printed by his grandson, Wang Shih-min. It seems that parts of the collection had been printed separately as the *Wang Wen-su kung tsou-ts'ao* 奏草, *wen-ts'ao* 文草, and *tu-ts'ao* 牘草. All three are listed in the catalogue of the prohibited books of the Ch'ing dynasty. An enlarged edition of a collection of Hanlin papers, the *Tseng-ting kuo-ch'ao kuan-k'o ching-shih hung-tz'u* 增訂國朝舘課經世宏辭, 15 *ch.*, is also listed under his name as editor-in-chief.

Both Wang Hsi-chüeh and his son, Wang Heng, were accomplished calligraphers, highly regarded by their contemporaries. In addition the father was known as a fancier of chrysanthemums.

Bibliography

1/218/4b, 8b; 5/17/157a; 18/15/1a; 64/己14下/1a; *Huang Ming wen-hai* 文海 (microfilm), 2/3/4, 5, 2/4/1; *Wang Wen-su kung wen-chi* (NLP, Wan-li ed., roll nos. 885–87); TSCC (1885–88), XIV: 277/11b, XXIII: 99/12b, XXIV: 124/8b; *T'ai-ts'ang-chou chih* 州志 (1919), 19/7b, 12a, 19a; MSL (1940), Shen-tsung, 156/2b, 237/5b, 256/3b, 266/6a, 267/1b, 273/6b; SK (1930), 56/6a, 78/2a, 178/7a, 179/14b; L. of C. *Catalogue of Rare Books*, 172, 977, 988, 1105, 1141; Sun Tien-ch'i (1957), 25, 216; Heinrich Busch, "The Tung-lin Academy and Its Political and Philosophical Significance," MS, XIV (1949–55), 51; W. Franke, *Sources*, 5.7.42.

Chou Tao-chi and Lienche Tu Fang

WANG Hsi-shan 王錫闡 (T. 寅旭, 昭冥, 肇敏, H. 曉庵), July 23, 1628–October 18, 1682, Ming loyalist and astronomer, was a native of Wu-chiang 吳江, prefecture of Soochow. He was seventeen when the Manchu troops overran his district in 1645. It is not recorded whether he took any active part in the local military resistance to the invaders (*see* Yeh Shao-yüan), but, according to one biographer,

he made several attempts at suicide and only resumed his normal way of life on his parents' pleas. In his own account, he reports that in 1649 he closed his door to all worldly pursuits, which included the taking of civil examinations under the alien regime. In an allegorical autobiography, "T'ien-t'ung-i-sheng chuan" 天同一生傳, he describes himself as the subject of the emperor Hsiu 休 (alluding to Ming from the common combination Hsiu-ming) and a student of the Odes, Changes, and Spring and Autumn Annals, while at the same time teaching himself mathematical astronomy and astrology; after the decline of the Hsiu regime he lived contentedly in obscurity and poverty, occasionally going out to the fields to look towards the south with sorrowful eyes, often being overcome with emotion. Apparently he was referring to the Ming troops then operating in the southwestern provinces (*see* Chu Yu-lang, ECCP). Thus he lived the life of a Ming loyalist awaiting in vain for the restoration.

He could hardly make ends meet, even by having a few pupils, particularly when his specialty was not a popular subject. In time, however, his scholarship won him acknowledgment among scholars, especially among like-minded loyalists to the Ming cause. About 1656 he was engaged by such a scholar, P'an Ch'eng-chang (ECCP), a historian who had assumed the task of writing a history of the Ming dynasty. Wang took charge of the compilation of the tables and probably also a treatise on astronomy. It was at P'an's home that Wang met Ku Yen-wu (ECCP). Meanwhile a wealthy Chuang family (*see* Chuang T'ing-lung, ECCP) invited a number of scholars to edit a Ming history which was published in 1660, with P'an listed as one of the editors. Three years later the Chuang work was adjudged seditious by the Manchu court and all writers and printers involved, some seventy persons including P'an, were condemned to death. It is recorded that Wang bravely paid a visit to the well-guarded

Hangchow prison disguised in the garb of a Buddhist monk, probably bearing messages to the loyalists inside.

In consequence of the Ming history case of 1663, most Chinese writers of that day were intimidated and became extremely cautious, but some reacted with a strengthened belief in the nationalistic cause. Thus Lü Liu-liang (ECCP) openly gave up his qualifications as an expectant to civil service under the Manchu regime and began to express in a subtle way his anti-Manchu ideas. Among Lü's friends at this time were Huang Tsung-hsi and Chang Li-hsiang (both in ECCP), who stayed at length in Lü's home to teach the Lü children. Later Wang also served as one of the instructors. In any case, he became strongly attracted to Chang as a teacher and to Lü as a Ming loyalist. In 1678 he wrote a letter to Ku Yen-wu recommending Lü highly as a worthy friend. In another letter (1680) Wang said that he expected a visit from Ku when they might discuss events of the last twenty years, and the nineteen reigns; this was his way of saying that the Ming dynasty did not end in 1644 with the sixteenth emperor, for there were three more reigns in south China until 1661. Meanwhile he repeatedly scolded P'an Lei (ECCP, half-brother of P'an Ch'eng-chang) for succumbing to the desire for fame and fortune by taking a special examination in 1679 to serve at the Manchu court. Wang wrote his letters to Ku and P'an in the ancient seal script, probably as a way to conceal such anti-Manchu sentiments. Similarly he and Ku both designated the years by the sexagenary stems and branches to avoid the use of Ch'ing reign names. In Ku's collected works there are poems, written in 1671 and 1680, addressed to Wang as kao-shih 高士, a high-minded scholar uncontaminated by desire for power and wealth. In an essay on contemporary scholars Ku paid Wang the highest compliment, holding him superior to himself in the study of heaven and man and in firmness of character(學究天人確乎不拔吾不如王寅旭).

Wang is described as slender and distinguished by his protruding teeth. He often complained of illness. Partially paralyzed in 1681, he died a year later. He had no son, so a former pupil took care of writing the inscription for the stone tablet buried in his tomb.

It seems that none of his writings was published during his lifetime. Shortly after he died most of his manuscripts were collected and preserved by P'an Lei who named the collection *Hsiao-an i-shu* 曉庵遺書. According to P'an's preface it included a collection of essays (printed in 1821 under the title *Hsiao-an hsien-sheng wen-chi* 文集, 3 *ch.*), and seven works on calendrical calculations, namely: 1) *Ta-t'ung-li hsi-li ch'i-meng* 大統麻西麻啓蒙, a summary of Chinese and western methods; 2) *Ting-wei li-kao* 丁未麻稿 (no longer extant), on the calendar for 1667 which Wang and P'an calculated together; 3) *T'ui-pu chiao shuo* 推步交朔, on predicting the particulars of the eclipse of August 24, 1681, calculated by Wang and his disciples, basing themselves on Chinese and western methods and on Wang's own method; 4) *Ts'e-jih hsiao-chi* 測日小記, recording the observations during the eclipse, which tallied most closely with Wang's method; 5) *San-ch'en-kuei chih* 三辰晷志 (no longer extant), on an instrument invented by Wang for the observation of the sun, moon, and stars; 6) *Yüan-chieh* 圜解, on trigonometry; and 7) *Li-fa* 麻法, 6 *ch.*, to which he appended twenty-four tables. The last item, embodying Wang's own system of calendrical calculations, was included in the *Ssu-k'u* library under the title *Hsiao-an hsin-fa* 新法, 6 *ch.*, without the tables. It was printed in 1838 in the *Shou-shan-ko ts'ung-shu* 守山閣叢書 which a year later included another of Wang's works, the *Wu-hsing hsing-tu chieh* 五星行度解, on the motions of the five planets.

In about 1890 Li Sheng-to 李盛鐸 (T. 木齋, 1860–1937) printed the *Hsiao-an i-shu* in his *Mu-hsi-hsüan* 木犀軒 *ts'ung-shu*, listing it under four main headings: "Li-fa" (P'an's no. 7), "Li-piao" 表 (the 24 tables), "Ta-t'ung li-fa ch'i-meng" (P'an's no. 1 without the *Hsi-li ch'i-meng*, probably no longer extant), and "Tsa-chu" 雜著, miscellany, including among other items P'an's nos. 3 and 4 and the *Wu-hsing hsing-tu chieh*.

Wang's lifelong aim was the synthesis of traditional Chinese and newly introduced Western astronomical techniques to form a system of computing phenomena based, in contrast to traditional Chinese systems, on a geometrically defined conception of the cosmos. Unlike his contemporary, Hsüeh Feng-tso (ECCP, p. 571), another of his generation's best astronomers, Wang was self taught in European astronomy, chiefly through study of the *Hsi-yang hsin-fa li-shu* (*see* Li T'ien-ching, ECCP), the collection of Jesuit treatises published by imperial order at the beginning of the Ch'ing. He probably did not have access to the entire collection, for in a letter (1673?) he asked P'an Lei to purchase for him in Peking several Jesuit works on the calendar including the *Wu-wei piao* 五緯表 (one of the works by Giacomo Rho, *q.v.*, printed in the *Hsi-yang hsin-fa li-shu*). In the same letter he also asked for a work by Ferdinand Verbiest (ECCP, p. 547), referred to here as *Nan-shih hsin-hai ch'i-cheng* 南氏辛亥七政. His mastery of old and new and his exceptional rigor in making observations and measurements to verify his calculations led him to make a number of criticisms on the clarity, consistency, and accuracy of the Jesuit writings.

By the 1630s most if not all of the missionaries had abandoned the obsolete Ptolemaic cosmology for that of Tycho Brahe (1546–1601), who had embodied most of the conceptual advantages of Copernicanism in a theologically innocuous and mathematically advanced system which retained some currency in Catholic Europe until about 1680. Because the Jesuits could not be wholly candid about the constraints in which the injunction against Galileo (1564–1642) in 1616 had

bound them, the Chinese were puzzled by the unexplained mixture of systems and constants in their writings. Wang Hsi-shan, in consistently choosing the most advanced of the available ideas, disproves the assertion of some recent historians that the traditional perspectives of Chinese astronomy would have made its practitioners incapable of appreciating Copernican cosmology even if the Jesuits had been free to introduce the new system before the mid-eighteenth century.

Wang's *Hsiao-an hsin-fa*, completed in 1663, presents his complete system of ephemerides computation, centered, as was the Chinese practice, about eclipse prediction. It gives techniques for predicting planetary occultations and solar transits for the first time in China, since the missionaries had discussed this problem only in principle. Some of his methods were later integrated into the imperially sponsored *Li-hsiang k'ao-ch'eng* of 1723 (*see* Ho Kuo-tsung, ECCP), which also incorporated post-Newtonian European data. The *Hsiao-an hsin-fa* was also copied into the Imperial Library. The *Ssn-k'u* editors knew so little about the book and its author that they thought it written before 1644. In his *Wu-hsing hsing-tu chieh*, completed in 1673, he gives a clear geometric explication of his world-model, based on a critical adaptation of Tycho Brahe's scheme. Most remarkable is an attempt to account for the planets' anomalous motions (*i.e.*, the fact that their orbits are not quite centered upon the sun) in terms of an asymmetric attraction exerted by the outermost moving sphere of the universe. Although this attraction is represented in terms of the ancient pneumatic ch'i 氣 concept, Wang explicitly likens the attraction of the "first moving sphere" (*primum mobile*) for a planet to "the action of a lodestone upon needles." Wang thus holds a secure place in the prehistory of gravitation, and one can only agree with Hsi Tse-tsung 席澤宗: "We can imagine, if Wang Hsi-shan had only come upon [the writings of Copernicus and Kepler, which the Jesuits in China had but did not disseminate], how much greater his contribution to astronomy would have been."

Bibliography

Yin-te 9: 4/132/13b, 18b, 19b; SK (1930), 106/8b; Juan Yüan (ECCP), *Ch'ou-jen chuan, ch.* 34–35; Hsi Tse-tsung, "Shih lun 試論 Wang Hsi-shan te t'ien-wen kung-tso" 的天文工作, *K'o-hsüeh-shih chi-k'an* 科學史集刊, 6 (1963), 53; Wang P'ing 王萍, *Hsi-fang li suan-hsüeh chih shu-ju* 西方曆算學之輸入 (Nankang, Taiwan, 1966), 78; *Ku T'ing-lin shih-wen-chi* 顧亭林詩文集, (1959), 140, 393, 428; *Sung-ling wen-lu* 松陵文錄, 15/8a, 16/1a; Joseph Needham and Wang Ling, *Science and Civilization in China*, III (Cambridge, England, 1959), 454.

N. Sivin and Chaoying Fang

WANG Ken 王艮 (T. 汝止, H. 心齋), July 20, 1483–January 4, 1541, thinker, a native of An-feng-ch'ang 安豐場, T'ai-chou 泰州 prefecture of Yangchow, came from a family of salt-farmers little acquainted with book learning. He was given the name Yin 銀, meaning silver, and he answered to it for thirty-eight years until it was changed by his master, the philosopher Wang Shou-jen (*q.v.*), to the scholarly name of Ken, one of the eight trigrams. At about the age of ten Wang Yin had to stop his schooling and help with the family tasks. A few years later his mother died. On one occasion he underwent training as a tradesman, accompanying his father to Shantung on several business trips. For a time he also tried to learn the art of an herb doctor. It is said that he did not give up the study of the classical texts which he kept in his sleeves, so that he could ask for help whenever he encountered a knowledgable person willing to explain difficult passages to him. At age twenty-five he visited the temple of Confucius in Ch'ü-fou 曲阜, and for the first time became aware that the great sage was, after all, just a man like himself. He began to practice seriously the Confucian teachings on personal conduct.

At home he manifested a special filial devotion to his father, taking his place in arduous labor during the winter. He spent his free time in silent meditation on the Classics, shut up in a small room. At times he even forgot to eat and sleep. In 1511, when he was twenty-eight, he saw in a dream the heavens falling and the people running about in panic, until he himself arose to push back the heavens and put the sun, moon, and stars in working order again, to the great joy of everyone. He woke up bathed in perspiration. Suddenly he became aware of a new openness in his heart, understanding it to be the place where Heaven and Earth and all things are one. He sought, thenceforth, to live always in this higher state of consciousness. His family, in the meantime, was prospering materially.

Fired with zeal for the reform of local customs, Wang counseled fellow villagers to give up and burn their Taoist and Buddhist images, and pay greater venerations to the ancestral cult. Above his own door he inscribed these words: "This Way (tao) comes from [the sages] Fu-hsi, Shen-nung, the Yellow Emperor, Yao, Shun, Yü, [Kings] T'ang, Wen, and Wu, the duke of Chou, and Confucius. To all who seek it, whether young or old, high or low, wise or ignorant, I shall transmit it." He took care to find in the Classics confirmation of his ideas, and to find in them the truth, without allowing commentaries on them to misinterpret what he sought. In conformity with certain prescriptions given in ancient ritual texts, he made for himself a long cotton gown, a ceremonial hat, belt, and tablets; alluding to the *Mencius* he said: "How can one speak the words of Yao, and perform the actions of Yao, without also wearing Yao's clothes?" (Cf. Legge, *Chinese Classics* II:205.)

In 1521 Wang Yin heard for the first time about Wang Shou-jen through a friend, who remarked upon the similarity of his teaching to that of the great man, then governor of Kiangsi, who already had a number of disciples. He reacted by saying that if Wang Shou-jen's doctrine of liang-chih was indeed the same as his own teaching of ko-wu (investigation of things), then Wang Shou-jen was clearly Heaven's gift to mankind, but that, if there were differences, he himself was Heaven's gift to Wang Shou-jen. He set out at once by boat to visit the governor. On arrival at the latter's residence he stood still at the middle gate, clothed in his ancient-style garments and holding aloft his tablet on which was inscribed a saying from the *Analects* (cf. Legge, *Chinese Classics*, I:114) until Wang Shou-jen himself came out to conduct him inside. Wang Yin took the seat of honor and spent some time debating with Wang Shou-jen, moving only to a lower seat to acknowledge his acceptance of the latter's greater understanding. He begged then to become a disciple. The next day, he regretted his earlier action, and returned to assume once more the seat of honor, until further debate convinced him of the governor's superior wisdom, and confirmed him in his desire to become a disciple. Much impressed, Wang Shou-jen told his other followers that he was more touched by "this man" than he had been at the capture of the rebel prince Chu Ch'en-hao (*see* Wang Shou-jen). It was then that Wang Shou-jen changed the new disciple's name to Ken.

After a short stay at home with his father, Wang Ken followed Wang Shou-jen back to the latter's home in Shao-hsing, Chekiang, and inquired about the kind of cart in which Confucius went around the then known world. He received in reply a simple smile. Wang Ken thereupon proceeded to build such a vehicle as he imagined it to have been, and rode in it to Peking, with the intention of submitting a long memorial to the throne. This was in 1522. At the capital his strange appearance and eccentric behavior attracted wide attention, until, urged by Ou-yang Te (*q.v.*) and other fellow disciples residing there, and by a letter from Wang

Shou-jen, he returned south. As punishment, he was refused an interview with the master for three days, although he waited daily by the gate. On the third day, on catching sight of Wang Shou-jen emerging, Wang Ken, on his knees, shouted out words of apology, and, when these met with no response, he loudly chided the master, reminding him that the *Mencius* (cf. Legge, *Chinese Classics*, II: 197) relates that even Confucius would not have carried things so far, namely, to an extreme of severity toward himself. Wang Shou-jen relented and invited him inside.

Wang Ken spent the next years close to Wang Shou-jen in Shao-hsing, learning from his words and example, and assisting him in the instruction of others. In 1523, during a local famine, he collected grain from the wealthy and asked for official help to distribute it to the needy. When an epidemic occurred, he occupied himself by compounding and dispensing medicine. Some of his writings were also completed during this period.

After the master's death in 1529, Wang Ken returned to T'ai-chou, opened a school there, and received a large number of disciples. He also traveled about to take part in the frequent scholarly sessions conducted by Wang Shou-jen's disciples. Wang Ken proved himself to be an excellent teacher, with a gift for imparting ideas and inspiration. Toward the end of his life, due to sickness, he was asked to teach in bed, assisted sometimes by Lo Hung-hsien (*q.v.*), who had built him a house. Although recommended several times for office, Wang Ken, however, remained a commoner all his life. He died at the age of fifty-eight. One of his sons, Wang Pi 襞 (T. 宗順, H. 東厓, 1511-87), had been selected by Wang Shou-jen himself to study under Wang Chi and Ch'ien Te-hung (*qq.v.*). Wang Pi assisted his father in his later teaching, taking his place after his death. Wang Ken's disciples included scholars as well as men of lowly station. Hsü Yüeh (*see*

Ho Hsin-yin) and Wang Tung 王棟 (T. 隆吉, H. 丁菴, 1503–81) were officials, whereas Chu Shu 朱恕 was a woodcutter and Lin Ch'un 林春 (T. 子仁) began life as a servant.

Wang Ken made much of his teaching of the "investigation of things." Huang Tsung-hsi called it the "Huai-nan 淮南 [Doctrine] of Investigation of Things." It is based on the Confucian concept of reciprocity, proceeding from individual self-cultivation to the government of society, as the fulfillment of man's basic moral responsibility. Wang employed the vocabulary of the Great Learning, saying that "things" have their "roots and branches," that one ought to proceed from the root—self-cultivation—to the branches— ordering of family, country, and world. The fundamental task was described as "giving peace [and security] to self" (an-shen 安身), with the emphasis on being natural (tzu-jan 自然). In a brief essay, "Ming-che pao-shen lun" 明哲保身論 he maintains that true wisdom (ming-che) or knowledge of the good (liang-chih) re-quires a genuine love for oneself and one's self-preservation, which is the starting-point for loving and respecting others and being loved and respected by them in return, extending to loving and protect-ing family, country, and the world. He protests therefore against that self-preser-vation which gives no place to loving others, as well as against that love of others which gives no place to proper self-love, and thus leads to extreme self-sacri-fice. For this, he has been criticized by Liu Tsung-chou (ECCP) who questioned his emphasis on an-shen in preference to an-hsin 安心 (giving peace of mind). Liu remarked that martyrdom might sometimes be necessary, and that Wang's ideas, while generally correct, might offer an excuse for the cowardly to prefer bodily preser-vation to taking risks.

Wang Ken, however, gave justifica-tions for his ideas in identifying self (shen) with the Way (tao) —ultimate reality—and with the Highest Good. He proclaimed especially that the self (man) should be the true center and focus of Heaven and Earth and all things, rather than vice versa. He also envisaged study to be a spontaneous and joyous work, by which selfish desires are removed and the person is awakened to his mind and its pure state. He celebrated this joy in a song, entitled "Lo-hsüeh ko" 樂學歌. He also saw this effort as that open to every man and woman (yü-fu yü-fu 愚夫愚婦). For he discovered in the ordinary person the possibility of greatness and heroism— that of being one with all things—, which is not the result of a forced effort, but presents itself in the form of a spontan-eous, joyous altruism.

Wang Ken did not develop a system-atic social and political theory. Neverthe-less, in a rather lengthy essay, he dis-cussed the Way of Kingliness (wang-tao 王道) in terms of its fundamental require-ment of self-cultivation, which demands a proper system of moral education. He advocated that a new subject of ethics be introduced in civil examinations in which students would be tested for knowledge of content as well as in personal conduct. He also manifested great concern for the practical improvement of the common man's lot. Moved by local injustices suffered by the salt farmers, he demanded for them in 1538 a more equitable distrib-ution of land in the An-feng region and won his point.

It was largely his influence as a teach-er and that of his fellow disciple, Wang Chi, which made of the philosophy of Wang Shou-jen an instrument of self-renewal and social consciousness in the whole lower Yangtze area. Wang Ken's teachings were propagated by several gen-erations of his descendants, especially by his son, Wang Pi. The T'ai-chou school, so named after Wang Ken's native place, produced a mass movement, exerting a deep influence on late Ming times, pro-voking critical and independent thinking as well as individualistic and eccentric behavior in many persons. Owing largely to its plebeian character and its role in social protest, it came to be called, in the twentieth, the "leftist" branch of the school of Wang Shou-jen. Some of its best-known adherents were Ho Hsin-yin, Lo Ju-fang, Li Chih (*qq.v.*), and Yen Chün (*see* Ho Hsin-yin).

Wang Ken's recorded sayings were published as *Hsin-chai yü-lu* 心齋語錄, 2*ch*. An abbreviated version of this exists as *Hsin-chai yüeh-yen* 約言 in the *Hsüeh-hai lei-pien* of Ts'ao Jung (ECCP). The first edition of his collected works, *Wang Hsin-chai ch'üan-chi* 全集, 6 *ch.*, printed by Wang Pi in the mid-16th century, does not seem to have survived. It was reprinted by his grandson, Wang Chih-yüan 之垣 with an appendix, *Shu-chuan ho-pien* 疏傳合編, 2 *ch.*, which includes a *nien-p'u* by his disciple, Tung Sui 董燧 (T. 兆時), and other related material by his great-grandson, Wang Yüan-ting 元鼎. It also has a preface by Chou Ju-teng (*q.v.*). A copy of this edition and a reprint of 1631 are preserved in the National Central Library in Taipei. There is also a 5 *chüan* edition credited to Wang Yüan-ting, which was printed in China in 1826, reprinted in Japan in 1847, and again in China in 1912. The above-emntioned *Shu-chuan ho-pien* was also appended to Wang Pi's collected works, *Tung-yai i-chi* 東崖遺集, 2 *ch.*, printed in the 1620s. Another full version of Wang's works has the title *Ming-ju* 明儒 *Wang Hsin-chai hsien-sheng i-chi* 遺集. It is in 5 *chüan* with a preface dated 1607 and was reprinted in 1910. The contents of these collections appear similar, but the arrangement is quite different. The 5 *chüan* work does not have Chou Ju-teng's preface. One copy of this is kept at the Kyoto Jimben Library.

Bibliography

1/283/13a; 3/185/18a ; 4/10/3b; 5/21/7a; 42/76/10b; 83/32/1a, 6a; SK (1930), 96/4a; Chou Ju-teng, *Sheng-hsüeh tsung-chuan* (preface 1606), 16/1a; Hou Wai-lu 侯外廬 *et al.*, *Chung-kuo ssu-hsiang t'ung-shih* 中國思想通史, Vol. 4B (1960), 958; Hsü Yüeh, *Wang Hsin-chai pieh-chuan* 別傳 in *Ming-ju* *Wang Hsin-chai hsien-sheng i-chi* (1910 reprint), 4/6b; Keng Ting-hsiang, "Wang Hsin-chai hsien-sheng chuan," *Keng T'ien-t'ai hsien-sheng wen-chi* (1958 ed., Taipei reprint, 1970), 14/1a; Li Chih, *Hsü ts'ang-shu* (Wan-li ed.), 22/14a; Sun Ch'i-feng (ECCP), *Li-hsüeh tsung-chuan* (1666 ed., Taipei reprint 1969), 21/36a; Tung Sui, *Nien-p'u* in *Ming-ju Wang Hsin-chai hsien-sheng i-chi* (1910 reprint), 3/1a; Wang Ken, *Hsin-chai yüeh-yen*, in Ts'ao Jung, comp., *Hsüeh-hai lei-pien*, Vol. 30; *id.*, *Ming-ju Wang Hsin-chai hsien-sheng i-chi*, with additions by Wang Yüan-ting (1631 ed., 1910 reprint); *id.*, *Wang Hsin-chai hsien-sheng ch'üan-chi*, with additions by Wang Yüan-ting (1631 ed.); Wang Shou-jen, *Wang Wen-ch'eng kung ch'üan-shu* (SPTK, lst series), *nien-p'u*, 33/950; Kyoto Jimben Kagaku Library *Catalogue of Chinese Books* (1963), 748; Kuo-hsüeh Library *Catalogue* (1934), 34/41b; National Central Library *Catalogue of Rare Books* (1967), 1055; Okado Takehiko 岡田武彦, *Ō Yōmei to Minmatsu no jugaku* 王陽明と明末の儒學 (Tokyo, 1970) 125; W. T. de Bary, "Individualism and Humanitarianism in Late Ming Thought," in de Bary, ed., *Self and Society in Ming Thought* (New York, 1970), 157.

Julia Ching

WANG K'o-k'uan 汪克寬 (T. 德輔, 仲裕, 德一, H. 環谷先生), February 13, 1304-December 7, 1372, native of Ch'i-men 祁門 hsien (Anhwei), is known primarily for his studies of the ancient writings on rites and his source study of the commentary by Hu An-kuo (1074–1138) on the Spring and Autumn Annals. Wang's *Ch'un-ch'iu Hu-chuan fu-lu tsuan shu* 春秋胡傳附錄纂疏, 30 *ch.*, was plagiarized by Hu Kuang (*q.v.*) who, under orders from Emperor Chu Ti (*q.v.*), directed the compilation of the *Ch'un-ch'iu ta ch'üan* 春秋大全, 70 *ch.* The plagiarism is noticed in the *Ching-i k'ao* of Chu I-tsun (ECCP), a notice which in turn is quoted by the editors of the *Ssu-k'u* catalogue.

It was chiefly due to Wang's ancestors that Sung philosophy, known as li-hsüeh, flourished in Ch'i-men during Yüan times. His grandfather and a distant great-uncle studied under the Sung philosopher, Jao Lu 饒魯, a leading disciple of Huang Kan (1152–1221), who in 1254 received an appointment as head of the prefectural school of his native place, Jao-chou 饒州, Kiangsi. Wang K'o-k'uan's father, Wang Ying-hsin 應新 (T. 元美, H. 中山, 1259–1338), as a teacher once submitted twenty suggestions to the Yüan government, urging that it act to "convenience the people," but his hope of having this series, entitled *Pien-min er-shih t'iao* 便民二十條, sent through channels to the Censorate was never realized.

Wang K'o-k'uan was a precocious child. His father passed on to him the teachings that he had received from Jao Lu, including records of questions and answers between student and teacher. He thus became immersed in Sung philosophy from his youth up. He acquired the version of the Four Books according to Chu Hsi (1130–1200), and, reading day and night, punctuated it himself. He then set out to read the Six Classics, the works of the philosophers, the official histories, and the *Tzu-chih t'ung-chien kang-mu* of Chu Hsi *et al.* Later he studied for four years (1322–26) under Wu Yü 吳迂 (T. 仲迂), another disciple of Jao Lu. In 1326 Wang passed the provincial examination for the *chü-jen*, but failed in the higher examinations in Ta-tu. He is said to have concluded that a government career at that time was not what he wanted. In 1328 he went to various places to meet several famous masters of Sung thought, such as Hsü Ch'ien (1270–1337) in Chin-hua 金華, Chekiang, and Chu Kung-ch'ien 朱公遷 (fl. 1341) in Jao-chou. According to report, the following year a Mongol official offered him a teaching post in the local government, but he declined; for he had decided to devote himself to private teaching and writing.

Wang completed his study of the commentary on the Spring and Autumn Annals by Hu An-kuo in 1334. Four years later the scholar Wang Tse-min (1273–1355), a fellow clansman, wrote a preface. Yü Chi (1272–1348) wrote a second preface in 1341 after having written a funerary inscription for Wang's father. The work was printed in 1346. When, in 1352, rebel Red Turban disturbances flared in southeast China, Wang, like many others, took to the hills in search of refuge. During the four years he spent in hiding, he frequently lectured, together with Cheng Yü (1298–1358), Yüan loyalist and fellow scholar. Wang, moved by Cheng's suicide, wrote his hsing-chuang (record of conduct). In 1356 Ch'en Yu-liang (*q.v.*) extended his power into the region and tried to press Wang into service. But Wang refused, and fled to T'ai-p'ing 太平, northeast of Ch'i-men, which had been taken by Chu Yüan-chang the year before. In 1358, when Chu made a tour through his area, he stopped off to invite Wang to expound on the Way of good government (chih-tao 治道). Wang, however, declined, asserting that he was ill.

Rebel disturbances continued in the region until Chu Yüan-chang finally succeeded in subduing his rivals in 1367. Wang's plans to live out his days in retirement came to an end when, in the following year, the emperor ordered that gifts be sent to Wang's residence, and that he be invited to help Sung Lien compile the official history of the Yüan. After six months' work in Nanking, the project reached partial completion and Wang made preparations to return home. When the ruler requested Wang to compile a work to be known as *Ta Ming chi-li* 大明集禮, Wang declined. He did, however, contribute his *Chou-li lei-yao* 周禮類要 (no longer extant), to Tseng Lu 曾魯 (T. 得之, 1319–72), the designated chief compiler of the new work, to use as reference. The emperor finally consented to Wang's wish to be sent home, and presented him with gifts of gold and silk. Before he left Nanking, Wang showed his work on the Chou rites to both Wei Su and Sung Lien (*qq.v.*). Their prefaces are still extant. According to Yü Chi's preface to *Ch'un-ch'iu Hu-chuan fu-lu tsuan-shu,* Hu An-kuo had compiled his study of the Spring and Autumn Annals in an attempt to revitalize

Chinese civilization, so that the country might withstand external threats. It therefore "sets forth what the ruler of men in his rightful performance of his duties must do," and "opens up what the minds of men in the world had long been ignorant of." Wang's study, Yü alleges, serves to elucidate Hu An-kuo sources for the benefit of candidates in the state examinations. (Hu's work on the Spring and Autumn Annals became part of the required reading for the examinations administered by the state in 1415.) The editors of the *Ssu-k'u* catalogue note this aspect of Wang's motivation in compiling his study of Hu's commentary, and state that Wang "was probably following the ways of the times." The editors also quote Ch'en T'ing 陳霆 (T. 聲伯, cs 1502), who criticized Wang for following Hu's interpretations too slavishly. Yet, while the editors quote Ch'en in agreement, they also praise Wang for having carefully elucidated the sources of Hu An-kuo's work. Wang himself boasts in his preface that "to know the strengths and weaknesses of the three commentaries (*i. e.* the commentaries to the Spring and Autumn Annals by Ku-liang, Kung-yang, and Tso), all the novice need do almost is to look here."

The second work copied into the Imperial Library, the *Ching-li pu-i* 經禮補逸, 9 *ch.*, is a synthetic compilation of passages dealing with ancient rituals concerned with good fortune, death, war, guests and weddings that are found in all the Classics and histories, in order to supplement the three collections of rites (*I-li*, *Chou-li*, and *Li-chi*), for, as he explained in his preface, books on ancient rites were incomplete even in the time of Confucius. His *Ching-li pu-i* was first printed about 1369 and reprinted in the *T'ung-chih-t'ang ching-chieh* (*see* Singde, ECCP).

Shortly before his death, Wang's students issued a prospectus soliciting contributions to print his books on the Classics. It mentioned two works that had

already been printed by a publisher in Fukien, namely, the *Ch'un-ch'iu tsuan-shu* 纂疏 and *Ch'un-ch'iu k'ao-i* 考異; that a work on history, the *Tzu-chih t'ung-chien kang-mu k'ao-i*, had been printed by the government school of Ch'i-men; and that among the as yet unpublished works were: *Chou-i chuan-i yin-k'ao* 周易傳義音考, 26 *ch.*, *Shih-chuan yin-i hui-t'ung* 詩傳音義會通, 30 *ch.*, and *Ssu-shu yin-cheng* 四書音證, 10 *ch.* Apparently none of these was printed. Wang's collected works, excluding his writings on classical studies, printed under the title *Huan-ku chi* 環谷集, 8+1 *ch.*, were included in the Imperial Library. A descendant of Wang, Wang Mou-lin 懋麟, edited and printed the *Huan-ku chi* in 1679 in a collection of works by three of his ancestors entitled *Wang-shih san hsien-sheng chi* 汪氏三先生集. This collection is sometimes found under the title *Ch'i-men san Wang chi* 三汪集. It incorporates both a record of conduct and a chronological biography written by a student of Wang K'o-k'uan, named Wu Kuo-ying 吳國英. The *Ching-li pu-i* is included in two different collectanea.

Bibliography

Yin-te 24: 1/282/5a; 5/114/13a; 24/1/26b; 32/36/7a; 40/5/1b; 61/111/2a; 88/9/44b; *Yin-te* 35: 22/236/11a; 23/34/37b; 25/88/19b; 28/4/7a; 29/二辛; SK (1930), 20/4a, 28/5a, 168/10b; Chu I-tsun, *Ching-i k'ao* (SPPY ed.), 134/1a, 199/1a; *id.*, *P'u-shu-t'ing chi*, 62/1a; Yü Chi, "Ch'un-ch'iu Hu-shih chuan tsuan-shu hsü" 春秋胡氏傳纂疏序, *Tao-yüan hsüeh-ku lu* 道園學古錄 (SPPY ed.), 31/5a; Huang Tsung-hsi (ECCP), *Sung Yüan hsüeh-an* (SPPY ed.), 83/12b; Wang Tzu-ts'ai 王梓材 and Feng Yün-hao 馮雲濠, *Sung Yüan hsüeh-an pu-i*, 83/316b; Sung Lien, "Wang [Tse-min] hsien-sheng shen-tao pei-ming," *Sung Wen-hsien kung ch'üan-chi* (SPPY), 5/2a; Wu Kuo-ying. *Huan-ku hsien-sheng nien-p'u*; Hsieh Ts'un-jen 謝存仁 ed., *Ch'i-men-hsien chih* (*1653 hsiu-pu* 修補 ed.), 3/91a.

John D. Langlois, Jr.

WANG K'o-yü 汪砢玉 (T. 玉水, H. 樂卿, 龍惕子), 1587–1645, art critic and historian, was by registry a native of Chia-hsing 嘉興, Chekiang, where his family, originally from She-hsien 歙縣 (Hui-chou-fu), had settled perhaps for several generations, engaging in the salt business. His father, Wang Chi-mei 繼美 (T. 世賢, H. 愛荊, 荊 筼, d. ca. 1628), led an extravagant life, befriending Buddhist monks, and collecting *objets d'art* which were housed in buildings called Ning-hsia-ko 凝霞閣 and Chen-shang-chai 眞賞齋 situated in a rock garden. There, famous artists and collectors often visited him, presented him their own works, and contributed colophons to the masterpieces in his collection. Among these friends were Hsiang Yüan-pien, Li Jih-hua (*qq. v.*), and Tung Ch'i-ch'ang (ECCP).

It was in such an affluent and aesthetic atmosphere that Wang K'o-yü was brought up. He became a student in the local school but, failing to pass any of the higher examinations, apparently purchased the rank of a scholar of the National University in Peking, where he was registered probably during the years 1623 to 1626. Somehow he managed to obtain the appointment to a judgeship (6B) in the Shantung salt distribution commission in Tsinan, the provincial capital, where he served for about a year from the autumn of 1626 to 1627. The fact that his appointment took place when the eunuch Wei Chung-hsien (ECCP) was all powerful, and was terminated abruptly after Wei's fall indicates the possibility that he was involved in the investigations of the eunuch party. In the colophon on a painting he writes that some scoundrel took away everything in his studio when he suffered a calamity in Shantung (余在東省遭艱被宥人罄齋頭物). This sounds very much like the confiscation of the properties of an official under investigation on very serious charges. It seems that his home in Chia-hsing was also affected, for he mentions in another colophon that during the calamity of 1627 the family collection of about a hundred miniature scenes, arranged with dwarf trees and unusual rocks in precious porcelain pots (bonsai ?), had suffered from want of care.

Wang K'o-yü was apparently rather proud of his short-lived official position in Tsinan, a city famous for its springs, and arrogated to himself the sobriquet, Ch'i-shih-er-ch'üan chu-jen 七十二泉主人 (Master of the seventy-two springs). Among his one hundred or so other sobriquets was also the one describing himself as an official of salt distribution in the ancient T'an viscounty (譚子國轉運臣). He compiled a history of the salt monopoly entitled *Ku-chin ts'o-lüeh* 古今鹺略, 9 *ch.*, with a supplement in 9 *chüan;* this receives mention in the *Ssu-k'u* catalogue.

Wang K'o-yü's principal contribution to scholarship is his collection of colophons and commentaries on calligraphy and painting, compiled in 1643 under the colorful title *Shan-hu wang* 珊瑚網 ([iron] net for coral) sometimes referred to as *Wang-shih* 汪氏 *Shan-hu wang*. It receives no mention in the bibliographical memoir of *Ming-shih*, but it was copied into the *Ssu-k'u* library. It existed only in manuscript until edited by Miao Ch'üan-sun (BDRC) and printed in 1916 in the *Shih-yüan* 適園 *ts'ung-shu*. The book is divided into two sections, one on calligraphy under the subtitle *Ku-chin fa-shu t'i-pa* 古今法書題跋, 24 *ch.*, and one on painting, *Ku-chin ming-hua* 名畫 *t'i-pa*, 24 *ch.* The calligraphy section consists of four parts: colophons (*ch.* 1-21); catalogues of famous collections, Shu-p'ing 書憑 (*ch.* 22); excerpts from expositions on the methodology of the calligraphic art, Shu chih 旨 (*ch.* 23), and gleanings from critical studies of great calligraphers, Shu-p'in 品 (*ch.* 24). The section on paintings is similarly divided into colophons (*ch.* 1-22), catalogues, Hua-chü 畫據 (*ch.* 23), criticisms Hua-chi 繼 (*ch.* 24), and methodology Hua fa 法 (Supplement). The last three items are included in the *Mei-shu* 美術 *ts'ung-shu* of 1913.

In his preface to the calligraphy section, written in 1643, he mentions that since childhood he had learned about collecting art from his father, and subsequently accumulated colophons and descriptions of masterpieces in more than twenty volumes, most of which consisted of unpublished pieces written by great artists or critics. Now that his wife had died and he in retirement had time on his hands he started to edit what he had copied, beginning with calligraphy. The section on paintings was edited at the end of the same year. Many of the items were in Wang's own collections, and his colophons often contain intimate opinions and details of his own life. Although a more systematic work than the *Ch'ing-ho shu-hua fang* by Chang Ch'ou (*q. v.*) published in 1616, the *Shan-hu wang* sometimes gives erroneous identifications based on second-hand information. The book's main contribution to the history of Chinese art is in the preservation of the colophons on various masterpieces, a practice imitated and improved upon by later compilers such as Pien Yung-yü (ECCP). Most histories of Chinese art mention the *Shan-hu wang* by title, but in general references to it are confined to one section in which the author, drawing from many but unidentified sources, undertook to define some of the technical terms in painting, especially the part in which he enumerated eighteen varieties of linear treatment 古今描法 employed by the figure painters of the past.

Besides being an art critic and historian, Wang K'o-yü was a poet of some note, and his name is mentioned in books on Ming poetry. Unfortunately only a few of his poems have survived, most of which were composed as colophons to works of art. A rare example of his calligraphy may be seen in a colophon he attached to a painting "Ssu lun t'u" 絲綸圖, done by the artist Liu Sung-nien (*ca.* 1150-1214十), now in the collection of the National Palace Museum, Taiwan, and reproduced as No. 30 in the *Illustrated Catalogue of Chinese Government Exhibits for the International Exhibition of Chinese Art in London* (1936), Volume III.

Wang K'o-yü also wrote a work about the West Lake of Hangchow, entitled *Hsi-tzu-hu shih-ts'ui yü-t'an* 西子湖拾翠餘談, 3 *ch.*, printed in 1893 in the *Wu-lin chang-ku ts'ung-pien* (*see* Ting Ping, ECCP). It consists of his personal accounts of various gardens, monasteries, and other points of interest around the lake which he visited during more than forty years, beginning in 1603 when he went to take the provincial examination for the first time. From 1630 on he went there often in the company of his son (Wang Yüan 淵 ?) when the latter began to sit for the examinations too. He reports in the preface that in 1645 he found these travel accounts after he had lost most of his manuscripts as a result of the battles in Chia-hsing during the Manchu occupation. This is the last dated reference to Wang K'o-yü. He was then fifty-eight years of age.

Bibliography

40/70/15a; 64/辛27下/3b; 86/19/39a; *Chia-hsing-hsien chih* (1906), 25/15a, 26/11b, 34/28b; SK (1930), 84/5a, 113/5a; Wang K'o-yü, *Shan-hu wang*; Huang Pin-hung 黃賓虹 and Teng Shih 鄧實, *Mei-shu ts'ung-shu*, Vol. 6.

Ch'en Chih-mai

WANG Kuang-yang 汪廣洋 (T. 朝宗), died January/February 1380, a native of Kao-yu 高郵, prefecture of Yangchow, served Chu Yüan-chang as a civil official from 1355 until his death. Although he was probably not a successful administrator, he was favored by the Ming founder with high offices in the Secretariat. The facts of his early life are obscure. He studied for a time under the Yüan loyalist and Hanlin academician Yü Ch'üeh (1303-58), and became proficient in Classics and history. He passed the civil service examinations at the end of the Yüan. Moving to T'ai-p'ing 太平 from his native Kao-yu around 1354, he was living there in July, 1355, when Chu Yüan-chang drove out the Yüan and invested the city. Wang was one of several scholars (see T'ao An) who joined Chu's staff at that time. He began as a clerk in the newly-established T'ai-p'ing prefecture, and by 1357 he rose to be an auditor (照磨). After Hu Ta-hai (q.v.) captured Chu-ch'üan 諸全 (Chu-chi 曁) in February, 1359, he was put in charge of military requisitions, and in the same year appointed to a censorial post. Two years later he became a bureau director in the Chiang-nan branch. When the central secretariat was founded in 1364, he was appointed a bureau director to assist Li Shan-ch'ang (q.v.).

During the years from 1362 to 1367, Wang was sent out of the capital on at least four temporary assignments. In May, 1362, Chu Yüan-chang dispatched him and several other officials to assist Chu Wen-cheng (see Chu Yüan-chang) in the control of the city of Hung-tu 洪都 (Nanchang) which had fallen to Hsü Ta (q.v.) the month before. In September, 1364, Ch'ang Yü-ch'un (q.v.) laid siege to Kan-chou 贛州 in southern Kiangsi. There he met stubborn resistance from Hsiung T'ien-jui (see Ch'en Yu-liang), a former follower of Hsü Shou-hui, and Ch'en Yu-liang (qq.v.). Chu Yüan-chang sent Wang to deliver instructions to Ch'ang and help him devise a successful strategy. Wang made the long voyage up the Yangtze and Kan Rivers in stormy weather, none too cheerfully, by his own account. On his arrival, he advised Ch'ang to make it clear to Hsiung that he and his troops would be allowed a safe and honorable surrender. It was not until February of the following year, however, that the city finally fell without much bloodshed. Wang remained at Kan-chou to help protect it until his promotion late in 1366 to the office of administration vice commissioner; he was sent off (May), this time to Shensi, where he helped establish the new branch secretariat in that province.

Wang soon became involved in the bitter struggle among contenders for power in the central government. Li Shan-ch'ang fell ill some time in 1369 and other hands were needed to take up his administrative burdens. Yang Hsien (see Empress Ma) was recalled from his post in Shansi in October, 1369, to serve as junior vice administrator. Yang was a northerner who had moved south with his father, a one-time Yüan official, in time to be caught in Chu Yüan-chang's net at Nanking in 1356. An aggressively ambitious man, he was enraged when, early in 1370, Wang was recalled from Shensi and appointed senior vice administrator. Yang proceeded to assume the full authority of the Secretariat while Wang stood passively by. Not satisfied with Wang's acquiescence, Yang caused the censor Liu Ping 劉炳 (T. 彥昺) to impeach him for having failed in his filial obligations to his mother. Chu Yüan-chang at first believed the charge and sent Wang back to Kao-yu, a turn of events about which the dismissed official was not altogether unhappy because, as he remarks in one of his poems, he had been away from home for sixteen years. Fearing that his victim might be reappointed in the capital and seek redress, Yang persuaded Liu Ping to send up another memorial, suggesting that this time Wang be sent all the way to Hainan. Chu, reportedly, prompted by a memorial from Li Shan-ch'ang suggesting that Yang was behind the charges, now tried Yang, and executed him. Wang was then reinstated as senior vice administrator and, in December, 1370, received the title Chung-ch'in-po 忠勤伯 (Loyal and diligent earl) with an annual income of 360 tan.

When in February, 1371, Li Shan-ch'ang retired as senior councilor, and Hsü Ta, the junior councilor, left for the north at the head of the army, Wang was promoted to the office of junior councilor. As the senior office was left unfilled, he stood alone for the next two years at the head of the Secretariat. What little evidence there is about the nature of his relationship with the emperor during this period suggests that it was probably a difficult one. On two occasions Chu Yüan-chang communicated to him his fear of being deceived and manipulated by his own subordinates. In the first instance (August, 1372) the emperor told him that he had learned from his study of history that rulers often allowed themselves to be flattered by officials who invented and reported good omens and suppressed bad ones. He accordingly commanded Wang to see to it that the Secretariat should thenceforth report only ill omens to him. On another occasion, the day before the emperor's birthday (which fell according to the lunar calendar on the 15th of October), Wang conducted his colleagues into the emperor's presence to ask him whether they might have the honor of performing the congratulatory rites. The emperor responded by telling them that his displeasure with the excessive gifts presented him on an earlier occasion had led him to abolish such ceremonies both for his birthday and for the mid-autumn festival. He would, instead, retire to his quarters, eat simple fare, and refuse all congratulations.

Suddenly out of favor again, Wang was dismissed from the Secretariat in February, 1373, on the ground of his meek personality and inattention to duty. He was then banished to the post of administration vice commissioner in the Kwangtung branch secretariat at Kwangchou. This left the office of councillor vacant for six months until the appointment of Li Shan-ch'ang's protégé, Hu Wei-yung (*q.v.*). In June, 1374, Wang was recalled to Nanking and appointed senior censor-in-chief. His activities in this post are largely unrecorded. He did, however, use his office to embarrass Li Shan-ch'ang. In September, 1376, Wang and his colleague, Ch'en Ning (*see* Hu Wei-yung), joined in impeaching Li and his son, Li Ch'i (*see* Li Shan-ch'ang), for disrespect towards the emperor and for their ingratitude for the many favors they had received. Wang's motives in thus injuring someone who had defended him against

Yang Hsien in 1370 are not disclosed. The emperor, in any case, forgave the two Li, saying that severity in minor matters would demoralize the other courtiers, and that Li Shan-ch'ang was a great official who had long been in his service. Late in the same year the emperor charged Wang with the revision of the law code which, he said, was unclear as originally drafted.

In October, 1377, Hu Wei-yung was promoted to senior councilor and Wang appointed to replace him. For the first time in more than six years, both councilor posts were now filled, but association with his new colleague was to involve Wang in his fate. According to the official versions of Wang's biography, the emperor expected him to watch Hu's conduct and keep him informed. His unwillingness or inability to do so was a disappointment to Chu. In September, 1379, a formal but possibly sarcastic letter to Wang advising him to overcome the heat sickness that had been his excuse for not attending court for a time may have been warning of trouble to come. Two months later palace eunuchs discovered that a tribute mission from Champa had arrived and not been properly received or reported. The emperor, in his anger, charged the Secretariat with having intentionally concealed the matter. Hu Wei-yung, Wang, and others were summoned before him to confess their error.

The end came for Wang early in 1380. The censor, T'u Chieh (*see* Hu Wei-yung), reported that Wang had known of Hu's alleged murder of Liu Chi (*q.v.*) in 1375, and had failed to report it. Wang, questioned by the emperor, denied the charge, but his denial was in vain and he was banished to Hainan. En route to his place of exile, he was overtaken by an imperial messenger bearing additional charges against him, and, according to different accounts of the matter, he either hanged himself or was executed on the spot. Several sources assert that after Wang had started on his journey the emperor had reflected bitterly on what he considered to have been Wang's failure to inform him either of Chu Wen-cheng's insubordinate conduct at Kan-chou some fifteen years before or of Yang Hsien's machinations. In February/March, 1380, moreover, when the emperor abolished the Secretariat, his edict contained a savage posthumous denunciation of Wang, whom he described as having been a slothful character who spent his days and nights in drunken carousing. This was Chu's last word on a man who may well have participated in the rebellion against his will. In his first encounter with the disorders in Kao-yu, some thirty years before, he had witnessed the abduction of his neighbor's wife by an unruly mob of rebels, and on that occasion had written a poem to record his sense of outrage. When he was sent to help Ch'ang Yü-ch'un at Kan-chou in 1364, his account of the mission almost ignores the purpose for which he was sent, and dwells at length on a happy chance meeting with an old man he had known in his youth. The ultimate tragedy of his relationship with Chu seems to have arisen quite naturally from his deeply reluctant performance in a role that he detested. Ten years after his own death, surviving members of his family were among the victims in the wholesale executions of Li Shan-ch'ang's associates in 1390.

Wang's collected poems, the *Feng-ch'ih yin-kao* 鳳池吟稿, 10 *ch.*, with a preface of 1371 by Sung Lien (*q.v.*), was reprinted in 1488 and 1497. A copy of the latter edition is preserved in the collection of the National Library of Peiping (microfilm no. 987). It has been reproduced (1971) in the *Ssu-k'u ch'üan-shu chen-pen* 珍本, 3d series. Besides his poetry, Wang is known for several styles of calligraphy.

Bibliography

1/127/6a; 5/11/12a; MSL (1962), T'ai-tsu, *ch.* 3–129; KC (1958), 579; SK (1930), 169/2a; Chu Yüan-chang, *Kao-huang-ti yü-chih wen-chi*, 2/18a, 7/26a; Wang Kuang-yang, *Feng-ch'ih yin-kao*, 1/24b, 8/2b; TSCC (1885–88), XIV: 282/2/5b, XXIV: 117/23/5a; *Kao-yu-chou chih* (1845, Taiwan reprint), 9/6a, 10/15b; *Ming-shih* (Taipei, 1963), 1616; L. of C. *Catalogue of Rare Books*, 896.

                                    Romeyn Taylor

WANG Meng 王蒙 (T. 叔明, H. 黃鶴山樵), *ca.* 1301-October 14, 1385, has been considered by critics since the 16th century one of the "Four Great Masters of Late Yüan Painting." Born in Hu-chou 湖州 prefectural city, Chekiang, he had prominent family connections. His grandfather on his mother's side was Chao Meng-fu (1254–1322), the most influential painter and calligrapher of early Yüan, whose wife Kuan Tao-sheng (1262–1319), was also an artist, known especially for her paintings of bamboo and orchids. Other members of this distinguished family were Chao Meng-fu's son, Chao Yung 雍 (1289-*ca.* 1360), grandson, Chao Lin 麟 (mid-14th c.), and great-grandson-in-law, Ts'ui Yen-fu 崔彥輔 (mid-14th c.), all noted painters. In addition, Wang was related to some of the literary figures in the Yüan, including Shen Meng-lin 沈夢麟, T'ao Tsung-i (*q.v.*), and especially Yü Yu-jen 俞友仁, whose sister he married. His father, Wang Kuo-ch'i 國器, was a poet and art collector. All these provided him with a rich heritage and background. In spite of this, however, very little is known about Wang Meng's life. Of his early years, especially before 1340, almost nothing is recorded. One source indicates that he was skilled in writing poetry and essays, in calligraphy and painting, all in the family tradition, and especially strong in historical studies. We learn that he visited the capital, Ta-tu (Peking), were he established friendships with prominent members of the court and earned their respect.

During the Yüan period, Wang served once as li-wen 理問, provincial prosecutor, a rather lowly position. The period of his service was probably quite short, for he

is known to have lived after the early
1340s at his house on Mt. Huang-hao 黃鶴
山, near Hangchow, and adopted his literary name, Huang-hao-shan ch'iao 樵 (Fuel
Gatherer of Yellow Crane Mountain). He
had connections with some of the leading
literary and artistic circles of that day.
Wang often visited Ku Ying (*see* Ch'en
Ju-yen), whose home in K'un-shan 崑山
was something of a cultural center in
late Yüan, with endless parties attended
by famous literati. He came to know
Huang Kung-wang (1269–1354) and Cheng
Yüan-yu (*see* Chou Chih), Ni Tsan (*q.v.*),
and other artists and poets of the Soochow area. In fact, during the 1360s, he
appears to have lived in Soochow or at
least visited that city quite frequently, as
shown by reference to his being there.
One of the most famous gatherings he
attended was the one at T'ing-yü-lou 聽雨
樓 (Rain-listening pavilion) in 1365, for
which he painted a scroll which has colophons by several well-known intellectuals
such as Ni Tsan, Chang Yü, Yao Kuang-
hsiao, and Kao Ch'i (*qq.v.*). He is said to
have executed some paintings jointly
with Huang Kung-wang and Ni Tsan. Perhaps his stay in Soochow during these
years was the result of the new political
and cultural atmosphere under the rule of
Chang Shih-ch'eng (*q.v.*), who set up his
headquarters in that city between 1356
and 1367. Although some of his best
friends, such as Ch'en Ju-yen and Chao
Yüan (*q.v.*), seem to have served under
Chang, he steered clear of political involvement.

After the establishment of the Ming,
Wang Meng was one of the first of the
literati to be appointed by the emperor. For
some ten years he served as prefect of
T'ai-an 泰安 in Shantung. One of the best
known episodes in his life at this time concerns his painting association with Ch'en
Ju-yen, who happened to be serving in the
same area. Wang had taken some three
years to complete a scroll of Mt. T'ai,
which could be seen from his office. One
day, when snow was falling, Ch'en came

for a visit. Looking at the painting and
the snow, they changed the picture into
a snow scene (*see* Ch'en Ju-yen).

The end of Wang Meng's life was
tragic. In 1380 Hu Wei-yung (*q.v*), the
prime minister, was executed for an
alleged plot against the life of the emperor, and thousands of people who were
related to or associated with him suffered
execution or imprisonment. It was reported that Wang Meng had visited the
prime minister's home with some friends
to see some of the paintings in his collection. For this link, Weng Meng was put
in prison, dying there in 1385.

Although Wang did write some poetry
during his life, no collection of his works
is known. A few of his poems, however,
were included by Chu I-tsun (ECCP) in
his *Ming shih tsung*. His fame lies solely
in his paintings. At present, while close
to a hundred paintings are attributed to
his name, a majority cannot be taken
very seriously. His best works may be
considered in relation to a two-phase development. His early works, most of which
are either datable or assigned to the 1340s
and the early 1350s, reflect the lineage of
his art. The "Hua-hsi yü yin" 花溪漁隱
(Fisherman on the flower stream) and the
"Ch'iu-shan ts'ao-t'ang" 秋山草堂 (Cottage
on an autumnal hill), both undated and
both in the Palace Museum, Taipei, and
both known to exist in several versions
or copies, seem to represent his earlier
style, showing indebtedness to his maternal grandfather's "Ch'iao Hua ch'iu se" 鵲
華秋色 (Autumn colors on the Ch'iao and
Hua Mountains) and "Shui-ts'un t'u" 水村
圖 (Water village). In this period he shows
an interest in more open river or lake
views with fore-, middle-, and back-grounds
separated horizontally and clearly in an
S-curve arrangement. The land strips,
rolling hills, willows, and pines are typical
motifs which seem to have come from
Chao's works. His brushwork is more
precise and defines forms more according
to nature. The "Hsia-shan yin chü" 夏山
隱居 (Hermitage on summer hill), dated

1354, in the Freer Gallery of Art, Washington, D. C., also belongs to this group. The later phase of his development may be seen in works generally datable to the 1360s. Among them are some of the best-known paintings from his hand, such as the "Ch'ing-pien 靑卞 yin chü" (Hermitage on Ch'ing-pien Mountains), dated 1366, now in the Shanghai Museum, the "Lin ch'uan ch'ing chi" 林泉清集 (Literary gathering in woods and springs) dated 1367, whereabouts unknown (reproduced in *Shina Nanga Shūsei* 支那南畫集成), and the "Hsia-jih shan-chü" 夏日山居 (Mountain villa on a summer day), dated 1368, Palace Museum, Peking. They show high mountains from a close range with large groups of trees in the foreground, in thick and busy brushwork and in complex composition. The main inspiration for these works came from two painters of the 10th century, Tung Yüan and Chü-jan. A number of other works, though undated, seem to be related to this phase. They include the "Ku k'ou ch'un keng" 谷口春耕 (Spring fields at the entrance of a valley), the "Hsi-shan kao i" 谿山高逸 (Mountain hermitage), and the "Chü-ch'ü lin wu" 具區林屋 (Scenic dwelling at Chü-ch'ü), all in the Palace Museum, Taipei. These works show that in this period he was able to blend together the elements of the art of Chao Meng-fu with those of Tung Yüan and Chü-jan to achieve a style of his own. Almost no work recorded comes from the period between 1370 and 1383, except the "Tai tsung mi hsüeh t'u" 岱宗密雪圖 (Snow on Mt. T'ai) mentioned in the episode referred to above, which was destroyed in the Ming period. Perhaps all the works completed while he served as prefect in T'ai-an failed to survive.

During his own lifetime and shortly after his death, Wang Meng's reputation as a painter does not seem to have been outstanding. He did, however, have some influence on a number of artists working in the Soochow area, such as Hsü Pen and Wang Fu (*qq.v.*). His ascendancy to the ranks of the great Yüan masters was mostly the result of interest in his works by members of the Wu school. In his early years, Shen Chou (*q.v.*) imitated Wang Meng for some time. But the artist who explored all the potentials of his personal style was Wen Cheng-ming (*q.v.*), whose art dominated Soochow during the 16th century. Through Wen and his numerous followers, Wang Meng became one of the most respected artists of the past.

Bibliography

Yin-te 35: 22/238/11b; 23/36/32b; 25/56/10a; *Yin-te* 24: 1/285/25a; 3/161/20a; 24/1/69b; 40/13/25b; 64/甲18/1a; 84/甲前/17a; 86/4/32; Hsia Wen-yen 夏文彦, *T'u-hui pao chien* 圖繪寶鑑 (*Hua-shih* 畫史 *ts'ung-shu* ed.), 5/135; Chiang Shao-shu 姜紹書, *Wu sheng shih shih* 無聲詩史 (same ed.), 1/3; Wang Fu, *Shu-hua ch'uan hsi lu*, 己上 27b, 己下 17b; Li Jih-hua, *Liu-yen-chai pi-chi*, 4/33a; Ku Ying, *Yü-shan p'u kao* 玉山璞稿 (in *Yüan shih hsüan* 元詩選, 辛); id., *Yü-shan ming sheng chi* 名勝集; id., *Ts'ao-t'ang ya chi* 草堂雅集; Pien Yung-yü (ECCP), *Shih-ku-t'ang shu hua hui k'ao*, Vol. 21; Lu Hsin-yüan (ECCP), *Jang-li-kuan kuo yen hsü lu*, 3/13a; *Hangchou-fu chih* (1579 ed.), 91/ 1246; Wen Chao-t'ung 溫肇桐, *Yüan mo ssu ta hua chia* 元末四大畫家, Hong Kong, 1960; P'an T'ien-shou 潘天授 and Wang Po-min 王伯敏, *Huang Kung-wang yü Wang Meng*, Peking, 1958; Wang Chi-ch'ien 王季遷 and Li Lin-ts'an 李霖燦, "A study of Wang Meng's masterpiece 'Hua-hsi yü yin-t'u'" 王蒙的花溪漁隱圖, *National Palace Museum Qu.* Vol. I, no. 1 (July, 1966), 63; Shen Shih-liang 沈世良, *Ni Kao-shih nien-p'u* 倪高士年譜, 1909; Ch'ang Pi-te 昌彼得, "T'ao Nan-ts'un hsien-sheng nien-p'u ch'u kao" 陶南村先生年譜初稿, *T'u-shu-kuan hsüeh-pao* (Tunghai University, Taiwan), VII (1966), 1, VIII (1967), 21; Weng T'ung-wen 翁同文, "Wang Kuo-ch'i wei Wang Meng chih fu lun" 王國器爲王蒙之父論 in the *Po pu* 百部 *ts'ung-shu*, Yi-wen Publishing Co., Taipei; Dōtani Norio 堂谷憲勇, *Shina bijutsushi ron* 支那美術史論 (Kyoto, 1944), 173; Max Loehr, "Studie über Wang Meng: Die datierten Werke," *Sinica*, XIV (1939), 273; Osvald Sirén, *Chinese Painting*, IV (New York, 1956-58), 85; Sherman E. Lee and Wai-kam Ho, *Chinese Art Under the Mongols: The Yüan Dynasty (1279-1368)* (Cleveland, 1968), nos. 255-258; Chuts-ing Li, "Stages of Development in Yüan Landscape Painting," *National Palace Museum Bulletin*, IV, no. 2 (May-June, 1969), 1, IV, no. 3 (July-August 1969), 1; Bo

Gyllensvard, "Some Chinese Paintings in the Ernest Erikson Collection," BMFEA, 36 (1964), 159, pls. 1 and 2; E. J. Laing, *Chinese Paintings in Chinese Publications, 1956-1968* (Ann Arbor, 1969), 137.

Chu-tsing Li

WANG Mien 王冕 (T. 元章), 1287-1359, painter and poet, was a native of Chu-chi 諸暨, Shao-hsing prefecture, Chekiang. The son of a farmer, he spent his youth doing many chores for the family, such as herding water buffaloes. From early childhood, however, he began to show a keen desire to study, as described in a number of anecdotes. It is said that a scholar in the same district, Han Hsing, (1266-1341), took Wang as a pupil and eventually trained him in the Classics, especially the Spring and Autumn Annals. Wang is reported to have had an impressive appearance; he was tall and had a bristling beard. He sat for the *chin-shih* examination, but failed to place. So he burned his essays, began to study the ancient military arts, and sought to find an outlet for his knowledge and artistic ability. He had difficulty, however, in demonstrating his talents, and became known as an eccentric.

In time several officials sought his acquaintance. A native of the same district, Wang Ken (1278-1348), especially came to respect him. Later, Wang Ken, then an inspector (chien-chiao 檢校, 7A) of Chekiang, paid Wang Mien a visit. Finding the latter in poor clothes and broken shoes with toes exposed, the official became concerned, left him a pair of straw shoes, and tried to induce him to accept an appointment as a civil servant. But Wang Mien refused. Some other officials also befriended him, and insisted that he take the position of a school instructor. Reluctantly he accepted but resigned after serving for a little over a year. Then he went to visit Wu (Soochow), where members of the gentry,

knowing him as a painter of plum blossoms and bamboos and rocks, sent him pieces of silk and asked for examples of his art. It is said that, although the silk pieces piled up high, he executed his pictures quickly. On each painting, he usually inscribed his poems to express his inner feelings. After some time there, he visited Chin-ling 金陵 (Nanking), where the officials also welcomed him.

In 1347 he traveled north to the Yüan capital city where he was invited to stay at the residence of the chief secretary of the court, T'ai-pu-hua (*see* T'ao Tsung-i), who had achieved fame for his administration of the prefecture of Shao-hsing several years previously. Though a number of officials offered to recommend Wang for various positions in the capital, he frightened them away, predicting the coming of rebellions and devastation.

Returning to the south in 1348, he stopped in Wu again and made the same predictions to his friends. Here he settled, bought a hundred *mou* of land on Mt. Chiu-li 九里 in K'uai-chi 會稽, and planted, among other things, a thousand plum trees. He made his home in a studio, wore old clothes and hats, and enjoyed himself by boating on Chien Lake 鑑湖, inviting friends occasionally to join him for wine and food. Among the people he came to know during his travels were some of the leading literati of late Yüan, such as Ts'ao Chih-po (1272-1355), Chang Yü (1277-1348), Wei Su (*q. v.*), and T'ao Tsung-i, Li Hsiao-kuang (1297-1348), and Wei Chung-yüan 魏仲遠.

In 1359 a group of rebel soldiers came to the neighborhood. At first they planned to kill him, but they spared him after he identified himself and boasted that he had some knowledge of military arts. They took him to see their chief, Hu Ta-hai (*q. v.*), a general under Chu Yüan-chang. It is said that later Wang was introduced to Chu at Wu-chou 婺州 (Chin-hua). Adopting the plan to capture Shao-hsing which Wang proposed, Chu asked him to take command in the assault. His scheme failed, however, resulting in heavy casualties. As a result, the rebels blamed him for their defeat. He died soon afterwards and was buried near the famous Lan-t'ing 蘭亭 (Orchid pavilion) in the same district, the site of the almost legendary gathering of the calligrapher Wang Hsi-chih and his friends in the 4th century.

The above version of this encounter with Chu Yüan-chang comes chiefly from the *Pao Yüeh lu* 保越錄, whose author, Hsü Mien-chih 徐勉之, a partisan of Chang Shih-ch'eng (*q. v.*), was quite unsympathetic to the cause of Chu Yüan-chang. Other versions tell the story differently. Hsü Hsien 徐顯, in his *Pai shih chi chuan* 稗史集傳, written in the Yüan period, which is the earliest source for Wang Mien's life, wrote of his offering moral advice to the rebel chief, urging him to give up looting and killing and to stop invading eastern Chekiang. Sung Lien (*q. v.*), in his biography of Wang Mien, mentions that Chu Yüan-chang, in planning his campaign to capture that area, sought the advice of Wang and appointed him a staff member, but does not go into further detail. It is likely that the version in the *Pao Yüeh lu* is the most reliable, while the other two sources, both written by his good friends, tried to cover up the real picture and even portrayed him as a hero.

There are several problems connected with the biography of Wang Mien. The first concerns the years of his birth and death. Because there were two persons by the name of Wang Mien in periods not far apart, his dates are given in such standard references as the *Hsü i-nien lu* 續疑年錄 as 1335–1407. These have been followed by many publications on Chinese art, causing some confusion. Another is that one of his earliest biographers was Sung Lien, the chief editor of the *Yüan-shih*. It is possible that Sung originally wrote his biography for that history, but later omitted it. Instead, he included it in his own collected writings. Perhaps because of the influence of this biography, later writers

came to respect Wang Mien as a model literatus. Huang Tsung-hsi (ECCP), the seventeenth-century philosopher, compared himself with Wang Mien in his introduction to the *Ming-i tai-fang lu*. Later Chu I-tsun (ECCP), who contributed a biography of Wang to the *Ming-shih*, carried this line further. Basing himself on Chu's biography, the novelist Wu Ching-tzu (ECCP), in his famous *Ju-lin wai-shih*, dramatized Wang Mien's life, making him a model scholar in his first chapter. In this fictionalization, however, numerous details of his life were changed, adding to the legendary character of Wang's life.

Wang is best known as a painter of plum blossoms, but known also as a poet and a seal-carver. As a painter, he seems to have absorbed the ink-plum tradition in his native prefecture, Shao-hsing, a tradition which began with the arrival there in the early 1130s of the Ch'an monk Chung-jen 仲仁, who is generally credited with the development of this technique. Wang Mien brought it to a high point. During the Yüan dynasty another famous painter of plums, Wu T'ai-su 吳太素, author of the *Sung-chai mei-p'u* 松齋梅譜 (completed in 1351), also lived in this area and might have been acquainted with Wang Mien. In the Ming period three of the best-known painters of plums, all considered followers of Wang Mien, are also connected with this region: Ch'en Lu 陳錄 (T. 憲章, fl. *ca.* 1440), a native of Shao-hsing, Liu Shih-ju 劉世儒 (T. 繼相, H. 雪湖), also a native, and Wang Ch'ien 王謙 (T. 牧之, fl. *ca.* 1500), a native of Hangchow, who lived in Shao-hsing for a time. In this whole stream of development of plum painting, Wang is generally regarded as supreme. He is also credited with developing the technique of using rouge to tint the blossoms which are otherwise in pure ink.

Among some twenty extant paintings attributed to him, the most interesting fall into two types. One, usually on silk, is larger in size and more ambitious in composition and execution; two of the finest examples are one called simply "Mo mei t'u" 墨梅圖, formerly in a private collection in China which depicts a branch of the plum in an L-shape (reproduced by O. Sirén), and another of the same title now in the Japan Imperial Household, which combines a rock and a branch of plum blossoms with the latter in a reverse C-shape (reproduced in *Sō gen no kaiga* 宋元の繪畫, pl. 86). On both of these his poems are inscribed. The other type is generally on paper, smaller and slenderer in format and more informal in treatment and less complex in composition. One such painting, now in the Nelson Gallery of Art in Kansas City, also entitled "Mo mei t'u," has been attributed to him, but is now considered to be by a contemporary, Tsou Fu-yüan 鄒復原 (reproduced in Harada, *Pageant of Chinese Painting*, pl. 385). Several other paintings, including a short handscroll of the same title, dated 1346 (Harada, pl. 387), two hanging scrolls of almost identical composition, one in the Masagi Museum 正木美術舘 in Izumi-Ōtsu 泉大津, Japan, and another in the former Shao Fu-ying 邵福瀛 collection in China entitled "Chao-shui ku-mei t'u" (Sirén, pl. 118), both dated 1355, and a fourth painting of the same date, called "Mei-hua t'u" 梅花圖 with five inscriptions of his own and many colophons by Ming literati, all show a standard arrangement—depicting the plum branch in a reverse S-curve. The "Chao-shui ku-mei t'u," bearing a long inscription which he wrote, called "Mei hsien-sheng chuan" 梅先生傳, is his way of giving the story of plum trees in China with some reference to himself.

Many of his poems have been collected in the *Chu-chai shih chi* 竹齋詩集, although originally he must have written many more than those in this volume. The first edition of this book was prefaced by Liu Chi (*q. v.*), who wrote that he first met the author in 1354 in the latter's native place. Liu praised Wang Mien's poetry for its straightforward expression, sincerity, solidity, and breadth.

In some of his poems, Wang attempts to compare himself with heroes of ancient times. In others, he shows his sympathy for the suffering of the people. A number of his oft-quoted poems go so far as to criticize the Mongols cynically. He wrote many poems for his paintings, referring to artists of the past and to others of his own time who must have inspired some of his works. Certain of his poems are included in a volume entitled *Tun chiao chi* 敦交集, which Wei Chung-yüan edited, incorporating poetic exchanges he had with his friends.

As a carver of seals Wang Mien is credited with the first use of the variegated hard soapstone 花乳石, largely replacing wood, copper, or ivory; this caused a minor revolution in the art. In his own paintings, he generally used two or more seals for his inscriptions.

Bibliography

Yin-te 35: 22/238/8a; 23/36/24b; 25/91下/12b; 29/2 庚; *Yin-te* 24: 1/285/5a; 3/266/4b; 5/116/18a; 6/1/ 2b, 5/24a, 7/22a, 45/37a; 23/17/8a; 32/49/3a; 61/ 151/16a; 64/18/6a; 65/7/9b; 84/甲前/8a; 88/10/1a; Wang Mien, *Chu-chai shih chi* (in *Shao-wu* 邵武 *Hsü shih* 徐氏 *ts'ung-shu*, 2/7); Hsü Hsien, *Pai shih chi chuan* (in *Li-tai hsiao shih* 歷代小史, 77), 9b; Sung Lien, *Sung hsüeh-shih wen chi* (SPTK ed.), 10/15a; Hsü Mien, *Pao Yüeh lu* (TsSCC ed.); Yeh Sheng, *Shui-tung jih-chi* (in Shen Chieh-fu, *Chi-lu hui-pien*, 138), 2/25b; Wei Chung-yüan, *Tun-chiao chi* (in *Yüan-jen hsüan Yüan-shih wu chung* 元人選元詩五種), 2b; Liu Chi, *Fei hsüeh lu* (in *Ku-chin shuo hai* 古今說海), 6b; K'ung Ch'i 孔齊 (fl. 1330–60), *Chih-cheng chih chi* 至正 直記, 4/6b; Chang Yü, *Ching chü chi* (SPTK ed.), 3/7b; Lu Jung 陸容 (1436–94), *Shu-yüan tsa chi* 菽園雜記 (in *Mo-hai chin-hu* 墨海金壺), 12/12a; Lang Ying, *Ch'i-hsiu lei kao*, 24/370; Li Jih-hua, *Tzu-t'ao-hsüan yu chui*, 1/16b; Huang Tsung-hsi, *Ming-i-tai-fang lu*, 1; Chu I-tsun, *P'u shu-t'ing chi* (SPTK ed.), 64/1a; Hsia Wen-yen 夏文彥 (fl. 1365), *T'u-hui pao-chien* 圖繪寶鑑 (*Hua-shih ts'ung-shu* ed.), 5/135; Chiang Shao-shu 姜紹書 (fl. 1644), *Wu-sheng shih shih* 無聲詩 史 (*ibid.*), 1/14; T'ao Yüan-tsao 陶元藻, *Yüeh hua chien wen* 越畫見聞 (*ibid.*), A/11a; T'ung I-chü 童翼駒, *Mo-mei jen-ming lu* 人名錄 (*ibid.*), 13; *Shan-yin-hsien chih* 山陰縣志 (1803 ed.),

16/21a; *Shao-hsing-fu chih* (1792 ed.), 54/23a; Hung Jui 洪瑞, *Wang Mien*, Peking, 1962; Osvald Sirén, *Chinese Painting* (New York, 1956-58), Vol. IV, 100, Vol. VI, pls. 118, 119, Vol. VII, 139; E. J. Laing, *Chinese Painting in Chinese Publications, 1956-1968* (Ann Arbor, 1969), 139; Sherman E. Lee and Wai-kam Ho, *Chinese Art under the Mongols* (Cleveland, 1968), 49, 98, pl. 250.

Chu-tsing Li

WANG Shen-chung 王愼中 (T. 道思, H. 遵巖居士, 南江仲子), 1509-59, a native of Chin-chiang 晉江, Fukien, and an official, is best known as a man of letters. It is said that he was capable of reciting poetry at the age of three. Certainly he must have been precocious, for when only seventeen he passed the *chih-shih* examination (1526) and was appointed secretary of a bureau in the ministry of Finance and then to an office in the bureau of the ministry of Rites. Among his colleagues, there were such scholars as T'ang Shun-chih, Li K'ai-hsien (*qq.v.*), and others who greatly stimulated his literary development. When an imperial edict appeared in 1533 ordering the selection of members for the Hanlin from among the officials at court, a number of people talked of recommending Wang. This was made known to the grand secretary, Chang Fu-ching (*q.v.*), who invited him for an interview, but Wang declined the invitation. Not surprisingly his name was passed over; instead, he received an appointment in the bureau of evaluation of the ministry of Personnel. In 1538 or 1539 he was transferred to Ch'ang-chou 常州 (east of Nanking) as assistant prefect. After serving in a number of other offices including that of administration vice commissioner of Honan, (1535) he resigned over a disagreement on policy with Grand Secretary Hsia Yen (*q.v.*) and retired (1541). His collected works, entitled *Tsun-yen chi* 遵巖集, 25 *ch.*, were copied into the Imperial Library in the 18th century, but his *Wan-fang-t'ang chai kao* 玩芳堂摘稿,

4 *ch.*, was merely listed by title in the Catalogue. Selections of his prose and poetry are included in various *ts'ung-shu*. In the judgment of his contemporaries he was a peer in literature of T'ang Shun-chih, Li K'ai-hsien, Ch'en Shu 陳束 (T. 約之, H. 后岡, cs 1529), Hsiung Kuo 熊過 (T. 叔仁, H. 南沙子, cs 1529), Jen Han 任瀚 (T. 少海, cs 1529), Chao Shih-ch'un 趙時春 (T. 景仁, H. 浚谷, 1509-67, cs 1526), and Lü Kao 呂高 (T. 山甫, H. 江峯, 1505-57, cs 1529), a group which came to be known as Pa-ts'ai-tzu 八才子 (eight men of talent).

Wang started his literary career by writing in the classical style. Influenced by the Ch'ien-ch'i-tzu (seven early masters) led by Li Meng-yang (*q.v.*), he began imitating the works of the people of Ch'in and Han as they did. He then came to the conclusion that no writing after the Han dynasty was of any value and clung to this opinion until he came across some of the essays of Sung writers. The works of Tseng Kung (1019-83), Wang An-shih (1021-86), and Ou-yang Hsiu (1007-72) particularly pleased him, but he disparaged the works of Su Hsün (1009-66), Su Shih (1037-1101), and Su Che (1039-1112)—father and sons—which he held to be vulgar. He then decided to burn all he had written in imitation of the literature of Ch'in and Han. His friend T'ang Shun-chih, witnessing his action, criticized it as excessive. He answered: "It is hard for me to explain the reasons behind my action, but you will feel it when you pick up your pen and do your writing." Indeed it came true that T'ang changed his view and like Wang started imitating the works of Tseng Kung and Ou-yang Hsiu.

From this point on T'ang and Wang banded together to promote the essays of these writers. They were convinced that a school which proposes to imitate slavishly the works of Ch'in and Han led by such people as Li Meng-yang and Ho Ching-ming (*q.v.*), had eventuated in the creation of literature that was both unreadable and distasteful. In this they were later joined by Mao K'un and Kuei Yu-kuang (*qq.v.*). Their combined assault put into eclipse the writings of the Ch'ien-ch'i-tzu.

The theory of literature which they advocated may be seen in the correspondence between Wang and T'ang, especially in an essay entitled "Ta Mao Lu-men (K'un) chih-hsien lun-wen-shu" 答茅鹿門（坤）知縣論文書 by T'ang, which is considered representative of the school and its principles. This essay outlines their key points: to express in any style a writer's direct feelings and emotion, this expression to be true in every sense; to oppose imitations of form and style, as readers would pass over such writing since they had the works of Shen Yüeh (441–513). In this essay T'ang explained that the reason why works of all schools in the pre-Ch'in and Han were preserved was because, in his view, each of them created its ideal and presented its own true expression. T'ang went on to say that the reason for the increasing neglect of essays of post-T'ang and Sung which discussed hsing-ming 性命 (nature and human nature) and tao-hsüeh 道學 (orthodox learning) was because they contributed nothing in themselves, being merely imitations of the ancients.

The literary pronouncements of Wang and T'ang sounded the death knell of renaissance led by Li Meng-yang and became the basis for the Kung-an p'ai sponsored later by Yüan Hung-tao (*q.v.*).

Bibliography

1/287/6b; 3/268/5a; 5/92/49a; 40/40/21a; 61/101/5b; 64/戊9/2b; 84/丁上/7b; 86/12/8b; SK (1930), 172/4a, 177/5a; *Ch'ang-chou-fu chih* (1886 reprint of 1695 ed.), 13/43a, 31/26a; *Honan t'ung chih* (1914), 31/25b; Kuo Shao-yü 郭紹虞, *Chung-kuo wen-hsüeh p'i-p'ing shih* 中國文學批評史 (1961), 307; Ho Ch'iao-yüan, *Ming-shan ts'ang*, 81/33b; TSCC (1885–88), XXIII: 102/90/10b.

Chin-tang Lo

WANG Shih-chen 王世貞 (T. 元美, H. 鳳洲, 弇州山人), December 8, 1526–1590, official and man of letters, was a native of T'ai-ts'ang 太倉, Nan-Chihli. He came from a distinguished family. His grandfather, Wang Cho 王倬 (T. 用檢, H. 質菴), a *chin-shih* of 1478, rose to be right vice minister of War in Nanking. Wang Shih-chen's father, Wang Yü 王忬 (T. 民應, H. 思質, 1507–November 17, 1560, cj 1531, cs 1541), served from 1552 to 1554 as assistant censor-in-chief and director of the coastal defense of Chekiang which was then being subjected to frequent raids by pirates. He next became governor of Shansi and a year later was appointed supreme commander of Chi-Liao in charge of frontier defenses north and northeast of Peking. When the imperial forces suffered a defeat by the Mongols in April, 1559, permitting the invaders to breach the Great Wall near Hsi-feng-k'ou 喜峯口 and plunder that area for five days, Wang Yü and several generals were held responsible for the disaster and sentenced to death. There are stories asserting that the reason for this harsh punishment of Wang Yü was the hostility between his son, Wang Shih-chen, and the chief minister of that time, Yen Sung (*q.v.*), who together with his son, Yen Shih-fan, had been looking for a pretext to destroy the Wang family. Wang Shih-chen personally appealed for mercy, but in vain, and late in 1560 his father was executed by imperial order. Only after Chu Tsai-hou (*q.v.*) ascended the throne and redeemed many who had been condemned during Yen Sung's heyday was Wang Yü posthumously rehabilitated (1567) in answer to a new petition of Wang Shih-chen. Twenty years later (1587), again on the son's request, Wang Yü was posthumously granted the title of minister of War.

It is said that at the early age of six Wang Shih-chen had memorized an astonishing number of characters. When only seventeen years of age, he passed the provincial examination and in 1547 he became *chin-shih*. Succeeding at the same time were Yang Chi-sheng, Chang Chü-cheng (*qq.v.*), and the poet Li Hsien-fang 李先芳 (T. 伯承, H. 東岱, 北山, 1511–94). Wang was at first named to a post in the Grand Court of Revision. In 1548 he was appointed an assistant secretary of the ministry of Justice. He stayed in Peking for about ten years, rising in rank in the ministry until in 1556 he received a transfer to the post of surveillance vice commissioner at Ch'ing-chou 青州, Shantung, where he arrived in 1557.

During his stay in Peking he laid the basis for his literary fame. On the recommendation of Li Hsien-fang in 1549, he joined a literary circle typical of the Ming period. Besides Li some of the members were Wang Tsung-mu (*q.v.*), Wu Wei-yüeh 吳維嶽 (T. 峻伯, H. 霽寰, 1514–69, cs 1538), and the Hou-ch'i-tzu 後七子 (seven later masters) including in addition to Wang Shih-chen, Hsieh Chen (*see* Hsü Chung-hsing), Tsung Ch'en (*q.v.*), Liang Yu-yü (*see* Huang Tso), Hsü Chung-hsing, and Wu Kuo-lun, as well as Li P'an-lung (*qq.v.*). At that time the leader of the group was Li P'an-lung, who already enjoyed a considerable reputation and who fascinated Wang Shih-chen (twelve years his junior) with his literary theories and his writings. Wang was obviously singled out by Li as the most talented. The backgrounds of the two men had been quite different, geographically and socially; this became evident only much later in the literary field, but until the death of Li P'an-lung in 1570 they collaborated in close friendship. Wang gradually became known in the capital and attracted the attention of higher officials. Together with Li, he became one of the leading figures of the renaissance movement, known as return to ancient style 古文辭運動. The ideas of this classicist school gradually gained acceptance. Its members condemned the contemporary t'ai-ko style (*see* Yang Shih -ch'i and Li Tung-yang) as well as the pa-ku-wen 八股文 style of the examination hall, in consequence of which the

literature of Sung Confucianism also came to be slighted. They advocated the "return to the ancient" and "revival of the ancient," taking as a model for prose the Ch'in-Han period and as model for poetry the Han, Wei, and mid-T'ang period. Thoughts which already had been formulated one generation earlier by Li Meng-yang, Ho Ching-ming (*qq.v.*), and others were now further developed. This preceding classicistic group became known as the Ch'ien 前-ch'i-tzu (seven early masters) of the Ming.

Around this time the dominant figure on the political scene was the chief minister Yen Sung. He tried to attract men of literary fame and to bring them under his influence, among them Wang Shih-chen, who, however, refused to take part in the general servility. In 1554 open hostility between Wang and Yen Sung broke out. Wang's friend, Yang Chi-sheng, second secretary in the War ministry, had presented a memorial to the emperor on the "ten major transgressions and five infamies" of Yen Sung, in which he boldly castigated the minister; as a consequence he was imprisoned and executed in 1555. Wang stood by him, defended him, and finally arranged for his burial. The result was that Yen Sung twice barred Wang's promotion and arranged to have him transferred to Ch'ing-chou, a prefecture notorious for its lawlessness.

The condemnation of his father in 1559 certainly left a deep mark on Wang. He immediately resigned and not only spent the "three years of mourning" in his native place but remained there until the enthronement of Chu Tsai-hou in 1567, in spite of the fact that Yen had been overthrown in 1562. During those years he began to design his gardens, which later became famous. The first of these was a small one laid out beside his dwelling within the town walls and was named Li-tzu-yüan 離薋園 (garden to keep off thorns). A second garden of about eleven acres was built inside the west gate

of T'ai-ts'ang, in which he erected a pavilion for his collection of sūtras. At first
this garden received the Buddhist name
of Hsiao-chih-lin 小祇林 or Hsiao-chih-
yüan 園, but later this was changed to
Yen-shan 弇山 yüan.

After the rehabilitation of his father,
for which occasion he returned (1567) for
a brief time to the capital, Wang went
back to his native place. In 1568 he accepted the position of surveillance vice
commissioner in Ta-ming 大名, Pei-Chihli.
Here he stayed only a few months during
the autumn and winter, because by the
end of that year he received orders to
transfer to Wu-hsing 吳興, Chekiang, to
replace Li P'an-lung. In 1570 Wang was
promoted to surveillance commisioner in
Shansi, but held the post barely three
months, for he returned home late that
year due to his mother's illness. After her
death three years of mourning followed.
Between 1573 and 1576 he held the posts
of surveillance commissioner of Hukuang
(1573), president of the Court of the
Imperial Stud (1574), and governor at
Yün-yang 鄖陽 (1574–76). When in the
autumn of 1576 he was called to take the
position of president of the Grand
Court of Revision, the censor Yang
Chieh 楊節 (cs 1568) denounced him,
forcing him to renounce the post. The
same thing happened when he was nominated as prefect of Nanking. On imperial
order he had to return home, where he
stayed for more than a decade.

It is highly likely that the frequent
transfers of Wang, which undermined his
influence, as well as the denunciation by
Yang, were due to Chang Chü-cheng.
Contemporary biographers indicate this.
The *Ming-shih* and other notices record
that Wang brought about the condemnation of the younger brother of Chang
Chü-cheng's wife and covertly accused
Chang Chü-cheng himself of being responsible for the earthquake in Ching-chou.
The main reason for this mutual hostility,
however, was probably that Wang, as a
well-known and independent scholar, exert-

ed considerable power; and a person in
Chang Chü-cheng's position was constrained to destroy this power as soon as it
ran into conflict with his own interests.
Wang seems to have written in a derogatory way about Chang, going so far, it
is said, as to describe the latter's indulgence in carnal debauchery in a letter to
his friends in the capital. In addition he
once remarked that such a man would
bring disaster to the empire. (Compare
Wang's biography of Chang Chü-cheng in
Chia-ching i-lai nei-ko shou-fu chuan 嘉靖
以來內閣首輔傳, *chüan* 7 and 8.)

About this time Wang Shih-chen had
begun to make an earnest study of Buddhist and Taoist thought. He wrote at one
point: "Earlier I said that there is nothing
to add to the Way of the saints. Now,
however, I realize that there is something,
the sūtras of the Buddha" (*Yen-chou-shan-
jen ssu-pu kao* 四部稿, 139/14b). When
he was in T'ai-ts'ang where his brother
and his friend, Wang Hsi-chüeh (*q.v.*),
were living, he became a devotee of the
latter's daughter, a Taoist known by the
name of T'an-yang tzu (*see* Wang Tao-
chen), whom the three often went to see
in 1580. Wang Shih-chen called himself
her disciple and wrote her biography after
her death. All three devotees were accused
of heterodoxy in 1581. Although this
matter was not pursued any further, this
also may be one of the deeper reasons
for the hostility between Chang Chü-cheng
and Wang Shih-chen. At this period Wang
was in his fifties; he was the most influential literary figure of the time, and
he had many followers, besides being an
official of some note.

In 1584 Wang declined a nomination
as right vice minister of Justice in Nanking
but four years later accepted the appointment as right vice minister of War in
Nanking, probably persuaded by Wang
Hsi-chüeh. He had completed in 1589 the
required years for rank 3a. When promoted to be minister of Justice in the southern capital, he obtained the rank 2a. At
that moment, however, the censor Huang

Jen-jung 黃仁榮 (cj 1558), an enemy of his for some time, denounced him, accusing him of dishonesty, reminding the court that Wang several times had had charges brought against him while he was holding rank 3a and so did not in fact serve a full term. In spite of this he was permitted to retain his rank and office, but he requested permission to retire. In the spring of 1590 his third petition was finally accepted. He died that autumn.

Wang had three sons, Wang Shih-ch'i 士騏 (b. 1554, cs 1589), Wang Shih-su 士騙 (1566-1601), and Wang Shih-chün 士駿 (1569-97). His great grandson, Wang Chien (ECCP), became known as a landscape painter. Wang Shih-chen's brother, Wang Shih-mou (q.v.), was also a scholar-official, and the brothers lived in a close and productive relationship.

Wang Shih-chen's literary output consists of some thirty titles, some of which are attributed to him, but apparently are not his work, for even during his own day publishers seem to have used his name for the purpose of increased sales. In any case his extraordinary productivity may be regarded as a significant feature of his life. Thus the editors of the Imperial Catalogue write: "Since ancient times nobody has surpassed him in abundance of writings." Some two thirds of his collected works are in the field of belles-lettres; his historical publications amount to another third; moreover, we find books on painting and calligraphy. Creative writings, criticism, and scholarly compilations are included. All of them reveal his broad education, his versatility, and the range of his talents. In the history of Ming literature he is ranked as the most prominent representative of the classicist school. Li P'an-lung introduced him to the school but Li was mainly concerned with promoting the ideas of his predecessor Li Meng-yang. It was Wang Shih-chen's remarkable accomplishment that he combined the northern and southern literary styles by adjusting the classicist tendency to the literary taste of the

south. He himself was a typical representative of the gentry-culture of the south, which may explain the influential position which he held throughout twenty years (from the death of Li P'an-lung in 1570 until his own passing). He was a poet who exerted an enormous influence in his own time and even on later Japanese scholars such as Ogyu Sorai 荻生徂徠 (1666-1728) and Hattori Nankaku 服部南郭 (1683-1759), a disciple of Sorai. As a youth he was passionate and arrogant, refusing to curry the favor of high officials and courageous enough even to oppose them. When he went to the north, he readily accepted the theories of the classicist school which were more in accordance with the austerity of the northern culture than with the over-refined literary culture of the south as developed after the Sung period. It so happened that both Li P'an-lung and Li Meng-yang were men from the north. Because Wang's cultural level was above that of Li P'an-lung, he did not promote the ideas of the classicist school as rigidly as did Li, and after the latter's death, he gradually parted from the original ideas of this school.

Wang, due to his more systematic way of thinking, was better able to formulate a new line of poetics than was Li P'an-lung. One of the most important and best-known books among his critical writings on poetry is *I-yüan chih-yen* 藝苑卮言 which later was included as *chüan* 144-55 in his *Yen-chou-shan-jen ssu-pu kao*. This work reveals Wang clearly as a follower of the classicist school; not surprisingly since the main part of it was written during his collaboration with Li, six *chüan* being composed between 1558 and 1565, and two additional *chüan* as well as four supplementary *chüan* being completed by 1572. Here the *ko-tiao* 格調 theory (or style based on the poetry of the Han, Wei, and mid-T'ang) is clearly manifested. While Wang in this work paid homage to Li P'an-lung, he gently criticised him, by making such remarks as "plagiarism and imitation are great illnesses in poetry."

In 1576, while at Yün-yang, Wang Shih-chen completed his outstanding work, *Yen-chou-shan-jen ssu-pu kao*, 174 *ch.*, which contains a preface dated 1577 by Wang Tao-k'un (*q.v.*); the four sections are: fu, shih, wen, shuo 賦詩文說. Later it was supplemented by the *Hsü-kao* 續稿, 207 *ch.*, edited by Wang Shih-chen's grandson, printed during the Ch'ung-chen period. These two works seem unquestionably his. The slow change in Wang's attitude towards the theory of the classicist school can easily be discovered by reference to the above-mentioned work and to the *Yen-chou-shan-jen tu-shu hou* 讀書後, 8 *ch.*, edited by Ch'en Chi-ju (ECCP) at the end of the Ming. Now Wang stated that the mere return to the ancients as had been demanded by Li Meng-yang and Li P'an-lung was not sufficient; basically, however, he remained a classicist. Wang also acknowledged the transformation of poetic forms during the different periods. He appreciated a poet like Po Chü-i (772–846) whom Li P'an-lung had completely neglected, and he warmly praised the poems of Su Tung-p'o (1037–1101) as shown by the preface to his own *Su Chang-kung wai-chi* 蘇長公外紀, 10 *ch*. Su was a poet whom Li P'an-lung had condemned as well. The official biography in the *Ming-shih* illustrates this development in Wang's thinking with the following anecdote: "When Wang Shih-chen was seriously ill, Liu Feng 劉鳳 (T. 子威, cs 1544) visited him and saw in his hands a book of Su Tung-p'o, which he zealously read and did not put aside." In his later life Wang did not deny a certain merit even in a contemporary opponent like Kuei Yu-kuang (*q.v.*), who once had called him pretentious and mediocre.

The renaissance movement may be credited with the promotion of Ch'in and Han works such as the *Shih-chi*. Wang indeed took an active part in this revival of classical literature. Indirectly this group also contributed to an increased esteem for literature by emphazising that it was the highest human accomplishment. As a result of this, fiction and drama enjoyed a prestige unknown before. Doubtless Wang was in contact with this movement; this may be concluded from the famous anecdote that he was the author of the novel *Chin P'ing Mei* 金瓶梅 and the drama *Ming-feng chi* 鳴鳳記. Possibly he had some connection with the writing of this play which deals in detail with the intrigues of Yen Sung and his son Yen Shih-fan as well as with the sufferings of their victims, such as Hsia Yen (*q.v.*) and Yang Chi-sheng. It vividly pictures the history and society of those days, a characteristic almost unique in the drama of that time, which was concerned largely with love affairs. [Editors' note: For English translations of the *Chin P'ing Mei* (partial and complete) *see* T'ien-yi Li, *Chinese Fiction* (New Haven, 1968), 122; for a brief discussion of the *Ming-feng chi, see* Josephine Huang Hung, *Ming Drama* (Taipei, 1966), 124.]

Among his other writings special mention may be made of *Wan-wei yü-pien* 宛委餘編, which is included in the *Ssu-pu kao*. Wang's collected poems are in this and also in the *Ssu-pu hsü-kao*. According to Yoshikawa Kōjirō 吉川幸次郎, "the style of many of Wang's poems, as well as that of Li P'an-lung, is somewhat stiff because both followed ancient patterns. But in contrast to Li, Wang's style is more flexible and picturesque, indicating his multifarious talents." Wang, for example, wrote some poems in the style of Po Chü-i. Most of Wang's historical writings are concerned with the Ming period. One may take it for granted that Wang made it his business to record historical events frankly and truthfully as he saw them, especially the happenings of his own time. As a result a number of his books came to be listed for partial or complete censorship in the 18th century; fortunately, copies of most have survived. Among his works in this genre are the *Yen-*

shan-t'ang pieh-chi 弇山堂別集, 100 *ch.* (preface dated 1590; also included in *Ssu-pu kao*), the first version of which was copied into the Imperial Library. According to the *nien-p'u* by Ch'ien Ta-hsin (ECCP), it was written in 1558. It is an important work on state affairs of the Ming period. Others are the *Chia-ching i-lai shou-fu chuan*, 8 *ch.* (preface of 1617), which treats the grand secretaries of the Chia-ching, Lung-ch'ing, and Wan-li periods (1522 to his own time), the *Chin-i chih* 錦衣志, 1 *ch.*, which deals with the Embroidered-uniform Guard, its leading officers and their practices, and the *Ku-pu-ku lu* 觚不觚錄, a collection of miscellaneous notes on the Ming dynasty, which the editors of the *Ssu-k'u* catalogue considered of importance to historians. The library of Columbia University is fortunate in possessing Ming editions of the following: *Yen-chou shan-jen ssu-pu-kao* (printed 1577), *Yen-chou shan-jen tu-shu-hou*, *Yen-shan-t'ang pieh-chi* (1590), *Yen-chou shih-liao* 史料, 30 *ch.*, and *Yen-chou shih-liao hou-chi* 後集, 100 *ch.*, the last two being edited by Tung Fu-piao 董復表 and printed in 1614.

Wang's concern wtih the arts is shown in the compilations *Wang-shih hua-yüan* 畫苑, 10 *ch.*, 4 supplementary *chüan* by Chan Ching-feng 詹景鳳 (T. 車圖, H. 白岳山人), and *Wang-shih shu-yüan* 書苑, 12 *ch.*, with 8 supplementary *chüan* by Chan Ching-feng. Both serve as important reference works for the history of Chinese art. An example of a work attributed to him spuriously is the *Shih-shuo hsin-yü pu* 世說新語補, 20 *ch.* (preface 1586), which is a combination of the collection of anecdotes by Liu I-ch'ing (403-44) and the *Ho-shih yü-lin* by Ho Liang-chün (*q.v.*). Through the influence of Ogyu Sorai this book came to be widely read in Japan.

Bibliography

1/287/17a; 5/45/85a; 15/10/20a; 63/26/31a; 84/丁上/60a; MSL (1965), Chia-ching, 7893, Wan-li (1940), 212/3b, 215/4b, 221/3a; KC (1958), 3861, 3920, 3949, 4624, 4643; SK (1930), 51/7a, 58/2b, 141/11b, 177/18b; *T'ai-ts'ang-chou chih* (1629), 19/1a; *Yen-chou-shan-jen nien-p'u* (in Ch'ien Ta-hsin, ECCP, *Ch'ien-yen-t'ang ch'üan-shu*), Peking, 1884; Huang Ju-wen 黃如文, "Yen-chou hsien-sheng wen-hsüeh nien-piao," *Wen-hsüeh nien-pao* 文學年報, 4, Peking, 1938; Sun Tien-ch'i (1957), 46, 57, 118, 129, 158, 175, 197, 202, 250; Hashimoto Jun 橋本循, "Ō-en-shu no bunshō-kan to sono bunshō" 王弇州の文章觀と其の文章, *Shina-gaku*, I (1921), 379–98M; atsushita Tadashi 松下忠, "Ō Se-tei no Kobunji-setsu yori no dakka nitsuite" 王世貞の古文辭說よりの脱化について, *Chūgoku bungaku-hō*, 5, 1956; Yoshikawa Kōjirō , "Gen-Min-shi gaisetsu" 元明詩概說, 1963; Barbara Krafft, "Wang Shih-chen, Abriss seines Lebens," OE, Jg 5, 1958; L. Carrington Goodrich, *The Literary Inquisition of Ch'ien-lung* (1935), 66, 256; W. Franke, *Sources*, 1.3.8, 2.2.6, 8, 8.1, 3.3.13, 4.3, 6.6, 4.2.3, 4, 6.2.10, 7.6.5.

[Editors' notes:

1) The *Yü* in the name of Wang Yü is pronounced also as *shu*.

2) Concerning the garden, Li-tzu-yüan, the character for *li* in the *Ssu-pu-kao* is also given as 蘺 (weeds), hence signifying "a garden of weeds and thorns." Perhaps he later considered the other reading as too offensive.

3) Wang Shih-chen's comment on Buddhism and Confucianism to the effect that the Buddhist sūtras have something additional to say, should perhaps be considered in the light of the rest of his statement, which severely qualifies it: "Precisely because there is something additional to say, in the end nothing is added. Hence the Way of our sage is limited while that of Buddha is limitless. How is it limited? By keeping to the middle." Apparently Wang liked Buddhist literature but considered the Confucian teaching which depends on evidence preferable to the Buddhist doctrines which require belief in an imagined world.

4) The sources differ as to Wang's dates of birth and death. The *Ming-shih* reports them as 1529–93; the *Kuo-ch'üeh*

records his death at the age of sixty-eight *sui* under date of February 17, 1591, which would make the date of birth *circa* 1524. We follow the epitaph of Wang Hsi-chüeh and the chronological biography by Ch'ien Ta-hsin (ECCP).

5) His trip by boat in 1574 from his home to Peking is recorded in eighty-two paintings in color, the first thirty-two by Ch'ien Ku (*q.v.*) depicting the scenic places from T'ai-ts'ang to Yang-chow, and the rest by Chang Fu 張復 (T.元春, 1546-*ca.* 1631), Ch'ien's student who accompanied Wang Shih-chen. It is said that Chang painted fifty scenes in ink and that later Ch'ien added color. These paintings in three albums are now preserved in the Palace Museum, Taipei.]

Barbara Yoshida-Krafft

WANG Shih-hsing 王士性 (T. 恒叔, H. 天台山元白道人), 1547-98, landscape devotee, geographer, and official, was a native of Lin-hai 臨海, T'ai-chou 台州, ,Chekiang and brought up almost like an adopted son by his distant uncle, Governor Wang Tsung-mu (*q.v.*). He became a *chin-shih* in 1557, and for the twenty-one years until his death held a variety of government positions in Peking and in the provinces. His career seems to have been solidly successful if without particular distinction. In his first post, as magistrate of Ch'üeh-shan 確山, Honan, he had the courage to extend hospitality to Ai Mu (*see* Chao Nan-hsing), an official banished for criticizing the then all-powerful grand secretary, Chang Chü-cheng (*q.v.*). In 1583 he became a supervising secretary in the office of scrutiny. After the period of mourning for his mother (1585-88) he was sent to Szechwan as director of the provincial examination of 1588. He then served as an intendant successively in Yunnan, Honan, and

Shantung. In 1595 he became vice minister of the Court of Imperial Stud but was soon transferred to be minister of the court of state ceremonies in Nanking where he died. For the greater part of his official life he exercised various functions of supervision and inspection which took him on journeys to many places in China and allowed him to indulge his taste for scenery and his catholic interest in geography.

This concern for the land was so strong as to become the driving force of his life. It is symbolized in a story which held that Wang was the reincarnation of a monk of Mt. Omei in Szechwan who before his death (which coincided with the moment of Wang's birth) had vowed in his next life to realize his unfulfilled desire to visit China's famous mountains. Wang admired Hsiang Chang 向長 of the Han dynasty for having climbed the Five Peaks; but he was doubtless drawn also by Hsiang's only recorded utterance: "I know that poverty is better than wealth, and low position preferable to high; but I still do not know how death compares with life"; —for Wang himself had a strong streak of eccentricity and, despite his official career, a liking for solitude that verged on misanthropy. He too succeeded in touring all of the Five Peaks and a large number of other places as well, including virtually all of China's most renowned scenic spots.

His writings grew out of these travels, and he believed that what was expressed in nature as landscape and in man as literature was one and the same irrepressible quintessence of things. His *Wu Yüeh yu ts'ao* 五岳游草, 12 *ch.*, is a collection of prose and poetry, printed in 1593. The *Ch'ien chih* 黔志 and *Yü chih* 豫志, two short regional sketches, were extracted by a book dealer and published as independent works. A later collection of his travels is his *Kuang yu chih* 廣游志, 2 *ch.* The *Kuang chih-i* 廣志繹, 5 *ch.*, the preface of which is dated 1597, contains further observations and reflections arranged by region. *Wu Yüeh yu chi* 五岳游記, 1 *ch.*, (probably completed in Yunnan in 1591) is a brief and polished account of Wang's trips to each of the Five Peaks. One source lists a *Yü hsien chi* 玉峴集 among his works, and one of his poems is included in the *Ming-shih tsung* of Chu I-tsun (EC CP).

Wang's preoccupation with the earth's surface was both mystical and esthetic; the *Kuang chih-i* reveals him also as a well-rounded physical and cultural geographer. His urge to visit personally all possible scenic places reveals his emphasis on personal observation and even experiment. But he was concerned as well with explanatory principles, especially for the regional differences he encountered on his travels. Thus he attempts to understand climates by considering north-south position, elevation, and soil, and to account for the historical rise and fall in the fortunes of various parts of China by geomantic theorizing about the country's three great dragons or mountain systems. The work contains discussions of land forms, tides, regional customs and dialects, the non-Chinese peoples of the southwest, the traders of Macao and their k'un-lun nu 崑崙奴 (black slaves), the question of sea transport of grain to the capital, regional disparities in taxation (on which he is quoted by Ku Yen-wu [ECCP] in *Jih-chih lu*), and many other matters.

His son Wang Li-ku 王立轂 (T. 紫芝) was a *chü-jen* of 1606, but aborted his official career to become a Buddhist monk.

Bibliography

1/223/17a; 3/206/13a; 40/53/10b; *Kuang chih-i*; *Wu Yüeh yu chi*; *T'ai-chou-fu chih* (1936), 103/9b; TSCC (1885–88), XXIII: 110/98/22b; *Chekiang t'ung-chih* (1934), 3152, 4069; Ch'ien Hsi-yen 錢希言, *Kuai yüan chih-i* 獪園志異 (preface of 1613), 8/1a; SK (1930), 78/1b.

Andrew L. March

WANG Shih-mou 王世懋 (T. 敬美, H. 麟洲, 東牆生, 損齋), 1536-August 5 (?) 1588, official, calligrapher, and man of letters, was a native of T'ai-ts'ang 太倉, northwest of Shanghai. He came from a prominent clan which for generations produced degree holders and officials. A story about his childhood relates that when his elder brother, Wang Shih-chen (*q.v.*), passed the provincial examination, Wang Shih-mou, then only seven, used to get up very early to study, explaining when asked that he did not want to lag behind his brother. At the age of nine he contracted tuberculosis which affected his health throughout his life. His father Wang Yü (*see* Wang Shih-chen) refrained from pressing him in his studies but the boy worked hard anyway, an attitude which delighted his father. Some years later he became a student in the National University in Peking, passing the provincial examination at the capital in 1558, and the *chin-shih* in the following year. Not long afterwards his father, for his defeat at the Luan River 灤河, was lodged in prison to await execution. Wang Shih-mou and his elder brother did their utmost to save him but to no avail. After their father's death, he and his brother stayed at home for about ten years. During this period he devoted himself to writing poetry and came to be considered a rising star in the literary circles of his day.

His reentry into civil service came one year after Emperor Chu Tsai-hou (*q.v.*) came to the throne. He received an appointment as a secretary in the bureau of ceremonies in the ministry of Rites, at Nanking. Shortly after he assumed office he achieved a certain reputation for criticizing the chief military commissioner in Nanking, Hsü P'eng-chü 徐鵬舉, the duke of Wei 魏國公 (enf. 1519, d. March 9, 1570), for the latter's attempt to make the son of his concubine his heir rather than the son by his first wife. In 1570 he was ordered transferred to a vice directorship in the ministry of Rites, but

Empress Liu (d. 1615), mother of Chu Yu-chiao and Empress Wang (d. 1619),
mother of Chu Yu-chien (1611–44)

Chu yu-chiao (1605–27)

PLATE 11

陽明先生像

Wang Shou-jen (1472–1529) by Ch'en Hung-shou (1599–1652), dated 1646

PLATE 12

was forced to decline because of illness. On his way home he received the news of his mother's death.

He returned to the ministry of Rites after the mourning period to fill a vacancy in the bureau of sacrifices. Later he became assistant minister in the seal office. Having only light official duties, he spent much of his time associating with men of letters, and formed a literary society. In 1576 he received the appointment of assistant administration commissioner of Kiangsi province, where he proved himself an able official. A censor who was impressed by his ability took him on tour to Kiukiang and Jao-chou 饒州 to assist in administrative business before the governor arrived. After that he was promoted to be provincial surveillance vice commissioner in charge of postal service in the lower reaches of the Yangtze valley; this was not an easy assignment and required a competent man. Wang proved able to control his staff effectively and reduce corruption. In the autumn of 1579 he was entrusted with the supervision of the provincial examination in Kiangsi. His fairness won him a promotion to be educational director in Shensi in the following year.

In 1580 he and his brother became devotees of the Taoist daughter of Wang Hsi-chüeh (q.v.). Although the accusation of heterodoxy lodged against them later caused them no real trouble, Wang Shih-mou felt obliged to resign his post. He retired to his native town in October, 1581, where he erected a villa called T'an-yüan 澹園, and devoted himself to writing and to gardening.

Three year later, due to his brother's urging, Wang accepted another appointment as educational director, this time in Fukien, a province where his father had participated in the defense against Japanese pirates in 1550. So he came to this area with a sense of mission, one purpose being to find young men of talent. He withstood the temptations of bribery, giving himself over during his first three months to reading papers of the provincial examina-

tion. This led him to be very careful to show no favoritism towards those whose family members were people of influence. He came to develop a genuine interest in Fukien. The customs of the local people, the activities of their literary circles, the mountain scenery, and the variety of the province's flowers, trees, and fruits (over eighty are mentioned)—all these he lucidly recorded in his *Min-pu shu* 閩部疏, *Hsüeh-p'u tsa-shu* 學圃雜疏, and other writings. He is said also to have protected Lin Chao-en (q.v.), known for his advocacy of the heterodox doctrine of three religions in one.

Shortly after his transfer to be administration vice commissioner in the Fukien provincial administration office, Wang was called to Peking to be chief minister in the Court of Imperial Sacrifices. Unfortunately ill health cut short his career. He returned home in the winter of 1587 and died a few months later.

His writings, collected and printed by his brother, were entitled *Wang Feng-ch'ang chi* 奉常集 (poetry, 15 *ch.*, prose, 54 *ch.*); the book contains three prefaces, dated 1589, by Wu Kuo-lun (q.v.), Li Wei-chen (see Hsieh Chao-che), and Ch'en Wen-chu (see Wu Ch'eng-en). His work of literary criticism, *I-p'u hsieh yü* 秇圃擷餘, and fifty-eight prefaces written for the books of certain friends, which are included in the above, deserve special mention. So too do others published during his lifetime, later collected under the title *Wang Feng-ch'ang tsa-chu* 雜著. Practically all of his writings (fifteen in number) are listed in the Imperial Catalogue, but only one, the *I-p'u hsieh yü*, was thought worthy of inclusion in the *Ssu-k'u ch'üan-shu*; another, the *K'uei-t'ien wai-ch'eng* 窺天外乘 (1 *ch.*), drew the criticism of other officials of the Ch'ien-lung era who ordered that a certain passage be torn out and burned. More recently, however, his descriptions of life, activities, and products of Fukien have received more favorable attention. Dr. Joseph Needham, for example, has noted his description of paper makers in Fukien who "mounted their trip-hammers in boats each with two water-wheels and furiously pounded away by the aid of the fast-flowing current of their rivers." Dr. Walter Swingle has remarked on his early (1587) description of maize in China. And Philip K. Reynolds and Mrs. C. Y. Fang have dilated on his comments on the varieties of the banana plant in Fukien; the mei-jen-chiao 美人蕉 of Foochow, Wang asserted, was the most beautiful in the banana family. He was noted too for his excellent calligraphy.

Wang had four sons and four daughters. His youngest daughter became the wife of the son of Chao Yung-hsien (*q. v.*).

Bibliography

1/287/20a; 5/70/81a, 58/24b; 22/10/50a; 40/47/27b; 43/4/4b; 64/巳7/1a; 84/丁上/62a; 86/14/6b; MSL (1965), Mu-tsung, 1034, Shen-tsung (1966), 2021, 2175; KC (1958), 3949, 4583; SK (1930), 64/3b, 127/7b, 144/4b, 178/6b; TSCC (1885–88), XIV: 277/361/25a, XXIII: 107/631/22b, XXIV: 124/652/36b; Chang Hsüan, *Hsi-yüan chien-wen lu*, 11/36b, 14/36a, 20/18b; Wang Shih-chen, *Yen-chou-shan-jen hsü-kao*, 140/1a; *id.*, *Yen-chou-shan-jen ssu-pu kao*, 150/17b; *id.*, *Yen-chou shih-liao*, 26/12b; Ch'ien Ta-hsin (ECCP), *Yen-chou-shan-jen nien-p'u* 年譜, 6a; Chao Yung-hsien, *Sung-shih-chai wen-chi*, 8/6a; Li Wei-chen, *Ta-mi-shan-fang chi*, 11/8b, Wang Tao-k'un, *T'ai-han fu mo*, 16/51a; Wang Shih-mou, *Wang Feng-ch'ang chi* 序/1a, 5/19a, 7/1a, 7/15b, 8/6a, 47/19b; Sun Tien-ch'i (1957), 27; Shimizu Taiji 清水泰次, *Mindai shi ronsō* 明代史論叢 (Tokyo, 1962), 438; Walter T. Swingle, *Report of the Library of Congress, Orientalia Added, 1932–33* (Washington, 1934), 10; Philip K. Reynolds and Mrs. C. Y. Fang, "The Banana in Chinese Literature," HJAS, V (1940–41), 170; Joseph Needham, *Science and Civilization in China*, IV: 2 (Cambridge, England, 1965), 410.

Mingshui Hung

WANG Shou-jen 王守仁 (T. 伯安, H. 陽明), October 31, 1472–January 9, 1529, philosopher and official, came from a family registered in Yü-yao 餘姚, Chekiang, but residing most of the time in the prefectural city of Shao-hsing. His father, Wang Hua 華 (T. 德輝, H. 實庵, 海日翁, 龍山公, 1453–March 9, 1522), chosen optimus in the examination of 1481, rose to be minister of Personnel at Nanking (1507). It is said that Wang Shou-jen was unable to speak until the age of four. He joined his father in Peking when he was ten years of age; his mother having died when he was thirteen, he remained there two more years. He began formal schooling at eleven and exhibited a developing spirit of adventure and a questioning of orthodox beliefs, characteristics that help to explain his future turbulent political career and dynamic thinking. At fifteen, when he visited the Chü-yung 居庸 Pass, north of Peking, he showed a keen interest in archery. At sixteen he went to Nanchang, Kiangsi, for his marriage. There is a story told that on the day of the wedding he went to visit a Taoist priest. Their discussion on the nourishing of life became so absorbing that he stayed in the temple throughout his wedding night. There are many comparable stories about his early years. The one on his wishing to volunteer to put down a rebellion, however, is obviously false for that particular uprising had already been suppressed six years before his birth.

An important event occurred in 1489 when he was seventeen. On his way home from Nanchang he visited Lou Liang (*q. v.*) at Kuang-hsin, Kiangsi, who told him about the doctrine of ko-wu 格物 (investigation of things) advocated by the Sung neo-Confucianists, and that one could become a sage through learning. This interview served to open up for him the broad vista of neo-Confucianism. In the following year his father arranged for him and his cousins to discuss the meaning of the Classics. In 1492 at the age of twenty he obtained the *chü-jen* degree and was again with his father in Peking. Most probably it was at this time that he tried to test the theory of Chu Hsi

(1130–1200), about the investigation of things, by sitting in front of some bamboos to try to discern their principles, only to fall ill after several days. This failure led him to devote his energy to literary composition but even that effort did not help him to pass the metropolitan examinations of 1493 and 1496. About this time he shifted his attention to the study of military arts in which he became quite expert, and of Taoist techniques for prolonging life. After further disillusionment with the study of Chu Hsi and with literary pursuits, and being in rather delicate health, he actually contemplated entering some Taoist retreat to search for ways of attaining longevity. In 1499, however, he passed the *chin-shih* examinations. Thereupon he received an appointment in the ministry of Works.

It happened that at this juncture the emperor issued an edict inviting recommendations. In response Wang memorialized the throne recommending eight measures for national defense and security. Although these recommendations were not implemented, they drew attention to him because of his sensible ideas on defense, strategy, finance, and the administration of the frontier, some of which he himself had the opportunity two decades later of putting into practice with signal success. In the following year he was appointed a secretary in the ministry of Justice. A year later (1501) he was ordered to check the records of prisoners in the prefectures north of Nanking, and is said to have corrected injustices in a number of cases.

Active involvement in government had now made him increasingly conscious of the errors in both Taoism and Buddhism as well as of the mistake of devoting himself to literary composition. His health declined and he had hemorrhages. Consequently, in the autumn of 1502, he received leave to return home for recuperation. He liked the Yang-ming 陽明 ravine in the K'uai-chi 會稽 range, situated twenty *li* southeast of Shao-hsing, so much

that he built a cottage there for his retreat and called himself Yang-ming tzu 子. Very likely he engaged in some sort of Taoist exercises for reasons of health, but there is no substance to the story that he became so expert in the Taoist art that he actually could foretell in detail the visit of friends, or that he contemplated deserting society altogether. In any event, when his health was fairly well restored two years later, he returned to Peking. In the autumn of 1504 he was invited to conduct the provincial examination in Shantung. Later he became a secretary in the ministry of War. The following year scholars began to come to him as students. He gave them lectures on the need to make up their minds to become Confucian sages and he attacked the habits of recitation and flowery compositions. Not unnaturally the conservative and the jealous accused him of courting popularity. Chan Jo-shui (*q. v.*), then a Hanlin bachelor, saw great promise in him, however, befriended him, and joined him in an effort to promote Confucianism. In the total record of Wang's intellectual development, this contact is fully as important as his earlier meeting with Lou Liang.

A critical event in his life occurred in 1506. The new emperor, Chu Houchao (*q. v.*), a youth of fifteen, fell into a situation in which the eunuch Liu Chin (*q. v.*) dominated the government. On February 10, a supervising censor in Nanking, Tai Hsien 戴銑 (T. 寶之, cs 1496), led a group in a joint memorial attacking the powerful eunuch. Liu Chin had him thrown into prison. Wang immediately presented a memorial in his defense, although Tai was a stranger to him. As a result he was imprisoned for about two months, and after suffering a beating of forty strokes in the palace, was then banished to northwestern Kweichow as head of the Lung-ch'ang 龍場 dispatch station. In the summer of 1507 he started on his way to the place of exile. When he reached the Ch'ien-t'ang 錢塘 River near Hangchow, he discovered that agents of Liu Chin were following him. Fearing the worst, he discarded his clothing on the river bank to suggest suicide, and thus escaped. After visiting his father at Nanking he went to Kweichow overland by way of Kuang-hsin and Changsha, arriving in the spring of 1508. Exciting accounts have been invented to dramatize his escape by reporting that after he eluded the agents, he boarded a merchant vessel and went to Fukien, where, after walking for tens of *li* at night, he was refused admission to a Buddhist monastery, spent the night in a deserted temple which a tiger dared not enter to devour him, and was advised by a strange person and by divination to return home. It was then, according to the myth, that he went to visit his father in Nanking.

Lung-ch'ang was inhabited by Miao and Liao aborigines, who liked him well enough to build his wooden structures to replace the straw huts provided at the station. Still conditions were primitive, so that his subordinates frequently fell sick, and he had to draw water, gather fuel, and do the cooking. He cheered his companions and himself by singing. Under these conditions of hardship and solitude he gave himself up to a period of intense thought. One night an understanding of the Confucian principle of the investigation of things suddenly burst upon him. Thus in 1508, at the age of thirty-six, he came to the realization that to investigate the principles of things is not to seek for them externally in actual objects, as Chu Hsi had taught, but to look for them in one's own mind. In his understanding, these things, although distributed throughout all matter, are not outside the mind. To him principles and mind are identical. In this he stands diametrically opposed to Chu Hsi who believed that principles exist independently of the mind. His doctrine was as new as it was revolutionary. To support his radical ideas and also to show that he did not deviate from the Classics, he wrote the *Wu-ching i-shuo* 五經億說

of which only thirteen passages have survived (in the *Wang Wen-ch'eng kung ch'üan-shu, ch.* 26). His ideas did not enjoy ready acceptance.

In the following year his thinking took another major step forward, namely, the formulation of the epoch-making theory that knowledge and action are one （知行合一）. The relationship between knowledge and action had always been a central thesis in the Confucian tradition, but from Confucius to Chu Hsi the emphasis had been on their correspondence and mutual dependence. Wang struck a new note in declaring that "knowledge in its genuine and earnest aspect is action and action in its intelligent and discriminating aspect is knowledge," that "knowledge is the beginning of action and action is the completion of knowledge," and that "fundamentally the task of knowledge and action cannot be separated." One knows beauty or filial piety, he argued, only when one experiences and acts upon it. He expounded this doctrine undoubtedly when vice commissioner Hsi Shu (*q. v.*) invited him to lecture at the Kuei-yang 貴陽 Academy and treated him as a teacher.

In 1510 Wang was promoted to be magistrate of Lu-ling 廬陵, Kiangsi, arriving in the spring. There he inaugurated the various measures that were to be prototypes in his later administrations and were to make him politically famous, namely, by issuing pronouncements (sixteen times) of moral admonition, selecting community elders to help instruct and direct the people, and establishing the ten-family joint registration system (保甲) in which the families are grouped together with joint responsibility for the prevention of crime and bandit infiltration. In the winter, seven months after Liu Chin had been executed, Wang was granted an imperial audience in Peking. A month later he received promotion to the office of secretary in the ministry of Justice at Nanking. The next year (1511) he was transferred to the ministry of

Personnel in the same city where he rose to become director of a bureau. Later in Nanking he became vice minister of the Court of the Imperial Stud (1512) and then chief minister of the Court of State Ceremonial (1514). During this period his pupil and brother-in-law, Hsü Ai 徐愛 (T. 曰仁, H. 橫山, 1487-1517, cs 1508), discussed with him the basic tenets of his philosophy, notably the investigation of things, the identity of mind and principle, the unity of knowledge and action, his differences with Chu Hsi over the interpretation of the *Ta-hsüeh* (Great Learning), and the contrast between the principle of Nature and selfish human desires, all of which are recorded in the first part of the *Ch'uan-hsi lu* 傳習錄. Meanwhile the number of his followers markedly increased. At places which he visited, such as Ch'u-chou 滁州, northwest of Nanking, several hundred people often gathered around him to discuss philosophical questions. He stressed the foundation of moral endeavor, the clear understanding of the substance of the mind, and man's original nature, as well as the practice of sitting in quiet meditation. Of Chan Jo-shui he spoke highly and urged his pupils to value their association with him. He attempted to reconcile the conflict between Chu Hsi, who advocated "pursuing extensive study," and Lu Chiu-yüan (1139-93), who advocated "honoring the moral nature," actually to bring Chu Hsi in line with his own philosophy.

As Wang grew in prominence and in influence, he became increasingly bored with the routine jobs he held in Peking and Nanking. A number of his followers in Ch'u-chou, moreover, did not adhere to his teachings and some even parroted his ideas without meaning them. Early in 1515, on the occasion of the regular evaluation of officials, he asked permission to resign. Seven months later he did so again, but both petitions were denied. On the recommendation of the War minister Wang Ch'iung (*q.v.*), he received a promotion on September 15, 1516, to be left

assistant censor-in-chief and governor of southern Kiangsi and adjacent areas. After visiting his home he arrived in Kan-chou 贛州 early the following year.

Under his jurisdiction were parts of four provinces where bandits and rebels had been in control for several decades. They numbered in the tens of thousands with over a hundred strongholds, and invaded government seats, kidnaped and murdered officials, even appointing their own administrators. Some of their leaders declared themselves kings. Repeated campaigns, one with some thirty thousand troops, failed to suppress them. When Wang arrived he immediately instituted the ten-family joint registration system to prevent infiltration and espionage, organized local militia, and in June reorganized government troops into clearly numbered units and definite lines of command. Within ten days after his arrival, he directed his attack against the rebels entrenched in Chang-chou 漳州, Fukien. His troops and those from Fukien and Kwangtung approached them from three directions, and in two months' time defeated them. In the autumn he turned on the rebels in Heng-shui 橫水 (in southwest Kiangsi) and defeated them in twenty days. Then he went in pursuit of those in T'ung-kang 桶岡, farther west, bordering Hukuang. This campaign lasted for some forty days. The next one, launched early in 1518, was in the Li-t'ou 浰頭 area in northernmost Kwangtung. It took a little over two months. In all, over a hundred strongholds were seized and fifteen thousand rebels killed or captured.

The success of the four campaigns was due chiefly to Wang's personality, intelligence, strategy, and his use of local troops instead of calling for support from great distances. He could thus stage surprise attacks whenever there was sufficient concentrated strength, and, when expedient, appease the enemy. One bandit leader from Li-t'ou was persuaded to surrender, rewarded, and permitted to join the government ranks; another hesitated, but was eventually induced to do the same. Wang feasted the latter, but finding him guilty of insincerity had him executed. Another important factor in Wang's success was the fact that he had greater authority than his predecessors. In the autumn of 1517 the court granted him the right to make decisions as situations required. As a reward for his accomplishments, he was promoted to be right assistant censor-in-chief and his son made a centurion (later a chiliarch) in the Embroidered-uniform Guard.

During these two years, 1517 and 1518, Wang was by no means devoting all his energy to military operations; he was also paying attention to social and political reforms as well as to philosophy. He established Ch'ung-i 崇義 and Ho-p'ing 和平-hsien (Kiangsi) to ensure pacification and reconstruction, extended the ten-family joint registration system, carried out relief, reduced taxes, readjusted official salaries, reformed former bandits (now called "new citizens"), opened community schools, repeatedly gave moral instruction to young and old, and, most significantly, set up the community compact (鄉約). In this institution, started in the autumn of 1518, good deeds were rewarded and evil deeds punished at open community meetings, following reports and confessions and preceding a banquet, with elected elders officiating.

In the field of philosophy Wang was concerned chiefly with Chu Hsi. Ever since going to Nanking in 1514 he had encountered sharp criticism because of his own questioning attitude and because of his opposition to Chu Hsi's school of thought which had controlled the civil service examinations for over a century. Partly to defend himself and partly to lessen the animosity, he published in the summer of 1518 the old text of the *Ta-hsüeh* as found in the *Li-chi* which had occupied his mind in his Kweichow days. Chu Hsi had rearranged the text and amended it to show that the investigation of things and the extension of knowledge

preceded the sincerity of the will, but Wang insisted on the original order, in which sincerity comes first. He also published his "Master Chu's final conclusions arrived at late in life" (now in the *Ch'uan-hsi lu*) which he had compiled three years before. In this short treatise he arbitrarily selected passages, each out of context, from letters Chu Hsi had written to others, in an attempt to show that Chu Hsi had changed his position late in life and had come around to views similar to those of Wang. This publication invited attack for several centuries. A month after its appearance, his disciple Hsüeh K'an 薛侃 (T. 尚謙, H. 中離, cs 1517, d. 1545), also published the *Ch'uan-hsi lu* (part 1 of the present work) in Kiangsi, which consists of conversations expressing Wang's basic ideas up to that time. This was later supplemented by part 2, compiled by Nan Ta-chi 南大吉 (T. 元善 or 原善, 1487–1533, cs 1511) in 1524, and part 3, compiled by Ch'ien Te-hung (*q.v.*) in 1535.

In the summer of 1519 Wang received orders to go to northern Kiangsi to suppress a rebellion in Fukien. When he reached Feng-ch'eng 豐城 in Kiangsi, he was informed that Chu Ch'en-hao 朱宸濠, prince of Ning (d. January 13, 1521), had rebelled. Wang had been in contact with the prince, having received Liu Yang-cheng 劉養正, the prince's aide, who came ostensibly to invite Wang to lecture. Instead of accepting the invitation Wang sent his pupil, Chi Yüan-heng 冀元亨 (T. 惟乾, H. 闇齋, d. 1521), to the prince to dissuade him from rebelling and to spy on him. According to one version, Wang himself decided to suppress the rebellion, escaped from the prince's pursuing agents in disguise, went to Chi-an 吉安, and consulted with the prefect, Wu Wen-ting 伍文定 (T. 時泰, cs 1499). Another version has it that he decided only at the prefect's urging. At any rate, to delay the prince from proceeding immediately to Nanking, which would surely fall, Wang fabricated documents indicating that large imperial armies were approaching and intimating that Liu Yang-cheng was a secret agent. After ten days of indecision and delay, the prince started from Nanchang and soon surrounded Anking (July 29, 1519). Wang then determined to attack weakly defended Nanchang. His armies, eighty thousand strong, entered the city on August 14, with Wu Wen-ting in the lead. Some records assert that many of Wang's troops were undisciplined "new citizens" who plundered and killed civilians. On hearing the news about Nanchang, the prince turned his entire army back and encountered Wang's armies on the 18th. After several retreats, he was defeated and captured on the 20th. It is not without interest that a retired official in Fukien, learning of the rebellion, dispatched some fo-lang-chi 佛郎機 (Portuguese cannon) to Wang for use against the prince but they arrived seven days too late.

Some historians have asserted that Wang originally had some understanding with the prince and fought him only after he had concluded that the latter would fail or because imperial armies were on the way. These accusations are the result of his unfriendly relations with eunuchs and officials at court for whom, except for the War minister, Wang Ch'iung, he never had any respect. In his earlier reports on the suppression of bandits, Wang Shou-jen gave credit to officials of the War ministry but not to eunuchs or to court officials, and he did likewise in reporting the defeat of the prince. The emperor, undoubtedly at the instigation of his favorites, decided to lead the imperial expedition himself on the pretext that remaining rebels had to be eliminated; actually, however, he undertook it so that he and his coterie might claim credit for the victory and handle the prince themselves. Reporting earlier on the rebellion Wang had advised the emperor not to leave the capital. Now he dispatched a special memorial urging the emperor to halt his expedition, but in this he failed. The

eunuch Chang Chung 張忠 had been sent to take over the prince, but Wang preferred to deliver him to the emperor himself. He left Nanchang on October 4. Chang Chung urged him to turn back but he refused and proceeded to Hangchow where the eunuch Chang Yung (q.v.) awaited him. The latter, who was instrumental in getting rid of Liu Chin and was therefore more acceptable, persuaded Wang to turn the prisoner over to him. Wang was made governor of Kiangsi and returned to Nanchang.

Wang's enemies in the capital had been accusing him of plotting rebellion himself. When the emperor was in Nanking early in 1520, Chang Chung and other eunuchs tested Wang's intentions by persuading the emperor to issue an edict ordering him to present himself, on the assumption that he would refuse and thereby betray his design. But to their astonishment he complied, having been duly tipped off by Chang Yung. To deny him an opportunity of seeing the emperor, imperial favorites stopped him on the way. After waiting for half a month, he proceeded to Chiu-hua 九華 Mountain (Anhwei). This helped to minimize the suspicion that he planned to rebel and he was ordered to return to Kiangsi. The emperor's favorites at Nanking were still demanding credit for the victory, however, and in August Wang reported it again, this time giving full credit to eunuchs and officials. This ended the crisis for him, but he failed to save his pupil, Chi Yüan-heng, who, together with his wife and two daughters, had suffered imprisonment. A year later, five days after his release, Chi died.

As governor of Kiangsi for a year and a half, Wang relieved the tax burden of the people, tried to repair the damage of floods, exempted the descendants of Lu Chiu-yüan from conscription, and gave them financial assistance for study. He also reviewed troops in Kan-chou obviously to impress his political enemies. When Chu Hou-ts'ung (q.v.) ascended the throne in 1521, he summoned Wang to court, but Grand Secretary Yang T'ing-ho (*q.v.*) blocked the move. In August the court appointed Wang minister of War at Nanking in the capacity of adviser and planner, the motive being to keep him from coming to Peking. Two months later he returned home to visit his ancestral graves. On December 7, he was awarded the title of earl of Hsin-chien (新建伯) with a hereditary salary of 1,000 piculs of rice and an imperial certificate exempting his descendants from criminal punishment; but neither the salary nor the certificate was issued. He declined the honors twice without effect. In March, 1522, his father died and he remained at home to mourn his loss. Supervisory secretary Mao Yü 毛玉 (T. 用成, cs 1505), instigated by higher officials, proposed his impeachment, but Wang's pupil, Lu Ch'eng 陸澄 (T. 原靜, 清伯, cs 1517), another secretary, prevented it.

For several years from this point on Wang was politically quiet. He even kept away from the bitter controversy in 1524 over the proper title to be conferred on the emperor's father (*see* Feng Hsi and Chu Hou-ts'ung). His first wife died in 1525, leaving no offspring. (Ten years earlier his father had designated a cousin's son to be Wang Shou-jen's heir.) He next married a Miss Chang 張, who bore him a son, named Wang Cheng-i 正億, toward the end of the following year.

These were the years of Wang's supreme philosophical achievements. Criticism of him by followers of Chu Hsi's doctrine rose to a high pitch, but his own following remained loyal. Wang Ken (*q.v.*) formally became his student in 1520, Ch'ien Te-hung in 1521, prefect Nan Ta-chi and sixty-eight-year-old Tung Yün 董澐 (T. 復宗, H. 蘿石, 白塔山人, 1457–1533) in 1524, and censor Nieh Pao (*q.v.*) in 1526 (though they performed no ceremonies until four years after Wang's death). Others numbered in the hundreds, particularly after 1523; they hailed from Kwangtung, Hukuang, Kiangsi, and Nan-Chihli. Hun-

dreds attended his lectures in Shao-hsing. In 1521, at the age of forty-nine, Wang enunciated his doctrine of the extension of innate knowledge (致良知). For years the idea of innate knowledge had been foremost in his thinking, an idea he described as "the original substance of the mind," which is "intelligent and clear." When one's will becomes sincere, he said, one will naturally extend this knowledge to the utmost, culminating in both understanding and action. Later, in 1527, he taught his pupils the Four Axioms to clarify the doctrine, saying:

In the original substance of the mind there is no distinction between good and evil.

When the will becomes active, however, such distinction exists.

The faculty of innate knowledge is to know good and evil.

The investigation of things is to do good and remove evil.

In regarding innate knowledge as the substance of the mind, Wang achieved a better understanding of the nature of man. The new concept gave Chinese thought a different outlook and a dynamic purpose. It shocked the Chinese intellectual community but it also brought fresh air. Wang said himself that it was "achieved after a hundred deaths and a thousand sufferings."

For more than five years Wang was not called to service and was able to devote his time to developing his philosophy. His friend Hsi Shu and his pupil Huang Wan (*q.v.*) recommended him unsuccessfully to be minister of War and similar positions. In June, 1527, however, he was brought out of retirement to suppress rebellions in Kwangsi in the capacity of left censor-in-chief and chief of military affairs in Kwangtung, Kwangsi, Hukuang, and Kiangsi. The tribal prefect of T'ien-chou 田州, Ts'en Meng 岑猛, had rebelled and was executed, but several campaigns had failed to dislodge his followers, who now captured Ssu-en 思恩,

Kweichow. Wang arrived in Wu-chou 梧州 at the end of the year. In the following month he was made provincial governor of Kwangtung and Kwangsi, for Yang I-ch'ing (*q.v.*) and other high officials had no wish to have him as a fellow official at court. The tribal chiefs wanted to surrender. Wang, arriving at Nan-ning 南寧 early in 1528, offered them especially lenient terms, for he appreciated their legitimate grievances. A month later (March 3) both Ssu-en and T'ien-chou were pacified without a fight. There were, however, still tens of thousands of aboriginal bandits and rebels in Pa-chai 八寨 in southwestern Kwangsi, who controlled three hundred square *li* of territory, having frustrated government troops from the beginning of the Ming dynasty. Wang had disbanded many of his soldiers and was sending the Hukuang army home. The rebel chiefs thought that he was not going to attack them. To their surprise, however, Wang's forces suddenly descended and in a month's time (mid-summer) overcame them. For a hundred years thereafter, peace reigned in this region. Wang's statesmanship at the conclusion of his campaign shows up here as elsewhere in his career. In one of his memorials he wrote that permanent peace among the aborigines could be achieved only by the appointment of two officials, one a Chinese, the other a tribal chief. "The duty of these officials would be to show them how to live, and how to irrigate their fields. The local government should supply the natives with seeds, livestock, and agricultural implements, which should be returned, together with one third of the harvest. Get more farmers to plant uncultivated land; induce more merchants to come to trade; but take as low taxes as possible so that the people can maintain their accustomed worship, travel as usual, and meet all their living expenses."

His coughing had bothered him for years, and now he was very ill. Part of the time during the Kwangsi campaigns Wang had to handle military affairs while traveling in a carriage. He asked to be relieved and started his homeward journey without waiting for an answer. He died in January in Nan-an 南安, Kiangsi. When his body was returned to his home, the traditional honors (a posthumous title and other awards) were withheld. Instead his earldom and other hereditary privileges were revoked, for Kuei O (*q.v.*), minister of Personnel and chancellor of the Hanlin Academy, hated him and accused him of leaving his post without permission, mishandling the rebels, disrespecting traditional doctrines, spreading false learning, and allowing his followers to be reckless. Some of those who protested were dismissed or banished. The "false learning" was severely proscribed.

Thirty-eight years later, however, in 1567, a new emperor honored him with the title of marquis of Hsin-chien and the posthumous title of Wen-ch'eng 文成 (completion of culture). A year later his son received the hereditary title of earl of Hsin-chien. In 1584 an imperial decree ordered that henceforth he be offered sacrifices in the Confucian temple. This constituted the highest honor it was possible to bestow on a scholar; it was granted to only four neo-Confucianists of the entire Ming dynasty.

Wang's philosophy, spreading all over China, dominated the intellectual scene for over a century until the end of the dynasty. But severe criticism developed and has persisted since, partly because of his opposition to Chu Hsi and partly because of his affinity with Ch'an Buddhism. Undoubtedly the Ch'an doctrine of sudden enlightenment influenced his theory of direct intuition. He frequently used Buddhist idioms and practiced Buddhist techniques, such as meditation, intentionally shocking his pupils. Some of his followers degenerated into "crazy Ch'an Buddhists," laying claim to any desire or passion as innate knowledge and even to depravity as innate action. Certain critics such as Ku Yen-wu (ECCP) have attributed the downfall of the Ming to belief in his school of thought. This is one-sided and exaggerated, of course. At its best Wang's philosophy produced men of sincere purpose and firm action. This was the case in Japan where his ideas were expounded by such outstanding thinkers as Nakae Tōju 中江藤樹 (1608-48), Kumazawa Banzan 熊澤蕃山 (1619-91), and Sakuma Shōzan 佐久間象山 (1811-64). The Yōmeigaku (Yang-ming school) has been recognized as a dominating force in Japanese thought, especially as manifested by its influence on many of the highly motivated and dedicated leaders during the Meiji restoration of 1868. In China too it inspired modern leaders such as Sun Yat-sen, particularly in the idea of action. In Taiwan since 1949 Wang's advocacy of sincere will and vigorous effort has made him a great source of inspiration. Discussions and publications there (including two commentaries on the *Ch'uan-hsi lu*) have paid more attention to him than he has received anywhere else. [Editors' note: The first collection of Wang's works appeared in 1536 under the title *Yang-ming hsien-sheng ts'un-kao* 存稿, consisting of *wen-lu cheng-chi* 文錄正集, 5 *ch.*, and a *wai* 外 *chi*, 9 *ch.*, and a *pieh-lu* 別錄, 10 *ch.* It was edited by Ch'ien Te-hung and Huang Hsing-tseng (*q.v.*) and printed in Soochow. It has a preface by Huang Wan written in 1536. There are several later editions; the one included in the *Ssu-k'u* library is the 1572 edition, entitled *Wang Wen-ch'eng kung ch'üan shu*, 38 *ch.* Li Chih (*q.v.*), who edited the philosophical works by Wang under the title *Yang-ming hsien-sheng tao-hsüeh ch'ao* 道學鈔, 7 *ch.*, was also the author of the life chronology *Yang-ming hsien-sheng nien-p'u* 年譜, 2 *ch.*, both works being completed in 1600 and printed in 1609.]

The reproduction of a Ming dynasty portrait of Wang appears as a frontispiece in Wing-tsit Chan's *Instructions for Practical Living*. Another informal portrait, painted in 1641 by Ch'en Hung-shou (ECCP), hangs in the Fogg Museum. For an example of his calligraphy *see* Wang Shih-chieh (BDRC), *et al.*, *A Garland of Chinese Calligraphy*, II (Hong Kong, 1967), 7.

Bibliography

1/195/1a; 3/185/1a; Hsieh T'ing-chieh 謝廷傑 (cs 1559), comp., *Wang Wen-ch'eng kung ch'üan-shu* 全書 (also entitled *Yang-ming ch'üan-shu*, 1572) including the *nien-p'u* 年譜 by Ch'ien Te-hung (*ch.* 32-36), the *Hsing-chuang* by Huang Wan (*ch.* 37), and the *Ch'uan-hsi lu* (*ch.* 1-3); Mao Ch'i-ling (ECCP), *Wang Wen-ch'eng chuan-pen*; Huang Tsung-hsi (ECCP), *Ming-ju hsüeh-an* (*ch.* 10); Yü Ch'ung-yao 余重耀, *Yang-ming hsien-sheng chuan-tsuan* 傳纂, 1923; Chang Hsi-chih 張希之, *Yang-ming hsüeh-chuan* 學傳, 1961; Takase Takejirō 高瀬武次郎, *Ōyōmei shōdan* 王陽明詳傳, 1915; Wang Yang-ming, *Instructions for Practical Living and Other Neo-Confucian Writings* (tr. of the *Ch'uan-hsi lu* by Wing-tsit Chan), New York and London, 1963; Chang Yü-ch'üan 張煜全, "Wang Shou-jen as a Statesman," *Chinese Social and Political Science Review*, Vol. 23 (1939-40), 30, 155, 319, 473; P. Pelliot, TP, 38 (1947), 202; W. T. Swingle, *Library of Congress, Orientalia Added, 1923-24*, 267; *Yenching University Library Bulletin*, no. 15, October 15, 1931.

Wing-tsit Chan

WANG Shu 王恕 (T. 宗貫, H. 介庵, 石渠老人), 1416-May 11, 1508, a celebrated minister of Personnel, was born into a well-to-do farming family of San-yüan 三原, Shensi. He was tall and stout, with a commanding voice like the sound of a large bell. During his long official career of forty-five years he served under four emperors, Chu Ch'i-chen, Chu Ch'i-yü, Chu Chien-shen, and Chu Yu-t'ang (*qq. v.*). It began in 1448 when he became a *chin-shih* and was selected to be a bachelor in the Hanlin Academy. Of the thirty bachelors of that year all came from north of the Yangtze River. It was the only time in the Ming dynasty that the Hanlin Academy had no one from the Wu dialect area of Chekiang and Nan Chih-li, nor from any other province south of the Yangtze River. This unique occurrence indicates a definite policy of favoring the northerners, which was adopted by the powerful eunuch Wang Chen (*q. v.*), perhaps with the consent of Emperor Chu Ch'i-chen. A year later, however, the emperor was captured by the Oirat in a battle in which Wang Chen lost his life. Under the new emperor, Chu Ch'i-yü, southerners like Shang Lu, P'eng Shih, Yü Ch'ien, and Yeh Sheng (*qq. v.*) came to power and another remarkable situation developed; only six of the bachelors of 1448 were retained as compilers in the Academy.

Late in 1449 Wang Shu was sent to the Grand Court of Revision as a judge. In 1454 he received a promotion to be prefect of Yangchow, where for five years he was in active service. He abolished unjust practices, distributed famine relief effectively, dispensed medicine to the poor, and established an academy supported by income from public land. When he left, the people of Yangchow erected a shrine in his honor.

In 1460, after being adjudged an outstanding official, Wang Shu was raised four grades to administration commissioner of Kiangsi. Four years later he was transferred to Honan, and in April, 1465, again received a promotion. Given the rank of a right vice censor-in-chief, he became governor of northwestern Hukuang in charge of resettling the immigrant population in the mountainous area. In September, when he asked for leave on account of the death of his mother, he was granted only two months and ordered to return immediately to his post, because a rebellion had erupted under the leadership of Liu T'ung (*see* Hsiang Chung). Wang's force at Ku-ch'eng 穀城 was inadequate and so troops were sent from nearby provinces and from Peking to fight the rebels. In August, 1466, Liu was captured and executed, but the rebellious conditions continued for several years. Meanwhile Wang Shu was transferred to be governor of Honan and promoted to left vice censor-in-chief.

Wang became senior vice minister of Justice in Nanking in March, 1468. A year later he retired on account of his father's death. On resumption of office in November, 1471, he was made senior vice minister of Justice in charge of conservancy of the Grand Canal. While there he compiled a history of the canal, entitled *Ts'ao Ho t'ung-chih* 漕河通志, which was printed about this time but is no longer extant. Much of it, however, is preserved in the later work, *Ts'ao Ho t'u-chih* (*see* Wang Ch'iung). From 1473 to 1476 Wang Shu served as vice minister of Revenue in Nanking. Then for one year he was sent to Yunnan, where as governor he had the unpleasant task of trying to check the illegal activities of the eunuch, Ch'ien Neng (*see* Chu Hou-chao), who was collecting precious stones for the emperor's favorite consort, Wan Kuei-fei (*q. v.*). Wang Shu succeeded in preventing the eunuch from trading directly with the Annamites and in confiscating some shipments of rubies and sapphires. In the end the eunuch remained in Yunnan while Wang himself was transferred. The emperor again sent him to Nanking, but gave him the higher rank of censor-in-chief with the added duty of serving as the civilian member of the triumvirate in supreme control of the southern capital, the other two being a chief eunuch and a central military commissioner (*see* Wang Yüeh).

In April, 1478, Wang Shu was made minister of War in Nanking while remaining a member of the triumvirate. From February, 1479, to May, 1484, he served as governor of Nan Chih-li; after that he was returned to the office of minister of War in Nanking and to the triumvirate. This time the chief eunuch was none other than the same Ch'ien Neng of Yunnan days. But Ch'ien gave him no trouble and voiced his high respect for Wang's honesty. In January, 1486, Wang received the honorary title of junior guardian of the heir apparent. Meanwhile he memorialized repeatedly expressing disapproval of the emperor's extravagance and misplaced confidence. To most of his memorials at this time the emperor paid no heed. Finally the monarch could tolerate him no more and, in the edict permitting another Nanking official to retire, added the remark that Wang Shu was too old and incompetent and was to be deprived of his honorary title and dismissed from office. Thus in September, 1486, at seventy years of age he was dishonorably discharged. But he was acknowledged in the empire as a courageous champion of right principles. There was a saying at the time to the effect that of the twelve ministers in the two capitals only Wang Shu stood out. A minor official who protested his dismissal was punished and demoted. About this time Wang published a biography of himself, entitled *Ta-ssu-ma San-yüan Wang-kung chuan* 大司馬三原王公傳. Accredited to a friend, it nevertheless contains most of Wang's memorials, including those which the emperor had disregarded.

One year after his retirement Wang Shu was recalled by the new emperor, Chu Yu-t'ang, and late in 1487 was appointed minister of Personnel in Peking. In January, 1488, he received the honorary title of grand guardian of the heir apparent. It was a heart-warming period for the conscientious officials of the day, for under the new regime many abuses of the previous reign were corrected, wrongdoers punished, and officials unfairly treated restored to office. For five years Wang as head of Personnel was able to promote and keep in office men of proven integrity, and performed his duties as he saw fit. In May, 1489, he was honored because of his years by being exempted from performing obeisance at court on days of rain or snow. When someone suggested that Wang be named a grand secretary, the emperor replied that, as head of Personnel, Wang was indispensible and, moreever, he could always be consulted on any matter of state. About this time, however, the emperor began to confide in certain eunuchs, grant favors to the family of the empress, and reject some of Wang's recommendations on the promotion or demotion of officials. Early in 1493,

after an evaluation of the entire bureaucracy of the empire, the ministry of Personnel and the Censorate jointly named some two thousand five hundred individuals for demotion or dismissal. The emperor commented in an edict that competent men were hard to find and so ordered that the less serious cases be reconsidered, with the result that over ninety men were permitted to remain in office. Wang regarded this as a show of distrust and memorialized that the joint recommendations were based on documented evidence following regulations strictly. He suspected that the emperor was under the influence of the new grand secretary, Ch'iu Chün (*q. v.*), whose book on statecraft, the *Ta-hsüeh yen-i pu*, had been recently published in Fukien with funds contributed by the emperor himself. The main idea in the edict was evidently the same as that expressed in Ch'iu's book. In April the head of the Imperial Academy of Medicine, Liu Wen-t'ai 劉文泰, accused Wang of showing disrespect to the previous emperor by printing memorials in which he criticized the emperor. In this way, Liu said, Wang's action was tantamount to revealing the deceased emperor's mistakes which he had not wanted publicized. As evidence Liu submitted Wang's biography mentioned above. In his defense Wang accused Liu of holding a personal grudge against him for having been denied a request for promotion. Wang also named Ch'iu Chün as the prime mover of Liu's act of revenge. In the final judgment in June the emperor refused to regard Ch'iu as being involved, and reduced Liu's position to that of physician in the Academy of medicine. The emperor, however, showed his disapproval of Wang by ordering the destruction of the printing blocks of his biography. When Wang protested by asking for retirement, he was permitted to leave. The emperor graciously granted him a monthly pension of two piculs of grain and the assignment of two servants from the office of his native district.

The feud between Wang Shu and Ch'iu Chün has usually been attributed to trivial matters, such as precedence in the line-up at court functions. Ch'iu as minister of Rites had ranked lower than Wang, the minister of Personnel, although he had the grade of 1B. When Ch'iu became a grand secretary (5A) in 1491, he thought he should precede Wang but the latter would not yield. According to Shen Chieh-fu (*q. v.*), Ch'iu was displeased when Wang announced that a man's character might be under suspicion if he had written an operetta; this was obviously in reference to the *Wu-lun ch'üan-pei* which Ch'iu had composed in his younger days. Actually it seems that the conflict between the two reflected the mutual distrust between northerners and southerners. Both men were able writers and perhaps they were jealous of each other. In 1491 the two probably secretly competed for the office of grand secretary which went to Ch'iu. In any case, after Wang was forced to retire people in general blamed Ch'iu. It is said that after Ch'iu died in Peking in 1495 and Liu Wen-t'ai came to offer condolences, Ch'iu's widow chased him out the gate and scolded the doctor for involving her husband in the controversy.

Wang Shu was seventy-seven years of age when he retired the second time. During the following fifteen years of his life he taught and studied and edited a collection of memorials of the past sixteen centuries, an enormous work in 120 *chüan*, which does not seem to be extant. He wrote a preface to his notes on the Classics when he was ninety. He died at ninety-two, when his fellow provincial, the eunuch Liu Chin (*q. v.*), was in power. Wang was posthumously honored with the highest title of grand preceptor. He was canonized as Tuan-i 端毅. His memorials for which he was particularly noted were first printed in 1482 under the title *Ta ssu-ma Wang-kung tsou-i* 奏議, probably together with the above-mentioned biography. This edition does not seem to have survived. In 1502 an admirer, Wang Hsien

(*see* Wang T'ing-hsiang), had it reprinted in Soochow under the new title *Wang Chieh-an* 介庵 *tsou-i*. This was apparently reprinted in 1547 as the *Wang-kung tsou-kao* 稿, 6 *ch.* Meanwhile a more complete edition, entitled *T'ai-shih* 太師 *Wang Tuan-i kung tsou-i*, 15 *ch.*, was printed in 1521 in San-yüan. This work was copied into the Imperial Library of the 18th century. He His collected works, *Wang Tuan-i wen-chi* 文集, 9 *ch.*, was printed in Honan in 1552. It includes in *chüan* 7 his notes on the Book of Changes, *Wan-i i-chien* 玩易意見 (copied into the *Ssu-k'u*), and from *chüan* 8 to 9 the notes on the other Classics, *Shih-ch'ü* 石渠 *i-chien*. The *Ssu-k'u* Catalogue records a separate edition of the latter work in 4 *chüan*, with two supplements each in 2 *chüan*. In these notes he expressed his doubts on the commentaries by Chu Hsi (1130–1200) and others officially proclaimed as correct and not to be deviated from; this shows the same spirit of independent judgment that prompted him to criticize those whom he considered mistaken, and recommend those who in his opinion were right. In the 1811 edition of his collected works an autobiography which he wrote in 1502, entitled *Shih-ch'ü lao-jen lü-li lüeh* 老人履歷略, was appended; in it he justified every action of his life, as if he had to have the last word.

Wang Shu had seven sons. The youngest, Wang Ch'eng-yü 承裕 (T. 天宇, H. 平川, cs 1493, 1465–1538, Pth. 康僖), rose to be minister of Revenue at Nanking (1527–29). He established an academy at San-yüan, known as the Hung-tao shu-yüan 宏道書院, which became as well known as the one established on his father's proposal, the Hsüeh-ku 學古 shu-yüan.

Bibliography

1/182/1a; 5/24/59a; 8/32/1a; 63/15/30a; 83/9/2a; MSL (1964), Hsiao-tsung, 1337, 1357, 1395, 1406, 1444, 1473, Wu-tsung (1965), 0881; KC (1958), 2646, 2915; *T'ai-shih Wang Tuan-i tsou-i*

(NLP microfilm, no. 42), *ch.* 13; *Wang Tuan-i wen-chi* (NCL microfilm), 1/1a, 15a, 2/4b, 10a, 11b, 6/16a; Ch'en Tzu-lung (ECCP), *Huang Ming ching-shih wen-pien, ch.* 39; *Yü-hsüan Ming ch'en* 御選明臣 *tsou-i* (1781), 4/20b; Shen Te-fu, *Yeh-hu-pien* (1959), 257, 300; *San-yüan-hsien chih* (1880), 13/19a, 15/16a; *Huang Ming wen-hai* (microfilm), 3/6/13; SK (1930), 7/4b, 34/1a, 55/6a, 56/2b, 175/11b; W. Franke, *Sources,* 5.4.18.

Chaoying Fang

WANG Ssu-jen 王思任 (T. 季重, H. 遂東, 謔庵, 稽山外史), August 26, 1575-October 30, 1646, poet, essayist, artist, and official, was born in Peking where his father, an indigent but ambitious herb doctor from Shan-yin 山陰 (Shao-hsing), Chekiang, was waiting for a government appointment. His mother was probably a second wife, for at his birth his father was already forty-five years of age and had a son in his twenties. Wang Ssu-jen describes dramatically in his autobiography how at his birth, a difficult one, with the midwife exhausted and his father kneeling in prayer, it was this eldest brother (a peddler in the Peking streets), who rushed in and used his strength to induce delivery. This is the only time he refers to this brother. In an entry written years later he mentions a second brother twice, both times describing him as unreliable and a trouble-maker. He never refers to these (half?) brothers, or his father, by name.

In 1579 his father received a temporary appointment as physician to the soldiers along the Great Wall, and then, after serving two years as a prison doctor in the ministry of Justice, was appointed in 1582 physician to the household of the prince of I 益王, Chu I-yin 朱翊鈏 (enf. 1580, d. 1603), in Nan-ch'eng 南城, Kiangsi. Before assuming his post he took his family, including Wang Ssu-jen, then seven years old, to Shao-hsing to visit his ancestral place. The family lived in Nan-ch'eng over four years, during which Wang Ssu-jen made spectacular progress in his studies preparing for the civil examinations. His promise was such that his father resigned from the princely establishment in 1587 in order to escort him to Peking to acquaint him with the ways of the government, its officials, and their sons. There was also the consideration that for a young man to take the examinations in the north afforded a better chance to succeed than in Chekiang where competition was much keener. A law proscribed an outsider from competing for a vacancy reserved by quota for the natives of the area, and it was strictly enforced by imperial order when Wang arrived in Peking in 1588. He was then engaged by Huang Hung-hsien 黃洪憲 (T. 懋中, H. 葵陽, 1541-1600, cs 1571), a reader in the Hanlin Academy, to be companion to his son in classical studies. This arrangement lasted for about a year, during which Wang benefited greatly from the elder Huang's teaching.

By regulation a candidate was listed according to his ancestral registry, not according to his place of birth; hence, legally Wang Ssu-jen was supposed to take his examinations in Shao-hsing. It so happened that a granduncle had been buried west of Peking in Wan-p'ing 宛平 district. The fact of owning an ancestral burial ground gave him a slender claim to compete for admission to the school of that district. At the examination of 1589 fellow students were outraged by his presence and approached him threateningly. He was saved from bodily harm by the magistrate, Hsü Ch'i-tung 徐啓東 (T. 養元, cj 1567), who shielded him. The same magistrate also prevailed upon the higher authorities to admit him to the prefectural school. There he suffered insults and attacks and had to conceal his brilliance by turning in inferior papers at regular tests.

As his father expected, in 1594 he passed the *chü-jen* examination and a year later, aged twenty, he emerged as a *chin-shih*. Then he was given official leave to marry. His bride was a granddaughter of Yang Wei-ts'ung 楊維聰 (T. 達甫, H.

方城, b. 1500, cs 1521, optimus, native of Ku-an 固安, south of Peking). The wedding party was attended by his fellow *chin-shih*, numbering over three hundred. Because his mother insisted on returning to Shao-hsing, he accompanied her, but had to rent a house, as the family had no place of its own.

In 1596 he went to Peking for his first appointment, which was as magistrate of Hsing-p'ing 興平, Shensi. For lack of money he arrived on a donkey. This and his youth gained him the appellation of "baby magistrate" (娃娃知縣). At first some of his staff slighted him, but their attitude changed as a result of his decisive and correct judgments. After a few months he had to retire on account of the death of his mother.

Late in 1599 he was appointed magistrate of Tang-t'u 當塗, forty miles southwest of Nanking. It was a lucrative post but, as a river port on the Yangtze, was frequently visited by superiors on business and dignitaries passing through. The harvests of the area depended on the dikes which held back the water at flood time. He made it his first task to strengthen and keep them guarded. As a result the district was blessed with good harvests during his six years in office. He thus had surplus funds for public works and new buildings. It was the time when Emperor Chu I-chün (*q.v.*), intent on exacting silver for his privy purse, was sending out eunuchs to open mines. In 1602 one of them, Hsing Lung 邢隆, came to Tang-t'u and all the officials were apprehensive. Wang alone calmly approached the eunuch and pleased him by claiming relationship, pointing out that his wife's family (Yang) had some connection in the past with the Hsing family. After gaining the eunuch's confidence, Wang warned him of the unpredictable consequences of opening mines in a region so near the tomb of the founder of the dynasty, for it might turn out to be a geomantic mistake. His warning persuaded the eunuch to refrain from opening any

mines and to agree to take an annual sum of silver from the people of the two prefectures south of Nanking. This saved the area from having houses demolished and ancestral tombs destroyed in search of veins of silver, as happened elsewhere.

After receiving twenty-four recommendations, Wang was summoned to Peking (1605) as an expectant censor, but the Censorate failed to confirm him. According to his own account, he had once arrested a man for shipping government salt without a license. The man turned out to be the son of the head of the Censorate, who now blocked his appointment. There was also the powerful governor in charge of grain transportation, Li San-ts'ai (*q.v.*), who denounced Wang to the ministry of Personnel as unethical for having entered the bureaucracy under false pretences. So he was given the least desirable promotion, that of a secretary in the ministry of Justice in Nanking. Arriving late in 1605, he received a warm reception from the scholar Chiao Hung (ECCP). His experience in judicial matters won him a temporary assignment as acting censor, which gave him the opportunity to show his talents. In a month he disposed of the accumulated cases of several years. His fellow censors showed their displeasure by attacking him in a memorial filled with accusations supplied by a former colleague at Tang-t'u, whom he had offended by an offhand witty remark. Late in 1606 he was relieved of office and demoted one grade. His father commented that the setback might prove a blessing if it could reduce his arrogance. On reaching home he learned that the people of Tang-t'u had erected a shrine to honor him.

Wang Ssu-jen lived three years in retirement in Shao-hsing. In 1608 he paid a long visit to the scenic T'ien-t'ai 天臺 and Yen-tang 雁蕩 mountains on the east Chekiang coast. His account of these travels, entitled *Yu-huan* 游喚 (Call of the wanderlust), was to become a classic of its kind. The following year, swallowing

his pride, he proceeded to the ministry of
Personnel in Peking to accept his demotion. His next assignment was in Taiyuan,
Shansi, to serve as deputy chief clerk in
the surveillance commissioner's office, a
nominal and transitional appointment. For
formality's sake he held the office a few
days, and then took the opportunity to
tour the Buddhist shrines on Mt. Wu-t'ai.
In the account of his visit there he describes the forest on the mountain's flanks.
Three hundred years later two American
scholars quote passages from it to show
conditions he found as compared with
those of recent years. While in Shansi
Wang amused himself by composing a
sham memorial listing the arrogant ways
and misdeeds of Li San-ts'ai whom he
blamed for causing him to be barred from
the post of censor. A friend who saw the
draft composition wrote a genuine memorial
to the throne based on it; this paved the
way for Li's dismissal (March, 1611).
Though Wang Ssu-jen gained some prestige in this way, he also incurred the
hostility of the Tung-lin partisans as Li
was then an active leader of that party.

Wang became a magistrate once more
in 1611, holding office in Ch'ing-p'u 青浦,
near Shanghai. Some of the leading citizens, such as Tung Ch'i-ch'ang and Ch'en
Chi-ju (ECCP), welcomed him, but certain others of the gentry resented his coming, for one of his initial acts was to
publish a list of owners of land and then
to grade the labor service accordingly.
This endeared him to the common people,
for he lessened their burdens. In less than
a year, however, he was forced out of
office by the censor in charge of tribute
grain transportation, P'eng Tuan-wu 彭端
吾 (cs 1601), whose unreasonable demands
he had resisted and publicly ridiculed. It
happened that P'eng was then hoping to
be admitted to the Tung-lin party and had
been a supporter of Li San-ts'ai, but his
name was never included in the party's list.

Late in the same year Wang left
Ch'ing-p'u to return to Shao-hsing. He
was now wealthy enough to enjoy retire-

ment. He liked friendly gatherings, and
loved wine, for which Shao-hsing was
famous. He built a house with a garden,
called Pi-yüan 避園 (Retreat). He also
erected a library, Tu-shu chia-shan-shui
lou 讀書佳山水樓 (Study amid beautiful
surroundings). Later he had a painting
of the library made on a scroll; it included the colophons of more than seventy poets written during a period of some
twenty years. Following the vogue of his
day he studied geomancy, and this knowledge probably augmented his income. He
also edited (for some publishers?) the examination papers of the *chü-jen* of 1612
and *chin-shih* of 1613, entitled *Jen-kuei
ho-che* 壬癸合轍 (Successful answers for
these two years), which had an extensive
sale. Reportedly, he edited another anthology, *Pai-chia lun ch'ao* 百家論鈔, 12 *ch.*
In 1617 he went to Peking to accept his
demotion for the second time. He was
appointed registrar in the administration
commissioner's office in Shantung. After
holding that office as a formality a few
days only, he was granted leave to go
home. In 1618 he received notice of his
appointment as prefectural judge of Yüan-
chou 袁州, Kiangsi, but declined the offer
in order to remain with his father,
then eighty-eight years of age. Four years
later his father died (1622). After the
mourning period he revisited Nan-ch'eng
and other places in Kiangsi where he had
lived three decades previously.

Wang went again to Peking (1626) to
apply for an appointment, but found the
atmosphere not to his liking and returned
home. It was the time when the eunuch,
Wei Chung-hsien (ECCP), was at the height
of his power and was persecuting members of the Tung-lin party. Wang did not
belong to any clique and had both friends
and enemies in the Tung-lin group. When
subsequent to Wei's downfall late in 1627
the Tung-lin members were rehabilitated,
many officials in retirement were examined
at the same time for reinstatement. Wang,
on the recommendation of his friends,
was also recalled to officialdom. In

1629 he went once more to Peking to apply for an appointment. At that time Ch'ien Ch'ien-i (ECCP) and Wen T'i-jen (q.v.) were contending for a seat in the Grand Secretariat. Ch'ien's supporters in the Tung-lin party forged a volume of poems praising Wei the eunuch, with Wen T'i-jen's name prominently inserted so as to discredit him. It was found that Wang had a poem in the volume too, and he was again placed under investigation. When the volume was proved spurious and the forgers were caught, Wang's name was cleared, and in September he was sent to Sung-chiang 松江 as director of the prefectural school. The following May he was promoted to instructor in the National University. There he gave a lecture which was attended by an earl accompanying the consort of a princess. The lecture was posted in a public place and widely acclaimed.

In March, 1631, Wang was appointed a secretary in the ministry of Works in Nanking. Late that year he was placed in charge of the lumber tax office at Wuhu where his policy of treating the merchants with fairness won him "praise all along the Long River." In 1633, after being first promoted to a bureau director, he was appointed assistant surveillance commissioner of Kiangsi assigned to Kiukiang as military intendant. He trained five hundred selected troops in archery and swimming under water, and with their help he put an end to piracy on Poyang Lake and stopped the practice of pillaging ships in distress. He also pacified two populous and mutinous clans by admitting the sons of their leaders to the government schools. Two years later word came that the bandits of the northern provinces under Chang Hsien-chung (ECCP), after burning the imperial ancestral tombs at Feng-yang 鳳陽, were moving south towards Huang-mei 黃梅, Hukuang, on the opposite bank of the Yangtze River from Kiukiang. When urgent requests came from Huang-mei for help, the Kiangsi authorities were at first hesitant to comply,

but Wang persuaded the governor, Hsieh Hsüeh-lung 解學龍 (T. 石帆, cs 1613), to send soldiers across the river to the rescue. They arrived just in time to quell an attempted uprising inside Huang-mei city and to hold off the attacking bandits. (*Kuo-ch'üeh* errs in saying that Huang-mei fell.) Soon after the enemy left, however, someone in Peking brought charges on irrelevant matters against Wang, and once more he was removed from office at a time when his extraordinary services should have been rewarded. Wang, serious and sensitive by nature, had to suffer all his life from injustices of this sort and to contend with mediocrity too. Perhaps his habit of responding to such misfortune with witticisms and sarcastic comments was his way of keeping his sanity. It may be said, however, that his swift rise from poverty to wealth seems to indicate that in financial matters he may well have been vulnerable.

He was then sixty years of age and ready to live the rest of his life in retirement. He now had a large family. His wife had died in 1617, but he had five concubines. It seems that he had eight sons, seven surviving him. The eldest, Wang Huai-ch'i 槐起, was born in 1616, the fourth died of smallpox in 1617, and the eighth was born in 1631. He is known to have had five grandsons as of 1639. That was the year he wrote his chronological autobiography, *Wang Chi-chung tzu-hsü nien-p'u* 王季重自叙年譜, a work hitherto unknown to the world of literature. Recently a manuscript copy was found in the Peking University Library, presumably once belonging to the Yenching University collection. A manuscript was made for the National Library of Peking, of which a duplicate is in Kyoto. A copy, xeroxed in 1971, is perhaps the only one in the West. It affords for the first time answers to most of the questions concerning Wang's life and serves to correct the inaccuracies in previous sketches about him.

At the end of the autobiography

Wang mentions that he had his properties divided among his sons, expecting to live with them by turn from then on. This situation was interrupted in 1645 when the conquering Ch'ing forces crossed the Yangtze and took Nanking, putting an end to the scandalous court of the Hung-kuang 弘光 emperor (Chu Yu-sung, ECCP) and his chief grand secretary, Ma Shih-ying (ECCP). When Ma announced that he was escorting the emperor's mother to Shao-hsing, Wang wrote an appeal to the empress-dowager and made a public declaration, both of them denouncing Ma for the misrule of the past year. Ma then went elsewhere.

Meanwhile the gentry of Shao-hsing gave their welcome to Prince Chu I-hai (ECCP), who set up court there in August. Wang Ssu-jen was summoned from retirement, given several promotions, and finally made minister of Rites. (According to Shao T'ing-ts'ai, ECCP, Wang was appointed vice-minister.) It soon became obvious that the prince was incompetent and by July, 1646, he fled south when the Ch'ing troops came to Shao-hsing. Wang escaped to the hills and died of illness or by fasting, in a hut by his family burying ground. His name came to be celebrated in the local shrine of worthy men.

The writings of Wang Ssu-jen were acclaimed in his lifetime, particularly his essays in the style of Yüan Hung-tao(q.v.) and Ch'en Chi-ju. His poetry and prose appeared in several anthologies of his day. His essays for the civil examinations were celebrated as models. His travels probably had some influence in inspiring the great explorer, Hsü Hung-tsu (ECCP). Wang wrote a biographical sketch of Hsü's father, in which he praised the son for his disdain of an official career or the pursuit of wealth, for his devotion to exploring mountains and rivers, and for his ability to write good prose.

Wang's poems were printed in two collections, *Pi-yüan ni-ts'un* 擬存 and *Er-er chi* 爾爾集. Ch'ien Ch'ien-i criticized his poems as brilliant but out of control. He greatly appreciated Wang as a humorist and predicted that his *I-lü* 奕律 (Chess code, being regulations for chess players humorously written in the serious style of the Ming code) would become a classic piece of literature. According to Ch'ien, even in Wang's last days, when he tried to escape from pursuing enemy troops, he took his chess set with him. A copy of Wang's humorous writings, entitled *Nüeh-an wen-fan hsiao-p'in* 謔菴文飯小品, 5 *ch.*, is preserved in the Naikaku Bunko, Tokyo.

His collected works, *Wang Chi-chung chi* 集, edited by himself, were published from time to time in a number of topical treatises, some in a complete form such as *I-lü* and *Yu-huan*, and some to be continued, such as *Pi-yüan ni ts'un* and *Er-er chi*. The National Peiping Library lists two editions, one issued about 1625 having eight topics and the second printed about 1635, with thirteen topics. In the 1625 edition (hitherto erroneously identified as a Wan-li ed.) the *Pi-yüan ni-ts'un* consists of 96 leaves of poems, but in the later edition it has 154 leaves. In the Library of Congress copy, with 16 topics, the *Pi-yüan ni-ts'un* has 157 leaves, indicating that it was printed several years after 1635, hence the latest edition known.

Wang Ssu-jen's writings in prose were collected in 4 *chüan* by P'an Hsi-en (ECCP) and included in his *Ch'ien-k'un cheng-ch'i chi* 乾坤正氣集, printed in 1828, reprinted 1881. In the early 1930s Wang suddenly became one of the popular essayists, probably because of promotion by Chou Tso-jen (BDRC), and other Shao-hsing writers. A collection of his works in ten topics, entitled *Wang Chi-chung shih-chung* 十種, appeared in 1936; it seems to be based on an incomplete copy of the 1635 edition.

Wang is also known as a painter and calligrapher. One of his paintings is represented in the *Tōyō bijutsu taikan* 東洋美術大觀.

Bibliography

1/99/20b, 104/17a; 36/4/13a; 40/58/5a; 59/42/2a; 64/庚7/7b; Ch'ien Ch'ien-i, *Lieh-ch'ao shih-chi*, 丁12/73a; *Wang Chi-chung tzu-hsü nien-p'u*; Chang Tai (ECCP), *Lang-hsüan wen-chi* (Taipei, 1956), 43, 56, 132; KC (1958), 5690; Shao T'ing-ts'ai (ECCP), *Ssu-fu-t'ang wen-chi*, 2/54a; Cha Chi-tso (ECCP), *Tsui-wei lu*; T'ang Pin-yin 湯賓尹, *Shui-an wen kao* 睡庵文稿 (preface, 1611), 4/1a, 10/1a; SK (1930), 114/10a, 193/4a; *Shan-yin-hsien chih* (1936), 14/31b, 26/6b; Naikaku Bunko *Catalogue*, 365; P'an Ch'eng-hou 潘承厚 ed., *Ming-chi chung-lieh ch'ih-tu ch'u-pien* 明季忠烈尺牘初編; Chu Chien-hsin 朱劍心, *Wan-Ming hsiao-p'in hsüan-chu* 晚明小品選注 (1936), preface, 74, 155; Sun Tien-ch'i (1957), 17, 164, 197, 226, 233; L. C. Goodrich, *The Literary Inquisition of Ch'ien-lung* (Baltimore, 1935), 256; Osvald Sirén, *Chinese Painting*, VIII (London, 1958), 255; L. of C. *Catalogue of Rare Books*, 1006; W. C. Lowdermilk and Dean R. Wickes, "History of Soil Use in the Wu T'ai Shan Area," monograph, JNCBRAS (1938), 10.

Chaoying Fang and
Mingshui Hung

WANG Tao-chen 王燾貞 (childhood name Kuei 桂), December 30, 1558-October 17, 1580, better known by her religious appellation T'an-yang-tzu 曇陽子, was a native of T'ai-ts'ang, Soochow, the second of three daughters of Wang Hsi-chüeh (*q.v.*) and an elder sister of Wang Heng (*see* Wang Hsi-chüeh). Her short life, filled with mystery and alleged miracles, ended with the announcement that she had ascended to immortality without passing through the stage of death. It is even said that both her names, Tao-chen and T'an-yang-tzu, were given to her by the immortals with whom she was associated before her own ascension.

The literature about T'an-yang-tzu is abundant, but factual data are scarce. It is also difficult to separate fact from fancy, intentional ambiguity from sincere belief, prejudicial judgment from reasonable conclusion. There are two biographies of Wang Tao-chen, one by the well-known and prolific writer Wang Shih-chen (*q.v.*), entitled *T'an-yang ta-shih chuan* 大師傳, which has been highly publicized and frequently referred to; the other, and little known and seldom mentioned, is by Fan Shou-chi (*q.v.*), under the title *T'an-yang hsien* 仙-*shih chuan*. Both men were older contemporaries but called themselves her disciples. While Wang Shih-chen was a good friend of her father, Fan was also an acquaintance. Apparently the materials for the biographies were supplied by Wang Hsi-chüeh. Besides the *T'an-yang ta-shih chuan*, Wang Shih-chen wrote the *Chin-mu chi* 金母紀 and the *T'an-luan* 鸞 *ta-shih chi* to supplement and to clarify certain allusions made in the principal biography. These accounts contain so much that is mystical, mysterious, and necromantic that they leave the reader with many questions and a great deal of doubt.

T'an-yang-tzu's life may be sketched as follows. It is said that as a child she did not enjoy the favor of her parents. An early engagement of a daughter was the custom of the day, yet her mother delayed it. Finally she was betrothed to Hsü Ching-shao 徐景韶 (d. 1574), a son of Hsü T'ing-kuan 廷裸 (cs 1559), then provincial assistant administration commissioner of Chekiang. Just before the marriage was to take place in 1574, her fiancé died. It is said that at first her parents tried to hide the news from her, but she told them that she had been aware of it before the messenger arrived. She then asked to be considered as Hsü's widow.

Ming society was a paradoxical one in many ways. On one hand, under certain circumstances, there was widespread indulgence in sensual activities; on the other, the Confucian ideal of chastity was upheld. For a wife to take her life shortly after her husband's death, or for a betrothed girl to refuse to marry another if her fiancé died, was always considered to be an honorable act, especially by the scholar-official class. In some cases, the girl being young and innocent, it was the parents who consciously or unconsciously made the decision. In such a situation, because of their possible feeling of guilt, the parents often became indulgent and permissive. Under the pretext of lack of space in her father's official residence in Peking, situated near the National University, T'an-yang-tzu begged for private quarters for herself; so in 1574 a small separate unit was built for her adjacent to the main house, and she began to lead a religious life of her own design. After living in Peking for some fifteen years, she returned with her grandparents to T'ai-ts'ang. A year later her father, anticipating antagonism from the powerful minister, Chang Chü-cheng (q.v.), retired from office and returned home with the rest of his family. The old house must have been a spacious one, for here Wang Tao-chen maintained her own quarters in a separate two-story unit, using the second floor as her place of worship. It was in these quarters that she is said to have received female immortals and deities, performed miracles, and learned by heart certain religious tracts, mostly mixtures of Buddhist and Taoist sayings. She also developed a beautiful hand, her personal seal style (篆). Later she copied pieces of religious literature, and many disciples received specimens of her calligraphy. She often made trips, presumably "out-of-body" excursions, and abstained from eating for long periods. Among her devoted disciples were her own father and Wang Shih-chen.

In the summer of 1580 she asked permission of her grandfather and father to visit her fiancé's place of interment, and hinted that she might soon ascend to immortality. A shrine (龕) was prepared for her. When she arrived at Hsü's grave, she cut off a coil of hair on the right side of her head as a sacrifice. For many days she stayed at the site. Then she preached to a multitude of people. Finally, on October 1, she retreated into the shrine, where it is said she underwent transformation, and made her ascent as an immortal. This final parting, say her biographers, was witnessed by a hundred thousand people. Later the shrine was taken to the T'ien-tan kuan 恬澹觀 (the Taoist

Temple of Peace and Serenity), built for the occasion by her father. (T'ien and tan were the two key words in her preaching.) Reportedly too, her pet snake, which she called her "guardian dragon" (護龍), also became an immortal with her. After this mysterious event both her father and Wang Shih-chen lived in the temple for some time. Besides Wang Shih-chen and his younger brother, Wang Shih-mou (q.v.), a number of contemporary scholars and poets were among her disciples. Millions of words must have been written in prose as well as in poetry to her and about her. Some even dreamed of the Ta-shih and recorded their dreams.

A few months later Wang Shih-chen wrote the biography, printed it, and distributed it to people far and wide, including some officials in Peking. It received severe criticism. In 1581 Niu Wei-ping 牛惟炳 (T. 承庵, cs 1574), a supervising secretary, and Sun Ch'eng-nan 孫承南 (T. 道可, cj 1567), a censor, simultaneously impeached Wang Hsi-chüeh and Wang Shih-chen for heresy. Fortunately for the two Wang, a fellow townsman, Hsü Hsüeh-mo (q.v.), then minister of Rites, helped to smooth the matter over.

The affair did not end there, however. About 1589 an imposter, asserting that she was T'an-yang-tzu, appeared in T'ai-ts'ang. This is recorded by both Shen Te-fu (q.v.) and Shen Tsan (see Shen Ching), who indicated that she was actually a concubine of the uncle of the real T'an-yang-tzu, who had run away. This story with its element of scandal must have spread rapidly. People drew varying conclusions. Some years later when T'an Ch'ien (q.v.) noted this occurrence in his Tsao-lin tsa-tzu, he did not regard the second T'an-yang-tzu as an imposter. One modern scholar has treated it simply as something which developed out of an illicit affair.

It is also said that, after her ascent to immortality, Wang Tao-chen went to the Mien-chu 緜竹 Mountains in Szechwan, where she dwelt in the company of another female immortal. As a consequence a temple of the same name (T'ien-tan-kuan) was built for her there. Another report has it that the temple in her native place was later destroyed by a stroke of lightning.

Because of the mysterious nature of her life and the lack of factual information about her death throughout the following centuries, the story of T'an-yang-tzu has fascinated many. Scholars such as Yang En-shou 楊恩壽 (T. 蓬海, H. 坦園, 1824-1891+) and Wang Kuo-wei (BDRC) have centered their attention on the relationship between her life story and the most popular Ming drama *Mu-tan t'ing*, written by T'ang Hsien-tzu (1550-1616, ECCP). To this day there is no decision as to whether T'ang modeled his heroine after T'an-yang-tzu; most critics have rejected the theory. The fact remains, however, that if one compares the two in detail, some obvious similarities do appear. As a contemporary, T'ang Hsien-tzu could not have failed to read the biography written by Wang Shih-chen, or to hear the story of the imposter. While it is true that he must have drawn upon numerous other sources for his play, it seems that the life story of Wang Tao-chen must have had a measure of influence upon the dramatist.

Was Wang Tao-chen a magician? If so, how did she acquire her skill? Was she mentally deranged? If so, to what extent? Did she possess extrasensory perception, or practice astral projection, if such things are really possible? How much was dream, how much was real in her professed relationship with the immortals? Or was she born with a superior intellect that enabled her to hoodwink her family and most people who came into contact with her? Probably the only conclusion we may safely draw is that the story of Wang Tao-chen reflects the temperament and psychology of Ming society at that stage, some aspects of which may remain mysterious forever.

Bibliography

64/己16/2028 (1936); TSCC (1885-88), IV/145/9a; KC (1958), 4390; T'an Ch'ien, *Tsao-lin tao-tsu* (*Shih-yüan ts'ung-shu* ed.), 576; Wang Hsi-chüeh, *Wang Wen-su-kung wen-ts'ao* (Wan-li ed.), 12/16b; Wang Heng, *Kou-shan hsien-sheng chi* (Wan-li ed.), 14/29b, 20/9a; Fan Shou-chi, *Yü-lung-tzu chi*, 22/3a, 5b, 70/4b; Wang Shih-chen, *Yen-chou shan-jen hsü-kao*, 66/1a, 17b, 78, and a number of shorter pieces of both poetry and prose (Ch'ung-chen ed.); Wang Shih-mou, *Wang Feng-ch'ang chi* (Wan-li ed.), 詩2/70a, 文8/13b, 12/13a, 49/17a, 50/18a, 19b; T'u Lung, *Po-yü chi* (Wan-li ed.), 詩1/18a, 6/6b, 8/7a, 文5/11a; Wu Yüan-ts'ui 伍袁萃 (cs 1580), *Lin-chü man-lu* 林居漫錄 (Wan-li ed.), 別集2/5b; Shen Te-fu, *Wan-li yeh-hu pien* (1959), 593; Shen Tsan, *Chin-shih ts'ung-ts'an* 近事叢殘 (1794), 1/21a, 4/36b; P'eng Shao-sheng (ECCP), *I-hsing-chü chi* (1921), 2/26b; Yang En-shou, *Tz'u-yü ts'ung-hua* 詞餘叢話 (*T'an-yüan ch'üan-chi* 坦園全集 ed.), 9; Wang Kuo-wei, *Lu-ch'ü yü-t'an* 錄曲餘談 (*Hai-ning Wang Ching-an hsien-sheng i-shu*, 6; Teng Chih-ch'eng 鄧之誠, *Ku-tung so-chi* 骨董瑣記 (1955), 1/29; Shen Tseng-chih 沈曾植, *Hai-jih-lou cha-ts'ung* 海日樓扎叢 (1962), 259.

Lienche Tu Fang

WANG Tao-k'un 汪道昆 (T. 伯玉, 玉卿, H. 南明, 南溟, 太函), 1525-93, poet, playwright, scholar, and high official who achieved fame in various lines, particularly in military affairs, was a native of She 歙-hsien, Hui-chou 徽州 (Anhwei). His grandfather, Wang Hsüan-i 玄儀 (d. 1548), and his father, Wang Liang-pin 良彬 (1504-80), were both salt merchants. A precocious child, Wang Tao-k'un received his initial education from his grandfather, who taught him ancient poetry when he was not yet three. It is said that he memorized about one hundred poems quickly and recited them at the request of his grandfather during banquets. After he became a *sheng-yüan* in the local school, Wang reportedly read the entire collection of some one hundred thousand *chüan* in the family's library. He remained an omnivorous reader throughout his life, on subjects ranging from classics, history, prose, and poetry, to Taoist texts and the

Buddhist canon. Above all he developed at an early age a profound interest in the science of military strategy; this was doubtless inspired by his father who almost embarked on a military career himself. Because of the sickness and subsequent death of his first wife, née Wu 吳, Wang did not participate until 1546 in the provincial examination. He passed and the following year achieved the *chin-shih*. Two of his classmates were Chang Chü-cheng and Wang Shih-chen (*qq.v.*). He had a chance to receive a good appointment at court, for the chief grand secretary, Hsia Yen (*q.v.*), expressed an interest in getting acquainted with him, but he did not respond. In 1548 he was made magistrate of I-wu 義烏, Chekiang. Then a young man slightly over twenty years of age, he proved to be competent, efficient, upright, and alert. Legalism and Confucianism both affected his administrative work. He set up and strictly enforced rules of reward and punishment. He also organized local militia, teaching tactics of defense and offense. This militia, known then as the I-wu ping 兵, later became the nucleus of the army of Ch'i Chi-kuang (*q.v.*). At the same time he did not neglect his studies, and vigorously promoted local education. As a result, there were fewer lawsuits, robbery declined, and powerful families preyed less on the poor. His performance left such an imprint that the local people erected a monument to honor him upon his departure.

In 1551 he was promoted to be secretary of the Kiangsi bureau in the ministry of Revenue, but after two years was tranferred to the bureau of operations in the ministry of War. The following year he became vice director of the bureau of provisions, and in 1557 director of the bureau of Personnel. The same year he was made prefect of Hsiang-yang 襄陽, Hukuang, where he remained until 1561; then he received a transfer to be surveillance vice commissioner in Fukien, and was charged with military responsibility

at Fu-ning 福寧. At this time the southeast coast was plagued by raids of the *wo-k'ou*. On arriving at his post, Wang immediately strengthened the military defenses, put down a mutiny, and continued to drill the soldiers diligently. In 1562 the pirates moved southward, occupying several towns along Fukien's coast. In response to his plea, Hu Tsung-hsien (*q.v.*) dispatched additional forces led by Ch'i Chi-kuang to go to his aid. Wang participated in strategic planning with both T'an Lun (*q.v.*) and Ch'i. Together they defeated the pirates after several difficult engagements. For his service Wang received special gifts from the emperor, was promoted in grade, and in the winter of 1563 became surveillance commissioner. On T'an Lun's departure the following year, Wang took his position and became right assistant censor-in-chief, and concurrently governor of Fukien. He and Ch'i continued their mission of destroying the remaining bandits and pirates, and on four occasions received imperial gifts of silver and silk. Wang and Ch'i, furthermore, developed a solid friendship which lasted throughout their lives. Ch'i was a great admirer of Wang's writings, which he considered to be one of the three treasures 三絕 of Fukien, the other two being his own army and the scenic Wu-i 武夷 Mountain. Later, when Wang was no longer in government service, Ch'i did not forget to ask Wang Shih-chen to write a congratulatory note to celebrate Wang's sixtieth (*sui*) birthday. Another important figure with whom Wang kept in close correspondence at this time was Chang Chü-cheng. They did not conceal their admiration for each other's talent and ability. Wang Tao-k'un met his first setback in his political career in 1566. One of his soldiers got into a fight with Ch'en Chin 陳謹 (T. 德言, H. 環江, optimus of 1553, 1525-66), then a compiler of the Hanlin Academy and concurrently right director of instruction, who was at home observing a period of mourning. Ch'en died of wounds from the altercation. As a consequence Wang was impeached and dismissed from office. In 1570 he was recalled to duty and appointed right assistant censor-in-chief, and concurrently governor of Hukuang. Although there is no clear evidence as to who was responsible for his recall, Wang's unusual enthusiasm in promoting the erection of an honorary gateway in his native place for Chang Chü-cheng, who by then had risen to be grand secretary, seems to offer an explanation. Two years later Wang was promoted to right vice minister of War, and the next year senior vice minister with specific instructions to inspect the frontier in Chi-chou 薊州, Liaotung, and Paoting. Serving in this capacity, he sent in a number of memorials concerning border defense. In particular, he suggested the enlistment of six hundred thousand soldiers to be stationed between Hsüan-fu and Chi-chou, as a special unit to protect the capital and to give aid in time of need. His suggestion was considered too costly and set aside. His other strategic suggestions likewise received lukewarm response. He must also have felt uneasy because Chang Chü-cheng had openly praised the congratulatory note he wrote to celebrate the seventieth (*sui*) birthday of Chang's father. For these reasons, he requested leave to serve his aging parents (1575). The request was granted, but the leave became a permanent one, for he never returned to court. Several reasons can be given to explain his action. He disapproved of Chang Chü-cheng's failure to observe the traditional mourning period for his deceased father (1577). His own parents died within three years of each other (1578 and 1581 respectively). When he had discharged his filial duties, he was plagued by disease, first a spleen ailment and then tuberculosis. Perhaps the deteriorating political climate following the death of Chang Chü-cheng may likewise have served as an excuse not to resume an official career. It is also possible that he felt that he had reached the peak polit-

ically and wanted to spend the rest of his days in leisure, writing and traveling. The drama *Wu-hu yu* 五湖遊, which he wrote about the retired life of Fan Li and Hsi Shih (both 5th century B.C.), may well be a reflection of his own desire.

Although his official career ended, his literary fame grew, particularly after the publication of his work *Fu-mo* 副墨, 9 *ch.*, published shortly after his retirement. Chang Chü-cheng's open praise of the above-mentioned birthday note doubtless also enhanced his literary reputation. According to the testimony of contemporaries, prior to this date Wang Tao-k'un had not enjoyed the same prestige in literary circles as Wang Shih-chen, although the latter's brother, Wang Shih-mou (*q.v.*), held Wang Tao-k'un's ku-wen 古文 in the highest esteem. On the other hand, Wang Shih-chen, his fellow graduate, had not yet achieved as impressive an official record. Seeing that it was a chance to elevate himself politically, Wang Shih-chen also openly praised Wang Tao-k'un's writings and brought the latter's prestige to his own level. Later in life, when his position and rank were above that of Wang Tao-k'un, Wang Shih-chen is said to have greatly regretted having uttered this praise.

Wang Tao-k'un lived some nineteen years in retirement. During this period he seems to have existed on the income from his writing of epitaphs, birthday notes, poems, and prose for others, particularly for merchants. Because of his own family background, Wang had considerable admiration and understanding of the merchants with whom he came in contact. He devoted a large part of *Fu-mo* and *T'ai-han chi* 太函集, 120 *ch.* (a copy of which is in the Library of Congress), published in 1591, to championing the merchants. With his fluid and lucid style and because of his fame as a literary figure and high official, Wang had no difficulty in winning their admiration. As one contemporary remarked, after Wang Tao-k'un's unusual praise, the virtues of merchants really could be compared with those of the ancient sages. Valuable parts of both the *T'ai-han chi* and the *Fu-mo* are his memorials (some of them on military matters) and his semi-official correspondence. Wang wrote besides on many themes, including card-playing, drinking games, and a description of the sacrifices to the god of literature, Wen-ch'ang 文昌.

In addition to writing, Wang frequently toured scenic spots and called on well-known Buddhist monks. One person who was constantly at his side wherever he went was his only brother, Wang Tao-kuan (*see* Fang Yü-lu), whom he considered talented but unlucky as far as success in the examinations was concerned. His love for his brother reached such a point that he gave him rather than his own son the yin privilege, upon special imperial permission; this enabled Wang Tao-kuan to enroll in the National University. When his brother later became a paraplegic, Wang Tao-k'un continued to care for him, entertaining him and taking him on his travels. His brother's death greatly saddened Wang, who died a year later.

Wang Tao-k'un made a selection of the best of his writings from *Fu-mo* and *T'ai-han chi* and named it *T'ai-han fu-mo* (preface 1591), 22 *ch.*, to be printed after his death. (A microfilm of the copy in the National Library of Peiping collection is available.) His family carried out his wish during the Ch'ung-chen period. He also wrote the *Ch'u sao p'in* 楚騷品, 1 *ch.* He was particularly noted as a dramatist, leaving a collection entitled *Ta-ya-t'ang tsa-chü* 大雅堂雜劇, with a preface written in 1560; but parts were probably printed one after another. According to Fu Hsi-hua 傅惜華, the Peking Library has a copy containing four of them. All are also included in the collection *Sheng Ming* 盛明 *tsa-chü*, but under more or less different titles, as shown below with the variant title in parentheses. The four are: *Kao-t'ang chi* 高唐記 (*Kao-t'ang meng* 夢), *Lo-shen* 洛神 *chi* (*Lo-shui-pei* 水悲),

Wu-hu chi (*Wu-hu yu*), and *Ching-chao* 京兆 *chi* (*Yüan-shan hsi* 遠山戲). Another tsa-chü by Wang, the *T'ang Ming-huang ch'i-hsi ch'ang-sheng-tien* 唐明皇七夕長生殿, does not seem to be extant. A ch'uan ch'i 傳奇 entitled *Tung-kuo* 東郭 *chi* is also attributed to him, though the authorship is still in doubt. The story, however, seems to reflect some episodes in Wang's own life, for the hero led a retired existence after he had achieved military distinction.

Bibliography

1/287/19b; 3/268/16a; 15/10/24a; 22/9/39a; 24/3/52a; 32/37/15a; 40/47/2a; 42/96/12a; 64/己3/7b; 84/丁上/65a; 86/13/43b; MSL (1965), Shih-tsung, 8983, Mu-tsung, 1040, 1532, Shen-tsung (1966), 0173, 0203, 0742, 0912; KC (1958), 4014; TSCC (1885-88), XIV: 282/36/46b, XXIII: 107/63/25a; *Chung-kuo chin-shih hsi-ch'ü shih* 中國近世戲曲史 (Peking, 1957), 193; Shen T'ai 沈泰, '*Sheng Ming tsa-chü, ch.* 1-4; *She-hsien chih* (1771), 8/28b, 10/6a, 7b, 11/9b; *Hui-chou-fu chih* (1699), 9/40a, 12/53a; *Hsiang-yang-fu chih* (1760), 19/6b; *I-wu-hsien chih* (1727), 9/31a, 10/12b; *Fukien t'ung-chih* (1737), 29/40b; *Yün-yang-fu* 鄖陽 *chih* (1870), 5/1/9b, 3/20b; Chang Chü-cheng, *Chang T'ai-yüeh wen-chi* (Ming ed.), 24/1b, 13b, 25/2b, 7a, 35/26a, 27a; T'u Lung, *Pai-yu chi* (Ming ed.), 11/6a, 12/11a, 13/15a; Huang-fu Fang, *Huang-fu ssu-hsün chi* (Ming ed.), 46/17, 56/19b, 61/7; Wang Shih-chen, *Yen-chou shan-jen ssu-pu kao* (Ming ed.), 62/17, 96/15; *id.*, *Yen-chou shan-jen hsü-kao* (Ming ed.), 34/8, 130/17, 152/15, 154/11; Yü Chün 喻均 (cs 1564), *Shan-chü wen-kao* 山居文稿 (Ming ed.), 6/10, 7/32b; Wang Tao-k'un, *T'ai-han fu-mo* (NLP microfilm, no. 863); *id.*, *Fu-mo* (ibid., no. 1046); Fu Hsi-hua, *Ming-tai tsa-chü ch'üan-mu* 全目 (1958), 103; Feng Meng-chen 馮夢禎 (1548-1605), *K'uai-hsüeh-t'ang kao* 快雪堂稿 (Ming ed.), 1/13b, 21/3b; Li Wei-chen 李維楨 (1547-1626), *Ta-pi shan-fang chi* 大泌山房集 (Ming ed.), 11/3, 35/5, 12/26b, 71/20b, 114/9b; Wu Kuo-lun, *Chan-ch'ui-tung kao* (Wan-li ed.), 28/20; Fang Yang 方揚 (1540-83), *Fang Ch'u-an hsien-sheng chi* 初菴先生集 (Ming ed.), 11/23b, 12/20; SK (1930), 177/19b; L. of C. *Catalogue of Rare Books*, 973; W. Franke, *Sources*, 5. 6. 23; R. van Gulik, "On the Seal Representing the God of Literature," MN, IV: 1, 35n.; Ping-ti Ho, *The Ladder of Success in Imperial China* (New York, 1962), 73.

Angela Hsi

WANG T'ing-hsiang 王廷相 (T. 子衡, H. 浚川), December 4, 1474–September 23, 1544, philosopher and official, was born in I-feng 儀封, Honan. His father, Wang Tseng 王增 (d. 1505), a native of Lu-an 潞安, Shansi, was for some offense sentenced to banishment and penal military service at I-feng, where by fortune or hard labor he became a successful landowner. It happened that in the I-feng area, some thirty miles east of Kaifeng, on the south bank of the Yellow River, there were large stretches of untaxed land, including some used as farms, once owned by the guards of the prince of Chou but left fallow after they moved to Peking in 1421 (see Chu Su). There was also the ownerless alluvial land created by the Yellow River. This stream, blocked by the highlands of Shantung, generally had the tendency to shift its course in that area; these shifts caused minor floods every year and serious disasters, frequently killing entire families and destroying official records. Wang Tseng probably profited from working on land of this sort. In any case he managed to provide an education for his son, who went on to become a *chü-jen* in 1495 and a *chin-shih* and a Hanlin bachelor in 1502. As a result of the son's success the father rose from the status of a convict soldier, first, to that of landowner, and then to membership in the gentry class.

In the Hanlin Academy Wang T'ing-hsiang wrote a paper on the defense of the frontiers which marked him as a military strategist. This led to his appointment in 1504 as a supervising secretary for war in the office of scrutiny. A year later his father died and he retired for the mourning period. In 1508, when he was about to resume his post, he was punished on a minor charge of negligence and sent to Po-chou 亳州, Nan-Chihli, as a judge, an office of the same rank (7B) but considerably lower in prestige. Probably he met with such reverses because of his friendship wish Ts'ui Hsien 崔銑 (T.

子鍾, 仲鳧, H. 後渠, 洹野, 少石, 1478–1541, cs 1505, Pth. 文敏), Li Meng-yang, Ho Ching-ming (*qq. v.*), and others of the group of talented younger officials disliked by the powerful eunuch, Liu Chin (*q. v.*). By controlling his resentment and performing his duties at Po-chou ably, Wang was promoted in 1509, first to the magistracy at Kao-ch'un 高淳, south of Nanking, and then to the Censorate in Peking. While a censor he served as salt inspector of Shantung (1510) and as regional inspector in Shensi (1511–12?). Shortly after his appointment as director of education of Pei-Chihli (1513?), he was accused of acts exceeding his authority while in Shensi by the avaricious eunuch, Liao T'ang 廖堂 (or 鐺), whose connections inside the palace made it impossible for Wang to lodge an appeal. He was arrested, tried, and downgraded to be a vice magistrate, and sent to the coastal district of Kan-yü 贛榆 on the border of Shantung, where he quietly lived for two years (1514–16). He then served for a year (1516) as magistrate of Ning-kuo 寧國, south of Nanking, and for a few months in 1517 as vice prefect of Sung-chiang 松江. Thereafter he held the offices of director of education in Szechwan (1517–21) and in Shantung (1521–23), surveillance commissioner in Hukuang (1523), and administration commissioner in Shantung (1524).

After three years in retirement to mourn the death of his mother, he returned to service in 1527, receiving in June an appointment as governor of Szechwan with the rank of vice censor-in-chief. At this time the central government was undergoing a reorganization in favor of the Chang Fu-ching (*q. v.*) faction which sided with the emperor in the *Ta-li i* controversy over the question of the posthumous elevation of the emperor's father to imperial rank. Wang T'ing-hsiang had from the beginning expressed his support of the emperor, and so became one of the in-group. In the following fourteen years he served as vice minister of War

(1528–30), as Nanking minister of War (1530–33), and as censor-in-chief in Peking (1533–41). Early in 1534, during the Tatung mutiny (see Liang Chen), when the minister of War, Wang Hsien 王憲 (T. 維綱, H. 荊山, cs 1490, d. 1537, Pth. 康毅), was ordered to give undivided attention to the suppression of the mutineers, his duty as civlian director of the Peking Integrated Divisions (團營) was given to Wang T'ing-hsiang. By concurrently heading the Censorate and the Integrated Divisions for seven years, Wang both demonstrated his political ability and confirmed the trust imposed in him by the emperor. He accompanied the latter on visits to imperial ancestral tombs north of Peking in 1536 and to the tomb of the emperor's father in Hukuang in 1539. In the latter case Wang first tried to dissuade the emperor from taking the tour, but when the emperor ignored the advice and appointed him to the entourage, he did his best to safeguard the monarch's person and see to it that the proper ceremonial was observed en route. In April he was given the rank of grand guardian of the heir apparent. He also received silver and other rewards for his part in supplying the laborers for the construction of the ancestral temples, the archive building (1536), and such a palace building as Tz'u-ning-kung 慈寧宮 (1538).

The success of Wang T'ing-hsiang in his official career was due partly to his belief that he could serve the emperor best by seeing that an atmosphere of harmony and congeniality prevailed at court. He seldom reported on his subordinates and cooperated well with his colleagues, especially those in the emperor's favor, such as Duke Kuo Hsün (q.v.), the military commander-in-chief of the Integrated Divisions. It happened that in May, 1541, the newly constructed imperial ancestral temple caught fire and burned to the ground, causing extreme distress and anxiety to the emperor who, being very superstitious, believed the disaster to be portentous. The emperor blamed his own conduct as cause for this show of heavenly displeasure, but at the same time looked for misdeeds among the men at court who might share the responsibility. Every official was ordered to submit a review of his conduct to ascertain his possible guilt. As a result twelve were dismissed (see Li K'ai-hsien). Wang T'ing-hsiang was directly questioned by the emperor for his failure to report on the presumed misconduct of his subordinates, especially the regional censors. Finally the emperor picked Kuo Hsün to be the greatest culprit. The emperor, after his illness late in 1533, had avoided conducting in person the sacrifices at the temples and altars. Most of the time Kuo Hsün was delegated as imperial representative, especially at the year-end sacrificial ceremony at the imperial ancestral temple, and so it was thought possible that something he had done had brought about its destruction. Just then Kuo was being bombarded by accusations. In one case it was found necessary to issue an edict ordering him to refrain from ignoring his colleagues and to manage the assignment of labor service jointly with his civilian counterparts, including Wang T'ing-hsiang. Kuo, however, arrogantly questioned the wisdom of the edict and refused to receive it. In the end he was accused of showing disrespect to the emperor by this act. Wang stood accused also of lese majesty and, even when he explained that he should not have been the recipient of an edict issued principally to Kuo, he was dismissed from office, reduced to commoner status, and sent home. Three years later, when the officials of Honan reported his death and recommended posthumous honors, the emperor ignored the request.

In June, 1567, half a year after the emperor's death, most of the decisions during his reign, now considered unjust, were reviewed and rectified. Wang was restored to his former ranks and awarded the posthumous name Su-min 肅敏. In his native place he was honored in the local school as a celebrity; two and a half centuries later, however, his district lost its identity in 1819 after a serious flood, and became a part of the Lan-i 蘭儀 district. The place has since been submerged several times, most seriously during the floods of 1855 and 1937.

During his life Wang was widely acclaimed as a poet, prose writer, and philosopher. Before 1530 he had probably printed his poems from time to time but it seems that none of these small collections has survived. In 1533 two disciples printed his collection of ethical and philosophical essays, *Shen-yen* 慎言, 13 *ch.* In 1636-37 his collected works appeared under the title *Wang-shih chia-ts'ang chi* 氏家藏集, 41 *ch.* which included poems(*ch.* 1-20), prose (21-32), essays (33-40), and the *Ta T'ien-wen* 答天問 in the final *chüan.* The last was his exposition of the ancient poem on mythology and legends, "T'ien-wen" (Heavenly questions), attributed to Ch'ü Yüan (*ca.* 340-278 B.C.). In 1539 a disciple of Wang printed his poems and prose written after 1533 and entitled the collection *Nei-t'ai chi* 內臺集 (writings as head of the Peking Censorate), 7 *ch.*, and in the same year his second collection of ethical and philosophical essays was brought out under the title *Ya-shu* 雅述, 2 *ch.* The Columbia University Library has a copy of *Wang-shih chia-ts'ang chi* to which are appended the *Nei-t'ai chi, Shen-yen, Ya-shu*, and a work on funeral rites, *Sang-li pei-tsuan* 喪禮備纂, 2 *ch.*, printed in 1561 by a fellow townsman and admirer, Chang Lu 張鹵 (T. 召和, H. 滸東, 1523-98, cs 1559).

There is another collection of Wang's works known as *Wang Chün-ch'uan so-chu shu* 浚川所著書 which includes the *Nei-t'ai chi*, 7 *ch.*, another *Nei-t'ai chi*, 3 *ch.* (probably the edition printed in 1538), *Chün-ch'uan tsou-i chi* 奏議集 (memorials), 10 *ch.*, *Chün-ch'uan kung-i chi* 公移集 (correspondence), 3 *ch.*, and *Chün-ch'uan po-kao chi* 駁稿集 (dissenting opinions on certain judgments), 2 *ch.*

In the history of literature Wang T'ing-hsiang is named one of the "seven early masters" (*see* Li Meng-yang) of the middle Ming period, who advocated a return to the style of T'ang and pre-T'ang in poetry and Han and pre-Han in prose; hence it is generally characterized as a renaissance movement. Of the seven, Wang was the most successful in his official career but as a poet he received adverse criticism from such writers as Ch'ien Ch'ien-i and Chu I-tsun (ECCP). His devotion to meditation and philosophical discourses also distinguished him from the others, as did his moderation, prudence, and consideration, reflected sometimes in his poetry and prose. Ch'ien Ch'ien-i, however, blamed him for lauding unduly both Li Meng-yang and Ho Ching-ming in his prefaces to their collected works. Actually Wang himself laid more stress on the theme and sentiment in poetry than on structure and style, and criticized his contemporaries for only mirroring the works of T'ang masters. In one letter to a friend he summarized the way to learn to write poetry: it should be done through four tasks (四務) and three understandings (三會). The four tasks are: deliberating on the subject matter (運意), determining the best style to convey the thoughts (定格), completing the piece (結篇), and refining the words and lines (鍊句). As the three understandings to improve one's art, he named the widening of knowledge to develop talent (博學以養才) the multiplying of production to increase confidence (廣著以養氣), and the accumulating of experiences to attain correctness in judgment (經事以養通).

These three understandings, especially the last one, indicate a mind always seeking the truth, which gives Wang the stamp of an original thinker. By observation he learned that a caterpillar found in a hornet's nest was not there for adoption but as food for the young, thus refuting a mythical belief found in the Book of Poetry. By learning calendrical calculations he rejected the Confucianists' belief in destiny and their assertion that some natural phenomena were heavenly warnings to the ruler. To him such ideas hampered the effective efforts to prevent such disasters as flood or holocaust. He refuted the theory of some Sung philosophers that principle (*li* 理) originated matter (*ch'i* 氣), and taught like Chang Tsai (1020-77) that all principles came from matter (萬理皆生於氣). In his thought, which may be characterized as materialistic human nature constitutes such principles, some of which are selected by sages as beneficial to society and called "good," and some as harmful and condemned as "bad." Hence human nature is subject to modification by learning and by education. He even regarded filial piety as not inherent in human nature, a conclusion he arrived at by observing that an adopted child could never recognize his natural father. In these respects his thought disagreed with that of Mencius and was closer to Hsün-tzu's. In his *Ya-shu* (1539) Wang states that under a self-righteous ruler most officials felt obliged to be circumspect and therefore found it difficult to maintain their integrity. This seems to have been prophetic, for when, in 1541, after the imperial ancestral temple was destroyed by fire, and Wang, like all officials at court, had to comment on his own conduct in a memorial, he too cited drought and flood as heavenly warnings. In that memorial he called the emperor's attention also to the prevalence of bribery condoned by grand secretaries and high officials at that time, saying that in previous reigns bribes of a hundred taels were considered excessive but the current amount had reached tens of thousands. This was resented by those in power, because Wang was known for his incorruptibility; the memorial therefore doubtless contributed to his dismissal five months later.

During the reevaluation of the thinkers of the past, which took place in Peking in the 1950s, Wang T'ing-hsiang, Huang Wan, and Lü K'un (*qq. v.*) received attention for their advocacy of "materialistic

monism" as opposed to the prevalent rationalistic school of Chu Hsi (1130-1200) and the idealistic school of Wang Shou-jen (*q. v.*). A volume containing selections from Wang T'ing-hsiang's philosophical writings entitled *Wang T'ing-hsiang che-hsüeh hsüan-chi* 哲學選集 appeared in 1965. Hitherto maligned by poetical critics and sometimes ignored by historians (perhaps for his membership in the Chang Fu-ching clique), Wang T'ing-hsiang seems at last to be receiving some appreciation four hundred years after his death.

Bibliography

1/194/24b; 3/178/21a; 5/39/36a; 8/48/21a; 40/31/18b; 43/2/9b; 64/丁3/1a; 83/50/1a; 84/丙/66a; *Wang-shih chia-ts'ang chi*, 33/1a, 8b, 14a, 18a; *Wang T'ing-hsiang che-hsüeh hsüan-chi*, Peking, 1965; Hou Wai-lu 侯外廬, *Chung-kuo ssu-hsiang t'ung-shih* 中國思想通史, IV (Peking, 1960), 912-57; *Ming ching-shih wen-pien* (1963?), 1468; James Legge, *The Chinese Classics*, IV (1871), 334.

Chaoying Fang

WANG To 王鐸 (T. 覺斯, 覺之, H. 嵩樵, 東皋長, 癡僊道人, etc.), 1592-April 25, 1652, calligrapher, painter, grand secretary at the end of the Ming, and minister of Rites under both the Ming and the Ch'ing, was a native of Meng-ching 孟津, Honan, a district northeast of Loyang, the famous capital of the Later Han dynasty and intermittently, of several short-lived dynasties from the third to the 10th century. Not much of his early life is known except that at seventeen he attended the Ho-tung Academy 河東書院 at P'u-chou 蒲州, in Shansi. In his youth he became interested in the stone monuments, some commemorating events of state but mostly sepulchral, erected at the historic burial ground on Mt. Pei-mang 北邙山, only a few miles from his native place. Most of the inscriptions were written by famous calligraphers, and rubbings from them have long been treasured. The scenery and these tablets probably influenced Wang To's style of painting and calligraphy, both of which he diligently practiced and in both of which he excelled. He averred that one must experience the feeling of climbing to the top of Mt. Sung 嵩山 to achieve the spirit of calligraphy in the grass style for which he became nationally known. He is also celebrated for his paintings of landscapes as well as orchids, bamboos, plum blossoms, and rocks.

In 1622 Wang passed the metropolitan examination with distinction, and became a bachelor, then (March, 1624) a compiler in the Hanlin. In the following year he received an appointment as acting head of the Hanlin Academy at Nanking. Early in 1637 he was recalled to Peking as a junior supervisor of instruction, and in August of that year, after the retirement of Wen T'i-jen (q.v.), was even named by the ministry of Personnel as one among thirteen candidates for the post of grand secretary. He did not get that position but was placed four months later on the staff for the education of the heir apparent. In July, 1638, he received the rank of a vice minister of Rites to supervise the instruction of Hanlin bachelors. Late in that year he submitted a memorial to the throne criticizing Yang Ssu-ch'ang (q.v.) for his handling of negotiations with the Manchus. Aside from this he seems not to have participated in any political debate. In November, 1640, he was promoted to be minister of Rites in Nanking. He remained in office for only two months, for he retired early in 1641 owing to the death of one of his parents. Three years later (April 15, 1644) Wang was recalled to the same office, this time in Peking, but before his arrival Li Tzu-ch'eng (ECCP) had already entered the capital and Emperor Chu Yu-chien (ECCP) had committed suicide (April 25). So Wang proceeded to Nanking where Chu Yu-sung, together with Ma Shih-ying as senior grand secretary and Shih K'o-fa as minister of War (all in ECCP), was in the process of setting up a new government.

In June Wang received the appointment of minister of Rites and grand secretary; in the following September he became successively junior guardian of the heir apparent and minister of Personnel. At midnight on June 3, 1645, Chu Yu-sung, hearing that the Manchus had crossed the Yangtze River, fled in secret. The next morning Ma Shih-ying followed suit, leaving Nanking without leadership. A mob gathered that afternoon to demand the release from prison, and enthronement, of Wang Chih-ming 王之明, who asserted that he was the heir apparent of Emperor Chu Yu-chien. Wang To, having previously denounced Wang Chih-ming as an imposter, attempted to escape but fell into the hands of the mob and was humiliated at the palace gate. He got away and, resuming his office, he joined Ch'ien Ch'ien-i (ECCP) and a number of other high officials in an ignominious surrender to the Manchus.

On March 14, 1646, Wang began to served the new regime in Peking as minister of Rites, and his younger brother, Wang Yung 鏞 (T. 仲和), was appointed surveillance vice commissioner in Shansi. In the same year his son, Wang Wu-chiu 無咎 (T. 藉茅), achieved the chin-shih and became a Hanlin bachelor. Three years later (February 18, 1649) Wang To was appointed a vice editor-in-chief of the Ch'ing T'ai-tsung shih-lu. In the last three years of his life he received further honors and was reappointed minister of Rites in Peking (April 11, 1652). A week before this he was dispatched to Mt. Hua 華山 to hold a ritual sacrifice on behalf of the new dynasty. The poems written on certain historical spots during this mission are revealing. Some are laments for the passing of the previous dynasty and express strong feelings of self-pity. He was given the posthumous name Wen-an 文安. His biography is listed in the Er ch'en chuan 貳臣傳 (On officials who served two houses).

He left a collection of his writings, entitled Ni-shan-yüan hsüan chi 擬山園選集,

54 *ch.*, printed in 1653. It was proscribed
in the 18th century, so is comparatively
rare. Sun Tien-ch'i reports three editions:
one in 82 *chüan* printed at the end of
the Ming, another with the title *Ni-shan-
yüan wen hsüan chi* 文選集, 32 *chüan*, printed in the first years of the Ch'ing, and
a third in 22 *chüan*, printed in 1658. Some
examples of his calligraphy reproduced in
rubbings are known as *Ni-shan-yüan t'ieh*
帖. Reproductions of his calligraphy and
painting may be found in many collections.

Bibliography

Ming-shih (Taipei, 1962), 1393, 1546, 3081, 3092;
KC (1958), 5772, 5786, 5792, 5811, 5816, 5878,
5882, 6038, 6066, 6087, 6134, 6154, 6189, 6198,
6206, 6208, 6211; MSL (1940), Hsi-tsung, 23/13a,
Huai-tsung, 10/6b, 11/10a; *Ta Ch'ing li-ch'ao shih-
lu* 大清歷朝實錄 (Mukden, 1937), Shih-tsu, 16/
21b, 19/3a, 23/12a, 25/22a, 26/23a, 42/3a, 9a, 46/
16b, 59/5b, 63/8b, 14a; *Ch'ing-shih lieh-chuan* 清史
列傳 (Shanghai, 1928), 79/13a; *Honan t'ung-chih*
河南通志 (1914), 59/54a, 73/50b; Honan fu-chih
府志 (1867), 43/23a, 95/22a, 24a, 98/62a, 99/46a,
101/37a; Ma Tsung-huo 馬宗霍 (1898-), *Shu-
lin chi-shih* 書林紀事, 2/76b; Chen-chün 震鈞
(1857–1920), *Kuo-ch'ao shu-jen chi-lüeh* 國朝書人
輯略 (1908), 1/9a; Ch'ien Ch'ien-i, *Mu-chai yu-
hsüeh chi*, 30/4a; Chang Keng 張庚 (1685–1760),
Kuo-ch'ao hua-cheng lu 國朝畫徵錄, 上/21; Cha
Chi-tso (ECCP), *Tsui-wei lu*, 紀/18/20a; Sun
Tien-ch'i (1957), 232; *Shina nanga taisei* 支那南畫
大成 (Tokyo, 1935), 3/24, 11/87; *Teihon shodō
zenshū* 定本書道全集, XIII (Tokyo, 1956), 24,
167; *Shodō zenshū*, XXI (Tokyo, 1962), illustrations, nos. 32–39, p. 152; *Min Shin no kaiga* 明清
の繪畫 (National Museum, Tokyo, 1964), 36,
40; Victoria Contag and C. C. Wang, *Seals of
Chinese Painters and Collectors* (rev. ed., Hong
Kong, 1966), 76, 644; Osvald Sirén, *Chinese
Paintings* (New York, 1956–58), V, 54, 56, 129,
VII, 255; E. J. Laing, *Chinese Paintings in Chinese
Publications, 1956–1968* (Ann Arbor, 1969), 200;
Tseng Yu-ho Ecke, *Chinese Calligraphy* (Phila-
delphia, 1971), #67.

Mingshui Hung

WANG Tso 王佐 (T. 孟輔), died September 1, 1449, minister of Revenue from
1442 to 1449, a native of Hai-feng 海豐,
Shantung, was born into a military family
which settled in Lin-an 臨安 (Hangchow),
during the early years of the 12th century.
His great-grandfather, a company commander under the Mongols, served in
the transportation of tribute grain. His
grandfather, also in the military service,
deserted the ranks at the collapse of the
Yüan in the 1360s and took the family
to Shantung. His father, Wang P'o 朴
(T. 子素, 1352–1431, cj 1372), the first in
the family to make a mark in scholarship, served as an instructor in the district
school of Pin-chou 濱州, Shantung. Apparently a wealthy man, he is said to have
been robbed of possessions worth a thousand taels of silver, and when partly compensated he contributed the amount to
local charities.

Following his acquisition of the
chü-jen in 1411, Wang was admitted to
the National University from which he
graduated in due course. In January, 1418,
he received an appointment as supervising
secretary of Personnel, being promoted to
be an assistant minister of Revenue in
September, 1427. Three years later he was
dispatched to investigate the reported
swindling in the government granaries in
Peking and those along the Grand Canal
in Lin-ch'ing 臨清 (Shantung), Huai-an
淮安, and Hsü-chou 徐州 (Nan-Chihli).
In July, 1431, he was sent to Huai-an to
review the proposal of Ch'en Hsüan 陳瑄
(*q.v.*, then in charge of the shipment of
grain to the capital), for an alternate
system of delivery to ease the burden on
the taxpayers. Under this scheme, the
people would bring their tribute rice and
a surcharge to a designated collection
station nearest their locality, where the
rice would be loaded onto grain boats by
the transport troops who would be paid
from the surcharge; the rice would then
be shipped to Peking. This recommendation was put into effect (1431).

Wang was assigned in April, 1432, to
oversee the dredging of the old section
of the canal system (known as Pai-ho

白河), which extended some 300 *li* from T'ung-chou 通州 to Chih-ko 直沽 (near Tientsin), to facilitate the transportation of tribute grain. In August of the following year he again assumed supervision of granaries in the capital area. In February, 1435, he and a general were sent to Honan as joint grand defenders; they found the soldiers short of rations due to the corruption of the officers in charge. To counteract this, Wang recommended that future supplies be sent directly from outside government granaries instead of drawing from local storage depots. In June he undertook an inspection tour in both Nan- and Pei-Chihli to scrutinize the conduct of local officials, returning to Peking two months later to receive promotion as senior assistant minister. He was ordered in November to Shensi to supervise the provisioning of the guards in Kansu and neighboring regions. He reported that many of them had nearly exhausted their grain reserves, and that the taxes imposed on the unoccupied land assigned to the soldiers for cultivation were far too excessive. He also observed that the army lacked horses for military training and for dispatching messages; whereupon he proposed to the court that it audit the stock of horses assigned to the various offices and that the extra ones be sent to the frontier for proper purposes. The ministry of Revenue subscribed to his first recommendation, but the ministry of War spurned his second suggestion since, they pointed out, according to the injunction laid down by Emperor Chu Ti (*q.v.*), the number of horses for official use was to remain secret.

In October, 1436, Wang Tso was one of the officials sent to oversee the disposal of salt in the Huai region, in Ch'ang-lu 長蘆 (Pei-Chihli), and in Chekiang as well where the commodity was handed over to the merchants in exchange for their service in supplying grain to the army. In these places Wang and his colleagues uncovered cases of official corruption and profiteering by merchants; they

restored the operation to normal shortly afterward. Resuming his duty in the ministry in April, 1438, Wang was again put in charge of the granaries in the capital area. In November, 1441, when the minister of Revenue, Liu Chung-fu 劉中敷 (1380-June 4, 1453), was imprisoned for violating the law by proposing (during a shortage of fodder in the capital area) to send the imperial horses and cattle to be fed in civilian stables, Wang became acting minister, and replaced Liu as minister in January of the following year.

Wang served as minister for eight years until his untimely death in 1449. During this period he demonstrated his caliber as a thoughtful, competent, and innovative minister. These were the years of financial instability caused by preparations for war against the Mongols, and the dwindling of supplies from the grain producing region in the lower Yangtze area as a result of natural calamities. Wang's chief preoccupation was the maintenance of a balanced economy and a rational distribution of resources to meet the needs of the various sectors of the country. He was concerned with the grain supply of the army in the frontier region, making frequent adjustments, and watching out for the possible illicit activities of those in charge. He also took into account the impact of the military undertakings on the economy; thus for example, in March, 1443, after the imperial forces became involved in the suppression of the rebellion of Ssu Jen-fa (*q.v.*) in Yunnan, he proposed reducing the stipend of the local officials as well as the material rewards granted them. Similarly, he watched carefully the changing rates of exchange in the transaction of grain into cash, and on several occasions introduced measures to prevent people who had to pay their share of tribute in cash from becoming the victims of a fluctuating money economy. In July, 1446, when there was a rise in the value of cash, he proposed that the rate of exchange in wheat (originally set at 80 *kuan* 貫 for 1 *shih*) be reduced to 60; and in May of the following year, as another step to maintain equilibrium of exchange, he memorialized the court to reduce the cash stipend of the officials from 25 *kuan* to 15. In addition, he attempted to maintain a balanced distribution of grain in the nation; to this effect he occasionally proposed changes in the quota to be shipped to the capital for storage in the granaries, and recommended that the portion that had to be kept in the provincial storage depots be used in accordance with local needs.

Wang's performance made a marked impression on Chu Ch'i-chen (*q.v.*), who began to favor him. The emperor invited him to join his entourage when making visits to the imperial tombs outside the capital and to take part in ceremonies; on several occasions when Wang was accused of certain offenses, the emperor treated him with leniency. One instance took place in April, 1446, when Wang was charged with shifting responsibility in the investigation of the case of Chang An 張安 (the third earl of An-hsiang 安鄉伯, d. December, 1449), who was indicted for embezzling the stipend of his younger brother, Chang Ning 寧. Wang was thrown into prison by the Embroidered-uniform Guard, but the emperor soon ordered his release. Then in April, 1449, a censor impeached Wang for violating the rule requiring that horses in the imperial stables be fed not with grain and hay from the capital area, but instead with fodder supplied by the peasants from Honan, Shantung, and Pei-Chihli. Having learned that Wang acted in order to relieve the plight of the local population from flood and drought, the emperor pardoned him. When, in August of that year, the eunuch Wang Chen 王振 (*q.v.*) persuaded the young emperor to take personal command of a campaign aginst the Oirat chieftain Esen (*q.v.*), Wang Tso was among those summoned to join the expedition, Together with many of his colleagues, Wang remonstrated against this hazardous undertaking, but the eunuch turned a deaf ear to his plea.

In the disastrous defeat at T'u-mu on September 1, the emperor and his retinue were taken prisoner, while many high officials, including Wang Tso, were killed in action.

Early in 1450, when the new emperor Chu Ch'i-yü (*q.v.*) bestowed lavish posthumous awards on the officials who perished in the campaign, Wang Tso was honored with the title of junior guardian. Two sons of Wang also benefited. The eldest, Wang Chen 震 (T. 道陽), received an appointment as secretary in the ministry of Revenue; the fourth son, Wang I 頤 (T. 道正), entered the National University through the yin privilege and achieved the *chin-shih* in 1456. Then in October, 1466, acting on the recommendation of the minister of Rites, Yao K'uei (*q.v.*), Emperor Chu Chien-shen (*q.v.*) granted Wang Tso the canonized name Chung-chien 忠簡 (loyal and unruffled). Wang Tso is a prominent example of one who rose to ministerial rank after having been merely a student in the National University; in his day it had not yet become the practice to require the *chin-shih* as a qualification for higher government positions.

During the Ming period there were several men with an identical name, but no other had so distinguished a career. (Cf. Harvard-Yenching *Yin-te*, 24, Vol. II, 76, 77, and *Ming-jen chuan-chi tzu-liao so-yin* 明人傳記資料索引, 34.)

Bibliography

1/167/4a; 3/152/4a; 5/28/30a; 8/22/6a; MSL (19 63), T'ai-tsung, 2047, Hsüan-tsung, *ch*. 30–115, Ying-tsung, *ch*. 1–181, Hsien-tsung (1964), 673; KC (1958), 1776; *Hai-feng-hsien chih* (1670), 7/3b, 10/7b, 11/3a; Li Shih-mien, *Chih Chung-wen ku-lien wen-chi* (NCL microfilm), 10/7a.

Hok-lam Chan

WANG Tsung-mu 王宗沐 (or Tsung-shu 宗沭; T. 新甫, H. 敬所, Pth. 襄裕), 1523–91, was born in Lin-hai 臨海, Chekiang province. Upon obtaining the *chin-shih* in 1544, he served as a secretary in the ministry of Justice and later as a vice director. A series of provincial assignments followed in a long official career. He became assistant surveillance commissioner in charge of education, Kwangsi, assistant administration commissioner, Kwangtung, and vice education intendant, Kiangsi (1556). Next he served successively as administrative vice commissioner, surveillance commissioner, and right administration commissioner of Kiangsi (1562). When insurgents in Fukien penetrated his territory, Wang directed the campaign of suppression, his troops defeating them at Yung-feng 永豐. Subsequently he was promoted to left administration commissioner, Shansi province.

Early in 1563, while still holding the last assignment, he submitted a memorial to Emperor Chu Hou-ts'ung (*q.v.*) in which he discussed the seriousness of the famine situation in Shansi. A major reason for the insufficiency of grain for the people, he wrote, was due to the necessity of supplying 670,000 piculs annually to the frontier defense posts and 850,000 piculs for the support of the imperial clansmen in the province. He pointed out that transportation costs of the army supplies often doubled the value of the grain forwarded. In conclusion he petitioned that the land taxes in Shansi in arrears be remitted and that the proceeds from the increased quota on the salt tax of Ho-tung in southwestern Shansi be retained to subsidize the imperial clansmen, thus alleviating the burden on the local population. This petition annoyed the emperor and Wang was reprimanded. He then asked for retirement, but the request was denied. In the end he received a transfer to Kwangsi province as left administration commissioner. In this position he did not stay long as his father's illness enabled him to return home on leave. After the death of his father and the three years' mourning, he became left administration commissioner of Shantung.

On November 2, 1571, he was promoted to the office of director general of grain transport at Huai-an 淮安. At this time Liang Meng-lung (*q.v.*), governor of Shantung, was championing the transportation of grain by sea, and Wang came enthusiastically to his support. Along with Liang he spoke in favor of the route skirting the Shantung coast instead of one which risked the hazards of the open sea. His argument prevailed but the operation did not last long.

Upon completion of his term at Huai-an, Wang was made right vice minister of Justice at Nanking (January 6, 1575); later he served in the same capacity in the ministry of Works. His last official position was left vice minister of Justice in Peking. When Chang Chü-cheng (*q.v.*) maneuvered Emperor Chu I-chün (*q.v.*) into suppressing his own critics, those who dared to criticize Chang were one after another flogged, jailed, or exiled. In 1576 an imperial censor, Liu T'ai (*see* Wang Tsung-tsai), who owed his career advancement to Chang, submitted a memorial impeaching his benefactor for usurpation of power and for corruption. The grand secretary in due course had Liu arrested and beaten. Exiled to Kwangsi for several years, Liu faced further misdemeanor charges. At this point it is said that Wang Tsung-mu spoke in his defense and thus antagonized Chang Chü-cheng. Wang suffered no overt reprisal. In 1579, several ministerial officials were dispatched to inspect the frontier army commands, Wang Tsung-mu among them. He toured Hsüan-fu, Tatung, and Shansi. Early in 1581, however, several supervising secretaries and censors, in both Nanking and Peking, initiated two separate k'ao-ch'a shih-i 考察拾遺 (supplementary miscellaneous impeachments). Wang's name, along with that of Fang Feng-shih (*see* Liang Meng-lung), minister of War, appeared on both bills. It is possible that Chang Chü-cheng was behind the impeachment actions, as Wang's biographer has asserted. On March 17, 1581, the emperor directed that Fang's services be retained; Wang, however, was ordered to retire. After Chang's death the following year, many of Wang's admirers suggested his recall, but he remained at home. Nine years later he passed away in Lin-hai and was posthumously awarded the title of minister of Justice.

Aside from being an efficient civil administrator, Wang Tsung-mu was also an assiduous promoter of education, a polished poet, a philosopher, and a prolific writer. He built several academies in Kwangsi and Kiangsi and sponsored the reissuance of the works of Wang Shou-jen (q.v.) and Lu Chiu-yüan (1139–93), writing prefaces for both collections. In his early years at the court he befriended Wang Shih-chen (q.v.), and, with five others, organized a poetry club. In the field of thought he belonged to the Chekiang branch of the Wang Yang-ming school. His personal vigor and promptness in action were reminiscent of that eminent figure.

Following the plan of history of Ssu-ma Kuang (1019–86), Wang Tsung-mu was one of those who extended Ssu-ma's chronicle to later times. He named his work *Sung-Yüan tzu-chih t'ung-chien* 宋元資治通鑑, 64 *ch*. Another historical compilation of his is entitled *Shih-pa-shih-lüeh* 十八史略. His belles-lettres are collected in *Ching-so wen-chi* 敬所文集, 30 *ch*. A collection of his memorials appears as *Wang Tsung-mu tsou-shu*, 4 *ch*., also known as *Ts'ao-fu* 漕撫 *tsou-shu*. The *Yüeh-shih san-chen lu* 閱視三鎮錄, which summarizes his observations on the frontier, seems to have disappeared, for it was listed for suppression in the 18th century. His plans and actions in the sea operation of 1572 resulted in the publication of the *Hai-yün chih* 海運志, 2 *ch*. The *Ching-so wen-chi* and *Hai-yün chih* are mentioned by title only in the *Ssu-k'u* catalogue. Two of his other works deal with the provincial administration; one is the *Kiangsi ta-chih* 江西大志, 7 *ch*., and the other is the *Tung-sheng ching-chih lu* 東省經制錄. The *Nan-hua-ching pieh-chuan* 南華經別傳 reveals his

interest in Taoism. Two final works are entitled *Ying-ning yü-lu* 攖寧語錄 and *Huang Ming ming-ch'en yen hsing lu* 名臣言行錄, 14 *ch*. The Harvard University library has a rare copy of the latter.

Now available in microfilm, the *Hai-yün chih* was originally published several years before Liang Meng-lung's *Hai-yün hsin-k'ao* (1579). It is less substantial than Liang's book; nevertheless, a number of identical documents may be found in both works. The *Hai-yün chih* discloses that the seafaring ships originally conceived by Wang have larger dimensions than those actually constructed. Each of these ships according to Wang's design would require fifty sailors to operate and would cost one thousand taels of silver. An instruction which Wang issued is reproduced in the above-mentioned work, and reveals his pseudo-scientific approach. He believed that the weather on the first day of each lunar month determined the outlook of the first ten days, that on the second day one could foretell the conditions of the middle ten-day period, and that on the third day one could predict what would prevail during the balance of the month. Wind direction, Wang explained, could be analyzed in terms of eight trigrams. If the wind's association with the particular trigram were determined, one could tell which hours during the day were favorable for navigation and which were not.

Despite his many pre-modern concepts, however, Wang seems to have established himself in history as something of a pioneer. His *Kiangsi ta-chih* discusses the province's land taxes, corvée labor, historical divisions and principalities, irrigation systems, military topography, native products, and the procelain industry. The single-whip method, as certain historians believe, may have risen as a spontaneous movement, devised simultaneously by a number of local officials in different districts in the mid-sixteenth century; Wang Tsung-mu, however, is credited as the first to have used the term in a publication and given it a precise definition.

P'ang Shang-p'eng (*q.v.*), who extended the single-whip method in Chekiang, reportedly followed in Wang's footsteps. Ku Yen-wu (ECCP), among several scholars, accepted this version and indicated that the second chapter of *Kiangsi ta-chih* marks the beginning of the single-whip method.

Wang's interest in collecting local information and his systematic approach to every problem were carried on by his four able sons. One, Wang Shih-sung 王士崧 (cs 1583), was a secretary in the ministry of Justice. He published a chronological biography of his father, *Wang Hsiang-yü kung-nien-p'u* 襄裕公年譜. A second son, Wang Shih-ch'i 琦 (T. 圭叔, H. 豐輿, 1551–1618, cs 1583), became governor of Tatung. His *San-yün ch'ou-tsu-k'ao* 三雲籌俎考 (4 *ch.*) is an intensive documentation of the frontier command that he administered; it embodies information on organization, military colonization, army supplies, and the tributary trade with Mongol tribes in the late sixteenth and early seventeenth centuries. A third son, Wang Shih-ch'ang 昌 (T. 永叔, H. 十溟, cs 1586), became governor of Fukien. The most distinguished member of the family was an adopted son, Wang Shih-hsing (*q.v.*), who passed on his father's methods and interests to Ku Yen-wu.

Bibliography

1/223/13b; 3/206/10b; 64/己8/12a; 83/15/2b; MSL (1965), Shih-tsung, 8203, 8335, Mu-tsung, 1504, Shen-tsung (1966), 0212, 2096; *Ming-shih i-wen-chih pu-pien fu-pien* (1959), 34, 43, 58, 86, 110, 629, 736, 1217; SK (1930), 84/2b, 177/17a; Yao Chin-yüan (1957), 55; *Kiangsi t'ung-chih* 江西通志 (1880), 12/40b, 48b, 127/40a; *Chekiang t'ung-chih* 浙江通志 (1934), 2849; *Shansi t'ung-chih* (1892), 12/13a, 86/40b, 103/39b; *T'ai-chou-fu chih* 臺州府志 (1936), 71/9a; Ku Yen-wu, *T'ien-hsia chün-kuo li-ping-shu* (SPTK), 39/88a; Wang Tsung-mu, *Hai-yün-chih* (NLP microfilm #534); Wang Shih-ch'i, *San-yün ch'ou-tsu-k'ao* (reprint, 1936); W. Franke, *Sources*, 3.3.4, 8.11.1.

Ray Huang

WANG Tsung-tsai 王宗載 (T. 時厚, H. 又池, cs 1562), a native of Ching-shan 京山, Hukuang, is best known for his service as overseer of the Ssu-i kuan (College of Translators; *see* Cheng Ho), and for his book on the institution, *Ssu i kuan k'ao* 考 (preface dated 1580). Following his graduation as *chin-shih*, Wang occupied a succession of posts: hsien magistrate of Hai-yen 海鹽, Chekiang (1562–66), censor, regional inspector in Fukien, and vice minister of the Court of Imperial Sacrifices. His appointment as overseer of the college came in 1578. This institution, never one to draw the best students, was then at a low point in its history. Only fifty of the seventy-five men appointed to it in 1566 remained. Presumably the selection of Wang was to invigorate it and attract more and better candidates.

It so happened that shortly before a flurry of excitement had been caused by the arrival in Peking of a mission sent by the king of Siam bearing, besides tribute, a memorial written on gold leaf which no one at court could read. According to the later account of Lü Wei-ch'i (*q.v.*), this display of ignorance embarrassed the government; whereupon Grand Secretary Chang Chü-cheng (*q.v.*) arranged for the setting up of a Siamese bureau at the Ssu-i kuan. (Up till this time the college had maintained nine bureaus: Mongol, Muslim [Persian, etc.] Tibetan, Uighur, Jurchen, Pai-i [or Yunnanese Thai], Burmese, Indian [Sanscrit?], and Chieng-mai [northern Siamese and Lao], with numerous subdivisions.) The leader of the Siamese mission, Wo-men-la 握悶辣, and two other fellow countrymen were drafted as instructors.

Wang Tsung-tsai, in the preface to his work, tells of arranging a meeting with the Siamese envoy to learn from him as much as possible about the geography, highways, commercial resources, language, and customs of the country. He then determined to compile a book which would contain translations made by each bureau of the college, informing readers as to the conditions under which foreign states had been formed or had disappeared, the degree of accessibility of mountains and streams in their territories, their resources, and the diversity of their ways of life and their speech. In addition he planned to provide a sketch of each country's relations with China, these to precede the special vocabulary of the different bureaus.

Wang's book was apparently never published. G. Devéria in 1878, after a search of six years, located an original manuscript copy in the library of the Russian Ecclesiastical Mission in Peking; Paul Pelliot in 1909 reported that Devéria had donated a copy of this to the École des Langues Orientales in Paris; a copy of a manuscript, with a note written by Lo Chen-yü (BDRC), was printed in Peking, 1924; and in 1940 Hsiang Ta (see Giulio Aleni) wrote of two others in China. Though bearing an identical sounding title it must, of course, be distinguished from the Ssu-i 譯 kuan k'ao of Chiang Fan 江繁 (T. 采白, fl. 1686-1702), published in 1695.

After four months as overseer of the college, Wang was made a vice minister of the Grand Court of Revision (March 26, 1579). In 1580 he was given the rank of an assistant censor-in-chief and appointed governor of Kiangsi, where he conducted the trial of a former censor, Liu T'ai 劉臺 (T. 子畏 , cs 1571, Pth. 毅思 granted in 1621), who happened to have offended Chang Chü-cheng. Liu was found guilty and sentenced to exile in April, 1581, and many believed that Wang had followed Chang's instructions in the trial. In May, 1582, the court recalled Wang to Peking to serve in the Censorate, but two months later Chang Chü-cheng died and a series of reversals in decisions of judicial cases followed. In March, 1583, Liu was posthumously given a higher rank, and seven months later Wang was cashiered and sentenced to banishment to a frontier guard as a common soldier. It is unknown when he received a pardon, but it seems that he died at home in the 1620s at the advanced age of eighty-one.

Bibliography

1/82/4a, 324/19b; 21/17/62a; MSL (1966), Shen-tsung, 1724, 1774, 1777, 2032, 2456, 2623; KC (1958), 4343, 4372, 4430, 4454; Ching-shan-hsien chih (1882), 11/20a, 19/11a, 21/11a; Hai-yen-hsien chih (1876), 2/23b; Kiangsi t'ung-chih (1881) 13/6a; Fukien t'ung-chih (1938), 10/5b; Chekiang t'ung-chih (1934), 2681; Hsiang Ta, "Note on the Sze-I-Kwan-K'ao" (in Chinese), T'u-shu chi-k'an 圖書季刊, n. s. II: 2 (June, 1940), 181; G. Devéria, "Histoire du Collège des Interprètes de Péking," Mèlanges Charles de Harlez (1896), 94; Paul Pelliot, BEFEO, IX (1909), 170; id., JA (1914), II, 180; id., TP, Vol. 26 (1929), 54, Vol. 38 (1948), 224; Norman Wild, "Materials for the Study of the Ssŭ I Kuan," BSOAS, XI (1943-46), 620, 625, 635, 637; W. Franke, Sources, 7. 1. 5.

Søren Egerod and
L. Carrington Goodrich

WANG T'ung-kuei 王同軌 (T. 行甫, or 行父), ca. 1530-1608十, man of letters, a native of Huang-kang 黃岡, Hukuang, was born into a prominent family which produced many degree holders, officials, and scholars. His grandfather, Wang Lin 麟 (T. 體仁, d. 1505), a chin-shih of 1499, was magistrate of Feng-ch'iu 封邱, Honan, in the years 1500 to 1505. His father, Wang T'ing-huai 廷槐 (T. 稚占), a chü-jen of 1528, died in his forties, never having held office. If one examines the rosters of degree holders in their local histories, one will notice that the names of men of this particular Wang clan appear often over a period of some two hundred years. Of these individuals the most celebrated was possibly Wang T'ing-ch'en 廷陳 (T. 稚欽), an uncle of Wang T'ung-kuei. After becoming a chin-shih in 1517, Wang T'ing-ch'en became a bachelor to receive further training in the Hanlin Academy. Because of his daring act of memorializing against the emperor's plan to make an imperial trip to the south in 1519 (*see* Chu Hou-chao), he was flogged and expelled from the Academy, and dispatched to Yü-chou 裕州, Honan, as magistrate. After two years of undistinguished service, he retired and lived at home for the rest of his life. Although his official career was short and without note, he became well known for his literary accomplishments, and was highly regarded by his contemporaries. In his *I-yüan chih-yen*, Wang Shih-chen (*q.v.*), praises both his poetry and his prose, and calls him a talented man (才子). His collected literary works, the *Meng-tse chi* 夢澤集, 17 *ch.*, may be found in the *Hu-pei hsien-cheng i-shu* 湖北先正遺書 (1923). This uncle apparently was an inspiration to Wang T'ung-kuei and influenced him in his literary development.

Early in life Wang T'ung-kuei became a *kung-sheng* (1552) and attended the National University in Nanking. He was unlucky in the examinations, however, and never obtained a higher degree. As a follower of his uncle, and a disciple of the poet Wu Kuo-lun (*q.v.*), he became known in literary circles, and his writings were respected. Probably it was in the early 1590s, when rather late in life, that he purchased a minor official post (9A) in Peking and was assigned to assist in the supervision of the palace poultry farm, the Fan-yü shu 蕃育署, which supplied chickens, ducks, and geese for the Court of Imperial Entertainment, under the directorate of imperial parks (上林苑). In 1599 he received a promotion to a slightly higher post (8A) in the office of transmission, and a year later he was accorded another promotion (7A) to a secretarial post in the Court of the Imperial Stud in Nanking.

During his stay in Peking he met a number of people, saw many things of interest, and heard a variety of strange stories. With a light touch and an intent to entertain he jotted down these anecdotes. The accumulation was printed in Peking in the mid-1590s under the title *Er-t'an* 耳

談 (譚). In 1597 a Nanking edition appeared. It became a best seller of the day. Then more editions were printed in Shensi and in Chekiang. With such encouragement and his continuing interest, Wang kept up his practice. By 1603 a classified edition much enlarged was brought out in Nanking under the title *Er-t'an lei-tseng* 類增. Like several similar collections by Ming authors, Wang's works are valuable to later students of Ming history. They are in a sense the periodical literature of their day, a record of the times, containing not only newsworthy reports, but also gossipy items.

The first edition of *Er-t'an* printed in Peking is in 5 *chüan*, and the *Er-t'an lei tseng* is in 54 *chüan*. Both are preserved in the rare book collection of the National Library of Peking. The subject matter of the anecdotes primarily concerns people and events of the day including some reports about members of his own family and even a few items about himself. With a large number of his stories, either at the beginning or at the end, he notes their origin in such words as "so-and-so said." Some of these tales were later copied into the *Ch'ing-shih lei-lüeh* by Feng Meng-lung (*q.v.*), and these in turn served as the plots of some of Feng's famous short stories in the collections known in abbreviated form as the *San-yen*. One good example is the story of Chin San and his wife. Identical versions may be found in *Er-t'an* under the title *Wu-ch'i-yü Chin San* 武騎尉金三, in *Er-t'an lei-tseng* under the title *Wu-ch'i-yü Chin San ch'ung-hun* 重婚, and in the *Ch'ing-shih lei lüeh* under the title *Chin San ch'i* 妻. Later this story received lengthened form in *chüan* 22 of the *Ching-shih t'ung-yen*, the *Sung hsiao-kuan t'uan-yüan p'o-chan-li* 宋小官團圓破氈笠. There are also stories which appear in both the *Er-t'an* and the *Ch'ing-shih lei-lüeh*, but which used different names and places in variant texts, such as the *Ch'ü-fu te-lang* 娶婦得郎 (*Er-t'an lei-tseng*, *ch.* 8) and *K'un-shan min* 崑山民 (*Ch'ing-shih lei-lüeh*, 2/9b). The expansion of this story constitutes *chüan* 8 of the *Hsing-shih heng-yen* of Feng Meng-lung, *Ch'iao t'ai-shou luan-tien yüan-yang p'u* 喬太守亂點鴛鴦譜.

It is not clear when Wang T'ung-kuei retired from his last post in Nanking, but at the time the compilation of the local history of his native district was initiated under magistrate Mao Jui-cheng (*q.v.*) he was invited to be the senior compiler. This earliest edition of the *Huang-kang-hsien chih* was completed and printed in 1608 and received praise for its excellence.

Wang's collected literary works, according to the local history, are listed under four separate titles: the *Ts'ang-ts'ang-ko ts'ao* 蒼蒼閣草, the *Ho-chiang-t'ing ts'ao* 合江亭草, the *Yu-yen ts'ao* 遊燕草, and the *Lan-hsin chi* 蘭馨集. As Li Wei-chen (*see* Hsieh Chao-che), Wu Kuo-lun, and Wang Shih-chen all left prefaces to the *Wang Hsing-fu* 行甫 *chi*, possibly the four books cited above were grouped together and known by the last mentioned title. The *Er-t'an* was not copied into the Imperial Library, but receives an incorrect notice in the *Ssu-k'u* catalogue. This notice, states that Wang T'ung-kuei was magistrate of Chiang-ning 江寧 (Nanking), which he never was. In this the editors of the catalogue confused him with Wang T'ung-ting 王同鼎 (T. 調甫), either a brother or a cousin, who was magistrate of Chiang-ning in the early 1620s (T'ien-ch'i period). It seems that this erroneous statement was taken from the *Lieh-ch'ao shih-chi* by Ch'ien Ch'ien-i (ECCP) without checking. The same notice includes one of the prefaces of *Er-t'an* and gives the author's name as T'ao Yeh 陶冶. Actually T'ao Yeh was only the calligrapher, the author of that preface being Li Wei-chen. In addition the notice criticizes Wang T'ung-kuei for paying respect to T'ao Chung-wen (*q.v.*), the Taoist adept, without realizing first, that T'ao was also from Hukuang, a compatriot of Wang T'ung-kuei, and second, that the attitude of many Ming people toward religious Taoism was different

from that of the 18th century, and that the *Er-t'an* does not profess to be political. Furthermore, the notice gives the number of *chüan* of *Er-t'an* as 15, which seems to indicate that the *Ssu-k'u* editors were not aware of the existence of the classified and enlarged edition.

Bibliography

64/庚30/11a; 84/丁中/23a; *Huang-kang-hsien chih* (1882), 7/29a, 10/8a, 34b, 12/3a, 23/63b, 58b; *Feng-ch'iu-hsien chih* (1937), 5/6b; *Yü-chou chih* (1740), 4/3a; *Chiang-ning-fu chih* (1880), 22/28a; Wang Shih-chen, *I-yüan chih-yen* (in *Yen-chou shan-jen ssu-pu kao*, Wan-li ed.), 148/16b, 150/1b; SK (1930), 144/6a; Feng Meng-lung, *Ch'ing-shih lei-lüeh* (1902), 1/7b, 2/9b; Wang T'ung-kuei, *Er-t'an lei-tseng* and *Hsin-k'o er-t'an* (NLP microfilm, nos. 18 and 537).

Lienche Tu Fang

WANG Wei 王褘 (sometimes incorrectly written I 禕, T. 子充, H. 華川), January 24, 1323-February 5, 1374, scholar and writer, was born into a prominent family of I-wu 義烏 in Chin-hua 金華 prefecture, Chekiang. His grandfather, Wang Yen-tse 炎澤 (January 7, 1254-1332), and father, Wang Liang-yü 良玉 (1289-1363), were Confucian teachers, the former, the head of Shih-hsia shu-yüan 石峽書院 in Ch'un-an 淳安, and the latter an instructor in the district school of Ch'ang-shan 常山, both in Chekiang. Among Wang Wei's teachers were Liu Kuan (1270–1342) and Huang Chin (1277–1357). Huang was considered the last in the line of famous scholars who made Chin-hua a major center of Confucian learning during the late Sung and Yüan periods. A *chin-shih* of 1315, Huang served six years as an erudite in the National University in the Yüan capital, Ta-tu, and retired in the 1330s. He was recalled in 1347 and Wang Wei followed him to Ta-tu, apparently in the hope of an appointment but without success. In 1348 Wang submitted a long memorial on current affairs, which those in power considered too outspoken. Feeling rejected and unhappy, he returned home in 1350. His despondency is reflected in some of his poems of this period.

As a prose stylist, however, Wang Wei was greatly admired, the number of commissioned and requested pieces—prefaces, funerary and other inscriptions, descriptive accounts, and the like—preserved in his collected works, testify to his popularity. Locally he became a prominent member of the group of Chin-hua writers such as Sung Lien, Su Po-heng (*qq.v.*), and Hu Han 胡翰 (T. 仲申, H. 仲子, 長山, 1307–81), all of whom later served in various literary capacities under Chu Yüan-chang.

The fall of Wu-chou 婺州 (also in Chin-hua-fu) to Chu Yüan-chang's forces in January, 1359, brought Wang Wei an appointment for the first time; in the establishment of a secretariat office in Wu-chou, he, with a number of other Confucian scholars, received a post as chief clerk. On the subjugation of Kiangsi in the winter of 1361, he presented a eulogy, *P'ing Chiang-hsi sung* 平江西頌, to Chu Yüan-chang who is said to have commended him highly. His next appointment in the spring of 1363 was as a sub-director in the office of education for the area controlled by Chu. He retired in June to mourn the death of his father. In the late spring of 1365 he returned to the court and was appointed gentleman-in-waiting in the ministry of Rites and concurrently commissioner for embassies. As such he is said to have had a major part in determining the ceremonies for the new dynasty. In the winter he moved to the new post of diarist. In the late summer of 1366 he was awarded a golden belt and sent as vice prefect to Nan-k'ang 南康, Kiangsi. This area included Lu-shan 廬山 with its celebrated scenic spots, and he reported in a preface to a series of "records of excursions" that the sites were over-grown and few tracks open as a result of the continual fighting since 1355.

He did not remain long in Nan-k'ang.

In the next year he was recalled to court to participate in the discussions over the proper ceremonies to be used in the enthronement of Chu Yüan-chang. (An entry in the *shih-lu* for April 30, 1367, indicates that Wang had returned to his former post as diarist.) He apparently, however, gave offense to the newly enthroned emperor and was sent in 1368 to Chang-chou 漳州 in Fukien as assistant prefect. His offense cannot have been very grave, for, by March of the following year, he was summoned back to the capital to serve with Li Shan-ch'ang (*q.v.*) and Sung Lien as chief editors of the *Yüan-shih*, based on the *Yüan shih-lu*. Because this work ended with the year 1333, he and Sung were further ordered to compile the history of the late Yüan period up to 1368. Meanwhile, when Sung became chancellor of the Hanlin Academy, Wang Wei received an appointment as Hanlin writer. Soon after the completion of the *Yüan-shih* in July, 1370, both men were reduced to the position of compilers for failing to attend an audience. Wang Wei, early in 1371, was sent as an envoy to Tibet, but was recalled after he had reached Lan-chou 蘭州 in Shensi. He took the opportunity to visit historical sites in the province, including the temple to the Duke of Chou (especially venerated by Confucians) at Ch'i-shan 岐山 (where, to his distress, the custodian was a Taoist and the observances were crude and incorrect), and the tomb of the Han emperor Wu, Mao-ling 茂陵. During the summer he stayed in the old capital of the Han and T'ang dynasties, Ch'ang-an (Sian).

In February, 1372, the court ordered him to undertake a new embassy. He was sent to Yunnan to call for the submission of the Yüan prince of Liang 梁王, Basalawarmi 把匝剌瓦爾密 (d. 1382). He reached Yunnan during the summer and presented the imperial edict. While the prince was apparently hesitating as to whether or not to comply, an emissary from the Mongol court at Karakorum came to strengthen his resistance. Wang

Wei failed in his mission and was killed. A repetition of Wang Wei's embassy occurred in 1375, when Wu Yün 吳雲 (T. 友雲, Pth. 忠節) was sent with a similar call to allegiance and suffered the same fate. The subjection of Yunnan had to wait until the end of 1381. In the following year Wang's son, Wang Shen 紳 (T. 仲縉, 1360-1400), made an unsuccessful journey to Yunnan to search for his father's remains. In 1400, on Wang Shen's application, Wang Wei received posthumously the title of chancellor of the Hanlin Academy and the name Wen-chieh 文節. This name was changed to Chung-wen 忠文 in 1441, in response to a memorial by Liu Chieh 劉傑 (T. 朝用, 1466-1516, cj 1483), vice magistrate of I-wu and editor of Wang Wei's collected works. During the Ch'eng-hua period it was decreed that a shrine be erected to him at Yun-nan-fu. Early in the next reign, through the initiative of Wang Chao 詔 (T. 文振, 1428-91), governor of Yunnan, Wu Yün was granted the title of minister of Justice and the posthumous name Chung-chieh 忠節, and commemorated in the same shrine, which then became known as Er-chung ssu 二忠寺 (Shrine of the two loyal ones). The original shrine was later destroyed, but a new one on a fresh site was built in 1692 to celebrate three martyrs, Wang, Wu, and Kan Wen-k'un 甘文焜 (T. 仲明, 1632-73). The last, as governor-general of Yunnan and Kweichow, committed suicide when Wu San-kuei (ECCP) revolted.

Wang Wei's wife, née Ho 何 (Miao-yin 妙音), survived him by three years, dying in 1377, aged fifty-six *sui*. (Sung Lien wrote her tomb inscription.) Of their two sons, the elder, Wang Shou 綬 (T. 孟縕), did not enter public service, but the family tradition was maintained through the younger, Wang Shen, in whom Sung Lien saw a likeness to his father. He became an erudite of the National Academy for a short period before his death, and was a contemporary and close friend of Fang Hsiao-ju (*q.v.*). Wang Shen's son, Wang T'u 稌 (T. 叔豐), and others at-

tempted to recover Fang's body for burial after his execution in 1402. Wang T'u was singled out for pardon for this offense because his grandfather died for the dynasty.

Wang Wei produced a continuation of the annotated chronology *Ta-shih chi* 大事記 by Lü Tsu-ch'ien (1137-81). This *Ta-shih chi hsü-pien* 續編 is said to have originally covered the years from 89 B.C. to A.D. 1276, but the extant version in 77 *chüan* extends only to 959; if the remainder of the work then existed, it would appear to have been lost by the time of the first printing in the Ch'eng-hua period. Wang wrote as well a short account of the eminent people who helped to found the Ming, entitled *Tsao-pang hsün-hsien lu lüeh* 造邦勳賢錄略. He also revised an astronomical work, *Ko-hsiang-hsin shu* 革象新書 (by a 13th-century author, Chao Yu-ch'in 趙友欽), perhaps under the influence of his mother. It is asserted that he condensed the *Ch'ung-hsiu* 重修 *Ko-hsiang hsin shu* to 2 *chüan* from the original 5, removing irrelevancies and contradictions, and that he put the work into logical order. Wang Wei collected his prose writings under the title *Hua-ch'uan chi* 華川集, with preface by Hu Han, and later made a second collection with prefaces by Sung Lien and Su Po-heng; his verse was probably originally kept separate. The two collections were combined, together with his verse, in an edition in 24 *chüan*, entitled *Wang Chung-wen kung chi* 公集, with a new preface by Yang Shih-ch'i (*q.v.*). The edition in 20 *chüan* to be found in the *Chin-hua ts'ung-shu* includes neither Wang Wei's verse nor his notes, *Ch'ing-yen ts'ung-lu* 青巖叢錄 and *Hua-ch'uan chih-tz'u* 巵詞; these were later extracted from the collected works as separate items in *Hsüeh-hai lei-pien*, compiled by Ts'ao Jung (ECCP). Some works listed under his name, however, may be spurious. Wang Shen's collected works were transmitted under the title *Hsü-chih-chai chi* 續志齋集; the edition copied for the *Ssu-k'u ch'üan-shu* was in 12 *chüan* with 1 *chüan* of appendices; earlier there had been an edition in 30 *chüan*. The record of Wang Wei's career, *Han-lin tai-chih Hua-ch'uan Wang kung Wei hsing-chuang* 待制華川王公 禕行狀, compiled by Cheng Chi 鄭濟 (T. 仲辨, fl. 1393), who had been a pupil of Sung Lien, is the prime source of most Ming accounts of Wang Wei and of the biography in the *Ming-shih*.

Bibliography

1/289/8a; 3/270/6b; 5/20/84a, 44/14a; 61/101/4a; MSL (1962), T'ai-tsu, 0073, 0153, 0327, 0783, 0849, 0965, 1061, 1314; KC (1958), 476; Huang Chin *Huang Chin-hua wen-chi*, 4/19a, 33/12a; *Sung Yüan hsüeh-an*, 70; Juan Yüan (ECCP), *Ch'ou-jen chuan*, 29; SK (1930), 47/12a, 106/3a, 124/3b, 169/2b; *Yün-nan-fu chih* (*Chung-kuo fang-chih ts'ung-shu* ed.), 16/5a; Fang Hsiao-ju, *Ch'ang-shan chiao-yü Wang fu-chün hsing-chuang* 教諭王府君行狀, *Hsün-chih-chai chi*, 21; *Tsao-pang hsün-hsien lu lüeh*, included in Huang Ch'ang-ling 黃昌齡, *Pai-ch'eng* 稗乘, Wan-li ed. (NLP microfilm, no. 536); F. W. Mote, *The Poet Kao Ch'i* (Princeton, 1962), 148, 158, 164, 179.

                                        A. R. Davis

WANG Wen 王問 (T. 子裕, H. 仲山), 1497-1576, painter, calligrapher, and poet, was a native of Wu-hsi, Nan-Chihli. After passing the metropolitan examination in 1532, instead of taking the palace examination immediately, he retired for six years, during which he cured himself of palpitation and gave occasional lectures on the Confucian Classics at a monastery near his home. Finally in 1538 he returned to Peking, where he qualified for the *chin-shih*. He was then made a secretary in the ministry of Revenue, and was later (1541?) sent to Hsü-chou 徐州 (Nan-Chihli), to inspect state granaries there. During his stay in Hsü-chou his mother died, so he went home to observe the mourning rites.

Returning to government employ, he requested that he be transferred to Nanking, a place not far from Wu-hsi, so that he might personally attend to his aging father. His petition granted, he was sent there in 1544 as a secretary in the ministry of War, but his father was still unwilling to move away from home and ordered him to prepare thirty fans, each with a sketch and a poem drawn and written by Wang himself. When he was away, therefore, the father could use one fan a day each month as a reminder of his absent son. Wang Wen's next appointment was as director of a bureau and soon afterwards he was appointed an assistant surveillance commissioner of Kwangtung. He started on the journey to the south but when half way through Chekiang, he was overwhelmed with sorrow for having left his father unattended. He composed twelve poems expressing his feelings, and, sending in his resignation, he returned home. The old man, in his early eighties, had a young son and daughter by a concubine. Wang Wen treated them with kindness and consideration as if they were his own children. In the spring of 1554, when the pirates looted Soochow and neighboring towns, Wu-hsi was in great danger. Wang Wen and his father escaped to Nanking where they stayed several months. It seems his father died shortly after they returned home. When the mourning period was over, Wang Wen was recommended on several occasions for government posts. Each time he declined. For the next twenty years or so, he avoided the cities and spent his life at Mt. Pao-chieh 寶界山 on the shore of Lake T'ai, about eight miles south of Wu-hsi city. There he built a villa, planted bamboos, trees, and flowers, and arranged some water courses and picturesque stones round about. He often sat alone, with his hands folded over his knees, burning incense, and reading the Book of Changes. Whenever he felt inspired, he would write poems and paint, or try his penmanship in the cursive 草書 and running 行書 styles. As he enjoyed an enviable reputation for his filial piety and integrity, people came from afar to call on him; generally he politely declined to see them, pleading illness. Those with whom he preferred to associate were mainly Taoist priests and local scholars. When he died, his pupils, many of whom were established scholars, gave him the unofficial posthumous name Wen-ching 文靜 (Learned and peaceful). A shrine (王斂事祠) was erected in his honor at a scenic spot on Mt. Hui 惠, surrounded by age-old pines and curved rocks, where he used to visit.

As an artist he excelled in figures, landscapes, flowers, and birds. His mature works are marked by ease and freedom. His mode of representation is more descriptive and closer to nature than that of his predecessors in the Sung and Yüan dynasties, since he drew on the actual scenery in the Wu-hsi area rather than from imagination. Eight scrolls of his landscape paintings are still extant in collections in Taiwan, Japan, and the United States. The most interesting one is a scroll entitled "Yü-lo t'u" 漁樂圖 (Joy of the fishermen) in Baron Iwasaki's 岩崎 collection. It represents an actual view as seen from his retreat on Mt. Pao-chieh. In the words of Osvald Sirén, "It is not a traditional combination of mountains and streams but a view over low marshy land, traversed by a river and enveloped by a misty atmosphere which is so dense that it almost obliterates the forms in the background. The leafy trees and bamboos in the foreground emerge like wavy plumes, and between them one may discover two small boats with fishermen and farther away the fishing hamlets on the shore, while the boats out on the river beyond are hardly more than faint shadows over the grey water." The motif is explained in a short poem:

At dawn, the lake shore is obscured by rosy clouds.
A line of fishing boats sets out from the distant shore, hurriedly rowing.
Don't be vexed at this life of solitude and hardship, For fishermen are exempt from taxation.

As Sirén so aptly describes it, "the whole thing is light and vaporous, rendered in a very sensitive impressionistic manner with thin washes and soft touches of the brush." It is most representative of Wang Wen's original style.

His poetry and calligraphy, though not to be compared with his paintings, are unaffected and spontaneous. They, together with his paintings, were much sought after by his contemporaries. Among his literary works, the *Ming-shih* lists his *Chung-shan shih-hsüan* 仲山詩選, 8 *ch.* Ch'ien Ch'ien-i (ECCP) regarded it highly and selected ninety poems to include in his anthology.

Wang Wen's son, Wang Chien 鑑 (T. 汝明, H. 繼山, 1520–90), became an established painter too. A *chin-shih* of 1565, he served as magistrate of the sub-prefecture Wu-ting 武定, Shantung, and after a series of promotions was made director of a bureau in the ministry of Personnel. He later gave up his career in order to be with his aged father. Several years after Wang Wen's death, Wang Chien resumed his old office following persistent summons from the government. When he finally retired in 1589, he was given the title minister of the Court of the Imperial Stud. He died a year later. He was a man of conspicuous virtue. After the death of his wife, née Pao 鮑, in the early 1550s he did not remarry. He is credited with the authorship of several books including a literary collection, *Pao-chieh chi* 寶界集.

Bibliography

3/268/9b; 5/73/31a, 99/160a; 22/8/39a; 40/42/28a; 64/巳17/5a; 65/6/9b; Ch'ien Ch'ien-i, *Lieh-ch'ao shih-chi*, 丁 3/12a; *P'i-ling jen-p'in chi* 毘陵人品記, 9/19下; *Huang Ming wen-hai* (microfilm), 13/4/18, 21; *Wu-hsi-hsien chih* (1881), 19/29a, 21/10a; *Wu-sheng shih-shih* 無聲詩史 3/39a; O. Sirén, *Chinese Painting* (London, 1956–58), VII, 256; id., *A History of Later Chinese Painting* (London, 1938), I, 66; *Palace Museum Weekly*, no. 122, 481.

Lee Hwa-chou

WANG Wen-lu 王文祿 (T. 世廉, H. 廉子, 海沂子, 沂陽生), 1503–86, bibliophile, was born into a military family of Hai-yen 海鹽, Chekiang. He was descended from Wang Chung 王忠, a Yüan soldier of the Qangli 康里 tribe of central Asia, who in the late 14th century became an officer in the Ming army. For meritorious services, the emperor, Chu Ti (*q.v.*), awarded him the Chinese surname Wang, and in 1410 made him regional commander of western Shensi on the Ninghsia and Kansu frontiers. In 1435 his grandson, Wang Kuei 貴, inherited the rank of an assistant guard commander and was assigned to the Hai-ning Guard 海寧衞 with headquarters in Hai-yen city. The main branch of the descendants of Wang Kuei inherited his rank for eight generations until the end of the Ming dynasty. His grandson, Wang Hsüan 軒 (T. 載之), second inheritor of the rank, was the grandfather of Wang Wen-lu.

Wang Hsüan, although a military officer, was a learned man and expert in divination. He lived at a time when the influential families of the Soochow-Hangchow area were expanding their landholdings. As one of the leading families of Hai-yen it became quite affluent. His first son inherited the rank. His second son, Wang Tso 佐 (T. 朝輔, H. 學圃, d. 1543), led a life of leisure and was noted for his skill in archery and horsemanship. He is credited with a small compilation, *Hui-t'ang chai-ch'i* 彙堂摘奇 (Choice pieces from the Hui-t'ang), which consists of reproductions of the inscriptions on three monuments, all obviously hoaxes. In his day forgeries flooded the market because of the demand by wealthy collectors of antiques. These three inscriptions, puzzled over by the curious as representing ancient scripts, were of such a kind. One of them, the so-called Koulou pei 岣嶁碑, ascribed to the legendary emperor Yü, was supposed to have been engraved about 1212 and "discovered" in 1534 by the prefect of Changsha, named P'an I 潘鎰 (cs 1521). Wang Tso was

apparently one of the first to consider it authentic. Among others of like mind may be mentioned Yang Shen, Chan Jo-shui, and Lang Ying (*qq.v.*). Although some scholars, such as Wang Shih-chen (*q.v.*) and Ku Yen-wu (ECCP), had expressed their incredulity concerning this inscription, the editors of the 1885 gazetteer of Hunan gave a long account of it but remained noncommittal.

Wang Tso married a member of a Lu 陸 family of Shanghai, possibly of the same clan as the scholar Lu Shen (*q.v.*). At the time of the birth of Lady Lu (1469–1538) her family had a turn in fortune, and so they named her Sai-chin 賽金 (as good as gold). She was well educated, loved and respected, and exerted great influence in the bringing up of her son, Wang Wen-lu. She taught him at an early age to value books, how to mend damaged ones, and how to correct the misprints. She was a remarkable woman, as witnessed by her son's devotion to her and by the epitaph written by Huang Hsing-tseng (*q.v.*). In later life Wang Wen-lu recalled how she told him anecdotes about the founder of the Ming dynasty, Chu Yüan-chang. Obviously from her he learned about the subordinate position of women as shown in the Confucian rules of conduct. Even in the case of the funeral rites, those for the mother had always been of a lower order than those for the father, until Chu Yüan-chang proclaimed them to be the same for both parents, and wrote this into the Ming code (*see* Chu Su).

As an only child in a well-to-do family, Wang Wen-lu was accorded the best in education. In 1516 he began to learn to play the lute. Four years later his father brought him to meet the father of Cheng Hsiao (*q.v.*), and in 1527 both father and son visited the academy established by Wang Shou-jen. The latter was then in Kwangtung as supreme commander, leaving oversight of the academy to his disciple, Wang Chi (*q.v.*), under whom Wang Wen-lu studied for a short while. In 1531, probably as a student in the National University in Nanking, he took the provincial examination there and became a *chü-jen*. He failed to pass the triennial metropolitan examination which, it is said, he faithfully tried repeatedly until the age of almost eighty. This would mean then that from 1532 to 1583, except for the periods of mourning for his parents (1538-*ca.* 1543), he went to Peking to take that examination at least sixteen times without success, perhaps a record in persistence but certainly a succession of repeated disappointments and a tragic waste.

In his case the wealth he inherited made life bearable, for he assembled a large library and engaged in reading, writing, and publishing. At first he wrote about his thoughts and observations of his neighborhood, as did some of his friends, including the above-mentioned Huang Hsing-tseng, a fellow *chü-jen*. The latter died in 1540 and left several short treatises, published by Wang, on rice, fish, the chrysanthemum, silkworm, and the taro, as well as an important work on government service in which he bitterly attacked the preference given to holders of the *chin-shih*. Later Wang himself became increasingly concerned over the misrule of the Chia-ching emperor, and wrote about the corruption, injustice, and lawlessness that were hurting the Soochow area. He was worried in 1550 when the Mongols raided up to the walls of Peking. Later he was personally affected by the pirates who in 1554 overran the Hai-yen region, killing thousands of people. He extended his studies to military and financial matters, and appealed to the authorities to stop the practice of exempting the influential from land taxes, thus adding to the burdens of the common folk. Wang himself had all his land properly registered for assessment, which he could have avoided had he not been so conscientious.

By 1555 Wang had published fifty treatises, including twelve by himself, several ancient works he edited with com-

ments, and the rest by his friends. Almost all were short ones, mostly of a few leaves each. The longest was his own work of miscellaneous notes, entitled *Hai-i-tzu* 海沂子, 5 *ch.* Among his other works may be mentioned the *I-hsien* 醫先 on preventive medicine, the *Lung-hsing tz'u-chi* 龍興慈記 on early Ming events as recounted by his mother and recorded from memory in 1551; the *T'ing-wen shu-lüeh* 庭聞述略, miscellaneous observations made by his father, the *Wen-mai* 文脈, a short work of criticism of Ming authors; the *Ch'iu-chih p'ien* 求志篇, on moral conduct in government service; and the *Wen-ch'ang lü-yü* 文昌旅語, a recording of conversations of a group of friends. He gave the fifty works the collective title *Ming-shih hsüeh-shan* 明世學山. Later the title was changed first to *Ch'iu-ling* 丘陵 *hsüeh-shan* in order to match the title of the Sung prototype *ts'ung-shu*, the *Po-ch'uan hsüeh-hai* 百川學海, compiled by Tso Kuei (fl. 1274), printed about 1265-75 and reprinted in 1501. Both titles came from a sentence in the *Fa-yen* 法言 of Yang Hsiung (53 B.C.-A.D. 18). About 1568 Wang changed the title of his collection to *Po-ling hsüeh-shan* in order to avoid the use of the word ch'iu, which happens to be the personal name of Confucius. Although a fire in 1565 destroyed his library of books, he continued writing and printing. More items were added from time to time, and by 1584 he listed in the table of contents one hundred titles (ninety-eight of which were printed). Among the later additions may be mentioned the following under Wang's own name: *Chu-hsia wu-yen* 竹下寤言, containing jottings of his thoughts, 2 *ch.*; *Ts'e-shu* 策樞, 5 *ch.*, an important work on reforms in military and financial matters; *Shu-tu* 書牘, 2 *ch.*, his letters on current affairs; and *Shih-ti* 詩的, literary criticisms.

Wang wrote also about geomancy and made comments on Taoist texts. He was likewise a believer in Buddhism. It seems that he, like his father, was susceptible to intellectual hoaxes. In 1564 he met the brilliant scholar and notorious fabricator of books in classical style, Feng Fang (*q. v.*), who handed him a copy of the "stone classic ancient text" of the Great Learning, under the title, *Ta-hsüeh shih-ching ku-pen* 大學石經古本. The official text of the Great Learning was the one edited by Chu Hsi (1130-1200). It was disputed by Wang Shou-jen who held the one in the Classic of Rites to be the original ancient text, calling it the *Ta-hsüeh ku-pen*; but these two texts differ only in the order of arrangement of the paragraphs. Feng Fang went further, rearranged the text in a, to him, more logical order, and asserted that it was based on old rubbings from the Classics engraved on stone in the Cheng-ho 政和 (*sic*) period of the Wei dynasty (220-64). These rubbings, according to Feng, had been handed down in his family for generations. It is known that the stones with the valuable inscriptions had been smashed to pieces soon after completion, and only a few fragments existed. Hence no one could effectively refute him, although the nonexistence of the Cheng-ho reign title should have been enough to warn an observant reader. Wang, however, was so credulous that he made some annotations and published the text and Wang Shou-jen's version as the first two items in the final edition of his *Po-ling hsüeh-shan*. This probably happened in 1584. A year later the scholar, T'ang Po-yüan 唐伯元 (T. 仁卿, cs 1574), submitted a copy of the *Ta-hsüeh shih-ching ku-pen* to the throne with the request that it be proclaimed as the official text to be followed in the examinations. At the same time T'ang raised heated objections to the placing of the commemorative tablet of Wang Shou-jen in the temple of Confucius. The emperor rejected T'ang on both counts and punished him by demotion. This, however, did not deter several other scholars from accepting the "stone classic" version as authentic, including Kuan Chih-tao (*see* Ku Hsien-ch'eng) and Liu Tsung-chou (ECCP).

Both Wang Wen-lu and Yüan Chiung (*q.v.*) stand out as pioneers in publishing collections (*ts'ung-shu*) that included works of a serious nature only. Just as Yüan started a succession of publishers of *ts'ung-shu* in the Soochow area, Wang had his followers in Hai-yen, such as Hu Chen-heng and Yao Shih-lin (*qq.v.*). Perhaps both also helped to pave the way for some enterprising dealers in Hangchow and Nanking.

Bibliography

64/庚 18/8a; 84/丁下/75a; *Hai-yen-hsien chih* (1876), 15/59b, 16/2b, 17/3b, 12b, 18b; *Chia-hsing-fu chih* 嘉興府志 (1877-78), 57/50a; *Ho-fei-hsien chih* (1920), 16/6b, 20/30b; *Chekiang t'ung-chih* (1934), 2471, 3116; *Hupeh t'ung-chih* (1934), 3474; *Hunan t'ung-chih* (1934), 5355; *Szechwan t'ung-chih* (1815), 127/46a, 146/43b; *Lu-chou-* (廬州) *fu chih* (1885), 28/6a; Sheng Feng 盛楓 (cj 1681), *Chia-ho cheng-hsien lu* 嘉禾徵獻錄 (*Tsui-li* 檇李 *ts'ung-shu* ed.), 37/13b; *Ku-ch'eng-hsien chih* (1921), 6/16b; *Ting-hsien chih* (1934), 9/29a; Yeh Ch'ang-ch'ih (BDRC), *Ts'ang-shu chi-shih shih* (1958), 3/160; SK (1930), 74/6a, 190/1a, 193/4b, 196/3a, 197/10a; Ch'ien Ch'ien-i (ECCP), *Ch'u-hsüeh chi* (SPTK ed.), 17/11a; Chu Liang-pi 朱良弼, *Yu-chi pien* 猶及編, 46/10b (*Yen-i chih-lin* 鹽邑志林 ed.); Chang Hsin-ch'eng 張心澂, *Wei-shu t'ung-k'ao* 僞書通考 (1954), 445; Yü Ta-kang 俞大綱, "Chu T'ang-yin t'ung-ch'ien," CYYY, Vol. VII, Part 3 (1937), 355; Louis Hambis, *Documents sur l'histoire des Mongols à l'époque des Ming*, (Paris, 1969), 21.

Chaoying and Lienche Tu Fang

WANG Ying-chiao 汪應蛟 (T. 潛夫, H. 登原, 蔚翔, Pth. 靖簡), d. 1628, who ended his career as minister of Revenue, was born in Wu-yüan 婺源, Nan-Chihli. Qualifying for the *chin-shih* in 1574, he first served as a secretary in the bureau of equipment (ministry of War), Nanking, was next promoted to director, and then transferred to the ministry of Rites in the same city. Later he became vice provincial surveillance commissioner, Fukien; education intendant, Szechuan; administrative vice commissioner, Shantung; provincial surveillance commissioner, Shansi.

In 1597 the Ming court, in promotion of its second campaign in Korea, created a new governorship at Tientsin with responsibility for coastal defense and the transportation of supplies for the expeditionary forces, and put Wan Shih-te 萬世德 (T. 伯修, cs 1568) in charge. Wang Ying-chiao, then military intendant at I-chou 易州, was transferred to Tientsin as the new governor's chief assistant. When Wan became commander-in-chief of the Chinese expeditionary forces in Korea the following year, Wang was promoted to right assistant censor-in-chief to take over the governorship. Upon the successful conclusion of the Korean campaign, Wang's name appeared in an order of commendation for his service in administering supplies for the army; this included an increase in salary. After the cancellation of the governorship at Tientsin in 1599 (it was not revived until 1621), Wang became governor of Paoting, where he assumed responsibility for the six southern prefectures of Pei-Chihli—a position he held until early 1602.

While Wang was governor at Tientsin and Paoting, Emperor Chu I-chün (q. v.) dispatched eunuchs to various parts of the empire to direct the mining of silver and to collect sales and transit taxes. These eunuchs caused a wave of civil disturbances. On several occasions Wang petitioned the throne to recall them, but to no avail. As a result of his intervention, however, a proposed increase in the tax quota in Pei-Chihli was reduced by half.

As governor Wang also recommended that the dry land within his territory be irrigated. Some of this land, he asserted, might be converted to rice paddies. After conducting experiments on five thousand mou (about 700 acres), near Tientsin, he declared that he had turned some forty percent of it into rice paddies. The land, after the water had been cleansed of its alkaline deposits, which previously had been considered infertile or uncultivable, now produced as much as four piculs of grain per mou. Hence he proposed a military farm of seventy thousand mou. The ministry of Works concurred in his

recommendation and it received the emperor's approval. For some unknown reason, however, the project was never carried out. Later in 1621 Tso Kuang-tou (q. v.) made a similar suggestion, also without effect.

Early in 1602 Wang received promotion to right vice minister of Works. He immediately requested leave on the ground that his parents were old and needed his attention. On July 26, 1602, the leave was granted and Wang returned to his native Wu-yüan. During his absence from the court, he was further promoted to left vice minister of War. Nevertheless, he extended his leave indefinitely. After the deaths of his parents he did not return to duty, nor did the court recall him. For about eighteen years his official status remained ambiguous, a not uncommon occurrence in the later years of Chu I-chün's reign.

Little has been recorded as to what occupied Wang in these eighteen years; he seems to have been instrumental, among other activities, in constructing a private academy in Wu-yüan. Education was one of his major concerns all through his life. In 1620 Emperor Chu Ch'ang-lo (ECCP) made an effort to recall the statesmen who were disgraced, banished, or dismissed by his father. Among them was Wang Ying-chiao, whom he appointed minister of Revenue at Nanking (August 30, 1620). About a year later (August 2, 1621) Wang was transferred to Peking to take over the ministry at the capital. Almost at once he involved himself in a series of controversies. When Sun Shen-hsing (ECCP) and Tsou Yüan-piao (q. v.) reopened the investigation into the sudden death of Emperor Chu Ch'ang-lo, more than a hundred courtiers were assembled. Under the leadership of the minister of Personnel, Chang Wen-ta (see Li Chih), it was agreed that Grand Secretary Fang Ts'ung-che (ECCP, p. 176), though cleared of the charge of murder, was responsible through negligence for the emperor's untimely death. After the conference Wang Ying-chiao and Chang Wen-ta joined in a petition requesting that Fang's name be removed from the official register, and that eunuch Ts'ui Wen-sheng (*see* Kao P'an-lung) and court physician Li K'o-shao (ECCP, p. 176) be condemned to death. The memorial also brought up Fang's failure to order Lady Li (*see* Kao P'an-lung) to evacuate the emperor's living quarters immediately after the imperial succession. The memorial though ignored had some effect. It touched on two of the three issues, which, academic and freakish as they seem to be, were to engulf the Ming court in partisan disputes for several years (*see* Wei Chung-hsien, ECCP), with tragic results. The new emperor's nurse, K'o 客, had besought Emperor Chu Yu-chiao (ECCP) to grant her a piece of government land for her future burial. As the request fell under the jurisdiction of the ministry of Revenue, it came to Wang, who regarded it as unwaranted and refused to comply. His refusal annoyed the emperor.

Wang's fiscal policies also brought him into disagreement with some of his colleagues. Hsiung T'ing-pi (ECCP), during his second term as commander-in-chief in Liaotung, conceived a strategy which called for the establishment of three bases of operation. His command was to have a total strength of 260,000 men, with an annual budget of 12,000,000 taels of silver. Wang demanded that the proposed strength be drastically reduced. He argued that he could not produce more than 7,160,000 taels for Hsiung's purposes. Those who disliked Wang charged that he was too old for the ministerial position. Unhappy at court, Wang requested retirement seven times before leave was eventually granted on January 29, 1623. With the now title of senior guardian of the heir apparent, Wang was allowed to return home with full honors. In his farewell message Wang warned the emperor of the danger of trusting eunuchs. Three years later he was disgraced along with members of the Tung-lin (*see* Ku Hsien-

ch'eng), but escaped personal prosecution.

Wang is credited with some thirteen works (*see Wu-yüan-hsien chih*). The titles cover a variety of subjects such as poetry, proverbs, commentaries on Confucian Classics, etc. A collection of fifty-seven of his memorials is available in microfilm; two among them were submitted while he was governor at Tientsin, thirty-one while governor at Paoting, and twenty-four while minister of Revenue. These papers shed much light on Ming government in the early 17th century in general and its fiscal administration in the 1620s in particular. From his memorials it may be observed that Wang's ideas are not always sound. For instance, he argued that cavalry might be partially replaced by wheeled vehicles and crossbows be substituted for firearms, frugality being his main consideration. His policy on taxation, on the other hand, is more enlightened. In his effort to raise state income, he refused to put any extra burden on farm land. Instead he recommended the creation of new revenues by taxing all pawnshops and by suspending the partial remission of tax payments on properties held by government officials; by selling provincial grain reserves and by requiring provincial governors, prefects, and magistrates to tighten their administrative budgets, and surrender the savings to the central government. Proceeds from the commutation of corvée labor, along with fines and confiscations, were likewise to be delivered in part to the imperial treasury. Ch'en Jen-hsi (*q. v.*) in his *Huang Ming shih-fa lu* (*ch.* 34) gives a detailed account of the amounts considered receivable by the ministry of Revenue, the original figures having been drawn probably from the ministry's file of 1623. The breakdown of items and the totals given agree in general with those appearing in Wang's memorial of 1622. This suggests that his recommendations had for the most part been put into effect.

Bibliography
1/241/5b, 9b, 259/12b; 8/79/9a; 37/2/1b; 39/16/19a;

MSL (1940), Shen-tsung, 314/6a, 323/9b, 339/9b, 340/3b, 369/2a, 373/7b, Hsi-tsung, 6/18a, 45a, 11/22a, 18/27b, 24/33a, 61/18b; KC (1958), 129; Li Yen 李棪, *Tung-lin-tang-chi k'ao* 東林黨藉考 (Peking, 1957), 71, 155; *Wu-yüan-hsien chih* (1920), 21/9b, 64/4a; Wang Ying-chiao, *Wang Ch'ing-chien kung tsou-su* 公奏疏 (NLP microfilm, roll no. 142); W. Franke, *Sources*, 5.7.46.

Ray Huang

WANG Yüeh 王岳, died November, 1506, a eunuch, was a native of Tsun-hua 遵化, Pei-Chihli, and a victim in a palace intrigue in the first year of the Cheng-te period. Nothing has been recorded concerning his origin, education, early career, and how he succeeded in reaching a high position within the eunuch heirarchy as a director of Rites and in charge of the Eastern Depot. His life and death, however, are closely connected with the final ascent to power of Liu Chin (*q.v.*).

We find him initially in the service of Chu Hou-chao (*q.v.*), probably beginning in 1492 when the latter was named heir apparent. The next concrete information recorded is that Wang was assigned to be one of the directors of ceremony and in charge of the Eastern Depot almost immediately following Chu Hou-chao's accession on June 19, 1505.

Wang must have enjoyed a good reputation in official circles, for different accounts describe him as one who followed the Confucian moral code: he was faithful, righteous, loyal, and pure, the type of eunuch that Chu Yu-t'ang (*q.v.*) as emperor would appoint in the household of his heir apparent.

The situation at the end of Chu Yu-t'ang's reign was not favorable for the young prince as his father's health was declining, and the heir apparent, now a boy of fourteen, began to show an increasing interest in hunting, music, and other pleasures rather than in state affairs. Certain eunuchs, such as Liu Chin, seized this opportunity to establish their influence, and they became the chief challengers of the position held by Wang Yüeh and his associates.

At the time of the young emperor's succession, probably with the support of the empress-dowager and definitely with the support of such court officials as Liu Chien, Hsieh Ch'ien, and Li Tung-yang (*qq.v.*), Wang's faction maintained their control. As late as May, 1506, near the end of Chu Hou-chao's first year on the throne, the evidence is clear that Wang had a post of influence. On May 25, when two positions were vacated (assistant commander of the guard and assistant director of the elephant house), Wang was asked to assume both.

As head of the Eastern Depot Wang had to work closely with the offices of Scrutiny and the Censorate. In dealing with official matters one record describes Wang as a person who upheld traditional ethical principles firmly, and followed the laws of the land closely. He often provided information concerning the emperor's activities to the officials, so that timely counsel might be proffered. He was especially praised for the fact that he treated people at court politely, a rare thing then for a powerful eunuch.

Meanwhile, the Eight Tigers (*see* Chu Hou-chao), who pandered to the young emperor's interest in military games and other amusements, had gained the emperor's confidence to such a degree that they were being placed in significant positions. On October 8, the Wang faction and the leading officials concocted a plan to put pressure directly on the throne the following day, and hopefully get rid of the Eight Tigers once and for all. At this critical point, a secretary of the ministry of Personnel, Chiao Fang (*q.v.*), because of his personal antagonism toward certain colleagues, leaked the plot to Liu Chin and his cohorts (*see* Chiao Fang). That same night the Eight Tigers went to the emperor, defamed Wang Yüeh and his group, and asked the emperor, "What harm does it to the empire if Your Majesty chooses to have a little fun with dogs, horses, and falcons?'' Further, they charged that Wang Yüeh intended to restrict the emperor's activities by exerting pressure on the court officials, and that the whole campaign by the bureaucracy against them was the work of Wang Yüeh. They then cunningly persuaded the young emperor to make a test himself the following morning to see whether their charges were true, simply by asking Wang Yüeh to strike an official with a stick when the officials came to have an audience. If Wang should plead for forgiveness of the official, that would prove that their charges were true.

The next morning, without questioning the relevance of such a method, the young emperor followed their suggestion. As soon as he gave the order, Wang immediately threw himself down in front of the emperor and pled for the official. His response was sufficient.

As a consequence, Wang and his associates were exiled to serve the imperial tomb in Nanking. Shortly after Wang's party left the capital, Liu Chin forged an imperial edict ordering his death on the way, and he was murdered when his boat reached Lin-ch'ing 臨清, Shantung.

When the governor of Shantung, Chu Ch'in 朱欽 (T. 懋恭, cs 1472), learned of this, he memorialized the throne arguing that it was not just to punish Wang Yüeh with death before his case had come to trial. He further proposed that, since Liu Chin had been responsible, it was he who should be punished. Unfortunately the memorial came into the hands of Liu Chin before it was placed before the emperor, and he withheld it.

Five years later (May 5, 1511), some months after Liu Chin's execution, a vice director of a bureau in the ministry of Justice, Su Chin 宿進 (T. 孺忠, cs 1508) memorialized the throne suggesting that Wang Yüeh and a few other victims of Liu Chin be compensated posthumously. The suggestion angered the emperor; Su was bastinadoed fifty times, and cashiered.

Bibliography

42/25/18a; 61/159/4b; *Ming-shih* (Taiwan ed.), 95/994, 186/2180, 188/2200, 304/3413, 3421; MSL (1964), Hsiao-tsung, *ch.* 53–61, Wu-tsung (1965), *ch.* 1–18; KC (1958), *ch.* 46, p. 2998; Ch'en Ho 陳鶴 (1757–1811), *Ming chi* 明紀 (SPPY ed.), *ch.* 21–24; Ku Ying-t'ai (ECCP), *Ming-ch'ao chi-shih pen-mo, ch.* 43; Hsia Hsieh (1799–1875?), *Ming t'ung-chien* (1900 ed.), *ch.* 43; Wang Shih-chen, *Yen-shan-t'ang pieh-chi*, 94/7b; Liu Jo-yü, *Cho-chung chih*, 5/2a; T'ang Shu 唐樞 (1497–1574), *Kuo-shen chi* 國琛集, II/43; Wu Ying 吳瀛, *Ming-shih pen-chi* 明史本紀, (Palace Museum ed., 1932), *ch.* 15; Yin Luan-chang 印鸞章 & Li Chieh-jen 李介仁 (eds.), *Ming-chien kang-mu* 明鑑綱目 (1936), *ch.* 5; Huang-fu Lu (*see* Huang-fu Fang), *Huang Ming chi-lüeh*; Kao Tai, *Hung-yu lu, ch.* 12. Yeh Ting-i 葉丁易, *Ming-tai t'e-wu cheng-chih* 明代特務政治 (Peking, 1951), 534.

Yung-deh Richard Chu

WANG Yüeh 王越 (T. 世昌), December 3, 1426-January 12, 1499, sometime earl of Wei-ning 威寧伯, was one of four civilians in the Ming dynasty awarded ranks of nobility for military exploits. The others were Wang Chi 驥, Hsü Yu-chen, and Wang Shou-jen (*qq.v.*). Wang Yüeh came from a farming family of Chün 濬-hsien in Ta-ming 大名 prefecture, south of Peking. (The district was assigned to Honan in 1725). Tall of stature, he had great strength and mastered archery on horseback. He was also well read and learned how to compose with dispatch both poetry and prose. In 1450 he became a *chü-jen* and a year later a *chin-shih*. There is a legend reporting that at the palace examination his composition was blown away by a tornado and he had to write a new one. A few months later a Korean embassy came to Peking bringing the lost document with the story that it had dropped out of the sky before the royal audience hall. In any case Wang Yüeh was soon appointed a censor and served a term as inspector in Szechwan (1453?). He then retired because of his father's death. In 1456 he was reinstated. His ability and resourcefulness greatly impressed his superior in the Censorate, K'ou Shen (see Wang Ao 翺), an exacting taskmaster who entrusted him with editing the memorials for the entire office. In 1460 he was given the steep promotion from 7A to 3A and made surveillance commissioner of Shantung.

In May, 1463, when a successor to Han Yung (q.v.) as governor of Tatung came under consideration, the emperor personally chose Wang Yüeh for the post. It is said that when Wang appeared at the audience he wore the regular court robe but with sleeves cut short to gain more freedom of action, and the emperor approved of his innovation. Appointed as right vice censor-in-chief he proceeded to Tatung. When his mother died, he was given a short leave in October, but ordered to hurry back to his post as the entire northern front was threatened by Mongol raids.

Since 1435, when there was instituted in Nanking a triumvirate composed of a general (commander), a civilian (chief of staff), and a eunuch representing imperial authority (see Huang Fu), it had become the organ to direct field commands of large expeditionary forces. The eunuch member, called chien-chün 監軍 or chen-shou 鎮守, usually acted as the supervisor but he was also responsible for firearms. After the defeat of 1449 (see Chu Ch'i-chen), more power was assumed by the civilian commander who was either a hsün-fu 巡撫 (governor or coordinator), a tsung-tu chün-wu 總督軍務 (supreme commander), or tsan-li 贊理 (sometimes ts'an-tsan 參贊) chün-wu (associate commander). It was the time when literary men like Han Yung, Yeh Sheng, and Hsiang Chung (qq.v.) distinguished themselves in military matters. Wang Yüeh was perhaps as ambitious as any of them.

Wang Yüeh served as governor of Tatung for eight years during which he held the concurrent post of governor of Hsüan-fu from October, 1467, to May, 1468. He began to be noticed by military commanders as an efficient assistant in logistics, and in March, 1467, he was given

the title of tsan-li chün-wu. At this time the Yen-sui 延綏 frontier on the northern and western Shensi border became active because the region in the Yellow River bend, known as Ho-t'ao 河套 (later also called Ordos after a Mongol tribe that settled there), which had been left unoccupied by order of Chu Ti (q.v.), was now used by the nomads (mostly Mongols) as pasture land. Recently some Bäg Arslan 乩加思蘭 tribes from west of Turfan began to camp there. In 1466, 1467, and1469 the Ming court had to send troops from Peking to defend the area. In February, 1470, Wang Yüeh was ordered to stay in Yü-lin 榆林 on the north Shensi border to supervise the supplies for the armies from Peking and elsewhere, and was reprimanded when, finding the front quieting down, he started to move back to Tatung on his own. In April he was made ts'an-tsan chün-wu to the chief commander Chu Yung (see Hsiang Chung). After some minor victories Wang was promoted in January, 1471, to right censor-in-chief. In the summer Wang and Chu were ordered back to Tatung but later in the year, when the Yen-sui front became threatened, they were told to return to Yü-lin. Wang was now relieved of his duties as governor in order to give his entire attention to the military situation at Yen-sui. In January, 1472, Chu, being recalled to Peking, left Wang as commander of more than forty thousand troops guarding a frontier of some three hundred miles. Just then ten thousand Bäg Arslan horsemen invaded the Ku-yüan 固原 and Ninghsia region, and in February dealt a crushing blow to Wang's pursuing troops.

The question then arose as to whether to clear Ho-t'ao of the nomads or to let them remain and defend the frontiers against their raids. For several months there were consultations between the court at Peking and the frontier commanders. In June a conference was held in the capital which Wang hurried back to attend. He and Yeh Sheng advised caution on the ground that an offensive would require an army so large it would be difficult to supply. The court, however, decided on action, appointing Marquis Chao Fu (see Han Yung) as commander-in-chief and Wang Yüeh as chief of staff with the title tsung-tu chün-wu. They were to fight the Bäg Arslan tribesmen with some eighty thousand men. Four months later Chao and Wang memorialized that their effective troops numbered only forty thousand for a task requiring four times as many, and that it would be better to build strong defenses along the border and retain part of the present troops as guards. Chao, accused of cowardice, in December was replaced by Earl Liu Chü (see Liu Yung-ch'eng). Wang Yüeh received a reprimand but was permitted to retain his post. In July, 1473, he was given the responsibility for the frontiers from Yü-lin to Ninghsia, while Liu Chü was stationed at Ku-yüan. For some minor victories Liu's earldom was made hereditary, but Wang had his title changed only to left censor-in-chief, no raise in rank. Probably Wang had long smarted over the injustice of a civilian commander sharing equally any punishment but receiving much less in rewards than the military officer on the same mission. Ever since he had gained independent command in 1472, he had been training his officers and men in field maneuvers and establishing an efficient network of intelligence. He was eager to win a spectacular victory by himself as commander.

The opportunity came when Wang received a report that the Bäg Arslan horsemen had slipped away to raid an area south of Ninghsia, leaving their tents at the Hung-yen ch'ih 紅鹽池 (Red Salt Lake) north of the Great Wall, about one hundred twenty miles west of Yü-lin. Quickly Wang led forty-six hundred picked horsemen riding day and night. They arrived there two days later on October 20, 1473. There was a short engagement that afternoon in which they routed the enemy guards, killing three hundred fifty-five and capturing seven. Then, looting the tents, they set them afire. The booty included seventeen thousand weapons, etc., one hundred thirty-three camels, thirteen hundred horses, five thousand head of cattle, and ten thousand sheep. Meanwhile Wang also sent out urgent orders to the generals in the Ninghsia region to waylay the main army of the tribesmen returning with their plunder. This they did, thus gaining a second victory early in November. When the defeated enemy returned to Red Salt Lake to discover their losses, they retreated from Ho-t'ao, moving north and west of the Yellow River. This left the Yen-sui borders quiet for a number of years, affording a breathing spell for Yü Tzu-chün (q.v.) to rebuild the Great Wall in that area, a task which he started in the following year (1474).

In the battle of Red Salt Lake Wang Yüeh gained the first sizable victory over the Mongols and their allies in half a century. It was especially notable following the defeat of 1449. What distinguished Wang even more was that he, a civilian commander, achieved this, for Liu Chü, the general, did not show up until the battles were over. Liu Chü was recalled early in 1474 and died that April. Meanwhile Wang's report was suspected of exaggeration and apparently it was played down by his detractors. Even his total strength of forty-six hundred soldiers divided into three columns was distorted in the official document (as recorded in the shih-lu) to make it appear that each group consisted of that number of men. Probably discouraged by such denigration, he asked for sick leave in March. Although in June he was rewarded with the title of junior guardian of the heir apparent, he repeated his request for leave, which was finally granted in August only after the eunuch in residence at Yü-lin spoke on his behalf.

After half a year of rest in Peking Wang Yüeh was appointed (March, 1475) head of the Censorate and commander of the twelve Peking training divisions. This was the time when the court underwent a subtle change, owing to the revelation that there was an heir apparent (*see* Chu Yu-t'ang), and to the rise in influence of the emperor's favorite, Wan Kuei-fei (*q.v.*). Emperor Chu Chien-shen placed his trust in the eunuch Wang Chih 汪直 (*q. v.*), appointing him to head the West Depot, a new secret service office and court of interrogation. When the minister of War, Hsiang Chung, contended unsuccessfully with Wang Chih in 1477, the eunuch's power became obvious. It seems that Wang Yüeh at this time began to cultivate a close relationship with him. Early in 1478, when he complained that he did not receive appropriate rewards for his victory at Red Salt Lake, he was given the additional concurrent rank of minister of War. Late that year the higher title of grand guardian of the heir apparent also came to him. In May, 1479, he served with Chu Yung and Wang Chih on a commission of five to select troops from the Peking training divisions for combat duty. Later the same year Wang Chih and Chu led these troops to Liaotung and, for an invasion of the Jurchen land, were highly rewarded, Chu being raised to duke.

Perhaps Wang Yüeh watched with jealousy, for he was eager for fame and confident of his own prowess. Soon he had his chance. Early in 1480, when the Mongols again raided Shensi, it was decided to send Peking troops to fight them. The emperor named Chu Yung as commander, Wang Chih as eunuch supervisor, and Wang Yüeh as chief of staff. Somehow Wang Yüeh maneuvered to have Chu Yung proceed to Yü-lin with the main army while he and Wang Chih led a light division to Tatung. There, reinforced by local troops to a total of twenty-one thousand, they went north of the Great Wall, and in five days' riding arrived at a point a few miles from the large Mongol settlement on the lake called Wei-ning-hai-tzu 威寧海子. The day, April 8, 1480,

broke, lashed by a heavy storm of snow mixed with rain. They surprised the Mongols and defeated them. Wang Yüeh reported suffering 38 casualties but returning with 437 heads, 12 standards, 171 captives, 1,085 horses, 31 camels, 176 cattle, 5,100 sheep, and over ten thousand articles of military equipment. On receiving the report, the emperor praised Wang Yüeh and the eunuch and rewarded the two bearers of the message with higher hereditary ranks. The two happened to be Wang Chih's foster son and Wang Yüeh's own son. The latter, Wang Shih 時, already a hereditary centurion of the Embroidered-uniform Guard, was now made a chiliarch.

After the victory Wang Yüeh returned to Peking and on April 18 was enfeoffed earl of Wei-ning with hereditary rights. He also held his concurrent posts as head of the Censorate and commander of the Peking divisions. A month later Duke Chu Yung returned in dejected mood, for he was obliged to report the loss of a third of his seventeen thousand horses. In October Wang Yüeh received an order to ready the Peking troops for an expedition to Liaotung, but the order was soon withdrawn. In January, 1481, he and Wang Chih were sent to Tatung where they gained several minor victories for which Wang Yüeh received the higher title of grand tutor of the heir apparent, and his son, Wang Shih, was promoted to be an assistant guard commissioner. Wang Yüeh, however, now lost his civilian status and his post in the Censorate. Instead he was made a central military commissioner and commander-in-chief of the Peking armies; but these titles were honorary, for he was not allowed back in Peking but ordered to remain at the frontier. His title was at first General to Suppress the Northern Barbarians (June, 1481) and later, Vanguard General to Invade the West (January 1482). On a report of victory in June, 1482, his stipends were increased. Yet obviously both he and the eunuch were fast losing the emperor's favor, and the generals, nobles, and courtiers who disliked them or were jealous of Wang Yüeh had gained their ends. In July, 1483, the eunuch was sent to Nanking and in September was reduced to the status of a palace attendant. Wang Yüeh, as the eunuch's cohort, was deprived of all ranks and titles, reduced to be a commoner, and banished to An-lu 安陸, Hukuang.

He lived in exile for four years. After the enthronment of Chu Yu-t'ang in 1487, he was pardoned and permitted to return to his home in Chün-hsien. Seven years later, after repeated memorials complaining of unjust treatment, he was given back his rank of censor-in-chief and allowed to retire. It is said that he again worked his way into the bureaucracy through a powerful eunuch. When he was once more named head of the Censorate, the order was rescinded because of many objections. In 1497, however, he was appointed supreme commander and governor of Kansu, and, at his own request, received command also of Yen-sui and Ninghsia troops. He was then seventy-one years of age. The following year he led an army to the north of Ninghsia and won a battle for which he was given the title of junior guardian. At this time he made a proposal to recover Hami, but before it was acted on he learned of the memorials at court censoring him for his associations with the eunuchs. He died in office at Kan-chou 甘州 and was honored with the posthumous name Hsiang-min 襄敏 and the title grand tutor.

The editors of the *Ming-shih* praise Wang as a strategist and a generous leader. Many generals and high officials owed their start to his recommendations. They cite a story that once he and Chu Yung were scouting in Mongol territory with a thousand cavalry when the enemy arrived in force. Wang stopped Chu from beating a hasty retreat, and lined up his horsemen in readiness for battle. This made the enemy hesitate. At nightfall he instructed his men to retreat slowly while he led the rear guard. After they had all returned to their fort safely, he told Chu

that any impatient move would have brought on disaster. Another tale describes him as the unconventional militarist who kept a troupe of female singers. A prince had given them to him, and once he unconcernedly allowed a worthy officer to choose one of them as a reward. The *Ming-shih* makes the unusual comment that alive he was blamed for being too ambitious, but after his death frontier troops suffered greatly for want of supplies and from corruption among their officers; no frontier commander of the Ming, it adds, was his equal.

The editors of the *Hsien-tsung shih-lu* (completed 1491), assuming that Wang Yüeh's career ended in 1483, included a long account of his life at the point reporting his loss of ranks and titles. Thus he had two biographies in the *Ming shih-lu*, the second one, also long, at the entry recording his death.

His collected works, *Li-yang* 黎陽 *Wang Hsiang-min kung chi*, 4 *ch.*, was printed in Soochow in 1530 and reprinted in Chengtu, 1585. A copy of the reprint was reproduced in Taipei in 1970. His poems are plain, unadorned, and uncluttered by illusions, for he wrote to please himself. Thus he produced many poems containing a message with impact. Most were written during the period when he was out of office and given to carousing, riding, and gardening. But some of his memorable poetry was written while commanding troops on the frontier. In one poem, dating from about 1480, he included a line: it is easy to talk military but difficult to command in the field (談兵容易用兵難). Perhaps this sample of his writing was shown the emperor by someone who accused him of criticizing His Majesty.

Bibliography

1/171/16b; 5/10/52a; 8/26/19a; 21/9/19a; 40/21/4b; 61/99/19a; 64/乙 18/13b; Li Chih, *Hsü ts'ang-shu* (1959), 270; Ch'ien Ch'ien-i (ECCP), *Lieh-ch'ao shih-chi*, 丙3/1b; *Ming kung-ch'en hsi-feng ti-pu* 明功臣襲封底簿 (Taipei, 1970), 189; KC (1958), 2727; MSL(1964), Hsien-tsung, 3523, 3534, 4106,

Hsiao-tsung, 2523; Cheng Hsiao, "Ming-ch'en chi," *Wu-hsüeh pien*, 24/15a; Louis Hambis, *Documents sur l'histoire des Mongols à l'époque des Ming*, 37; D. Pokotilov, *History of the Eastern Mongols from 1368 to 1634* (tr. by R. Loewenthal), *Studia Serica*, Ser. A, pt. 1 (Chengtu, 1947), 76; W. Franke, "Addenda and Corrigenda," *ibid*. Ser. A, pt. 2 (Chengtu, 1949), 48.

Chaoying Fang

WEI Chi 魏驥 (T. 仲房, H. 南齋), 1374–October 3, 1471, scholar and official, was a native of Hsiao-shan 蕭山, Chekiang. A *chü-jen* of 1405, he was appointed assistant instructor in 1406 of the Sung-chiang 松江 prefectural school and served in this capacity for twelve years. He taught with care and enthusiasm and set a fine example to the students, some of whom proved successful in their later careers. During these years he also helped with the preparation of the *Yung-lo ta-tien* (*see* Chu Ti). Later he served as an erudite in the Court of Imperial Sacrifices. In 1426 became a vice director of the bureau of evaluation in the ministry of Personnel. After officiating as vice minister at the Court of Imperial Sacrifices in Nanking, he was appointed in 1438 a vice minister of Personnel on probation. The following year the appointment was confirmed. Five years later (1443) he received a transfer to be vice minister of Rites in Peking, and then of Personnel in Nanking. In 1448 he became minister of Personnel in the southern capital. Two years after this, when he was seventy-seven years of age, he received leave to retire.

During his years at court he acted as a director of the metropolitan examination three times, and of the provincial examination in Kiangsi twice. Throughout his life he upheld the principles of justice and rectitude, and refused to become involved in any party strife. Even when the eunuch Wang Chen (*q. v.*) was in power he showed respect to Wei Chi. Following his retirement Wei exercised frugality and lived harmoniously with the people in his native place. His most important contribution to them was the rebuilding of the dikes and deepening of the ponds and lakes. The people were grateful to him for his aid. In 1471 he died at home, aged ninety-seven, and was buried nearby. He was the oldest one among the officials in Ming history; the posthumous name accorded him was Wen-ching 文靖.

Wei left a collection of memorials and other writings which is probably not extant, but a selection entitled *Nan-chai hsien-sheng Wei Wen-ching kung chai-kao* 南齋先生魏文靖公摘藁, 10 *ch*. + 1 *ch*., is still available. The first four *chüan* were written during his years as an official, the remaining were completed after his retirement. The editors of the *Ssu-k'u* catalogue mention the work, but did not include it in the Imperial Library. He is also said to have been partly responsible for an early edition of the *Sung-chiang chih* 志.

Wei Chi had a brother, Wei Ch'i 騏, a *chin-shih* of 1404, who became a Hanlin bachelor, and rose to be the secretary of a bureau in the ministry of Justice.

Bibliography

1/158/9a; 5/27/5a; MSL (1964), Hsien-tsung, 1811, 2089; SK(1930), 175/6b; Cheng Hsiao, *Wu-hsüeh-pien*, 22/la; *Hsiao-shan-hsien chih kao* 志稿 (1935), 14/7b; Teng Yüan-hsi 鄧元錫, *Huang Ming-shu* 皇明書 (1606), 21/7a; Chu Ta-chao 朱大韶 (1517-77), *Huang-ch'ao ming-ch'en mu-ming* 皇朝名臣墓銘 (NCL microfilm), 3/33a; *Chekiang t'ung-chih* (1934), 2305, 2370, 2838, 4063, 4902; Ch'en Hsün (*see* Lü Yüan), *Fang-chou wen-chi* 芳洲文集 (NLP microfilm), roll 978, 3/7b; *Nan-chai… chai-kao* (NCL microfilm).

Liu Chia-chü

WEI Kuei 韋貴 (T. 崇勳), 1413–October 12, 1493, eunuch, was a native of Kwangsi, probably of aboriginal origin from Wu-yüan 武緣. He entered the palace of Emperor Chu Chan-chi (*q. v.*) in 1433 at the age of twenty. During the reign of Chu Ch'i-chen (*q. v.*), he was sent (1459) to Chekiang to supervise the manufacture of paper. In June, 1464, Emperor Chu Chien-shen (q. v.) summoned him to oversee the erection of a memorial tablet in honor of his late father in the imperial mausoleum north of Peking, after which Wei was made a palace attendant (feng-yü 奉御, grade 8B).

In May, 1469, Wei Kuei was entrusted with the repair of the temples and shrines on Mt. T'ai-yüeh T'ai-ho 太嶽 太和 (formerly known as Wu-tang shan 武當山), a Taoist center in northwestern Hukuang built in 1418. Wei mobilized, in addition to local peasants, thousands of troops for this purpose. To ease their burden, he obtained permission to relieve the soldiers from regular duties and exempt the conscripted laborers from corvée service. This accomplished, Wei Kuei was promoted to be an assistant eunuch in charge of the state ceremonies there and in the defense of that area. In December, 1470, he assumed direction, together with Hsiang Chung (q. v.), the censor-in-chief, of the effort to suppress the bandits in the Ching-Hsiang 荆襄 area where the provinces of Hukuang, Honan, Shensi, and Szechwan meet. For this Wei received (June, 1472) promotion to be senior assistant eunuch, and subsequently deputy eunuch. Four months later the emperor dispatched a senior eunuch and others to T'ai-ho-shan to install an image of the deity Chen-wu 眞武. In anticipation of the rugged journey, Wei ordered the construction of several suspension bridges over the mountain passes leading to the peak; this facilitated the ascent and spared the local population undue involvement. As a reward the emperor honored him with the rare gift of a costume with dragon design.

Acting on the recommendation of Liu Fu 劉敷 (T. 叔榮, 1421-1502, cs 1451), the governor of Hukuang, the emperor appointed Wei in April, 1476, to supervise the administration of the Hukuang and Ching-Hsiang prefectures, with headquarters in Wu-tang district, concurrent with his duties on T'ai-ho-shan. A year later, accep ting the proposal of Hsiang Chung that the immi-

grants in the Ching-Hsiang area be legalized by registration as tax-payers and put under proper jurisdiction, the court again dispatched Wei Kuei, together with the associate censor-in-chief, Yüan Chieh (see Hsiang Chung), to supervise the registration and create a new prefecture, named Yün-yang 郧陽-fu. For this performance Wei advanced to the rank of senior eunuch; later, he was appointed grand defender of the Hukuang branch administration, his final post. There he undertook the repair of fortified sites, the erection of schools, and the strengthening of local defenses against possible banditry. His dedication earned him the esteem of the local inhabitants and rich rewards from the emperor, who also extended his favor to several members of Wei's family.

Following the enthronement of Chu Yu-t'ang (q. v.) in 1488, Wei Kuei submitted a request for retirement, but this was denied. Late in 1490, after an outbreak of banditry in Szechwan, the court again sent him, along with Tai Shan (q. v.), the censor-in-chief, to take charge of the suppression. Mobilizing the troops of the Chün-chou 均州 guard, they succeeded in restoring order within two months. Thereupon Wei Kuei returned to his post in Wu-tang, where he died three years later, at the age of eighty. He was survived by six adopted sons, all of whom served as junior military officers.

His close friend Hsü P'u (q. v.), then senior grand secretary, who composed an account of his life and his epitaph, extols him for his noble conduct, integrity, frugality, and dedication to duty, which set him markedly apart from those eunuchs who were known for their vices.

Bibliography

MSL(1964), Hsien-tsung, 1336, 1948, 2046, 2767, 3549, 4264; Hsiao-tsung, 572; Hsü P'u, Hsü Wen-ching kung Ch'ien-chai Chi (NCL microfilm), 5/2a, 8/49a.

Hok-lam Chan

WEI Liang-fu 魏良輔, flourished 16th century, musician, is said to have been a native of K'un-shan 崑山, near Soochow. He appeared at T'ai-ts'ang 太倉 near K'un-shan about 1540, and is closely connected with the origin and development of k'un-ch'ü 崑曲, the flower of the southern drama and the most prestigious of all theatrical forms in China for three hundred years. The term k'un-ch'ü (musical songs and plays of K'un-shan) or K'un-shan ch'iang 腔 (tunes of K'un-shan) denotes a style of opera. It is reported that Wei turned to the study of southern songs and lyrics after he had been surpassed in the northern drama by a friend, Wang Yu-shan 王友山. He devoted himself so completely to this art that one legend relates that he did not leave his study for ten years.

It is at this particular time that Wei seems to have had a hand in the final shaping of the k'un-ch'ü into its unique form through a process of adaptation, blending, and innovation within a number of local styles. During this period, the southern opera was divided into four basic musical modes, each of which was related to the manner and dialect of the particular district in which it originated: 1) the I-yang 弋陽 ch'iang (Kiangsi), 2) the Yü-yao 餘姚 ch'iang (Chekiang), 3) the Hai-yen 海鹽 ch'iang (Chekiang), and 4) the K'un-shan ch'iang (Nan-Chihli). When Wei arrived at K'un-shan, the southern drama, with its gentler, more melodic tunes, had begun to vie with the northern drama in prestige and popularity. Nevertheless, Wei was not satisfied with any of the four styles of the south, as they seemed to lack aesthetic beauty and form. He saw some potential in the K'un-shan ch'iang, however, even though it was the least known and performed of all the styles. It was conducted in the Wu dialect, a soft, pleasant-sounding, but unusual speech which was incomprehensible to the other regions of China. Linguistic limitations, then, restricted performances in this style to the Wu

district (or Soochow region), an area extending eastward from Ch'ang-chou 常州 to Shanghai.

The K'un-shan style which Wei Liang-fu chose as the basic pattern for his innovations had obviously existed for some time. A statement by Chu Yün-ming (q.v.) in his *Wei t'an* 猥談 (Vulgar talks) indicates it was created long before Wei's appearance on the scene. Other evidence in the *Ching lin hsü-chi* 涇林續記 by Chou Yüan-wei 周元暐 reveals that the K'un-shan ch'iang was known as early as the Hung-wu period. A recently discovered handwritten copy of the *Nan tz'u yin cheng* by Wen Cheng-ming (q.v.) shows that Wei himself attributed its creation to a man of the late Yüan dynasty by the name of Ku Chien 顧堅. Thus it is likely that the K'un-shan ch'iang had been performed as an operatic art for several decades, perhaps for over a hundred years. It appears then that Wei did not originate the K'un-shan ch'iang, but only elaborated upon it and brought it to perfection.

As Wei improved the provincial music and folk songs of this area, he combined them with various musical techniques and the best elements from the Hai-yen, I-yang, and even northern tunes. In forming a new musical style from existing modes and rhythms, he refined his articlation and vocalization in the pronunciation of sounds so that his artistic matching of tones with tempo and pitch enthralled his audiences. His new product was also called shui mo tiao 水磨調 (tune of the water mill), for the smooth and steady waves of sounds were restrained, just like the water flowing through the mill. The elegance, grace, and superb mastery of Wei's music both surprised and fascinated the other song masters of Soochow, all of whom acknowledged that it was far superior to the other styles.

Wei Liang-fu was assisted in his work by other musicians, namely, Yüan Jan 袁髯, Yu T'o 尤駝, and the famous master Kuo Yün-shih 過云適, but perhaps the most important person was his son-in-law, Chang

Yeh-t'ang 張野塘 (a native of Anhwei).
Chang was also an expert in northern
songs and lyrics, and had come to T'ai-
ts'ang as an exile. When Wei heard Chang's
singing, he not only engaged him as an
assistant, but also proposed that Chang
marry his daughter. Chang's contribution
was important, because he was able to
help Wei improve the instrumentation for
his music.

Northern drama used the hsien 絃 or
stringed instruments to provide the leading
musical accompaniment, whereas the southern drama had the kuan 管 or wind
instruments. By combining instruments
from both operatic styles Wei produced
a symphony with wind, string, and percus-
sion to orchestrate fully the beautiful
songs in his repertoire. He took the ti-tzu
笛子 (the horizontal flute) as the leading
instrument and harmonized it with the
sheng 笙 (reed or bamboo wind organ),
the p'i-pa 琵琶 (lute), san 三 hsien (man-
dolin), yüeh ch'in 月琴 (moon guitar),
hsiao 簫 (vertical flute), and finally a small
drum and wooden clapper to mark time and
accentuate the rhythm. Wei also used a
musical scale of seven notes instead of the
ancient five.

This improvement in orchestration and
accompaniment produced a strong, plain-
tive sound which stressed the soft, pliant
tones of the flute. The notes were not
only even, harmonious, and correct, but
they were longer and fuller with more
variation in phraseology, subtlety, and
style. Under Wei's direction, strict attention was given to the rules of prosody
and length of measure in union with the
sweet sounding instruments. The combination of the north-south musical accompaniment with the lyrical song resulted in
such a moving dreamy style that it was
considered a novel and outstanding contribution to the musical theater.

Although Wei perfected the k'un-ch'ü
as an elegant, romantic, musical drama
with songs sung to the flute, the final
artistic touch necessary was the addition
of poetic lyrics and narrative. Wei's new
style was purely a musical form without
any acting or dancing, for he was not a
playwright but a scholar with musical training. Consequently, the k'un-ch'ü was produced formally as a theatrical medium only
when it was adopted by Liang Ch'en-yü (q.v.)
for his play, Huan-sha chi 浣紗記 (which
Josephine Huang Hung calls the Beauty
Trap, and Colin Mackerras the Laundering
of the Silken Stole).

Wei and his collaborators achieved
fame when the k'un-ch'ü eclipsed other
operatic forms as the chief dramatic presentation in China. But it is Wei, the musical
master and key member of a team which
guided this dramatic style to its ultimate
form, to whom we must give much of the
credit. For the k'un-ch'ü style certainly
changed the nature of theater entertainment and encouraged an impressive
number of great playwrights to create a
voluminous treasury of dramatic literature.
This made the Ming opera a literary, as
well as a performing, art, and one of the
great glories of Chinese opera.

[Editors' note: It so happens that a
near contemporary of the same name, a
native of Hsin-chien 新建, Kiangsi, is
often confused with him. This second Wei
Liang-fu (T. 師召, H. 尚泉, 此齋) came
not only from a gentry family but was
also a chü-jen of 1516 and a chin-shih of
1526, later holding official positions as
high as surveillance vice commissioner of
Kwangsi (1550) and administration commissioner of Hukuang (1551?). A long
eulogy by Wang Tsung-mu (q.v.) written
in 1551 describes him as an elderly official, scholarly and upright. He must have
been near sixty at that time, too late to
start a new life in music.]

Bibliography

Shen Te-fu, Yeh-hu-pien (1959 ed.), 646; Lo
Chin-tang 羅錦堂, "Ts'ung Sung Yüan nan-hsi
shuo tao Ming tai te ch'uan-ch'i" 從宋元南戲說
到明代的傳奇, Ta-lu tsa-chih 大陸雜誌, Vol. 28,
no. 3 (February 15, 1964), 71; no. 4 (February
29, 1964), 125, no. 5 (March 15, 1964), 165;
Ch'en Wan-nai 陳萬鼐, Yüan Ming Ch'ing chü-

ch'ü shih 元明淸劇曲史 (Taipei, 1966), 340; Liu Wen-liu 劉文六, *K'un-ch'ü yen-chiu* 崑曲研究 (Taipei, 1969), 17; Meng Yao 孟瑤, *Chung-kuo hsi-ch'ü shih* 中國戲曲史, 2d ed., Vol. 2 (Taipei, 1967), 265; Yao Hsin-nung 姚莘農, "The Rise and Fall of the K'un-ch'ü," THM, Vol. II, no. 1 (January, 1936), 65; Josephine Huang Hung, *Ming Drama* (Taipei, 1966), 108; A. C. Scott, *Traditional Chinese Plays*, 2 vols. (Madison, 1967 & 1969); Colin Mackerras, "The Growth of the Chinese Regional Drama in the Ming and Ch'ing," *Jo. of Oriental Studies*, IX: 1 (January, 1971), 74; Harold Acton, tr., "Lin Ch'ung Yeh Pen," THM, Vol. IX: 2 (September, 1939), 181. For the second Wei Liang-fu: *Hsin-chien-hsien chih* (1871), 32/32b, 40/17b, 25b; *Hupei t'ung-chih* (1934), 2885; *Hunan t'ung-chih* (1934), 2443; *Shantung t'ung-chih* (1934), 1704; Wang Tsung-mu, *Ching-so hsien-sheng chi* (1574), 3/19a.

Dell R. Hales

WEI Su 危素 (T. 太樸 or 朴, H. 雲林), 1303–February 27, 1372, scholar and historian, was a native of Chin-ch'i 金谿, Fu-chou 撫州-fu, Kiangsi. The Wei family, originally from Honan, settled in Kiangsi in the early seventh century when one of its distinguished ancestors became the governor of Fu-chou. The genealogical line, however, ended in the middle of the 13th century when the last descendant produced no heir and adopted the son of a Wang family who became Wei Su's grandfather. The latter served as a chief administrator of the branch secretariat of Kiangsi under the Yüan and had a son who was Wei Su's father.

A precocious child, Wei Su began his studies under the instruction of his grandfather; by the age of fifteen, he is said to have had a good knowledge of the Classics. Then he went to Lin-ch'uan 臨川, a neighboring district, to seek enlightenment from Wu Ch'eng (1249–1333), the doyen of late Yüan neo-Confucianism, and Fan Heng (1272–1330), also a leading Confucian scholar. It is said that the two were so impressed by his scholastic achievement that they treated him as an equal and sought his advice on many subjects.

Wei Su's reputation in literary circles eventually came to the attention of Chang Ch'i-yen (1285–1353), then head of the Censorate of the southern court; later, Chang brought him to Ta-tu (modern Peking), the Yüan capital. In 1342, upon his mentor's recommendation, he was given charge of the selection of Confucian Classics for presentation at the audience of Emperor Toγon Temür (*q.v.*). This belated start at the age of forty was to inaugurate for Wei Su a long and remarkable official career. In 1347 he received an appointment as a scholar-in-waiting at the Hanlin Academy, and served as a compiler in the national history office. Following this, he memorialized the court on the urgent need to compile the history of the Sung, Liao, and Chin dynasties, and was successful. The court commissioned the officials in the two former Sung capitals, Kaifeng and Lin-an (Hangchow), to search for the archives of the Sung dynasty, and appointed him one of the compilers of the projected Sung history. In addition, he labored on the national history, producing chapters of the biographies of the empresses and ladies-in-waiting and of the dynasty's meritorious officials; these became the basis of the Yüan history project inaugurated during the early Ming (*see* Sung Lien). The emperor also entrusted him with the preparation of an annotated text of the *Er-ya* 爾雅, an ancient dictionary, and other early writings now lost, which he completed within a few months.

In the following decade, until the end of the Yüan, Wei Su had a series of rapid promotions in various ministries. He served successively as an erudite of the Court of Imperial Sacrifice (1351); a proctor of the National University, and a vice director of the ministry of War(1353), a director of bureaus in the Censorate (1355), ministries of Works, Agriculture, and in the end as minister of Rites (1357). He then entered the Secretariat (1358) in charge of the presentation of lectures to the emperor, and advanced to be a counselor (1360), a post which he held for five successive years. In these various capacities, Wei Su distinguished himself as an upright, scrupulous, capable, and energetic official. When he served in the Court of Imperial Sacrifices, he occupied himself with the rectification of rituals; in the National University, he labored on the printing of the Classics; in the ministry of War, he supervised the development of waste land into farmland; in the Censorate, he was an alert and outspoken critic of injustice; in the ministry of Works, he constantly remonstrated against unnecessary, expensive undertakings; in the board of Agriculture, he attended to the cultivation of the area near the capital to ensure a steady supply of grain for the population; in the ministry of Rites, he devoted himself to ritual matters concerning the state and to the promotion of public education; when he was a counselor in the Secretariat, he sought out the talented and recommended them to office. His long and distinguished career thus earned him an honored position in Yüan officialdom.

In 1364 Wei was appointed a first-class bachelor (ch'eng-chih 承旨) in the Hanlin Academy, concurrently in charge of the drafting of imperial edicts and memoranda and the compilation of national histories. Late in this same year he was transferred to be a vice administrator in the branch secretariat of the Ling-pei 嶺北 province (in outer Mongolia), withdrew a year later, after the authorities repeatedly ignored his remonstrances, and retired to Fang-shan 房山 (southwest of modern Peking). During this time, the fortunes of the Yüan were rapidly declining as the Mongols were repeatedly defeated by the rebels in the south, while the army of Chu Yüan-chang was advancing towards the north. In September, 1368, under the pressure of the Ming forces, Toɤon Temür deserted Ta-tu and fled in the direction of Shang-tu, appointing Tämür-buqa, the prince of Huai 淮王 (d. 1368), minister in charge of the state. At this juncture, the prince recalled Wei

to the Hanlin Academy, but after only one day in office, Ta-tu fell to the advancing Ming forces of Hsü Ta (*q.v.*), and his career under the Yüan came abruptly to an end.

When Hsü's forces entered Peking, Wei reportedly planned to die for his master by drowning himself in a well near his residence; he was prevented, however, by friends. They pointed out that, since he had been out of office before the fall of the Yüan, it would not be a disgrace for him to live as an ex-Yüan official; furthermore, he should survive for the sake of the Yüan history about which he knew so much. This is said to have convinced him. Aware that the Ming army might violate the national archives, he pleaded with the official in charge to remove them from the history office to a safe place; in this way, the Yüan *shih-lu* was rescued from possible destruction. In September, 1368, together with a number of former Yüan officials, he went to call upon Hsü Ta, then commanding general, to offer his services to the new regime. Through Hsü's arrangement the group arrived at Nanking in February, 1369, and was received in audience by Chu Yüan-chang who, delighted at the presence of the officials, granted them lavish gifts and titles. Wei became an expositor-in-waiting in the Hanlin Academy and was entrusted with the composition of the Huang-ling pei (Epitaph for the imperial tomb; *see* Chu Yüan-chang), which he completed a month later. Shortly afterwards he was temporarily suspended from office, because of absenting himself from the imperial audience, but was reinstalled in May, 1370, and subsequently appointed a scholar in the newly instituted college of literature (弘文舘). During this time, the emperor often summoned him to the palace to inquire about events in the previous dynasty, particularly the reasons for its downfall. On one such occasion, Wei spoke to the emperor on the urgency of recovering the remains of the Southern Sung emperors whose tombs were violated by the notorious Tibetan lama Yang-lien-chen-chia 楊璉眞伽, or Byaṅ-spriṅ 1Caṅ-skya (d. 1292), and others around 1285. Chu Yüan-chang promptly commissioned authorities in the area to recover what imperial remains they could, and accord them a proper burial in a newly constructed mausoleum called Yung-mu ling 永穆陵 in Shao-hsing, Chekiang; this was completed in 1370. Because of his fairly advanced age, Wei Su held no official position, but he occasionally received summons from the emperor to offer counsel on state matters. Although he professed a title and was respected for his literary talents, he served the Ming with mixed feelings since the emperor looked down on him as an ex-Yüan official begging for service in the new regime. Probably for this same reason, he was relatively ignored by his contemporaries. Late in 1370 a certain censor rebuked him for serving two dynasties and recommended his dismissal, Acting on this recommendation, Chu Yüan-chang banished him to Han-shan 含山, Ho-chou 和州, as the custodian of the temple honoring Yü Ch'üeh (1303-58), the Yüan commander of Anking who committed suicide when the city fell to the rebel forces late in 1357. This was intended apparently as a reminder of his own disloyalty to his former master. After living in exile for a year, he died at the age of sixty-nine; later his body was brought back to his native place for burial. He was survived by two sons; the eldest, Wei Yü 於, a chin-shih of 1360, served as an instructor in a Confucian school in Anking; the youngest, Wei Yu 游 (d. 1371), served the Yüan as a proctor of the Confucian academy in the Ta-tu circuit.

Wei Su earned the epithet of "lao-ch'en" 老臣 (venerable minister) for his long and distinguished official career under the Yüan, but suffered from prejudicial treatment in his service with the Ming. Although admired for his scholarship and literary achievement, he was in the end indifferently received by the emperor and his colleagues. Except for Sung Lien, his colleague in the history office who gave a balanced appraisal of him in an epitaph, Ming writers were generally less favorably disposed. They stigmatized him for deserting the Yüan to serve the Ming, and were seemingly unconvinced by the story that he decided not to die for his master because he felt obliged to record the Yüan history. He became a subject of mockery, for example, in the *Ju-lin wai-shih* (The Scholars), the famous 18th century satirical novel by Wu Ching-tzu (ECCP), who characterized him as a senile official who depended on his past record and made little contribution.

Wei Su was a belle-lettrist and prolific writer. His prose writing is characterized by a balanced, elegant classical style, while his poetry is considered spirited and rhythmic. The number of commissioned or requested pieces—imperial edicts, memoranda, private epitaphs, tomb-inscriptions, and other essays—some of which are preserved in his collected works, supply important information on the events and personages of the late Yüan and early Ming. His calligraphy was prized among his contemporaries, while his particular style is said to have inaugurated a distinctive school. He was, moreover, a literary critic. As a prose stylist, he advocated a return to the archaic models of the pre-Han period, but he shared the view of Yang Wei-chen (*q.v.*), his distinguished contemporary, that it was the style, rather than the spirit, that should be imitated. In this sense, as a modern scholar sees it, Wei might be considered a precursor of the school of "seven early masters" in Ming literature who espoused a return to the archaic models of pre-T'ang writers (*see* Li Meng-yang).

Despite his popularity, only a fraction of his writings, especially those composed during the Ming, has been preserved. This is because, although he enjoyed wide fame in the Yüan, for reasons stated above, he was relatively neglected by Ming authors as were his writings. His collection of poetry written during the

Yüan, entitled *Yün-lin chi* 雲林集, 2 *ch.*, was printed in 1337, with sequels of *pu-i* 補遺 and *hsü* 續 *pu-i*, 2 *ch.* His other collection of prose and poetry, mostly written during the Yüan, called *Yüeh-hsüeh-chai kao* 說學齋稿, is said originally to have contained 50 *chüan*, but only a small portion in 4 *chüan* was recovered by Kuei Yu-kuang (*q.v.*) from early Ming manuscripts. The National Library of Peiping has a manuscript copy of this work, unclassified, which appears to have been based on Kuei Yu-kuang's transcription. (Both the *Yün-lin chi* and *Yüeh-hsüeh-chai kao* have recently been reproduced in the *Ssu-k'u chen-pen*, ser. 3. The latter was based on a manuscript, 13 *ch.*, preserved in the National Central Library. They were put together in a single collection known as *Wei hsüeh-shih chi* 學士集, 14 *ch.*, in 1748.) Through the recovery of additional writings, another collection of Wei's writings, entitled *Wei T'ai-p'u* 太僕 *chi*, 25 *ch.*, was printed by Liu Ch'eng-kan (ECCP, p. 321) in 1914; in addition to the *Yün-lin chi*, it includes a collection of essays, 10 *ch.*, incorporating parts of the *Yüeh-hsüeh-chai kao*, with a sequel, 10 *ch.*, and an appendix of biographical and bibliographical material, 1 *ch.*—by far the most complete collection of Wei Su's literary works.

Wei was also the author of other independent works. The best known, the *Lin-ch'uan Wu Wen-cheng kung (Ts'ao-lu) nien-p'u* 吳文正公（草廬）年譜, 1 *ch.*, a chronological biography of Wu Ch'eng, his mentor, is included in the *Wu Wen-cheng kung ch'üan-chi* 全集(1448). Among other works, the *Ming-shih* lists him as the author of the *Er-ya lüeh-i* 略義, 19 *ch.*, probably the same work done under the auspices of Emperor Toγon Temür, which is now lost. To him is also attributed the authorship of the *Yüan hai-yün chih* 元海運志, 1 *ch.*, a short account of the history of maritime trade under the Yüan dynasty. This is found to be a fabrication in his name, for a similar version is contained in the section "hai-yün" in the encyclopedic *Ta-hsüeh yen-i pu* by

Ch'iu Chün (*q.v.*). There is a chronological biography of Wei Su entitled *Wei T'ai-p'u nien-p'u*, by the late Ch'ing scholar Tsou Shu-jung 鄒樹榮; it is included in his *I-su-yüan* 一粟園 *ts'ung-shu*, printed in 1922.

Bibliography

1/285/7a; 61/144/13a; 84/甲/16b; 88/7/48a; *Yüan-shih* (*po-na* ed.), 45/18a, 113/10b; MSL(1962), T'ai-tsu, 776, 788, 1007, 1008, 1050, 1323; KC (1958), 436; Sung Lien, *Sung hsüeh-shih chi*, 59/3b; Ho Meng-ch'un 何孟春, *Yü-tung hsü-lu chai-ch'ao* 餘冬序錄摘抄, in *Chi-lu hui-pien* ed. by Shen Chieh-fu, 148/17b; Liao Tao-nan, *Tien-ko tz'u-lin chi*, 6/9a; Teng Ch'iu 鄧球, *Huang Ming yung-hua lei-pien* 皇明泳化類編 (Taipei, 1965), 110/1b; Ho Ch'iao-yüan, *Ming-shan ts'ang* (Taipei, 1970 ed.), 3224; SK (1930), 60/1a, 84/1b, 169/3a, 175/2a; TSCC (1885–88), XIV: 46/3b, XXIII: 91/79/3b; *Chin-ch'i-hsien chih* (1870), 24/5b; Ch'ien Mu (BDRC), "Tu Ming-ch'u K'ai-kuo chu-ch'en shih-wen chi," 讀明初開國諸臣詩文集, *Hsin-ya hsüeh-pao* 新亞學報 6:2 (August, 1964), 289; Shunjō Nogami 野上俊靜, "Sōka to Yō-ren-shin-ga" 桑哥と楊璉眞伽, *Ōtani daigaku kenkyū nempō* 大谷大學研究年報, 11 (1958), 1; Naoaki Maeno 前野直彬, "Min shichi-shi no sensei Yō I-tei no bungakukan ni tsuite," 明七子の先聲楊維楨の文學觀について, *Chūgokū bungaku hō* 中國文學報, 5 (1956), 41; *The Scholars*, tr. by Yang Hsien-yi and Gladys Yang (Peking, 1964), chap. 1.

Hok-lam Chan

WEN Chen-meng 文震孟 (original *ming* 從鼎, T. 文起, H. 湛持), 1574-July 5, 1636, scholar-official, was born into a celebrated literary family of Wu 吳-hsien (Soochow). The Wen clan traced its ancestry back to the Han dynasty, while one of Wen Chen-meng's direct forebears, Wen T'ien-hsiang (1236-January 3, 1283), was the last prime minister of the Southern Sung, finally executed for his continued intransigence towards the Mongols. His great-great-grandfather, Wen Cheng-ming (*q.v.*), grandfather, Wen P'eng, and his granduncle, Wen Po-jen (for both *see* Wen Cheng-ming), were all well-known

Ming artists. At the age of seventeen he obtained the *chü-jen* in Soochow, specializing in the *Ch'un-ch'iu*. In spite of his family background, Wen was not successful in the metropolitan examination until his tenth attempt. Then at forty-eight (1622) he placed first in the palace examination and was appointed a compiler in the Hanlin Academy. Not long after assuming this position, he submitted a memorial sharply critical of Wei Chunghsien (ECCP) and vigorously defending Tsou Yüan-piao and Feng Ts'ung-wu (*qq.v.*). Both of these men had been senior censors and were foremost leaders of the Tung-lin movement (*see* Ku Hsien-ch'eng). Their enemies had impeached them for having established an academy, Shou-shan shu-yüan, in Peking (*see* Tsou Yüan-piao), not unlike the Tung-lin. Tsou and Feng were forced to retire. Wen compared the persecution of these men to the harassment of the philosopher Chu Hsi (1130-1200) by Han T'o-chou (d. 1207). Infuriated, Wei Chung-hsien secured from the emperor an order to have Wen Chen-meng beaten eighty blows in court. Such a punishment would have been terminal and was vigorously opposed by the grand secretary, Han K'uang (*q.v.*), and numerous other officials. In the end Wen was merely demoted; he returned home without accepting an inferior position. In retrospect this may have been a blessing in disguise, for in 1624, the year Yang Lien (ECCP) impeached Wei Chung-hsien, Wen was not in office and thus escaped the sanguinary penalties dealt out to many of the Tunglin sympathizers.

In the winter of 1626 a fellow townsman of Wen, Sun Wen-chai 孫文豸, wrote a poem grieving for the heroic general, Hsiung T'ing-pi (ECCP). Since Hsiung had been a victim of Wei Chung-hsien's acts of terrorism and had been executed, Sun's poem was viewed as treasonous and he was subsequently seized by the warden's office. It later transpired that Wen and other Tung-lin sympathizers, Ch'en Jen-hsi (*q.v.*) and Cheng Man (ECCP), were also involved in this case. Men K'o-hsin 門克新 (cs 1619), a censor and partisan of Wei Chung-hsien, promptly impeached them, with the result that their names were all erased from the rolls.

The situation changed markedly in the autumn and winter of 1627 with the death of Chu Yu-chiao (ECCP) and the subsequent departure and suicide of Wei Chung-hsien. Within the next few months a committee of high officials was ordered to investigate and determine the degree of culpability of those who had cooperated with the eunuch; numerous Tung-lin partisans too were recalled to service, Wen Chen-meng among them. In the spring of 1629 a list was submitted called "the roster of traitors"(逆案). Although Wang Yungkuang (*see* Wen T'i-jen), then minister of Personnel, was certainly one of the eunuch's henchmen, the emperor did not cashier him. Wen vigorously memorialized against Wang. In defense Wang suggested to the emperor that Wen had personal and partisan motives for this impeachment, which may well have been true. The emperor, desirous of preventing one clique from ever dominating the government again, retained Wang and dropped the matter.

As senior director of instruction, Wen daily lectured the young ruler on the Classics and their application to contemporary government. His humorless approach to this duty is touched on in his official biography. One day during the lectures, the emperor was leisurely sitting with his foot up resting on one knee. When Wen, in reading the *Shu ching* came to the passage, "The ruler of men: how can he be but respectful," he looked over at the emperor's foot. The latter promptly put his sleeve over it and slowly put his foot down.

After a short time in office, Wen, coming into conflict with powerful antiTung-lin ministers, retired to his home rather than take a lower appointment. In 1632, however, he returned as a junior supervisor of instruction. Two years later the emperor ordered his ministers to recommend an eminent scholar to lecture on the Spring and Autumn Annals, which he thought would be an aid in pacifying rebellions. Traditionally, this work had not been included in the list of Classics discussed before the emperor because of the numerous incidents of improper relationships, *i.e.*, inferiors killing superiors. Wen Chen-meng was renowned for his knowledge of this Classic, having specialized in it at an early age. But Wen T'i-jen, an opponent of the Tung-lin group and the chief grand secretary, did not suggest his name. Ch'ien Shih-sheng (*q.v.*), who had recently (October, 1633) become a grand secretary, however, was favorably disposed towards Tung-lin partisans and recommended Wen Chen-meng. Wen T'i-jen could not but concur in the nomination. In February, 1635, when the rebels were ravaging the imperial tombs at Feng-yang (*see* Chang Hsien-chung, ECCP), Wen submitted a memorial suggesting various administrative reforms. He was especially critical of the triennial evaluations of the ministry of Personnel and of the favoritism and partisanship evident in the promotion of officials. The grand secretaries, Wen T'i-jen and Wang Ying-hsiung 王應熊 (T. 非熊, H. 春石, cs 1613), however, effectively thwarted any constructive changes. In July of the same year the emperor determined to increase the number of grand secretaries. Although Wen Chen-meng, pleading illness, asked not to be considered, he was appointed in August to be vice minister of Rites and concurrent grand secretary. Within three months he came into sharp conflict with Wen T'i-jen over the naming of a new chief minister of the Court of Imperial Sacrifices. Both Ho Wu-tsou 何吾騶 (T. 龍友, H. 家岡, cs 1619) and Wen Chen-meng, as the two most pro-Tung-lin grand secretaries, recommended a like-minded official, Hsü Yü-ch'ing 許譽卿 (T. 夷實, 霞城, H. 公實, cs 1616). Wen T'i-jen, naturally opposed to Hsü, persuaded his henchman, the minister of Personnel, Hsieh

Sheng (ECCP), to impeach him. When Wen and Ho attempted to defend Hsü and others who were included in the impeachment, the emperor rebuked them for "favoritism and causing confusion." Ho Wu-tsou was dismissed and Wen Chen-meng, dropping his commission, retired (December 15, 1635).

A few months later, his nephew and close companion from childhood, Yao Hsi-meng (*see* Ch'ien Shih-sheng), who had himself been forced into retirement shortly before Wen, expired. Wen, grief stricken, followed his beloved nephew not long afterwards. This was in the summer of 1636. In almost all of the conflicts recorded in the *Ming-shih* in which Wen became involved, Yao played some collateral or tangential role. Indeed, it would seem that of the two Yao was by far the more vigorous Tung-lin partisan. According to Chu I-tsun (ECCP), in his *Ching-chih-chü shih-hua*, Wen was the most outspoken of the fifty grand secretaries of the Ch'ung-chen period.

In 1639 and 1642, as posthumous awards, Wen's former office was restored to him and then he was named minister of Rites. During the reign of Chu Yu-sung (ECCP), he was canonized Wen-su 文肅. Wen had a younger brother of some note, Wen Chen-heng 亨 and two sons, Wen Ping 秉 and Wen Ch'eng 乘 (T. 應符); the last died defending the dynasty against the Manchus. The younger brother, Wen Chen-heng (T. 啓美, H. 木雞生, Pth. 節愍, 1585–1645), a tribute scholar in the National University during the T'ien-ch'i era, served for a time in the last years of the Ming as a drafter in the central drafting office of the Wu-ying hall 武英殿. He is better known, however, as a talented lute player, calligrapher, landscapist, and author of the *Ch'ang wu chih* 長物志, 12 *ch.*, which—unlike his brother's best-known works—was included in the *Ssu-k'u ch'üan-shu*. It is noteworthy for its study of everyday life in his own time. The twelve *chüan* are divided as follows: 1) the house, 2) flowers and trees, 3) water and rocks, 4) birds and fishes, 5) painting and calligraphy, 6) tables and couches, 7) miscellaneous (including household utensils, combs, stationery, lutes), 8) costumes and bedding, 9) boats and wheeled vehicles, 10) arrangement of household objects, 11) fruits and vegetables, and 12) incense and tea. The *Wu-hsien chih* records also a number of other pieces by Wen, among them the *Wen-sheng hsiao-ts'ao* 文生小草, 1 *ch.*; this was listed for destruction in the 18th century, but Sun Tien-ch'i reports the existence of an old manuscript copy. Wen may also be the author of the vivid account of the uprising at Soochow in the spring of 1626, entitled *K'ai-tu ch'uan-hsin* (*see* Chou Shun-ch'ang), translated by Charles O. Hucker. Wen refused to live under the Manchu rule and starved himself to death at the age of sixty.

Wen Ping (T. 蓀符, H. 大若, 1609-69), the elder son, hid in the mountains at the collapse of the Ming. When captured and urged to enter official life, he refused, remarking: "I dare not disgrace my father." Eventually he committed suicide, his wife, née Chou 周, following him in death. Wen Ping left several books of some significance for understanding events of his day. There is the *Lieh Huang, hsiao-shih* 烈皇小識, 6 *ch.*, which Ch'en Shou-yi 陳受頤 has called "Brief notes on Emperor Ch'ung-Cheng," and from which he has culled several passages dealing with the sectarian rivalry at the court at the end of the Ming. A second, entitled *Hsien-po chih shih* 先撥志始, 2 *ch.*, records events of the years 1573-1624 and 1625-29, stressing the "three cases" (*see* Kao P'an-lung) which plagued the dynasty near its end, and the misdeeds of the eunuch Wei Chung-hsien. To the printed copy of the K'ang-hsi period has been added, in manuscript, notes on the last emperor's attempt to quell the rebellions of his time (19 pages), the *Tung-lin lieh-chuan* (11 pp.) by Ch'en Ting (*see* Tao-chi), and an account of the building of a temple by Wei Chung-hsien (2 pp.). (This rare copy is in the National Library of Peiping.) The *Ssu-k'u*

editors describe the book but did not include it in the Imperial Library, as the title was put on the proscribed list. A third work is his account of the years of the Manchu take-over, *Chia-i shih-an* 甲乙事案, 2 *ch.*; it commences with the 4th lunar month of 1644 and ends with the 12th lunar month of the following year (actually January 17-February 15, 1646). This too was proscribed. Finally there is Wen's book on the internal history of the Wan-li years, *Ting-ling chu-lüeh* 定陵注略, 10 *ch.*, in which the factional strife is clearly described; it was written after the collapse of the Ming. This is known only in manuscript, on microfilm, or in photocopy.

A number of Wen Chen-meng's literary contributions have survived. His *Ku Su ming-hsien hsiao-chi* 姑蘇名賢小記 (Notes on famous personages of old Soochow), 2 *ch.*, and (*Nien yang hsü kung*) *ting shu chi* (念陽徐公) 定蜀記 (Notes on Szechwan), 1 *ch.*, have been made widely available through various collectanea; so also two short Taoist works which he edited: *Tao-te-ching p'ing-chu* 道德經評注 and *Lao-tzu hui-han* 老子彙函. Wen left as well a draft collection of poetry entitled *Yao-p'u* 藥圃 (A garden of herbs) and the *Ts'e-hsüeh yüan chi* 策學圓機, which was proscribed in the following century, and seems no longer extant. Chu I-tsun remarks that Wen's poetry was "level and elegant...intricate yet clear and perspicuous."

Bibliography

1/251/17b; 3/235/16b; 4/12/10a; 8/87/1a; 27/x/10a; 39/23/1a; 40/66/1a, 70/3b; 64/ 辛 6 下 /2b, 辛 18/2b; 65/5/3b; 86/19/30a; 87/2/19a; MSL *fu-lu* 附錄 (1967), Ch'ung-chen, 0083, 0284; KC (1958), *ch.* 85-95; *Wu-shih fu-ch'en k'ao* 五十輔臣考, 3/7; *Wu-hsien chih* (1933), 12/14b, 57/10a, 67/37b, 69 下/4b; Ku Ying-t'ai (ECCP), *Ming-ch'ao chi-shih pen-mo* (1658), 66/19; Hsia Hsieh 夏燮 (1799-1875?), *Ming t'ung-chien* 明通鑑, 3151, 3243, 3259; SK (1930), 54/5b, 62/8a, 123/2b; Yao Chin-yüan (1957), 105, 159; Sun Tien-ch'i (1957), 23, 54, 70, 108; Chou Ch'üeh 周愨, "Kuan-ts'ang Ch'ing-tai chin-shu shu-lüeh" 舘藏清代禁書述略, *Kiangsu sheng-li Kuo-hsüeh t'u-shu-kuan ti-wu nien-k'an* 江蘇省立國學圖畫舘第五年刊, V (Nanking, 1930), 11; V. Contag and C. C. Wang, *Seals of Chinese Painters and Collectors* (rev. ed., Hong Kong, 1966), 23; Sir Percival David, "A Commentary on Ju Ware," *Trans. of the Or. Ceramic Soc.*, 14 (1936–37), 41; C. O. Hucker, "Su-chou and the Agents of Wei Chung-hsien," *Silver Jubilee Volume of the Zinbun-kagaku-kenkyusyo* (Kyoto, 1954), 227; W. Franke, *Sources*, 1.4.10, 2. 8.14, 17, 4.6.8; Ch'en Shou-yi, "The Religious Influence of the Early Jesuits on Emperor Ch'ung-cheng of the Ming Dynasty," THM, VIII: 5 (May, 1939), 407, 418.

L. Carrington Goodrich
and Donald L. Potter

WEN Cheng-ming 文徵明 (original *ming*: Pi 璧, *tzu*: Cheng-ming, and 徵仲, H. 衡山), November 6, 1470–1559, painter, calligrapher, and scholar, was a native of Wu-hsien (Soochow). He was a descendant of the same clan as Wen T'ien-hsiang (1236–January 3, 1283), the noted last-ditch defender of the Sung, and traced his ancestry far back in Chinese history. In recognition of this fact he took as his *hao* the name of the district in Hukuang, Heng-shan, where the Wen family established itself shortly after the year A.D. 1000. Not until the time of Wen Cheng-ming's great-grandfather, Wen Hui 文惠, who belonged in the military officer category, did the family move to the area of Soochow.

Relatively early in his long life Wen Cheng-ming dropped his given name, Pi, in favor of his *tzu*. It was not, however, a youthful change. Evidence from dated paintings finds him still using the name Pi in his mid-forties. The year 1515 (or possibly 1516) is the last clear date that he employed both Pi and Cheng-ming for his signature or seal. When he was young he appeared to some to be a very dull boy. Only his father, Wen Lin 林 (T. 宗儒, 1445–99, cs 1472), differed, having faith, we are told, that the boy's talents would in time reveal themselves. The father died suddenly while serving as prefect of Wen-chou 溫州, Chekiang, and though Wen Cheng-ming rushed to his side, he arrived three days too late. The accounts, such as his biography in the *Ming-shih*, asserting that Wen was sixteen *sui* at this time, are in error.

The story is told that at the time of Wen Lin's death, his colleagues collected a sum of money to present to the son, but that the latter refused to accept it. This sense of family pride and independence becomes a constant theme that is stressed in all accounts of Wen Cheng-ming's life. There is another story about his relative poverty at this time. Yü Chien 俞諫 (T. 良佐, 1453–1527, cs 1490), who held the title of censor and was a friend of Wen's uncle, Wen Shen 森 (T. 宗嚴, 1462–1525, cs 1487, his father's younger half-brother), wished to give him some money. But when the uncle questioned the adequacy of his food, the young scholar asserted that he had enough gruel to eat; when asked as to his clothes, Wen insisted that the spots on them were caused by rain and were temporary, and when finally the uncle suggested that something should be done to clear the drain before his living quarters, Wen replied that such action would damage the houses of his neighbors. Yü Chien then gave up his attempts to render aid.

Wen devoted himself early in life to acquiring the learning and artistic skills for which he was to become so famous. He was helped by several of his father's close friends. Wu K'uan (*q. v.*), who achieved the *chin-shih* in the same year as Wen Lin, is said to have guided his prose, and sometimes also his poetry and calligraphy; Li Ying-chen 李應楨 (T. 貞伯, 1431–93) helped him with his calligraphy; and Shen Chou (*q. v.*) was his master in painting. In addition he was close to others of his own generation who shared the same scholarly and artistic interests; they helped make Soochow China's major cultural center at this time. These were Chu Yün-ming (*q. v.*), Soochow's leading calligrapher; T'ang Yin (*q.*

v.), the painter; and Hsü Chen-ch'ing (*q. v.*), the leading literary personality. While the great figures of the day are usually cited as excelling in some branch of the arts, they most certainly were gifted in more than one. Thus Wen wrote a good deal of poetry, which has found its way into standard anthologies, and in his collected writings, *Fu-t'ien chi* 甫田集, there are some seven hundred forty-one poems preserved.

By this time in China's history, cultural attainments were constantly compared to or contrasted with those of earlier days. Styles of the past were of vital importance in forming one's own. Accordingly writers brought forth great names when discussing Wen's artistic work. Chao Meng-fu (1254–1322), an artist of high accomplishment, was his most admired model. As Wen's pupil, Ch'en Tao-fu (*q. v.*), wrote of the "Seven Junipers" that Wen painted with the Yüan master in mind: "In his lines and washes, delicate and lush, he attained the essence of Chao Meng-fu's genius." Li Kung-lin (1049 –1106) is sometimes named as another influence. As we now look critically at Wen's existing paintings, we can affirm that his interest in the painting of the past ranged far more widely than standard esthetics of the literati would indicate.

Early in life Wen had not followed a course leading to the official examinations, and attempts to involve him in government service after he had acquired some fame met with indifferent success. In 1519–20, when the prince of Ning, Chu Ch'en-hao (*see* Wang Shou-jen), led a revolt in Kiangsi, he tried unsuccessfully to enlist the services of Wen, then in his late forties. Wen, refusing his invitation and offer of money, pleaded illness.

At the age of fifty-three *sui* he was recommended to Peking for an official post by the governor, Li Ch'ung-ssu 李充嗣 (T. 士修, H. 梧山, 1462–1528, cs 1487). His trip north during the spring of 1523 along the Grand Canal was memorable enough to inspire a series of poems, the first from Yangchow. On being examined by the ministry of Personnel, he obtained the rank of consultant (9B) in the Hanlin Academy and worked on the *shih-lu* of the Cheng-te period. He was awarded the "golden belt" for his services when the history was completed (1525). He is said to have had to petition the throne three times for retirement. Finally, in 1526, after approximately three years in the north, he was allowed to return home. Since it was winter, he waited for the spring thaw to permit his return by boat.

From this time on, the rest of his long life was spent in his native Soochow where he earned lasting fame as an independent scholar-painter. Although some accounts indicate that he now built for himself a special dwelling or studio, calling it Yü-ch'ing shan-fang 玉磬山房 (Jade-chime mountain-dwelling), it seems to have been in existence before his trip north; an example of his calligraphy (in Kansas City's Nelson Gallery) written at the Yü-ch'ing shan-fang is dated in the eighth month of 1516. Another important studio was the T'ing-yün-kuan 停雲館 (Hall of the lingering clouds), mentioned, for example, on paintings of 1517 and 1538.

It is clear that an artist-scholar like Wen was far more important for his writing, his calligraphy, and his painting than for his activities in office. There is thus little about his long life in Soochow that offers significant material for standard Chinese biographies. Fortunately a large number of scrolls by Wen have been preserved. Occasionally inscriptions on them give us insights into his career. Thus we know that in 1497 he was still under the tutelage of Shen Chou, who asked him to copy a painting by Chao Meng-fu. Toward the end of 1507 he painted a small hanging scroll for a certain Lai-shih 瀨石 who was going north (for official service). This travel present is perhaps Wen's earliest dated preserved scroll. In 1508 he visited nearby T'ien-p'ing Mountain 天平山, which was a rather frequent goal of local expeditions. Another important local pilgrimage spot must have been West Island on Tung-t'ing Lake 洞庭西山. We know from a painting that Wen was there in 1543. The memory of his travels to the north stayed with him. In 1527, on his return, he had been sufficiently impressed by the northern pine trees to become involved in a painting of this theme, finished only by 1531. As late as 1537, fourteen years after his journey to Peking, he wrote out the series of poems—mentioned above—that he had composed on the trip. In his later years he was very close to Hua Hsia華夏, a collector and scholar in Wu-hsi無錫. In 1549 Wen painted a picture of Hua's studio; later he sent Hua a magnolia painting in return for the hospitality shown while visiting him there. The Soochow artist painted the studio again eight years later in 1557. His interest in the theme of old age, particularly in painting rocks and ancient trees is important at this time (1549-51). Yet the most significant fact about his advancing years seems to have been not the weakening of his powers, but a constant vigor and strength. The careful precise brushing of small k'ai-shu script continued to the end of his life. At the age of eighty-six he carefully copied the *Ch'ih-pi fu* 赤壁賦 (Red Cliff) by Su Shih (January 8, 1037-1101) in this style to pay back a wager for having lost a game of chess. One of the greatest examples of his calligraphy in a bold standard style comes from the final year of his life when he was eighty-nine. He died peacefully while writing a friend's tomb inscription; putting aside his brush he sat motionless, going, we are told, like an immortal.

As might be expected, Wen seems to have had a model family. His wife was a daughter of Wu Yü 吳愈 (T. 惟謙, H. 遜庵, 1443-1526, cs 1475). She was born the same year as her husband, but died at the age of seventy-two in 1542. They had three sons and two daughters. We know most about two of the sons who were important artists in their own right: Wen P'eng 彭 (T. 壽承, H. 三橋, 1489-1573), the eldest, and Wen Chia 嘉 (T. 休承, H. 文水, 1501-83), his second son. A nephew, Wen Po-jen 伯仁 (T. 德承, H. 五峯, 1502-75), was also one of the leading artists of his day. The skills of the family continued for several generations and thus one finds a grandson, Wen Ts'ung-ch'ang 從昌 (T. 南岳, 夢珠, 1574-1648), and a great-granddaughter, (Chao) Wen Shu (趙) 淑 (1595-1634), often listed among the names of later artists.

Wen Cheng-ming's influence spread to a whole circle of pupils and friends. In this group one may mention Ch'en Tao-fu, Wang Ch'ung, Lu Chih (qq. v.), Wang Ku-hsiang 王穀祥(T. 祿之, H. 酉室, 1501-68), Ch'ien Ku, Chü Chieh (qq. v.), and Lu Shih-tao 陸師道 (T. 子傳, H. 元洲, cs 1538). Wen is one of the first artists in Chinese history from whom we have such a rich store of surviving painting and calligraphy. Not until the Ch'ing dynasty do we appear to have comparable bodies of material that we can with confidence associate with individual artists. While we have something of the same phenomenon in the case of Shen Chou, teacher of Wen, for thelatter even more is available and many of the finest works are carefully dated. While Shen may always stand as the figure who made Soochow synonymous with the greatness of scholar-painting in the Ming period, Wen distilled his master's more blunt beginnings to the point of a refined and clearly conscious art. We surely do not yet know enough about this art to select with certainty all authentic paintings from the great mass of attributed works. But since Wen's life was so much his painting—a seemingly endless stream of creativity—no account of that life would be complete without a substantial, although not definitive, list of scrolls known now either in relatively available originals or through existing reproductions. A starting point for an understanding of Wen's art is the list of paintings given by Osvald Sirén. For the seals on some of his paintings see Victoria Contag and C. C. Wang.

Bibliography

1/287/1b; 3/267/1b; 34/11/12b; 40/38/1a; 64/丁 11/10a; 65/3/12b; 84/丙/56a; MSL (1964), Wu-tsung, Introduction; *Wen Cheng-ming ch'üan-chi* 全集 (Shanghai, 1935); Chang An-chih 張安治, *Wen Cheng-ming*, Shanghai, 1959; Chiang Shao-shu 姜紹書 (17th cent.), *Wu-sheng-shih shih* 無聲詩史 (Shanghai, 1962), 2/27a; *Hua-yüan to-ying* 畫苑掇英 (Shanghai, 1955), III: 3, 1, *Ku-kung shu-hua lu* 故宮書畫錄 (Taipei, 1956), 1/104, 2/8, 3/77, 4/184, 5/334, 6/43; *Liao-ning sheng po-wu-kuan ts'ang-hua chi* 遼寧省博物舘藏畫集 (Peking, 1962) pls. 25–31; *Shang-hai po-wu-kuan ts'ang-hua* (Shanghai, 1959), pl. 55; *Su-chou* 蘇州 *po-wu-kuan ts'ang-hua chi* (Peking, 1963), 2 vols., pls. 12, 13; *Sō Gen Min Chin meiga taikan* 宋元明清名畫大觀, I (Tokyo, 1932), pls. 115–23; *Tō* 唐 *Sō Gen Min meiga taikan* (Tokyo, 1929), 2 Vols., pls. 285–98; *Chinese Art Treasures* (exhibited in the United States [Washington, 1961–62]), pls. 97, 98; R. Edwards, *The Field of Stones* (Washington, 1962), 46; Sherman E. Lee, *Chinese Landscape Painting* (Cleveland, 1954), 79, pls. 53a–56; Max Loehr, "A Landscape. Attributed to Wen Chengming," AA, XXII (1959), 143; Wang Shih-chieh *et al*, *A Garland of Chinese Calligraphy*, II (Hongkong, 1967), nos. 9, 10; L. C. S. Sickman (ed.), *Chinese Calligraphy and Painting in the Collection of John M. Crawford, Jr.* (New York, 1962), 134, pls. 37, 38; L. C. S. Sickman and A. Soper, *The Art and Architecture of China* (Harmondsworth, 1956, 1960), 157, 161, 165, 177, 182, 184, 187, pls. 135–36; Osvald Sirén, *Chinese Painting* (New York and London, 1956–58), IV: 172, VII: 257; E. J. Laing, *Chinese Paintings in Chinese Publications, 1956–1968* (Ann Arbor, 1969), 201; Tseng Yu-ho, "The Seven Junipers of Wen Cheng-ming," ACASA, VIII (1954), 22; V. Contag and C. C. Wang, *Seals of Chinese Painters and Collectors* (rev. ed., Hong Kong, 1966), 19, 636.

Richard Edwards

WEN T'i-jen 溫體仁 (T. 長卿, H. 圓嶠), died August 9, 1638, the favorite and most controversial minister of the last Ming emperor, was a native of Wu-ch'eng 烏程 Chekiang. A *chin-shih* of 1598, he was selected to be a Hanlin bachelor, later rising to compiler. From 1612 to 1615 he served as director of studies at the National University in Nanking. In 1622 he became junior vice minister of Rites. Two years later he was made senior vice minister, but due to the death of one of his parents he retired before assuming the post. Early in 1628 he became minister of Rites in Nanking, but he had hardly entered on his duties when he was posted to Peking to serve as grand supervisor of instruction with the concurrent title of minister of Rites. In November, 1628, the grand secretary, Liu Hung-hsün (*see* Chou Yen-ju), a leading Tung-lin partisan, was dismissed and banished to the frontier. The next month the emperor ordered the nine ministers, chief supervising secretaries, and censors to recommend candidates to fill the vacated office. Eleven names were suggested, including the junior vice minister of Rites, Ch'ien Ch'ien-i (ECCP) junior vice minister of Personnel, Ho Ju-ch'ung (*see* Liu Ching-t'ing); the censor-in-chief, Ts'ao Yü-pien 曹于汴 (T. 自梁, H. 貞予, 1558–1634, cs 1592); and the minister of Personnel, Wang Yung-kuang 王永光 (cs 1592). The committee which named these men was dominated by members of the Tung-lin politico-literary group. It is not surprising that they recommended chiefly their associates or those sympathetic with their views. Wang Yung-kuang seems to be the only exception. Reportedly Ch'ien Ch'ien-i worked hard to have himself named first on the list because customarily such a designation assured a man the appointment. Two men who considered themselves better qualified, and were angered by their exclusion, were Chou Yen-ju and Wen T'i-jen. They at once conspired to discredit the committee. It so happened that in 1621, while supervising the provincial examination in Chekiang, Ch'ien Ch'ien-i had become involved in a bribery scandal concerning one of the candidates. Ch'ien was apparently innocent, and he himself had exposed the suspect in a memorial; moreover, the case had long been decided and the guilty parties appropriately disciplined. Wen, however, memorialized against selecting a man of Ch'ien's record for the post of grand secretary. The emperor promptly summoned Ch'ien and Wen to a hearing at a court session, during which Wen eloquently convinced the emperor of his own loyalty and honesty and of the conspiracy of Ch'ien and the Tung-lin group. Ch'ien was sent home and later his name was struck from the official roll. Most of his supporters were punished, one being imprisoned; several, including Ch'ü Shih-ssu (ECCP) and the censor, Fang K'o-chuang 房可壯 (T. 陽初, H. 海客, 1579–1653, cs 1604), being demoted to various provincial offices.

For having antagonized the Tung-lin group Wen became the target of repeated denunciations and accusations which, however, were either petty or could not be substantiated. This further strengthened the emperor's suspicion that the memorials against Wen were largely motivated by partisan concern. Wen also was careful about his own conduct so as to avoid any cause for suspicion. Though he was not appointed to the Grand Secretariat for another year, his arguments carried the day.

In the winter of 1629 the Manchus invaded north China by way of Mongolia. Yüan Ch'ung-huan (ECCP), who enjoyed considerable Tung-lin support at court, was forced to withdraw from Liaotung in order to defend the capital. Whereupon the anti-Tung-lin faction led by Wang Yung-kuang seized this opportunity to accuse Yüan Ch'ung-huan of treason for having made a truce with the Manchus in September, 1626. They also impeached Yüan's sponsor, Grand Secretary Ch'ien Lung-hsi (see Ch'ien Shih-sheng). Ch'ien. barely escaping execution, and another grand Secretary, Han K'uang (q.v.), were both forced to resign in February, 1630—a major setback for the Tung-lin. Yüan was condemned to dismemberment in the market place, and later his major Tung-lin supporter, Ch'ien, was arrested.

In the same year both Wen and his colleague Chou Yen-ju were appointed grand secretaries. At the end of the year Wen received the honorary distinction of junior guardian of the heir apparent as a reward for his efforts in completing the *Shen-tsung shih-lu*. This, together with the *shih-lu* of the T'ien-ch'i period, probably completed in 1637, is the only literary work associated with the name of Wen T'i-jen. In 1632 the chief grand secretary, Chou Yen-ju, was impeached by Tung-lin censors. Wen, who coveted Chou's position, secretly worked to undermine his influence, and in July, 1633, Chou was forced to resign, his dissimulating friend succeeding to his rank. In August, Ho Ju-ch'ung, a Tung-lin partisan who had resigned from the Grand Secretariat two years earlier, declined to accept an imperial summons to return to his office. Whereupon the supervising secretary Huang Shao-chieh 黃紹杰 (or 傑, cs 1625) suggested to the emperor that the reason for Ho's preference for retirement was the reluctance of a superior man to associate with his opposite. Angered by such criticism, Wen promptly managed to have the censor demoted and assigned to a provincial post. In similar ways he succeeded in removing many Tung-lin men and in promoting their opponents.

In February of the following year, at Wen's instigation, an opportunist from Ch'ang-shu 常熟, Nan-Chihli, Chang Han-ju 張漢儒, impeached his fellow townsmen Ch'ien Ch'ien-i and Ch'ü Shih-ssu. Wen attached to the memorial the suggestion that both men be imprisoned. Ch'ien Ch'ien-i then sought help from the director of ceremonials, Ts'ao Hua-ch'un 曹化淳, the leading palace eunuch. It so happened that when Wei Chung-hsien (ECCP) murdered Wang An (see Kao P'an-lung), the eunuch friendly to the Tung-lin party, Ch'ien wrote the inscription for his tomb. Wang An had sponsored Ts'ao so that it was natural for the latter to be favorably disposed towards Ch'ien. Chang Han-ju, however, discovered this collusion and reported it to his patron. Whereupon Wen secretly memorialized the emperor intimating that Ts'ao Hua-ch'un was guilty of a crime. The emperor showed Ts'ao this memorial; the latter, protesting his innocence, urged an investigation of the charges. The machinations of Wen and Chang accordingly came to light. The emperor ordered Chang to be confined in a cangue until dead. From then on one memorial after another denounced Wen. In June he begged to retire on the grounds of ill health, perhaps expecting an imperial reply begging him to remain. To his surprise, the emperor granted his request. Wen was dining when the order came. So great was his consternation that he dropped his spoon and chopsticks. It seems, however, the imperial trust in him did not waver for, after his death, the emperor conferred on him the posthumous rank of grand tutor and the designation Wen-chung 文忠.

Little is known of Wen's family. Because of his office, however, his great-grandfather, grandfather, and father all received posthumous honors and are mentioned in the gazetteer of Wu-ch'eng. His younger brother, Wen Yü-jen 育仁 (T. 幼貞), through the yin privilege, received official preferment. Wen T'i-jen's three sons, Wen Yen 儼 (T. 公望), Wen K'an 侃 (T. 公俊), and Wen Chi 佶 (T. 公端). received minor offices in the capital by virtue of the position of their father. Wen Yen was given the office of vice minister of the seal office, while the other two served as drafters (rank 7B) in the central drafting office, positions commonly reserved for those who entered the civil service by means other than the literary examinations.

The official biography of Wen T'i-jen is included in a section of the Ming-shih entitled "Chien-ch'en" 奸臣, which may be rendered as "treacherous ministers." There are only six major biographies in this section. Three of these treat officials of the late Ming: Wen T'i-jen, Chou Yen-ju. and Ma Shih-ying (ECCP). None of these

three may be properly considered traitorous. Furthermore, even his arch enemies grudgingly conceded Wen's incorruptibility. It seems that the only characteristic common to these three was their opposition to the Tung-lin. In view of this, some questions as to their judgment fall upon the writers of Ming history.

The Ming-ch'ao chi-shih pen-mo, compiled by Ku Ying-t'ai (ECCP) and first printed in 1658, was one of the earliest attempts at writing the history of the previous dynasty. Its chapter on the Tung-lin group, "Tung-lin-tang i" 黨議, chüan 66, was reportedly written by Wu Ying-chi (ECCP, p. 52), a member of the Fu-she (idem., p. 52), the politico-literary group most strongly opposed to Wen T'i-jen. Another important influence on historians of the Ming in early Ch'ing was Ch'ien Ch'ien-i, Wen's long-time enemy. Ch'ien himself had finished a draft Ming history which was destroyed by fire before publication. Even more important in the intellectual milieu of the mid-17th century was Huang Tsung-hsi (ECCP). His father had been one of the early victims of Wei Chung-hsien, while he himself was among the most active members of the Fu-she. It is reported that when Chu Yu-chien (ECCP) came to the throne in 1627, Huang Tsung-hsi made his way to the capital with an awl in his sleeve for the purpose of avenging his father. Huang's partisan commitment can hardly be doubted. Considering the fact that the Ming-shih kao was compiled by a pupil of Huang, Wan Ssu-t'ung (ECCP), the pro-Tung-lin bias is not surprising. Wan T'ai (ECCP), the father of Wan Ssu-t'ung, was a student of a leading Tung-lin partisan, Liu Tsung-chou (ECCP), and, of course, a close friend of Huang Tsung-hsi. With this background, one finds it hard to see how Wan could have dealt differently with anti-Tung-lin subjects. The biography of Wen T'i-jen in the Ming-shih is only a slightly abridged version of the one in the Ming-shih kao.

All the biographies of Wen T'i-jen

are filled with memorials of Tung-lin members criticizing him. Furthermore, since Wen was a grand secretary from 1630 to 1637, chief grand secretary from 1633 to 1637, and since his collaborator. Hsüeh Kuo-kuan (ECCP, p. 53), was chief grand secretary from 1637 to 1640, as was Chou Yen-ju from 1640 to 1643, historians are fond of observing that Wen's maladministration was largely responsible for the fall of the Ming. It is true that of the fifty grand secretaries of the Ch'ung-chen period Wen T'i-jen was the most powerful and held office the longest. Yet it is highly doubtful that the blame heaped upon him is justified. Certainly the lax administration of the Wan-li emperor and the eunuch disaster of the T'ien-ch'i period cannot be laid at his door. What steps the favorite grand secretary of the last emperor might have taken to stem the tide of decline are not recorded in the incomplete dynastic records. Only biographies written by vindictive partisans allotting "praise and blame" remain.

[Editors' note: As a controversial figure in history Wen T'i-jen warrants closer study. An analytical examination of the personalities and events he dealt with may throw more light on the man himself, and perhaps also present a plausible explanation of the sharply different opinions about him offered by his contemporaries as well as by later writers. He impressed his emperor as a minister entirely trustworthy and well versed in literature, and a competent and loyal secretary, warranting the posthumous name of Wen-chung which the emperor must have chosen deliberately. This is in diametrical opposition to Wen's designation as a treacherous or perfidious minister in the official Ming-shih. It is interesting to note that in August, 1644, four months after the fall of Peking to the rebels, the prince of Fu (Chu Yu-sung, ECCP), in an investigation as to who might be held responsible for the disaster, found Wen T'i-jen as much to be condemned as the two grand secretaries, Chou Yen-ju and Hsüeh

Kuo-kuan, both of whom had been sentenced to death. The Nanking regime deprived all three of posthumous honors but, because Wen was the only one who had received any, the verdict affected him alone. The name Wen-chung was accordingly withdrawn. But half a year later the case was reopened and this coveted canonization restored to him.

T'an Ch'ien (q.v.), a contemporary of Wen, rebutted public opinion which judged Wen a usurper and perpetrator of treacherous acts. In T'an's opinion the emperor (Chu Yu-chien) was not a ruler who could have tolerated such a minister. T'an, however, said that Wen followed the emperor's wish to pursue a policy of harsh treatment of those considered guilty and, in order to avoid being censored himself, kept free from any taint of bribery. Another contemporary, Li Ch'ing (ECCP), recorded that Wen was an accomplished writer of imperial comments on memorials, and lamented that on reflection the two grand secretaries. Wen and Chou, and the War minister Yang Ssu-ch'ang (q. v.), had all been denounced for bringing on the ruin of the empire. Although many seem to think that the emperor, who made the decisions and chose the men to carry them out, had only himself to blame, nevertheless, they were reluctant to say so plainly, probably out of consideration of the fact that the emperor did redeem himself by committing suicide.]

Bibliography

1/308/28a; 3/237/6b; 27/x/16a; *Wu-shih fu-ch'en k'ao* 五十輔臣考, 2/28; *Li Kuang-t'ao* 李光濤, "Lun Ch'ung-chen er nien [chi-ssu lu-pien]" 論崇禎二年「己已虜變」, CYYY, 18 (1948), 470; Liu Po-han 劉伯涵, "Lun Yüan Ch'ung-huan yü Tung-lin tang ti kuan-hsi" 論袁崇煥與東林黨的關係, LSYC, 4 (April, 1958), 16; Hsia Hsieh 夏燮 (1799–1875?), *Ming t'ung-chien* 明通鑑, 3154, 3157, 3197, 3201, 3209, 3214, 3241, 3272, 3274, 3548; KC (1958), 5460, 5468, 5537, 5541, 5563, 5729, 5732, 5737, 5743, 5760, 5813, 6131, 6139, 6185, 6192; Yeh T'ing-kuan 葉廷琯, *Ou po yü hua* 鷗波漁話, 4/2a; Hsieh Kuo-chen 謝國楨, *Ming Ch'ing chih chi tang-she yün-tung k'ao* 明清之際黨社運動考

(1934), 72; *Wu-ch'eng-hsien chih* (1881), 10/27a, 32b, 34/8b; Ku Chieh-kang, "A Study of the Literary Persecution During the Ming" (tr. by L. Carrington Goodrich), HJAS, III (1938), 291; Wolfgang Franke, *Sources*, 1.1.13.

Donald L. Potter

WU Ch'eng 吳成, original name Mai-lü 買驢, died January 15, 1434, a native of Liao-yang 遼陽 in Liaotung, served as a military commander under five emperors during the fifty years of his career. Mai-lü's father, probably of Mongol origin, served in the late Yüan period as an administrative assistant of the Liao-yang branch province but submitted to the Ming court in 1388, presumably at the call of the Mongol general, Kuan-t'ung 觀童 (the duke of Ch'üan-kuo 全國公), following the latter's surrender in July, 1387. Mai-lü, who accompanied his father to China, was subsequently appointed a platoon commander of the Yung-p'ing 永平 guard, east of Peiping, and rose to become a company commander. When Chu Ti (*q.v.*), then prince of Yen, started his rebellion against Chu Yün-wen (*q.v.*) in the autumn of 1399, Wu submitted to the prince with his Mongol soldiers and was rewarded with a promotion to be a regional vice commander of Peiping. During the next three years he took part in several major campaigns and gained the confidence of Chu Ti.

In January, 1403, shortly after Chu Ti's enthronement, Mai-lü adopted the Chinese name Wu Ch'eng and advanced to the rank of commander. He was periodically dispatched to the northern frontier to oppose the intrusion of Mongol tribesmen. In March, 1410, Wu was selected to join the expeditionary force, led by Chu Ti against the Mongol tribes of Bunyaširi and Aruγtai (*q.v.*), in the Kerülen River valley in revenge for an earlier defeat (*see* Qorγočin). Wu distinguished himself in battle and was promoted (in September) to be an assistant commissioner in the military headquarters. In the following decade Wu resumed duty on the northern frontier with headquarters at K'ai-p'ing 開平 (the Yüan summer capital), to be on the alert for Mongol invaders; here he eventually rose to the rank of commissioner. Beginning in 1422, as Aruγtai renewed his depredations, Wu Ch'eng became actively involved in campaigns against him. Wu's initial encounter, however, ended in disaster. In April of this year, while he was assuming the defense of Hsing-ho 興和 north of Kalgan, Aruγtai, taking advantage of his absence on a hunting trip, overran the fortress and carried away his wife and children as hostages. The emperor reprimanded Wu for his neglect of duty, but gave him no other punishment.

In reprisal for the attack, Chu Ti immediately organized another expeditionary force against Aruγtai; leading a huge army in person, he put Wu Ch'eng and several Mongol officers in command of the vanguard units. This time the Chinese succeeded in crushing the enemy's resistance. Three years later, Emperor Chu Kao-chih (*q.v.*), following the policy of his father, sent Wu Ch'eng to join the command of Hsüeh Lu (*see* Chu Chan-chi) to round up remnants of Aruγtai's followers in the Kerülen River area. The two scored another victory over the enemy and brought back many prisoners and much booty. On August 8 of this year, the emperor rewarded Wu Ch'eng with the hereditary title of earl of Ch'ing-p'ing 清平伯, carrying an annual stipend of 1,100 bushels of rice.

Following the enthronement of Chu Chan-chi, Wu Ch'eng continued to serve on the northern frontier. In August, 1426, however, he was recalled to Peking, together with Hsüeh Lu, to join an expedition under the emperor's personal command against Chu Kao-hsü (*q.v.*). The Mongol soldiers under Wu proved their effectiveness, and helped suppress the attempted *coup d'état* against the throne. A year later Wu Ch'eng was appointed deputy commander of the K'ai-p'ing region to assist Hsüeh Lu in the defense of that area. In August the Chinese repelled a major intrusion by the enemy and scored a spectacular victory, for which they were richly rewarded. Two months after this Wu and Hsüeh took part in another expedition commanded by the emperor, this time against the Mongol tribes from the Uriyangqad commanderies outside the Great Wall. The Chinese forces won a victory at K'uan-ho 寬和, about twenty miles northeast of Hsi-feng-k'ou 喜峯口 (*see* Chu Chan-chi). About this time the Mongols returned Wu's wife and children. Shortly after his return, Wu was again honored, on March 29, 1429, with the title of marquis of Ch'ing-p'ing. Two years later (August, 1431), the court granted him 400 *mou* (*ca.* 60 acres) of unoccupied land in Pao-ti 寶坻 hsien, Shun-t'ien 順天 prefecture, to pasture his herds. He continued his service on the northern frontier in various capacities until his death two and a half years later. He received the posthumous rank of duke of Ch'ü-kuo 渠國 (the *Ming-shih* table and *Kuo-ch'üeh*, however, give the title as Liang 梁 -kuo), and the canonized name Chuang-yung 壯勇.

A year after Wu Ch'eng's death, as his son did not survive him, Emperor Chu Chan-chi appointed his grandson Wu Ying 英 to inherit the title of earl of Ch'ing-p'ing, with the same amount of stipend. When Wu Ying died in May, 1450, his son succeeded to the title fourteen years later (October, 1464) when he reached maturity. Among the later inheritors of the earldom, the best known is Wu Ch'eng's great-great-grandson, Wu Chieh 傑 (T. 漢臣, d. July, 1531), who became a registered taxpayer of Ho-fei 合肥 (Anhwei) and succeeded to the title in April, 1508. Pursuing a distinguished military career, he rose to the rank of general in charge of pacification of the insubordinate tribesmen in the Hukuang region. The last earl was Wu Tsun-chou 遵周 (T. 盤銘), who inherited the title in October, 1610. He died in 1644 in the defense of Peking against the rebels under Li Tzu-ch'eng (ECCP), and was awarded the canonized name Chieh-min 節愍.

Bibliography

1/107/3a, 156/4a; 61/99/2b; MSL(1963), T'ai-tsung, 281, 1383, 2221, 2331, 2351, 2403, Jen-tsung, 113, 201, 243, Hsüan-tsung, 496, 725, 768, 1160, 1232, 1768, 1880, 2394; KC(1958), 1462; Cheng Hsiao, *Wu-hsüeh pien*, 19/18b; Chang Hung-hsiang 張鴻翔, "*Ming-shih* chüan i-wu-liu chu-ch'en, shih-hsi piao," 明史卷一五六諸臣世系表, *Fu-jen hsüeh-chih* 輔仁學誌, Vol. 5, nos. 1–2(1936), 14; Henry Serruys, "Mongols Ennobled during the Early Ming," HJAS, 22 (1959), 226.

Hok-lam Chan

WU Ch'eng-en 吳承恩 (T. 汝忠, H. 射陽山人), *ca.* 1506-*ca.* 1582, poet and writer of fiction, was a native of Huai-an 淮安, the district seat of Shan-yang 山陽 and the prefectural seat of Huai-an, at the point where the Grand Canal crossed the Yellow River during the Ming and a major part of the Ch'ing dynasties. His great-grandfather and grandfather both served as minor education officials in Chekiang. His father, Wu Jui 吳銳(1461–1532), however, had the reputation of a fool in his locality for being overly credulous and easily taken in or bullied. Poor and without hope in scholarship, Wu Jui married a wealthy man's daughter and worked in the family's silk shop as a clerk. A daughter resulted from this marriage. Probably in his middle forties Wu Jui took a concubine(née Chang 張), who gave birth to Wu Ch'eng-en. A precocious child, Wu Ch'eng-en once felt cut to the quick when he overheard someone refer to him as "the fool's son," but his father, true to character, advised him to face reality. Years later, apparently after Wu Ch'eng-en had gained recognition as a promising student and a potential official, those who had once ridiculed, cheated, or insulted his father came to the old man respectfully for advice. Even the prefect, Ko Mu 葛木(T. 仁甫, H. 厄山, cs 1517), honored him as guest at the annual ceremonial feasts given by the officials to the local gentry (1530 or 1531).

Accomplished as he was as a writer, Wu Ch'eng-en failed time and again to pass the provincial examination at Nanking. In 1544 he was selected as the tribute student for that year of the Huai-an prefectural school and so qualified to reside in Nanking as a scholar of the National University. For the next eighteen years, except for a brief visit to Peking in 1550, he lived chiefly in Huai-an and Nanking, continuing to try his luck at the examination hall. He made a living through the remuneration he received from literary compositions, many examples of which can be found in his collected works. Particularly noted is the kind of composition in vogue in his day called chang-tz'u 障詞, consisting of a poem in the tz'u style with a long introduction, usually conveying a congratulatory message on a birthday or on a promotion. The composition was as a rule written in beautiful calligraphy and attached to a screen or a piece of silk. He probably also received remuneration for editing or compiling books for others, of which the following are definitely known to be at least partly his: *Ch'un-ch'iu lieh-chuan* 春秋列傳, 5 *ch.*, by Liu Chieh 劉節(T. 介夫, H. 梅國, 1476 –1555, cs 1505), and *Huai-chün wen-hsien chih* 淮郡文獻志, 26 *ch.*, bio-bibliographical history of Huai-an by P'an Yün 潘塤 (T. 伯和, H. 熙臺, 1476–1562, cs 1508). Liu Chieh served as director of Grain Transport from 1530 to 1533. P'an Yün, after being cashiered from the governorship of Honan in 1529, lived the rest of his life in retirement in Huai-an, and the inscription on the monument at his tomb was composed by Wu Ch'eng-en. In sponsoring Wu, P'an followed the general pattern practised between the wealthy gentry and young promising literati of a locality. Other such families of Huai-an included those of Wu's contemporaries and friends, Shen K'un (*see* Lin Jun) and Li Ch'un-fang (*q.v.*), each a *chuang-yüan* (first on

the list of *chin-shih* for his year). In Nanking too Wu was accepted by the men of letters of the day, either native residents such as Hsü T'ien-hsi 徐天錫 (T. 申之, 1485–1562, a descendant of Hsü Ta, *q.v.*), or incumbent officials such as Ho Liang-chün (*q.v.*).

Sometime around 1562 Wu gave up hope of passing the provincial examination and went to Peking to register as a scholar in the National University in order to qualify for an appointment to a minor office. It was about this time that he wrote a long poem in the fu style, entitled *Ming-t'ang fu* 明堂賦, to commemorate the completion of the rebuilding of the three main halls in the imperial palace destroyed by fire in 1557. He must have written this fu before September 28, 1562, because on that day the names of the three halls were changed by imperial order; in the fu, however, they were designated by their old names. It may, of course, have been written as a paper required of the students of the National University. This and an essay written (for someone else) in 1562 congratulating Grand Secretary Hsü Chieh (*q.v.*) on his sixtieth birthday should have enhanced Wu's fame as a writer and contributed to his chance for an appointment.

Some two years later Wu was appointed vice magistrate of Ch'ang-hsing 長興, Chekiang, a district on the southeast shore of the lake, T'ai-hu. Probably when he was in Hangchow (about 1564) to receive instructions from the governor, Liu Chi 劉畿 (T. 子京, H. 羽泉, 1509–69, cs 1550), he wrote a preface to Liu's work on military leaders in history, *Chu-shih chiang-lüeh* 諸史將略. How long Wu served in Ch'ang-hsing is not definitely known. The local gazetteer praises him for his integrity and remembers him as associating only with those of the local gentry who were of high moral standards, naming especially Hsü Chung-hsing (*q.v.*), known as one of the "seven later masters" (*see* Li P'an-lung). In 1565 there came to Ch'ang-hsing as magistrate the famous essayist, Kuei Yu-kuang(*q.v.*), under whom Wu probably served for more than two years until Kuei was promoted in 1568. Curiously, nothing in the collected works of either of these two great writers indicates that any relationship ever existed between them. Recently (1950s?), however, a discovery was made in Ch'ang-hsing of two monuments, the inscriptions of which were composed by Kuei but both written on the 10th day of the 10th month, Lung-ch'ing 1st year (1567), in the hand of Wu. The calligraphy of Wu follows the style of Chao Meng-fu (1254–1322), pleasing, and graceful. It seems that Wu left Ch'ang-hsing about the time he brushed these inscriptions or shortly thereafter.

Little is known about the last years of Wu's life. One source says that after Ch'ang-hsing he served as a tutor (chi-shan 紀善) in the palace of the prince of Ching 荊王 (probably the sixth prince, Chu I-chü 朱翊鉅, d. 1570). In that case he should have resided in the prince's establishment in Ch'i-chou 蘄州, Hukuang, during his term of office, possibly 1568-70. He died in Huai-an in or before 1582. He is known to have had a daughter but no son. After his death it was the son of a cousin, Ch'iu Tu 邱度 (T. 志中, H. 正岡, 汝洪, cs 1577), who collected and edited his poems and essays and printed them in 1589 under the title *She-yang hsien-sheng ts'un-kao* 射陽先生存稿, 4 *ch.*, with a supplement in 1 *chüan*. There is a preface to this work written in 1590 by Ch'en Wen-chu 陳文燭 (T. 玉叔, H. 五岳山人, cs 1565), who served as a prefect of Huai-an from 1570 to 1573. In the preface Ch'en relates that Wu died almost ten years earlier, which in Chinese reckoning might mean nine or even eight years.

Wu's collected works received little notice following their publication and, except in the local gazetteers, remained practically unknown for three hundred forty years. In 1777, when a scholar of Huai-an tried to assemble Wu's writings, he was able to turn up only a few essays; this small collection

was printed by Mao Kuang-sheng (*see* Mao Hsiang in ECCP) in 1921 but still it received scant attention. In 1923, when the great scholar Hu Shih (BDRC) wrote the *Hsi-yu-chi k'ao-cheng* 西遊記考證 identifying Wu as the author of the *Hsi-yu-chi*, Wu emerged as a celebrity in Chinese literature and a writer of distinction; his life story too became a subject for almost feverish inquiry. Even so it was six years after this, late in 1929, that someone discovered in the Palace Museum in Peiping a copy of the *She-yang hsien-sheng ts'un-kao* of 1529, perhaps the only extant copy of the first edition, and printed it in installments in the Museum weekly, *Ku-kung chou-k'an* 故宮週刊. The following year the Museum printed a two-volume edition. A fresh edition with supplements and a chronology of Wu's life by Liu Hsiu-yeh 劉修業 appeared in 1958 under the title *Wu Ch'eng-en shih-wen chi* 詩文集.

In the *She-yang hsien-sheng ts'un-kao* two of the essays are prefaces to works compiled by Wu himself. One was written for a collection of anecdotes and ghost stories composed when he was a young man fond of fictional writing in all its forms. This collection, entitled *Yü-ting chih* 禹鼎志, is unfortunately lost. The other work, for which he himself wrote a preface, is an anthology of poems in the tz'u style, which he compiled by rearranging, with some supplementation, the two foremost anthologies of tz'u, *Hua-chien-chi* 花間集 of the 11th century and *Ts'ao-t'ang shih-yü* 草堂詩餘 of the 13th century. Perhaps whimsically he named his anthology the *Hua-ts'ao hsin-pien* 花草新編. This involves a pun literally meaning a new work on flowers and grass but really signifying a modern arrangement of the two older works, each represented by the first character of its title. He described his method of arrangement in the preface in this redundant fashion, i ta-hsiao ch'a hou-hsien, i tuan-ch'ang wei hsiao-ta 以大小差後先以短長爲小大, meaning an arrangement by order of length, *i. e.*, number of characters. About 1583 there appeared in print an anthology of tz'u under the title, *Hua-ts'ao ts'ui-pien* 粹編, 12 *ch.*, with the editor's name given as Ch'en Yüeh-wen 陳耀文 (T. 晦伯, cs 1550) and a preface signed by Ch'en dated in the winter of 1583. A comparison of the two prefaces shows clearly that Ch'en's version was based on the one by Wu with changes and substitutions. In Ch'en's, Wu is indicated as a local student whose library was available to Ch'en about the year 1559 when he was serving as prefectural judge of Huai-an; as to the anthology, however, Ch'en claimed it as his own. Concerning the method of compilation as noted in the sentence quoted above, Ch'en substituted the characters shih-tz'u 世次 (chronological order) for ta-hsiao (length or size). Since the book totally disregards any order by time, this substitution, although an improvement in literary style, is contrary to fact and reveals the spurious nature of Ch'en's claim to authorship. It seems that after Wu died Ch'en or his agent purchased the manuscripts of the anthology and published them in 1583 as his work, never suspecting that only a few years later someone would edit a collection of Wu's writings and include the original preface. This is a conjecture but, if correct, serves to corroborate the year of death of Wu as approximately 1582.

The work that contributes most to the fame of Wu Ch'eng-en as a writer is the above-mentioned *Hsi-yu-chi* in 100 chapters. Yet, for over three hundred years in all its numerous editions since the first published by Shih-te-t'ang 世德堂 in 1592, its authorship is given as anonymous, or placed under a pseudonym, or written incorrectly. Only in the *Huai-an-fu chih* 府志 of 1625 and other local gazetteers is the fact that Wu had a work by the title *Hsi-yu-chi* cursorily recorded. It was only after Hu Shih wrote his introduction to the Ya-tung 亞東 Bookstore edition of 1923 that Wu's authorship of this great piece of fiction came to be firmly established. Although no reference to Wu's con-

nection with it can be found in his own writings or in those of his acquaintances, this may be explained by the conjecture that he composed it at home during the last ten years of his life, and that his other writings of that period had disappeared. On the other hand he did give a description of his keen interest in fiction from childhood on and his attempts at imitating some early short story writers. Perhaps he or his family had to conceal his connection with it because in his day an official and one-time tutor to a prince would have been castigated or ostracized for being so eccentric. In any case, since 1923 his name has been prominently given as author in all important editions of the *Hsi-yu-chi* and his admirers have filled volumes on his life and works. Some have studied the bibliographical history of *Hsi-yu-chi*, trying to trace earlier works that could have provided the author with inspiration and to compare the different later editions. Of the latter, *Hsi-yu-cheng-tao-shu* 證道書 edited about 1690 by Wang Hsiang-hsü 汪象旭 (T. 憺漪), the *Hsi-yu chen-ch'üan* 西遊眞詮 edited about 1696 by Ch'en Shih-pin 陳士斌 (T. 允生, H. 悟一子), and the *Hsin-shuo* 新說 *Hsi-yu-chi* edited in 1748 by Chang Shu-shen 張書紳 (T. 南薰) are the three versions on which most later editions have been based. Since about 1932 several Ming editions have come to light, especially the one in 1592. It was then discovered that in the Ch'ing editions the original chapters 9–12 had been compressed into three (10–12) and a new chapter 9 added. This was curdely done, without regard to sequence and internal contradictions.

Hsi-yu-chi (Journey to the West) is a masterful epic novel depicting the experiences of Tripiṭaka when he journeys to India to obtain Buddhist scriptures. He is shielded and protected in a mythological setting by the courageous, worldly-wise, and heroic Monkey. It is written in vernacular prose and many of the poems which are used for descriptive purposes, or which advance the action, are enjoyably fresh and free of pedantry.

[Editors' note: In 1964 the English scholar, Glen Dudbridge, published an article in Chinese on the early editions of the *Hsi-yu-chi*, in which he expressed some doubt as to its authorship. In a subsequent study in English, published five years later, he emphasized this with the statement that he remained "sceptical about this ascription (to Wu) chiefly because the evidence to support it is ultimately thin and dubious." The evidence in question, the listing of *Hsi-yu-chi* among the titles credited to Wu in the *Huai-an-fu chih* of 1621–27, seems indeed inconclusive. The only other middle seventeenth-century bibliography linking Wu's name with a book entitled *Hsi-yu-chi* is the *Ch'ien-ch'ing-t'ang shu-mu* by Huang Yü-chi (ECCP), who, however, places it in the geography section among travels. Hence it cannot be entirely ruled out that Wu wrote an account of a journey or voyage which happened to have the same title as the fictional work. The identity of the author of the novel is thus still open to question. As to Wu Ch'eng-en, he probably would have remained in oblivion had it not been for this possibly erroneous ascription.]

Readers of Chinese, not only in China but also in Korea and Japan, have enjoyed the *Hsi-yu-chi*. A Japanese paraphrased edition, started about 1758 by Kutsuki Sannin 口木山人 and continued by others, was completed by Takizawa Bakin 瀧澤馬琴 (1767–1848) under the title *Ehon Seiyūki* 繪本西遊記, and called one of the four remarkable books (*Shidai kisho* 四大奇書). This was included in the Teikoku Bunko 帝國文庫 edition of 1896. Several Japanese translations have been attempted since; the only nearly complete one is the *Chūgoku koten bungaku zenshū* 中國古典文學全集 edition of 1960 by Ōta Tatsuo 太田辰夫 and Torii Hisayasu 鳥居久清. There are also several abridged English versions, of which the best is the one paraphrased by Arthur Waley and published under the title *Monkey* in 1942.

The 1943 edition of *Monkey* includes an introduction by Hu Shih.

Bibliography

Wu Ch'eng-en shih-wen chi, with illustrations showing Wu's calligraphy, Peking, 1958; Lu Hsün, *A Brief History of Chinese fiction*, tr. by Yang Hsien-yi and Gladys Yang (Peking, 1959), 198; *id.*, *Hsiao-shuo chiu-wen ch'ao* 小說舊聞鈔, 56; Hu Shih, "*Hsi-yu-chi* k'ao-cheng" 考證, *Hu Shih wen-ts'un*, II(Taipei,1962), 354; Chao Ts'ung 趙聰, "Ch'ung-yin 重印 *Hsi-yu-chi* hsü 序", *Hsi-yu-chi*, I, Hongkong, 1961; *Hsi-yu-chi yen-chiu lun-wen-chi* 研究論文集, Peking, 1957; Liu Ts'un-yan, "Ssu-yu-chi te Ming-k'o-pen" 西遊記的明刻本, *Hsin-ya hsüeh-pao*, Vol. 2 (1963), 323; Su Hsing 蘇興, "Kuan-yü 關於 *Hsi-yu-chi* te 的 chi-ko 幾個 wen-t'i 問題", in *Wen-hsüeh i-ch'an tseng-k'an* 文學遺產增刊, 10 (1962), 134; Glen Dudbridge, *The Hsi-yu-chi: a study of the Antecedents to the sixteenth-century Chinese novel*, Cambridge, England, 1970; Anthony C. Yu, "Heroic Verse and Heroic Mission: Dimensions of the Epic in the *Hsi-yu-chi*," JAS, 31: 4 (August, 1972), 882.

Liu Ts'un-yan

WU Chung 吳中 (T. 思正 or 司正), 1372–August 3, 1442, a native of Wu-ch'eng 武城, Shantung, served as minister of Works for more than twenty years in the first half of the 15th century. He came from a scholarly family. His grandfather and great-grandfather had served as minor officials in the Yüan dynasty.

In 1398 Wu Chung, then a student in the National University, was named administrator of the rear colony guard at Ying-chou 營州, Peiping. Subsequently he was promoted to be the administrator of the commandery at Ta-ning 大寧. When Chu Ti (*q.v.*) started his rebellion and led his troops to Ta-ning, Wu surrendered and was kept at his post there. Wu was one of a number of northerners who gained Chu Ti's confidence and rose to prominence after the latter ascended the throne. He was employed in a number of positions—in the Peiping provincial administration office, in the Grand Court of

Revision (1403), and in the Censorate (1404). His principal employment, however, was in the ministry of Works, where he held the title of minister off and on from 1407 to 1442.

Within a year of his conquest of Nanking, and in the first month of his reign (1403), Chu Ti renamed his old fief Peking. Over-all development of the new capital was placed under the responsibility of a trusted official, Ch'en Kuei (see Juan An), who was accompanied to the north by the emperor's eldest son. In August, 1406, orders were given to secure lumber from various provinces, gather supplies, assemble work forces, recruit artisans, and cast bricks and tiles so that the construction in Peking could begin the following year. On February 11, 1407, Wu Chung was named minister of Works. Little was accomplished in this early construction effort at Peking, presumably because of the inadequacy of supply transport to north China, and also perhaps because Ming armies were busy in Annam. Wu Chung accompanied the emperor north to Peking in 1410/11 and again in 1415 /16. He helped in the transportation of military supplies during the emperor's expeditions against the Mongols.

In 1416, when the decision was made to commence construction of the western palace at Peking, Wu Chung was still in mourning for his mother. It is said that he told the emperor that it would be inappropriate for him to undertake such an auspicious project while in mourning attire. Probably for this reason he was transferred in September to be minister of Justice, a position which he held all through the construction efforts in Peking. As minister Wu Chung was primarily concerned with providing manpower for grain shipment and labor service, since the commutation of criminal sentences was one of the principal sources of labor available to the throne.

Late in 1421, when the emperor began preparation for his third military campaign beyond the Great Wall, Wu Chung, along with the minister of Revenue, Hsia Yüan-chi (q.v.), and the minister of War, Fang Pin (see Hsia Yüan-chi), objected to the expedition on the grounds that it would be impossible to supply his needs. Wu and Hsia were imprisoned for their insubordination, and Fang Pin committed suicide (December). Wu remained in prison until Chu Ti's death. He was released in September, 1424, as soon as Emperor Chu Kao-chih (q.v.) took the throne, and was restored to his old position as minister of Justice. Two months later he was concurrently made a supervisor of instruction, then transferred to the post of minister of Works and given the honorary title of junior guardian of the heir apparent. Wu held this post with minor interruptions until his death.

Wu was a capable official who spoke his mind at court and was repeatedly and richly rewarded for his service. He was fond of worldly pleasures and accumulated considerable wealth and numerous concubines. He was afraid of his wife, however, who on one occasion at least publicly twitted him about venality. In July, 1428, he was found to have misappropriated building materials for the private use of a eunuch. In consideration of his long service, Emperor Chu Chan-chi (q.v.) treated him leniently, taking away his title as junior guardian and fining him one year's salary.

The principal accomplishments of Wu Chung's career were the construction of palaces in Peking and the first three imperial tombs north of the city. Major reconstruction was undertaken at Peking in the Cheng-t'ung period. Between 1437 and 1439, the builders did extensive work on the outer walls. They erected towers on all of the nine main gates together with enceintes at each of them, and other towers on the four corners of the main wall. Arches were erected outside each gate. They deepened the moat and faced its sides with brick and stone. The old wooden bridges were replaced by stone ones, and nine sluice gates regulated the water as it entered the moat at the northwest corner of the city, circulated the walls, and flowed out at the southeast corner.

Early in 1440 Wu Chung and the censor, Shen Ch'ing 沈清 (created earl in 1441, d. May 12, 1443, Pth. 襄榮), were charged with construction of the palaces. The work force was set at seventy thousand men, civilians and military. The major items of construction were the Feng-t'ien 奉天, Hua-kai 華蓋, and Chin-shen 謹身 audience halls (which had been burned down in 1421), and the Ch'ien-ch'ing 乾清 and Ch'ien-ning 寧 palaces. They completed the work in the autumn of 1441. The principal honors went to the eunuch Juan An, who may have been the over-all planner of the city's construction. Wu was accorded the honor of junior preceptor.

The completion of the palace buildings marked the emergence of Peking as the primary capital of the Ming empire. Although the emperor formalized its primacy in 1421, his decision was reversed by his short-lived successor, Chu Kao-chih; the move back to Nanking, however, was never carried out. Consequently, from 1425 to 1441, official documents referred to government agencies at Peking as part of a "temporary" capital. This usage was changed on November 14, 1441. Such scrupulousness illustrates the extreme importance which the Ming state vested in ceremonial and symbolic forms. Before undertaking reconstruction at Peking, Wu Chung was delegated by the emperor to sacrifice to the spirits of the gates and walls concerned. In building the halls Wu and others conducted sacrifices upon the arrival of the roof beams.

The effort expended in building the palaces may well have left Wu Chung exhausted. He was ill from 1441 on, and, even though he continued to receive a salary as the minister of Works, management of the ministry was taken over by another official in September. In May of the following year, upon completion of the work, he told the emperor that he was still sick and asked to be replaced. The emperor granted his request. Two months later he died. The minister of Rites was sent to honor his spirit, and court business was suspended for one day. He received the posthumous title earl of Ch'ih-p'ing 茌平伯 and the name Jung-hsiang 榮襄. His son, Wu Hsien 賢, was appointed a secretary in the ministry of Works upon his father's death. Another son was made a hereditary centurion in the Embroidered-uniform Guard.

Bibliography

1/111/11a, 151/10b; 5/50/10a; MSL (1963), T'ai-tsung, *ch.* 22–243, Jen-tsung (1963), 24, 147, Hsüan-tsung, 1084, Ying-tsung, *ch.* 54–94.

Edward L. Farmer

WU Hui 吳惠 (T. 孟仁, H. 天樂翁), 1400–July 29, 1468, envoy to Champa in 1441, was born into a peasant family in a village south of Soochow. Owing to the recognition and encouragement of the magistrate, Wu was admitted to the district school. He then became a *chü-jen* in 1426 and achieved the *chin-shih* a year later—the first from his village to acquire such a high honor. His initial appointment was as messenger and he was to become a dedicated, outspoken official.

On July 29, 1441, Wu and Shu T'ung 舒瞳 (cs 1433), the supervising secretary of the messenger office, were appointed special envoys to Champa to invest the regent as the legal successor. The appointments followed the arrival in June of the messenger of Prince Mo-ho-pen-kai 摩訶賁該(Mahā Vijaya, r. 1441–46), a member of the royal family, who informed the court of the death of King Chan-pa-ti-lai 占巴的賴 (Champâdhirâja, also known as Jaya-Simhavarman V, r. 1400–41). The messenger then reported that the officers surrounding the late king's nephew, Mahā Quí-lai 貴來 (r. 1446–49), an infant who was the legal claimant to the throne, agreed to his abdication in favor of the prince who begged to receive the investiture as king of Champa. The court approved and subsequently dispatched the mission.

Accordingly Wu and his partner embarked from Tung-kuan 東莞, Kwangtung, on February 3, 1442, arriving in Champa on the 9th, and left the country on June 13 upon the completion of their assignment. After seven days at sea, when the party reached Ch'i-chou yang 七洲洋 off Hainan Island, the ship was caught in a storm and almost capsized. The crew was frightened, but Wu maintained his composure. As the story has it, Wu wrote a poem and dropped it into the sea as an offer of sacrifice to the goddess of Heaven; a few hours later, the wind subsided and they proceeded on their way, sighting the coast of Kwangtung on the 22d. We owe this precise information to an excerpt from Wu's diary which is fortunately preserved in the *Chen-tse chi-wen* by Wang Ao 王鏊 (*q.v.*). In addition to a day-by-day record of the voyage, Wu left a vivid description of his visit to the royal palace, the investiture ceremony, and the customs of the inhabitants. One which he noted, among other interesting items, was the observation of the shang-yüan (上元) festival on the fifteenth day of the first moon in the lunar calendar (February 25, 1442). This is one of the few surviving eyewitness accounts by a Chinese envoy of his mission to a foreign country since the flurry of diplomatic intercourse in the days of Cheng Ho and Ch'en Ch'eng (*qq. v.*).

On his way back, Wu passed through Wei-hui 衞輝 prefecture, Honan. He found the assessments on land, once cultivated by migrants but now abandoned, to be higher than necessary. At his suggestion the rate of taxation was appropriately reduced. He also found the prefecture to be overburdened by the demands of foreign envoys from western regions en route to Peking. The court, recognizing the correctness of his views, reinforced the regulation limiting the retinue allowed each envy at the Shensi frontier before they were permitted to enter the country.

Having observed the mourning period for his father, who died shortly after his return, Wu was promoted to be the prefect of Kweilin, Kwangsi, a position which he held for ten years (*ca.* 1447-*ca.* 1457). Kweilin was an under-developed prefecture and the scene of frequent revolts of tribespeople. There was, moreover, the custom of settling disputes by dueling with swords or knives; numerous judicial cases also awaited attention. Wu promptly dismissed the cases, freeing all the prisoners involved, and concurrently banning the custom of dueling. Late in 1451, the T'ung 侗 tribes of I-ning 義寧, in collusion with the Miao 苗 tribesmen in southern Hukuang, seemed on the verge of rebellion. The authorities contemplated the use of force, but Wu convinced them to try persuasion. It is said that Wu went to the rebels' camp in person, accompanied by only a score of guards, and succeeded in inducing the chieftain to renounce the plans to revolt.

Meanwhile, another band of rebels from Wu-kang 武岡-chou, Hukuang, crossed the border and seemed on the point of inciting the T'ung people to join them. Wu again ventured into the chieftain's presence and secured his pledge of allegiance. The rebels were thus foiled in their attempt. Late in 1452, however, he received a reprimand from the ministry of War for his defense of Wu I 武毅, the assistant commander-in-chief of Kwangsi, who, having been posted there since 1446, had recently been demoted for his failure to pacify the rebels. In his memorial, Wu Hui pointed out Wu I's meritorious performance and the adverse conditions under which he executed his duties, but the authorities branded Wu Hui as a member of the general's clique and dismissed his plea. His testimony, nevertheless, seems to have produced the desired effect, for two months later the commander was

restored to his former title. Wu Hui
was apparently quite successful in his administration, for reports have it that during
his decade in office Kweilin enjoyed considerable peace. Among his achievements
he received credit for the reprinting, in
1450, of the local gazetteer, *Kwei-lin chün
chih* 郡志, 32 *ch.*, compiled by Ch'en Lien
陳璉 (T. 廷器, H. 琴軒, 1370-1454), during the Hsüan-te period. It is said that,
when the officials of the ministry of
Personnel evaluated the record of the
prefects of the nation, they were so
pleased with Wu's performance that they
ranked him at the top. His service, unhappily, was terminated by the death of
his wife.

Following his term as prefect, Wu
should have been promoted to grade 3A, but
as there was no vacancy, he was appointed
to a 3B post and given a 3A stipend. This
post, assumed in January, 1458, was the
office of administration vice commissioner
of Kwangtung. While he was so employed,
the bandits of Kwangsi, roaming across
the border, constantly made depredations
on the northwestern region of Kwangtung.
In October, 1460, one band attacked Kwangchou 廣州 -fu (Canton), but Wu had
been on the alert and successfully repelled
it with the assistance of the local defense
corps. It is not certain how long he remained in Kwangtung, but he is said to
have asked permission to retire after a
few years in office.

Wu was a man of both courage and
determination, and reportedly also a generous friend, one who would not hesitate
to share his means with his needy clansmen without distinction. Wu left a few
poems which are preserved in the *Ming-
shih chi-shih* 明詩紀事 by Ch'en T'ien (*see*
T'ien Ju-ch'eng). Two pieces deserve attention. One is the poem which he composed
as an offer of sacrifice to the goddess
of Heaven mentioned above; the other
describes his encounter with the Kwangsi
tribesmen. Besides being a poet, he
apparently achieved some success as a
calligrapher.

Bibliography

5/99/24a; 34/3/9b; 64/乙 16/2a; MSL(1963), Ying-
tsung, 1618, 4487, 6101, 6462; TSCC (1885-88),
XI: 601/1/11a; Chu Hao 祝灝 (1405-83), *T'ung-
hsüan chi* 侗軒集 (NCL microfilm), 4/12a; Ts'ai
Yü 蔡羽 (d. 1541), *Lin-wu chi* 林屋集 (NCL
microfilm), 18/3a; Wang Ao, *Ku-su chih* (Taipei,
1965), 52/35b; *id.*, *Chen-tse chi-wen* (Taipei, 1965),
上/25b; *Kwangtung t'ung-chih* (1934), 353; *Kwangsi
t'ung-chih* (Taipei, 1965), 25/20b, 247/9b;
Yen Ts'ung-chien 嚴從簡, *Shu-yü chou-chih lu* 殊
域周知錄 (1934), 7/6b; Chu Yün-ming, *Su-ts'ai
hsiao-tsuan* 蘇材小纂, in Yüan Chiung, *Chin-sheng
yü-chen chi* (Peking, 1959), bk. 5, 29b; *Chung-
kuo pan-k'e t'u-lu* 中國版刻圖錄 (Peking, 1960),
66; Georges Maspero, "Le Royaume de Champa," TP, XIV (1913), 169.

Hok-lam Chan

WU K'uan 吳寬 (T. 原博, H. 匏菴, 玉延
亭主), January 17, 1436-August 19, 1504,
poet and calligrapher, was a native of
Ch'ang-chou 長洲, Nan-Chihli. His grandfather, Wu Shou 壽, and his father, Wu
Yung 融 (T. 孟融, H. 東莊老人, 1399-1475),
were both members of the gentry engaged in the textile business. The family
started to accumulate some wealth under
his father's successful management. Wu
K'uan's elder brother carried on the family
business. Wu K'uan himself and a younger
brother, Wu Hsüan 宣 (H. 拙脩居士, 1438-
85), were encouraged to pursue an education. Wu K'uan came to distinguish himself in classical studies even when he was
a tribute student at the National University. After becoming a *chü-jen* in 1468,
Wu K'uan achieved first place in the *chin-
shih* examinations of 1472. His first appointment was as a compiler in the Hanlin
Academy. When his father died in 1475,
he went home to observe the mourning
rites. Following his return to Peking, he
served again as compiler in the Hanlin;
then, in 1481, he was promoted to be
right chief adviser of the heir apparent,
Chu Yu-t'ang (*q.v.*). After the latter's
enthronement, Wu became left chief secretary of the new heir apparent. In 1490

he took part in the preparation of the veritable records of the preceding emperor, *Hsien-tsung* 憲宗 *shih-lu*, while he held the concurrent positions of grand supervisor of instruction and expositor-in-waiting in the Hanlin. Three years later he became right vice minister of Personnel. When his stepmother died at the end of 1494, he was compelled to retire again, but returned to the capital in 1496 with the same title, and was promoted to be left vice minister in 1498. In 1500 he was assigned the additional concurrent duty of associate editor of the *Ta Ming hui-tien* (*see* Hsü p'u). Upon the completion of this work in January, 1503, he was appointed minister of Rites. In this year he was assigned to the compilation of the *Li-tai t'ung-chien tsuan-yao* (*see* Li Tung-yang). In the following year he requested leave on account of his health, but his plea was ignored. He died soon afterwards, and received the canonized name Wen-ting 文 定 (cultured and serene).

In March, 1495, after the death of Ch'iu Chün (*q.v.*), Wu K'uan should have been selected, both by merit and seniority, to succeed him in the Grand Secretariat, but, because Wu was still in mourning, Hsieh Ch'ien (*q.v.*) and Li Tung-yang were appointed. Upon his return to the capital in 1496, Hsieh Ch'ien spoke earnestly on Wu's behalf, hoping that he would also be appointed; but Wu was never elevated to the Secretariat. In fact, during his thirty-year service in the bureaucracy, even though he was noted for his integrity and literary excellence, others often passed him in securing promotions. Many of his friends were indignant, but Wu remained serene and unperturbed. In an account in which he gives his reasons for the selection of P'ao-an 匏菴 as his *hao*, he reveals clearly his modesty and his philosophy of life. According to him, P'ao (bottle gourd) has two different meanings. On one hand, it is an utterly useless thing—something which can be suspended as a decoration, but cannot be eaten. On the other hand, it is of use

since one can cross a river on it. Moreover, since, when struck, it produces one of the eight musical sounds 八音, and also is the material for making a reed-organ 笙簧, it can be employed at court or in the ancestral temple of the imperial family. It is therefore useful. He thus named his dwelling place P'ao-an and consequently made it his cognomen. He took the "uselessness" to symbolize himself and the "usefulness" as a personal goal to which he aspired.

While he was serving in the Hanlin he built a garden and a pavilion called Yü-yen-t'ing 玉延亭, east of his house. There he planted trees and flowers, and there he would sometimes go to read. At other times he invited friends who would compose poems with him. On one occasion, June 12, 1499, he joined with nine other respected officials in a function at the Bamboo Garden belonging to Chou Ching (*q.v.*). An even-tempered man, Wu was loved and admired for his non-partisan attitude, his understatements, and his compassion for the weak and the poor. When his childhood friend, Ho En 賀恩 (the top *chü-jen* in the provincial examination of 1468), became very ill in the capital, Wu took him home, and personally attended to his needs day and night. After Ho's death, he observed a mourning period of one month. His family had an estate of several hundred *mou* in Ch'ang-chou. At the time of the yearly collection of rents, he often helped ease the financial burden of his poor relatives and acquaintances by giving out parts of his share of the land. His portrait appears among the nine grandees in the volume *Chu-yüan shou-chi-t'u* (*see* Chou Ching).

Unlike that of his contemporaries who wrote in highly mannered styles, such as the t'ai ko-t'i (*see* Li Tung-yang), Wu's prose and poetry are unadorned and simple. They are marked by a natural grace. A great admirer of Su Shih (1037–1101), perhaps the finest of the Sung poets and calligraphers, Wu displayed skill in calligraphy which clearly show his debt

to Su Shih, while at the same time he did
not slavishly imitate him. In other words,
he developed a style of his own. A very
rare example, a collection of six of his
poems in his own handwriting, entitled
Wu K'uan chung chu shih 種竹詩, was
reprinted in Shanghai in 1964. Among his
literary works, he is remembered for his
P'ao-weng chia-ts'ang chi 匏翁家藏集, 77＋1
ch. A copy of this is in the Naikaku Bunko, Tokyo. The *P'ing-wu lu* 平吳錄, 1 *ch*.,
an account of the rise and fall of Chang
Shih-ch'eng (*q.v.*) from 1353 to 1368, is
also credited to him.

Bibliography

1/184/11b; 3/168/8a; 5/18/3a; 6/2/9a, 7/5a, 13b,
12/27b, 13/9b, 19/22b, 20/8a, 30b, 45/12b; 12/21/
6b; 16/16/2a, 29/33b; 40/24/24b; 43/2/4b; 61/128/
22a; 84/丙/30b; Shen I-kuan, *Ming chuang-yüan
t'u-k'ao*, 上/51; *Chiang-nan t'ung-chih* 江南通志
(1736), 148/10b; *P'ao-weng chia-ts'ang chi* (SPTK
ed.); MSL (1964), Wu-tsung, 1064.

Lee Hwa-chou

WU Kuo-lun 吳國倫 (T. 明卿, H. 川樓, 南
嶽山人), February 25, 1524-July 21, 1593,
poet, essayist, and official, was a native
of Hsing-kuo-chou 興國州, Hukuang, his
ancestors belonging to the military category. His elder brother, a successful business man, supported Wu Kuo-lun in his
studies; moreover, he found a bride for
him from the Ch'en 陳 family. Shortly
after the marriage, this brother died but
the young wife helped him continue his
studies by selling her dowry and jewelry.
Wu Kuo-lun, however, was fond of gam-
bling. In anger she burned his gaming
equipment and scolded him. This had the
desired effect. He studied harder and in
1549 took first place in the provincial
examination, graduated as *chin-shih* the
following year, and was made a drafter
in the central drafting office in 1551. The
position was then a clerical one. Because
of his obvious qualifications, both Yen
Sung and Hsü Chieh (*qq.v.*) planned to
promote him, but at this juncture his
wife died, so he received permission to
go home for the funeral. On his return,
Wu was promoted to the position of supervising secretary in the War ministry
with the help of Yen Sung and his son.
While in this post he dared to criticize
Yen, and in 1555 joined Wang Shih-chen
(*q.v.*) in defending Yang Chi-sheng (*q.v.*)
for his courageous action in accusing Yen
of major crimes against the state. For this
he was transferred out of the capital and
his ensuing posts were in the provinces.
The first was as clerk of surveillance commission, Kiangsi, the next as prefectural
judge of Nan-k'ang 南康 in the same
province. Despite his demotion he was
philosophical enough to enjoy life. He
traveled much in the area. Yen Sung
wanted to dismiss him, but Hsü Chieh supported him and had him shifted to Kuei-te
歸德, Honan, where he served in the same
capacity for two years. He then returned
home.

On the ousting of Yen Sung as chief
grand secretary (1562), Wu came back
into official life as, successively, vice prefect of Chien-ning 建寧, Fukien, and prefect of Shao-wu 邵武 (also in Fukien).
He was considerate and fair and paid
much attention to education there. In the
year 1564 he enlarged and rebuilt the
provincial college in Shao-wu. In this post
he had his parents honored with the official title of his own rank. He also had
his deceased wife (Ch'en-shih) and his
new wife (Shu-shih 舒氏) honored with
the title kung-jen 恭人. Next he became
prefect of Kao-chou 高州, Kwangtung
(1569-71), where he was known as a strict
official. At this southern river port he
distinguished himself in the defense of
the city against outlaws and pirates. When
he decided to fight as leader at the front,
he said farewell to his wife and gave his
family servant a package of his writings,
asking him to send it to a friend in case
he died. Kao-chou was eventually saved,
and Wu was praised by the townspeople,
who erected a shrine in his honor while

he was still alive. He had two more appointments, both brief; one as surveillance vice commissioner in Kweichow (1572) and then, as left vice commissioner of Honan before he was cashiered on the occasion of the national scrutiny. He spent the rest of his life in literary activity and came to be known as one of the seven later masters along with Li P'an-lung (*q.v.*), Wang Shih-chen, and others.

During his retirement Wu built a garden named Pei-yüan 北園, the first garden existing in his native place. It served as a literary salon where he played the role of generous host and where much literary activity took place. Pei-yüan was located at the foot of Shih-shan 獅山 (Lion Mountain) to the north of Hsing-kuo-chou and was bordered by two lakes, Ts'ang-lang hu 滄浪湖, and Fu-ch'uan 富川 hu. There was already a pond of about 100 *mou* called Hsiao 小 Ts'ang-lang in the garden, but he made another pond by diverting water from the Ts'ang-lang lake. In the center of this artificial pond, in addition to a rock which stood there, he arranged more stones into three ranges of thirty-six peaks, called Hu-ling 壺嶺. The hollows in the latter were called Tan-sui tung 甔甀洞 and that is why he entitled his anthology *Tan-sui-tung kao* 稿. He also built two small bridges to reach the two islands in the pond. Then he acquired a boat to sail around Hu-ling with literary friends. Sometimes they rowed out to the Fu-ch'uan lake in the moonlight. He also constructed pavilions one of which was built in the middle of the lake known as Hsia-ou-t'ing 狎鷗亭 (Playing with gulls pavilion). The title derives from a Taoist allusion ascribed to a passage in the original *Chuang-tzu*. So here we find in him Taoist manifestations which are in strong contrast to his former official attitudes. This is shown even more strikingly on the occasion of the death of his second wife in 1592. When burying her, besides making an open grave for himself on her left, he wrote on the two pillars

of the tomb pavilion a couplet concerning two literary figures, T'ao Ch'ien (375?–427) and Liu Ling (221–300), known for their Taoist understanding of life and death. His end came the following year (1593), after he had enjoyed a longer life span than any of the other members of his literary group. In 1614, twenty-one years after his death, on the recommendation of the prefect Kao Wei-yüeh 高維岳 (T. 君翰, cj 1573), his name was listed among those who were to receive sacrifices at the shrine in honor of local worthies.

Wu was not only a prose artist but also a poet. He was known for his five- and seven-word regular poems. As one of the most popular writers of his time, he was invited to indite many epitaphs for his contemporaries. Most of his literary pieces are included in his anthology *Tan-sui-tung kao*, 54 *ch.*, and *hsü* 續 *kao*. The work was prohibited two centuries later, but has survived, at least in part. The National Central Library in Taipei and several libraries in Japan possess incomplete copies. A few other writings were collected in the *Wu-ch'uan-lou* 吳川樓 *chi*, 1 *ch.*, and the *Hsü Wu-ch'uan-lou chi*, 1 *ch.*, and may now be found in the *Sheng Ming pai-chia shih ch'ien-pien* 盛明百家詩前編 and *hou-pien* 後編. Besides these, he also wrote two short historical works, one on the rebellions of Ch'en Yu-liang and Chang Shih-ch'eng (*qq.v.*), and another on that of Fang Kuo-chen (*q.v.*), entitled respectively *Ch'en Chang pen-mo lüeh* 陳張本末略, 1 *ch.*, and *Fang Kuo-chen pen-mo lüeh*, 1 *ch.* They were both criticized as unreliable by the editors of the *Ssu-k'u* catalogue. The former is now available in several collectanea.

Bibliography

1/287 /17a; 3/268/14a; 40/46/30a; 64/己 2/15a; 84/丁上/58a; 86/13/42a; TSCC (1885–88), XXIII: 106/94/8b,113/101/12a; *Hsing-kuo-chou chih*(1889), 1/2b, 3/13b, 15a, 14/8a, 21b, 20/9b, 32/6b, 34/16a, 19a, 59a, 35/2a, 4a, 5b, 8a, 9a, 23b, 31a; *Kwang-*

tung t'ung-chih (1934), 4376; *Kuei-te-fu chih* (1893),
4/2b; *Shao-wu-fu chih* (1897), 12/2b, 14/6b; *Kao-chou-fu chih* (1889), 19/13a; *Kweichow t'ung-chih* (1741), 17/23b; SK (1930), 66/9b; Sun Tien-ch'i (1957)239; Yamane and Ogawa, *Ming-jen wen-chi mu-lu* 明人文集目錄(Tokyo, 1966), 39; *Huang Ming wen-hai* (microfilm), 9/7/16, 10/7/7, 8, 11/4/5, 12/1/13, 13/2/9, 8/11, 14/8/4, 15/6/5, 19/3/25; Wang Shu-min 王叔岷, *Chuang-tzu chiao-shih* 莊子校釋 (Shanghai, 1947), 1; *Hsüan-ch'eng* 宣城 *-hsien chih* (1888), 13/28b, 18/12a; NCL *Catalogue of Rare Rooks*, 1079; Seikado Bunko *Catalogue*, 730; Naikaku Bunko *Catalogue*, 354.

L. Carrington Goodrich and Yang Chin-yi

WU No 吳訥 (T. 敏德, 克敏, H. 思庵),
1372–April 9, 1457, official, practitioner
of medicine, and thinker, was a native of
Ch'ang-shu 常熟, in the lower Yangtze
delta. His father, while an assistant magistrate of Yüan-ling 沅陵, Hukuang, was
arrested after false accusations, and sent
to prison in Nanking (*ca.* 1392). Wu No
hastened to the capital to enter an appeal
offering to take his father's place. But
he was too late; the father died in prison
before the case could be settled. To add
to his misfortunes, Wu No's stepmother
and grandmother likewise passed away.
He did not allow these losses, however,
to interfere with his studies, and he
gradually achieved some reputation both
as scholar and physician. Although offered
the post of assistant instructor in two
local schools he declined. Later on, as a
result of recommendations by local authorities, for his skill as a physician, he was
summoned to Nanking, where he was
received with favor by the heir apparent,
Chu Kao-chih (*q. v.*), and established
himself as an instructor, tutoring the sons
of officials of rank in Nanking. Even the
emperor (Chu Ti, *q.v.*), is reported to
have taken some notice of him, making
him an adviser during the last years of
his reign. On the accession of Chu Kao-
chih (1425) Wu received an appointment
as censor in Peking. Later he served as
inspecting censor in Chekiang and Kwei-

chow. By the year 1430 he was promoted
to junior assistant censor-in-chief in Nanking and in 1435 became senior vice censor-in-chief and acting censor-in-chief.

The care with which he performed
his duties, together with his incorruptibility, gained him not only a good reputation but also trouble. He tried to protect
law-abiding officials and bring to justice
those who were not. In the early years of
the Cheng-t'ung period he impeached
Tung Cheng 董正, an assistant minister
in the Court of Imperial Entertainment,
for misappropriation of public goods.
Forty-four officials involved in the matter
were punished. When he cautioned Li
Chen 李畛, a junior transmission commissioner, to be more careful in his work,
the latter struck back with counter charges, accusing Wu of delaying imperial
mandates. Both received prison sentences
late in 1437, but were released not long
afterwards. Wu No retired from public
office in 1441 and gave himself up to
study and writing in his native place.

Though respected for his knowledge
of medicine, he himself was much more
interested in philosophy. The life he lived
was a frugal one, and he demanded the
same of his associates. One day, when his
grandson, Wu Ch'un 淳 (T. 原伯, cs 1448),
also a censor, appeared wearing silk
clothes, he ordered him to change to
cotton dress. On another occasion, when
the same grandson returned to the vicinity
of his home on official business, Wu No
would not allow him to stay at home on
the ground that public affairs should be
his first concern. To promote the thought
of the Sung school, he edited the *Hsiao-
hsüeh chi-chieh* 小學集解 (Collected commentaries on the *Hsiao-hsüeh* of Chu Hsi),
10 *ch.*, and submitted it to the emperor,
Chu Ch'i-chen (*q. v.*). A copy of this in
6 *chüan* is preserved in the Kiangsu Provincial Library. He also compiled and
edited Chu Hsi's poems and essays, entitled
Wen-kung shih-wen ch'ao 文公詩文鈔, as
well as an edition of the writings of the
philosopher Wu Ch'eng (1249–1333), *Wu*

WU Pin

[1492]

Wen-cheng wen-ts'ui 吳文正文粹. Another
philosophical work, his commentaries on
various writings by the Sung thinkers, is
the *Hsing-li ch'ün-shu pu-chu* 性理羣書補注.
Only 6 *chüan* of this book are extant. Wu
has likewise to his credit a literary collection, the *Wen-chang pien-t'i* 文章辨體, 50
ch., with a supplement in 5 *chüan*. It is
an anthology of prose and poetry, pre-
Ming and early Ming, grouped according
to their genres, with explanations. As Wu
himself acknowledged, it was modeled
after the *Wen-chang cheng-tsung* 正宗 of
the Sung thinker, Chen Te-hsiu (1178-
1235). Wu's own writings were published
as the *Ssu-an hsien-sheng* 思庵先生 *wen-ts'ui*,
11 *ch.*

Another of Wu's interests was the
judicial process; to that end he brought
out an edition of the *T'ang-yin pi-shih* 棠
陰比事 originally compiled by Kuei Wan-
jung (cs 1196) in 1211, and published
around 1222 and 1234. (This has been
rendered into English by R. H. van Gulik.)
Wu reduced Kuei's 144 cases to 80, and
rearranged the order according to the
seriousness of the offenses committed; he
also deleted an earlier commentary and
added a shorter and less helpful one of
his own. His sequel consisted of 23 cases
of his own selection. His final text, dated
1442, contained 27 additional cases, which
he incorporated in his *Hsiang-hsing yao-
lan* 祥刑要覽, 2 *ch.* This work was meant
to be useful for administrators and judges.

Following his death at the age of
eighty-five, Wu No was canonized as
Wen-k'o 文恪 and his tablet, together with
that of Chang Hung 洪(*q. v.*), was placed
in the shrine honoring Yen-tzu-yu, the
disciple of Confucius, in Ch'ang-shu. His
great-grandson, Wu T'ang 堂 (T. 子升, cs
1499), served for a time as the vice minister of the Grand Court of Revision.

Bibliography

1/58/8a; 3/148/6a; 5/64/49a,50a; 8/19/14a; *Ch'ang-
Chao ho-chih* 常昭合志 (1898), 8/42b, 12/70b;
Ch'ang-Chao ho-chih kao 稿 (1904), 24/11a; SK
(1930), 101/3a, 5a, 191/7b; MSL (1963), Ying-
tsung, 0709; Wu No, *Hsing-li ch'ün-shu pu-chu*
(Ming ed.), NLP microfilm, no. 565; *id.*, *Wen-
chang pien-t'i hsü-shuo* 序說 (Hong Kong reprint),
1965; Wang Shih-chen, "Wu Wen-k'o kung No
chuan-tsan" 贊, *Huang Ming wen-hai* (microfilm),
ch. 68; NCL *Catalogue of Rare Books* (Taipei,
1967), 3, 1010; R. H. van Gulik, *T'ang-yin-pi-
shih, Parallel Cases from under the Pear Tree*
(*Leiden, 1956*), 22, 66, 191.

Huang P'ei and Julia Ching

WU Pin 吳彬 (T. 文中, or 仲, H. 質先),
fl. 1591-1626, painter of landscapes and
figures, was a native of P'u-t'ien 莆田 in
Fukien. The dates of his birth and death are
unknown; his works, however, belong to
the period given above. A painting bearing a date equivalent to 1568, attributed
to him in a catalogue, seems to be too
early to be authentic. Judging from extant
paintings, his early training must have
been in the landscape styles of the Wu
吳 school (the tradition of Wen Cheng-
ming, *q.v.*, and other Soochow artists) and
Buddhist figure painting of a traditional
kind. During the early part of the Wan-li
reign, probably in the 1570s, he was called
to the southern court at Nanking and
given the position of drafter in the central drafting office. According to another
source he held the position of secretary
of a bureau in the ministry of Works.
Emperor Chu I-chün (*q.v.*) is said to have
admired his paintings. On one occasion
Wu memorialized the emperor, saying:
"The only scenery that your subject has
had a chance to see is the mountains and
valleys of the south; his vision is restricted to that region. He desires to travel to
Shu 蜀 (Szechwan) in the west to see
the scenery of the Chien Pass 劍門, the
Min 岷 and O 峨 [-mei 眉] Mountains.
His painting might well then attain
some new perceptions." His request was
granted; he made the trip, after which
his painting became "even more remarkable than before."

He probably executed for the court such works in a finely detailed manner as the handscroll "Greeting the spring" (dated 1600, now in the Cleveland Museum of Art) and a famous album of landscapes with figures representing festivals of the twelve months (now in the National Palace Museum, Taipei). He also specialized in paintings of arhats, whom he represented with a grotesquerie that seems to reflect a partly facetious archaism. Extant examples include a hanging scroll representing arhats in a landscape, dated 1601, and an album of pictures of arhats (both in the National Palace Museum).

At the Nanking court he came into contact with other painters, notably Mi Wan-chung (ECCP), who were attempting to revive in their works the monumental landscape tradition of the Northern Sung period, and earlier. This direction in painting was consciously opposed to the Southern Sung doctrine of Tung Ch'i-ch'ang (ECCP). Mi Wan-chung "questioned and learned from Wu Pin morning and night, so that their manners of painting grew to be similar." From certain passages in Wu's painting, it is apparent that he was aware of European art, probably through the prints and paintings brought to China by Matteo Ricci (q.v.), who was in Nanking during the last years of the 16th century.

Beginning some time in the first decade of the 17th century, Wu Pin painted the landscapes that are his major surviving works. Ostensibly done in imitation of early masters of the monumental landscape, they in fact introduce to painting a new element of fantasy, forcing geological formations beyond the bounds of possibility to a point where they can be experienced only as visions of a dream world, or an interior landscape. Excellent examples are in the National Palace Museum in Taipei (*Ku-kung shu-hua chi*故宮書畫集, no. 34, dated 1609, and another in the same volume, mistakenly captioned "Anonymous Sung") and in the Hashimoto

Collection, Takatsuki, Japan (dated 1615).

During the T'ien-ch'i era Wu Pin fell victim to the political tension of the time. Upon reading the decree, posted on a city gate, which apparently the eunuch, Wei Chung-hsien (ECCP), issued on his own authority, Wu expressed his disapproval aloud and was overheard by a spy. He was seized and imprisoned, and his rank and salary stripped from him. Nothing is known of his fate thereafter.

Although Wu Pin's works were evidently much in demand during his lifetime, he has been undervalued by most critics, both Chinese and foreign. Chinese writers generally stress the technical skill and decorative aspects of his painting, as does Sirén.

As a painter of figures, he was given faint praise as being "able to hold his own against Ting Yün-p'eng" (q.v.), who is actually a far less original and interesting master. One who held a higher opinion of him was his contemporary and fellow provincial, Hsieh Chao-che (q.v.), who in his *Wu tsa tsu* writes: "Wu sets his thoughts in motion and creates unusual scenes; the products of his brush are mysterious and fine. When he comes to do figures and Buddhist images, even though he doesn't presume to approach the level of [Wu] Tao-tzu [d. 792] in the distant past, his strength suffices to match [Chao] Sung-hsüeh [Meng-fu, 1254–1322] in the recent past. When [Wu's art] passes on to future generations it will undoubtedly be worth [the ransom of] two cities." Also "In recent times, Wu Wen-chung 文中 [Pin] alone has learned from [the figure painters] Ku [K'ai-chih, 344-406?], and Lu [T'an-wei, *ca.* 440-500]; the place of prominence in his century will assuredly belong to this man." [Editors' note: Three examples of landscapes and one of flora by Wu Pin have also been reproduced in the fourth (Ming) volume of *Chung-kuo li-tai ming-hua chi* 中國歷代名畫集 (Palace Museum, Peking, 1965) and in *T'ien-ching-shih i-shu po-wu-kuan ts'ang-hua chi* 天津市藝術博物舘藏畫集 (1963). In comparing Wu with Tung

Ch'i-ch'ang, Hsieh Chao-che remarks that while Tung imitated earlier artists Wu was original and creative. Any judgment of Wu's art, however, seems to be premature without a study of his painting of figures on which Hsieh has lavished such high praise. Hsieh's prediction that Wu was going to be recognized as the leading artist of his century was not fulfilled. It was definitely Tung's century.]

Bibliography

P'u-t'ien-hsien chih (1758), 30/2b; *Fukien t'ung-chih* quoted in *P'ei-wen-chai shu-hua p'u* 佩文齋書畫譜, 57/27b; *Hua-shih ts'ung-shu* 畫史叢書 (1963), I; Hsieh Chao-che, *Wu tsa tsu*, VII (Chung-hua shu-chü reprint, p. 196). *See* Hsü Pang-ta 徐邦達, *Li-tai liu-ch'uan shu-hua tso p'in pien-nien-piao* 歷代流傳書畫作品編年表 (1963), 90, and Kuo Wei-ch'ü 郭味蕖, *Sung Yüan Ming Ch'ing shu-hua chia nien-piao* 宋元明清書畫家年表 (1958 index, p. 18), for lists of dated works, extant or recorded; *see also* Osvald Sirén, *Chinese Painting*, Vol. V, p. 49, Vol. VI, pl. 298, and Vol. VII, p. 269 (New York 1956-58) and E. J. Laing, *Chinese Paintings in Chinese publications, 1956-68* (Ann Arbor, 1969), 206, for lists of known exant works, to which many more can be added.

James Cahill

WU Sheng 吳甡 (T. 鹿友, H. 岢愚, 柴庵), 1589-1644+, a native of Hsing-hua 興化, prefecture of Yangchow, was one of the fifty grand secretaries of the Ch'ung-chen period (1628-44). A *chü-jen* of 1609 and a *chin-shih* of 1613, he became magistrate of Shao-wu 邵武, Fukien, for three years. At the end of his first term of office he received the most favorable grade. After an imperial audience early in 1616, he was promoted to the magistracy of Chin-chiang 晉江, Fukien, a more important district. In the middle of the same year, his father having died, he retired to observe the mourning rites. At their conclusion (1619) he became magistrate of Wei-hsien 濰縣, Shantung.

Early in the T'ien-ch'i reign, Wu Sheng was selected to go to Peking to wait for appointment in the central government, and within a few months (1622) was made a censor. Before long, however, he found himself at odds with the all-powerful eunuch Wei Chung-hsien (ECCP), and late in 1623 was back at home ostensibly to care for his aging mother. On the accession of Chu Yu-chien (ECCP) as emperor in 1628, he was reinstated as censor. The following year he went on an inspection tour of Honan, and in 1631 supervised relief work in Shensi. After successive promotions, he became governor of Shansi, coordinating and commanding the military forces of the Yen-men 鴈門 pass and the northern border. While in Shensi, he made the acquaintance of Shih K'o-fa (ECCP), and later in Shansi of Yüan Chi-hsien (ECCP), both of whom later became renowned as Ming loyalists. Wu regarded them highly and was responsible for recommending them to the court; both came to his rescue when he was in trouble some years later.

Because of his success in administration and in defense, Wu Sheng earned a reputation as a military expert. By 1638 he became junior vice minister of War and in 1640 senior vice minister, and two years later was given the special charge of overseeing the troops stationed in and around the capital. About the same time (July 16, 1642) he was elevated to be grand secretary and concurrently minister of Rites. In April of the following year, on his transfer to head the ministry of War, the emperor ordered Wu to be commander-in-chief to put down rebels who were then overrunning central China. Without an army of his own, he realized how impossible the mission was. He therefore begged for time to assemble a military force. For his apparent hesitancy he was accused of cowardice. His appointment was recalled and he was forced to retire (July 7)). A few months later in 1643, the emperor decided that he deserved harsher punishment; so he exiled Wu to Chin-ch'ih 金齒, a garrison outpost on the extreme border of Yunnan.

In the meantime the political condition of the whole country was deteriorating. When Wu reached Kiangsi on his way to the southwest, his old friend Yüan Chi-hsien, then governor general of several provinces, persuaded him to stay at Nan-k'ang 南康, and wait for changes in the situation. Peking fell shortly afterwards (April, 1644). A few months later the Ming government at Nanking granted him full pardon. Apparently Wu lived quietly at home under the succeeding dynasty until his death.

His sons, Wu Yüan-lai 元萊 (T. 北海) and Wu Hsiang-feng 翔鳳 (T. 夢祥, 珏園), are both recorded in the local history of their native place, the *Hsing-hua-hsien chih.* The elder was a *kung-sheng* of 1660 and officiated in both Peking and the metropolitan area in the Shun-chih period (1644-61), while the younger became known for his literary ability and for his painting.

Wu Sheng left several works. The *Ch'ai-an shu chi* 柴庵疏集, 20 *ch.*, probably the most important, is a collection of his memorials, arranged chronologically, printed in 1644 in south China. To this work are appended two other items, the *Wu-yen* 寤言 (miscellaneous notes), 2 *ch.*, and the *I-chi* 憶記 (a memoir), 4 *ch.* The memoir, dated August/September, 1644, was written apparently for the primary purpose of vindicating himself for his cautious attitude when given the military command. Yet this short work offers information too on the last days of the Ming dynasty. Certain data, such as the local conditions at Shao-wu at the time of his magistracy, and his description of the Wen-yüan hall 文淵閣 in the Ch'ung-chen years, provide interesting sidelights. These three works were all proscribed in the 1780s but copies are available in Taipei, and on microfilm.

The editors of the *Ssu-k'u* Catalogue (ts'un-mu 存目 section) draw attention to his work on famous ministers and generals who flourished from Han to Sung times, entitled *An-wei chu* 安危注, 4 *ch.*, which emphasized the different responsibilities of civil and military officials. It upheld the theory that while the country is at peace it is the civil officials' responsibility to rule, but when the country is in danger it is the military officials' responsibility to defend and pacify. If this is true, the *An-wei chu* must also have been composed for the purpose of vindicating himself, and so must have been written in or after 1644.

Shih K'o-fa, who contributed a preface to Wu Sheng's memoir, the *I-chi*, also submitted a memorial on Wu's behalf in 1643 (the text being included both in the memoir and in the *Ch'ai-an shu chi*). These two pieces, however, are not found in Shih's collected works. For future students of Shih's writings, their discovery in Wu Sheng's memoir may be of some interest.

Bibliography

1/252/14a; 64/庚 23/1a; MSL(1967), Ch'ung-chen period; KC (1958), 5930, 5967, 5977; *I-chi*, 1645; *Ch'ai-an shu chi*, 1644; SK (1930), 62/6a; *Hsing-hua-hsien chih* (1852), 列傳 8/15a, 27b, 文苑 8b, 9/書目 3a, 古文 13b; Li Fu-tso 李福祚 (compiler), *Chao-yang shu-chiu pien* 昭陽逑舊編 (Hsien-feng period, 1851-62), 1/9b; Sun Tien-ch'i (1957), 117, 219; C. O. Hucker, *The Censorial System of Ming China* (Stanford, 1966), 220, 224.

Lienche Tu Fang

WU T'i 吳悌 (T. 思誠, H. 疏山), 1502–1568, official, cartographer, thinker, was born in Chin-ch'i 金谿, Fu-chou-fu 撫州府, Kiangsi, the prefecture famous as the birthplace too of Lu Chiu-yüan (1139–93). In 1531 he passed the provincial examinations and obtained the *chin-shih* the following year. His first assignment was as magistrate of Lo-an 樂安, Shantung, where he remained one year. His service in Hsüan-ch'eng 宣城 (south of Nanking) is remembered particularly for his aid in a time of famine; he brought in grain from elsewhere, and made it available for purchase. In 1537, as censor in Kwangsi, he frequently made suggestions for improvement in administration. On one occasion when the court was displeased with the results of an examination held in Nanking, allegedly because of veiled criticisms in the papers submitted, Wu T'i lodged a memorial with the emperor pleading the cause of the examination candidates who had been forbidden to sit for the metropolitan examination in Peking. For this he himself was put in prison, but in the course of time his suggestion was adopted. Two years later Wu was back in office, and dispatched to the region north of the Yangtze delta to inspect the salt monopoly. There he made friends with the philosopher Wang Ken (*q.v.*), whom he recommended for office, but in vain. As the people in the area were suffering from a flood and consequent deficiencies, he made a distribution of rice destined for tribute without troubling to gain imperial permission. After this he resigned to take care of his mother.

In 1543 he returned to Peking, and received an appointment as a censor. This was the era when Yen Sung and Hsia Yen (*qq.v.*) held the reins of power in the central government. Though they were his fellow-provincials, Wu refrained from making contact with them, and even handed in his resignation, remaining out of office for over twenty years. Not until 1566 did he return to public life, at the persuasion of the local authorities. He served a brief term as censor in Shansi, then was quickly promoted as vice minister of the Court of Imperial Sacrifices, as chief minister of the Court of the Imperial Stud in Nanking, and finally of the Grand Court of Revision there, all within a year. There were at that time in Nanking three men of distinction serving in the ministries of Personnel and Justice, namely: Hu Sung (*see* Cheng Jo-tseng), who rose to be minister of Personnel in Peking during the last six months of his life, and was canonized as 莊肅; Mao K'ai 毛愷 (T. 達和, 遠和,

H. 介川, 節齋居士, December 26, 1506–October 8, 1570, cs 1535), who served as minister of Justice in Peking from 1567 to 1570, and was canonized as 端簡; and Wu Yüeh 吳嶽 (T. 汝喬, 1504–70, cs 1532), who became minister of Personnel in Nanking, and was canonized as 介肅. These three, together with Wu T'i, came to be known as "Nan-tu ssu chün-tzu" 南都四君子 (the four gentlemen of Nanking). After the accession to the throne of Chu Tsai-hou (*q.v.*) in 1567, Wu was made junior vice minister of Justice in the subordinate capital, remaining there until his death the following year.

Wu T'i published in 1536 a map of the Ming empire entitled *Huang Ming yü-ti chih t'u* 皇明輿地之圖. It was reprinted in 1631 by Sun Ch'i-shu 孫起樞. Two copies of this second edition are known to be extant, both in Japanese libraries, one at the Sendai Tōhoku University and the other at the Ise Jingū. He also left one book entitled *Wu Shu-shan chi* 疏山集, 17 *ch.* According to the Imperial Catalogue this work originally was one of 3 *chüan*, to which his disciple, Li Yüeh 李約, added a fourth recording his words and deeds; the rest is due to later compilers. There is, however, a 12 *chüan* version extant in Tokyo University's Tōyō Bunka Kenkyūsho 東洋文化研究所, entitled *Wu Shu-shan hsien-sheng i* 遺 *chi*.

Fifty-three years after his death Wu T'i was canonized as Wen-chuang 文莊. The people of Fu-chou, Kiangsi, erected a shrine, known as Wu-hsien tz'u 五賢祠 (Hall of five sages), at which he was accorded sacrifices along with Lu Chiu-yüan, Wu Ch'eng (1249–1333), Wu Yü-pi (*q.v.*), and Ch'en Chiu-ch'uan 陳九川 (T. 惟濬, H. 明水, 1494–1562, cs 1514).

His son, Wu Jen-tu 仁度 (T. 元重, 繼疏, cs 1599), first became a drafter in the central drafting office, then a director in the ministry of Justice in Nanking, and finally, after a number of promotions, the governor of Shansi, where he served for four years until sickness forced his resignation late in 1616. In 1621 he was recalled to Peking and in 1624 became junior vice minister of Works. As his sympathies lay with the members of the Tung-lin party (*see* Ku Hsien-ch'eng), he fell into the bad graces of the eunuchs in power and was forced out.

Bibliography

1/283/19b; 5/25/50a, 27/44a, 42/92a, 45/49b, 54b, 49/35a, 94/75a; 15/6/43a; 83/19/28a; SK (1930), 60/3b; *Huang Ming wen-hai* (microfilm), 7. 2. 8; *Kiangsi t'ung-chih* (1880-81 ed.), 153/3b; *Fu-chou-fu chih* (1876), 51/15a, 56/15b; *Shantung t'ung-chih* (1934), 2379; *Shansi t'ung-chih* (1892), 12/11b; Hirosi Nakamura, "Les cartes du Japon qui servaient de modèle aux cartographes européens au début des relations de l'Occident avec le Japon," *Monumenta Nipponica*, 11: 1 (1939), 104, 121 (n. 20), and fig. 2.

Huang P'ei and Julia Ching

WU Yü-pi 吳與弼 (T. 子傳, H. 康齋), January 6, 1392-November 20, 1469, thinker, was born into an official-scholar family of Ch'ung-jen 崇仁, Fu-chou 撫州 prefecture, Kiangsi. His ancestors, who came from Honan, began to settle in the Fu-chou area in the 10th century. His grandfather was the first to move to Ch'ung-jen. His father, Wu P'u 溥 (T. 德潤, H. 古厓, 1363 -October 3, 1426), passed first in the metropolitan examination of 1400, fourth on the *chin-shih* list, and was appointed a Hanlin compiler by the ill-fated emperor Chu Yün-wen (*q.v.*). Two years later the rebel prince, Chu Ti (*q.v.*), conquered the capital city and usurped the throne. Wu P'u joined the new court and was raised to be a first class compiler in the Hanlin Academy. It is said that the promotion was the reward for his participation in the compilation of the first revised edition of the *T'ai-tsu shih-lu* of 1403 (*see* Hsieh Chin). Late in 1404 he was named one of the twenty deputy chief compilers of the *Yung-lo ta-tien* (*see* Yao Kuang-hsiao). From October, 1408, to the day he died (eighteen years) he served as the director

of studies in the National University at Nanking, earning the reputation of a devoted teacher who remained poor.

Wu Yü-pi was three years old when his father left home to study in the National University. It seems that at about this time his mother died and his father remarried. When he went to Nanking in 1402, he and his father at first hardly recognized each other. He then studied under him for seven years in preparation for the civil examinations. This instruction was interrupted in 1409 when Wu Yü-pi, at nineteen *sui*, suddenly renounced any further participation in the civil examinations. The usual explanation is that, on reading *I-Lo yüan-yüan lu* 伊洛淵源錄, by Chu Hsi (1130–1200), the account of the beginning of Sung neo-Confucianism, Wu decided to educate himself to become a sage. It is said that his father evinced strong disapproval and rebuked him, but he was adamant and so was permitted to live as a hermit in the second story of a building in order to concentrate on meditation and the study of the Classics. Two years later he was sent home for his marriage. From then on until summoned by imperial order in 1458, a period of forty-seven years, he led the life of a poor country teacher, attending to his own farm and subjected to labor service like a peasant.

As an official's son and a member of the gentry, his behavior seems strange indeed, and there has been no satisfactory explanation in the literature about or by him. Only in the writings by his disciple, Hu Chü-jen (*q.v.*), may one find a clue. Hu at the age of twenty-two went to study under Wu, and then and there, like his mentor, renounced participation in the civil examinations; this amounted to declaring his refusal to serve at the court. In Hu's collection of random thoughts, *Chü-yeh-lu* (*see* Hu Chü-jen), there are two entries denouncing any emperor who usurped the throne and murdered its rightful occupant, declaring that men of talent and virtue would never serve such a ruler. In another entry Hu specifically pointed out that in the Yunglo period (the reign of Chu Ti), one could find no scholar reputed to have sense and honor; there appeared in numbers, however, clever fellows gifted in writing elegant poetry and prose. The implication of these statements is that Hu disapproved of Chu Ti's claim to the throne and preferred to have nothing to do with such a court. If this be true of the disciple, then it must have been true of the master too. Wu Yü-pi went to the capital the year that Chu Ti usurped the throne, causing the death of the emperor and executing the latter's faithful followers. After his intensive study of the Classics, and having learned the meaning of Confucius' teachings about loyalty and faithfulness, Wu probably came to the realization that a true follower could not serve Chu Ti. Then he read the teachings of the Sung philosophers who laid emphasis on living by one's principles and practicing one's beliefs. Hence his announcement that he would completely cut himself off from officialdom. His father must have been thoroughly alarmed by this declaration, which, if discovered, could mean death to the entire family. So he kept Wu Yü-pi secluded for two years, and when the son would not repent sent him home and severed their relationship.

If this were the case, then the mysterious letter which Wu Yü-pi sent to his father in 1421, which was to puzzle the editors of his collected works, becomes entirely clear. In this letter he confessed that his lack of consideration was the reason why his father had punished him and cut him off; that last year (1420) he went to Nanking to see his father but was rejected; that this summer he was again on his way towards Nanking when he felt discouraged and turned westward to Wuchang; and that he decided to send his father this letter now (July or August), because, after reading the Four Books continually for half a year, he thought he had finally found the entrance to the path of sagehood. The letter brought about the desired reconciliation between father and son, which took place later that year.

Subsequently Wu became more relaxed, managing the family farm at the village, Hsiao-p'o 小坡, while teaching and studying. After the harvests in 1423, he studied Chu Hsi's edition of the annotated text of the Analects, discovering here and there passages which gave him inspiration. In a letter to his father he said that since the eighth moon (September, 1423) he felt that he had gained a great deal in improving himself by exercising self examination. It appears that later his father sent to him his three younger halfbrothers to study with him. At this time his determination to achieve sagehood is manifested in his dreams of having conversations with Confucius, King Wen of Chou, and Chu Hsi. Even his wife had a dream of Confucius appearing at their gate for a visit. By 1430 so many students had come to receive his instruction that he instituted some rules for the younger ones. Several entries in his diary reveal that he was at first disturbed by the incongruity of his lowly status as a peasant and his achievement in scholarship, and had to find consolation in the passage in the Doctrine of the Mean, "In a poor and low position he does what is proper to a poor and low position." As the son of an official he may be regarded as relatively poor for he led a simple life and occasionally had to borrow some grain from a neighbor. On the other hand, he had an income from the students, in addition to owning a house and some land. From his own writings it is evident that he had bond servants and farm hands. Perhaps he sometimes worked on the farm to help out with the harvest or to show his students the use of farm tools; some tales later exaggerated this, saying that he not only tilled the land himself but also made his students work for him. There is a story of his winnowing in the early morning and scolding his new student, Ch'en Hsien-chang (*q.v.*), for not rising before day-break as one in pursuit of sagehood should. This appears to be true, for Ch'en did stay in Wu's home to study. It happened in 1454, when Ch'en was on his way back to Kwangtung after failing to pass the metropolitan examination in Peking. Later Ch'en reported that he received instructions on many subjects from Wu, and described the latter as a responsible teacher with an unyielding and upright personality. In later life Wu Yü-pi gained such a wide reputation as a teacher that he was several times recommended to the throne as worthy of an official appointment. This happened in 1446, 1450, 1452, 1454, and finally in 1457. On the last occasion the one who recommended him to the emperor was the general Shih Heng (*q.v.*), who then wielded great power as the chief supporter of Chu Ch'i-chen (*q. v.*) in his restoration. The emperor sent a special messenger to bring Wu to Peking. Arriving in June, Wu received the imperial order appointing him a director of instruction of the heir apparent; but he refused to accept it, and repeatedly requested retirement on account of illness. He stayed in Peking two months, during which he received much assistance from Grand Secretary Li Hsien (*q.v.*) and Shih Heng. For the latter's family genealogy Wu wrote a preface, signing himself correctly as a scholar under Shih's sponsorship. Finally permission to leave came. Before his departure he submitted a memorial giving ten pieces of advice to the emperor; these the latter accepted graciously. Wu was accorded various honors and a stipend for life. Thus honored by the emperor Wu spent his last eleven years in contentment, almost elation, as shown in his poems. He was respected not only in his own native place but everywhere he went. In 1461 he traveled to Shih-shou 石首, Hukuang, to pay his respects at the tomb of Yang P'u (*see* Yang Shih-ch'i), who had taught him for a short while back in 1410. In 1462 Wu went to Fukien to honor the memory of Chu Hsi. At

various times he also took short trips about his native province. His poems, which are arranged chronologically, reveal his activities and the growth of his thought. Plain and unadorned, his poetry, like himself, presents an honest record of the simple life of one who had achieved peace of mind. It is interesting to note that almost half of it was written after 1457 when he was in a serene mood. His last poem bears the date equivalent to November, 1469, a few days before the end.

His collected works, *Wu K'ang-chai wen-chi* 康齋文集, were first printed in 1494 in 4 *chüan*; this book is no longer extant. The second and enlarged edition of 1526 was printed by the prefectural office of Fu-chou by order of the governor of Kiangsi. This is the parent copy of the 1590 and other later editions. It includes his poetry, 7 *ch.*, memorials, letters, and miscellaneous essays, 1 *ch.*, prefaces, 1 *ch.*, records, 1 *ch.*, and his "notes" (jih-lu 日錄), 1 *ch.*, and epigraphs, sacrificial essays, and the like, 1 *ch*. Of these, the most "philosophical" section would be the notes. These are full of references to his dreams, as well as to the poverty he experienced, and the efforts he made to perfect his character. His style is simple and straightforward. The editors of the *Ssu-k'u* Catalogue comment that Wu was able to integrate in himself the good points of both Chu Hsi and Lu Chiu-yüan (1139-93), to endure hardships, and to succeed in the cultivation of a noble character.

Wu achieved in his last years a genuine tranquillity. He has been nonetheless severely criticized for two events in his life. The first concerns his ancestral burial grounds where some person, probably a cousin, planted a grave site without obtaining his authorization. This was not a dispute over property rights, but a serious offense against the geomantic belief of feng-shui 風水, *i.e.*, that an ancestor's grave could influence the destiny of the descendants. Wu appealed to the local officials to no avail, and in 1440 sent a half-brother to carry his letter to the provincial director of education, asking the latter to exert his influence in the case. Apparently nothing came from the effort, for it seems that the case was finally settled by the prefect, Chang Kuei 張瑰 (T. 德潤, cs 1457). A fantastic story circulating at the time accused Wu of suing his own half-brother and suffering indignities at Chang's court, for he appeared in the dress of a commoner. The story must have been invented by a maligner, for Chang held office in Fu-chou for two or three years beginning only in 1467, when Wu was in his late seventies and had long before received the honor of a one-time guest of the emperor. Hence he could not have appeared before Chang as a commoner. Another version of the story describes Chang as the culprit who forced Wu's half-brother to sue him so Chang could have him arrested. This is an obvious fabrication for Chang, an honest and just official, could not have perpetrated an act of such meanness. Yet the editors of the official *Ming-shih* took the story to be a true one. As to the second story, it concerns the preface to Shih Heng's family genealogy written in 1458, in which Wu acknowledged Shih as his sponsor. The preface was later included in his collected works. The teller of the anecdote ridiculed Wu as obsequious to Shih, and, after Shih lost the emperor's favor in 1459, as indiscreet. Actually Wu was stating a fact when he acknowledged Shih's sponsorship in 1458, a year before the latter's downfall, and afterwards was honest enough to publish it without modification. The first person to record these pieces of gossip was Yin Chih (*see* Yang Ming) who, in his book of notes, *Chien-chai so-chui lu* 謇齋瑣綴錄, related them with relish for, according to the *Ming-shih*, Wu had slighted him at a banquet in 1458. Yin was a *chin-shih* of 1454 and a Hanlin compiler, but Wu was given the rank of a director of instruction, one grade higher than Yin. Yin, moreover, was a junior

fellow provincial by almost thirty years. There was no reason for him to be offended by being assigned a lower seat. Thus the anecdotes about Wu, as told in the *Chien-chai so-chui lu*, must be pronounced untrue. Yet these fabrications were repeated in Wu's time, probably by people prejudiced in favor of those holding the *chin-shih* degree.

After Wu's death these derogatory tales persisted to blemish his memory. He had a son and three daughters, and is known to have had two great-great-grandsons. But the family inheritance in land, pitifully small from the start, was soon reduced to nothing. Forty years after his death the shrine at his tomb in Ch'ung-jen was burned down, and the farmland deeded to its maintenance had been sold. His great-great-grandsons were penniless and starving. In 1517 or 1518, when Wang Shou-jen (*q.v.*) was governor of southern Kiangsi, he proposed the rebuilding of Wu's shrine. Apparently there were doubts about Wu's relationship wlth Shih Heng, for Wang explained at length how Wu's refusal to accept the official appointment revealed his wisdom in foreseeing Shih's impending disaster. It seems that Wang's proposal met with some obstruction and passed through various offices before imperial sanction finally came to Kiangsi. Then the local officials checked the registers and recovered one eighth of the original estate, amounting to about three acres of barren ground yielding less than one picul of rice a year. They assigned that pittance to the support of Wu's shrine on which the emperor had bestowed the designation Ch'ung-ju-tz'u 崇儒祠, or shrine in honor of a Confucian scholar. On completion of the rebuilding of the shrine in 1526 the officials erected a monument in praise of the emperor, recording that in the one hundred fifty odd years since the founding of the dynasty never had such favor been bestowed on a commoner. In 1584 Wu's disciples, Hu Chü-jen and Ch'en Hsien-chang, received the honor of being celebrated in the Temple of Confucius, in sharp contrast to Wu's being practically ignored by the court after 1526.

Wu Yü-pi is usually judged to have been self-taught. Ever since 1409, when he renounced an official career to devote himself to self-cultivation to become a sage, he concentrated on meditation and the studying of the Four Books, the Five Classics, and the recorded dialogues of the Sung thinkers, seeking at the same time to put into living practice their counsels. In part through such efforts, he was gradually able to correct his own character defects, especially a tendency toward stubbornness and anger, which he himself readily admitted and had difficulty in overcoming. He showed a significant lack of interest in purely metaphysical speculations, leaving no recorded discussion of such subjects as the relationship between li 理 and ch'i 氣, which the Sung thinkers had discussed. His extant notes reveal rather a constant preoccupation with virtuous conduct. He spoke also of the cultivation of the mind and heart (hsin 心) through a life of reverence (ching 敬) and of hard labor. In his memorial giving advice to the emperor, he included the duties of the emperor to honor the ancient sages and their teachings, to observe the example of their virtues by acting as father and mother of his people, by being cautious in his commands, by promoting moral education, by employing worthy officials, and by working in union of mind and heart with his subordinates.

Huang Tsung-hsi (ECCP) placed Wu Yü-pi at the head of his history of Ming philosophy, probably, as is often said, because of the influence which Wu exerted, through his disciples, Ch'en Hsien-chang and Lou Liang (q.v.), on the development of the thought and character of Wang Shou-jen. Besides Ch'en and Lou, Wu's most important disciple was Hu Chüjen. When the individual contributions of these disciples are considered, it is quite clear that each man developed different areas of thought and character of the master.

Where Ch'en Hsien-chang shows remarkably pro-Buddhist sympathies, especially through his love of contemplation, Hu manifests a greater attention to righteous action.

Bibliography

1/98/1a, 5/114/20a,24b; 8/37/3a; 14/6/24b; 83/4/1b, 5a, 8a, 11b; KC (1958), 2069, 2071, 2275; *Fuchou-fu chih* (1876), 50/10a, 56/11b; Jung Chao-tsu 容肇祖, *Ming-tai ssu-hsiang shih* 明代思想史 (1941), 19; *Wu P'in-chün nien-p'u* 吳聘君年譜 in *Shih-wu chia* 十五家 *nien-p'u*, Vol. 9, ed. by Yang Hsi-min 楊希閔 (1878 ed.), 2b, 3b, 5a, 10a; SK (1930), 170/12b; Wu Yü-pi, *Wu K'ang-chai wen-chi* (NLP microfilm, 1594 ed.), 8/14b, 25a; Hu Chü-jen, *Chü-yeh lu* (1866), 4/4a, 7a, 16b; Honda Shigeyuki 本田成之, "Min-gaku gairon" 明學概論, *Takase hakushi kanreki kinen shinagaku ronsō* 高瀬博士還暦紀念支那學論叢 (1931), 248; Hellmut Wilhelm, "On Ming Orthodoxy," MS 29 (1970-71), 9.

Chaoying Fang, Julia Ching, and Huang P'ei

YANG Chi 楊基 (T. 孟載, H. 眉菴, 鹿場居士), *ca.* 1334-*ca.* 1383, poet, minor painter, and official, was born into a family which hailed from Szechwan, later settling in Soochow, then known as P'ing-chiang 平江, where his grandfather had been an official in the Yüan government. Yang's birth date is not to be found in any document. Although there are several of his undated poems which give his age as forty, and one of them even mentions his grandmother as ninety years of age at the time he was forty, it is difficult to fix the year in which they were written. Since the date of his dismissal from his post in Kiangsi has been established as in the spring of 1373, a study of the context of these undated poems enables us to fix them in that year. Thus his birth occurred probably in 1334, as shown by the author in a recent article cited below.

Yang Chi was said to be a child prodigy. As a boy of nine, he was reportedly able to recite the Six Classics in their entirety. When barely twenty, he wrote a book of history of more than a hundred thousand characters, entitled *Lun-chien* 論鑒. His early talent in poetry is revealed in a famous anecdote told in connection with Yang Wei-chen (*q.v.*), the popular poet of that period whose *hao* was T'ieh-ti-tzu 鐵笛子 because he owned an iron flute. Once when Yang Wei-chen was on a visit to Soochow, it fell to Yang Chi to write a poem on the subject of the flute. In response, he composed one in Yang Wei-chen's own style. Yang Wei-chen, surprised at its excellence, announced to everybody that the youth was superior to himself in the art of poetry. Subsequently, Yang Chi came to be called Hsiao-Yang 小楊 (Yang junior) to distinguish him from Yang Wei-chen who was known as Lao 老-Yang (Yang senior) in literary circles of the day. He was also regarded as one of the "Four outstanding figures of Soochow," which included Kao Ch'i, Hsü Pen, and Chang Yü (*qq.v.*).

In spite of his literary talent, Yang Chi failed in the examinations and was obliged to make a living in a village in Ch'ih-shan 赤山 teaching school. After the rebel leader Chang Shih-ch'eng (*q.v.*) occupied Soochow and it became the capital of his territory, Yang served for some time as secretary in Chang's government, and was later under the patronage of the influential and cultured Jao Chieh (*see* Hsü Pen), to whom he dedicated a number of poems.

From 1366 onward, Chang's territory suffered encroachment by the armies of Chu Yüan-chang, Soochow being taken after ten months of resistance in 1367. This led to the execution of Jao Chieh and the banishment of a large part of the population of the city. The members of Yang Chi's family, about twenty in number, were among those affected. Yang Chi himself and some of his friends were sent to Hao-liang 濠梁, the present Feng-yang 鳳陽 (Anhwei). There Yang Chi and Hsü Pen shared a rustic house which Yang named Meng-lü-hsüan 夢綠軒, be-

cause once Hsü dreamed of the verdure to the south of the Yangtze. In the autumn of 1368, Yang Chi was forced to go to Ta-liang 大梁, present day Kaifeng in Honan. His long poem composed there under the title "Liang-yüan yin-chiu ko" 梁園飲酒歌 was to a certain extent an autobiographical sketch of his life to that point. Besides a lament over his own misfortunes, it reveals also the unhappy condition of the people after the war.

Following his release early in 1369, Yang Chi was appointed magistrate of the district Ying-yang 榮陽 in Honan, but by the end of the year he gave up the assignment and went to the capital (Nanking), where he made his home for the next two years, without any position. Although in poor circumstances, he frequently took trips to surrounding regions such as Chü-jung 句容. At the beginning of 1372 he proceeded to Nanchang as an auxiliary official in the Kiangsi provincial government. On being implicated in the case of his superior, he was dismissed from his post in the following spring. (This chronology is based on his dated poems; Ch'ien Ch'ien-i [ECCP], who dates his dismissal before 1371, seems to be in error.) He returned to Nanking, but by the autumn was given another mission, and sent to Hunan and Kwangsi.

Following his return to the capital, Yang Chi served for some time as vice director of a bureau in the ministry of War. In July, 1374, he was appointed a surveillance vice commissioner of Shansi, eventually receiving a promotion to surveillance commissioner. Some time later he suffered false accusations, was dismissed, and condemned to hard labor. This punishment led to his death in Nanking. Since there are the poems of Chang Yü deploring his demise, and Chang Yü himself died in 1385, this must have happened not long before 1385.

Yang Chi's poetic work entitled *Mei-an chi* 眉菴集, 12 *ch.*, +1 *ch.*, was edited by Chang Hsi (*see* Hsü Pen) in 1485. Although there are the editor's notes appended to different groups of poems to designate their place of composition, some of the notes are not always reliably attributed; a study of the context of these poems shows that they were written while Yang Chi was staying elsewhere.

Only one of Yang Chi's paintings has been recorded in older catalogues. As to the "Chiang-shan wo-yu t'u" 江山臥遊圖, ascribed to him, reproduced in the *I-yüan i-chen* 藝苑遺珍, it is obviously a fake because seven characters "庚子七十四老人" are prefixed before his name.

Bibliography

1/185/20b; 3/266/17a; 5/97/64a; 84/甲/10b; MSL (1962), T'ai-tsu, 1577; Yang Chi, *Mei-an chi* (SPTK, 3d ser.), 1/17a, 23b, 29a, 3/2b, 10b, 4/1a, 11a, 9/6a, 10/7b; Chang Yü, *Ching-chü chi*, 6/12b, 18a; SK (1930), 169/22a; P'ang Yüan-chi 龐元濟, *Hsü-chai ming-hua lu* 虛齋名畫錄, 8/1; John C. Ferguson, *Index of Artists*, 354a; Weng T'ung-wen, "Yang Chi sheng-nien chi ch'i shih chung 'mu ju tou' wen-t'i" 生年及其詩中 '木入斗' 問題, *Nanyang Univ. Jo.* 6 (1972), 162; *I-yüan i-chen*, Vol. 2, pl. 39 (Hong Kong, 1967); F. W. Mote, *The Poet Kao Ch'i* (Princeton, 1962), 100.

T'ung-wen Weng

YANG Chi-sheng 楊繼盛 (T. 仲芳, H. 椒山), June 16, 1516-November 12, 1555, an official who came to be greatly honored for his courage and loyalty, was a native of Jung-ch'eng 容城, prefecture of Paoting. He was the youngest of two brothers, born to his father's wife, née Ts'ao 曹, and one half-brother, born to his father's concubine, née Ch'en 陳. When he was four years of age his mother, who could no longer tolerate the treatment meted out to her by her husband's favorite, separated from him. As a result two-thirds of the family property went to Yang's father, concubine, and half brother, and one third to his mother, her two sons, and one daughter. A year later the latter's property was re-divided, the older brother and his wife getting one share, the mother, Yang Chi-sheng, and his sister receiving another. Under these circumstances all three

(mother, sister, and son then aged six) had to work in the field, his task being to tend to the cattle. About the same time (1522) his mother died, probably from tuberculosis. In spite of these difficulties he somehow acquired sufficient schooling to become a *chü-jen* in 1540. Four years later he began to study in the National University where he came under the influence of Hsü Chieh (*q.v.*). In 1547 he achieved the *chin-shih* and received an appointment as secretary in the bureau of honors of the ministry of Personnel in Nanking. While there he became a student of musical theories, astronomy, geography, military tactics, etc., taught by Han Pang-ch'i (*q.v.*), then minister of War in the southern capital. In the field of music he worked with Han on devising a musical instrument on the basis of Han's theories. His next office was in Peking, where he served as vice director of the bureau of equipment in the ministry of War. At this time (1551) Altan-qaγan (*q.v.*) was subjecting the northwest to repeated and punishing raids, even menacing Peking. Ch'iu Luan (*q.v.*) as commanding general inadvisedly attacked the retiring Mongols near the Great Wall, and, following his defeat, recommended that they be placated by having the court accede to their demand for tribute-trade arrangements. When approval came (April 9, 1551), Yang protested violently (April 20), setting forth his reasons in cogent and forceful fashion. The emperor could not brook his opposition and had him packed off (after severe flogging), first to prison and thence to Ti-tao 狄道 (in present-day Kansu) as jail warden 典史. Here Yang found the local population suffering from military depredations and eunuch harassment and did much to alleviate their distress. Among other things he helped the people open up a coal mine, and founded an academy known as Ch'ao-jan shu-yüan 超然書院. On Ch'iu Luan's fall from grace, followed by his death a year later, Yang was recalled. In quick succession he served as magistrate in Chu-ch'eng 諸城,

Shantung, secretary of the Yunnan bureau in the Nanking ministry of Finance, vice director of the Hukuang bureau in the ministry of Justice, and then of the bureau of personnel in the ministry of War in Peking. Yen Sung (q.v.) tried to win his allegiance, but to no avail. Yang saw the injury Yen was doing to the state, and, after considerable soul searching and careful preparation, in a second memorial denounced him for ten major crimes and five infamies. Towards the end of the memorial he held that the emperor could verify the accusations by asking his own sons, the two princes. Unfortunately the emperor assumed that such a reference to the princes was an attempt to involve them in court politics. By imperial order Yang was sent to the court of the Embroidered-uniform Guard to be questioned under torture as to whether anyone was in collusion with him. Again on imperial order he was severely beaten before being delivered to the jail of the ministry of Justice. In his autobiography he describes in detail how, with only a piece of broken porcelain, he made an incision on his bruised buttocks to release clotted blood, and cleaned the area down to the bone. Miraculously he survived but, on the charge of an offense amounting to "fraudulently transmitting a forged princely order," was sentenced to death. For three years he languished in jail, in spite of the emotional appeal of his wife, née Chang 張, who offered to die in his place—a plea written by Wang Shih-chen (q.v.). Yang eventually met his end at the age of thirty-nine, reportedly inditing a four-line stanza on his way to execution at the market place, a poem which in essence bespeaks his utter loyalty to the throne. (The Ming-shih errs in recording his death on October 15. That was the day of his sentencing. The shih-lu reports that he was executed, together with Chang Ching and Li T'ien-ch'ung (qq.v.), four weeks later.) Wang saw to the removal of Yang's body to his native place, whence in 1602 it was transferred to a tomb in the neighboring district, Ting-hsing-hsien 定興縣, where he had gone to school. In the following reign, over a decade later, Yang received the posthumous rank of a vice director of the Court of Imperial Sacrifices, and the name Chung-min 忠愍 (loyal and regretted). Even the first Manchu emperor in Peking, just 101 years after his death (1656), commemorated Yang's loyalty.

Yang Chi-sheng's two memorials and the entreaty of his wife were later collected by Li Chih (q.v.) and Yü Yün-hsieh 俞允諧 in a book entitled Yang Chiao-shan tsou-shu 椒山奏疏, 1 ch., published a few decades after his death in San i-jen wen-chi 三異人文集, and frequently reprinted. The latter also includes Yang's will, his injunctions to his descendants, and other writings, in 3 chüan. Besides his oft-repeated poem, his memory was kept green by an ancestral hall erected in his honor in Paoting and another put up on the former site of the ministry of Justice in Peking (the south end of Ssu-fa-pu chieh 司法部街). Report has it too that both a bridge and a lane in the capital, Cha-tzu ch'iao 乍子橋 and Cha-tzu hu-t'ung 衚衕, remind people of the moment when, be being on his way to deliver his memorial of denunciation of Grand Secretary Yen, his wife besought him to desist. On June 25, 1937, a bare fortnight before the Japanese attack at Lu-kou 蘆溝 ch'iao, a memorial service was conducted in Yang's honor. Henri Maspero is the authority for the assertion that he became known after his day as the ch'eng-huang 城隍 (tutelary god) of Peking.

In addition to his memorials several short works are credited to Yang. The Ssu-k'u ch'üan-shu includes his Yang Chung-min chi 集 in 3 + 1 ch., but the editors thought poorly of the San i-jen chi, 22 ch., because one of its compilers was Li Chih, and listed it by title only in the Imperial Catalogue. Yang's Yen hsing lu 言行錄 (words and deeds) was published in 1932, and his own chronological record (nien-p'u 年譜) appeared in 1856.

Bibliography

1/209/21a; 3/193/12a; 5/41/55a; 8/56/8a; 14/5/17a;
32/5/2b; 40/43/30a; 42/92/1a; 53/3/14a; 61/108/13b;
63/23/32a; 64/己 9/7a; 86/13/4b; MSL (1965),
Shih-tsung, 6621, 6628, 6903, 7391; SK (1930),
172/7b, 192/9b; KC (1958), 3861; Li Chih, *San
i-jen wen-chi*; *Pao-ting-fu chih* (1894), 11/11b, 43/
22b, 44/12a, 57/6b, 67/4a; *Chi-fu t'ung-chih* 畿輔
通志 (1934), 316, 1171, 6250, 7736; *Ch'ing-chou-
fu chih* 青州府志 (1859), 36/18b; *Yang Chung-min
kung nien-p'u*; Lu Chiu-kao 陸九皋, "Chieh-shao
介紹 Ming Yang Chi-sheng...mo-chi shou-chüan"
墨迹手卷, *Wen-wu* no. 3 (1963), 18; H. Serruys,
*The Tribute System and Diplomatic Missions
(1400–1600)*, (Brussels, 1967), 62; W. Franke,
Sources (1968), 5.5.34; H. Maspero, "Mythologie de la Chine moderne," *Mythologie asiatique
illustrée* (Paris, 1928), 263; L. C. Arlington,
"China's Heroes of the Past," *T'ien Hsia
Monthly*, 5:5 (December, 1937), 471; A. R.
Davis (ed.), *The Penguin Book of Chinese Verse*
(Baltimore, 1962), 59.

*Sun Yüen-king and
L. Carrington Goodrich*

YANG Ch'i-yüan 楊起元 (T. 貞復, H. 復
所), 1547-October 7, 1599, thinker and
official, was a native of Kuei-shan 歸善,
Kwangtung. He came from an educated
family; his father, Yang Ch'uan-fen 傳芬
(H. 肖齋, d. 1592), had been a disciple of
Chan Jo-shui (*q.v.*) and passed on to Yang
Ch'i-yüan a deep interest in philosophical
matters. Yang Ch'i-yüan was a studious
youth, achieving the *hsiu-ts'ai* at the age
of fourteen. Five years later he showed
unusual calm and composure when
captured by local bandits who eventually
set him free. The following year (1567) he
ranked first in the provincial examinations. He had some difficulty in the metropolitan tests, but remained undaunted in
spite of three failures. Acquaintance with
Li Yün-ju 黎允如 (a native of Chien-
ch'ang 建昌, Kiangsi), a disciple, relative,
and fellow countryman of Lo Ju-fang (*q.v.*),
greatly stimulated him, and, in 1577, the
year Yang finally acquired the *chin-shih*,
he was much pleased to meet Lo Ju-fang
himself, who happened to be at the capital.

Although Lo was then out of favor,
having resigned from official tasks after
an impeachment which had probably been
occasioned by the displeasure of Chang
Chü-cheng (*q.v.*), then holding the reins
of power, Yang did not hesitate to associate with him. That same year Yang was
made a Hanlin bachelor, and then a compiler (1579). In 1586 he took the occasion
offered by official business to travel
south, visit his family, and, on his way
back to Peking, stop in Kiangsi to spend
some time with Lo Ju-fang at his study,
the Ts'ung-ku shan-fang. He became
formally Lo's disciple and absorbed all he
could from Lo's teaching. During the rest
of his life Yang was greatly attached to
Lo, whom he considered a sage, much in
the same manner as Lo considered Yen
Chün (*see* Lo Ju-fang).

Yang had a fairly successful official
career. In 1589 he became director of
studies at the National University and, in
1591, librarian of the Imperial Library in
charge of the compilation of records
concerning the imperial genealogy. The
following year he returned to his native
place for his father's funeral, and remained
there during the prescribed mourning
period. On its completion he was
named chancellor of the National University, and then successively vice minister
of Rites (1596) and of Personnel (1597)
in Nanking. In 1598 he was summoned to
Peking to serve as vice minister of
Personnel and reader-in-waiting, but was
prevented from going by the death of his
mother, which occurred in Nanking. He
returned to Kwangtung to bury her, but was
shortly afterwards overtaken by sickness,
and followed her in death, at the age of
fifty-two. He was honored posthumously
with the title Wen-i 文懿.

As a follower of the T'ai-chou branch
of the Wang Yang-ming school (*see* Wang
Shou-jen), Yang Ch'i-yüan understood
hsin 心 (mind) to be the One behind the
Many, without equal or opposite. He
sometimes called it ming-te 明德 (illustrious virtue), which, he said, was the same

in all, and cannot be obscured by the individual physical endowment or by passions. He believed that sagehood could be attained through an inner realization of this truth, without the need of effort and self-exertion. His definition of hsin obliterated all distinction between hsing 性 (nature) and ch'ing 情 (emotions, sensations), or between self and others. He also acknowledged openly his indebtedness to Ch'an Buddhist insights. During his sojourn in Nanking, Yang conducted lectures jointly with other thinkers of the time, especially Chou Ju-teng (*q.v.*) and Hsü Fu-yüan (*see* Hsü Chieh). He was present at the debate (*ca*. 1592) which took place between Chou and Hsü on the subject of the mind being beyond good and evil. It is said that Wu Tao-nan (*see* Ch'en Yü-pi), who rose to be minister of Revenue and grand secretary, was one of his disciples.

Yang was the author of a number of books. These include *Cheng-hsüeh p'ien* 證學篇, 4 *ch*., with supplement, 1 *ch*., a personal testimonial of his thought; *Chu-ching p'in-chieh* 諸經品節, 20 *ch*., a compilation including sixteen Taoist and twelve Buddhist classics. There is also a 12 *chüan* collection of his works, entitled *Yang Wen-i chi* 集, edited by his grandson, Yang T'ing-ch'un 廷春. A smaller collection, *Yang t'ai-shih* 太師 *chi*, 4 *ch*., appears on the list of books to be suppressed, but a copy of this in 8 *chüan*, printed in the Wan-li period, the *Yang Fu-so hsien-sheng* 復所先生 *chia-ts'ang* 家藏 *chi*, is preserved in the Naikaku Bunko, which also possesses the *Yang Fu-so ch'üan*全-*chi*, 22 *ch*. (Ming ed.). Yang likewise edited and published a treatise written by Lo Ju-fang, the *Shih-jen p'ien* 識仁篇, 2 *ch*.

Bibliography

3/183/20a; 5/26/75a; 8/70/6a, 7a; 16/162/4a; 32/112/7a; 63/22/51a; 83/34/22a; KC (1958), 5185, 5232; SK (1930), 125/1a, 4a, 132/1b, 179/8a; *Kwangtung t'ung-chih* (1934), 3990; Naikaku Bunko *Catalogue*, 358, 587; Sun Tien-ch'i (1957), 183.

Julia Ching and Huang P'ei

YANG Chüeh 楊爵 (T. 伯修 [珍], H. 斛山, 1493-October 27, 1549), official and scholar, was a native of Fu-p'ing 富平, Shensi. He came from a poor family, and did not begin formal schooling until the age of twenty *sui*. He had the opportunity, however, of studying with the renowned Shensi philospher Han Pang-ch'i (*q.v.*); as a consequence he and Yang Chi-sheng (*q.v.*) became known later as the Two Yang, disciples of Han (韓門二楊).

In 1529 Yang Chüeh became a *chin-shih*. His first appointment in the messenger office was followed by promotion to censor. About 1531 he returned home on account of illness. Then his mother died. After the observance of the traditional period of mourning, he was recalled to Peking in 1539 to resume his old post. On March 1, 1541, he submitted a strongly worded memorial on five topics of admonition. He attacked Grand Secretary Hsia Yen and Duke Kuo Hsün (*qq.v.*), pointing out the irrationality of spending large sums of money to build the Altar of Thunder (雷壇), while many people were dying from cold and hunger. And he counseled the emperor, Chu Hou-ts'ung (*q.v.*), that the Son of Heaven should hold court, receive his ministers in audience, quit spending all his time in the company of Taoist priests and believing in their superstitions, and cease meting out punishments of such severity to censors who crossed his path that they often resulted in death. This memorial made the emperor extremely angry. On the following day Yang was thrown into the Embroidered-uniform Guards' prison. On the night of March 10, he was flogged and on the night of March 14, was again questioned and tortured. Because of the seriousness of his case, he was put in chains; as a result other people, both prisoners and the men who worked in the jail, were apprehensive and dared show him no kindness, those doing so being punished. Contrary to Yang's expectation of death, he amazingly not only survived all the initial miseries, but also endured two consecutive terms of imprisonment lasting seven long years. He lived to tell the story.

In the meantime, two other officials died in the same prison because they spoke out for him. About two and a half months after Yang was punished and imprisoned, on April 30, 1541, a fire broke out in the palace area, damaging the imperial ancestral temple. For this misfortune, the emperor issued an edict as a repentant gesture asking the officials to criticize the government. A young secretary of the ministry of Revenue, Chou T'ien-tso 周天佐 (T. 字弼, H. 磧山, cs 1535), either took the imperial edict too seriously, or resolved to brave death for justice and achieve a name for himself; in any case he submittted a memorial asking for Yang's release. After arrest and confinement in the Embroidered-uniform Guards prison, Chou was flogged on May 30, 1541, and died in three days from the wounds inflicted. Later in the same year another man, P'u Hung 浦鋐 (T. 汝器, H. 竹塘, cs 1517), followed Chou's example. As censor, in 1540, P'u had been made regional inspector of Yang's native province, Shensi. Perhaps he felt it his duty to rescue a man from the region where his official duties lay. His memorial provoked the same violent reaction. P'u was immediately arrested, taken to Peking, and incarcerated on December 30, 1541. Flogged on January 15, 1542, he died, possibly from an infection, on the 21st of that month, in the same cell where Yang was held, after the latter failed in a desperate effort to save him. To their memory and in gratitude for their courageous memorials on his behalf, Yang wrote their biographical sketches.

Yang had little difficulty in finding worthy companionship in the prison. One fellow inmate was the famed philospher and scholar, Ch'ien Te-hung (q.v.), a follower of Wang Shou-jen (q.v.). For his impeachment of Duke Kuo Hsün, Ch'ien was jailed in the winter of 1541. Ch'ien and Yang were old friends and happy to see each other. Together they discussed ancient classics and phillosophy, and encouraged each other in the pursuit of sagehood. It was in the prison that Yang began his serious study of *I-ching*, the Book of Changes. After Ch'ien's release, two other scholars arrived. These were Liu K'uei 劉魁 (T. 煥吾, H. 晴川, cj 1507), and Chou I 周怡 (T. 順之, H. 都峯, 簡莊先生, 訥溪先生, 1506-1569, *chin-shih* of 1538). The former was punished in 1542 for his memorial suggesting the postponement of the construction of the Altar of Thunder so that the money might be redirected towards border defense; the latter for his impeachent of Yen Sung (*q.v.*), the then all powerful grand secretary. This comradeship in misery not only boosted the morale of all three, but also stimulated their interest in learning and the discussion of the Classics and conduct of life. There were also two police serving in the eunuch controlled investigation office (tung-ch'ang 東廠) who were ordered to spy on Yang and report every five days. One named Su Hsüan 蘇宣 (T. 延詔) saved Yang's legs from the pressure of the stocks by protecting his ankles with curved tiles. The second was Yang Tung 楊棟 (T. 國用), who requested permission to have food taken to Yang.

Early in the autumn of 1545, during the seance of divining by planchette (扶乩 or 扶鸞), the spirits revealed to the emperor that Yang Chüeh, Liu K'uei, and Chou I were punished unjustly. Thereupon the three were released together on September 17 of that year. Unfortunately an unfavorable incident occurred which made the emperor change his mind. In less than a month following their release, he issued a secret order to bring them back. After being home for only ten days, Yang was required to return to Peking. On November 28 he reached the capital and re-entered the same prison. For Liu K'uei and Chou I, it was even more tragic, the rearrest of Liu being made before he reached home, and Chou I having barely a single visit with his aged mother. They too were incarcerated in the same prison on the night of December 14, 1545. It was their fate that the three friends would be confined together for another two years.

The long punishment of the three must have weighed on the emperor's mind. On December 4, 1547, another fire broke out in the imperial palace. In the sound and fury of the fire, the emperor imagined that he heard a voice calling out the names of these three men. This time he could not stand the strain any longer, and ordered their release for good.

On his two imprisonments and all the suffering he experienced and witnessed, Yang left two essays, the *Ch'u-k'un chi* 處困記 and the *Hsü* (續) *ch'u-k'un chi*. Although many other Ming officials had similar experiences they either did not live to tell the tale, or did not care to do so after their release. These two essays, therefore, are unusual documents on Ming judicial conditions. Furthermore, between the lines of seemingly traditional expressions, one can sense the feeling of protest in Yang's prose, for he was a northern scholar of vigorous personality. Forty-three years after his death the posthumous name of Chung-chieh 忠介 was finally bestowed (1592) on Yang Chüeh.

As a philosopher Yang is regarded as one of the San-yüan 三原 School, established by the Honan scholar Hsüeh Hsüan (*q.v.*), and known for its members' outspokenness against injustice with their emphasis on practice rather than speculation. Repeatedly Yang expressed the belief that once a man sees what is right, he should neither waver nor be influenced by personal gain or loss. His life truly exemplified his philosophy.

The *Ssu-k'u ch'üan-shu* includes two of Yang's works: the *Chou-i pien-i* 周易辨疑, a work of 4 *chüan* on the Book of Changes, and the *Chung-chieh chi* 忠介集, his collected literary works of 16 *chüan*. The *Ming-shih* reports a work by him on the Doctrine of the Mean, the *Chung-yung chieh* 中庸解. An abridged collection of his literary works under the title of *Hu-shan chi* 斛山集 was printed in the *Kuang li-hsüeh*

pei-k'ao 廣理學備考 in 1835. And eighty-five poems and twenty essays of his may be found in the *Kuan-chung liang-ch'ao shih wen ch'ao* 關中兩朝詩文鈔, an anthology of poetry and prose writings by Shensi authors during the Ming and Ch'ing dynasties, compiled by Li Yüan-ch'un 李元春, printed in 1832.

Bibliography

1/209/8b, 12b, 13b, 14b, 16b; 3/193/5a; 5/30/78a, 31/108a, 65/97a, 129a, 70/37a; 83/9/7b; SK (1930), 5/2a, 172/5a.

Lienche Tu Fang

YANG Hsüan 楊塤 (T. 景和), fl. 1426-64, lacquer-maker and artist, was descended from a family specializing in lacquer-ware in the Yang-hui 楊滙 village in Hsieh-t'ang 斜塘, Chia-shan 嘉善, prefecture of Chia-hsing 嘉興, Chekiang. Hsieh-t'ang, popularly known as Hsi 西 -t'ang, had been a thriving center of lacquer-ware manufacturing in the lower Yangtze valley since the 12th century, following the emigration of craftsmen from the north after the fall of the Northern Sung. It had produced during the Yüan dynasty such well-known names in the industry as Chang Ch'eng 張成, P'eng Chün-pao 彭君寶, and Yang Mao 茂.

Yang Mao, a pioneer of the Yang-hui School and presumably an ancestor of Yang Hsüan (or of the same clan), acquired a reputation for his carved works in red lacquer, called t'i-hung 剔紅, during the late Yüan and early Ming; although some of his wares were marred by thin and fragile coating, they found a ready market in Japan and the Liu-ch'iu (Ryū-kyū). Some of the wares produced by Yang Mao and Chang Ch'eng were reportedly brought back to China by the envoys of these two countries, during the middle years of the Yung-lo period, as part of their tribute. When Emperor Chu Ti (*q.v.*) learned of this, he summoned them to the capital, but by this time both had passed away. He then appointed the son of Chang Ch'eng, Chang Te-kang 德剛, to be an assistant director (8A) of the bureau of construction in the ministry of Works, in charge of the production of lacquer-ware in the Kuo-yüan factory 果園廠. There seems to be no record as to a similar appointment for Yang Mao's descendant. Yang Hsüan's father, whose name is not recorded, was also a lacquerer. During the Hsüan-te period, a number of Chinese workmen went to Japan to study the latest technique in colored laquer developed by the Japanese. It is not certain whether the Yang father and son also studied there, but Yang Hsüan skillfully applied the Japanese technique to produce new styles of colored lacquer-ware. During the reign of Chu Ch'i-chen (*q.v.*), Yang was enlisted as an artisan in a government agency in Peking, presumably as a lacquerer. He would have remained obscure, like many other artisans and craftsmen in Chinese history, had it not been for his involvement in a political squabble towards the end of the T'ienshun period.

It happened late in 1463 when Men Ta (*see* P'eng Shih), the powerful assistant commander of the Embroidered-uniform Guard, who had lately assumed charge of the department, tried to implicate his colleague, assistant commander Yüan Pin (*see* Esen), with false accusations. Yüan Pin, who gained the favor of Chu Ch'i-chen for his loyal service during the emperor's captivity in the camp of Esen (*q.v.*) in 1449, was one of the few officials who dared to flout Men's wishes. Before this Men Ta had indicted his rival on several occasions on unfounded charges, but none succeeded in damaging him. This time Men Ta placed Yüan under arrest, accusing him, *inter alia*, of having misappropriated government properties to construct a residence for the eunuch Ts'ao Ch'in (*see* Ts'ao Chi-hsiang) and another for General Shih Heng (*q.v.*), and of having seized girls from decent families

to be his concubines.

When the news became known, Yang Hsüan, a public spirited individual who had little connection with Yüan Pin, spoke out in his defense. He submitted a petition, outlining Yüan's meritorious service and the dubious nature of the charges, and pleaded with the court to conduct an open trial to ensure justice. Undaunted, Men Ta had Yang arrested, and made him testify that he had acted on order of Li Hsien (*q.v.*), the Hanlin chancellor whom Men Ta also wished to oust from office because of earlier grudges. Yang Hsüan complied under torture; but when he appeared before the court he laid bare the facts and exposed Men Ta's scheme. Li Hsien was thus spared. The judicial authorities nevertheless, reluctant to offend the powerful commander, recommended capital punishment for both Yüan Pin and Yang Hsüan. At this point the emperor intervened, and the two received lighter penalties. Yüan Pin was to retire to Nanking on pension, retaining his title, while Yang Hsüan was later released from prison. This incident is reported by the Hanlin compiler Yin Chih (*see* Yang Ming), and was subsequently recorded in the *Ying-tsung shih-lu*. Because of this courageous act, historians and biographers hailed Yang as a "righteous man" (義士). The contemporary scholar-poet Chang Pi (*q.v.*) later wrote a laudatory account of his life; it was included in Chang's collected works and provides the main source for Yang's biography.

In the field of lacquer, Yang Hsüan's major contribution was his skillful application of the Japanese technique of mixing gold or silver powder in lacquer, known as ni-chin 泥金, to produce a multi-colored coating distilled from various ingredients, called piao-hsia 縹霞 or ts'ai-ch'i 彩漆, which made the articles more colorful, shining, and durable. Yang's multi-colored wares, ranging from screens, furniture, to different types of utensils, moreover, were decorated with elegantly drawn designs or paintings of landscape, figures, flora, and birds, often accompanied by graceful calligraphy. His gift as an artist, which was rare among the lacquer workmen, added to the beauty of his works. As a result, Yang Hsüan's wares were not only well received in China, where people dubbed him Yang Wo-ch'i 楊倭漆 (Yang the Japanese-lacquer master), but were also prized items among Japanese connoisseurs who considered his artistry superior to their own masters'.

The craftsmanship of the Yang family as perfected by Yang Hsüan was inherited by his descendants. One of them, Yang Ming 明 (T. 清仲), who flourished during the late Ming, produced an annotation of a valuable treatise on lacquer entitled *Hsiu-shih lu* 髹飾錄, 2 *ch.*, compiled by Huang Ch'eng 黃成 (T. 大成, fl. 1567–72), a lacquer master from Hsin-an 新安, Hui-chou 徽州 prefecture, with Yang's preface dated 1625. Yang Ming indicates the technical innovations introduced by his ancestors, but he makes no mention of their names, nor does he give details of their particular skills. A modern edition of the *Hsiu-shih lu*, with Yang Ming's notes, was printed in 1926 (reprinted 1959) by the modern scholar Chu Ch'i-ch'ien 朱啓鈐, from a manuscript dating back to the early Ch'ing (preserved in Japan), with an appendix of "elaborate verification" (箋證) of the text by K'an To 闞鐸. The value of this work lies in the fact that it is the only extant text on Chinese lacquer of the Ming period, and is therefore indispensible for a study of this subject. Unfortunately it deals only with the technical aspects of the craft, giving scant information on the historical development.

[Editors' note: In some Ming accounts, Yang Hsüan's given name is erroneously written as 瑄 or 琯, hence easily confusing him with two contemporary scholar-officials who had the same name Yang Hsüan (*q.v.*) but with their given names variably written as 瑄 or 宣.]

Bibliography

5/113/23a;6/27/21a; 32/2/44a; 65/8/2b; MSL(1963), Ying-tsung, 7143; KC(1958), 2157; T'ao Tsung-i, *Cho-keng lu* (SPTK), 30/13b; Ts'ao Chao 曹昭, *Ko-ku yao-lun* 格古要論 (preface 1387), in Chou Lü-ching 周履靖, ed., *I-men kuang-tu* 夷門廣牘 (1940 ed.), 6/51a; Yin Chih, *Chien-chai so-cho lu* 謇齋瑣綴錄, in Li Shih 李栻, ed., *Li-tai hsiao-shih* 歷代小史 (1940 ed.), 93/25a; Shen Meng 愼蒙 (1510–81), *Huang Ming wen-tse* 皇明文則 (preface 1573), 12/40a; Kao Lien 高濂, *Yen-hsien ch'ing-shang chien* 燕閒淸賞箋, in Teng Shih 鄧實, ed., *Mei-shu* 美術 *ts'ung-shu* (1947), 3d ser., Vol. 10, 35a; *Hsiu-shih lu* (1926 ed.); Liu T'ung and Yü I-cheng, *Ti-ching ching-wu lüeh* (1957 ed.), 68; TSCC (1885–88), XVII: 785/19/6b; *Chia-hsing-fu chih* (1878), 33/29a; *Chia-shan-hsien chih* (1918), 26/1b; Ōmura Seigai 大村西崖, *Chung-kuo mei-shu shih* 中國美術史, tr. Ch'en Pin-ho 陳彬龢 (1928), 218; Wang Shih-chen, *Chin-i chih* (TsSCC), 15; Suo Yu-ming, "A study of carved red lacquer" (in Chinese), *National Palace Museum Qu.*, VI:3 (1972), 11; Teng Chih-ch'eng 鄧之誠, *Ku-tung so-chi* 骨董瑣記 (1936), 5/19b; Cheng Shih-hsü 鄭師許, *Ch'i-ch'i k'ao* 漆器考 (1936), 35; Chu Ch'i-ch'ien, *Ch'i-shu* 書 (1957), 4/36b, 5/50a, 6/63a; *Wen-wu ts'an-k'ao tzu-liao* 文物參考資料, October, 1956, and July, 1957, issues; Edward F. Strange, *Catalogue of Chinese Lacquer* (Victoria and Albert Museum, London, 1925), 3; Fritz Low-Beer, "Chinese Lacquer of the Early 15th Century," BMFEA, 22(1950), 145; *id.*, "Chinese Lacquer of the Middle and Late Ming Periods," BMFEA, no. 24 (1952), 27; Harry M. Garner, "Lacquer and Furniture," in *The Arts of the Ming Dynasty* (London, 1958), 33, plates 58–75; *id.*, "The Export of Chinese Lacquer to Japan in the Yüan and Early Ming Dynasties," *Archives of Asian Art*, XXV (1971–72), 7; Sir Percival David, *Chinese Connoisseurship, the Ko ku yao lun, the Essential Criteria of Antiquities* (London, 1971), 146.

Hok-lam Chan

YANG Hsüan 楊瑄 (T. 廷獻), 1425-July 29, 1478, scholar-official, was a native of Feng-ch'eng 豐城, Nanchang prefecture, Kiangsi. It is said that Yang's family name had originally been Wang 王. One of his distinguished ancestors, who settled in Wu-ning 武寧 of the same prefecture, was a senior statesman at the court of the the T'ang dynasty late in the ninth century. Yang Hsüan's great-great-grandfather, who still bore the name Wang,

moved the family to Feng-ch'eng during
the last years of the Yüan. When his descendants came to be registered as taxpayers at the beginning of the Hung-wu
era, they claimed for some unknown reasons the name Yang which the family
subsequently adopted. Yang Hsüan's father, Yang Tzu-jung 子榮 (original *ming*
Hsien 顯), the first in the family to
acquire a literary degree, served as a
secretary in the princely fiefdom of Shu
蜀 in Chengtu, Szechwan.

Following his acquisition of the *chü-
jen* in 1453 and *chin-shih* a year later,
Yang Hsüan received an appointment as
censor in 1456. In April he was sent to
Pei-Chihli and Shantung to take charge
of the branding of government horses.
Early in February, 1457, as Emperor Chu
Ch'i-yü (*q.v.*) was gravely ill and the heir
apparency still vacant, Yang was one of
a score of officials planning to plead with
the emperor to designate a successor.
Yang himself confided that he had already
vowed with two other censors that, if
their requests were ignored, they would
submit their resignations. On the morning
of February 11, as they were awaiting an
audience with the emperor, they found
that the eunuch Ts'ao Chi-hsiang, his associate Shih Heng (*qq.v.*), and others had
already reinstalled the ex-emperor, Chu Ch'i-
chen (*q.v.*). Thus they had to forgo their
plan and Yang Hsüan stayed on as censor.
In June he surprised the court by making
charges against Ts'ao Chi-hsiang and Shih
Heng. It happened that during his tour in
Pei-Chihli, he learned that a sizable
amount of fertile, productive land had been
misappropriated from the local inhabitants
by the families of these two imperial
favorites. On the 14th he memorialized
the throne on their wrongdoings and
demanded immediate action against the
offenders. The emperor, pleased with his
courage, ordered an investigation into the
matter.

In the meantime, members of the
Censorate in the capital, headed by Chang
P'eng 張鵬 (T. 騰霄, H. 拙菴, 1423-94, cs

1451, Pth. 懿簡), acting on Yang Hsüan's
complaint, supported his accusation against
Ts'ao and Shih. Before they made the
move, however, the news reached Ts'ao
through one of his informers; so he anticipated them by making a countercharge
that Chang P'eng (a nephew of the late
eunuch Chang Yung 永, executed February
16, as a member of the clique of Yü
Ch'ien, *q.v.*), sought to slander him to
avenge his uncle. The emperor subsequently ordered the arrest of both Chang
P'eng and Yang Hsüan. On the 23d, members of the Embroidered-uniform Guard
further revealed that the latter had a
prior understanding with the censors-in-
chief, Keng Chiu-ch'ou (*q.v.*) and Lo Ch'i
(*see* Li Shih); as a result they too were
cashiered and put in jail. In due course,
two other officials, Grand Secretary Hsü
Yu-chen and Minister of Personnel Li
Hsien (*qq.v.*), were also accused of being
coconspirators; five days later, they received similar sentences.

It is said that Yang had been tortured to confess that he had acted under
the order of certain high officials (presumably the above-mentioned) who wished to
discredit Ts'ao Chi-hsiang and his cronies,
but he refused to comply. He was first
sentenced to death and his colleagues to
exile. By coincidence, on the 28th a sudden storm ripped through the capital,
inflicting serious damage. The judicial
authorities, sensing that this was an indication of Heaven's displeasure, recommended a reduction in sentences for the
offenders. Yang Hsüan was then banished
to the T'ieh-ling 鐵嶺 guard, Liaotung;
several of his colleagues, including Keng
and Lo, were given lighter punishments,
and others, such as Hsü and Li, were
exonerated. Before long a general amnesty
was pronounced, enabling Yang to return
to the capital; because of his continued
hostility towards Ts'ao and Shih, however,
he again suffered exile, this time to the
Nan-tan 南丹 guard, Kwangsi. He languished there for the next five years, and
did not regain his freedom until after

the execution of Ts'ao Chi-hsiang in August, 1461. Three years later (April, 1464), following the enthronement of Chu Chien-shen (*q.v.*), Yang was reinstated as censor; sometime later he was promoted to be a surveillance vice commissioner of Chekiang and served there until his death.

During his tenure in Chekiang, Yang Hsüan devoted himself to improving the judicial system in the province, lightening the financial burden of the people by reducing the share of cash payment (in lieu of supplying paper) to the central government, and to reorganizing the coastal defense against the raids of the *wo-k'ou*. His major achievement, however, lay in the improvement of irrigation in several districts, and the repair of the sea wall to prevent tidal waves from innundating the land. He was responsible for dredging West Lake which supplied water for the irrigation of over sixteen hundred thousand *ching* (*ca.* 2.4 million acres). In 1477 he supervised the repair of the sea wall in Hai-yen 海鹽-hsien which had become dilapidated. In this endeavor Yang applied the model which Wang An-shih (1021–86) introduced in Yin 鄞-hsien, changing the wall from perpendicular to sloping to make it more resistant to tidal erosion. The length of the new sea wall came to twenty-three hundred *chang* (*ca.* 5 miles), and it was popularly called P'o-t'o 陂陀 (declivity). Unfortunately Yang's model proved ineffective, approximately one third of the wall crumbling about ten years later. The local magistrate, charged with the repair, then modified Yang's design by blending it with the traditional model, and strengthening the embankment with an inner wall having rectangular pillars. In September of 1477 Yang received promotion to be surveillance commissioner; he died less than a year later, at the age of fifty-three. Following this, the people of Hai-yen, in gratitude to Yang Hsüan for his work in flood control, erected a shrine on the embankment in his memory. After its destruction in 1575, the administrative officials of Chekiang petitioned for a new shrine. Upon its completion three years afterwards, the court granted the name Pao-kung 報功.

Yang Hsüan was the author of *Fu-pi lu* 復辟錄, 1 *ch.*, a narrative of the political events during the reinstallation of Emperor Chu Ch'i-chen in 1457, which he completed some time after his appointment as surveillance vice commissioner of Chekiang. His purpose, Yang stated, was to provide source materials for the records of this period, which the historiographers engaged in compiling the chronicles of the T'ien-shun era found to be lacking. In this undertaking Yang supplemented his own reminiscences with the writings of his contemporaries, such as Ch'en Hsün (*see* Lü Yüan), Li Hsien, Yeh Sheng (*qq.v.*), and others.

Yang Hsüan's son, Yang Yüan 源 (T. 貴溪, 本清), an astrologer, served as a secretary in the Court of the Imperial Stud during the reign of Emperor Chu Yu-t'ang (*q.v.*). In 1495, when the emperor issued an edict requesting frank opinions after receiving reports of earthquakes from several provinces, Yang submitted a memorial. Because of his junior status, however, Yang was charged with superseding his authority, and was demoted to be a clerk in the administration office of T'ung-jen 銅仁-fu, Kweichow. Sometime later he was recalled and appointed an asistant calendar officer (五官監候, grade 9A) in the directorate of astronomy.

In October, 1506, Yang Yüan stunned the court by submitting a memorial sharply critical of the young emperor Chu Hou-chao (*q.v.*) for associating with the group of eunuchs headed by Liu Chin (*q.v.*) and neglecting his normal duties. Telling of his observation of the abnormal celestial configurations which he considered ominous, Yang prophesied a state of disorder as a result of the emperor's indulgence in diversions, excessive construction work, imposition of heavy levies, and abdication of authority. He then urged him to pay more attention to state affairs, abstain from

excesses, suppress the eunuchs and syco-
phants, and avail himself of the counsel
of his senior statesmen. His remonstrance
pleased the court officials, but the emperor
ignored him.

Late in this year, citing another example of ominous cosmological signs, Yang
memorialized again, censuring imperial
favorites for misguiding the monarch and
superseding their authority. This time he
stirred the wrath of Liu Chin who, acting
ostensibly in the name of the emperor,
had him punished with a flogging of
thirty strokes. In September of the following year, undaunted, Yang presented yet
another memorial, again citing the cosmological warning, urging the emperor to
withdraw the authority delegated to his
subordinates, alluding especially to Liu
Chin. Seeing this, Liu was outraged; he
ordered Yang's arrest, gave him a flogging
of sixty strokes, and had him exiled to Su-
chou 肅州, Kansu. He died of his wounds
in a postal station in Meng 孟-hsien,
Huai-ch'ing 懷慶 prefecture, Honan, where
he was buried. In 1598 the governor of
Honan petitioned for the erection of a
shrine on the site of his grave; the court
approved and later granted it the name
Hsien-chung 顯忠. Emperor Chu Yu-chiao
(ECCP) conferred upon him (1621) the
posthumous name Chung-huai 懷. The
gazetteer of Feng-ch'eng credits him with
the authorship of a treatise on astrology
entitled *Hsing-hsüeh yüan-liu* 星學原流, 20
ch., which, however, does not seem to
have survived.

Yang Hsüan, whose given name appears frequently in the variant form of
宣, is easily confused with his fellow *chin-
shih* graduate, Yang Hsüan, whose *ming*
was 宣, but which was often written as
瑄. This Yang Hsüan (T. 振方, July
14, 1425-November 3, 1497), was a native
of Hsin-ch'eng 新城, Paoting-fu. He served
successively as censor (1456-58), assistant
minister and minister of the Court of
State Ceremonial (1458-75), and assistant minister of Rites (1476). He was
cashiered in August, 1478, on account of

incompetent performance.

Bibliography

1/162/19a; 5/84/52a; 9/21/22b; 61/107/4a; MSL
(1963), Ying-tsung, 5706, 5961, 5968, 5974, Hsien-
tsung (1964), 74, 85, 114, 151, 3085, Wu-tsung
(1965), 527, Shen-tsung (1966), 6048; KC (1958),
2403, 2897, 5184; *Feng-ch'eng-hsien chih* (1873),
8/28a, 17/4b, 24/6b; *Huang Ming wen-hai* (microfilm), 12/2/8; *Hai-yen-hsien chih* (1876), 6/40b,
11/35a; Yang Hsüan, *Fu-pi lu* in *Chi-lu hui-pien*,
ch. 21; Li Hsien, *T'ien-shun jih-lu* in *Chi-lu hui-
pien*, 22/3b, 26a; W. Franke, *Sources*, 2.5.5. For
Yang Hsüan II: 5/76/2a; 32/4/24b; MSL, Ying-
tsung, 5662, 5885, 6290, Hsien-tsung, 375, 2729,
3049, 4884, Hsiao-tsung (1964), 2301; *Hsin-ch'eng-
hsien chih* (1935), 9/4b.

Hok-lam Chan

YANG Hsün-chi 楊循吉 (T. 君謙, H. 南峯.),
1458-1546, scholar, poet, and bibliophile,
was a native of Soochow. The family had
lived earlier in K'un-shan 崑山, but in the
last years of the Yüan dynasty it made the
move to avoid hostilities on the part of
groups contending for mastery of the
region. When his great-great-grandfather,
a soldier, died in action, his widow née
T'ao 陶 was left with five sons. In the
early years of the Hung-wu period she
either willingly or by coercion found
service in the imperial palace. Yang Hsün-
chi gives as her title Nei-t'ing mu-mu 內
廷姥姥. In her old age she was allowed
to return home. It seems that on her account the family became well-to-do. Of the
five sons, the eldest, Yang Hsün-chi's
great-grandfather, placed in the category
of wealthy citizens (富民), moved to
Nanking on government order in an effort made by the emperor to redistribute
the rich families and to bring prosperity
to the capital. This branch of the family
presumably did not settle in Nanking, but
returned later to Soochow. The second
son was a merchant, engaged in commerce in Fukien, who possessed large
holdings of real property; the third son was
his associate. The two younger sons were

both given posts in the palace through their mother's instrumentality, the older becoming a eunuch who served in the directorate of woodcraft and bookcraft (御用監), and the fifth acting as supervisor of the Taoist temple of ceremonial music and dance (神樂觀).

In spite of the favorable financial situation of the family, no member elected to pursue an official career through the examinations until the time of Yang Hsün-chi. The change of social status was quite obviously brought about by the distaff side. Yang Hsün-chi's maternal uncle, Liu Ch'ang 劉昌 (T. 欽謨, H. 椶園, 1424–80, cs 1445), who rose to administration vice commissioner of Kwangtung, was an accomplished scholar and poet. It was under this uncle's inspiration and guidance that Yang, who was endowed with natural gifts, became a serious student and had little difficulty in achieving success in the examinations. A *chü-jen* of 1477, he obtained the *chin-shih* in 1484, and received the appointment of a bureau secretary in the ministry of Rites. His official career, however, was short. As he was absent from his duties too often, pleading illness real or fancied, he received a reprimand. When he asked to be transferred to a teaching post so that he might be near his home, his request was refused. In 1488, at the early age of thirty, he left office and returned to Soochow. In retirement he devoted his time to studying, writing, and building up his library.

A common practice in book collecting of the time was to borrow rare works and copy them by hand. Two of Yang's poems, one on his bookcases, and one on copying books, give a vivid picture of his life as a bibliophile, his enjoyment, and his concerns. He complained of the lack of interest in books on the part of his family, and expressed the wish that he might give them away to his friends before his death, so that his precious collection might not be dispersed or destroyed. From his collection it is said that he produced a classified encyclopedic hand-

book, the *Hsi-nang shou-ching* 奚囊手鏡 (13 *chüan* according to one source, 20 *chüan* according to another), which the editors of the *Ssu-k'u* catalogue praised for its bibliographic comprehensiveness.

In 1489, owing to a palace fire, the emperor, Chu Yu-t'ang (*q. v.*), asked in a decree for frank comments from his subjects. Yang, still at home, submitted a memorial suggesting the restoration of the Chien-wen 建文 reign title in order that historical facts might be put in their proper order. No reply came, nor was his suggestion adopted; his sense of and interest in history, however, are thus revealed (*see* Ch'en Yü-pi). For the compilation of the *Hsiao-tsung shih-lu* in 1506, the ministry of Rites issued orders to the provinces to supply relevant materials. The responsibility for collecting data from Soochow fell to Yang. The result was the *Su-chou-fu tsuan-hsiu chih-lüeh* 蘇州府纂修識畧 in 6 *chüan*. Perhaps a by-product of this labor resulted in the *Wu-chung wang-che chi* 吳中往哲記, also known as *Wu-chung ku-shih* 故實, a short biographical work about forty-one eminent men of Soochow of the early years of the Ming. These brief biographies were later supplemented (*hsü-chi* 續記 and *pu-i* 補遺) by another Soochow scholar, Huang Lu-tseng (*see* Huang Hsing-tseng). Yang left two other historical works, the *Liao hsiao-shih* 遼小史, 1 *ch.*, and the *Chin* 金 *hsiao-shih*, 8 *ch.* As these deal with the Khitan and Jurchen, they were banned in the Ch'ing dynasty, and very few copies of the original editions (*ca.* 1609) have survived; in the early 1930s, however, they were reprinted in the first series of the *Liao-hai ts'ung-shu* 遼海叢書. Among his unfinished works, according to some sources, was also a projected history of the Sung dynasty, *Sung chi* 宋紀.

Ma Chin 馬金 (T. 汝礪, cs 1484), a graduate of the same year as Yang Hsün-chi, who became prefect of Lu-chou-fu 廬州府, Nan-Chihli, in 1504, invited Yang to be chief editor of a local history of his district. After a stay of four months in Lu-chou, Yang found himself in disagreement with the editorial policies of his host. He left, therefore, and returned home, but two years later he wrote his recollections of Lu-chou in a brief work entitled *Lu-yang k'o-chi* 廬陽客記, which may now be found in the *Shuo-fu hsü*, part 26 (*see* T'ao Tsung-i). Some years later, in 1529, he completed a gazetteer of his native place, the *Wu-i chih* 吳邑志, in 16 *chüan*, which has survived; so too has a work entitled *Chin-shan tsa-chi* 金山雜記, 1 *ch.*, about the mountain west of Soochow, where in his youth he pursued his studies in a Buddhist monastery. He also left two short collections of anecdotes of human interest about his native Soochow, the *Su-t'an* 蘇談, 1 *ch.*, and the *Wu-chung ku-yü* 吳中故語, 1 *ch.*

In 1520, when Emperor Chu Hou-chao (*q. v.*) was on his excursion to Nanking, Yang was recommended for his poetic achievements and invited to join his entourage. The emperor took a fancy to his songs and lyrics and retained him for four and a half months. After the monarch returned to Peking, Yang was again summoned north, and remained in the capital until after the emperor's death. As to the one who made the recommendation to the emperor, several Ming authorities, including Wang Shih-chen (*q. v.*), assert that it was the emperor's favorite actor, Tsang Hsien (*see* Chu Hou-chao). T'an Ch'ien (*q. v.*), however, in his *Tsao-lin tsa-tsu* objects, showing the assertion to be chronologically out of the question. Because of Tsang Hsien's involvement in the rebellion of Chu Ch'en-hao (*see* Wang Shou-jen), he fell out of favor, was punished, and later murdered (1519) before the emperor's trip to the south. The possibility should not be excluded, however, that Yang made the acquaintance of Tsang Hsien some time earlier, and that the emperor had heard Yang's name from Tsang. Wang Shih-chen also reports that the emperor made Yang wear military attire and treated him just as he did the actors; as a consequence Yang felt ashamed and begged to be relieved, but Wang fails to mention that Yang was summoned to Peking later.

In 1536 Yang Hsün-chi again presented to the throne a literary piece (頌) in praise of the erection of the new imperial ancestral temple, and a Taoist book, the *Hua-yang ch'iu-ssu chai-i* 華陽求嗣齋儀, 10 *ch.*, as the emperor, Chu Hou-ts'ung (*q.v.*), was a Taoist devotee and then concerned over the lack of an heir. At the age of eighty-five *sui*, Yang Hsün-chi prepared his own burial place, and wrote his own epitaph (生壙碑). Apparently he passed on none of his scholarly and literary attributes to his descendants. Perhaps it is equally true that he left them little of the family property, which he inherited, for sources indicate that in his old age he lived in straitened circumstances.

As a poet he has received tribute from most later critics for the freshness of his approach and his easy and lucid style. His own theory for writing good poetry is that it must come primarily from one's heart, and should be understandable "even to women and children." His collected literary works, entitled the *Sung-ch'ou-t'ang chi* 松籌堂集, is noted in the *Ssu-k'u* imperial catalogue as a book of 12 *chüan*, but it also appears in 5 *chüan*, or 22 *chüan* in other lists. The National Central Library has a 5 *chüan* handwritten edition (a microfilm of which is available) with five subtitles: 1) The *Tu-hsia tseng-seng shih* 都下贈僧詩, a collection of poems presented to Buddhist monks, written in 1488. In that year the government issued one hundred ten thousand certificates to the Buddhists and Taoists. Among the Buddhist monks who went to Peking to qualify for the certificates were some of his acquaintances from Soochow. To each of these monks, at the time of his leaving Peking, Yang presented a poem. 2) The *Chü-hua pai-yung* 菊花百詠, one hundred poems singing the praises of a hundred varieties of chrysanthemums. 3) The *Teng-ch'uang mo-i* 燈窗墨藝 and 4) The *Tsuan-mei chi* 攢眉

集, two collections of essays. 5) The *Lu-yang k'o-chi*, a short gazetteer of Lu-chou mentioned above. The *Ming-shih* lists eight titles and the *Ssu-k'u* catalogue notes thirteen by Yang Hsün-chi. Some sources state that he left works totaling nearly one thousand *chüan*, many of them no longer extant. In his autobiography (epitaph) he mentions that he had on hand at that time a few finished and unfinished works, and that he was editing them. Perhaps he never completed the effort, which explains why the extant editions of the *Sung-ch'ou-t'ang chi* all differ in content as well as in number of *chüan*.

Bibliography

1/286/15a; 5/35/66a, 99/28a; 40/25/15a; 64/丙8/8b; 84/丙/35b; TSCC (1885–88 ed.), XIV/231/13b, XXIII/100/1b; *Huang Ming wen-hai* (microfilm), 5/5/7, 8; MSL(1964), Wu-tsung, 163/1a, 177/12b; KC (1958), 2519, 3151; SK (1930), 53/3b, 60/4a, 64/2a, 73/2b, 76/1b, 77/5a, 131/4b, 175/17b; Yeh Ch'ang-ch'ih (BDRC), *Ts'ang-shu chi-shih* (1958), 89; Sun Tien-ch'i (1957), 81, 95, 107, 212, 223, 245.

Lienche Tu Fang

YANG I-ch'ing 楊一清 (T. 應寧, H. 石淙, 邃菴, 三南居士), December 24, 1454-September 6, 1530, official and scholar, was born at Hua-chou 化州, Kwangtung, where his father, Yang Ching 景 (cj 1423, d. 1473), was then serving as vice magistrate. The ancestral home of the family was at An-ning 安寧, Yunnan; but on leaving office in 1460, the father retired to Pa-ling 巴陵, Hukuang. Yang I-ch'ing was an exceptional student, being made a special member of the Hanlin Academy at the age of seven; he qualified for the *chü-jen* in 1468 and the *chin-shih* in 1472. The following year his father died and, since Yunnan was too far away, he was buried at Tan-t'u 丹徒, Nan-Chihli, where his daughter lived. From that time on, Tan-t'u became Yang I-ch'ing's place of residence. About 1476, after completing the period of mourning, Yang became a drafter in the Grand Secretariat. Several years later, he was made assistant surveillance commissioner of Shansi province. In 1491 he received the appointment of commissioner of education in Shensi, where he served about eight years. During this time, he established an academy at Sian, named Cheng-hsüeh shu-yüan 正學書院. At the same time he applied himself to the study of frontier affairs, becoming especially interested in the horse superintendency.

After serving as vice minister of the Court of Imperial Sacrifices (1498–1501) and then as minister of the same court in Nanking (1501), he was ordered to proceed to Shensi with the rank of vice censor-in-chief to supervise the management of horses. He soon felt the need for more and better mounts for the army, and urged the court to provide more land for breeding and pasturing the animals. When the Mongol invaders under Batü Mönke (*q.v.*) captured Hua-ma-ch'ih 花馬池, Ning-hsia, Yang was designated governor of Shensi. Shortly after Chu Hou-chao (*q.v.*) ascended the throne in 1505, Yang suggested the appointment of a supreme commander of ministerial rank to direct the defense areas of Yen-sui 延綏 (northern Shensi), Ning-hsia, and Kansu. In February, 1506, on the recommendation of War Minister Liu Ta-hsia (*q.v.*), Yang himself was appointed supreme commander of these three western frontier defense areas. Eight months later he presented to the throne a memorial suggesting repairing and strengthening the frontier walls, originally built by Hsü T'ing-chang 徐廷璋 (T. 公器, H. 拙菴, cs 1451, governor of Yen-sui in 1464–65), and building more fortifications along the frontier. His plan was promptly approved, and funds issued, but the then powerful eunuch Liu Chin (*q.v.*), provoked by his independence, prosecuted him on the charge of wasting public money. He was thrown into the prison of the Embroidered-uniform Guard. At this point the grand secretaries, Li Tung-yang and Wang Ao 王鏊 (qq.v.), exerted themselves on his behalf, so that he gained his release, but resigned from office in April, 1507.

In May, 1510, the prince of An-hua, Chu Chih-fan (see Yang T'ing-ho), launched his rebellion. Yang was reappointed supreme commander to suppress it, while the eunuch Chang Yung (q.v.) was ordered to supervise Yang's army. A few days later, before Yang had reached Ning-hsia, the rebellious area, Chu Chih-fan was captured by General Ch'iu Yüeh (see Ch'iu Luan). At that time Yang was on friendly terms with Chang Yung. Ascertaining that Chang was jealous of Liu Chin, Yang encouraged the eunuch to overthrow the latter. His words had the desired effect; Liu Chin was put to death on September 27 of the same year, and Chang Yung rose in the estimation of the court. For this reason Chang Yung felt grateful to Yang. On the 30th of the same month, Yang received the appointment of minister of Revenue. Five days later his rank was raised to that of junior protecter of the heir apparent; in the meantime Ch'iu Yüeh received the title of earl of Hsien-ning 咸寧.

Yang I-ch'ing was made minister of Personnel in January, 1511, and in 1514 was given the rank of shao-fu 少傅. At the end of March, 1515, the grand secretary, Yang T'ing-ho, took leave because of his father's death; and two months later Yang I-ch'ing, continuing in the post of minister of Personnel, became concurrently a grand secretary. When Yang entered the Grand Secretariat, Chang Yung had been put out of the way, while Ch'ien Ning (see Sayyid Ḥusain) had risen high in the emperor's favor. At first Ch'ien's relations with Yang were satisfactory but they soon deteriorated. In 1516, on the occasion of an extraordinary astronomical phenomenon and a flood, Yang I-ch'ing criticized the court, remarking that the administration was controlled by a few men of lowly origin; that men who were fully armed and untrustworthy

were constantly seen at court; and that the defense measures in the capital were in a state of collapse. Assuming that this memorial criticized them, both Ch'ien and Chiang Pin (q.v.), favorites of the emperor, were incensed. In August they bade their men accuse Yang of a supposed affront to the throne. Accordingly, on September 11, Yang was removed from office, and he returned to Tan-t'u.

Three years later the emperor started a tour of the south and arrived at Nanking on January 15, 1520. On September 23 he left Nanking and on the 29th reached Tan-t'u and stayed for two days at Yang I-ch'ing's house, where Yang entertained him lavishly. The emperor delighted in composing verses with Yang and in examining his collection of books. When he departed for Peking, he took with him Yang's copies of the Wen-hsien t'ung-k'ao 文獻通考 in 60 volumes and the Ts'e-fu yüan-kuei 册府元龜 in 202 volumes. Chu died a few months later and was succeeded by his cousin, Chu Hou-ts'ung (q.v.). While the latter was a boy in An-lu 安陸, Hukuang, he heard his father remark that there were three outstanding persons in the middle and lower Yangtze valley: Liu Ta-hsia, Li Tung-yang, and Yang I-ch'ing; this characterization had impressed itself on Chu Hou-ts'ung's mind. Shortly after he ascended the throne (March, 1521), he sent off messengers with gifts to tender his compliments to Yang, then the only survivor of the three. A few months later the titles to be granted to the parents of the new emperor came up for discussion (Ta-li i). Having read the copy of Chang Ts'ung's (Chang Fu-ching, q.v.) memorial submitted to the throne on August 4, 1521, Yang wrote a letter to his disciple Ch'iao Yü (see Huang Hsing-tseng) in which he held that Chang was right. In the meantime he urged Chang and certain other officials of like mind to proceed to the capital to support the emperor. In July, 1524, Chang complied; soon after, his proposal was ratified, and as a consequence the emperor held him in high esteem. On January 21, 1525, with the support of Chang and Kuei O (*q.v.*), Yang I-ch'ing was again appointed supreme commander of the three frontiers of Shensi with the titular ranks of minister of War and censor-in-chief. This was the first time that a former grand secretary was ordered to superintend frontier military affairs.

Early in 1525, when some ten thousand horsemen in Ch'ing-hai invaded Kansu, Yang directed his men in putting them to flight. At the end of the year, when a distinct coolness developed between Chang Ts'ung and Grand Secretary Fei Hung (*q.v.*), Yang was summoned to court, and within six months appointed a grand secretary with the rank of minister of Personnel and junior preceptor. He was given further honors on the completion of the *Jui-tsung hsien-huang-ti shih-lu* 睿宗獻皇帝實錄 (the Veritable Records of Chu Yu-yüan; *see* Chu Hou-ts'ung) in August of that year. After Fei Hung's removal from office in March, 1527, Yang became senior grand secretary; his rank was elevated in September of the same year to that of a first-class official, and Left Pillar of State. As the senior grand secretary, he reported to the throne in November that most of the land in the eight prefectures close to the metropolitan district had been taken over by eunuch bureaus, imperial relatives, and powerful families, and suggested that this situation be investigated and brought to a stop. At the end of 1527, with the support of Yang I-ch'ing and Chang Ts'ung, the eunuch Chang Yung, who had been in disgrace for more than ten years, was made superintendent of the Integrated Divisions (training center for troops in Peking).

In October, 1527, Chang Ts'ung was appointed grand secretary, and in March, 1529, Kuei O was given a like appointment. Because of disharmony in the Grand Secretariat, Yang was removed from office on October 20. Even so, Chang still harbored resentment against him and early in 1530 bade his men accuse Yang of having taken bribes from the late eunuch Chang Yung and his younger brother, Chang Jung (*see* Chang Yung), in return for helping them achieve higher appointments in the palace. As a result, on March 3 of that year, Yang was stripped of his honors. He died six months later. In 1548 the court restored his ranks and granted him the posthumous name Wen-hsiang 文襄.

Yang is said to have been impotent, yet he married but had no issue. He was versatile and able to adapt himself to various circumstances. A man of extensive learning, he was especially expert in frontier affairs. His memorial of 1505 on the trade of tea for horses on the Shensi border was considered especially constructive. He liked to draw out a man's talents. Many men of his day, such as Ch'iu Yüeh, Wang Shou-jen, and Wang T'ing-hsiang (*qq.v.*) owed their rise in office to his recommendation and support. In point of ability, hardly anyone among his contemporaries excelled him. For this reason he was compared by some to Yao Ch'ung (651–721). He wrote a number of books, most of them extant; among them are the *Hsi-cheng jih-lu* 西征日錄 (record of a trip made by the author to inspect the border regions in Shensi, Ning-hsia, and Kansu, and of military enterprises against the Mongols in these areas), 1 *ch.*; the *Chih-fu tsa-lu* 制府雜錄 (Miscellaneous notes on his times); the *Shih-tsung wen-kao* 石淙文稿, 14 *ch.*, first printed in 1526; the *Shih-tsung shih-kao* 詩稿, 19 *ch.*; and the *Kuan-chung tsou-i ch'üan-chi* 關中奏議全集 (a collection of his memorials), 18 *ch.*, first printed in 1550. A copy of this in 10 *chüan* was copied into the Imperial Library. He also supervised the compilation of the *Ming-lun ta-tien* 明倫大典, 24 *ch.*, which included various papers written in justification of granting imperial honors to the emperor's father. A copy of the original edition of 1528 is in the Library of Congress.

Bibliography

1/198/1a; 3/176/9a; 5/15/70a; 7/41/4a; 63/12/23a; 64/丙 2/1a; 84/丙 /15b; 86/8/22a; MSL (1963), Wu-tsung, 0283, 0522, 0657, 1367, 1462, 1563, 2482, 2762, 3598, Shih-tsung (1965), 0162, 1193, 1480, 1509, 1647, 1755, 1830, 2489, 6151; KC (1958), 3107; *Tan-t'u-hsien chih* (1879), 26/6b; *Li-pu hsien-na kao* 吏部獻納稿 (NLP microfilm, no. 65); SK (1930), 55/6b, 175/15b; W. Franke, *Sources*, 2.6.1, 5.4.20, 6.4.2.; L. of C. *Catalogue of Rare Books*, 150; Morris Rossabi, "The Tea and Horse Trade with Inner Asia," *Jo. of Asian History*, 4:2 (1970), 155.

Chou Tao-chi

YANG Jung 楊榮 (original *ming* 子榮, T. 逸仁), 1371–1440, a native of Chien-an 建安, Fukien, was one of the famous "three Yang" under whom the Grand Secretariat emerged as a distinctive and powerful governmental institution (*see* Yang Shih-ch'i). Known later as the Eastern Yang, he served at the court of five successive emperors, and for more than forty years he was an intimate, influential counselor of Chu Ti, Chu Kao-chih, Chu Chan-chi, and Chu Ch'i-chen(*qq.v.*). His long career of uninterrputed favor despite maximum exposure was a rarity in Ming times.

Yang placed first in the Fukien provincial examination of 1399 and then in 1400 graduated high enough in the metropolitan examination to be selected for service as a compiler second class in the Hanlin Academy. When Chu Ti overthrew his nephew and seized the throne in 1402 Yang was among the court officials who welcomed him to the capital, Nanking, and even changed his name to celebrate the event. Chu Ti quickly chose him to be one of seven Hanlin officials, Yang Shih-ch'i among them, who were assigned to the Wen-yüan hall 文淵閣 as a personal secretariat. He was the youngest and, according to Yang Shih-ch'i, the cleverest of the seven; the emperor made him a favorite companion. He was associated with the latter during frequent periods of residence at Peking while it was being readied as a new capital, was entrusted with tutoring the imperial heirs Chu Kao-chih and Chu Chan-chi; he also accompanied both Chu Ti and later Chu Chan-chi on military expeditions into Mongol territory to the north and northwest—in 1410, 1414, 1422, 1423, 1424, 1428, and 1434. He was present when the third emperor died on campaign in 1424, and took the news to the heir apparent in Peking. A year later he received deathbed instructions from Chu Kao-chih and escorted a new heir apparent to Peking. He was a chief compiler of the *shih-lu* of the first four reigns and came to be Chu Ti's principal personal adviser about military affairs. In 1426 he planned and took an important personal part in Chu Chan-chi's campaign against the rebellious prince Chu Kao-hsü (*q.v.*), and in 1426–27 served as a leading architect of the unpopular peace policy that caused Chinese withdrawal from Annam. In his last years he, Yang Shih-ch'i, and Yang P'u (*see* Yang Shih-ch'i) were nearly a three-man regency for young Chu Ch'i-chen.

Throughout his career Yang Jung enjoyed an unbroken succession of promotions. By 1407 he became successively Hanlin compiler first class, Hanlin expositor-in-waiting, and expositor-in-waiting and concurrently mentor in the supervisorate of imperial Instruction. In 1407 he was made Hanlin expositor-in-waiting and concurrently secretary of one of the directorates of instruction in the supervisorate of imperial instruction. The next year, when his father Yang Po-ch'eng 伯成 (T. 士美) died, Chu Ti waived his mourning obligation and recalled him to duty immediately after the funeral; and in 1410 the emperor would not allow him to enter into mourning for his mother because of the imminence of a northern campaign. In 1416 Yang was promoted to the chancellorship of the Hanlin Academy, remaining concurrently a secretary in the supervisorate of imperial instruction. In 1419 he was named grand secretary and concurrently Hanlin chancellor. Under

Chu Kao-chih, in quick succession he was promoted to be chief minister of the Court of Imperial Sacrifices, then was named junior tutor of the heir apparent, and finally held three titles and received three salaries concurrently as junior tutor of the heir apparent, minister of Works, and grand secretary of the Chin-shen tien 謹身殿. Chu Chan-chi continued these honors. Then in 1430 Yang became junior tutor, with concurrent offices and salaries as before; and in 1439, under Chu Ch'i-chen, he became junior preceptor, with concurrent titles and salaries as before. Upon his death in the Hangchow area the following year, while he was returning to duty from a trip to inspect family graves at home, he was given the eminent posthumous title grand preceptor, great officer of the Court of Imperial Entertainments, and Pillar of the State, and canonized Wen-min 文敏.

Despite these successive titular embellishments, Yang Jung's substantive duty from 1402 on was to be in regular attendance upon his ruler. As later Chinese were to point out in awe, for forty years Yang was never absent from the ruler's side. Not only did he receive three concurrent salaries in his later years, but he was also showered with imperial gifts on every suitable occasion. It appears that the Yang family of Fukien was left in comfortable circumstances at his death, and it prospered for generations, producing a minister of Personnel, Yang Tan 旦 (T. 晉叔, H. 偲菴, cs 1490), a minister of War, Yang Chao 兆 (H. 晴川, cs 1556), a bibliophile, Yang Shih-ching 仕儆 (T. 敬甫, H. 直菴, 1437-96, cj 1460), and the 16th-century scholar Yang Ying-chao 應詔 (T. 天游, cj 1531), compiler of an intellectual history of Fukien province called *Min-hsüeh yüan-liu* 閩學源流. The family also had some troubles. Yang Jung's son, Yang Kung 恭, who held a minor post in the Seal Office, reportedly was beaten and reduced to commoner status in Chu Ch'i-chen's reign for quarreling with neighbors about property; and in

1477 Yang Jung's grandson Yang T'ai 泰 and great-grandson Yang Pi 畢 (possibly Yang Hua 華), who successively held a hereditary military rank in the Chien-ning Guard, were implicated in murder charges by the favored palace eunuch Wang Chih 汪直 (*q.v.*). Yang Pi died in prison before the case was tried. Yang T'ai was sentenced to death, but as the result of a subsequent judicial review he was released to be a commoner. More than a hundred of Yang T'ai's clansmen were imprisoned because of the charges against him, and almost all the property of the Yang T'ai family was confiscated by the government.

Of the "three Yang," historians have been inclined to praise Yang Shih-ch'i for his learning and character, Yang P'u for his integrity and constancy, and Yang Jung for his skillful discernment. Yang Jung's reputation has suffered from relatively faint praise and worse. Some later Ming writers denounced him for his role in the withdrawal from Annam and his failure to prevent the rise of eunuch influence, and the criticism was frequently voiced that he was quick-witted, shrewd, and canny in an unprincipled way. He is reported to have said, "I am always upset about ministers who get into trouble by being forthright. For serving a ruler there is a certain style, and for remonstrating with superiors there is a certain technique. Suppose, for example, I were reading the Thousand-character Classic with the emperor and he were to say, 'Heaven is black and Earth is red' [that is, misreading the opening statement of the work]. I wouldn't be hasty in speaking up. How can I be sure he isn't testing me? How can I know where his notions come from? How can I be certain 'black and yellow' cannot be 'black and red'? There is no advantage in speaking out too soon. I'd wait a while. Then, if he asks questions about it, I'd say, 'It seems to me that when I read the Thousand-character Classic as a boy the text said, "Heaven is black and Earth is yellow," but I don't know if that's so or not.'" It is no doubt because of anecdotes such as this that later Ming writers remarked, "Whereas Yang Shih-ch'i was upright and not crafty, Yang Jung was crafty and not upright (譎而不正)."

It would appear that, although Yang Jung might indeed have been adroit in staying in imperial favor, he was a commonsensical, decisive, and trustworthy counselor. When authorities in Chekiang province requested a military expedition to exterminate rebellious mountaineers, Yang persuaded Chu Ti that the so-called rebels were no doubt impoverished, oppressed people who had no alternative but to make a commotion; they should be soothed, he suggested, not attacked. The emperor sent a commissioner to reason with the rebels, and they all submitted. On another occasion Yang persuaded the monarch that he could not rightfully recall to service in a border expedition conscripts who had long before been given their discharges. Yang convinced a reluctant Chu Chan-chi that he must personally take the field to demonstrate and assert his authority when it was challenged by Chu Kao-hsü. Against the wishes of a strong war party at court, he later strengthened the emperor's inclination to abandon China's long and costly effort to control Annam. It is also said that Yang repeatedly used his artfulness in keeping emperors in a good humor to save the lives of eminent ministers who angered them. He seems on the whole to have been an influence for stability and reasonableness, and it appears appropriate to give him some of the credit for China's domestic tranquillity and prosperity during the 1420s and 1430s.

Yang owned a beautiful pleasance in Peking, known as Hsing-yüan 杏園 (Apricot garden). Here on April 6, 1437, he gathered together eight of his colleagues, all men of high office, including Yang Shih-ch'i and Yang P'u, for a spring party. Each of them composed a poem celebrating the occasion, and a court painter of the day, Hsieh Huan (*see* Wang

Chih 王直), depicted the scene on a scroll. Both poems and reproductions of the painting are preserved in a volume entitled *Hsing-yüan ya-chi t'u* 雅集圖 bearing a preface by Yang Shih-ch'i and a postscript by Yang Jung.

Yang Jung wrote in the clear, simple, official style called t'ai-ko 臺閣 (literally, the style of the Censorate and the Grand Secretariat), which the 18th-century *Ssu-k'u* editors defended in a distinctly patronizing tone. His collected writings, *Yang Wen-min-kung chi* 公集, in 25 *chüan*, were repeatedly published by the Yang family in Ming times. The Kiangsu Provincial Library has two copies and the National Central Library in Taiwan has a single copy of the 1445 edition, with an appendix in 1 *chüan*; the latter also has an incomplete 1515 edition with a 2 *chüan* appendix, which is available on microfilm. This work, which suffered partial excisions in the 1780s, was nevertheless copied into the Imperial Library. The National Central Library also has a Yang Jung compendium called *Liang-ching lei-kao* 兩京類稿, 20 *ch.*, published by his family in 1448. More generally accessible is Yang's day-by-day record of the 1424 expedition on which Chu Ti died, called *Pei-cheng chi* 北征記, 1 *ch.*, which is preserved in several collectanea including the *Chi-lu hui-pien* by Shen Chieh-fu (*q.v.*), but is mentioned by title only in the *Ssu-k'u* catalogue. Other writings called *Yü-t'ang i-kao* 玉堂遺稿 and *Hsün-tzu pien* 訓子編 seem to have been lost and may never have been published. A biography of Yang, *Yang Wen-min-kung-nien-p'u* 年譜, in 4 *chüan*, was published in 1552.

Bibliography

1/148/8b; 3/138/8b; 5/12/22a; 61/120/18a; 63/10/29a; MSL (1962), T'ai-tsu, introd., 4, T'ai-tsung (1963), 0166, 0535, 1013, 1071, 1126, 1152, 2189, 2471, Hsüan-tsung 1539, Ying-tsung 0801, 1216, 1329, Hsien-tsung (1964), 2957, 2994; KC (1958), 887, 1357, 1590; SK (1930), 52/10a, 170/5b; Shen Te-fu, *Yeh-hu pien*, 18/6b; *Kiangsu Provincial Library Catalogue* (Nanking, 1933), 34/10a; Sun Tien-ch'i (1957), 183; L. of C. *Catalogue of Rare Books*, 1065; Tilemann Grimm, "Das Neiko der Ming-Zeit von den Anfängen bis 1506," OE, I (1954), 139; Wolfgang Franke, *Sources*, 7.3.3; Arthur W. Hummel, *Annual Report of the Librarian of Congress, Division of Orientalia* (Washington, 1941), 163.

Charles O. Hucker

YANG Lien 楊廉 (T. 方震, H. 月湖, 畏軒), August 25, 1452-April 5, 1525, official, scholar, and thinker, was a native of Feng-ch'eng 豐城, Kiangsi. His father, Yang Ch'ung 崇 (T. 尙賢, H. 復庵, cj 1450, d. 1508), who served as prefect of Yung-chou 永州, gave the son a careful education in the Confucian Classics. Yang Lien became a *chü-jen* in 1477. The following year he failed the metropolitan examination, and returned home to teach in his native place. In 1486 he assisted in the compilation of the local gazetteer. A year later he ranked third in the metropolitan examination and was made a Hanlin bachelor. Pleading illness, however, he returned home. In 1490 he was appointed supervising secretary in the office of scrutiny in Nanking. An earthquake occurred the next year, and Yang launched accusations against several high officials and recommended others to the attention of the court, in particular Li Tung-yang, Wang Ao 鏊, and Wu K'uan (*qq.v.*). He also defended Wang Shu (*q.v.*), then minister of Personnel, against false accusation. In 1493 he went into mourning on the death of his mother. When this was concluded, he was reinstated as supervising secretary in Peking. As a result of his memorial in 1496, a shrine was built to honor Hsüeh Hsüan (*q.v.*), and the latter's writings were printed by imperial order. Then at his own request he was transferred to Nanking, in order to be nearer his aging father (1498). In 1500 he received the appointment of vice minister of the Court of Imperial Entertainments in Nanking. Four years later he was put in charge of the provincial examinations in Chekiang. Promoted to be vice minister of the Court of the Imperial Stud in Nanking in 1507, he was able to serve only two years as the death of his father sent him into mourning for the second time. In 1511 he returned to public life as a transmission commissioner, but the following year was transferred to be governor of the metropolitan prefecture, Peking. He returned to Nanking (1515) as a junior vice minister of Rites. Four years after this he took charge for a while of the ministry of Works. On the occasion of the visit to Nanking (1519) of Emperor Chu Hou-chao (*q.v.*)—a tour which Yang, together with many others, had opposed—he requested that the Imperial order instructing officials there to wear military attire while in audience be canceled, and won his point. After the accession to the throne (1522) of Emperor Chu Hou-t'sung (*q.v.*), Yang was promoted to be minister of Rites in Nanking. The following year he requested retirement from office, giving old age as an excuse. It is possible that he was unhappy with the young emperor's wish to grant posthumous honors to his deceased father, Prince Chu Yu-yüan (*see* Chu Hou-ts'ung), for he had written eight memorials on that subject, citing the philosophers Ch'eng I (1033-1107) and Chu Hsi (1130-1200); he had also vigorously opposed the suggestions of those who wished to see the prince further honored. In this his position was close to that of his friend Lo Ch'in-shun (*q.v.*), who too retired soon from public life. Reportedly the emperor sought to keep Yang in office, but failed. He died two years later at the age of seventy-three.

Yang Lien was a versatile scholar, with interests broad enough to cover various disciplines, including the Classics, philosophy, mathematics, astronomy, and even medicine. His reverence for the Sung thinkers, Chou Tun-i (1017-73), Ch'eng Hao (1032-85), Ch'eng I, Chang Tsai (1020-77), and Chu Hsi, was such that he memorialized the emperor in 1499, suggesting that their tablets be put before those of the Han and T'ang in the

Confucian Temple. This yielded no result. According to his disciple, Sun Ts'un 孫存 (T. 性甫, H. 豐山, cs 1531, 1491–1547), Yang Lien was also esteemed by his great contemporary, Wang Shou-jen (*q.v.*).

Yang was a prolific author, with over twenty works to his credit. There is a detailed list of these in the biographical account written by Sun Ts'un, in the *Kuo-ch'ao hsien-cheng lu* of Chiao Hung (*q.v.*). The following titles are enough to indicate the breadth of his scholarship: the *T'ai-chi-t'u tsuan-yao* 太極圖纂要, 1 *ch.*, *Shu-hsüeh t'u-chüeh fa-ming* 數學圖訣發明, 1 *ch.*, *Lü lü tsuan-li t'u-shuo* 律呂纂例圖說, *Li-yüeh shu* 禮樂書, 1 *ch.*, *Hsüan-chu feng ya yüan-liu* 選注風雅源流, 1 *ch.*, *I-hsüeh chü-yao* 醫學舉要, 1 *ch.*

One of his historical works, the *Huang Ming ming-ch'en yen-hsing lu* 名臣言行錄, 2 *ch.*, has become one of the important biographical sources for the Ming period. There is another work, the *Wan-yen lu* 琬琰錄, included in the *Shuo-fu hsü* (*see* T'ao Tsung-i). Yang Lien was very fond of the Great Learning, and of the explanations of the text by the Sung thinker, Chen Te-hsiu (1178–1235), entitled *Ta-hsüeh yen-i* (*see* Ch'iu Chün). He compiled an abridged version of this work, *Ta-hsüeh yen-i chieh-lüeh* 節略, 20 *ch.*, which he presented to the emperor. The editors of the *Ssu-k'u* Catalogue mention only one work by Yang Lien, the *Yüeh-hu chi* 月湖集, 48 *ch.*, and describe it as consisting essentially of his personal writings, those in prose style resembling recorded dialogues, while his poems are said frequently to contain philosophical themes.

After his death, Yang Lien was honored with the posthumous title of junior guardian of the heir apparent, and was canonized Wen-k'o 文恪. Following one of his last requests, Lo Ch'in-shun composed his epitaph. One of his sons became an assistant magistrate through imperial favor.

Bibliography

1/160/14a, 182/7a, 282/25b; 5/24/52a, 36/32a, 35a, 37b; 14/5/25a; 16/42/29b; MSL(1940), Shih-tsung, 51/16b; Lo Ch'in-shun, "Mu-chih ming" 墓誌銘 in *Huang Ming wen-hai* (microfilm), 5/6/6; SK (1930), 175/19a; *Kiangsi t'ung-chih*(1880), 28/19a, 137/27b, 31a; *Fu-chou-fu chih* 撫州府志 (1876), 56/12b; *Hunan t'ung-chih* (1934), 2424; Huang Yü-chi (ECCP), *Ch'ien-ch'ing-t'ang shu-mu* (1913 ed.), 2/13b, 3/41a, 11/5a; *Shuo-fu hsü* (1646), 8; W. Franke, *Sources*, 3.3.3.

Julia Ching and Huang P'ei

Yang Ming 楊銘 (original name Ha 哈-ming), *ca.* 1433–October 3, 1503, an officer in the Embroidered-uniform Guard, served under three emperors as interpreter and envoy to the Mongol camp during the fifty years of his career. Yang's early years are obscure. From his original name Ha (a partial transcription of Ḥajjī), he appears to have been a Muslim of possible Uighur-Mongol origin. His personal name Ming, however, is Chinese. His father, Ha-chih 只 (a full transcription of Ḥajjī; referred to as Yang Chih by his son after the latter adopted the Chinese surname), a junior officer in the Chinese army, was promoted to be a chiliarch late in 1449. Owing to his command of both Chinese and Mongol, Ha-chih was recruited to accompany the envoy Wang Hsi 王喜, a commander in the Embroidered-uniform Guard of Korean origin, to the Oirat court of Esen (*q.v.*) in March, 1448. Ha-ming, then a young lad, joined the retinue. In March of the following year the Ḥajjī were again members of an embassy to the Oirat under the chief envoy Wu Liang 吳良(original name Ölje-temür, 1376–1474), a commander of Jurchen birth in the Embroidered-uniform Guard.

On this occasion the Ming embassy was not permitted to return home. Esen apparently held its members in custody in reprisal for the detention by the Ming court of some of his own delegates. Only a certain Wu Chün 吳俊 succeeded in escaping and returning to China. Meanwhile Esen had been moving southward, and, after the capture of Emperor Chu Ch'i-chen

(*q.v.*) in September, 1449, the Chinese prisoners, including the two Ḥajjī, were allowed
to meet with the captive emperor and stay
with him. In October, when Esen brought
his captive to the vicinity of Peking
and was refused admittance, Ha-chih went
in as a messenger and remained after
being promoted to a chiliarch. Ha-ming,
however, stayed with the emperor throughout his captivity, serving him at times like
a personal attendant. He also carried messages between the Oirat and the Ming
court, accompanied the emperor whenever
the Oirat moved, and kept him in good
spirits. Upon Chu Ch'i-chen's release in
September, 1450, Ha-ming received from
the new emperor (*see* Chu Ch'i-yü) the
rank of constable in the Embroidered-
uniform Guard.

In February, 1457, following Chu Ch'i-
chen's restoration to the throne, Ha-ming
was promoted to asssitant commander in
the Guard and served on a mission to the
Oirat, headed by Ma Cheng 馬政, a commander (of Uighur origin) in the same
Guard. In May the Chinese envoys met a
Mongol attack in northern Shansi and
were taken captive, but Ha-ming and Ma
Cheng's son, Ma Chien 鑑, escaped and
succeeded in reaching Chinese territory.
The two men came under suspicion and
were subjected to interrogation, but they
received no punishment. In March, 1459,
because of a mishap, Ha-ming was
demoted to be a chiliarch in the Kweichow
guard. He probably received a pardon
shortly afterwards for, according to his
reminiscences, he took part in the suppression of the rebellion of Ts'ao Ch'in (*see*
Ts'ao Chi-hsiang) and was awarded the
rank of vice commander. Then in February, 1466, he joined the expedition headed
by Chu Yung (*see* Hsiang Chung) against
the bandits of Liu Ch'ien-chin 劉千斤 in
Hukuang, and in October of the following
year received a further promotion to be
commander.

All this time he was known as Ha-ming;
he is first mentioned as Yang Ming in the
shih-lu of June, 1471, when he was sent
to Tatung as interpreter to receive and
investigate a Mongol tribute mission and
escort it to Peking. In subsequent years
this task was assigned to him several
times, and from 1478 on he is regularly referred to as grand interpreter.
He was charged in August with clearing
up a difficulty stemming from the fact
that some Jurchen chieftains had assumed
higher ranks than they actually held and
expected rewards and presents accordingly.
In May, 1484, observing that the Mongols
in the Uriyangqad commanderies were
under pressure from the northern tribes to
join their cause, Yang Ming recommended
sending an embassy to ensure their loyalty; the ministry of War, however, rejected
his proposal as premature. Emperor Chu
Yu-t'ang (*q.v.*) accorded him the rare
honor in April, 1491, of making his rank
as commander hereditary. In September,
1499, when trouble flared up in the commanderies, Yang Ming undertook an investigation and reported that many recent
border incidents were provoked by Chinese troops from Liaotung. Two months
later he was put in charge of the soldiers
in Liaotung (with the rank of high commander) to guard against possible attacks
by the settlers of the commanderies. On
at least two occasions, June, 1495, and
April, 1500, he had to deal with Tibetan
tribute envoys, and warned them that
they could not ask for more presents
than were customarily distributed on such
occasions. We know nothing more of
Yang Ming until the report of his death
in 1503. His son, Yang Ts'ung 琮, who
inherited the rank of commander in the
Embroidered-uniform Guard, continued to
serve as interpreter.

Besides his official services Yang
Ming is known as the author of the *Cheng-
t'ung lin-jung lu* 正統臨戎錄, 1 *ch.*, an
account of his experiences with Emperor
Chu Ch'i-chen from September, 1449, to
the autumn of 1450. Written in colloquial
language, it contains interesting observations on the Oirat attitude toward the
captive emperor and the relation of the

latter to the Ming court during this period. Judging from the brief autobiographical statement appended to the end of his reminiscences, one may assume that Yang wrote this some time after 1491. The *Cheng-t'ung lin-jung lu* is highly rated as a source for the study of this episode, more valuable than the *Pei-cheng shih-chi* 北征事蹟, 1 *ch.*, a similar account by his contemporary Yüan Pin (*see* Esen), an officer in the Embroidered-uniform Guard who also stayed with the captive emperor. The letter appears actually to have been written by Yin Chih 尹直 (T. 正言, H. 謇齋, 1427-1511, cs 1454), a Hanlin compiler, who (basing it on Yüan's report) submitted it to the court in 1465. There is a rifacimento of Yang's account in the literary language, entitled *Cheng-t'ung pei-shou* 狩 *shih-chi*, prepared by an unknown writer on the basis of the original version. Both works are included in the *Chi-lu hui-pien*, edited by Shen Chieh-fu (*q.v.*).

The *shih-lu* under dates of 1472 and 1473 mentions another Yang Ming, an assistant commander-in-chief serving in Shensi, who was exiled to Kweichow for corruption in the army, in June, 1473, but was exonerated later.

Bibliography

1/167/10a; MSL (1963), Ying-tsung, 5820, 5859, 5920, 5938, 6377, Hsien-tsung(1964), 1770, 1963, 2039, 2087, 2250, 2957, 3244, 4244, Hsiao-tsung (1964), 368, 914, 996, 1844, 2709, 2770, 2877, 3780; KC (1958), 1807, 1810, 1819, 1841, 1847, 1869, 1872; Chang Hung-hsiang 張鴻翔, "Ming wai-tsu tz'u-hsing k'ao" 明外族賜姓考, *Fu-jen hsüeh-chih* 輔仁學誌, 3:2 (1932), 19; Wada Sei 和田清, *Tōashi kenkyū (Mōko hen)* 東亞史研究 (蒙古篇), Tokyo, 1959), 923; Henry Serruys, *Sino-Mongol Relations During the Ming, II: The Tribute System and Diplomatic Missions* (Brussels, 1967), 577; W. Franke, *Sources*, 2.5.3, 4.

Hok-lam Chan

YANG Po 楊博 (T. 惟約, H. 虞坡), June 11, 1509-September 7, 1574, noted minis-

ter of War, was a native of P'u-chou 蒲州, Shansi. His father, Yang Chan 瞻 (T. 叔後, H. 舜原, d. 1555, cj 1519), rose from a local magistrate to assistant surveillance commissioner of Szechwan. After qualifying as *chin-shih* in 1529, Yang Po received an appointment the following year as magistrate of Chou-chih 盩厔 in the prefecture of Sian. Though only twenty years of age, he showed unusual wisdom and ability. Later he was transferred to the city of Sian, where he made an impressive record, for which he was promoted to secretary and later director of the bureau of provisions in the ministry of War. During the last assignment he went with the grand secretary, Chai Luan (*see* Yen Sung), on a tour of inspection of the entire length of the northern frontier from Liaotung to Kansu. The mission lasted from March, 1539, to February, 1540. Everywhere they went Yang made a careful study of the towns, strategic areas, local customs, and the morale and size of the army. The grand secretary was greatly impressed by the young staff officer whose quick-witted action once saved an awkward situation. At Su-chou 肅州 several hundred tribesmen came clamoring for gifts. Having brought nothing for them, Chai was helpless and afraid of a riot. Yang, however, immediately cowed the tribesmen by accusing them of failing to arrive on time to welcome his excellency, thus putting them in the wrong and changing an unruly mob to one beseeching pardon. In his report to the throne Chai recommended that Yang be entrusted with important affairs. He was then transferred to be director of the bureau of operations. About this time (1542) Altan-qaɣan (*q.v.*) was making overtures, looking towards improved trade relations. Yang thought well of the idea but the court did not, executing Altan's unlucky envoy and offering a reward for the capture or death of his master. Minister of War Chang Tsan 張瓚 (T. 延獻, cs 1505, 1473-1542, Pth. 恭襄) was ordered to take charge of the expulsion of the invaders; Chang in turn relied on Yang for tactical and strategic planning and execution. After Mao Po-wen (*q.v.*) took over the ministry of War, he requested Yang to remain. When important memorials on military matters were referred to the ministry for comment, it relied on Yang to draft replies. Some of these drafts were regarded as models of their kind. While in charge of the bureau of operations, Yang was responsible not only for the strategy to defend the northern frontiers but also for the planning of the pacification of Annam (*see* Mao Po-wen). Late in 1543 Yang was promoted to surveillance vice commissioner in Shantung in charge of education. In May, 1545, he was raised to be the administration vice commissioner in the same province.

The court summoned him a year later to be right assistant censor-in-chief and concurrently governor of Kansu, where he involved himself in reconstruction work in Su-chou and Kan 甘 -chou, digging canals, promoting and improving agriculture, and repairing fortifications. He also directed the resettlement of the same tribal people he intimidated in 1539. These were the ones who, escaping from the Turfan raiders about 1528, had been permitted to live at Su-chou for more than twenty years. Because they were semi-nomadic and frequently had disputes with the Chinese, who were chiefly farmers, Yang Po persuaded their leaders to agree to move about fifty miles southwest of Su-chou where there was open land for pasture. For their protection Yang built or strengthened seven walled forts and some watch towers. In this way he resettled 3,454 persons in 706 yurts.

For several victories over Mongol raiders, Yang Po was rewarded in September, 1549, with the promotion of two grades in rank, to be a titular vice censor-in-chief. In the summer of 1550 he left Kansu and returned home to mourn the death of his mother. So he was forced to be inactive while Esen (*q. v.*) and his hordes broke through the Great Wall and overran the area north of Peking. It is said that Yang was recommended as an expert on northern frontier warfare, but the then powerful general, Ch'iu Luan (*q.v.*), whom he had once censored, barred his recall. In October, 1552, the court summoned him to Peking to serve as junior vice minister of War. From March to August, 1553, he held the *ad hoc* title of ching-lüeh 經略 to serve as head of a mission to inspect the frontier north and northeast of Peking in order to formulate a plan to rebuild the defenses against any future Mongol raids. While on the mission he was promoted to senior vice minister of War. On his recommendation the Ch'ao-ho-ch'uan forts (*see* Ch'en Ti) were constructed as the second line of defense inside the Ku-pei 古北 pass. Some strategic posts northwest of Peking were also strengthened. In January, 1554, he received the appointment of supreme commander of the northeastern frontier (Chi-Liao tsung-tu 薊遼總督, as recorded in Ming shih-lu; Kuo ch'üeh misses a line). In October he went to the front to direct the defense against intrusions by the Mongols under Pa-tu-er 把都兒 (younger brother of Altan), and held them off at Ku-pei pass, where the fortification had been strengthened at his suggestion in the preceding year. After a daring night attack he forced the Mongols to retreat. For his success in this battle he was promoted to titular senior censor-in-chief, and concurrently junior vice minister of War, and awarded the hereditary rank of a battalion commander of the Embroidered-uniform Guard. In March, 1555, the emperor, displeased with the then minister of War, Nieh Pao (*q.v.*), for his lack of efficiency, dismissed him and appointed Yang Po in his stead. Early in the following year Yang had to return home on account of the death of his father. The emperor (March, 1558) recalled Yang as titular head of the ministry of War but immediately sent him out to serve as supreme commander of Hsüan-fu and Tatung. There his greatest contribution was the rebuilding of the

Great Wall, parts of which still stand to this day. In November, 1559, he was summoned to the capital to resume his duties at the ministry of War. This time he continued in that office for seven years. In 1563 the supreme commander, Yang Hsüan 楊選 (T. 以公, H. 東江, cs 1544), disobeyed his instructions and shifted the troops eastward, thus weakening the northern front. This resulted in another breakthrough by the Mongols who once more raided as far as the suburbs of Peking. The emperor ordered Yang Hsüan executed and was about to punish Yang Po too when the grand secretary, Hsü Chieh (*q.v.*), interceded for him and saved him from disgrace.

Yang Po was transferred (November, 1566) to head the ministry of Personnel, and so was in a strategic position in the struggle for power between Hsü Chieh and Kao Kung (*see* Chang Chü-cheng); in this Yang sided with Hsü. Under the new emperor, Chu Tsai-hou (*q. v.*), Hsü ousted Kao (June, 1567) and held great power for over a year until he himself was forced to resign. Meanwhile Yang served as minister of Personnel with dignity and efficiency. Tall and portly and bearded, he made an impressive figure at court. He had come from a well-to-do family, and among his relatives were Chang Ssu-wei and Wang Ch'ung-ku (*qq.v.*), fellow-townsmen whose families made their fortunes in the government salt monopoly. Thus he could maintain his impartiality without financial worries. Court politics, however, finally caught up with him. Early in 1570, because he defended P'ang Shang-p'eng (*q.v.*) from unjust accusations, he was charged with trying to deceive the emperor with false reports,and forced to resign. Immediately Kao Kung was recalled as grand secretary and, in an unprecedented way, given the concurrent charge of the ministry of Personnel to succeed Yang. Apparently Kao appreciated Yang's ability, and in April, 1571, recommended his recall from retirement to serve once more as minister of War. It was

a time of grave decisions, for, although peace had just been concluded with the Mongols (*see* Altan-qaγan and Wang Ch'ung-ku), it could only be insured by strong defenses on the frontier. Yang was credited with transferring more Chekiang troops to strengthen the northern border (*see* Ch'i Chi-kuang and T'an Lun). When, in July, 1572, Kao Kung was forced out of office by the intrigues of the eunuchs and Chang Chü-cheng (*q.v.*), Yang was again made minister of Personnel. For his long service he was given the honorary title of junior preceptor. A year later he fell ill and in October, 1573, retired. When he died a year later, he was given posthumously the title of grand tutor and the name Hsiang-i 襄毅.

Yang Po is said to have left a literary collection, *Yü-p'o-chi* 虞坡集, 10 *ch.*, as well as two *chüan* of poems and four more of miscellaneous works. His main contribution in writing, however, consists of his memorials, printed in a collection at the conclusion of each mission or after leaving an office. Huang Yü-chi (ECCP) lists seven of these collections and Wolfgang Franke, six, but the only extant ones seem to be those in the Naikaku Bunko and the Sonkeikaku. The *Ming ching-shih wen-pien* (*see* Ch'en Tzu-lung, ECCP), contains five *chüan* of his memorials, all important documents on military matters.

He had five sons. The eldest, Yang Chün-min 俊民 (T. 伯章, H. 本庵, cs 1562, d. 1599), served as minister of Revenue during the difficult years from September, 1591, to May, 1599, when the country was at war with the Mongols in the north and northwest (*see* Li Ju-sung) and against the Japanese in Korea (*see* Konishi Yukinaga). The latter campaign, which lasted seven years (1592-99), proved a serious drain on the treasury. In addition, there were the extravagant demands both by the irresponsible emperor, Chu I-chün (*q.v.*), and his mother Li-shih (*q. v.*), for personal expenses. In all these matters Yang seems to have served the empire

well. When he died shortly after his retirement, he was granted the title of junior guardian. There is a long memorial
under his name in the *Huang Ming ching-
shih wen-pien*. Among Yang Po's other
sons may be mentioned Yang Chün-shih
士 (cs 1574), and Yang Chün-ch'ing 卿
(military cj 1568), the one who inherited
the military hereditary rank awarded in
1554, and who rose to be a commander
of the Embroidered-uniform Guard.

Bibliography

1/97/19a, 214/1a; 3/198/1a; 5/25/54a,29/66a; 8/65/
1a; 13/14/18a; 16/116/10b, 130/31b; 24/2/141b; 32/
100/49b; 40/41/8b; 64/ 戊 17/5a; MSL (1965),
Shih-tsung, 7212, 7281, 7440, 9027, Mu-tsung,
0992, 1371, Shen-tsung (1966), 0030; KC (1958),
3905, 4254, 4839; SK (1930), 56/5a; *Chou-chih-
hsien chih* (1925), 5/6b; *P'u-chou-fu chih* (1754), 8/
8b, 28a, 12/28a, 14/27b, 20/20a; TSCC(1885–88),
XI: 582/34/2b; Ho Ch'iao-yüan, *Ming-shan ts'ang*
(1971), 5025; D. Pokotilov, *History of the Eastern Mongols during the Ming Dynasty from 1368
to 1634*, tr. by R. Loewenthal (Chengtu, 1947),
118; H. Serruys, *Sino-Mongol Relations during the
Ming*, II (Brussels, 1967), 57; L. Hambis, *Documents sur l'histoire des Mongols à l'époque des
Ming* (Paris, 1969), 57; W. Franke, *Sources*, 5.
6.26.

Angela Hsi and Chaoying Fang

YANG Shan 楊善 (T. 思敬), 1384-June 11,
1458, official who held the longest service
record of any Ming official (over five
decades) in the Court of State Ceremonial,
and who headed a successful mission
to Esen (*q. v.*) in 1450, was born at Ta-
hsing 大興 (later Peking). In 1400, while
a student, Yang was introduced to Chu
Ti (*q.v.*), then prince of Yen, who subsequently put him in charge of ceremonial
matters. Yang followed him during his
campaign to unseat his nephew, Chu Yün-
wen (*q. v.*), and gained his trust. Shortly
after Chu Ti's enthronement, Yang was
appointed an usher in the Court of State
Ceremonial, and promoted two years later
to be a conductor of ceremonies. He be-

came a director of the bureau for entertaining guests (1409), and was selected to
be an attendant of the heir apparent, Chu
Kao-chih (*q.v.*). In May, 1418, he received
a promotion to be assistant minister of
the same court. While holding the rank
of a secretary in the ministry of Rites
(1421), he was sent to Fukien to supervise
the funeral of the ruler of Ku-ma-la-lang
古麻剌朗 (Cabarruyan Island?), who had
visited Peking the previous year. Shortly
after Chu Kao-chih's assumption of power,
Yang Shan was made minister of the
Court of State Ceremonial (October, 1424).
Though not accomplished in scholarship,
Yang has been described as alert and
intelligent. Another gift was his ability
to enunciate loudly and distinctly, which
made him well suited for the conduct of
ceremonies.

Yang Shan served in the same court
under the next two emperors and gained
their confidence. During this period he
was twice indicted, in November, 1431,
and in September, 1441, respectively, for
minor offenses, but through imperial support suffered no punishment. Early in
1449 Yang was promoted to be vice minister of Rites, concurrently serving as
head of the Court of State Ceremonial.
In August of that year, when Emperor
Chu Ch'i-chen (*q.v.*), urged on by the
eunuch Wang Chen (*q.v.*), took personal
command of an army against the Oirat,
Yang was ordered to join the expedition.
In the disastrous defeat at T'u-mu, during
which the emperor was captured and
scores of officials perished, Yang was one
of the few who managed to return safely.
Reinstated in his old post, he was promoted to be a vice censor-in-chief and
recruited (October) by Yü Ch'ien (*q. v.*)
to take part in the defense of the capital
against enemy raids. Two months later he
became a censor-in-chief, alternating his
duties in the military defense with those
in his regular office.

In August of the following year, as
the Ming court and Esen were trying to
normalize their relations, Yang Shan re-

ceived a summons to head a special mission
to the Oirat court. Several official exchanges had been made earlier but they
produced little result as Esen, now holding
the Chinese emperor as hostage, was
eager to exploit the situation. The new
emperor, Chu Ch'i-yü (q.v.), on the other
hand, was uncertain about Esen's motives
in his expressed willingness to release his
prisoner, and also over the possible reper-
cussions attendant on the return of the
former monarch. Before Yang's appointment, Chu Ch'i-yü had already sent Li
Shih (q.v.) to the Oirat camp to explore
Esen's intention and the mood of his
elder brother. It appears that the new
emperor too was waiting until such time
as might be advantageous to him; thus he
tried to play down the negotiation by
sending junior officials as emissaries and
by shying away from the question of his
brother's return. Shortly after Li Shih's
departure (August 8), however, an Oirat
embassy arrived in Peking reiterating
Esen's desire for a peace settlement and
urged the court to send an envoy of ministerial rank to assure the Oirat chief of
China's genuine interest in his proposal.
Urged on by the court officials, Chu Ch'i-
yü reluctantly sent Yang to head another
mission. The fact that Yang was chosen
for this task was not only because he
was mentioned by the Oirat envoy as
one of the acceptable candidates, but
also because of Yang's experience and his
skill as a shrewd negotiator.

Yang Shan left the capital on the
25th of August at the head of a delegation
that included his deputies Chao Jung 趙
榮 (T. 孟仁, H. 三省, 1412-75), a vice
minister of Works of central Asian origin,
Wang Hsi 王息, a military officer of
Korean descent, and T'ang Yin-chi 湯胤勣
(T. 公讓, d. November 9, 1466), a commander of the Embroidered-uniform Guard,
the great-grandson of T'ang Ho (q.v.).
Four of Yang's sons also accompanied
him. Before he departed the emperor gave
Yang the same instructions that he had
given Li Shih earlier; the order did not
include negotiation for the return of the
ex-emperor, nor did the emperor make
available any gifts for Esen, or item of
daily necessity for the former monarch.
It is said that Yang had to defray the
expense of a few gifts for presentation
from his own purse. Yang had little knowledge of the situation in the Oirat camp
when he and his party set out; at T'u-mu,
however, they met Li Shih's group on
its way back. Yang then learned two
items of news important to the success
of his own mission: first, that Esen had
indicated his willingness to release the
imperial captive in return for China's
goodwill; second, that the ex-emperor had
declared that he intended to retire after
his return to Peking. This intelligence
was not known to the court until Li presented his report on the 28th; the emperor
then dispatched a messenger to inform
Yang of these developments, yet he gave
no instruction on the return of the imperial captive. It appears that the emperor
was reluctant to make a decision until
after Yang Shan's return, pending further
deliberation on the implications of Esen's
offer. He must have been astonished to
have Yang escort Chu Ch'i-chen back to
Peking without obtaining his approval.

Yang and his party arrived at the
Oirat camp on September 5, but were
unable to meet Esen until the 7th when
he returned from a hunting trip. The
meeting was cordial as Esen was eager
for the arrival of a senior Chinese envoy
with whom he might arrange the release
of his hostage in return for the restoration of tributary relations with the Ming
court. During their conversation Esen,
surprised by the lack of worthy gifts and
failure to mention the release of the ex-
emperor in the imperial decree, questioned
Yang on the intention of his master. To
ease Esen's suspicion, Yang tactfully responded that the Chinese deliberately omitted these in order to demonstrate their
belief that the Oirat chief was not avaricious, and that his release of the imperial
captive would not be due to the acceptance

of ransom. Esen, said to be flattered by Yang's remarks, ordered his men to prepare for the return of his hostage, though he may have already made up his mind on this count. Yang was then escorted into the presence of Chu Ch'i-chen; there he greeted him in the etiquette required of a minister to a reigning monarch. The party set out on its return trip on September 13, arriving in Peking on the 20th. Meanwhile Chu Ch'i-yü had already learned of the release, and unquestionably had mixed feelings about his elder brother's return, as this would pose a challenge to his legitimacy as emperor. For this reason he did not reward Yang Shan to the degree that Yang had expected on the ground that he had acted on his own initiative. Nevertheless, as a modest gesture, he promoted Yang one grade, making him a senior censor-in-chief. Later Yang wrote an account of his trip to the Oirat court; this is no longer extant, but much of it has been incorporated into the *P'i-t'ai lu* of Liu Ting-chih (*q.v.*).

Piqued over the treatment received, Yang secretly gave support to a group of officials and eunuchs who were plotting the reinstallation of the former monarch; these included Ts'ao Chi-hsiang, Shih Heng, Hsü Yu-chen (*qq.v.*), and others. Early in 1457, taking advantage of the serious illness of the emperor, they skillfully executed a coup and put the ex-emperor back on the throne. Once returned to power, Chu Ch'i-chen richly rewarded those who had brought about his reinstatement. On February 25 Yang Shan received the hereditary title of earl of Hsing-chi 興濟伯, with an annual stipend of 1,200 bushels of rice. A few days later he was once more made head of the Court of State Ceremonial, and in April became concurrently minister of Rites. In the following month his four sons who had taken part in the restoration also received awards of military ranks.

Yang Shan now enjoyed a prestigious position and was able to exercise some influence in court politics. It is said that he played a role in the nomination of Li Hsien (*q.v.*) to the Grand Secretariat. His rise in power, however, invited the enmity of his colleagues, notably Shih Heng and Ts'ao Chi-hsiang, who began attacking him in the emperor's presence. Before they succeeded in outmaneuvering him, Yang died, thus escaping the impeachment suffered by some of his fellow plotters a few years later. He received the posthumous name Chung-min 忠敏, and the earldom was subsequently (October 19) passed on to his son Yang Ts'ung 琮, who had also taken part in the coup. Yang Ts'ung, however, lost this distinction when, in July, 1465, certain officials invoked the precedent taken in 1460 against Shih Heng and several other members of the restoration group. On that occasion, along with the sentence meted out against the culprits, an imperial edict decreed that their descendants be denied the privilege of inheriting their fathers' titles. Acting on their recommendation, Emperor Chu Chien-shen (*q.v.*) stripped Yang Ts'ung of his title, but in tribute to his father's meritorious service, he appointed him a vice commander of the Chin-wu 金吾 guard in the capital.

Most of Yang Shan's biographers, though praising his skill as a diplomat, express contempt for his character. They charge him with employing various schemes to advance at the expense of his colleagues. They also report that, when Yang was jailed early in 1403 for an offense, he happened to have as fellow prisoner Chang P'u 章樸 (T. 原質, cs 1404), a Hanlin bachelor incarcerated on unspecified charges. Later Yang discovered that Chang possessed a manuscript copy of the writings of Fang Hsiao-ju (*q.v.*), whose literary works had been condemned and banned from circulation. When Yang reported this, Chu Ti had Chang executed for violation of the law and as a member of Fang's clique, and released Yang in reward for his information. The biographers, moreover, contend that Yang had much to do with Chu Ch'i-chen's decision, after he had regained the throne, to punish those officials loyal to Chu Ch'i-yü, men such as Yü Ch'ien, Wang Wen (*q.v.*), and Ch'en Hsün (*see* Lü Yüan).

Bibliography

1/171/11a; 5/10/38a; 8/26/11a; 32/1/6a; 61/99/4b; 63/13/9a; MSL (1963), T'ai-tsung, 2079, 2271, Hsüan-tsung, 1929, Ying-tsung (1964), *ch.* 83–291, Hsien-tsung, 374; Liu Ting-chih, *P'i-t'ai lu*, Li Shih, *Pei-shih lu*, Yang Ming, *Cheng-t'ung lin-jung lu*, Li Hsien, *Ku-jang tsa-lu*, all in Shen Chieh-fu, *Chi-lu hui-pien*, 16/6a, 17/10b, 19/21b, 23/10a; Hsia Hsieh 夏燮, *Ming t'ung-chien* 明通鑑 (1959), 652.

Hok-lam Chan

YANG Shen 楊慎 (T. 用修, H. 升庵, 博南山人), December 8, 1488-August 8, 1559, eldest son of Grand Secretary Yang T'ing-ho (*q.v.*) and a native of Hsin-tu 新都, Szechwan, was a brilliant student, scholar, and an authority on Yunnan. Selected optimus in the palace examinations of 1511, he entered the Hanlin as a compiler. In August, 1517, he was one of the officials who vigorously protested the emperor's absence from the capital and excursions to military posts on the northern frontier (*see* Chu Hou-chao). Later in that year he pleaded illness and obtained permission to return to Szechwan to recuperate. He resumed his office in Peking late in 1520 in time to assist his father during the 1521 crisis over the selection of the succeeding emperor, Chu Hou-ts'ung (*q.v.*). At the first tutoring session of the youthful emperor in September, 1521, Yang Shen gave a lecture on a passage in the *Book of History*, explaining that punishment for serious crimes should be carried out and not be reduced in any way. It was general knowledge at court that Yang's lecture was a protest against the permission granted to two eunuchs to redeem themselves from death sentences. In 1522 he was sent on a mission to offer sacrifices to the spirit of the Yangtze River and to the ancestors of the prince of Shu 蜀 at Chengtu, Szechwan. He wrote an acount of his ten months' journey, entitled *Chiang-ssu chi* 江祀記. This marked the height of his official career, which was abruptly terminated in 1524.

In the controversy known as the *Ta-li-i* (*see* Feng Hsi), when Emperor Chu Hou-ts'ung, insisting on the elevation of his deceased father to full imperial status, wrathfully meted out punishment to the hundreds of memorialists who voiced opposition, Yang Shen was one of the group of one hundred thirty-four who received beatings in prison on August 14. Five days later they were all bastinadoed in public in the imperial courtyard; this resulted in the deaths of at least eighteen of them. Yang somehow survived the ordeal and was sentenced to exile. He and two others were each given another beating and a heavier sentence: to become exiled convicts on "permanent" (永遠) military service as common soldiers, Yang to serve at Yung-ch'ang wei 永昌衞, a guard near the western border of Yunnan, about the most distant outpost of the empire.

The selection of this guard for Yang's service may have had a more sinister intent. The administration had for seventy years been placed in the hands of a resident eunuch and a guard commander, much to the disadvantage and distress of the native population, chiefly Shan tribesmen. Ho Meng-ch'un (*see* Li Tung-yang), who served as governor of Yunnan from 1519 to 1521, made a strong appeal to the throne to abolish the eunuch's office and return the administration to its former status of a chün-min fu 軍民府 or frontier prefecture governing both miltary and civilian families. Ho's memorial came up for consideration in the central government at a time when Yang Shen's father was in power and in a position to override opposition by the eunuchs and military men and to approve Ho's proposal. In this way civilian rule was reestablished at Yung-ch'ang, the order specifying that a *chin-shih* of proven ability be appointed prefect. Local opposition came from those who had profited from the military and eunuch command. They threatened a riot but were restrained by provincial authorities. Yang T'ing-ho even composed an essay commemorating the conversion of the eunuch's office to headquarters for the prefect. The essay was inscribed on a monument erected in 1524, probably after Yang T'ing-ho had already lost favor at court and been forced to resign; this took place in March of that year. Emperor Chu Hou-ts'ung regarded Yang as leader of the opposition in the *Ta-li i* controversy and held a grudge against him. Hence, the emperor's choice of the Yung-ch'ang guard as a place for the son's banishment may well have been a deliberate move on his part to give the local profiteers a chance to vent their feelings against the father through the son. The emperor never relented his vindictiveness against the two Yang. When Yang Shen reached the age of sixty-five *sui*, the legal age for retirement from military service, he requested permission to return to Szechwan, leaving his son as substitute. The petition was denied. Once (1558?), when he was in Szechwan on a visit, he was arrested and brought back to Yunnan in chains by order of the governor, Wang Ping 王昺 (T. 承晦, H. 杏里, 1491–1566, cs 1523). Some governors, however, treated him with courtesy, sending him on special missions to Szechwan. During one mission in 1540 he was appointed an editor of the Szechwan provincial local history. In twenty-eight days he completed the anthology section, which came to be the only part of the gazetteer that has survived. This is the *Ch'üan-Shu i-wen-chih* 全蜀藝文志, 64 *ch.*, printed in 1541 and reprinted in 1796, 1812, and 1891.

The thirty-five years of life in exile afforded Yang the opportunity to become one of the most widely read and prolific scholars in history. Not that he had failed to exercise his talents earlier; while in the Hanlin Academy he had helped edit the *Wen-hsien t'ung-k'ao* 文獻通考 (1524 ed.) and to compile the *Wu-tsung shih-lu* (*see* Chu Hou-chao). Now, however, he was an independent scholar, able to write whatever he wished; a stream of compositions flowed from his brush. He himself revealed that he delighted in reading on all subjects. He assembled many unusual books, which he read diligently, making notes and recording his thoughts and the results of his research. The accumulation, when published, came to over a hundred titles. One of his admirers, Chiao Hung (ECCP), with the help of the bibliophile Ts'ao Hsüeh-ch'üan (*q.v.*), compiled a bibliography of 138 items, grouped under cheng-chi 正集 (Yang's own poems and prose, 15 titles), wai-chi 外集 (study notes, 38 titiles), and tsa-chi 雜集 (works edited and selections from earlier authors, 85 titles). Some of his works were published during his lifetime, including anthologies, such as the one of ancient poets, *Feng-ya i-pien* 風雅逸編, 10 *ch.*, about 1535; several collections of miscellaneous notes, such as *Tan-ch'ien tsung-lu* 丹鉛總錄, 27 *ch.*, in 1554; several collections of literary criticism, chiefly the *Sheng-an shih-hua* 升庵詩話, 4 ch. (date unknown), and its supplement, *pu-i* 補遺, 3 *ch.*, in 1556; and several works on phonology, etymology, and studies of the Classics. Some prompt books for writers of poetry are also attributed to him. Among the books he edited or annotated the following may be mentioned: the *Shui-ching* 水經; the *Yüeh-chüeh shu* 越絕書, the author of which he identified as Yüan K'ang (fl. A.D. 40); the T'an-kung 檀弓 section of the Book of Rites; and the *Shan-hai-ching* 山海經.

Already nationally known as Yang chuang-yüan 狀元, or optimus Yang, and because of the unjust sentence he had to serve for life, Yang in exile became the object of general interest, and perhaps some jealousy, which was enhanced by his publications. Wang Shih-chen (*q.v.*), basing himself on hearsay, reported that Yang paraded in the street with flowers in his hair in the company of students and women; probably this occurred on the occasion of a traditional festival of that locality, unacceptable to Confucianists. One author, Ch'en Yüeh-wen (*see* Wu Ch'eng-en), published a work in 4 *chüan* listing one hundred fifty errors, mostly minor, found in Yang's writings; hence the title, *Cheng Yang* 正楊 (Rectification of [the mistakes of] Yang Shen). It was published in 1569, ten years after Yang's death. The interest in his life and works was aroused even more by such attacks. The prolific writer, Hu Ying-lin (*q.v.*), gave titles to some of his own books in imitation of Yang.

In 1582 the governor of Szechwan, Chang Shih-p'ei 張士佩 (T. 玫夫, H. 濾濱, 1531–1609, cs 1556), edited Yang's writings with the help of his nephew, Yang Yu-jen (*see* Yang T'ing-ho), and published (as of that time) a complete collection, *T'ai-shih sheng-an wen-chi* 太史升庵文集, including a sketch of his life, *Sheng-an nien-p'u* 年譜, 11 *chüan* of prose, 29 *chüan* of poems and 41 *chüan* of miscellaneous notes, making a total of 81 *chüan*. It was reprinted in 1592 and in 1601. As more manuscripts came to light, a supplementary collection was edited by a grandson (by adoption ?), Yang Wu 鋙 (T. 宗吾), and published in 1606 by another governor of Szechwan and admirer, Wang Hsiang-ch'ien (ECCP). This is the *Sheng-an i-chi* 遺集, 26 *ch.* The above mentioned Chiao Hung collected still more of Yang's unpublished works and edited the miscellaneous notes covering twenty-six topics, running from astronomy to fauna and flora. This is the *Sheng-an wai-chi*, 100 *ch.*, published in 1616. Of the three collections, the first was reprinted in 1795 under the title *Sheng-an ch'üan* 全 *-chi*, and the other two were reprinted in 1844.

Of special interest are Yang's memoirs on Yunnan, about which he became well informed. He traveled widely in the province and occasionally to his native place in Szechwan, mostly on official duty, but once to attend the burial of his father.

These pieces include the *Yunnan shan-ch'uan chih* 山川志, 1 *ch.*, on mountains and streams; the *Tien-ch'eng chi* 滇程記. 1 *ch.*, which is concerned largely with geographical matters; the *Tien-tsai* 載 *chi*, 1 *ch.* (completed in 1543), which is historical; and the *Tien-hou* 候 *chi* on the climate and other aspects of Yunnan that differed from the rest of China. One other work, usually attributed to Yang, is the *Nan-chao yeh-shih* 南詔野史 (Unofficial history of Nan-chao), 1 *ch.*, an expanded 1776 edition of which was translated into French by Camille Sainson. The editors of the *Ssu-k'u* catalogue, however, have expressed grave doubts as to this attribution, pointing out that others also had a hand in it, especially Juan Yüan-sheng 阮元聲 (cs 1628, a native of Ch'ü-ching 曲靖, Yunnan), and that an edition of 1633 includes events occurring in 1585 (after Yang's death). There is no doubt, however, about the authorship of the *Tien-tsai chi* which apparently served as a base for the *Nan-chao yeh-shih*, for it was incorporated in *Ku-chin shuo-hai* by Lu Chi (*see* Lu Shen), completed in 1544.

Yang in his sketches incorporates materials which might otherwise have disappeared. He details the geographical divisions of the province, deals with antique remains, examines the customs of the people, and treats their history. The last starts from ancient times and relates the curious legend that the first native chief was a third-generation descendant of Aśoka, emperor of India in the 3d century B.C.; the author also emphasizes the expansion into southwest China of Buddhism, which displaced an ancient belief in the nāgas, and records the interesting fact that in 1201 the Sung court sent the prince of Ta-li 大理 a complete copy of the Chinese translation of the *Tripiṭaka*. Curiously he makes no mention of the penetration of Islam under the Yüan.

In another contribution, a preface to a work by Mu Kung 木公 (fl. 1526–53) on the history of the Na-khi chiefs of Li-chiang 麗江, dated November 9, 1545,

Yang gives a genealogy of the Mu clan which he starts with the founder of the Yeh 葉 family in the 7th century, and brings down to the time of Mu Te (*see* Mu Tseng), who in 1382 submitted to the Ming general, Fu Yu-te (*q.v.*), and collaborated with him in overcoming some of the recalcitrant tribespeople. This list is of interest for, beginning with the second name and running through to the twenty-first, the first character of each one reproduces the last character of the name of his predecessor. As Edouard Chavannes and Lo Ch'ang-p'ei have remarked, this is a practice also followed in the kingdom of Nan-chao, among the Mo-so 麼些 of Wei-hsi 維西, and among the Burmese. The clan name of Mu was novel with Mu Te; his forebears had used the name Mai (or Mo) 麥, which, probably transliterating a name with the initial sound of mak or mok, may well represent the name of the tribe, which gradually came to be considered the name of the family. Hsü Hung-tsu (ECCP) a century later remarked that the first Ming emperor was responsible for changing the name Mai to Mu.

Yang lived not only in Yung-ch'ang but also in a number of other places in Yunnan (as well as in Szechwan) as revealed in the poems in his *nien-p'u*. Eventually he built a villa at the foot of Pi-chi shan 碧雞山, a picturesque spot west of Kunming. Here he did much of his literary work, and here, after his death, the grateful people of the province erected in his memory both a shrine and an academy, known as Pi-yao shu-yüan 碧嶢 書院. (For illustrations of the shrine, his statue, and an ancestral tablet, *see* Joseph F. Rock, cited below. Another imaginary portrait appears in the *Ming chuang-yüan t'u-k'ao*.) On his death his remains were transported to his native place and laid to rest by the grave of his grandfather, Yang Ch'un (*see* Yang T'ing-ho), where his father likewise is buried. He was survived by two sons by concubines and by his second wife, Huang O (*q.v.*). They were married in 1519 but lived apart during most of his exile. They exchanged poems, however, especially in the form of ch'ü 曲 of which she left a collection. His yüeh-fu, entitled *T'ao-ch'ing yüeh-fu*, were brought together with her ch'ü in a single volume in 1934.

Many of Yang's publications are extant. Seven printed in the Ming dynasty belong to the National Library of Peiping and are available in microfilm; others are known to be at the National Central Library, Harvard, the Library of Congress, Columbia, and elsewhere. A fictional piece, the *Han tsa-shih pi-hsin* 漢雜事祕辛, which he declared he had discovered, has from the beginning been suspected as from his brush, and has been characterized as a fake by as recent a critic as Paul Pelliot. Three others were sent up to the capital during the period of Ch'ien-lung for possible censorship. One of these escaped completely —the *Nien-i shih t'an tz'u* 廿一 史彈詞, 2 *ch.*, printed at the end of the Ming, and again in 1701. (Yang's authorship of this work, however, is doubtful.) The other two suffered from excision. The *Tan-ch'ien yü* 餘 -*lu*, 17 *ch.*, was even copied into the Imperial Library, presumably after the passage in the 14th *chüan* had been deleted, while the *Li Cho-wu tu* 李卓吾讀 *Sheng-an chi*, 20 *ch.*, suffered deletions in *chüan* 2 and 7 for its characterization of the Mongols as i 夷 (barbarians) and the Khitan and Jurchen as chieh hu 羯胡(rank smelling Hu). A copy of the latter is preserved at Columbia University.

In 1567, a year after Emperor Chu Hou-ts'ung died, Yang Shen was posthumously restored to officialdom and given the rank of vice minister of the Court of Imperial Entertainment. Early in 1621, he was one of seventy-one men of the dynasty awarded posthumous names, his being Wen-hsien 文憲. By his admirers, especially his fellow provincials, he was ranked with the T'ang poet, Li Po (701-62), and the Sung scholar, Su Shih (1037-1101), as t'ien-ts'ai 天才 (genius). Wang Shih-chen considered him an expert on classical references but not always reliable in interpretations, proficient in anecdotes but neglecting the official histories, interested in the history of poetry while ignorant of its principles, and given to transcendent thoughts but occasionally missing the obvious. Ch'ien Ch'ien-i (ECCP), after repeating his remarks, expressed his agreement with Wang. A Ch'ing scholar, Li Tz'u-ming(ECCP), recorded in his diaries of 1854 his study of Yang's collected works during half a month's time, and, after copying down the worthy passages, made some observations on both Yang's discoveries and his errors.

Bibliography

1/192/1b; 3/267/21a; 5/21/51a; Shen I-kuan (*q.v.*) *et al.*, *Ming Chuang-yüan t'u-k'ao* (1875), 2/14a; Ch'ien Ch'ien-i, *Lieh-ch'ao shih-chi*, 丙 15/la, 閏 4/9a; KC (1958), 330; TSCC (1885–88), XXIII: 101/89/5b; *Yunnan t'ung-chih*(1894), 88/27b; *Hsin-tu-hsien chih* (1929), 1/17a, 5/14b, 33b, 6/14a; SK (1930), 24/la, 66/10a, 119/1a, etc.; NCL *Index*,60, 514, 655, 712; Li Tz'u-ming, *Yüeh-man-t'ang tu-shu-chi* 越縵堂讀書記, II (1963), 668; Camille Sainson, *Nan-tchao ye-che, Histoire particulière du Nan-tchao* (Paris, 1904); Paul Pelliot, BEFEO, 4 (1904), 1094; *id.*, TP, 23 (1924), 181; Edouard Chavannes, TP, 5(1904), 473; *id.*, TP, 13(1912), 566; *id.*, TP, 17 (1916), 137; Joseph F. Rock, *The Ancient Na-khi Kingdom of Southwest China* (Cambridge, Mass., 1947), 162, pls. 47, 48, 49; Thomas Watters, *Essays on the Chinese Language* (Shanghai, 1889), 81; J. Bacot, *Les Moso* (Leiden, 1913), 186, pl. 38, fig. 14; Ch'iu K'ai-ming 裘開明, CHHP, n.s. II: 2 (1961), 101; *id.*, *Chung-kuo wen-hua yen-chiu so hsüeh-pao*, II: 1 (Chinese Univ. of Hong Kong, 1969), 49; L. of C. *Catalogue of Rare Books*, 279, 287, 627, 720; Gest Oriental Library *Catalogue* (Peking, 1941), 31; Lo Ch'ang-p'ei, "The Genealogical Patronymic Linkage System of the Tibeto-Burman Speaking Tribes," HJAS, 8 (1945), 349.

*L. Carrington Goodrich
and Chaoying Fang*

YANG Shih-ch'i 楊士奇 (*ming* Yü 寓 until 1398, H. 東里), 1365–April 2, 1444, grand secretary from 1421 to 1444, was a native of T'ai-ho 泰和, Kiangsi. He, Yang Jung (*q.v.*), and Yang P'u (see below), grand secretaries during the first half of the 15th century, later became known as the San Yang 三楊 (Three Yang), who represented the halcyon days before the T'u-mu debacle of 1449 (*see* Wang Chen). Yang Shih-ch'i was descended from an old Kiangsi gentry family, which had flourished during the Sung and the Yüan dynasties. His great-grandfather, Yang Ching-hsing 景行 (T. 可賢, cs 1315), had been Hanlin compiler under the Mongols. The family at the end of the Yüan, however, had become impoverished, and Yang Shih-ch'i, losing his father at an early age, was temporarily adopted into a Lo 羅 family. [Editors' note: Yang Shih-ch'i was sixteen months old when his father died, according to a eulogy of his mother written in 1412. The author of the eulogy reports that it was as a result of the ravages of the war that the Yang clan was scattered and certain members of it lost their lives; also that its properties were broken up or destroyed, and that the mother and infant son were reduced to destitution. It seems that his mother had to live at first with her own family, surnamed Ch'en 陳. About 1369, in desperation, she went to live in the house of a local scholar, Lo Hsing 羅性 (T. 子理, *ca.* 1326–*ca.* 1395), probably as a concubine if not a maid. Yang Shih-ch'i, then four years old, became Lo's foster son and took the surname Lo. Meanwhile Lo became a *chü-jen* (1371?) and served a term as vice prefect of Te-an 德安, north of Wuchang (1372–75?). For some irregularity he was punished by being banished to Shensi where he died about twenty years later. Yang Shih-ch'i, while receiving the same education as the other sons of Lo, was puzzled over finding himself excluded from ceremonies of ancestral worship. He later found out from his tearful mother about his own progenitors. It is said that at the age of seven or so he began to conduct the worship of his ancestors at a secret place. Learning this, Lo restored Shih-ch'i's

surname to Yang and before departing to
his place of exile sent him and his mother
back to the Yang clan in T'ai-ho, but
continued to take an interest in the boy,
exhorting him through correspondence to
be faithful in his studies. Later Yang
wrote a sketch of Lo's life, expressing
gratitude for his upbringing and for being
treated as a son (*Tung-li wen-chi* 文集, 22/
10a). The part played by Yang's mother
would have been looked on as scandalous
in a later era when neo-Confucian tenets
regarding female conduct became more
strictly applied in the generally stabilized
scholar-official society. In the early years
of the Ming, however, it was not unusual
for a widow of high birth to remarry or
even for a woman to be the mother of
two *chuang-yüan* of different surnames, as
in the case of Ma To 馬鐸 (T. 彥聲, H.
梅巖, cs 1412, d. 1423) and Li Ch'i 李騏
(T. 德良, cs 1418, d. 1425)]. While still
a youth Yang started teaching. Even
at this time he won local attention for
his literary skill. When working as a private tutor at Wuchang in Hukuang province, he was summoned in 1398 to the
capital to help compile the draft of the
first version of the *T'ai-tsu shih-lu* (completed 1402). Without going through the
regular examinations he was put in the
first rank after a special examination
guided by the then minister of Personnel,
Chang Tan 張紞 (T. 昭季, H. 鷃菴, d.
1402), who promoted him to be associate
secretary in the administration office of
the prince of Wu 吳, Chu Yün-t'ung 朱允
熥, third son of the heir apparent, Chu
Piao (*q.v.*), who was enfeoffed in 1399
and died 1415.

Though high officials at the court of
Chu Yün-wen (*q.v.*) had been his sponsors, Yang Shih-ch'i was among the first to
welcome the prince of Yen (Chu Ti, *q.v.*)
when he subdued Nanking and usurped
the throne. He soon entered the group of
learned advisers whom the new emperor
selected, and received an appointment as
a secretary in one of the directories of
instruction to serve as tutor to the heir

apparent, Chu Kao-chih (*q.v.*). This rather
precarious position brought him and his
colleagues into favor and danger at the
same time, because the emperor never
ceased to distrust the southerners for
opposing him. During the emperor's absence in the north, one of the princes, Chu
Kao-hsü (*q.v.*), added fresh cause for suspicion by preparing to rebel. Yang twice
(1414 and 1422) awaited trial in prison.
His attitude, however, was such as to
cause the emperor to pardon him on both
occasions. While he often tried to protect
fellow officials from the imperial flashes
of rage, he was quite ready to advise on
burning the books of anyone who dared
to criticize the Sung neo-Confucianists.
When the emperor died in Mongolia in
1424, Yang and a few colleagues, Yang
Jung, Chien I, Hsia Yüan-chi (*qq.v.*), and
others became the leading group at the
court of Chu Kao-chih.

Yang Shih-ch'i rose to the positions
of a junior guardian, a grand secretary,
and an honorary minister, first of Rites
and then of War. The stories circulating
about his activities during that time deal
with his strong stand in matters of ritual
and an official's right to speak openly. He
seems to have had close relations with
the emperor, his former pupil, but his
obstinate judgments on right and wrong
often caused the emperor to sigh. Yang
Shih-ch'i's influence, together with that of
his colleagues, Yang Jung and others,
rose during the Hsüan-te and early Cheng-
t'ung reigns. The background of this
phenomenon has surely to be seen in the
unique combination of talents that the
Hsüan-te period witnessed; with such
efficient politicians as Chien I and Hsia
Yüan-chi, Yang Jung, and Ku Tso (*q.v.*),
the Ming consolidated itself and had all
the aspects of an enduring dynasty. Yang
Shih-ch'i was just one of this group.
After the rebellion of the prince of Han,
Chu Kao-hsü, in 1426, it was his un-
swerving stand against punishment without
clear evidence that saved another imperial
uncle's life. This led to a difference of

opinion with Yang Jung. But in 1427 it was the voices of both Yang Shih-ch'i and Yang Jung which led to withdrawal from Annam in opposition to those of the war party under Chang Fu (*q.v.*) and others.

In his capacity as a chief adviser to the emperor, Yang Shih-ch'i often took the opportunity to press for reform measures. In 1432 the sponsorship system for selecting officials was reintroduced to secure effective government in central and local administration. Altogether he was a man who shaped but did not carry out political measures; time and time again his influence brought him into conflict with various officials. In his old age, when his son, Yang Chi 稷, was tried for criminal actions at home in Kiangsi, many voices rose against the old, successful, but unloved pleader and critic. He died, aged eighty *sui*, showered with such honors as only imperial China could bestow.

Together with Yang Jung he had laid the foundations for that central government agency later to be known as the Nei-ko 內閣 (inner cabinet or grand secretariat). Though it is true that, after 1382, the year of institutional reform under the first emperor, and again after 1402, when Chu Ti formed his new government, several scholar-advisers had served the emperor as private secretaries, only the tutorial group around the heir apparent, Chu Kao-chih, was able, it seems, to institutionalize what had at best been a temporary practice. Probably it was the fact that the tutors of Chu Kao-chih, united with Chu Ti's trusted secretaries, Yang Jung and others, gave the practice of memorializing within the palace its regularity and stability. The later Nei-ko institution could build upon this rather stable political influence of the two Yang, which was a contrast to the conduct of official business by the powerful eunuch Wang Chen (*q.v.*).

At the same time Yang Shih-ch'i exercised some influence in the literary field. His fondness for and imitation of Sung masters of prose and his easy and plain poems helped to create the so-called t'ai-ko-t'i 臺閣體 (Grand Secretariat style, *see* Li Meng-yang). This style was judged "simple and reasoned, agreeable and manifest" by its acclaimers, but barren and spiritless by its critics. Rather a pedagogue than a scholar, though widely read and especially apt in correcting documents, Yang Shih-ch'i seems to have sunk his literary spirit into the drafting of documents and writing the history of his time. The *shih-lu* of four emperors and the edicts of the Hsüan-te and early Cheng-t'ung periods demonstrate this. About 1416 he compiled with others a collection of selected memorials dating from earliest times through the Yüan, entitled *Li-tai ming-ch'en tsou-i* 歷代名臣奏議, 350 *ch.*, classified under 64 headings. He also sponsored the compilation of a catalogue of the Imperial Library called *Wen-yüan-ko shu-mu* 文淵閣書目 in 4 *chüan* (recent editions are in 20 *chüan*), which was presented to the throne in 1441. His own collected works were published under the title *Tung-li ch'üan-chi* 東里全集, 97 *ch.*, *pieh-chi* 別集, 4 *ch.* These were all copied three centuries later into the *Ssu-k'u ch'üan-shu*. Four other works are listed by title only in the eighteenth-century imperial catalogue. A second edition of the *Tung-li ch'uan-chi* contains only the *Tung-li wen-chi*, 25 *ch.*, to which is appended a *Tung-li pieh-chi*, consisting of three titles: *Sheng-yü lu* 聖諭錄, *Tsou-tui lu* 奏對錄, and *Tai-yen lu* 代言錄. The second edition had four printings, 1445, 1618, 1678, and 1877.

It seems appropriate to add here a few words about the third of the "Three Yang." Yang P'u 楊溥 (T. 弘濟), 1372-August 6, 1446, grand secretary from 1436 to 1446, was a native of Shih-shou 石首, Hukuang. After acquiring the *chin-shih* degree in 1400, he entered the Hanlin Academy to become instructor to the heir apparent, Chu Kao-chih, shortly after Chu Ti had gained the throne. He was thrown into prison in 1414 for alleged conspiracy, together with other high officials. While several died in prison, the most prominent being the grand secretary, Hsieh Chin (*q.v.*), Yang P'u managed to stand the ordeal by "reading the Classics, histories, and philosophers several times." Only after ten years was he set free by Chu Kao-chih (now emperor), whom he served as special adviser. He then took various secretarial posts, until he was advanced to the Grand Secretariat after the accession of Chu Ch'i-chen (*q.v.*) to the throne. His calm firmness and utter devotion to work earned him praise exceeding his true political stature. While his two Yang colleagues were not without fault, Yang P'u seems to have died regarded by all as just and honest. He was accorded the posthumous name of Wen-ting 文定. Like the other two Yang he too is associated with the compiling of the early *shih-lu*.

Most accounts, laudatory or critical, add a few remarks about the three as a group. The *Ming-shih* compilers after more than two hundred fifty years felt safe to praise the "Three Yang" in terms of time honored models of China's great past. In this they were anticipated by later Ming authors, who felt that the two centuries of Ming rule had been made possible by the efforts of the three and their colleagues. But other sources indicate what must have been felt among officials more nearly contemporaneous. Ch'iu Chün (*q.v.*) asked about forty years later whether the "wise men of the time could possibly escape the judgment of history." Even a fellow townsman of Yang Shih-ch'i, Yin Chih (*see* Yang Ming), in his *So-chui lu* 瑣綴錄, forthrightly accused the "Three Yang" of having abused their power, thereby playing into the eunuchs' hands. This leads to a critical appraisal of the system: "Those learned servants handled the documents and offered advice, they secretly assisted at state affairs, but still as officials they were nothing but secretaries." The relative peace and prosperity of the time offered ground for fame, the critic adds, yet this condition did not always result from good politics. This was to be the weakness of the system: mere orthodoxy and technical skill in handling the bureaucracy never compensated for genuine political talent.

Bibliography

1/148/1a; 3/138/1a; 5/12/28a; 8/17/9a, 31b; 61/120/2395; 63/10/43b, 46a; MSL (1963), T'ai-tsung, 0156, 0535, 1013, 1168, 1793, 1985, 2247, 2349, Jen-tsung, 0025, 0145, Ying-tsung, 0800, 0978, 1197, 2300, 2828; SK (1930), 53/1a, 55/10b, 85/3b, 170/5b; Ho Ch'iao-yüan, *Ming-shan ts'ang* (Ch'en-lin chi, Yung-lo ch'en 1), 1a; Cheng Hsiao, *Wu-hsüeh pien*, 27/1a; Liao Tao-nan, *Tien-ko tz'u-lin chi*, 1/5b; *Huang Ming wen-hai* (microfilm), 1/4/16; *Tung-li ch'üan-chi*; L. Carrington Goodrich, "Maternal Influence," HJAS, XII (1949), 226–30; W. Franke, *Sources*, 1.1.2, 3, 4, 2.4.1.

Tilemann Grimm

YANG Ssu-ch'ang 楊嗣昌 (T. 文弱, 文若, 子微), March 25, 1588-April 10, 1641, scholar and official, was a native of Wu-ling 武陵, Hukuang. He was the son of Yang Ho 楊鶴 (T. 修齡, cs 1604, d. 1635). A *chin-shih* of 1610, Yang Ssu-ch'ang was appointed instructor in the prefectural school in Hangchow and later a lecturer in the National University at Nanking. In 1622, while serving as a bureau director of the ministry of Revenue in Nanking, he went on leave and did not return to government office until 1628, when he was appointed director of education of Honan. In the following year when the Manchus attacked Peking, he went to its defense and was appointed intendant at Pa-chou 霸州, south of Peking. In 1631 he was transferred to Shanhaikuan. At this time his father, Yang Ho, who had served two years (1629-31) as supreme commander of the Shensi Frontier Area was found guilty of misjudgment in dealing with the bandits in his province, and sentenced in 1632 to exile. Two years later, when Yang Ssu-ch'ang

was appointed supreme commander of the
Hsüan-fu and Tatung frontier area, he
pleaded for his father's pardon but to no
avail. The following year Yang Ho died
in his place of exile and the son left his
post in November, 1635, for the period
of mourning. Within a year he received
a new appointment and, in spite of repeated requests for permission to complete
the observance of the mourning rites, was
compelled by imperial order to go to Peking and assume office (April, 1637). Had
he strictly observed the code he would
have had to wait until 1639 to take up
official duties because his father's second
wife died in the autumn of 1636. Although
the emperor (see Chu Yu-chien, ECCP)
recalled him on the justifiable excuse of
military duty in a time of emergency,
many officials at court, especially those
belonging to the Tung-lin party (see Ku
Hsien-ch'eng) who were opposed to Yang,
continually embarrassed the emperor by
alluding to Yang's failure to observe his
filial duties.

Widely read and eloquent, Yang impressed the emperor as a diligent administrator attending personally to details and
as a practical-minded official. They probably also shared a dislike of the querulous-
ness of the censors with their advice
and carping criticism. As minister of War,
Yang advocated a policy of keeping on
the defensive in the northeast or even of
opening trade relations with the Manchus,
citing the peace treaty of 1571 with the
Mongols as a precedent; his idea was to
gain time so that the government might first
suppress the rebellion. He never succeeded
in securing peace with the Manchus partly
due to objections raised at court but
mainly because the enemy was militarily
stronger. The failure of peace negotiations
forced the Ming government to fight on
two fronts, with the result that each time
the suppression of the rebels seemed imminent troops had to be transferred to
protect Peking against the Manchus, thus
permitting the rebels to regain their
strength. Yang could do no more than make

plans and hope for the best. About the
middle of 1637 he submitted a strategic
plan for the establishment of a line of
defense to encircle the bandits in the
central plain, and for the creation of
a large mobile army for their annihilation.
This plan was called the "four main and
six auxiliary lines of defense," ssu-cheng
liu-yü 四正六隅 or a "net of ten sides,"
shih-mien chih wang 十面之網. It designated the armies in Shensi, Honan, Hukuang, and Chiang-pei 江北 (i.e., present
northern Anhwei) as one which should
hold the principal lines of defense because
the bandits were then operating in these
areas. It also designated the armies in
Yen-sui (northern Shensi), Shansi, Shantung, Kiangsi, Szechwan, and Chiang-nan
(江南, present southern Anhwei) as the
ones to control the areas on the perimeter to block all escape routes. For the
command of the mobile troops Yang recommended Hsiung Wen-ts'an (q.v.), who
was to direct the campaign from Yün-
yang 鄖陽 on the Han River, controlling
Honan on the north and east, Shensi and
Szechwan on the west, and Hukuang on
the south. To finance the campaign Yang
recommended the raising of 2.8 million
taels, of which over seventy percent was
to come from a surtax on land for one
year. The plan was adopted, and after
preparations for half a year, was publicly
announced on January 10, 1638. Yang
promised to have the bandits crushed in
three months. Hsiung, however, after
some initial victories, pursued a policy of
trying to entice Chang Hsien-chung
(ECCP) and other rebel leaders to surrender by promising them commissions and
land to farm. Each was to be permitted to
keep his own men as a unit, on the assumption that others might thus be attracted.
The mobile campaign, supposed to take
three months, was protracted without
explanation and the surtax for one year
was continued and came to be known as
the chiao-hsiang 剿餉 or military fund for
suppressing the bandits.

Yang continued to enjoy the emperor's

confidence. On May 29, 1638, the observatory reported that Mars was hidden by the moon and became invisible, portending disaster. The emperor blamed himself and took to fasting. Yang, however, cited historical antecedents to prove that when the ruler is virtuous such signs could mean only that it would be unlucky to fight a border war. His meaning, of course, was clear: namely, that a policy of appeasement towards the Manchus should be pursued. This explanation pleased the emperor who, two months later, awarded Yang the high rank of grand secretary while he served concurrently as minister of War. This promotion provoked more attacks on Yang by Huang Tao-chou (ECCP) and others of the Tung-lin party. Meanwhile, as an award for the victories in Shensi in that year, Yang was given the hereditary rank of a centurion in the Embroidered-uniform Guard.

In October, 1638, the Manchus disdained Yang's peace offers and crossed the border in force, starting a devastating raid into Pei-Chihli and Shantung that lasted five months, during which they took and pillaged over seventy cities. Had precedents been followed, Yang should have been held responsible and executed (*see* Hsia Yen and Ch'iu Luan). Yet he was punished only by being stripped of his titles for a short period; furthermore, he was ordered to conduct the court martial of the officials and generals who had failed to ward off the Manchu invaders. More than thirty men were sentenced to death while Yang still held his offices. As a result more abuse was heaped on him. At this time the court adopted a plan to have the frontier military areas made responsible for giving intensive training to selected men as combat troops and to make certain prefectures and districts responsible for the training of militia so that the local communities might defend themselves when attacked. The training program was to be financed by another surtax of 7.3 million taels, called lien-hsiang 練餉, or fund for training. This,

together with the fund for combating the bandits and an earlier one for fighting the Manchus (the Liao-hsiang 遼餉 imposed since 1618), is called san-hsiang 三餉, or the three military funds. These funds constituted a total surtax of 16.7 million taels, which was four times the normal annual tax in silver. The collection of these taxes and the increased abuses involved in the procedure became a heavy burden on the people and contributed to the downfall of the dynasty. Yang was often blamed for his part in proposing two of the three funds.

Meanwhile Hsiung Wen-ts'an failed to keep the surrendered bandits under proper surveillance. In June, 1639, Chang Hsien-chung and his followers, nourished and rested, rose again in rebellion. In September Yang Ssu-ch'ang volunteered to assume field command. Holding the highest rank of a commander, Grand Secretary Yang received from the emperor a sword as symbol of authority, silver and warrants to distribute as awards, as well as a feast in the palace and a poem in the emperor's own hand. Invested with full powers, he arrived in October, 1639, at his headquarters in Hsiang-yang, Hukuang, to assume command of over a hundred thousand men. When in March, 1640, one of his generals, Tso Liang-yü (ECCP), won a signal victory over Chang Hsien-chung in T'ai-p'ing (modern Wan-yüan) on the Szechwan-Shensi border, Yang gained in prestige and imperial confidence. He tried to hold Chang Hsien-chung and other bandits in Szechwan and sent his armies to pursue them. In order to direct the campaign more efficiently he moved his headquarters in August, 1640, south to I-ling 夷陵 (present I-ch'ang) on the Yangtze River. At the same time he complained to the ministry of Revenue over the delay in sending him pay and supplies, the cost of which came to over two hundred thousand taels per month.

In October, 1640, Yang moved west to Wu-shan 巫山 inside the Szechwan border. His strategy, however, gave the advantage to the rebels who traveled light and pillaged for food. In February, 1641, at K'ai-hsien 開縣 Chang Hsien-chung turned on the exhausted government troops and defeated them. This victory gave him the chance to slip through the cordon and move eastward to attack the defenseless cities in Hukuang. At the same time (February, 1641) another bandit leader, Li Tzu-ch'eng (ECCP), captured Loyang and executed the first prince of Fu (see Cheng Kuei-fei). A month later Chang Hsien-chung captured Hsiang-yang, killing the 7th prince of Hsiang (i.e., Chu I-ming 朱翊銘). Yang tried unsuccessfully to save the situation by hurrying back to I-ling. Realizing the serious responsibility for such disasters, he became despondent and died. Most probably he committed suicide, as reported in various accounts. Although blamed by most of the court for the resurgence of the bandits in 1641, he was exonerated by the emperor and about a year later given posthumously the high title of grand tutor of the heir apparent. In 1643, when Chang Hsien-chung came to Hukuang and took Wu-ling, he so hated Yang that he violated the burial grounds of the Yang family. Later Yang's skull was found and reburied.

In all contemporary sources as well as in the official histories of the Ming period, such as the *Ming-shih*, Yang is reported as vain, stubborn, overly self-confident, and inclined to trifling, and is blamed for raising taxes and failing to suppress the rebels. The *Ming-shih* records that he tried to balance the power of the general, Tso Liang-yü, by raising the rank of another general, but did it so clumsily that both officers distrusted him, with the result that Tso disobeyed Yang's orders to fight Chang Hsien-chung. Tso, however, is known to have said that the rebels should not be entirely eliminated in order to present the court, ruthless and without compunction, from turning on the generals once the former were no more. Hence it probably did not make any difference. Yang's reputation suffered chiefly because he had antagonized and tried to ignore members of the Tung-lin, who were articulate and the writers of history.

One contemporary official, Li Ch'ing (ECCP) who served as a supervising censor (1638-40) while Yang was minister of War, after recording many of the misdeeds of Yang and three other high officials, Chou Yen-ju, Wen T'i-jen (qq.v.), and Ch'en Hsin-chia (see Hu Chen-heng) finally conceded that, however inadequate these men were, they still were far superior to others who held comparable positions in their day. The writer, P'eng Shih-wang (1610-83, ECCP, p. 847), wrote a long poem explaining his change of opinion of Yang from detestation to respect after he had evaluated all the facts. The 18th-century historian, Chao I (ECCP), considered Yang's plan of encirclement a sound one. Except for these few instances, the only writers favoring Yang were his own descendants and some fellow provincials. The first one to protest against his detractors was his son, Yang Shan-sung 山松 (T. 忍古), who went to Peking in 1669 to appeal to official historians not to sully his father's name, —and who in 1680 wrote a protest entitled *Ku-er yao-t'ien lu* 孤兒籲天錄, 17 ch., to refute the unjustified criticism of his father. There are two shorter works by Yang Shan-sung, both printed in the *Tun an ts'ung-pien* 遯盦叢編 in 1913. One entitled *Chao-tui chi-shih* 召對紀實 describes the two audiences at court in 1638 (July 28, August 13) when Huang Tao-chou, hoping to be appointed a grand secretary himself, tried to discredit Yang as a competitor but became involved in an argument with the emperor. After Yang was promoted to grand secretary and Huang demoted, Yang became the target of abuse by members of the Tung-lin party, and a distorted version of the audience was circulated. In the *Chao-tui chi-shih* Yang Shan-sung presented an account to correct this version. The other work, entitled *Pei-nan chi lüeh* 被難紀略, is an account of the violation of Yang's tomb by the rebels under Chang Hsien-chung in 1643, and the narrow escape from their hands by Yang's three sons. Another son, Yang Shan-tzu 梓 (T. 仲子), also wrote a treatise defending his father, entitled *Pien-pang lu* 錄. About 1740, when the official history of the Ming dynasty was just completed, a great-great-grandson, Yang Ch'ao-tseng 超曾 (T. 孟班, 1693-1742, cs 1715, minister of War 1738-41, Pth. 文敏), composed a memorial requesting some changes to be made in the biography of his ancestor. It seems that memorial was not submitted.

Yang Ssu-ch'ang was a prolific writer. About 1621 he had already printed three collections of poetry and prose, namely, *Shih-t'o* 詩籜, *Yeh-k'o-ch'ing-hsieh chi* 野客青鞋集, and *Ti-kuan chi* 地官集. Towards the end of his life he printed his memorials in the collections *Fu-kuan tsou-i* 撫關奏議, *Hsüan-yün* 宣雲 *tsou-i*, *Chung-shu* 中樞 *tsou-i*, and *Tu-shih tsai-pi* 督師載筆. A fourth collection, never printed, which contains memorials he presented during the years 1617-41, together with answers to imperial questions and semi-official correspondence, is entitled *Yang Wen-jo hsien-sheng wen-chi* 文弱先生文集, 57 ch. Manuscript copies are preserved in both Tokyo and Peking. His later poems were printed in the collection *Lo-chi-yüan shih-chi* 樂饑園詩集. The printing blocks were destroyed about 1646 but incomplete sets have been reported to be still extant. Forty-five pieces of his writings, including thirty-two memorials, may be found in the Hunanese anthology of prose writings, *Hunan wen-cheng* 湖南文徵 of 1871, and thirty-six of his poems in the anthology *Yüan-hsiang ch'i-chiu chi* 沅湘耆舊集 of 1843. These documents indicate that many of the unfavorable remarks about him in various books should be discounted.

There is a *Wu-ling ching-tu lüeh* 武陵競渡略 attributed to Yang under the pen name of Ch'ing-ling t'ing-chang 青陵亭長. It is a small treatise on the Dragon-boat festival in Wu-ling, and is incorporated in the 28th *chüan* of the *Shuo-fu hsü* 說郛續.

Bibliography

1/252/1a; 3/243/4b; 27/X/17b; 41/2/20a; 64/22/6a; Chang Tai 張岱, *Shih-kuei-shu hou-chi* 石匱書後集 (Shanghai, 1959), 1/22; Cheng Ta 鄭達, *Yeh-shih wu wen* 野史無文 (Shanghai, 1960), 4/15-17; *Ming chi* 明紀 (Shanghai, 1935), 54/562, 571, 578; *Ming-chi pei-lüeh* 明季北略 (Shanghai, 1936), 15/201-202); *Ming-ch'ao chi-shih pen-mo* 明朝紀事本末 (Shanghai, 1935), 72/42, 43, 45; *Ming t'ung-chien* 明通鑑 (Shanghai, 1959), Vol. 4; KC(1958), 5890-91 *passim*; T'an Ch'ien, *Tsao-lin tsa-tsu* (Shanghai, 1935), 252; Wen Ping 文秉, *Lieh-huang hsiao chih* 列皇小識 (Shanghai, 1940), 7/192; WMSCK, *chüan* 7, 8; Li Ch'ing, *San-yüan pi-chi* 三垣筆記 (Chia-yeh-t'ang, 1927), 上/10a, 13a, 坿上/20b, 坿中/14b; Li Wen-chih 李文治, *Wan-Ming min-pien* 晚明民變, 72; Chao I (ECCP), *Nien-er-shih tsa-chi*, *chüan* 36; *Ming-mo nung min ch'i-i shih-liao* 明末農民起義史料 (Peking, 1952), 281; *Ming Ch'ing shih lun-ts'ung* 明清史論叢 (Wuhan, 1957), 106; W. Franke, *Sources*, 5.8.46.

Chaoying Fang and Albert Chan

YANG T'ing-ho 楊廷和 (T. 介夫, H. 石齋), October 15, 1459-July 25, 1529, scholar and onetime grand secretary, was a native of Hsin-tu 新都, Szechwan. His father, Yang Ch'un 楊春 (T. 元之, H. 留耕, 1436-1515, cs 1481), rose to be assistant surveillance commissioner of education in Hukuang. Yang T'ing-ho became a *chü-jen* at the age of eleven, and when only nineteen (1478) qualified for the *chin-shih* degree, and was appointed Hanlin bachelor. Some time later he went home to marry. Upon his return to the capital in 1480 he resumed work in the Hanlin Academy, and aided inter alia in the preparation of various imperial compilations such as the *Hsien-tsung shih-lu* 憲宗實錄, completed in 1491, and the *Ta Ming hui-tien* 大明會典 (Collected institutes of the Ming dynasty) completed in 1503. During these years he received frequent promotions, rising to be chancellor of the Hanlin Academy (1505). In the following year he was elevated to grand senior supervisor of instruction while still holding the post of chancellor; in addition he became vice director-general

for the compilation of the *Hsiao-tsung* 孝
宗 *shih-lu*. Early in 1507 he was made
responsible for the drafting of imperial
decrees and rescripts, and soon afterwards
transferred to Nanking as left vice minister
of Personnel. His elevation to be minister fell on July 1 of the same year, but
he held that post only a few months, being
recalled to Peking as minister of Revenue
and concurrently grand secretary of the
Wen-yüan hall. A succession of higher
titles followed, including that of Kuang-lu
ta-fu chu-kuo 光祿大夫柱國 (Pillar of State)
in 1509. At that time, the eunuch Liu Chin
(*q. v.*) was in the ascendancy at court,
while his followers, Grand Secretary
Chiao Fang (*q. v.*) and Minister of Personnel Chang Ts'ai (*see* Chu Hou-chao), a
fellow townsman of Liu, were powerful
too. Although Yang and Li Tung-yang
(*q.v.*) were also members of the Nei-ko,
little could be done to check their machinations.

In 1510 Chu Chih-fan 朱寘鐇, the
prince of An-hua 安化王 (4th generation
descendant of Chu Yüan-chang, enf. 1492,
executed 1510), and his men rose in revolt
against the government under the pretext
of destroying Liu Chin's influence. Yang
T'ing-ho asked Emperor Chu Hou-chao to
assign General Ch'iu Yüeh (*see* Ch'iu Luan)
to suppress the rebellion. This was done
and Ch'iu succeeded in accomplishing his
mission and taking Chu Chih-fan captive.
At the same time the eunuch Chang Yung
(*q.v.*) informed the emperor of Liu Chin's
malpractices. Liu was put to death in
September of the same year and Yang
again favored with higher titles. Later in
November the rebellion headed by Liu Liu
劉六, Liu Ch'i 七, and Ch'i Yen-ming 齊
彥名 broke out. Ma Chung-hsi 馬中錫 (T.
天錄, 1446-June 1, 1512, cs 1475), recommended by the minister of Revenue, Yang
I-ch'ing (*q.v.*), received orders to crush it,
but Ma's efforts proved in vain. Whereupon Yang T'ing-ho proposed that the emperor put Lu Wan (*see* Chu Hou-chao) in
Yang I-ch'ing's place; in the meantime, he
recommended P'eng Tse (*see* Mansūr) as

the one to lead the government troops to
attack the rebels, headed by Chao Sui 趙
燧, who were overrunning Honan. Some
time later (September, 1512), these rebels
were exterminated. The grand secretary,
Li Tung-yang, resigned on February 2,
1513; whereupon Yang T'ing-ho became
head of the Grand Secretariat.

Following the execution of Liu Chin,
Chang Yung tended to be overbearing.
Once he arrested a man branded with
dragon marks on his arms, and proposed
as a reward for himself that he be granted
the title of marquis. Yang, however,
refused to give his consent, thus thwarting
Chang's ambition. When P'eng Tse was
about to attack (1514) the rebel Yen Pen-
shu 鄢本恕, he sought Yang's counsel.
Yang remarked: "It will be easy for you
to defeat him; after the victory, however,
you would be well advised to go slow in
withdrawing your troops." P'eng Tse,
disregarded this counsel. Immediately
after he had defeated the enemy and
killed Yen Pen-shu, he pulled back his
men but some of the enemy suddenly
renewed the attack. As a consequence,
P'eng Tse had to reassemble his army and
lead them back into battle. He then came
to appreciate Yang's wisdom.

On February 10, 1514, a fire broke
out in the Ch'ien-ch'ing palace 乾清宮
where the emperor lived. Yang asked the
emperor to issue a decree of self-reproach
and the emperor complied. Yang also
advised him to attend the court on time,
to disband useless troops, to appear at lectures given in the palace, and to close the
imperial store located in the palace. His
advice, however, was disregarded. When
Yang's father died (March 23, 1515), he
begged the emperor to allow him to return
home to attend to the funeral arrangements. His petition was not approved until
he had repeated his request time and
again; when it was granted he remained
in his native place for more than two
and a half years. Among the grand secretaries of the Ming dynasty, he was the
first permitted to stay home to complete

the mourning period for his parents. Late in 1517, recalled to Peking, he again served concurrently as minister of Personnel and grand secretary. At that time the emperor was making a tour through Hsüan-hua 宣化, from which he returned in mid-February, 1518. During this tour, the emperor frequently went hunting in the region of Tatung, Shansi, Yen-sui 延綏, Shensi, and so on. There were many occurrences of misrule in the court because the emperor seldom attended to official business. The eunuchs, such as Ku Ta-yung (*q.v.*), Wei Pin (*see* Chu Hou-chao), and Chang Hsiung 張雄, exceeded their prerogatives; so too did the emperor's favorites Ch'ien Ning (*see* Sayyid Ḥusain) and Chiang Pin (*q.v.*) to both of whom the emperor had granted the imperial surname. Although Yang was the senior grand secretary and often remonstrated with the emperor, it was of little use. Faced with this situation, he repeatedly applied for retirement but his requests were disallowed. Since he did not then insist on his opinions about state affairs, the eunuchs and imperial favorites treated him with some consideration. On July 10, 1519, Chu Ch'en-hao (*see* Wang Shou-jen), rebelled. The emperor wanted to appoint himself commander-in-chief and personally lead the army against the rebels. Yang and certain others at court opposed the plan, but the emperor was adamant. On September 15 the emperor left Peking for the south. (By this time, Wang Shou-jen had already captured the rebel prince, but the emperor was ignorant of that fact.) He ordered Yang and another grand secretary, Mao Chi 毛紀 (T. 維之, Pth. 文簡, 1463–1545, cs 1487) to remain at the capital and take charge of general affairs. Although the emperor received the report that Wang had gained a complete victory, he did not stop, arriving in Nanking on January 15, 1520. In spite of his absence the government functioned well, and as a result Yang's reputation rose. He frequently entreated the emperor to return, but the latter paid no

attention. Not until January 18, 1521, did the emperor go back to Peking. During the first part of his return journey, the emperor became indisposed. Suddenly he had a hemorrhage, as he was sacrificing to heaven in the southern suburb of the capital. A few weeks later, his sickness worsened and he died at the Pao-fang 豹房 (Leopard House) on April 20, 1521. The eunuchs Ku Ta-yung and Chang Yung promptly went to the Nei-ko and raised the problem of succession with the grand secretaries. Yang showed them the *Huang Ming tsu-hsün* (*see* Chu Yüan-chang) and said, "According to these precepts, in case an emperor who has no son dies, his brother is to succeed him. Now Chu Hou-ts'ung (*q.v.*), the eldest son of Chu Yu-yüan (*see* Chu Hou-ts'ung), is the grandson of Emperor Chu Chien-shen (*q.v.*), the nephew of Chu Yu-t'ang, and Chu Hou-chao's cousin. He is the one in line for the throne." The other grand secretaries, Liang Ch'u (*q.v.*), Chiang Mien (*see* Liang Ch'u), and Mao Chi all agreed and promptly ordered the eunuchs to report this to the Empress-dowager (née Chang), wife of Chu Yu-t'ang, and announce it to the various officials.

As the senior grand secretary, Yang T'ing-ho followed tradition by issuing an edict in the name of the new emperor, proclaiming a general pardon and attaching thereto a broad outline of general policies to be followed and actions to be taken. The edict dealt not alone with correcting the abuses of the reign just concluded but also with the inauguration of reforms in the new. This document is the longest and most detailed of any comparable pronouncement. Yang appears to have considered in it all the problems of the empire. Throughout the nearly half century to follow, the government benefited from his guidelines. Among the actions which he took during the thirty-seven days he was in sole control were such measures of economy as dismissal of a reputed 148,700 superfluous personnel in Peking and reduction of taxes by some

1,532,000 *shih* of grain. He sent away a
host of Taoist priests, packed off the
envoys of Hami, Turfan, and Portugal
(*see* Tomé Pires), disbanded useless military, and discharged many of the women
sent to the palace. Besides, he managed
to arrest Chiang Pin, who was executed
three months later. All of these steps were
widely applauded.

On May 27 of the same year Chu Hou-
ts'ung arrived in Peking from his estate
and was duly enthroned. In addition to
continuing in his high office Yang was
appointed in November one of the direc-
tors-general for the compilation of the
Wu-tsung 武宗 *shih-lu*. Subsequently he
was honored with the title of Left Pillar
of State. At first the new emperor treated
Yang well. Through the controversy known
as *Ta-li i* (*see* Chu Hou-ts'ung), however, his standing declined as he differed
with the emperor. Yang even went
so far as to reprimand him and reject
the edicts which the latter issued. His
rigidity led certain officials to speak ill
of him. Later both the supervising secretary, Shih Tao 史道 (T. 克弘, H. 鹿野,
1484-June 6, 1553, cs 1517), and the
censor Ts'ao Chia (*see* Li Meng-yang)
accused him of several offenses. Although
the emperor punished Shih Tao and Ts'ao
Chia lightly in order to save Yang's face,
his dislike of Yang increased.

Because the emperor liked to perform
Taoist sacrifices, Yang memorialized in
1523, remonstrating against this practice.
In the same year, the emperor wanted to
send certain eunuchs to Soochow and
Hangchow to supervise the silk factories
and collect materials for him; again Yang
protested but the emperor paid no attention. About the same time, the title of
grand tutor was given him; but Yang refused to accept it. Yang repeatedly begged
to be retired, but was ordered to remain
at his post, and did so for a few more
months.

Immediately after his retirement
(March 15, 1524), a discussion of the titles
for the emperor's parents was resumed,
and two months later the emperor got
the court to agree to all that he wanted.
In 1528 many officials suffered punishment for having opposed him in the *Ta-li i*
controversy; Yang among them was stripped of his honors and reduced to the
rank of commoner. He died the following
year.

A few years later, the emperor questioned the grand secretary, Li Shih 李時
(T. 宗易, H. 序菴, Pth. 文康, 1471-January
5, 1539, cs 1502), as to the amount of
grain the imperial granary had accumulated. Li replied: "The grain now stored up
is enough to meet several years' demand.
It results from the government's having
weeded out many superfluous officials
and having practiced strict economy
in the early years of Your Majesty's
reign." At this the emperor sighed and
said: "This was due to Yang T'ing-ho's
meritorious service which we should not
forget."

Yang liked to study historical records,
the condition of the people, frontier affairs, and the ideas of the school of law.
He wrote a number of books, among
them the *Shih-chai chi* 石齋集, 8 *ch.* His
memorials were collected in a work entitled *Yang Wen-chung kung san lu* 文忠公
三錄, 7 *ch.*, which was copied into the
Imperial Library. The first portion of this
in 4 *chüan* is preserved in the Library of
Congress, while the Naikaku Library owns
a complete copy. Yang was economical
and brought his children up strictly. He
had four sons and two daughters. The
sons were Yang Shen (*q.v.*), Yang Tun 惇
(cs 1523), Yang Heng 恆, and Yang
Ch'en 忱. Both Yang Shen and Yang Tun
achieved the *chin-shih*, the former being
accorded first place in 1511, while Yang
Ch'en became a *chü-jen*. His grandson
Yang Yu-jen 有仁 was also a *chin-shih*
(1577). In 1567 Yang T'ing-ho's honors
were restored and the official title of
grand guardian and canonization Wen-
chung 文忠 also awarded.

Bibliography

1/190/1a; 3/176/1a; 5/15/1a; 6/2/16a, 5/17a, 6/35b, 16/25b, 20/11b, 23/10b, 31/37a, 42/2b, 46/39b; 7/19/17a; 8/41/10a; 14/3/10a; 17/1/1a; 18/3/1a; 42/69/1a; 61/127/17b; 63/12/1a; 64/丙 7/8a; 84/丙 15a; Li Chih, *Hsü fen shu*, 3/8a; *id., Hsü ts'ang-shu*, 12/4a; Wang Shih-chen, *Yen-chou shih-liao ch'ien chi, ch.* 28; Wang Ch'iung, *Shuang-hsi tsa-chi,* 24a; Ku Ying-t'ai (ECCP), *Ming-ch'ao chi-shih pen-mo, chüan* 50; MSL (1965), Wu-tsung, *ch.* 31–197, Shih-tsung, 0010, 0181, 0285, 0899; KC (1958), 2892, 2901, 2980, 3220, 3244, 3255, 3272, 3380, 4041; Chang Wei-hua 張維華, "*Ming-shih* fo-lang-chi Lü-sung Ho-lan I-ta-li-ya ssu chuan chu shih" 明史佛朗機呂宋和蘭意大利亞四傳注釋, YCHP, mon. 7 (1934); SK (1930), 55/6b; Naikaku Bunko *Catalogue*, 157; L. of C. *Catalogue of Rare Books*, 166; Paul Pelliot, "Le Ḥōja et le Sayyid Ḥusain de l'Histoire des Ming," TP, 38 (1948), 83; W. Franke, *Sources*, 5.5.35.

Chou Tao-chi

YANG Tung-ming 楊東明 (T. 啓修, H. 晉安 [or 菴] ,惜陰居士), 1548–1624, official and thinker, was born into a well-to-do family of Yü-ch'eng 虞城, Honan. A *chü-jen* of 1576 and *chin-shih* of 1580, he first obtained an appointment as drafter in the central drafting office. In 1589 he became a supervising secretary. Like a number of others at court, he was critical of conditions and frequently memorialized the throne. His criticisms, though praised by his fellow-officials, met with no response. When the people in Nan-Chihli, Honan, and Shantung suffered from a flood (1594), he submitted an illustrated memorial to the throne. This is said to have moved the emperor to appropriate a large sum of money for relief. In the following year he served as an examiner in the metropolitan examination. Although several graduates on this occasion rose to prominence in later years, he avoided coming into closer relation with them as he felt it his duty to select talent for the state, not to deflect any advantage to himself. About the same time he accused Shen Ssu-hsiao (*see* Ku Hsien-ch'eng) of coming to the support of a censor included in the list of people to be dismissed. As this case was involved in the factionalism then rife at court, Yang found himself demoted to be a chao-mo 照磨, or commissary of the records office, in the provincial administration office in Shensi. Shortly afterwards he retired.

By nature Yang was a man of action. He disliked living a life apart from the common folk. During his years at home he devoted himself to the welfare of the people of his district. He adopted a public granary system 社倉, in order to level the price of grain, and acquired some land for the poor to cultivate. When flood destroyed a dike in 1601, he joined with others in the work of repair. In addition, he gave attention to education. Early in 1596 he established a free school for poor boys, taught disciples said to have numbered over a hundred, and also made other contributions to his native place. His earnestness in public affairs won him a score of commendations to the throne by local authorities. The reign of Chu Ch'ang-lo (ECCP) lasted only a few weeks, yet in this period Yang received three appointments. He served first as a vice minister of the Court of Imperial Sacrifices, second as chief minister of the Grand Court of Revision, and finally as chief minister of the Court of Imperial Entertainments. After the accession to the throne in 1621 of Chu Yu-chiao (ECCP), he received the appointment of transmission commissioner in Nanking. Before leaving for the south, however, he became a junior vice minister of Justice (the previous appointment having been allowed to lapse). In this office he never forgot to maintain his guiding principle: to uphold the law without distinction between weak and powerful, poor and rich. In the same year, according to Sun Ch'i-feng (ECCP), he became partly responsible for the founding of the Shou-shan Academy in Peking (*see* Tsou Yüan-piao), where it was customary for a while for certain high officials, connected with the Tung-lin party, to meet for discussion. They contributed measurably to the revival of neo-Confucianism. A year or so later he retired from office for the last time.

Yang Tung-ming was a friend of many followers of the school of Wang Shou-jen (*q.v.*), including especially Tsou Yüan-piao, Keng Ting-hsiang, Yang Ch'i-yüan, and Feng Ts'ung-wu (*qq.v.*). Through discussions with such men, he learned the main tenets of Wang Shou-jen's philosophy, and became one of the few scholars of Wang's school in the north. Yang attacked the Sung thinkers for separating human nature into two parts, moral nature (i-li chih-hsing 義理之性) and physical nature (ch'i-chih 氣質 chih-hsing), the former being good and the latter leading to evil. Instead, he reinterpreted the doctrine of li 理 and ch'i 氣, describing them as one and integral, with ch'i being the creative force, and li the order in creation. The only nature is thus that of ch'i, which is totally good in its pristine purity, but becomes ambiguous and differentiated as individual endowments vary in degrees of "purity." To the Tung-lin critics of Wang Shou-jen's First Maxim regarding the mind-in-itself being beyond good and evil (*see* Wang Shou-jen and Wang Chi) Yang Tung-ming replied that Wang was speaking not of nature, the goodness of which was beyond doubt, but of mind. He explained that goodness refers, in its absolute sense, to man's original nature, and, in its relative sense, to man's activity. According to him, in describing the mind-in-itself as being "neither good nor evil," Wang Shou-jen regarded it as the source of dynamic activity, which is distinct from nature-in-itself, the principle of tranquillity.

The *Yü-ch'eng-hsien chih* lists ten titles attributed to his authorship, but only one of these seems to be available, the *Shan-chü kung-k'o* 山居功課, 10 *ch.*, a copy of which, printed in 1624, is in the Naikaku Bunko. The *Ssu-k'u* catalogue records two of his books by title only, the *Ch'ing-so chin-yen* 青瑣藎言, 2 *ch.*, and *Chi-min t'u-shuo* 饑民圖說, 1 *ch.* Sun Ch'i-feng men-

tions altogether four of his works, and drew especially from *Lun hsing i yen* 論性臆言, as did also Huang Tsung-hsi (ECCP).

Yang had a son named Yang Ch'un-yü 春育, who served for a while as an assistant surveillance commissioner by imperial favor. Yang Tung-ming passed away at the age of seventy-six. Four years after his death he was accorded the posthumous title of minister of Justice, and his tablet was placed in the sacrificial hall of Yü-ch'eng.

Bibliography

1/241/14a; 3/226/12a; 39/13/24a; 61/134/2683; 83/29/8b; KC (1958), 4722, 5424; *Yü-ch'eng-hsien chih* (1895), 3/12b, 5/10a, 15b, 24a, 26a, 6/12a, 15b, 8/6b, 24b, 31b, 66b, 9/62a; *Chi-fu t'ung-chih* (1934), 4488; SK (1930), 56/7b, 64/4b; Ch'en Chien and Shen Kuo-yüan (*see* Ch'en Chien), *Huang Ming ts'ung-hsin lu* (1620), 37/37a; T'ang Pin 湯斌, *Lo-hsüeh pien* 洛學編 (1688), 4/80a; Sun Ch'i-feng, *Li-hsüeh tsung-chuan*, 23/58a; Naikaku Bunko *Catalogue*, 365; H. Busch, "The Tung-lin Academy and Its Political and Philosophical Significance," MS, XIV (1949-55), 62.

Huang P'ei and Julia Ching

YANG Wei-chen 楊維楨 **or** 禎 (T. 廉夫, H. 鐵崖, also 鐵笛子, etc.), 1296-June 19, 1370, poet, somewhat eccentric literary figure, and minor Yüan official, was born in K'uai-chi 會稽, Chekiang, into a family that had not recently produced any officials. Yang Wei-chen's early years were spent in study and travel around the regions near his home. His father, not satisfied with his son's academic progress, locked him up in an elevated studio on T'ieh-yai 鐵涯 Mountain for five years, and, as the story goes, fed and supplied him by means of some system of pulleys. This secluded study of the Classics and History bore fruit in 1327 when Yang was among eight-five successful candidates in the chin-shih examination, specializing in the Ch'un-ch'iu (Spring and Autumn

Annals).

As a serious student of the *Ch'un-ch'iu* from his days as a youth, Yang became known in his lifetime as a teacher of this Classic; he attracted a number of students, none of whom, however, made any particular mark in their own right. Yang's several works on the *Ch'un-ch'iu* are no longer extant; in fact, only one volume of three *chüan*—*Ch'un-ch'iu ho-t'i chu-shuo* 春秋合題著說—is listed by title only in the Catalogue of the *Ssu-k'u ch'üan-shu*. Nevertheless, from the reconstruction of the Yüan *I-wen-chih* (or bibliography), we know that he did write several other studies on the *Ch'un-ch'iu* and the *Tso chuan*, and on other Classics, but they seem to have disappeared, and judging from the available comments they make no original contribution. Of Yang's historical works, Sung Lien (*q.v.*) in his tomb inscription mentions both the *Pu-cheng san-shih kang-mu* 補正三史綱目 (which is not referred to in other sources) and the *Li-tai shih-yüeh* 歷代史鉞 (which Yang in his autobiographical sketch says was a work of 200 *chüan*). Yang's *Shih-i shih-i* 史義拾遺, 2 *ch.*, still available, is a collected miscellany of brief stories and episodes ranging from the Hsia dynasty through the Sung, which he amended by setting up hypothetical situations showing how events should have or could have taken place. This work, thus, is not a serious piece of historical scholarship, but it does contain many of Yang's moral judgments on famous personages and occurrences.

Yang is not easily identifiable with a particular philosophical school. Huang Tsung-hsi and Ch'üan Tsu-wang (both in ECCP) in their *Sung Yüan hsüeh-an* do not locate him very firmly in any one tradition. Only through loose association is he grouped in the school of Hsüeh Chi-hsüan (1125-73), the Sung philosopher whom Ch'üan Tsu-wang credits as being one of the fountainheads of the utilitarian Yung-chia 永嘉 school. Yang is on the periphery of Hsüeh's school, being the penultimate in the line of transmission of one of its branches. His mentor is recorded as Ni Yüan 倪淵, an insignificant Yüan thinker. Apparently by virtue of the fact that it was known that Yang purchased and studied, when he was young, the *Huang-shih jih-ch'ao* 黃氏日抄, of Huang Chen (1213-80), he is also mentioned in connection with the latter's school, although again not in the direct line of transmission.

Yang's career as an official was not particularly remarkable and was beset with frustrations. His first post, to which he was appointed shortly after earning the *chin-shih*, was the magistracy of T'ien-t'ai 天台 in Chekiang near the coast; he was faced here with a clique of corrupt clerks whom he attempted to punish and bring under control, but to no avail. So he resigned. His next post was in the salt administration of Ch'ien-ch'ing 錢清 on Hangchow Bay, where the salt taxes were so burdensome that the people could not meet their quota. Yang's persistent pleading with his superiors about this problem resulted in only partial alleviation. Although there is some discrepancy in the sources about the chronological sequence of events for this period in Yang's life, it now seems that some time during his tenure in this office his father died, and he went into mourning. For the next ten years after coming out of retirement, approximately from 1334 to 1343, Yang was not assigned another post, because, as he himself believed and wrote, some officials felt that he exhibited excessively uncompromising ideals. There is no doubt some truth in this, for Pei Ch'iung 貝瓊 (T. 廷琚, 廷臣, d. 1379), one of Yang's more accomplished poetry students of long standing, says that his mentor was so straightforward and unhesitatingly candid that some considered him eccentric. These years without official appointment were spent in traveling around the lower Yangtze valley, part of the time with a fellow poet, Chang Yü (*q.v.*), and in literary pursuits, often accompanied by carousing.

In 1343 Yang was summoned to the capital, together with some thirty other scholars, to exert a final effort at completing the Sung, Liao, and Chin dynastic histories. An impasse over the thorny problem of which dynasty (or dynasties) should be invested with cheng-t'ung 正統 (orthodox succession) had impeded previous compilation attempts. Some scholars favored having the transmission of legitimacy pass solely through the Sung, that is, from Northern Sung to Southern Sung and then directly to the Yüan, with the Chin and Liao dynasties being treated as illegitimate barbarian states. Others argued for making the Liao history Pei-shih 北史 (Northern history), because the Liao was established prior to and coexisted for a time with the Sung. In this case, the history of the Northern Sung would be called simply Sung-shih 宋史 and the Southern Sung history Nan 南 Sung-shih because the Liao and Chin, whose history would be entitled Pei-shih, had control of the northern half of country. The editor-in-chief of the three histories, Toqto (1313–55), finally had to resolve this dilemma arbitrarily by decreeing that, as in the history of the Three Kingdoms, none of the three dynasties would have sole claim to legitimacy but each would still have its own reign-names 年號. The theory was that the Yüan gained cheng-t'ung after uniting the empire under one imperial house by subjugating both the Chin and the Sung. Yang was not at all satisfied with this compromise solution and privately wrote a long essay—Cheng-t'ung pien 辨—positing that only the Sung dynasty conveyed legitimacy to the Yüan. This disquisition, which was probably written after the histories were officially accepted, made him an instant celebrity and his position was often praised and even accepted long after his death as the definitive statement on the problem.

Yang sustains his arguments primarily with the theory of cheng-t'ung developed in the T'ung-chien kang-mu by Chu Hsi (1130–1200), who himself derived his principles from the concept of Great Unification 大一統 found in the Ch'un-ch'iu. Briefly put, Yang asserted that under the Chin there was no "cheng," for the affairs of state were not upright and correct; furthermore, there was no "t'ung," because the entire realm was not unified. On the other hand, the Southern Sung acquired its legitimacy directly from the Northern Sung. To substantiate his argument further, Yang introduced a new dimension to the theory of cheng-t'ung: the Chu Hsi-influenced concepts of tao-t'ung 道統 (moral succession) and chih-t'ung 治統 (political succession), which actually are interrelated and indivisible. Pursuing this line of reasoning, Yang traces the transmission of tao from Yao and Shun through various stages eventually to Chu Hsi and then finally to the Confucianist, Hsü Heng (1209–81), maintaining that the tao succession never passed through the Liao and Chin. Consistent with his principle, Yang does not use the posthumous names of the Liao and Chin rulers in his essay, but rather their personal names. In sum his essay is quite daring; he does not veil his criticism of the historical board, and he implies that the Yüan rule prior to 1279 was somehow illegitimate.

The fame, or notoriety in some quarters, that Yang gained from his essay was of little value for advancing his career in officialdom. Even though his superior on the historical board, Ou-yang Hsüan (1283–1357), wanted to recommend him for a post, some unknown officials in the capital objected. Yang instead returned for a two-year interlude to private life as poet and teacher; he traveled throughout the general region between Wu-hsing 吳興, Chekiang, and Soochow, and at one point is recorded as having become a teacher of the Ch'un-ch'iu to the children of a prominent family in Sung-chiang 松江. In 1348 he received appointment as the Ssu-wu t'i-chü 四務提舉 in Hangchow, where he is described as heavily burdened with official duties. From this post he was transferred to that of judicial official in the prefectural government of Chien-te 建德 (Chekiang). He was assigned his last and highest official position in 1352, educational supervisor in Kiangsi province, but because of the disorders in the area he was unable to assume this office. Caught in the seesaw fighting of various competing rebels and Yüan troops, Yang and his family fled to Fu-ch'un Mountain 富春山 and then later to Ch'ien-t'ang 錢塘, both in the general vicinity of Hangchow.

Contemporaneous with Yang's retreat to the relative safety of isolated areas was the rise of the bandit-rebel Chang Shih-ch'eng (q.v.), whose control extended throughout this region. In 1358, a short time after Chang "surrendered" on his own terms to the Yüan and accepted the title of grand commandant, he approached Yang to join his retinue. It would have been a great coup for Chang to have won his allegiance, then certainly one of the best-known literati of the region, if not the empire. But Yang rebuffed Chang's approaches and, being the unflinching critic that he was, dared to write five essays (no longer extant) and a letter castigating and admonishing Chang. In essence, Yang expressed concern that Chang was not getting the right advice from his officials and associates, who he thought, were more interested in their own welfare and prosperity than Chang's.

During the eighteen years between 1352 and the second year of the Ming rule, a period when Yang had no official responsibilities, he was at the height of his literary career; the influence of his poetic style was widely felt. His talents as a poet, essayist, and teacher were in great demand. Residing mostly in the Sung-chiang district, he attracted a long train of followers and friends. Among his more noteworthy literary acquaintances were Chang Yü, Ku Te-hui (see Ch'en Ju-yen), Ni Tsan (q.v.), and Li Hsiao-kuang (1297–1348). This varied group frequently engaged in literary critique sessions or in poetry contests, and often indulged in what some people of that

time and later considered rather bizarre frivolity. Yang was never one to be self-conscious about his own behavior nor one to abstain from wine, women, and song. In 1369 Emperor Chu Yüan-chang summoned him to Nanking to participate in the compilation of the *Li yüeh shu* 禮樂書. Yang refused this initial invitation, reportedly replying, "How can a widow almost in her coffin manage to marry again?" A second invitation sent with gifts early in the following year at first met with a declination, but finally Yang consented to journey to the capital on the condition that he not be made an official and thereby violate his loyalty to the former dynasty under which he had served. He remained in the capital 110 days, long enough to help establish the principles or guidelines for compiling this monograph on the rites and music. Pleading illness, he returned to his home with the consent and appreciation of the emperor. Two or three months later he died of some sort of liver ailment at the age of seventy-four.

In the eyes of his contemporaries and later traditional scholars and in our estimation today, Yang's reputation clearly rests on his poetic talents and accomplishments. Just as Yang the man was a controversial figure, however, so his poetry and essays have also received very mixed critical appreciation. Perhaps this is to be expected given his theory of poetics. He believed that a poem could be no greater than the temperament or nature (性情) of the poet; therefore, the poet should remain free to cultivate his own individuality and nature. Only then should a style be selected from the models of the past, a style that would adequately suit the poet's needs and artistic objectives. More crucial to the success of a poem than its style or form was the spirit it conveyed. Style should in no way encumber this spirit, or, for that matter, the nature or temperament of the poet. The stylistically unsophisticated but emotion-laden poems in the feng 風 section of the *Shih-ching* tes-

tify to this principle, Yang often wrote.
The works of most later poets, especially
those of late T'ang, Sung, and Yüan
times, were overlaid with stylistic conceits
and verbal voluptuousness that often
concealed petty sentiments.

The most severe attack against both
Yang and his poetry was voiced by a
younger contemporary, Wang Wei (q.v.),
who accused him of being a literary
devil (文妖). Yang's writings, he remarked,
were not only literarily reprehensible but
also morally degenerate, rending asunder
jen 仁 (altruism) and i 義 (righteousness)
and upsetting name and reality. The
Ssu-k'u editors, assuming a less extreme
moralistic view, do not fully concur
in this judgment. They hold that Yang's
essays are flowing and powerful. Ch'üan
Tsu-wang, however, points out that Yang's
prose style did not follow the simple
straightforward one predominant from
the mid-twelfth century on; Yang sought
effects in the unusual and the ornate. As
for his poetry, the Ssu-k'u editors thought
that at its best it excelled anything of
the time, but at its worst merited Wang's
and others' criticism. In seeking fresh
meaning and freedom in his poetry, Yang
sometimes resorted to excessive allitera-
tion and to shocking references to weird
objects. His style in the hands of less
talented students and imitators, furthermore, often sank into wild exoticism. Chao
I (ECCP), writing several hundred years
later, said, "In the late Yüan and early
Ming, Yang Wei-chen was the dominant
figure, but in his startling eccentricities he
imitated Li Ho (791–817), while in his
bewitching seductiveness he imitated Wen
T'ing-yün (ca. 812–70) and Li Shang-yin
(813–58). Thereby he established his own
style, to be sure, but in the end, it failed
to open a strong and vigorous new course
to poetry." A Japanese scholar, Maeno
Naoki 前野眞彬, has, however, found Yang
to be an unconscious precursor to such
later Ming poets as Li Meng-yang and
Ho Ching-ming (qq. v.) who, like Yang,
harked back to the spirit and models of

Han and pre-Han poetry.

Yang's style was known as t'ieh-yai-
t'i 體. Of all the poetic genres in which
he composed, he is most widely known for
and considered himself most accomplished
in yüeh-fu 樂府. This form, which had
long been divorced from music, allowed
the kind of lyric freedom suitable to
Yang's temperament and artistic purposes.
While he did not totally abandon the
traditional metric patterns, he did employ
new ones and often utilized highly original unorthodox, or contemporary subjects.
In the opinion of the Ssu-k'u editors,
Yang's yüeh-fu style is indebted to Li Po
(701–62) and Li Ho; according to Yang,
the contemporary poet most kindred to
him in spirit and style was Li Hsiao-
kuang. Yang's shih 詩 (poems) were also
well known and respected in his time, as
were his yung-shih 詠史 which deal with
historical episodes up through the Sung.
He considered his fu 賦 poems, most of
which he composed when very young,
unworthy of being published, but unbe-
knownst to him they were collected and
printed.

Yang was a prolific prose and poetry
writer, but comparatively few remnants
of his work survived long after his death;
even these are not all conveniently brought
together. Tung-wei-tzu wen-chi 東維子文
集, 31 ch., contains many of his miscellaneous prose compositions and only two
chüan of his shih; however, his most famous essay, Cheng-t'ung pien, is not to be
found in this collection. The fact that it
is included in the Ch'o keng lu, chüan 3,
of T'ao Tsung-i (q.v.), completed in 1366,
is indicative of the respect in which it
was held by Yang's contemporaries; this
essay is also incorporated in Pei Ch'iung's
biography of Yang. [Editors' note: It is
not without interest that Yang wrote a
preface for T'ao's important work on its
completion.] In his autobiographical
sketch Yang mentions that the essay was
some 5,000 words in length, but the versions extant today are only 3,000 words
long. Another edition (1502) of Yang's

wen-chi in 5 chüan, titled T'ieh-yai wen-chi, and located in the National Central Library in Taipei, has a number of pieces not in the Ssu-pu ts'ung-k'an edition. Yang's work of historical criticism, Shih-i shĭh-i, although located in a third Ming edition of his wen-chi (5 ch., also dated 1502 and available in the National Central Library), is most readily found today in the Ch'ing-chao-t'ang ts'ung-shu 青照堂叢書. Two very brief narratives—Ya-ch'ang chih 啞倡志 and Nan-lou mei-jen chuan 南樓美人傳 — are both printed in the anonymous compilation, Lü-ch'uang nü-shih 綠窗女史; a third tale, Chu-ch'a meng-chi 煮茶夢記, is included in the Shuo-fu hsü (弓 43) of T'ao T'ing (see T'ao Tsung-i). Ch'u hung p'u 除紅譜, a short work about a dice game, has often been spuriously attributed to Yang (for example, by T'ao Tsung-i and by Ch'ien Ta-hsin [ECCP] in the latter's reconstruction of the Yüan I-wen-chih), but the late bibliophile Yeh Te-hui (BDRC) has conclusively shown that Yang wrote just the preface to the volume.

It is recorded that Yang destroyed many of his poems, particularly those he composed when relatively young; but thanks to the efforts of his student, Wu Fu 吳復(T. 見心), many have been preserved. Two collections of his yüeh-fu in 10 chüan have been reprinted, entitled respectively T'ieh-yai ku 古 yüeh-fu chu 注, the notes being by the Ch'ing scholar and fellow provincial, Lou Pu-ch'an 樓卜瀍(T. 西濱, fl. 1774), and T'ieh-yai hsien-sheng ku yüeh-fu. An appendix to the Ssu-pu ts'ung-k'an edition includes six chüan of Yang's Fu-ku shih 復古詩, with notes by Chang Wan 章琬 of the Yüan dynasty. In the Ssu-pu pei-yao edition are also T'ieh-yai yung-shih chu 詠史註 and T'ieh-yai i-pien chu 編註, both of 8 chüan and annotated with prefaces (1774) by Lou. Yang's fu are assembled in a work of four chüan entitled Li-tse i-yin 麗則遺音, which may be found today in an appendix to a Mao Chin (ECCP) edition of Yang's yüeh-fu; a copy of this volume may be found in the National Central Library, Taipei, and another in the Naikaku Bunko, Tokyo.

During his lifetime Yang possessed some local fame as a calligrapher and to a lesser extent as a painter. (His elder brother, Yang Wei-han 維翰 [T. 子固, 1294–1351], was a minor painter and calligrapher of the period.) Although he certainly was not outstanding, his calligraphic style is individualistic; critics have commented also on its mature strength. He was frequently called upon to inscribe poems and colophons on paintings. A number of samples of his brushwork are readily available today in various catalogues and art compendia. There is a long colophon to the painting "Yu-yü-hsien t'u" 有餘閒圖 (Leisure to spare) by the 14th-century Yao T'ing-mei 姚廷美, now in the Cleveland Museum of Art; the painting is reproduced and the colophon translated in a catalogue by this museum, and both the painting and colophon reproduced in a compilation by Cheng Chen-to (BDRC). A. G. Wenley reproduces and translates a poem and colophon composed by Yang in 1361 for a little-known late Yüan painter's work, now in the Freer Gallery of Art. Finally, a scroll painting by Yang of a solitary pine tree, entitled "Sui-han 崴寒 t'u" (Cold of the season), is in the National Palace Museum in Taiwan.

Bibliography

Yin-te 24: 1/285/2a; 3/266/2a; 5/115/15a, 20a; 22/1/25a; 32/49/12a; 61/145/2a; 84/ 甲前 /10b; 88/10/21a; Yin-te 35: 22/238/10a; 23/36/23a; 24/47/24b; 29/初辛; Pei Ch'iung, Ch'ing-chiang Pei hsien-sheng wen-chi 清江貝先生文集(SPTK), 2/3a, 7/1a; Shao-hsing-fu chih 紹興府志(1792), 54/22a, 58/9b, 60/12a; SK (1930), 30/2a, 168/12a; Chu I-tsun (ECCP), P'u-shu t'ing-chi (Kuo-hsüeh chi-pen ed.), ch. 64; T'ieh-yai hsien-sheng wai-chi 外紀 in ms.; T'ao Tsung-i, Ch'o keng lu (SPTK), 3/1a, 23/4a, 30/14a; Yeh Sheng, Shui-tung jih-chi (Taiwan reprint, 1965), 3/4a, 24/7b; Lang Ying, Ch'i-hsiu lei-kao (Taiwan, 1963), 320; Ho Liang-chün, Ssu-yu-chai ts'ung-shuo (Peking, 1959), 231; Ch'u Jen-huo 褚人穫, Chien-hu er-chi 堅瓠瓜二集, ch. 4; Ho Ch'iao-yüan, Ming-shan ts'ang (1641),

95/2a; Huang Tsung-hsi and Ch'üan Tsu-wang, *Sung Yüan hsüeh-an*, ch. 47; *Sung Yüan hsüeh-an pu-i* 補遺 (Taiwan, 1962), 52/30a; Ch'iao Yen-kuan 喬衍琯, "Yang Wei-chen shih wen-chi pa-chung" 詩文集八種,*Kuo-li chung-yang t'u-shu-kuan kuan-k'an* 國立中央圖書館館刊, n.s., II:2 (October, 1968), 80; *id.*, "Yang T'ieh-yai hsien-sheng wai-chi," *ibid.*, I: 4 (April, 1968), 86; Lo Pao-ts'e 羅寶冊, "Ming-tai chih ch'u-ch'i wen-hsüeh 明代之初期文學, *Shih-ta yüeh-k'an* 師大月刊, no. 2 (1933), 251, 273; Ch'ien Chi-po 錢基博, *Ming-tai wen-hsüeh* 明代文學 (Shanghai, 1939), 2, 74; Ma Tsung-huo 馬宗霍, *Shu-lin ts'ao chien* 書林藻鑑 (Shanghai, 1936), 277b; *Yüan Yang Wei-chen shu ch'eng-nan ch'ang-ho shih* 書城南倡和詩 in *Ku-kung po-wu-yüan ts'ang li-tai fa-shu hsüan-chi* 故宮博物院藏歷代法書選集, Peking, 1963, first series, ts'e 16; *Yüan Yang Wei-chen chen-ching-an mu-yüan shu* 眞鏡庵募緣疏, Peking, 1965; *Yün-hui-chai ts'ang T'ang Sung i-lai ming-hua chi* 韞輝齋藏唐宋以來名畫集, compiled by Cheng Chen-to (BDRC), Shanghai, 1947; Sun Yüeh-pan 孫岳頒, *P'ei-wen-chai shu-hua p'u* 佩文齋書畫譜 (1708), 39/1a, 79/57b; *Ku-kung shu-hua lu* 故宮書畫錄 (Taiwan, 1965), ch. 5, 228; Shimonaka Yasaburō 下中彌三郎, ed., *Sodo zenshū* 書道全集, Vol. 17 (Tokyo, 1956), 167, 187, pl. 48, 49; A. G. Wenley, " 'A breath of spring,' by Tsou Fu-lei," *Ars Orientalis*, Vol. 2 (1957), 459; Maeno Naoki, "Min shichi shi no sensei—Yō Itei no bungakukan ni tsuite" 明七子の先聲―楊維楨文學觀について, *Chūgoku bunga-ku hō* 中國文學報, no. 5 (October, 1956), 40; F. W. Mote, *The Poet Kao Ch'i* (Princeton, 1962), 195, 245; P. Pelliot, "Quelques remarques sur le Chouo Fou," TP, 23 (1924), 169; Sherman E. Lee and Wai-kam Ho, *Chinese Art under the Mongols*: *The Yüan Dynasty (1279–1368)*, (Cleveland, 1968), catalogue no. 260.

Edmund H. Worthy

YANG Ying-lung 楊應龍 (d. July 21, 1600) was an aboriginal official of Po-chou 播州, an area of extended size, somewhat indefinite borders, and rugged terrain located mainly in northeastern modern Kweichow. His position was a hereditary one, having been passed down in the family since the late ninth century. His earliest known ancestor, Yang Tuan 端, a native of Shansi, had arrived in the Po-chou area during the reign of T'ang Hsi-tsung (r. 874–889), responding to a strange dream and to an imperial appeal for recruits to suppress a Nan-chao rebellion. Yang Tuan had established himself as the dominant force in the region, was accorded official recognition, and inaugurated the practice of transmitting power from generation to generation within his own clan.

The Yang family submitted to the Ming dynasty early in the Hung-wu era, presented tribute to the emperor in 1372, and was confirmed in its hereditary position. Upon several subsequent occasions, the family rendered valuable service to the dynasty, usually in the form of suppressing outbreaks among various southwestern aboriginal peoples. Its control of Po-chu, however, was by no means absolute during the Ming period. By this time, seven other local families, T'ien 田, Chang 張, Yüan 袁, Lu 盧, T'an 譚, Lo 羅, and Wu 吳, had become prominent and in important matters their opinions had to be sought. An assistant prefect was stationed at Huang-p'ing 黃平, Kweichow, however, to supervise Po-chou taxation affairs.

Yang Ying-lung, described as cruel even as a child, succeeded his father in 1572, and at first showed no disposition to deviate from the loyalty which his ancestors had rendered to the Ming. In fact, he achieved considerable success fighting Tibetan tribes and was rewarded with ceremonial clothing, gold, and a promotion.

Though the sources contain no direct discussion of the question, it may be conjectured that the most general cause of the uprising was reverse acculturation, *i. e.*, Yang's identification with aboriginal interests. Undoubtedly Yang's ancestry was partly non-Chinese and he may have come to regard himself as an upholder of aboriginal, primarily Miao, values in the struggle against the spread of Chinese influence. At the same time it seems certain that Yang's motives in rebelling were partly personal in origin, because, after having come to favor a concubine, née T'ien 田, and to suspect his wife, née Chang 張, of infidelity, he killed the latter

(1587). Subsequently he went on to kill several other members of the Chang family. These brutal actions aroused uneasiness among seven of the eight prominent families of the area, and a split between them and Yang occurred.

Finding himself increasingly isolated, Yang joined forces with an aboriginal group known as the Sheng Miao 生苗 (uncivilized Miao) and began outright looting. Such actions finally prompted the paternal uncle of Yang's slain wife to join with two local officials in presenting to the provincial authorities a report which charged Yang with rebellion. The report evoked two variant ways of solving the problem presented. One was to suppress Yang through the forthright use of military force and the other, apparently most favored by provincial officials and the gentry families in the general Kweichow-Szechwan border area, advocated the employment of political means. The latter eventually prevailed and no military moves against Yang were undertaken. Instead, he was persuaded to submit himself to judicial proceedings, and, after refusing to appear before any tribunal in Kweichow, he consented to go to P'eng-shui 彭水, Szechwan, in 1590.

At the conclusion of the P'eng-shui trial, undoubtedly much to his surprise, Yang was sentenced to death by beheading. The sentence was forthwith appealed to Peking, Yang promising to pay twenty thousand taels of silver if he were granted his freedom. While his petition was being considered, the Japanese invasion of Korea occurred and an imperial edict was circulated throughout the country calling for recruits. Seizing upon this opportunity, Yang promised to supply five thousand troops in exchange for his release. Eventually his offer was accepted and he was allowed to resume his position in Po-chou. Once back in the familiar fastnessess of his native area, Yang refused to live up to his promise. Even worse, he killed several officials dispatched to remind him of his obligation, and sought to evade responsibility for the slayings by blaming them on the "uncivilized" Miao.

Early in 1594, the governor of Szechwan, Wang Chi-kuang 王繼光 (H. 泉皋, cs 1577), and others, organized an expedition to crush Yang, and forces were dispatched to Po-chou from the north, east, and south. When the Szechwanese contingent, arriving from the north, reached the vicinity of the strategic Lou-shan Pass 婁山 關, Yang pretended to surrender and negotiations ensued. During them, however, Yang launched a surprise attack and badly defeated one section of the Szechwanese force. Following this defeat, the entire expedition was suspended and a censor was dispatched with instructions to reach a settlement with Yang through negotiation; but all attempts at appeasement failed.

Late in the same year the central government gave increased priority to the problem of suppressing Yang and appointed Hsing Chieh 邢玠 (T. 式如, cs 1571) as supreme commander and concurrently vice minister of War. Hsing arrived in Szechwan and sent Yang a letter promising that he would not be condemned to death if he surrendered, but warning that if he refused to submit, a price of ten thousand taels of silver would be placed on his head. Furthermore, Hsing ordered some of the government forces withdrawn from Ch'i-chiang 綦江 in southern Szechwan as a sign of official goodwill and the sincerity of the government's desire to reach an accommodation. By this time groups on both sides had formed whose interests demanded that the rebellion continue. The seven prominent local families did not want a surrender, preferring to see Yang and the special position of his family destroyed. On the other side, Yang's associates realized his surrender would bring about their own destruction and consequently put pressure on him to persist in the rebellion. Finally, Hsing Chieh managed to establish contact with Yang who agreed to negotiate provided an official was sent to assure him that he would not be ambushed after his surrender.

The prefect of Chungking, Wang Shih-ch'i (*see* Wang Tsung-mu) was appointed to conduct the final negotiations with Yang and persuaded him eventually to come to An-wen 安穩 in Ch'i-chiang, Szechwan, for trial. Yang arrived dressed as a prisoner and accompanied by twelve leading figures associated with him in rebellion. These men were surrendered to the authorities and immediately sent to Chungking where they were beheaded in a public execution. Yang's trial ensued and at the end of it he received his freedom though at a heavy price: he was required to pay forty thousand taels of silver and to assist the local authorities in lumbering activities; he was deprived of his office, which was handed over to his eldest son Yang Ch'ao-tung 朝棟; his second son was to be detained at Chungking as a hostage; and he had to vow that he would never again disturb the public peace. The administration of Po-chou too was reorganized so that a considerable portion of the power exercised hereditarily by the Yang family was bestowed upon officials in the regular local bureaucracy.

With the conclusion of Yang's trial, it seemed that peace in the southwest had been restored. Hsing Chieh returned to Peking, where he was rewarded for his services by being named censor-in-chief, and the full attention of the central government could now turn once more to the Korean emergency. Yang's acceptance of the peace terms was half-hearted at best, however, and tension between the authorities and himself soon reasserted itself.

Though technically deprived of his position in favor of his eldest son, Yang resumed full power and proceeded to employ it in several oppressive ways, one of the most objectionable of which was the execution of wealthy local citizens after charging them with trivial crimes and confiscating their property. Furthermore, he consolidated his position of influence with the various Miao tribes. Outside his native area, his relations with provincial officials worsened even more rapidly following the death of his second son, apparently of natural causes, in Chungking. Nor was Yang's mood improved when the authorities refused to return the body of his son until he had paid the forty thousand taels imposed upon him as a fine at his trial. Thus, Yang again moved toward outright rebellion and one of his more imaginative advisers attempted to persuade him to strike boldly at Chungking and Chengtu, capture the prince of Shu 蜀王, Chu Ch'üan 朱銓 (enf. 1578, d. 1615), who would be held as a hostage, and increase his demands for additional grants of power from the government. But Yang rejected these suggestions and continued to confine his activities to the familiar Szechwan-Kweichow border region.

During 1596, 1597, and 1598 Yang made raids over a wide area in northern Kweichow and southern Szechwan, where, according to the sources, he and his Miao troops were guilty of murder, rape, looting, and desecration of tombs of a particularly outrageous sort. No effective measures against him were taken, however, because the attention of the central government was still focused on Korea.

Early in 1599, following the Japanese retreat from Korea, the governor of Kweichow dispatched an army of three thousand to attack Yang, but after an apparent initial success, the force was virtually annihilated. The defeat provoked increased counter-measures on the part of the government which then named an ex-censor, Li Hua-lung (*q.v.*), minister of War, and ordered him to take personal charge of military affairs in Szechwan, Hukuang, and Kweichow. Before adequate forces could be assembled by the government, however, Yang had already pressed farther northward in Szechwan. Some indication of his military strength and its relative sophistication is provided by his capture of the town of Ch'i-chiang and his use of a type of cannon during the attack.

Following the fall of Ch'i-chiang, he proclaimed that the border of his area should be advanced closer to the Yangtze.

Possessing inadequate forces to meet the immediate emergency, Li Hua-lung pretended to advocate a policy of negotiations and peaceful settlement, a stance which produced the desired effect on Yang, who halted his expansion. At the same time, Li was secretly planning a major military push and collected forces from southern Hukuang and Kwangsi. In addition, the government position was considerably strengthened by the return to Szechwan of the famed general, Liu T'ing (*q.v.*), who had been serving on the northeastern frontier. There was considerable suspicion about Liu's reliability, since his connections with the southwest were longstanding and previously he had had close ties with Yang. Li Hua-lung, nevertheless, established good relations with Liu, convinced him that his best interests lay in the direction of loyal service to the Ming, and entrusted him with considerable military authority.

During the latter part of 1599 and early 1600, having become aware that Li Hua-lung's offer of peace was a cover-up, Yang launched a major military effort in Kweichow, burning the towns of Tung-p'o 東坡 and Lan-ch'iao 爛橋, and threatening communications with the southern sector of the province and with Yunnan. By early 1600 Li Hua-lung's plans for a massive attack were complete, and on March 26 a force said to consist of two hundred forty thousand troops (of whom 30 percent were Chinese and 70 percent were aboriginal tribesmen) converged on the troubled area from three directions: north (Szechwan), east (Hukuang), and south (Kweichow). Li directed general operations from his headquarters at Chungking and issued orders that the rebels should be crushed mercilessly outside the traditional border of Po-chou, but that military operations should be limited inside the traditional borders.

The tide of war went against Yang virtually from the beginning of the campaign, with the first major rebel defeat coming on the northern (Szechwan) front. The overwhelming might of the government forces made a profound psychological impact upon the rude Miao tribesmen who constituted the bulk of Yang's army. Morale sagged badly in the rebel ranks and desertion became rampant. Yang's efforts, increasingly desperate, to win back the loyalty of his troops with generous monetary rewards ended in failure. His cause did receive a last-minute boost when one of the government commanders defected. The sense of relief proved to be only temporary, however, and the rebels soon found themselves once again being pushed toward their doom.

On July 21, 1600, Yang hanged himself, all rebel resistance collapsed, and the power of the Yang family was destroyed after having endured for over seven centuries. The government had succeeded in crushing the long-continuing uprising after a campaign of almost four months during which it reportedly had slain twenty thousand rebels and captured over a hundred. The captives included Yang's brother and eldest son.

Early in 1601 Yang's corpse was cut to pieces and his brother and son executed in Peking as a warning to all the southwestern aboriginal peoples. This drastic action ended a reign of twenty-nine generations. Subsequently, Po-chou, as a governmental entity, was abolished and its territory divided up to form two new administrative units: Tsun-i 遵義 prefecture in Szechwan (now in Kweichow) and P'ing-yüeh 平越 prefecture in Kweichow.

Bibliography

1/228/10b, 312/1a; Ku Ying-t'ai (ECCP), *Ming-ch'ao chi-shih pen-mo*, 64; KC(1958), 4726, 4830, 4832, 4839; *Tsun-i-fu chih*(1841), 31, 40; Li Hua-lung, *P'ing Po ch'üan shu* (TsSCC ed.); Okano Masako 岡野昌子,"On Yang Ying-lung's Revolt at Po-chou of the Late Ming Dynasty," *Tōhōgaku*, 41 (March, 1971), 63.

James B. Parsons

YAO K'uei 姚夔 (T. 大章, H. 損菴), 1414–
March 7, 1473, minister of Rites from
1463 to 1469 and of Personnel from 1469
to 1473, was a native of T'ung-lu 桐廬,
Yen-chou 嚴州 prefecture, Chekiang. The
Yao family, originally from Kaifeng,
settled in Chekiang at the beginning of the
12th century and earned a reputation for
its tradition of learning. The first in the
family to distinguish himself was Yao
K'uei who gained a first in the prefectural
examination of 1438, and acquired the
chin-shih in 1442. In April, 1443, he
received an appointment as supervising
secretary in the office of scrutiny of Personnel. Thereupon, he submitted an eight
point memorandum urging the court to
pay close attention to the appointment of
civil servants, and to the operation of
government agencies, to abrogate the
practice of putting eunuchs in charge of
goverment depots, and to make an effort
to promote public education. Some of his
recommendations are said to have been
adopted by Emperor Chu Ch'i-chen (*q.v.*).

After the capture of the emperor by
the Oirat tribesmen in the battle of T'u-
mu on September 1, 1449, Prince Chu
Ch'i-yü (*q.v.*), was appointed acting head
of administration and then regent. Two
weeks later Yao K'uei was among the
leading civil and military officials who
urged the prince to assume the imperial
title. He also spoke eloquently on the
need of defending Peking at all costs
against further raids by the Oirat; he proposed mobilizing the imperial forces in
Hsüan-fu and Liaotung to launch a coun-
teroffensive in the enemy's rear, so as to
ease the pressure on the front. In March,
1450, following the inauguration of the
new reign, Yao received an appointment
as junior vice minister of Justice, and
was transferred to Nanking a year later.

In May, 1453, Yao returned to Peking
to serve in the ministry of Rites, after
which he was ordered to make an inspection tour to Yunnan to investigate the
conduct of the local officials. When Emperor Chu Ch'i-yü fell ill (February, 1457),

the designation of an heir apparent
became an urgent matter. The idea of
naming a successor did not please the
emperor, but leading officials kept pouring
in memorials pleading with him to reconsider. At this juncture, together with Shang
Lu (*q.v.*), his mentor, Yao submitted a
memorial urging the emperor to appoint
the descendant of Emperor Chu Chan-chi
(*q.v.*) to perpetuate the lineage of his
father. But before the memorial received
attention, the coup of Hsü Yu-chen (*q.v.*)
and others had succeeded in reinstating
the ex-emperor. Because of his opposition
to General Shih Heng (*q.v.*), who became
powerful due to his part in the restoration of the throne, Yao was transferred
(in March) to Nanking, but shortly afterwards the emperor recalled him to be the
senior vice minister of Rites (October),
and a year later appointed him to the
ministry of Personnel.

In February, 1463, Yao received a
promotion to be minister of Rites. In the
following year he submitted a number
of memorials remonstrating with the
emperor on his failure to give attention
to state affairs and outlining proposals for
various reforms. In September of this
year, he pleaded with the emperor to
remember to be frugal and restrained,
refrain from military adventures, and attend to state affairs. He submitted (April,
1467) a ten-point memorandum with proposals to end the state of laxity in the
schools and the irregularities in the examination system. In May of the following
year, taking advantage of the appearance
of ominous cosmological phenomena, Yao
submitted another memorial proposing
that the emperor consider appointing an
heir apparent, suspend the construction of
costly temples in the capital, and banish
the Buddhist monks from the western
regions. The emperor is said to have been
impressed by his remonstrances and proposals.

In July, 1468, Empress Ch'ien, wife
of Emperor Chu Ch'i-chen, died. According
to the will of the late emperor, she was

to be buried with him in the imperial tomb, but the idea was scorned by the emperor's surviving consort née Chou, mother of Emperor Chu Chien-shen(*q.v.*), who proposed a separate burial. The ministers, however, voiced objection. Emperor Chu Chien-shen subsequently called a conference to discuss the matter. Yao took the lead in opposition, submitting three successive memorials defending the original decision, citing the ancient code of rites. As the emperor remained indecisive, Yao dramatized the case by leading a group of officials to wail in front of the Wen-hua 文華 gate of the imperial palace. The emperor is said to have been so deeply moved by the loyalty of the ministers to their late master that he finally succeeded in convincing the empress dowager to change her mind.

Although enjoying Chu Chien-shen's confidence, Yao was not without enemies, most of whom were officials of northern origin jealous of the position enjoyed by a southerner. A censor criticized him in July, 1468, for example, for appointing an official, a southerner, who had previously been involved in an offense, and again in October by a group of censors who falsely charged him with corruption. Under these circumstances, Yao asked for relief from duty by pleading ill health, but the emperor intervened by dismissing all the charges and even cashiering his accusers.

A year later Yao was appointed minister of Personnel succeeding Ts'ui Kung (*see* Shen Chou) on the recommendation of Shang Lu. This concluded a decade of bitter factional strife between the nothern and southern aspirants. Following the death (in 1467) of Wang Ao 翱(*q.v.*), the powerful northerner who had been minister for over a decade (1453–67), the two factions started to compete for this influential and rewarding appointment. After much contention, Li Ping (*see* Han Wen), a protégé of Wang, succeeded to the post, but was ousted from office by the intrigue of the southerners in February, 1469. The same fate befell Ts'ui Kung who stayed in office for only four months (February-June). Yao's appointment, therefore, signaled the new interest of the emperor in the southerners. For this reason, although he was known for impartiality, Yao recommended scores of southerners to various government positions. Hence, in the following years until his death, he was constantly under slanderous attack by the northerners. With imperial support, however, he held his ground. In October, 1471, the emperor bestowed on him the honorary title of junior guardian of the heir apparent. Shortly afterwards, he begged permission to retire on grounds of failing health, but the emperor ignored his plea. He died a year later, at the age of fifty-nine, and received the posthumous name Wen-min 文敏 (cultured and earnest).

Yao K'uei's contemporaries acclaimed him as a man of integrity and determination, an insistent and purposeful critic of government affairs. They also cited his competence in ritual matters and the management of government, and praised him for his effort in recruiting men of talent to government service, although the contemporary northerners charged him with prejudice. Many of Yao's memorials outlining his suggestions and criticisms of state affairs are preserved in his collection of writings. This was first engraved by his family under the title of *Yao Wen-min kung i-kao* 公遺稿, 10 *ch.*, in the early 1490s. A copy of the original edition is preserved in the National Central Library, Taipei. It was reprinted by Yüan Ch'ang (ECCP) in 9 *chüan* (the 10th *chüan* and the appended biographical material of the original is missing), plus an appendix of collated notes in his *Chien-hsi ts'un-she ts'ung-k'o* (1898).

Yao K'uei had a son, Yao Pi 璧 (cj 1456, cs 1464), who served as director of a bureau in the ministry of War. He became involved in June, 1477, in the case of Hsiang Chung (*q.v.*), the minister who made an unsuccessful bid to oust the eunuch Wang Chih 汪直 (*q.v.*). He was thrown into prison and then demoted to be a vice prefect of Ssu-ming 思明 -fu in Kwangsi. He contracted a disease there and was unable to perform his duties; he died a few years later at home after obtaining permission to retire.

Bibliography

1/177/16b; 5/24/45a; 8/28/10a; 40/20/12b; MSL (1963), Ying-tsung, 2060, 3880, 4537, 4977, 5837, 6112, 7010, Hsien-tsung, 814, 916, 1076, 1119, 1184, 1186, 1269, 1353, 1413, 1831, 2191, 3010, 3024; KC (1958), 2254, 2265, 2325; P'eng Hua 彭華, *P'eng Wen-ssu kung wen-chi* 彭文思公文集 (NCL microfilm), 7/37a; SK (1930), 175/10b; *Yen-chou-fu chih* (1898), 15/43a, 18/4b, 16a, 19/19b; Ch'en Lun-hsü 陳綸緒 (Albert Chan), "Chi Ming T'ien-shun Ch'eng-hua chien ta-ch'en nan-pei chih cheng" 記明天順成化間大臣南北之爭, *Sinological Researches* 中國學誌 (Tokyo), no. 1 (1964), 102.

Hok-lam Chan

YAO Shih-lin 姚士粦 (or 麟, T. 叔祥), 1561 -*ca.* 1651, a native of Hai-yen 海鹽, Chekiang, principal compiler of the *Yen-i chih-lin* 鹽邑志林, had an unusual background for a scholar. Yao never competed in any examination, nor did he ever enter the bureaucracy. Apparently he issued from a poor family and supported himself as a young man by portrait painting. He declared that at nineteen years of age he was still illiterate. It was on the 6th day of the 4th moon of 1580 (April 29), while he was working in Te-ch'ing 德清, Chekiang, that he began his formal education with his employer, Chiang Hai-jih 姜孩日. Four years later a relative employed him. The young son of the family, Lü Chao-hsi 呂兆禧 (T. 錫侯, 1573-90), who became a *hsiu-ts'ai* in 1588 but failed to qualify as a *chü-jen* in 1589, was a book collector. Although a difference of twelve years lay between Yao and Lü, they became fast friends, largely because they studied together and were both bibliophiles at heart.

Sources on Yao's life are scanty. From his own notes it seems that he traveled widely in northwest China as well as along the southeast coast. He served as secretary to Shen Ssu-hsiao (*see* Ku Hsien-ch'eng) when the latter was provincial governor of Shensi (1591-92), and witnessed the insurrection of Pübei (*see* Li Ju-sung). By 1597 we find him in Nanking editing the *Sung-shu* 宋書 by Shen Yüeh (441-513), and preparing under the direction of Feng Meng-chen (*see* Chu Lu), chancellor of the Nanking National University, a new edition of the histories of the Southern and Northern dynasties.

Later in the 1620s he was back in his native place participating first in the compilation of the local history, and then taking charge of the collection of works by Hai-yen authors at the request of the magistrate, Fan Wei-ch'eng (*see* Hu Chen-heng). The *Yen-i chih-lin*, which undoubtedly developed out of the local history, comprising 41 titles, was completed in 1623, and printed under Fan's name as editor-in-chief. In 1937 it was photolithographically reprinted as one of the ten reproduced Yüan and Ming rare editions by the Commercial Press, and entitled *Yüan Ming shan-pen ts'ung-shu* 元明善本叢書. A number of interesting items are included, and so is Yao's own work, the *Chien-chih pien* 見只編, comprising 3 *chüan* of notes, which ranks as one of the most informative among this category of books by Ming authors. It includes anecdotes about officials and literary people of his age, and articles about mutinies, Japan, piracies, salt mines, the examination system, etc.

Ch'ien Ch'ien-i (ECCP) mentions a visit Yao Shih-lin paid him in 1640, and remarks on the latter's advanced age and high spirits. Both delighted in discussing the poets of their day. To commemorate the occasion Ch'ien wrote a poem of sixteen stanzas. According to Ch'ien, some time after 1644 Yao died in poverty, aged over ninety *sui.*

Later scholars have asserted that Yao Shih-lin produced works under the names of earlier writers. This practice seems to have been not uncommon with Ming authors. The two works usually attributed to him are: 1) the *Yü-ling-tzu* 於陵子, a philosophical work of 12 *p'ien* 篇, which he attributed to T'ien Chung 田仲 (Ch'en Chung-tzu 陳仲子) of Ch'i 齊 of the period of Warring States; 2) the *Hsin-shih* 心史,a literary collection including historical notices about the last days of the Sung dynasty, in which he cited the Sung patriot Cheng Ssu-hsiao (1239-1316) as author. (A man allegedly discovered it while digging a well in a Soochow monastery in 1638.) The former work was included in the *Pi-ts'e hui-han* (*see* Hu Chen-heng), and the latter was first printed in 1639. The consensus is that both were probably written by Yao, but together with his friends and collaborators, Hu Chen-heng and Shen Shih-lung (*see* Hu Chen-heng).

Yao's name appears in no fewer than eight entries in the *Ssu-k'u* catalogue, but only a small compilation of notes of Lu Chi (early 3d century A. D.) on the *I-ching* was copied into the Imperial Library.

Bibliography

40/71/3a; 84/ 丁下 /75a; *Hai-yen-hsien chih* (1876), 17/3b, 末/12b; *Chekiang t'ung-chih* (1934), 3118; Chu Liang-pi 朱良弼, *Yu-chi-pien* 猶及編, *Yen-i chih-lin* ed., 46/10b; Yeh Ch'ang-ch'ih (BDRC), *Ts'ung-shu chi-shih shih* (1958), 160; SK (1930), 1/2b, 66/10a,74/6a, 78/1b, 124/1a, 134/3b, 174/15a, 192/13b; Chang Hsin-ch'eng 張心澂, *Wei-shu t'ung-k'ao* 偽書通考(1954), 834, 975; Sheng Feng 盛楓 (cj 1681), *Chia-ho cheng-hsien lu* 嘉禾徵獻錄 (*Tsui-li* 檇李 *ts'ung-shu* ed.), 46/2b; *Huang Ming wen-hai* (microfilm), 5/10/9.

Lienche Tu Fang

YAO Shou 姚綬 (T. 公綬, H. 丹丘子; 穀庵, 雲東逸史, etc.), 1423-May 4, 1495, painter, calligrapher, and poet, was a native of Chia-hsing 嘉興, Chekiang. Yao's father, Yao Fu 黼 (T. 廷章, d. 1446), was himself a poet, calligrapher, painter, and collector of antiques. Yao Shou became a *chü-jen* in 1453 and a *chin-shih* in 1464. [Editors' note: A fire broke out in the examination halls on February 26, 1463, resulting in a heavy loss of life among the assembled candidates. This prevented holding the triennial tests until six months later. The palace examination took place in April, 1464.] His first official assignment was as an apprentice in the ministry of Works. Four months later he was transferred to the Censorate to learn how to review judicial cases. Soon he was sent out to inspect the government's salt gabelle at Yangchow. During the two years he was on this mission, many people were saved from famine because of his relief measures. Resuming his office in the Censorate in 1467 he was demoted the following year to magistrate of Yung-ning 永寧, Kiangsi, an unpleasant place. He resigned within a year, pleading the necessity of attending his aging mother. In March, 1469, he returned to Chia-hsing. For the next twenty-six years he lived quietly at home, with occasional excursions to nearby regions. In 1477 he even built a large, well-decorated boat, furnished it with books and paintings, in the fashion of the shu-hua ch'uan 書畫船 (books and paintings houseboat) of Mi Fu (1051-1107), and set off along the waterways. Often while relaxing on the boat he composed poems and painted. His representations of landscapes, bamboos, and birds, some in color and some in ink, are known in China, Japan, and in the West. In his "Chu-shih" 竹石 (Bamboos and rocks), dated July 2, 1470, in ink, in the Shinosaki collection, the bamboos are shown hanging from the projecting cliffs, and the leaves are long and sharp like spearheads, as Osvald Sirén so aptly describes the painting. Another representative painting, "Solitude in the mountain hermitage," is reproduced in a recent catalogue of the Musée Cernuschi. A collection of his calligraphy and paintings, done chiefly in 1494, which he took great pride in naming *Shang-hsin ts'e* 賞心册(That which delights the heart), is now reproduced in the 9th *ts'e* of *Wen-ming ying-yin hua-ts'e er-shih-liu chung* 文明影印畫册二十六種 (published 1921-36). His calligraphy and poetry also won some attention in his day.

As to his literary works, he is especially remembered for his *Ku-an chi* 穀庵集, 14 *ch.*, a copy of which is available in microfilm. The *Ta-i t'ien-jen ho-chih* 大易天人合旨, 10 *ch.*, a study on the Book of Changes is also credited to him.

One of Yao Shou's sons, Yao Hsün 旬 (T. 用宣), was installed in Jen-shou palace 仁壽殿 by Emperor Chu Chien-shen (*q.v.*) because of his skill in calligraphy. Among his several grandsons, the second, Yao Ch'in 芹 (T. 惟誠) was known as a skillful calligrapher and painter.

Bibliography

32/44/20a; 40/22/30b; 64/丙 10/1a; 65/3/1b; 84/乙/32b; 86/8/2a; *Chia-hsing-hsien chih* (1906), 36/26b; *Chia-hsing-fu chih* (1879), 50/27b; Hsia Wen-yen 夏文彥 (fl. 1365) and Han Ang 韓昂 (fl. 1519), *T'u-hui pao-chien* 圖繪寶鑑, 6/161; Chiang Shao-shu 姜紹書 (fl. 1640), *Wu-sheng shih-shih* 無聲詩史, 2/20; *Chung-kuo li-tai ming-hua chi* 中國歷代名畫集, IV (Peking, 1965), pl. 20; *Ku-kung shu-hua lu* 故宮書畫錄 (Taipei, 1956), 中/290; *T'ien yin-t'ang ming-hua hsüan* 天隱堂名畫選, I (Tokyo, 1963),pl. 14; *Nihon genzai Shina meiga mokuroku* 日本現在支那名畫目錄 (Tokyo, 1938), 140; E. J. Laing, *Chinese Paintings in Chinese Publications, 1956-1968* (Ann Arbor, 1969), 207; O. Sirèn, *A History of Later Chinese Painting*, I (London, 1938), 37; Yao Shou, *Ku-an chi* (NLP microfilm, no. 992); Musée Cernuschi, *Peintures chinoises* (Paris, 1967), no. 3 and pl. 3.

Hwa-chou Lee

YAO Kuang-hsiao 姚廣孝 (monastic name: Tao-yen 道衍, T. 斯道, H. 逃虛子, 獨庵禪師), 1335-May 3, 1418, Buddhist monk, poet, official, was a native of Ch'ang-chou 長洲 in the prefecture of Soochow. Al-though his family had followed the practice of medicine for generations, Yao preferred the monastic life, and at the age of thirteen entered Miao-chih-an 妙智庵 in Wu-hsien 吳縣 in the same prefecture. In his early years he studied Ch'an Buddhism under several masters, including Hsü-pai-liang 虛白亮 and Chih-chi 智及 (H. 愚庵, 1311-78), at a number of monasteries located in the lower Yangtze valley. When he became convinced that Ch'an teachings were too abstract for him, he turned to the Pure Land Doctrine 淨土宗. In addition he read the Confucian Classics and the works of China's earliest thinkers, and trained himself in the writing of poetry and prose. He studied under Hsi Ying-chen 席應眞 or 珍 (T. 心齋, H. 子陽子, 1301-81), a Taoist at the Ling-ying kuan 靈應觀, where he learned the theories of yin-yang, the arts of divination, fortune-telling, and physiognomy, which he was to use with remarkable success in his later years. He also became much interested in military science, and associated with such poets and scholar-officials as Kao Ch'i, Sung Lien, and Su Po-heng (*qq.v.*). Yao's first years as a monk are little known. It is said that in 1373 he asked the ministry of Rites for an official monastic certificate and assignment to the Chüeh-lin ssu 覺林寺 (another name for the Miao-chih monastery). A year later, when Chu Yüan-chang summoned monks versed in Confucian doctrine, Yao responded and passed the examination supervised by the ministry of Rites, but did not accept an office. The emperor then granted him a monastic robe and allowed him to return to his monastery. By 1381 Yao had compiled at least two Buddhist works. In a postscript to one of them, the monk Ta-yu 大佑 (H. 遽菴, 1334-1407) testified that Yao had changed allegiance from T'ien-t'ai to Ch'an, and that at this time he was practicing the Pure Land Doctrine.

The year 1382 marks a turning point in Yao's life. In September Empress Ma (*q.v.*) died. In order to arrange for the funeral ceremonies, the emperor requested his ministers to recommend qualified monks employed at his court and at those of the imperial princes to recite sūtras for the deceased empress. On the recommendation of Tsung-lo (*q.v.*), Yao was one of those thus enlisted and was later assigned to the court of the prince of Yen, Chu Ti (*q.v.*), in Peiping to reside at the Ch'ing-shou 慶壽 monastery (later renamed Ta-hsing lung 大興隆 ssu). With his broad learning and temporal interests he made a good impression on Chu Ti, and their friendship grew. From this time on Yao became Chu Ti's most trusted counselor in civil and military affairs. Such a mixture of Yao's religious and political sophistication at the court of the prince of Yen is no ground for surprise. Chu Yüan-chang at Nanking too surrounded himself with a number of high-ranking Buddhist monks, such as Tsung-lo and Ju-ch'i (*see* Tsung-lo), who frequented the imperial court, where they held Buddhist conferences and conducted religious ceremonies on a large and imposing scale, wrote memorials to the throne on state problems, and not infrequently denounced Confucian scholars and officials to their considerable annoyance.

For the next sixteen years, from 1382 to 1398, Yao's activities at the court at Peiping are unrecorded. The historical sources report rather dramatically that Yao tried to instill into the mind of his prince through his skills in persuasion, divination, and physiognomy, a conviction of his imperial destiny. There is a story that during one of the first meetings with Chu Ti, when both were still at Nanking, Yao said to him: "Great Prince, your bodily figure is quite extraordinary, your powerful personality is without peer.... Let me serve you at your court and I shall put a white hat on your rank" (meaning 白 above 王＝皇). Yao later asked permission to introduce the famous physiognomist Yüan Kung (*q. v.*) who, during an earlier meeting with Yao, had reportedly foretold his rise to power by calling Yao a Liu Ping-chung (1216-74) a Buddhist priest

who served Qubilai Khan as adviser and confidant. Yüan, it is said, recognized Chu Ti in disguise in a tavern and prophesied that, when his beard would reach to his navel, he would become emperor.

In June, 1398, Chu Yüan-chang died and was succeeded by his grandson, Chu Yün-wen (*q.v.*), who, on the advice of Ch'i T'ai and Huang Tzu-ch'eng (*see* Lien Tzu-ning), adopted the policy of centralizing military power by reducing the princedoms. After four had been thus eliminated, Chu Ti who, as guardian of the northern marches against the Mongols, had a much larger army under his command than any other remaining prince, felt that his turn was coming. Yet he is reported to have been irresolute and unable to plan for his self-defense. According to the official version of Chu Ti's rebellion, Yao felt obliged to take the initiative and stir the prince to action, again with the help of divination, and seconded by Yüan Kung, the physiognomist. Yao reminded the prince that his imperial father liked him best, that he held him to be better qualified to rule the empire than his other sons, and that he had wanted him to come to Nanking before he died. His army was well trained and stationed in a rich part of the country. Actually, it seems that, even without any advice from Yao, the prince was too intelligent, ambitious, and energetic to be caught napping. After the plan to rebel was set, Yao built new arsenals in the labyrinthine sections of the palace and surrounded them with high fences. When the blacksmiths made too ominous a noise with their hammers and anvils, he brought large flocks of geese and ducks near the arsenals so that their clamor would drown out the noise. He trained soldiers in the palace grounds, and in the countryside. He recommended capable man for leadership in the army, and at the same time had to dispel fits of despondency and even despair of his prince.

The rebellion started in July, 1399, and after three years of fighting the capital city (Nanking) was taken (*see* Chu Yün-wen). During the war Yao remained in Peiping and, together with the eldest son of Chu Ti, guarded the city. He continually offered advice to the prince in the field. Certain accounts unfavorable to Yao have charged him with manipulating Chu Ti like a marionette, and being almost entirely responsible for instigating the rebellion with all its attendant atrocities and hardship. The prince, become emperor, could not well be accused of rebellion and usurpation of the throne. So history found in Yao a suitable scapegoat whom T'an Ch'ien (*q.v.*) in his *Kuo-ch'üeh* could call "an evil man." Chu Ti himself, perhaps unwittingly, blackened the image of his adviser in the eyes of loyal officials by praising him as the most meritorious official of the war. Although it is difficult to ascertain his precise role in the usurpation, Yao undoubtedly exerted great influence on Chu Ti. The latter found in him a resourceful adviser, a wholehearted supporter of his policies, and a loyal official with great foresight and courage. But the initiative was with Chu Ti who, for example, did not hesitate to liquidate over eight hundred members of the opposition in Nanking, with the scholar Fang Hsiao-ju (*q.v.*) among them. It is said that Yao had insistently asked the prince to spare Fang. Yao's opponents among the loyal officials could not ignore the occasionally good advice he gave the prince. But his connection with the usurpation sullied his reputation as a faithful official and Buddhist monk. The records report two episodes highly embarrassing for Yao. In July, 1404, a serious flood and subsequent famine plagued Soochow and Chekiang. The emperor entrusted Yao with relief measures. On that occasion he met his elder sister whom he had not seen since 1382. She did not mince words in expressing her contempt for his having disgraced his monkish calling. The same thing happened to Yao when he visited his friend of old, the hermit Wang Pin 王賓 (T. 仲光, H. 光菴), who, ignoring his repeated

calls, finally dismissed him, saying: "You have taken the wrong stand!" These anecdotes may be spurious, but are ones historians and scholars repeated to show what many upright and loyal officials and pious Buddhist monks, especially those sympathetic to Chu Yün-wen, thought of him.

In July, 1402, Chu Ti ascended the throne and in November of the same year he appointed Yao head of the central Buddhist registry, making him the first monk of the whole empire. Two years later (May) the emperor elevated Yao to the rank of junior preceptor of the heir apparent; then he asked him to return to secular life, and to use his family name to which he added by special mandate the name Kuang-hsiao (to broaden filial piety) by which he is best known in history. He gave Yao a residence and two palace ladies, but Yao refused everything. He stayed in his monastery, wore his Buddhist habit, and only when he went to an audience did he don his official robe. The emperor continued to favor him and affectionately addressed him as junior preceptor instead of calling him by his name.

Late in the same year the emperor received a report from Hsieh Chin (*q.v.*) about the compilation of the thesaurus, *Wen-hsien ta-ch'eng* 文獻大成, and charged Yao and others with its revision. The huge work was considered finished in 1407, and on December 14 of this year Yao submitted his report to the throne. The emperor then changed its name to *Yung-lo ta-tien* 永樂大典, and one year later contributed a preface in which the number of *chüan* is given as 22,937. During these busy years the emperor also appointed Yao (May, 1407) tutor to his grandson Chu Chan-chi (*q.v.*). In October, 1411, Chu Ti entrusted Yao with the supervision of the second revision of the *T'ai-tsu shih-lu*. Nine years earlier Li Ching-lung (*see* Li Wen-chung) had been charged with the revision of this *shih-lu* with the purpose of eradicating references that might challenge the legitimacy of Chu Ti's replacement of his nephew as the imperial successor. When the revised text was submitted to the throne (1411), the emperor was displeased with its contents and also found it hastily done and incomplete. Although Yao had retired from official life (September, 1412), the emperor called him back, together with others, to undertake its rewriting; this was presented to the throne in June, 1418, a month after Yao's death. This revision the emperor accepted.

In the spring of 1418, when Yao felt his end approaching, he left Nanking for Peiping to take leave of his imperial master. Chu Ti came to his bedside twice and on the second occasion asked Yao about his last wishes. Yao requested him to release from prison the monk P'u-hsia 溥洽 (T. 南洲, 1348–1426), who had reportedly cursed Chu Ti while he was still prince for his rebellion. His request was immediately granted. Yao died shortly afterward, aged eighty-three. He was ennobled as duke of Jung-kuo 榮國, and given the posthumous name Kung-ching 恭靖. The emperor granted him a state funeral according to Buddhist rites. His ashes were buried at T'ai-p'ing-li 太平里, 40 *li* northeast of Fang-shan 房山-hsien, Pei-Chihli. The emperor wrote a tomb inscription, and the stele was set up at Yao's grave in 1426. A month later he ordered Yao's name tablet placed in the T'ai-miao 太廟 along with the image of three other meritorious officials in Chu Ti's service. Late in 1530 Yao's tablet was removed to his former residence, the Ta-hsing-lung monastery (*see* Liao Tao-nan). Eight years later, after a fire destroyed the monastery, it was removed to the Ta-lung-shan huo-kuo ssu 大隆善護國寺, the former residence of the late Yüan chancellor, Toγto. Yao had an adopted son named Yao Chi 繼, whom Emperor Chu Kao-chih (*q.v.*) appointed (April, 1425) vice minister of the Seal Office.

Yao Kuang-hsiao was the author of three short treatises on Buddhism and of two collections of belles lettres. The *Ching-t'u chien-yao lu* 簡要錄, a treatise on rebirth in the Pure Land with a preface and a postscript dated 1381, gives numerous details about Yao's life. The *Chu Shang-shan-jen yung* 諸上善人詠 praises some 123 men believed to have gained rebirth in the Pure Land. He finished it the same year. Both works are included in the *Dai Nihon zōkuzōkyō* 大日本續藏經. The *Tao-yü lu* 道餘錄, a treatise refuting the neo-Confucian arguments against Buddhism by the philosophers Chu Hsi (1130–1200), Ch'eng Hao (1032–85), and Ch'eng I (1033–1107), was written toward the end of his life and first printed in 1619 with funds contributed by Ch'ien Ch'ien-i (ECCP). A copy of this edition is preserved in the National Central Library in Taipei. Because of its unorthodox nature, the *Tao-yü lu* was denounced by later Confucian scholars and had a limited circulation. It was reprinted by Sun Yü-hsiu 孫毓修 in *Han-fen-lou pi-chi* 涵芬樓祕笈 in 1925, and Heinz Friese recently published a partial translation into German. The *T'ao-hsü tzu shih-chi* 逃虛子詩集, 10+1 *ch.*, contains Yao's poems. The Naikaku Bunko treasures a manuscript copy, a microfilm of which is available in the Princeton University Library. Another manuscipt copy is preserved in the National Central Library. The *T'ao-hsü lei-kao* 類稿, 5+1 *ch.*, contains Yao's miscellaneous essays. A manuscript copy is preserved in the former Kiangsu Provincial Library, Nanking. A portrait of Yao in Buddhist costume, looking quite impressive, is reproduced in the *Ku-kung* 故宮 (Palace Museum Monthly, February, 1930).

Japanese monks, before returning from their visits to Chinese monasteries, frequently asked Yao for a preface or postscript to their memoirs or literary collections (*see* Zekkai Chushin). Apparently they regarded him as a model among monks of his time. Future research will have to determine how much initiative and encouragement Yao gave to the printing and distribution of many sūtras and

Buddhist writings, and also how deeply he influenced his imperial master in his policy with respect to Buddhism.

Bibliography

1/145/1a; 3/134/1a; 5/6/52a; 40/17/1a; 61/160/6b; 63/9/1a; 84/閏/12a; MSL (1963), T'ai-tsung, 534, 573, 627, 926, 1016, 1516, 2073, Hsi-tsung, 267, 270, Hsüan-tsung, 457, Shih-tsung (1965), 2759; Anon., *Ching-nan kung-ch'en lu* 靖難功臣錄 (TsS CC), 1; Wang Shih-chen, *Ming-ch'ing chi-chi*, 3/3a; Liu T'ung, *Ti-ching ching-wu lüeh* (1957), 8, 64; Ho Ch'iao-yüan, *Ming-shan tsang* (1970 ed.), 3317; Wen-hsiu 文琇, *Tseng-chi hsü Ch'uan-teng lu* 增集續傳燈錄, 5/4356 (Dai Nihon zōkuzōkyō ed.); Huan-lun 幻輪, *Shih-chien ch'i-ku lüeh hsü-chi* 釋鑑稽古略續集, 3/132a; *Chiang-su sheng-li kuo-hsüeh t'u-shu-kuan tsung-mu* 江蘇省立國學圖書館總目 (Nanking, 1933–35), 34/9b; Wang Ch'ung-wu, 王崇武, *Ming ching-nan shih-shih k'ao-cheng kao* 明靖難史事考證稿 (1948), 39; Wu Han 吳晗, "Chi 記 *Ming shih-lu*," in *Tu-shih cha-chi* 讀史劄記 (1957), 190; Makita Tairyō 牧田諦亮, "Dōen den shōkō" 傳小稿, TK, 18 (October, 1959), 173; David B. Chan, "The Role of the Monk Tao-yen in the Usurpation of the Prince of Yen," *Sinologica*, VI (1959), 83; H. Friese, "Der Mönch Yao Kuang-hsiao (1335–1418) und seine Zeit," OE, 7 (1960), 158; *id.*, "Das Tao-yü-lu des Yao Kuang-hsiao," OE, 8 (1961), 42; L. Carrington Goodrich, "More on the Yung-lo ta-tien," JRASHKB, 10 (1970), 18.

Eugen Feifel and Hok-lam Chan

YAO Shun-mu 姚舜牧 (T. 虞佐, H. 承庵), December 20, 1543–1627, scholar, teacher, official, was a native of Wu-ch'eng 烏程, Chekiang. For generations his ancestors were farmers, but his father Yao Jang 讓 (H. 滽庵), orphaned when young, became a cloth tradesman, and saw to it that his son received an education. Yao Shun-mu was thus made to think from boyhood on that to become a scholar-official was the highest ambition in life. He acquired the *chü-jen* in 1573, but failed six times in the metropolitan examination. In August, 1592, he received an appointment as magistrate of Hsin-hsing 新興, west of Canton in Kwangtung; here he made his mark (1592–97) as an efficient and upright official, taking especial interest in education and the public welfare. The grateful people erected a shrine in his honor. In his final year in this magistracy Yao compiled the *Hsin-hsing-hsien chih*, apparently no longer extant as a separate work, but parts are included in his collected writings. Somehow he incurred the displeasure of the former magistrate, then a higher official. Though supported by others, he expected that he would be affected by this man's annoyance and be demoted. At this juncture, however, his mother died; so he returned home for the funeral.

In 1600 he received the lower appointment to registrar (7A to 9A) in the record bureau of the provincial surveillance office in Kwangsi. That same winter he was reassigned to be acting prefect of Ch'üan-chou 全州 in the same province. Becoming outraged by the greed and illegalities of the eunuch tax collectors in the prefecture, he asked for and received an assignment as a messenger. When he returned in 1602, he requested no further assignment and devoted his time to the study of the Spring and Autumn Annals. This done (1603), he was recommended for a promotion and became the magistrate of Kuang-ch'ang 廣昌 in Kiangsi, serving until 1605. Here, too, the people put up a shrine in his honor.

Yao Shun-mu was a convinced follower of Confucius, at the same criticizing Taoist priests and Buddhist monks, and deprecating the famous Seven Sages of the Bamboo Grove (third century A. D.) for their individualism. In his *Chia-hsün* 家訓 (Family instructions), he directed his descendants on one hand to let no Taoist or Buddhist practitioners appear at his funeral, or at that of any other member of his family, and on the other to take loving care of their ancestral tombs. It is no wonder, therefore, that during his later years, as he taught and labored on the Classics, he should record a dream in his autobiography about the master. It happened on October 29, 1613. He asked Confucius to show him a jade seal. Confucius produced five or six pieces of jade. Yao, gazing at them in some surprise, assembled them into a seal about three inches long on each side. But one corner of the seal remained incomplete. Yao suggested that the seal be inlaid with gold so that it might last for a long time. Confucius smiled and remarked, "That is exactly what I intend to do." The master then ascended a platform which stood about two feet above the ground, whereupon Yao duly made his obeisance. Yao was surprised to note that Confucius' hair was yellow. When Yao awoke he realized that the dream must have happened because he had exhausted himself day and night in writing about the Classics and was eager to have his work approved by the master.

Yao had a number of students, two of whom, Liu I-hun 劉一焜 (T. 元丙, cs 1592) and Yang Ho (see Yang Ssu-ch'ang) helped him in 1614 to build a home for his books. Yao wrote voluminously on the canon. His books deal with the Changes, 12 ch., the Documents, 12 ch., the Odes, 12 ch., the Rites (Li Chi), 12 ch., the Spring and Autumn Annals, 12 ch., the Book of Filial Piety, 1 ch., and the Four Books, 11 ch. Each title included the expression i-wen 疑問 (difficult questions), for he took up problems which he doubtless encountered in his teaching and tried to resolve. Of these seven works, all of which received notices in the Ssu-k'u catalogue, only the one on the Odes, the Shih-ching 詩經 i-wen, was admitted to the Imperial Library. (This is reproduced in the Ssu-k'u chen-pen, ser. 3). Another of his works is the Lo-t'ao yin ts'ao 樂陶吟草, 3 ch., published in 1673 by his great-grandson Yao Ch'un-hsien 湻顯 (T. 子濳). It too receives a notice in the catalogue. A lengthy exposition of neo-Confucian principles, Hsing-li chih-kuei 性理指歸, 28 ch., Yao reedited in 1610, and another grandson, Yao Ch'un-ch'i 起 (T. 子雲, H. 胥山),

revised, supplemented, and published in 1656. A copy is preserved in the Library of Congress. A collection of Yao's essays, 16 ch., and poetry, 3 ch., entitled Yao Ch'eng-an chi 承庵集, printed near the end of his life (1626), was partially proscribed a century and a half later because of various minor points. This work, also known as Lai-en-t'ang ts'ao 來恩堂草, 16 ch. (preface of 1613), printed about 1626, is available on microfilm. It contains Yao's autobiography. Finally one may mention a brief collection of proverbs, Yao yen 藥言, which may be found in the Chih-chin-chai ts'ung-shu, series 1, of Yao Chin-yüan (ECCP, p. 902).

When Yao was seventy-eight years of age, his third wife died, to be followed in death shortly afterwards by his two concubines. His health declined and he passed away at the age of eighty-four. He had six sons and at least nineteen grandsons, several of whom gave good accounts of themselves in the next dynasty. During his lifetime, the eldest, Yao Tso-tuan 祚端 was his greatest joy, for he became a chinshih in 1607 and was made magistrate of Chiang-tu 江都 (Yangchow), serving from 1607 to 1613; once, on the occasion of a quarrel between residents on the seacoast and the people engaged in making salt, the administration vice commissioner of the prefecture asked him to resolve the conflict, and this he did to the general satisfaction. He was promoted to censor in 1614 and in the summer of 1620 received an appointment as inspector of affairs in Shensi. In 1624 he was made surveillance vice commissioner of Szechwan and ordered to serve as intendant at Chungking; he pleaded illness, however, and returned home to be with his father. The following year he was recalled to serve once more as censor.

Bibliography

40/52/8a; 86/15/13a; Wu-ch'eng-hsien chih (1881), 9/20a, 10/2b, 3b, 14/31a, 15/5b, 25b, 31/9b; Hu-chou-fu 湖州府 chih (1874), 10/39a, 12/19b, 26a, 59/9a, 72/61a, 73/8b, 75/16b; Chien-ch'ang-fu chih 建昌府

志 (1909), 6/21a, 47a; *Chekiang t'ung-chih*(1934), 3061, 4040; *Kwangtung t'ung-chih* (1934), 4341; *Yang-chou-fu chih* (1874), 37/24b; 44/45a; *Chao-ch'ing*肇慶 *-fu chih* (1876), 12/36b, 16/51a; SK (1930), 8/1b, 14/1a, 16/4a, 24/2b, 30/4b, 32/5a, 37/4b; Sun Tien-ch'i (1957), 130; Yamane and Ogawa, *Ming-jen wen-chi mu-lu* 明人文集目錄 (Tokyo, 1966), 125; NCL *Catalogue of Rare Books* (Taipei, 1967), 1103; L. of C. *Catalogue of Rare Books*, 458.

Yang Chin-yi and L. Carrington Goodrich

YEH Hsiang-kao 葉向高 (T. 進卿, H. 臺山), 1562–1627, scholar and onetime grand secretary, was a native of Fu-ch'ing 福清, Fukien. He was born in a hovel where his mother at that moment was taking refuge from Japanese pirates. His father, Yeh Ch'ao-jung 朝榮, served for a time as subprefecture magistrate of Yang-li 養利, Kwangsi. After qualifying for the *chü-jen* in 1579 and the *chin-shih* in 1583, Yeh Hsiang-kao was made a Hanlin bachelor, subsequently promoted to be compiler, and then transferred to Nanking as director of studies at the National University. In his capacity as left deputy supervisor of instruction (1598), he tutored the future emperor, Chu Ch'ang-lo (ECCP), who nicknamed him Fei-hsü hsien-sheng 飛鬚先生 (Mr. Flying Beard). The following year he was promoted to the post of right vice minister of Rites in Nanking, and then made right vice minister of Personnel there. When the case of the yao shu 妖書 (weird pamphlet) developed at the end of 1603 (*see* Cheng Kuei-fei), he sent a letter to Grand Secretary Shen I-kuan (*q.v.*) suggesting that he act with more discretion. Shen was not amused, and Yeh was to remain at Nanking without promotion for several years. In 1606 two grand secretaries, including Shen I-kuan, were removed, only one remaining. The following year Yeh Hsiang-kao was appointed concurrently minister of Rites and grand secretary; at the same time, Wang Hsi-chüeh, Yü Shen-hsing (*qq.v.*), and Li T'ing-chi 李廷機 (T. 爾張, H. 九

我, Pth. 文節, secundus in 1583, also from Fukien, d. December 28, 1616) were given like appointments. When Yeh assumed office at the beginning of 1608, Yü Shen-hsing had just died. Wang Hsi-chüeh flatly declined to accept the appointment, and Li T'ing-chi attended office for only a few months, although he continued to be nominally a grand secretary. On January 4, 1609, the senior grand secretary, Chu Keng (*see* Shen I-kuan), died and Yeh succeeded him.

At that time Emperor Chu I-chün (*q. v.*) had reigned for almost forty years. The administration was honeycombed with corruption, and occurrences of misrule at the court were all too common. As the senior grand secretary, Yeh on one occasion presented the emperor with a memorial which may be summarized: Currently certain conditions are putting the country in a dangerous situation. These are not calamities from heaven, or the work of robbers, bandits, enemies, and the like. They are as follows: 1) many posts of importance in the government are unfilled, and numerous officials are not qualified for their posts; 2) Your Majesty does not understand the plight of the people, and those at court lack opportunity to report directly to Your Majesty about state problems; 3) the educated classes often act without due consideration and are interested only in their own selfish ends; 4) the court always wants to add to its wealth and the people are too heavily taxed; 5) demoralization and immorality prevail throughout the country. Under such circumstances Your Majesty must be determined to exert an effort to appoint men of ability and substance to every office, and to eradicate those practices which have been causing mischief; then the government will be in good order and the country will be safe from danger. The emperor, however, paid no attention. Concerned for his country and its people, Yeh often made similar remonstrances, but only in two or three cases out of ten were his suggestions accepted and carried out, in spite of the emperor's respect for him. Being unable to realize any of his goals, Yeh repeatedly asked permission to resign, even going so far as to say: "Your Majesty should accept the suggestions of a grand secretary. If you do not want to adopt them, what is the use of my remaining in office?" But he was not allowed to leave.

Early in 1612 Yeh was ill for about a month; during that time all memorials and reports were brought to his home for scrutiny. In March, 1613, as grand secretary he was required to take reponsibility for the metropolitan examination; at the same time he had to draft proposed rescripts for the throne. Because of this dual responsibility he was forced to do his work in the examination hall itself. These two situations, especially the latter one, were considered unusual and had seldom happened previously under the Ming. From the beginning of 1609, the Grand Secretariat in reality had a single grand secretary, Yeh Hsiang-kao. So in the course of the following years Yeh frequently requested the emperor to enlarge the Secretariat. Finally, on October 31, 1613, the emperor appointed Fang Ts'ung-che (ECCP, p. 176) and Wu Tao-nan (see Ch'en Yü-pi).

At the end of 1612 a lavishly constructed palace was put up in Loyang for the prince of Fu, Chu Ch'ang-hsün (see Cheng Kuei-fei). The ministry of Works submitted a memorial to the throne strongly supported by Yeh requesting the emperor to let the prince of Fu move there immediately; the emperor, however, refused to comply. Pressed by many officials who made the same request, the emperor finally replied (1613) that the prince of Fu would not be ordered to go to his domain unless four million *mou* of fertile land was made ready for him. This order Yeh vigorously opposed and he made use of every opportunity to admonish the emperor. Eventually in May, 1614, the prince left Peking for Loyang. At the same time his domain was limited to one million nine hundred thousand *mou*—even this provision of course added greatly to the burden of the people.

In spite of numerous honors bestowed during the years 1611 and on, Yeh's sense of frustration increased. In 1614 he applied for retirement more insistently; at last on September 26 of the same year he was permitted to resign. As soon as Chu Ch'ang-lo mounted the throne (1620) Yeh was recalled to Peking, but he refused to go. About a month later, the emperor died, to be succeeded by Chu Yu-chiao (ECCP). Yeh was again summoned to court, but remained at home. Only on December 7, 1621, did he arrive at the capital to serve as titular minister of Personnel and concurrently grand secretary.

At the beginning of his reign, the new emperor appointed a number of able men to high office, and the hope was widespread that a genuine reform in government would ensue. The emperor, however, was less than fifteen years of age and his immaturity gave the eunuch Wei Chung-hsien (ECCP) his opportunity. In May, 1621, Wei tentatively accused another eunuch Wang An (see Kao P'an-lung), his rival and a friend of the Tung-lin party, of a supposed affront to the throne. Shortly afterward, Wang An was put out of the way and subsequently murdered by Wei's followers. Early in 1622 Wei managed the dismissal of the minister of Personnel, Chou Chia-mu (q.v.). A few months later the minister of Justice, Wang Chi 王紀 (T. 惟理, Pth. 莊毅, cs 1589), the minister of Rites, Sun Shen-hsing, and the censor-in-chief, Tsou Yüan-piao (qq.v.), were all attacked and removed from office at the instigation of Wei. Yeh made every effort to put a stop to these developments, but even his influence was of no avail. As a consequence he too fell afoul of the unscrupulous eunuch.

In 1623 Supervising Secretary Ch'en Liang-hsün 陳良訓 (cs 1613) presented a memorial to the throne attacking Wei and his followers. As there was a sentence in the memorial that read "the country's fortunes are reaching their nadir," Wei put Ch'en in jail and wanted to inivolve many men in the case and punish them with equal severity. Yeh strongly opposed his move declaring that if Wei did this he would resign from office instantly. This halted Wei but only momentarily. Ch'en Liang-hsün suffered simply the penalty of forfeiting some of his salary, and Wei's threats were not carried out. Because those officials who were opposed to Wei always relied on Yeh for support, Wei detested him, and by making use of every pretext made trouble for him again and again. Yeh repeatedly begged to be retired but permission was not granted.

In the summer of 1624 Wan Ching (*see* Ch'ien Shih-sheng), a vice director in the ministry of Works, Was condemned to be flogged in the court because of an accusation he brought against Wei. Although Yeh exerted himself in Wan's behalf, the sentence was carried out and Wan died as a result of the beating. A few days later, a fellow townsman of Yeh, Censor Lin Ju-chu 林汝翥 (T. 大葳, 沁泓, d. 1647), fearing similar punishment for whipping a eunuch, fled to Tsun-hua 遵化, Pei-Chihli. Since it was said that Lin was Yeh's son-in-law, Wei had his men make a strict search of Yeh's residence in Peking. Ultimately Lin was seized at Tsunhua and was flogged in the court, but he survived the ordeal. In the face of this situation, Yeh more insistently asked for retirement, and on August 22, 1624, his petition was granted. After his departure, Wei and his followers became all-powerful, and the members of the Tung-lin party lost a very important supporter at court. In 1625 Wei, by means of false accusations, brought about the death of vice censor-in-chief Yang Lien (ECCP) and assistant censor-in-chief Tso Kuang-tou (*q.v.*). At the same time many other officials of like mind were demoted, dismissed, or exiled.

After the middle of the Ming dynasty, especially after the Cheng-te era, those officials who committed offenses and incensed an emperor were often brought before the Wu-men 午門 (Meridian gate)

in front of the palace to be bastinadoed. This was called t'ing-chang 廷杖 (flogging in the court). Being inalterably opposed to this punishment, Yeh strove for its abolition. While he served as grand secretary, it was seldom imposed except in a few cases such as those of Wan Ching and Lin Ju-chu. Immediately before his retirement in 1624, Yeh once again spoke his mind to the emperor about it. From that time on, although the offending officials sometimes died of maltreatment in jail, this punishment was not resorted to.

Yeh died in the autumn of 1627 (about the same time as the emperor, whose death occurred on September 30), but the news of his passing was not reported to the court until May 8, 1628. In the following year he was posthumously given the official title of grand preceptor of the emperor and canonized as Wen-chung 文忠 (cultured and loyal). He was buried on Mount T'ai-ling 臺嶺山 in Min-hsien 閩縣, Fukien. Later a shrine called Yang-chih tz'u 仰止祠 was erected in his honor at the foot of Feng-huang shan 鳳凰山 near Fu-ch'ing.

Yeh Hsiang-kao was a man of justice and prudence. For years he stood high in the estimation of the people; he was considered also a true friend of the Tung-lin party. At the same time he was a patron of the Catholic missionaries. Though he did not actually enter the Church, he was favorably disposed towards its doctrine. He was on especially close terms with Giulio Aleni (*q.v.*); it is said that much of Aleni's success in Fukien was due to Yeh's influence.

During the Ming period, most Fukienese could speak only their own dialect, which many other Chinese do not understand. After Yang Jung (*q.v.*) and Ch'en Shan 陳山 (T. 汝靜, 半溪, native of Shahsien 沙縣, Fukien, 1365–1434) served in the Grand Secretariat—the former from 1402 to 1440 and the latter from 1427 to 1429—there was no Fukienese who entered it until Yeh Hsiang-kao and Li T'ing-chi were appointed in 1607.

Yeh was the author of a number of books, the more important being *Ts'ang-hsia ts'ao* 蒼霞草, 20 *ch.*, *Hsü-ts'ao* 續草, 20 *ch.*, *Yü-ts'ao* 餘草, 14 *ch.*, *Ssu-i k'ao* 四夷考, 8 *ch.*, and *Chü-pien* 蘧編 (the last being a chronological record of his own career). An interesting feature of the *Yü-ts'ao* is a section on the dialect of Liao tung (Liao yen 遼言 in *chüan* 14). All five of these came to be listed in the catalogue of prohibited books over a century later; fortunately copies of each are still extant. He also supervised the compilation of the *Kuang-tsung shih-lu*, 8 *ch.*, completed in 1623. A manuscript copy of this version is said to be in Seoul. It was later revised twice. Yeh's memorials, some 850 all told, were collected under the title *Lun-fei tsou-ts'ao* 綸扉奏草, 30 *ch.*, hsü 續 *ts'ao*, 14 *ch.*; this item too was to be prohibited, but copies have been preserved in Peking, Foochow, Tokyo, and the Library of Congress (the last part only).

Yeh had a son named Yeh Ch'eng-hsüeh 成學 (T. 汝習), who served as executive assistant in the seal office. In the year 1607, when his father became grand secretary, Yeh Ch'eng-hsüeh, together with the magistrate of his native place, Ling Han-ch'ung 凌漢狆, began the erection of a pagoda called Jui-yün t'a 瑞雲塔. It was not completed until 1615, however, a year after the older Yeh had resigned for the first time. This monument, "constructed nearly throughout of magnificent green-stone," writes Gustav Ecke, "constitutes one of the landmarks of the town."

Bibliography

1/240/1a; 3/200/1a; 8/72/5a; 30/2/9a; 39/17/1a; 40/54/13b; 64/庚 14/2b; 84/丁中/69a; 86/15/32a; KC (1958), 5288, 5428; *Fu-chien t'ung-chih* 福建通志 (1936), 列傳 27/23a; Sun Tien-ch'i (1957), 58, 199, 203; Gustav Ecke, "Two Ashlar Pagodas at Fu-ch'ing in Southern Fu-chien, with Some Additional Notes on Prime-Minister Yeh Hsiang-kao," *Bull. of the Catholic University*, no. 8 (December, 1931), 49; Heinrich Busch, "The Tung-lin shu-yüan and Its Political and Philosophical Significance," MS, XIV (1949–55), 51; C. O. Hucker, "The Tung-lin Movement of the Late Ming Period," in *Chinese Thought and Institutions* (edited by John K. Fairbank, Chicago, 1957), 147; id., *The Censorial System of Ming China* (Stanford, 1966), 167; L. of C. *Catalogue of Rare Books*, 173, 397, 650, 1019; P. M. d'Elia, *Fonti Ricciane*, II (Rome, 1949), 42, 300, 588; W. Franke, *Sources*, 1.1.12, 5. 8.47, 7.1.8.

Chou Tao-chi

YEH Hsien-tsu 葉憲祖 (T. 美度, 相攸, H. 六桐, 桐柏, 檞園居士, 檞園外史, 紫金道人), 1566–1641, scholar, official, and dramatist, was a native of Yü-yao 餘姚, Chekiang. His family originally lived in Soochow and claimed Yeh Meng-te (1077–1148) as their ancestor. Yeh Hsien-tsu's grandfather, Yeh Hsüan 選 (cs 1538), had served as a bureau director in the ministry of Works and his father, Yeh Feng-ch'un 逢春 (T. 叔仁, H. 和齋, February 19, 1532-September 12, 1589, cs 1565), had a number of appointments, rising to be prefect of Lu-chou 廬州 (Anhwei) in 1578, and prefect of Yün-yang 鄖陽, Hukuang, in 1582. When in the last post, on the occasion of a flood of the Han River 漢水, he opened the official granaries to provide food for the refugees, without first getting permission from the court. He was accused of disobeying the regulations. Then, while in mourning over his father's death, he was dismissed (1586). His collection *Kung-pu chi* 工部集, 16 *ch.*, does not seems to be extant.

Yeh Hsien-tsu grew up in a literary environment. Passing the provincial examination in 1594, he did not graduate as *chin-shih* until 1619. He was first appointed magistrate of Hsin-hui 新會, Kwangtung, where people had suffered from piratical depredations for years. His initial act was to arrest the leader of the pirates, to ensure local security. He also tried to promote education by establishing the Mo-ch'ing kuan 摩青館 for selected students. His eldest daughter, Yeh Pao-lin 寶林 (1609–76), married Huang Tsung-hsi (ECCP), son of Huang Tsun-su. As the latter had been one of those opposed to Wei Chung-hsien. and was to suffer death (July 24, 1626) in consequence, this connection naturally had an adverse effect on the son-in-law at that time. In spite of his good reputation in Hsin-hui, Yeh received no promotion. Instead, Wei Chung-hsien saw to his transfer from Hsin-hui, first to serve as a judge of the Grand Court of Revision, and then to be secretary in the bureau of forestry and crafts of the ministry of Works, where he was put in charge of the mint. During his service in the ministry, the Huang-chi palace 皇極殿 was under construction and at the same time the town of Ning-yüan 寧遠, attacked by the Manchus, was successfully defended. It fell to Yeh to provide supplies both for construction and for military defense. When the Huang-chi palace was completed in 1626, more than nine hundred officials received promotion, Yeh among them. He was upgraded two ranks, and was given the appointment of vice minister of the Court of the Imperial Stud, while still in charge of the mint. In the same year, when the the first shrines were being erected in Chekiang and other places, in honor of Wei Chung-hsien, and another was ordered for Peking, Yeh moved from the area, for he was ashamed to live near it; he also refused to serve as a superintendent of the construction work. Wei's dislike of him turned to hatred. In the following year the minister of Works, Hsü Ta-hua 徐大化 (cs 1583), was dismissed on the ground of misappropriating funds. Yeh supported Hsü by providing him with the necessary money. This led to his own dismissal.

After Chu Yu-chien (ECCP) came to the throne, Yeh was brought back to the bureaucracy as a secretary in the ministry of Justice in Nanking (1630), and later was placed in charge of the protection of Shun-ch'ing 順慶 (Szechwan). He was then promoted to be surveillance vice commissioner of the military defense circuit of the prefectures of Ch'en-chou 辰州 and Yüan-chou 沅州 (Hukuang). His

successful defense of the area against Miao 苗 rebels reported to the court by the supreme commander, Chu Hsieh-yüan (see Ch'i Ch'eng-han), led to his promotion to be administration vice commissioner of Szechwan to guard Chien-ch'ang 建昌. His last appointment was that of surveillance commissioner of Kwangsi, but he did not accept the post. Five years after his retirement, he died at home at the age of seventy-five.

Yeh's main claim to fame was not that of an honest official, but as dramatist and poet. Some of his close friends, such as the Buddhist monk Chan-jan (q. v.). and Yüan Yü-ling (see Yüan Chih), were also dramatists. His plays included the Luan-pi chi 鸞鎞記 (The barb of love), Chin-so 金鎖 chi (The golden lock), and Ssu-yen 四豔 chi (The four wantons). The first is based on a story of the T'ang dynasty, and reflects the difficult years he himself endured studying for the advanced degree. The second, co-authored by Yüan Yü-ling, is an adaptation of an early Yüan dynasty lyrical drama by Kuan Han-ch'ing (ca. 1220/30–1300/10). (For an English rendering see Arlington and Acton, *Famous Chinese Plays*.) The third is actually a cluster of four plays, each one telling a romantic story. It has come down in two editions. One copy, printed in the last days of the Ming, preserved in the National Peking Library, has been reproduced in the *Ku-pen hsi-ch'ü ts'ung-k'an* 古本戲曲叢刊, series 2. Several others of his ch'uan-ch'i 傳奇 plays are known by title only. Of those called tsa-chü 雜劇, Yeh is said to have composed twenty, but only eight have survived. These include ones with Buddhist, romantic, and historical themes. Two of them are considered outstanding: *I-shui-han* 易水寒 (Everlasting fame), which is woven around the story of Ching K'o (d. 227 B.C.), would-be assassin of the king of Ch'in, and *Ma-tso* 罵座 chi (A tale of scorn). Of his other writings two have survived, both reproduced in the *Li-chao-lu* 黎照廬 ts'ung-shu; they are entitled

Ch'ing-chin-yüan fu-ts'ao 青錦園賦草, 1 *ch.*, and *Kuang-lien-chu* 廣連珠, 1 *ch.* A scattering of his poetry is also extant.

Bibliography

5/89/54a; 24/4/31a; 32/51/57a; 40/61/20b; MSL (1966), Hsi-tsung, 4038; KC (1958), 5339, 5340, 5371; *Shao-hsing-fu chih* (1792), 31/42b, 46b, 52a, 32/40b, 47b, 57b, 49/19a, 53/41a, 54/32a, 56/1a; *Yü-yao-hsien chih* (1899), 19/63b, 67a, 193/9b, 12b, 24a, 31b, 23/12/10a, 23/13/27b; Ch'i Piao-chia (ECCP), *Yüan-shan-t'ang Ming ch'ü-p'in chü-p'in chiao-lu* 遠山堂明曲品劇品校錄 (Shanghai, 1955), 173, 190, 202, 129; Huang Wen-yang 黃文暘, *Ch'ü-hai tsung-mu t'i-yao* 曲海總目提要 (Hong Kong, 1967), 344, 339, 623; Lü T'ien-ch'eng 呂天成, *Ch'ü-p'in* 曲品, 305, 322; Fu Hsi-hua 傅惜華, *Ming-tai ch'uan-ch'i ch'üan-mu* 明代傳奇全目 (Peking, 1959), 160, 352; *id.*, *Ming-tai tsa-chü ch'üan-mu* (Peking, 1958), 116, 138, 169, 171; *Ku-pen hsi-ch'ü ts'ung-k'an*, Vol. 2 (microfilm 1955); Mao Chin (ECCP), *Liu-shih-chung ch'ü* 六十種曲 (Shangai, 1935), Vol. 3; Shen T'ai 沈泰, *Sheng Ming tsa-chü*, Vols. 1 & 2 (Peking, 1958); *Yüan* 元 *Ming tsa-chü* (Peking, 1958); Chang Ch'üan-kung 張全恭, "Ming-tai te nan-tsa-chü" 明代的南雜劇 in *Ling-nan hsüeh pao* 嶺南學報, Vol. 6, no. 1 (1937), 50; Josephine Huang Hung, *Ming Drama* (Taipei, 1966), 79, 198; L. C. Arlington and Harold Acton, *Famous Chinese Plays* (Peiping, 1937), 94.

Ching-hwa Ho Jen

YEH Po-chü 葉伯巨 (T. 居升), died late in 1376 or early in 1377, was a native of Ning-hai 寧海, Chekiang. Two items of information are recorded about his youth: one, that he became an expert on ritual, and by his early twenties was already known for that throughout his district, households conducting a wedding or a funeral frequently consulting him on forms and proprieties, and asking him to serve as master of ceremonies; two, that he was apparently somewhat officious about correcting anyone's lapses in behavior or morality, but people all recognized his sincerity and lack of malice, and therefore were not angered.

Because he demonstrated expert knowledge of the Classics, Yeh Po-chü was sent as a student to the National University at Nanking by direct recommendation, one of the standard means of recruitment in his day. He did not study there long. At that time the National University had thousands of students, and served as a vast talent pool from which the central administration was accustomed to draw for many kinds of service. Its students frequently were sent on special missions, or appointed directly to office. On April 9, 1375, the emperor ordered that university students found to be "older and of superior virtue" be selected for assignment to district or prefectural schools in the north as teachers. Yeh must have been among the three hundred sixty-six sent off at that time. He was assigned to P'ing-yao 平遙, southwest of Taiyuan in Shansi. It is said that during the year and a half that he served there, his students came to hold him in respect and affection. It was while in that post that the event occurred for which he is known in history.

The *shih-lu* records a number of exceptional astronomical phenomena during the year 1376. Court experts considered them inauspicious. The emperor, whether on his own initiative or on that of counselors hoping to use such circumstances to influence his behavior, on October 22 issued an edict noting the "disastrous prodigies" and seeking "frank words" about his rule. This was an opportunity for serious-minded scholar-officials or commoners to express deeply felt criticisms; these the emperor generally took quite seriously. By far the most noteworthy response came from Yeh Po-chü. It was a "ten thousand word memorial" discussing at length three faults that had become apparent to him during the nine years of the new dynasty and which he felt were leading to grave problems. These were: 1) the scale of enfeoffment of the imperial princes was excessive; 2) harsh punishment was too heavily relied upon; and 3) the government was seeking too hasty improvement resulting from its rule. It was a perceptive and courageous memorial. Historians have quoted it at length from Ming times onward, regarding it as an important document in political history, but mostly stressing the first section of it, which discussed the system of enfeoffing the imperial princes, because that seemed to foretell the troubles of the following reign. That is the part, moreover, which aroused the emperor's fury, and caused Yeh's death. But all three sections of the memorial merit consideration in an assessment of early Ming rule.

In 1370 eight important fiefs (or nine, counting one which ceased to exist after its prince died) had been created for the sons of the founder born by that year, excluding of course the eldest, the heir apparent. This established the expectation that all of the imperial princes would be granted similar fiefs. To Yeh Po-chü this seemed to be a dangerous division of the central power, "weakening the trunk to enlarge the branches." Yeh held that Chu Yüan-chang, in trying to prevent the isolation of the throne, had gone too far; he assumed that Chu had in mind the history of the recent Sung and Yüan dynasties during which the central power had not possessed reliable bases of support on the borders and in the provinces. Yeh was looking farther back into history. He said that the regional power exercised by the Ming princes could easily grow to the point where it would threaten the center, and that, if later it should become necessary to reduce the power of these feudatories, the center might not be able to act quickly or powerfully enough. Some advisers to the throne, he anticipated, were sure to counter with the argument that all the fief-holders were the Son of Heaven's own flesh and blood (or, in the Chinese idiom, bones and flesh), and that fact assured their loyalty. Not so, explained Yeh, for when one looks into history one finds too many instances where imperial kinsmen in similar situations had defied the central

authority and attempted, sometimes successfully, to displace it. He made specific reference to Han and Chin history, especially to the Rebellion of the Seven Feudatories in the Former Han; this was a favorite historical subject in early Ming court discussions of the lessons of history, and one used again in analyzing the crisis of 1399 (see Chu Yün-wen). The lessons of history are clear, Yeh concluded; therefore it would be appropriate now to alter the system, reduce the number and scope of the fiefs, take away their local administrative authority, decrease the size of their garrisons, and finally, divide their fiefs equally among the princes' sons and grandsons rather than let one inherit all.

On reading this, Chu Yüan-chang had one of his fits of blazing fury, roaring: "He is trying to stir up dissension within my own family." He was expressing no doubt his genuine fear for the security of his dynasty. Yeh was brought from Shansi, but by the time he arrived in chains at the capital a chief minister was able to delay notice of his coming until the emperor was in good spirits and then propose that Yeh be turned over to prison authorities rather than have the emperor confront him in person. Some accounts have it that Yeh's memorial was received in the 11th moon (December 12, 1376-January 9, 1377), a not unreasonable lapse of time following the October 22 edict, considering the distance from Nanking to P'ing-yao. Yeh died of starvation in prison not long afterwards.

The *Ming-shih* appends to Yeh's biography a comment that Yeh, in criticizing the system of imperial princedoms, described powers and responsibilities and levels of staffing and support that were not in fact accurate. The contemporary scholar Huang Chang-chien 黃彰建 has discussed Yeh's memorial in relation to the *Huang Ming tsu-hsün* (Ancestral Instructions; see Chu Yüan-chang) and the changes in the system of enfeoffment. He agrees that some of the points raised by Yeh were inaccurate; they referred to an earlier system that had been promulgated in 1373, and already altered early in 1376. Huang concludes that Yeh, teaching far off in Shansi, simply had not learned about the latest revision of the Ancestral Instructions. The main points of Yeh's criticism still applied, nevertheless, and the emperor's anger was not aroused by those discrepancies of detail, however important. The system of strongly garrisoned princedoms endured, and many later historians have credited Yeh with having foreseen the situation leading to the civil war and usurpation by Chu Ti (*q.v.*). Probably because of this, Yeh was among the early Ming officials posthumously awarded rank and name (Chung-min 忠愍) by the Southern Ming court at Nanking in 1645.

The other two parts of Yeh's long memorial reveal much about the conditions of government in the early years of the Hung-wu era. The second section stresses the special significance of a dynastic founder's reign in establishing the precedents that will become fixed in practice. "The emperor in establishing the dynastic foundations leaves a model that will endure for a hundred generations; his every action will have binding force upon his sons and grandsons." And successful dynastic founders, he cautions, have always employed virtue to solidify the people's acceptance of their rule; to rely heavily on punishments with which to intimidate the people is to lose their confidence. There follows a lucid analysis of the ways in which harsh punishments induce faults in administration, destroy the effectiveness of public servants, undermine public morality, and in the long run defeat their purpose. Of particular interest is Yeh's outspoken comment on a situation widely recognized but seldom mentioned in the early years—reluctance of qualified persons to accept office. He notes the government's urgent need for talented recruits to officialdom and goes on to criticize the ill-considered ways of

recruiting persons.

The last section notes how long it took for the glorious ages in the past to achieve their ultimate perfection, and how patient the sage-like model rulers were in leading their people gradually into upright ways and harmonious government. In fact, the Ming success in these first nine years has not been inconsiderable, Yeh notes. The empire is at last unified and at peace, the standards have been corrected, and the disintegration of the previous era has been reversed. Therefore, he suggested, don't be overhasty in demanding results of each new governmental measure; don't constantly express anger at failures, intervene to slaughter those who have erred, issue new laws and revised regulations, and by intimidation try to bring about instant success. He maintained that continued good influence from the radiant imperial personage would gradually transform the society, as the warm sun of springtime gradually melts the ice at the edges of the ponds. That does not happen quickly, Yeh reminded the ruler, but it happens surely.

Yeh Po-chü was particularly critical of the educational system in relationship to recruitment of officials; he felt that the government was misusing the system in its eagerness to recruit talent for service. Many vacancies in schools for both teachers and students existed, he noted, and their functioning was seriously impaired. The best students merely had time to indicate an aptitude, but never to acquire sound learning, before their studies were disrupted by appointment. In effect Yeh was criticizing the path by which he himself had risen quickly to official status. Early Ming government has often been praised for its broad base of selection, rapid upward mobility for talented men, and for the greatly expanded National University where students could be drawn directly into positions and responsibility. Yeh praised the Sung dynasty for the excellence of its educational system and the high level of public morality that it achieved, and blamed the Mongol Yüan for having undermined all of that. This resentment against Mongol influence on traditional Chinese standards of behavior was a popular point with Chu Yüan-chang and, in fact, expressed an attitude quite generally held among the literati of early Ming. On this point and in the other criticisms of government Yeh's remarks were not greatly different from those expressed by others, and often accepted by Chu Yüan-chang (*see* Lien Tzu-ning. and Hsieh Chin). Only his comments on the imperial household system went beyond the point that the emperor could tolerate, it would seem, although he was beginning to display the erratic suspicion and uncontrollable anger that came increasingly to mark his reign.

Yeh Po-chü's biography has often been coupled with that of a fellow native of Ning-hai, Cheng Shih-li 鄭士利 (T. 好義), who also submitted a memorial of criticism in October, 1376, and who likewise died as a consequence. Fang Hsiao-ju (*q.v.*) wrote a joint biography of the two early in the Chien-wen era, linking their histories, and many subsequent historians have continued to do the same. Fang, also a native of Ning-hai, was interested in Yeh and Cheng for that reason, but also for other reasons. Yeh's warnings about the princedoms justified the attitudes of Fang and other loyalists toward Chu Ti in his efforts to usurp the throne. And Cheng Shih-li's memorial dealt with the injustice done to over a hundred loyal and upright officials caught in a technical impropriety in the use of official seals, and all sentenced to execution or banishment just at that time. Fang's father, serving as a magistrate in Shantung, had been one of those executed. Cheng Shih-li's elder brother Cheng Shih-yüan 元 was another. Known as the k'ung-yin an 空印案 (the case of the pre-stamped documents), it concerned an administrative practice that had grown quite general. The documents used for reporting tax revenue shipments from localities to the central government were pre-stamped with the official seals of the responsible magistrates, but the spaces indicating precise amounts were left open until the ministry in Nanking had checked out actual receipts and could give final figures. The practice was made necessary by the time and distance separating the sending offices and the receiving ministry, by difficulties in calculating the amounts used in transit, and by the fact that the slightest discrepancy would render a document invalid. In order to obviate the necessity of canceling documents and sending messengers back and forth to deliver corrected ones, a special form of the magistral seals was devised to be used for this purpose only, and the documents were stamped with it. When the emperor learned of this practice, technically improper but both reasonable and firmly fixed in practice, he again was enraged at what he thought might be collusion to conceal official cheating. To make an example to officialdom, he ordered all district and prefectural officials whose names were among those found on pre-stamped documents to be executed, whether or not charges of cheating could be made against them. Many superior officials were done away with, but no high official within the central government was willing to risk the emperor's anger and plead their case.

Cheng Shih-li was aware of a limitation in the criticisms invited by the emperor in his edict of October 22, 1376: no one was allowed to use the occasion to plead a private cause. Therefore Cheng worded his memorial with that in mind, saying that, by preventing the emperor from making a great error that would affect the whole administration, he was serving a public cause. The emperor, however, who was always suspicious of a plot among his underlings, first attempted to discover who had engineered Cheng's action. Finding no organized conspiracy, he ruled that Cheng was merely pleading for a family member, and sentenced him to perform hard labor at P'u-k'ou 浦口

(north of Nanking) where he died later. Cheng's memorial also details aspects of early Ming administration, and is a document of considerable interest to the historian of Ming institutions.

Bibliography

1/139/2a; 5/113/13a; 42/39/3a; 61/101/22b; 63/25/8a; MSL (1962), T'ai-tsu 1809; KC (1958), 540; Ho Ch'iao-yüan, "Ch'en-lin-chi" 臣林記, 4, *Ming-shan-ts'ang*; Cha Chi-tso (ECCP), *Tsui-wei lu*, "Chuan" 13 上/15a, 18a; Hsia Hsieh 夏燮, *Ming-t'ung-chien* 明通鑑, *chüan* 6; Wu Han (BDRC), *Chu Yüan-chang chuan* 傳 (1948), 203; Huang Chang-chien, "Lun Huang Ming tsu-hsün-lu pan-hsing nien-tai ping lun Ming-ch'u feng-chien chu-wang chih-tu" 論皇明祖訓錄頒行年代並論明初封建諸王制度, CYYY, Vol. 32 (July, 1961), 129; *Ming-ch'en tsou-i* 名臣奏議 (*Chü-chen-pan ts'ung-shu* 聚珍版叢書 ed.), 1/1a; Chu Kuo-chen (ECCP), *Yung-chuang hsiao-p'in* 湧幢小品 (1959), 5/114; Ku Chieh-kang, "A Study of Literary Persecution during the Ming,"tr. by L. Carrington Goodrich, HJAS, III (1938), 269.

F. W. Mote

YEH Shao-yüan 葉紹袁 (T. 仲韶, H. 天寮), December 31, 1589-November 11, 1648, poet, came from a distinguished family whose home was situated near Lake Fen 汾湖 in the southern part of Wu-chiang 吳江, south of Soochow. His father, Yeh Chung-ti 重第 (d. 1599), became a *chin-shih* in 1587 in the same class as Yüan Huang(*q.v.*), a close friend from childhood. The two families lived not far apart, although the Yüan properties were located in the contiguous district of Chia-shan 嘉善, Chekiang province. In 1589, when Yeh Chung-ti and his wife were on their way to Peking for an assignment, Yeh Shao-yüan was born in an inn on the Grand Canal at Lin-ch'ing 臨清, Shantung. It seems that an astrologer made a comment to the effect that the child could not survive his tenth birthday. According to popular belief, when the messenger of death called a name, the one who answered to it would be taken away. Hence any child whose death at a certain age was predicted could, by being adopted by foster parents, live under an alias until he had passed that age. The prediction was made early in 1590, at the time when Yeh Chung-ti began his term as magistrate of Yü-t'ien 玉田, east of Peking, and while Yüan Huang was occupying a similar post in the adjoining district, Pao-ti 寶坻. Yeh Shao-yüan's parents took him at the age of four months to Pao-ti to live with Yüan Huang as his foster son. In 1592 Yüan, before going to Korea to fight the Japanese, sent his family back to Chia-shan with the Yeh child in their care. It was after his birthday in 1598 that the boy returned to his own family and began to live under his own name, Yeh Shao-yüan, which means the Yeh who carries on the Yüan tradition—an expression of gratitude. After his father died a year later, he again received help and instruction from Yüan Huang and was practically brought up with his son, Yüan Yen (*see* Yüan Huang). The two passed the provincial examination in the same year (1624), Yüan in Hangchow and Yeh at Nanking. Then both qualified for the *chin-shih* in Peking a year later; so also did a cousin, Yeh Shao-jung 顒 (T. 季若, d. *ca.* 1670). Of the three Yeh Shao-jung fared best in his official career, serving as censor inspector in Kwangtung (1633-35) and Shansi (1638), and minister of the Grand Court of Revision (January 1641-42), accumulating wealth as he did so. Yüan Yen went in 1626 to Kwangtung to act as a magistrate and died there a year later.

Yeh Shao-yüan's term in the bureaucracy was brief. After serving as an instructor in the military school at Nanking (1627) and in the National University in Peking (1628) he held for two years the post of a secretary in the ministry of Works (1628-30). During the Manchu invasion of 1630 he took part in the defense of Peking, being responsible for the deepening of the moat along the east wall and for control of the military supply depot, K'uei-chia ch'ang 盔甲廠, in the southeastern corner of Peking. The behavior of the eunuchs supervising public works at this time of national crisis greatly disheartened him; he found them abusing the people and busily lining their own pockets. He also witnessed the firing of new guns, some of which exploded because the officer in charge, who had received a bribe, tampered with the powder in order to put the blame on the minister of Works, Nan Chü-i (*q.v.*). According to Yeh's autobiography, the cannon, presented by Hsü Kuang-ch'i(ECCP), exploded at that time too, because the emperor, who was present, ordered the use of an excessive amount of gunpowder. After the disaster the emperor ordered strict observation of Hsü's directions on the use and care of western style firearms.

Late in 1630 Yeh Shao-yüan asked for leave to be with his mother who was then over seventy years of age. He had been in charge of supplying the government with military equipment worth over forty thousand taels and made an accurate account of all transactions. In the end he could not even finance his own passage home without a loan from his wife's younger brother, Shen Tzu-cheng 沈自徵 (T. 君庸, H. 漁洋, 1591-January 31, 1633), whose income in Peking as a private adviser on military affairs to high officials was better than his. Yeh knew that his honesty had exasperated his predecessors, superiors, and expectant successors, who thought him a fool, but he could not have acted otherwise. He related how in 1625 a friend promised him appointment to the Hanlin Academy on the payment of sixteen hundred taels instead of the regular price of two thousand, and when he refused the friend called him too impractical (太迂).

Early in 1631 Yeh arrived home two days before the lunar New Year's Day, and so was able to celebrate it with his entire family together. His wife, Shen I-

hsiu 宜修 (T. 宛君, 1590-1635), a noted poet, was the daughter of Shen Ch'ung 珫 (T. 季玉, H. 懋所, 1562-1622, cs 1595), a second cousin of Shen Ching (*q.v.*). Their marriage in 1605 was a celebrated event in the Soochow area, for they were known as a well-favored and talented couple. They had eight sons and four daughters. The three older daughters, Yeh Wan-wan 紈紈 (T. 昭齊, 1610-January 31, 1633), Yeh Hsiao-wan 小紈 (T. 蕙綢, b. 1613), and Yeh Hsiao-luan 鸞 (T. 瓊章, 瑤期, 1616-32), were gifted and versed in poetry. The eldest daughter married a grandson of Yüan Huang; the second daughter married Shen Yung-chen 永楨, a grandson of Shen Ching.

The third daughter, Yeh Hsiao-luan, was brought up by her uncle, Shen Tzu-cheng, also a poet, as was his wife, Chang Ch'ien-ch'ien 張倩倩 (1594-1627). When Yeh Hsiao-luan left the Shen household in 1625 to return home, she surprised her parents by her pleasing appearance and gracious manners. Two years later, at the age of eleven, she began to study the art of poetry; at thirteen came the game wei-ch'i 圍棋, and at fifteen, painting and music. Her father commented on her looks as unsurpassed. Her mother, in a sketch of Hsiao-luan's life, summarized the girl's appearance as one of unusual beauty. At that time she was betrothed to a certain Chang Li-p'ing 張立平. Five days before the wedding she passed away. Her parents, grief stricken, wrote eulogies of her and believed that she became a Taoist goddess. Seventy days later her eldest sister, Wan-wan, died of a disease of the lung, but probably her unhappy marriage affected her health, for her husband completely ignored her. In April, 1635, Yeh Shao-yüan's second son, Yeh Shih-ch'eng 世偁 (T. 聲期, b. 1618) succumbed to heart failure after failing in the examination required for entrance to the local school, while his elder and a younger brother succeeded. Half a year later their mother also died.

Yeh Shao-yüan, grieved by these

losses, was determined to perpetuate their memory. It was rather unusual for a girl to be educated, and Yeh was appreciative of the extraordinary fact that so many of his female kinsfolk had learned the art of poetry. From 1632 to 1636 he edited and published their works and the eulogies about them, his own included, in a collection known as *Wu-meng-t'ang chi* 午夢堂集 consisting of the following titles: *Li-ch'ui* 鸝吹 and *Mei-hua shih* 梅花詩 by Shen I-hsiu; *Ch'ou-yen* 愁言 by Yeh Wan-wan; *Fan-sheng-hsiang* 返生香 by Yeh Hsiao-luan; *Yüan-yang meng* 鴛鴦夢, a drama by Yeh Hsiao-wan; *Yao-wen* 窈聞 and *Hsü* 續 *yao-wen*, accounts by Yeh himself relating that Yeh Hsiao-luan had become a goddess or "immortal" and telling of a séance at which she appeared; *I-jen ssu* 伊人思, selected writings of forty-four women, edited by Shen I-hsiu; *Po-wen ts'ao* 百旻草, by Yeh Shih-ch'eng; *Ch'in-chai yüan* 秦齋怨, eulogies of his mother, wife, daughters, and sons, by Yeh Shao-yüan; *Ch'i-yen ai* 屺雁哀, eulogies of Shen I-hsiu by her sons and daughters; and *T'ung-lien hsü-so* 彤奩續些, more eulogies. The following items were added later: *Ling-hu chi* 靈護集, writings by another son, Yeh Shih-jung 世倅 (T. 威期, 1619–40), and *Ch'iung-hua ching* 瓊花鏡, describing a séance in 1642 during which Yeh Shao-yüan learned that his deceased wife and daughters had all become goddesses.

Yeh Shao-yüan did not remarry; in 1636, then forty-seven years of age, he arranged marriages for the last two slave girls in the family. In 1637, after seeing his father's name entered into the Wu-chiang district shrine of local worthies, he completed his autobiography, *T'ien-liao tzu-chuan nien-p'u* 天寥自撰年譜. A supplement, *Nien-p'u hsü* 續, concludes with entries dated in August, 1645, when the Manchus crushed all resistance in the area and enforced the order to shave the forehead and braid the hair in a queue. Yeh finished his autobiography on the day that he left his home and entered a monastery to be tonsured as a Buddhist monk, a symbolic way of showing resistance to the alien conquerors. He took no active part in the military resistance under the fellow townsman, Wu Yang (ECCP, p. 102), but tried to keep a record of those who did, among whom were some of his own relatives. When he died in 1648, he left a diary which he kept from September, 1645, to October, 1648, entitled *Chia-hsing jih-chu* 甲行日注, 8 *ch.* written under his Buddhist name, Mu-fu 木拂 (H. 華桐流衲); also a collection of anecdotes, entitled *T'ien-liao nien-p'u pieh-chi* 別記. For two hundred years his writings remained in manuscript; only in the 19th century were the autobiography and an imperfect edition of the diary printed. The autobiographical material, anecdotes, and a work entitled *Hu-yin wai-shih* 湖隱外史 first appeared in 1906, being published by Teng Shih 鄧實 in his *Kuo-ts'ui ts'ung-shu* 國粹叢書. Later the autobiography, supplement, and the diary were included in Liu Ch'eng-kan's 劉承幹 *Chia-yeh t'ang* 嘉業堂 *ts'ung-shu* (1918).

In the 1930s, when the late Ming style of impressionistic prose came into vogue, Yeh Shao-yüan's writings became popular too. An edition of his autobiography and supplement is included in the *Chung-kuo wen-hsüeh chen-pen* 中國文學珍本 *ts'ung-shu* of 1936, where, together with the anecdotes and the diary, they are given the collective title *Yeh T'ien-liao ssu-chung* 四種. The same collection also incorporates a new edition of the *Wu-meng-t'ang ch'üan-chi*, thus furthering the popularity of the poems of Yeh's wife and daughters. Their poems in tz'u style may also be found in the anthology *Hsiao-t'an-luan-shih kuei-hsiu tz'u* 小檀欒室閨秀詞, under the following titles: *Li-ch'ui tz'u* by Shen I-hsiu, *Fang-hsüeh hsüan* 芳雪軒 *tz'u* by Yeh Wan-wan, and *Shu-hsiang ko* 疏香閣 *tz'u* by Yeh Hsiao-luan. They are obviously copied from the *Wu-meng-t'ang chi*.

In the late Ming period, perhaps more than at any other time, the belief in communication with the deceased, in reincarnation, and in the transformation to a god or immortal after death, was quite prevalent. Ch'ien Ch'ien-i(ECCP), himself a believer, records that in the Soochow area there were séances, at which Yeh's wife and eldest daughter appeared as Ch'an Buddhist spirits of the T'ien-t'ai 天台 sect; Yeh Hsiao-luan, at first as a Taoist spirit, is supposed to have been converted later to that sect too. Among the fourteen poems by Yeh Hsiao-luan in Ch'ien's anthology of Ming poetry, *Lieh-ch'ao shih-chi*, three are described as composed after death and revealed during séances. The *Wu-meng-t'ang chi*, of course contains many more such poems. An ink slab supposedly belonging to Yeh Hsiao-luan came into the possession of a certain Wang Shou-mai 王壽邁; he printed a collection in 1856, entitled *Yen yüan chi-lu* 硯緣集錄, which included descriptions of her and the ink slab, and some reports of séances in which she is said to have appeared.

Yeh Shao-yüan left two collections of poems, *T'ien-liao chi* and *Lü-chu chi* 櫚塵集, which do not seem to be extant. Some of his writings may be found in the *Wu-meng-t'ang chi* and several other anthologies. They were conspicuously left out by Ch'ien Ch'ien-i in his anthology which, however, included some poems by Yeh's wife and daughters. A collection of poems, entitled *Ts'un-yü ts'ao* 存餘草 by his second daughter, Yeh Hsiao-wan, was printed about 1684 by her younger brother, Yeh Hsieh 燮 (T. 星期, H. 己畦, 橫山, 1627–1703); he was Yeh Shao-yüan's sixth son. It appears that he registered under his original name, Yeh Shih-kuan 世倌, when he became a student in the school of the neighboring district, Chia-shan. After 1648 he changed his name to Yeh Hsieh, became a student of the prefectural school of Chia-hsing 嘉興, and proceeded to take the civil examinations until he became a *chin-shih* in 1670. During his first and only assignment, as magistrate of Pao-ying 寶應 on the Grand Canal north of Yangchow (1675–January, 1677),

he tried to serve conscientiously but was in the end cashiered. It was the time of the San-fan war when troops and supplies were transported continuously on the canal, making excessive demands on the post stations; yet the Manchu government had just ordered a general reduction in allowances, which resulted in the people in each district supplying more service on a smaller budget. This meant that the Chinese people were forced to finance the alien military power to conquer themselves, with Yeh Hsieh as one of the agents. It happened that the people of Pao-ying had been suffering from floods for several years and could not bear any additional tax burden. When Yeh Hsieh was discharged on the ground that he lacked the ability to meet the situation, he had to assume the deficit of the post station as his personal debt. It took him years to pay it off by teaching students at home and by occasionally serving as adviser to officials as far away as Kwangtung and Shensi. He left a literary collection, *Chi-ch'i chi* 己畦集, 33 *ch.*, and a work on poetry, *Yüan-shih* 原詩, 4 *ch.* These and a number of critical remarks on the writings of Wang Wan(ECCP), entitled *Wang wen chai-miao* 汪文摘謬, were reprinted by Yeh Te-hui (BDRC) in 1915–17.

Bibliography

40/66/13b, 86/21b; 43/5/9b; *Lieh-ch'ao shih-chi* 閏, 4/46b; *Su-chou-fu chih* 蘇州府志 (1862), 104/23b, 105/13b, 17a, 25a, 27a, 106/12b; *Chiang-su shih-cheng* 江蘇詩徵; Yeh Te-hui, *Hsi-yüan tu-shu chih* 郋園讀書志 (1928), 4/15b, 10/9a, 15/39b; Yin Tseng 殷增, ed., *Sung-ling shih-cheng ch'ien-pien* 松陵詩徵前編 (1883), 6./1a, 4b, 6a, 8/1a, 9a, 12/2a, 7a, 10a; Yeh *T'ien-liao ssu-chung*; Yeh Hsieh, *Chi-ch'i shih* 詩, 5/13a, 9/14b; *Chi-ch'i wen* 文, 8/29a, 9/1a, 13/6a, 14/1a; Kuo Shao-yü 郭紹虞, *Chung-kuo wen-hsüeh p'i-p'ing shih* 中國文學批評史 (1961), 43; Ling Ching-yen 凌景埏, "Yü-yang shan-jen nien-p'u" 漁洋山人年譜 (about Shen Tzu-cheng) in *Wen-hsüeh nien-pao* 文學年報, no. 7, 1941; Portrait in *Kuo-ts'ui hsüeh-pao*, 3d year (1907); SK (1930), 197/12a.

Chaoying Fang

YEH Sheng 葉盛 (T. 與中, H. 仲盛, 蛻庵, 涇東道人，澱東老漁, Pth. 文莊), 1420–74, official, scholar, and bibliophile, was a native of K'un-shan 崑山 in the prefecture of Soochow. After becoming a *chin-shih* in 1445, he was appointed a supervising secretary in the War ministry's office of scrutiny. During the crisis of 1449, when Emperor Chu Ch'i-chen (*q.v.*) was captured by the Mongols, Yeh began to be noticed for his outspokenness. He first proposed the punishment of all those who had abandoned the emperor and slipped back to the capital. Then he proposed the selection of officers to train new troops in preparation for the launching of a counterattack. When the emperor's younger brother, Prince Ch'eng 郕王 (Chu Ch'i-yü, *q.v.*), ascended the throne, Yeh protested against the custom of bestowing presents and honors in a new reign, in the light of the recent catastrophe. Later in the same year, when the Mongols threatened Peking, Yeh again offered his counsel on various military and strategic matters.

After the crisis had eased, he received a promotion to chief supervising secretary, and was sent to rehabilitate the refugees in Honan (1450). When the new monarch reportedly tended to indulge more in pleasure than in public business, Yeh succeeded in persuading him to hold additional audiences at noon. In official conferences Yeh frequently expressed his opinions freely, paying little heed to the fact that his own status was a junior one. Some senior officials resented his forwardness, and gave him the nickname of Yeh Shao-pao 葉少保, or Yeh the Junior Guardian, mocking him for his bravado. At the same time, however, they recognized his ability.

In 1451 he received the appointment of right administration vice commissioner of Shansi with the specific duties of supervising military supplies for the frontier troops in Hsüan-fu, northwest of Peking. While holding the same rank he was later given the duties of a consultant to regional commander Sun An 孫安 (d. 1471), native of Kao-yu 高郵 in the lower Yangtze valley, who was then assistant commissioner-in-chief stationed in Hsüan-fu. The northern part of this area had been abandoned during the emergency of 1449. In cooperation with Sun An, Yeh helped to resettle eight forts, the most prominent among them being Tu-shih 獨石. They provided for agricultural projects, improved transportation facilities, and established local schools and medical services. In his years in Hsüan-fu, Yeh contributed no small part to the stabilization of the northern frontier. In the latter part of 1456, when his father died, Yeh retired from office and returned home to observe the mourning period. This interruption in his official career may have been a very timely one, because it prevented him from becoming involved in the restoration of Chu Ch'i-chen (February, 1457).

Yeh was summoned to be assistant censor-in-chief in 1458 and to proceed to the south as governor of Kwangtung and Kwangsi. At this time these two provinces were troubled by bandits and the rebellious Yao 猺 tribe of Lung-shui 瀧水, Kwangtung. Following the pacification of the region, a governor of Kwangsi was appointed with Yeh assuming responsibility for Kwangtung alone. Three years later, after the enthronement of the new emperor (Chu Chien-shen, *q.v.*), Yeh returned to Peking for consultation. Then he was appointed left assistant censor-in-chief, and once more set out for Hsüan-fu, this time as governor. During his administration over seven hundred forts underwent repair, large areas of land were brought under cultivation, the living conditions of the settlers improved, and the defenses of the frontier made more secure. In 1467 he received promotion to right vice minister of Rites. Two years later he was transferred to a similar post in the ministry of Personnel. About this time certain high officials proposed to settle and fortify the Ordos region which had been abandoned to the Mongols for decades. Yeh received orders (1472) to look into the matter and to exchange opinions with those concerned. He advised against the proposal, and held that no offensive action should be taken unless the defenses were strong. Later such action, however, was taken, and proved unsuccessful (*see* Tseng Hsien). Two years before his death he became left vice minister of Personnel. He died in office (March 25) and received the posthumous name Wen-chuang.

If there ever was a typical pattern for a successful censorial career, Yeh Sheng's would certainly be so classified. He was once criticized for excessive slaughter in suppressing the Yao tribesmen and the bandits in Kwangtung and Kwangsi. He explained his actions, however, and received no reprimand. It is said that in court he had one antagonist in his famous contemporary, Ch'iu Chün (*q. v.*). Could it be that Ch'iu, being a native of Kwangtung, had received unfavorable reports, substantiated or not, about Yeh's administration in his own province, and thus nursed a grudge against him?

Yeh is said to have admired several Sung scholar officials for their attainments: in prose he emulated Ou-yang Hsiu (1007–72), in calligraphy he followed the style of Su Shih (1037–1101), and in administrative skill he looked up to Han Ch'i (1008–75) and Fan Chung-yen (989–1052), particularly the last, who also happened to be a fellow townsman from Soochow. Fan's portrait was reportedly found hanging in his working and living quarters; all through Yeh's life he regarded Fan as his model and master.

Among Yeh's writings, his *Shui-tung jih-chi* 水東日記 has always been valued as an important source for Ming history, containing information on institutions in Peking, the northern frontiers, and southern China. The *Ssu-k'u* Imperial Library includes a 38 *chüan* edition, and recently a 40 *chüan* K'ang-hsi edition was photo-lithographically reproduced (1965) in Taiwan. There are also three abridged editions: a one *chüan* edition of 77 notes appeared as early as the mid-sixteenth century in the *Chin-sheng yü-chen chi* 金聲玉振集, reprinted 1959 in Peking; another one *chüan* edition under the title *Shui-tung chi-lüeh* 記略 printed in 1646 in the *Shuo-fu hsü* of T'ao T'ing (*see* T'ao Tsung-i); and a seven *chüan* edition entitled *Shui-tung jih-chi chai-ch'ao* 摘抄 printed in 1617 in the *Chi-lu hui-pien* by Shen Chieh-fu (*q.v.*) and later reprinted by the Commercial Press in 1938. An index of the 40 *chüan* edition is included in the *Chūkoku zhihitsu zatsucho sakuin* 中國隨筆雜著索引 (Kyoto, 1960). His memorials entitled *Yeh Wen-chuang kung tsou-shu* 葉文莊公奏疏, printed about 1631 in 40 *chüan*, are subdivided chronologically into four parts: the *Hsi-yüan tsou-ts'ao* 西垣奏草, 9 *ch.*, the *Pien-tsou ts'un-kao* 邊奏存稿, 7 *ch.*, the *Liang Kuang tsou-ts'ao*, and the *Shang-ku* 上谷 *tsou-ts'ao*, 8 *ch.* Twenty-five of his memorials arranged in two *chüan* may also be found in the *Huang Ming ching-shih wen-pien* which has recently been reprinted both on the mainland and in Taiwan. His collected literary works, the *Lu-chu-t'ang chi* 菉竹堂集, consist of two *chüan* of prose and one *chüan* of poetry. Two catalogues of Yeh Sheng's library were reprinted in the *Yüeh-ya-t'ang ts'ung-shu* 粵雅堂叢書 (15th series, 1854), one of books, the *Lu-chu-t'ang shu-mu* 書目, and one of rubbings, the *Lu-chu-t'ang pei* 碑目.

In the preface to the catalogue of his books, Yeh describes his library as one holding over 4,600 titles in approximately 22,700 *chüan*. The motto he composed to be carved on his book cabinet is perhaps the most quoted by later bibliophiles:

Read with attention,
Lock up securely,
Put away with care,
And the shelving must be high (and airy).
Sons, grandsons, and their sons
Must read and learn.

To lend books to irresponsible parties
Is also lack of filial piety.

It is fortunate that he had good descendants who contributed either to the building of his library, or to the editing and printing of his works. During his lifetime as he moved from place to place in government service he never had a home for his books, although he had named his library Lu-chu-t'ang. It was not until the time of his great-great-grandson, Yeh Kung-huan 葉恭煥 (T. 伯寅, H. 括蒼 山人, b. 1523, cj 1546), that a structure was put up in K'un-shan for the books, and Wang Shih-chen (q.v.) was asked to write an essay to commemorate the occasion.

Another man of the same name, Yeh Sheng (T. 昌伯, H. 虛室, 1435-94), who was a native of Lan-ch'i 蘭谿, Chekiang, graduated as *chin-shih* in 1475 and officiated as subprefectural magistrate of Chüchou 莒州, Shantung.

A renowned censorial official and a contemporary of the first Yeh Sheng was Lin Ts'ung 林聰 (T. 季聰, H. 見庵, Pth. 莊敏, 1417-October 6, 1482, cs 1439), a native of Ning-te 寧德, Fukien, who rose to be minister of Justice. In their early years they often collaborated and acted in concert. The editors of the *Ming-shih* cite Yeh and Lin together as exemplary members of the surveillance agencies of their time.

Bibliography

1/177/23b; 5/26/13a; KC (1958), 2338; TSCC (1885-88), XI: 798/18b, XIV: 549/13b, XXIV: 120/5a; SK (1930), 38/11a, 56/2b, 87/1a, 175/11a; *Yeh Wen-chuang-kung tsou-shu* (NCL microfilm); Yeh Ch'ang-ch'ih (BDRC), *Ts'ang-shu chi-shih shih*(Shanghai, 1958), 79; Wang Shih-chen, "Lu-chu-t'ang chi," in *Yen-chou shan-jen ssu-pu kao*, 95/13b; C. O. Hucker, *The Censorial System of Ming China* (Stanford, 1966), 94; W. Franke, *Sources*, 4.1.1, 5.3.4. For Lin Ts'ung, *see* 1/177/ 20b, 5/44/40a; TSCC(1885-88), XI: 354/6a, XIV: 359/6a.

Lienche Tu Fang

YEH Tsung-liu 葉宗留, died November/ December 1448, ringleader of an insurrection resulting in the devastation of a large part of the Chekiang-Fukien-Kiangsi region from 1447 to 1448, was a native of Ch'ing-yüan 慶元, Ch'u-chou 處州 -fu, Chekiang. A youth of robust physique, unlettered, but skillful in the military arts, Yeh worked for a while as a servitor in the prefectural office. This being unrewarding, he found it more profitable to steal from the local government-controlled silver mines. In time he organized a small band of disaffected miners who were poorly rewarded for their labor, and hardpressed to fulfill their annual quota. Under his leadership they secretly looted the mines in the border region of Chekiang and Fukien.

Yeh and his band eventually caught the attention of government authorities in August, 1444, when they began to work the Fu-an 福安 mines and clashed with the local security force, killing the administration vice minister of Fukien. They successfully eluded the police, however, and in the following years expanded their activities to a number of mines in Chekiang and Fukien, especially those at Ch'ing-yüan and Cheng-ho 政和. In October, 1447, despairing of the profit they made from the depleted silver mines, they came out openly as outlaws. Yeh proclaimed himself their king, distributed forged heretical texts, then led his men in pillaging Cheng-ho, and returned to Ch'ing-yüan, attracting a large following from among the villagers and miners.

Yeh's band was reportedly well organized and trained in the use of weapons. It is said that Yeh recruited an expert on military arts, a certain Yeh Ch'it from Lung-ch'üan 龍泉, to instruct his followers. In the ensuing months, operating from Cheng-ho, bands of rebels pillaged the neighboring districts in the northwest, then raided Chien-ning 建寧 -fu to the southwest. Everywhere they looted and burned down houses, but distributed booty to those who would join their cause; in this way they attracted even more followers, and alarmed the whole province (Fukien). Meanwhile Yeh's band roamed across the border into Kiangsi, where they occupied the mountain passes of Ch'e-p'an-ling 車盤嶺, obstructing the traffic between Kiangsi and Fukien, and threatening the major mining center of Ch'ien-shan 鉛山hsien in Kiangsi. The government became genuinely disturbed.

During this time a large section of Fukien had fallen prey to the insurgents under Teng Mao-ch'i (q.v.), with whom Yeh was reportedly in frequent contact. The authorities then took steps for their suppression. In September, 1448, the court ordered Chang K'ai (see Teng Mao-ch'i), an associate censor-in-chief, to lead a command against them. Mobilizing his troops from Kiangsi, Chang was blocked from entry into Fukien on the border of Ch'ien-shan. At this point, Han Yung (q.v.), then a censor in Kiangsi, urged Chang to take immediate action. After much hesitation and indecision, Chang sent Commander Tai Li 戴禮, who volunteered for the task, to head a unit of five hundred to meet the challenge; later he sent Commander Ch'en Jung 陳榮 to lead a still large supporting force. On November 30 (according so Chang Hsüan [q.v.]) the government contingent met the rebels in Huang-po-p'u 黃栢舖 near Ch'ien-shan, and heavy fighting ensued. Yeh, who was dressed in red, was killed in action but his body was not immediately identified. A later official report, however, asserts that he fell victim to his fellow headman Ch'en Chien-hu 陳鑑胡, who killed him in a drunken brawl. Ch'en, who later proclaimed himself king of the T'ai-p'ing 太平 state, was executed in December, 1449, along with his fellow leaders.

Having lost their chief, the rebels retreated into the mountains of Ch'ienshan and realigned their forces, while the government troops pressed hard on their heels. Under the command of Yeh Hsi-pa 希八, their new leader, the rebels successfully ambushed their pursuers near P'u-

ch'eng 浦城 on the Kiangsi-Fukien border, killing both Tai Li and Ch'en Jung. Following up their victory, they invaded Chekiang, ravaging several districts, and bolstered their strength by recruiting displaced villagers and bands of criminal elements, numbering, it is said, more than a hundred thousand men. In April, 1449, after being informed of the debacle, the court ordered Shih P'u (see Yü Ch'ien), minister of Works, to head a special punitive force, concurrently commanding Chang K'ai to stand by for a joint maneuver against the insurgents. Before the relief force arrived, however, they had laid siege to Ch'u-chou and terrorized the city for several months. Eventually, the reinforcements of Chang K'ai arrived from Chekiang in June after considerable delays on the way. Executing a carrot-and-stick policy, Chang secured the surrender of several rebel headmen, including Yeh Hsi-pa, while ruthlessly crushing the recalcitrant die-hards. The insurgents were finally suppressed in August, though remnants remained active in the ensuing years. Notwithstanding this performance, Chang K'ai on his return in November was sharply criticized by the censors for inept leadership, and was stripped of his title by Emperor Chu Ch'i-yü (q.v.). When Emperor Chu Ch'i-chen (q.v.) regained the throne in 1457, however, he forgave Chang and restored his title.

The aftermath of the uprising was significant. The dislocation of the rural population, as in the case of Ch'u-chou, prompted the authorities to grant them a three-year period of exemption from corvée labor. But more important, this popular uprising aroused concern in the court for the plight of the miners. As a consequence, the court reviewed its mining policy, and in October, 1449, ordered a considerable reduction of the output quota imposed on them, and abolished the death penalty for theft in the mines a decade later.

Bibliography
61/161/10a; MSL(1965), Ying-tsung, ch. 136–185;

KC (1958), 1752; Chang Hsüan, *Hsi-yüan wen-chien lu*, 92/33b; Ku Yen-wu (ECCP), *T'ien-hsia chün-kuo li-ping shu* (SPTK, 3d ser.), 31/15b, 34/52a (here the character *liu* in Yeh Tsung-liu is rendered as *liu* 劉); Li Lung-chien 李龍潛, "Ming Cheng-t'ung chien Yeh Tsung-liu Teng Mao-ch'i ch'i-i ti ching-kuo chi t'e-tien" 明正統間葉宗留鄧茂七起義的經過及特點, *Li-shih chiao-hsüeh* 歷史教學 (1957), no. 3, 11; Tanaka Masa-toshi 田中正俊, "On the Historical Records Concerning the Rebellion of Teng Mao-ch'i" (in Japanese), *Studies on the Ming Period Presented to the Late Taiji Shimizu* (Tokyo, 1962), 637; Lucia Caterina, "Per una nuova interpretazione della rivolta di Yeh Tsung-liu," *Annali dell' Istitute universitario Orientale di Napoli*, nuova Serie, XX (1970), 369.

Hok-lam Chan

YEN Chen-chih 嚴震直 (T. 子敏), 1344-October 7, 1402, official, was the son of rich peasants of Wu-ch'eng 烏程, Hu-chou 湖州 -fu, Chekiang. A youth of robust physique, Yen disdained scholarly pursuits but became skilled in accounting and the management of his estate. After the founding of the Ming dynasty Emperor Chu Yüan-chang initiated the system whereby the collection of taxes in a specified area was assigned to a leading family, conferring on it the title of liang-chang 糧長. Yen Chen-chih represented his family in their area. His duties included the collection of tribute grain and its delivery to government granaries. He performed these duties with dispatch. Impressed by his performance, Chu Yüan-chang summoned him to the capital and offered him an official position. In 1390 he served as assistant administration commissioner of the office of transmission, and a year later became director of a bureau in the ministry of Revenue in charge of the Kiangsi region. Early in 1393 he was appointed vice minister of Works and in July, minister.

During his tenure in office Yen was credited with the improvement of the service system for artisans. As part of the establishment of voluntary service, all male adults were required to register in the artisan households, then estimated at around 230,000, and to report to the capital for a three-months' tour of duty, once in every three years. Due to mismanagement, however, many men found that no work was assigned to them. As a corrective, Yen required a member from each household to submit a vita with such details as name, occupation, and special skill. With this information in hand, the authorities were able to tap the services of available manpower in accordance with the schedule and the needs of specific projects, without causing unnecessary hardship. In October Yen became involved in the case of misconduct of his younger brother and nephew. Acting on the charges of the local people, the court ordered Yen to conduct a public hearing. He pronounced a fair judgment, it is said, and sentenced them accordingly. Pleased with Yen's sense of justice, the court commuted his relatives' sentence and ordered their release. On January 3, 1394, owing to a slight offense, Yen was demoted to be a censor. In this new capacity he reexamined a number of dubious judicial cases and so spared many innocent people punishment, often at the risk of incurring the displeasure of the authorities. In September, 1395, Yen was appointed, together with minister of Rites Jen Heng-t'ai 任亨泰 (T. 大雍, cs 1388), to serve on an embassy to Annam. Their mission was to inform the Annamite king of the court's punitive action against Chao Tsung-shou 趙宗壽 (fl. 1388–95), the rebellious aboriginal official of Lung-chou 龍州, Kwangsi, who had been charged with usurping his title. They counseled the king not to side with the usurper and informed the Annamites of the Chinese intentions so that the presence of troops in that area would not alarm the population. In April, 1396, acting on the proposal of T'ang To 唐鐸 (T. 振之, 1329–97, Pth. 敬安), minister of War, the court sent Yen to Kwangsi to take charge of the dredging of the sixty *li* Ling-ch'ü 靈渠 Canal in Hsing-an 興安, which connected the Li 灕 with the Hsiang 湘 River, and had been an important link since 219 B.C. Under Yen's supervision, the local population was mobilized, and in less than two months they successfully dredged the canal, built reservoirs, embankments, and flood gates, cleared the rocks from the river bed, and renovated existing facilities. This accomplished, the canal became navigable for transport of military supplies as well as a source for the irrigation of nearby farms.

Yen submitted a memorial in March, 1397, proposing a change in the system of shipment of salt from Kwangtung to the merchants of Kwangsi in exchange for the supply of grain for the military guards in their province. The merchants of Kwangsi, a province which was now impoverished, failed, however, to absorb the assigned quota of salt, the bulk of which was left in storage in Kwangtung. It was reported that, in the span of almost one year, out of a total quota of some 850,000 lots (yin 引) of salt, only one tenth was disposed of in Kwangsi. Yen then proposed storing some 308,000 lots of the quota in Kwangtung, offering the merchants who provided grain in Kwangsi the privilege of disposing of the salt in the four southern prefectures of Kiangsi. The court approved his recommendation, and to Yen's credit Kwangtung salt then became available in the markets in southern Kiangsi.

In May Yen received a promotion to be associate censor-in-chief; then in September he was reappointed minister of Works. In the following spring, pleading old age, he obtained permission to retire. When Chu Yün-wen (*q.v.*) succeeded to the throne, Yen declined an official appointment; as a reward for his long service, the emperor kept him in the capital. Shortly after Chu Ti (*q.v*) ascended the throne, Yen was brought to his attention. In August, 1402, he and one of several other officials were appointed to undertake an inspection tour of the provincial offices in Shantung, Shansi, Honan, Shensi, and other regions, and make recommendations for improvements in local administration. While on that mission he died in Tsechou 澤州, Shansi, in October.

Some biographers, however, give a different picture of his last years. They report that, following the outbreak of the rebellion of Chu Ti, Emperor Chu Yün-wen appointed Yen to take charge of the supply of rations destined for the imperial forces in Shantung. While serving in this capacity he was captured and taken to Peiping as prisoner. Some accounts hold that he was later executed by Chu Ti. Others report that the emperor appointed him minister of Works and head of a mission to Annam. On his homeward journey through Yünnan, he ran into the deposed emperor Chu Yün-wen. Grieved over the plight of his former ruler, he committed suicide by swallowing ingots of gold. Perhaps because of this information, when the regional inspector, Huang Chung 黃鐘 (T. 律元, H. 麗江, 1540–1608, cs 1577), proposed the erection of a shrine in Yen's honor in Wu-ch'eng in 1591, he mentioned in his recommendation that Yen had died for his loyalty to Emperor Chu Yün-wen. This assertion, however, was challenged by Yen's descendant, Yen Chih 祗 (T. 文昭), who, decades later refuted the account of his ancestor's death on a memorial tablet at the shrine, holding that this account, rather than honoring the dead, would only falsify the true standing of his ancestor.

Yen Chen-chih was not a man of letters and left few writings. The *Wuch'eng-hsien chih* lists him as the author of three works, none of which seems to have survived. His collection of poetry entitled *Ch'ien-hsing chi* 遣興集 is also lost, but fragments are preserved in such anthologies of Ming poetry as the *Ming-shih tsung* by Chu I-tsun (ECCP).

Bibliography

1/151/2b; 40/4/16b; 61/116/9b; 63/5/39b; MSL (1962), T'ai-tsu, 3327, 3354, 3367, 3486, 3583,

3617, 3646, T'ai-tsung (1963), 169; KC (1958), 880; Cheng Hsiao, *Wu-hsüeh pien*, 58/1b; Wu K'uan, *P'o-weng chia tsang chi* (SPTK ed.), 43/8b; Lu Ts'an 陸粲, *Keng-ssu pien* 庚己編 in *Chi-lu hui-pien*, 173/7b; *Wu-ch'eng-hsien chih* (1881), 6/26a, 14/5a, 30/16a, 31/5b; *Kwangsi t'ung-chih* (1800), 117/7b; *Huang Ming wen-hai* (microfilm), 61/7/2/18; *Ming-shih* (Taipei, 1963), 1850.

Hok-lam Chan

YEN Sung 嚴嵩 (T. 惟中, 介谿, 勉庵), 1480-1565, a grand secretary from 1542 to 1562, was a native of Fen-i 分宜, Kiangsi. His family was classified in the artisan cetegory. A *chin-shih* of 1505, he was appointed a Hanlin bachelor and then a Hanlin compiler. Owing to ill health, he received permission to return home and there for ten years devoted himself to study, earning a reputation for his writing of prose and poetry. After his return to government service, he first held the appointment of expositor-in-waiting, then served as acting chancellor of the Hanlin Academy at Nanking, after which he received a transfer to the post of director of the National University in the capital. According to one source, Yen in fact had insufficient qualifications for the latter position, but one of the grand secretaries, a fellow townsman of Yen, favored his appointment. In 1528 he became vice minister of Rites and later vice minister of Personnel. Early in 1532 he was promoted to be minister of Rites in Nanking and then (June 30, 1533) minister of Personnel in the same city.

After a five-year stay in the southern capital, he returned to Peking to take part in the celebration of the birthday of the emperor. It happened that the government had just decided to revise the Sung history 宋史; so the authorities requested that Yen be permitted to stay on in charge of the revision, and he was given the titular appointment of minister of Rites with the concurrent title of chancellor of the Hanlin Academy (May 20, 1536). According to one

source, the then minister of Rites, Hsia Yen (*q.v.*), who later became Yen's rival, initially patronized him and had much to do with his entry into the charmed circle of actual power. Later (February 4, 1537), when Hsia Yen became a grand secretary, Yen took his place as minister of Rites. It was in this capacity that Yen began to find favor with the emperor and to win his trust. Then on September 24, 1542, when Yen was sixty-two, the emperor appointed him grand secretary; he remained in that post for almost twenty years until dismissed from office on June 20, 1562.

Of all the leading political figures of the Ming dynasty, Yen has been one of those most maligned and unfairly treated in historical writings. In the *Ming-shih* Yen is placed in the chapter labeled "Treacherous Ministers." According to its introductory remarks, treacherous ministers are those who "usurped imperial power, engaged in rebellious activities, shook the dynastic foundations, butchered and harmed the loyal and good, were wicked both at heart and in deed, and cruel throughout their lives." Specifically, Yen Sung and his son, Yen Shih-fan 嚴世蕃 (T. 求德, H. 東樓, 1513-April 24, 1565), were singled out as both wicked and insatiably greedy. There are many reasons for this; yet a closer examination of contemporary writings shows why Yen and his son have been represented in such a bad light.

First, the Veritable Record of Shih-tsung (Chu Hou-ts'ung, *q.v.*) was compiled under the editorship of Yen's political foes; hence information about Yen and his son was both censored and twisted. Second, Yen's biography in the *Ming-shih* is almost entirely based on the writing of Wang Shih-chen (*q.v.*), whose father's death is said to have been caused by Yen Sung. Third, the rivalries among the grand secretaries often generated heated factional strife, which resulted in a number of memorials to the throne recommending impeachment. Yen, of course, suffered from these developments. Fourth, the grand secretaries, especially the chief grand secretaries, during the Chia-ching reign, came to assume greater authority than before and tended to encroach upon the prerogatives of the six ministries. This situation brought upon the chief grand secretary the wrath of many officials who wanted to maintain the traditional administrative system wherein the ascendancy of various ministries remained intact. Fifth, the reigning emperor, especially during his later years, became so absorbed in his selfish search for such Taoistic favors as health and longevity that he came gradually to rely for the conduct of public business on the chief grand secretary. In the eyes of officials and common people, Yen illegally assumed imperial prerogatives. The emperor, on the other hand, knew well how to preserve his power and very often, by playing one grand secretary against the other, made sure that his ministries would look to him for the delegation of authority. On top of all these, Yen Sung and his son could not resist the temptation of securing their political power by planting their followers in important official positions and at the same time by excluding or getting rid of those who were unfriendly and critical. Last, Yen, and especially his son, could not rise above the practice of the time—accepting presents and feathering their own nests through the use of their influential positions. This naturally provided strong ammunition for their foes.

It is not fair to say, as do the critics, that Yen Sung had no competence for the grand secretaryship but obtained and held it because of his obsequiousness. No doubt he won the monarch's trust because he complied on many an occasion with the whims and fancies of the strong-willed sovereign. When the emperor wanted very much to honor his own father by placing him on an equal footing with the previous dynastic rulers and by conferring on him a posthumous imperial reign title (*Ta-li i*; *see* Feng Hsi), Yen

after offering token resistance knuckled under. Yen also pleased the emperor greatly by announcing the appearance of propitious clouds (慶雲), a token of heavenly blessing, and personally wrote a congratulatory rhyming essay for the occasion. The emperor selected him and several others to escort him on a tour to the Ch'eng-t'ien 承天 prefecture, Hukuang (the emperor's former princedom)—a sign of imperial favor. As time went by the emperor became dissatisfied with the chief grand secretary, Hsia Yen, who in various minor matters antagonized him. Very soon a rivalry developed between Hsia and Yen, resulting in the dismissal of the former (1542).

In his years in high office, Yen served the emperor loyally, diligently, and circumspectly. Knowing that the latter was deeply interested in Taoistic arts and practices, he spared no effort in the composition of the Taoist offering-prayers (青詞), and recommended to the emperor some people who had knowledge of Taoist health techniques. Even his critics admitted that Yen often worked hard in his palace office, not even returning to his private quarters for needed rest, and that Yen won the emperor's trust through his tactfulness and astuteness. Although he was in his sixties, he was as active and energetic as a man in his prime. The emperor was so pleased that he permitted Yen to be released from ministerial duties and conferred on him a silver seal bearing an inscription which read "loyal, diligent, sagacious, and wise," and not long afterwards the honorary title of grand tutor to the heir apparent. After the departure (September 14, 1544) of Grand Secretary Chai Luan 翟鑾 (T. 仲鳴, H. 石門, 1477-November 16, 1546, cs 1505, Pth. 文懿), which Yen engineered, he became the chief grand secretary, assuming all responsibilities of the Grand Secretariat.

Yen, however, was not secure in the new position. Feeling that Yen had assumed too much power, the emperor

(October 22, 1545) summoned Hsia back to his old post. The rivalry revived at once. In his capacity as chief grand secretary Hsia began to act overbearingly toward Yen and even dismissed some of Yen's men from office. For fear that Hsia might make trouble for his son, Yen Shih-fan, who as vice minister of the seal office acted somewhat arrogantly towards the high-ranking officials, Yen took his son to see Hsia and they knelt before him begging his forgiveness. To avoid trouble, Yen sent his son home on the pretext that he was needed to tend the ancestral graves. Knowing that Hsia had antagonized Marquis Ts'ui Yüan 崔元 (T. 懋仁, H. 岱屏, Pth. 榮恭, 1478-1549), Commander Lu Ping, and Marquis Ch'iu Luan (*qq.v.*), all of whom were the emperor's favorites at the time, Yen conspired with them for Hsia's downfall. When they sensed that Hsia had fallen into disfavor, Yen and his plotters seized upon the issue of recovering the Ordos region in the great bend of the Yellow River, an issue strongly advocated by Hsia and Tseng Hsien (*q.v.*), and succeeded in bringing about their dismissal and execution (October 31, 1548). With Hsia out of the way, Yen again became the chief grand secretary and the sole power in the cabinet.

The *Ming-shih* is responsible for the generalization that for almost twenty years Yen was the most influential man in the government. Both before and after Hsia left the scene, several other favorites of the emperor played their parts in the deliberation of state affairs. Besides Ts'ui Yüan, Lu Ping, and Ch'iu Luan, mentioned above, there were such people as Duke Kuo Hsün (*q.v.*), Duke Chu Hsi-chung 朱希忠 (T. 貞卿, Pth. 恭靖, 1516-72), and the Taoist practitioner T'ao Chung-wen (*q.v.*) to whom he turned for counsel. It is a fact, nonetheless, that for a number of years Yen seems to have played the leading role, since the emperor trusted him and let the court take care of itself after 1539.

On the whole Yen discharged his duties ably, considering the circumstances at that time. Even one of his bitter critics had to concede his diligence and devotion in high office. He also deported himself with humility. When scholars and officials came to see him he always had kind words for everyone and tried his best to please them. Besides, he was ably assisted by his son, Yen Shih-fan, who also enlisted a number of men of talent. Neither the father nor the son could be charged with excluding able men from government, for they did recruit many. Yet, since there was always rivalry among high ranking officials, Yen and his son, in order to secure their own position, undeniably were hostile to those who refused to become subservient to them.

Unlike his father, who was thin and lean and possessed of a stentorian voice, Yen Shih-fan was short-necked, corpulent, and blind in one eye. Lacking any pretense to scholarship he did nevertheless develop competence in office and in the course of time, as his father advanced in age, the latter relied on him more and more. No one but the son could make out the written instructions of the emperor and no one could fathom the imperial mind so well. Naturally Yen Shih-fan came to be consulted at all times on matters important or trivial. He received his first official appointment through the yin (廕) privilege. Then he became a vice minister of the seal office, later promoted first to chief minister of the Court of Imperial Sacrifices, and then to junior vice minister of Works, with concurrent duties in the seal office. Even his hostile critics conceded that Yen Shih-fan was versed in the history of the dynasty, knew current issues thoroughly, had a retentive memory, and was conversant with the administration, economy, and strategic significance of both the central government and the provinces. According to the same sources, however, there was another side to Yen Shih-fan's personality. He was boastful, saying that throughout the empire, only two men, Lu Ping and Yang Po (*q.v.*), were his equals in ability. He enjoyed high life and developed an insatiable appetite for antiques and paintings. Worst of all, he engaged in corrupt practices. In the years when Yen Sung was most influential, he and his son were often charged with selling official positions. They controlled the government to such an extent that the director of the bureau of appointments (ministry of Personnel) and the director of the bureau of operations (ministry of War) were called by the critics Yen's kuan-chia 管家(household stewards).

It happens that the period of time during which Yen Sung was most influential, *i.e.*, from 1548 to 1558, was also a time when Ming China was rocked by both the Mongol incursions in the northwest and *wo-k'ou* (or Japanese pirates) in the southeast. These occurred when the Chinese, inured to a long period of peace, neglected both land frontier and coastal defenses. For the early reverses on both fronts Yen Sung naturally was blamed. For instance, when the Mongol tribes under Altan qaγan (*q.v.*) raided the metropolitan area and demanded the establishment of tribute-trade relations, the exposure of gross neglect of frontier defenses led many critics to censure Yen for his corrupt management of governmental affairs. The emperor was infuriated and demanded the heads of those who had been responsible for military operations in the region. The then minister of War, Ting Ju-k'uei 丁汝夔 (T. 大章, cs 1521, d. October 6, 1550), became a victim of imperial wrath. Yen's critics, however, ascribed his execution to treachery on Yen's part, saying that it was the latter who had advised Ting not to risk a fight with Altan Qaγan near the capital in order to cover up Yen's failure to give adequate attention to the nation's frontier defenses in the north. Again Yen was criticized for his part in failing to provide against piratical raids on the coast. Upon Yen's recommendation, one of his able protégés, Chao Wen-hua (*q. v.*), was dispatched to the southeastern provinces to tackle the piracy problem when it became a serious menace. Chao in his turn recommended such able men as Hu Tsunghsien and T'ang Shun-chih (*qq. v.*). When these people ordered the raising of revenue locally for the support of troops, they stirred many to accuse them of pocketing large sums of money for themselves and for Yen and his son. The emperor, angered by the ineptitude and inefficiency of some of the military commanders, ordered the execution of certain ones such as Chang Ching (*q.v.*) and Li T'ien-ch'ung (*see* Hu Tsung-hsien). Here too his critics held Yen responsible. Actually it was Yen's junior colleague, Grand Secretary Hsü Chieh (*q.v.*), who recommended that the officers be held to account. Despite the fact that both situations came under control during the remainder of Yen's tenure as chief grand secretary, not a single word of commendation appears in traditional historical writings.

Yen is also one of the most denounced political figures in the *Ming-shih*. What is more, quite a number of the accusers came to public notice just because of their intrepid stand against Yen. As early as the time when he served as minister of Rites at Nanking, they charged him with taking bribes. Later when his star was in the ascendant, he incurred more criticism. Since he had already won the emperor's trust, almost all of his accusers suffered for their hardihood; they were demoted, cashiered, exiled, or deprived of their official status; a few were even sentenced to capital punishment. The main accusations made against Yen and his son may be summarized briefly as follows: Yen's usurpation of imperial power, his encroachment on the prerogatives of the ministries, his and his son's sale of official appointments, his efforts to gag official critics, his responsibility for the death of a number of good people, and his indulgence of his son's highhanded actions. In view of the circumstances, it is apparent that some accusers were motivated by political rivalries, some by the concern for the deterioration of the traditional political structure, and some by the corrupt practices of Yen Shih-fan. There is no doubt at all that the latter, able as he was, went too far, and was thus highly vulnerable. On the other hand, the political foes of father and son resorted to any means whatever to bring about their downfall and a number of the denunciations were so motivated. Nonetheless the Yen unquestionably brought hatred upon themselves. They were responsible for the deaths of both Yang Chi-sheng and Shen Lien (*qq.v.*) who, in their memorials and attacks, demanded the end of the entire Yen faction. The Yen, thus goaded, took extreme measures.

As time went on, Yen Sung gradually lost the emperor's favor and found a formidable rival in his junior colleague, Hsü Chieh. Yen Shih-fan did nothing to help, for he antagonized ever more people, even his former ally Lu Ping. On one occasion, three of Hsü's supporters savagely attacked Yen in their memorials in an attempt to oust him from his influential position. Even though they failed and were punished, the emperor could not help but entertain doubts about his onetime favorite. Yen tried his best to incriminate Hsü, but to no avail.

Then in 1561 Yen's wife died. At Yen's request, the son was permitted to stay in the capital to take care of his father, instead of accompanying the coffin back to his native district. As he was observing mourning for his mother, however, he was not permitted to enter the palace to help his father. Left alone in the palace office, the octogenerian was often at a loss over what to do with the emperor's instructions and failed to satisfy him. Even Yen's Taoist offering-prayers, now ghost-written by his aides, no longer pleased the emperor.

About this time, fire broke out in the palace and destroyed the emperor's living quarters. Yen suggested that the monarch temporarily stay in the imperial lodge where the former emperor Chu Ch'i-chen

(*q.v.*) had once lived during his younger brother's reign. Being highly superstitious, the emperor was not pleased at all. He wanted to rebuild the burned palace. Yen did not approve, maintaining that the cost would be too high. Hsü Chieh, however, devised a scheme for rebuilding it reasonably. This delighted the emperor. From then on he consulted Hsü on almost everything and trusted Yen only with sacrificial matters. Yen now began to sense the insecurity of his position and hoped that his junior colleague would not turn against him.

At this time too the emperor had come under the influence of a Taoist adept, Lan Tao-hang 藍道行 (d. 1562), who boasted that he had the power to invoke the gods through the planchette. Lan was hostile to the Yen and in his planchette messages urged the emperor to get rid of both. The emperor hesitated. Learning of this suggestion through some eunuch connection, Censor Tsou Ying-lung (*see* Lin Jun) dispatched a memorial to the throne attacking them, especially the son, Yen Shih-fan. As a result, Yen Sung was dismissed from office (1562) and ordered back to his native district via the official postal service, with the understanding that he be annually supplied with a hundred piculs of rice by the authorities. Yen Shih-fan, however, was placed under investigation. After trial he was found guilty of the charge of corruption and, together with his two sons, Yen Ku 鵠 and Yen Hung 鴻, and his confidant, Lo Lung-wen 羅龍文 (H. 小華 道人), was sentenced to a term of banishment on the remote frontier. His servant, Yen Nien 嚴年, known among the literate as Master O-shan 鄂山先生, was also imprisoned for the part he played in soliciting bribes. Still taking pity on Yen Sung for his long and loyal service, the emperor decreed a special pardon for Yen Hung, making him a commoner so that he might take care of his grandfather.

Knowing that the emperor still had some feeling of compassion for Yen Sung, his opponents made further efforts to eradicate his influence so as to protect themselves. Unfortunately for Yen, his son provided them with a good pretext. Yen Shih-fan, instead of going to Lei-chou 雷州, Kwangtung, his place of exile, secretly returned to his native district. Rather than stay quietly at home, he attracted attention by putting up more buildings on his own estate and hiring additional domestic servants for the protection of the family property. Under the leadership of Hsü Chieh, Yen's rivals seized upon this opportunity to charge Yen Shih-fan, Lo Lung-wen (a relative of the notorious deceased pirate leader, Wang Chih 王直, *q.v.*), and others (falsely as it happened) with attempting to connive with the Japanese pirates. Probably as a result of this charge, a story accusing Yen Shih-fan of collusion with the pirates appeared, and found its way into the collection entitled *Ku-chin hsiao-shuo*, edited by Feng Meng-lung (*q.v.*) and published in 1621. Yen Shih-fan and Lo were executed and their properties confiscated. Yen Sung and his grandsons were all degraded to the status of commoner. From then on Yen's name became taboo among the officials; he was shunned by all others, and all his friends and supporters in the government were either cashiered or degraded. At the age of eighty-five, Yen died in a graveyard shelter and did not even have a decent burial.

Yen Sung wrote the *Ch'ien-shan-t'ang chi* 鈐山堂集 (35 *ch.*). Although the editors of the *Ssu-k'u* catalogue praised it for the elegance of its composition, they refused to give the work a place in the Imperial Library on the ground that the author had misused his political power. He also was responsible for the *Nan-kung tsou-i* 南宮奏議 (30 *ch.*) and the *Li-kuan piao-tsou* 歷官表奏 (15 *ch.*) which contain his memorials presented during the years 1537 to 1542 and 1527 to 1554, respectively. The Library of Congress has a copy of the first collection and Seikadō a copy of the second. Other memorials of his

are included in the *Chia-ching tsou-tui lu* 奏對錄 (13 *ch.*), a copy of which is among the rare books of the Peiping Library. An abridged version of the *Nan-kung tsou-i*, entitled *Nan-kung shu-lüeh* 疏略 (8 *ch.*) printed in 1547, is listed in the rare book catalogue of the National Central Library, Taipei. Yen Sung's poetry is preserved in the *Nan huan kao* 南還稿, a copy being available in microfilm. An interesting example of Yen's calligraphy may be noted on a stone tablet which stands (or used to stand) in the courtyard of a monastery west of Peking, known as the Chi-lo ssu 極樂寺; it extols the beauty of the shrine and of its setting.

One of the accusations brought against Yen and his son was the inordinate tribute they exacted for favors. The booty they amassed was all confiscated on their dismissal from office; a list of these treasures appears in *T'ien-shui ping-shan lu* 天水冰山錄, printed in the *Chih-pu-tsu-chai ts'ung-shu* (*see* Pao T'ing-po, ECCP) and in later collections. It is possible, of course, that the list was exaggerated by their enemies.

Bibliography

1/308/10a; 3/286/15a; 5/16/44a; MSL (1965), Shih-tsung, *chüan* 87–509; Yen Sung, *Nan huan kao* (NLP microfilm); Cha Chi-tso (ECCP), *Tsui-wei lu*, ts'e 55/*ch.* 30; Ch'en Tzu-lung (ECCP), *Huang Ming ching-shih wen pien*; Chu Kuo-chen (ECCP), *Huang Ming ta-shih chi*, 36; id., *Yung-ch'uang hsiao-p'in* 9; Hsia Hsieh 夏燮 (fl. 1862), *Ming t'ung-chien* 明通鑑; Hsü Chieh, *Shih-ching-t'ang chi*; Hsü Hsüeh-mu, *Shih-miao chih-yü lu*; Ku Ying-t'ai (ECCP), *Ming-ch'ao chi-shih pen-mo*, 50; *Yün-chien tsa-chih* 雲間雜誌, 1/1b, 3/11b; Sun Ch'eng-tse (ECCP), *Ch'un-ming meng-yü lu*; T'an Hsi-ssu, *Ming ta-cheng tsuan-yao*, 51; Wang Shih-chen, *Yen-chou shih-liao*, part 2, 9; id., *Yen-shan-t'ang pieh-chi*, 45; *Huang Ming yung-hua lei-pien* 皇明泳化類編, 62/7a; Ch'ien Ch'ien-i (ECCP), *Lieh-ch'ao shih-chi* (1652), 丁11/1b; SK (1930), 176/5a; W. Franke, *Sources*, 5.5.36.

Kwan-wai So

YI Hon 李琿, also known as Kwanghaegun 光海君, November 23, 1575-August 7, 1641, was the fifteenth king of the Yi dynasty in Korea, reigning from March 17, 1608, until his dethronement on April 12, 1623. The second son of King Yi Yŏn 李昖 (temple name: Sŏnjo 宣祖, 1552–1608) by a concubine, Kongbin 恭嬪 (née Kim 金, d. 1577), Yi Hon is described as an eager pupil and diligent in his Chinese studies. In June, 1592, on the approach of the Japanese invaders to Seoul, he was named crown prince and charged with leading a separate court to conduct the war while the king escaped north to the border. In Korean society of the Yi dynasty a concubine ranked as low as a slave, and the son of a concubine was stigmatized as sŏŏl 庶孽 (illegitimate). In the order of succession, when a queen had no son the throne went to the eldest surviving son by a concubine. In this emergency Yi Hon was chosen over his elder brother, Yi Chin 津 (1574–1609), also known by his title Imhaegun 臨海君, who had acquired an unsavory reputation for both his conduct and his lack of interest in study.

During the war, which lasted from 1592 to 1598, Yi Hon performed his duties well. Several times the king announced his intention to abdicate in his favor, but each time he was persuaded by the court to continue to reign. Yi Hon and his branch court moved from one place to another in the northern provinces, encouraging the enlistment of volunteer soldiers by the local gentry while supervising the supplies to the Chinese troops who came to fight the Japanese. After the king returned to Seoul late in 1593, Yi Hon stayed outside the capital in the southern provinces for two more years. While Chinese commanders were defending Korea in the field, the crown prince's presence there allayed any criticism.

In time, however, Yi Hon found his position as crown prince threatened because in 1602 his father remarried and his second queen gave birth in April, 1606, to a son, Yi Ŭi 李㼁 (d. 1614), better known by his title, Yŏngch'ang taegun 永昌大君. Since, according to the rigid cus-tom of the Korean aristocracy, no son by a concubine could inherit his father's rank and perquisites when there was a son by the legitimate wife, the faction at court which did not favor Yi Hon supported Yŏngch'ang taegun as legally the sole claimant to the throne. Taegun as a title was reserved for the son of a queen, while the son of a concubine could receive only the title "kun" (often pronounced "gun" in combinations). In this instance, however, the king could not very well demote a crown prince of fourteen years' standing in favor of an infant. Yet there was always the question in many people's minds as to whether in time Yi Hon would be replaced, especially because his status as crown prince, although reported to the Chinese court from the beginning in 1592, had never been formally confirmed by the Chinese emperor. When the king was on his deathbed, he sent one message to the crown prince and another to seven officials related to the royal family entreating them to look after the infant prince with love and to protect him from harm. In this way, amid an atmosphere of doubt and suspicion, Yi Hon ascended the throne. He came to it obviously with apprehension, surrounding his palace with troops whom he kept on guard long after he had had his brother, Yi Chin, arrested and exiled on the charge of plotting a military uprising. An investigation by envoys sent from China ruled in his favor, and this resulted in his confirmation as king of Korea, but he never felt secure in his position. Every report of a treasonous plot was investigated exhaustively. In some serious cases Yi Hon personally conducted trials at the court, employing various tortures which either forced confessions warranting execution or resulted in death from maltreatment.

In 1613, during the trial of one treason case, a prisoner declared that the plot was instigated by the family of the dowager queen in favor of her son, Yi Ŭi. Yi Hon took the opportunity to have the dowager queen deposed and confined, the prince imprisoned on Kanghwa Island where he died of starvation in March, 1614, and the rest of her family exterminated.

In the fifteen years of his reign, however, Yi Hon was able to do much towards the reconstruction of the country in the wake of Japanese occupation and war. Seoul he restored during the years 1611 to 1616 to a state of royal grandeur. In 1610 and later he instituted population and labor-service registration, reformed the taxation system, enshrined certain fifteenth- and sixteenth-century Korean scholars of the Confucian tradition as sages, and saw to the reprinting of a number of Korean compilations (encyclopedic, historical, geographical, poetic, biographical, and educational), among them the important *Koryŏ sa* 高麗史, 139 *kwŏn*, and Chinese classics with translation into Korean vernacular. He ordered too the importation and reprinting of various books from China: six of the dynastic histories which were of special interest to Korean scholars, the literary collection *T'ai-p'ing yü-lan*, and a work containing the memorials of noted ministers throughout the past, *Li-tai ming-ch'en tsou-i* (*see* Yang Shih-ch'i). Under his sponsorship there appeared (1610) the compilation of an encyclopedia, *Tong'ŭi pogam* 東醫寶鑑, in 25 *kwŏn*. [Editors' note: The time of printing of the brass movable type edition of *Samguk sagi* 三國史記 has never been definitely ascertained. It is devoid of any preface or colophons and lacks any other clue to its identification. The suggestion that its typography shows similarity to that of the *Hyŏnjong sillok* 顯宗 實錄 seems inconclusive. Another theory may be advanced for consideration: that the book was printed with a new font at the end of Yi Hon's reign, immediately before the *coup d'état* of 1623 and the succession of Yi Chong (*see* Ch'en Chien) to the throne, and that the prefaces or colophons by Yi Hon were destroyed; this was the case with the *Tongguk sinsok samgang haengsil* 東國新續三綱行實, engraved between 1614 and early in 1616, which

may have been secretly saved by someone who treasured its excellent woodcuts. This conjecture about the *Samguk sagi* is proffered here with the hope that it may induce some interest and discussion.]

In foreign affairs his main concern was the growing menace of the Manchus, known as Chin or Later Chin (*see* Nurhaci, ECCP). Having every desire to remain aloof from the conflict of the two giants, Ming China and the Chin, he was forced to proceed with the utmost caution, to keep from irritating Nurhaci by his maintenance of friendly relations with China, and to persuade Peking that he could give no more than token aid in view of the debilitating results of the war with Japan. His policy of virtual neutrality had many antagonists at his court who felt that the country owed its existence to the help of the Chinese two decades earlier; yet Yi Hon, overriding the opposition, strengthened the armies on the border, accumulated food supplies, and worked for the improvement and increase of explosive weapons. In 1618, pressed by both the Chinese court and his own advisers, he sent a force of ten thousand men to aid the former in its defensive war, but the result was a disaster. The Korean general surrendered to Nurhaci without a fight. Yi Hon followed up this loss by placating Nurhaci with supplies, and trying to ward off Chinese accusations with excuses. At the end of 1621 a Chinese officer, Mao Wen-lung (ECCP), crossed the Korean border to harass the Chin army's rear (which he continued to do until 1627), and the following year another Chinese, Liang Chih-yüan 梁之垣 (cs 1607, a native of Teng-chou 登州, Shantung), came by sea to demand supplies of food, firearms, and military support. These involvements led inevitably to Manchu penetration of the peninsula (1627 and 1636), fighting on Korean soil, and eventual subjugation.

In the meanwhile a palace revolution brought an end to Yi's career as king, and his exile to islands off the coast. It was probably during his reign that tobacco was introduced from Japan.

Bibliography

Kwanghaegun ilgi 日記, *Chosŏn wangjo sillok* 朝鮮王朝實錄, *Vols.* 26–33; Hong Hŭi 洪熹, "Heishu Kōkaikun ron" 廢主光海君論, *Seikyū gakusō* 青丘學叢, Vol. 20 (1935); Yi Pyŏngdo 李丙燾, "Kwanghaegun ŭi tae Hugŭm chŏngch'aek" 光海君의對後金政策 (*Kuksasang ŭi che munje* 國史上의諸問題), Vol. 1 (1959); Inaba Iwakichi 稻葉岩吉, *Kōkaikun jidai no Mansen kankei* 光海君時代の滿鮮關係, 1933.

Hŏ Sŏndo, Cha Chuwhan,
and Chaoying Fang

YI Pang-wŏn 李芳遠 (T. 遺德), June 13, 1367–May 30, 1422, born in Hamhŭng 咸興, was the fifth son of Yi Sŏng-gye (*q. v.*). In 1382 he took the *chinsa* 進士 degree, and in the following year passed the final civil service examination (文科). He then received the office of milchiksa taeŏn 密直司代言 (senior 3d rank) in the Koryŏ court. After his father had staged the *coup d'état* of 1388 and had marched back from Wihwa Island, he worked zealously for his father's cause, helping to consolidate the power of the Yi family.

He was a farsighted strategist, and it was he who persuaded his father to eliminate the major opposition to the Yi party at court, Chŏng Mong-ju (*see* Yi Sŏng-gye). On his way to receive the returning heir apparent of Koryŏ, Wang Sŏk 王奭, at Hwangju 黃州, Yi Sŏng-gye held a hunt at Haeju 海州. His horse slipped and he fell, hurting himself (April 9, 1392). Chŏng Mong-ju, taking advantage of Yi's injury, planned to crush his party. Before Chŏng could carry out his plan, however, Yi Pang-wŏn and his henchmen murdered Chŏng, who was returning home after a sick call on Yi. Like Li Shih-min (599–649), to whom Yi Pang-wŏn is often compared, he played an important and decisive role in placing his father on the throne.

Despite his services, not he, but his half-brother Yi Pang-sŏk 碩, the eighth and youngest son of Yi Sŏng-gye, born to Yi Pang-wŏn's stepmother, née Kang 康 (Queen Sindŏk 神德王后, d. September 15,1396), became heir apparent (September 7, 1392). [Editors' note: This naming of the youngest son as heir is undoubtedly the practice of ultimogeniture, which the Manchus are known to have followed in the 15th to 17th centuries. The ancestors of the Manchu imperial house were Jurchen tribal chieftains who, in the late 14th and early 15th centuries, lived on the Tumen River. It seems that Yi Sŏng-gye's father and other ancestors had lived in that area too. This common practice of ultimogeniture may suggest the possibility that the Yi family was closely related to the Jurchen. (*See* Fang, Chao-ying, "Ch'ing-ch'u man-chou chia-t'ing-li ti fen-chia-tzu ho wei-fen-chia-tzu" 清初滿洲家庭裏的分家子和未分家子, *Kuo-li Peiching ta-hsüeh wu-shih chou-nien chi-nien lun-wen chi* 國立北京大學五十周年紀念論文集, 1948.)] Under the false pretext that Chŏng To-jŏn (*q.v.*) and Nam Ŭn 南誾 plotted with the heir apparent to harm other princes, he initiated a coup on the night of October 6, 1398, killed Chŏng and Nam, and had Yi Pang-bŏn 蕃 and Yi Pang-sŏk slain on their way to exile. Thus he eliminated his half-brothers and cleared the way for his own rise. The court proposed that Yi Pang-wŏn be named heir apparent, but he refused in order to incur no suspicion, and instead had his second brother Yi Pang-gwa (*see* Yi Sŏng-gye) declared heir apparent. It was only after the second princely feud over succession that he accepted the nomination. Yi Pang-gan 幹, the fourth son of Yi Sŏng-gye, was persuaded to take arms against his younger brother, Yi Pang-wŏn (February 22, 1400). But Yi Pang-gan lost and was banished to Tosan 兎山. On February 25, with his father's approval, Yi Pang-wŏn finally became heir apparent. His brother, knowing Yi

Pang-wŏn's prestige and ambition, abdicated in his favor. Thereupon the latter ascended the throne on November 28 at Such'ang Palace in Kaesŏng.

During eighteen years of reign, Yi Pang-wŏn not only established the political structure of the Yi dynasty, but also consolidated and secured the throne for his descendants. The capital was moved again in 1399 to Kaesŏng, but the king finally decided on Hansŏng 漢城 as his capital. With this return to Hansŏng in 1405, it became the political and cultural center of Korea. New palaces and pavilions were constructed and civilian houses roofed with tiles. The government improved the sewage system (completed in 1412), built arcades (行廊) on both sides of the streets to be used as markets, and constructed a wall in between for fire prevention.

With the disbanding of private soldiers (May, 1400), the government effected the centralization of military power. The king also clearly defined the nature and function of the State Council (議政府) and Six Boards, and improved the local administration system by establishing two new provinces, Yŏnggil 永吉 in the northeast and Pyongyang in the northwest. The bureau of royal household administration (敦寧府) was established in 1414 to guarantee the rights of the royal family and its members. In the capital, five (later reduced to four) colleges were established (1411), and the palace examination system was initiated (1414). A large drum called the sinmun'go 申聞鼓 was placed in the palace gate (1402) so that anyone who had grievances might appeal directly to the throne. Yi ordered the printing of paper money (1401) and (1403) the casting of new copper type, known as kyemi 癸未.

Yi Pang-wŏn was an ardent believer in Confucianism and worked to promote it. During 1406-7 land owned by monasteries and temples was confiscated to be used as a military fund, and the number of slaves belonging to the temples was drastically reduced, and they were turned over to public offices. He abhorred anything that was unorthodox from the Confucian viewpoint. He frowned on the observance of praying for rain. He personally examined the contents of songs to be included in the bureau of music and rejected those based on popular tradition. For instance, the monggŭmch'ŏk 夢金尺 and suborok 受寶籙, composed by Chŏng To-jŏn in 1392 to praise the auspicious omens foretelling the rise of Yi Sŏng-gye, were assigned a subordinate place because of their fantastic content. When Ha Yun (see Yi Sŏng-gye) presented two poems in March, 1412, one was rejected for the same reason. Further, in January, 1419, he based his dislike for another song, the Hujŏn chinjak 後殿眞勺, on similar grounds. In 1417 he ordered the books on divination and geomancy in the bureau of astronomy (sŏungwan 書雲觀) burned, and he confiscated similar books owned by the people. He was also persuaded by a group of rigid Confucianists to introduce the concept of subjugation of women, especially prohibition of their remarriage and prohibition of the sons of remarried women from entering the civil service.

Yi Pang-wŏn was, however, not altogether anti-Buddhist. His measures against the religion were chiefly political and economic; personally he was sympathetic to this faith, and often overtly encouraged its activities. The first reason for his sympathy was, according to some historians, his father's illness and subsequent death. When Yi Sŏng-gye was ill from early in 1408, Yi Pang-wŏn brought monks to the palace, prayed for the recovery of his father, and offered his royal robe to the Buddhist god of medicine. Upon his death, the funeral was according to the *Chu-tzu chia-li* 朱子家禮, but Buddhist masses were also held to pray for the repose of the dead. Yi Pang-wŏn had reasons for this move. He hoped to atone for his crimes and obtain forgiveness from his deceased father, who had been alarmed by his son's cruelty and thirst for power. In June, 1413, when his consort, Queen Wŏn'gyŏng 元敬王后 (July 28, 1365-August 18, 1420), had become seriously ill, he appealed to the power of the same god of medicine. In April of that year he ordered the Haein monastery 海印寺 to run off another copy of the *Tripiṭaka* (the blocks for which had been cut during the years 1236-51). In the same year he granted rice and beans to temples. He also allowed construction and repair of temples and pagodas.

Another reason for his change in attitude was ascribed to the influence of the Ming court and its envoy. The preference for Buddhism of Chu Ti (*q.v.*) was well manifested by his demands: collection of copper Buddha images, Śarīra and paper for the printing of the *Tripiṭaka*. His envoy to Korea, Huang Yen 黃儼, was a fanatical Buddhist. Huang, officer in the directorate of ceremonial and a senior eunuch, was a menace in the Korean capital, and is described by the annalist as "rude, impolite, arrogant, and corrupt." He went there first in 1403 and wished to make an excursion to the famed Kŭmgang san 金鋼山 (Diamond Mountains). Asked for the reason, Huang replied that "it was because the shape of the mountains resembled that of a Buddha image." In 1406 he carried away three copper images of Buddha, preserved in the P'ophua monastery 法華寺 on Cheju 濟州 (Quelpart) Island; and in 1407, 800 Śarīra and another image of Avalokiteśvara from the Kwangni 廣利 monastery in Kaesŏng. He arrived in the capital again in September, 1411, and requested ten thousand sheets of paper for the publication of the *Tripiṭaka*. Sensing Chu Ti's feeling for Buddhism, the Korean court did not wish to appear anti-Buddhist, at least while a Ming envoy was on Korean soil.

Yi Pang-wŏn's efforts for the improvement of Sino-Korean relations must be termed commendable. As early as 1394 he went to China to free Korea from false charges made by the first Ming emperor (his party leaving the capital in July and returning in December, 1394). His mission was successful, and the Liaotung border, hitherto closed to Korean envoys, was reopened. But soon after his enthronement, Chu Ti seized Nanking (July, 1402) and usurped the throne. Two months later he dispatched Yü Shih-chi 俞士吉 (T. 用貞, d. 1435), the assistant censor-in-chief, and informed Korea of his accession. Thereupon Yi Pang-wŏn sent Ha Yun to congratulate him and to request a new seal and investiture; both were granted in 1403.

Normally the tribute articles consisted of ginseng, mats, lacquerware, brushes, leopard and seal skins, and the like. The emperor's "gifts in reply" included silk, porcelain, medicine, books, musical instruments, and writing materials. The books granted included *Wen-hsien t'ung-k'ao* by Ma Tuan-lin (*ca.* 1223-1289), *Yüan-shih*, *Lieh-nü chuan*, attributed to Liu Hsiang (77-6 B.C.), *T'ung-chien kang-mu*, by Chu Hsi and his disciples, *Jen-hsiao huang-hou ch'üan-shan shu* (*see* Empress Hsü), and *Hsiao-tz'u huang-hou chuan* (biography of Empress Ma). Among the items of annual tribute, the heaviest burden on Korea until 1429 was 150 ounces (liang) of gold and 700 of silver. In order to meet this demand, the court not only encouraged mining but also restricted the domestic use of these metals. In 1409 Sol Mi-su 偰眉壽 (d. 1415) and others were sent to request the substitution of local products. Chu Ti, however, insisted on conforming to the established practice, but finally in 1429 a successor, Emperor Chu Chan-chi (*q.v.*), permitted Korea to substitute oxen, horses, and cotton. Often Chu Ti's demands were unexpected and unreasonable, however. Sometimes, he would order the collection of copper images of Buddha (1406, 1407) and eunuchs and young prospective eunuchs (almost yearly from 1403 onward). His demand of 1408 was the most shocking [although he was in fact continuing a practice common under the Yüan]: he asked Korea to offer beautiful maidens.

Upon receiving this order, the court sent
out officials to the provinces to recruit
girls from thirteen to twenty-five *sui*.
Among the three hundred chosen, the
Ming envoy, again Huang Yen, personally
selected five. When they were forced to accompany the returning envoy, "the wailing
of their parents and relatives," writes the
historian, "overwhelmed the streets." In
1409 the same envoy returned to ask for
more maidens. This practice continued
until 1436, in the reign of Chu Ch'i-chen
(*q.v.*). Once in China, the Korean girls
either entered the imperial harem or
worked in the palace. In this connection
we should note that the mother of Chu
Ti is thought to have been a Korean.

On the other hand, Korean-Jurchen
relations were more complicated and event-
ful. After the fall of the Mongols Liaotung became the object of dispute among
the Chinese, the Koreans, and the Mongols. Ming influence in the area increased
after the surrender of Naɣaču (*q.v.*) in
1387, and extended from the south of
K'ai-yüan 開源 to the Liaotung plain, west
of the Yalu. Korea, too, used the divide-
and-rule policy. As a conciliatory measure
Jurchen chiefs were given titles, encouraged to enroll in the royal guards in the
capital, and to intermarry with Koreans.
They were also supplied with houses, servants, clothes, saddles, and food. In May,
1406, trade centers were established in
Kyŏngsŏng 鏡城 and Kyŏngwŏn 慶源, and
salt and iron were exchanged for Jurchen
oxen and horses.

Towards the end of the Koryŏ period
the court established the Kilchu 吉州 myriarchy in the Tumen River basin. The same
area was pacified and controlled by Yi
Sŏng-gye, and his father before him. They
had been raised in this region and had
genuine understanding of Jurchen manners and customs. The Uriyangqad 兀良哈
of the Mao-lien 毛憐 guard and the Odoli
斡朶里 of the Chien-chou 建州 left guard
were subservient to Yi Sŏng-gye before
and after his enthronement. In 1410,
however, the Wu-ti-ha 兀狄哈, together

with the Uriyangqad and Odoli, raided
Kyŏngwŏn with three hundred cavalry,
and the Korean military commander was
killed in action. Cho Yŏn 趙涓, the Ch'al-
lisa 察理使, mobilized the army in Kilchu,
crossed the Tumen, and utterly routed the
Uriyangqad and killed their chief. As the
Jurchen raids became more frequent and
the defense of the area became more difficult, the court transferred the tombs of Yi
An-sa (*see* Yi Sŏng-gye) and his wife, née
Yi, in Kongju 孔州 (modern Kyŏnghŭng
慶興) to Hamju 咸州 (modern Hamhŭng)
and the town of Kongju itself to Kyŏngsŏng. It was only during the reign of
King Yi Do 世宗 (May 7, 1397-March 30,
1450, r. 1419-50), successor of Yi Pang-
wŏn, that the court took a firm attitude
towards the northern problem. King Yi
Do and his able minister, Kim Chong-sŏ
金宗瑞 (d. October 31, 1453), developed
an offensive policy, advancing the line
farther north, beyond Punyŏng 富寧. In
1434 the king established the so-called six
garrisons 六鎭 there.

The southern bank of the lower reaches of the Yalu, the so-called northwest,
already belonged to Korea at the end of
the Koryŏ period. On the southern bank
of the upper reaches of the Yalu, the
northeast, the Kapchu 甲州 (modern Kap-
san 甲山) myriarchy was established in
1391, and by 1416 the area west of Kapchu came under Korean control. In the
time of King Yi Do, however, Jurchen
raids became frequent, and the Uriyangqad of the Chien-chou guard, with its
chief, Li Man-chu (*q.v.*), often plundered
Liaotung. Soldiers and citizens in Liaotung, both Chinese and Jurchen, sought
refuge in Korea, and by 1423 their number
reached over five hundred. When they
were returned to China, according to the
Ming order, the Jurchen bore Korea a
grudge. In January, 1434, Li Man-chu
with four hundred cavalry, raided the
southwest of Yŏyŏn 閭延 (modern Chasŏng
慈城 in north Pyongyang province). After
four months of preparation, the king
ordered the subjugation of the Jurchen.

An army of 15,500 men marched north and defeated them on the Po-chu 婆豬江 (T'ung-chia) River. The victory was reported to Peking on June 19, and to the royal ancestral temple on June 21, 1434. In 1437 Yi Ch'on 葳, the military commander of Pyongyang province, crossed the Yalu with eight thousand men and destroyed the enemy strongholds in Wu-la shan-ch'eng 兀剌山城 (also written 亏羅, 五老, and 五女) and Wu-mi fu 吾彌府 (modern Huai-jen-hsien). Later the king established the so-called four commanderies (四郡) along the Yalu.

On September 7, 1418, Yi Pang-wŏn abdicated in favor of his third son, Yi Do. Yi Pang-wŏn died four years later. He had twelve sons and seventeen daughters. In August, 1422, the board of Rites gave him the temple name T'aejong 太宗. He was buried in the Hŏnnŭng 獻陵, on September 21, west of Kwangju 廣州, and the spirit path stele, composed by Pyŏn Kye-ryang 卞季良 (1369-May 15, 1430), was erected in October. The Ming envoy arrived on May 24, 1423, to confer his posthumous name Kongjŏng 恭定.

The compilation of the veritable records of the king, T'aejong sillok 太宗實錄, was begun in March, 1424, by Yun Hoe 尹淮 (1380-March 29, 1436), Sin Saek 申穡, and Pyŏn Kye-ryang (upon his death, Hwang Hui 黃喜 [d. February 28, 1452]), and Maeng Sa-song 孟思誠 (d. 1438), and completed in April, 1431, in 36 chapters. It was revised in 1442.

Bibliography

Chŏng In-ji, et al., Yongbi ŏch'ŏn ka; Yun Hoe, et al., T'aejong sillok, 1/30b; No Sa-sin 盧思愼 and Yi Haeng 李荇, Sinjŭng Tongguk yŏji sŭngnam 新增東國輿地勝覽 (Kojŏn kanhaeng hoe ed., 1958), 6/14b; Yi Kŭng-ik 李肯翊, Yŏllyŏsil kisul 燃藜室記述 (1912-14 ed.), 1/70, 2/114; Yi Pin-sŭng 李斌承, Chosŏn T'aejo silgi 朝鮮太祖實紀 (1927), 62a; Han U-gŭn 韓沽劢, "Yŏmal Sŏnch'o ŭi pulgyo chŏngch'aek," Seoul taehakkyo nonmunjip 6 (1957), 1; Ikeuchi Hiroshi, "Sŏn-sho no tōhokukyo no Jurchen tono kankei," Mansen rekishi chiri kenkyū hōkoku 滿鮮歷史地理研究 報告, 2 (1916), 203, 4 (1918), 299, 5 (1918), 299, 7 (1920), 219; Yi In-yŏng 李仁榮, "Sŏnch'o Jurchen muyŏk ko," Chindan hakpo 震檀學報, 8 (1937), 1; Yi Sang-baek 李相佰, Hanguk munhwasa yŏn'gu non'go 韓國文化史研究論考 (1954), 76, 173, 251; id., Hanguk sa: kŭnse chŏn'gi p'yŏn 韓國史近世前期篇 (1962), 72, 107, 116.

Peter H. Lee

YI Sŏng-gye 李成桂 (later name Tan 旦, T. 仲潔, 君晋, H. 松軒), October 27, 1355-June 18, 1408, founder of the Yi dynasty, was born in Yŏnghŭng 永興, the second son of Yi Cha-ch'un 子春 (temple name 桓祖, October 27, 1335-June 23, 1361). Yi's family, originally of Chŏnju 全州, traced its origin to Yi Han 翰, who served the Silla dynasty as the master of Works (司空). Yi Sŏng-gye's great-great-grandfather, Yi An-sa 安社 (temple name: 穆祖, d. April 18, 1274), was said to be an 18th generation descendant of Yi Han. Yi An-sa moved from Chŏnju to Ŭiju 宜州 (modern Tŏgwŏn 德源) and served the Koryŏ dynasty as prefect of Chŏngju 定州. He then moved farther north to Odong 斡東 (10 miles east of modern Kyŏnghŭng 慶興), and became commander of five thousand households (五千戶達魯花赤) under the Yüan. His fourth son, Yi Haeng-ni 行里 (temple name: 翼祖), born in Tŏgwŏn, continued to serve the Mongols as a chiliarch. The latter's fourth son, Yi Ch'un 椿 (temple name: 度祖), was born in Hamhŭng 咸興 and died on August 25, 1342. The Koryŏ court granted him the posthumous title Ch'ansŏngsa 贊成事. The Koryŏ sa 高麗史 mentions Yi Cha-ch'un for the first time in 1355, when, as the chiliarch of Ssangsŏng 雙城, he arrived at the capital to pay homage to King Kongmin (see Kwŏn Kŭn). When the king, in order to free himself from the Mongol yoke and to regain the Korean territories in the north, ordered Yu In-u 柳仁雨 to attack the Mongol commissioner in Ssangsŏng, Yi Cha-ch'un followed the king's instructions and assisted Yu in his successful campaign (1356). Koryŏ then regained Ssangsŏng and the area north of Hamhŭng. Subsequently (1361) Yi Cha-ch'un was honored with several titles until he was made military commander of the northeastern region. Thus Yi Sŏng-gye's ancestors were Koryŏ nationals who served the Mongols in the northeast. Because of geographical proximity, they were in contact not only with the Mongols but also with the Jurchen tribes, and were familiar with their manners and customs. Yi was raised amid such surroundings, and is said to have excelled in equestrian archery from his boyhood.

The first Koryŏ office Yi Sŏng-gye held was that of the kimowi sangjanggun 金吾衛上將軍 (senior 3d rank) in 1361. In the same year, as the myriarch of the northeast, he subjugated the rebellious Pak Ŭi 朴儀, and in December repulsed the Red Turbans. When the latter occupied the capital (1362) Yi, together with other officers, recaptured it. During this campaign, he and his men are said to have slain one hundred thousand rebels. In August he annihilated the forces of Naɤačư (q. v.) in Hamhŭng. Two years later Ch'oe Yu 崔濡, a Koryŏ traitor who fled to the Mongols, crossed the Yalu with ten thousand men and devastated the north. Yi, together with Ch'oe Yŏng 瑩, first defeated them in the northwest and then turning his troops to the northeast regained the lost territory. For this distinguished service he was awarded the rank of milchik pusa 密直副使 (senior 3d rank) and granted certain laudatory epithets (March 5, 1364). On January 7, 1370, he was promoted to general of the northeast region and chi munhasŏng sa 知門下省事 (junior 2d rank). In the same month Yi, with five thousand cavalry and ten thousand infantry, marched north to destroy the Tongnyŏng pu 東寧府 and sever relations with the Northern Yüan. His troops went deep into enemy territory, up to the right bank of the T'ung-chia River 佟家江, and captured the enemy stronghold there. As a consequence of these campaigns,

his name became dreaded by Mongol and Jurchen alike.

His military skill was equally manifested in his campaigns against the Japanese pirates in the south. The coastal raids of these corsairs, which began in 1223, became more frequent and disastrous from the time of Sin U 辛禑 (r. 1365–1375, 1388–d. 1389). On August 13, 1371, when the Japanese pillaged the area along the Yesŏng River 禮成江, he, as the regional commander of the Western River, defeated them. On July 24, 1372, King Kongmin named him the hwanyŏng puyun 和寧府尹, and ordered him as general of the army to attack the pirates. Yi drove them out on July 26, 1377, from Kyŏng-sang province 慶尙道, and in June annihilated them below Mt. Chii 智異山; in the following months he subdued others at various ports and towns. During May, 1378, Japanese ships arrived at Sŭngch'ŏn pu 昇天府 (modern Kaep'ung 開豐 in Kyŏnggi province 京畿道). General Ch'oe Yŏng was unable to stand against them until Yi came with his picked cavalry to wipe out those who had landed. The most famous campaign against the pirates was at Mt. Hwang 荒山 (1380). General Yi attacked them at Unbong 雲峯 (modern Namwŏn 南原 in north Chŏlla province 全羅北道), cornered them at Mt. Hwang and crushed them. He and his victorious army were welcomed at the Ch'ŏnsu monastery 天壽寺 (near modern Changdan 長湍) by court officials including General Ch'oe Yŏng. In August, 1382, he was nominated to be the regional commander of the northeast, and in September of the following year he fought a successful battle against a Jurchen chief on the plain of Kilchu 吉州. He was then appointed to other high offices. In October, 1385, for his subjugation of the Japanese pirates, he received more honors. In the beginning of 1388 he was promoted to be vice chancellor; his name and fame were now firmly established both at court and abroad.

Perhaps Yi's most dramatic decision

taken before his enthronement was his refusal to march north to drive out Ming garrisons in Liaotung. Instead, he withdrew from Wihwa Island 威化島, and gave the *coup de grâce* to the waning Koryŏ dynasty. Discussion of the chain of events and open conflicts between the pro-Mongol and pro-Ming parties at court is in order. King Kongmin, the thirty-first monarch of Koryŏ, came to the throne in the last years of Mongol rule. In China major rebel leaders were emerging in an effort to assert their power and destroy the weakening and disunified house of Yüan. The king's ambition was to drive out the Mongol military commission from Ssangsŏng established first in 1258 to govern the territory north of Ch'ŏllyŏng 鐵嶺, and to recover the land in the north. Yi Cha-ch'un and Yi Sŏng-gye appeared at a propitious moment to render service in the recovery of the northern area. In the same year that Chu Yüan-chang seized Nanking (1356) the king discontinued the use of the Mongol reign-title; and in the year that Chu captured Peking, driving out To-γon Temür (*q.v.*), he sent envoys to the founder of the Ming. From August, 1370, he began to use the Ming reign-title of Hung-wu, thus initiating friendly relations between Ming and Koryŏ.

But two events that took place in 1374 overshadowed the otherwise friendly Sino-Korean contacts. First was the assassination of King Kongmin by eunuchs on the night of October 19; and second was the murder of the returning Ming envoy, Ts'ai Pin 蔡斌, by a Korean escort. Because of these events, Chu Yüan-chang became suspicious of Koryŏ's sincerity, and ordered the exclusion of Korean envoys. When sent to request the posthumous title for the murdered king and the investiture of the new king, they were repeatedly turned back at Liaotung. Koryŏ, in order to demonstrate its sincerity, stopped using the Mongol reign title of Hsüan-kuang 宣光 (which was adopted in March, 1377), and from October, 1378,

took the title Hung-wu. When in November of the same year Sim Tŏk-pu 申德符 (1328-January 28, 1401) was sent as the New Year's felicitation envoy, Chu Yüan-chang reprimanded him and demanded punishment of the regicides. Learning that some Koryŏ officials were still communicating with the Northern Yüan, the Ming emperor continued to exclude Korean envoys either at Liaotung or at Teng-chou 登州 (Shantung), and until 1385 imprisoned or banished those who managed to reach Nanking. Despite the emperor's ill-treatment of envoys and his exorbitant demand for tribute horses, Koryŏ continued to demonstrate its goodwill and dispatched Chŏng Mong-ju 鄭夢周 (1337-92) in August, 1384, as the birthday felicitation envoy. This time the emperor restrained his temper, received Chŏng, and returned the exiled or imprisoned Koreans. Finally in October, 1385, on behalf of the emperor, the envoy conferred the posthumous title on King Kongmin; and invested Sin U as king of Korea.

At the end of the next year, however, Chu again made an unreasonable demand, the purchase of five thousand Korean horses. Korea did its utmost to meet it, but envoys were again rejected at Liaotung twelve months later. The emperor reissued orders to the Liaotung military commission to forbid Koreans from crossing the border. The reasons given for his action were: 1) Korean ministers are insincere and cannot be trusted; 2) their envoys do not come at the right time; 3) tribute horses are weak and run down and unusable. To make the Sino-Korean relations worse in March, 1388, the Ming court introduced another urgent problem. It explained that, since the territory north, east, and west of Ch'ŏlyŏng was once occupied by the Mongols, the Ming-Korean border should be drawn along Ch'ŏllyŏng, on the border of present Kangwŏn and Hamgyŏng 咸鏡 provinces. This news threw the Koryŏ court into great commotion. At emergency meetings it was decided unanimously that

Korea could not relinquish her territory north of Ch'ŏllyŏng. The pro-Mongol chancellor Ch'oe Yŏng and equally pro-Mongol king, Sin U, decided to march to Liaotung to destroy Ming garrisons there. Sin U, therefore, mobilized the army and made preparations for the expedition. Chancellor Ch'oe, the stanch supporter of it, was made the generalissimo, Cho Min-su 曹敏修 (d. 1391) commander of the left Army, and Yi Sŏng-gye of the right.

Before the departure for the Yalu on May 7, Yi Sŏng-gye pointed out four objections to the mobilization: 1) it is difficult for a small state to attack a large country; 2) mobilization in the heat of the summer is inadvisable; 3) it will give Japan an opportunity to invade Korea if troops are transferred to the north; and 4) the rainy season will rust the points of the arrows, and cause the soldiers to fall sick. Yi, nevertheless, reluctantly joined the march, but ordered his troops (June 26) to recross the Yalu and march back to the capital. He then banished the war advocates, Ch'oe Yŏng and Sin U, and again from July 7 on adopted the reign-title Hung-wu, and had Sin Ch'ang 辛昌, son of Sin U, placed on the throne.

Yi became the U si jung 右侍中 and took the helm of state affairs. He and his progressive pro-Ming party, consisting chiefly of students of neo-Confucianism, set out to remove the sources of future trouble. First, under the pretext that they were descendants of Sin-ton 辛旽, a favorite monk of King Kongmin, and hence not of the legitimate Wang line, Sin U and Sin Ch'ang were banished and later executed. Instead, Wang Yo 王瑤 (d. 1392), the seventh generation descendant of King Wang Tak (1144–1204), was enthroned on December 2, 1389, the last monarch of the Koryŏ dynasty. Second, they had already enforced land reform in October, and then burned land registries a year later. Third, they assassinated the last Koryŏ loyalist, Chŏng Mong-ju, in April, 1392, thus removing another obstacle in their way. On July 31 the last

Koryŏ king was sent into exile and on August 5, Yi Sŏng-gye ascended the throne at the Such'ang Palace 壽昌宮 in Kaesŏng 開城 as the first ruler of the Yi dynasty.

His enthronement meant the victory of the pro-Ming and anti-Buddhist party, the members of which generally upheld the newly imported neo-Confucianism. The new dynasty, therefore, rejected Buddhism, which had been the state religion for over eight hundred years, as subversive of public morality, and adopted neo-Confucianism as its official philosophy. This gave a metaphysical justification for kingship and for society organized in a pattern of well-defined social positions. Founders of the new dynasty also brought in the Confucian idea of "heavenly mandate" as a means of emphasizing its legitimacy. Deserving subjects, who assisted in the revolution and framed the new government, set out to compose eulogies to win the minds of men. The poems so composed praised not only the cultural and military accomplishments of the founder but also the beauty of the city of Hansŏng 漢城 (modern Seoul), the new capital as of 1394. In 1396 walls were constructed around the city. He and his ministers remodeled political and cultural institutions, and reinstituted and improved the civil service examinations. In order to legalize new systems and institutions, Chŏng To-jŏn (q.v.) compiled the *Chosŏn Kyŏngguk chŏn* (1394) and Cho Chun (*see* Chŏng To-jŏn) the *Kyŏngje yukchŏn* 經濟六典 (later revised by Ha Yun 河崙 [1347–1416] and others). Envoys from the Liu-ch'iu Islands arrived in 1392 (August and September), 1394, and 1397; and those from Siam in 1393.

Soon after his accession Yi Sŏng-gye sent envoys to Nanking informing the Ming court of the dynastic change. He also requested the emperor to select a new name for Korea. Thereupon Chu chose Chosŏn 朝鮮 as the most beautiful and fitting, and it was adopted March 27, 1393. Owing to problems, however, concerning Korean-Jurchen contacts and yearly tribute, friendly relations were not easily established. The Ming emperor accused Korea of influencing Chinese border officers, of enticing the Jurchen to cross the Yalu and violate Ming territory, and once again of sending unfit horses as tribute. Nam Chae 南在 (d. 1419) was sent to free Korea of these charges (July 10). Chu was adamant, and ordered border officials once more to close the Liaotung frontier. When Yi repeatedly sent missions to ask for his favor, the emperor finally ordered Yi to send one of his sons to give an explanation. Thereupon Yi Pang-wŏn (*q. v.*), accompanied by Cho Pan 趙胖 (d. 1401) and Nam Chae, went to Nanking. As a consequence Chu accepted their explanations and ordered the reopening of the border. When, however, Chŏng Ch'ong (*see* Kwŏn Kŭn) was dispatched to request investiture, the emperor found disrespectful phraseology in the diplomatic missives, and asked Yi to send their writer. When Chŏng To-jŏn, originator of the missives in question, refused to proceed to Nanking, Kwŏn Kŭn, Ha Yun, and others went instead. Their plea and literary talents so moved the emperor that he returned the imprisoned envoys, and praised the sincerity of Yi Sŏng-gye. Sino-Korean relations were, however, normalized only in 1401 when Ming envoys brought investiture and the golden seal inscribed "the King of Chosŏn."

Another moot point in Sino-Korean relations concerned the genealogy of Yi Sŏng-gye. When on May 25, 1394, the Ming envoy, Huang Yung-ch'i 黃永奇, arrived and sacrificed to the mountains and rivers, the sacrificial prayer contained a passage to the effect that Yi Sŏng-gye was a descendant of Yi In-im 李仁任, a powerful and corrupt pro-Mongol minister. This assertion was due to two Korean nationals who fled to China towards the end of Koryŏ (1390). Despite repeated entreaties for correction, the Ming court did not consider it important, and continued to make the same error. This matter

of genealogy was not settled until the 16th century. When the notice of investiture arrived belatedly in 1401, Yi Sŏng-gye had abdicated three years previously in favor of his second son, Yi Pang-gwa 芳果 (temple name: 定宗, Pth. 恭靖大王, 1365–1420). Yi Sŏng-gye was honored as the Sangwang 上王 until his fifth son, Yi Pang-wŏn, succeeded Yi Pang-gwa on November 28, 1400, as the third king of the dynasty. From that day until his death Yi Sŏng-gye was honored as the T'aesangwang 太上王. He died in 1408 in the Ch'angdŏk Palace 昌德宮 in Seoul. In August he was given the traditional temple name for a dynastic founder T'aejo 太祖 (Grand progenitor). He was buried on September 28 in the mausoleum known as Kŏnwŏn nŭng 健元陵, south of Yangju 楊州, near Seoul. On October 18 the Ming envoy arrived with the posthumous epithet of K'ang-hsien 康獻 by which he was often referred to in Korean records (*i.e.*, as Kanghŏn taewang 大王). The spirit way stele 神道碑, the text of which was composed by Kwŏn Kŭn and calligraphed by Sŏng Sŏng-nin (*see* Chŏng To-jŏn), was erected on May 27, 1409. Yi Sŏng-gye had eight sons and five daughters.

Yi Pang-wŏn ordered the compilation of the veritable record of his reign, *T'aejo sillok* (October 6, 1409). The work, begun by Ha Yun and others on February 14, 1410, was completed on April 22, 1413. The manuscript was revised four times, 1438, 1442, 1448, and 1451. It was later printed with movable type, and was reproduced as the first part of the *Chosŏn wangjo sillok* 朝鮮王朝實錄 (1893 *kwŏn*, 1955–58).

Another invaluable source for the study of the life and time of Yi Sŏng-gye is the *Yŏngbi ŏch'ŏn ka* 龍飛御天歌, compiled in 1445 to praise the founding of the Yi dynasty. This eulogy-cycle, consisting of 125 cantos, assigned altogether eighty-one to Yi Sŏng-gye.

Bibliography

An Chŏng-bok 安鼎福, *Tongsa kangmok* 東史綱目 (1915 ed.), 14B, 50, 290; Chŏng In-ji 鄭麟趾, *et al.*, *Koryŏ sa* 高麗史 (1955 ed.,), 38/30a, 47a, 133/1a, 45b; *id.*, *Yongbi ŏch'on ka*; Ha Yun, *et al.*, *T'aejo sillok*, 1/1a, 14b; No Sa-sin 盧思愼 and Yi Haeng 李荇, *Sinjŭng Tongguk yŏji sŭngnam* 新增東國輿地勝覽 (1958 ed.), 11/10a, 39/42a, 48/12a; Sŏ kŏ-jŏng 徐居正, *Tongguk t'onggam* 通鑑 (1912 ed.), 46/210, 605; Yi Kŭng-ik 李肯翊, *Yŏllyŏsil kisul* 燃藜室記述 (1912–14 ed.), 1/1, 76, 2/89; Akiyama Kensō, "Yi-si Chosŏn to Ryūkū tono kōtsū," *Shigaku zasshi*, 41:7 (1930), 788; Fukaya Toshikane, "Sŏn-sho no dochiseido no ippan-iwayuru kadenhō o chūshin to shite," *ibid.*, 50:5 (1939), 609, 736; Ikeuchi Hiroshi, "Yi-chō no shiso no densetsu no sono kōsei," *Tōyō gakuho*, 5: 2 (1915), 229, 5: 3, 328; *id.*, "Koryŏ Sin U-chō ni okeru Ch'ollyŏng no mondai," *ibid.*, 8:1 (1918), 82; *id.*, "Koryŏ Kongmin wang no Yüan ni taisuru hankō no undō," *ibid.*, 7: 1 (1917), 117; *id.*, "Koryŏ Kongmin wang-chō no Tongnyŏngbu seibatsu ni tsuiteno kō," *ibid.*, 8: 2 (1918), 206; *id.*, "Koryŏ matsu ni okeru Ming oyobi Pei-Yüan tono kankei," *ibid.*, 29 (1918), 56, 161, 251, 372; Sin Sŏk-ho 申奭鎬, "Yŏmal Sŏnch'o ui woegu wa ku taech'aek," *Kuksasang ŭi chemunje*, 3 (1959), 103; *id.*, "Chosŏn wangjo kaeguk tangsi ŭi taemyŏng kwangye," *Shigaku zasshi*, 1 (1959), 93; Yi Pin-sŭng 李斌承, *Chosŏn T'aejo silgi* 朝鮮太祖實記 (Seoul, 1927), 1a; Yi Pyŏng-do 李丙燾, *Koryŏ sidae ŭi yŏn'gu* (1954), 377; Yi Sang-baek 李相佰, *Yijo kŏn'gukŭi yŏn'gu*, 1954; *id.*, *Hanguk munhwasa yŏn'gu non'go* 韓國文化史研究論考 (1954), 3, 173; L. Carrington Goodrich, "Korean Interference with Chinese Historical Records," JNCBRAS, 68 (1937), 27.

Peter H. Lee

YIN Shou-heng 尹守衡 (T. 用平, H. 冲玄, 嬾翁), died *ca.* 1634, aged eighty-three *sui*, scholar, was a native of Tung-kuan 東莞, Kwangtung. From an early age he was fond of study. He passed the *hsiu-ts'ai* examinations at fifteen and in 1582 received the *chü-jen*. Thereafter he took the metropolitan examination six times without success. In or about 1592, as a *chü-jen* applying for an appointment, he was selected acting instructor in the district school of Ch'ing-liu 清流 in the western mountainous region of Fukien.

He took his position seriously and stimulated his students' interest in scholarship. In 1594 he was assigned to temporary duty in Wuchang as an assistant examiner in the provincial examination of Hukuang, and the following year tried again for the *chin-shih*. Except for these journeys it seems that he remained in Ch'ing-liu during the period 1592 to 1598. There he became acquainted with a local dignitary, P'ei Ying-chang 裴應章 (T. 元周, H. 澹泉, 1537-1609, cs 1568), who later served as a vice-minister of Personnel (1596-1600). In 1598, when Yin was very despondent after his sixth failure at the metropolitan examination, P'ei persuaded him to apply for a magistracy and, apparently with P'ei's help, he was appointed to that office in Hsin-ch'ang 新昌, Kiangsi, where he served for two years. According to his own account, he incurred the displeasure of his superiors because he refused to observe the custom of sending them gifts. Late in 1600 his sponsor, P'ei Ying-chang, was transferred from the powerful office in the ministry of Personnel by being promoted to be minister of Works in Nanking. Soon Yin too lost his magistracy by being named chief judge in the princedom of Chao 趙 at Chang-te, Honan, which was an office higher in rank but reserved for deadwood. He at once resigned and retired to his home, being then about fifty.

For over thirty years thereafter Yin Shou-heng devoted his life to the compilation of a history of the reigning dynasty, to which he gave the title *Shih-ch'ieh* 史竊 (Unauthorized history), for he considered himself one who had taken on unasked the responsibility of an official historian. In writing such a contemporary history he was often laughed at and sometimes suspected as a bearer of grudges. At one point he felt dejected and wanted to give up but was encouraged to continue by his friend, Chang Hsüan (*q.v.*), and brought the work to near completion. Eventually the book received much praise. One magistrate of Tung-kuan helped him in collecting references and conferred on him a tablet with the inscription, *Ch'ing-ch'ao i-shih* 清朝逸史 (Unofficial Historian of our Pure Dynasty). Hence Yin sometimes called himself *i-shih*, "the unofficial historian."

The *Shih-ch'ieh*, originally designed to comprise 105 *chüan*, was still short of four *chüan* when Yin died, the four to consist of the record of empresses and the treatises on government organization, taxation, and grain transport. The final version includes records, 8 *ch.* (one missing), treatises, 6 *ch.* (3 missing), ten hereditary families, 8 *ch.*, biographies, 82 *ch.*, and autobiography, 1 *ch.* In 1636 his eldest son, Yin K'uei-ch'ang 魁昌 (T. 昌廷), became a *chü-jen* and, with the help of friends, undertook the first engraving of the book (*ca.* 1637–39) under the title *Huang Ming shih-ch'ieh*. During the wars of the following decade the printing blocks were lost. The third son, Yin Yü-ju 玉如, purchased a first edition from which he produced (*ca.* 1647) a second engraving. A third and collated edition was published some sixty years later by a grandson, Yin Shao-hsüan 紹宣 (T. 淑之, cj 1702), with the help of the magistrate of Tung-kuan (1705–8), Li Ssu-hang 李思沆 of Fu-p'ing 富平, Shensi, who contributed a preface dated 1706. The title of this edition was modified to *Ming shih-ch'ieh* and sometimes, *Shih-ch'ieh*. The repeated engravings of this book by the Yin family reveal not just a pride in the authorship of an ancestor but perhaps also an interest in some profit from its circulation. By the late 18th century, however, it was placed on the list of banned books. Whether or not the printing blocks were destroyed at that time is not recorded. In any case there is a complete set of blocks preserved in the Tung-kuan municipal museum library; an examination of a copy from these blocks shows that they were probably engraved in the late 19th or early 20th century. [Editors' note: The Columbia University copy includes a biography of the author by Juan Yüan (ECCP), then the governor general.]

As a history of the Ming dynasty Yin's book is short on facts, probably because he did not have access to an adequate library. His comments on various matters, on the other hand, frequently show good judgment and are worth consulting. For example, in his treatise on military affairs, the Chün-fa-chih 軍法志, he points out several causes for the decline of Ming military power, such as the misuse of soldiers for menial labor and the subordination of the military to incompetent civil officials in field command. Occasionally Yin gives his personal experience to substantiate a point, such as the demand for bribery by a censor on regional inspection when he was serving as magistrate of Hsin-ch'ang. It is interesting to note that the popular contemporary history of the Ming period, the *Huang Ming t'ung-chi*, was by Ch'en Chien (*q.v.*), another native of Tung-kuan. Yin Shou-heng is said to have left a literary collection, *Lan-an chi* 嬾庵集.

Bibliography

42/79/8b, 105/1a; *Tung-kuan-hsien chih* (1911), 59/14a; Yao Chin-yüan (1957), 59, 225; Sun Tien-ch'i (1957), 121; *Huang Ming wen-hai* (microfilm), 4/4/5; Wolfgang Franke, *Sources*, 2.1.4.

Albert Chan

YON-tan-rgya-mts'o, February, 1589-January, 1617, the fourth Dalai lama, was born in the Köke-nuur region, the son of Altan-qaɣan's grandson Sümir Daičing. The man responsible for the conversion of the Mongols, the third Dalai-lama, bSod-nams-rgya-mts'o (*q.v.*), had died in the midst of his new followers, and the heads of the Yellow sect in Tibet gladly seized on the occasion to knit even more closely the interests of the family of Altan-qaɣan (and the Mongol princes in general) with those of the dGe-lugs-pa. The Tibetan churchmen who had accompanied bSod-nams-rgya-mts'o to Mongolia recognized the child as the latter's incarnation; on their representations, the K'ri Rin-po-c'e (elective abbot) of dGa'-ldan and other high dignitaries of central Tibet confirmed the choice. The whole proceeding meant, as it were, that a seal of approval had been placed on the new international position of the Dalai-lamas. The official recognition took place only in 1601, however, when a large commission of Tibetan churchmen and nobles traveled to Köke-qoto and paid obeisance to the boy. In the following year they brought him to Tibet in a ceremonial progress. As a sort of compensation to the Mongols for the loss of the head of the Yellow Church, a high-ranking substitute was created among them on this occasion; it was the first Maidari Qutuqtu (rJe-btsun Dam-pa) of the Qalqa.

The education of the young Dalai-lama, already commenced by the Tibetans who surrounded him at Köke-qoto, was completed at 'Bras-spuṅs; it was, of course, completely Tibetan, and the boy must have remembered little, if anything, of his Mongol home and milieu.

The arrival of Yon-tan-rgya-mts'o in Tibet was followed by a period of uneasy truce; the Red sects and their protectors held back, awaiting further developments. In the meantime the young Dalai-lama, following the example of his predecessors, started on extensive propaganda tours all over the country, not excluding gTsaṅ (south central Tibet), where he visited the great dGe-lugs-pa monastery of bKra-śis-lhun-po. But soon the latent hostility came out into the open. In 1605 the P'ag-mo-gru-pa attacked the governor of the Lhasa district. In 1607 the Mongol army, acting presumably in favor of the dGe-lugs-pa, invaded central Tibet, but was beaten back by the gTsaṅ troops. In 1612 the rulers of gTsaṅ, supporters of the Red sect of the Karma-pa, confronted a real coalition, headed by the sNe'u-gdoṅ chief, a P'ag-mo-gru-pa belonging to the family of the former rulers of Tibet. The decision of arms went against the coalition; the P'ag-mo-gru-pa lost their old capital sNe'u-gdoṅ, which they never recovered, and they ceased to be a power in Tibetan politics. This of course meant a serious blow to the Dalai-lama, whose Tibetan party had collapsed; as a consequence, he was thrown back almost completely on Mongol support.

Yon-tan-rgya-mts'o went back to 'Bras-spuṅs in 1611. Nearby Lhasa was visited in the same year by the gTsaṅ ruler P'un-ts'ogs-rnam-rgyal, and thus in that year the Karma-pa excluded the Yellow sect from their great smon-lam festival; it was an ominous sign. P'un-ts'ogs-rnam-rgyal made a gesture of conciliation by asking the Dalai-lama to grant him a mystical initiation; but the latter, after some wavering, refused. This, of course, increased the tension, and Yon-tan-rgya-mts'o chose to get out of the way of possible harm by shifting his residence to the ancient royal temple of bSam-yas, to the southeast of Lhasa. As a matter of fact, he was growing up as a serious and deeply religious young man, who cared little about worldly matters. These were entrusted to the capable hands of the p'yag-mdzod (treasurer), dKon-mc'og-c'os-'p'el (1573–1646), who played a most important political role during the last years of the fourth and early years of the fifth Dalai-lama. In 1616 he received a Chinese embassy, headed by the Tibetan Lama bSod-nams-blo-gros, supposed to have been sent by Emperor Chu I-chün (q.v.), to bestow a title and presents on the Dalai-lama. At least, this is the account in the Tibetan biography; but the Chinese sources seem to be silent about the matter. [Editors' note: Chu I-chün's mother was a devout believer in Buddhism and frequently sent messengers to various monasteries in the empire to present alms, sūtras, and images. These, however, were purchased at her own expense and were not recorded in official annals. She died in 1614. She possibly made a vow to send some presents to the Dalai-lama, and after her death her son may have fulfilled it as an act of filial piety.]

In these years the power of the gTsaṅ ruler was at its zenith and the dGe-lugs-pa faced a most serious crisis. Its outcome could not yet be foreseen, when the Dalai-lama died at the young age of twenty-eight.

Bibliography

Nag-dban-blo-bzan-rgya-mts'o (fifth Dalai-lama, 'Jig-rten-dbaṅ-p'yug t'ams-cad-mk'yen-pa Yon-tan-rgya-mts'o-dpal-bzaṅ-po'i, rnam-par-t'ar-pa nor-bu'i-p'reṅ-ba, Vol. Ña of his collected works; G. Tucci, Tibetan Painted Scrolls (Rome, 1949), 50; G. Schulemann, Die Geschichte der Dalai-Lamas (Leipzig, 1958, 2d ed.), 215; L. Petech, "The Dalai-Lamas and Regents of Tibet: A Chronological Study," TP, 47 (1959), 372.

Luciano Petech

YÜ An-ch'i 俞安期 (early *ming*: Ts'e 策, T. 公臨; changed *ming* to Hou 後, and T. to 羨長), *ca.* 1551-*ca.* 1618, a native of Wu-chiang 吳江, prefecture of Soochow, was a poet and encyclopedist of note. According to Shen Tsan (*see* Shen Ching), Yü's grandfather had been employed by Shen's family as an accountant, and Yü's uncle sold himself to the family as a bond servant. After Yü's father died, he lived for a time with this uncle. Shen Tsan recalled that about this time (1563 or 1564) he and Yü used to play together. Yü was some eight or nine years older; so he was probably humoring the son of the master. A few years later Yü left his uncle to live with a Chou 周 family, probably as companion to its sons. He was so gifted and studious that he became informed about many subjects and could write poetry well. Before long he struck out to live independently. On one occasion he attracted the attention of Wang Shih-chen (*q.v.*) by sending him an effusion of one hundred fifty lines.

Wang's praise of the piece quite naturally contributed to Yü's reputation.

This occurred when Yü was about twenty-nine years of age, around the year 1580. A few years later Wang sent Yü a poem when the latter went to live in Wu-hsi 無錫, west of Soochow. Apparently at this time Yü had gained a reputation for integrity and fidelity. On one occasion he attended to the needs of a former benefactor in distress and at another time took care of the son of a deceased friend. The said benefactor was Lung Tsung-wu 龍宗武 (T. 君揚, H. 澄源, 1542-1609, cs 1571), one-time prefectural judge of Soochow, assistant prefect of T'ai-p'ing 太平-fu (*ca.* 1578), and an administration assistant commissioner of Hukuang (*ca.* 1583). Late in the 1570s Lung had befriended Yü and came to regard him as a protégé. It happened that in 1578 a man accused of having written derogatory accounts about the powerful grand secretary, Chang Chü-cheng (*q.v.*), died while awaiting trial in the T'ai-p'ing prison under Lung's jurisdiction. There were rumors that Lung's superiors, trying to please Chang, ordered Lung to have the man secretly put to death. By 1583, when an imperial decree posthumously denounced Chang, Lung and his former superior were formally charged with responsibility for the man's death, and sentenced to permanent exile on the frontier. Yü voluntarily went to Hukuang to help in Lung's defense, and after the sentencing sent him off. It was indeed a gallant act, but it probably made him feel insecure in his native place. In any case for some reason he changed his residence to Wu-hsi. He apparently had to give up hope of entering government service too, for in the poem of 1584 Wang Shih-chen addressed him as a shan-jen 山人, indicating that he had adopted a way of living that included a wide range of superior professionals, from artists to philosophers. Yü's specialties included poetry and geomancy. In 1587 he published a collection of his poems (28 *ch.* ?, later expanded to 40 chüan), entitled *Liao-liao chi* 寥寥集. Shen Tsan, who was serving as a secretary in the ministry of Works in Nanking, records that Yü came to pay a visit, and surprised him with his change in appearance and dignified carriage—an entirely different person from the youth he had known; also that this collection had greatly enhanced his prestige. But certain poems in this work displeased the Manchu court two centuries later; so they were ordered expunged. On Yü's poetry the *Ssu-k'u* editors quote with approval a disparaging remark by Chu I-tsun (ECCP): Yü's poems are like colored paper flowers, pretty but without roots.

Both poetry and geomancy are arts that could be rendered as services to the affluent and influential—poetry for entertainment and geomancy to satisfy the selfish desire to prolong the enjoyment of wealth and power in the family. As a shan-jen, Yü traveled to various places for more than ten years. It is not at all, as one of his biographers suggests, that he was away from home because of wanderlust; he appears always to have been employed for one or another of his talents. For instance, in 1571, he was engaged as a guest companion and teacher by an imperial clansman in Sian, Shensi. A fellow townsman from Wu-hsi, by the name of Li Ying-hsiang 李應祥 (T. 善徵, cs 1577), who was serving there as assistant administration commissioner, had compiled a gazetteer of Shensi and Kansu, entitled *Yung-sheng lüeh* 雍勝畧, 24 *ch.* Yü was asked to be an editor and to enrich it with quotations from famous poets and writers. His contribution was so highly regarded that his name appears in the book as a joint compiler.

A few years later Yü returned south and began to publish his own books in Nanking. His first compilation was a classified encyclopedia, *T'ang lei-han* 唐類函, 200 *ch.*, printed in 1603. It lists as collator the name of Hsü Hsien-ch'ing 徐顯卿 (T. 公望, H. 檢庵, cs 1568), who had died in 1602. As Hsü was one-time vice minister of

Personnel (1588–90), perhaps his name did lend some prestige to the book. Actually Yü did not need it, for the work, an intelligent rearrangement of cullings from several T'ang compendia, answered the need of writers for ready reference to words and phrases, and became very popular. Later Yü published a series of similar compilations such as the aid to poets, *Shih-chün* 詩雋 *lei-han*, 150 *ch.*, printed in 1609, listing the names of Mei Ting-tso as supplementer and Ts'ao Hsüeh-ch'üan (*qq.v.*) as editor. Another book in the series is a guide to letter writing, *Ch'i* 啓-*chün lei-han*, 102 *ch.*, with a table of contents, 9 *ch.*, and a supplement, *Chih-kuan k'ao* 職官考, 5 *ch.*, which gives a list of titles and government offices, and serves as a reference to proper or fancy ways of addressing important persons. In addition to listing Ts'ao Hsüeh-ch'üan again as an editor, and Li Kuo-hsiang 李國祥 (T. 休徵) of Nanchang as the original compiler (輯撰), Yü put his own name down as the assembler (彙編) of the *Ch'i-chün lei-han*, probably because Li had an earlier compilation of which Yü made extensive use. A third one in the series is the *Lei-yüan ch'iung-ying* 類苑瓊英, 10 *ch.*, which seems not to have survived. None of these works was included in the *Ssu-k'u* library, but all received notices in its catalogue. By imperial order in 1710 the *T'ang lei-han* was expanded by a commission to include post-T'ang works. This was printed in 450 *chüan*, under the title *Yüan-chien lei-han* (*see* Wang Shih-chen, ECCP).

Little is known about Yü's later life except that about 1608 he bought a house with a garden in Nanking. In 1618, when he planned to retire, he sold the printing blocks of *T'ang lei-han* to another publisher, Ch'eng K'ai-hu 程開祜, who, instead of following the common practice of making changes on the blocks to list the new owner as the compiler, left the original authorship intact and merely supplied a preface. Yü is sometimes recorded as having had a son, Yü Nan-shih 南史 (T.

無殊), a poet. Actually he had two sons the elder being the renowned Ch'an master, T'ung-wen 通問 (T. 箬庵, 1604–55), author of *Hsü teng ts'un-kao* 續燈存稿, 12 *ch.*, a work on the biographies and teachings of Ch'an monks from the late 12th to the 17th century.

Bibliography

40/63/14b; 64/ 庚 25/18b; 84/ 丁下 /52a; 86/18/8b; SK(1930), 138/5b, 178/10b, 193/9a; P'an Ch'eng-chang (ECCP), *Sung-ling wen-hsien*(1693), 9/17b, 11/7a; Wang Shih-chen, *Yen-chou shan-jen hsü-kao*, 7/6a; Ku Ch'i-yüan, *Lan-chen ts'ao-t'ang chi*, 7/10a; Ch'en Yüan (BDRC), *Ch'ing-ch'u seng-cheng-chi*, 3, 6, 12; Shen Tsan, *Chin-shih ts'ung-ts'an*, 1/37a; TSCC (1885–88), XXIII: 113/101/9b; *Soochow-fu chih* (1862), 105/18b; Sun Tien-ch'i (1957), 147; Ch'iu K'ai-ming 裘開明 in CHHP, n.s. II: 2 (June, 1961), 107; *Ming-shih i-wen-chih pu-pien fu-pien* 藝文志補編附編 (Shanghai, 1959), 84, 113, 119, 120, 704; Naikaku Bunko *Catalogue*, 295, 301, 426; L. of C. *Catalogue of Rare Books*, 727, 728, 1137; *Yung-sheng lüeh* (NLP microfilm no. 384); A. Wylie, *Notes on Chinese Literature* (1867, rpr. of 1922), 188.

Chaoying Fang

YÜ Ch'ien 于謙 (T. 廷益, H. 節庵 or 闇), May 13, 1398–February 16, 1457, statesman and military man, was born in Ch'ien-t'ang (Hangchow), Chekiang. The original home of the Yü family was in Honan province. The family lived in Hangchow, however, as Yü Ch'ien's great-grandfather was stationed there during the late Yüan period, and had died while in office. Yü is reported to have been a strong-willed and straightforward boy showing a particular admiration for the late Sung patriot and hero, Wen T'ien-hsiang (1236–83). In 1417 Yü became a *hsiu-ts'ai*, in 1420 a *chü-jen*, and in 1421 a *chin-shih*. In 1418 he married the daughter of the Hanlin scholar Tung Yung 董鏞(T. 孟聲, cs 1404), also from the Hangchow region.

In 1422 Yü received an appointment as a censor in Peking. Four years later, he participated in the punitive camaign of Emperor Chu Chan-chi (*q.v.*) against his rebellious uncle Chu Kao-hsü (*q.v.*). As a censor Yü became known for the keen judgment, the high resolve, and the integrity he exhibited in prosecuting culprits as well as in defending those unjustly accused. Promoted to the rank of a vice minister of War in 1430, he served concurrently as governor of Honan and Shansi. Except for a short interruption he held this position for sixteen years. In 1441 he was mistakenly indicted and imprisoned, being taken for a censor of the same name who had ventured to oppose the powerful eunuch Wang Chen (*q.v.*). After the discovery and rectification of the error, he remained for a short time as vice minister of the grand court of Revision in the capital, but returned during the same year to his former position as governor of Honan and Shansi. This reappointment was due mainly to the requests made on his behalf by the officials and the people, as well as by the imperial princes residing in the two provinces. He fulfilled his official duties responsibly and impartially to the benefit of the local population. His merits are stressed in the biographies to be found in the local histories of these two provinces. In Kaifeng a shrine to his memory was erected during the Ch'eng-hua period.

Because of the death of his father in 1447 Yü had to resign from all his positions. The court did not permit him to stay at home for the whole mourning period, however, recalling him to Peking during the same year as right vice minister of War. As a result the opportunity came to play a crucial role in the fate of the empire, enabling him to share in saving the dynasty from an early downfall. When in August, 1449, the emperor set out on his ill-fated campaign against the invading Oirat, a great number of leading officials, including the minister of War, K'uang Yeh (*q.v.*), had to follow. Fortunately Yü had remained behind as acting head of the ministry.

After the news of the catastrophe reached Peking, consternation and confusion prevailed in government circles. In a heated debate Hsü Yu-chen(*q.v.*) proposed to move the administration from Peking to Nanking. Yü, together with the minister of Rites, Hu Ying (*q.v.*), strongly opposed this suggestion and referred to the disastrous experience of the Sung court when it shifted the capital from Kaifeng southward in 1127. And, as K'ou Chun (961–1023) recommended in 1004, Yü asked the death penalty for those advocating the removal. The government's decision to remain at Peking and to defend it by all means was thus probably due in large measure to Yü Ch'ien's firmness. As action proceeded against the clique of Wang Chen, turmoil developed within the palace and fighting broke out between followers of Wang and his enraged opponents resulting in the death of several people. The horrified regent, the prince of Ch'eng, Chu Ch'i-yü (*q.v.*), and some leading officials were about to leave the scene precipitately, but were deterred by Yü who prevailed upon the prince to issue an edict ordering the punishment of Wang Chen's collaborators. A few days later, on September 7, Yü was promoted to minister of War. By his resoluteness in a most critical situation he emerged as the strongest man within the government. He is said also to have played a decisive role in the plan to proclaim the regent as the new emperor in order to stabilize the critical situation as well as to deprive the Oirat leader, Esen (*q.v.*), of the prestige of keeping a Chinese emperor as his prisoner. The prince regent agreed only after Yü had remarked: "Your subjects are certainly concerned with the state; it is not for selfish reasons that we wish Your Highness to extend aid in an emergency in order to tranquillize the spirits of land and grain and to comfort the minds of the people."With the installation of a new ruler the imperial captive lost his former value and Esen was no longer in a position to exploit his prisoner as a means of political pressure on China.

In addition to his post as minister of War, Yü had the responsibility of defending Peking against the Oirat. With the assistance of Shih Heng (*q.v.*), he succeeded in reorganizing some of the demoralized Chinese troops and in preparing the city for an anticipated siege. His actions, added to Esen's temporizing, frustrated the latter's take-over of the capital. For his accomplishments during this crisis, the most serious which the dynasty had so far experienced, Yü received the title of a junior guardian and concurrently the appointment of tsung-tu chün-wu 總督軍務 (supreme commander of military affairs) with responsibility for the reorganization of the army. Yü considered it his main task to reinforce the neglected fortifications along the Great Wall and to strengthen the fighting power of the largely disorganized and demoralized armed forces to prevent once and for all a recurrence of the events of 1449. Since the existing army organization of the three large training divisions had deteriorated beyond the possibility of efficient reorganization, the emperor approved in 1453 Yü's proposal to introduce the so-called system of t'uan ying 團營 (integrated divisions) for the metropolitan garrison. One hundred fifty thousand men were selected from the metropolitan troops to make up ten training divisions of fifteen thousand men each headed by a tso-ying tu-tu 坐營都督 (divisional commissioner-in-chief). With this entirely novel organization, newly qualified officers could be put in charge of each unit, and Yü hoped to train a new striking force to be sent to the border in case of an emergency. The remaining units of the three large training divisions were to stay behind for the protection of the metropolitan area. Yü's careful military precautions combined with a rather uncompromising policy resulted in the cessation of further major Mongol incursions during the Ching-t'ai period. Besides the protection of the northern frontier Yü had to deal with various minor struggles and military measures against the not yet fully integrated natives living in the southern and southwestern provinces: Kwangtung, Kwangsi, Hukuang, Kweichou, Yunnan, and Szechuan. He realized, however, that the pacification of these people posed not merely a military problem. Well aware that the confrontations with the inhabitants of the south were of local importance only and could never seriously threaten the empire as a whole, as the Mongols had proved capable of doing, he directed his main efforts to the defense of the northern frontier.

Yü's wife had died in 1445, but he never remarried nor did he take a concubine. He lived an unpretentious, almost frugal, life. His official duties consumed by far the major part of his time and energy. Worry over the problems to be solved often prevented his sleeping at night. Occasionally he indulged in painting and calligraphy, and wrote poems and essays. He even achieved some note as a poet. His character is reflected most clearly in a short colophon he wrote on a portrait of himself, entitled Hsiao-hsiang tzu-tsan 小像自贊:

> His eye though clear-sighted is not able to see the right moment for action.
> His belly [as the center of feeling] though big is not able to be tolerant.
> His appearance is not above the average.
> His virtue is insufficient to adorn the person.
> Although his nature is rustic, his feelings are upright.
> Most precious to him are a good name and reputation.
> Most important to him are his ruler and his parents.
> He does not demand comfort in his home.
> He cares not whether his clothes are old or new.

> Not immaculate and not corrupt; not submissive and not haughty.

In 1455 he fell seriously ill. The emperor even sent his personal physician to take care of him. Shih P'u (see Chin Ying) was ordered (January 21) to act for him as minister of War. (Early in 1454 Yü had tendered his resignation, but it was not accepted.) Apparently Yü never regained his former strength and energy. Prior to his illness his name often appears in the Veritable Records, but he is scarcely mentioned after 1454, and none of the extant memorials dates later than that year. Thus he was probably physically not in a position to prevent the *coup d'état* of 1457. By his uncompromising and strict attitude in administering his office and by his lack of tolerance in dealing with the shortcomings of others, Yü had made not a few enemies. Shih Heng, originally his collaborator, became gradually his rival and considered Yü an obstacle to his personal ambitions; Hsü Yu-chen could not forget the humiliation he had suffered for his suggestion to move the capital in 1449, a suggestion which had proved to be a serious handicap in his official career. The eunuch, Ts'ao Chi-hsiang (*q.v.*), had wanted to play a role similar to that of Wang Chen and found Yü in his way. Chang Yüeh· (see Chu Ch'i-yü) had been charged by Yü with corruption and other crimes and had suffered punishment. Not surprisingly therefore, after the restoration of Chu Ch'i-chen, Yü was at once arrested and indicted for high treason. He was forced to sign a dictated or drawn-up confession of crimes he had never committed. In particular he was improperly charged with having encouraged Chu Ch'i-yü to name his own son heir apparent and his consort empress in 1452, and with instigating the installation of a prince from outside the capital as heir apparent when the emperor fell ill in 1457. The minister of Personnel, Wang Wen 王文 (T. 千之, d. 1457, cs 1421), who was on trial together with Yü, tried to argue against the unjust indictment, but Yü replied: "It is the intention of Shih Heng and his clique to kill us; what is the use of arguing." It is said that the emperor, Chu Ch'i-chen, agreed to sentence Yü to death only after Hsü Yu-chen had remarked: "If Yü is not killed there would be no justification for this *coup d'état*." The accusers had first asked for the lingering death, but the emperor commuted the sentence to decapitation. On February 16, 1457, Yü was publicly executed along with Wang Wen and four eunuchs. One other charge made against Yü was that he had misused his official position for the benefit of himself and of his family. But when after his death his property was conficated, it was found to consist only of some ordinary household effects and a few presents he had received from the emperor.

In 1466 the court cleared Yü's name of all charges and restored him posthumously to all his former offices. Later, as the result of a petition by Yü's eldest son (1489), an imperial edict granted the erection of a memorial shrine at his grave near Hangchow and the bestowal of the posthumous title Su-min 肅愍, changed to Chung-su 忠肅 early in 1590. Another memorial shrine was erected on the street known later as Hsi piao-pei hu-t'ung 西裱褙胡同 in the eastern part of Peking. To the end of the Ch'ing period candidates from Yü's home province coming to Peking for the metropolitan examinations enjoyed spending a night in the shrine. They hoped that his spirit might appear in their dreams and give them some indication as to their possible success in the examination. There developed a popular belief that the spirits of guiltless people put to death would have a particular influence upon the fate of others.

Yü had three sons. The eldest, Yü Mien 冕 (T. 景瞻, 1422-1500), became an official through the yin privilege in 1450 and rose to the position of prefect of Nanking. He died without issue. The second son died in early childhood; the third, Yü Kuang 廣 (born in 1441), managed with the help of a eunuch to escape after his father's execution to K'ao-ch'eng 郜城, Honan, the original home of the Yü family. His descendants settled there. Yü Ch'ien's only daughter, Yü Ch'iung-ying 瓊英 born in 1429, later married Chu Chi 朱驥 (T. 尚德, d. 1490).

Yü Ch'ien's collected writings, *Yü Chung-su-kung chi* 于忠肅公集 in 12 (13) *chüan*, were published during the T'ien-ch'i period; another edition, *Yü Chieh-an chi* 于節闇集, in 9 *chüan*, is contained in the *San i-jen chi* 三異人集, edited by Li Chih (*q.v.*) during the Wan-li period. A new edition of his prose writings and of a collection of poems on the plum blossom, *Yü Chung-su-kung wen-chi* 文集, was published by his descendants during the 1720s and reprinted with some additions in 1802. The memorials, *Yü-kung tsou-i* 于公奏議, 10 *ch.*, were also published separately, first in 1476, and reprinted in 1541, and then in *Wu-lin wang-che i-chu, hou-pien* 武林往哲遺著後編, 1899-1900. There is likewise an early Korean reprint of the memorials. The poems and essays (without memorials) are collected separately in *Yü Su-min-kung chi*, 8 *ch.* (original edition of 1527, reprint in *Wu-lin wang-che i-chu, hou-pien*, and an abridged edition in *Ch'ien-k'un cheng-ch'i chi* 乾坤正氣集, 1848 and 1866). A new selection of his poems, *Yü Ch'ien shih-hsüan* 詩選, was published in Hangchow, 1958.

Bibliography

1/170/1a; 5/38/37a, 75/26a; MSL (1963), Ying-tsung, 5806; KC (1958), 2023; Ting Ping 丁丙, *Yü-kung-tz'u mu lu* 祠墓錄, 12 *ch.* (in *Wu-lin chang-ku ts'ung-pien* 掌故叢編, 1900); Lai Chia-tu 賴家度 and Li Kuang-pi 李光璧, *Yü Ch'ien ho Pei-ching* 和北京 (Peking, 1951 and 1961); *Ming ching-shih wen-pien* (1964), 229; Ch'ien Ch'ien-i (ECCP), *Lieh-ch'ao shih-chi*, 乙, 4/15b; Tung K'ang 董康, ed., *Pi-pu chao-i* 比部招議 (1935); *Yü Chung-su-kung nien-p'u* 年譜, appendix of *Yü Chung-su-kung wen-chi*; W. Franke, "Yü Ch'ien, Staatsmann und Kriegsminister, 1398-1457," MS, XI (1946), 87; id., "Ein

Dokument zum Prozess gegen Yü Ch'ien i.J.
1457," *Studia Serica*, VI (Chengtu, 1947), 1, 93.

Wolfgang Franke

YÜ Hsiang-tou 余象斗 (T.仰止; also known
as Yü Shih-t'eng 世騰, T. 文台, H. 三台山
人), fl. 1588-1609, of Chien-yang 建陽,
Fukien, was an obscure but interesting
figure connected with the history of
Chinese fiction. Yü Hsiang-tou has come
to the attention of scholars mainly
because of his vocation as a printer
and publisher, and because of his interest
in selling popular novels and stories.
The firm was known both as San-t'ai
kuan 三台館 (Triple-terraced house) and
as Shuang-feng t'ang 雙峯堂 (Double-peak
hall), the two names often appearing
together on the same title page.

The trade had been in the Yü family
for centuries, being handed down from
father to son since the Sung dynasty. In
fact, Chien-yang, a district in the prefecture of Chien-ning 建寧 (formerly in
the circuit of Chien-an安),was the largest
commercial book center in China during
the greater part of the Ming period. Two
towns in this district, Ma-sha chen 麻沙
鎮 in Yung-chung li 永忠里 and Shu-fang
chen 書坊 (book market), also known
as the Shu-lin 書林 (forest of books)
in Ch'ung-hua 崇化 li are important
names in the history of Chinese printing,
for they were prominent in the
industry from the early years of the Sung
dynasty until the end of the Ming. The
latter town, Shu-fang or Shu-lin, obviously
derived its name from the old terms
meaning "book-dealers" or "publishers"
because of the large number of printing
firms there. Shu-fang had been a
significant book mart as far back as the
T'ang dynasty, and the Yü family was
th most important publisher in this town,
being identified collectively as the Yü
family of Chien-an and individually by
separate shop names.

Yü specialized in publishing illustrated
novels, dramas, and popular manuals,
and his business was evidently a prosperous one because, in addition to his own
production, there is evidence that he
printed at least eleven novels and one
anthology of short stories. According to
these publications, he was most active
during the years from 1588 to 1609. His
interest in publishing, however, was primarily financial, and not scholarly, for he
was unscrupulous in appropriating and
plagiarizing the works of others for his
personal gain. His own literary creations
consisted of at least three: *Huang Ming chu-
ssu kung-an chuan* 諸司公案傳; *Wu-hsien-
ling-kuan ta-ti Hua-kuang t'ien-wang chuan*
五顯靈官大帝華光天王傳; *Pei-fang Chen-wu
hsüan-t'ien shang-ti ch'u-shen chih chuan*
北方眞武玄天上帝出身志傳. The first was a
collection of detective stories and the latter
two were Taoist fantasies and supernatural
tales. The last two titles are significant
because they indicate that the Yü
family definitely had some relationship
with the work *Ssu-yu chi* 四遊記 (The
four pilgrimages), a collection of four
separate earlier publications. The two
adventures appear with different titles in
various extant editions. For example, Sun
K'ai-ti 孫楷第 finds that the *Wu-hsien-ling
kuan ta-ti Hua-kuang t'ien-wang chuan* is
the same as *Nan* 南 *yu Hua-kuang chuan*.
The tale was published in 1830 in the
Ssu-yu ch'üan 全 *chuan* and the *Ssu-yu ho*
合 *chuan*. Liu Ts'un-yan reports that the
Yü family probably had some connection
with the unique copy (1571) of this tale,
entitled *Ch'üan hsiang* 像 *Hua kuang t'ien-
wang nan-yu chih chuan* (Prince Hua-kuang),
now in the British Museum. As for the
*Pei-fang Chen-wu Hsüan-t'ien shang-ti ch'u-
shen chih chuan*, Sun K'ai-ti lists another
Pei yu chi Hsüan-ti ch'u-shen chuan 北遊記
玄帝出身傳,also in the Tao-kuang editions
of the *Ssu-yu ch'üan chuan* and the *Ssu-yu
ho chuan*. There is in addition a unique
copy (1602) of this work in the British
Museum under the title *Ch'üan hsiang pei-
yu chi Hsüan-ti ch'u-shen chuan* (The dark

god Chen-wu), probably published by the Yü family. The recent Shanghai reprint (1956) of the *Ssu-yu chi* now carries the Hua-kuang and the Chen-wu adventures as *Nan-yu chi* (Pilgrimage to the south) and *Pei-yu chi* (Pilgrimage to the north) respectively. The important fact to note here is that Yü Hsiang-tou accounted for two of the three novelettes in the series (four in all) which were printed in the Wan-li period. Liu's conclusion is that a complete version of the the Four Pilgrimages might have actually been printed during the Ming, though no known copy exists, and that the Yü family was involved in some way with the publication. Liu furthermore suggests that the fourth novelette "Hsi 西 yu chi" (Pilgrimage to the west) in the series and the famous novel with the identical title by Wu Ch'eng-en (*q.v.*) may both have derived from the same source.

Yü also compiled a study on Chinese poetry under the title *San-t'ai hsüeh yün shih-lin cheng-tsung* 三台學韻詩林正宗, and is believed to have been responsible for the compilation as well as publication of the work *Wan-yung cheng-tsung pu-ch'iu-jen ch'üan pien* 萬用正宗不求人全編, rendered by Arthur Hummel as "The 'Ask No Questions' Complete Handbook for General Use" (1609). Using the name of Wen-t'ai 文台, Yü gives credit for gathering the material to a 14th century Taoist mystic, Lung-yang-tzu 龍陽子. This work is a kind of Ming encyclopedia with illustrations of farming, weaving, and strange countries. It covers a variety of subjects with each subdivision being initiated with a full page illustration of some general heading. Other topics such as astronomy, geography, medicine, architecture, music, painting, calligraphy, archery, husbandry, chess, and dominoes are illustrated separately with maps or pictures.

Perhaps Yü's most famous contribution was his edition of the *Shui-hu chuan* (*see* Lo Kuan-chung). Using the edition published by the marquis of Wu-ting,

Kuo Hsün (*q.v.*), about 1550, Yü brought out a shorter version of the book in 1590 which included two new sections on the expeditions against the rebels T'ien Hu 田虎 and Wang Ch'ing 王慶. Yü's motive in this publication, however, was his desire for quick profit from the popularity of the *Shui-hu*. Apparently Yü's new edition stimulated sales, partly because of the lower sale price resulting from savings on paper and labor in the abridged work.

Illustrations were a distinctive feature of Yü's publication format, especially in his fiction. The commentary, if any, would usually appear at the top of the page, the illustration in the center with a continuous caption or colophon on each side, and the text proper underneath. The illustration would occupy the upper half of the page while the lower half would be devoted to the text, which, according to extant works, generally consisted of twelve to fifteen lines with about twenty or so characters in a line.

In literary terms, however, Yü's abridgment is reportedly not a good one. Aside from the stylistic loss resulting from the shorter narrative, his interpolations and additions contain certain flaws which are discussed in detail by Richard Irwin in his study of the novel. But as the publication was popular, it created interest in the work and became the forerunner of an entire series of abridged versions. Yü's edition, however, was the most important one because of its lasting effect on the final revised and complete form of the *Shui-hu*. The title of his printing was: *Hsin-k'an ching-pen ch'üan-hsiang ch'a-tseng T'ien Hu Wang Ch'ing chung-i Shui-hu ch'üan-chuan* 新刊京本全像插增田虎王慶忠義水滸全傳. The title blatantly advertises the expanded section of the novel: the T'ien Hu and Wang Ch'ing campaigns in which Sung Chiang (fl.1117-21) tries to pacify the rebels. These stories show some color, imagination, and interest due to the greater use of the supernatural element than is found in the original text. But these episodes are characterized by narrative gaps, careless composition, and structural weaknesses, while the rest of Yü's contribution seems to be a poor imitation of campaign battles and sieges. The book is poorly edited and appears to be, in Irwin's words, "the hasty, slipshod writing of a relatively illiterate bookseller."

These additions suffered drastic revision in subsequent, improved editions of the *Shui-hu*. They were too inferior to occupy such a prominent place in the expanded version. Most of the T'ien Hu story has been eliminated in the revised form as well as the venture against Wang Ch'ing. What is important, however, is that Yü's efforts helped to popularize one of China's great novels and possibly promoted scholarly interest in the revisions which followed his publication. The changes by Yü denote, moreover, the end of a long process of story accretion in the *Shui-hu*, and they are preserved, if in name only, in all the later editions of the "complete" novel.

The established list of publications by Yü Hsiang-tou's firm, in addition to those already mentioned, include: *Hsin-k'an ching-pen ch'un-ch'iu wu-pa ch'i-hsiung ch'üan-hsiang Lieh-kuo chih-chuan* 春秋五霸七雄全像列國志傳; *Ching-pen t'ung-su yen-i an-chien ch'üan Han* 通俗演義按鑑全漢 *chih-chuan*; *San-kuo* 三國 *chih-chuan*; *Hsin-chien* 鐫 *ch'üan-hsiang tung-hsi liang Chin* 東西兩晉 *yen-i chih-chuan*; *Hsin-k'o* 刻 *an-chien yen-i ch'üan-hsiang T'ang-shu* 唐書 *chih-chuan*; *Ch'üan-hsiang an-chien yen-i nan-pei liang Sung* 南北兩宋 *chih-chuan*; *Ta Sung chung-hsing Yüeh-wang-chuan* 大宋中興岳王傳; *Ying-lieh-chuan* 英烈傳; *Ching-pen tseng-pu chiao-cheng* 增補校正 *ch'üan-hsiang chung-i Shui-hu chih-chuan p'ing-lin* 評林; *Wan-chin ch'ing-lin* 萬錦情林; and *Hsin-k'an pa-hsien ch'u-ch'u tung-yu chi* 八仙出處東遊記.

Bibliography

Ssu-yu chi, Shanghai, 1956; Cheng Chen-to (BD RC), "Shui-hu-chuan te yen-hua" 的演化, *Chung-kuo wen-hsüeh lun-chi* 中國文學論集 (Shanghai, 1934), 230; Sun K'ai-ti, *Chung-kuo t'ung-su hsiao-shuo shu-mu* 通俗小說書目 (Hong Kong, 1967), 24, 28, 33, 40, 51, 59, 112, 170, 184, 185, 320; id., *Jih-pen Tung-ching Ta-lien t'u-shu-kuan so chien* 日本東京大連圖書館所見 *Chung-kuo hsiao-shuo shu-mu t'i-yao* 提要 (Shanghai, 1953), 55, 59, 76, 97, 158, 179, 239; *Chien-yang-hsien chih* (1929), 12/28a; C. T. Hsia, *The Classic Chinese Novel: A Critical Introduction* (New York, 1968), 78; Arthur W. Hummel, Division of Orientalia, *Annual Report of the Librarian of Congress, 1940* (Washington, 1941), 165; Richard Gregg Irwin, *The Evolution of a Chinese Novel: Shui-hu-chuan* (Cambridge, 1966), 68, 73, 82, 102, 114; K. T. Wu, "Ming Printing and Printers," HJAS, VII (1942–43), 236; Liu Ts'un-yan, *Buddhist and Taoist Influences on Chinese Novels*, Vol. 1 (Wiesbaden, 1962), 78, 108, 132, 136, 152; id., *Chinese Popular Fiction in Two London Libraries* (Hong Kong, 1967), 48, 68, 116, 143.

Dell R. Hales

YÜ Shen-hsing 于愼行 (T. 可遠, 無垢, H. 穀山), 1545-January 30, 1608, scholar and onetime grand secretary, was a native of Tung-a 東阿, Shantung. His father, Yü P'in 玭 (T. 子珍, H. 册川, cj 1528), served as vice prefect of P'ing-liang 平凉 (in present day Kansu) about 1559–62. After qualifying as *chü-jen* in 1561 and *chin-shih* in 1568, Yü Shen-hsing received an appointment in the Hanlin Academy, first as bachelor and then (1570) as compiler. After a year at home he was summoned (1572) to return to aid in the compilation of the *Shih-tsung shih-lu* (completed 1577) and the *Mu-tsung shih-lu* (completed 1574). For the satisfaction he gave in this performance he was promoted one grade. During these same years he served as an assistant examiner in the metropolitan examination of 1574. While acting as expositor (appointed 1576) he was one of several at court who criticized Grand Secretary Chang Chü-cheng (*q.v.*) for his failure to observe properly the period of mourning following his father's death (1577). This led to Yü's retirement

(1579) on the ground of poor health.
Recalled to service in 1583, he became a
counselor of the heir apparent and served
in 1585 as one of the directors of the
chü-jen examination in Nanking, and as
an editor of the *Liu ts'ao chang tsou* 六
曹章奏 (Memorials of the six ministries),
and of the *Ta Ming hui-tien* (*see* Shen
Shih-hsing) in 1585. His next duty was
to serve as expositor of the Classics to
the emperor. He chose to lecture on the
history of the T'ang dynasty—the reasons
for its successes and its failures. Early in
1578 the emperor produced twenty-six
paintings from the imperial collection and
divided them among the six lecturers with
the order that each painting was to have
a colophon in the form of a poem. Four
paintings were assigned to Yü: a snow
landscape, a rainy misty scene, a depiction
of quail, and another of the white egret.
The last was from the hand of the
Hsüan-te emperor (*see* Chu Chan-chi). Yü
followed orders, but because his calligraphy was inferior he asked a friend to
write his poems, duly reporting this fact
at the time of presentation. His honesty
pleased the emperor. On August 9, 1586,
he became a minister of Rites, and three
years later minister and concurrently chancellor of the Hanlin. Beginning in 1590,
at the time when Emperor Chu I-chün (*q.
v.*) was hesitating over whom to appoint
as heir, Yü entreated him several times to
announce his decision, much to his annoyance. Yü was permitted to retire on
November 1, 1591, after being accused of
revealing the name of the chief examiner
for the provincial civil service tests in
Shantung. Sixteen years later (June 9,
1607), he was one of seven men recommended to fill three posts in the Grand
Secretariat; ten days later,he, Yeh Hsiang-
kao, and Li T'ing-chi (*qq.v.*) were announced as the emperor's choice. Yü went
to Peking but soon fell ill and retired (January 3, 1608); before long he succumbed.
He was accorded the posthumous name
Wen-ting 文定.

Yü's learning was said to be profound;
it was reported that, of all the members of the Hanlin Academy of his day,
he and Feng Ch'i (*q.v.*) were considered
to be the best scholars. According to the
local history, Yü wrote nine books, but
only four of these seem to be extant. His
collected poems, the *Ku-ch'eng shan-kuan
shih chi* 穀城山館詩集, 20 *ch.*, with preface
of 1604. is the only one copied into the
Imperial Library. A companion work is
his *Ku-ch'eng shan-kuan wen* 文 *chi*, 42 *ch.*
There is a Nanking edition of both printed
in 1607. The third is his *Ku-shan pi-chu*
穀山筆塵, 18 *ch.*, printed in 1613. There
is a 1625 edition edited by his son, Yü Wei
緯. This contains, as W. Franke writes,
"miscellaneous notes on political, institutional, and other subjects, beginning from
early times, including the Ming period to the
author's lifetime." A third edition appeared in 1677. In the following century
it was banned, but the work has been preserved. An often quoted pronouncement
which Yü makes in this book concerns
the Sui emperor, Yang(r. 605–18), famous
for his part in the extension of the Grand
Canal: "He shortened the life of his
dynasty by a number of years, but benefited posterity unto ten thousand generations. He ruled without benevolence, but
his rule is to be credited with enduring
accomplishments." The fourth of Yü's
books is the *Tu-shih man-lu* 讀史漫錄, 14
ch., giving his reflections after reading
the history from earliest times to the
Mongol period. The *Ssu-k'u* critics dismiss
it rather airily with the comment, "there
is nothing seriously wrong with his discussion, nor anything original either." At
the same time that these editors were
writing it was ordered partially expunged.
Certain passages dealt with incidents in
the history of the Liao, Chin, and Yüan
dynasties. This work as expurgated, but
with 6 *chüan* added by Huang En-t'ung
(ECCP, p. 132), was printed in 1840 and
reprinted twice (1844, 1895). He also
left two short pieces in one *chüan* each,
the *So-yen meng yü* 瑣言夢語 and *Tsa-chi*
雜記, both being preserved in the *Kuang*

K'uai shu 廣快書, published by Ho Wei-jan 何偉然 in 1629. The local history of Tung-a includes rescripts 制勅 written (for the emperor?) between 1573 and 1607, memorials 奏疏 sent to the throne in the 1590s, including his pleas to the emperor over the problem of succession, letters 書, prefaces 序, notes 記 about his travels to scenic spots, the local examinations for the two hundred years before his day, repair of a stele by a local bridge, reconstruction of two monasteries and a single Taoist phalanstery, and the like, epitaphs 墓誌銘 and inscriptions on tablets 墓表. Yü was the editor of the *Yen-chou-fu chih* 志, 52 *ch.*, published in 1596. This is rare but two copies are known to exist in Japan, one in the imperial collection and the other in the Sokeikaku Bunko 尊經閣 文庫.

Bibliography

1/217/11b; 3/200/10a; 5/17/203a; 8/72/17a; 32/95/61b; 40/51/5b; Ch'ien Ch'ien-i (ECCP), *Lieh-ch'ao shih-chi*, 丁:11/23b; MSL(1966), Shen-tsung, 3229, 3992, 8197, 8345, 8375; *Tung-a-hsien chih* (1829), 12/5a, 10b, 13/10b, 14/3a, 15/3a, 16/14b, 30b, 17/2b, 7b, 18/9b, 20/8a, 22/3a, 29b; *Shantung t'ung-chih* (1934), 4733; *Huang Ming wen-hai* (microfilm), 2/4/1, 15/6/3; TSCC (1885–88), XI: 247/67/12a; SK (1930), 90/12a, 125/3a, 172/12a, 179/1b; Sun Tien-ch'i (1957), 209, 250; Yamane and Ogawa, *Ming-jen wen-chi mu-lu* 明人文集目錄 (Tokyo, 1966), 2; L. of C. *Catalogue of Rare Books*, 622, 960; *Title Index to Independent Chinese Works in the Library of Congress* (3d ed., 1932), II, B 367; W. Franke, *Sources*, 4.3.14; Chi Ch'ao-ting, *Key Economic Areas in Chinese History* (London, 1936), 122.

L. Carrington Goodrich

YÜ Ta-yu 俞大猷 (T. 志輔, H. 虛江), July 7, 1503–September 16, 1579, of Chin-chiang 晉江, Fukien, military officer, was known primarily for his contributions in suppressing the *wo-k'ou* on the coasts of Chekiang, Fukien, and Kwangtung in the mid 16th century. Born into a hereditary military family, as a young man Yü studied both the *I-ching* and the military classics. When his father, Yü Yüan-tsan 原瓚, died, Yü assumed the family hereditary post as a centurion of the Ch'üan-chou 泉州 Guard. This was the post originally awarded to Yü Min 敏, founder of the family, for his services rendered to Emperor Chu Yüan-chang.

Yü Ta-yu passed the military *chü-jen* examination in 1534, and received the military *chin-shih* in the following year. Subsequently he was promoted to a chiliarch and appointed battalion commander (5A) on Chin-men 金門 (Quemoy Island), where he served five years. As an eager junior officer he offered his advice to a provincial civil official who, offended at what he considered audacity, had Yü beaten and his rank taken away. Not easily daunted, Yü successively offered his advice and services to the minister of War on Annam policy (in 1540?; *see* Mac Dang-dung) and to the supreme commander of the Hsüan-fu and Tatung area on northern frontier policy (1542), but was rebuffed on both occasions. Appointed T'ing-chang 汀漳 post commander stationed at Wu-p'ing 武平, Fukien, he combined discussing the *I-ching* with the local literati and teaching his soldiers the tactics of warfare. In mid 1544 he tasted defeat at the hands of the *wo* but later (1546) succeeded in posting victories over the pirate K'ang Lao 康老, and then received a transfer (1548) to the Kwangtung regional military commission as acting assistant commissioner (3A). He was instrumental in suppressing uprisings there, and was eventually (1550) given the tactical command of assistant commander 參將 at Yai-chou 崖州 in the same province.

In 1552 the *wo-k'ou* raids on the Chekiang coast began to mount in intensity, and, as an experienced field commander, Yü was shifted (1554) to the post of assistant commander of the prefectures of Ningpo and T'ai-chou 台州. T'ang K'o-k'uan and Lu T'ang (*qq.v.*) were also assistant commanders in the area at this time. In the seven years (1552-59) Yü was in the middle of the fray in the battles against the *wo-k'ou*, and was one of the outstanding military officers on the coast. His early achievements as a field commander, however, were uneven. After initial victories against the sea raiders, Yü suffered a reverse and lost his salary. (He won it back after burning fifty of the enemy's boats.) This was the first of six "crimes" in this seven-year period; the seventh resulted in his imprisonment in the capital.

In one engagement he lost three hundred men and a military *chü-jen* for which he was tried, convicted, and ordered to "manage the bandits"; in another he lost his rank; in still another he lost the right to the hereditary yin privilege, later retrieved. Nevertheless he continued up the ladder of ranks and won positions of increasing responsibility. In June, 1555, he received the post of regional vice commander of the area south of the mouth of the Yangtze River, and a year later, on April 26, was appointed Chekiang regional commander, the first of five such commands he would hold. As a reward for his defeat of the Chinese pirate Hsü Hai (*see* Chao Wen-hua) he was promoted in the winter of 1556 to assistant commissioner-in-chief (2A), a major step from regional to central administrative rank. After promotion to acting vice commissioner-in-chief (1B) for victories on the Chekiang coast, he was accused and found guilty of failure in an assault on the *wo-k'ou* base on Chusan Island (March, 1558). In the following year, Hu Tsunghsien (*q.v.*) blamed both him and Ch'i Chi-kuang (*q.v.*) for failing to contain the pirates. For this he lost his rank and his yin privilege, and in April he was incarcerated in the prison of the Embroidered-uniform Guard in Peking.

Freed through the intercession of Lu Ping (*q.v.*), Yü was sent to the northern frontier to redeem himself. While in the Tatung defense area he built a device described as a wheelbarrow(獨輪車)which

was used to keep the enemy's horses at bay (*see* Ch'en Ti). It worked so well that his plans were sent to the capital, and a wheelbarrow division was established in the capital army.

As a result of a successful stratagem against the Mongols, which resulted in a signal victory, Yü was given back the yin privilege, and after reassessment of merit for the capture of Wang Chih (*see* Lu T'ang), he was forgiven his "crimes" and put on the appointment list. He was assigned to Chen-kan 鎮筸, Hukuang, as assistant commander, and in August, 1561, was transferred to the Nan-kan 南贛 area encompassing the borders of Kiangsi, Kwangtung, and Hukuang provinces. As a result of his victories there he was made regional vice commander, and then chosen to be the Fukien regional commander where he cooperated with the Chekiang regional vice commander, Ch'i Chi-kuang in recapturing the prefectural city of Hsing-hua 興化 and the P'ing-hai 平海 Guard (May, 1563). Late in the same year he was shifted back briefly to his post at Nan-kan, now as regional commander, and in July, 1564, was posted at the same rank to Kwangtung. Once again he joined with the now Fukien regional commander, Ch'i Chi-kuang, in coordinating land and sea attacks against the bandit Wu P'ing (*see* Lin Tao-ch'ien), who had taken refuge on the island of Nan-ao 南澳 near the Fukien-Kwangtung border. Wu slipped away and Yü, who was responsible for the naval aspects of the engagement, was held responsible, tried, and divested of his rank. After further victories this was restored, and he was appointed Kwangsi regional commander with the seal of "General who quells the Man" (cheng-Man chiang-chün 征蠻將軍) in November, 1567. There he gained many victories against local bandits, and was promoted to acting vice commissioner-in-chief (1B), then junior commissioner-in-chief (1A), and his yin privilege was advanced to that of guard assistant commander (4A).

Yet once again he was impeached, this time for disloyalty and avarice, and ordered home (April, 1572) to await investigation. Later recalled to take a post in the southern capital, he refused it, returning instead to the coast as Fukien regional commander. He lost this in a few months, and the autumn of 1572 found him at home. He came out of retirement once again, to accept a post in the rear military commission where he controlled the training of the barrow divisions in the capital army which he had been instrumental in creating.

A cursory glance at his record reveals that Yü Ta-yu was one of the most important military commanders of the mid-16th century. In over thirty years of military service he rose to the rank of junior commissioner-in-chief and served as regional commander in five of the major defense areas in the southeast from Chekiang to Kwangsi. A student of both civil and military classics and a holder of the military chin-shih, Yü was an adept officer in the field known for his careful planning. He was versed in the use of naval and land forces, the use of deception, ambush on the battlefield, and spies in the enemy's camp. He had a reputation for loyalty towards the dynasty and honesty with his troops. At his death he was promoted to senior commissioner-in-chief and given the posthumous title of Wu-hsiang 武襄. His son, Yü Tzu-kao 咨皋, became Fukien regional commander. Yü's writings, including maps and illustrations, are collected in Cheng-ch'i-t'ang chi 正氣堂集, which includes his first collection, Cheng-ch'i-t'ang chi, 16 ch., printed in 1565, with two supplements, a Cheng-chiao Ku-t'ien shih-lüeh 征剿古田事略 (designated as chüan 16B), printed in 1571, and a Chen-Min i-kao 鎮閩議稿, printed in 1572; his second collection, Cheng-ch'i-t'ang hsü 續 chi, 7 ch., published in 1578; a third collection, entitled Cheng-ch'i-t'ang yü 餘 chi, 4 ch. (also recorded as 5 ch.). He wrote as well the Hsi-hai chin-shih 洗海近事, 2 ch., published 1569,

a record of his military activities on the southeast littoral. In 1841 a second edition of the Cheng-ch'i-t'ang chi appeared. In 1934 the Kuo-hsüeh Library in Nanking reproduced the Ming edition with a postface by Liu I-cheng (BDRC).

Bibliography

1/212/1a; 3/196/1a; 5/107/43a, 50b; 61/141/10a; 63/14/33a; MSL (1965), Shih-tsung, 7470, 7904, 8028, 8263, 8379, 8523, 8688, Mu-tsung, 1623; KC (1958), 3852; Kwangtung t'ung-chih(1934), 705, 709, 3444; SK (1930), 53/7a; Chin-chiang-hsien chih (1765, repr. 1967), 144, 200; T'ing-chou 汀州-fu chih (1752), 20/16a; Kan 贛-chou-fu chih (1873), 40/4a, 45/2a; Ch'iung 瓊-chou-fu chih (1890), 30/13b; Naikaku Bunko Catalogue, 83, 356; W. Franke, Sources, 7.2.2, 8.12.

James F. Millinger

YÜ T'ung-hai 俞通海 (T. 碧泉), 1330-May 19, 1367), was a native of Ch'ao-hsien 巢縣 (Anhwei). During the rebellions at the end of the Yüan, Yü, together with his father and younger brothers, belonged to the group of pirates on Lake Ch'ao headed by Chao P'u-sheng (see Hsü Shou-hui). In 1355 Chu Yüan-chang was at Ho-chou 和州 intending to cross the Yangtze River, but lacked boats; at the same time the pirates were being driven from the lake by the warlord Tso Chün-pi (see Chang Shih-ch'eng). Chu Yüan-chang solicited their aid, but Chao P'u-sheng persuaded most of them to join the forces of Ch'en Yu-liang (q.v.); nevertheless a minority led by the Yü together with Liao Yung-an and Liao Yung-chung (qq. v.), provided Chu with the boats which he needed. Yü participated in the fighting which led to the capture of Nanking in 1356 and to the founding of Chu Yüan-chang's regime there; he was given the post of commander of the Ch'in-huai wing 秦淮翼, a designation which then comprised the reserve elements of Chu's fleet. He was subsequently promoted to executive officer of the branch bureau of military affairs, and led a flotilla against General Lü Chen (*see* Chang Shih-ch'eng) on Lake T'ai, in which battle he lost his right eye. In April, 1359, he defeated his former leader, Chao P'u-sheng, near Anking, and received a promotion to assistant commissioner of the bureau of military affairs.

The surrender of the rest of the Lake Ch'ao group, as a result of the great victory near Nanking in July, 1360, made the adherents of Chu Yüan-chang a significant naval power for the first time. For his part in defeating the forces of Ch'en Yu-liang near Ts'ai-shih 采石, Yü was promoted to deputy commissioner of the bureau of military affairs. The following year he accompanied the fleet which once again defeated Ch'en Yu-liang, captured Kiukiang, and blockaded Wuchang. In 1363 Yü and Liao Yung-chung commanded the two wings of the fleet during the Poyang Lake campaign. On August 30, the first day of the naval battle, he took advantage of the direction of the wind to destroy several of Ch'en Yu-liang's ships by fire (this is probably not an instance of the use of firearms, though there are other undoubted examples of this during the same period), and afterwards rescued Chu Yüan-chang when the latter's flagship ran aground and came under heavy attack. On the following day he and Liao Yung-chung organized an attack by their fireships, employing seven small boats containing explosive powder wrapped in reeds; this tactic allegedly destroyed several hundred ships. The enemy was so weakened by these losses that two days later Yü and Liao were able to lead a squadron directly through the center of their battle line, a feat which greatly encouraged Chu's supporters. Despite these successes, however, the enemy ships remained too numerous and individually too formidable to be destroyed. On the night of September 2 Chu's fleet withdrew and sailed to a new anchorage at the southern end of the straits, blocking egress from the lake. The enemy soon followed and anchored facing them. While this situation endured, Yü urged upon Chu the desirability of moving to a position upstream from Hu-k'ou 湖口 on the Yangtze. Chu eventually agreed, and in the final battle on October 3 Ch'en was killed and most of his fleet surrendered.

The following year Yü took part in the capture of Wuchang and was promoted to administrator of the secretariat along with Ch'ang Yü-ch'un (*q.v.*). Afterwards he was placed in charge of the Chiang-Huai 江淮 branch secretariat established at Lu-chou 廬州, and won further victories in the war against Chang Shih-ch'eng. At the siege of Soochow he was again severely wounded by arrows, taken to Nanking, and there he died. He was posthumously made duke of Yü 豫國公, which title was changed in 1370 to duke of Kuo 虢 with the honorific appellation chung-lieh 忠烈 (loyal and bold).

Yü's father, Yü T'ing-yü 廷玉, ultimately attained the rank of assistant commissioner of the bureau of military affairs, but predeceased his son and was posthumously ennobled as duke of the commandery of Ho-chien 河間郡公. As Yü T'ung-hai had no sons, his younger brother, Yü T'ung-yüan 通源 (T. 百川, d. April 5, 1389), succeeded to his offices and distinguished himself as a commander in the conquest of the north China plain and Shensi. In 1370 he received the rank of marquis of Nan-an 南安侯 with a stipend of 1,500 *shih*. In 1371 he fought in the Szechwan campaign. After a long military career he was ordered to retire in 1389 and was given a house in Ch'ao-hsien. Soon afterward he died. As his son, Yü Tsu 祖, was too sickly to inherit, and Yü T'ung-yüan himself was afterwards implicated in the Hu Wei-yung (*q.v.*) affair, the marquisate terminated.

Yü Yüan 淵 (d. September 24, 1399), originally named Yü T'ung-yüan 通淵, the younger brother of Yü T'ung-hai and Yü T'ung-yüan, rose to the rank of assistant commissioner-in-chief, and, because of Chu

Yüan-chang's regard for Yü T'ung-hai and their father, did not suffer when his brother posthumously lost the marquisate. In 1392 he was created marquis of Yüeh-sui 越嶲侯 with a stipend of 2,500 *shih*. He was disgraced and sent into exile the following year as a result of the Lan Yü (*q.v.*) episode, but in 1399 Emperor Chu Yün-wen (*q.v.*) restored his titles so that he might take part in the army mobilized against his uncle, Chu Ti (*q.v.*). Yü Yüan was killed in the battle of the Po-kou River 白溝河. His son, Yü Ching 靖, inherited the title, but lost it as a result of Chu Ti's victory in the civil war.

Bibliography

1/133/3a; MSL (1962), T'ai-tsu, *ch.* 30, 44, 51, 54, 83, 157, 329; KC (1958), 274, 276, 284, 330, 380; Ku Ying-t'ai (ECCP), *Ming-ch'ao chi-shih pen-mo* (1658), *ch.* 3; Ch'ien Ch'ien-i (ECCP), *Kuo-ch'u ch'ün-hsiung shih-lüeh, ch.* 4; L. Carrington Goodrich and Feng Chia-sheng, "The Early Development of Firearms in China," *Isis,* 36 (1947), 114.

Edward L. Dreyer

YÜ Tzu-chün 余子俊 (T. 士英), 1429–March 23, 1489, scholar-official, who served with distinction as minister of War and Revenue under Emperors Chu Chien-shen and Chu Yu-t'ang (*qq.v.*), was a native of Ch'ing-shen 青神, Szechwan. The Yü family, which originally hailed from Ching-shan 京山, Hukuang, moved to Szechwan to seek shelter from the rebel uprisings against the Yüan government in the early 1360s. Yü Tzu-chün's father, a bureau director in the ministry of Revenue, died when his son was only nine years of age. Achieving the *chin-shih* in 1451, Yü Tzu-chün received an appointment as secretary in the ministry of Revenue. In January, 1455, he attracted attention by submitting a memorial criticizing the excessive spending by the functionaries in the Court of Imperial Entertain-

ment and by the monks and Taoists in conducting religious festivities. In August of the following year he rose to be a vice director of the Fukien bureau in the same ministry, and became magistrate of Sian four years later (March, 1460). One of his notable achievements there was the supervision of an irrigation project (1465) to provide sufficient fresh water which was then in short supply due to the silting of the old canal (*see* Keng Ping-wen). Instead of dredging the existing waterway, Yü bored an underground canal leading the water of two streams into the city from the east, and letting it flow to the west. The water was made available by means of a series of shafts with a masonry lining extending to a length of 1,550 *chang* (over 3 miles). As a reward for his performance Yü was promoted to be an administration vice commissioner twenty months later (October, 1467). Early in 1470 he was transferred to be administration commissioner of Chekiang where he officiated until his promotion to be vice censor-in-chief and governor of Yen-sui 延綏 (Shensi) in February, 1471.

Yü Tzu-chün's new appointment high-lighted the immense problem facing the Chinese defenders in formulating schemes to resist the increased depredations of the Mongol tribesmen under the leadership of P'o-lai (*see* Hsiang Chung). During the previous year, the vice censor-in-chief in charge of the defense of Yen-sui, Wang Jui 王銳 (cs 1439), proposed the erection of defense walls along the frontier at Yü-lin 榆林 to be equipped with fortresses and beacon-fire towers. Wang's recommendation was supported by Ma Wen-sheng (*q.v.*), governor of Shensi; the matter was discussed at court, but no immediate action taken in view of the enormous cost. In August, 1471, seven months after he assumed duty, Yü submitted a lengthy memorial in which he reiterated the previous proposals for the construction of a wall along the ridges of the mountainous region of Yen-sui and Ch'ing-yang 慶陽 in northern Shensi and Kansu. This wall ,he said, would be 2.5 *chang* (*ca.* 30 ft.) in height, complete with fortresses and beacon-fire towers, and he proposed to undertake the construction during the months of September and October, requesting a work force of fifty thousand men. The senior officials, led by the minister of War, Pai Kuei (*q.v.*), however, dissented arguing that this undertaking would be too costly and burdensome for the local population, and recommended further study. In the following months, the Mongols intensified their offensive against Yü-lin, and, as the government failed to repel the enemy from the Ordos region, the situation became critical, and the proposal in favor of defensive measures gained popularity.

Late in October, 1472, Yü Tzu-chün submitted another memorial outlining his earlier plan for the construction of the wall, arguing its merit against the raiders, and that such an investment would eventually reduce the annual defense budget. This time he received support from the emperor as well as from senior military officials such as Chao Fu (*see* Han Yung) and Wang Yüeh(*q.v.*), over the opposition of Pai Kuei and others; the building started under his supervision in the spring of 1474. In August, Yü reported that the wall was almost completed. It extended from Ch'ing-shui-ying 清水營 in northeastern Shensi to Hua-ma-ch'ih 花馬池 in northwestern Ning-hsia, running to the southwest for about two thirds of its length and then to the northwest. This wall, 1,770 *li* long (nearly 600 miles)was erected along or close to the tops of the mountain chain, with fortresses, beacon-fire towers, and sentry posts, totaling over eight hundred units; with a labor force of over forty thousand, it took several months to complete, at a cost in excess of a million taels of silver. It provided not only a permanent barrier against the intrusion of the Mongols, but also a shelter for the cultivation of military farms which reportedly yielded an income of over sixty thousand bushels of grain in reve-nue. The result of Yü's labor was first tested in July, 1482, when the Chinese defenders, barricaded behind the wall, successfully nullified a major offensive by the Mongols. During the next century, several attempts were made to repair and strengthen it: by Yang I-ch'ing (*q.v.*) in 1507, by Fan Chi-tsu (*see* Liang Ts'ai) in 1541, by Weng Wan-ta (*see* Wang Chiu-ssu) in 1546, and by Wang Ch'ung-ku (*q. v.*) in 1574. The over-all effectiveness notwithstanding, this wall also produced negative aspects with regard to the Chinese defense on the northern frontier. It created a barrier, physically and psychologically, in northern Shensi and Ning-hsia, which limited the Chinese to a defensive policy and discouraged them from venturing into the Ordos region (*see* Tseng Hsien); as a result it subsequently fell under Mongol domination to the detriment of Chinese interests.

Late in December, 1475, Yü Tzu-chün received a transfer to be governor of Shensi. He then submitted a seven-point formula dealing with defense matters and with the improvement of the well-being of the local population, still threatened by sporadic Mongol invasions. He petitioned the court to exempt military conscripts registered in Shensi and Kansu from being assigned to the sourthern provinces, and took personal command of campaigns against the rebellious Ch'iang 羌 tribesmen in Kansu. He also resumed work on his irrigation project in Sian, dredging the underground canal. This canal, when completed, came to be popularly known as Yü-kung 余公 ch'ü (Mr. Yü's canal). In September, 1477, in recognition of his performance, the emperor appointed him minister of War, and awarded him the honor of junior protector of the heir apparent a year later (November, 1478).

In his new capacity Yü Tzu-chün devoted his attention to the defense of the northern frontier; he refrained from adventurous campaigns and improved the condition of the armed forces to raise their combat effectiveness. In November,

1477, he promulgated ten guidelines for the military, giving instructions to strengthen the discipline of the armed forces, promoting the morale of the soldiers by standardizing rewards and punishments, eliminating red tape, and encouraging the rapport between the military and the local administration. At the same time he remonstrated against unwarranted provocations against the tribesmen in the border regions. For instance, he rejected the request of Ch'en Yüeh, a protégé of the eunuch Wang Chih 汪直 (q.v.) and governor of Liaotung, to launch a campaign against the Jurchen settlement in Chien-chou 建州 because of minor incidents. He also spurned the proposal made by Ch'en Yen 儼 (T. 時莊, cs 1454), governor of Kweichow, to mobilize a massive army drawn from three provinces to crush a rebellion of the Miao 苗 tribesmen in his own province. It was in the fromer instance that he antagonized Wang Chih, who subsequently rose to dominate the court. Wang connived with his cronies for Yü's removal; but before their plan materialized, Yü had left office to mourn the death of his mother (February, 1481), thus sparing himself possible disgrace.

In August, 1483, after completing the mourning requirement, Yü Tzu-chün was recalled to be minister of Revenue, but was instructed seven months later to serve concurrently as governor of Hsüan-fu and Tatung in charge of defense and military supplies, with the additional title of grand protector of the heir apparent. In September, 1484, he submitted a scheme for the manufacturing of a special kind of war chariots, totaling fifteen hundred, with a thousand assigned to Tatung and five hundred to Hsüan-fu, each of which was to be manned by ten soldiers. These chariots, he said, would be effective in encountering the Mongol horsemen on the flat land of the frontier. The emperor approved, but the new vehicles were far from perfect, and the plan had to be temporarily abandoned. Late in this year, with the enemy retreating, Yü returned to

Peking to resume charge of the ministry of Revenue. Two months later (February, 1485) he submitted a memorial complaining about the inadequacy of grain reserve at the frontier, urging the court to increase the supply from the reserve in the capital circuit, at the same time reducing expenses in the inner court. A month later, as the Mongols renewed their offensive, the emperor ordered him back to the frontier, giving him the rank of vice censor-in-chief, and appointed Yin Ch'ien 殷謙 (T. 文撝, H. 遜齋, 1417–1504, cs 1439) as minister of Revenue. In August Yü Tzu-chün submitted a plan for the repair and erection of walls in Hsüan-fu and Tatung, for 1,321 li (about 440 miles), encompassing the entire frontier from the bend of the Yellow River to the coast of Liaotung. He proposed the construction of 440 new beacon-fire towers, each estimated at 3 chang (ca. 35 ft.) in height and width, and requiring six hundred men working six out of every seven days. The over-all scheme required a total of 86,000 laborers, and eight months to complete, at an estimated cost of 150,000 bushels of grain, 77,000 taels of silver, and 250,000 piculs of salt. In view of the effectiveness of the walls at Yensui, the emperor approved his plan, and commanded that construction be started in May of the following year. Unlike his earlier project which he had personally supervised, Yü left the task this time to his subordinates in order to give them experience. The assignment, however, was complicated by the disparity between planning and execution, and consequently placed great burden on them. Following a dispute with him they memorialized the court charging Yü with inadequate leadership and waste of funds; as a result, the emperor reassigned him (November, 1485) to be governor of Tatung, with the rank of censor-in-chief. Earlier the eunuch Wei Ching 韋敬, then grand defender of Ning-hsia, had accused Yü of improperly exercising his authority to effect the transfer and promotion of certain officials in charge of the defense of the frontier. Wei did this apparently because of his grudge against Yü for having revealed his misrule while he was grand defender of Yen-sui, which had resulted in Wei's transfer to his present post. Acting on this and the previous charges, the emperor ordered several officials to the frontier to conduct an investigation (*see* Juan Ch'in). Upon their return they reported Yü innocent of the charge, but considered his project wasteful of funds and burdensome to the population. To placate the opposition, the emperor revoked (March, 1486) his title of grand guardian of the heir apparent, and sent him into retirement.

In August, 1487, the emperor recalled Yü to be minister of War and restored his honorary title, but a month later the monarch died. When Chu Yu-t'ang ascended the throne, Yü thrice submitted a request to retire (October, November, and February, 1488), but the emperor asked him to remain. In February of the following year he submitted a four-point memorandum in which he proposed the adoption of a scheme for the equal distribution on a regional basis of candidates for civil service appointments, increasing the grain reserve in the provinces, improving the frontier defense and the firearms units, and to ensure justice scrutinizing the penalties used in criminal cases. His recommendations were accepted. In March, 1489, stricken by ill health, Yü again pleaded for permission to retire, but the emperor declined. He died at the end of this month, at the age of sixty. The emperor granted him the posthumous rank of grand protector, and the canonized name Su-min 肅敏 (majestic and earnest), and appointed his grandson Yü Ch'eng-tsu 承祖 a hereditary battalion commander of the Embroidered-uniform Guard, but the latter died shortly afterwards. The emperor then appointed (May, 1493) Yü Chen 寊 (T. 世臣, H. 青野, cj 1483), Yü Ch'eng-tsu's father, a chiliarch commander of the Embroidered-uniform Guard, and later (April, 1502) granted his descendants

the privilege of inheriting the rank of battalion commander. Following his new appointment, Yü Chen erected a shrine in his native place in honor of his father. During the next reign, shrines in honor of Yü Tzu-chün were erected in several places along the frontier in Shensi and Ning-hsia. Some of his memorials were collected in the *Yü Su-min kung tsou-i* 奏議, 6 *ch.*, which was proscribed during the 18th century but has survived. A copy of an incomplete version used to be preserved in the former Institute of Humanistic Studies, Peiping. Portions of this collection have been copied into the *Huang Ming ching-shih wen-pien* of Ch'en Tzu-lung (ECCP).

Yü Tzu-chün's son, Yü Chen, after being appointed chiliarch commander of the Embroidered-uniform Guard in 1493, was sent to Kweichou to take part in the suppression of a Miao rebellion, and was subsequently promoted to be an assistant commander. Four years later, summoned to Peking, he was appointed a regional commander, and held this post for over a decade until his confrontation with the eunuch Liu Chin (*q.v.*) during the early years of Emperor Chu Hou-chao (*q.v.*). He then sought permission to retire on the pretext of ill health to prevent possible disgrace; presumably his hereditary military rank was abrogated at this time. Three years later, shortly after Liu Chin's execution, he was recalled but was soon ordered to retire to Nanking, retaining his title and stipend, until his death in 1517. Being childless, he adopted his cousin's eldest son Yü Ch'eng-en 恩 (T. 懋忠, H. 鶴池) as his heir.

Yü Tzu-chün had an adopted son, Yü Huan 寰 (1463–1506), born to his younger brother. Entering the National University (October, 1476) through the yin privilege, Yü Huan achieved the *chin-shih* in 1499 and became a bureau secretary in the ministry of Revenue. In August of the following year he submitted a three point memorandum on defense in which he argued for the efficiency of the chariots and beaconfire towers introduced by his uncle, and urged the court to manufacture the former and repair the latter along the defense walls. His recommendations were accepted. Yü Huan later advanced to be an assistant bureau director of the same ministry, and died while in office at the age of forty-three.

Yü Huan had three sons who also made a mark in the official service. His eldest son Yü Ch'eng-en entered the National University through the yin privilege. He was first appointed an assistant commander of the Embroidered-uniform Guard at Nanking (1519), next regional assistant commander of Hukuang (1525), and then of Szechwan (1528), distinguishing himself in the suppression of the local tribesmen. Four years later (1532) he rose to be a mobile commander of Mao-chou 茂州, Szechwan, where he erected walls along the outer perimeter of his prefecture to block the rebellious natives. Following this he became an assistant commander (1536) in charge of the pacification of the tribesmen on the border of Szechwan and Kweichow, but retired a year later because of illness. He died at the age of fifty-three.

The second son, Yü Ch'eng-hsün 勛, a *chin-shih* of 1517, was appointed a compiler in the Hanlin Academy, where he officiated until his implication in the *Ta-li i* controversy during the early years of the reign of Chu Hou-ts'ung (*q.v.*). He then retired and spent the next forty years in scholarly pursuits. He served as editor of the local gazetteer *Ch'ing-shen-hsien chih*, 6 *ch.*, completed in 1551 (revised in 1606), which is still extant.

The third son, Yü Ch'eng-yeh 業 (T. 草池), a *chin-shih* of 1523, first served as prefect of Teng-chou 鄧州, Honan, and was promoted to be vice prefect of Yunnan-fu, in 1531. He then officiated in such capacities as vice bureau director in the ministry of Revenue, bureau director in the ministry of Justice (1533), and assistant surveillance commissioner of Yunnan (1534). In 1543 he went to Peking to petition for the reinstatement of

the hereditary military rank granted to the descendants of his uncle Yü Chen, which had been abrogated during the early years of the Cheng-te reign. Following this, he was transferred to a similar post in Honan, and received promotion to be assistant administration commissioner of Hukuang (1544). He reached his highest post—surveillance vice commissioner of Yunnan—in the following year, and died some time later.

Bibliography

1/178/10a; 3/161/9a; 5/38/68a; 8/31/8a; 16/32/8a, 47/54a, 123/5b, 127/30a, 128/9a; 32/109/17a; 61/124/15a; MSL (1963), Ying-tsung, 4555, 5380, 5687, 6554, Hsien-tsung (1964), *ch.* 1–293, Hsiaotsung, *ch.* 1–186, Wu-tsung (1965), 522, 980, Shih-tsung (1965), 5674; KC (1958), 2582; Li Tung-yang, *Huai-lu-t'ang wen hou-kao*, 11/6b; Liu Ch'un 劉春 (cs 1487), *Tung-ch'uan Liu Wen-chien kung chi* 東川劉文簡公集 (NCL microfilm), 15/26b; Chang Hsüan, *Hsi-yüan wen-chien lu*, 52/18a, 54/2b, 60/18b, 61/10a, 62/10b, 75/31b, 83/1a; Ho Ch'iao-yüan, *Ming-shan ts'ang* (Taipei, 1970 ed.), 3799; *Huang Ming wen-hai* (microfilm), 13/7/10, 17/2/17; *Ch'ing-shen-hsien chih* (1606), *ch.* 5 下; *Hsi-an-fu chih* 西安府志 (1779, 1970 ed.), 5/8b, 7/13b; *Szechwan t'ung-chih* (pref. 1815), 37/11a, 51/35a, 124/18b, 125/58b, 150/52a; Li Shu-fang 李澂芳, "Ming-tai pien-ch'iang yen-ko k'ao-lüeh" 明代邊牆沿革考略, *Yü-kung* 禹貢, 5:1 (March, 1936), 1; Ku Chieh-kang (BDRC), *Shih-lin tsa-shih (ch'u-pien* 初編) (Peking, 1963), 79; I Chih 伊志, "Ming-tai 'ch'i T'ao' shih-mo" 「棄套」始末, in Pao Tsun-p'eng 包遵彭 ed., *Ming-tai pien-fang* 邊防 (Taipei, 1968), 141; Sun Tien-ch'i (1957), 85; W. Franke, *Sources*, 175; Joseph Needham, *Science and Civilization in China*, IV:3 (Cambridge, 1971), 335.

Hok-lam Chan

YÜ Yu 余祐 (or Yü Hu 祜, T. 子積, H. 認齋), 1465–1528, thinker and official, was a native of Po-yang 鄱陽, Kiangsi. His grandfather, Yü T'ai 泰, served as magistrate in Fu-ch'ing 福清, Fukien. Yü Yu himself became a student of Hu Chü-jen (*q.v.*) in 1483, and shortly afterwards married his teacher's daughter. In 1486 he qualified for the *chü-jen* and in 1499 the *chin-shih*. He was appointed a secretary in the ministry of Justice, Nanking, later rising to the directorship of a bureau. A decision he made in a judicial case, however, displeased the powerful eunuch Liu Chin (*q.v.*); this led to his dismissal from office in 1508. After Liu's death (1510), Yü was recalled to government service and made prefect of Foochow. He was then appointed surveillance vice commissioner of Shantung, but was prevented by the death of his father from assuming office. After completing the mourning period, he was sent to Hsü-chou 徐州, Nan-Chihli, as surveillance vice commissioner in charge of the military defense circuit. He made efforts to control the activities of the eunuchs in charge of court tribute, who frequently demanded excessive payments and unusual favors from local officials, thus exposing himself to their vengeance. Under a false charge, Yü was arrested, put into the notorious prison of the Embroidered-uniform Guard, and demoted as assistant prefect to Nan-ning 南寧, Kwangsi. Shortly afterwards, he was transferred as prefect to Shao-chou 韶州, Kwangtung, but declined the promotion and resigned from official duties. On the accession to the throne (1521) of Emperor Chu Hou-ts'ung (*q.v.*), Yü Yu was summoned back to official service and later promoted to be provincial surveillance commissioner in Honan. He served in the same position in Kwangsi, until he was named administrative commissioner, first of Hukuang and then of Yunnan. In 1527 Yü Yu received the appointment of chief minister of the Court of the Imperial Stud. Before he had time to report to office, he was promoted to be vice minister of Personnel. But the good news never reached him. At the age of sixty-three Yü Yu was overtaken by sickness and died in Yunnan.

Probably the best known of Hu Chü-jen's disciples, Yü Yu sought to be scrupulously faithful to his master's teachings.

He considered himself an exponent of the philosophy of Ch'eng I (1033–1107) and Chu Hsi (1130–1200), and gave emphasis to reverence (ching 敬) and sincerity (ch'eng 誠) in the quest for sagehood. He published a selection of Chu Hsi's writings on political, social, and economic affairs, under the title *Wen-kung hsien-sheng ching-shih ta-hsün* 文公先生經世大訓, 16 *ch.* According to the editors of the *Ssu-k'u* catalogue, this work, completed in 1514, presents selections from Chu's recorded sayings and writings without developing the ideas incorporated. Yü also edited Chu's comments on literature in the *Yu-i lu* 遊藝錄, 1 *ch.*, which is known besides as *Yu-i chih-lun* 至論.

Yü Yu expressed his own philosophical ideas in the *Hsing-shu* 性書, 3 *ch.*, which he wrote while in prison. This book seems to be no longer extant, but there still exists a long letter from Yü's good friend, Wei Chiao (*see* Cheng Jo-tseng), who voiced disagreement with Yü's interpretation of nature (hsing) as being composed of li 理 and ch'i 氣, the former being simple and integral and the latter diverse and divided. Wei prefers to see both as whole and integral, but with manifold manifestations. He maintains, moreover, that nature belongs entirely to the realm of li, which is full of goodness, while the emotions (ch'ing 情) refer to that of ch'i, which is morally ambiguous and gives occasion to evil desires. Thus it would appear that Wei Chiao sought to correct Yü Yu for departing from certain views of Ch'eng I and Chu Hsi, and to lend firm support to his view of li.

Yü Yu was a contemporary of Wang Shou-jen (*q.v.*). He criticized the latter for his presentation of the allegedly "mature views" of Chu Hsi. Yü declared that Chu held to the importance of the cultivation of the mind and heart (hsin 心) during his youth, but changed his views twice: first after meeting in 1158 with Li T'ung (1093–1163), and then after discussing the philosophy of Hu Hung (1105–55) with Chang Shih (1133–80) around

1166/67. According to Yü, Chu's "mature views" regarded nature (hsing) in its "unstirred" (wei-fa 未發) and "stirred" (i-fa 已發) moments, that is, the recovery of the original equilibrium and the maintenance of the harmony of the emotions.

Bibliography

1/282/1a; 3/263/12a; 5/26/29a; 16/29/4b, 150/3b, 16b; 32/59/33b; 83/3/9a; SK (1930), 95/10b; Hu Chü-jen, *Chü-yeh lu* (TsSCC, lst ser.), 1; *Hu Wen-ching kung nien-p'u* 胡文敬公年譜 in *Shih-wu chia* 十五家 *nien-p'u*, ed. by Yang Hsi-min 楊希閔 (1878 ed.), 9/20a; Huang Yü-chi (ECCP), *Ch'ien-ch'ing-t'ang shu-mu*, 11/5a; *Jao-chou-fu chih* 饒州府志 (1872), 14/47b, 18/13a, 26/65a; Wei Chiao, *Wei Chuang-ch'ü hsien-sheng chi* 莊渠先生集 (Shanghai, 1937), A/3; Wang Mou-hung (1668-1741), *Chu-tzu* 朱子 *nien-p'u* (Taipei reprint, 1966), 1A/13, 1B/36.

Julia Ching and Huang P'ei

YÜAN Chih 袁袠 (T. 永之, H. 胥臺), November 25, 1502-June 29, 1547, scholar, was born into a wealthy family of Soochow. The youngest of four brothers, all known as excellent writers, he was the only one to succeed in the civil examinations, becoming a *chin-shih* in 1526. He passed fourth on the list and was among the twenty selected to be bachelors in the Hanlin Academy. In November, 1527, the emperor ordered a reexamination of the Hanlin academicians. As a result, Yüan Chih, one of the twenty-two to receive new assignments, was sent to the ministry of Justice as a secretary. In September, 1528, he went to Honan as co-director of the provincial examination. One of the candidates he passed was the future powerful minister Kao Kung (*see* Chang Chü-cheng).

In 1531, while serving as a secretary in the bureau of personnel of the ministry of War, Yüan Chih was held responsible for a fire that destroyed the building housing the bureau, and received a sentence of banishment to the Hu-chou 湖州 Guard as a common soldier. This seems to have been a rather unusual punishment, for the Guard was situated only forty miles from his native place. In any case he was pardoned in 1533 and seven years later was reinstated as a secretary in the Nanking ministry of War. In 1543 he served a term as assistant surveillance commissioner of Kwangsi in charge of education, and then retired. About this time he wrote a work on political economy consisting of twenty essays, each on certain practices in the Ming government which he thought should be changed. The book entitled *Shih-wei* 世緯, 2 *ch.*, was almost lost to sight (it was not even listed in the bibliographical section of the *Ming-shih*) until a copy (perhaps the only one then extant) turned up in the 1770s and was included in the Imperial Library. In 1787 a clansman (Yüan T'ing-t'ao, ECCP, p. 417) made a special request to the *Ssu-k'u* commission to have a copy made for the Yüan family library. It was later printed in the 15th series of the *Chih-pu-tsu-chai ts'ung-shu* (*see* Pao T'ing-po, EC CP).

Among other works by Yüan Chih may be mentioned the *Huang Ming hsien-shih* 皇明獻實, 40 *ch.*, consisting of 180 biographies of Ming personages. A manuscript copy of this work is preserved in the National Central Library, Taipei. He is known to have written a number of biographies of famous men of Soochow. A collection of his writings, *Yüan Yung-chih chi* 永之集, 20 *ch.*, was printed about the time he died. It was reprinted in 1584 under the title *Hsü-t'ai hsien-sheng* 胥臺先生 *chi*, a copy of which is in the Library of Congress. He was also an accomplished calligrapher, as evidenced by the xylographically reproduced preface in his handwriting to the collection of correspondence entitled *Sheng-ch'eng-chi* 聲承籍, edited by Chao Han 趙漢 (T. 鴻逵, H. 漸齋, b.1488, cs 1511). The preface was written in 1546, a year before Yüan died.

Yüan Chih had a son, Yüan Tsun-ni

尊尼 (T. 魯望, 1523-74, cj 1543, cs 1565), who rose in March, 1572, to be surveillance vice commissioner of Shantung in charge of education. It is said that he owed his promotion to his father's student Kao Kung. When Kao was no longer in power, this relationship became a liability to Yüan Tsun-ni. So, as the story goes, he tendered his resignation late in 1573 when he learned that the Shantung governor, Fu Hsi-chih (*see* P'an Chi-hsün), was about to make an unfavorable report about him. He left a collection entitled *Yüan Lu-wang chi* 魯望集, 12 *ch.*, printed *ca.* 1575. A descendant, Yüan Pao-huang 寶璜 (T. 珍夏, H. 渭漁, 1846-96, cs 1892), was the author of a bibliography of writings of the Yüan family, entitled *Yüan-shih i-wen chin-shih lu* 藝文金石錄, 2 *ch.*

As to Yüan Chih's brothers, each of the three purchased the rank of a student of the National University. The eldest, Yüan Piao 表 (T. 邦正, H. 陶齋), also purchased the rank of a police officer and served in that capacity successively in Peking (1531-33) and Nanking (1533-39). Later he rose to the post of assistant prefect of Lin-chiang 臨江, Kiangsi (1540). He is often confused with his contemporary of the same name, the Yüan Piao (T. 景從, cj 1558) of Fukien, and thus erroneously credited with the latter's anthology of twelve Fukien poets. The second, Yüan Chiung (*q.v.*), and the third, Yüan Pao 褒 (T. 與之, H. 鏡機子, 卧雪, 1499-1576), were both noted bibliophiles. Yüan Pao's son, Yüan Nien 年 (T. 子壽, H. 德門, 1539-1617, cs 1577), served as prefect of Ch'ing-chou 青州, Shantung (1587-91), intendant of western Kiangsi (1591-95), intendant of southern Yunnan (1595-98), and surveillance commissioner of Shensi. A grandson of Yüan Nien was the noted writer of musical drama, Yüan Yü-ling 于令 (T. 令昭, H. 鳧公, 籜庵, 1592-1674).

Two cousins of Yüan Chih achieved some fame as poets, namely, Yüan Kun 袞 (T. 補之, H. 虛谷, cj 1528, cs 1538), who rose to be deputy director of a bureau in the ministry of Rites, and Yüan Ch'iu 裘 (T. 紹之, H. 志巳). About 1680 the Ch'ing scholar, Wang Wan (ECCP), whose wife was a descendant of Yüan Chih, wrote biographical sketches of the six Yüan cousins, collected under the title *Yüan-shih liu-chün hsiao-chuan* 氏六俊小傳.

Yüan Chih also had five sisters, the youngest of whom married a fellow townsman, Wu Hsiao-kuang 伍孝光 (also known as Wu Ch'ing-chung 卿忠, fl. 1585-89, son of Wu Yü-fu 餘福, T. 君求, H. 寒泉, cs 1517). For a time her husband was involved in a lawsuit and imprisoned. Probably because of this she had her son brought up as a member of her own family, passing under the name of Yüan Ts'ui 袁萃 until he became a *chin-shih* in 1580, when he officially changed his name to Wu Yüan-ts'ui (T. 聖起, H. 寧方, fl. 1550-1608). He served as magistrate of Kuei-hsi 貴溪, Kiangsi (*ca.* 1580-86), as secretary, then associate bureau director, in the ministry of War (*ca.* 1591-95), as intendant of the Hangchow circuit, and later as director of education of Chekiang (December, 1595-June, 1598), as assistant administration commissioner of Hukuang (1598-*ca.* 1600), and as intendant of the Hai-pei circuit (海北道), Kwangtung (1604-6). He is best known for his four collections of miscellaneous notes, *Lin-chü man-lu* 林居漫錄, *ch'ien-chi* 前集, 6 *ch.*, *pieh* 別 *chi*, 9 *ch.*, *ch'i* 畸 *chi*, 5 *ch.*, and *to* 多 *chi*, 6 *ch.*, all published between 1606 and 1608. His caustic comments on government policies, sharp critiques on current affairs, and relentless exposition of the wrongdoings of some of his contemporaries read as though written in modern journalistic style.

Bibliography

1/287/3a; 5/101/66a; Ch'ien Ch'ien-i (ECCP), *Lieh-ch'ao shih-chi*, 丁 3/8b; KC (1958), 3442, 3487; *Huang Ming wen-hai* (microfilm), 14/3/8, 9; *Yüan Lu-wang chi* (NLP microfilm, roll 869; *Hsü-t'ai hsien-sheng chi* (NLP microfilm, roll 933); Wang Wan, *Tun-weng wen-lu*, 13/41a; Shen

Te-fu, *Wan-li yeh-hu pien*, 631; SK (1930), 93/6a, 177/4a.

Chaoying Fang

YÜAN Chiung 袁褧 (T. 尙之, H. 謝湖, 懶生, 藏亭), October 18, 1495-July 25, 1560, bibliophile, was the second of four brothers in a wealthy Soochow family, the best known of whom was the youngest Yüan Chih (*q.v.*).

Yüan Chiung took the provincial examination perhaps eight or ten times without success and ended up with the rank of a student in the National University, obtained by purchase. As a book collector and publisher, however, he should be regarded as one of the foremost in the Ming dynasty. Book collecting in his family began in the middle of the 15th century, apparently after his ancestors, like other prominent families of that area, had become affluent. His own library, named Chia-ch'ü-t'ang 嘉趣堂, appears in the imprint of most of his publications.

About 1534 Yüan began to publish some of the treasures in his collection, as well as the current writings of his friends, in a series entitled *Chin-sheng yü-chen chi* 金聲玉振集, one of the earliest *ts'ung-shu* ever printed. It was obviously planned as a series, as evidenced by the positioning of the serial title and by a class designation under the title of each work. Another innovation, the notation of chia-pu 甲部 (group one), appears only once and was then abandoned for reasons unknown. There are also mistakes due to indifferent proofreading, as in the case of the biographical work, *Kuo-pao hsin-pien* 國寶新編, printed in 1536 as soon as its author, Ku Lin 顧璘 (T. 華玉, H. 東橋, cs 1496, 1476-1545), had completed it; the work has two prefaces, one by the author and the other by Yüan Chih, but the engraver carelessly transposed the signatures. In spite of such errors, the *Chin-sheng yü-chen chi* still ranks among the most important serial publications in the Ming period; this is chiefly because more than forty of its fifty-five titles are treatises on history and geography, some being printed for the first time. It started a trend in such publications as the *Chi-lu hui-pien* (*see* Shen Chieh-fu), which helped to preserve some important sources on Ming history.

Yüan Chiung added to the series from time to time accounts of current events. In 1550 he printed four works dealing with the transportation of tribute grain from south China by the sea route. This was then a timely issue as the Yellow River frequently, with its load of silt deposited in the channel, blocked the passage of boats on the Grand Canal. In 1538 the surveillance vice commissioner of Shantung, Wang Hsien (*see* Wang Chiu-ssu), had made a start on the opening of a new canal, called Chiao-lai 膠萊河, to cut across the Shantung peninsula in order to shorten the sea route; he was forced to leave, however, when the project was still in its initial stage. Soon after Yüan's publication of these four books, several officials recommended a resumption of the work on this canal. In October, 1554, a censor, Ho T'ing-yü 何廷鈺 (T. 潤夫, H. 熙泉, cs 1550), received imperial sanction to conduct a survey of the terrain. The survey came to an inconclusive end, but a member of his staff, Ts'ui Tan 崔旦 (T. 伯東), wrote an enthusiastic memoir on the feasibility and advantages of such a canal, entitled *Hai yün pien* 海運編, 2 *ch*. This memoir, published by Yüan directly after its completion late in 1554, seems to have been an attempt to influence a decision on the matter. In this sense, Yüan's serial publication served as a political tract of the day. This is even more evident in the case of the three articles on the pirates, namely, the *Hai-k'ou-i* by Wan Piao (*q.v.*), the *Hai-k'ou hou-pien*, with a colophon in Yüan's name dated early in 1560, and the *Hai-k'ou hou-pien hsia* 下 by Mao K'un (*q.v.*), with the colophon also in Yüan's name but dated in 1565. All three works and the two colophons have since been referred to as fundamental sources on the pirates of that period. It was in the course of writing this biography that Yüan's dates of birth and death were located in the genealogy of his family, where the records indicate that he died in July, 1560. It follows that the colophon to Mao's work must be regarded as a forgery (see Mao K'un). Apparently after Yüan's death and the transfer of the printing blocks to a new owner, the serial continued for some time to be published as if it were still under his editorship.

In the series is another work printed in 1550 under Yüan's own name as compiler. This is the *Feng-t'ien hsing-shang lu* 奉天刑賞錄 on the rewards and punishments ordered by Chu Ti (*q.v.*) after his usurpation in 1402. The compilation reveals the favoritism shown by the Yung-lo emperor to his partisans in sharp contrast to the sadistic punishments visited upon his opponents (not recorded in the official histories). Yüan Chiung assembled these records from various sources, especially the *Jen-wu kung-ch'en chüeh-shang lu* by Tu Mu (*q.v.*).

Two Sung editions which Yüan reproduced in facsimile have been highly treasured by collectors. One is the *Shih-shuo hsin-yü* 世說新語, 3 *ch.*, of Liu I-ching (403-44), reproduced in 1535 from the 1188 edition. The other is the six annotators' edition of the anthology *Wen hsüan* 文選, 60 *ch.*, of Hsiao T'ung (501-31), reproduced from a Sung printing. From Yüan's colophon one learns that the engraving took fifteen years, from 1534 to 1549, and was done by carefully selected xylographers. Two of the engravers even left their names, one in 1547 at the end of *chüan* 44 and the other a year later at the end of *chüan* 56. As soon as it was published in 1549, the book became a treasure. Some unscrupulous dealers, by deleting Yüan's imprints and in some cases substituting fake colophons or forged seals, passed the book off as an original Sung edition. The Imperial Library in the Ch'ing dynasty owned no fewer than ten copies of Yüan's 1549 edition, nine of

which revealed such tampering.

Yüan Chiung was also the publisher of three series of anecdotes, each consisting of forty titles in 40 *chüan*, known as *Ssu-shih chia hsiao-shuo* 四十家小說 differentiated by the prefixes *ch'ien*, *hou*, and *kuang* 廣.

As an artist Yüan is said to have excelled in depicting flora and birds. Lu Shih-hua (*see* Hsiang Sheng-mo) records a painting by Yüan entitled "Ch'ing-hsiang tz'u-ti t'u" 清香次第圖. Its theme is the four stages of the plum flower—the bud, its opening, blooming, and wilting. Yüan was highly regarded for his poetry; very few of his poems, however, are extant.

Bibliography

Wu-hsien chih 吳縣志 (1933), 56A/16b, 66A/2b; Ch'ien Ch'ien-i (ECCP), *Lieh-ch'ao shih-chi*, IV, 8/20b; *Wu-men Yüan-shih chia-p'u* 吳門袁氏家譜 (1919), *ch.* 6; Yeh Ch'ang-ch'ih 葉昌熾, *Ts'ang-shu chi-shih shih* 藏書紀事詩 (1958), 108; Yeh Te-hui (BDRC), *Hsi-yüan tu-shu chih* 郎園讀書志 (1928), 6/29a; *T'ien-lu-lin-lang shu-mu* 天祿琳琅書目 (1884), 10/30a; *Ming-tai pan-pen t'u-lu ch'u-pien* 明代版本圖錄初編 (1940), 6/34a; Lu Shih-hua, *Wu-yüeh so-chien shu-hua lu* 吳越所見書畫錄, 5/95a; Shioya On 鹽谷溫, "Min no shosetsu san-gen ni tsuite" 明の小說「三言」に就て in *Shibun* 斯文, Vol. 8 (1926), nos. 5, 6, 7; W. Franke, *Sources*, 3.6.5, 7.8.7, 9.4.1.

Chaoying Fang

YÜAN Chung-ch'e 袁忠徹 (T. 公達, 靜思), 1376-1458, a native of Yin-hsien 鄞縣, Chekiang, was a physiognomist, quite as well known as his father Yüan Kung (*q. v.*) before him. Legends and stories which testify to the excellence of his skill are even more numerous than those about his father in Ming writings.

Accompanying his father to Peiping in 1397, Yüan Chung-ch'e met Chu Ti (*q. v.*), the prince of Yen, for the first time. Yüan is said to have read many faces clearly and accurately and earned high praise from the prince. Two years later the prince again summoned him for consultation on the insecure political situation under his nephew's newly inaugurated rule. Yüan advised the prince to be cautious and reticent, and that eventually the will of Heaven would prevail. As the arsenals in Peiping were busy manufacturing weapons day and night, he suggested that the prince have them moved underground so that they would be neither seen nor heard. At an official banquet the prince asked him to read the faces of the assembled officials secretly. For certain ones among them appointed by Nanking, Yüan predicted that their fate would be capital punishment. The prince was reportedly elated, and was further confirmed in his decision to make a military move.

After the prince ascended the throne Yüan first received an appointment as usher in the Court of State Ceremonial, and later as assistant minister of the seal office with occasional duties as counselor on other matters. In 1406 he became a drafter in the central drafting office. He was frequently found in the emperor's company on the imperial trips to Peiping or the expeditions to the northwest, such as those of 1410, 1414, and 1422. When the heir apparent incurred the displeasure of his imperial father, Yüan was one among a group sent to investigate the frightened prince. Following the favorable report by this group, the position of the heir apparent became less precarious. By 1414 Yüan Chung-ch'e returned to his old post in the seal office, and by 1416 was promoted to be vice minister of that branch of the central government.

The emperor had unreasoning faith in the curative powers of the deities of the Ling-chi kung (靈濟宮), whereas actually the so-called hsien fang 仙方 (supernatural prescriptions) were devised by the Taoists of that temple. Some of the drugs brought on shortness of breath and rising phlegm, which made the emperor susceptible to fits of temper. No official except Yüan dared to speak against his belief. When Yüan did so, the emperor angrily ordered him flogged but later he calmed down and Yüan suffered no further punishment. It is said that Yüan also spoke out against the dispatch of missions to faraway lands to collect treasures.

In 1422 both Yüan and the prognosticator Huang-fu Chung-ho 皇甫仲和 (native of Sui-chou 睢州, Honan) accompanied the emperor on an expedition to Mongolia. No Mongols were encountered so the emperor wanted to turn back. When he asked Yüan and Huang-fu for their prognostication both said that the Mongols would appear in force that afternoon. Apparently that was not what the emperor hoped would occur; he accused the two of collusion, had them handcuffed, and threatened them with execution if they were mistaken. The Mongols, however, came that day in considerable strength; the opposing forces became locked in battle, but a sandstorm soon stopped the fighting. The emperor again wanted to retreat, but Yüan and Huang-fu advised him to hold on for they predicted that the Mongols would surrender the following day. Their prediction proved correct.

In 1425 under the new reign of Chu Kao-chih (*q.v.*), Yüan was forced to retire. In 1426, however, the next emperor Chu Chan-chi (*q.v.*) reinstated him in his old post of vice minister of the seal office. The record states that as soon as Yüan saw the paleness of the new monarch's complexion, he announced that within seven days a member of the imperial house would rise up in arms, which, of course, came to pass in the ill-fated rebellion of Chu Kao-hsü (*q.v.*).

Yüan finally received permission to retire in 1439. In his later days in court, it is said that he once confided to Pai Kuei (*q.v.*) that both Wang Wen (*see* Yü Ch'ien) and Yü Ch'ien had the countenances of men destined for beheading. Wang had an exceptionally pallid face, a condition known in physiognomy as li-hsüeh-t'ou 瀝血頭 (dripping blood head), and Yü's eyes always turned upward, a state known as wang-tao-yen 望刀眼 (eyes gazing at the sword). After the restoration of 1457, both were executed.

Yüan's son, Yüan Ying-hsiang 應驤, achieved no special distinction but several descendants later held minor offices.

Yüan Chung-ch'e left some works on physiognomy. The *Ku-chin shih-chien* 古今識鑑, 8 *ch.*, a collection of stories on physiognomy from ancient times to his own day, is noticed in the *Ssu-k'u* catalogue, though not included in the Imperial Library. In this notice, mention is made of another title by him, the *Jen-hsiang ta-ch'eng* 人相大成, which was not available to the editors at the time. Yüan's *Fu-t'ai wai-chi* 符臺外集, 2 *ch.*, was recently reprinted in the seventh series of the *Ssu-ming* 四明 *ts'ung-shu*. He also wrote a poetic essay, the "Jen-hsiang fu" 人象賦, which was appended to the *Ku-chin shih-chien* according to one bibliographic source, and was the editor if not the author of a work entitled *Shen-hsiang ch'üan-pien* 神相全編, 12 *ch.*, attributed to the tenth-century Taoist priest Ch'en T'uan.

In historical works as well as in random notes by Ming authors, many stories about Yüan Chung-ch'e's skill in physiognomy are told and retold. The best known is probably the story of a bond-servant, a boy who worked in the home of one of Yüan's friends. After seeing the boy on a visit, he advised his friend not to keep him for the boy had an unlucky face. The friend followed his advice very reluctantly because the boy had a good appearance and conducted himself well. Leaving his master, the boy lived from hand to mouth with no permanent place to stay. Upon taking shelter one night in a temple, he noticed an old garment in a corner. When he investigated he found pieces of gold and silver wrapped up in it, amounting to a sum of four or five hundred taels. He quickly checked his first inclination to make off with the money, and decided to stay and wait for the rightful owner. Reason told him that his life had been unlucky enough;

should he engage in any wrong-doing his future might be even darker. After daybreak a weeping woman returned to the temple looking for her lost money. The woman's husband, a soldier at a guard post, was in prison awaiting execution. She had sold all their possessions in order to pay his ransom and save him. In her anxiety and worry, she had forgotten to take the money with her after resting in the temple. The boy returned the money and refused any reward. After accomplishing her purpose, the woman told her husband about the boy's kind deed and he in turn told his superior officer, the commander of the guard. As the latter had no son, he located the youth and adopted him. A few years later, on the death of the commander, the adopted son succeeded to his position. Later as the new commander he visited his old master, the man who had adhered to Yüan Chung-ch'e's advice. The master decided that Yüan had been mistaken in his prediction. To make a test, he asked the young man to don his old clothes and serve tea when Yüan came to visit. As soon as Yüan saw him, he remarked with surprise, "You are now an officer of the third grade; you must have done some exceptionally good deed." For it was the common belief that good deeds merited improvement of one's fate. Then the young man told his story and the friend's faith in Yüan's skill was restored.

Different versions of this story, including the *Huan-chin t'ung-tzu* 還金童子 by Lu Ts'an (*see* Kuei O), had existed probably before it was expanded into the most mature form as *chüan* 21 in the *P'ai-an ching-ch'i* by Ling Meng-ch'u (*q. v.*); this work is one of the celebrated collections of Ming short stories. The title in Ling's work is "Yüan shang-pao hsiang-shu tung ming-ch'ing, Cheng she-jen yin-kung tao shih-chüeh" 袁尙寶相術動名卿, 鄭舍人陰功叨世爵; in it the youth is given the surname Cheng.

[Editors' note: There are many cases of magicians like Yüan in Chinese history.

Only the most intelligent and sharp-witted can be proficient in charlatanism; the success of a physiognomist depends as well on clever publicity. Perhaps some of the stories about Yüan were invented by himself or his friends, and further embroidered when retold.]

Bibliography

1/299/10b, 14b; 5/77/17a; TSCC (1885-88), XVII: 650/14b; SK (1930), 111/8b; *Yin-hsien chih* (1877), 32/30a, 33a, 34/44b; Lu Ts'an, *Keng-ssu pien* 庚巳編, 3/4b, 5a (in Shen Chieh-fu, *Chi-lu hui-pien, ch.* 166); Chu Yün-ming, *Chih-kuai lu* 志怪錄, 26b (*in Chi-lu hui-pien, ch.* 210).

Lienche Tu Fang

YÜAN Huang 袁黃 (T. 坤儀, H. 學海, 了凡, 趙田逸農), December 26, 1533-1606, official and scholar, who resuscitated the Taoist merit and demerit system, was a native of Wu-chiang 吳江 (Soochow), but his ancestral home was Chia-shan 嘉善, Chekiang. His great-great-grandfather, known as Yüan Ch'i-shan 杞山, was implicated in the abortive attempt of 1402, led by Huang Tzu-ch'eng (*see* Lien Tzu-ning) to resist Chu Ti (*q. v.*). As a result he had to leave home and went to live in Wu-chiang. It was also for this reason that no one of the Yüan family for the three following generations ever embarked on an official career, or took part in the examinations. In Wu-chiang his great-grandfather, Yüan Hao 顥 (T.孟常, H. 菊泉), married into the family of Hsü Yu-chen (*q. v.*). Because of his sense of loyalty toward Chu Yün-wen (*q.v.*), Yüan Hao wrote a treatise entitled *Chu-te p'ien* 主德篇, in appreciation of that dethroned monarch. He and his son, Yüan Hsiang 祥 (T. 怡杏), and his grandson, Yüan Jen 仁 (T. 參坡), all followed the medical profession, although they were scholars as well and left writings on various topics. Another tradition of the Yüan family was its beliefs in various popular practices, such as geomancy and physiognomy, and also in religious Taoism.

Yüan Huang broke with this heritage, however, and emerged as the first of his family to pursue an official career. He became a *hsiu-ts'ai* in 1550, but not until 1567 was he selected to be a *kung-sheng* in the National University, Peking. In 1570 he obtained the *chü-jen*, but another decade and a half elapsed before he passed the metropolitan examinations (1586) and was made a *chin-shih*. He received his first appointment as a magistrate of Pao-ti 寶坻 in the Shun-t'ien prefecture 順天府, where he took up his official duties in the summer of 1588. Being a conscientious official, he studied the problems of the administration and the ills of the people. The most celebrated of his achievements in Pao-ti was the lowering of the land tax from .237 to .146 taels of silver per *mou*. As Pao-ti was practically in the shadow of Peking, the transportation of tribute grain and choice timber for construction in the palace area became an additional burden for the people. Yüan, concerned with the alleviation of their ills, worked to solve these problems and others involving the floods and droughts that sometimes damaged the area. Yüan, because of his wide interests, also directed his attention to problems of national urgency, such as frontier defense, ocean transportation, and the preparation of young students prior to their sitting for the civil examinations.

When the Japanese invaded Korea (1592), the Korean king urgently pled for Chinese help. The court in Peking first appointed Sung Ying-ch'ang (*see* Li Ju-sung) as governor-general of Chien-chou 建州 and Liaotung and Li Ju-sung as field commander. About this time Yüan was promoted to secretary in the ministry of War. He and another member of the same ministry, Liu Huang-shang 劉黃裳 (T. 玄子, cs 1586, 1527-93+), were posted as military councilors to the expeditionary force to Korea. Neither of them was young, Yüan nearly sixty, Liu over sixty. Early in 1593 they crossed the Yalu River and arrived in Korea. Following Li Ju-sung's initial victory, they moved to Pyongyang. Unfortunately the victory was not followed by further success; reverses, squabbles between the northern and southern forces, scandals and indecision in Peking, followed. Consequently, both Sung Ying-ch'ang and Li Ju-sung were ordered back to Peking in July, 1593. Yüan and Liu too were relieved of their responsibilities and retired from office, sharing the blame for these failures. Some years after his death, however, in a later reign, Yüan Huang was posthumously awarded the title of a vice minister of the Seal Office for his services in Korea.

The *Chosŏn wangjo sillok* 朝鮮王朝實錄 gives some interesting information about Yüan not found in Chinese sources: the Korean king was informed that Yüan gazed at the sky every morning, and that he allegedly declared that the atmosphere about the king's palace was favorable; hence, there was no doubt that the lost territories would be recovered. Prognostication involving study of the atmosphere (wang-ch'i 望氣), a feature of Chinese geomancy, quite bewildered the Korean king. He also learned that in Kaesŏng 嘉山, Yüan had seen the Korean government statutes (會典) and made certain inquiries. This disturbed the king greatly, as shown by his repeated orders to the Korean officials to keep the work out of the reach of Yüan, lest it be taken to China. It is clear that the Koreans were critical and suspicious of the Chinese officials.

Yüan with his background and as a man of his time was, like many intellectuals of the sixteenth century, both a Confucian scholar and one deeply involved in Buddhistic beliefs, Taoist practices, and many folk cults as well. He promoted the amalgamation of the three teachings, and reintroduced the merit and demerit system. In a way, he and Lin Chao-en (*q.v.*) were the two chief revivers of religious Taoism in the late Ming in spite of the fact that the Buddhists always laid claim to him as one of their followers.

At the age of sixty-eight, Yüan wrote a work of instructions for his son, Yüan Yen 袁儼 (T. 若思, H. 素水, cs 1625, 1581–1627, magistrate of Kao-yao 高要, Kwangtung), which was later printed and reprinted many times and bore varied titles, such as *Hsün-tzu yen* 訓子言, *Liao-fan ssu-hsün* 了凡四訓, etc. The first of the four chapters of this work contains especially interesting autobiographical detail. Yüan Huang relates that after his father's death, while still in his 'teens, he took his mother's advice and ceased to prepare for the examinations, taking up the study of medicine instead. Then he met a Mr. K'ung 孔 from Yunnan, a Taoist prognosticator. Mr. K'ung told him that he was predestined to serve in officialdom and would become a *hsiu-ts'ai* in the following year. Thereupon Yüan abandoned medicine and returned to the pursuit of an official career. In the next year, indeed he passed all the qualifying examinations as K'ung predicted and at the exact rank foretold. Mr. K'ung then made a prognostication covering his whole life: his limited career in the bureaucracy, his death at fifty-three *sui*, and his fate of having no son. For some twenty years subsequently, everything happened as Mr. K'ung had said, even to the exact amount of stipend rice he would receive from the government. In accordance with the predictions, he became a *kung-sheng* and went to the National University at Peking. After one year in the capital, he was transferred (1569) to the National University of Nanking. Before reporting to the university, however, he visited the well-known Buddhist monk Fa-hui 法會 (T. 雲谷, 1500–79) in the Ch'i-hsia 棲霞 mountains northeast of Nanking. For three days and three nights the learned monk and Yüan sat quietly face to face. Then Fa-hui started questioning Yüan on his life, ideas, and beliefs. Yüan confessed to being a fatalist, because of the accuracy of Mr. K'ung's predictions. To arouse him from this state, the monk drew on the Buddhist law of ethical causation, on the Confucian belief that one might escape from heavenly calamities but not from those brought on by oneself, and finally on the Taoist creed of self-discipline through the system of merit and demerit. Yüan was so moved that then and there he made the decision to seek rebirth through reason. To indicate this personal triumph, he changed his original *tzu* of Hsüeh-hai 學海, to Liao-fan 了凡, meaning "to end being average," for the monk had told him that only average people allowed themselves to be bound by predetermination.

Perhaps it is appropriate to note here that while the Buddhist monk Fa-hui was teaching Yüan about the Taoist system of merit and demerit, another famous monk, Chu-hung (*q.v.*), in his youth (*ca.* 1550s) had reprinted the *Kung-kuo ko* 功過格 and later adapted it to Buddhist usage, publishing this new and revised edition in 1604 under the title *Tzu-chih lu* 自知錄. It shows how much the three teachings, by the sixteenth century, had become fused, the interpenetration being a threeway affair.

Following the encounter with Fa-hui, Yüan broke away from the spell produced by Mr. K'ung's prognostications. Vowing and successfully achieving three thousand good deeds, or merits, he passed the provincial examinations and became a *chü-jen* (1570). After this, he resolved to achieve another three thousand to fulfill his wish for a son, and a son was born to him in 1581. Then he concentrated on the desire to obtain an advanced degree, and a *chin-shih* he became (1586). Finally he reached the age of fifty-three *sui*, still hale and hearty, and lived on for many years more. The slow progress toward accomplishing the ten thousand merits of his later vow worried him after he had taken office as magistrate in Pao-ti. One night in a dream an immortal told him that his single official act of lowering the land tax could already be counted as ten thousand good deeds. While he was still

in doubt about this interpretation a monk from Mt. Wu-t'ai 五臺山 substantiated this statement informing him that by his act ten thousand people must have benefited.

Yüan left a number of works which can be classified under three categories: government-administrative writings, moral-religious writings, and reference books mostly aimed at students preparing for the examinations. In 1605 eleven of his shorter works were printed under the collective title *Liao-fan tsa-chu* 雜著, of which four may be considered as in the first category, namely the *Ch'üan-nung shu* 勸農書 on agriculture, the *Huang-tu shui-li* 皇都水利 on water conservancy in the capital area (noticed in the *Ssu-k'u* catalogue), the *Li-fa hsin-shu* 曆法新書 on the calendar, the *Pao-ti cheng-shu* 政書 on the administration of Pao-ti, where he served. The second category included his instructions for his son and the *Ch'i-ssu chen-ch'üan* 祈嗣眞詮, the essentials for praying for an heir, which also received a notice in the Imperial Catalogue. In the third category was *Li-shih kang-chien pu* 歷史綱鑑補, an outline history of China, first printed in 1606, and later in the Ch'ing period reprinted together with the *Kang-chien hui-tsuan* 綱鑑會纂 by Wang Shih-chen (*q.v.*) under the title *Yüan Wang kang-chien ho-pien* 合編 probably published by a bookdealer primarily for commercial gain. This work later became very popular among the Japanese. According to Morohashi Tetsuji 諸橋轍次 in the *Daikanwa jiten* 大漢和辭典, when modernization came to Japan, the term li-shih was adopted for the history course in the new schools. It is rather ironical that apparently the Chinese readopted it from the Japanese for the same purpose later. Another general reference work entitled the *Ch'ün-shu pei-k'ao* 群書備考, with some notes made by his son, was compiled chiefly for the benefit of degree aspirants. It is not clear when it first appeared, but a 4 *chüan* edition, supplemented and published by Shen Ch'ang-shih 沈昌世 (T. 文甫, native of Hangchow), was printed in 1642 with the variant longer titles, *Tseng-ting* 增訂, *ch'üan-ch'ang* 全場, or *Tseng-ting er-san-ch'ang* 二三場 *ch'ün-shu pei-k'ao*. This work caught the attention of the Ch'ien-lung commissioners who ordered the excision (from *chüan* 4) of the maps of the northern frontier; fortunately complete copies have survived. A prose anthology, also directed to examination participants, entitled *P'ing chu pa-tai wen-tsung* 評註八代文宗, 8 *ch.*, likewise receives a notice in the *Ssu-k'u* catalogue.

Yüan Huang's collected literary works, the *Liang-hsing* (or *hang*) *chai chi* 兩行齋集 in 14 *chüan*, which is a useful source for the study of his opinions and beliefs, was probably printed soon after his death. For example, a letter to Sung Ying-ch'ang reveals that Yüan originally did not favor the sending of an expeditionary force to Korea. And the rarely quoted biography of Wang Ken (*q.v.*), the eccentric disciple of Wang Shou-jen (*q.v.*), further evinces his relationship with the Wang Yang-ming school. One source suggests that the term Liang-hsing, which he chose for his studio name and then as the title of his collected literary works, connotes the idea that besides being a Confucian scholar he followed the two ways of both Taoism and Buddhism.

Besides the popularization of the system of merit and demerit, a work on quiet meditation, the *Ching-tso yao-chüeh* 靜坐要訣 (1929), has also been attributed to him. Yüan is said to have been a philanthropist, contributing every year many *shih* of grain, seventy percent of which went to Buddhist monks and thirty to his relatives and acquantances.

Bibliography

40/55/12a; 43/4/7b; 64/庚 15/5a; 86/16/13b; TSCC (1885–88), XIV: 153/8b, XXII: 532/1b, XXIII: 111/2b; SK (1930), 12/4b, 17/3a, 28/8a, 53/4b, 75/3b, 125/3a, 193/2a; Chu Ho-ling 朱鶴齡, *Yü-chai hsiao-chi* 愚齋小集 (1930), 14/7a, 15/5b; P'eng Shao-sheng 彭紹升, *Chü-shih chuan* 居士傳 (1878), 45/1a; Feng Meng-chen 馮夢楨, *K'uai-hsüeh-t'ang chi* (microfilm, Wan-li ed.), 6/2b; *Chia-shan-fu chih* (Kuang-hsü ed.), 54/9b; *Su-chou-fu chih* (T'ung-chih ed.), 105/13b; *Pao-ti-hsien chih* (1917), 8/4a; Mao I-po 毛一波, Draft biography of Yüan Huang in Chinese; Sun Tien-ch'i (1957), 185, 209; *Chosŏn wangjo sillok*, Vol. 21 (1593), 596, 599, 602, 613, 639, 644, 651, 655, 667, Vol. 22 (1594), 289, Vol. 23(1598), 470; Kenneth Ch'en, *Buddhism in China* (Princeton, 1964), 436; L. Carrington Goodrich, *The Literary Inquisition of Ch'ien-lung* (1935), 153, 260; Liu Ts'un-yan, "Yüan Huang and His 'Four Admonitions,'" *Jo. of the Or. Soc. of Australia*, V (1967), 108.

Lienche Tu Fang

YÜAN Hung-tao 袁宏道 (T. 中郎, 無學, 六休, H. 石公, 石頭居士), 1568-October 22, 1610, official and essayist, was the second of the three famous Yüan brothers of Kung-an 公安, Hukuang, the others being Yüan Tsung 宗-tao and Yüan Chung 中-tao (*see* below). Their ancestors had been military officials for generations, but their grandfather began turning the attention of the clan to books. Their mother was the daughter of Kung Ta-ch'i 龔大器 (T. 容卿, H. 春所, cs 1556) who served as an administration commissioner of Honan. Yüan Hung-tao's nickname was "Yüeh" 月 (or the moonchild) because at the time of his birth his mother dreamed of the moon. He showed his aptitude for literature at an early age when, as a student of fifteen, he organized and headed a literary society in the city. He became a *chü-jen* in 1588 and a *chin-shih* in 1592, but was less desirous of government appointment than of a continuance of his literary and philosophical studies and discussion with his two brothers. He made two trips in the meantime to Huang-chou 黃州 to seek the independent thinker Li Chih (*q.v.*). On the second occasion (1593) his brothers accompanied him. Among the three, the eldest Yüan Tsung-tao, then on leave from the Hanlin Academy, had recently embraced Ch'an Buddhism and was advocating the oneness of Buddhism and Confucianism; hence his thinking was in harmony with that of Li Chih. Yüan Hung-tao, while agreeing with his brother on fundamental matters, took issue with him for making compromises in the interest of self-preservation. "A phoenix would not share the same nest with an ordinary bird, and a man of mettle should set his own pace and go his own way instead of laughing and crying with the world and allowing others to pierce his nose and rope his head," he argued. Li Chih praised both brothers but placed his hope in Yüan Hung-tao whose "incomparable intellectual capacity and courage mark him out for undertakings of great spiritual depth." All the brothers advocated a more lively style in prose writing which came to be known in Chinese literature as the Kung-an p'ai (派).

In 1595 Yüan Hung-tao received an official appointment as magistrate of Wu-hsien 吳縣 (Soochow), which he vacated after a year. He then visited West Lake and roamed the hills and mountains of Chekiang, and discussed his literary views with Hanlin academician T'ao Wang-ling 陶望齡 (T. 周望, H. 石簣, b. 1562, cs 1589) and other scholars. From these encounters came a fresh, spontaneous verse and prose style that "flowed out of his true nature" and set the mode by "sweeping aside the cloud and mist" of the prevailing imitative classicism of Li P'an-lung and Wang Shih-chen (qq.v.), against which his elder brother had already raised the cry with his Hanlin colleague, Huang Hui 黃輝 (T. 平倩, 昭素, cs 1589).

In 1598, when his elder brother was serving in Peking as a tutor to the emperor's eldest son, and his younger brother was a student at the National University, Yüan Hung-tao joined them at the capital as an instructor in the metropolitan prefectural school and later as an instructor in the National University. There the three brothers organized a literary society at Ch'ung-kuo ssu 崇國寺, in the western part of the city, which they named P'u-t'ao she 蒲桃社 (Grape society). Two years later, in 1600, Yüan became a secretary in the bureau of ceremonies in the ministry of Rites. He served only a few months, however, and returned home, presumably for reasons of health.

At this time the eldest brother died. The news so saddened Yüan Hung-tao that he abstained from meat for years to add to the merit of the deceased, and retired with his younger brother and some Buddhist monks to a tract of land south of his native city where he planted thousands of willow trees, and applied himself to the subtleties of Buddhism. He made excursions to Lu-shan 廬山 and to the remote parts of Kiangsi and southern Hukuang, his writing developing with his added spiritual insight and gaining in vigor and naturalness.

Yüan Hung-tao resumed his duties with the ministry of Rites in 1606. After another visit home he was made a secretary in the bureau of honors in the ministry of Personnel in the late spring of 1608. He then received a transfer to the bureau of appointments, and became vice director of the bureau of evaluations, in which office he instituted the annual efficiency rating of the clerks (書吏) in the central government. In September, 1609, he conducted the provincial examination in Shensi. Late in that year, after having been promoted to director of the bureau of records, he went on leave and spent the last months of his life with his younger brother in Sha-shih 沙市 near their native place. After his death, at the age of forty-two, his memory was preserved in the shrine for Kung-an's men of note and in Wu-hsien's shrine for distinguished officials.

Yüan Hung-tao's essays and poems were collected under the titles *Hsiao-pi-t'ang chi* 瀟碧堂集, 20 ch., *Chin-fan* 錦帆 *chi*, 4 ch., *Chieh-t'o* 解脫 *chi*, 4 ch., and *P'ing-hua-chai* 瓶花齋 *chi*, 10 ch., printed in Soochow during the years 1602–10. In 1629 there appeared a classified edition, entitled *Li-yün-kuan lei-ting Yüan Chung-lang ch'üan-chi* 梨雲館類定袁中郎全集, 24 ch., which was reprinted in Japan in 1696.

There was another early seventeeth-century edition entitled *Yüan Chung-lang chi*, of which little is recorded. The *Hsiao-pi-t'ang* and *Yüan Chung-lang chi* were both listed on the Index Expurgatorius of the Ch'ien-lung period. The *Yüan Chung-lang ch'üan-chi* was reprinted in June 1935, with a preface by Su Yüan-lei 蘇淵雷, which calls attention to Yüan Hung-tao's humor, and also to his popularity in the cataclysmic 1930s when the national situation was not unlike that of the late Ming, and the mood of the intelligentsia had also turned from involvement to diversion to bitterness.

Yüan Hung-tao's more serious works included one on Ch'an Buddhism, *Tsung-ching she-lu* 宗鏡攝錄, 12 *ch.*, listed in the bibliographic section of the *Ming-shih*, and another on Pure Land Buddhism, *Hsi-fang ho-lun* 西方合論, 10 *ch.*, with a preface by Yüan Tsung-tao dated April 6, 1600 (the year of his death). The latter is collected in the *Ching-t'u shih-yao* 淨土十要 of Chih-hsü (*q.v.*), and included in *Taishō Daizō-kyō* (no. 1976). As an admirer of Li Chih, who put the erotic *Hsi-hsiang chi* 西廂記 (The western chamber) and the picaresque *Shui-hu chuan* (*see* Shih Nai-an) on a par with the quintessence of Ch'in, Han, and Six Dynasties literature, Yüan Hung-tao for his part ranked the *Shui-hu* and the *Chin P'ing Mei* (*see* Wang Shih-chen) with the Classics, and wrote a historical romance, *Tung-Hsi-Han yen-i* 東西漢演義. Columbia University library has an original Ming edition of the work in 24 *ts'e* 冊. Also extant is his revised edition of a drama, *Hung-mei chi* 紅梅記 by a Chou Ch'ao-chün 周朝俊. Yüan's *P'ing-hua-chai tsa-lu* 雜錄, 10 *ch.*, is a miscellaneous work which ranges in subject matter from Chinese medical formulae to comparisons of Confucianism and Taoism. Like his collected works, it did not meet with favorable comments by the orthodox editors of the *Ssu-k'u*, who blamed the Kung-an brothers for being partly responsible for the decadence of Ming society by "parading their talents and exceeding the bounds of orthodoxy."

Yüan Hung-tao's monograph on flower arrangement, *P'ing-shih* 瓶史, 1 *ch.*, included in his collected works, is indicative of his outlook on life and mode of living. It made its way to Japan probably in the 18th century and was then reprinted there, and resulted in the initiation of a sect. The Kōdōryū 宏道流 of flower arrangement in Japan is said to be currently in its twenty-fourth (teacher-disciple) succession. The style of this school is simple and natural, using mainly three, and sometimes five, stems of three height levels.

His elder brother, Yüan Tsung-tao (T. 伯修, H. 石浦, 香光居士), March 12, 1560–1600, obtained the *chü-jen* degree in 1579 and headed the *chin-shih* list in 1586 at the age of twenty-six when he became a bachelor and then a compiler in the Hanlin Academy. At first he was an earnest practitioner of the Taoist methods of Lin Chao-en (*q.v.*). In 1589 he turned to Ch'an Buddhism, and received inspiration from the monk, Shen-yu 深有, a disciple of Li Chih. He pored over the works of the Ch'an masters Tsung-kao (1089–1163) and Ming-pen (1262–1323) and opened up new vistas for his two younger brothers, with whom he spent some nine years. From 1597 to 1600 he served as a tutor to the emperor's eldest son (later the heir apparent). He was made posthumously grand supervisor of instruction and a vice minister of Rites when Chu Ch'ang-lo (ECCP) ascended the throne in 1620. His close friend and associate Huang Hui wrote his epitaph. His literary associate Tung Ch'i-ch'ang (ECCP), when director of education of Hukuang, honored his memory in the shrine for Kung-an's men of distinction in 1601. Yüan Tsung-tao named his studio Po-Su-chai 白蘇齋 after the poets Po Chü-i (772–846) and Su Shih (1037–1101), whom he admired. The collection of his works, entitled *Po-Su-chai chi*, 22 *ch.*, was printed shortly after he died; of this edition several copies are extant although it was listed for censorship in the 18th century. It was also reprinted in Shanghai in 1935.

He is reported to be the author of two dramas.

The younger brother, Yüan Chung-tao (T. 小修, H. 上生居士), 1570–1624, headed the *chü-jen* list in 1603, but did not attain the *chin-shih* until 1616. He then received an appointment as instructor in the prefectural school of Hui-chou 徽州 (Anhwei), and subsequently became an erudite in the National University in Peking. At his own request he was transferred to Nanking as a secretary in the bureau of ceremonies in the ministry of Rites, whence he rose to director of the bureau of appointments in the southern ministry of Personnel in 1624. He was the author of a Buddhist work, *Ch'an-tsung cheng-t'ung* 禪宗正統, 1 *ch.*, listed in the *Ming-shih* bibliographic section, and a diary entitled *Yu-chü fei-lu* 遊居柿錄, 20 *ch.* His collection of essays and poems, *K'o-hsüeh-chai* 珂雪齋 *chi*, 24 *ch.*, printed in 1618, including his travelogues and correspondence, was also listed among the prohibited books. There was besides a *K'o-hsüeh-chai chi-hsüan* 集選, 24 *ch.*, printed in 1622. Sun Tien-ch'i reports a *K'o-hsüeh-chai wai* 外 *chi*, 11 *ch.* The Naikaku Bunko has the *wai-chi* but in 15 *chüan*. The *K'o-hsüeh-chai chin* 近*-chi*, believed to be the original 24 *chüan* edition referred to in the diary, was reprinted in Shanghai in 1935, in 6 *chüan*, with a preface by Chang I-p'ing 章衣萍, dated December 15, 1935. The diary, *Yu-chü fei-lu*, was also reprinted in Shanghai in 1935. In an entry in August, 1610, Yüan Chung-tao noted the death of Matteo Ricci (*q.v.*), whom he had "met several times in Hung-tao's office." A devout Buddhist, Yüan Chung-tao showed his admiration for the Jesuit scholar "who is said to be a celibate. His country worships heaven," wrote Yüan, "and is unacquainted with Buddhism, but practices the ten virtues, and cherishes friendship, with many people committed to celibacy." Matteo Ricci's description of the earth fascinated him. "There are worlds in all directions. People living on top and people living underneath stand feet to feet. Those underneath are like flies and insects walking upside down on a roof beam. It is all very strange," he remarked. "But it coincides with the words of the *Tsa-hua ching* 雜華經 (*Hua-yen* 華嚴 *ching*): 'There are worlds above, and worlds below, and worlds all around.'"

Bibliography

1/288/12b; 3/269/8b; 40/55/5a, 57/18b, 61/8b; 64/庚 5/1a; 84/丁中/84a; A-ying 阿英(Ch'ien Hsing-ts'un 錢杏邨), "Yüan Chung-lang yü cheng-chih" 與政治, *Jen-chien-shih* 人間世, Vol. 7 (July, 1934),13; Chang Ju-chao 張汝釗, "Yüan Chung-lang te fo-hsüeh ssu-hsiang" 的佛學思想, *Jen-chien-shih*, Vol. 20 (January, 1935), 14; Biography of Yüan Hung-tao in *Ching-t'u shih-yao* 淨土十要 (1894); Chung-shu 中書, "Yüan Hung-tao yü Jih-pen ch'a-hua" 與日本插花, *Ta-kung pao* 大公報, Hong Kong, February 1, 1966; Jen Wei-k'un 任維焜, "Yüan Chung-lang p'ing-chuan" 評傳, *Shih-ta yüeh-k'an* 師大月刊, Vol. 2 (January, 1933), 158; *K'o-hsüeh-chai chin-chi*, 下册 (1935) Biography, preface, and 下册, 44; *Kung-an-hsien chih* (1874), 6/17b; Liu Ta-chieh 劉大杰, *Chung-kuo wen-hsüeh fa-chan-shih* 中國文學發展史, 下册, 114; *Ming-shih i-wen-chih* 藝文志, 3/21a, 4/19a; SK (1930), 116/7a, 128/4b, 179/12b; Sun Tien-ch'i (1957), 62, 111, 243; *Yu-chü fei-lu* (*Yüan Hsiao-hsiu jih-chi* 日記, 1935), 106; *Yüan Chung-lang ch'üan-chi*(1935), 文鈔 45, 隨筆 19 and 25; André Lévy, "Un document sur la querelle des anciens et des modernes *more sinico*," TP, LIV, no . 4–5 (1968), 266; L. Carrington Goodrich, *The Literary Inquisition of Ch'ien-lung* (Baltimore, 1935), 260; P. M. d'Elia, *Fonti Ricciane*, II (Rome, 1949), 67; L. of C. *Catalogue of Rare Books*, 911, 912, 986, 1106, 1198; Kuo Shao-yü 郭紹虞, *Chung-kuo wen-hsüeh p'i-p'ing-shih* 中國文學批評史 (1961), 363, 382, 400, 421.

C. N. Tay

YÜAN Kung 袁珙 (officially known by his *tzu* T'ing-yü 廷玉, H. 柳莊), 1335-December 30, 1410, physiognomist, was born into a family that had settled in Yin 鄞-hsien, Chekiang, beginning with the early years of the 12th century, and had a distinguished record of civil service and scholarship. A precocious boy, Yüan Kung was well read in the classical literature and broadly informed in pseudo-science subjects, but he did not prepare himself for the civil service examination. Instead, as he attained adulthood, he develped a penchant for travel, often making trips to out-of-the-way places. On one occasion, when visiting a monastery on P'u-t'o 普陀 Island off the coast of Ting-hai 定海, Chekiang, he met a physiognomist named Pieh-ku-yai 別古崖, who was a monk. Impressed by Yüan's features, the monk persuaded him to study physiognomy, saying that through this skill he would become prosperous. As the story goes, the monk's instructions were as follows: first, he asked Yüan to gaze at the sun until he became almost blind, and then try to find some black beans in a dark room. Next, the monk hung some colored threads outside the window and asked him to identify the colors in the moonlight. After Yüan was found capable of doing all this, the monk taught him the secrets of his art. His method was to light two torches in a dark room at midnight or before dawn, then send for a client and ask Yüan to examine his features and complexion. Next, he had to consult the date of birth. Only then could a prediction be reached.

During the chaotic years of the early 1360s, except for occasional travel, Yüan Kung spent his time at home, where he planted willow trees around his house, which he called Liu-chuang 柳莊; and so he came to be known as Master Liu-chuang. After he had achieved some repute in physiognomy, many distinguished people came to visit him for advice, and, according to report, he accurately foretold the fortunes of several prominent personages of the late Yüan and early Ming. Some people credited him with, among other things, persuading the monk, Yao Kuang-hsiao (q.v.) to come out from his monastic seclusion to serve the state. Reportedly Yüan met Yao in Sung-shan monastery 嵩山寺, Nan-Chihli, in the early years of the Hung-wu period. Noticing his peculiar features, Yüan remarked:

"You are no ordinary monk. You are the equal of Liu Ping-chung." [Liu Ping-chung (1216-74) was a Buddhist priest who served Qubilai Khan (r. 1260-94) as adviser and confidant.] In 1397 Yao Kuang-hsiao, who had lately gained the confidence of Chu Ti (q.v.), then prince of Yen, recommended Yüan Kung (known at that time as Yüan T'ing-yü) to the prince; the latter subsequently summoned him to Peiping for an audience.

The story of his meeting with Chu Ti (April, 1398) is dramatic indeed. The prince, intending to test Yüan's knowledge, did not call him directly to his presence, but chose to meet him incognito. Disguising himself as a guard, he mixed with nine others who resembled him in appearance and went to a drinking quarter where Yüan was called to study their features. At the meeting, Yüan had no difficulty in identifying the prince. Unhesitatingly he fell on his knees, addressing him as "Your Majesty," and spoke in a tone as though the prince were the real emperor. Chu Ti, wary of arousing suspicion, tried unsuccessfully to stop him; then the party broke up. Later Yüan was called to Chu's quarters. There Yüan pointed out that the prince possessed the features of a Son of Heaven, and predicted that he would become emperor at the age of forty, and that he would enjoy a twenty-year peaceful reign. Yüan's prognostication, it is said, strengthened Chu Ti's determination to usurp the throne. The story, however, may also have been invented by Chu himself in an effort to create an aura of mystery to justify his usurpation of power. Though flattered, Chu could not keep him long in his quarters, for he feared that Yüan might spread the story, thus exposing his own seditious intent and jeopardize his position. So after rewarding Yüan with a sizable gift, Chu sent him home; three months later, however, he summoned Yüan's second son, Yüan Chung-ch'e (q.v.), also a skillful physiognomist, to Peiping for a similar meeting, but gave him no position.

Early in 1400, while at home, Yüan Kung and his son were charged by a local official with being implicated in Chu Ti's plot. They were arrested and dispatched to Nanking, but Emperor Chu Yün-wen (*q.v.*) pardoned them and sent them home. A year later, at the emperor's request, they returned to the capital to present a treatise on physiognomy.

Shortly after Chu Ti's enthronement in July, 1402, recalling Yüan Kung's prognostication, he sent for him and his son again, appointed Yüan Kung (September) assistant minister of the Court of Imperial Sacrifice, and lavished gifts on them. Late that same year, however, Yüan was clapped into prison over a minor offense, but gained release after five months following a plea by Yüan Chung-ch'e. In subsequent years, Yüan Kung and his son continued to frequent the emperor's quarters, and they reportedly influenced him in his decision to designate the heir apparent. It is said that, when the emperor was about to build a palace for the heir apparent, he could not decide which of his sons deserved the honor and called upon Yüan Kung to study their features. Yüan's verdict, so we are told, carried considerable weight in the naming of Chu Kao-chih (*q.v.*) in 1404, and Chu Chan-chi (*q.v.*) as the latter's successor. In the winter of 1409, three years after he had chosen Peiping as a temporary residence, Chu Ti invited Yüan to his new palace, but shortly afterward, because of hts advancing years, Yüan begged leave to retire. He died at home late in 1410, at the age of seventy-five. (The *shih-lu*, followed by the *Kuo-ch'üeh*, however, records his death on January 28, 1411, probably the date the court received the news.) Mourning Yüan's passing, Chu Ti granted a sizable sum for his burial, and commanded Yao Kuang-hsiao to compose a biography for his tomb inscription. Seven years later (April, 1418), through the petition of Yüan Chung-ch'e, the emperor raised Yüan Kung's rank posthumously to vice minister of the Court of Imperial Sacrifices. Yüan had four sons; at least two of them were also physiognomists; of particular interest is the second, Yüan Chung-ch'e.

Yüan Kung was not merely a professional physiognomist; he practiced his art with a high moral concern. His aim, it is said, was to expose man's wickedness so that those who became aware of their shortcomings might undertake to reform themselves. Yüan was quite a lively figure. He loved poetry, drinking, singing, and enjoyed painting bamboos. People at that time compared him to Shao Yung (1011-77), a mathematical philosopher, and gave him the sobriquet of Master K'ang-chieh 康節先生 after his predecessor. This comparison was made because Shao had written a book called *Huang-chi ching-shih shu* 皇極經世書, devoted to discussing the mystical relations between cosmological phenomena and human physiology. Yüan left a collection of poetry entitled *Liu-chuang hsien-sheng shih-chi* 詩集, 1*ch.*, compiled and engraved a year after his death by Yüan Chung-ch'e, with a preface by Yao Kuang-hsiao dated 1411. A copy of this edition is in the Naikaku Bunko, Tokyo. A manuscript transcription is preserved in the collection of the National Library of Peiping, and is available on microfilm (no. 982).

A younger brother of Yüan Kung, Yüan K'uei 珪 (T. 廷圭, H. 清白生, 1336-1417), became, at the end of the Yüan dynasty, an instructor in Hsiao-shan 蕭山 and Hai-ning 海寧 in his native province of Chekiang. In 1382 he received an appointment as magistrate of Mao-ming 茂名, Kwangtung, but later was exiled to Szechwan over a minor offense. Through the recommendation of his nephew, Yüan Chung-ch'e, he was employed (*ca.* 1397) as an adviser by the prince of Yen, and became a supervising secretary in the office of scrutiny for rites (1402-3). His last post was as prefectural judge of Ho-chou 和州, Nan-Chihli (1411), where at the conclusion of his term of three years he retired (*ca.* 1415), and died two years later at the age of eighty-one.

Bibliography

1/299/9a; 3/281/12b; 5/70/47a; 84/2/18b; MSL (1963), T'ai-tsung, 178, 1430; KC (1958), 1056; Tai Liang, *Chiu-ling shan-fang chi* (SPTK), 18/5a, 27/18a; Tsou Chi 鄒濟 (1358–1425), *I-an wen-chi* 頤菴文集 (NCL microfilm), 4/54b; Huang Jun-yü 黃潤玉 (1389–1477), *Nan-shan Huang hsien-sheng chia-chuan chi* 南山黃先生家傳集 (NCL microfilm), 50/1a; Lu Jung 陸容 (1436–97), *Shu-yüan tsa-chi* 菽園雜記; Lu Ts'an (*see* Kuei O), *Keng-ssu pien* 庚巳編 (in Shen Chieh-fu ed., *Chi-lu hui-pien*, 164/2b, 184/23b); Wang K'o-yü, *Wang-shih shan-hu wang hua-chü*, 23/30b; *Yin-hsien chih* (1877), 31/6b, 32/28a, 33a, 56/24b, 64/3b, 65/19a; *Huang Ming wen-hai* (microfilm), 20/1/11; Wang T'ing-yen 王亭彥 ed., *P'u-t'o lo-chia hsin-chih* 洛迦新志 (1924?), 6/35b, 9/2b; Yüan Fou 袁阜, *Chung-kuo li-tai pu-jen chuan* 中國歷代卜人傳 (Canton, 1948), 8/29.

Hok-lam Chan

YÜEH Shao-feng 樂韶鳳 (T. 舜儀, 致和), fl. 1355–80, scholar-official, was a native of Ch'üan-chiao 全椒 (Anhwei). Yüeh's early years are obscure. He appears to have had a good knowledge of the Classics and an aptitude for military arts. During the rebel uprisings in the 1350s, Yüeh and several of his fellow townsmen saw their opportunity, and sided with their particular hero. When Chu Yüan-chang, then a subordinate officer under Kuo Tzu-hsing (*q.v.*), occupied Ho-chou 和州 in the spring of 1355, Yüeh and his friends proceeded to Chu's quarters to offer their services. Impressed by his promise, Chu recruited Yüeh to his staff, and invited him to take part in the campaign across the Yangtze that autumn. Yüeh's duties were apparently to give counsel on military affairs and help the rebel leader with secretarial matters. In 1357 Chu Yüan-chang appointed him an administrator in the Kiangsi branch province, whence he rose to become a regular member of the new government in Nanking.

Yüeh Shao-feng remained out of the limelight until sometime after Chu's enthronement. Early in 1370 he was appointed a diarist, then transferred to be a supervising secretary, and became a vice minister of War in the following year. He rose to minister of War in 1372, and subsequently was put in charge of a program to drill soldiers so as to prevent them from suffering demoralization in time of peace. In August, 1373, he was transferred to the Hanlin Academy as an expositor; whereupon he began to play an active role in literary matters and distinguish himself as a scholar and teacher. He was soon charged, together with Chan T'ung (*q.v.*), with rewriting the six songs to the music played during the sacrificial offerings to Confucius. In October he was made a member of the commission, headed by Chan T'ung and Sung Lien (*q.v.*), to compile the day-by-day records of the court; when completed in June, 1374, these became known as the *Ta Ming jih-li*, 100 ch. (*see* Chan T'ung). Subsequently the emperor entrusted him with the compilation of a compendium of memorials composed by T'ang and Sung officials to provide guidance on format and style for his ministers when they planned to make similar presentations.

About this time the emperor also ordered the Hanlin members to compose songs for the music played in front of the imperial procession on its return from offering sacrifices outside the capital city. The songs used to be in praise of imperial achievements, but the emperor wanted them changed to words warning people to be wary. In October, 1374, Yüeh and his associates drafted thirty-nine changes of such music, together with appropriate songs and dancing patterns aimed at inspiring moral awareness. Yüeh's talent in phonology also found an outlet when late in that year the emperor, dissatisfied with the infelicities in the system of rhymes based on the dialects of the Yangtze valley, appointed him and Sung Lien compilers of a standard rhyme book or phonetic dictionary, taking the north

China pronunciation as the norm. When this was completed in April,1375, it came to be known as the *Hung-wu cheng-yün* 洪武正韻,16 *ch.*, and contained about 12,000 characters. The compilers reduced the number of rhymes in the four tone groups from 107 (in the *Li-pu yün lüeh* 禮部韻畧 of Liu Yüan 劉淵, published 1252) to 76. They took into account a wide variety of dialects from both north and south, and drew from earlier lexical sources. Their work fell short of their goal, however, as most of the compilers hailing from the Yangtze valley were unfamiliar with the northern pronunciation, and were too conservative to overhaul the traditional system. In 1390 the emperor ordered a revision of the text; this became the standard reference for later phonological works until its modification by Mei Ying-tso (*q.v.*). In October the emperor again entrusted Yüeh with the revision of rites for sacrifices at the imperial tombs. Making adaptations of T'ang and Sung practices, Yüeh subsequently submitted a new set of rites which the emperor accepted.

After taking a short leave of absence due to illness, Yüeh was recalled (1376) to become a director of studies of the National University at Nanking, and promoted to be the chancellor in March, 1379. In his new capacity he also served as instructor of the heir apparent, Chu Piao (*q.v.*), and was responsible for drawing up a code of etiquette for his correspondence with his brother princes. Yüeh's tenure at the National University was brief; stricken by ill health, he obtained permission to retire in 1380. He is said to have died shortly afterwards.

Yüeh Shao-feng's career was almost unique in that he was one of the few persons in the entire dynasty who held both the posts of minister of War and chancellor of the National University. He enjoyed the confidence of the emperor. Together with Sung Lien, Chan T'ung, and Wu Ch'en (*see* Chan T'ung), Yüeh became known as one of the ssu hsüeh-shih 四學士 (four scholars) of his time.

In addition to the above-mentioned official works, he was responsible, together with Sung Lien, for the compilation of the first edition of Chu's collected writings, 7 *ch.*, completed in 1374 (later expanded to 20 *ch.*, *see* Chu Yüan-chang). Yüeh's own compositions, however, do not seem to have survived. Ch'en T'ien (*see* T'ien Ju-ch'eng), who records only one of his poems in the *Ming-shih chi-shih*, makes a rather reserved comment on his poetic achievement. Yüeh's immediate descendants are not recorded; but he is known to have had five younger brothers, all of whom held government positions.

Bibliography

1/136/14a; 5/38/5a; 16/19/35a, 46/10b, 158/17b; 64/甲 5/4b; MSL (1962), T'ai-tsu, 1447, 1488, 1507, 1678, 1984; *Ch'üan-chiao-hsien chih* (1920), 10/2a; Chu Yüan-chang, *Kao-huang-ti yü-chih wen-chi*, 7/35a; Liao Tao-nan, *Tien-ko tz'u-lin chi*, 5/4a; Yang Yü-t'ing 楊遇庭(cs 1580), *Yang Tao-hsing chi* 楊道行集 (NLP microfilm, no. 812), 23/9b; SK (1930), 42/6a; Li Chin-hua 李晉華, *Ming-tai ch'ih-chuan shu k'ao* 明代勅撰書考 (Peiping, 1932), 7, 11, 23; Wang Li 王力, *Han-yü yin-yün hsüeh* 漢語音韻學 (Peking, 1956), 505; Paul Pelliot, article on Lexicography in *Encyclopaedia Sinica* (Shanghai, 1917), 300.

Hok-lam Chan

ZEKKAI Chūshin 絶海中津(H. 蕉堅道人), November 13, 1336-April 5, 1405, a priest of the Rinzai Sect 臨濟宗 of Zen, but better known as a poet, served both in Japan and in China. During the Kamakura 鎌倉 and Muromachi 室町 periods, Chinese poems and writings were popular among Zen priests both in Kamakura and in Kyoto. These priests not only loved to read Chinese poems and writings, but also wrote some themselves. This kind of literary activity was known as Gozan Bungaku 五山文學 and Zekkai was an outstanding figure in the group. People called him one of a pair of bright jewels in it, the other being Gidō Shūshin (*see* Tsu-shan), who was highly respected for his learnng and his compositions.

Zekkai was a native of Tsuno 津能 in Tosa district 土佐. At the age of twelve, he went to live in Tenryū-ji 天龍寺 in Kyoto without taking the tonsure, but soon moved to Saihō-ji 西芳寺. Here he studied under a high priest named Musō 夢窓 (1275-1351) who took note of his talent and encouraged him to read, but Zekkai refused, remarking that the way to enlightenment was not in books. Much impressed, Musō continued to take a special interest in him and after two years Zekkai was ordained.

While studying under Musō Zekkai developed a close friendship with Gidō. When Zekkai was seventeen, Musō retired from the world, so he and Gidō went to Kennin-ji 建仁寺 to study under Ryūzan Tokuken 龍山徳見, remaining under his tutelage for twelve years. There was a young man then in Kamakura named Ashikaga Motouji 足利基氏 (1340-67), the first general controller of the Kanto provinces 關東管領, who was highly intelligent and liked to associate with Zen priests who he hoped might help him govern. He invited Gidō to his house and Zekkai accompanied him. Zekkai lived at Kenchō-ji 建長寺 and Enkaku-ji 圓覺寺 and helped to train younger members of the order.

After five years Zekkai seized the opportunity to go to China and left with Jorin 汝霖 and other priests. There were at this time in China a number of monks known for their literary craftsmanship such as Ch'üan-shih 全室, Ch'u-shih 楚石, Meng-kuan 夢觀, and Chu-an 竹庵. Zekkai made friends with some of them and stayed with Ch'üan-shih at Mt. T'ien-chieh 天界山 in Hangchow. Ch'üan-shih appreciated Zekkai's poetic ability and later, when he moved to Mt. Ching 徑山, invited Zekkai to go there and tried to appoint him to the position of head priest, but Zekkai refused the appointment.

After staying at Mt.Ching for several months, he started on an extensive tour of China. Together with Chūjo 忠恕, Hakuei 伯英, and others who arrived in China after he had, he wandered around Wu 吳 and Ch'u 楚 (the Yangtze valley), took passage for Mt. Pei-ku 北固山, where he ascended a storied structure named To-ching-lou 多景樓 in Kan-lu-ssu 甘露寺; from there he went to Nanking, the capital.

In 1376, when Ch'üan-shih was invited to an audience, he made the name of Zekkai known to the emperor, who thereupon summoned him too. When Zekkai appeared, the emperor spoke to him warmly and led him to another hall where he showed him a map of Japan and asked him the location of the ancient shrine where Hsü Fu was buried. According to report Hsü had gone to Japan to search for the elixir of life by order of the first Ch'in emperor (259-210 B.C.) and had died at Kumano 熊野. Then the emperor asked him to improvise a poem. Zekkai complied with one (七言絶句) and the emperor himself composed one that was similar. On his departure the emperor gave him a cane and some gold, and offered special conveniences for his return to Japan.

Zekkai reached Japan in 1379 and lived at Unkyo-an 雲居庵 in Kyoto. The following year he went to Kōshū district 甲州 and established Keirin-ji 慧林寺. Adoring him for his virtues, many people came to see him at the temple. After living there for three years, he returned to Tenryū-ji.

In 1384 Akamatsu Yoshinori 赤松義則 built a monastery called Hōun-ji 法雲寺 in Hanshū district 播州 and asked Zekkai to be the abbot; but instead Zekkai suggested Jorin, who had also returned. Now Zekkai had written a statement in which he criticized the tendency of such powerful people as Akamatsu and Shōgun Yoshimitsu (*see* Chang Hung) for their indulgence in extravagances without regard to the people's troubles. This infuriated the shōgun, whereupon Zekkai fled to

Zenigahara 錢原 in Settsu district 攝津, where Hosokawa Yoriyuki 細川賴之, also detested by Shōgun Yoshimitsu for similar remonstrances, greeted him. Yoriyuki built a monastery called Hōkan-ji 寶冠寺 in Awa district 阿波 in 1385 and asked Zekkai to be the abbot.

Gidō, who by this time was in the confidence of the shōgun, besought him to reconsider his attitude toward Zekkai. The shōgun relented and asked Gidō to send for Zekkai, but when he failed to respond, the shōgun himself wrote a letter to Hosokawa Yoriyuki asking him to use his influence with Zekkai. Yoriyuki did so and finally Zekkai agreed to go to Kyoto to see the shōgun. After that the shōgun respected Zekkai, and when Yamana Ujikiyo 山名氏清 rose in revolt against him, the shōgun asked Zekkai for one of his robes and wore it under his armor. After suppressing the rebellion, the shōgun is said to have shown Zekkai's robe to the people, remarking that he had won because of its protection.

Zekkai from that time on took part in public affairs and became the writer of the sovereign's messages to foreign lands. The shōgun allowed him to live in Shōkoku-ji 相國寺 which he promoted to be first among the temples in Kamakura.

Zekkai died at the age of sixty-nine. After his death, one of his disciples, Gakuin Egaku 鄂隱慧奯, collected his poems and writings and published them under the title *Shōkenkō* 蕉堅稿. According to the preface of the book which Zekkai's Chinese friend Tao-yen 道衍 (Yao Kuang-hsiao, *q.v.*) wrote, Zekkai's poetic talent won him favorable attention among Chinese poets.

Bibliography

Kitamura Sawakichi 北村澤吉, *Gozanbungaku shikō* 五山文學史稿 (Tokyo, 1941), 345–413; Uemura Kanko 上村觀光, "Gozan shiso den" 五山詩僧傳, *Gozanbungaku zenshū* 全集, 5 (Tokyo, 1936), 452; *id.*, preface of "Shōkenkō," *Gozanbungaku zenshū*, 2 (Tokyo, 1936), 1022.

Toyoko Y. Chen

INDEX OF NAMES

INDEX OF NAMES

INDEX OF TITLES OF BOOKS

INDEX OF TITLES OF BOOKS

INDEX OF SUBJECTS

INDEX OF SUBJECTS

089584